P9-BZQ-236

CONVENTION DECISIONS
AND VOTING RECORDS

Studies in Presidential Selection
TITLES PUBLISHED

CONVENTION DECISIONS AND VOTING RECORDS

Second Edition

RICHARD C. BAIN *and* JUDITH H. PARRIS

Studies in Presidential Selection
THE BROOKINGS INSTITUTION
Washington, D.C.

Copyright © 1973 by
THE BROOKINGS INSTITUTION
1775 Massachusetts Avenue, N.W., Washington, D.C. 20036

Library of Congress Cataloging in Publication Data:
Bain, Richard C
  Convention decisions and voting records.

  (Studies in presidential selection)
  Includes bibliographical references.
    1. Political conventions.   I. Parris, Judith H.,
joint author.   II. Title.   III. Series.
JK2255.B3 1973   329'.0221   73-1082
ISBN 0-8157-0768-1

9 8 7 6 5 4 3 2 1

THE BROOKINGS INSTITUTION is an independent organization devoted to nonpartisan research, education, and publication in economics, government, foreign policy, and the social sciences generally. Its principal purposes are to aid in the development of sound public policies and to promote public understanding of issues of national importance.

The Institution was founded on December 8, 1927, to merge the activities of the Institute for Government Research, founded in 1916, the Institute of Economics, founded in 1922, and the Robert Brookings Graduate School of Economics and Government, founded in 1924.

The Board of Trustees is responsible for the general administration of the Institution, while the immediate direction of the policies, program, and staff is vested in the President, assisted by an advisory committee of the officers and staff. The by-laws of the Institution state, "It is the function of the Trustees to make possible the conduct of scientific research, and publication, under the most favorable conditions, and to safeguard the independence of the research staff in the pursuit of their studies and in the publication of the results of such studies. It is not a part of their function to determine, control, or influence the conduct of particular investigations or the conclusions reached."

The President bears final responsibility for the decision to publish a manuscript as a Brookings book or staff paper. In reaching his judgment on the competence, accuracy, and objectivity of each study, the President is advised by the director of the appropriate research program and weighs the views of a panel of expert outside readers who report to him in confidence on the quality of the work. Publication of a work signifies that it is deemed to be a competent treatment worthy of public consideration; such publication does not imply endorsement of conclusions or recommendations contained in the study.

The Institution maintains its position of neutrality on issues of public policy in order to safeguard the intellectual freedom of the staff. Hence interpretations or conclusions in Brookings publications should be understood to be solely those of the author or authors and should not be attributed to the Institution, to its trustees, officers, or other staff members, or to the organizations that support its research.

Foreword

ONCE DISMISSED as political sham, presidential nominating conventions increasingly have been recognized as forums for serious contests over major public issues as well as representative assemblies for choosing candidates for high office. One indication of this new perspective is the parties' full-dress debates at recent conventions—the Republican platform fights in 1964 over civil rights, civilian control over nuclear weapons, and the condemnation of political extremism, and the Democratic debates over Vietnam policy in 1968 and a plethora of issues in 1972. In addition, each party has seen fit in the last decade to alter its convention apportionment formula, delegate selection methods, and procedural rules. More than ever, the national party conventions are worth the attention of students of the American democratic system.

This is the second edition of a book originally published by Brookings in 1960, not long after national television first opened up convention proceedings to a viewing audience numbering tens of millions. The first edition, which covered the history of national conventions through the 1956 election, evolved from research done by Paul T. David, Richard C. Bain, and Ralph M. Goldman that resulted in *The Politics of National Party Conventions,* also published by Brookings in 1960. In compiling information, the authors discovered that no comprehensive history existed of past presidential nominating conventions. Scholars thus had to rely on the printed proceedings, but complete sets of these party records were few and for many researchers access was difficult. The idea of the book, therefore, was to compile in one volume thorough but succinct histories of the conventions of both major parties plus compilations of the roll call votes taken.

By 1972, the first edition was long since out of print but not forgotten. Its value as a tool for scholarly research, as a convenient point of reference for convention officials, and as a kind of almanac of conventions for politically concerned laymen was underscored as the book literally became a collector's item.

The present edition is related logically to a second wave of Brookings research on presidential politics. Books in the series that have been published thus far examine the electoral college, campaign finance, reform of convention procedures, and various issues of presidential selection treated in a volume of essays. Studies in progress deal with minor parties and with the politics of major party presidential nominations.

The author of the new material in this edition, a Research Associate in the Governmental Studies program at Brookings, benefited from helpful comments on her manuscript by Gilbert Y. Steiner, Director of Governmental Studies, and Stephen Hess, William R. Keech, Daniel A. Mazmanian, Richard P. Nathan, Richard M. Scammon, and James L. Sundquist. Sara Sklar typed the manuscript; Elizabeth H. Cross edited it. The painstaking work necessary to produce the voting records since 1960 was undertaken by Edna M. Birkel. Mrs. Parris is grateful for all of these contributions.

As always, the views, opinions, and interpretations in this book are solely those of the authors and should not be ascribed to other staff members, officers, or trustees of the Brookings Institution.

KERMIT GORDON
President

April 1973
Washington, D.C.

Contents

Introduction

DECISIVE CHOICES ABOUT the leadership and principles of national politics are made at national party conventions. There the presidential and vice-presidential nominees are selected, the platform is written, rules for governing the party are established, and the initial rally of the election campaign is held. In a sense, the collective decisions of convention delegates are more important than the collective decision of the electorate in November; because of the customary dominance of the two major parties, the convention decisions, except in unusual years like 1912 and 1968, reduce the range of popular choice to the Democratic ticket, the Republican ticket, and abstention from voting.

At conventions the choice of a presidential nominee has been the main item of public attention, the principal concern of many politicians, and the major story followed by journalists. Much of convention events is shaped by the strategic situation surrounding the presidency. When the party has a president in power, his wishes about the vice-presidential nomination, the platform, party rules, and any other issues that arise are usually followed. This is particularly the case if he is seeking renomination. When the party does not have an incumbent president, manifest controversy is more likely at the convention as candidates and party factions vie for power.

As 1972 clearly demonstrated, the vice-presidential nomination has not been the object of equivalent attention. Customarily, vice-presidential selection has been a prerogative of the presidential nominee, based on his judgment of who will add the most political appeal to the ticket (or detract the least); the convention delegates have simply ratified his choice. Historically, many politicians, including some vice-presidents, have emphasized the insignificance of the office; yet eleven of the vice-presidential nominees have become president—eight by succeeding a chief executive at his death, and three by subsequent election.

Scoffing about the platform has become widespread. Writing in the late nineteenth century, the Russian scholar Ostrogorski called the platform "the biggest farce of all the acts of this great parliament of the party."[1] One candidate for president, Wendell Willkie, called platforms "fusions of ambiguity." To this day, commentators assert that platforms are vague rather than specific in order to appeal to as many interest and voting groups as possible and that their content is forgotten by all concerned as soon as it has been written and approved by the convention. This conclusion is overstated. Platforms are written by party activists familiar with public issues and mindful of the party tradition. The sources of the statements they write are not simply the wishes of lobbyists or the ephemeral tactics of candidates but also existing party documents, measures sponsored by the party's President or legislators, and similar proposals. Moreover, as Gerald Pomper has concluded from his intensive study of the content of party platforms, those party promises are significant, mostly specific, statements about public policy; the substance of the Democratic and the Republican platforms does differ; and a very high percentage of the pledges made in platforms have in fact been adopted.[2] Small

1. M. Ostrogorski, *Democracy and the Organization of Political Parties*, Vol. 2: *The United States*, edited and abridged by Seymour Martin Lipset (Quadrangle Books, 1964), p. 138.
2. Gerald M. Pomper, *Elections in America: Control and Influence in Democratic Politics* (Dodd,

wonder that political leaders at conventions take the platform deliberations seriously.

Party rules are widely considered an arcane matter except by politicians. The national convention is *the* governing body of the national party; between conventions, its authority is delegated to the national committee. Procedures for constituting and running the convention may affect the fortunes of the candidates and the participants; they are ignored at political peril.

Generally, all decisions made by a national convention reflect the state of a political party at a particular point in time. They mirror the relative strength of the party factions contending for power, the issues with which they are concerned, the extent of party unity and the dimensions of diversity, and the nature of appeals for popular support. Together, the Republican and Democratic national conventions represent two political visions of the United States of America. Like any perceptions of exterior reality, the visions are not simply momentary; they are grounded in past experience and traditions, and they provide some precedents for future behavior.

EVOLUTION OF THE
CONVENTION SYSTEM

Although the strategies and tactics of presidential nominations have been in some ways remarkably similar over the years, the *conventions* that nominated Henry Clay and Andrew Jackson for president in 1832 were very different from those that selected Richard Nixon and George McGovern 140 years later. Most of the changes reflect the growth and development of the U.S. political party system, which was in a very rudimentary stage at the time conventions began. And many of the trends parallel emerging patterns in U.S. government generally. Since 1832, conventions have been routinized, na-

tionalized, and (in various ways as defined by a contemporary understanding of the term) democratized.

Routinization

By today's standards, the 1832 meetings were haphazard affairs. Leaders of the National Republican movement sought to demonstrate broadly based support for Clay in nominating him by the new device that the ephemeral Anti-Mason party had used in 1831—a national nominating convention. With little formal planning, the four-day National Republican gathering began with 130 delegates and continued with others who straggled in. Each state delegation judged its own credentials. The convention nominated Clay as the candidate of those who opposed Jackson, selected Pennsylvanian John Sergeant as Clay's running mate, appointed a committee to draft an "address to the people" on the issues, and adjourned. The Democratic convention was similar except that the committee to draft an address recommended that instead the individual delegations issue their own reports to their constituencies.

By 1972 conventions had been institutionalized in a regular cycle of activities. Permanent records were kept in year-round national committee offices. The Republican National Committee had a full-time convention director, and the less affluent Democrats hired one many months before their delegates met in Miami Beach. By long-established custom, the national committees, acting on recommendations of their site-selection committees, chose the convention cities approximately a year in advance. Each of the national committees issued an official call to the national convention that was sent to the state and territorial parties six months or more before the convention assembled. The call set forth the time and place of the convention, the method of apportioning convention votes among the delegations, rules of delegate selection, procedures for the filing of credentials and carrying on challenges to delegations, and—in the Democratic party —requirements of state party loyalty. Logis-

Mead, 1970), pp. 149–70; and "Controls and Influence in American Elections (Even 1968)," *American Behavioral Scientist,* Vol. 13 (November–December 1969), pp. 223–28.

tics and physical amenities for the convention participants were worked out by the convention director and an arrangements committee of the national committee, other staff members, local officials, those in charge of the convention hall, hotel officials, and representatives of the news media—particularly the television networks. The parties' platform committees held hearings and began deliberations at least a week before the convention. Depending on how much controversy was anticipated, the panels on credentials, rules, and permanent organization also started their work so that it would be finished before the official convention opening. Formal, written rules of procedure for Democratic conventions were approved for the first time at the 1972 Democratic convention; until then, the party had relied on a compilation of precedents recorded by the long-time parliamentarian of the convention, Congressman Clarence Cannon of Missouri. Written Republican rules dated back to the nineteenth century, although they had since been elaborated.

Nationalization

The development of this apparatus is a national phenomenon. Although it was long a truism of politics and political science in the United States that the Democratic and Republican parties were simply a collection of state Democratic and Republican parties, the situation has changed. There now exists not only a formal party organization—the convention and the national committee—but also a growing staff bureaucracy, a body of increasingly complex and specific rules, and *national standards,* enforceable by the convention, for state party behavior.

As of this writing, the most important aspect of the national standards concerns methods of selecting and seating delegates. The initial breakthrough came as a result of the Republican delegate contests of 1952, when Taft and Eisenhower forces contended for access to GOP caucuses and conventions in several southern states. The "Eisenhower Republicans"—often former Democrats—claimed that they had been shut out of dele-

gate selection caucuses; the Taft regulars charged that the Eisenhower partisans were not Republicans or at least not qualified to take part in GOP gatherings under their state party rules. After a convention credentials fight that Eisenhower won, thereby ensuring his nomination, the Republicans wrote specific delegate selection procedures into their national convention rules and have continued to adapt them as needed. Similarly, the Democrats, after a credentials contest waged by the Mississippi Freedom Democrats in 1964, established national rules against racial discrimination in delegate selection. Again, after the numerous seating challenges in 1968, the Democratic convention voted to create what became the McGovern-Fraser Commission on Party Structure and Delegate Selection, which wrote eighteen procedural guidelines to be followed by the state parties. Panels in both parties will monitor the delegate selection process in advance of the 1976 conventions.

What strikes many observers is that the state parties have abided by the national party rules. Evidently they have decided that it is in their interest to do so. After all, the national committees that voted to establish the rules were composed of state politicians. Their authority to act collectively for the party throughout the nation has been given legitimacy by the acceptance of nearly all the state leaders.

It may be ironic that national party organization and authority is growing at a time when party organizations around the country have declined and voters' party loyalty clearly has slipped. But perhaps the decline in power of the state and local organizations has made their leaders less inclined to defy their fellow partisans; and perhaps the loss of party influence over the voters has motivated the leaders to enhance whatever party solidarity remains. Loyalty, not defiance, is the basis of party organization and strength.

Influence of Polls and Primary Elections

Early conventions were gatherings of party leaders whose own judgments about the candidates and bargaining with one another determined the identity of nominees. In more recent times, popular attitudes about the candidates have played an increasingly important role.

Since systematic national polling was instituted in 1936, almost every presidential nominee has been the candidate who was ahead in the last Gallup poll before the convention. An exception came in the Democratic party in 1952, when Estes Kefauver led decisively but Adlai Stevenson was nominated. In the Republican party in 1964, the final poll gave Senator Barry Goldwater 22 percent, former Vice-President Richard M. Nixon 22 percent, Ambassador to Vietnam Henry Cabot Lodge 21 percent, and Governor William W. Scranton 20 percent; and Goldwater, of course, was nominated. Although the relationship between polls and nominations is not directly causal, it is more nearly influential than spurious.

Presidential primaries also have increased both in importance and number. Particularly since John F. Kennedy in 1960 succeeded in demonstrating his strength at the polls and minimizing the alleged drawbacks of his relative youth and Roman Catholic faith, candidates have attempted to emulate his sweep of the primaries as a path to victory. No one else has done it quite Kennedy's way, although Richard Nixon won all the Republican primaries in 1968. In any case, some major primary victories are regarded as highly desirable, if not entirely necessary for nomination. In 1972, there were many more presidential primaries than previously: twenty-three primaries in twenty-two states and the District of Columbia. The increased number resulted principally from changes in state laws needed to conform to the delegate selection guidelines of the McGovern-Fraser Commission. Whether the number of primaries will decrease again as it did after their early heyday in the Progressive Era is an open question. Many Democratic politicians have been vociferously unhappy with the experience of the 1972 primaries, concluding that candidates' physical and financial resources were strained, that the primary states

did not receive expected economic boosts despite the added publicity, and that "centrist" candidates suffered while "radicals" gained. Even though the number of primaries may be reduced, however, their collective influence is certain to remain, for they are the best indication before the convention of whether a candidate can win the election.

Judicial Regulation

Another aspect of the democratization of conventions has been the apparently increasing willingness of the courts to apply constitutional safeguards to them. Long reluctant to enter "the political thicket," the Supreme Court in 1944 ruled that political parties could not hold primary elections that were limited to white people because such a procedure violated constitutional provisions guaranteeing equal voting rights to persons of all races. During the 1960s, the Court wrote a series of decisions requiring the apportionment of legislative bodies on the basis of population, so that each district represented approximately equal numbers of voters. By implication, the apportionment of party bodies was a justiciable issue.

Between 1968 and 1972, lawsuits were filed applying those principles to conventions. In first the Democratic and then the Republican party, suits charged that the formula for apportioning the national convention was not based, as the plaintiffs argued that it should have been, on the number of party voters in preceding elections. In January 1972 the Supreme Court refused to review an appellate court decision reversing a district court ruling that struck down the Democratic National Committee's apportionment formula for 1972. A suit against the Republican formula for 1976 is still pending as this is written.

Redress from the courts has also been sought in recent seating contests. The most notable instance came at the 1972 Democratic convention over the constitutionality of California's traditionally winner-take-all primary election. The lower courts were willing to entertain the issues, but the Supreme Court declined to consider the case and one of the justices stayed an appellate court order awarding the disputed delegates to one of the parties. Although the courts remain averse to intervention in party affairs, they have done so in cases of invidious discrimination. Their future course is as yet uncharted.

Television

The ubiquity of the news media, and particularly of television, at conventions has accompanied their democratization. Conventions are more public than they used to be. While reporters have been permitted at the quadrennial gatherings from the beginning, they have enjoyed increasing access to the decision-making process.

Since the television networks began what they call gavel-to-gavel coverage in 1952, the innermost workings of conventions have been revealed to a vast new audience. Whenever politicians have attempted to keep television reporters out of meetings, the reporters have had the opportunity to broadcast a powerful image—the picture of themselves, the representatives of the public, standing outside a closed door. Not surprisingly, fewer doors have been closed since the advent of television.

Television has been partially responsible for many "cosmetic" changes in recent conventions—shorter speeches, more restrained oratory, fewer demonstrations, more decorum, increasing use of professionally prepared party films, and so forth. Scheduling has been planned to put the party's best foot forward during prime-time televiewing hours and delay the unpleasantness of intraparty battles until other times. Success in such efforts varies with the political situation: in 1972 the Republican convention that harmoniously renominated the Nixon-Agnew ticket had an actual script that was followed almost to the letter, but the far more divided Democratic convention ran until after midnight at each session.

Increasing scrutiny of the internal operations of conventions has also contributed to more substantive changes. Those who have called for "fair play," from the Eisenhower credentials contestants in 1952 through the strident Democrats of 1968 and the more genteel dissidents of both parties in 1972, might have pursued their cause without the presence of the TV cameras. Certainly the GOP dissidents of 1912 did. But the opportunity to take a cause to a national television audience means that there is a powerful motive to make conventions and all the party procedures related to them *look fair*.

Apportionment and Voting Rules

Three specific rules that have been changed since conventions began reflect changing democratic norms. At the 1832 Democratic convention, each state was given as many votes as it had in the electoral college—a reasonable enough measure of the state's share of the party's presidential constituency. The initial Republican convention in 1856 allocated each state six votes at large and three for every congressional district. As voting patterns across the nation became established, however, one-party areas developed. As a result, the convention apportionment rules did not reflect the extent of party support in each state. After the fight over apportionment in 1912, the Republicans adjusted their rule to give some recognition to party strength. The Democrats did not change their formula until President Franklin Roosevelt began looking for a convention bonus for the "solid South." As already noted, the battle still rages over the appropriate principles of convention apportionment; at issue is the question of which formula is most "fair" and "democratic."

Voting rules also have been changed for similar reasons. At President Roosevelt's request, the Democrats in 1936 agreed to abandon their traditional rule (never used by the Republicans) requiring a two-thirds majority for presidential and vice-presidential nominations, adopting instead the simple majority required for other votes. The southern states, which enjoyed considerable potential as a bloc under the two-thirds rule, accepted its abandonment in exchange for more convention representation under new apportionment rules that gave a bonus for party support. Again, the Democrats in 1968 voted to abolish the unit rule, under which all of a delegation's votes must be recorded as the majority decides. The rule was believed to interfere with a right to vote however one chooses. The unit rule has been banned at all levels of the Democratic party. The Republicans have never enforced the unit rule at their conventions, but it has operated at times; some Republicans have called for a rule against it as undemocratic in principle.

Size

Conventions are much bigger than they used to be. Changes in the apportionment rules have expanded an institution originally about the size of Congress to one with 1,348 votes in the 1972 Republican gathering and 3,016 in the Democratic conclave. New Republican rules will bring its 1976 total to around 2,000 votes. And in the Democratic party, the tradition of fractional voting has meant considerably more delegates than votes.

The major reason for increased size has been the desire of more and more people to participate, augmented by the growth in national population since 1832 and the bonus votes to reward party support. Moreover, virtually everyone active in party politics would like to attend the national convention; and those who cannot attend would like at least to be represented. Hence the inexorable trend has been toward larger conventions. It is easier to give votes than to take them away. Although journalists, political scientists, and other observers have criticized conventions as inefficient and unwieldy, they are unlikely to get any smaller because the desire to participate in them is unlikely to decline.

THE APPROACH OF THIS BOOK

This is the second edition of a book originally published by Brookings in 1960. Essentially similar in format to its predecessor, this edition has some differences based on experience with the use of the book and research done on presidential politics since

1960. The content of the chapters from the preconvention era through 1956 and the tables of voting records through 1956 have not been changed in any way. The new historical chapters and tables of roll call votes follow the same general pattern as the initial edition. Thus each narrative begins with a discussion of the political context of the two conventions—issues, candidates, salient events, records of the primary elections and public opinion polls. The two conventions are then described in roughly chronological order, with occasional pauses to explain the background of important convention decisions. Each chapter concludes with a statement of the election results, but there is no attempt to analyze the postconvention campaign.

One feature of the original edition that is not found in the later chapters is a statistical analysis of certain roll call votes. In the earlier edition, tetrachoric correlation coefficients were calculated in order to compare the voting on the presidential nomination with voting on other matters that the author considered significant. This analysis showed the extent to which delegates voting together on a contested presidential nomination also voted together on another controversial issue. As Richard Bain noted in the introduction to the original edition, such analysis could be done only when the decision of both the roll call votes was considerably less than unanimous—a closer division than 90 percent to 10 percent.[3] This is a

3. As Bain explained in the first edition, the calculations were made as follows. Delegations were classified as higher or lower than the average for the winning side of the issue vote selected. Thus in the 1844 Democratic convention, in which approximately 56 percent of the vote was cast for adoption of the two-thirds rule, all delegations that cast at least 56 percent for the rule were classified as high, and those that cast less than 56 percent were classified as low. In this instance, fourteen delegations, holding a total voting strength of 120, were high, and eleven delegations, with a voting strength of 146, were low.

The subsequent votes of the high delegations cast for other issues or on nomination ballots were counted. In the above instance, the high delegations cast 15 for Van Buren and 105 for other candidates on the first nominating ballot. Similarly, the low delegations voted 131 for Van Buren and 15 for other candidates. These figures were then entered in a matrix as follows:

fruitful method of analysis, and the calculations made for the first edition have been preserved. In keeping with the principal use of the volume as a reference work, however, calculations have not been done for the most recent conventions. The many possibilities of statistical analysis—particularly in the numerous roll calls of the 1968 and 1972 Democratic conventions—are left to the reader.

In the earlier chapters, some of the nominating roll calls are identified as "critical ballots." This term refers to the vote for the winning candidate when the real decision is reached—before the switches of votes and the bandwagon effect. For most single-ballot nominations, the critical ballot is the vote at the end of the roll call, even though a majority may be supplied only through subsequent switches, as in the 1952 Eisenhower nomination. For multiballot nominations where the final ballot is unanimous (that is, more than 90 percent for the winner), the previous ballot is defined as the critical ballot. For those multiballot nominations where the winner receives less than 90 percent of the votes before the shifts, the final roll call before the shifts is considered the critical ballot. At all the conventions from 1960 through 1972, except for Lyndon Johnson's nomination by acclamation in 1964, the presidential candidate was nominated on the initial roll call ballot.

	First ballot	
	Van Buren	Others
High for majority side of issue	15 (a)	105 (b)
Low for majority side of issue	131 (c)	15 (d)

The tetrachoric coefficient of correlation was then calculated as follows:

$$\frac{bc}{ad} = \frac{105 \times 131}{15 \times 15} = \frac{13{,}755}{225} = 62.5.$$

The estimated correlation coefficient for this ratio was obtained from a table of values of estimated tetrachoric correlation based on Pearson's "cosine methods" for various values of bc/ad. For this instance, the value of 62.5, as calculated above, equaled the estimated correlation coefficient of 0.94, indicating a very high relationship between these two votes. See Allen L. Edwards, *Statistical Methods for the Behavioral Sciences* (Rinehart, 1954).

The narrative histories of the conventions in this book are followed by three appendixes. The first lists presidential and vice-presidential nominees of the major parties from 1832 through 1972. The second lists the major convention officers of the parties during the same years. In the final and longest are found the delegation-by-delegation roll call votes of the conventions. The Democratic roll calls are presented chronologically, followed by the roll calls of Whig and Republican conventions. For conventions with less than ten presidential nominating ballots, all are listed; for those with more than ten, sampling was done. All the ballots since 1864 on issues other than the presidential nomination are listed. Incomplete records at some earlier conventions made it impossible to present all the roll call breakdowns. A brief preface to the appendix containing the roll call tabulations explains in greater detail the methods that were used in preparing it.

Omitted from this edition is an appendix that gave thumbnail biographical sketches of several hundred prominent convention participants. Reactions to the book have made it clear that the identification of persons in the text is sufficient for a general orientation to their background.

Except for scholarly references in this chapter and certain notations in the tables, the new material in this edition contains no footnotes. All the quotations and factual information were obtained from official printed convention proceedings, newspapers, and other readily available sources.

The narratives and statistical tables in this book provide a record rather than an analysis of each of the past national party conventions. They describe the issues that were debated at the conventions, not why those issues rather than others were debated or how satisfactory the resolution of the debates turned out to be. But by delineating who, what, when, and where, the book can serve as a resource for those asking the questions why and how.

THE CONVENTIONS

1789-1828

The Preconvention Years

WHEN THE ELECTORS of the ten states participating in the first American presidential election met in their respective states in February 1789 to cast their ballots, they were found to be agreed in general on two points. Almost all were staunch supporters of the new Constitution and saw in it a hope for strong federal government; all saw George Washington as the one man who could best guide the new government through its period of infancy.[1]

On the question of the Vice Presidency, the electors exercised the freedom of choice envisaged by the Constitution, and the verdict was by no means unanimous. The choice was John Adams, who received but 34 of a possible 69 votes, and the balance of the votes were scattered among ten other candidates. There was apparently no formal nomination of Adams, and his vote seems to have been by virtue of his generally accepted availability as a well-known northern statesman who would balance Washington's southern background.

PARTISANSHIP DEVELOPS

In this first election, partisan division was at a minimum, for only those who tended to support the new Constitution took part in the proceedings, and among these, clear lines of partisanship had not yet developed. By the second election, not

[1] Rhode Island and North Carolina had not yet ratified the Constitution and did not participate in the election. New York was unable to decide in the relatively short time available how its electors should be chosen, and therefore failed to select any.

only had the number of participants increased, but there was a beginning of factional divisions that were soon to develop into political parties. The main line of division was between those who preferred a strong central government and those who preferred a strong states rights position. Alexander Hamilton was the acknowledged leader of the Federalist partisans; James Madison and Thomas Jefferson were outstanding among the Antifederalists. Washington inclined toward the Federalists, despite his efforts to maintain a neutral position, but was considered far enough above the factional fight to be unopposed for re-election in 1792. In fact, Jefferson himself urged the President to run a second time on the basis that his leadership was essential to the stability of the new republic.

Partisan lines developed on the vice-presidential selection for 1792, however. John Adams' candidacy as a Federalist was taken for granted, and he seems to have received more nearly the solid support of that faction than in either the previous or the succeeding election. The Antifederalists, then in process of adopting the name "Republican" to illustrate their opposition to the monarchial tendencies they charged to John Adams and the Federalists generally, backed George Clinton for the Vice Presidency. Clinton seems to have been selected by virtue of his upset victory in winning the New York governorship on the Republican ticket; no clear record has been found as to the method by which Clinton was designated, but it seems probable that the party leaders in and out of Congress made the choice. Madison and Jefferson, the real party leaders, undoubtedly preferred to wait until the top position was open before making the race. Adams received 77 of the 132 electoral votes.

NOMINATION BY CAUCUS

In 1796, with Washington's declaration against a third term, the contest was open for both offices. The Federalist candidates, John Adams and Thomas Pinckney, and the Republican candidates, Thomas Jefferson and Aaron Burr, were designated by informal caucuses of the congressional members of the respective parties. The Federalist electors who gave 71 votes to Adams supported Pinckney with only 59 of their second votes. The Republican support for Burr was proportionately less—30 votes to Jefferson's 68. As a result, the President and the Vice President were from different parties, since the Constitution provided that the individual receiving the second highest number of votes would be the Vice President.

For the election of 1800, President Adams and Vice President Jefferson were the acknowledged leading presidential candidates for their respective parties; Charles C. Pinckney and Aaron Burr were named as their respective running mates by informal caucus of party leaders in Congress. Party lines held much more firmly, with the result that Republicans Jefferson and Burr were tied for first place with 73 votes each. Although it was generally accepted that the vote was intended to make Jefferson the President, Burr apparently made no strong move to protest his own selection for the higher office. When the decision thus went into the House of Representatives, many of the lame-duck Federalist members saw in the situation a chance to humiliate the hated Jefferson by voting for Burr. However, largely due to the influence of Hamilton, better council prevailed

and Jefferson was given his rightful place. As a result of this near debacle, the Constitution was amended to insure that electors would designate the presidential and vice-presidential candidates on their ballots.

The Republicans used the congressional caucus as their general nominating method during the period of their dominance between 1800 and 1820, though it was never accepted without protests. But the Federalists, as their membership in Congress dwindled, found it necessary to use other methods—among them, in 1808 and again in 1812, a nominating convention. These meetings were, however, quite unlike the conventions subsequently introduced in the Jacksonian period; small groups of Federalist leaders, designated in widely different ways, met in secrecy. Although the gatherings did provide a measure of legitimacy to the candidates they named, during this period no Federalist candidate stood much chance of success.

By 1824 the so-called "Era of Good Feelings" was nearing its end and the dominant Republican party was on the verge of splitting into warring factions. Several major candidates were ready to make the presidential race, but with the congressional caucus almost wholly disapproved, there was no single established method by which nominees might be selected. Therefore each candidate used the method that seemed best for him.[2]

Henry Clay of Kentucky, Andrew Jackson of Tennessee, and John C. Calhoun of South Carolina were each nominated by their state legislature. John Quincy Adams was designated by several legislatures in New England. All of these gentlemen were subsequently endorsed by legislatures of other states. William H. Crawford, Secretary of the Treasury and the administration favorite, in addition to nomination by the Virginia legislature, was endorsed by a caucus of as many members of Congress as could be induced to support him. Only 68

[2] For discussion of the congressional caucus as a nominating instrument, see David, Goldman, and Bain, op. cit., pp. 17, 96, 159.

of the 261 members of Congress attended the caucus, and a substantial number of states were totally unrepresented. It is doubtful that the caucus endorsement did Crawford much good, though the effect of a serious illness he suffered shortly before the election complicates the analysis. In any event, the bitter attacks upon the caucus as a nominating device had effectively destroyed its usefulness, and it was never employed again.

None of the nominees received a majority in the election, and the decision was again thrown into the House of Representatives. Out of the ensuing battle John Quincy Adams emerged as the victor. Andrew Jackson, as the loser under conditions that at least appeared to justify the claims of his followers that he had been defrauded, was clearly the man Adams would have to fight in the election of 1828.

Jackson technically became a candidate for the 1828 race almost as soon as the 1824 decision was reached; the Tennessee legislature again nominated him in October 1825. Adams' renomination was taken for granted; if he received a formal nomination, it was given little attention and has been lost in obscurity. An interesting aspect of 1828 was the support given by the Jacksonians to the vice-presidential renomination of John C. Calhoun, Vice President under Adams. Adams himself supported his Secretary of the Treasury, Richard Rush, as his running mate; Rush was nominated by an informal convention held in Harrisburg, Pennsylvania, apparently attended mostly by Pennsylvanians.

Jackson's victory in 1828, aside from being decisive, was important because the division between Adams and his supporters was based upon more than differences between the personalities of the candidates. Important geographical and economic patterns emerged; if institutionalized, they presaged development of programmatic parties. Jackson, at least, was able to institutionalize his coalition.

1832

THE CONTEST IN 1828 had been between loose coalitions with no more than rudimentary party organization in either camp. John Quincy Adams' defeat was followed by almost complete dissolution of his coalition; Andrew Jackson, on the other hand, tightened the reigns on his and organized the first national party worthy of the name. Not all elements of the coalition were willing to accept his firm leadership, and substantial groups, including key leaders, turned to opposition. However, Jackson's winning margin had been big enough to withstand these losses, and he looked to the election of 1832 with considerable confidence—a confidence justified by an opposition so divided that it was unable to combine on a single ticket.

The first candidate in the field was presented by the short-lived Antimason party, and the method by which he was selected established a precedent. The party, beginning as a collection of local groups in 1827 in upper New York State, had spread rapidly to other parts of the state and in 1830 burst its bounds to become a national organization. In September 1831 it held a national nominating convention in Baltimore, Maryland—the first such open convention for a major party.

The decision to hold a national meeting for the purpose of selecting a candidate was undoubtedly dictated by need. The young party was frankly sectional and had so little representation in Congress that it could not have nominated by congressional caucus had it desired to do so. Nomination by state legislature was possible, but would not have focused national attention upon the candidate. Further, since various

groups among the party members were by no means in agreement as to who the candidate should be, a forum was needed where candidacies could be discussed and a decision reached. This same forum could be used to facilitate a national organization and to project a national party image.

Thirteen states were represented, none south of Maryland. To give as much appearance of unity as possible to the nomination, three quarters of the total vote in the convention was set as the nominating majority. Although many respected political leaders had indicated sympathy for the Antimason cause, very few were willing to accept the new party's nomination. William Wirt, United States Attorney General under John Quincy Adams, finally accepted, but only after declaring that he had once been a Mason, knew of nothing invidious about Masonry, and would willingly resign if, after hearing his statement, the convention determined that another candidate would be preferred. His nomination was allowed to stand.

THE NATIONAL REPUBLICAN CONVENTION

Most of those who cooperated in the National Republican movement were drawn together by common opposition to

1 The National Republicans are selected as constituting the second major party of the two-party system on the grounds that they polled the second highest vote in the 1832 election and that they were in several ways most nearly the lineal precursors of the Whigs.

For brief biographical data on key figures of both 1832 conventions—and the conventions of all ensuing years—see Appendix B.

Andrew Jackson's positions on the tariff and/or internal improvements.[1] The leading champion for anti-Jacksonians on both these issues was Henry Clay of Kentucky. For the industrial East, he espoused high protective tariffs; for the expanding West, he urged sale of public lands and use of the revenues from these sales for roads, canals, and other public improvements. However, although these were the issues around which the coalition first was formed, the issue that was actually dominant in the campaign concerned the National Bank—should it be rechartered or not?

Clay also was the congressional leader in the fight against Jackson's attempt to destroy the Bank and probably more than any other was responsible for the question becoming a campaign issue. The Bank charter was not due to expire until 1836, but, largely at the insistence of Clay, Congress passed a rechartering act in 1831, which Jackson vetoed. In the fight that followed, the major antagonists were Clay and Jackson.

Although the new party had no problem in selecting a candidate, as Clay was the obvious choice, it did face the problem of how to present him as a truly national candidate backed by a national organization against the well-organized administration party. The old method of nomination by state legislature would not serve the purpose. Accordingly, the device used by the Antimasons was adopted, and a national nominating convention was called.

Baltimore, Maryland, December 12, 13, 14, 15, 1831

The first and only national meeting of the new party was held under inauspicious conditions. The weather throughout the eastern coastal area was so bad that roads were almost impassable, and many delegates were delayed. When the convention was called to order at noon on December 12, only 130 delegates were present, but stragglers kept arriving throughout the proceedings and even after the nominations had been completed. Eventually, before the convention adjourned, all states then in the Union except Tennessee were represented, although in disproportionate numbers.

Convention Organization

The temporary chairman was selected by motion from the floor, and the convention turned its attention to the question of the legitimacy of its membership. No committee on credentials was appointed, but by resolution the question was left to each state to decide for itself. The resolution read:

That the delegations of the several States represented in this convention be requested to examine the credentials (or the evidence of appointment) of the members of their respective States, and report a list of their names tomorrow at 12 o'clock.[2]

The next question related to the press. Objection was raised to a motion "inviting" editors to seats on the convention floor, and the suggestion was made that instead they be "permitted" to take seats. Evidently hostile members of the press were present, and in a period when most publications were highly factional in their treatment of political news many delegates questioned the advisability of "inviting" bitter critics to hear the convention deliberations; if they must be allowed in the hall, it should be on sufferance. The original motion carried, however, and the press was "invited."

A committee of five was appointed to select permanent officers, and chose former Governor James Barbour of Virginia as permanent chairman. Barbour recognized

[2] *Niles' Register*, Vol. 41, Dec. 24, 1831, p. 301. This influential weekly journal, published in Baltimore by Hezekiah Niles, featured government and political news. It served as quasi-official reporter for the earliest conventions and is therefore used in this book as the chief source for the proceedings up to 1856.

the many factions present and urged the need for subordination of special interests for the good of the whole.

In a display of patriotism, the convention invited Charles Carroll of nearby Carrollton, venerable signator of the Declaration of Independence, to attend, but he was unable to come because of his ill health and the inclement weather.

The Presidential Nomination

The nominating proceedings began with a motion:

That the convention do *now* proceed to nominate a candidate for the office of president of the United States, to be supported by those who are opposed to the re-election of Andrew Jackson.[3]

The wording of the resolution was significant in its negative rather than positive tone, for the National Republicans—as the Whigs after them—were never able to become a positively oriented party. After the resolution passed, a letter from Clay was read. He urged the delegates to disregard commitments to him and to make whatever choice they thought best. He assured them that he would support the convention choice.

With no pre-established ground rules for taking the vote, it was agreed that each member's name should be called, whereupon he would announce his own vote. Every delegate, as was expected, announced for Henry Clay.

The Vice-Presidential Nomination

The same procedure was followed in nominating the vice-presidential candidate. With equal unanimity former House member John Sergeant of Pennsylvania was nominated.

Following Sergeant's nomination, a committee was suggested to determine the costs of running the convention and to arrange to pay for it. A Baltimore delegate assured the convention that Baltimore citizens would take care of all costs for the hall and its operations. However, it was pointed out that other costs, such as printing and postage, were not included in this generosity, and a committee was therefore appointed.

There being no formal party organization such as is now supplied by the national committees, a temporary recommendation was made by resolution:

Resolved, That a central state corresponding committee be provisionally appointed in each state where none are now appointed. And that it be recommended to the several states to organize subordinate corresponding committees in each county and town, in their several respective states.[4]

The Platform

No platform, in the modern sense, was prepared, but a committee "to prepare an address to the people of the United States" was appointed. While the committee was working, the convention recessed and proceeded in a body to the residence of Charles Carroll to pay its respects. Meanwhile, letters of thanks were received from both nominees, as well as their promises to conduct an energetic campaign.

The address to the people consisted primarily of an attack on Jackson and his administration. It pointed out that Jackson had entered the White House under unusually favorable conditions: his majority had been overwhelming, the country was prosperous, and there were no sharply divisive interests to plague him. According to the address, all this had changed—he had fought with factions within his party as well as outside his party. He had fought with Congress and with the courts. The national economy had fallen sharply as the result of his policies. The country was now divided on many issues. What was needed to correct the nation's ills, the address concluded, was a change of the man in the White House.

[3] *Ibid., p.* 302.

[4] *Ibid., p.* 305.

FIRST DEMOCRATIC CONVENTION

With his own re-election almost a certainty, President Jackson's major concern was the selection of his running mate. The brilliant but erratic South Carolinian, John C. Calhoun, elected as Jackson's Vice President in 1828, had been one of the first leaders to fall out of the coalition. Subsequent events increased the acrimony between the two men, and the peak of enmity was reached when Calhoun's was the deciding vote against the confirmation of Martin Van Buren as Minister to England. As a result, Jackson was determined to push Van Buren into the Vice Presidency in 1832, with the further resolve that he should succeed to the Presidency in 1836.

To ensure Van Buren's selection as the vice-presidential candidate, Jackson could not depend with certainty on either of the nominating methods used in the past, such as endorsement by congressional caucus or by state legislature. Jackson himself had already been nominated for 1832 by the state legislatures, as he had been also in his former two campaigns. But if the vice-presidential nomination were made by this method, there was a strong probability that several candidates would be offered by various legislatures, making the ultimate choice of Van Buren uncertain. What Jackson needed was a means by which party leaders in all the states could be committed to one candidate. Borrowing a leaf from the opposition, he arranged to call his own nominating convention.

Baltimore, Maryland,
May 21, 22, 23, 1832

The convention met in response to a call promulgated by the New Hampshire legislature. The meeting was called to order by a representative of that state who declared that the

. . . object of the people of New Hampshire who called this convention was, not to impose on the people, as candidates for either of the two first offices of the government, any local favorite; but to concentrate the opinions of all the states. . . . They believed that the example of this convention would operate favorably in future elections; that the people would be disposed, after seeing the good effects of this convention in conciliating, the different and distant sections of the country, to continue this mode of nomination.[5]

Convention Organization

Most of the basic features of future Democratic conventions were found in this first one. A slight hitch occurred in selecting the temporary chairman when it was announced that the original choice was confined to his room by sudden indisposition. Another was chosen from the floor. A committee of one member from each state was appointed "to report to the convention the names of the delegates in attendance." Apparently the only question before the committee was the status of the District of Columbia delegation. The committee dodged the issue by recommending to the convention that "they should be admitted as members, under such regulations as the convention should deem proper," whereupon by a vote of 126 to 153 (the roll call is not given by state) the convention refused the delegation the right to vote. However, subsequent to the nominating ballot, and after a resolution declaring Van Buren to be the unanimous nominee for the Vice Presidency, a resolution was passed permitting the District of Columbia vote to be recorded in his favor.

Permanent Organization and Rules

The committee on rules acted also as a committee for selecting the permanent officers of the convention. Robert Lucas of Ohio was chosen as permanent chairman, and four vice presidents and three secretaries were also selected. The rules were brief but of great importance to future Democratic conventions. They read:

[5] *Ibid.,* Vol. 42, May 26, 1832, p. 234.

Resolved, That the delegates from each State in this Convention, be entitled to as many votes in selecting a suitable person for the office of Vice President, as such State will be entitled to in the Electoral College for the choice of this officer, equally to the apportionment bill, recently passed by the Congress of the United States; and that two thirds of the whole number of votes given be required to a nomination and on all questions connected therewith.

Resolved, That in taking the vote, the majority of the delegates from each state designate the person by whom the votes for that state shall be given.

Resolved, That the meetings of the convention be opened by prayer, and that the rev. clergy of this city be respectfully invited to perform the duty.

Resolved, That the candidate for the vice presidency shall be designated by the ballot or ballots of the person or persons selected for this purpose, by the respective delegations, without nomination in convention—and that if a choice is not had upon the first ballotting, the respective delegations shall retire and prepare for a second ballotting, and continue this mode of voting, until a selection is made.[6]

No debate on the resolutions is recorded, and no evidence is given of any opposition being voiced. The principle of apportionment on the basis of electoral college strength was retained in pure form in subsequent Democratic conventions until 1940, when a bonus system was added. The second part of the first rule—the two thirds rule for a nominating majority—established a precedent which, though a recurring source of controversy, lasted until 1936. Part of the future controversy resulted from the ambiguity of the phrase: "two thirds of the whole number of votes given." This subsequently was interpreted variously to mean two thirds of the apportioned strength of the convention, whether or not all were present and voting, or two thirds of those actually present and voting.

The second resolution established the principle that the vote of a delegation should be announced by its chairman rather than by each delegate voting independently. An interesting feature of the fourth resolution is the restriction against nominating speeches—a restriction long since abandoned. Since Van Buren supporters controlled the convention, the probable purpose of the rule was to prevent disruption of the established voting line-up by inflammatory oratory. The resolution was not presented with the first three, but just before the resolution to proceed with the nomination.

The Presidential Nomination

The convention did not actually nominate Jackson for the presidential candidacy, contenting itself with the following resolution:

That the convention repose the highest confidence in the purity, patriotism and talents of Andrew Jackson, and that we most cordially concur in the repeated nominations which he has received in various parts of the union, as a candidate for re-election to the office which he now fills with so much honor to himself and usefulness to his country.[7]

The Vice-Presidential Nomination

Van Buren was nominated on the first ballot with 208 votes to 49 for Philip P. Barbour and 26 for Richard M. Johnson. The convention then recessed. When it reconvened, the Virginia delegation, which had voted for Barbour, presented a resolution of support to Van Buren, and the nomination was declared unanimous.

The Platform

At this late stage, a committee was appointed "to draft an address to the people of the United States." After deliberation, this committee reported that it was deemed advisable for

. . . the several delegations in this convention, in place of a general address from this body to

---

[6] *Proceedings of a Convention of Republican Delegates, Baltimore*, 1832, pp. 6-7.

The name "Democratic" was not officially used until 1840. In 1832 the Jacksonian party was still at times called Republican, but more usually Democratic-Republican.

[7] *Proceedings*, 1832, p. 7; *Niles' Register*, Vol. 42. May 26, 1832, p. 235.

the people of the United States, to make such explanation by address, report, or otherwise, to their respective constituents of the objects, proceedings and result of the meeting as they may deem expedient.[8]

The committee further recommended that the president of the convention appoint a "general corresponding committee from each state." This was adopted. The committee appointed varied from three to eighteen members from each delegation, but the number appointed for each state did not necessarily reflect the size of the state; New York was represented by only three members, compared to eighteen each for

[8] *Niles' Register*, Vol. 42, May 26, 1832, pp. 235-236.

Pennsylvania and Virginia and fifteen for Tennessee.

The account of the proceedings in *Niles' Register* closes with the note that the list of delegates would be published in subsequent editions. However, the space requirements of onrushing events precluded this, and succeeding volumes frequently deplored that much that should be reported was omitted because of lack of space. A list of delegates is included in *The Proceedings of a Convention of Republican Delegates from the Several States of the Union, Baltimore,* printed by Samuel Harker in 1832. However, this account does not provide as much other detail as *Niles' Register*.

Presidential Election, December 4, 1832

ANDREW JACKSON (D) : popular vote, 707,000; electoral vote, 219
HENRY CLAY (NR) : popular vote, 329,000, electoral vote, 49

1836

DURING HIS TWO TERMS Andrew Jackson did much to stabilize the unorganized coalition that won him his first election. Inevitably, in the process of forcing competing factions into a party framework, he antagonized some—who departed to join the ranks of the opposition. Jackson's own stature was indicated, and the opposition's lack of cohesion illustrated, by the fact that the Democratic party of the day was best known as the Jacksonian party, and the opposition, composed of heirs of the old Federalists, dissident Democrats, and a hodgepodge of others, found their one common ground in being anti-Jacksonians.

Despite the division of the opposition, Jackson had no easy time during his administration. His own proclivity for seeing every issue as black or white encouraged him to take positive stands on almost everything; his powerful will, accompanied by complete faith in his own decisions, made bitter conflict with all other sources of power inevitable. Some of the charges made against him in the National Republican address to the people were close to the truth: he fought with Congress; he fought with the courts; he fought with other political leaders who disagreed with him.

He was backed, however, by a group of politically acute followers, who despite being sorely tried on occasion, were almost fanatical in their loyalty to him. He also was backed by the voices and the votes of thousands of citizens, particularly of the less privileged classes, who were equally fanatical in their loyalty. Had he wished to try, he almost certainly could have won a third term. However, he was plagued by ill health throughout his tenure, and this alone may have been enough to persuade him not to make the effort—in any case, he did not, but being the man he was, he fully intended to dictate his successor.

SECOND DEMOCRATIC CONVENTION

In 1832, Andrew Jackson had found the national nominating convention to be a suitable device for confirming his choice for Vice President, Martin Van Buren. The question then became one of finding the best way to confirm the same man for the presidential succession in 1836. Jackson was enough of a politician to recognize storm clouds when he saw them, and he knew that there would be much objection to Van Buren's nomination. To deprive this opposition of time to develop an effective strategy and to settle upon one candidate to oppose Van Buren, Jackson called a nominating convention over a year before the election.

Baltimore, Maryland,
May 20, 21, 22, 1835

No call is printed in the proceedings of the convention as reported in *Niles' Register,* but the report of the first day is preceded by the following statement:

Proceedings of a convention of delegates appointed by the "democratic republicans" in the several states of the union, assembled in the city of Baltimore, May 20, 1835, for the purpose of nominating candidates for the offices of president and vice president of the United States.

The delegations were irregular in size, the numbers apparently being determined more by distance than by voting strength

20

of the states. South Carolina, Tennessee, Alabama, and Illinois did not send delegations, but one resident from Tennessee, who was in Baltimore on other business, was allowed to cast the 15 votes allotted to his state. The other three states did not vote. Other delegations were as follows:

State	Number of Delegates	Votes Allowed
Maine	16	10
New Hampshire	20	7
Massachusetts	18	14
Vermont	7	7
Rhode Island	8	4
Connecticut	6	8
New York	42	42
New Jersey	63	8
Pennsylvania	60	30
Delaware	14	3
Maryland	188	10
Virginia	100	23
North Carolina	15	15
Georgia	3	11
Kentucky	13	15
Tennessee	1	15
Ohio	18	21
Indiana	11	9
Mississippi	2	4
Missouri	2	4
Louisiana	3	5
Michigan Territory	2	0
Arkansas Territory	1	0

Convention Organization

Andrew Stevenson of Virginia was selected both as temporary and permanent chairman. Two committees were appointed, one "to report rules for the government of the convention," the other to provide "a list of names of the members from the several states." The only contest before the latter concerned the Pennsylvania delegation, in which two opposing groups claimed to be the properly constituted representatives from that state. Both delegations were accepted by the convention to share the vote of the state, a compromise which, in the words of the reporter, "satisfied neither party." Both factions voted together in the two nominating ballots, but split on at least one other vote. In the course of the debate on the Pennsylvania credentials, the important question arose as to whether Pennsylvania should be allowed to vote on questions pertaining to organization of the convention prior to the credentials question being settled. After discussion, the convention was unwilling to make a final decision, and cut the Gordian knot by resolving that the Pennsylvania delegates be *excused* from serving on the credentials committee.

The rules committee had more difficulty, although the parts of its report that provided for six vice presidents to aid the permanent chairman and four secretaries to record the proceedings, and that adopted the rules of the House of Representatives so far as applicable to govern the proceedings met no objections. However, three important questions arose with respect to voting: (1) What should be the relative voting strength of the several delegations? (2) How should the delegation votes be cast? (3) What should constitute a nominating majority?

Proposed answers to these questions were provided in two resolutions presented by the chairman of the rules committee.

Resolved, That in taking the vote for the nomination of president and vice president, a majority of the delegation from each state shall designate the member or members who shall give the vote of the state.

Resolved, That the delegates from each state in this convention be entitled to as many votes in selecting suitable persons for the offices of president and vice president, as such state is entitled to in the electoral college for the choice of the officers by law, and that two thirds of the whole number of votes given be required for a nomination, and all questions connected therewith.[1]

The first resolution recognized the delegations as representatives of federal units rather than as individuals. No discussion appears in the account of the convention given in *Niles' Register*; the resolution was apparently accepted without serious ques-

[1] *Niles' Register*, Vol. 48, May 30, 1835, p. 227.

tion. The same appears to be true for the first part of the second resolution, directing that the delegation from each state be given the same number of votes held by the states as electoral college votes. But a sharp debate arose over the question of the majority to be required for nomination. Those supporting the original resolution stressed the need for an appearance of solidarity in the nominations. One of the supporters of the two thirds majority requirement, Romulus M. Saunders, insisted:

. . . no one had the most remote desire to frustrate the proceedings of the conventions; and provided a majority should on the first or second ballot, fix upon an individual, it was reasonably to be expected that the minority would be disposed to yield and unite with the majority, so as to produce the effect contemplated.

Ironically, Saunders was to become a key figure in the group that stopped the nomination of Van Buren in 1844 despite the fact that Van Buren received a majority on the first ballot. According to the reporter for *Niles' Register:*

The two thirds principle was probably intended to affect the nomination of vice president—and to keep out Mr. R. M. Johnson; many being willing, as we understand, to make no nomination rather than accept of [sic] him.[2]

An amendment changing the nomination requirement to a simple majority was accepted by a vote of 231 to 210, the vote apparently being taken by individual delegates instead of by electoral college weight, since the total electoral vote was only 265. Subsequently, however, the majority rule clause was reconsidered, and the two thirds rule reimposed by voice vote.

One other aspect of the rule was important in future conventions as it could have been in this, although nothing in the proceedings indicates any question being raised. The wording of the resolution that "two thirds of the whole number of votes given be required for a nomination" was apparently interpreted by the convention as two thirds of the votes present in the

convention. Since South Carolina, Alabama, and Illinois were unrepresented this was quite a different thing from two thirds of the entire electoral vote—an important difference when the vote for Johnson is noted. The unrepresented states held a total of 23 electoral votes, which, added to the 265 votes actually present in the convention, amounted to a total of 288 votes.[3]

The Nominations

No question arose on the roll call for Martin Van Buren as the presidential candidate, for he received all of the 265 votes present. But Richard M. Johnson received only 178 votes, 1 vote more than two thirds of the strength of the delegates present in the convention, and 14 less than two thirds of the 288 votes constituting the electoral vote of all the states then in the Union.

The proceedings in *Niles' Register* do not report any question being raised on this point, but do record a question on the problem of the unit rule. Immediately following the roll call on the vice-presidential nomination, a delegate from Ohio stated that some of that delegation were for former Senator William C. Rives of Virginia, but that they had been operating under the misapprehension that the delegation must vote as a unit. Shortly thereafter a Michigan delegate stated that if the unit rule prevailed, the entire Michigan vote, which had been split 4 for Johnson and 10 for Rives, should go to Rives. Neither vote change was allowed, but if the convention had ruled either way and allowed a corresponding vote change, a second ballot would have been required. This would also have been true if the convention had ruled that a two thirds majority meant two thirds of all states in the Union (the convention of 1860 did so

<hr/>

[2] *Ibid.*, p. 228.

[3] Michigan and Arkansas, with 3 votes each, were in territorial status at the time of the convention, but joined the Union in time to vote in the election.

rule). All states but Virginia finally agreed to support the full ticket; Virginia held out against the nomination of Johnson.

As in 1832, a committee was appointed to draft "an address to the people of the United States, or resolutions, to be submitted to the convention or both as the committee shall think most advisable."[4] Also as in 1832, it was resolved that each session be opened with prayer, that the balloting for nominees proceed without nominating speeches being made, and that there be repeated balloting, if a first ballot was unsuccessful.

Almost all of the questions that would plague future Democratic conventions from then on were raised in one form or another, and many of the 1836 arguments for or against particular interpretations of important rules would be heard repeatedly through the years. Some of the decisions reached by the 1836 delegates emerged fairly well crystallized, although they were retested in subsequent conventions before they found final shape; others apparently were made without much thought—their potentiality as trouble spots being perceived only dimly as the delegates passed on quickly to what seemed more important business. But every convention since has been played against the backdrop of this one—the first convention in which a modern politician might have felt somewhat at home.

[4] *Niles' Register,* Vol. 48, May 30, 1835, p. 228.

THE ANTI-JACKSON NOMINATIONS

Neither the National Republicans nor the Antimasons had been able to follow up their attempts to develop stable national parties, and in 1836 the emerging Whig party was still in the infant stage. Many eminent men were among the Whig leaders; the new party had already made important gains in state and local offices, but it possessed neither the organization nor the central unity of purpose necessary for a national campaign. Accordingly, the Whig leaders decided to make a virtue of necessity, by adopting a strategy that seemed best for the occasion: instead of nominating by a convention, they would attempt to run a strong sectional candidate against Van Buren in each of the various areas of the country, in the hope that these candidates could between them win a majority of the electoral vote and thus throw the election into the House of Representatives.

In Massachusetts, Daniel Webster was the candidate. Throughout most of the South the candidate was Senator Hugh L. White of Tennessee. In most of the other states General William Henry Harrison was named on the ballot. By the criterion of total success, the strategy did not work, but the combined vote of the anti-Jackson or Whig candidates indicated a nationally balanced electorate for the Whig party if all of the elements could somehow be brought together into one camp.

Presidential Election, December 6, 1836

MARTIN VAN BUREN (D): popular vote, 765,483; electoral vote, 170

WILLIAM HENRY HARRISON (W): popular vote, 549,567; electoral vote, 73; total Whig or anti-Jackson popular vote, 739,795

1840

SHORTLY AFTER TAKING the oath of office in 1837, Martin Van Buren was confronted by a serious national depression—a depression blamed by anti-Jacksonians on Jackson's fiscal policies and particularly upon his destruction of the National Bank. In a day when the responsibilities and potentials of the federal government for intervening in economic crises were even less understood and far less acceptable than they are today, Van Buren took little effective action—an especially understandable procedure for the leader of a party whose every platform throughout the pre-Civil War period denied the right of the federal government to undertake internal improvements and insisted upon a strict states rights interpretation of the Constitution.

FIRST WHIG CONVENTION

The Whigs' 1836 strategy of running sectional favorites against Van Buren to throw the election into the House of Representatives had failed in its immediate objective. Nevertheless, analysis of the vote disclosed widespread anti-Jacksonian strength. Could this strength be focused upon one candidate? The problem was difficult, for the only common ground held by the many factions was opposition to Jackson and his followers, now nominally led by Van Buren.

One of the larger of these factions was led by Henry Clay, but the very fact that he was a factional leader militated against him as a coalition choice, some factions of which were almost as opposed to Clay and his program as they were to Jackson himself. Other leaders, among them Daniel Webster, were similarly handicapped, and the situation was ripe for nomination of someone whose name was well known, but whose political record did not alienate any of the important factions. Two such potential candidates were in the field—General Winfield Scott, and General William Henry Harrison.

Clay was not to be beaten without a struggle, for his supporters mustered considerable delegate strength. His opposition concentrated on the cry "Clay can't win." The leader of the Clay opponents, Thurlow Weed, a shrewd and powerful New York politician who had formerly been a leading Antimason, attacked Clay support wherever he could. His work in New York State was particularly effective. One strategy used there was the so-called "triangular correspondence" whereby men professing to be Clay supporters wrote to men in other parts of the state and expressed regrets that Clay had no strength in the writer's part of the state. The recipients, who were also in on the scheme, showed the letters to real Clay supporters and expressed their regrets in turn that it appeared Clay could not carry the state. The device shook the confidence of the Clay people, but was not enough to persuade them to support his nearest competitor—Harrison. Weed accordingly urged them to support General Scott as an interim measure, and between the true Harrison strength, the true Scott strength, and the Clay partisans who agreed to support Scott as a compromise measure, Weed was successful in keeping New York out of the Clay column.

Harrison had run well against Van Buren in several states in 1836, at a time when relative prosperity favored the administration party. In the states where the two men faced each other, Harrison won nearly 49 per cent of the popular vote, and he did this without taking a firm stand upon any issue—nor had he taken any stand since. Winfield Scott was by far the weakest of the three Whig candidates. At the opening of the convention part of his delegation strength, particularly in the New York delegation, was willing to shift to Harrison if the latter showed real strength.

Harrisburg, Pennsylvania,
December 4, 5, 6, 1839

Approximately 254 delegates were listed as authorized delegates in the report of the proceedings. Although this total was the same as the total number of electoral votes in the states represented, some of the delegations did not reflect their state's exact electoral college voting strength but over represented or under represented it. On the whole, however, both the Whig convention and the Democratic convention indicated increased acceptance of the principle of a direct relationship between the number of delegates and electoral college apportionment.

During the reading of the roll, a contest was announced in the Pennsylvania delegation; after a short debate, further discussion was postponed, and the roll continued. No committee on credentials appears to have been appointed, and it was announced at the next session that the contest had been compromised, apparently by action of the delegation itself. A committee was appointed to nominate permanent officers for the convention, following which a motion was made to recess until three o'clock that afternoon. After debate, the motion was amended to change the time of reconvening to ten o'clock the next morning. Justification for the change in

time was "to give the members of the convention an opportunity of communicating together. . . . Evil consequences were very apt to succeed hasty action." The motion was approved as amended.

The report of the committee on permanent organization was read and accepted on the morning of the second day, and following an acceptance speech by the permanent chairman, James Barbour of Virginia, the real business of the convention began. The first issue was whether the Louisiana delegation should be allowed to cast the Arkansas votes by proxy. In view of the liberality of the convention in allowing the full vote to delegations with partial representation, it seems possible that the Arkansas request might have been granted had it not been that the letter from Arkansas party members making the request also stipulated the votes were to be cast for Clay and Tyler. Since Clay opponents controlled the convention, it is not surprising the letter was tabled.

The next subject was critical to the final decisions of the convention: the manner in which the nominations were to be made. The unusual arrangement finally adopted was prompted by the Clay opposition's fear that Clay could not be stopped if the vote were taken openly in the convention, without application of the unit rule. Clay's popularity was so great that many delegates were only willing to vote against him if they could do so anonymously. Furthermore, strong pro-Clay minorities existed in several delegations, notably among them the New York delegation, and these might turn the tide if recognized. The rule adopted appears to have been the culmination of Thurlow Weed's cleverly contrived campaign.

The original motion was made by a member of the pro-Harrison Pennsylvania delegation. He proposed that one or more members from each state should be designated as a committee; the individuals would caucus with their delegations on the nomination and report the results to the committee. If no majority resulted, new caucuses were to be held and the procedure repeated until the majority was reached. During the debate, the intention became clear that the full vote for a delegation should be cast by the majority—unit rule, in other words.

A pro-Clay amendment to the motion proposed that the results of the state caucuses be submitted to the convention, and that the minority votes be recorded. This was supported by a pro-Clay member of the New York delegation, who pleaded that minority votes should be counted. Boies Penrose of Pennsylvania, who had been working closely with Weed, countered with an argument supporting the committee proposal, and adding that states without full delegations should be allowed to vote the full electoral strength. Based upon the delegate list in *Niles' Register*, this would add slightly more to Harrison strength than to Clay. Debate was long and general, but in the end the anti-Clay group got all that it wanted. Since the rule is unique in convention history, it is quoted here in full:

Ordered. That the delegates from each state be requested to assemble as a delegation, and appoint a committee not exceeding three in number, to receive the views and opinions of such delegation, and communicate the same to the assembled committees of all the delegations, to be by them respectively reported to their principals; and that thereupon the delegates from each state, be requested to assemble as a delegation, and ballot for candidates for the offices of president and vice president, and having done so, to commit the ballot designating the votes of each candidate and by whom given to its committee; and thereupon all the committees shall assemble and compare the several ballots, and report the result of the same to their several delegations, together with such facts as may bear upon the nomination, and said delegation shall forthwith re-assemble and ballot again for candidates for the above offices, and again commit the result to the above committees, and if it shall appear that a majority of the ballots are for any one man for candidate for president, said committee shall report the result to the convention for its consideration; but if there shall be no such majority, then the delegations shall repeat the balloting until such a majority shall be obtained, and then re-

port the same to the convention for its consideration.

That the vote of a majority of each delegation shall be reported as the vote of that state; and each state represented here shall vote its full electoral vote by such delegation in the committee.[1]

The Presidential Nomination

The committee deliberations do not appear in the proceedings, but some information was gleaned from members present and reported elsewhere. The results of the first committee ballot indicate the success of the scheme. Clay led with 102 votes; Harrison followed with 91; and Scott trailed with 57.[2] The 42 New York votes were recorded for Scott, and clearly held the balance of power; with 128 votes required for a majority, the New York delegation could nominate either of the leaders.

Nevertheless, no nomination was made for over twenty-four hours, while the convention cooled its heels. Thurlow Weed's explanation, and he should have been in as good a position to know as anyone, was that this time was used in an effort to placate the Clay supporters in the hope of gaining more effective support for the election campaign. Finally, New York moved. On the final ballot presented to the convention Harrison led with 148 votes to Clay's 90, and Scott's 16. Following the usual speeches, Harrison was declared the unanimous nominee.

The Vice-Presidential Nomination

After such a bitter struggle, the exigencies of "availability" called for selection of a running mate drawn from the Clay ranks. The convention choice fell unanimously upon Clay's friend John Tyler of Virginia. His assets for the ticket included his residence in a southern state; he was also a

[1] *Niles' Register*, Vol. 42, Dec. 14, 1839, pp. 249-250.
[2] Nathan Sargent, *Public Men and Events* (1875), Vol. 2, p. 91. This account indicates that Kentucky voted 14 instead of 15 in accordance with the electoral vote, and that Michigan did not vote.

recent convert from the Democratic party—if he was a convert at all—and as such could be expected to attract non-Whig support.

The Platform

Nothing was said of platform or principles throughout the convention. Even in the course of the speeches, the theme was anti-Van Buren and anti-Democratic rather than pro-anything at all specific. Thus, with no platform, with an elderly gentleman whose fame rested upon obscure military exploits of a generation before, and with a converted Democrat as his running mate, the Whig party moved toward its first national victory.

THIRD DEMOCRATIC CONVENTION

Despite depression within the nation and jealousies within his party, the renomination of the incumbent President, Martin Van Buren, would have been difficult to stop even if anyone had tried—which nobody did. This did not mean that Van Buren could control the convention completely—certainly not to the extent of dictating his choice of running mate. It may, however, have been with his acquiescence, if not by his suggestion, that the convention took the extraordinary steps it did regarding the vice-presidential nomination.

Baltimore, Maryland, May 5 and 6, 1840

As in 1831 and 1835, the convention of 1840 was called by the Democratic members of the New Hampshire legislature. Twenty-one of the twenty-six states then in the Union were represented, no delegations appearing from Connecticut, Delaware, South Carolina, Virginia, or Illinois. New Jersey sent an oversized delegation, fifty-nine in all, to share the 8 votes allotted the state. Only one delegate was present to cast the 14 votes for Massachusetts and one for the 3 votes from Arkansas, and these

must have been busy men if they fulfilled proper functions as members of the platform, permanent organization, and nominating committees. Several other states also were under represented, but since each delegation was given its state's full electoral college vote, the number of individuals in the delegation made little difference.

Convention Organization

The convention moved smoothly through the organizational phases, perhaps because of past experience, or because it was quite generally agreed at the outset what the decisions were to be. Isaac Hill of New Hampshire was named temporary chairman. After the credentials and permanent organization committees reported, with no apparent difficulties, a committee was appointed "to prepare resolutions declaratory of the principles of the Republican party of the Union," another "to prepare an address in support of the principles of the Republican party of the Union," and a third, consisting of one member from each state, "for the purpose of taking into consideration, and reporting at the next session of the Convention, upon the subject of the nominations of President and Vice-President of the United States."

The Platform

The brief platform contained essentially the same statements that had been made in previous "addresses" and that would constitute the party program for some years to come. It advocated strict construction of the Constitution; opposed federal concern with internal improvements, such as highways and canals; and bitterly opposed a national bank. The resolutions were read and passed without comment, but the reading of the address was delayed somewhat by a discussion as to the propriety of its being read before the nominations were made, since it mentioned the name of the probable nominee. When assurance was tendered that only the presidential nominee was mentioned, objection was withdrawn and the address was read and approved. In content and in form it resembled the keynote speeches of more modern days—and was a very long document. Addressed *To the People of the United States,* it began with a dissertation on the principles of the Democratic party; discussed in detail how Van Buren had followed those principles in his administration and the progress made during his term and Jackson's; outlined the dangers of turning the government over to the opposition; and closed with the plea:

Freemen of the United States, choose between these parties and these candidates! The decision is yours and the stake is yours!

The Nominations

The nomination for President and Vice President was entrusted to a committee appointed for the purpose, subject to approval by the convention. This unusual procedure apparently was dictated by the realization that, while no contest would be made for the presidential nomination, disagreement on the vice-presidential candidate was almost certain—and could precipitate an open convention fight so bitter and disruptive as to endanger the party prospects. A committee operating in closed session might resolve the problem, without exhibiting the extent of the party split.

The committee presented two resolutions, each with an explanatory preamble. The first, recommending the renomination of President Van Buren, was accepted without dissent. The second recommended that no candidate be selected by the convention for the Vice Presidency. Its argument was based upon the fact that several states, including some not represented in the convention, were presenting candidates for Vice President. In view of the fact that all the proposed candidates

. . . have filled the various public trusts confided to them, ably and faithfully, and have thereby secured for themselves the confidence of their republican fellows, . . . the Convention deem it expedient at the present time not to choose between the individuals in nomination, but to leave the decision to their republican fellow-citizens in the several states, trusting that before the election shall take place, their opinions shall become so concentrated as to secure a choice of a Vice-President by the electoral colleges.[3]

Objection was made by the partisans of Vice President Johnson, and a roll call vote was demanded. Nowhere in the proceedings is mention made of rules or of a committee on rules. Even during the discussion of the resolution not to nominate a candidate for Vice President, no question was raised as to the majority by which the committee approved the decision. The only question raised referred to the number of votes allowed each state. Once the delegates were satisfied that electoral college weights were used, and that their own states had voted in accordance with the state caucus, no further objection was made, and the resolutions were approved by voice vote.

Throughout, the terms "Republican" and "Democratic" were used interchangeably, as were "Whig" and "Federalist" for the opposition. The proceedings were published under the title *Proceedings of the National Democratic Convention;* on the title page the resolutions were termed "Expressive of the sentiments of the Democratic Party of the Union."

[3] *Proceedings of the National Democratic Convention,* 1840, p. 19.

Presidential Election, December 2, 1840

WILLIAM HENRY HARRISON (W): popular vote, 1,274,624; electoral vote, 234
MARTIN VAN BUREN (D) : popular vote, 1,127,781; electoral vote, 60

1844

THE WHIG ATTEMPT in 1840 to broaden the party's base of potential support by nominating an anti-administration Democrat for Vice President was successful in the election, but soon backfired. After barely a month in office, the aged Harrison died, and John Tyler succeeded. Throughout his political career Tyler had shown strong traits of independence, and he did not change when he became President. He soon broke with his erstwhile Whig supporters over the issue of the National Bank, and after he had vetoed Whig attempts to re-establish the Bank all of his Cabinet except Daniel Webster resigned. For the balance of the term, his support depended upon an uneasy coalition of anti-Van Buren Democrats, a few liberal Whigs, and a scattering of independents with no party affiliation. His prospects for renomination as the candidate for either major party were never very great.

As the election year approached, the Texas question increasingly absorbed the interest of the nation. Since 1836, when Texas proclaimed its independence from Mexico, there had been continued pressure for annexation to the United States both by citizens of Texas and by groups within this country. Nothing was done during the Van Buren administration or during the early part of the Harrison-Tyler administrations, primarily because of opposition in the North to the addition of so large an area in which slavery was already entrenched. With the threat of intervention by Great Britain and France in 1843, however, matters came to a head; early in 1844 an annexation treaty was presented to the Senate.

The question was one upon which most leaders were forced to take a stand—and certainly presidential candidates were called upon to do so. In what may have been a coordinated effort, the outstanding candidate for each major party, Henry Clay and Martin Van Buren, declared against annexation. The declaration was to be more costly for Van Buren among the Democrats than for Clay among the Whigs.

SECOND WHIG CONVENTION

Henry Clay had been sidetracked by a cleverly conducted prenomination campaign in 1840, but he was not to be denied this time. After the break between President Tyler and the majority of the Whig party, he had become the undisputed leader of the congressional Whigs, a factor which, when added to his great popularity with many voters throughout the country, made successful opposition to his candidacy next to impossible.

Had his position been less strong, his stand against annexation of Texas might have encouraged opposition. For various reasons, however, his prospects were not badly damaged in his party. His closest followers were apparently not greatly surprised by his stand, and although the most ardent proponents of annexation were the southern slaveholding states, which must be reckoned with because they held something over one third of the voting strength in the convention, Clay could not be stopped by a one third veto, since Whig rules specified a simple majority for nomination. Thus, his position on the Texas matter did not jeopardize his nomination—but it did make his chances for election more remote.

Baltimore, Maryland, May 1, 1844

All states then in the Union were represented in the convention, but there was little relationship between the number of delegates and the authorized electoral college voting strength. Tennessee, for example, with 13 electoral votes was represented by five delegates; Indiana, with 12 electoral votes sent sixty-one.

Convention Organization

It appears from the proceedings that credentials were accepted and a committee appointed to select permanent officers for the convention before the convention was officially organized. When Reverdy Johnson of Maryland, after calling the convention to order, announced that the committee, consisting of two members from each state, was ready to report the slate of convention officers, a member of the committee arose to suggest that it was "according to the usage in such cases" that the committee should recommend a temporary preliminary organization of the convention, and that Arthur S. Hopkins of Alabama was proposed for temporary president.

The tenure of the temporary president was evidently quite short; immediately following a prayer, he announced the proposed permanent officers of the convention, who were approved by the delegates.

The Presidential Nomination

After an address by the permanent chairman, Ambrose Spencer, a motion to nominate Henry Clay passed by acclamation, amid enthusiastic cheering. It was then proposed that Mr. Clay address the convention and the citizens of Baltimore the next day, but a letter from Clay stated that he could not reconcile an appearance at the convention with his "sense of delicacy and propriety."

The Vice-Presidential Nomination

The convention then turned its attention to the question of the vice-presidential nomination. Before any discussion, letters were read from two potential candidates, George Evans of Maine and John M. Clayton of Delaware, in which they withdrew their names from any consideration. The convention accepted the letters, and directed they be entered upon the journal along with the statement of the convention's approval for the high motives with which the two had acted. Following this resolution, another letter was read withdrawing the name of John McLean of Ohio.

With the field thus narrowed down, the delegates addressed themselves to the question of how the vice-presidential nominations should be made. Several plans were rejected, among them the one used to nominate Harrison for the Presidency in 1839, by which each state delegation had decided upon a candidate in caucus and then voted as a unit for that candidate. In the procedure finally adopted

. . . the roll was called in order; and as the name of each delegate was called out by one of the secretaries, he voted, *viva voce*, for the candidate he preferred.[1]

Thus, in successive conventions the Whigs employed diametrically different nomination methods, neither of which was again used in a major-party convention.

Four candidates were presented for the nomination: John Sergeant of Pennsylvania, Millard Fillmore of New York, John Davis of Massachusetts, and Theodore Frelinghuysen of New Jersey. Frelinghuysen led on the first ballot with 101 out of 275 votes cast. John Davis was runner-up. On the second ballot Frelinghuysen gained to 118, Sergeant and Davis dropping, and Fillmore gaining slightly. Following the second ballot, Sergeant withdrew, and his votes, accompanied by part of Fillmore's strength, moved to Frelinghuysen, who was then nominated with a total of 155 votes. Friends of the other candidates pledged

[1] *Niles' Register*, Vol. 46, May 4, 1844, p. 148.

their support to the nominee, and the nomination was made unanimous.

The Platform

Following the nominations, several resolutions were passed, most of them laudatory of Clay, Frelinghuysen, and the Whigs in general, but including at least one attempt to summarize the principles upon which the campaign should be based.

Resolved, That these principles may be summed up as comprising, a well regulated national currency; a tariff for revenue to defray the necessary expenses of the government, and discriminating with special reference to the protection of the domestic labor of the country; the distribution of the proceeds of the sales of public lands; a single term for the presidency; a reform of executive usurpations:—and, generally—such an administration of the affairs of the country as shall impart to every branch of public service the greatest practicable efficiency, controlled by a well regulated and wise economy.[2]

FOURTH DEMOCRATIC CONVENTION

At the time Van Buren declared against immediate annexation of Texas, many delegates had already been selected and pledged to him. His pronouncement created a dilemma for many of these: should they follow their mandate and thereby assist in nominating a man who stood against the one thing they most desired? Or should they reject the mandate and work toward nominating another man who believed as they did about Texas?

From the moment Van Buren's Texas letter was published, correspondence both open and confidential began among Democrats throughout the country. What should be done? If Van Buren were to be stopped, how could it best be accomplished? Who should be nominated in his stead? Several were ready and willing to be chosen.

Always available during this period was Lewis Cass of Michigan, recently U.S. Minister to France, whose expansionist views had been well known for a long time.

[2] *Ibid.,* p. 148.

Richard M. Johnson of Kentucky, the controversial former Vice President, was more than willing to try for the larger job and had a considerable personal following. Senator James Buchanan of Pennsylvania was presented as a favorite son. One candidate openly sought the Vice Presidency— James K. Polk, former governor of Tennessee.[3]

Baltimore, Maryland, May 27, 28, 29, 1844

The proceedings as printed in *Niles' Register* are unusual in that the delegates were listed, with a statement of the pledges by which they were bound by their electing constituencies, and in some cases the actual resolution by which they were bound.[4] All states then in the Union except South Carolina were represented.

Convention Organization

Shortly after selection of the temporary chairman, the battle began. The opening gun was a proposal to adopt the rule of the 1832 convention stipulating "a two thirds majority of the votes given" for nomination; the rule, a speaker said, had led to success in that year. Objection was made that rules should not be adopted until all credentials questions had been settled, and

[3] How deliberately it was done in this case remains an open question, but the stratagem of running for Vice President in a situation of potential stalemate for the presidential nomination has many advantages, and deserves more attention than it has received. A vice-presidential candidate can have telling points made for him that are essentially the same as for a presidential candidate, without appearing to compete with others for the higher position. Negotiations for mutual support can be carried out on an open and legitimate basis, with not just one of the presidential candidates but with as many as desired. Whatever Polk himself may have had in mind, it seems evident that some at least of his supporters were thinking of the presidential nomination while talking of the vice-presidential. Even Andrew Jackson, from his retirement in The Hermitage, quietly gave his blessing. When the deadlock became evident to all, Polk was brought forward and the convention accepted him as it could not have accepted anyone who had been actively in the midst of the fight against Van Buren.

[4] *Niles' Register,* Vol. 46, June 1, 1844, p. 211.

a substitute motion was made to appoint a credentials committee. The debate, which generated "much confusion," was interrupted by a prayer, then was immediately resumed.

Credentials Committee

The motion on rules was finally withdrawn, and an amended motion to appoint a credentials committee of one member from each state was passed. The committee was directed to report both the number of delegates from each state and the number of votes, based upon the electoral vote, to which each delegation was entitled, and to authenticate the credentials of the delegates.

Following appointment of the committee, discussion arose as to how the committee should function. One point of view was that each of its members should examine the credentials of his own delegation and report the results; in a sense, this envisaged the committee as twenty-six separate committees. The opposition viewpoint held that the committee should act as a whole on the credentials of each state delegation. The latter viewpoint prevailed, after an exciting session but one in which "there was no breach of gentlemanly courtesy on the part of the members." The convention then adjourned to permit the committee to do its work.

Early in the afternoon of the same day the committee reported that its members were "unanimously of opinion that the delegates now present were entitled to seats in that capacity." The committee noted, however, that Louisiana, which was entitled to six delegates, had only two in attendance. A resolution was proposed providing that each state be allowed its full electoral college vote regardless of how many delegates were in attendance, but was immediately withdrawn. Louisiana nevertheless cast its full 6 votes on the subsequent roll calls; whether more Louisiana delegates arrived in the meantime or whether the con-

vention gave either tacit or overt approval is not stated in the published proceedings.

Rules

After approving a motion to appoint a committee of one from each state to nominate permanent officers and appointing the committee, the convention turned once again to the crucial question of the two thirds rule. The debate waxed so warm that one delegate

. . . recalled the convention to a recollection that they were acting in the presence of the American people,—in the presence of whig reporters, for whig papers,—and entreated that they would act calmly and dispassionately.[5]

One side cited the precedents of 1832 and 1835. The other side not only denied the force of those particular precedents, but discounted the importance of precedents generally: "And where would the gentleman find a precedent for the Declaration of Independence? Where a precedent for the constitution of the United States?" The speaker grew so excited at one point that, in the words of the *Niles'* reporter, "he leaped from the floor and stamped with involuntary and enthusiastic energy, as if treading beneath his feet the object of his loathing."

The debate was again interrupted, this time for the election of the permanent officers. The morning of the second day H. B. Wright of Pennsylvania, the permanent chairman, took the chair and the argument over the two thirds rule was resumed. Van Buren supporters tried to refer the question to a committee on rules to be appointed for the purpose but were strenuously opposed, and the two thirds rule was adopted by a vote of 148 to 118. Several delegations pledged to Van Buren split their vote evenly on the two sides of the question—enough to change the balance. By this technique, with the votes being given by states, individual delegates may

---

[5] *Ibid.*, p. 214.

have hoped to escape direct censure, since it would be difficult to tell how each delegate voted if delegations agreed to keep caucus deliberations secret.[6] After the vote a recess was taken.

The Presidential Nomination

When the convention reconvened, balloting began, and seven ballots were taken without important interruption. Van Buren started with 151 votes on the first ballot, a clear majority of the 266 votes cast. His nearest opponent was Cass with 84 votes; Johnson received 24, and four others shared 13 scattered votes.

On each subsequent ballot Van Buren lost votes. On the seventh ballot he was down to 99, and Cass, who received most, but not all, of Van Buren's losses, had risen to 123. Johnson held 21 votes and James Buchanan 22. At this point a Van Buren supporter attempted to force the issue by a motion to nominate Van Buren, on the grounds of his majority vote on the first ballot, and threatened to leave the convention if the motion was not approved. The acting chairman refused to entertain the motion, holding that it was a virtual rescission of the rules adopted during the morning session, that a two thirds majority would be required to change the rules, and that a vote could be taken only if requested by two individuals who had voted with the majority on the morning vote.[7]

This did not satisfy the Van Buren supporter, identified in the proceedings as a Mr. Miller of Ohio, for he "leaped upon the bench and—in a loud voice—insisted upon being heard." Much confusion followed. One delegate proposed that Andrew

Jackson receive the unanimous vote of the convention as its nominee—a proposal that "was received with mingled applause and good humored laughter." This resolution also was declared out of order. Some of Miller's fellow Ohio delegates and other Van Burenites scattered throughout the convention hall demanded that Miller be heard, and he finally was recognized, but only after "a scene of violent commotion and disorder."

Miller appealed the decision of the chairman and gave a review of the arguments against the two thirds rule. This reopened the debate, which continued until the convention adjourned for the night.

When debate was resumed the next morning, Wright, the permanent chairman, interrupted the speaker "to explain, that he did not occupy the chair at the time the decision was made, and intimated that the resolution to nominate Van Buren by majority votes would require a notice of one day." The acting chairman of the previous day explained his decision and reaffirmed it, and his stand was endorsed by Wright.

At this point in the proceedings a curious change took place. First, Governor Thomas W. Bartley of Ohio, who had been supporting Miller and his demand for an appeal, announced that, had he thought his friend respectfully treated, he would have requested that Miller withdraw the appeal. He went on to speak generally on the subject of "trampling upon rights, and want of courtesy upon the part of gentlemen who had attempted to lord it over them." The appeal against the decision of the chairman was then immediately withdrawn; the withdrawal of Johnson and Buchanan as candidates followed—all, or so the speakers declared, in the interests of harmony.

Some of Van Buren's supporters, unwilling to join a "harmony drive" that obviously was not going to help their candidate, charged that many delegates, particularly those from Pennsylvania, were violating

---

[6] See *Analysis of Key Votes*. (For each convention that lends itself to this analysis—as described in the Introduction on page 9—the key vote or votes will be flagged thus with a footnote. The discussion will be found in each case at the end of the respective convention narrative.)

[7] The permanent chairman had turned the convention over to a substitute, apparently under the impression that nothing out of the usual order was apt to occur.

their clear instructions to "vote for and use every means to obtain the nomination of Martin Van Buren." Others tried "to pour oil upon the troubled waters."

The eighth ballot finally was taken. Van Buren's vote rose to 104 and Cass dropped to 114; the balance went to the erstwhile vice-presidential candidate, James K. Polk. Immediately after the results were announced, Virginia received permission to leave the hall for caucus. New York also asked permission, but when its chairman included the stipulation that no vote be taken in the delegation's absence, objection was raised; the chairman of the New York delegation then announced that the delegation "will stay and *watch* the proceedings."

Amidst confusion so great that the chairman said it was impossible for him to preserve order, a Pennsylvania delegate explained his voting record in the convention. He declared that he had discharged his obligation to Van Buren by voting for him three times, had then turned to Buchanan, but now was going to vote for Polk. A New Yorker then sharply charged the delegations, particularly from the South, that had been instructed for Van Buren but failed to carry out their instructions, with "fiddling while Rome is burning," and said that if they persisted in nominating a candidate favorable to the annexation of Texas they would be accused of corrupt bargaining and intrigue. The entire Texas question, he continued, had been thrown into the limelight by the aspiring ambitions of a man like Nero; he refused, however to name the man. He then offered a resolution to rescind the two thirds rule, but the resolution was ruled out of order.

The New York delegation obtained permission to caucus. Another wild scene occurred as it withdrew, the New Yorkers exchanging insults with southern delegates. Men from both sides of the Mason-Dixon line tried to quiet the disturbance, and the governor of New Hampshire urged the nomination of Polk as the one way to harmonize the convention.

During the course of the ninth ballot

several states passed, but by the time one third of the votes had been cast the trend to Polk was clear: there were 74 votes for Polk to 20 for Cass, all others having dropped out of the race. At this point the Virginia delegation returned from caucus but refused to announce a decision until the New Yorkers returned. With the arrival of New York, the Virginia chairman, despite his delegation's consistent vote for Cass, asserted his great affection for Van Buren; in the interests of party harmony, however, he stated that he would now cast the 17 Virginia votes for Polk.

A Van Buren floor manager announced that he had in his possession a letter from his candidate authorizing withdrawal if party harmony demanded it. He said he had consulted with many of Van Buren's friends, and it had been decided that the time had come when the letter should be used, and Van Buren's name withdrawn. New York's 38 votes were then cast for Polk. Confusion again reigned as states that had passed now gave their votes to Polk; others that had split their vote or given it entirely to Cass were permitted to change. Finally, Polk was the unanimous choice of the convention. Twenty minutes later, congratulations to the convention were received from the Democratic members of Congress in Washington by means of the new Morse Electro Magnetic Telegraph, opened for use on May 24.

The Vice-Presidential Nomination

Senator Silas Wright of New York, a close friend of Van Buren, was placed in nomination by a speech which stated that it was New York's due, under the circumstances, to provide the candidate for the second place. Others seconded him, and no other name was mentioned. On the roll call, Wright received the nomination with all but 8 votes. Mr. Morse's Telegraph then again became a feature, for Wright was notified a few minutes after the vote was announced and promptly returned a message declining the nomination. Requests that he reconsider were fruitless, and the convention adjourned for the night to permit a delegation to visit him personally. (One story has it that many delegates distrusted the new-fangled invention and thus insisted that Wright's refusal be verified through a face-to-face visit.)

The next morning a firm refusal from Wright was read to a depleted convention, which then proceeded to do the job again. On the first ballot seven candidates received votes. Governor Fairfield of Maine, with 107 votes, headed the list; none of the others had as many as 50. Far down the list, with 13 votes, was George M. Dallas of Pennsylvania, former U.S. minister to Russia. During the balloting and after the results were announced, questions were raised as to the candidates' stands upon such questions as Texas and the National Bank. Dallas's stand on the latter came under particular scrutiny, since he apparently had supported the Bank charter as a Senate member during Jackson's first term. His explanation that he had then been acting in accordance with instructions from his state legislature but had since consistently opposed the Bank seemed to satisfy most of the questioners, for on the second ballot he received 220 votes and the nomination. On a motion for a unanimous nomination, "only one negative vote was heard, but that was very loud."

The Platform

No platform was drawn up by the convention, but following Wright's nomination a committee "of one from each state was appointed to draft resolutions and prepare an address." A resolution supporting a single term for the Presidency was offered and referred to the committee, as were several other resolutions.

In the final session, "a central committee of fifteen was appointed, and an immediate and full organization of the party throughout the Union recommended."[8] This was an early forerunner of the Democratic national committee.

Analysis of Key Votes[9]

The critical vote was the one sustaining the two thirds rule. It was highly candidate-oriented, with a correlation of $-.94$ between the majority side of the issue and Van Buren's first ballot vote, and $+.94$ with the combined votes of the other candidates. In various recitals of this convention, much has been said of the action of the delegates pledged to Van Buren who voted with the majority to support the rule and thereby ensured Van Buren's defeat, and there is certainly no question that at least thirty-four of them did so, for that many who voted for Van Buren on the first ballot, in which he received a clear majority, also voted for the two thirds rule. Few chroniclers have said much in their justification. Yet, political considerations aside, the fact is that even at this early date the rule was an established precedent—and the Van Buren people therefore were defying precedent when they attempted to overthrow it. On several occasions after 1844 similar attempts to overthrow precedent were met and defeated on the grounds that it was unfair to change the rules of the contest after the contest had started, and more than one candidate abandoned the effort when he saw the furor it raised. An excellent recent example was Franklin D. Roosevelt's quick withdrawal of his attempt to change the two thirds rule in 1932.

[8] *Niles' Register*, Vol. 46, June 1, 1844, p. 218.
[9] For an explanation of the calculation of the correlation coefficients used in the analysis of key votes, see the Introduction, pp. 9-10.

Presidential Election, December 4, 1844

JAMES K. POLK (D): popular vote, 1,338,464; electoral vote, 170
HENRY CLAY (W): popular vote, 1,300,097; electoral vote, 105

1848

THE MEXICAN WAR had been fought and won between 1844 and 1848 and thousands of square miles of new territory had been added to the nation's frontier. With the new acres came the problem of what to do with them, and particularly how to handle the slavery question while the lands were being occupied by settlers. Southern demands that the new areas be completely open to slavery were met by increasing opposition from northern antislavery advocates. The question had first come to a head in 1846 when the so-called Wilmot Proviso was appended to an appropriations bill connected with negotiations with Mexico. Stipulating that slavery be forever excluded from all territories that might be acquired from Mexico, the Proviso set off an angry debate between the Whigs and Democrats in Congress that had repercussions in every part of the land. It was passed as part of the appropriations bill in early 1847 by the House of Representatives, where the greater northern population could exert its weight, but was rejected by the Senate, where the balance between slave and non-slave states was more equal.

From this time until the Civil War, the slavery question dominated the political scene. No man considered at all hostile to slavery could hope to gain southern support for the Presidency. The North was less solid on the subject, and this division enabled the southerners to exert greater influence than the relative population size of their region justified—an influence exploited to the full in Congress, in the conventions, and in the elections.

FIFTH DEMOCRATIC CONVENTION

President Polk stated early in his term that he did not intend to seek renomination, and it was obvious by 1848 that he would keep his word, whether he wanted to or not. For the Democrats the Mexican War had been a failure from the political point of view: it had produced two Whig military heroes, but no Democratic equivalents. The Democrats were thus obliged to look for their potential candidates in the ranks of the political activists—most of whom had committed themselves so far on one side or the other of the slavery issue as to weaken their availability.

Among the more available was Lewis Cass, who had been Van Buren's leading competitor in 1844 until the convention stampeded to Polk. Since then he had served in the Senate, where he opposed the Wilmot Proviso and advocated popular sovereignty in its stead. This record made him acceptable to many southerners but decreased his popularity in some of the northern states, particularly in his own northwestern region. He was further handicapped by Van Buren's belief that he had been the agent of Van Buren's defeat in 1844.

James Buchanan, Polk's Secretary of State, had considerable northern support but was not popular in the South, and he apparently received little encouragement from the President—who, in fact, encouraged no candidate. Judge Levi Woodbury of New Hampshire was considered favorably despite his New England residence by many southerners as "a northern man with southern principles"—an important availability factor for the time.

Baltimore, Maryland, May 22, 23, 24, 25, 1848

All states then in the Union were represented in the convention. South Carolina's delegation consisted of but one man, to cast the state's 9 votes. The New England and Middle Atlantic states, with the exception of New York, generally adhered to the principle of one delegate for each electoral vote, and several states in other sections followed suit. Other states sent oversized delegations, among them Virginia with 69 delegates for 23 votes; North Carolina, 22 delegates, 11 votes; Louisiana, 18 delegates, 6 votes; Kentucky, 32 delegates, 12 votes; and Indiana, 27 delegates, 12 votes. All were admitted to seats in the convention, though references in the proceedings suggest that the hall was overcrowded.

The Credentials Committee

New York sent two complete delegations, one from each of the bitterly contesting factions, the Hunkers and the Barnburners, that divided the New York Democrats of the period. The contest as to which delegation would be accepted was triggered by a resolution to establish a credentials committee consisting of one delegate from each state. Objection was made that it would be impossible to choose one New York delegate, and a substitute was offered which spelled out the duties of the committee in somewhat greater detail, but which also allowed for two New York members—one delegate from each of the contesting delegations. This was objected to in turn on the grounds that it doubled the committee voting strength of New York. After a series of parliamentary moves, the substitute was adopted with the amendment that the two New York factions be allowed committee representation without voting rights.

During the roll call to appoint members to the credentials committee, the member named for Florida stated in unequivocal terms that he was prejudiced against the Barnburners and offered to resign if, on the basis of this being known, the convention did not consider him a competent juror. The convention did not see fit to reject him.

The committee subsequently reported on each delegation except New York's, but the report was not accepted immediately, owing to a question about the voting rights of the single delegate from South Carolina. This delegate had been selected in a mass meeting, apparently conducted for only one congressional district, but his credentials stated that he was to cast the entire vote of the state if there were no other delegates. South Carolina had for some time been a trouble spot in the party; it had not sent delegates in 1836 or in 1844, and this fact was used by the delegate in substantiating his claim to the full 9 votes:

> Let me, however, warn the democratic party that they should act in this case with all deliberation. The State of South Carolina, I regret to say, has been somewhat remiss; and the action of this convention will exercise a most important influence upon her conduct hereafter.[1]

Whether because of this threat or for other reasons, he was allowed to cast the full vote of South Carolina.

Rules and Permanent Organization

With the New York contest still hanging fire, the report of the committee on organization was submitted and approved, and the convention then adjourned for the day. On the second day, following a speech by the permanent chairman, Andrew Stevenson of Virginia, the delegates considered the rules by which the convention would be governed. The first question was the method of voting; up to this point voting had been by voice, thus giving undue weight to the oversized delegations. To correct this, the convention adopted a resolution which restricted each delegation to

---

[1] *Niles' Register,* Vol. 74, Aug. 2, 1848, p. 73.

the number of votes to which the state was entitled in the electoral college and provided that the manner in which the vote was cast should be determined by the individual delegations.

A following resolution to adopt the rules of the 1844 convention inevitably raised the question of the two thirds rule. Parts of the 1844 rules were adopted without difficulty, but the two thirds rule was reserved to be acted upon separately. Objection was made by New York that a decision should not be made upon the question until the New York seating contest was settled and that state given a voice. The first roll call vote was taken on the question of tabling the two thirds rule until after the report by the committee on credentials; tabling lost 133 to 121, New York not voting.[2] In the course of the roll call the right of the South Carolina delegate to the full electoral vote of the state was again challenged, but upheld by the convention. The vote on the main question of adopting the two thirds rule passed 175 to 78, New York not voting, and the convention adjourned until five o'clock that evening.

Credentials Committee (continued)

The evening session and all of the next day, including an evening session, were occupied with the New York question, which was not settled finally until the fourth day. The committee recommended seating of the Hunker delegation. During the first session of the New York debate, a resolution was passed permitting two speakers from each side of the question to present their case, each speaker to be limited to one hour. Following the presentations, considerable parliamentary skirmishing occurred, in the course of which several roll call votes were taken. A motion was made to recommit the New York contest to the committee "with instructions to inquire into and report the facts." A second mo-

tion struck out all of this after *resolved* and substituted the following:

Resolved, That both sets of delegates now present and asking admission from the State of New York be, and they are hereby, admitted to a full participation in all the privileges and proceedings of this convention, and be authorized to cast seventy-two votes for the State of New York, being the whole number of delegates claiming seats from that State, and that the vote and strength of every other State be relatively increased.[3]

An amendment was next offered to the substitute providing that each of the New York factions receive half the electoral vote, and that the vote of the other states remain unchanged. This amendment passed 126 to 125, according to the original announcement of the vote—which was later changed to 126 to 124. The convention then adjourned for the night. On the morning of the fourth day the substitute, as last amended, passed 130 to 120, and the credentials report, as amended, by 133 to 118. Thus both delegations were seated, with half votes.

This did not finish the matter, for a final attempt was made by the Syracuse, or Hunker, delegation to oust their rivals from the convention by the following motion:

Resolved, That the New York delegation, known as the Syracuse delegation, are rightfully entitled to cast the vote of said State in this Convention.[4]

This resolution was tabled 157 to 95.

The Presidential Nomination

The compromise satisfied no one. Both New York factions refused to vote or to cooperate in any other way. Their behavior gave rise to an amusing interlude during the brief nominating speech for James Buchanan:

I nominate [the speaker said], in the name of the Democracy of my State, the distinguished son of Pennsylvania, James Buchanan. (Applause.) And, as an omen of success and har-

---

[2] See *Analysis of Key Votes.*

[3] *Niles' Register,* Vol. 74, Aug. 2, 1848, p. 77.
[4] *Ibid.,* Vol. 74, Nov. 22, 1848, p. 326.

mony, allow me to direct your attention to the red and white rose blended. (Loud Applause.) Here it is, sir! (Exhibiting the beautiful emblem.) It is the gift of a lady to this Convention, and I beg to present it to our New York friends. (Applause.)

The roses were handed to the New York delegations, but both declined to receive the offering.[5]

The refusal of the New York delegations to vote resulted in a curious application of the two thirds rule, which apparently received no attention at the time. The total voting strength on the electoral college basis was 290, of which New York held 36 votes. Thus, the maximum voting in the convention was 254. On the first ballot Lewis Cass received 126, Buchanan 55, and Woodbury 53, with scatterings for the others. Cass moved to 133 on the second ballot, to 156 on the third, and to 179 on the fourth ballot—whereat he was declared to be nominated, "having received two thirds of the whole number of votes cast." His fourth-ballot vote was actually 15 short of two thirds of the total electoral vote, and 9 more than two thirds of the total vote cast. Although this was the first occasion on which less than two thirds of the authorized convention vote was cast on the final presidential nominating ballot, no protest or question appears to have been raised. (As already noted, a less than two thirds vote had occurred on a vice-presidential nomination, due to the fact that not all states were represented on that occasion. But here, New York was represented, and delegates from one of the factions were present when the vote was taken.)

The Vice-Presidential Nomination

In the evening session following the nomination of Cass, a committee was appointed, "to prepare and report such resolutions as they may deem proper for the adoption of this Convention." The convention then proceeded to nominate a vice-

presidential candidate. On the first ballot General William O. Butler of Kentucky took a substantial lead with 114 votes, his only near competitor being General John A. Quitman of Mississippi with 74. Only 252 votes were cast on this ballot, and the two thirds requirement is given in the proceedings as 168. On the second and final ballot 253 votes were cast, Butler receiving 169, just over two thirds of the total cast. That he was considered nominated is indicated by the following:

Before the ballot was announced upon the second ballot, it appearing that William O. Butler had received two thirds of the whole number of votes, those States which had not voted unanimously for William O. Butler, were allowed to change their votes, and to give them unanimously for that distinguished individual.[6]

The Platform

The fifth and final day was devoted primarily to the report of the committee on resolutions, but prior to the report a resolution was presented, recommending that no state send more delegates to future national conventions than entitled by its electoral votes. This was tabled.

The platform, as presented by the resolutions committee, demanded strict construction of the Constitution, opposed federal involvement in such internal improvements as roads and canals, and in general took a strong states-rights position. Tariff should be for revenue only, and not be used to protect and foster selected industries. These stands were common to all Democratic platforms of the era.

Following the report, William L. Yancey, the pro-slavery firebrand from Alabama, proposed an amendment to the platform on the growing question of the right of Congress to interfere with slavery, either in the existing states or in the territories.

Resolved: That the doctrine of non-interference with the rights of property of any portion of the people of this confederation, be it in the

[5] *Ibid.*, p. 327.

[6] *Ibid.*, p. 328.

States or in the Territories, by any other than the parties interested in them, is the true republican doctrine recognized by this body.[7]

The amendment was rejected 216 to 36, with all affirmative votes coming from southern delegations, as might be expected. However, a number of nays were recorded by southern states as well, among them Virginia with 17, North Carolina 11, Mississippi 6, Louisiana 6, Texas 4, Tennessee 12, and Kentucky 11. The report in its original form was then adopted with 249 yeas and no nays, and the convention adjourned.

One act of this convention was to have lasting significance. A committee was formed, consisting of one member from each state, to guide the party through the election and the years intervening before the next convention. This was the first national committee.

Analysis of Key Votes

The key vote on the parlimentary question of tabling the motion to adopt the two thirds rule pending the report of the credentials committee is a curious one. It appears to be highly candidate-oriented, yet relatively unrelated to the question of either rules or credentials. The motion to table clearly was defeated by the supporters of all the candidates except Cass, all but 16 of whose 133 first-ballot votes came from delegations that supported the motion to table. On the other hand, 96 per cent of the Buchanan first-ballot voters, 91 per cent of Woodbury's, and 71 per cent of the minor candidates' support came from delegations that voted to act upon the two thirds rule immediately. The correlation with Cass's first-ballot vote is −.94; with his critical ballot (the third) it is −.85.

When the vote to table is correlated with the vote on the two thirds rule, the result is .08—almost no correlation; when correlated with the vote to admit both New York delegations, the one important ques-

[7] *Ibid.*, Vol. 74, Nov. 29, 1848, p. 348.

tion before the credentials committee, the result is only .30.

A possible explanation of this shift from high to low relationship on matters that would seem to be interrelated is that the Cass leaders may have thought it possible to seat the one New York delegation that they favored and, with this addition, clearly to control a majority in the convention. Defeat on the question of tabling the two thirds rule may well have given them pause, and induced them to adopt thereafter a strategy of neutrality. With his first-ballot strength coming as equally as it did from slave and non-slave areas, Cass obviously could run into trouble if he backed either side of the New York contest, which had slavery question overtones.

THIRD WHIG CONVENTION

The preconvention situation in the Whig party resembled 1840, and memories of that year's victory undoubtedly influenced the strategy followed. Henry Clay retained much of his old stature but his losses were remembered too; in addition, many anti-slavery Northerners objected to him, and he was again labeled with the slogan, "Clay can't win."

Daniel Webster, despite his powerful oratorical efforts, was unable to muster more than sectional strength, and other veterans of the political wars were similarly handicapped in competition with the Whig generals newly returned from their Mexican War triumphs. Of the two best-known of these, General Winfield Scott and General Zachary Taylor, the latter quickly assumed the lead.

Taylor's campaign for the nomination received early impetus through endorsements by state legislatures and other groups. His positions on issues were ambiguous, and there was even question whether he was a Whig—but ambiguity in 1848 was more of a help than a hindrance, particularly in a party that had never been able to determine a clear set of principles.

When asked for his views on various subjects, Taylor answered freely enough, but nothing very concrete ever emerged from his answers. He was, he said, a Whig, but not an ultra Whig.

Philadelphia, Pennsylvania,
June 7, 8, 9, 1848

All states were represented in the convention; however, the Texas delegates did not appear in person, and a proxy for their votes presented by the Louisiana delegation was honored by the convention. Most delegations appeared to have been limited to one delegate for each electoral vote, the notable exception being the Indiana group of forty delegates with a voting strength of only 12. Immediately after selection of the temporary chairman, the roll of delegates was read. The propriety of the Texas proxy with respect to voting on questions before the convention and to membership on committees was challenged, but no final decision was reached in the first session. A motion to bar membership of a Louisiana delegate as well as the Louisiana representative for Texas on the committee to select permanent officers was ruled out of order. Immediately before the close of the first session, the rules of the House of Representatives were adopted as the rules of the convention so far as they were applicable.

Convention Organization

The question of the Texas vote arose again in the evening session of the first day, with respect to the vice presidents of the convention. The recommendation of the committee for the permanent chairman, John M. Morehead of North Carolina, was approved unanimously, but a division of the question with respect to approval of the list of the vice presidents was demanded. After somewhat confused debate, the convention accepted the sensible suggestion of one delegate who pointed out that the post of convention vice president

was merely honorary and did not prejudice the more important question of the right to exercise the Texas vote. Following this, a motion to appoint a committee to examine the credentials of the delegates was amended to retain the same committee that had selected the permanent officers.

Considerable difficulty was experienced during the first day because of the crowded condition of the hall and disorder among the spectators in the gallery. Twice, motions to clear the galleries were rejected, and the convention adjourned on the note that something should be done to improve the situation. According to the *Niles'* reporter, the committee made new arrangements before the opening of the second-day sessions and conditions were considerably improved, though not ideal.

The first question raised on the second day was the manner of voting—relevant to the oversized Indiana delegation. It was moved that only as many delegates should be seated in the regular section for delegates as a state was apportioned in the electoral college and that others, including alternates, be seated at the rear of the hall. The Indiana delegates assured the convention that they would cast only 12 votes as entitled, but requested that the entire delegation be allowed to sit together "for mutual advice and consultation." In view of this and of the announcement that the committee on credentials was considering the problem, the motion was tabled.

Credentials Committee

Six resolutions were presented by the credentials committee. The first allowed honorary seats to the Washington, D. C., delegation and was passed. The other five, presented as a group, encountered objection, and were then acted upon separately. The first of the five was defeated by a roll call vote, 156 to 120.[8] It had resolved:

That the majority of delegates from States not fully represented, be authorized to vote for

[8] See *Analysis of Key Votes.*

districts from which there are no delegates, and be authorized to fill vacancies.[9]

The second resolution designated which of the members of the Louisiana delegation were to cast the vote of Louisiana and which were to vote for Texas and was accepted. The third related to the right of one delegate from Missouri "to give the vote to which his district is entitled on the floor of the Convention." Although the question was discussed on the floor, no details are given, but in view of the fact that eight Missouri delegates were present, with an electoral college vote of 7, this apparently was an attempt by one delegate to ensure himself a full vote. The resolution was tabled.

The next stipulated:

That the delegates from all the States be requested to select the number of delegates which each State is entitled to represent said State on the floor, and that the alternate or supernumerary delegates have seats provided for them as honorary members.[10]

The Indiana delegation proposed an amendment that voting delegates be selected, but that all be allowed to retain seats. The claim was made that the big delegation was the result of factional problems within the state, and that the original resolution, if passed, would cause difficulties that could jeopardize Whig victory in November. The chairman of the credentials committee proposed a compromise, striking out the words "supernumerary" and "honorary," and in this amended form the resolution was passed.

The last resolution permitted Louisiana to cast the Texas vote, and backed the recommendation with a resolution made by the Texas state Whig convention. Although considerable objection was voiced, some of it by Clay supporters despite the known preference of Louisiana and Texas for Clay, the resolution was accepted, after which the convention adjourned.

Although the convention reconvened behind closed doors, the *Niles'* reporter somehow obtained information as to what occurred. A motion to reconsider the Texas question was defeated by tabling, 154 to 113, but no state-by-state vote is available. Additional resolutions provided that delegation votes should be limited to the state's electoral vote, and that a majority vote should constitute a nomination. Immediately before the nomination speeches began, the doors were opened.

The Presidential Nomination

Six candidates figured in the voting on the presidential ballots, though only three received a substantial vote. Zachary Taylor led on the first ballot with 111 votes, followed by Clay with 97; Scott was far behind at 43. Taylor's strength was greatest in the southern states, although he received scattering votes from all sections of the Union. Clay's support concentrated in the Middle Atlantic and New England sections, with nominal support from the West, relatively little from the South, and less than half the vote of his own state, Kentucky. All of Scott's vote came from the Middle Atlantic states and the West. Taylor and Scott gained slightly on the second ballot, with 118 and 49 respectively, Clay declining to 86. This pattern continued, with Taylor reaching 171 votes and the nomination on the fourth ballot, Scott in second place with 63 votes, Clay third with 32. Considerable confusion ensued.

The Vice-Presidential Nomination

Because of the confusion, several attempts were made to adjourn the convention for a brief period before considering the vice-presidential candidates. The attempts were unsuccessful, and the chair called for nominations. Nine names were mentioned, but only two received substantial support. On the first ballot Millard Fillmore of New York led with 115 votes; on the second he received the nomination with 173 votes. Abbott Lawrence of Massa-

[9] *Niles' Register*, Vol. 74, Dec. 6, 1848, p. 356.
[10] *Ibid.*

chusetts, with 109 votes at the start, retained the respectable total of 87 on the final ballot.

A motion to make the nominations unanimous set off a round of speeches, some of them indicating dissatisfaction with the results. The dissaffected elements insisted that they did not know where Taylor stood, and especially whether he was in support of Whig principles. One delegate cried, "Give us a pledge of that kind—that these principles for which we have suffered so much—are received by him, and that he will live or die in sustaining them." When it became obvious that the motion for unanimity could not be passed, it was withdrawn. After a series of oratorical gestures, many of them avowals by anti-Taylor men that they would support the ticket, the convention adjourned without a unanimous nomination and with no statement of party policy.

Analysis of Key Vote

The vote defeating the motion to permit the majority of delegates from states only partially represented to cast the entire vote of the state was candidate-oriented. Nearly 70 per cent of the Clay votes on the first nominating ballot came from delegations that had voted higher than average on the negative side of the early issue, and an even higher per cent of Scott's vote—nearly 80 per cent—came from the same delegations. Taylor's first-ballot support, on the other hand, was almost entirely from delegates who had voted for the amendment, and the scattering support received by others was split fairly evenly. Thus, the vote could be considered a defeat for Taylor—particularly if the Clay and the Scott supporters could combine.

Taylor was in a strategic position on the first ballot, however, for he needed only 31 votes—exactly the total polled by the minor candidates—for the nominations. On the other hand, the total Clay and Scott support on the first ballot, if combined, would still require some help from supporters of minor candidates if Taylor's lines held firm. Since many of Clay's first-ballot votes were more or less complimentary to an old party leader, it was unlikely that they were under sufficient control to be turned over to Scott. In the event, Taylor's total moved up on each ballot as scattered supporters of Clay and of minor candidates moved either to Taylor or Scott. The clear candidate-orientation of the key vote is shown by the fact that the correlation with the Taylor first-ballot vote is −.69, remaining at −.66 on the critical ballot. Most of his additional vote obviously came from the same delegations that tended to support him originally.

Presidential Election, November 7, 1848

ZACHARY TAYLOR (W): popular vote, 1,360,967; electoral vote, 163
LEWIS CASS (D): popular vote, 1,222,342; electoral vote, 127

1852

THE GREAT TERRITORIAL expansion after the Mexican War brought tremendous opportunities to the young nation—and equally tremendous problems. The question of slavery in the new territories became a burning issue, since the provisions of the Compromise of 1820, which had kept an uneasy lid on the question for so many years, were not adequate to meet the new problems. From the southern point of view, the balance in the Senate between free and slave states was a critical point, for the rapid growth of the industrial North made it impossible for the South to keep pace in the House of Representatives where population determined apportionment. A second critical point was the Presidency; the South could not support anyone who was not considered sympathetic to slavery.

The struggle over the question of the extension of slavery in the newly acquired territories came to a head in 1850 and could easily have burst into open conflict. Gifted leaders, particularly the aged Henry Clay and Daniel Webster, fortunately were available to effect a compromise that—though all too briefly—reduced the tension. But the Compromise of 1850 did not relieve southern determination to prevent anyone opposed to the southern point of view from reaching the White House.

had produced great confusion in the Whig ranks. The Democratic nomination had thereby been made a valuable prize. The defeated candidate of 1848, Lewis Cass, was very much in the race, as was James Buchanan of Pennsylvania, who had also received convention attention in the past. Another elder statesman, William L. Marcy, ex-senator and ex-governor of New York and Secretary of War under Polk, completed the list of major candidates who were over 60 years of age. Opposed to them was the youthful Senator Stephen A. Douglas of Illinois, making his first serious try for the presidential nomination.

Working quietly in the background was a small group who saw the probability of a deadlock and the need for a noncontroversial compromise candidate upon whom the warring factions might unite. The man they picked was Franklin Pierce, whose modest record as a congressman and senator from New Hampshire had ended ten years before, thus dropping him from the conflict on the national scene. His more recent experience in the public eye as a minor general in the Mexican War could be exploited. Known as a "northern man with southern principles," he had not been publicly involved in the recent political fight, and accordingly was not handicapped by enemies, as were most of the other contenders.

SIXTH DEMOCRATIC CONVENTION

The death of President Taylor in July 1850 and the succession to the Presidency of Fillmore, who had been selected upon grounds of electoral expediency rather than compatibility with the head of the ticket,

Baltimore, Maryland,
June 1, 2, 3, 4, 5, 1852

The convention was called to order by the first national chairman of a major party, Benjamin F. Hallett of Massachusetts. Hallett's first problem was one that

44

has plagued chairmen ever since—the assignment of seats to the delegates. Seats had been provided on the basis of each state's electoral strength, but several states sent oversized delegations. Hallet requested these groups to select from their number those to be seated in the space assigned, with the balance to be seated at the rear of the hall. He pointed out that the convention call specified that delegates be restricted to the same number as the electoral votes held by the state "and no more," as the national committee had been directed by resolution in the 1848 convention.

In his opening address, Hallett stated that the purpose of the convention was to consummate "the union of the democratic party throughout the Union, to preserve and maintain the Union."

Convention Organization

Romulus M. Saunders of North Carolina was nominated from the floor as temporary chairman. He too stressed the need for harmony. Under his chairmanship, the convention authorized a committee "to select the permanent officers" and one "to examine and report on credentials." Georgia was represented by two full contesting delegations, and apparently by voluntary action did not appoint members to the committees, each faction selecting one representative "to advocate before the committee their claims for recognition." A rules committee was also appointed. The convention then recessed, to permit the committees to go to work.

The rules of the 1848 convention were followed in the report of the rules committee, including the wording which specified that nominations could only be effected by "two thirds of the whole number of votes given." A motion to reconsider the two thirds rule was tabled, without recorded debate, by an overwhelming vote: 269 to 13. John W. Davis of Indiana was selected permanent chairman.

A resolutions committee was appointed on the evening of the first day, and on the second day a motion to wait for approval of the platform before making the nominations was tabled after considerable discussion.

Credentials Committee

With the exception of the two contesting Georgia delegations and a highly questionable set of credentials held by an individual seeking to cast the vote for South Carolina, the problems before the credentials committee were restricted to individual district delegate contests in Maine, Massachusetts, and Vermont, and the majority report was approved 194 to 83. However, during discussion of the credentials questions, a telegram was received announcing that three additional delegates from Tennessee "whose votes may control the entire action of the delegation" had been named and were soon to arrive. The question of Tennessee was recommitted to the committee, but no further mention of action on it appears in the proceedings.

The Georgia case was compromised by admitting both contesting groups of twenty-one and seventeen delegates respectively, with the provision that "said delegation thus united, cast the vote of the State." A South Carolina delegate, carrying a paper from "a group of citizens . . . authorizing him to give such vote or votes . . . as the signers of said paper would be entitled to," was not admitted.

The Presidential Nomination

After further discussion as to whether the nominations should precede adoption of the platform, it was decided to nominate first, and the long series of roll calls began on the morning of the third day. On the first ballot Cass led with 116 votes, followed by Buchanan with 93, Marcy 27, Douglas 20; six other candidates had scattered votes.

Eight ballots were taken during this session, in the course of which Cass, after first gaining slightly, fell slowly back to 113.

Buchanan also lost slightly, Marcy remained steady, and Douglas ended with 34. The next two sessions, ending with the 26th ballot, were characterized by steady erosion of the Cass vote, until it had fallen to a mere 33. Buchanan assumed the lead on the 20th ballot and held it thereafter, with about a hundred votes on each of the last few ballots. Marcy remained steady, but Douglas rose to a peak of 80 on the 26th ballot. On the 21st ballot, a new name had broken into the group of leaders when 13 votes were cast for William O. Butler of Kentucky, the vice-presidential nominee of 1848, who closed with 24 on the final ballot before adjournment.

Butler dropped out of the race after a brief run during the evening session of the fourth day. Cass made another spurt and reached a new crest of 123 on the 33rd ballot—the highest figure yet reached by any of the candidates. Marcy again remained steady, as Buchanan and Douglas lost much of their gains. Cass continued to gain after the recess, reaching 130 votes on the 34th ballot. On this ballot, Virginia transferred from Buchanan to Daniel Dickinson of New York. Dickinson immediately declined, but took the opportunity to request Virginia to vote for Cass to help break the deadlock. Instead, Virginia voted for Franklin Pierce on the 35th ballot—the first time his name had been mentioned.

From the 36th to the 46th ballots, Marcy enjoyed a run, finally receiving 98 votes on the 46th; most of his gains were recorded out of Cass support. During this period Pierce received 29 or 30 votes on each ballot. Relatively little change was recorded on the next two ballots, but as the 49th ballot began Maine and New Hampshire voted for Pierce, and Vermont for Douglas. The Massachusetts chairman announced the vote of his delegation as 7 for Pierce and 6 for others, but before he sat down he made the vote unanimous for Pierce. The states between Massachusetts and New York in the roll call went solidly for Pierce; New York split its vote among three other candidates, and withdrew for caucus shortly

thereafter. North Carolina announced for Pierce with an accompanying plea for his support from the entire convention on the grounds that he was the most suitable compromise. From then on, all resistance vanished, and Pierce became the unanimous nominee.

The Vice-Presidential Nomination

Maine accepted the honor to its favorite son by stating, when called as the first state for vice-presidential nominations, that the delegation did not want to suggest a candidate "and were willing that their southern friends should have their choice."[1] The speaker then finished by suggesting Senator William R. King of Alabama. King was far in front on the first ballot with 125 votes, no rival receiving more than 30. On the second ballot, following withdrawal of most of the minor candidates, King was nominated with 277 votes. Illinois cast its vote for former Senator Jefferson Davis of Mississippi; his name was withdrawn immediately by the Mississippi delegation, but Illinois refused to change the vote.

The Platform

Strict construction of the Constitution was again stressed in the 1852 platform and the federal government was denied the power to "commence and carry on a general system of internal improvements." On the tariff, the platform was anti-protectionist, advocating tariff for revenue only. It opposed a National Bank. On the slavery question, it declared that the "democratic party will resist all attempts at renewing, in Congress or out of it, the agitation of the slavery question"; the Compromise of 1850 must be upheld.

[1] Prior to 1868, states were called in an order based partly on geographic location and partly on order of entrance into the Union. Maine, as one of the states in the Union at the time the convention system began, headed the list, followed by the New England states; the geographic order then moved southward and westward. As new states were added to the Union, they took their place at the bottom of the list.

Prior to final adjournment, a resolution was offered authorizing the national committee to apportion twice the number of electoral college votes as the voting and delegation strength for the next convention. Requests were entered that the motion be withdrawn, to which the national committee chairman responded that it would be impossible to conduct a deliberative convention if states continued to send as many delegates as they wished. A motion to table the resolution was defeated 136 to 152, and the resolution itself was approved 195 to 68.

FOURTH WHIG CONVENTION

The second unfortunate experience of the Whig Party in having a President die in office came at a time when there was no dominating figure of national stature to which the party could turn—as it had turned to Henry Clay in 1844. Millard Fillmore worked hard for a nomination in his own right, and had the advantages which incumbency always enjoys; however, his difficulties with other Whig leaders created a bitterness that precluded them from compromising in his direction under any circumstances, and these same conflicts had become so well known among the rank and file of the party membership that delegates came to the convention either entirely for Fillmore or completely opposed to him. Most of Fillmore's delegation strength, despite his New York residence, came from the South.

His major opponent, from the standpoint of committed delegation strength, was General Winfield Scott, of long-time military fame. Scott, despite his Virginia heritage, was the selection of the West and much of the Northeast. Daniel Webster had the rest of the support, mostly from New England. Scott and Webster had long been in the presidential picture, each having figured in previous conventions, and each was well past his prime—Scott was 66 and Webster 70.

Baltimore, Maryland,
June 16, 17, 18, 1852

The Whigs had not yet established a national committee, and the convention was called by the Whig delegation in Congress. The time set for the meeting was at 12 noon on June 16, 1852. Fifteen minutes before that hour, an individual delegate called the convention to order and put a motion to elect George C. Evans of Maine as temporary chairman. The motion carried, though by no means unanimously.

Convention Organization

The new chairman took the rostrum at once and as the first order of business entertained a motion to establish a committee to select permanent officers. Objection was made that the entire proceedings to this point were irregular, because the time set in the call had not arrived and many delegates were not yet present. Nevertheless, the motion to appoint the committee was approved, as also was one for a credentials committee, following which the chairman declared a motion to adjourn carried, "amid a storm of noes."

The convention reconvened that evening, only to hear that the credentials committee was not ready to report and "didn't know when—maybe for days." Someone proposed that a prayer be offered, and an argument developed as to whether this should be done before or after the permanent organization had been completed. The chairman stated that "a Reverend gentleman had been in attendance at the convention all day for the purpose of offering prayer." Despite this plea, the "Reverend gentleman" was not allowed to discharge his function.

The argument then switched to the question whether action should be taken on the report of the committee on permanent organization before the credentials report had been approved. Finally, the chairman of the committee on permanent organization read the report, adding that "he didn't care whether the convention acted on it or not." General John G. Chapman of Maryland was recommended as permanent chairman. A motion was made to table the report on the grounds that many states were over represented—Virginia for example, having 45 delegates present—and others were under represented. After a long argument, the report was approved. The permanent chairman pleaded for harmony, asked for a prayer, and the session adjourned.

The Platform

The next day, rules were adopted restricting the voting rights of delegations to their electoral college strength regardless of the number of actual delegates present. A motion to draft a platform stipulated that the platform be adopted before the nominations were made. In introducing the motion the speaker said:

> We want to know who we are, and whether we are all of one party or not. We want to know if our principles are your principles, and your principles ours. If they are not, and your principles and doctrines are different from ours; it is better we should know it now at once. . . . We desire to know from gentlemen whether or not we cannot agree upon a platform broad enough and strong enough to ensure the union and success of the principles of the Whig party of the whole Union.[2]

The motion carried with relatively little opposition. More difficulty was encountered in deciding how the platform committee should be appointed and how it should operate. A first motion authorizing the appointment of a committee passed by 200 to 96. A second directed that the members be selected by each delegation, to which an amendment was offered authorizing the representative of each delegation to vote the full electoral college weight in the decisions of the committee; the motion as amended was adopted 149 to 144.[3] Soon a warm discussion broke out over the question of reconsidering the voting strength

[2] *Baltimore Sun,* June 18, 1852.
[3] See *Analysis of Key Votes.*

and changing it back to the customary method of one vote for each delegation. The question was of such great interest that members of the credentials committee suspended their work and refused to leave the convention hall, and an adjournment was taken to enable them to complete their work.

Credentials Committee

Considering the time elapsed between the appointment of the credentials committee and its report, there were surprisingly few contests, involving only four scattered district delegates in New York and one in Vermont. The committee's solution for one of the contests brought a roar of laughter from the delegates: both contestants were granted the right to seats and to "cast the vote in all cases in which they can agree." A minority report urging seating of one set of contestants was rather roughly handled by the credentials chairman, who somewhat arbitrarily called a vote on the previous question.[4] The minority evidently had substantial support, however, for the previous question was ordered by a majority of only 164 to 117. This was sufficient, for the minority acquiesced in a voice vote approving the majority report.

The Platform (continued)

The platform question was complicated by previous action of the southern delegates, who had formulated a full platform which had been printed and distributed the day before. This gave the southerners a substantial edge in the forthcoming committee deliberations, since they could present an agreed-upon solid front against the relatively disorganized northern representatives. This advantage would be furthered if the committee voting was on the basis of one vote for each state, thus discounting

[4] A parliamentary motion designed to limit debate and speed getting to the vote on the main issue.

the weight of the large northern states. By themselves, the southerners could not muster a majority in the convention, but on this question the small northern states, since their relative influence also was involved, tended to side with the South. The southerners won their point; when the convention reassembled, the decision was made to withdraw the electoral college voting weight, and the committee was appointed.[5]

The platform deviated furthest from the Democratic platform in a modest suggestion that the federal government could legitimately be involved in some internal improvement matters, particularly in harbors and rivers. It followed the Democratic line in urging strict construction of the Constitution and approval of the fugitive slave law. It also urged against further agitation of this latter issue. International alliances were opposed. Federal governmental expenses were to be defrayed by income from imposts, direct taxation being opposed.

Additional resolutions were offered from the floor. One would bind the convention "to nominate no man for President or Vice President who has, by his public acts and recorded opinions, left anything to be misunderstood of his opinions on the compromise." Since this could be interpreted to mean that a candidate could be accepted only if he were clearly for or against the Compromise of 1850, it evidently was aimed at General Scott, whose views were the most ambiguous of the three major candidates. The resolution was tabled.

The same fate met a resolution to support in good faith the nominee of the convention, whoever he might be. During the debate on these two resolutions and upon the platform itself, southern delegates demanded that agitation of the slavery issue be permanently barred from politics. Scott was charged with exploiting the subject as part of his effort to get the nomination. In Scott's defense, a letter from him was read in which he stated his aversion to further agitation. Southerners retorted that he had written other letters, with a different slant

[5] See *Analysis of Key Votes.*

that attempted to appease the Free Soilers and other anti-slavery factions. The platform finally was adopted in its original form by 227 to 66. Most of the negative vote was cast by Free Soil Whigs from the northern states. Despite complaints that the plank on the Compromise was too weak, all southern delegates voted for it.

When the secretary read the results of the roll call, he was charged with using the wrong tone of voice. He declared that there was so much noise in the hall that he had to "use his lungs to their utmost extent" and if the convention wanted to censure him, this was its privilege. The matter was dropped after a motion was made to proceed with the nominations.

The Presidential Nomination

As originally presented, the motion to nominate included a stipulation that the nominating majority be "a majority of all the votes given." This was amended to read "a majority of the electoral college," and passed in that form. The difference was a real one, for a few districts were not represented, and both Scott and Fillmore held about 45 per cent of the convention strength on the first ballot, Scott receiving 132 votes, Fillmore 133, and Webster the remaining 29 votes cast.

Six ballots were taken before adjournment, Scott varying between 131 and 134 votes, Fillmore between 130 and 133, with Webster remaining constant. The next day was spent in balloting, and the ranks of all three candidates remained almost unbroken. Scott varied between 130 and 136, reaching a peak on the 38th ballot; Fillmore between 127 and 133, with his low point coming on the 46th ballot, the last for the day; and Webster between 28 and 32. During the balloting charges were made that absent delegates were being voted, but nothing was done about it. After the 31st ballot a three-clause resolution was offered stipulating (1) that the delegates pledge support to the nominee if "they occupy substantially the platform adopted by this Convention"; (2) that the convention remain in session, except for Sunday, until nominations were made; and (3) that after the 50th ballot the highest candidate be named the winner. Only 3 votes were cast in favor of this resolution.

After the 34th ballot, on an attempt to force a roll call on a motion to adjourn, a question was raised as to how many delegates were required to enforce a roll call demand. The chairman responded that "the convention had all along acted upon a rule of allowing the vote by States when demanded by a single delegate," but he didn't think this was the rule. Since there was no provision for a vote by states in the rules of the House of Representatives, he would enforce the one fifth rule for a roll call of individual representatives.

His ruling was challenged on the grounds that a rule had been passed by the convention, but it was pointed out that a rule had been proposed but not passed. The question was not really settled, but the roll was called for a motion to adjourn, which was defeated 126 to 76. Shortly thereafter, the convention got completely out of hand. Attempts were made to adjourn permanently, while charges were made and denied that a deal had been arranged whereby the Scott supporters in the North had given way on the platform in return for eventual southern support for Scott. The voting continued amidst great confusion through a 46th ballot, after which the convention finally adjourned by a roll call vote of 176 to 116.

On the morning of the final day, in an attempt to forestall the numerous attempts to adjourn that had occurred in the previous session, a motion was passed arranging an automatic recess from 1:30 to 4:00 p.m., with the stipulation that no other motion to adjourn be entertained before 1:30. The fight over the purported Scott deal broke out again, the occasion being an article written by Henry J. Raymond, editor of the *New York Times,* who held a seat by proxy in the convention. He charged that Georgia, Tennessee, and Vir-

ginia were involved. Anti-Scott delegates attempted to deprive Raymond of his seat and expel him from the convention, but their motion was dropped after long and bitter argument. The balloting continued.

On the 48th ballot the break began, with the shift of three Missouri delegates to Scott, giving him a new peak of 139. As individual delegates moved, the 49th ballot tended in the same direction, and the roll call was interrupted frequently by speeches for the candidates as delegates tried variously to hold the line or to increase the break.

To add to the already intense excitement, a bench broke during a roll call and panic was narrowly averted. On the 53rd ballot New Hampshire shifted to Scott, whereupon the dam finally gave way, and speaker after speaker pledged support to Scott despite previous opposition. A telegram from Scott pledged support to the platform, making it easier for others to give him their backing. The session closed on a mournful note, with a resolution of regret for the imminent passing of Henry Clay, who lay on his deathbed.

The Vice-Presidential Nomination

Reconvening after a brief recess, the convention passed resolutions praising the Fillmore administration and also Daniel Webster. There seemed to be no anxiety to get to the business of selecting the vice-presidential candidate, and when the nominations began, no candidates seemed to want them. Maine announced for a Tennessean, New York for a Georgian, and so on—but most of those who were named refused immediately. Finally, Secretary of the Navy William A. Graham of North Carolina was declared the unanimous nominee by the chairman, but the confusion was so great that many delegates may not have known what was going on.

The convention closed on a provision for the future—a future that was not to be. On a motion to authorize the national committee to select a site and issue the call for the next convention, an amendment was offered designating Louisville, Kentucky, as the next meeting place in honor of Henry Clay. The amendment failed and the original motion was passed—but by 1856 most of the delegates would have turned to other parties and other conventions and the Whig convention would be only a minor third-party meeting.

Analysis of Key Votes

The roll call vote assigning electoral college weight to voting in the platform committee—subsequently reversed—was supported heavily by Scott supporters and opposed almost equally by supporters of the other candidates. The correlation of the aye vote on this issue with Scott's first ballot vote is +.89; with Fillmore's −.77, and with Webster's −.79. Webster held the balance of power between the other two candidates, each of whom held about 45 per cent of the convention vote. However, Webster believed that his service to the South in persuading the North to accept a new fugitive slave law as part of the Compromise of 1850 entitled him to consideration from that section—and that this consideration would take the form of votes from southern delegates which were then being cast for Fillmore.

The action of the pro-Webster New England delegations in opposing the motion, along with most of the southern delegations, is compatible with Webster's general strategy of doing nothing to alienate the southerners. Webster refused to give up, and when the break came it began with minor shifts from Fillmore to Scott and swelled to a flood as Webster lost control of his own people.

Presidential Election, November 2, 1852

FRANKLIN PIERCE (D) : popular vote, 1,601,117; electoral vote, 254
WINFIELD SCOTT (W) : popular vote, 1,385,453; electoral vote, 42

1856

THE COMPROMISE of 1850 had served the immediate end of reducing the conflict level on the slavery issue, but it was by no means a final solution of the problem. As settlers poured into the new territories, sharp conflicts arose between northerner and southerner. The fight between the frontiersmen was quickly taken up by those who remained at home, and while basically sectional in nature affected the parties differently.

When the Kansas-Nebraska Act in 1854 nullified the Compromises of 1820 and of 1850, serious schisms appeared in both parties. The Democrats were numerous enough to absorb losses; the Whigs were not. The Whig party had always been divided on slavery, and partially for that reason could never develop an integrated party philosophy. The bitter fight in the 1852 convention, followed by a record-breaking defeat at the polls and by the deaths of key leaders, had weakened the party to extinction.

Many dissident Whigs and Democrats were attracted temporarily to the short-lived Native American or "Know-Nothing" party, which for a time appeared destined to be the major opposition to the Democrats. The Know-Nothings, however, suffered from a weakness opposite from that of the Whigs. Whereas the Whigs had no basic philosophy, the Know-Nothing philosophy was too narrow in scope to attract and hold the loyalties of a majority of the electorate; in addition, this party too was soon split on the question of slavery.

During the period between the election of 1852 and the presidential campaign of 1856, the Know-Nothings reached their peak, but a new party was soon to absorb them, as well as Whig remnants and fragments of other parties, including many Democrats. In 1854 the Republican party was officially born; by 1856 it had grown big enough to enter the national field.

FIRST REPUBLICAN CONVENTION

Although several men with presidential aspirations were associated with the new party, the preconvention period was characterized more by negotiations between factional groups—in an effort to establish basic policy and develop a working organization—than by campaigns directed towards winning the nomination. A long fight in the Thirty-Fourth Congress for the speakership of the House gave opportunity for many of the leaders to work together, and to cooperate with the leaders of the Native American party, many of whom soon would become Republicans. The first concrete step toward a national organization was a call issued jointly by the Republican state chairmen in Ohio, Massachusetts, Pennsylvania, Vermont, and Wisconsin, inviting "Republicans of the Union" to an informal convention for organizing a national party and authorizing a national nominating convention.

Delegates from sixteen northern and eight southern states met in Pittsburgh on February 22, 1856. Although some of the leaders counseled moderation, the general tenor of the meeting, as reflected in its declaration of policy, was strongly anti-slavery so far as the territories were concerned and bitterly opposed to the Pierce administration. Despite the radical overtones and the flamboyant oratory, the convention did not neglect the serious business of party organization. A national committee of one member from each state was established under the chairmanship of Edwin D. Morgan of New York, who, in addition to being a successful merchant and banker, had shown himself to be an able politician. The new committee was authorized to organize and call a nominating convention.

Most of those prominently mentioned as potential presidential nominees were, for obvious reasons, closely identified with one or the other of the splinter groups composing the new party. Governor Salmon P. Chase of Ohio had won his office through a coalition in which Know-Nothings were strongly represented. Senator William H. Seward, former governor of New York, had on the other hand alienated the Know-Nothings by his defense of Catholics and foreigners, especially concerning their rights to education. Seward was also considered radical in his opposition to slavery. John McLean of New Jersey, an associate justice of the Supreme Court, represented the views of the more conservative Whigs. Selection of any one of these three men, or of any other prominent leader identified with a definite segment of the new and still unstable combination, might have alienated so many others as to kill the new party before it really started.

One prominent candidate, John C. Frémont of California, was not identified with any of the splinter groups. His national reputation was based on his military exploits during the Mexican War and on his colorful exploration trips which had earned him the name "Pathfinder." His political career was limited to one undistinguished term in the Senate, during which he had done nothing to alienate important elements of any party.

Philadelphia, Pennsylvania,
June 17, 18, 19, 1856

The call to the first Republican convention carefully omitted the word "Republican." According to contemporary accounts,

the wording of the call was considered so important that two days were reportedly spent in its composition. In full, it read:

To the People of the United States:

The People of the United States, without regard to past political differences or divisions, who are opposed to the repeal of the Missouri Compromise, to the policy of the present Administration to the extension of Slavery into the Territories, in favor of the admission of Kansas as a free State, and of restoring the action of the Federal Government to the principles of Washington and Jefferson, are invited by the National Committee appointed by the Pittsburgh Convention of the 22nd February, 1856; to send from each State three delegates from every Congressional District, and six delegates at large, to meet in PHILADELPHIA, *on the seventeenth day of June next,* for the purpose of recommending candidates to be supported for the offices of President and Vice-President of the United States.[1]

The convention membership was clearly sectional. All the northern states were represented, and the Territory of Kansas was admitted with full voting rights in recognition of the symbolic importance of "Bleeding Kansas." Of the slaveholding states, only Delaware, Maryland, Virginia, and Kentucky were represented, and even these only by partial delegations.

Although this first convention of the new party was composed of highly diverse groups, some of whom had been in conflict with each other, and although its tone was almost evangelical, it was well organized. In his opening remarks the chairman of the national committee, Edwin D. Morgan, stated the main question before the convention and the people of the United States to be:

. . . not whether the South is to rule, or the North to do the same thing; but whether the broad national policy our fathers established, cherished and forever maintained, is to be permitted to descend to her sons, to be the watchword, the text and the guiding star of all her

[1] *Proceedings of the First Three Republican National Conventions of 1856, 1860 and 1864,* p. 14. Over the years, the official proceedings of the conventions of the two major parties have varied in title, format, and publishing auspices. In this book, they will be cited simply by date and as RNC (or DNC), *Proceedings.*

people. Such is the magnitude of the question submitted. In its consideration, let us avoid all extremes.[2]

The speech of the temporary chairman, Judge Robert Emmet of New York, a former Democrat, also urged a calm approach.

But fellow citizens, let us not get excited upon this point. [Laughter] We come to treat Slavery not as a moral question. . . . Slavery is, so far as our functions are concerned with it, a political evil; and we do not come here to discuss whether, according to the great abstract principles of right and wrong . . . Slavery be right or wrong. Whether it is moral or immoral, it exists here among us, and we must manage it as well as we can. . . . We must prevent it from being, as its nature always urges it to be, aggressive. [Loud cheers] We must keep it back.[3]

And with respect to how slavery should be repressed, he said:

. . . there is not a man . . . but hopes to see the day, when such a thing as human bondage shall not exist in the world. . . . I trust that day will come. I am not for convulsing our country with efforts to force it—[or] forstall it.

He argued against over representation of southerners in the administration and the judicial branch, and deplored the southern tendency in Congress to thwart the will of the northern majorities.

Convention Organization

A committee on credentials, rules, and appointment was established to check credentials, report lists of delegates and their addresses, and to prepare rules for the convention. Committees also were formed for platform and permanent organization. Concurrent with the resolution authorizing the platform committee, a resolution was adopted that no ballot be taken for President or Vice President until after the platform was reported and adopted. With the divergent views on many subjects held by the potential candidates, this was a sensible safeguard. A Seward nomination, for example, could have precipitated a fight by the erstwhile Know-Nothings for a platform

[2] RNC, *Proceedings,* 1856, p. 15.
[3] *Ibid.,* pp. 19-20.

plank to offset Seward's known sympathies toward foreigners and other minority elements.

The committee on permanent organization reported promptly at the opening of the second session, and Henry S. Lane of Indiana, a former Whig, was unanimously elected permanent chairman. Immediately following his acceptance speech, which castigated the Democratic party for destroying the Compromises of 1820 and 1850 and perpetrating the Kansas outrages, the committee on credentials and on rules for the government of the convention reported. The only contests were in Pennsylvania, and the committee's recommendation was apparently accepted without debate. The rules for the convention were simple. States were to be called in order, each being allowed three times its electoral vote, except that no more delegates could be counted than were actually present. Kansas was to be treated as a state, despite its territorial status. The rules of the House of Representatives should govern actions in the convention wherever applicable. In response to a question as to whether the two thirds rule had been considered, the chairman stated that he supposed that Republicans were willing to abide by the will of the majority.

The Platform

The platform was reported the second day and accepted by voice vote, with only a minor change. After reciting the main points in the convention call, it declared adherence to the principles of the Declaration of Independence, particularly with respect to the inalienable right of men to life, liberty, and the pursuit of happiness. It declared that Congress had full sovereign power over the territories, with both the right and duty to prohibit polygamy and slavery in them. Violations of the constitutional rights of citizens for protection of life, liberty, and property in Kansas were itemized. Immediate admission of Kansas under the "free" constitution was demanded.[4] In anticipation of James Buchanan's nomination by the Democrats, his record as Minister to Great Britain was criticized. A transcontinental railroad and highway and river and harbor improvements subsidized by the federal government were advocated.

The Presidential Nomination

Immediately after the platform was adopted, a motion was made to take an informal ballot for the presidential nomination. Several delegates objected that more time was needed for deliberation, but a suggestion to appoint a committee "for interchange of opinion" failed to pass. During the discussion, announcements were made that Seward, McLean, and Chase were withdrawing from the race; despite this and the passage of the motion to take an informal ballot, the convention agreed to adjourn until evening.

Before the informal ballot was taken, McLean's withdrawal was itself withdrawn. No nominating speeches are recorded in the proceedings, and Frémont's name was mentioned first during the roll call on the informal ballot on which he received a substantial majority—359 to McLean's 190, with 4 votes scattered. A motion to declare Frémont the unanimous nominee was objected to and dropped without a vote. On the formal ballot McLean fell to 37 votes, and 1 vote was cast for Seward. Frémont, with 520 votes, was nominated.

Prior to the informal roll call, a communication had been read from the convention of the National American party, one of the northern segments resulting from the Know-Nothings' division over the slavery question. The communication included a copy of the proceedings of the National American convention, in which Nathaniel Banks of Massachusetts, Speaker of the House, was nominated as its presidential

candidate. Contemporary accounts suggest, and the logic of the situation appears to confirm, that Banks' nomination was inspired by pro-Frémont men already in the Republican party or expecting soon to enter it. Nomination of Frémont by the Know-Nothing convention might have alienated the foreign and Catholic vote. Banks, however, as one of the original Frémont supporters could be relied on to withdraw in his favor once Frémont had been nominated by the more representative group in the Republican convention, and this he promptly did.

At first the convention refused to accept the communication, and it was tabled; after the informal presidential ballot was taken, it was reconsidered. In the debate, Seward representatives took the lead, subordinating their own and Seward's distaste for the Know-Nothings in the interests of harmony within the new party, and the communication was accepted before the final ballot was taken on the presidential nomination.

The Vice-Presidential Nomination

The convention reassembled the following morning for the final business—selection of the vice-presidential nominee. Former Senator William L. Dayton of New Jersey was presented in an unusual speech that was primarily a quotation of a speech he himself had given as chairman of a New Jersey Republican convention. Other nominees were Abraham Lincoln of Illinois, Judge David Wilmot of Pennsylvania, author of the Wilmot Proviso when he served earlier in the House, and John A. King, of New York. An informal ballot was taken, in which Dayton led with 253 votes; Lincoln followed with 110, Banks 46, Wilmot 43, Charles Sumner, who had not been presented as a candidate, 35. Ten minor candidates shared the balance of the votes.

On the formal ballot, 20 votes stayed with Lincoln and 11 were spread among several candidates. Dayton received all the

[4] Two provisional governments, each with its constitution, had been formed in Kansas, one permitting slavery, the other abolishing it. Each had been submitted to Congress as the regular territorial government and constitution.

rest; immediately following the ballot, votes were transferred to make the nomination unanimous.

SEVENTH DEMOCRATIC CONVENTION

The problem facing the Democrats was similar to that faced by the newly organized Republicans, but whereas the Republicans needed to draw as many factions into their group as possible, the Democrats needed to retain dissident factions. Both were handicapped by the identification of their leaders with one side or the other of the slavery issue—an issue so dominant that no man whose stand was clear for either side could expect second- or third-choice support from those opposed to his viewpoint. For the Democratic leaders, the hazard was great; under the two thirds rule, where division on the issue was less than two to one, it would be mathematically impossible for anyone committed to a clear position to be nominated.

President Pierce was the leading victim of the situation. His position as a "northern man with southern principles" lost him much northern support. As a member of the administration, Secretary of State William L. Marcy was tarred by the same brush, even though Marcy actually did not subscribe to the President's position. Lewis Cass, still in the picture despite his 74 years, had voted in the Senate along with Stephen A. Douglas for repeal of the Missouri Compromise, thus alienating many northern delegates. Of the leaders opposed to repeal of the Compromise, Senator Sam Houston was about the only one of a stature sufficient to merit serious consideration for the nomination. Houston had been the only southern senator to vote against repeal. Although this may have gained him votes in the North, it effectively eliminated southern support.

One perennial candidate for the Presidency, James Buchanan of Pennsylvania,

was luckier than the rest. His previous experience in the Senate and in Polk's cabinet as Secretary of State were useful qualification factors, and he had had the good fortune to be safely in London, as Minister to England, during the turbulent years of the Pierce administration.

Cincinnati, Ohio, June 2, 3, 4, 5, 6, 1856

Since this was an era when physical altercations occurred even in the august halls of the United States Senate, it was not surprising that the convention had hardly been called to order when the members of a contesting delegation from Missouri brushed aside the doorkeepers and forced their way into seats set aside for the contested New York delegation. After some difficulty, the intruders were removed and the business of the convention resumed.

The convention call was notable for its brevity. The text in full as issued by the national committee was as follows:

Voted, That the next Democratic National Convention be held at Cincinnati, in the State of Ohio.

Voted, That in constituting the future National Convention, the Democratic Committee, in order to secure the respective rights of the States, each State shall be entitled to twice the number of delegates as it has in the Electoral College, and no more; and the Democratic Committee, in making arrangements for the next Democratic Convention, provide such number of seats, and secure the same to the delegates elect.[5]

It became immediately obvious that the instructions were not universally followed, for the chairman of the national committee announced that several states were substantially over represented. Oversized delegations were urged to select the proper number from their ranks, and Mississippi, for one, complied. Missouri and New York could not reach agreement, and their contests were left to the convention.

[5] DNC, *Proceedings,* 1856, p. 3.

Convention Organization

Samuel Medary of Ohio was selected unanimously as temporary chairman. Three committees were appointed: credentials, permanent officers, and platform were established, the last only after a motion to table was defeated 177 to 84. The vote had no sectional pattern, states from all sections voting on both sides of the question. New York did not vote, nor was a New York representative listed on any of the committees.

At the opening of the second day's session, the committee on permanent organization reported, and a southerner, John E. Ward of Georgia, was elected permanent chairman. New York was not listed in the roll call of convention vice presidents and secretaries. The committee on credentials reported that all states except New York were represented by duly elected delegates, the committee having decided that, of the two contesting Missouri delegations, the one originally seated by the committee on arrangements was entitled to permanent seats. The defeated delegation was led by B. Gratz Brown, who was to be a controversial figure in many future Democratic conventions.

The committee reported that hearings on the Missouri case had been so lengthy that the New York case had not yet been fully heard. Following this partial report of the committee, a motion from the floor that delegates be admitted from the District of Columbia was tabled "by a large majority." A series of resolutions regarding the galleries followed. The first, as amended, resolved:

That the galleries on the right of the President be appropriated exclusively for the use of the ladies, and gentlemen accompanying them.[6]

This was tabled 159 to 103. A second resolution, as amended, read:

That the galleries be cleared, and that the Committee on Organization be instructed to

issue one ticket to each delegate of the Convention, for distribution.[7]

This also was tabled, by 136 to 126. Other resolutions ranging from opening the galleries to all spectators to clearing them altogether were tabled or defeated, and the subject was dropped temporarily after a statement by the national committee chairman that the committee on arrangements was doing the best that it could. The overcrowding arose from requests by 300 "members of the press," most of whom were spurious, and from the lack of an adequate hall in the city.

Despite the space problem, the first business of the afternoon session was a motion to admit fifteen or twenty members of Congress who happened to be in the city. This was amended to include members of state legislatures who happened to be present. After a statement by one delegate that "this convention has no time to send out and collect the balance of mankind," the motion was tabled.

The Platform

The main theme of the platform was limitation of federal power and retention by the states of all powers not expressly given the central government by the Constitution. The principle was applied to several areas of government, but for the area of greatest interest it was emphasized in a phrase capitalized in the *Proceedings*: "NON-INTERFERENCE BY CONGRESS WITH SLAVERY IN STATE AND TERRITORY, OR IN THE DISTRICT OF COLUMBIA." Federal power to make internal improvements, such as roads and canals, or to charter a national bank was denied. Distribution to the states of proceeds from sale of federal public lands also was opposed. The party advocated tariff for income only, and opposed the principle of a protective tariff. Opposition was declared to groups such as the Know-

---

[6] *Ibid.*, p. 19.

[7] *Ibid.*

Nothing party that were based upon anti-Catholicism and denial of the rights of minorities.

A division was demanded between the domestic and the international sections of the platform. The domestic portion was approved unanimously, then the five sections of the international portion were treated separately. In order of reading they were as follows:

Resolved: That there are questions connected with the foreign policy of this country which are inferior to no domestic questions whatever. The time has come for the people of the United States to declare themselves in favor of free seas and progressive free trade throughout the world, and, by solemn manifestations, to place their moral influence at the side of their successful example.

Resolved: That our geographical and political position with reference to other States of this continent, no less than the interests of our commerce, and the development of our growing power, requires that we should hold as sacred the principles involved in the Monroe doctrine; their bearing and import admit of no misconstruction; they should be applied with unbending rigidity.

Resolved: That the great highway which nature, as well as the assent of the States most immediately interested in its maintenance, has marked out for free communication between the Atlantic and the Pacific Oceans, constitutes one of the most important achievements realized by the spirit of modern times and unconquerable energy of our people. That result should be secured by a timely and efficient exertion of the control which we have the right to claim over it, and no power on earth should be suffered to impede or clog its progress by any interference with the relations it may suit our policy to establish between our government and the governments of the States within whose dominion it lies. We can, under no circumstances surrender our preponderance in the adjustment of all questions arising out of it.

Resolved: That in view of so commanding an interest, the people of the United States cannot but sympathize with the efforts which are being made by the people of Central America to regenerate that portion of the continent which covers the passage across the Interoceanic Isthmus.

Resolved: That the Democratic party will expect of the next administration that every proper effort will be made to insure our ascendency in the Gulf of Mexico, and to maintain a permanent protection to the great outlets through which are emptied into its waters the products raised out of the soil, and the commodities created by the industry of the people of our Western valleys and the Union at large.[8]

The first section was passed by 230 to 29; the second by 239 to 21 after a vote shift by Mississippi. The third also passed, but by a reduced margin—180 to 56. Section four passed 221 to 38, and section five, the last on the regular platform, passed 229 to 33.

An auxiliary proposal presented by the platform committee, but not as an integral part of the platform, was tabled 154 to 120:

Resolved: That the Democratic party recognizes the great importance, in a political and commercial point of view, of a safe and speedy communication by military and postal roads, through our own territory, between the Atlantic and Pacific coasts of this Union, and that it is the duty of the Federal Government to exercise promptly all its constitutional powers for the attainment of that object.[9]

The intent of this resolution obviously was somewhat at odds with the spirit of the resolution in the main section of the platform denying the authority of the federal government to engage in internal improvements. However, rapid development of the Pacific Coast was increasing the pressure for transcontinental highways such as could not be met by individual state action, and the extent of this pressure is indicated by the size of the minority vote.

Despite tabling of a motion to reconsider the international resolutions by a vote of 171 to 79, one last effort was made by the objectors—particularly the Virginia delegation—through a motion:

That the resolutions in regard to the foreign policy of this Government are the expressions of opinion of this Convention, and are not to be exacted as articles of party faith.[10]

The chair ruled that this resolution must be referred to the committee on resolutions, whereupon a Virginia delegate moved the rules be suspended; the motion lost by roll

8 *Ibid.,* pp. 30-31.
9 *Ibid.,* pp. 31-32.
10 *Ibid.,* p. 32.

call vote, 171 to 74. Virginia particularly objected to the third resolution pertaining to the "highway" between the Atlantic and Pacific oceans, and from the distant view of a full century, it appears that the minority was right. President Pierce had extended recognition to a revolutionary government established by a colorful adventurer in Nicaragua. This was but the last of a series of incidents, not always to our credit, in the Caribbean—most of which involved us in one way or another with England, France, or both. The Nicaraguan filibuster government did not last long, however, and dreams of a canal implicit in the platform resolution were to wait half a century.

Upon completion of the platform business the convention adjourned until the following afternoon, since the credentials committee was still arguing the New York case. When finally completed, the majority report recommended that the New York delegation be split forty-four to twenty-six between the factions, giving the larger share to the "soft" contingent led by Secretary of State Marcy. A minority report proposed to divide the delegation equally between the "hards" and the "softs," and this amendment was accepted 137 to 123,[11] following which the amended report passed by voice vote.

The entrance of the New York delegation was followed by another attempt to reconsider portions of the platform. After first authorizing New York to cast a vote for the platform, which the delegation did unanimously, an attempt to take from the table the defeated resolution on overland communication between the Atlantic and Pacific coasts was defeated 175 to 121. Throughout the votes on the platform, no definite regional patterns appeared.

The Presidential Nomination

James Buchanan was the first candidate to be presented, followed by Franklin Pierce, Lewis Cass, and Stephen A. Douglas.

11 See *Analysis of Key Votes.*

No speeches were made (if the printed proceedings are correct), a single sentence sufficing in each instance. All four men had been candidates before. On the first ballot Buchanan led with 135½ votes; Pierce had 122½, Douglas 33 and Cass 5. Through the fifteen ballots that followed, the general pattern was a gradual erosion of Pierce support, some moving to Buchanan and some to Douglas. At the 10th ballot the score stood: Buchanan 147½, Pierce 80½, Douglas 62½, Cass 5½. There was very little change on the next four ballots, but on the 15th nearly all of Pierce's delegates left him, most of them for Douglas; the vote on this ballot was: Buchanan 168½, Pierce 3½, Douglas 118½, Cass 4½. The 16th ballot recorded no significant change other than the movement of the balance of Pierce's vote to Douglas, but after the roll call was completed a Douglas manager withdrew his candidate as authorized by a telegram from Douglas.

The convention refused to accept a motion to make the nomination unanimous, and insisted upon a roll call. All votes were cast for Buchanan, but the roll call provided an opportunity for numerous speeches, most of which eulogized defeated champions and pledged full support to the winner. California, however, whose vote consistently had gone to Lewis Cass, seized the opportunity to make a final plea for another vote on the question of the transcontinental highway. The plea was successful; the measure was reconsidered and passed substantially as offered originally— 205 to 87.

The Vice-Presidential Nomination

Contrary to the single-sentence nominations for the first place on the ticket, short speeches were made for most of the vice-presidential candidates, who included former Speaker of the House Linn Boyd of Kentucky; Representative John A. Quitman, Mississippi; former Representative John C. Breckinridge, Kentucky; Senator

Benjamin Fitzpatrick, Alabama; former Governor A. V. Brown, Tennessee; James A. Seddon, Virginia; Secretary of the Navy James C. Dobbin, North Carolina; Governor Herschell V. Johnson, Georgia; Senator Thomas J. Rusk, Texas; Senator James A. Bayard, Delaware; and Trusten Polk of Missouri. Breckinridge personally requested that his name be withdrawn on the grounds "that promotion should follow seniority." He was but 35 years of age. Others who withdrew, or were withdrawn by their friends, were Seddon, Rusk, and Polk.

Every man but Seddon received votes on the first ballot, with Quitman leading at 59, followed by Breckinridge, despite his attempted withdrawal, with 51, Boyd 33, Johnson and Bayard 31 each, and the rest under 30. On the second ballot the Maine and New Hampshire delegations gave Breckinridge their solid vote, although they had given him no votes on the first. Vermont voted solidly for him, as it had on the first ballot. Massachusetts gave him 11 out of 13, Rhode Island its solid vote, and New York half its total vote. When Delaware, Maryland, and Virginia gave their unanimous support for him, the end was obvious and all other names speedily were withdrawn with "appropriate speeches in announcing the change of the vote."

Since the new candidate was present—a rarity in conventions even up to very modern times—he was called upon to speak. "At last the manly form of Mr. Breckinridge stood above the surrounding crowd," as he promised full cooperation with his running mate and support for the platform.

Before adjournment, and in the course of clearing up the last-minute business, the convention made a fateful decision: the site of the next Democratic convention was designated as Charleston, South Carolina—the hottest hotbed of the South.

Analysis of Key Votes

On the minority credentials report, a high percentage (71 per cent) of the delegates in delegations that voted above average on the Aye side of the issue also voted for Buchanan on the first ballot, and he received 72 per cent of his vote from these delegations. Pierce, on the other hand, received 80 per cent of his votes from delegations opposing the issue. The correlation for Buchanan with the majority on the credentials vote is .68, and for Pierce—.65. Scattered support for others was almost equally divided between the delegations supporting or opposing the report.

By the 16th ballot, when the issue had been clearly joined between Buchanan and Douglas, Buchanan's vote correlated .79 with the Aye side of the credentials vote, and Douglas —.81. It is clear from these figures that Buchanan received most of his added support from those delegations that had supported the credentials report, and that delegates in delegations low in support on the issue vote had almost solidly gravitated to Douglas.

Presidential Election, November 4, 1856

JAMES BUCHANAN (D) : popular vote, 1,832,955; electoral vote, 174
JOHN C. FRÉMONT (R) : popular vote, 1,339,932; electoral vote, 114

1860

THE DIVISIVE FORCES present in 1856 were even more active in 1860, having been intensified by new incidents and new developments in the interim. Kansas remained a burning issue, not to be resolved until 1861. Further complicating both the Kansas problem and the slavery question in all the territories, was the Dred Scott decision of 1857, by which the Supreme Court declared the Missouri Compromise unconstitutional and denied the authority of Congress to prohibit slavery in a territory. In reaching this decision, the Court deliberately went beyond the facts of the case and dealt with overriding constitutional questions. Undoubtedly the Court's intention was to settle the issue once and for all —but the results provided the new Republican party with a focal issue and at the same time split the Democrats more deeply, since many northern Democrats objected to the extension of slavery. As a by-product of the decision, the principle of "popular sovereignty," by which the voters of a territory could settle the slavery question for themselves, was outlawed. This brought Stephen A. Douglas, leading proponent of popular sovereignty, even more in conflict with the administration than he already was, for President Buchanan made it clear that he supported the Dred Scott decision.

The temper of the times was perhaps best reflected by the furor raised over a relatively unimportant incident. In October 1859 a small group of men led by the fanatical John Brown raided Harpers Ferry with the intent to arouse southern slaves to insurrection. The affair, which was backed by a handful of abolitionist extremists, was poorly organized but it served to intensify southern fears and to push the South into an even more extreme position. Brown's subsequent execution made him a martyr in the North. Thus, the rift between the sections was deepened and the possibility of compromise was further reduced.

Although in different proportions, and in different depths of intensity, the slavery question affected both major parties—and many people refused to affiliate with either. The Constitutional Union party was formed out of various elements that sought an ideology they believed was not provided by the existing parties—Whig remnants, moderate southerners who sought to preserve the Union at any cost, and northerners not ready to take as strong a stand as the Republicans were expected to take.

The one and only Constitutional Union convention was held in Baltimore on May 9, 1860. Delegates attended from nearly all states, but with credentials of widely varying validity. The southern delegates supported Governor Sam Houston of Texas, but he received little support from the northern delegates. Former Senator John Bell of Tennessee was nominated on the second ballot. Edward Everett, famous orator from Massachusetts, was the only candidate presented for the Vice Presidency; he was nominated unanimously.

EIGHTH DEMOCRATIC CONVENTION

Certainly no man in public life in 1860 could escape entanglement with one side or the other of the slavery issue—the only question was the degree of entanglement. In any case, President Buchanan was quite clearly out of the candidacy picture; Stephen A. Douglas was quite clearly in it. But Douglas could expect little support from the South and faced bitter opposition even in the North. The opposition, centered, however, not around other candidates, but around factional and sectional interests. Those who supported Douglas did so with a fervor seldom matched. Those who opposed him offered no realistic alternatives; they simply would not take Douglas.

Charleston, South Carolina, April 23-May 3, 1860

The convention, called to order by David A. Smalley of Vermont, the chairman of the national committee, was to prove unusual in many respects. Its very location was unusual; no other convention had been held south of Baltimore (and no other would be until 1928). The site was chosen, it is reported, by the northerners as a gesture to the aroused southern delegates, in the hope that the latter would approach the problems in a more conciliatory mood if the meeting ground were deep within their own territory. If such a hope did exist, it was quickly frustrated. The Charleston meeting proved to be the most violent of all conventions, one of the longest in terms of time, and the only one, to date, unable to complete its business.

Convention Organization

Thompson B. Flournoy of Arkansas, a known Douglas partisan, was elected temporary chairman in one of the few unanimous acts of the meeting. As his first duty he called for prayer, immediately after which the first storm broke. This centered on a contest in the New York delegation, and began when a southern delegate requested permission to read a letter supporting the claims of one of the contesting delegations, whereupon objection was made. The pattern of the dispute that followed

was to be repeated regularly throughout the convention. Motion was followed by motion and countermotion; every parliamentary device was employed. Delegates repeatedly were challenged as out of order; rulings by the chairman were appealed and personalities frequently indulged in—all in an atmosphere of such confusion that the chairman himself was sometimes unable to remember his own rulings or the order of business. Finally a resolution was offered that combined acceptable features of the several preceding motions and substitutes. It provided for appointment of two committees, one on permanent organization and one on credentials. New York and Illinois, the two states presenting contesting delegations, were to be represented in the credentials committee, but neither could vote on its own contest. The resolution passed 255 to 48, negative votes being cast by southern states plus California and Oregon—another pattern to be repeated many times during the following days.

This did not quite finish the matter, however. Another motion was made to deny the New York and Illinois delegations that had been seated by the temporary roll further participation in convention proceedings until their cases were decided. This was tabled without debate by a roll call vote, 259 to 44. The pattern of the vote was exactly the same as that on the earlier resolution, except that Virginia voted with the minority and Georgia with the majority on the first vote, and reversed their stands on the second.

The report of the committee on organization was then presented, nominating the permanent officers, with Caleb Cushing of Massachusetts as permanent chairman. Also included in the report was an addendum that proposed the following rule:

That in any State which has not provided or directed by its State Convention how its vote may be given, the Convention will recognize the right of each Delegate to cast his individual vote.[1]

[1] DNC, *Proceedings*, 1860, p. 10.

This raised a second storm. After heated debate, the question was divided.[2]

The part of the report pertaining to the officers passed "with one dissenting voice." With Cushing in the chair, a motion to strike out the addendum rule was defeated 197 to 103½, and the rule was then "adopted by an almost unanimous vote." As an additional indication of the climate in the convention, on this and most motions, immediate motion was made to reconsider the vote and to lay the motion to reconsider on the table—a parliamentary device to make it more difficult for the vote to be changed.

Caleb Cushing's selection as permanent chairman was by no means a victory for the North. Cushing, whose remarkable career as a lawyer, businessman, soldier, congressman, diplomat, and writer included several transitions in party affiliation, had recently made a transition from an anti- to a strong pro-slavery position. The combination of this bias and his unquestionable ability was to prove important throughout the convention.

The next vote was taken on the question of tabling a resolution providing for adoption of the platform before balloting for the presidential nomination. It lost by the decisive margin of 270½ to 32½, the minority votes coming mostly from northern delegations. The previous question was moved, which would have restricted the time of speaking on any question to fifteen minutes, but the motion was defeated 182 to 121 in one of the few votes where the North-South split was not clearly evident.[3]

After the hot discussion on the first day of the convention, the resolution of the credentials problem was almost anticlimactic. The majority report seated the pro-Douglas delegation from New York. A minority report, signed by only six states, recommended that each of the contesting New York delegations be given 17 of the 35 votes apportioned, and that the remaining vote be cast alternately by the two factions; the report was defeated 210½ to 55, the basic division of the early votes reappearing.

By this time three days had passed, and a fourth was spent waiting for the platform committee to report. During the wait, several resolutions were read, mostly presented by southern delegates and mostly concerned with the slavery question; each was referred to the platform committee without debate. The only substantive act on the fourth day was selection of a committee "to report rules and regulations for the guidance of the next National Executive Committee."[4]

When the platform was finally presented it was accompanied by a minority report signed by fourteen states, and subsequently endorsed by New York. The minority signators actually represented a substantial majority in the convention, where the weight of population was reflected in the apportionment, but each counted only one vote in the committees, where the defection of the free states of California and Oregon to the pro-slavery coalition gave the slave states a slim majority.

Both proposals endorsed the Cincinnati platform of 1856, but differed in an added clause. The majority clause read:

Resolved, That the National Democracy of the United States hold these cardinal principles

[2] The problem appeared to center around the Pennsylvania delegation, in which a substantial minority existed. The incident is illustrative of the sharpness of tactical detail employed by the combatants in this convention, and also of the importance a minor slip can assume in political conflict between astute antagonists. The majority in the Pennsylvania delegation no doubt could have named one of its own number to the committee on permanent organization; instead, apparently on the assumption that the decisions of that committee would be routine, the majority faction gave it to one of the minority members and assigned one of the majority delegates to what seemed the more important credentials committee. The minority Pennsylvania delegate was elected chairman of the committee on organization. During the regular meeting of the committee, a resolution similar to that appended to the report "had only been voted down by a small majority." Subsequently, the chairman "labored hard to get the whole of the Committee together, again to consider this question of rules." He did not get them all, but those who came passed the addendum to the report.

[3] See *Analysis of Key Votes.*
[4] DNC, *Proceedings,* 1860, p. 35.

on the subject of Slavery in the territories: First, That Congress has no power to abolish slavery in the territories; Second, That the Territorial Legislature has no power to abolish slavery in any territory, nor to prohibit the introduction of slaves therein, nor any power to exclude slavery therefrom, nor any power to destroy or impair the right of property in slaves by any legislation whatever.[5]

This represented about as extreme a position as could have been taken by the southern contingent. The minority—or northern —proposal was moderate, but on the other hand, it did not quite meet the issue.

Resolved, That all questions in regard to the rights of property in States or Territories, arising under the Constitution of the United States, are judicial in their character; and the Democratic party is pledged to abide by and faithfully carry out such determination of these questions as has been or may be made by the Supreme Court of the United States.[6]

Other amendments were offered, and the entire day was spent in debate. The next day, an attempt to cut the Gordian knot was made by presentation of a substitute proposal containing substantially the same clauses as the two originals except the controversial ones, which were changed thus:

Resolved, That the government of a Territory, organized by an act of Congress, is provisional and temporary, and during its existence, all citizens of the United States have an equal right to settle in the Territory, without their rights, either of person or property, being destroyed or impaired by Congressional or Territorial legislation.

Resolved, That the Democratic party stands pledged to the doctrine that it is the duty of Government to maintain all the constitutional rights of property of whatever kind, in the Territories, and to enforce all the decisions of the Supreme Court in reference thereto.[7]

The motion proposing these resolutions directed that the majority and minority reports previously submitted be referred back to the committee, and the committee be directed to report back the new resolu-

tions as the committee report within an hour. A new debate broke out, and when a vote finally was called for, the question was divided. The resolution to commit the resolutions back to the committee was approved by the extremely close margin of one vote—152 to 151.[8] Although the slave states predominately favored recommital and the non-slave states were predominately opposed, some votes from each group crossed the line. The instructions binding the committee to report the proposed compromise were tabled by a decisive margin, and the committee in effect was left free to its own devices.

After adjournment, majority and minority reports were again submitted, the minority in this instance signed by but four states. The majority report included the first paragraph of the proposed compromise resolution, but added other clauses.

That it is the duty of the Federal Government, in all its departments, to protect, when necessary, the rights of persons and property in the Territories, and wherever else its constitutional authority extends.

That when the settlers in a Territory having an adequate population form a State Constitution, the right of sovereignty commences, and being consummated by admission into the Union, they stand on an equal footing with the people of other States; and the State thus organized ought to be admitted into the Federal Union, whether its Constitution prohibits or recognizes the institution of slavery.[9]

The minority report proposed that:

Inasmuch as difference of opinion exists in the Democratic party as to the nature and extent of the powers of a Territorial Legislature, and as to the powers and duties of Congress, under the Constitution of the United States, over the institution of slavery within the territories,

Resolved, That the Democratic party will abide by the decision of the Supreme Court of the United States upon these questions of Constitutional law.[10]

Following presentation of the reports,

[5] *Ibid.,* p. 37.
[6] *Ibid.,* p. 38.
[7] *Ibid.,* p. 41.

[8] See *Analysis of Key Votes.*
[9] DNC, *Proceedings,* 1860, p. 47.
[10] *Ibid.,* p. 48.

three roll calls were taken on the question of adjournment, with an intervening roll call defeating a motion to table the entire platform question. The adjournment votes were not solidly sectional, though most of the southern states supported them. All were lost. However, after a motion to put the main question passed by a heavy majority, 272 to 31—all the minority being from the South—the session adjourned without a record vote being taken.

Actual voting on the platform began on the seventh day. The first vote was taken on an amendment proposed by Benjamin F. Butler of Massachusetts, for endorsement of the Cincinnati platform of 1856, with no further reference to the slavery question. It was defeated 198 to 105.[11]

During the roll call, a New Jersey delegate questioned whether his delegation was committed to the unit rule; resolutions of the state convention had *instructed* the delegates to vote for a favorite son for Vice President, but merely *recommended* that they cast their votes as a unit. Chairman Cushing had ruled previously that the Georgia delegation was bound to the unit rule on the basis of a similarly worded resolution, and he now ruled the same way. The ruling was appealed, and two roll call votes were required to settle the matter. On the first, a motion to table the appeal was defeated 150 to 146; the chair was then overruled 151 to 145. On both votes the chairman received the solid support of the southern delegations and their California and Oregon allies, plus the anti-Douglas delegates from northern states.

On the vote to substitute the minority for the majority report, the North voted almost solidly in favor, the final vote being 165 to 138, but this was not followed, as would usually have been customary, by adoption of the platform as amended. A division was demanded, and each plank was voted on separately. The plank accepting the Cincinnati platform was passed easily,

11 *Ibid.,* p. 50.

even some southerners voting for it. On a vote to table the balance of the resolutions the southerners again were joined by some northern anti-Douglas delegates, but were defeated 188 to 81.

The minority plank resolving that the Democratic party would abide by the decision of the Supreme Court was then decisively defeated 238 to 21. Roll call votes on the less controversial planks followed, and all were passed—some unanimously, including a plan condemning enactments of state legislatures to defeat the execution of the Fugitive Slave Act. When the voting finally was completed, the platform stood with respect to the slavery question exactly as the Cincinnati platform had—essentially, the question was avoided. This was not enough for the southern delegates.

Immediately following the last vote the chairman of the Alabama delegation demanded recognition. He first read the resolutions passed by his state convention outlining the minimum slavery position satisfactory to the Alabama party, and instructing the delegation to withdraw from the convention if this minimum were not incorporated in the platform. The minimum established was full aceptance of the southern point of view on the slavery question. He then read the first and second majority reports, each of which was somewhat short of the prescribed minimum from Alabama's point of view, but either of which might have been acceptable. The points at issue between the northern and southern Democracy were, he said:

1st. As regards the status of slavery as a political institution in the territories, whilst they remain in the territories, and the power of the people of a territory to exclude it by unfriendly legislation.
And 2nd. As regards the duty of the Federal Government to protect the owner of slaves in the enjoyment of his property in the Territories, so long as they remain such.
This Convention has refused by the platform adopted to settle either of these propositions in favor of the South. We deny to the people of a Territory any power to legislate against the

institution of slavery, and we assert that it is the duty of the Federal Government, in all its departments, to protect the owner of slaves in the enjoyment of his property in the territories.[12]

The Alabama delegation then withdrew, followed by part or all of the delegations from Mississippi, Louisiana, Florida, Texas, Arkansas, and Georgia. In those instances where a minority of the delegation remained in the convention, delegates were permitted to cast their individual votes if the delegation was not bound by the unit rule. But if a delegation had been bound by its state convention, the chairman ruled, and was upheld by the convention, the majority in withdrawing bound the minority to withdraw and delegates remaining in the convention accordingly could not vote.

Withdrawal of a substantial number of delegates raised the important question as to what constituted a nominating majority, and a resolution was presented declaring:

That the President of the Convention be and is hereby directed not to declare any person nominated for the office of President or Vice President unless he shall have received a number of votes equal to two thirds of the votes of all the Electoral Colleges.[13]

Objection was raised that this recommended a change in rules, and as such could not be voted upon unless held over one day. The rule as previously adopted read:

Resolved, That two thirds of the whole number of votes given shall be necessary to a nomination of a candidate for President and Vice President by this Convention.[14]

Aside from the technical arguments made by both sides, two political arguments were stressed: on the one side, it was argued that the precedent could enable one third of future conventions to break up the convention by abstaining; on the other, it was held that this was a lesser danger than that a nomination made by two thirds of a fraction of a convention be imposed upon

[12] Ibid., p. 59.
[13] Ibid., p. 71.
[14] Ibid., p. 72.

the party. Chairman Cushing took the latter view in a vigorous speech, and ruled the proposed resolution to be in order. He was upheld in a significant vote in which many Douglas supporters joined the upholders—thereby effectively preventing any possibility of Cushing's nomination by the truncated convention. The vote to sustain the chairman's ruling resulted in 144 Yeas, 108 Nays, and the resolution itself passed by almost the same margin, 141 to 112.[15]

The Presidential Nomination

The nominations were made in single sentences, such as the following:

I put in nomination, before this Convention, as a candidate for the office of President of the United States, STEPHEN A. DOUGLAS.[16]

James Guthrie of Kentucky, Daniel S. Dickinson of New York, Andrew Johnson of Tennessee, and General Joseph Lane of Oregon were nominated with equal brevity, and several others received votes in the long parade of roll calls that followed.

Under the ruling of the chair, 202 votes were required for nomination. Douglas received 145½ on the first ballot, followed by Guthrie with 35 and Robert M. T. Hunter of Virginia with 42; others had scattered votes. Twelve ballots were taken before adjournment for the day, with very little change; on the 12th ballot, Douglas received 150½, Guthrie 39½, Hunter 38.

Balloting continued with no significant change throughout the next day, the ninth day of the convention. Douglas never dropped below 149 or rose above 152, although considerable variation occurred among the lesser candidates as fruitless attempts were made to find someone upon whom the anti-Douglas people could unite and who also could win enough Douglas

[15] Previous convention preceedings do not reveal that any question had ever been raised as to the meaning of the rule. On two previous occasions—1840 and 1848—when a substantial number of delegates abstained from voting, nominations were assumed to be completed after two thirds of the votes given, although less than two thirds of the electoral college vote had been cast for one nominee.
[16] DNC, Proceedings, 1860, p. 74.

support to break the deadlock. On the 26th ballot, for example, North Carolina switched its 10 votes from Hunter to Dickinson in a vain hope that the New York delegation would be tempted to vote for a fellow New Yorker. But nothing could break the deadlock.

On the tenth day an attempt was made to resume balloting, but a resolution to lay the pending order of business on the table passed overwhelmingly—199 to 51. By this vote the convention substantially agreed to adjourn until a later day, the only question being when and where. After brief discussion, Baltimore was agreed upon, and by a vote of 194½ to 55 it was resolved to meet there on the 18th day of June, 1860.

Analysis of Key Votes

The vote on the motion to recommit the minority and majority platform reports to the committee, resulting in a defeat for the pro-Douglas people by the narrow 152 to 151 margin, was representative of several votes that revealed the deepest split in the convention. Delegations voting above average on the majority (or anti-Douglas) side of the issue subsequently gave Douglas only 17 per cent of their votes on his maximum ballot, compared to 92 per cent given Douglas by those delegations that voted against recommitting the reports. The correlation between the majority vote on this issue and the Douglas vote on the 50th ballot is −.93.

On those votes where the North-South split was clearest, the correlation with Douglas is in almost all cases a perfect one, for he received no votes from the southern states. Only on one vote was there no correlation, that on limiting the time of speakers, when New York and Ohio, as well as scattered votes from other Douglas delegations, joined forces with many southern delegations to defeat the motion. Both the delegations voting above average on the issue and those voting below average were equally split between Douglas and non-Douglas on the 50th ballot. Many of the

non-Douglas votes were bolters who did not participate on the nomination ballots.

SECOND REPUBLICAN CONVENTION

The Republicans had almost no strength south of the Mason-Dixon line, and no expectation of developing any. However, Frémont's respectable showing in the North and West in 1856 and the substantial subsequent gains in state, local, and congressional elections—coupled with the almost certain break-up of the Democratic party—made the Republican nomination a valuable prize. The best-known and most open candidate was Senator William H. Seward, ex-governor of New York. As in 1856, Seward's supporters were extremely loyal, but he was faced by a numerous, if somewhat unorganized, opposition. A substantial number of the Republican leaders believed Seward to be too extreme on the slavery question; the Know-Nothing elements in the party and other groups believed that his nomination would drive thousands of voters from Republican ranks in the most critical states.

Several others received preconvention support. Ex-Governor Salmon P. Chase of Ohio was an avowed candidate; Judge Edward Bates of Missouri was considered a possible compromise candidate despite his 67 years, as was Supreme Court Justice John McLean, who was even older. Quietly behind the scenes, a group was working for Abraham Lincoln, the Illinois lawyer fresh from his famous series of debates with Douglas. Despite the victory of Douglas in the senatorial race, the debates had given Lincoln nationwide publicity. Lincoln managers won an early tactical victory when they persuaded the national committee to select Chicago as the convention site.

Chicago, Illinois,
May 16, 17, 18, 1860

The call for the convention differed from that of 1856 on several counts. The convention was designated "A National Republican Convention," an indication that the party had achieved a measure of stability that made it no longer necessary to avoid the name. The call was addressed not only to Republican electors but also to

the members of the people's party of Pennsylvania and of the opposition party of New Jersey, and all others who are willing to cooperate with them in support of the candidates which shall there be nominated, and who are opposed to the policy of the present administration, to federal corruption and usurpation, to the extension of slavery into the territories, to the new and dangerous political doctrine that the Constitution of its own force carries slavery into all the territories of the United States, to the opening of the African slave trade, to any inequality of rights among citizens; and who are in favor of the immediate admission of Kansas into the Union, under the Constitution recently adopted by its people, of restoring the federal administration to a system of rigid economy and to the principles of Washington and Jefferson, of maintaining inviolate the rights of the States and defending the soil of every State and Territory from lawless invasion, and of preserving the integrity of this Union and the supremacy of the Constitution and laws passed in pursuance thereof against the conspiracy of the leaders of a sectional party, to resist the majority principles as established in this government even at the expense of its existence.[17]

Representation was reduced to two, instead of three, delegates from each congressional district, and four, instead of six, delegates at large. All northern states were represented, as also were the territories of Kansas and Nebraska, the District of Columbia, and the slave states of Maryland, Delaware, Virginia, Kentucky, Missouri, and Texas. As the call suggested, delegates came from many parties and splinter groups, some still maintaining a semblance of organization, some moribund.

The convention met under circumstances very different from those of 1856. Instead of a small hall in staid Philadelphia, the meeting place was in the immense new Wigwam, the first structure to be built especially for a nominating convention, located in the burgeoning new city of

[17] RNC, *Proceedings*, 1860, pp. 83-84.

Chicago. In 1856 the Democrats had been able to select a conservative compromise nominee; in 1860 they were so deeply split that they had been unable to select a nominee at all in the Charleston convention. As a result, even the most pessimistic Republican delegate believed that the nominee of his convention would be the next President of the United States. Accordingly, major candidates were in no mood to withdraw as quickly as in 1856.

Convention Organization

David Wilmot, the temporary chairman, and other temporary officers were elected without incident, and committees on permanent organization, credentials, and order of business were appointed. The rules of the House of Representatives were adopted as the temporary rules. Appointment of a committee on resolutions was deferred until the convention was organized permanently, on the grounds that a platform might be adopted by a majority of the delegates seated on the temporary roll before their credentials were approved.

During the brief evening session the permanent officers were installed, with George Ashmun of Massachusetts in the chair. The platform committee was also appointed, despite protests that the credentials committee had not yet reported, and a national committee was authorized to consist of one member from each state and territory.

At the opening of the first session on the second day the chair received a communication requesting speakers to address the "twenty thousand Republicans and their wives, outside the building," an indication of the hectic conditions under which the convention was held. The report of the credentials committee was given and precipitated a debate over a problem that was to plague the Republican party in one form or another from then on. The report listed the states represented and their authorized number of votes; included were Texas, Maryland, Kentucky, and Virginia, none of which could be expected to poll a significant Republican vote. Immediately following this portion of the report, it was moved that the part relating to Texas be referred back to the committee, and an amendment added Maryland, Kentucky, and Virginia also for reconsideration. In a somewhat impassioned speech, David Wilmot of Pennsylvania declared:

This is not a mass convention, in which a mere numerical majority of all who chose to attend control the result, but this is a Convention of delegates representing a constituency and having constituents at home to represent.[18]

In counterargument, a fellow Pennsylvanian said:

Sir, shall they be disfranchised in this Convention of Republicans by Pennsylvania, New York, or New England, because they have the courage to stand up in a slave state for Republicanism and for free thought?[19]

Members of the threatened delegations painted lurid pictures of what it cost to be a Republican under these conditions:

I faced a mob in Baltimore; I faced the mob urged on by the aristocracy of the custom house, menial hirelings of this corrupt Administration. I went to my home and found that I had been burned in effigy and suspended by the neck, because I dared avow myself the friend of freedom.

I come here to tell this people that they have trodden down the Republican party with the iron heel of despotism, worse and more tyrannical than that of Russia or the Austrian empire. What has not the Buchanan Administration done? Why, sir, they have gone into the workshops of the government to seek out a Republican and turn him out to grass, taking the bread from his family, if he did not bow down to the slave power.[20]

As the debate progressed, it became clear that the consensus was to seat delegates from southern states and also from the territories, which had been brought into the discussion, but to reduce their quotas. The report was recommitted to the committee by a roll call vote, 275½ to 172½. For

reasons that are not entirely clear, this vote appears to have been perceived as candidate-oriented, for it was supported substantially by anti-Seward delegations and opposed by those that supported him, although Seward had little strength in the delegations to be reduced in strength.[21]

In the afternoon session the committee presented a report reducing the delegations from the southern states and the District of Columbia. Maryland, for example, was allowed 11 instead of 16 votes, and Virginia 23 instead of 30. This report was accepted without further discussion.

Rules

The rules committee presented five rules, three of which were passed without discussion. The first of these three established the order in which states should be called on roll call, the states that were in the Union when the convention system began being arranged in rough geographic order beginning with Maine, followed by the additional states in order of their entrance into the Union, and finally by the territories and the District of Columbia. The second provided that the report of the committee on platform and resolutions should be acted upon before balloting, and the third confirmed the rules of the House of Representatives, where applicable, as the convention rules.

A fourth resolution was quickly disposed of. As originally presented, it allotted each state four votes at large and two for each congressional district, but objection was made that this was in apparent conflict with the report of the credentials committee in which the apportionment of certain states was reduced. An amendment added, "provided that this rule shall not conflict with any rule reported by the Committee on Credentials and adopted by the Convention," and in this form the rule was passed by voice vote.

The fifth rule was another matter, for it

---

[18] *Ibid.*, p. 111.
[19] *Ibid.*, p. 112.
[20] *Ibid.*, pp. 113, 114.

[21] See *Analysis of Key Votes.*

was directed at the critical question as to what constituted a nominating majority. Both a majority and a minority report were made; respectively, they read:

Three hundred and four votes, being a majority of the whole number of votes when all the States in the Union are represented in convention according to the rates of representation prescribed in rule 2 [the rule on apportionment], shall be required to nominate the candidate of this convention for the offices of President and Vice-President.

That the majority of the whole number of votes represented in this Convention, according to the ratio prescribed by the Indiana rule, shall be required to nominate candidates for President and Vice-President.[22]

In supporting the majority version, the speaker warned that a candidate would be subject to the charge of being a sectional candidate if nominated by representatives of less than a majority of the electoral college. The minority report showed that application of the rule proposed by the majority was equivalent to a two thirds rule, since 304 votes was nearly two thirds of the total vote authorized in the credentials report. By roll call, the minority report was substituted for the majority, 358½ to 94½. Only Missouri voted solidly against the substitute, the other negative votes being minority split-offs from many delegations.

The Platform

The platform in general was an expanded version of the convention call. It included passages subscribing to the Constitution, and castigating the Democrats for crimes against the nation. Among certain other clauses of special historical interest, one placed the party clearly on the side of states rights:

That the maintenance inviolate of the rights of the states, and especially the right of each state to order and control its own domestic institutions according to its own judgment exclusively, is essential to the balance of powers on which the perfection and endurance of our

political fabric depends; and we denounce the lawless invasion by armed force of the soil of any state or territory under whatever pretext, as among the gravest of crimes.[23]

Without mention by name, the Dred Scott decision was attacked and its principles declared revolutionary. The authority of Congress or of any other body to legalize slavery in a territory was specifically denied.

Other less inflammatory planks were presented to encourage businessmen, workers, farmers—including the pioneers in the new lands—and even immigrants to support the new party. The West, on both sides of the Rocky Mountains, was specifically wooed by recommendations for river and harbor improvements and a transcontinental railroad.

Immediately after the report was read the committee chairman moved the previous question, but was overruled 301 to 155. Following the roll call, Joshua Giddings, a venerable and much-respected delegate from Ohio, proposed a passage from the Declaration of Independence as an addition to the platform. He was rather roughly handled, one delegate going so far as to say:

. . . it is not the business, I think, of this Convention, . . . to embrace in its platform all the truths that the world in all its past history has recognized. Mr. President, I believe in the ten commandments, but I do not want them in a political platform.

Giddings' amendment was defeated, and contemporary accounts describe his pathetic figure slowly leaving the convention. Subsequently, another delegate resubmitted the amendment, asking if it was the intention of the convention to go on record as having voted down the words of the Declaration. The amendment was accepted, and Giddings returned in triumph.

The Presidential Nomination

Immediately following passage of the platform, it was moved that balloting for the presidential nomination begin. Others

---

[22] RNC, *Proceedings*, 1860, p. 126.

[23] *Ibid.*, p. 131.

called for adjournment, and the question was settled when the chairman noted that the tally sheets were not ready. Subsequently, it was charged that failure to have the tally sheets ready was a trick on the part of the stop-Seward people in order to gain time, and some claimed that Seward almost certainly would have been nominated if a ballot had been taken at once. Whatever the truth of the charge, the delay probably did Seward no good and did provide more time for his opponents to negotiate. (It also set the stage for a coup by the Lincoln followers, who packed the convention hall while Seward supporters were parading the next morning.) However, Seward supporters did not press very hard for an immediate ballot, which they might well have done in view of the chairman's statement that the tallies would be available in a few minutes. The truth of the matter more probably is that, if the Seward leaders realized the danger of delay, they were hesitant about pushing too hard after the leader of the important—and uncertain —Ohio delegation said, "I call for a division by ayes and nays, to see if gentlemen want to go without their supper."

The next morning the candidates were presented in a series of one-sentence statements, Seward first, then Lincoln, William L. Dayton, favorite son of New Jersey, General Simon Cameron, favorite son of Pennsylvania, and Salmon P. Chase of Ohio. After a few equally brief seconding remarks, the first ballot was taken. Seward led, as expected, with 173½ votes; Lincoln was a respectable second at 102. The rest of the votes were spread among ten candidates, of whom only Bates (48), Cameron (50½), and Chase (49) received more than 15.

During the balloting the question of unit rule was raised. A majority of the Maryland delegation insisted that the delegation had been *instructed* by its convention to vote as a unit, while a minority insisted this had been merely a *recommendation*. The permanent chairman ruled that he was bound to receive the report made

by the delegation chairman unless the convention ruled otherwise; he then put the question to the convention. By voice vote, the question was decided in the negative, and the unit rule was therefore denied.

On the second ballot Seward moved up slightly to 184½ votes, but was almost caught by Lincoln with 181. Bates with 35 and Chase with 42½ were the only other significant contenders. On the third ballot, in the words of the reporter who prepared the proceedings, the following happened:

The progress of the ballot [third] was watched with most intense interest, especially toward the last, the crowd becoming silent as the contest narrowed down, when, before the result was announced, Mr. Cartter, of Ohio, said, "I arise, Mr. Chairman, to announce the change of four votes of Ohio from Mr. Chase to Abraham Lincoln." [24]

The switch put Lincoln over the top with ½ vote to spare, and delegation after delegation then clamored to get on the bandwagon. However, 100 votes had still not transferred before the motion came to make the nomination unanimous.

The Vice-Presidential Nomination

Immediately following celebrations by the victors and speeches by leaders of the losing factions, a proposal was made that chairmen of the delegations meet at the headquarters of the New York delegation before the convention resumed its work that evening. Obviously, the purpose of the meeting was to discuss the vice-presidential nomination, the only business still before the convention. This is one of the few cases in convention history where a specific caucus on the nomination is mentioned in the proceedings, although doubtless these meetings have been frequent.

When the convention resumed, Pennsylvania presented Congressman John Hickman as favorite son; Ohio named Senator Hannibal Hamlin of Maine; Massachusetts, its favorite son, Nathaniel P. Banks; and Indiana, Cassius M. Clay of Kentucky. On

[24] *Ibid.*, p. 153.

the first ballot Hamlin led Clay 194 to
101½, none of the others being near the
front-runners. New York gave half its vote
to Hamlin and split the balance between
six others. On the second ballot Hamlin,
owing to the order of the roll, first received
the solid support of the three small northern New England states, as he had on the
first ballot, then the transfer of the solid
Massachusetts vote, mostly from Banks,
followed by New York's full 70 votes indicated the trend. He was nominated with
357 votes, and the nomination was then
declared unanimous.

Before adjournment the convention ratified the new national committee and passed
the usual courtesy resolutions. One new
item of business was introduced, although
it was tabled. An Ohio delegate proposed
a resolution that the national committee
be instructed to draw up an apportionment
rule in which the basis of convention representation would be,

as near as may be in proportion to the number
of Republican electors found to reside, at the
last general state election preceeding the nomination, in each congressional district throughout the Union.[25]

Analysis of Key Votes

The vote to recommit the report of the
credentials committee passed 275½ to
172½. Probably because they wanted to
get quickly to the nominations, the pro-
Seward people opposed this motion. Since
Seward's first-ballot vote did not disclose
much strength in the delegations affected,
there seems no further reason, but the correlation between the vote on this issue and
Seward's first-ballot vote is −.89. For Lincoln, the correlation is +.67; for the others,
+.57.
As an indication of the tendency for subsequent nominating coalitions to be presaged by early non-nominating votes, the
correlation between this issue and the
second ballot is interesting. The correlation with Seward's vote remains almost

[25] *Ibid.,* p. 168.

exactly the same, −.88. Lincoln's correlation moved sharply upward to +.87, while
the correlation for other candidates dropped to +.11. The inference from these
figures is that Lincoln's additional strength
(he moved from 102 to 181 votes) came
almost altogether from delegations that had
supported the side of the issue favored by
his original followers. This trend continued; on the final nominating ballot,
after vote-shifting, Lincoln's correlation
with the issue vote had risen to +.90.

RESUMED DEMOCRATIC CONVENTION

Tempers had not cooled during the
interim between the May 3 adjournment
at Charleston and the June 18 opening of
the convention at Baltimore; if anything,
they had heated more. At Charleston in
May the bolters had met immediately following their withdrawal and authorized a
convention to meet at Richmond, Virginia,
the week before the Baltimore meeting.
Many of the southern states qualified the
Charleston delegates to represent them at
both Richmond and Baltimore. South
Carolina and Florida decided against sending delegates to Baltimore and qualified
them only to the rump convention in
Richmond. The question of how seceding
delegates should be treated at Baltimore
was obviously to be a major issue, and the
more staunch of the Douglas supporters
were in no mood to compromise.

Since the Baltimore meeting was a continuation of the Charleston meeting, Caleb
Cushing was in the chair. Before calling
the convention to order, he directed that
the roll be called to see which delegations
were present. Most of the northern states
were fully represented. South Carolina was
the first of the bolting states to be called;
at this point in the roll Cushing ruled that
only those states present when the Charleston convention was adjourned should be
called. As a result, South Carolina, Georgia, Florida, Alabama, Louisiana, Mississippi, and Texas were omitted.

The convention was then called to order. The opening prayer included these words:

May the hatchet of strife be buried and the damps of its sepulchre destroy its temper and corrode its edge, and the calumet of fraternal peace pass continually from hand to hand throughout the States and Territories of our beloved Confederacy.[26]

Cushing gave a brief review of the Charleston proceedings, and then raised the question of how credentials should be handled. The resolution adjourning the Charleston convention had recommended to the state parties that they "make provision for supplying all vacancies in their respective delegations to this convention when it shall reassemble." The chairman confessed that he could find no authority to guide him, but begged the delegates to put aside factional bitterness and to avoid mere technicalities in approaching the problem. A border state delegate moved:

That the President of this convention direct the Sergeant-at-Arms to issue tickets of admission to the delegates of the convention as originally constituted and organized at Charleston.[27]

A motion to table followed. Although this motion was not debatable, the chairman with consent of the convention permitted a question from the floor, and gave a lengthy answer. The question asked why all delegates qualified at Charleston were not equally eligible whether they had bolted or not. The chairman defended his action on the grounds that the closing resolution of the suspended convention provided that all vacancies be fulfilled, and that he had no way

. . . to discriminate upon the question whether these credentials came from a new State Convention called anew, and that Convention vacating anterior commissions; or whether they emanate from a Convention called anew and simply confirming anterior commissions;—in either case if the Chair had gone into the question it would have been necessary for him to hold hearings and investigations of credentials and

of facts in regard to eight states of the Union, as to which he had no more power under the rules of the House of Representatives than any other member of the Convention.[28]

The motion to table was withdrawn to permit a Douglas delegate to propose a substitute, whereby the lines were clearly drawn.

That the credentials of all persons claiming seats in this Convention made vacant by the secession of delegates at Charleston be referred to the Committee on Credentials, and said Committee is hereby instructed, as soon as practicable, to examine the same and report the names of persons entitled to such seats with the district—understanding, however, that every person accepting a seat in this Convention is bound in honor and faith to abide by the action of this Convention and support its nominations.[29]

During the confused discussion, obviously hindered considerably by the galleries as well as by disorder on the floor, the southerners tried to force an adjournment, but were defeated 178½ to 73½. They were more successful in defeating a motion for the previous question, for they were joined by a considerable number of northern delegates. The convention then reversed its previous decision and adjourned until the evening.

The entire evening session was taken up with debate on these and other alternatives proposed, but without conclusion before adjournment. The next morning a compromise was reached; the substitute amendment was adopted after first deleting the offending clause binding delegates to support the decisions of the convention. Other than to replace several delegates who indicated that they did not desire to serve on the credentials committee, no further work was done, although it took four motions, including a roll call and a great deal of discussion, to set the time of meeting after adjournment. Not enough time was allowed, for at the evening session the credentials committee announced that it would not be able to report that day, and,

[26] DNC, *Proceedings*, 1860, Baltimore, p. 94.
[17] *Ibid.*, p. 97.

[28] *Ibid.*, p. 98.
[29] *Ibid.*

until it could report, nothing could be done. The convention again adjourned.

Twice more it met, only to adjourn immediately. The committee finally was ready on the morning of the fourth day. Shortly after the opening prayer, another delay intervened.

... just at the moment when the most intense anxiety prevailed as to the presentation of the report of the Committee on Credentials . . . a loud crash proceeded from the center of the floor.[30]

A segment of the temporary floor over the orchestra pit had given way about three feet in the center, "throwing the settees and those who were on them, within a circle of about fifty feet, into one wedged mass, from which they extracted themselves as rapidly as possible, and fled in all directions to distant parts of the house." No one was injured, and the damage was repaired within about two hours.

Before reading the report, the credentials chairman attempted to explain some of the technical problems raised by the lack of precedent for the situation faced by the committee. Objection was raised; after a sharp exchange, Cushing ruled that all remarks should be postponed until the report had been read.

The committee ruled that delegations from Alabama, Mississippi, Louisiana, Texas, and Florida had become wholly vacant by reason of the secession of the entire original membership, and that delegations from Georgia, Arkansas, and Delaware were partially vacated. Florida presented no problem, for no delegates requested admittance from that state. Only one set of delegates each had appeared from Mississippi and Texas, and the committee recommended their admittance. Both sets of contesting delegates from Arkansas and Georgia were recommended, the votes to be split between them—with the additional proviso that if either set refused to accept the agreement the other would have full voting privileges. Decisions were made for specific contestants in the other cases.

[30] *Ibid.*, p. 111.

A complete minority report signed by nine members, with partial concurrence by a tenth, corroborated the majority report with respect to Delaware, Texas, and Mississippi, recommended for one set of contestants each in Arkansas and Georgia, and reversed the recommendation in the other cases. In addition it recommended that the Florida delegation accredited to the Charleston convention be invited to join the convention with full rights. In general, the minority report found for the Charleston delegates, and said that by withdrawing from the convention these delegates had not resigned; accordingly, it was argued, the clause in the resolution of adjournment providing for filling vacancies did not apply to them, but was intended to apply only to delegates who could not or would not go to Baltimore. The majority report was declared inconsistent, calling as it did for Charleston delegates in some instances, and other contestants in others. These and other arguments were incorporated in the minority report itself. A second minority report, subsequently withdrawn, signed by but one committeeman, agreed with all the majority recommendations except for Alabama.

The previous question was ordered, but, on the grounds that a majority of the delegates had not had time to consider the report, the convention adjourned until early evening. Evidently this did not provide enough time, for in the evening the New York delegation reported that it was not yet ready to vote and wanted more time. By roll call vote the convention adjourned until the next morning.

The minority leaders tried to capitalize upon the fact that most of the arguments generally brought out in debate were included in the minority report itself, and attempted to shut off all debate by parliamentary maneuver; they very nearly succeeded. However, Chairman Cushing ruled that the remarks made by the committee chairman following reading of the majority report constituted debate, and since debate had actually started, it could not be shut off within the limits allowed by the previous question. The speaker for the majority then argued that the resolution adjourning the Charleston convention intended the clause on filling vacancies to apply to those delegates who had bolted the convention. He stated that the principle upon which the majority had made its decision was consistent—that the decisions were based upon the validity of the credentials, which in turn were based upon action of state parties subsequent to the Charleston adjournment. If by these actions the same delegates were reselected, the majority moved their acceptance; if by valid state party action others were accredited, the claims of the latter were preferred over the claims of Charleston delegates.

The minority report was defeated 100½ to 150, but its supporters were not willing to accept the defeat as final. Roll call votes were taken upon each clause in the report, and most of the clauses affecting southern states, other than those in which the two reports were in agreement, were passed by approximately the same margin—150 to 100. Motions to reconsider and to table the motion to reconsider each of these votes were called for, but only one by roll call vote. This passed by a similar margin—150½ to 99.

The Presidential Nomination

The credentials question having finally been settled, motion was made to proceed with nominations for President and Vice President. A southern delegate immediately countered with a motion to adjourn *sine die,* but subsequently withdrew it. Virginia then started the exodus of the hard core of the defeated faction, mostly from the South but including some from the North. As each contingent left, its spokesman explained the motives; generally a spokesman for part of the delegation remaining in the convention then made a counter explanation. The withdrawals went on into the night, and con-tinued after the convention reconvened the following morning.

Repeated attempts were made in the morning to force a vote on the motion to nominate, and finally further withdrawal speeches were cut off for that purpose. Before taking the vote, however, Cushing announced his resignation from the chairmanship, stating that he would rejoin the Massachusetts delegation and would abide by whatever decision the delegation made as to further participation in the convention.

David Tod of Ohio then took the chair. As the first order of business, he ordered the call of the states on the pending question—a call repeatedly interrupted by the Massachusetts delegation. Finally, when Massachusetts was called, a protest signed by part of the delegation, including Cushing, announced the withdrawal of the signators. As the roll call continued others took the opportunity to announce that they were going, or were remaining. When the first presidential ballot was completed, only 190½ of the original 303 votes in the convention were cast. Douglas received 173½, the balance being scattered among six others.

Three more votes were added on the second ballot, still short of the 202 required for a two thirds nomination based upon the whole convention; Douglas received 181½, and the rest were divided between two candidates. It being obvious that it was impossible to get 202 delegates to vote, much less all for one candidate, a Virginia delegate moved and a Missourian, who stated that he had at no time voted for Douglas, seconded a resolution stating:

Resolved unanimously, That Stephen A. Douglas, of the State of Illinois, having now received two thirds of all the votes given in the Convention, he is hereby declared, in accordance with rules governing this body, and in accordance with the uniform customs and rules of former Democratic National Conventions, the regular nominee of the Democratic party of the United States, for the office of President of the United States.[31]

[31] *Ibid.,* p. 169.

After some discussion as to the propriety of the resolution, the vote was taken. The negative vote was called for and there being no response, the chairman said:

Gentlemen of the Convention, as your presiding officer I declare Stephen A. Douglas, of Illinois, by the unanimous vote of this Convention, the nominee of the Democratic party of the United States, for President. And may God, in his infinite mercy protect him, and with him this Union.[32]

The Vice-Presidential Nomination

Choice of a vice-presidential nominee was left to a caucus of the remaining southern delegates, who announced that they unanimously nominated Benjamin Fitzpatrick of Alabama. Their choice in turn was unanimously backed by those convention delegates who voted at all, a total of 198½ votes, and Fitzpatrick was announced as the nominee. He almost immediately refused the honor, but not before the convention had adjourned. The national committee filled the vacancy on June 25, selecting Herschel V. Johnson of Georgia by unanimous vote.

Shortly before the convention adjourned, a report from a special committee on rules

[32] *Ibid.*, p. 169.

and regulations was presented. It provided a mechanism whereby the gaps caused by bolting members could be filled: the national committee could appoint replacements in cases where the state party did not recommend replacement within a suitable period of time. It also recommended that the number of delegates in any delegation be restricted to not more than double the electoral vote of the state.

*   *   *

The nomination story for this hectic year was not yet finished. The delegates who bolted the Baltimore convention subsequently joined those of the Charleston bolters who had never gone to the resumed official meeting at Baltimore, and the combined groups staged another convention meeting in Charleston on June 28. After rejecting the platform adopted at the original Charleston convention before the bolt, the delegates of this highly sectional meeting nominated Vice President John C. Breckinridge of Kentucky for President. As vice-presidential nominee they chose one of the Charleston bolters, General Joseph Lane, expatriate southerner then living in Oregon.

Presidential Election, November 6, 1860

ABRAHAM LINCOLN (R): popular vote, 1,865,593; electoral vote, 180
STEPHEN A. DOUGLAS (D) : popular vote, 1,382,713; electoral vote, 12
JOHN C. BRECKINRIDGE (D) : popular vote, 848,356; electoral vote, 72
JOHN BELL (CU): popular vote, 592,906; electoral vote, 39

1864

THE HEROIC public image of Lincoln commonly held today makes it something of a shock to many to learn that doubt existed about Lincoln's renomination and re-election in 1864. Important groups worked diligently to prevent both, and Lincoln himself expressed doubts that he would be re-elected. Much hinged upon the conduct of the war, which, after the battle of Gettysburg and the capture of Vicksburg in July 1863, followed by Union defeat at Chickamauga in September and victory at Chattanooga in November, had settled down to what seemed a never-ending stalemate. In May 1864, Grant and Lee faced each other in the bitter but unspectacular Wilderness campaign; during the early part of the summer, Sherman's army was "lost" in the middle of the South. What the public did not know was that Sherman was breaking the back of the Confederacy and would capture Atlanta before the election; Mobile would fall to Farragut; and Sheridan would repay Early for his audacity in threatening Washington by defeating him in a series of battles in the Shenandoah Valley.

This good news was in the future during the preconvention period and at the time the conventions opened, and Lincoln was being widely criticized by many leaders within his own party. Secretary of the Treasury Salmon P. Chase, despite his anomalous position as a member of the Cabinet, was an avowed candidate to replace Lincoln. Other dissident elements grouped around Frémont. Still others proposed General Grant as the candidate, though he apparently gave them no encouragement. Not only was the Presidency at stake, but also control of the party, the conduct of the war, and the policies to be pursued when the war finally was won.

Most of the opposition to Lincoln within his own party came from party leaders who believed he should pursue a more radical policy with respect to slavery, who were disgruntled because they did not receive the patronage they wanted, or who feared he would be too tolerant of the defeated South when the war was over. The split did not cut deeply into the rank and file of the party, most of whom liked Lincoln and accepted him as a man who was doing the best he could under the circumstances. Lincoln himself was too good a politician to leave the nomination to chance. His supporters therefore busied themselves in state legislatures, many of which endorsed him and his administration, and in state conventions, where solid Lincoln delegations were selected; their success in Ohio, Chase's home state, effectively knocked Chase out of the running.

The Democrats were even more divided, for their division permeated the entire party and they did not have a focal point about which to unite such as Lincoln and his policies provided for the Republicans. On the one hand, large numbers of Democrats were ready for peace at almost any price; on the other, a perhaps larger group insisted the war should be fought to the bitter end, but believed it could be ended more quickly under their leadership. The Peace Democrats, popularly called Copperheads, were led by Clement Vallandigham of Ohio, who, despite his arrest for seditious activities and banishment to the Confederacy, was nominated as governor

of Ohio and subsequently allowed to re-
enter the North and participate in the
convention. Among the War Democrats,
the best-known figure was Governor Horatio Seymour of New York. However,
neither he nor Vallandigham was a candidate for the presidential nomination. Most
of the preconvention discussion centered
on George B. McClellan, whose ouster as
commander of the Union troops and banishment to obscurity by Lincoln encouraged
the Democrats to present him as a martyr.

NATIONAL UNION CONVENTION
(THIRD REPUBLICAN CONVENTION)

Shortly after the outbreak of war, in an
attempt to close ranks for its conduct, the
Republicans began to drop their official
designation and to use the term "Union"
in its stead. In some states, Republican
committees invited Democrats to join them
in local conventions and to nominate nonpartisan slates. Although Democratic organizations generally refused the invitation,
many individual Democrats, including
some important leaders, accepted and
joined hands with their erstwhile opponents. Accordingly, the Republican national committee when issuing the call to
the 1864 convention carefully avoided the
name Republican. The call in full was as
follows:

The undersigned, who by original appointment, or subsequent designation to fill vacancies, constitute the Executive Committee created
by the National Convention held at Chicago,
on the 16th day of May, 1860, do hereby call
upon all qualified voters who desire the unconditional maintenance of the Union, the supremacy of the Constitution, and the complete
suppression of the existing rebellion, with the
cause thereof, by vigorous war, and all apt and
efficient means, to send delegates to a Convention to assemble at Baltimore, on Tuesday, the
7th day of June, 1864, at 12 o'clock noon, for
the purpose of presenting candidates for the
offices of President and Vice-President of the
United States. Each State having representation in Congress will be entitled to as many
delegates as shall be equal to twice the number

of electors to which such State is entitled in the
Electoral College of the United States.[1]

Baltimore, Maryland
June 7 and 8, 1864

All of the states that had remained in the
Union were represented, and delegations
also appeared from Virginia, Tennessee,
Louisiana, Florida, Arkansas, and South
Carolina, as well as the territories. Contesting delegations were presented by
Missouri and the District of Columbia.
Considerable confusion attended the formation of the temporary roll because of
disagreement as to what should be done
about the delegations from the states that
had seceded. The problem was finally resolved by accepting the credentials of the
northern states that were not contested,
and referring all others to the credentials
committee for recommendations.

Convention Organization

In establishing the various committees,
only those states whose delegations were
uncontested were given representation. The
committee on permanent organization reported in the evening session of the first
day, and former Governor William Denni-
son of Ohio was presented as the permanent chairman. A committee on rules and
order of business was appointed when it
was noted that it had been forgotten in the
afternoon session. The rest of the session
was devoted to speeches.

The rules committee reported at the beginning of the next day. The first rule
detailed the order in which states should
be called, following the pattern of previous
conventions. This was objected to by the
Kansas delegation—because West Virginia,
the new state created out of the western-
most counties of Virginia that had refused
to secede with the rest of Virginia and was
admitted to the Union in 1863, was listed
ahead of Kansas. (The objection was mild;
however, in 1868 both parties changed to

[1] RNC, *Proceedings*, 1864, p. 175.

the alphabetic listing that has been used ever since.) The order of business was carefully stipulated: credentials were to be dealt with before platform, and the platform report was to precede the nominations. A problem that had been raised in 1860 was disposed of by a rule that stipulated the nominating majority as a majority of the votes authorized by the credentials committee. The question of unit rule was handled thus:

In a recorded vote by States, the vote of each State shall be announced by the chairman of the respective delegations, and in case the vote of any state shall be divided, the chairman shall announce the number of votes cast for any candidate, or for or against any proposition.[2]

Another new rule established regular procedure for a record vote by providing that the chairman should order the roll called if a majority of the delegates from any two states demanded it. (This rule remained in force until 1924, when the requirement was raised to six states.) Provision was made that the previous question should be ordered if demanded by a majority of one delegation and seconded by a majority of two others. Speakers were limited to one five-minute speech on each question, without unanimous approval of the convention. Where specific convention rules were not applicable, the rules of the House of Representatives were to apply.

Credentials

Three questions were involved in the report of the credentials committee. The first concerned the Missouri contest; a Radical Union delegation and an Unconditional Union delegation each sought admission. The committee reported for the Radical Union delegation. The background of the fight was complicated; part of it related to an insurgent movement against the Blair family, who had dominated Missouri politics for years. On the national level, the Blairs were one of the focal points of Radical Union antagonism

to the administration. Montgomery Blair, as Postmaster General, was a particular target, and extreme pressures for his removal from the Cabinet were exerted on Lincoln throughout the campaign; late in September, Lincoln finally did request his resignation.

The convention disposed of the contest by a roll call vote, but only after an extremely bitter and lengthy debate. The final vote was 440 to 4 in favor of the Radical delegation, only three Pennsylvanians and one Kentuckian voting in the negative. The vote is particularly interesting, since the convention contained a great many people who were opposed to the Radicals; credence must be given to the supposition that Lincoln's managers encouraged the admission of the Radical delegation in the interests of harmony and to prevent a bolt.

The second credentials question related to the delegations from Virginia, Tennessee, Louisiana, Florida, Arkansas, the territories, and the District of Columbia. The committee recommended that these be admitted with all convention privileges except the right to vote. A minority report stipulated that they be given full convention privileges, including the right to vote, and a roll call was taken on the question of Tennessee. The amendment was accepted 310 to 151, and a second roll call approved full privileges for Arkansas and Louisiana, 307 to 167. By voice vote, full convention rights were extended to the territories of Nebraska, Colorado, and Nevada, but the majority report was accepted for Virginia and Florida.

The third question, that of South Carolina, was disposed of without much comment. The committee recommendation excluding the delegation was approved.

The Platform

The platform was forthright in its statements declaring for full prosecution of the war, to be ended only by unconditional surrender of the South, and for the com-

[2] *Ibid.* p. 203.

plete extirpation of slavery, to be ensured by an amendment to the Constitution. It was less forthright when in one passage it expressed complete approval of Abraham Lincoln, his acts, and his policies, and in the next, in but slightly veiled terms, demanded revision of his Cabinet—by which was meant the expulsion of Montgomery Blair. It approved the administration's protests against Maximilian's seizure of the government of Mexico with the backing of French troops. The platform was accepted without debate.

The Presidential Nomination

The next order of business was nomination of the presidential candidate. In an attempt to stampede the convention into renominating Hannibal Hamlin as Lincoln's running mate, Simon Cameron of Pennsylvania, former Secretary of War replaced by Stanton in 1862, moved that both Lincoln and Hamlin be nominated jointly by acclamation. This threw the convention into an uproar, and a confused series of proposals and counterproposals followed.

Finally, after a reasoned speech by Henry J. Raymond of New York, newspaper editor and close friend of Lincoln, in which he urged that the roll be called on the grounds that "the moral effect of that vote will be greater than one taken originally by acclamation," the convention agreed to call the roll. Except for Missouri's 22, which under instruction went to Ulysses S. Grant, the votes of the entire convention—484—were cast for Lincoln. Immediately after the ballot Missouri changed its vote to Lincoln and moved that the vote be declared unanimous.

The Vice-Presidential Nomination

Many conflicting stories have been told of Lincoln's part in the selection of his running mate in 1864. They range all the way from flat statements that he kept hands off completely, to assertions that he had privately indicated War Democrat Andrew Johnson of Tennessee as the man he

wanted. Only one thing is certain—he did not publicly announce his preference. However, since it seems clear that Lincoln was genuinely worried about the outcome of the election, Johnson, or someone like him, was a more logical choice than Hamlin. It is true that Hamlin too had once been a Democrat, but that fact was obscured by his four-year service as a Republican officeholder. He was from Maine—a state and a section in which Lincoln expected to win anyway—and was in this respect therefore not likely to add materially to victory. Johnson, on the other hand, not only was a recent Democrat, but came from a border state, was on record as a fighter, and had a background that matched Lincoln's own in its appeal to the common man.

Besides Johnson and Hamlin, the candidates named were General L. H. Rousseau of Kentucky and Daniel S. Dickinson of New York; six others received one or more votes on the first ballot. Johnson led with an even 200 votes, followed by Hamlin with 150 and Dickinson 108. Rousseau received only the vote of his own state, and while the clerks were tallying the first ballot, the chairman of the Kentucky delegation transferred this vote to Johnson to start the band wagon. Most of the other delegations followed suit, Johnson finally receiving 494 votes on the adjusted tally.

NINTH DEMOCRATIC CONVENTION

The Democrats delayed their convention until the unprecedented date of late August in the hope that war developments would work further to their advantage. From a strictly political viewpoint, the party prospects looked very good on the day the convention opened. The bloody battles of the Wilderness and Cold Harbor had been followed by a long summer in which nothing seemed to be happening despite the steady lengthening of the casualty lists. The general feeling of weariness throughout the nation, amounting almost to despair, gave the arguments of the Copperheads—the "Peace" Democrats—their greatest potency of the entire war. Had they had a first-rate candidate within their ranks, they might well have carried the entire convention; as it was, they were forced to content themselves with writing the platform. They did not yet know—nor did anyone else—of the spectacular victories then in the making, the first of which would be announced while the convention was in session; the entire mood of the country was to change within the next week or ten days.

No name other than that of General George B. McClellan received really serious consideration. The major leaders of the party, among them Horatio Seymour, were unavailable for one reason or another. Selection of Seymour, who by most standards was the leading party figure, would have alienated the soldier vote, as well as the vote of thousands of others who felt that the war must be pushed to final conclusion, because his handling of the 1863 draft riots in New York City had earned him the label of "Peace" Democrat. His many acts of cooperation with the war effort paled into insignificance beside the dramatic publicity emanating from the riots. For those who looked behind this publicity, it was obvious that Seymour was not a "Peace" Democrat. Actually he believed that the war should be prosecuted more vigorously, and that under a Democratic administration it would be. This, of course, made him unavailable in the view of the Copperheads.

Chicago, Illinois,
August 29, 30, 31, 1864

The chairman of the national committee, August Belmont of New York, opened the convention with a plea for unity based upon the conservative position. Although he did not specifically press for continuance of the war, he urged the selection of "a tried patriot, who has proved his devotion to the Union and the Constitution," and asked that the convention "strive to bring [the nation] back to its former greatness and prosperity, without one single star taken from the brilliant constellation that once encircled its youthful brow." In a single phrase, he castigated both the Republican administration and the rebellious South:

. . . the sacred cause of the Union, the constitution and the laws, must prevail against fanaticism and treason.[3]

The temporary chairman, William Bigler of Pennsylvania, elected unanimously after Belmont's opening speech, was more explicit about how the nation was to be preserved. The present administration must be overthrown, so that another administration could

. . . directly and zealously, but temperately and justly, wield all the influence and power of the government to bring about a speedy settlement of the national troubles to the people, the fountain of political authority, and to the States under the forms of the Constitution; one which shall stand unfalteringly by civil and religious liberty; one which, instead of relying solely on its own peculiar dogmas and doctrines and the ravages of the sword shall refer the national troubles to the people, the fountain of political authority, and to the States under the forms of the Constitution; one which shall have no conditions precedent to the restoration of the Union, but which shall diligently seek that result as the consummation of permanent peace among the States and renewed fraternity among the people.[4]

This quite clearly suggested settlement of the war by negotiation, even at the risk of conceding to the South most of the war aims.

Convention Organization

After some discussion as to the right of representation for the territories and the southern states, representation being opposed by Samuel J. Tilden of New York, among others, the question was referred to the credentials committee. This committee was then appointed, as were the committees on permanent organization and resolutions.

[3] DNC, *Proceedings*, 1864, pp. 3-4.
[4] *Ibid.*, p. 4.

After hearing a series of resolutions, most of which attacked the administration for purported violations of civil and states rights, the convention adjourned.

The next day the single contest before the credentials committee, two full delegations from Kentucky, was decided by admitting both and splitting the vote equally. The official list of delegates included none from the seceded South or from any of the territories; nothing was said about the question in the report of the committee. Horatio Seymour was selected as permanent chairman, and the 1860 rules were adopted as the rules of the convention. Nothing was said about the disagreement in the 1860 convention over whether the nominating majority meant two thirds of the electoral college or two thirds of those present and voting, but since the figure given in the published proceedings as required for a choice is based upon the number of delegates present, there had apparently been tacit agreement that the seceded states should not be counted.

Seymour's speech of acceptance reiterated the statements of Bigler that the party had no conditions for the restoration of the Union. He indicted the administration and Lincoln for destroying states rights and civil liberties. The armies in the field had done a magnificent job, he said, but the lack of wise statesmanship by administration leaders had deprived them of the fruits of victory.

The Platform

The platform was a short document, consisting only of six resolutions. The second of these was the crucial one:

Resolved: That this convention does explicitly declare, as the sense of the American people, that after four years of failure to restore the Union by the experiment of war, during which, under pretense of a military necessity, or war power higher than the Constitution, the Constitution itself has been disregarded in every part, and public liberty and private right alike trodden down and the material prosperity of the country essentially impaired—justice, humanity, liberty and the public welfare demand that immediate efforts be made for a cessation of hostilities, with a view to an ultimate convention of the States, or other peaceable means, to the end that at the earliest practicable moment peace may be restored on the basis of the Federal Union of the States.[5]

According to the reporter, this was greeted by a reception that "battles all description." No one spoke against the platform report, although a delegate attempted to have another resolution added —the text of the first of Thomas Jefferson's Kentucky Resolutions, which defined the Federal Union as one in which all rights and powers not explicitly allocated to the central government by the Constitution remained vested in the states and reserving to the individual states the right to decide which powers were properly exercised by the federal government and the form of redress the individual states should take if, in their opinion, the central government transcended its rights. The motion was referred to the credentials committee without action by the convention.

The Presidential Nomination

The speech nominating General George B. McClellan for President was short and pleasant; what followed was neither short nor pleasant. Matters started out quietly enough with a seconding speech for McClellan and the presentation of Senator Lazarus W. Powell of Kentucky, Thomas H. Seymour, former governor of Connecticut, and ex-President Franklin Pierce of New Hampshire as candidates. The storm broke when a Maryland delegate, in seconding the Seymour nomination, stated: ". . . the strong arm of the military has been over us, and as it rests upon us now, it was instituted by your nominee."[6] Other in-

[5] Ibid., p. 27.
[6] The reference was to McClellan's seizure of part of the Maryland legislature and suspension of the writ of habeas corpus early in the war. The members of the legislature allegedly proposed to pass an act of secession as a prelude to invasion by a southern force massed nearby, and McClellan acted to prevent this.

dictments against McClellan, including his failure as a military commander, followed amidst constant interruptions from the delegates and the galleries. McClellan's friends leaped to his support, defending his actions as the only ones possible under the circumstances.

A Connecticut delegate disavowed any connection between Thomas Seymour and the attacks by the Copperheads on McClellan. Neither the Connecticut delegation nor Seymour himself, he said, had authorized presentation of his name, and its use in the convention was without Seymour's prior knowledge or permission. Lazarus Powell then withdrew his name, and a delegate from New Hampshire withdrew Pierce's name. After long wrangling, the convention adjourned until the next day.

In the relative calm of the morning after, the roll was called for the nomination. McClellan received 174 votes on the roll call, Thomas Seymour 38, and Horatio Seymour 12, before vote shifting. Upon completion of the call, a delegate from Ohio proposed that each delegate be allowed to stand and declare his vote personally; upon being denied the proposal, he requested time for the Ohio delegation, which had split its vote, to caucus. This was allowed, and during the interim Horatio Seymour made his first, but not last, protest against receiving votes as the presidential nominee. He stressed again the need for forbearance and unanimity within the party. Ohio's return set off a chain of vote shifting, and on the final ballot McClellan received 202½ votes, Thomas Seymour, 28½. Although no record appears in the printed proceedings of a vote on a motion to approve the nomination unanimously, this doubtless was an oversight, for such a motion was made by Clement Vallandigham, the outstanding leader of the Copperheads, and seconded by others who were late in getting on the band wagon.

The Vice-Presidential Nomination

Congressman George H. Pendleton of Ohio was presented for the Vice Presidency by a leader of the Copperheads. Although the presentation was made in but four short sentences, the chairman immediately afterward "suggested" that "the gentlemen who bring the names of candidates before the Convention will introduce the name without remarks or comment. . . . No man will be named here whose reputation will not be known to us all."[7] Other candidates were Congressman Daniel W. Voorhees of Indiana; George W. Cass of Pennsylvania; James Guthrie of Kentucky, Secretary of the Treasury under Pierce; former Senator Augustus C. Dodge of Iowa; Judge John D. Caton of Illinois; Lazarus W. Powell of Kentucky; former Congressman J. S. Phelps of Missouri.

All received votes on the first ballot, Guthrie leading with 65½, Pendleton and Powell following with 55½ and 32½. Caton, who had received only the Illinois vote, withdrew in favor of Pendleton, and New York and Kentucky, who had provided most of Guthrie's support, followed. This precipitated a wholesale switch, and Pendleton became the unanimous nominee. Pendleton, who was present, made a short acceptance speech, after which the convention soon adjourned.

[7] DNC, *Proceedings*, 1864, p. 54.

Presidential Election, November 8, 1864

ABRAHAM LINCOLN (R): popular vote, 2,206,938; electoral vote, 212
GEORGE B. MCCLELLAN (D): popular vote, 1,803,787; electoral vote, 21

1868

FEW PERIODS IN American political history have been as turbulent as the years between Lincoln's second election in 1864 and the election of 1868. Even in the midst of the 1864 campaign, some of the Radicals declared open war upon Lincoln's reconstruction policies, and others supported his candidacy only with reluctance. After Lincoln's death the fight between congressional and administrative elements of the party grew in fury when it became evident that Andrew Johnson, as President, intended to follow Lincoln's relatively liberal southern reconstruction policies. Throughout his administration Johnson received little support from Republicans, and was to all intents and purposes a Democratic President —as was attested by the size of his following in the Democratic convention of 1868.

The confusion of the political situation is further indicated by the fact that Salmon P. Chase and Ulysses S. Grant were each seriously considered for the presidential nomination by both parties. Chase, whom Lincoln had appointed Chief Justice of the Supreme Court in late 1864 and whose background included the governorship of Ohio, service in the Senate, and the post of Secretary of the Treasury under Lincoln, had one of the most kaleidoscopic political careers in U.S. history. A National Republican at the time of Henry Clay's campaign in 1832, he moved to the Whigs, thence to the Liberty, Free Soil, and Democratic parties in subsequent years, and was one of the founders of the Republican party. Despite his position in Lincoln's Cabinet, he offered himself as a candidate against Lincoln in 1864; in June 1864 he resigned from the Cabinet because of his opposition to Secretary of State Seward. Following Lincoln's death, Chase

first indicated support of Johnson, then gravitated to the Radicals, only to break with them on the issue of Johnson's impeachment. His statesmanlike and judicious conduct as president of the Court of Impeachment endeared him to the Democrats nearly as much as it infuriated the Radicals, and by April 1868 his name was being prominently mentioned by leading Democrats as a possible candidate.

The background and experience of General Grant were as nearly the opposite of Chase's as could be imagined. His political experience was limited to a vote cast for Buchanan in 1856—reportedly because he, Grant, "knew Frémont"—and a vote for Lincoln in 1864. For a period after Lincoln's death Grant was friendly with Andrew Johnson, who appointed him Secretary of War in April 1867 as a move in the struggle with the Radicals. Even before this, the Democrats, in looking for a candidate who could win, had fastened on Grant as a possibility. When, however, under heavy pressure from the Radicals, Grant turned back the keys of his office to deposed Secretary Edwin M. Stanton in January 1868, enmity quickly developed between the President and the General, who then became the darling of the Radicals. From then on, Grant's nomination as the Republican presidential candidate was virtually assured.

FOURTH REPUBLICAN CONVENTION

Only Grant and Chase were seriously considered for the Republican presidential nomination during the preconvention period, and by the time of the convention Grant stood alone.

The vice-presidential nomination was another matter. The succession of a Vice President after Lincoln's death had made the office more tempting than it had been for many years, and a number of men who were deterred from trying for the presidential nomination by Grant's superior availability were willing to take the second spot. Shortly before the convention opened, Benjamin F. Wade of Ohio, president *pro tem* of the Senate and heir to the remainder of Johnson's term if the impeachment proceedings were successful, was a definite front-runner. Many delegates were pledged to him, all fully aware that he might enjoy the powers of the presidential office for several months before a newly elected president would be inaugurated; no one doubted that "Bluff Ben" Wade would know how to make the most of this position. Others prominently mentioned were Governor Reuben E. Fenton of New York, Senator Henry Wilson of Massachusetts, and Speaker of the House Schuyler Colfax of Indiana.

Chicago, Illinois,
May 20 and 21, 1868

The official call used the designation "National Union Convention," and invited "the co-operation of all citizens who rejoice that our great civil war has happily terminated the discomfiture of rebellion."[1]

The first session was called to order by Governor Marcus L. Ward of New Jersey, chairman of the national committee. Newspaper editor Carl Schurz of Missouri was elected temporary chairman; his opening speech eulogized the party, its program, and its leaders, and made only a brief reference to the struggle between Congress and Andrew Johnson.

Convention Organization

Considerable time was taken in naming the committee on credentials. There were three questions. The first related to the

representation on the committee of states in which there were contests: two states were involved, one seat from California, and half the Maryland delegation contested. California was allowed a seat on the committee; Maryland voluntarily declined to name a member. The second question concerned the unreconstructed southern states. On the first calling of the roll, Alabama, Arkansas, and Georgia were omitted, and the call was interrupted by a protest.

The temporary chairman then announced that the unreconstructed states had not been officially invited, the intent being that the convention should determine what to do about them. It was decided that they should be called, and that the question of inclusion or exclusion be settled on an individual basis. All were accepted.

The third question, the status of territorial delegations, was raised by a protest from Colorado when its name was omitted on the roll call. The status of Colorado was unusual; its admission as a state had been approved by Congress but vetoed by Johnson. In a convention composed almost exclusively of enemies of Johnson, this undoubtedly was enough to ensure Colorado's acceptance. In any event, the delegation was given full voting and committee rights. The question of what should be done with the other territories and the District of Columbia was referred to the credentials committee.

The roll call for naming members to the committee on permanent organization was interrupted twice, first by a motion to reconsider the previous action on the unreconstructed states. The motion was tabled. The second interruption was a motion to adjourn for one hour. After its defeat, an attempt was made to simplify the procedure by having each state send the name of its nominee to the chair, thus dispensing with the roll call, but the chairman ordered the roll call continued. Maryland again waived right of membership.

Although another attempt was made to simplify the cumbersome procedure, the committees on resolutions and rules were appointed by the same process. The contesting Maryland delegates apparently could agree on members for these committees, for names were submitted.

The committee on permanent organization was first to report, and named General Joseph R. Hawley, former governor of Connecticut, as permanent chairman. Immediately following his acceptance speech, an attempt to nominate General Grant by acclamation was greeted by cries of "Too early," and was withdrawn after brief debate.

The credentials committee report was accepted without discussion. Territories and the District of Columbia were given seats without voting rights, as were the losing delegates in the Maryland contest. Pennsylvania's fifty-nine delegates were all given seats and authorized to cast the 52 votes allowed in any way they saw fit.

The rules committee spelled out the order of business in considerable detail. A majority of the delegations from any two states was set as the minimum requirement for a roll call demand. The custom that had originated in the first convention was institutionalized in a provision that in no case should the roll call for the presidential nomination be dispensed with, and up to the present day the custom has held firm. Before adoption of the rules report, another attempt to nominate Grant by acclamation was made; it failed, and the report was adopted.

The Platform

The committee on resolutions was still in session when the convention convened for the second day. Time was filled by reading resolutions—contrary to the rule previously passed that all resolutions be referred to committee without reading. Objection was made on that basis, but somewhat pointlessly, for it came after the resolutions had been read. The committee was still not ready; to fill time further, several delegates

were called upon to speak. One, after accepting, said:

Mr. President, I do not believe that this Convention is in humor now to hear a discourse on the political questions of the day. I was not prepared to make a speech, and I do not wish to interfere with the business of the Convention, and would rather be excused until that is over.

With but little urging he then obliged the convention with a speech that required over eight pages of fine print in the published proceedings.

More speakers were called upon, another attempt was made to suspend the rules and proceed with the nomination, the band played "The Star-Spangled Banner," "Hail Columbia," and "Columbia the Gem of the Ocean." Finally, the resolutions committee was ready to report.

The platform congratulated the country on the success of the Radical reconstruction policy, and insisted upon equal suffrage to all loyal men of the South, but specifically insisted that the question of suffrage in the "loyal States properly belongs to the people of those States." Hard money and economy in government were spoken for. Johnson received a round share of condemnation, and Lincoln a slender share of praise. The "brave soldiers" and the "widows and orphans of the gallant dead" were assured the "bounties and pensions provided by law."

Following acceptance of the platform, two resolutions were added by Carl Schurz and adopted. The first recommended removal of disqualifications and restrictions imposed upon late rebels, "in the same measure as the spirit of disloyalty will die out." The second recognized the principles of the Declaration of Independence as the true foundation of democratic government —a rather odd action on the part of those who were celebrating defeat of a rebellion, and whose primary concern at the moment was how best to establish rigid political control over the defeated areas.

The Presidential Nomination

The nominating speech was brief. It was delivered by Congressman John A. Logan, who, greeted by cries of "Bully! John!" said *in toto:*

Then, sir, in the name of the loyal citizens, soldiers and sailors of this great Republic of the United States of America; in the name of loyalty, of liberty, of humanity, of justice; in the name of the National Union Republican party; I nominate, as candidate for the Chief Magistracy of this nation, Ulysses S. Grant.[2]

The unanimous roll call quickly followed.

The Vice-Presidential Nomination

For the first time in the convention, real differences of opinion broke to the surface. When the demonstration following Grant's nomination had subsided, a motion to adjourn was made and defeated. A Virginia delegate gained the floor to nominate Henry Wilson, making a short speech in the process. The nominations that followed were also accompanied by short speeches. Next on the list was Schuyler Colfax, then Benjamin F. Wade, whose position as a front-runner had received a severe shock a few days before when the vote on the first test article of impeachment of President Johnson went against the Radicals. New York presented its governor, Reuben E. Fenton, as a favorite son with considerable support outside his own state. Among other favorite sons and minor candidates named were Andrew J. Curtin, former governor of Pennsylvania, and Hannibal Hamlin, Lincoln's first running mate.

On the first ballot Wade was the front-runner, as expected, with 147 votes. Three others were over the hundred mark: Fenton 126, Wilson 119, and Colfax 115. The others, with the exception of Curtin, whose 51 votes included 48 from his home state, were far out of the running. On the second ballot most of the formerly scattered votes concentrated upon the four leaders, all of whom gained except Wilson, who dropped two votes. Wade led with 170; Colfax had 145 and Fenton 144.

On the third and fourth ballots Colfax and Wade continued to gain, mostly at the expense of Wilson and Curtin, the latter having withdrawn; Fenton continued to hold his own. On the fifth and final ballot Wade gained only one vote, reaching his peak of 207, while Colfax picked up 40 votes over his previous ballot to pass Wade with 226—99 short of a nominating majority. Most of the Colfax gain came from Wilson. At the end of the roll call, and before the totals were announced, a bandwagon vote change began, in the course of which things became confused. Several delegations moved that the nomination of Colfax be declared unanimous, but the chairman refused to accept the motions. Before announcing the results of the previous call and while delegations were seeking to be recognized so that they could change their vote, the chairman directed the secretary again to call the roll. The call got as far as California, and was almost unanimous for Colfax, when a delegate from New York stated that the people near him did not know what was going on, and insisted on hearing the ballot results.

The chairman suggested that calling the roll was the easiest way to permit changes to be made, but there were so many interruptions and objections that he finally abandoned the call and recognized individual delegations. Fenton retained 69 votes and Wade 38, in each case nearly all from their respective home states of New York and Ohio. Then New York moved the nomination of Colfax be made unanimous, whereupon Ohio's spokesman said:

Was there ever such a race as this, in which Ohio had the leading nag in the race, and nearly had the leading horse on the home stretch, and yet is denied the poor privilege of congratulating the winner?[3]

[2] *Ibid.,* p. 72.

[3] *Ibid.,* p. 109.

He then seconded New York's motion, and
the nomination was declared unanimous.
The convention adjourned shortly thereafter.

TENTH DEMOCRATIC CONVENTION

Where the Republican alternatives had
been reduced to one potential nominee,
the Democratic alternatives remained numerous. The Chase candidacy had become
an undercover operation, and the principal
source of his strength, the New York delegation, entered the convention behind a
local stalking-horse, Lieutenant Governor
Sanford E. Church. The real leader was
the vice-presidential candidate of the previous election, George H. Pendleton of
Ohio, although President Johnson, seeking
to justify his regime by gaining the Democratic nomination, held considerable preconvention strength.

Pendleton had become the leading
apostle for the "Ohio Idea," a fiscal plan
for discharging, by the issuance of greenbacks, all of the national debt that did not
specifically call for payment in specie. In
an era when monetary valuations had not
yet been stabilized, greenbacks were not redeemable at par, and additional issue for
the purpose would further devaluate them;
accordingly, the burden of debt upon the
farmers and other debtors would be materially lessened, both by the provision of a
devaluated currency with which they could
pay their obligations and by the reduction
of the national debt. The losers, of course,
would be the holders of the bonds and of
other forms of indebtedness, and since
these tended to be concentrated in the
East, Pendleton received little support from
that section. The soft-money men undoubtedly held a majority of the strength
in the convention, as became evident in the
phrasing of the platform; the two thirds
rule, however, provided an opportunity to
use favorite son and stalking-horse tactics
to stalemate the nomination of the leading
proponent of soft money—an opportunity
quickly seized upon. Besides Church, other

favorite sons and stalking-horses were Governor James E. English of Connecticut,
former Governor Joel Parker of New Jersey, former Congressman Asa Packer of
Pennsylvania, and Senator James R. Doolittle of Wisconsin.

A candidate of national stature was General Winfield Scott Hancock, whose record
as a military commander of a reconstructed
southern district had brought him at odds
with the Radical controlling elements.
Frequently mentioned also, but with little
pledged support at the time the convention
opened, was Senator Thomas A. Hendricks
of Indiana. Always behind the scenes were
Horatio Seymour, New York's war governor, who once again insisted that he was
not a candidate, and Chase, whose supporters were watching for an opportunity.

As usually happens when the presidential
question is wide open, little thought was
given to possible candidates for the second
half of the ticket.

New York City,
July 4, 5, 6, 7, 8, 9, 1868

August Belmont, opening his second consecutive convention as chairman of the national committee, developed one prong of
what was to be a two-pronged Democratic
strategy: he launched into a bitter attack on
the reconstruction policies of the congressional Radicals and the general suppression
of civil rights. This theme was further
emphasized by selection of Independence
Day as the first day of the convention,
despite its being a Saturday. The temporary chairman, Henry L. Palmer of Wisconsin, contented himself with thanking
the convention for the honor, and stating
the hope that the deliberations of the convention would result in election victory.

Convention Organization

The routine proposal that the temporary
rules of the convention be the rules of the
House of Representatives met with unprecedented objection: "there are many
gentlemen in the Convention who do not

recognize the rules of the present House of Representatives"—a slap at the Republican-controlled Congress. The proposed rule was amended to provide that the temporary rules would be the rules of the last Democratic convention.

The question of giving representation to the territories was again a problem, and finally was decided in the negative by a roll call vote, 184 to 106. Committees on credentials, organization, and resolutions were appointed without additional difficulty. A series of resolutions that were read and referred to committee castigated the recent impeachment proceedings and called for a constitutional change removing right of impeachment from the Senate and placing it in the hands of the Supreme Court. The Declaration of Independence was read, and the convention adjourned until the following Monday morning.

The committee on permanent organization was first to report, and the second half of the team that had guided the deliberations in 1864 — Horatio Seymour — was named permanent chairman. The rules of the 1864 convention were adopted as the permanent rules. A question was raised as to whether the two thirds rule was to be based on votes cast or on the total electoral college; the chairman ruled that interpretation of the rules was not under consideration at the time, and the question was left open.

The credentials committee reported full representation from every state in the Union, and no contests. It recommended that three delegates from each territory and four from the District of Columbia be allowed to have the privilege of the floor but without voting rights. This subsequently was amended to permit all ten delegates from the District to have floor privileges.

Following the report of the credentials committee, several resolutions were offered with varying success; most of them pertained to matters properly in the sphere of the committee on resolutions, to which they were referred, but some involved rules and order of business. Among the latter, a resolution binding all delegates and all candidates to support the eventual nominees was adopted. A rule proposing that the nominating majority be a majority of all the votes in the electoral college in all future conventions was referred to the committee on resolutions.

It being obvious that the committee on resolutions would not report for some time, the following resolution was proposed:

I move that the Convention do now proceed to nominate a candidate for President of the United States.[4]

Despite protestations from the delegate making the motion that he did not intend any balloting to take place before adoption of the platform, an amendment was offered and passed by a roll call vote, 189½ to 90½, New York and Maine abstaining, that directed:

. . . no steps be taken towards the nomination of a candidate for the Presidency until after the Platform shall have been presented.[5]

Shortly thereafter, the convention adjourned until later in the day in the hopes that the platform would be ready for consideration. After it reconvened, considerable time was taken with a delegation from the Conservative Soldiers and Sailors Convention meeting in the same city, and with mutually laudatory speeches. It being evident that the platform still was not ready, motion was made to reconsider the previous vote barring action on the nominations. An attempt to table the motion to reconsider was defeated 172 to 142, and the motion to reconsider passed 179½ to 137.[6] After considerable parliamentary wrangling, the original motion to nominate was passed by a voice vote, but the motion lost its point when the convention voted 209 to 106 to adjourn for the day.

The Platform

On the following day the resolutions committee, after its long labor, was able to announce a unanimous report, which reit-

[4] DNC, *Proceedings*, 1868, p. 42.
[5] *Ibid.*, pp. 42-43.
[6] *Ibid.*, pp. 50-52. For the vote on tabling, see *Analysis of Key Votes.*

erated the theme first stated by national committee Chairman Belmont in opening the convention—a demand for guarantees of civil and states rights. A second theme, representing victory for the proponents of soft money, and therefore for Pendleton, called for payment of all obligations of the national government in "lawful money of the United States," except where the law under which the obligations were contracted specifically called for payment in coin. Another clause called for "one currency for the government and the people, the laborer and the office-holder, the pensioner and the soldier, the producer and the bond-holder."[7] Without debate, the platform was adopted by "an unanimous and tremendous vote."

The Presidential Nomination

Before settling down to the business of the nominations, the question as to what constituted a nominating majority was resumed. The chairman did not attempt to rule on the question, but asked the convention to make its own decision. A motion was then made by a delegate:

That two thirds of all the votes cast shall be required to nominate a candidate for President and Vice-President of the United States.[8]

The delegate accompanied his motion with a statement that he considered the two thirds rule the "most mischievous rule ever adopted by the Democratic party," and promised to move that majority rule be adopted for future conventions once the present nominations were made. After discussion, the motion was withdrawn, and the chairman declared that he would interpret the rule as it had been in the 1860 convention—that two thirds of the total electoral college vote be required to nominate.

On more than one occasion during the discussion about nominating procedure, hints were dropped indicating that certain of the delegates were not to be surprised

by the final action of the convention on the presidential nomination. The clearest of these occurred just before the roll was called for nominations, when the chairman was asked to state explicitly how he would rule if candidates were brought forward during the balloting who were not officially nominated on the regular roll call. It is not certain whether the delegate had Seymour or Chase in mind, but almost certainly it was one or the other. The chairman replied: "The Chair understands that this Convention has a right, at any time, to bring forward any new candidate it may see fit."[9]

James E. English, favorite son of Connecticut, was the first nominee. Hancock, Pendleton, Parker, Church, Packer, Johnson, and Doolittle were introduced in short order, most of the speeches being relatively brief. Just before the first ballot a delegate from the territories attempted to introduce a resolution allowing the territories to vote. He was declared out of order by the chair.

The first ballot showed Pendleton in the lead as expected. His 105 votes (212 being required to nominate) were followed by 65 for Johnson. Hancock and Church were the only others above 30. Eleven candidates received mention.

Johnson's vote evidently was largely complimentary, for it began to erode on the second ballot, as he dropped to 52; Pendleton lost a vote, and Hancock gained most of what Johnson lost. Twelve candidates in all received votes. As the balloting continued, Johnson continued to lose as Pendleton began a steady rise that continued with only minor breaks until he reached a peak of 156½ on the eighth ballot. Thereafter Pendleton's vote began a gradual decline until it broke sharply on the 16th ballot and disappeared entirely with his withdrawal on the 19th. Immediately following the 16th ballot an attempt to adjourn, undoubtedly stimulated by Hancock's big jump, was defeated 174½ to 142½.[10]

---

[7] DNC, *Proceedings,* 1868, p. 58.
[8] *Ibid.,* p. 62.

[9] *Ibid.,* p. 65.
[10] See *Analysis of Key Votes.*

In the meantime Senator Hendricks, who had received only token support on the early ballots, began a slow but steady rise until he received a total of 132 on the 21st ballot —only 3½ behind Hancock, whose vote had begun to climb when Pendleton's broke. Hancock's previous vote had varied roughly between 30 and 50 votes.

As the 22nd and final ballot began, a strong trend toward Hendricks was obviously in the making. When the roll had been called down through North Carolina, he had gained about 30 votes over the same point on the previous ballot, excluding Kentucky and Massachusetts, who passed on the 22nd roll call. Neither of these states had given him much support. Assuming no further gains, but that he would have held the same vote on the balance of the roll call, Hendricks' total would have surpassed the highest received by any candidate on any previous roll call. Ordinarily, at a point such as this, the bandwagon swing increases as the roll is called, and thus Hendricks would have been nominated unless something drastic occurred. Something drastic did.

When Ohio was called, the delegation chairman announced that, with the unanimous approval of the delegation including Pendleton, "and of every public man in the State," Ohio placed the name of Horatio Seymour in nomination and cast a unanimous vote for him. The convention broke into an uproar, and it was some time before Seymour could make himself heard. In an impassioned speech, he assured the convention of the sincerity of his many statements that he was not and would not be a candidate; in closing he said, "Gentlemen, I thank you, and may God bless you for your kindness to me; but your candidate I cannot be."[11]

His protests did no good. Ohio delegate Vallandigham stated that the declination could not be accepted and that Ohio's vote stood. New York gave her blessing, although protesting that her delegates had had nothing to do with the new movement, and would take no active part in it—"We leave it in the hands of others, as we are constrained to do." This probably was the plain truth, for contemporary accounts indicate that the New Yorkers had intended to do for Chase just what Ohio did for Seymour, but that they waited too long. Ohio did not want Chase, despite the fact that he was a citizen of that state, and had been its governor and U.S. senator; faction-torn New York, on the other hand, was considerably less than unanimous for its own ex-governor.

The roll continued to be called, with little further change from the 21st ballot until the last state, Wisconsin, was reached. Wisconsin cast its vote for Seymour, and was followed by the two states that had passed, Kentucky and Massachusetts. North Carolina was the first to switch its vote, and then, in the words of the reporter, "a scene of the wildest enthusiasm followed," as delegation after delegation sought the attention of the chairman *pro tem,* Seymour having been relieved of the chair. Finally, Samuel Tilden of New York gained the attention of the chairman; after carefully checking to see whether every other state had changed its vote, he switched the New York vote to make the nomination unanimous.

The Vice-Presidential Nomination

A recess for at least half an hour to deliberate was proposed by a delegate, because "the nomination for Vice President will be an important part of the coming election." His proposal was objected to by several, but in the end calmer counsel prevailed and the convention suspended activities for an hour. After the recess, the roll of states was resumed. Illinois nominated a favorite son, General John A. McClernand, who promptly withdrew. Iowa followed with its favorite son, Senator A. C. Dodge. Kansas nominated its citizen, General Thomas Ewing, Jr. Kentucky presented the name of General Francis P. Blair

11 DNC, *Proceedings,* 1868, p. 153.

of Missouri, whose nomination was then seconded by many states. New York passed on the roll call, but upon its completion placed the accolade upon Blair's head by seconding his nomination. Ewing and Dodge promptly were withdrawn, the vote became unanimous for Blair, and after routine closing business was completed, the convention adjourned.

Analysis of Key Votes

The most deeply split vote was taken on the question of tabling a motion to reconsider a motion previously passed to bar any action on the nominations before the platform had been passed. The motion was rejected 172 to 142, but the candidate-orientation was low. Correlation with the Hancock and Johnson first-ballot votes was −.43 and −.36 respectively and with Pendleton's votes, +.26. Correlation with the vote for others on the first ballot was +.18.

There was almost no relationship between the voting line-up on this vote with the final ballot before the shift to Seymour began. The correlation with Hendricks' vote at this point was −.08; with Hancock, −.01 and with others +.11.

The vote taken on a motion made by Tilden of New York to adjourn before the 17th ballot was more clearly candidate-oriented. The correlation between this vote and the vote on the 22nd ballot before the vote shifting to Seymour was: Hancock +.74; Hendricks −.40; others −.38. The motion was therefore defeated by quite solid opposition on the part of Hancock's supporters combined with uncertainty by many of the others. This is understandable in view of the fact that Hancock, for some ballots past, had been gaining steadily; his supporters naturally were interested in continuing the balloting in the hopes that this trend would continue. He was still too far from a two thirds majority, however, to seriously alarm the other delegates.

Presidential Election, November 3, 1868

ULYSSES S. GRANT (R) : popular vote, 3,013,421; electoral vote, 214
HORATIO SEYMOUR (D) : popular vote, 2,843,446; electoral vote, 80

1872

GRANT'S FIRST TERM was still young when the first major scandal broke. A group of speculators developed a corner in the gold market, basing their gamble upon their ability to obtain advance notice of administrative action in financial matters from members of Grant's family, and upon Grant's tendency to accept advice on financial matters from those he trusted. This corner could have been broken at any time by government sale of gold reserves, but Grant was persuaded it was better for the economy if the Treasury did not interfere. When the Treasury did begin to sell, the bottom dropped out of the market, but not before some, at least, of the conspirators had reaped a handsome profit. The culmination of the panic on September 24, 1869—"Black Friday"—ruined thousands of less advantaged speculators.

As the months rolled on, others took advantage of Grant's trust, and nearly every department of the government became infiltrated with grasping appointees bent upon mulcting public funds by all legal and extralegal means available. Many of the thefts did not come to light until much later, but enough was known at the time to have justified a major public revolt. The public, however, was in an expansionist mood. As the railroads pushed westward, new frontiers were opening; in a very real sense, the entire nation at that time was a frontier, and frontiersmen notoriously have taken law somewhat lightly. Fortunes could be made anywhere, if a man were quick enough and ruthless enough. A great many people were so busy trying to get their share of the new wealth that they could spare little thought to others engaged in the same scramble—un-less some of the others interfered quite directly with their own pursuits.

But some did protest. Within the Republican ranks a substantial movement began, fostered in its infancy by honest idealists but soon joined by others whose motivations were less noble. At the beginning the main theme of the group, which was soon to be known as the Liberal Republican party, was the liberation of the South from the chains of carpetbagging; as it grew, the theme expanded to an attack on special privilege generally.

Since the group was too few in numbers to hope to win in a three-way battle, Liberal Republican leaders devised a plan whereby they would nominate a presidential candidate acceptable to the Democrats—who would then nominate the same candidate. It was hoped that this joining of forces would produce the electoral majorities that were necessary throughout the North to offset the administration's advantage in its control of the southern states.

One candidate prominently mentioned as acceptable was Charles Francis Adams of Massachusetts, Minister to England under Lincoln and Johnson. Another was Judge David Davis of Maryland, appointed to the Supreme Court by his close friend Lincoln and whose decision in *ex parte Milligan* in 1866 had endeared him to both the Democrats and the Liberal Republicans. A third was Senator Lyman Trumbull of Connecticut, who had in 1864 introduced into Congress the resolution that was the basis for the Thirteenth Amendment and who was one of the few Republican senators who voted against the impeachment of Andrew Johnson. Others of lesser stature, all of whom had once been Democrats or had for some reason become attractive to Democratic partisans, were favorites of one or another of the groups attempting to form the new party.

Unfortunately, when the Liberal Republican convention opened in Cincinnati on May 1, 1872, the real leaders of the movement lost control to a group of political opportunists, and Horace Greeley of New York, brilliant but eccentric reformer and editor, was nominated as the presidential candidate. One of the prime movers of the convention steal, former Senator B. Gratz Brown of Missouri, was given the second place on the ticket.

Since, in effect, this convention nominated the Democratic ticket and wrote the Democratic platform, it deserves additional attention. According to contemporary commentators it was "a mixture of a town meeting and barbecue of national proportions." Without a nationwide formal organization, the Liberal Republican delegates came with all kinds of credentials, and in widely varying numbers in relation to state electoral strength. An attempt was made to bring order out of this chaos by directing the delegations to select twice the number of the electoral strength from their ranks, and name them as the official delegates. The tactic was not altogether successful, but did determine the relative voting strengths.

Prior to the convention, an informal arrangement had made among a group of prominent editors, including Horace White, Chicago *Tribune,* Murat Halstead, New York *Tribune,* Henry Watterson, Louisville *Courier-Journal,* and Samuel Bowles, Springfield (Mass.) *Republican,* to join hands to prevent the nomination of Judge Davis. Carl Schurz, who became the permanent chairman of the convention, shared their views. The editors' group, known as the "Quadrilateral," supported Adams, but they suddenly found the ground cut out from under them by the professional politicians, led by B. Gratz Brown and Senator Francis P. Blair, the latter having made a hurried trip from Washington to rally the forces opposed to

Adams. The professionals turned their support to Horace Greeley and to the great surprise of the nation—and particularly the Democrats—he became the convention nominee on the sixth ballot. The nomination of Brown followed quickly, many delegates having left in disgust before the second, and nominating, ballot, was taken.

ELEVENTH DEMOCRATIC CONVENTION

The strange actions of the Democratic leaders in 1872 will perhaps never be fully explained. Seymour's defeat in 1868 had been anything but abysmal—as biased an opponent as James G. Blaine spent several pages in his memoirs lamenting and trying to explain away the closeness of the results. The mid-term elections showed substantial gains for the Democrats in Congress. Some of the men who had been considered in the 1868 convention were probably too old in 1872, but not all were. Two of the 1868 candidates, in fact, were to receive strong support in the subsequent conventions: Hancock would be nominated for the Presidency eight years later, and Hendricks would be nominated and elected Vice President twelve years later. Whatever the explanation, the fact remains that in 1872 no Democratic leader made a strong enough plea to rally support against the surrender of leadership to a relatively small and poorly organized group of insurgents from the opposition party.

It is true that most of the delegates to the Democratic convention were already selected before the surprise results of the Cincinnati convention became known. It may also be true that had the Cincinnati convention selected a more suitable ticket, it might have been accepted by the Democrats with enthusiasm and victory might have resulted. However, the adjustments in making a workable administrative team would have been most difficult, though this probably was given little thought when the plans originally were laid. In any case, there was too little time after the period of shocked surprise following the Cincinnati nominations for any Democratic candidate to build the necessary following. The delegates came to the convention knowing what they had to do, whether they liked it or not.

Baltimore, Maryland,
July 9 and 10, 1872

The convention was called to order by August Belmont who, after twelve years as national committee chairman, announced that he was performing this duty for the last time. The temporary chairman, octogenarian Thomas Jefferson Randolph of Virginia—a grandson of Thomas Jefferson—then took the chair.

Convention Organization

During the early part of the proceedings, a certain amount of confusion was indicated, which could have been the consequence of a weak temporary chairman (not impossible in view of his advanced age), or of strong pressures being exerted on delegates to keep in line when many did not wish to do so, or a combination of both. The confusion was kept to little points, however, and on the main points, convention business proceeded as obviously desired by the managers. Committees were appointed for credentials and permanent organization, but not for resolutions; when a demand was made for appointment of this committee at the customary time, a delegate cried out: "We do not want any such committee yet." As the convention wore on, it became increasingly obvious that the management of the convention preferred as little discussion as possible.

James R. Doolittle of Wisconsin was selected permanent chairman in the short afternoon session, and he made it quite clear in his acceptance speech just what the duties of the convention were. The candidates and the platform of the Liberal Republican convention were to be endorsed— and that was all. Doolittle noted that no committee on resolutions had been appointed, and this omission was quickly repaired. Lest anything controversial in

the way of conflicting resolutions be presented from the floor, a motion was passed to refer all resolutions to the committee without debate and without reading.

The credentials committee reported no contests, and accorded territories the right to be seated but not to vote. After election of the national committee, the convention adjourned until the next day. The combined time spent in the first two sessions was less than three hours.

The Platform

Immediately following the prayer the next morning, the platform was presented. Except for a short preamble, the Cincinnati resolutions were given word for word. In the same breath that he moved the adoption of the resolutions the chairman of the platform committee moved the previous question, to restrict debate.

The call for the previous question was opposed energetically, but was sustained by a roll call vote 574 to 158, a substantial part of the negative vote coming from the southern states. The vote undoubtedly would have been closer, had not the unit rule been imposed in some instances; for example, the New York chairman, when announcing the delegation's vote, stated that several of the delegates, including himself, voted Nay. Nevertheless, the full 70 votes were recorded as Aye.

In the debate that followed, the platform chairman announced that he would take no part in the discussion and would yield his time to others. The main attack was carried by Senator Thomas F. Bayard of Delaware, who pleaded with the convention to place its own platform before the people and not "without crossing a *t*, or dotting an *i*, force down our throats without mastication or digestion the action of other men who have not been called into our councils." The burden for the defense was carried by a delegate from South Carolina and one from Texas, both of whom defended the clause in the platform opposing any reopening of the questions settled by the Thirteenth, Fourteenth, and

Fifteenth Amendments—a strange position for southern Democrats to take. Nothing whatever was said about the clause demanding a speedy return to specie payments or other almost equally sharp reversals from previous policy.

Although the committee chairman was lenient in the distribution of his time, the permanent chairman quite firmly shut off all debate at the close of the stipulated hour. He also refused to divide the question, and a roll call was taken on the entire platform. It was adopted 670 to 62, most of the negative votes again coming from southern states. As before, it was clear that some states were operating under the unit rule.

The Presidential Nomination

. Nominations were ruled out of order, and the roll was called for the vote. Alabama's vote for Greeley was accompanied by the outburst generally accorded a nominating speech. The roll call again was interrupted by a long speech from the chairman of the New York delegation in which he attempted to justify the action of a major party in following the lead of others instead of doing its own leading. In any event, only a scattered few failed to follow the lead: Bayard received 15 votes; Jeremiah S. Black of Pennsylvania, 21; William S. Gresbeck of Ohio, 2; and 8 votes were wasted by delegates as a register of their protests. Horace Greeley received the remainder—686 votes.

The Vice-Presidential Nomination

The same procedure was followed for the nomination of the vice-presidential candidate, except that interruptions were fewer and not as long. B. Gratz Brown received 713 votes, Senator John W. Stevenson of Kentucky the 6 votes of intrepid little Delaware, and 13 votes were not cast. It did not take long to finish up the odds and ends of work, and the convention adjourned after about six hours total time in actual session.

FIFTH REPUBLICAN CONVENTION

Whatever Grant's failings as a President, the public's memory of him as a military hero remained sufficiently strong to ensure that his renomination would be popular. Since those controlling the party mechanism had no reason to oust him—in fact every reason to want to retain the magic of his name at the top of the ticket—there was never any doubt as to the convention choice. Those who opposed him either gave up before the convention and quietly went along with the tide, or broke entirely with the party to join the Liberal Republicans in selecting a ticket of their own.

One who had suggested that he might like to run in Grant's place was his Vice President, Schuyler Colfax, or at least Grant had received that impression. Furthermore, two years before the convention Colfax had written a letter stating that he did not intend to run again for the Vice Presidency, thus opening the door for others to seek commitments even from Colfax's friends. This seriously weakened his position when the convention met.

Philadelphia, Pennsylvania, June 5 and 6, 1872

The call as issued by the national committee was again an invitation to the "National Union Convention," but the designation was changed by the convention itself to the National Union Republican Convention. In addition to stipulating the number of delegates allotted to each state—two for each member of Congress—the call recited a long series of purported achievements, of which the following are examples:

In calling this Convention, the Committee remind the country that the promises of the Union Republican Convention of 1868 have been fulfilled. The States lately in rebellion have been restored to their former relations to the Government. The laws of the country have been faithfully executed, public faith has been preserved, and the national credit firmly established. . . . The defenders of the Union have been gratefully remembered, and the rights and interests of labor recognized. . . . Equal suffrage has been engrafted on the National Constitution; the privileges and immunities of American citizenship have become a part of the organic law, and a liberal policy has been adopted toward all who engaged in the rebellion. . . . Corruption has been exposed, offenders punished, responsibility enforced, safeguards established.[1]

Morton McMichael of Pennsylvania was named temporary chairman. In his opening speech he hit the Liberal Republicans and the Democrats jointly:

The malcontents who recently met at Cincinnati were without a constituency; the Democrats who are soon to meet at Baltimore will be without a principle. The former, having no motive in common but personal disappointment, attempted a fusion of repelling elements, which has resulted in explosion; the latter, degraded from the high estate they once occupied, propose an abandonment of their identity, which means death.[2]

Convention Organization

Appointment of the regular committees was accomplished in but a few minutes. Then, as frequently happens in conventions where most of the business is decided in advance, the convention amused itself—in this case by hearing speeches from several of the more eminent leaders present, and for good measure from some of the colored delegates.

The committee on permanent organization reported at the end of the first session. A North Carolinian, Judge Thomas Settle, was selected permanent chairman. Early in the second session, substantially the same rules as in 1868 were adopted by a unanimous vote. A single minor contest for seats involved a Mormon and a non-Mormon delegation from the territory of Utah; the spokesman for the credentials committee assured the convention that the contest had been decided for the non-Mormon delegation without regard to religious affiliation. Moreover, the Mormons had refused an offer to seat both delegations with a split vote. The credentials committee report was approved "with a single dissenting voice."

[1] RNC, *Proceedings*, 1872, p. 119.
[2] *Ibid.*, p. 123.

The Presidential Nomination

The resolutions committee still being in session, more speeches were heard from distinguished delegates, the series being interrupted by an attempt to proceed with the nominations. This was objected to on the grounds that the order of business stipulated that the platform be adopted before the nominations were made. After more speeches, since there was no indication that the platform would soon be ready, the convention suspended the rule, and Grant's name was presented in a very brief speech. During the ensuing demonstration, while the band played "Hail to the Chief," "a life-size equestrian portrait of Grant came down (from the Balcony) as if by magic." The roll call followed shortly, and was unanimous.

The Platform

The platform was not presented until most of the speeches for the vice-presidential nominations were completed. It is a remarkable document from several standpoints, but most of all for its liberal tone, in view of the known records of the party leaders whose approval it must have had. In 1868, the platform had restricted recommendations for Negro suffrage to the southern states; in 1872, it took this position:

Complete liberty and exact equality in the enjoyment of all civil, political and public rights should be established and effectually maintained throughout the Union.[3]

This should be brought about "by efficient and appropriate State and Federal Legislation." On the question of civil service, the platform declared:

Any system of the civil service under which the subordinate positions of the Government are considered rewards for mere party zeal is fatally demoralizing, and we therefore favor a reform of the system by laws which shall abolish the evils of patronage, and make honesty, efficiency, and fidelity the essential qualifications for public positions, without practically creating a life-tenure of office.[4]

[3] *Ibid.*, p. 176.
[4] *Ibid.*

Abolishment of the franking privilege was recommended, laws to protect labor were urged, and extension of amnesty to late rebels was favored. Although not ready to recommend that the suffrage be extended to women, the convention agreed that women had a right to try to win it for themselves.

The Republican party is mindful of its obligations to the loyal women of America for their noble devotion to the cause of freedom. Their admission to wider fields of usefulness is viewed with satisfaction, and the honest demand of any class of citizens for additional rights should be treated with respectful consideration.[5]

Without discussion or opposition, the platform was approved.

The Vice-Presidential Nomination

The speech by a Pennsylvanian presenting Senator Henry Wilson of Massachusetts for the Vice Presidency was florid even for that day. One sentence will illustrate its general tone:

God forbid, sir, that by even so much as a fragment of a syllable, I should utter any sound derogatory to the gallant and noble spirits who at the signal-gun of the war, from rolling prairie and rushing river, from the silence of the forest and the depths of the mine, from the glow of the furnace, from the din of the factory, and from the bustle of the mart, from church and college, swarmed to the defence of the national capital.[6]

Much of the speech was filled with a complaint that Pennsylvania, in view of its excellent Republican record, had been badly treated by the party. Not only had the state been denied the Vice Presidency in the previous convention but later was unrepresented in the Cabinet; patronage demands were disregarded. When a Pennsylvanian had been mentioned in a journal

article as a possible candidate for the Vice Presidency in 1872, other papers met the proposition with sneers, the speaker said, and quoted one Boston paper as remarking: "Pennsylvania, as usual, comes forward with the demand, looking as much like a threat as a demand, about Presidential candidates." This finally brought him back to the business in hand, and he closed:

And now, as a fitting reply to the insinuations that the paper contained, I am here, under the unanimous instructions of the Pennsylvania delegation, to present the name of a statesman known to the country as an honest, upright, able man, who has labored, and is laboring still, earnestly in behalf of the laboring masses of the country, and for the good of the whole country; I mean Henry Wilson, of Massachusetts.

The presentation of Schuyler Colfax was accompanied by the plea to keep the winning ticket of 1868 intact. In general, Colfax's seconding speeches were from the West, Wilson's from the Northeast, and the southern seconds were equally split. Favorite sons were presented from Virginia, Texas, and Tennessee before the platform was reported; after its acceptance, delegates from Ohio seconded both major candidates.

On the roll call Wilson received 364½ votes, with 375 necessary for a majority. Colfax received 321½, and the remaining 66 votes were scattered among five others. Virginia, whose 22 votes had been cast for its favorite son, transferred to Wilson, giving him a majority. Indiana moved that the nomination be made unanimous. Colfax must have felt quite sure of the outcome; almost immediately after the results were announced a telegram was read, in which he congratulated the party upon the ticket after first thanking the Indiana delegation for its efforts. Soon thereafter, the convention adjourned.

[5] *Ibid.*, p. 177.
[6] *Ibid.*, p. 167.

Presidential Election, November 5, 1872

ULYSSES S. GRANT (R) : popular vote, 3,596,745; electoral vote, 286
HORACE GREELEY (D) : popular vote, 2,843,446; electoral vote, 66

1876

GRANT'S SECOND administration was marked by one scandal after another, sometimes involving men in high places and even close to Grant himself. A financial panic in 1873 further shook public faith in the administration, and the 1874 midterm elections resulted in impressive Democratic gains, including control of the House of Representatives. Whatever Grant's own thoughts may have been about the third-term tradition, others, including members of the Radical faction, saw the impossibility of his candidacy, and in December 1875 the House of Representatives overwhelmingly passed a resolution against a third term.

In most southern states, whites had regained political control or were in process of doing so, and carpetbaggers could not be depended upon to deliver as many southern Republican votes as in the past two elections. Thus, the Republicans were driven to greater dependence upon the electoral votes of the North and West—where votes had to be won against active competition. With the spirit of reform in the air, nomination of a Radical or of anyone close to Grant's administration would almost automatically ensure defeat. The Radicals nevertheless remained a force to be reckoned with in the convention.

The Democratic party, on the other hand, was recovering from its low point of 1872. The elections of 1874 had increased the number of Democratic governors and other elected officials, who became thereby potential presidential material, and this electoral success, plus the obvious failure of the administration, raised party morale to the highest pitch since before the Civil War.

The Republican convention was split between three relatively equal groups: the Radicals, led by Senators Roscoe Conkling of New York and Oliver P. Morton of Indiana; the so-called Half-Breeds, supporters of Speaker of the House James G. Blaine of Maine, who were drawn largely from regular Republican ranks and whose loyalty to their dynamic and colorful, if somewhat discredited, hero has seldom been equaled; and the reformers, most of whom preferred Secretary of the Treasury Benjamin H. Bristow of Kentucky.

With the temper of the times calling for reform, the Radicals could not hope to gain support from reform elements for a Radical candidate; their only hope to nominate one of their own number was to win a majority of Radical delegates during the preconvention period, which they were unable to do. Relations between the Radicals and Blaine's Half-Breeds were such that there was little hope of a transfer vote between the two groups, especially between Blaine and Conkling, who were bitter enemies. Blaine similarly had antagonized Bristow, and therefore Bristow's followers. Further, not long before the convention he had been implicated in the Union Pacific scandal, when the so-called "Mulligan letters" written by him were turned up by a congressional investigating committee. The letters contained allusions strongly suggesting improper use of his influence as Speaker of the House, and, despite his brilliant explanation on the floor of the House of Representatives, many remained unconvinced of his innocence. Even so, he was clearly the front-runner and might have been nominated if he had not suffered a severe physical collapse three days before the convention— a collapse that was exploited to the full by the opposition.

Cincinnati, Ohio, June 14, 15, 16, 1876

The call recognized the split between liberal and regular Republicans in 1872 by recommending that the committees of the several states invite "all Republican electors, and all other voters, without regard to past political differences or previous party affiliations, who are opposed to reviving sectional issues." A long recitation of the virtues of the proposed electorate followed, including subscription to "the full and free exercise of the right of suffrage without intimidation and without fraud." It especially invited all "who hold that the common-school system is the nursery of American liberty, and should be maintained absolutely free from sectarian control."[1]

The chairman of the national committee, Edwin D. Morgan, called his fourth convention to order (he missed those of 1868 and 1872). In a short speech he urged a sound-money platform plank, but otherwise avoided controversial issues. Theodore M. Pomeroy of New York, the temporary chairman, reiterated the hard-money theme, and at the same time warned the delegates that they, by their own folly, could bring about party defeat, whereas the opposition, acting as wisely as it might be capable, could not do so.

Convention Organization

All committees were appointed by a blanket motion directing delegation chairmen to name all committee members as the roll was called. During the roll call, a motion was passed denying committee membership to states with contests. Because of the obvious confusion in an unusually noisy

hall, another motion directed that names be sent to the chairman instead of being read.

The last speech before the committees began to report was an extraordinary one by Frederick Douglass, a prominent Negro leader. It was a bitter speech, in which he contrasted the freeing of his race with the freeing of the Israelites and the emancipation of the Russian serfs. The Israelites, he said, were provided with means to subsist; the Russian serfs, when emancipated, were given a few acres of land on which they could live and earn their bread.

> But when you turned us loose, you gave us no acres; you turned us loose to the sky, to the storm, to the whirlwind, and, worst of all, you turned us loose to the wrath of our infuriated masters.[2]

Permanent Organization

The report of the committee on permanent organization was accepted only after a minor protest that, since the convention was not yet officially constituted, the credentials committee had not reported. Edward McPherson, Pennsylvania lawyer and editor, was elected permanent chairman, and the convention adjourned until the next day.

At the opening of the next day's morning session, a memorial from Susan B. Anthony was presented to the convention by a woman speaker. The memorial urged that the convention resolve:

> That the right to the use of the ballot inheres in the citizens of the United States.[3]

The resolution was referred to committee— a not unusual fate for such attempts in those years.

The report of the rules and order of business became the occasion for some parliamentary jockeying by supporters of various presidential candidates. The Blaine people were anxious for an early nomination, and the chairman of the Maine

<hr>

[1] RNC, *Proceedings*, 1876, p. 231.

[2] *Ibid.*, p. 251.
[3] *Ibid.*, p. 257.

delegation objected to a rule requiring acceptance of the platform report before nominations were made.

Separate votes were taken on the order of business and the balance of the report, but both were adopted after some debate. To a proposal that the convention take a half hour recess after each ballot until some candidate received a majority of the vote, one delegate suggested that the motion be amended to direct each delegation or chairman to be suitably labeled as to what they asked, and whether they take "cash" or "country produce." The motion, plus its facetious amendment, was tabled.

Contests from Alabama, Florida, and the District of Columbia were presented and a division of the report, all except the Alabama recommendation, passed by voice vote. The majority report on Alabama found for a delegation that subsequently proved to be almost solidly for Blaine, with a few members for Bristow. A minority report proposed to admit a group reportedly pledged to Morton, the report being signed by the Indiana committee member who led the debate supporting it. Maine supported the majority report. The contest was sharply candidate-oriented, and this was reflected in the vote.[4] The minority report was defeated 375 to 354, most of the Blaine and Bristow delegations voting against it. Blaine had won the first round.[5]

The Platform

The carefully worded platform skirted some decisive issues, but spoke fairly clearly

in favor of reform. One plank defined the respective responsibilities of the administration and Congress regarding appointments to public service, then went on to define ideal appointment policy.

The senate is to advise and consent to appointments; and the house of Representatives is to accuse and prosecute faithless officers. The best interest of the public service demands that these distinctions be respected; that senators and representatives who may be judges and accusers should not dictate appointments to office. . . . The invariable rule for appointments should have reference to the honesty, fidelity, and capacity of appointees, giving to the party in power those places where harmony and vigor of administration require its policy to be represented, but permitting all others to be filled by persons selected with sole reference to the efficiency of the public service and the right of citizens to share in the honor of rendering faithful service to their country.[6]

The party "rejoiced in the quickened conscience of the people concerning political affairs," and pledged unsparing efforts to prosecute public officials who betrayed the public trust. The party once again agreed that the demands of the women for greater rights "should be treated with respectful consideration." The "bloody shirt" was not forgotten—the Democratic party was charged as "being the same in character and spirit as when it sympathized with treason."

With the exception of two planks, the platform was accepted without difficulty. The first to be questioned was:

It is the immediate duty of congress fully to investigate the effect of the immigration and importation of Mongolians on the moral and material interests of the country.[7]

The cautious wording of this clause indicates considerable compromise from what had been proposed by the West Coast delegates. It was strong enough, however, to precipitate a floor fight led by a Massachusetts delegate who demanded deletion on the grounds that the plank violated the basic principles of the Republican party—

[4] Delegates from Alabama were selected by the state central committee, but in this case the state committee, originally constituted of twelve members by the previous state convention, had been augmented to twenty-four through the process of the committee itself electing new members. This action had been ratified by a state-wide meeting, the representativeness of which was judged differently depending upon which political faction was favored. When time came to select delegates, six of the original members of the committee joined with the twelve new members in selecting the slate of delegates listed in the majority report, while the other six originals elected the minority slate.

[5] See *Analysis of Key Votes*.

[6] RNC, *Proceedings*, 1876, p. 280.

[7] *Ibid.*

a party that stood for equality of all the races. He received some support in debate, but on a roll call vote was defeated 532 to 215.

The second plank to be questioned pledged "to make provision at the earliest practicable period for the redemption of the United States notes in coin." A minority member of the committee wanted to tighten up the wording to state clearly that it was the duty of Congress to ensure that resumption of specie payment "may not be longer delayed." He received little support, and his measure was defeated by voice vote.

The Presidential Nomination

The relatively pedestrian efforts of the speakers who nominated Postmaster General Marshall Jewell, favorite son of Connecticut, Oliver P. Morton, and Benjamin H. Bristow were followed by what was, according to most contemporary accounts, a remarkably effective speech by Robert G. Ingersoll. Widely known as a master in a day when oratory was a highly prized skill, Ingersoll likened Blaine to "an armed warrior, like a plumed knight," who bravely attacked treason wherever he found it. The following speaker, who nominated Roscoe Conkling, acknowledged each of the previous nominees in turn and admitted their very high qualifications—until he came to Blaine. He contented himself with commiserating with Blaine's family and friends for the Congressman's recent illness, thus at one and the same time avoiding saying anything good about him and pointedly reminding the convention that this candidate was ill.

Former Governor Rutherford B. Hayes of Ohio was next presented—as a man with a habit of defeating Democratic aspirants for the presidency, since he had, at one time or another, defeated fellow Ohioans Allen G. Thurman, George H. Pendleton, and William Allen. In addition, and probably no less important, "He has no personal enmities." The last nominee, Governor

John F. Hartranft, favorite son of Pennsylvania, must have had mixed emotions when he heard or read the nominating speech presenting his name. His advocate freely conceded "to the gentlemen named [the other candidates] a great intellectual superiority over my candidate." But Hartranft, he said, was willing to follow good advice, was patriotic and honest, and "the people of Pennsylvania love him."

It was only five o'clock in the afternoon when the nominating speeches were completed, but a motion was made by an Indiana delegate to adjourn until the next morning. A roll call vote was demanded but was interrupted after the first two states had been called, when Blaine's manager asked if the hall could be lighted and was informed that the lighting system was in an unsafe condition. In view of this, the convention adjourned.

It was widely claimed at the time that Blaine sentiment was running strong, especially after Ingersoll's speech, and that he would almost certainly have been nominated had the roll been called then. Many charged that the lights had been tampered with deliberately to prevent an evening and night session. However, it can also be said that several speeches had followed Ingersoll's, including one by a colored gentleman seconding Blaine that was so full of obvious inaccuracies that it must have been highly amusing to the delegates. Since laughter is a strong antidote for strong emotions, the effect of Ingersoll's speech must have been considerably reduced by the time the adjournment was taken.

The next morning, before a noisy gallery, the first roll call began. Blaine led the field with 285, more than the sum of his next two opponents—Morton with 124 and Bristow with 113. Conkling received 99, Hayes 61, and Hartranft only the 59 votes of Pennsylvania. On the second ballot Blaine registered a minor gain, but the order of the major candidates did not change. However, during the course of the roll call, an important conflict occurred on the question of the unit rule. The chairman of the Pennsylvania delegation announced the vote as 59 for Hartranft, as on the first ballot. This was challenged by one of the delegation, who stated that he and a colleague wanted to vote for Blaine. They subsequently were joined by two others. McPherson, the convention chairman, ruled that "it is the right of any and of every member equally to vote his sentiments in this convention." An appeal to this decision was put to the convention and McPherson's decision was declared sustained, whereupon an argument broke out between Pennsylvania delegates and McPherson, in which the latter was charged with deliberately disregarding a demand for recognition before taking the vote. McPherson retorted in kind, until the argument was broken up by an intermediary, who reminded both parties that their conduct was unseemly.

A motion to reconsider was offered by a delegate for the stated purpose of allowing the Pennsylvania chairman to state his case, since such a motion would reopen debate. The argument on one side was based upon the action of the Pennsylvania convention binding the delegation to vote as a unit, and the second and fourth rules of the national convention. The important clause in the second rule read: "The votes of each delegation shall be reported by its chairman;" and in the fourth: " . . . and when any state had announced its vote, it shall so stand until the ballot is announced, unless in case of numerical error."[8] Although the delegate conducting the debate for the majority of the Pennsylvania delegation had also been chairman of the rules committee, he conveniently did not mention a clause in the sixth rule stipulating that when the vote in any delegation was divided, "the chairman shall announce the number of votes cast for any candidate, or for or against any proposition."

The other side of the case rested upon the fact that the delegates had been elected originally by a congressional district con-

vention that had instructed them for Blaine, and it was contended that each delegate was responsible to his own constituency rather than to the state convention. In any event, the speaker insisted that he had discharged any duty owed the state convention by voting for Hartranft on the first ballot. The pros and cons of Pennsylvania politics and party procedure were argued at length. A roll call vote to reconsider the motion upholding the decision of the chair carried 381 to 359, but only after a voice vote first had been declared the other way by the chairman.

A new debate broke out, this time on fundamental issues of representation and delegation. To the argument by one side that "the simple question before this convention is, whether each delegate has a right to vote as he believes the people he represents wish him to vote, or whether he can be . . . tied by party machinery," the other stated: "The simple question to be now decided by this convention is this: whether after we have been sent here by our state conventions, under instructions from them, we have the individual right to violate those instructions."[9]

The second major question was whether the convention was the supreme authority, or whether the states individually had the right to establish laws binding upon the national convention. On the roll call, the decision of the convention chairman was again sustained 395 to 353.[10]

At the time, the vote was hailed as a major victory for Blaine. But more important from the long-range viewpoint, the principle of representation by congressional district was institutionalized in Republican conventions—a principle that was to be challenged seriously only one more time, and by many of the very people who supported it in 1876.

For the next few ballots, there was very little change. On the fifth Blaine stood at 286, Bristow at 114, Morton at 95, but Hayes had been creeping steadily upward

[8] *Ibid.*, pp. 258-259.

[9] *Ibid.*, p. 316.
[10] See *Analysis of Key Votes.*

and was now in third place with 104 votes. At this point, delegations became restive and attempts were made to recess. Demands were made that time be given to caucus, but the sixth roll call continued. Blaine made his biggest gain so far, moving to 308, 70 votes short of nomination. Hayes replaced Bristow, 113 to 111, all others losing slightly. Further attempts were made to adjourn—all unsuccessful.

As the seventh roll call reached Indiana, Blaine had made impressive gains. His total on the sixth ballot through Illinois had been 81; it was now 105, and the addition of these 24 votes through the first third of the list brought him very close to the nomination. However, Indiana withdrew Bristow and cast all but 5 of its votes for Hayes. Kentucky followed suit. When New York was reached, its Conkling vote was added to the Hayes column. Pennsylvania split 28 for Hayes, 30 for Blaine; this was a critical division, particularly in light of the previous debate. Had the unit rule question not been raised by the Blaine faction, and had the Pennsylvania delegation continued to operate under the unit rule, Blaine presumably would have received the full Pennsylvania vote. Since the final vote on the seventh ballot was Hayes 384 and Blaine 351, it would appear that a minor victory in a preliminary skirmish paved the way to ultimate defeat.

On motion by the Blaine floor manager, the nomination of Hayes was declared unanimous.

The Vice-Presidential Nomination

Following the presidential nomination, several delegates caught the eye of the chair and presented candidates—Congressman William A. Wheeler of New York, Postmaster General Marshall Jewell of Connecticut, and former Congressman Stewart L. Woodford of New York—before the usual motion was passed to call states in alphabetical order. Kentucky presented General Joseph R. Hawley of Connecticut, and New Jersey its own favorite son, Senator Frederick T. Frelinghuysen. Woodford withdrew, and on the roll call his colleague from New York was so clearly ahead by the time South Carolina voted that the call was suspended, and Wheeler was nominated by acclamation.

Analysis of Key Votes

The key votes selected are those on the minority credentials report, rejected 369 to 360, and on sustaining the chairman's ruling by which the unit rule was defeated 395 to 353. The first of these seated an anti-Radical Alabama delegation, mostly for Blaine but some for Bristow, instead of a Radical group favoring Morton. Indices of correlation for this vote are tabulated below.

Thus, delegations voting above average with the majority rejecting the minority credentials report also supported Blaine strongly, and to a lesser extent the other

Candidate or Issue	Positive	Negative	Per Cent of Convention
Blaine first ballot	.74	.29	37.4%
Morton first ballot			16.8
Conkling first ballot			13.5
Bristow first ballot	.21		15.4
Others first ballot	.15	.97[a]	17.0
All except Morton and Conkling first ballot	.98[a]	.96[a]	69.7
Sustain Chair on Unit Rule	.49		
Hayes seventh ballot			52.2

[a] Less than five cases in one cell in the matrix.

candidates except Morton and Conkling. The latter two received almost no votes from delegations voting against the minority report. When the votes for all candidates other than Morton and Conkling are combined, the correlation index rises to +.98, and, since these candidates totaled nearly 70 per cent of the total convention strength, it is obvious that they controlled the convention and presumably could have named the candidate.

However, on Hayes' seventh-ballot nominating vote, the index of correlation is −.29, indicating that a large part of the nominating coalition consisted of Morton and Conkling supporters. The break in the solidarity of the anti-Radicals is indicated by the +.49 index of correlation between the minority credentials vote and the vote to sustain the chairman on the unit rule. Further analysis of the unit rule vote indicates what happened. The indices of correlation on this vote are:

of Hayes' electoral victory over Tilden, does much to explain Hayes' difficulties during his administration.

TWELFTH DEMOCRATIC CONVENTION

Well before convention time, Samuel J. Tilden of New York had achieved a strong front-runner position as a "reform" candidate. His qualifications for this title were of relatively recent origin, for, although he had been active in politics since his college days, until 1874 he had never held elective office higher than that of delegate to the New York Assembly. As a first-rate corporation lawyer, he had accumulated an immense fortune, and it would have been surprising if he could have done so were he handicapped by a demonstrably higher level of business ethics than those with whom he was in competition. Most of his political work was in party affairs and as

Candidate or Issue	Positive	Negative	Per Cent of Convention
Blaine first ballot	.88		37.7%
Morton first ballot		.33	16.4
Conkling first ballot		.83	13.1
Bristow first ballot		.17	14.5
Others first ballot		.67	17.9
Hayes seventh ballot		.56	52.2
Blaine seventh ballot	.51		46.4

The correlation between this vote and the first ballot for candidates reveals high and opposite correlations for Blaine and Conkling as on the other vote, but negative correlations of lower order for all the other candidates. In other words, the entire convention had shifted away from Blaine, except of course his own loyal support. The correlation of −.56 for Hayes' seventh-ballot vote, with which he received the nomination, indicates that his support was a mixture of Radical and anti-Radical votes opposed to Blaine. This combination of odd bedfellows, plus the contested nature

a party officer. His first real claim to being a reformist came as a leading figure in the exposure and destruction of the Tweed Ring in New York City—a group with which he had on occasion cooperated.

His activities against the Ring led to his election in 1874 as governor of New York, in which office he quickly added to his stature as a reformist by a methodic and successful attack upon another ring that had been exploiting the state in the operation of the canals. These exploits endeared him to, among others, the die-hard remnants of the Liberal Republicans, who endorsed his candidacy in a small convention held a few months before the Democratic convention. His main strength lay in the East, for he was an advocate of hard money; the West, where inflationary ideas predominated, preferred other candidates.

The principal soft-money candidate was Thomas A. Hendricks of Indiana, who had been a strong contender in 1868. A second was ex-Governor William Allen of Ohio, despite his defeat for re-election as governor by the new Republican presidential nominee, Rutherford B. Hayes. Another contender also had been in the 1868 race, Winfield Scott Hancock. The field was rounded out by a number of favorite sons and minor candidates.

St. Louis, Missouri, June 27, 28, 29, 1876

For the first time in the history of either party, a national convention met west of the Mississippi. The first act after the address by the chairman of the national committee, Augustus Schell of New York, was the selection of the Kentucky editor, Henry M. Watterson, as temporary chairman.

Convention Organization

The convention gave early signs of being disorderly; even the adoption of temporary rules and appointment of the regular committees was accompanied by an unusually large amount of parliamentary maneuvering and bickering. Much worse was to follow. John A. McClernand of Illinois was selected permanent chairman, and despite his long experience in the Illinois legislature, in the House of Representatives, and as a judge, he proved unable to control the convention. Throughout the two days he was chairman, the delegates and the galleries were in an almost constant state of uproar.

The committee on credentials reported no contests, but a resolution allowing delegates from the territories to be seated without voting rights was passed only after considerable confusion.

The Platform

Two minority reports were presented following reading of the platform, both related to the same problem. In 1875 the Republican-controlled Congress had passed an act providing for resumption of specie payments in discharging the bond obligations resulting primarily from the Civil War, and for reduction of the amount of greenbacks, also issued during that period. Many of the war bonds did not stipulate whether they were redeemable in gold or in paper, and since paper money had deteriorated badly in terms of gold value, the question of redemption became highly charged politically. A high percentage of the bonds were held by easterners, and accordingly specie payment was generally well supported in that area. On the other hand, westerners and southerners felt it to their advantage to have the bonds redeemed with cheaper paper money; in addition, they favored a large money supply, since most were debtors who would benefit by an inflated economy.

The majority platform denounced the Resumption Act of 1875 and demanded its repeal. The first minority report, signed by five eastern states, moved that this clause be deleted, but made no other suggestions. Delegates from seven midwestern states plus Pennsylvania countered with an attempt to strengthen the platform statement by deleting the clause as worded, and substituting the following:

The law for the resumption of specie payments on the first of January, 1875, having been enacted by the Republican party without deliberation in Congress or discussion before the people, and being both ineffectual to secure its object, and highly injurious to the business of the country, ought to be forthwith repealed.[11]

The western report, which was voted upon first, was defeated 515 to 219, western delegations providing most of the minority.[12] The vote on the eastern amendment was announced by the secretary as 219 Ayes

[11] DNC, *Proceedings*, 1876, p. 100.
[12] See *Analysis of Key Votes*.

and 550 Noes, but the detailed vote is not recorded in the proceedings. The original platform was then adopted by a roll call vote 651 to 83, with most of the minority vote from the West.

The Presidential Nomination

Governor Thomas A. Hendricks of Indiana, Governor Samuel J. Tilden of New York, and General Winfield Scott Hancock of Pennsylvania were placed in nomination, along with favorite sons from Ohio, Delaware, and New Jersey. Tilden, the front-runner, was bitterly opposed by part of his own delegation—an opposition that was voiced in a manner seldom heard.

The leader of the opposition, John Kelly of Tammany Hall, received recognition immediately following Tilden's nomination and proceeded to make a bitter speech against him, charging that he could not carry the critical western states. Interrupted frequently, Kelly was permitted to continue only because members of the New York Tilden faction repeatedly requested the delegates to hear him out. (Earlier in the convention he had attempted to torpedo the Tilden boom by obtaining the floor to state that a number in his delegation had requested him to read off a list of the names of men from New York who were opposed to Tilden—so that the convention could judge the character of men who formed the opposition; he was ruled out of order.)

Tilden, with 404½ votes, was far ahead of his nearest rival on the first roll call, although considerably short of the 492 votes required for nomination. Immediately following the roll, and before the totals were announced, Missouri shifted an additional block to Tilden, giving him 417½ total. Hendricks and Hancock trailed with 140½ and 75 respectively; the rest of the votes were scattered. An attempted adjournment was overruled by the chairman, and the second ballot followed immediately. Tilden went well over the two thirds requirement with 535; Hendricks and Hancock retained 85 and 58. The nomination was then made

unanimous, following several pledges of loyalty to Tilden from supporters of defeated candidates.

The Vice-Presidential Nomination

Following an overnight recess, the convention took up the question of the Vice Presidency. The proceedings were unusual. The roll was called as far as Indiana without response. The chairman of the Indiana delegation, after asserting that Indiana would support Tilden despite the fact that Hendricks had been the choice of the delegation, announced that the delegation could not undertake the responsibility for putting Hendricks' name on the ticket. He was followed by a series of speakers urging Hendricks' nomination, and there were demands that the rules be suspended to nominate without a roll call. A motion to this effect was lost, but on the roll call the vote of the entire convention, except for eight not voting, was cast for Hendricks.

The delegates then called for John Kelly, who had protested so bitterly against Tilden. Kelly did his job well; despite his previous opposition, he pledged to work for the ticket and urged others to do so.

At this stage—when most conventions consider their real business completed—an important resolution was presented, recommending abolishment of the two thirds rule in future conventions.

Resolved, that it be recommended to future National Democratic Conventions, as the sense of the Democracy here in Convention assembled, that the so-called two-thirds rule be abolished as unwise and unnecessary, and that the States be requested to instruct their delegates to the National Democratic Convention to be held in 1880, whether it be desirable to continue the two-thirds rule longer in force in the National Convention, and that the National Committee insert such request in their call for the Convention.[13]

A roll call taken on a motion to table was defeated by the narrow margin of 379 to 359. Surprising in terms of modern political divisions, six of the southern states voted against tabling, thus keeping

[13] DNC, *Proceedings*, 1876, p. 166.

the matter alive, although reversal of the vote of any one of them would have killed the measure. The resolution was then adopted without a roll call, separate votes being taken on the first clause down to "unwise and unnecessary" and on the remainder of the paragraph. The national committee, however, did not see fit to accept the recommendation, and no further action was taken.

Analysis of Key Votes

Despite the fact that the proposal by certain western states to go further than the majority platform draft on the monetary question was defeated by so large a majority, the pattern of the vote indicates definite candidate-orientation—and of course sectional-orientation as well, since the candidates were to a large extent sectionally supported. Tilden's index of voting correspondence on the first ballot with the majority side of the issue was a relatively high +.81 compared to Hendricks' index of −.46. The index for the other candidates, also drawing mostly from western sources of strength, was −.55.

The position of the others suggests that most would have preferred to go with Hendricks, at least so far as his position on the money question was concerned, but Tilden's heavy lead made Hendricks' prospects rather poor. On the first ballot Tilden polled a clear majority of 55.1 per cent, with Hendricks receiving only 19.0 per cent and the others 25.8. Tilden's second ballot nomination majority came almost entirely from those who had voted with the majority in rejecting the extreme soft-money amendment, as is indicated by his very high correlation index of +.95.

The Contested Election

As in 1824, election day did not finish the matter—though for very different reasons than on the earlier date. Republican party chiefs, faced with what seemed a hairbreadth defeat by Tilden, suddenly saw the opportunity to reverse the decision by claiming victory in certain southern states in which they controlled the electoral machinery, and therefore the official count. Minority counts were presented by Democratic members of the electoral boards, and the election depended upon which of the sets of returns were accepted by the President of the Senate, in the presence of both houses of Congress as directed by the Constitution. With a Republican Senate and a Democratic House, it was unlikely that agreement could be reached between them; therefore it was decided to form an Electoral Commission made up of five members from each house of Congress and five Supreme Court justices. While a tense nation waited, all contests, including one for a single elector in Oregon, were decided in favor of the Republicans. Hayes became President by the margin of 1 vote—plus the remarkable willingness of the American people (particularly those of Democratic persuasion in this instance) to abide by the winner-take-all majority rule principle even under highly strained conditions.

Presidential Election, November 7, 1876

RUTHERFORD B. HAYES (R) : popular vote, 4,036,572; electoral vote, 185; declared elected on March 2, 1877

SAMUEL J. TILDEN (D) : popular vote, 4,284,020; electoral vote, 184

1880

THE CIRCUMSTANCES surrounding the Democratic party's defeat in 1876 gave substance to its claims that Tilden and Hendricks had been robbed of the election, but these same circumstances made it more difficult for the party to unite upon the kind of candidate for 1880 who could make the most of the complaints. The contributions of southern conservatives to Rutherford B. Hayes' election, in return for which the carpetbaggers were withdrawn throughout the South, began a pattern that has persisted to this day. Against anything but a solid North and West, southern influence on Democratic presidential politics became crucial, and the "northern candidate with southern principles" again became an important factor. In Republican presidential politics, the agreements reached in 1876 and faithfully carried out by Hayes permitted the southern conservatives to emasculate the Republican party in the South—to make it, in effect, an appendage of the administration when the Republican party was in power, or the prey of able (and wealthy) political manipulators when it was not.

The President and the Democrats' titular leader, Tilden, had declared themselves out of the running at an early date, so the fields were wide open. Both fields were soon filled by familiar figures.

SEVENTH REPUBLICAN CONVENTION

Not only had Hayes removed himself from the running, but by his removal of controls over the southern states, his handling of patronage, his support of the civil service, and various other actions, he had alienated so many in his party as to limit his influence in the convention. His weakness as a party leader was clearly shown in 1876 during the post-convention struggle over the chairmanship of the national committee; his preference was disregarded in favor of a pro-Grant "Stalwart" candidate, Zachariah Chandler. When Chandler died in 1879, his replacement was Don Cameron, another member of the group who favored Grant for 1880.

Grant returned from a triumphant tour of Europe in the fall of 1879, and quickly became the center of a well-organized renomination campaign. The crux of the strategy planned by his supporters involved restoration of the unit rule that had been the subject of so much discord in the 1876 convention. If they could ensure the selection of a temporary chairman who would make a favorable ruling at the critical moment, the Grant men believed they could count the votes that were necessary to control the convention and the nomination.

Supporters of the other two major candidates, James G. Blaine, in the Senate since 1876, and John Sherman of Ohio, Hayes' Secretary of the Treasury, discovered the plot in time, and, by threatening to remove Cameron from the national committee chairmanship if he persisted, were able to force nomination of a neutral temporary chairman. Thus, the question of the unit rule was left to the convention rather than to the mercies of a biased chairman.

Chicago, Illinois,
June 2, 3, 4, 5, 7, 8, 1880

The convention call was much shorter than previous calls. Apparently the national committee judged the Republican party now sufficiently stable to permit the call to be addressed simply to Republicans —without extending a blanket invitation to "those who subscribe to the principles, . . . regardless of past political differences," and other such phrases common in earlier calls. This also may have been a reflection of the desire of the chairman and other national committee members to keep the base of representation in the convention as "regular" as possible.

The convention, the longest and in some respects the most bitterly contested of all Republican conventions, opened quietly enough, with acceptance of the committee's recommendation for temporary chairman, Senator George F. Hoar of Massachusetts. Hoar stayed on safe ground in his opening remarks, contenting himself with a reminder that the convention faced a grave responsibility in choosing its ticket, and with an attack on the Democrats as the party of rebellion and of the Ku Klux Klan, among their other attributes that were anathema to Republicans.

Convention Organization

The factional divisions within the convention began to appear during the roll for membership on the basic committees. Louisiana and the territory of Utah were not included in the lists. William P. Frye of Maine, a Blaine floor leader, moved that Utah be called. Senator Roscoe Conkling, Grant's floor leader, objected and demanded that if Utah were called, Louisiana should be called as well. After a sharp altercation, Conkling accepted Frye's statement that the omission of Utah was inadvertent and contrary to agreement reached in the national committee, but that Louisiana had been left off by agreement. For by no means the last time in

the convention, Conkling went out of his way to be sarcastic, even in accepting the situation. Shortly afterward, he moved that the convention adjourn until the next morning, whereupon another Blaine leader, in a rare gesture, agreed with him, and the meeting adjourned.

Conkling's optimistic hope that all the committees would be ready to report the next morning proved to be just that— optimistic. Only one, the committee on permanent organization, was ready. Conkling was not willing that any committee other than credentials should report, and moved to adjourn until six o'clock that evening. Since a time was stipulated in the motion to adjourn, the chairman ruled it debatable, and a Blaine floor leader made a speech urging that the committee on permanent organization be asked to report. Conkling's reply was an example of the sharpness of the repartee that ran throughout the convention, most of it stimulated by Conkling.

I find, Mr. Chairman, that I have been able to establish an unexpected claim to the gratitude of the Convention. But for the little motion which I had the honor to submit, the Convention and the country would have been deprived of the eloquent speech of my distinguished friend from Maine.[1]

The "distinguished friend from Maine" came back in kind.

Now one thing more, Mr. Chairman. I shall not enter with the gentleman the field of irony and sarcasm, in which he is so expert. The little power that I have has been cultivated in other directions. I leave that to him, only saying that if I am less raspish than he this morning, and am more amiable than he, this vast audience knows why it is so.[2]

The convention decided to proceed with the report of the committee on permanent organization, and Senator Hoar was retained as permanent chairman.

Although the committee on rules had completed its work, the convention honored a resolution made by that committee

[1] RNC, *Proceedings*, 1880, p. 393.
[2] *Ibid.*, p. 395.

that its report not be made until after the credentials report had been acted upon. Thus, action was delayed upon the important question of interpretation of the unit rule, and the convention recessed until that evening.

The committee on credentials was still unable to report when the evening session opened, and again a debate started as to whether other business should be transacted. The major argument against receiving the rules committee report, at least according to the statements of the protagonists, was that one rule proposed a five-minute limitation on speeches. A motion that the rules committee be instructed to report was amended to insert credentials committee in the place of rules. The amendment, which was supported by Conkling, was defeated 406 to 318.[3]

Twice during the roll call vote, the unanimous vote of a state was challenged, and in each instance the chairman ruled that the minority votes be recorded as the individual delegates indicated. The basic motion, that the rules committee be required to report, was then tabled after a statement by a delegate from a neutral delegation that many had voted against the amendment who would also vote against the main motion, since they felt that neither committee should report until after the committee on credentials. The convention then adjourned.

In the morning the convention was quickly brought into a state of uproar, again by the irascible Mr. Conkling, when he introduced a resolution stating:

Resolved, as the sense of this Convention that every member of it is bound in honor to support its nominee, whoever that nominee may be; and that no man should hold a seat here who is not ready to so agree.[4]

When negatives were heard on a voice vote, Conkling demanded a roll call in order to identify those who had so answered. However many may have voted "No" in the safe ambiguity of the voice

vote, on the roll call, only three from West Virginia did so. Conkling moved that these three be ousted from the convention. In the debate, he received support from relatively neutral sources, and it looked as if the resolution might succeed. However, Congressman James A. Garfield of Ohio swung the convention back to a more moderate stand in a reasoned speech that also provided Conkling with a reasonable face-saving position, which Conkling—no doubt having weighed the vote—promptly took. Some contemporary accounts say that Conkling, at this point, sent a note to Garfield congratulating him on his potential nomination.

The credentials report still not being ready, the convention decided to hear the report of the rules committee without, however, acting upon it. The only important departure from previous rules was the new section on the right of individual delegates to vote as they saw fit, regardless of unit rule. It read as follows:

In the record of the vote by States, the vote of each State, Territory, and the District of Columbia shall be announced by the chairman; and in case the vote of any State, Territory, or District of Columbia shall be divided, the chairman shall announce the number of votes cast for any candidate, or for or against any proposition; but, if exception is taken by any delegate to the correctness of such announcement by the chairman of his delegation, the President of the Convention shall direct the roll of members of such delegation to be called, and the result shall be recorded in accordance with the votes individually given.[5]

A minority report signed by eleven states, most of them southern, recommended the deletion of all after "for or against any proposition." Discussion on both reports was suspended until after the credentials report, which finally was ready.

The chairman of the credentials committee attributed the long delay to the fact that over fifty cases had been considered. The report was a long one, the minority report even longer. Much time was wasted on small details and in deciding how to

---

[3] See *Analysis of Key Votes.*
[4] RNC, *Proceedings,* 1880, p. 410.

[5] *Ibid.,* p. 419.

attack the massive problem before the convention finally got down to the real debate. The first long debate occurred on a decision of the majority report to seat the delegates at large from Illinois against objection that their seats should be declared vacant. The objection was raised, not in the minority report, but on the convention floor by the delegates whose seats were thus authenticated. The objectors were bothered because the mere inclusion of a statement that objection to their seating had been dismissed suggested that some irregularity might exist.

A strange debate raged for what must have been more than an hour, with the representative of the majority of the committee insisting that the clause certifying the delegates as properly seated should remain in the report, while the delegates concerned insisted it should be removed. When a rather serious name-calling stage was reached, a motion was carried limiting further discussion to no more than one minute per person, following which a motion to delete the offending clause was passed.

After a well-earned recess, the convention spent a considerable amount of time—more than seemed necessary from the difference between the proposals in question —on the question of how much time should be allowed each side for debate of the first contest to be considered, that of Alabama. The time finally was set at twenty minutes for each side. The weakness and obvious lack of organization of the party in southern states made contests such as this common throughout the period. The question probably could not have been settled on its merits—it was settled politically, the minority substitute being defeated 449 to 306 and the majority report being accepted by a voice vote.

The Illinois district delegate contest was another matter, for it involved leaders of one of the most experienced state organizations in the party. This, in fact, was the trouble: the conflict arose from charges that the party managers in the state con-

vention had disregarded choices made in several district caucuses, and selected others by a special committee. Members of the second group, since they were Grant men, had been seated by the national committee. The credentials committee, composed of a majority of anti-Grant men, reversed the national committee; the minority report of the credentials committee proposed to reverse the majority recommendations.

Before the question was put to a vote, an adjournment was defeated 653 to 103, and soon thereafter a vote was taken on the proposal to substitute the minority for the majority report for the first district of Illinois. The minority report was defeated 387 to 353. With the vote as close as it was, the minority refused to give up, and demanded a roll call on the adoption of the majority report on the same district. The vote was almost identical, the majority report being adopted 384 to 356. On both votes Kansas voluntarily passed, on the grounds that the same question was involved in her own contest. All of the Illinois delegation, except for the two first district delegates involved, voted in each instance, and solidly with the minority.

Still not satisfied, the minority insisted upon voting upon each district contest separately. On the vote for the contest in the third district, the second not being under contest, the majority report was accepted 385 to 353, Kansas still abstaining and the Illinois vote reflecting settlement of the previous contest in the two votes cast for the majority side. Only after another roll call, with the same pattern persisting, did the minority agree to settlement of the balance in favor of the majority report by a voice vote.

The Kansas case was taken up the next day. The majority proposed a compromise whereby ten delegates would share 6 votes. The conflict arose in a somewhat similar way as in Illinois, the state convention having elected a full slate of delegates, and caucuses in two districts having elected different representatives for their respective districts. As in Illinois, the conflict was closely tied to presidential preference, but evidently many delegates considered the minority to have less justification in this case, for the vote was much more in favor of the majority—476 to 184.

The West Virginia case came next. The same basic question was involved—should delegates elected by districts be seated in preference to those selected by a state convention? In each previous case a majority of the credentials committee had decided for delegates elected by district caucus, and their decision had been upheld by the convention, albeit the vote was highly partisan in most instances. In the West Virginia case, however, the committee reversed its policy and recommended seating of the state convention contestants. Early in the debate a member of the credentials committee who had previously voted with the majority frankly admitted he did not know why he and others had done so, "unless it be that we heard this case about four o'clock in the morning when a great many of us were tired." For the first time, the action of the majority was reversed, and the minority report substituted 417 to 330.

The final contest was from the territory of Utah. It involved a delegation selected by the state central committee without benefit of a state convention, and another selected by a convention called by individuals who objected to this procedure. The problem was further complicated by the fact that one delegation was Mormon and the other not. The minority report, in favor of the non-Mormon delegates elected by the convention, was approved by a vote closely paralleling the vote on West Virginia—426 to 312.

The next order of business was the report of the rules committee. The reports were read again, following which the Grant people tried once again to forestall final decision on the unit rule by moving to proceed at once with the nominations. Garfield led the debate in support of the majority report and of the committee

chairman. The attempt to start the nominations immediately without passing any rules was beaten 479 to 276, some of the Grant people voting with the majority. This was accepted as a test vote, and the votes to reject the minority report and to adopt the majority were taken by acclamation.

In an attempt to prevent future credentials difficulties of the kind that had plagued this convention, an amendment was proposed from the floor to direct the national committee to appoint a committee to devise a method for election of delegates to the 1884 convention. The motion specifically provided that such rules should provide for election of district delegates in their respective districts. It was passed by voice vote.

The Platform

Although the platform consisted mainly of a routine recital of Republican virtues and Democratic failings, two planks were of lasting interest.

The Constitution of the United States is a supreme law, and not a mere contract. Out of confederated States it made a sovereign Nation. Some powers are denied to the Nation, while others are denied to the States; but the boundary between powers delegated and those reserved is to be determined by the National, and not by the State Tribunal.

The work of popular education is one left to the care of the several States, but it is the duty of the National Government to aid that work to the extent of its constitutional power. The intelligence of the Nation is but the aggregate of the intelligence in the several States, and the destiny of the Nation must be guided, not by the genius of any one State, but by the aggregate genius of all.[6]

The platform itself was passed without debate and by voice vote, but an amendment created a considerable stir. This endorsed President Hayes' stand on the civil service, and demanded active cooperation between administrative and legislative branches in passing laws to ensure

[6] *Ibid.,* p. 533.

a strong merit system. The debate was characterized by frankness on the part of some of the civil service opponents. Said one delegate from Texas:

There is one plank in the Democratic party that I have ever admired, and that is, "To the victors belong the spoils." After we have won the race, as we will, we will give those who are entitled to positions office. What are we up here for?[7]

A Grant leader from Pennsylvania, with respect to Democratic officeholders still in office despite recent Republican administrations, said:

. . . they are incrusted like rats in their holes, and we cannot get them out. They are full of rebels—rebel soldiers; some of the rebel officers; and I, for one, do not want this civil service to be put too strongly upon us until we are allowed to turn out the rebel brigadiers and rebel captains, and put in Union soldiers. I simply want to get them out and make way for our one-legged and one-armed Union soldiers.[8]

Despite these realistic appeals, the measure was adopted.

The Presidential Nomination

The speaker presenting James G. Blaine as a candidate probably did Blaine little good, as the speaker, himself, admitted might be true. He began thus:

I shall never cease to regret that circumstances have been such as to impose the duty upon myself to make the nomination of a candidate to this Convention. . . . If, therefore, words of mine are important for the candidate who shall be proposed, they will benefit him but little.[9]

According to the memoirs of Chauncey Depew, the speaker closed with a final inepitude: "I have the honor to present to this Convention . . . James S. Blaine, of the State of Maine." The proceedings, however, were edited to show Blaine's correct middle initial.

The second major nomination was that of Grant, and the speaker, Roscoe Conkling. The speech, in its own way a classic

equal to Ingersoll's "Plumed Knight" speech in 1876, began:

And when asked what State he hails from,
    Our sole reply shall be,
He hails from Appomatox,
    And its famous apple tree.

He stressed the idea that Grant could carry the doubtful states, and vigorously attacked the arguments against the third term:

There is, I say, no department of human reason in which sane men reject an agent because he has had experience, making him exceptionally competent and fit.[10]

Taken by itself, the speech was extremely able. Unfortunately, not only had Conkling's persistent sarcasm throughout the convention alienated everyone not closely tied to his group, but memories of the unmentioned failings of his candidate were very fresh in the minds of his listeners.

Blaine's speaker did a poor job for his man, and Grant's a brilliant one; John Sherman's speaker, James A. Garfield, scarcely mentioned his candidate. Having first reminded the delegates of the solemnity of their task, he gave a brief history of the Republican party, a short dissertation on the need for party harmony, and a description of the kind of man needed. Up to this point, he could have been nominating anyone or no one. He finally outlined Sherman's career, but without naming him until the last sentence. When he did, he was somewhat less enthusiastic than Conkling had been for Grant:

I do not present him as a better Republican or a better man than thousands of others that we honor; but I present him for your deliberate and favorable consideration. I nominate John Sherman of Ohio.[11]

Others receiving nominating speeches were Senator William Windom of Minnesota, Senator George F. Edmunds of Vermont, and Elihu B. Washburne of Illinois, formerly Minister to France. It being

----

7 *Ibid.,* p. 536.
8 *Ibid.,* p. 537.
9 *Ibid.,* p. 546.

10 *Ibid.,* p. 552.
11 *Ibid.,* p. 557.

nearly midnight, the convention adjourned before taking a roll call.

Balloting began shortly after 10:00 a.m. and continued without interruptions until after 3:30 p.m., when a brief recess was taken. On the first ballot the three front-runners were Grant with 304 votes, Blaine 284, and Sherman 93. Something over 70 votes were distributed among the lesser candidates. With 756 delegates, 379 votes were required to nominate. When New York was called on the first ballot, Conkling requested that the roll of the individual delegates be called, stating that, although he had received instructions as to the vote of the delegation, some delegates preferred to have their individual votes recorded. This was allowed; thereafter, such roll calls were common throughout the convention and for the first time were printed in the proceedings.

Seventeen ballots were taken during this session, with the three major candidates hardly varying throughout and ending with almost the same vote as on the first ballot. The 17th ballot read: Grant 303, Blaine 284, and Sherman 90. From the 2nd through the 13th ballot, Garfield's name was kept constantly before the convention with 1 vote from a Pennsylvania delegate, who was joined during two ballots by an Alabama delegate and during three others by a Maryland vote; he dropped out on the 14th through the 17th roll calls.

During the evening session, the Pennsylvania vote for Garfield reappeared and stayed through the 28th ballot, when the convention adjourned for the night. From the 23rd ballot on, Garfield's supporter was joined by a delegation colleague. The three leaders continued to fluctuate within a very small range of votes; on the 28th ballot Grant had 307, Blaine 279, and Sherman 91. Conkling objected to the adjournment, but a roll call resulted in a 446 to 303 vote in favor. Although the negative vote was almost exactly the same as Grant's strength, it was partly coincidence, since some on each side of the Grant fight crossed over.

Sherman's managers must have spent a busy night, for he registered the first significant gain of the convention on the 29th ballot taken the next morning, when he rose to 116, the new strength coming from the previous Edmunds vote. Grant at 305 and Blaine at 278 remained stable. Garfield's faithful 2 votes from Pennsylvania stayed with him. On the 34th ballot Grant broke his previous ceiling with 312 votes, Blaine remaining at 275 and Sherman slipping back from his previous top of 120 to 107. On this same ballot Wisconsin, whose delegates had been distributing their 20 votes among four candidates, suddenly concentrated 16 votes on Garfield. Garfield rose to a point of order: "No man has a right, without the consent of the person voted for, to announce that person's name, and vote for him in this Convention." He was ruled out of order by the chairman.

On the 35th ballot, twenty-seven delegates accepted the cue and voted for Garfield, who finished that ballot with 50 votes. Grant moved up to 313, his top figure in the convention, Blaine dropped to 257 and Sherman to 99. It was all over on the next ballot—a ballot punctuated by many roll calls of individual delegations and much confusion. None of Garfield's strength came from the Grant people— Grant's vote stayed at 306—but Blaine and Sherman dropped out of the picture almost entirely. Garfield finished with 399 votes. Conkling, caustic to the last, moved for a unanimous Garfield nomination:

The Chair . . . anticipates my motion; but, being on my feet, I avail myself of the opportunity to congratulate the Republican party of the United States upon the good nature and the well-tempered rivalry which has distinguished this animated contest.[12]

The Vice-Presidential Nomination

The nomination for the presidential candidate was completed about 2:30 p.m., and the convention recessed for some two and a half hours to consider the question

[12] *Ibid.,* p. 628.

of the vice-presidential nomination. Following the recess, the first to be nominated was Elihu B. Washburne, who had received as many as 44 votes during the balloting for the first place on the ticket. The fact that his vote had come from as many as nine states indicated fairly general support. Marshall Jewell of Connecticut, a minor candidate for President in 1876, was nominated next, followed by Judge Thomas Settle, ex-Confederate of North Carolina, who had joined the Republicans immediately after the war.

New York passed on the roll call—negotiations apparently not yet having been completed—but requested attention after Tennessee named its favorite son, Horace Maynard. On behalf of "a large number of the New York delegation," Chester A. Arthur of New York was presented, and immediately seconded by the "radical" Ohio delegation, followed by New Jersey, Illinois, Mississippi, Maryland, and Missouri. In the face of this important indication of support, Texas nevertheless went through a token nomination of its former governor, Edmund J. Davis, but withdrew him when Settle's name was withdrawn and several states added their seconds to Arthur.

An attempt was made to nominate Arthur by acclamation, but a substantial number of delegates preferred to register their protests, and the roll was called. Arthur led by a wide majority with 468 votes to Washburne's 193. Seven other candidates received from 1 to 44 votes each. The nomination was then declared unanimous by motion of Blaine's floor manager, the chairman of the Maine delegation. Maine had voted against Arthur.

Analysis of Key Votes

The key vote selected—the vote rejecting Conkling's amendment to substitute "credentials committee" for "rules committee" in a motion requesting the latter committee to report—is typical of several roll calls in the convention. On most of these, the Grant supporters voted solidly together. In the present instance, the correlation with the majority side of the issue is $-.91$ for Grant; $+.61$ for Blaine; $+.23$ for Sherman; and $+.87$ for others. Most of the votes on the majority side of the issue, other than those of the die-hard Blaine group, eventually gravitated to Garfield, but very few of those who voted with the minority did. Garfield's correlation with the issue on his 36th-ballot vote is $+.78$. Grant's correlation on the 36th remains about the same as for the first ballot.

The coalition nominating Arthur for Vice President was quite different from the Garfield coalition, and more nearly resembled that of Hayes in 1876. Arthur's correlation with the issue vote is $-.47$, with Garfield's vote, $-.54$. These figures reflect the fact that Arthur was nominated by the ex-Grant supporters plus a relatively small portion of the Garfield vote turned over in a gesture of party solidarity, the most substantial block of which was provided by Garfield's own Ohio delegation.

THIRTEENTH DEMOCRATIC CONVENTION

The circumstances of Samuel J. Tilden's election defeat in 1876 should have made him the logical candidate in 1880, for the Democrats could have capitalized heavily upon the prevailing belief of millions that he had been unfairly defeated. However, disclosure of certain irregularities on the part of his own supporters weakened his cause, for Republicans could point out, with some justification, that both sides were playing the same game, and that Tilden's complaints were accordingly hypocritical. In addition, Tilden was opposed by Tammany Hall in his own state. But even these handicaps probably could have been overcome had Tilden not lapsed into one of his unaccountable periods of indecision. His failure to make a firm statement as to whether he would or would not accept the nomination left his followers in a position where they could neither push his cause energetically nor rally wholeheartedly about an acceptable alternative candidate.

With the prospects for victory good and Tilden's intentions uncertain, a large field entered the lists. Two of them, General Winfield Scott Hancock of Pennsylvania, still popular Civil War veteran, and Senator Thomas F. Bayard of Delaware, shared almost all the southern support between them. This was critical to the nomination, for, with the final ousting of the carpetbaggers following the 1876 elections, southern Bourbons once more were in control of their states. The mathematics of the convention under the two thirds rule ensured that no candidate receiving less than 90 per cent of the northern vote (that is, of all states except the eleven southern states that had seceded) could be nominated without some support from the South.

Other major candidates were Senator Allen G. Thurman of Ohio, now past his prime but with a strong following nevertheless, and Supreme Court Justice Stephen J. Field of California, whose support was modest but widely distributed throughout the nation. Favored by many Tilden backers, if their idol definitely were to withdraw from the picture, was Speaker of the House Samuel J. Randall of Pennsylvania. When the convention opened, none was considered far in front of his fellows and all were engaged in negotiations for support.

Cincinnati, Ohio,
June 22, 23, 24, 1880

The brief call to the convention was addressed to:

All Democratic conservative citizens of the United States irrespective of past political associations and differences, who can unite with us in the effort for pure, economical and constitutional government.[13]

[13] DNC, *Proceedings,* 1880, p. xv.

The call made no mention of territorial representation, but, in accordance with a resolution passed in the 1876 convention, states were requested to instruct their delegates upon whether it was desirable to continue the two thirds rule.

The chairman of the national committee presented Judge George Hoadly of Ohio as the nominee for temporary chairman. In his opening remarks, Hoadly spoke mostly of the "theft" of the previous election—a theme to be reiterated throughout the convention and the campaign to follow.

Convention Organization

Committees on organization, credentials, and resolutions were authorized and appointed, but a suggestion that a committee on rules be appointed was denied on the basis that there was no precedent for such a committee. In the midst of considerable confusion, a motion was offered to provide press tickets to bona fide editors of Democratic newspapers, but was defeated after it was pointed out that from three to four hundred of the best seats in the hall already had been assigned to the press. A series of resolutions regarding representation of the territories was referred unread to the committee on resolutions.

Shortly after the convention convened on the second day, the committee on permanent organization recommended former Senator John W. Stevenson of Kentucky as permanent chairman. As an auxiliary report to the list of officers for the convention, this committee stated that the memorials regarding territorial representation (which presumably had been turned over to them by the committee on resolutions) had been considered; it was recommended that two delegates be admitted from each territory and the District of Columbia with all privileges except the right to vote. Action on the report was delayed until after the report of the committee on credentials.

The credentials report confirmed the

action of the national committee with respect to a minor contest affecting one district in Pennsylvania and a New York contest for the entire delegation. In the case of Massachusetts, the report recommended seating of both delegations with the vote divided between them. A minority report on the New York contest recommended that one faction be given 50 votes and the other 20, each faction to determine how the votes would be apportioned among its respective group of delegates. On a roll call, New York declining to vote, the previous question was ordered, 361 to 297.[14] In response to a question, however, the chairman confessed he did not know just what the previous question entailed. Concerning rules of previous conventions, he said: "If anybody knows what those rules are, I will thank him to come up and state them himself." The best precedent, he stated, indicated that the rules provided for limitation of speeches to five minutes, and this he would enforce. "That is all I know about it."[15]

Following the roll call, the point of order was made that, under the rules of the House of Representatives, the previous question restricted the debate to one hour. Since the House rules had been adopted as the temporary rules of the convention, the point of order was accepted. The chairman of the committee granted forty minutes of the total time to the minority, the representatives of Tammany Hall. The first speaker for this group, though assuring the convention that "we do not use this in a threatening way," clearly warned that the party was courting loss of New York if his delegation did not receive the 20 votes demanded. A second speaker was more conciliatory, basing his argument upon precedents, of which there had been several, in which contesting delegations from New York had both been seated.

The principal majority speaker charged that the Tammany delegates had bolted the state convention only after they saw

that a candidate to whom they were opposed would receive the gubernatorial nomination, and that their leader, John Kelly, had stated they would bolt the national convention if Tilden were nominated. He recited cases in the past in which Tammany had "knifed" the Democratic cause. Convention precedents of the past did not apply to this contest, he said, since previous differences had been based upon important issues, not merely the choice between men, as in this case. A speaker for the minority pleaded that only fifteen of the seventy contesting delegates were from Tammany, but it did no good. The minority report was defeated 457 to 205½, New York again abstaining. The majority report was then adopted by voice vote. As a gesture of conciliation, a motion was passed to permit the rejected New York delegates to take seats in the hall.

The report of the committee on permanent organization was then taken from the table and passed, following which the permanent chairman took the rostrum. Since the resolutions committee was still in session, the convention decided to expedite matters by proceeding to nominate, but not to vote for, the presidential candidates.

The Presidential Nomination

Alabama and Arkansas not having candidates, Judge Stephen J. Field had the honor of first nomination, California being his place of legal residence. He received many seconding speeches during the proceedings, since his support was widely scattered. The speaker for Thomas F. Bayard stressed his broadly based appeal: "His is no sectional fame." Allen G. Thurman's long experience was stressed, then, lest this remind listeners of his age, the speaker added, "but he has not yet finished his course of usefulness and glory." To Winfield Scott Hancock's military record as a northern general was added his popularity in the South, which was the result of the fair treatment given the

[14] See *Analysis of Key Votes*.
[15] DNC, *Proceedings*, 1880, p. 28.

Southern people when he was military governor of Texas and Louisiana.

When the speeches for these and others had been completed, the platform committee was still in session; it was therefore suggested that one ballot be taken to "see how we stand." Objection was raised, and an attempt to adjourn until morning was defeated after a roll call vote that was necessitated in large part by gallery interference. The vote was 395½ to 317½ against adjournment, and the convention then decided to call the roll for the presidential nomination.[16] Hancock (171) and Bayard (153½) were far out in front, the third man being Henry G. Payne of Ohio, with 81 votes. Payne had not been nominated, and his votes came from Tilden people, who were trying to assess the strength of the convention before making a serious move. A scattering of votes went to sixteen other candidates, the highest received being 68½. The convention then adjourned until the next morning.

Immediately after the convention was next called to order, the New York delegation presented a long letter from Tilden in which he appeared to be attempting to justify his entire career, especially his actions during the contest of 1876. He concluded with a statement that, whereas in 1876 he had been willing to undertake the tremendous clean-up job required after years of Republican misrule, he no longer had the strength for the job. In introducing this letter, the speaker said that "the present sentiment of the State of New York [was] in favor of the Speaker of the House of Representatives—Samuel J. Randall." Thus, somewhat belatedly, the Tilden supporters received a relatively clear message from their leader.

The second ballot was then taken, and at the end of the call, Hancock had risen to 320, followed by Randall at 128½. Hancock was far short of the necessary 492 votes required by the two thirds rule—which was never discussed in the convention despite the statement in the call—but

the deficiency was soon supplied. Wisconsin made the first change, adding 10 votes to Hancock's total, after permission for a change of vote was authorized by vote of the convention. New Jersey added 11 more, Pennsylvania 27—and the flight was on.

The critical point was passed with the transfer of New York's 70 votes; shortly thereafter, to avoid the confusion of the numerous requests for changes, a motion to call the roll anew was carried. On the new call, Hancock received 705 of the total 738. Indiana stayed with its favorite son Thomas Hendricks, whose candidacy had never gotten off the ground.

The decision having been reached, one after another the representatives of the losing candidates took the stand to assure support. Finally, even Tammany's John Kelly was called to the platform, where he gave full assurances of his cooperation.

And in regard to New York, the man who once refers to the history of the past, and the political animosities which have existed in that State, let him, whoever he may be, be looked upon as a traitor to the cause.[17]

With the delegates in this happy mood of unanimity, Susan B. Anthony was permitted the rostrum. Not for the first time, she said, did the women make these demands: in 1868 alone and in 1872 with a colleague, she herself had appeared before the convention; in 1876, other representatives had presented the women's claims. She demanded that the Democratic party pledge itself "to use all its powers to secure to the women of the Nation protection in the exercise of their rights of suffrage."[18]

The Platform

The platform, passed after the presidential nomination, decried centralization in government and called for home rule. It was conservative on the money question, supporting paper money only backed by

---

[16] See *Analysis of Key Votes.*

[17] DNC, *Proceedings*, 1880, p. 123.
[18] *Ibid.*, p. 127.

specie. The position on the tariff question may have cost the election, for the platform called for a tariff for revenue only— a plank well designed to produce objection from labor as well as from manufacturers. On the other hand, importation of Chinese labor, through immigration, was specifically opposed. The issue that "precedes and dwarfs every other," the platform asserted, was the "great fraud of 1876-77" by which the defeated candidate was declared President. A more sacred duty was imposed upon the people of the Union "than ever addressed the consciences of a nation of freemen" to see that this crime was punished. The platform was adopted without debate and by unanimous vote.

The Vice-Presidential Nomination

It quickly became obvious that William H. English of Indiana, who had not been in public life since he retired from the House of Representatives in 1861, was the selected nominee. Nominated by Alabama, he was seconded by state after state; only one other name was mentioned, and that quickly was withdrawn. The rules were suspended, and English was nominated by acclamation.

Analysis of Key Votes

The vote ordering the previous question, thus limiting debate on the New York credentials question, was of relatively low candidate-orientation, but evidently was a minor defeat for Hancock, with whose vote on the second and nominating ballot the correlation was −.37. The vote to adjourn before balloting for the presidential nomination was more clearly candidate-oriented, and was supported generally by those who subsequently voted for Hancock. The vote on adjournment correlates +.57 with Hancock's nominating vote. Evidently the Hancock leaders wanted more time for negotiation, and were able to get it. Bayard's supporters were more or less on the fence, for the correlation with his top vote on the first ballot was +.18; but the supporters of minor candidates tended to oppose the adjournment. The first ballot correlation between the adjournment vote and the vote for others was −.40. Most of the opposition subsequently voted for Randall; on his second-ballot vote before vote shifting, every Randall vote came from delegations that had voted below the convention average on the vote to adjourn.

Presidential Election, November 2, 1880

JAMES A. GARFIELD (R) : popular vote, 4,453,296; electoral vote, 214
WINFIELD SCOTT HANCOCK (D): popular vote, 4,414,507; electoral vote, 115

1884

EARLY IN HIS TERM President Garfield was shot by a disappointed office seeker, and died after weeks of agony. This brought Chester A. Arthur, whose entire political career had been associated with machine politics and the spoils system, into the Presidency. There, his performance seemed completely inconsistent with his previous reputation, for he proved most circumspect in his appointments, fought against pork-barrel legislation, and sponsored civil service reform. In these actions, he was frequently at odds with large elements of his own party, particularly those with whom he had been most intimate.

Throughout his administration, investigation of scandals from past administrations kept the public in a turmoil, and added fuel to the fires being set by the reform elements in both parties. In the 1882 mid-term elections, the Democrats captured control of the House of Representatives and won several governorships, notably New York's. With two very close presidential contests in the recent past, the prospects were that the contest of 1884 also would be close. The unification of the "solid South" was further advanced, and the effects peculiar to each party had become an increasingly important element in the nominating politics. For the Republicans, many delegates from the weak southern parties were on the bargain and sale counter. For the Democrats, it was understood even more clearly than in 1880 that no candidate could be nominated against solid southern opposition without at least 90 per cent of the northern vote in the convention.

EIGHTH REPUBLICAN CONVENTION

Although Arthur's administration record has stood the test of history very well, it won him few friends at the time. His refusal to grant the patronage demands of his erstwhile intimates, the Stalwarts, lost him the wholehearted support of that group, although most of them voted for him in the convention—for want of anyone more acceptable. The reform elements could not forget his past, despite his more statesmanlike recent actions. Backed by the patronage power, he was able to enter the convention with substantial support from the southern delegations, but he could not expect to hold it if the tide turned against him.

The kind of popularity that Arthur never attained came easily to James G. Blaine, who had so narrowly missed the nomination in 1876 and 1880. The high degree of loyalty he had inspired for years in a large nationwide following survived even the 1876 charge of connection with highly questionable financial operations—an episode that would have ruined the political careers of most men. Appointed Secretary of State by Garfield in 1881, he resigned when Arthur succeeded to the Presidency. Now in 1884 the common belief—even on the part of his enemies—was that "It's Blaine's turn" to win the nomination.

Acceptance of the probability of Blaine's nomination by his opponents was doubtless fostered by the fact that the opposition was split among such widely different elements as the Stalwarts and the reformists. There was no candidate about whom these diverse groups could unite, since they could not unite on Arthur. Senator George F. Edmunds of Vermont was the choice of many of the eastern reformists, but could get no support from the Stalwarts. Senators John A. Logan of Illinois and John Sherman of Ohio were little more than favorite sons of their states, though each was a good possibility in case of a deadlock and supporters of each aided the stop-Blaine coalition by voting against organizational and procedural motions made by Blaine supporters during the convention.

Chicago, Illinois,
June 3, 4, 5, 6, 1884

The convention call reverted to previous practice and included a statement of the sentiments presumed to be shared by those selecting delegates to the Republican convention.

. . . The Republican electors of the several States, and all other voters without regard to past political differences, who are in favor of elevating and dignifying American labor, protecting and extending home industries, giving free popular education to the masses of the people, securing free suffrage and an honest counting of ballots, effectually protecting all human rights in every section of our common country.[1]

It also included, for the first time, explicit directions on the selection of delegates and on the method for handling contests—a reflection of the credentials difficulties in the previous convention.

The delegates-at-large shall be chosen by popular State conventions, called on not less than twenty days' published notice, and not less than thirty days before the time fixed for the meeting of the National Convention.

The Republicans of the various Congressional districts shall have the option of electing their delegates at separate popular delegate conventions, called on similar notice, and held in the Congressional districts at any time within the fifteen days next prior to the meeting of the State Conventions, or by subdivisions of the

State Conventions into District Conventions; and such delegates shall be chosen in the latter method if not elected previous to the meeting of the State Conventions. All district delegates shall be accredited by the officers of such District Conventions.

Notices of contests shall be given to the National Committee, accompanied by full printed statements of the grounds of contests, which shall also be made public; and preference in order of hearing and determining contests shall be given by the Convention according to the dates of the reception of such notices and statements by the National Committee.[2]

Convention Organization

Powell Clayton, ex-senator from Arkansas, was the nominee of the national committee for temporary chairman, but Henry Cabot Lodge of Massachusetts immediately proposed a colored delegate from Mississippi, John R. Lynch, as a substitute. Various interpretations of this move have been advanced. According to Senator George F. Hoar of Massachusetts, Clayton was a Blaine man, and a coalition of Blaine's opponents decided that substitution of a colored delegate for chairman would weaken Blaine's appeal to other colored delegates. Melville E. Stone, a journalist, states that Clayton originally was selected by the Arthur people, but that he subsequently moved into Blaine's camp when Arthur refused him a postmastership as reward for support; accordingly, the Arthur supporters wished to punish him.

Both suggestions may be correct so far as they go, for Lynch was nominated and seconded by members of the pro-Edmunds reformist bloc, and was supported by the Stalwarts, and these two groups, with assistance from favorite son delegations, elected him. The splits from the Ohio and Illinois delegations, both of which divided fairly evenly, provided the balance of power; the vote was Lynch 424, Clayton 384. It was the last victory but one for this coalition.[3]

Immediately following appointment of

[1] RNC, *Proceedings*, 1884, p. 4.

[2] *Ibid.*, pp. 4, 5.
[3] See *Analysis of Key Votes.*

the four standing committees, a motion was passed after some discussion:

That the subject of a revised apportionment of delegates to future National Conventions, and of a revised apportionment of members of the National Committee, be referred to the Committee on Rules and Order of Business, with leave to report before the ballot for President.[4]

The convention shortly thereafter adjourned. On the second day, this resolution was presented:

Resolved, as the sense of this Convention, that every member of it is bound in honor to support its nominee, whoever that nominee may be; and that no man should hold a seat here who is not ready to so agree.[5]

This precipitated an animated debate in which the arguments for and against a similar resolution presented by Roscoe Conkling in 1880 were renewed. It was finally withdrawn.

No difficulty arose over the selection of the permanent officers, other than a protest that they should not be approved until the committee on credentials had reported. General John B. Henderson of Missouri was elected permanent chairman and despite the protests assumed the chair immediately, but since the credentials committee was still in session the convention adjourned soon thereafter. During a short evening session the committee again reported it was not ready, and after a short argument over a motion to issue extra tickets to veterans, permitting them to sit in seats not occupied by regular ticket holders—a motion that was defeated—the convention again adjourned.

On the morning of the third day the credentials committee submitted a unanimous report which the convention accepted without debate. Nine contests involving individual congressional districts were settled in favor of the delegates seated on the temporary roll, as was the contest for the full delegation of Virginia. In two other district contests, one in New York and one

in Kentucky, the committee recommended seating both sets of contestants with a split vote.

The rules committee reported immediately thereafter. In general the format developed by Garfield in 1880 was followed, but several changes were made. For general parliamentary procedure, Cushing's Manual was adopted as the authority instead of the rules of the House of Representatives. The ten-minute restriction on nominating speeches was removed, and the time limit left open—a change some speakers took advantage of.

The most important rule changes related to the national committee. In the first place, officeholders were proscribed from membership by a clause specifying that only those eligible for membership in the electoral college might be members of the committee. And whereas the rules of the 1880 convention had authorized the national committee to issue a call and to prescribe methods for selection of delegates, the new rule provided definite instructions as to how delegates should be selected. Delegates in congressional districts should be selected in the same manner that congressional candidates were nominated; delegates at large were to be selected by state conventions.

With respect to the instructions received in the resolution referred by the convention during the first session, an auxiliary majority report was submitted, providing:

That in the future Republican National Conventions representation by delegates shall be as follows:
First—Each State shall be entitled to four delegates-at-large and to two additional delegates-at-large for each representative-at-large, if any, elected in each State at the last preceding Congressional election.
Second—Each Territory and the District of Columbia shall be entitled to two delegates.
Third—Each Congressional District shall be entitled to two delegates.[6]

This was a simple restatement of the previous apportionment rules. A minority report was then proposed.

[4] RNC, Proceedings, 1884, p. 28.
[5] Ibid., p. 37.

[6] Ibid., pp. 83-84.

Resolved, That in future Republican National Conventions representation by delegates shall be as follows:

First. Each State shall be entitled to four delegates-at-large and to one additional delegate-at-large for each Representative-at-large, if any, elected in said State at the last preceding Presidential election.

Second. Each Territory and the District of Columbia shall be entitled to two delegates-at-large.

Third. Each Congressional district shall be entitled to one delegate, and an additional delegate for every 10,000 votes, or majority fraction thereof, cast for the Republican Presidential electoral ticket at the last preceding Presidential election.

Fourth. The Republican National Committee shall, within the year following each Presidential election, ascertain and certify the representation to which each State and District will be hereby entitled in the next following National Convention.[7]

The minority report was signed by the committee members from eight states, including the large states of New York, Indiana, Massachusetts, Michigan, and New Jersey. The debate that followed brought out most of the points featuring debates on the subject in succeeding conventions. Southerners claimed they were being disenfranchised by the North because the "Bourbons" of the South illegally prevented them from voting, and that the resolution, in effect, sanctioned these voting frauds. It was pointed out that the provision for delegates at large gave considerable advantage to small states such as Rhode Island. Adoption of the minority report, it was suggested—a suggestion not too far from a threat—would result in additional losses in Congress and the probability that Republicans in the South would cease in their efforts altogether.

In defense of the minority report, only the factual point was made that the current method of apportionment resulted in serious inequalities in the relationship between the number of delegates and the number of Republican voters represented. Probably more to the point in reaching a decision on the matter, during the debate it

[7] *Ibid.,* p. 84.

was revealed that there would be a split in the New York delegation. Iowa was fully opposed, as was Missouri, and at least some objection would be found in Ohio and other northern states. As a result, the minority report was withdrawn without a vote, and the majority report accepted.

The Platform

In the opening address, the chairman of the national committee spoke of the "comparative lull of party strife which distinguishes the present condition of National politics" and suggested that it was a time when the selection of candidates was more important than issues. This point of view was reflected in the platform.

Tariff reform was pledged, with an inference that tariffs would be reduced, since the question was coupled with the need for reduction of the Treasury surplus. However, the reduction was to be not "by the vicious and indiscriminate process of horizontal reduction," but in line with protective principles. Regulation of the railroads and enactment of laws protecting labor were "favored," and reform of the civil service "should be completed." However, strong phrases, such as "we pledge" or "it is the duty of Congress," were reserved for such questions as exclusion of Chinese labor and the abolition of polygamy.

The Presidential Nomination

The speakers for James G. Blaine stressed his strength in the North, where the battle must be won. "The odds of the solid South are against us. Not an electoral gun can be expected from that section." Speakers for other candidates all managed to refer by indirection to the scandals with which Blaine had been connected, particularly the speakers for George F. Edmunds, the reform candidate. Arthur's principal speaker aptly, if not prophetically, pointed out that all successful Republican nominees had received a second term if they desired it, and failure to honor Arthur in the same way would be resented by the people. He concluded by quoting Robert S. Hawker's ballad, somewhat inaccurately but ringingly:

"And shall Trelawney die? And shall Trelawney die?/Then thirty thousand Cornishmen will know the reason why"—then cried, "Strike down Mr. Arthur, and not 30,000 Republicans but thirty times 30,000 will know the reason why."

It was well after midnight when the last speaker was finished, but many wanted to take a ballot before adjourning. A motion to adjourn until 10 a.m., supported largely by Blaine people, was defeated by the narrow margin of 410 to 391, but the Blaine leaders immediately followed with another motion to adjourn until 11 a.m. Again the roll was called, but finally those who favored an immediate presidential ballot gave up, and the roll was suspended after nine states had responded, despite the fact that the negative vote was stronger than at the same point on the previous roll call. The explanation probably lies in the confusion in the hall, for the proceedings are interspersed with such statements as, "It is utterly impossible to know or hear what is going on."

The next morning the chairman directed that the roll be called of those states that had not yet filled their positions on the national committee. Some delegations still had not made their selections, and a delegate from the District of Columbia admitted that his delegation had not agreed. To this, a colleague added, "And I am satisfied we won't agree."

The first ballot showed Blaine and Arthur far out in front of the field, which included six other names. Blaine led with 334½, Arthur polled 278, with Edmunds a poor third at 93. The second call began immediately after the totals for the first were announced; Blaine gained 14½ votes, taking 2 or more from each of the other four leading candidates. He increased his lead even more on the third ballot as he jumped to 375, again at the expense of all the other four. An attempt at this point

was made to adjourn. The motion was made by Senator Logan's Illinois delegation, and the vote presaged further gains by Blaine, whose supporters solidly opposed the motion. The respective supporters of Logan, Sherman, and Edmunds split on the issue, while Arthur's mainly stood fast for adjournment. The motion was defeated 450 to 364, and was followed by an abortive attempt to nominate Blaine by acclamation.[8] The fourth roll call was ordered; following a shift led by Logan's supporters, it proved to be the final one. The result was Blaine 541, Arthur 207, Edmunds 41, with 24 votes spread among three others. New York made the motion for unanimous nomination of James G. Blaine, "in behalf of the President of the United States, and at his request."

The Vice-Presidential Nomination

Only one name—John A. Logan of Illinois—was presented formally for the vice-presidential nomination, and a motion to suspend the rules and nominate by acclamation was actually passed. However, the Illinois delegation demanded that the roll be called—for what purpose it is not clear, unless to smoke out opposition to their favorite son. The roll was called, and Logan was nominated. He received 773 of the 820 votes in the convention, 7 being cast for others and the balance not cast. Most of those not cast appeared to belong to the Edmunds people, who had left the hall following the presidential nomination.

Analysis of Key Votes

The two roll call votes taken prior to the presidential balloting both resulted in defeats for the Blaine supporters. The vote on the majority side of the ballot for temporary chairman correlated −.69 with Blaine's third-ballot vote, and the motion to adjourn before calling the roll for the first nominating ballot correlated −.73 with the same ballot. Despite this second

[8] See *Analysis of Key Votes.*

defeat, the Blaine leaders were able to accomplish their purpose and force an adjournment. The leaders had things better under control when an attempt was made by the opposition to adjourn after the third ballot, the vote on this roll call correlating +.72 with Blaine's third-ballot vote. The willingness of some of the previous opposition to join in defeating the adjournment presaged the Blaine victory that came on the next ballot.

FOURTEENTH DEMOCRATIC CONVENTION

In an era of close national elections, nomination to represent either party was worth seeking. For the Democrats in 1884, it was particularly valuable, since not only had the mid-term elections netted them a majority in the House, but the nomination of Blaine a month before had been followed promptly by repudiation of the nominee by a number of influential Republicans. These dissidents, soon to be known as "Mugwumps," made it clear that they were ready and willing to support a Democratic nominee if he had a good "reform" record.

The Democratic list of available candidates was thin. As occasionally happens in the leadership development process, few aggressive new leaders had achieved sufficient stature to take over from the aging leadership of previous decades. Tilden, his health broken and past his seventieth birthday, quickly removed himself, despite the loyalty of his friends. General Hancock, the titular leader, was never seriously considered. Former Senator Allen G. Thurman of Ohio, though older than Tilden, was definitely in the running, as was the equally aged perennial candidate from Indiana, Thomas A. Hendricks. In addition to their age, both these latter candidates were further handicapped by their soft-money records, and by the fact that there was little in their records to attract the independent and reform vote. Thomas F. Bayard of Delaware was more available from this standpoint, but his residence in one of the smallest states was a handicap, as also was his affiliation with the Copperheads during the war. One man stood out—Grover Cleveland, "reform" governor of New York. In addition to his creditable record in his short term of office, the fact that he was known to have Tilden's backing probably was definitive.

Chicago, Illinois,
July 8, 9, 10, 11, 1884

The convention performed before what was perhaps the largest convention audience up to its time, the hall reportedly holding over 12,000 people. It was called to order by the chairman of the national committee, William H. Barnum of Connecticut. Richard B. Hubbard, of Texas, the temporary chairman, combined a ringing call for a reform ticket and platform with a plea for harmony within the convention.

That all was not to be harmonious was demonstrated immediately when a Tammany Hall delegate countered a motion to adopt temporary convention rules with an amendment. The conflict apparently was introduced deliberately by the majority in the convention to obtain an early test of strength, for in addition to the usual recommendation to adopt the rules of the last convention, a clause in the original motion stated:

That in voting for candidates for President and Vice-President no State shall be allowed to change its vote until the role of the States has been called and every State has cast its vote.[9]

The Tammany amendment read:

And when the vote of a State, as announced by the Chairman of the Delegation from such State, is challenged by any member of the Delegation, then the Secretary shall call the names of the individual Delegates from the State, and their individual preferences, as expressed, shall be recorded as the vote of such State.[10]

[9] DNC, *Proceedings*, 1884, p. 9.
[10] *Ibid.*, p. 9.

The point at issue was the unit rule, and the conflict resulted from the fact that, although Tammany Hall had been allowed representation on the New York delegation by the anti-Tammany majority in the state convention, the delegation had then been bound by the unit rule. In the course of the debate, one delegate made the reasonable point of order that the subject should be handled by the rules committee, but was ruled out of order by the chairman. Subsequently a motion to refer the question to the rules committee, when appointed, was lost.

The majority rested their case on precedent and the principle of state sovereignty. The minority argued that a state convention had no right to bind district delegates. In addition, they said, the unit rule has "always been the potent device by which political managers and political engineers have sought to give a false expression to the opinion of the voters of the State and pervert rather than to express their voice upon the floor of a deliberative body"—an interesting argument coming from a leader of that era's Tammany Hall.

Amidst considerable confusion, to which the galleries contributed, a roll call was demanded. The announcement by the delegation chairman from New York that 72 votes were cast against the amendment was challenged.

When the temporary chairman ruled that the vote should stand he based the ruling upon the interesting grounds that the question presented was the subject matter of the vote being taken. He graciously added that a protest was always in order and would be so recorded. Protests from Tammany that this did its cause no good were disregarded, and the amendment was defeated 463 to 332.[11]

The original motion was then put to a voice vote and adopted. Following this flurry, the convention settled down and appointed the usual committees without further incident.

11 See *Analysis of Key Votes.*

Convention Organization

On the morning of the second day the resolutions committee reported that it would not be able to report until the following day, which left the convention with a relatively thin agenda. A number of resolutions were read to the convention and referred without debate to the committee in accordance with a rule previously adopted. Among these was one amending the previous day's action on the unit rule, to restrict it only to delegations from states which had instructed their delegations to vote as a unit.

The committee on credentials reported settlement of a minor contest in Massachusetts, and recommended a new precedent in Democratic conventions by allotting seats and voting rights to two delegates in each of the territories and the District of Columbia. A motion to deny voting privileges to these delegates was defeated by voice vote, and the committee report was adopted.

Another series of resolutions was read and referred to committee—a series broken only by an unsuccessful effort to proceed with nominations, and terminated by announcement that the committee on permanent organization was ready to report. William F. Vilas of Wisconsin was elected permanent chairman. In his long speech of acceptance he reiterated the reform theme, and begged the forbearance of the delegates as he sought to carry out his assignment.

Reading of resolutions continued, and another motion was made to proceed with nominations. This time, the roll was called upon a motion to table and it was defeated 523 to 281. Again the solid vote of New York was challenged, and again it was allowed to stand. The convention then approved the motion to nominate, but with the stipulation that no vote be taken until after the report of the platform committee. Several attempts were made to adjourn, all of which were lost, and the chairman directed the secretary to call the roll of the states for presidential nominations.

The Presidential Nomination

Thomas F. Bayard of Delaware was the first to be presented. The second nomination probably was—and remains—without parallel in convention history. The name of Joseph E. McDonald of Indiana, a relatively obscure former senator, was presented as Indiana's favorite son by the man who obviously was the real choice of his delegation and a definite candidate on a national plane—Thomas A. Hendricks. In a very long speech, Hendricks demonstrated his own broad grasp of national problems, and pleaded for recognition of Indiana despite the fact that it was a "safe" state. Everything he said of his nominee's qualifications fitted himself quite as well, and he was followed by a seconding speech which could have been seconding Hendricks' own nomination by simply inserting his name in place of McDonald's. Hendricks was not placed in nomination officially. The next major candidate to be nominated was Allen G. Thurman who was presented by a representative of his own Ohio delegation.

The nominations of these and minor candidates were accomplished without unusual display, but when it became Cleveland's turn the situation changed. He was presented by a member of the New York delegation in a speech detailing his qualifications, but making no reference to the split in the delegation. This subject was introduced by a delegate from Illinois in a seconding speech, when he attacked the Tammany strategem of declaring that Cleveland could not win New York. He was followed by Thomas F. Grady, Tammany leader. Grady seized the "can't win" thesis, and proceeded to detail why. He was interrupted by demands that he be declared out of order since he was attacking a candidate, not making a nominating or seconding speech, and was allowed to continue only on motion made by a representative of his opposition faction in New York. The galleries were not so amenable, and he had considerable difficulty in proceeding,

despite threats from the chairman that the galleries might be cleared. Aside from opposition to Cleveland, Grady stated no choice and in effect seconded the nomination of all the other nominees.

Grady was followed by a colleague, Bourke Cockran. Opening with a statement that he intended to second a nomination, Cockran, too, launched into an anti-Cleveland speech. He, Cockran, was "too warm a friend of his [Cleveland's] to desire his promotion to an office for which I do not believe he has the mental qualifications." He dwelt at length on the politics of New York, but kept his word by finally seconding the nomination of Thurman. Following a pro-Cleveland speech from another New York delegate, the convention adjourned.

The next morning, seconding speeches and nominating speeches for minor candidates continued. The repercussions of the New York squabble were evident in many of them, as individuals took one side or the other, but a climax occurred when General Edward S. Bragg of Wisconsin in seconding Cleveland said:

They love him, gentlemen, and they respect him, not only for himself, for his character, for his integrity and judgment and iron will, but they love him most of all for the enemies he has made.[12]

At this point, Grady stepped directly in front of the chairman's desk and said: "Mr. Chairman, on behalf of his enemies, I reciprocate that sentiment, and we are proud of the compliment."

A few speeches later, the platform not yet being completed, the convention adjourned until evening, at which time the platform was presented.

The Platform

The first resolution presented by the committee on resolutions was different from the usual declarations of party policy, for it dealt with an important question of party organization. In the past, most chair-

---

[12] DNC, *Proceedings*, 1884, p. 176.

men of the national committees had been
selected primarily on the basis of their own
wealth or of their contacts with the
wealthy, and their role, except where individuals made it otherwise, was primarily
that of fund-raising. The resolution recognized the changing requirements of party
leaders; its preamble states the question
better than any synthesis could:

> Whereas, the Chairman of the National Dem-
> ocratic Committee is necessarily intrusted with
> such large powers in the arrangement and con-
> duct of the political campaign that upon his
> knowledge, prudence, and ability the successful
> execution of the plan of the party largely de-
> pends; and whereas, it is therefore highly im-
> portant that the National Democratic Com-
> mittee in selecting their Chairman should have
> the Democracy of the whole Union to choose
> from; therefore, resolved, that the National
> Democratic Committee be not restricted in its
> selection of a Chairman to the members of the
> Committee.[13]

The resolution was adopted without
debate.

A resolution was offered from the floor to
abolish the two thirds rule and to institute
majority rule in subsequent conventions.
When an overwhelming trend toward
agreement to table the resolution was revealed on the call of the first seven states,
the call was suspended, and the motion
indefinitely postponed. The committee on
resolutions then presented the regular platform.

The first part of the platform detailed
the purported difference between Republican statements and Republican performance in a series of brief sentences of which
the following are typical:

> It [the Republican Party] demands the res-
> toration of our Navy. It has squandered hun-
> dreds of millions to create a navy that does not
> exist.
> It professes to protect all American indus-
> tries. It has impoverished many to subsidize a
> few.[14]

A Democratic program was then detailed. It proposed a cautious approach to
tariff questions, pledging to revise the

tariff, but stating that "every step [must be]
regardful of the labor and capital thus involved." It proposed to rely upon the
tariff for all expenses of government and
opposed continuations of "taxation known
as 'Internal Revenue'," except to pay the
war debt and provide such things as pensions for veterans and their widows. The
previous position on money was reversed,
for the platform called for "honest" money,
convertible to specie. As so frequently was
the case during this period in the platforms
of both parties, a strong position was taken
on the rights of American citizens abroad,
including naturalized citizens. The platform closed with a statement of regret that
Tilden could not once again be called upon
to lead the party.

A lengthy minority report was presented
by Benjamin F. Butler of Massachusetts,
once a genuine power in the Republican
party and soon to accept the nomination
of two abortive minor groups, the Anti-
Monopoly and the Greenback parties.
Although Butler's proposal included resolutions on labor, monopoly, public corporations, civil service, and currency, in addition to the tariff, he specifically stated that
he would ask for a vote only on the tariff
resolution. This did not prevent him from
making extensive comments upon other
aspects of his proposals, and in discussing
the currency question, he probably did
Thurman's candidacy no good when he
said: "I represent many Greenback men,
good and true Greenback men like Allen
G. Thurman."[15] In a convention so obviously controlled by hard-money advocates,
most of whom were Cleveland men, this
alone might have justified allowing so much
time to a political renegade with so little
real claim on the convention.

Butler's program differed relatively little
from the majority, except that it opposed
all direct taxation except in case of dire
necessity. Where the majority wording
stated that tariffs should bear heaviest on
articles of luxury and least on articles of
necessity, Butler's proposed that luxury

---

[13] *Ibid.*, pp. 191-192.
[14] *Ibid.*, pp. 196-197.

[15] *Ibid.*, p. 209.

items be taxed to the utmost, and that materials used in manufacture of necessities not produced in this country enter entirely free. He also demanded greater recognition of the need to foster American labor through tariff schedules. On the record vote, Butler was able to secure only 96½ votes against 721½ for the majority report. The residue of his proposal was disposed of by voice vote, and the majority report adopted by the same method.

The Presidential Nomination (continued)

After an attempt to delay the proceedings until the next morning, which was defeated 628½ to 190½, the roll call for the presidential nomination began. The solid New York vote again was a matter of contention on the delay vote, but stood as it had before. On the first ballot for president, however, the New York chairman announced that his delegation cast a solid vote for Cleveland but that only 49 of the 72 votes actually were for him—which seemed temporarily to placate the opposition, for nothing more appears in the proceedings. On this ballot, Hendricks protested a vote cast for him—in the tradition of Seymour and Garfield. He similarly was overruled.

Ten candidates received one or more votes on the first ballot. Cleveland was far in the lead with 392, followed by Bayard, 170; Thurman, 88; Samuel J. Randall, veteran member of Congress and favorite son of Pennsylvania, 78; McDonald, 56; the balance of the vote scattering, Hendricks receiving only one.

A roll call was then taken on a motion to adjourn until the next morning; the motion's close defeat—412 to 404—was protested on the grounds that there was an obvious discrepancy in the vote. Six Illinois delegates had failed to vote, yet the vote as announced indicated only 4 less than the authorized 820 votes. The roll was called again for purposes of verification; the tally showed 412 to 401, with 7

votes not cast, and the motion was defeated —but immediately thereafter, at 1:16 a.m., the convention adjourned until 10:00 a.m., by voice vote. If it was sleep the delegates wanted, they probably wasted more than half an hour on the roll call and the subsequent bickering.

On the morning's next roll call "a determined and possibly a preconcerted attempt to 'stampede' the Convention to Mr. Hendricks" occurred following announcement by Illinois that one of its votes was cast for that gentleman. The official recorder, who may have been biased for Cleveland, stated:

. . . at no time was there any marked participation in the confusion by the body of Delegates. A careful computation made by the official Stenographer during the thirty minutes of uproar revealed the fact that, when the tumult was at its height, not more than twenty-five per cent of the Delegates were upon their feet or in any way joining the galleries in their demonstration.[16]

When the demonstration had run its course, the chairman of the Indiana delegation, who had ascended the platform in the meantime, was given recognition. He stated that the chairman had reminded him that nominations were not then in order, but he could announce by unanimous decision of his delegation that the name of McDonald was withdrawn for the purpose of casting the solid vote of Indiana for Hendricks "at the proper time." The rest of the Illinois votes were finally announced —38 among them for Cleveland, which opened the door for a demonstration by Cleveland followers.

Hendricks jumped into third place on the ballot, with 123½ votes. Cleveland moved up strongly to 475; Bayard and Thurman dropped, to 151½ and 60 respectively, while Randall nearly disappeared from the balloting. Before the results were announced Illinois and Kansas made minor corrections to their vote, but when North Carolina was recognized, it transferred its entire vote from Bayard to

[16] *Ibid.*, p. 237.

Cleveland. Virginia, whose vote had been widely split, consolidated all but 1 vote on Cleveland, and the band wagon was in full swing.

At 12:42 the first gun was fired on the Lake Front . . . by which the outside world was made aware . . . for a single instant there was a hush: then as the meaning of the salute was understood, the demonstrations were renewed.[17]

When the switching was completed, Cleveland held 683 of the 820 votes in the convention, small hard cores remaining with Hendricks and Thurman, and 10 votes split between three other candidates. The motion to make the nomination unanimous was approved, and the convention adjourned before taking up the business of selecting the second half of the ticket.

The Vice-Presidential Nomination

The proceedings for selection of the vice-presidential nominee were relatively short but nonetheless interesting. General John C. Black, of Ohio, received nominating and seconding speeches, whereupon he stood up on his chair and declined the honor. Another Civil War veteran, and one who was perhaps more widely known, General William S. Rosecrans, was nominated and seconded by West Coast states, he having moved to California and having at one time been that state's representative in Congress. When Indiana was called, the chairman announced that the delegation

"has no candidate for the Vice-Presidency, neither will it present any." Kansas presented a favorite son. Finally, Pennsylvania brought matters to a head with the nomination of Hendricks, immediately seconded by the Governor of Connecticut.

The chairman of the Indiana delegation protested immediately: "Thomas A. Hendricks is not and will not be a candidate for the Vice-Presidency . . . let not this Convention do that which it may have to meet and do again." When asked whether he was authorized to say that Mr. Hendricks would not accept a unanimous nomination, he replied: "I will answer that gentleman on my left by saying, in the language of Mr. Hendricks himself, that he is not and will not be a candidate for the Vice-Presidency."[18]

The protests were to no avail; state after state endorsed Hendricks and other names were withdrawn. On the roll call, Indiana passed until all others had cast their votes, whereupon its 30 votes were cast for Hendricks and the nomination declared unanimous. Shortly thereafter, the final adjournment was moved.

Analysis of Key Votes

The vote on the Tammany amendment to the temporary rules, which in effect upheld the unit rule, was clearly candidate-oriented. The correlations between this vote and subsequent ballots for candidates is as follows:

Candidate	First Ballot		Second Ballot Before Shift	
	Correlation	Per Cent of Convention	Correlation	Per Cent of Convention
Cleveland	.50	47.8%	.59	57.9%
Bayard	−.16	20.7	−.22	18.5
Thurman	−.74	10.7	−.79	7.3
Hendricks[a]		0.1	−.45	15.1
Others[b]	−.19	20.7		1.2

[a] First-ballot vote too small to correlate.
[b] Second-ballot vote too small to correlate.

[17] *Ibid.*, p. 244.

[18] *Ibid.*, p. 261.

On the first ballot, supporters of Cleveland and Thurman were clearly on opposite sides of the question. Bayard and the miscellaneous candidates also tended to oppose the side of the issue favorable to Cleveland, but to a much less degree than the Thurman delegates. On the second ballot before vote shifting, Cleveland's gain clearly came from delegations that had voted with his supporters on the unit rule question, for his correlation rose to +.59. A small part of his added support came from delegates who had voted for Bayard, and most of the balance from others, and in Bayard's case, the increase in the negative correlation indicates that most who left him must have voted with the majority on the unit rule. The similar rise in Thurman's negative correlation indicates the same thing for his vote. The attempt to "Garfield" the convention for Hendricks appears to have been largely backed by delegations who voted with the minority on the unit rule.

Presidential Election, November 4, 1884

GROVER CLEVELAND (D) : popular vote, 4,918,507; electoral vote, 219
JAMES G. BLAINE (R) : popular vote, 4,850,293; electoral vote, 182

1888

CLEVELAND'S MARGIN of victory over Blaine in 1884 was narrow, in terms of both the popular and the electoral vote. As the first Democratic President since the Civil War, Cleveland had certain problems that were undoubtedly more acute than they would have been for a Republican President. This certainly was true of patronage. "Regular" organization Democrats had been denied access for a long time to the rich fountain controlled by the administration, and they rushed to drink; however, they formed only part of the coalition that had contributed to Cleveland's victory, and every job obtained by a member of their troop was resented by the reformist wing of the coalition. The regulars, in turn, were infuriated by every failure to receive a job that they considered a legitimate part of the spoils of victory. No matter what Cleveland did in patronage matters, someone was offended.

Furthermore, on the dominant issue of the day—the tariff question—Cleveland had the misfortune to lead a party that was more deeply split than the opposition. The split was the more serious because throughout Cleveland's term the Republicans held a majority in the Senate, and after the 1886 mid-term elections the Democratic majority in the House was very small. Thus, the President's hand was restrained from every side. The one act that seemed to bring universal approbation was his marriage in 1886, for this White House wedding was one of the sensations of the time. Had the wedding taken place nearer to election time, its emotional glow might have bettered Cleveland's electoral chances; by 1888, however, Cleveland and his wife were no longer a romantic bridal pair, but merely another man and wife.

FIFTEENTH DEMOCRATIC CONVENTION

No one but Cleveland received real consideration for the Democratic nomination. This was not, however, because he was the universal choice of a unified party, for there were many opposed to him. The patronage problem earned him the dislike of many disgruntled office seekers—actually, a perennial source of difficulty for first-term presidents—his persistent vetoes of private pension bills that he regarded as raids on the Treasury alienated many veteran groups, and his forthright handling of other issues created other groupings of opposition. But these were all peripheral to the opposition roused by the main center of contention—the tariff. He literally split the party with his annual message to Congress in 1887, in which he took a firm stand for lower duties sufficient only to meet the needs of the government; the proponents of high protective tariffs turned solidly against him. But the power inherent in the presidential office, plus the fact that it is never an easy matter for a faction within the party to overthrow an incumbent eligible for renomination without discrediting the party, made opposition futile. In any event, none appeared in the convention.

The vice-presidential nomination was open, the venerable Thomas A. Hendricks having died early in his term.

St. Louis, Missouri,
June 5, 6, 7, 1888

The slate of temporary officers recommended by the national committee was presented by the national committee chairman and approved by the convention. For the first time in Democratic convention history, a Pacific Coast resident was selected as a convention officer when Stephen M. White was named temporary chairman. As could be expected under the circumstances in which the convention met, White's opening speech eulogized Cleveland and his administration, and blamed the Republicans in Congress for obstructing the administration program. He particularly blamed the Republicans for preventing a reduction of the tariff, and for the resulting "enormous surplus in the Treasury"— a strange problem to modern ears.

Convention Organization

The rules of the previous convention were adopted, including the clause restricting vote changes on the nominating roll calls to the end of the call. Nothing was said of the unit rule question which had been so controversial in the previous convention. The regular committees were appointed under a blanket resolution, but, by separate motion, the territory of Dakota was denied representation on the committees until a contest in its delegation had been settled, at which time committee members were added.

Before adjournment until the next day, a long discussion broke out over the perennial problem of tickets for spectators. The question was introduced by a motion to seat all members of the uniformed Democratic clubs that were present in the convention city—apparently many hundreds of them had arrived from ten or twelve states. The gentleman making the motion was evidently not aware of some of the more practical elements of the politics surrounding selection of convention cities, for he objected to the fact that a large block of tickets had been assigned to the Chamber of Commerce of St. Louis. A member of the national committee assured him that some 2,000 tickets had already been assigned the uniformed clubs. Another delegate suggested that a motion be passed to give the sergeant at arms "the power to increase the capacity of this hall," if the motion to admit all uniformed club members were passed, since the hall at present was filled to capacity. The question finally was referred to the national committee, and no more was heard of it.

The report of the credentials committee, including its solution of the Dakota contest, was approved without question, as also was the report of the committee on permanent organization. This latter report reaffirmed the rules for the convention as previously passed, and named Congressman Patrick A. Collins of Massachusetts for permanent chairman. In his acceptance speech Collins warned the party that the coming contest would be close, despite the excellence of Cleveland's administration: "Let no man here or elsewhere belittle or underestimate the strength or the resources of the opposition."

Shortly after Collins had taken the chair a petition was received from a women's convention held recently in Washington; the request that a representative of that convention be heard was approved. The lady, Mrs. E. A. Merriwether of St. Louis, was most forthright in her demands for women's suffrage. Having described the position of women as political slavery, she suggested that, if the convention did not see fit to endorse political recognition of women, it should pass a resolution stating:

Whereas, All history proves that education unfits human beings for the condition of subjugation, and awakens in the human soul aspirations for larger liberties and a higher life,

Whereas, During the last fifty years, we, the rulers of this land, have committed the great mistake of permitting a subjected class to enter schools of learning, thereby expanding their brains and quickening their thoughts, and breeding disaffection against our time-honored rule, these women going to and fro over the land, knocking at legislative doors, demanding to know why the glorious doctrines of Democracy should not apply to women as to men; and

Whereas, All history proves that the greater and denser the ignorance in which a class is held—

Resolved, That we, the Democratic men of America in Convention assembled, advise and urge the Legislature of every State in this broad Union to enact such laws as will forever put a stop to the education of the women of this land, and thereby put a stop to the clamor for equal rights, as will forever close the doors of every school, public or private, to the female children of this country; we advise and urge that it be made a penal offense, punishable by fine and imprisonment, to teach any girl or child the letters of the alphabet; and that any woman convicted of reading a newspaper or book, or entering lecture halls, whether as a listener or speaker, be severely punished by law.[1]

The men were not pleased. Mrs. Merriwether was interrupted repeatedly and actually not allowed to finish; the latter part of the resolution was taken down from her manuscript.

The Presidential Nomination

The afternoon being young when the resolutions committee announced that it could not report until the next day, many delegates wanted to proceed with the nomination. Others preferred to wait, but an attempt to adjourn was defeated and the roll was called for the presidential nomination. Alabama deferred to New York, whereupon Cleveland was nominated and seconded in a series of speeches. The rules were then suspended and Cleveland was nominated by acclamation—the first nomination without a roll call since Van Buren's in 1840.

All of this had taken so little time that some wanted to proceed with the vice-presidential nomination. Others wished to adjourn. One motion to adjourn until 10:00 a.m. the next day was voted down before it was discovered that the motion actually intended was written on the other side of the same piece of paper—calling for adjournment only until 8:00 p.m. that evening.

Although a motion to adjourn is not debatable, the chairman allowed considerable discussion before putting the vote. Unable to decide the majority on the voice vote, he ordered a roll call, and the motion was defeated 430 to 387. The previously defeated motion for adjournment until

[1] DNC, *Proceedings*, 1888, p. 73.

10:00 the next morning was then put to a roll call vote. By the time Florida was called, all but one delegate had voted for the motion, but an attempt to dispense with the call and move unanimous adjournment was refused by the chairman. The roll continued. When New York was called, the score stood 500 to 19 for adjournment; the chairman finally put the motion for unanimous adjournment to the backs of the few remaining delegates in the hall.

The Platform

In its first paragraph the platform reaffirmed the platform of 1884, and endorsed both the low tariff recommendations made by Cleveland in his annual message of 1887 and the attempts being made by congressional Democrats to reduce taxation. The balance of the platform consisted of a eulogy of the Cleveland administration and a castigation of Republican obstructionist tactics, particularly in the Senate where the Republicans had a majority. In a demonstration of unanimity, the platform was endorsed by Senator Arthur P. Gorman of Maryland, a representative of the protectionist faction of the party, and was passed without opposition by voice vote.

The Vice-Presidential Nomination

Allen G. Thurman of Ohio, a major opponent of Cleveland in the 1884 convention, was the first to be presented for the vice-presidential nomination. General John C. Black of Illinois was the next; the presenting speaker read a communication in which Black stated quite frankly that he would like the honor, but that he believed the sentiment of the convention had crystallized upon Thurman, and he therefore requested that his name be withheld. His friends refused to carry out the request, however; having in mind the death of elderly Thomas A. Hendricks shortly after he assumed the Vice Presidency, they believed that someone younger than the 75-year-old Thurman should be nominated.

Indiana nominated and pleaded for its governor, Isaac P. Gray. The plea was based more upon the grounds that it was important to carry Indiana (the reverse of the argument made for an Indiana nominee four years before when the plea was that that state should not be disregarded because she seemed safe) and relatively little was said about the nominee. The large number of seconding speeches for Thurman and the paucity of such speeches for others clearly presaged the result of the single ballot: Thurman received 684 votes, Gray 101, and Black 36. When the result became obvious, "Everybody produced a red bandanna, and every guidon in the hall was decorated with one." Throughout the convention, the bandanna was the symbol for Thurman, who reportedly always carried one. The nomination was made unanimous.

The closing business of the convention included passage of a resolution that indicated the end of an era—an expression of regret for the passing of so many old party leaders since the last convention. In addition to Hendricks, whose death had already been memorialized, Winfield Scott Hancock, Samuel J. Tilden, Horatio Seymour, and George B. McClellan, all of whom had carried the party's national banner, had died. On this sad note, the convention adjourned.

NINTH REPUBLICAN CONVENTION

For the first time since 1860, the Republicans faced the problems of the out-party against an intrenched incumbent; they also faced the first convention in sixteen years in which James G. Blaine was not an avowed candidate. Blaine's spirit nevertheless hovered over the convention, and it would have required but a word from his vacation place in Italy, where he was recuperating from a stroke, to set his followers to work. He had, however, sent home an adamant refusal to run even though nominated by a unanimous draft. The resulting open field was filled with hopefuls, none of whom possessed an outstanding lead over his fellows. John Sherman led, but his prospects indicated much less than a majority on the first ballot. The breadth of the field is indicated by the fact that on the first ballot, no less than fourteen individuals received votes, and none but Sherman had as much as 15 per cent of the total.

The convention, therefore, was quite unlike the previous three—in which one or more giants were in the lists. This was a battle of secondary leaders, whose differences in ideology and personality were scarcely distinct enough to excite the passions of the delegates. The Stalwarts were dispersed, their leaders dead. Since everybody now gave at least lip service to reform, the conflicts generally amounted to little more than bickering about different ways of saying approximately the same things. Probably no other convention has been so filled with petty squabbling over procedural and other details.

Chicago, Illinois,
June 19, 20, 21, 22, 23, 25, 1888

The call included the instructions regarding selection of delegates included in the resolutions passed by the previous convention, and recommended additional delegates for Dakota (the territory had not yet been split) and Washington—recommendations subsequently approved by the convention.

Convention Organization

The chairman of the national committee presented John M. Thurston of Nebraska as the temporary chairman, and without taking a vote turned the chair over to him. A Kansas delegate then asked whether the temporary chairman had been elected, to which the sergeant at arms replied: "The Temporary Chairman is Mr. John M. Thurston." The Kansan protested on behalf of his delegation, saying that his delegation regarded it as a "very great mistake," and that it would vote for another if the roll were called. The protest appears to have been completely disregarded, for Thurston proceeded with his opening speech.

Following his remarks, a motion was made to "elect as the officers of its temporary organization the various persons respectively recommended for those positions by the national committee." Thurston then said:

The Chair understands, the Chairman of the National Committee having recognized no objection on the floor of the convention, that the temporary organization has been accepted by the convention.[2]

The Kansas delegate again objected, and again was disregarded. The delegate who made the motion to elect the temporary organization withdrew it in light of the explanation of the temporary chairman.

The motion directing appointment of the standing committees proposed that the lists be sent to the chair rather than go through a roll call as in past conventions, and was accepted. Meanwhile, the convention called on a number of dignitaries, the more eminent of those who responded being the party's first standard-bearer, General John C. Frémont. The actual acceptance of the committee appointments was accompanied by a particularly bitter fight between contesting members of the Virginia delegation for seats on the committees—a fight characterized by such dialogue as the following:

Mr. Wise. I charge you with the frauds by which I was cheated out of my seat.
Mr. Mahone. Your charge is false.
Mr. Wise. Again I charge it.
Mr. Mahone. It is as false as you are foul.
Mr. Wise. I will put the stamp where it belongs at the proper time.

After the arguments had been thrown back and forth for some time, it was suggested that the whole discussion was pre-

mature, and the question one for the credentials committee to decide. A motion to exclude membership on the committees for all states having contests was tabled after a short debate, during which it was pointed out, as it had been before and would be in later conventions, that this would open the door to irresponsible or spurious contests that would disenfranchise legitimate delegations.

After the customary brief argument that no committees should report before the credentials committee did, the convention agreed to receive the report of the committee on permanent organization. Morris M. Estee, prominent California lawyer and politician, was selected permanent chairman. The first business to be conducted under his chairmanship was acceptance of the report of the committee on rules and order of business. The rules included only two important changes: the rules of the House of Representatives were established as the basic authority for parliamentary questions instead of Cushing's *Manual*, and an executive committee of nine members was established "to conduct the affairs of the party." It was to be appointed by the national committee, and formally recognized as an informal arrangement of some duration.

The report of the credentials committee included a minority report on the Virginia contests. The majority found for the delegates at large headed by William Mahone, leader of the "Readjuster" party—a coalition party now on the downgrade but which had enjoyed a brief period of power and office—and for the district delegates headed by John S. Wise, Mahone's opponent. The ninth congressional district was adjudged to have no legally selected delegates. The minority report differed from the majority with respect to some of the contested districts, and the exclusion of the delegates from the ninth district.

The question was divided, and separate votes were taken on different districts. By standing vote, the pro-Mahone delegates were accepted from the ninth district, but only after long debate. This did not finish the matter. On the grounds that many delegates did not understand on what they were voting, it was moved that the question be reconsidered. Much more parliamentary wrangling followed before another standing vote was taken on the question of tabling the motion to reconsider. It was tabled 252 to 174.

By this time, everybody was confused, including the chairman, and the next few pages of the proceedings are filled with discussion as to what was the order of pending questions. A roll call vote finally was taken on the minority report for the second congressional district; after it was decisively defeated 514 to 249½, the balance of the majority report was adopted by voice vote.[3]

The Platform

On the morning of the third day, the platform was presented. Characteristically for a party out of power, the words used in the recommendations were much stronger than those used during the long period of party supremacy. Such forthright statements and specific measures as the following were seldom found in platforms written when the party was in power.

We are uncompromisingly in favor of the American system of protection.

We condemn the proposition of the Democratic party to place wool on the free list.

The Republican party would effect all needed reduction of the National revenue by repealing the taxes upon tobacco.

We declare our opposition to all combinations of capital organized in trusts.

We demand the reduction of letter postage to one cent per ounce.

The Presidential Nomination

For the last time, Union generals were paraded up and down the battlefields of the war between the states, as they had

[3] See *Analysis of Key Votes.*

been in almost every convention since the conflict. Walter Q. Gresham, now an Indiana judge but presented for nomination by Illinois, "finally fell, pierced by a minnie ball, while leading his division into the shot and shell of the enemy at the bloody fight of Legget's Hill"; Benjamin Harrison, also of Indiana, "was in the thick of the fight at Resaca and Atlanta," though the fact that his grandfather was William H. Harrison, ninth President of the United States, seemed at least an equal factor of availability. Russell A. Alger of Michigan was one whose "bravery is written upon the blood-stained pages of his country's history." Ohio's candidate, Senator John Sherman, had the unfortunate handicap of serving in Congress during the war, but it was carefully pointed out that his brother was General William T. Sherman, famed for the march through Georgia. Chauncey Depew of New York and Senator William B. Allison of Iowa could not claim even this much.

Despite Sherman's relatively weak military assets, he led by a substantial margin on the first ballot with 229 of the required majority of 416. He was followed by Gresham, 107; Depew, 99; Alger and Harrison at 84 and 85; and Allison at 72. Eight others received scattered votes.

The field was reduced to twelve on the second ballot, Sherman picking up 20 votes as all the leaders held even or gained. Alger made the biggest jump, from 84 to 116. Twelve remained on the third ballot, with Sherman revealing weakness as he lost 5 votes, and Gresham returning to second position with 123—a lead of one vote over Alger. Allison and Harrison made slight gains, and Depew dropped slightly. The convention adjourned until evening, no protest being noted in the proceedings.

Immediately after the new session was called to order, Chauncey Depew was recognized and made a remarkable statement. He was not, he said, a serious candidate, but was merely serving as the vehicle for unanimity within the New York State party to keep it from breaking into a factional fight between supporters of the various more serious candidates. The agreement had originally been that the delegation would persist in a unanimous vote for him as long as the balloting continued. However, after searching his conscience, he had decided that national considerations were more important than personal or even state party problems, and accordingly, he had asked to be excused from the agreement.

A Sherman delegate immediately requested an adjournment until the next morning, and this was seconded by other delegates who had been predominately for Sherman or Allison on the previous vote. Confusion and disorder in the galleries precluded an accurate voice vote, and the roll was called. Indiana opposed, as did a majority of the New York delegation; Ohio, Iowa, and a majority of the Illinois delegation supported the adjournment. The motion carried 531 to 287.

The Saturday morning session opened with the fourth roll call, during which William B. McKinley withdrew his name. This was a somewhat gratuitous gesture, since McKinley had not been nominated, and previously had received no more than 8 votes on any ballot. It did, however, permit him to put in a plug for Sherman, whom he was pledged to support. Although the field remained at ten, on this ballot the race began to take the shape of a two-man fight. Sherman's vote dropped to 235, and Harrison climbed to 216—far over his previous total of 94. The fifth ballot, the last of the session, saw both leaders drop a few votes and Alger gain a few, whereupon a short adjournment was declared by a roll call vote, which was suspended after the call of Missouri when it became evident that the affirmative vote predominated.

The convention met again at four o'clock in the afternoon. The first order of business was a motion to adjourn until Monday morning, which carried 492 to 320, and the delegates separated to begin an intensive week end of caucuses. This adjournment evidently was an attempt to stop Harrison, for it was supported heavily by Sherman delegations, with considerable support from Allison; Harrison delegations mostly were on the negative side.

On Monday morning, the delegates were assured by letters from the railroads that their round-trip tickets would be honored even though they had been written to expire after one week. Two telegrams were then read from James G. Blaine, whose followers had kept him before the convention with a few votes, a high of 48 on the fourth ballot. The telegrams clearly stated that he wanted his previous statements to be respected—he was not a candidate.

Stories abound as to what had happened over the week end, and of the deals attempted or made. The famous telegram from a close Blaine associate in Europe is often quoted: "Take Harrison and Phelps." Certainly the major leaders must have had frequent meetings at which agreements were made, and it is entirely possible, if not probable, that Harrison was picked at these caucuses. Even if the decision were made, it would not necessarily be implemented immediately, for faces had to be saved in some instances, and in any case even strong political bosses cannot always "direct" their delegates as in a military organization.

Comparison between the fifth and sixth ballots for Harrison reveals that he gained or lost a vote or two in many states, but that the movement of the balance of the New York delegation to his column pushed him forward enough to keep pace with Sherman, who also gained. On the seventh ballot the real move began, with Harrison heading Sherman for the first time, 279 to 230, much of the gain coming from delegates who had been casting votes for Blaine. The eighth ballot, though far from unanimous, resulted in a clear majority of

544 for Harrison. Sherman still held 118, Alger 100, and Gresham 59, while 9 votes stayed with Blaine and McKinley, both of whom, despite their protests, had received some votes on every ballot.

Ohio led the motion for unanimity for Harrison, "who had the good sense to be born in Ohio." Representatives of the other candidates followed, and the seal was put on by the chairman of the Maine delegation who, because "the circumstances under which we have assembled seem to render it proper," pledged the full support of Maine's first citizen, James G. Blaine. In the love feast that followed, even Wise and Mahone of Virginia shared the platform.

The Vice-Presidential Nomination

When order was restored—at least to a degree—William O. Bradley of Kentucky was presented as the southern candidate for the Vice Presidency. The long opening speech was followed by a series of seconds, as the southern delegates seized their opportunity to be heard. Before continuing with further nominations, the convention adjourned, since "we can afford to finish the further labor of this convention with deliberation." The chairman at first refused to allow the motion on the grounds that nothing could interrupt a roll call, but subsequently failed to hear the objection duly recorded in the proceedings when it became obvious that a substantial majority wanted to adjourn.

At the evening session, Congressman William Walter Phelps was presented by New Jersey, and received a large number of seconds from various quarters. New York then offered Levi P. Morton, former Minister to France, who received more seconds than any, including a highly amusing one by a crippled colored delegate who "beheld on this floor the magnanimous magnanimity of the Empire State." One delegate, in seconding a favorite son candidate who immediately withdrew, gave the convention some sound advice:

Those who tell you that [despite Harrison's popularity in the South] it is possible to carry a State in the South are mistaken. My advice to you is, do your level best to carry them all; but be careful to make your arrangements to do without any of them.[4]

Morton received 592 votes on the single roll call, with Phelps and Bradley splitting something over 200 votes between them. A dozen votes were cast for two others.

Even after all the business had been completed, this convention could not adjourn without another tempest in a teapot. As an addition to the platform the chairman of the Maine delegation presented a resolution that was compounded of about as many platitudes as could be packed in a few paragraphs. The following is typical:

The Republican party stands before the country for the protection of the ballot, for the protection of American industry, and for the protection of the purity of the home. The altars of Republicanism in this country stand by the firesides of the American people. The very foundation of this grand organization of ours is in the sobriety, the morality and the virtue of the common people. . . . It stands today, if it stands for anything, as the standard bearer of every principle that tends to elevate our common humanity, and eradicate the evils which threaten the body politic.[5]

Some five or six pages later in the proceedings, undoubtedly representing considerable time, the convention decided to suspend the rules and adopt the resolution by standing vote, 828 to 1. The convention then adjourned.

Analysis of Key Votes

The roll call rejecting the minority report on the Virginia credentials contest is an excellent illustration of the tendency for groups that subsequently form the nominating coalition in a highly fragmented convention to vote together in other matters in the early stages of the convention. The correlation between this vote and subsequent nominating ballots is shown in the tabulation on the next page.

[4] RNC, *Proceedings*, 1888, p. 229.
[5] *Ibid.*, p. 236.

Candidate	First Ballot		Seventh Ballot	
	Correlation Coefficient	Per Cent of Convention	Correlation Coefficient	Per Cent of Convention
Allison	.38	8.7%	.32	9.1%
Alger	−.11	10.1	.05	14.4
Depew	.47	11.9	—	—
Gresham	.62	12.9	.59	10.9
Harrison	.40	10.2	.46	33.5
Sherman	−.76	27.5	−.76	27.6
Others	.13	18.8	a	4.5

[a] Frequency too small to correlate.

Supporters of candidates whose first-ballot vote correlated positively with the vote on the credentials contest clearly held a solid majority in the convention, and insofar as the credentials vote reflected the relative compatability or incompatability of the contesting factions, it would appear probable that the eventual nominee would come from a candidate whose vote correlated positively. By the seventh ballot, Harrison had taken the lead from Sherman, and the rise in his correlation figure indicates that more of the added support came from delegations correlating positively with the issue vote. Harrison's seventh-ballot vote actually came partly from Depew's early support and partly from others. On the eighth ballot, upon which Harrison received a majority, his correlation dropped to +.24, reflecting in part a band-wagon swing. It is noteworthy that over three quarters of the vote that refused to join the band wagon stayed with Sherman and Alger, both of whose first-ballot votes correlated negatively with the issue vote.

Presidential Election, November 6, 1888

BENJAMIN HARRISON (R): popular vote, 5,447,129; electoral vote, 233
GROVER CLEVELAND (D): popular vote, 5,537,857; electoral vote, 168

1892

BENJAMIN HARRISON'S victory over Grover Cleveland in 1888 had been a close one. Harrison actually received about 100,000 votes fewer than his defeated rival, and the winning margin in the electoral college hinged upon a razor-thin margin in New York, giving Harrison the 36 electoral votes of that state. In office, Harrison did little to endear himself to the voting public, and much to antagonize important factional elements within his own party. The very fact that his administration carried out a substantial part of the platform pledges—particularly with respect to the tariff, which was raised substantially, and to the Treasury surplus, which was speedily reduced through somewhat reckless distribution of pensions and through other expenditures—only served to embarrass Harrison.

The tide began to turn in the mid-term elections of 1890, when the House of Representatives went sharply Democratic. Rising prices seemed to vindicate Cleveland's staunch stand against high protective tariff rates. Other signs of discontent were evidenced in the rise of third-party movements among the farmers and others who did not participate in the prosperity enjoyed by some elements in the nation.

TENTH REPUBLICAN CONVENTION

Despite Harrison's unpopularity with many of the party leaders and his lack of appeal to voters generally, he nevertheless was far out in front in the preconvention campaign. In part, as for Cleveland in 1888, this was due to the general reluctance of a party in power to repudiate the ad-ministration of its own choice, but, in very considerable part, it also was due to the lack of genuine availability of potential candidates. James G. Blaine, despite his age and general bad health, remained the darling of a substantial group, and had been again much in public view as Harrison's Secretary of State. Blaine himself confused the issue by a somewhat bizarre action just before the convention, when he suddenly resigned from the Cabinet for reasons never fully explained, although the break with Harrison was made clear.

If Blaine's action was connected with any hopes for nomination, it came too late, and in any case most of his support depended upon the remnants of an older generation in process of being supplanted by a new one. The new generation, on the other hand, among whom Governor William McKinley of Ohio stood out, was not yet ready, and its members were content with flexing muscles in preparation for 1896. Between these two groups were the many party faithful, who for one reason or another were loyal to the organization—a somewhat heterogeneous group, but one that was effectively, if not brilliantly, led.

Minneapolis, Minnesota,
June 7, 8, 9, 10, 1892

The call to this convention more nearly resembled those of more recent conventions than any of its predecessors. It was addressed to "The Republican Electors of the United States," and opened thus:

In accordance with usage and the instructions of the Republican National Convention of 1888, a National Convention of delegates representative of the Republican Party will be held.[1]

There followed a simple statement of place, time, purpose, and the rules for selecting delegates and handling contests.

Convention Organization

J. Sloat Fassett of New York, secretary of the national committee, was selected temporary chairman, and the standing committees were appointed during the first session. Fassett's stay in the chair was brief, for when the convention convened the next day, William McKinley was elected permanent chairman and immediately took the chair. This, according to contemporary accounts, was the first Harrison coup of the contest, for McKinley was thus kept off the floor, where he could mingle with the delegates. By this means, it was believed, he could most effectively be prevented from "Garfielding" the convention.

The rules committee made minor changes in procedural regulations, and deleted the phrase incorporated in the rules of the 1888 convention that prohibited officeholders from becoming members of the national committee. This deletion was not mentioned when the chairman of the committee informed the convention of the changes that had been made, but no one questioned the omission.

The credentials committee did not report until the evening of the third day, and the report was accompanied by a minority report supported by a substantial number of states. The majority report found for the delegates seated by the national committee, except for four delegates at large and two delegates from the ninth congressional district of Alabama. The minority report, signed by sixteen members of the committee, among them the representatives for New York and Pennsylvania, recommended the seating of delegates on the original roll as presented by the national committee. A long and confused debate

followed, much of which had little to do with the relative merits of the manner in which the contesting delegates were selected.

At one point in the debate, Senator Edward O. Wolcott of Colorado stated: "I hold in my hand, Mr. Chairman, a list of 130 odd office-holders, who are delegates to this Convention, nine-tenths of whom live in States where there is a hopeless Democratic majority."[2]

To this, Powell Clayton of Arkansas retorted that senators were officeholders too; if officeholders were to leave the convention, Senator Wolcott would have to accompany them. Clayton made a point of the fact that he, himself, was not an officeholder, to which Wolcott retorted: "If he does not hold office, he drags a beautiful lot of them always in his train." Powell replied:

If every delegate in this hall who does not represent a Republican constituency were to leave this hall, we would have a very great scattering indeed, and some of the largest and greatest of states of them all would have to go out with us from the South.[3]

Chauncey Depew thereupon broke up the controversy with a witticism which permitted the chairman to get the convention back on the track.

In the course of the balloting on the question of substituting the minority report, the question was raised whether the contested delegates could vote upon their own case. McKinley first ruled, then stated his own dilemma.

Every delegate who was seated in this Convention by the National Committee is entitled to enjoy the privileges of the Convention [applause] until by a majority vote they shall have been unseated. . . . A question more serious, probably, than the one I have just stated is whether a delegate could vote in his own case [cries of "that is the question exactly"], and upon that question the Chair is very much embarrassed.[4]

After referring to the House of Representa-

---

[1] RNC, *Proceedings*, 1892, p. 10.

[2] *Ibid.*, p. 42.
[3] *Ibid.*, p. 44.
[4] *Ibid.*, p. 53.

tive's rule providing that every member shall vote unless he has a direct personal or pecuniary interest in the question, McKinley stated that he would be very glad to hear from others on the problem.

Many of the arguments presented in the course of the succeeding debate were to be heard again in 1912 and in 1952. Among these were:

... it is a universal law the world over ... that no man shall be a judge in his own case.

We are working under the rules of the 51st Congress, which state that no man can vote in a case in his own interest.

If the position of Senator Spooner of Wisconsin is correct, then the proceedings of a Convention could be, at any time, brought to naught by any sufficient number of conspirators who chose to make a contest in each delegation.

... the National Committee has been recognized as the supreme tribunal for the making up of the roll ... and until all contests are settled, and we have a permanent organization, the roll of the National Committee ought to be the roll called, and the names thereon ought to be permitted to be answered to, by their owners.[5]

Fortunately for the harmony of the 1892 convention, though perhaps unfortunately for the later history of the party, the question was resolved by the voluntary abstention of the contested Alabama delegates at large. This could be done the more easily since the votes were few and not decisive to the result as they were in later conventions when the same question arose.

On a roll call correlating with the subsequent ballot for the presidential nominees, the minority report on the delegates at large was defeated 463 to 423½.[6] Generally, after a clear-cut vote on a minority report, the vote on the majority report is permitted to be taken by voice, but in this instance, a roll call was demanded by a member of the minority, Senator Matthew Quay of Pennsylvania, whose political acumen should have stood him in better stead. The results, probably reflecting band-wagon movement after the first test

vote, was an even greater victory for the Harrison forces. The majority rose to 476 and the minority dropped to 365½, as some of the minority joined the majority, and others withheld their vote. At this point the credentials problems were temporarily laid aside, and the platform was adopted in a highly irregular way. When the convention once again turned its attention to the credentials report, the minority, with Quay as its spokesman, discreetly withdrew from further voting on the Alabama case. The majority report was accepted insofar as the other contests were concerned.

The Platform

Following acceptance of the majority report on the Alabama delegates at large, the chairman of the committee on resolutions had requested unanimous permission to read the platform resolutions "without debate" stating that "there is a reason why this should be done." Permission was granted without further explanation and the resolutions were read, following which the committee chairman moved their adoption; when protest was made, he acknowledged that he had received unanimous consent on the grounds that the resolutions would be read but not voted on at that time. The convention chairman nevertheless put the question, and declared the platform adopted.

The platform contained little that was controversial or that was related to interfactional struggle for the nomination, unless it was the closing paragraph eulogizing Harrison's administration. The orthodox stand on the tariff was again endorsed; the gold and silver issue was straddled by a plank favoring the use of both metals and the maintenance of parity between them by "appropriate legislation."

The Presidential Nomination

The nominating speaker for Blaine had a series of difficult problems. First he had to assure the convention that it was better

[5] *Ibid.,* p. 53, 54.
[6] See *Analysis of Key Votes.*

to nominate "the best man" even if by doing so it seemed to repudiate the administration; second, he had to persuade the
delegates that Blaine's health and strength
were fully recovered; third, he had to dis-
count Blaine's age—though it was only 62,
the illnesses had made him seem older.
These things the speaker tried to do
by eulogizing Blaine's accomplishments
throughout his long period of service.

Harrison's first speaker, in contrast that
probably was deliberate, was very brief. He
did not propose "to eulogize [Harrison's]
history or his life before this Convention,"
but simply wished to nominate him. Two
seconding speeches for Blaine followed.
Then came the main speech for Harrison,
by his floor manager, Chauncey Depew of
the New York delegation.

Depew, who was one of the most popular
speakers and raconteurs of his day, deftly
pointed out that victory would be won or
lost upon the record of the four years immediately past, not upon a reputation
gained prior to Cleveland's victory in 1884.
As for the claims made for Blaine's recent
record as Secretary of State, he said that
when he was told that the credit for the
brilliant diplomacy of this administration
belonged exclusively to the Secretary of
State, and other achievements in the various departments exclusively to the heads
thereof, "I am tempted seriously to inquire,
who, during the last four years has been
President of the United States, anyhow?"[7]
Among the many additional seconding
speeches, one for Blaine contained a direct
appeal to McKinley to await his turn:

I recognize in the distinguished chairman
here, one who is all fairness, and I want to say
now to him, in view of what I have said here
about others: make no pledges, and when four
years more roll around, we will [turning to
McKinley] make you President of the United
States.[8]

The roll call vote was interrupted frequently by challenges, requiring the tedious calling of the names of individual dele-

gates. By the time the call reached Texas,
it was obvious that Harrison would have a
majority, and Chairman McKinley apparently decided that he should drop his careful pose of neutrality and put himself
personally on the Harrison band wagon.
Turning the chair over to another delegate,
he moved that the nomination be made
unanimous. Objection was made by a
delegate who previously had voted for
Blaine; after a brief discussion, McKinley,
having made his point, withdrew his motion, and the roll call continued. The
final count stood Harrison 535⅙, Blaine
182⅙, McKinley 182, with 5 votes divided
between two other candidates and the balance of votes not cast.

The Vice-Presidential Nomination

In a convention that renominated an
incumbent President, with an incumbent
Vice President available, it might have been
expected that the question of the vice-
presidential candidate would have been
settled beforehand. However, Levi P.
Morton had done little to ensure his own
renomination, apparently on the basis that
he wanted to be drafted rather than to
appear to be a seeker after the office.

The presidential selection having been
made early in the afternoon, there was
plenty of time to finish the convention
business without recess, but Chauncey Depew requested one. As leader of the vic-
torious Harrison forces, he was not easily
denied. In the interim period, the New
York delegation caucused, and in the absence of strong support for Morton, friends
of Whitelaw Reid, famed editor of the
New York *Tribune* and presently U. S.
Minister to France, were able to persuade the delegation to back Reid. The
rest of the convention was apparently
willing to accept New York's selection, but
a minor hitch developed when a Tennessee
delegate nominated Congressman Thomas
B. Reed of Maine. The nomination was
withdrawn when a member of the Maine
delegation requested that no one vote for

7 RNC, *Proceedings*, 1892, p. 100.
8 *Ibid.*, p. 106.

Reed without first having received his permission. Reed was present at the convention, but the proceedings do not record whether he refused permission, or was even asked. Whitelaw Reid was nominated by acclamation—the first nominee of a Republican convention to be named without a roll call vote.

Analysis of Key Votes

The votes on the Alabama credentials were clearly candidate-oriented, delegations voting with the majority on the issue also tending to support Harrison. The correlations between the first vote and the votes on the single nominating ballot were: Harrison +.66, Blaine −.44, and McKinley −.70. Harrison received some votes from every southern state and a majority of these delegations in every state but Virginia. Most of the balance of the southern vote went to Blaine. Of Harrison's nominating majority, 35 per cent came from these states—a fact probably noted carefully by one interested participant of the convention, Marcus A. Hanna of Ohio. The southern vote added to what his friend William McKinley received without even being formally nominated would have been nearly enough for victory.

SIXTEENTH DEMOCRATIC CONVENTION

Grover Cleveland probably considered himself through with public office after his defeat in 1888, but the later apparent vindication of his stand upon the tariff, to which his 1888 defeat had generally been attributed, made him the obvious one to carry the banner in a campaign in which the tariff would be the dominant issue. Otherwise, in the rather thin crop of Democratic presidential hopefuls, the one who seemed most likely to succeed was David B. Hill, who as lieutenant governor of New York had taken over the governor's chair when Cleveland left it for the White House in 1885. Now in the Senate, he was the presidential candidate of Cleveland's long-time political enemy, Tammany Hall.

As an anti-Cleveland move, the New York state central committee, which was controlled by Tammany, had called a February convention for selection of delegates—April or May was customary. This was done to exploit both Cleveland's delay in making up his mind to run and the resulting lack of organization on the part of Cleveland's friends. The so-called "Snapper" convention selected a pro-Hill delegation with no difficulty, but the obvious unfairness of the maneuver raised such a popular outcry that Cleveland probably actually benefited. For one thing, it awoke Cleveland's friends to the fact that they had a battle on their hands. These friends held a later convention at which an "anti-Snapper" delegation favoring Cleveland was selected, but it was not seated in the convention.

Chicago, Illinois,
June 21, 22, 23, 1892

The convention was held in a huge temporary structure hurriedly put together for the purpose. Throughout the meetings the building was buffeted by storms, and the proceedings were frequently interrupted because the noise of thunder and the rain pounding on the thin roof made it impossible for speakers to be heard. Leaks in the roof developed, and the dripping water added to the discomfort of the delegates. At one point a large electric light broke from its mooring and fell toward the New York delegation, but fortunately did not go all the way.

Man-made disturbances in the midst of all this added further to the confusion. Most of the difficulty centered about the bitter opposition of the New York delegation to Grover Cleveland. Six hundred Tammany "braves" accompanied the delegation and took their places in the galleries, where they did their best to out-shout the nearly 20,000 other spectators, most of whom were for Cleveland. Th strongest of chairmen would have had difficulty keeping order in such a convention; unfortunately, the permanent chairman proved incapable of doing so, and things frequently got almost completely out of control.

Convention Organization

The convention opened quietly enough. William C. Owens of Kentucky was selected as temporary chairman, temporary rules were adopted, and the committees were appointed without incident in the afternoon session of the first day. The next day, the committees on credentials and permanent organization reported, and their recommendations were accepted without debate and without opposition. The ease with which the credentials report was passed was due to the decision of the contesting "anti-Snapper" delegation from New York to withdraw from the contest, despite the bitterness between it and the "Snapper" delegation. This decision was made by the Cleveland strategy board, and was based upon confidence that Cleveland had the necessary two thirds of the delegates for a first-ballot nomination without the New York delegation. To precipitate a fight might result in loss of more than could be gained even if the fight were won; if there were to be a fight, they reasoned, it was better that it be started by the minority.

The Platform

The first open division within the convention occurred over a matter not directly connected with the question of the nomination, and which resulted in a highly unusual vote pattern. The platform committee reported a tariff plank that recognized the principle of protection of industry, but restricted its application to "the difference between the cost of labor here and labor abroad." A substitute was offered that declared:

. . . it to be a fundamental principle of the Democratic party that the Federal Government has no constitutional power to impose and collect tariff duties except for the purposes of revenue only, and demand that the collection of such taxes shall be limited to the necessities of the government when honestly and economically administered.[9]

The substitute, which reflected Cleveland's views, was offered by an Ohio delegate and supported by Henry Watterson of Kentucky; Ohio and Kentucky were states from which Cleveland hoped to receive support. The speakers for the original plank were Cleveland men. The debate was very bitter, the proceedings highly disorderly. The New York delegation, despite animosity to Cleveland, supported the substitute. From the voting pattern, it seems clear that almost all who voted against the substitute subsequently voted for Cleveland, despite their opposition to his stand on the issue. The substitute was adopted 564 to 342.[10]

The Presidential Nomination

The roll call of the states for nominations for president followed immediately. Arkansas yielded to New Jersey, whose governor presented Cleveland's name; an unusual feature of the presentation speech was the mention of his own candidate's principal opponent, permitting a demonstration for Hill ahead of the Cleveland demonstration.

The nominating and seconding speeches continued—despite frequent suspension because of the noisy storm outside and the disorderly galleries within, and despite attempts to adjourn and interruption of speakers by delegates. Governors David B. Hill of New York and Horace Boies of Iowa were presented.

The call was finally completed at about two o'clock in the morning, at which point Bourke Cockran of New York was granted the floor on the basis that New York had been passed during the regular roll call. When his attempt to persuade the delegates to recess until the next morning

---

[9] DNC, *Proceedings,* 1892, pp. 82-83.
[10] See *Analysis of Key Votes.*

failed, Cockran launched into a remarkable diatribe against Cleveland. The burden of his complaint was that Cleveland was not an "organization man" and that his supporters, and particularly his appointees, could not be depended upon to support the party at all times and under all conditions. His bitter attack against the independents, or Mugwumps, culminated in the following realistic passage:

The Democratic party cannot fuse with the party that despises it, which derides its principles. The Republican party differs with us on principles. They differ with us on theories. We march against them in serried hosts. We take from them everything they have in the way of political property. We leave not sticking in their hands one single office which we can take from them. In this we may violate the abstract ethics of civil service reform, but we strengthen the Democratic party. We have to-day in the State of New York a Capitol in which every executive officer is a Democrat, in which both Houses of the Legislature are Democratic; in which there is not a single person, I believe, employed who is not a Democrat. We have produced in that Capitol such a political atmosphere that no Republican can breathe it and live. And every hour our Democratic forces grow stronger.

But while these Republicans go down before us, we respect them and they respect us. We ask no quarter and we give none when the Lord delivers the Philistines into our hands. But with the Mugwump there can be no treaty of peace nor implied faith. He has no weapon but slander and abuse. He does not want to enter the Democratic party; he wants to own it. He wants you to lend him this party organization to accomplish his own purposes, and not for the good of the Democratic party.[11]

Following Cockran's long speech, another attempt to adjourn until the next morning was defeated. The ballot was then taken for the presidential nomination. The estimates of Cleveland's strategists proved remarkably accurate — Cleveland received 617⅓ votes, barely 10 more than needed for nomination. Hill received 114 and Boies 103, with the balance scattered among eight other candidates. Following a statement by Cockran that New York now participated in the vote to make the nomina-

tion unanimous, the convention adjourned shortly before five o'clock in the morning.

The Vice-Presidential Nomination

In the final session later in the day with the atmosphere much calmer both inside and out, the convention proceeded to the final business of nominating a vice-presidential candidate. Former Governor Isaac P. Gray of Indiana, Adlai E. Stevenson of Illinois, Allen B. Morse, chief justice of the Michigan supreme court, and Congressman John L. Mitchell of Wisconsin were presented. At the end of the roll call, Adlai Stevenson led the field. Assistant Postmaster General during Cleveland's first administration, Stevenson had proven himself an able dispenser of party patronage, and, in view of the reverse record of Cleveland, this may have had a great deal to do with his nomination. In any event, it did with at least one delegate who, in his seconding speech, after admitting he was one of those who had been doubtful about Cleveland, stated:

I support Illinois' candidate because I understand he is a Democrat who believes that to the victor belong the spoils. Because he believes further, that there are honest and competent men enough in this Democratic party to fill all the offices, and I make the assertion that if he is placed in this high position Mugwumps and Republicans will receive no quarter at his hands.[12]

Immediately after the roll call, with Stevenson leading Gray 402 to 343, the Iowa delegation changed its vote to Stevenson, thus precipitating a band-wagon movement resulting in his nomination. After the changes had been recorded, Stevenson held 652 votes, Gray retaining 185 and the balance being divided between two others.

With the difficulties presented by a disorderly gallery in mind, a delegate put a motion that the national committee provide accommodations for delegates, alternates, members of the press, and members

11 DNC, Proceedings, 1892, pp. 151-152.

12 Ibid., p. 166.

of the national committee—and *none others* for the next convention. A roll call on the resolution was demanded, but it was at this point that the electric lighting fixture fell. In the ensuing confusion, a delegate stated: "I think it must be apparent to all the delegates here, that even a roll-call of the States cannot now be taken with that deliberation necessary to the proper proceedings of this Convention."[13] His recommendation that the resolution be referred to the national committee "with affirmative recommendation of this Convention and with full power to act" was approved by a voice vote. The convention adjourned shortly thereafter.

Analysis of Key Votes

The unusual relationship between the vote on the tariff substitute and the ballot for the presidential nomination is clearly shown by the correlation figures. Hill's correlation is +.56, Boies' +.52, and that of the combined minor candidates +.30. The correlation with Cleveland's vote, on the other hand, is —.52, Cleveland actually receiving more votes from delegations that had voted below the convention average on the issue than he did from delegations supporting the majority side that he favored.

The truth of the matter probably is that there was no Democrat of stature who was even mildly protectionist around whom

[13] *Ibid.,* pp. 180-181.

the minority could rally. Faced with the choice available, most of the minority preferred to go with Cleveland, whom they knew best and whom they thought had the best chance to win the election, rather than to take a chance on a lesser-known figure. Furthermore, the preconvention activities of Cleveland's supporters had undoubtedly been more intensive and more national in scope than those of his rivals.

Despite the fact that the substitute tariff plank was more in line with Cleveland's known position, it is probable that he would have preferred to avoid a convention fight. He almost certainly had approved the original plank as a compromise, for the chairman of the platform committee, who defended the plank and others who spoke for it were known Cleveland men. All contemporary reports remark upon the highly confused conditions within and without the convention hall, and it is entirely possible that communications among Cleveland's followers had broken down. Contemporary accounts also indicate that this opportunity to embarrass Cleveland, and possibly to split his support, was seized upon by his enemies, particularly Tammany Hall, and this is substantiated by the fact that the New York delegation voted for the substitute despite the fact that it was contrary to the historical stand of industrial New York. The split did not develop, however, for reasons indicated above. The protectionists had no one to vote for.

Presidential Election, November 8, 1892

GROVER CLEVELAND (D) : popular vote, 5,555,426; electoral vote 277
BENJAMIN HARRISON (R) : popular vote, 5,182,690; electoral vote, 145

1896

PRESIDENT CLEVELAND called the years of his second administration, particularly the latter part of it, the "luckless years," and it was an apt phrase. Following the serious depression of 1893, a wave of strikes swept the nation, culminating during the summer of 1894 in the Chicago labor war arising out of a strike of the workers of the Pullman Palace Car Company which spread to the railroads. When violence broke out in late June, Cleveland authorized intervention by federal troops, basing his act upon a statute passed in 1871 to curb the Ku Klux Klan, which empowered the President to use federal forces to suppress domestic violence whenever it obstructed or hindered the execution of the law; since the strike affected the passage of the United States mails, it affected the federal government. Cleveland was bitterly attacked by some and fervently supported by others for this act. The "luckless years" also presented Cleveland with the problems of large deficits, mounting tensions on the gold and silver question, and a series of severe international crises. To compound his difficulties, he lost the support of large elements of his own party, and, in the mid-term election of 1894, the Republicans gained a majority in both houses of Congress.

As a result of these difficulties, and particularly because of the bitter division between the Gold men and the Silverites, by 1896 the country was in a state of extreme tension. Substantial groups were ready for open revolt, and the rising Populist movement, particularly in the West and the South, seemed to show prospects of supplanting one or the other of the two major parties. On the other hand, conservatives were desperately searching for a sedative that would bring calm to the situation.

ELEVENTH REPUBLICAN CONVENTION

The story of the 1896 Republican convention—and the nomination of William McKinley—must begin with a description of the activities of Mark Hanna, for the convention was dominated, and its decisions largely predetermined, by the careful plans and preconvention work of this remarkable businessman-turned-politician. There was little new in his methods; his contribution to politics was a synthesization of time-tested techniques into a single system, which he employed with the methodical care and attention to detail of a successful businessman. In a very real sense, he raised the manipulative and technical aspects of politics and campaigning to the level of a profession. He incorporated the national vision of a Thurlow Weed with the attention to political detail practiced by such local bosses as Quay and Platt, and superimposed upon this composite an efficient fund-raising and budget-control procedure never before equaled in any national campaign. With all of this, he still found time to consider and to guide major decisions in party policy.

In the cold light of retrospect, it is probable that McKinley was the logical candidate for the Republican party in 1896. Certainly none of his opponents could present as rounded a claim as he. He had an honorable record in the House of Representatives; he had proven his vote-getting ability by his election and re-election as governor of a large critical state in the face of a Democratic tide; he was well liked and well known; and even his political opponents were not in general bitter in their opposition. His leading opponent, Speaker of the House Thomas B. Reed of Maine, although very able, lacked color, came from a small safe state, and received most of his support from one section of the country. The other candidates were little more than favorite sons, and in the cases of Matthew Quay and Levi P. Morton, even that title should probably be placed in quotation marks. Certainly none of the favorite sons were of presidential stature, and even the political bosses might have given pause before acquiescing in their nomination.

Thus, it appears highly probable that McKinley would have been nominated without Hanna's very considerable help, and the fact that such professionals as Quay and Thomas C. Platt allowed Hanna to get ahead of them in collecting southern delegates tends to substantiate this thesis. Southern delegates had received the careful attention of the professional politicians for a generation or more, and it is extremely doubtful that Hanna's early activities went unnoticed. It is more probable that Quay, Platt, and others of their kind simply had no suitable candidate around whom to collect support, and that they had no desire to make a real battle on grounds where their defeat was certain. Accordingly, they resigned themselves to a token fight, after trying unsuccessfully to trade their support to McKinley in return for recognition in the administration.

However, the probability that McKinley might have been nominated without Hanna's efforts does not detract from the reality of Hanna's contribution. The management of every campaign from that day to this has been conducted on a more professional plane as a result of his work.

St. Louis, Missouri,
June 16, 17, 18, 1896

The call to the convention generally followed that of 1892, and consisted mainly of instructions as to the number and method of selection of delegates and alternates by the respective states. Territories were "advised" to elect four delegates each, and admission of these delegates was "recommended" to the convention.

Convention Organization

The recommendation of the national committee for temporary chairman was accepted unanimously, and Charles W. Fairbanks, Indiana lawyer, took the chair. His opening speech dwelt lingeringly upon the difficulties and failures of the incumbent Democratic administration, compared to the virtues and accomplishments of its Republican predecessor. A substantial part of his speech dealt with the highly charged silver question. He objected strenuously to the unlimited coinage of silver, or to the establishment of coinage on a 16-to-1 ratio unless this were done on an international basis. Unilateral action by the United States, when the current international ratio was about 30 to 1, he said, would quickly destroy the international and internal financial relations of the country. Thus he set a "gold standard" tone for the convention, although leaving a slight crack in the door for the silver supporters.

The rules of the previous convention were adopted as the temporary rules, and the standing committees appointed without incident. In the opening session of the second day, the only committee ready to report was that on permanent organization. After considerable protest, based upon the argument that no formal business should be transacted until the credentials had been approved, firm action on the part of the chairman enabled the report of the permanent organization to be heard and approved. Senator John M. Thurston of Nebraska was named permanent chairman.

Immediately after the new chairman took his place, a letter was received from the credentials committee announcing that it had not completed its work, and the convention adjourned until the afternoon, when the credentials report was heard.

Although a large number of contests had been presented to the committee, only the contests in Delaware and Texas were mentioned in the majority report, the balance being covered in a blanket recommendation:

As to the other matters of contests presented to your Committee . . . we recommend that the role of delegates and alternates to the Convention from the several States and Territories and the District of Columbia, as prepared by the National Committee for the Temporary Organization, be approved and adopted as the permanent roll of delegates and alternates to this Convention.[1]

A minority report charged that none of the 160 cases presented to the national committee had been granted hearings in the committee, and that the temporary roll presented to the convention by the committee had clearly been understood to be a prima facie roll. It had been the understanding of the minority in the national committee that all contestants would have an opportunity to be heard by the credentials committee of the convention, and it was charged that, with the exception of the Texas and Delaware contests, none of the contestants were heard. The minority report recommended reversal of the decisions on the Texas and Delaware contests, and recommittal of the rest of the majority report to the credentials committee for further action.

The previous question was moved and ordered by a roll call vote, 551½ to 359½.[2] During the roll call the convention chairman ruled against a protest that delegates involved in the contest should not vote. With the safe margin indicated by the first test vote, the majority of the committee did not find it necessary to spend much time in justifying their actions, and did not do so. The

minority committee members protested vigorously in a series of speeches, limited by the previous question as to total time, and then contented themselves with a division of the question without demanding a roll call on either the Delaware or Texas question or upon the balance of the report as divided.

The report of the committee on rules confirmed the recommendation of the call by allowing the territories to vote, but contained no other important changes from the rules of 1892.

The Platform

The platform was presented on the morning of the third day. The only controversial plank was the one relating to the gold and silver question. The majority report reiterated the stand taken by Fairbanks in his introductory speech:

We are therefore opposed to the free coinage of silver, except by international agreement with the leading commercial nations of the earth—which agreement we pledge ourselves to promote, and until such agreement can be obtained the existing gold standard must be maintained.[3]

A minority plank recommending free and unlimited coinage of silver and gold at a ratio of 16 to 1 was presented by Senator Henry M. Teller of Colorado, and, in deference to his long and faithful service to the party, he was allowed to speak in support of his substitute. The long and somewhat pathetic speech was in effect his farewell to the party, for it closed with the statement that he would perhaps never again address a Republican convention. Immediately following the speech, the Gold men quickly cut off any further debate with a motion to table the substitute, which carried by a margin of eight to one. The Silverites demanded a second roll call on the majority plank with approximately the same result, following which a few delegations and scattered individual delegates left the convention,

[1] RNC, *Proceedings,* 1896, p. 48.
[2] See *Analysis of Key Votes.*

[3] RNC, *Proceedings,* 1896, p. 83.

whereupon the chairman remarked, "Gentlemen of the Convention: there seems [sic] to be enough delegates left to transact the business of the Convention." The substitute was then tabled 818½ to 105½.

Despite the proportions of this defeat, the Silverites were not yet willing to give up passively, and a second roll call vote was held on the adoption of the financial plank. The pattern remained the same: 812½ to 110½.

After the balance of the platform had been adopted by voice vote, the chairman permitted the delegates who were bolting the convention to give explanations for their action. The speakers frequently were interrupted by hisses and boos, but the chairman insisted that they be heard, and they were. Some of the protesting delegates announced that they would remain, despite the fact that they could not support the financial plank. Those who left, left not only the convention hall but also the party. Most of them were found in Bryan's column on election day.

The Presidential Nomination

The nominating speeches were long and somewhat tedious. Joseph B. Foraker, former governor of Ohio, a rival of McKinley and a political foe of Hanna, nominated McKinley in a speech deriding the Democratic party and proposing that the need of the country was a businessman leader. Upon mention of McKinley's name in the middle of his speech, Foraker was interrupted by a twenty-five-minute ovation.

Among others named was Senator William B. Allison of Iowa, whose main claim to the nomination seemed to be that James G. Blaine, who had died since the last convention, had once said of him:

He is true, kind, reasonable, fair, honest and good. He is methodical, industrious and intelligent, and would be a splendid man to sail along with smoothly and successfully.[4]

Thomas B. Reed was presented by Senator Henry Cabot Lodge of Massachusetts.

[4] Ibid., p. 106.

Chauncey Depew, in the name of New York, presented Levi P. Morton, Vice President under Harrison and, subsequent to his failure of renomination with Harrison in 1892, governor of New York. Pennsylvania's favorite son was Senator Matthew Quay.

None came close to McKinley on the ballot. He received 661½, with Reed, Quay, Morton, and Allison following with less than 250 votes among them. Colorado and Idaho had withdrawn completely from the convention, and several other states from the silver area cast only a partial vote.

Chauncey Depew and Henry Cabot Lodge gracefully acknowledged defeat in the love feast following the roll call. Quay was called for, but had left the convention. Not without justice, the convention then called for Mark Hanna, who acknowledged the call with a short and modest statement.

The Vice-Presidential Nomination

Only two candidates received serious consideration in the voting for the second place on the ticket. The first of these was Garret A. Hobart of New Jersey; the other, with strong southern and border-state backing, was Henry Clay Evans, who recently had been defeated for governor of Tennessee in a disputed election. Ohio split her vote on the roll call, but the solid votes of New York and Pennsylvania removed any doubt as to the results. Hobart was nominated with 533½ votes. Evans received 280½, the balance of about 90 votes being scattered among seven others.

Analysis of Key Votes

How well Hanna had done his work is shown by the figures on the vote on the previous question on the credentials report, and the relationship between this vote and the presidential ballot. Delegations voting above the convention average on the majority side of the issue were almost solid—90 per cent voting together. These same delegations were even more solid for McKinley, giving him 95 per cent of their vote, probably a reflection of band-wagon effects after the clear results on the test vote. The correlation between the two votes is +.89. Included with the majority on both the issue vote and the McKinley vote was a substantial majority of every southern delegation.

SEVENTEENTH DEMOCRATIC CONVENTION

Although the silver question was to be the main issue in 1896, divisions on other questions greatly complicated the factional conflict during the preconvention period, particularly from the point of view of the factions favoring gold. For example, some among those supporting Cleveland on the gold issue opposed him on the tariff question. As always during this period, divisions within the New York Democrats were a handicap to national leaders whose base was in that state. Cleveland helped obscure the succession question by avoiding questions about the possibilities of his trying for a third term. Perhaps most important of all, no established leader close to the administration was of sufficient stature to develop a strong pro-administration candidacy.

The Silverites were in somewhat better state, although not by much. Their most noteworthy leader, Illinois Governor John P. Altgeld, was ineligible by reason of foreign birth. Richard P. Bland of Missouri had been identified almost exclusively with the silver question during his long stay in Congress, but he was in his sixties— somewhat old to become the standard-bearer of a coalition bent on a volatile new crusade. Former Governor Horace Boies of Iowa also had the possible handicap of being in his sixties. Senator Henry Teller, who had bolted the Republican party during the convention in June, received surprising preconvention support in

view of his short tenure as a Democrat, though this did not materialize in votes in the convention. Behind all these was a young man, yet in his thirties, who knew very well where he wanted to go and who had carried on a quiet personal campaign to get there. All William Jennings Bryan needed was a little luck.

Chicago, Illinois, July 7, 8, 9, 10, 11, 1896

Prior to preparation of the convention call, the national committee had rejected the proposal referred to it by the 1892 convention recommending that the 1896 convention be held in a smaller hall where only the delegates, alternates, members of the national committee, and the press could be accommodated. Accordingly, the convention was held in the Chicago Coliseum, with the usual accommodations for spectators. The spectators soon found entertainment, for immediately after the opening prayer, the national committee's nomination of Senator David B. Hill of New York as temporary chairman was opposed by a minority report offering Senator John W. Daniel of Virginia for the post. This precipitated the critical struggle for control of the convention.

Convention Organization

Hill was the candidate of the Gold Democrats—Daniel of those who supported silver as a monetary base. Actually, the Silverites predominated in the convention; that supporters of the gold standard dominated the national committee was due primarily to the fact that the committee had been elected four years before, when the silver movement was not nearly so strong. The debate was bitter, though neither side doubted the outcome. The Gold minority based its case upon precedent—no recommendation of a Democratic national committee had ever been rejected before—and upon the need for party harmony. Threats were combined with pleading. One Gold Democrat cried:

> Gentlemen, you are going to do it, will you? You will do it, will you? Listen a minute. I want to say one word to you about the Eastern Democrats. We will stand everything from a Democrat—very little from a Republican—but we are not worms. Treat us badly, as you mean to do, . . . and I will tell you just what we will do. There is no threat about it. We will do this. We will fight you for your indignities and insults. In Southern phrase, we will fight you here and elsewhere, and we will fight you until you are sorry for your indiscretion of this day.[5]

The Silverite majority, knowing its strength, demanded the right to control the convention machinery. By a vote of 556 to 349, it exercised that right, and Senator Daniel was elected.[6] From then on, the question was not whether a Gold or a Silver man would be nominated, but which of the Silver men it would be.

The customary committees were appointed, and the committee on credentials was the first to report. The most important contest involved the seating of the Nebraska delegation in which the slate headed by William Jennings Bryan was recommended by the committee, reversing the ruling of the national committee. This recommendation was approved by the convention without a roll call vote. On the contest in two congressional districts in Michigan a roll call vote was held. Here again the majority report of the credentials committee reversed the ruling of the national committee. A minority report, recommending that the delegates seated on the temporary roll be given permanent seats, was defeated by 558 to 368, with four absent or not voting. This vote correlated closely with the vote on the temporary chairmanship, and again indicated the strength of the Silver group.

Stephen M. White, senator from California, was elected permanent chairman—and was presented with a symbolic silver gavel. He had many occasions to use it.

[5] DNC, *Proceedings*, 1896, p. 77.
[6] See *Analysis of Key Votes*.

The Platform

The report of the platform committee touched off acrimonious debate as several minority planks were proposed. The main debate centered upon the monetary plank. It was begun by Senator Ben Tillman of South Carolina, who supported free silver; featured Senator David B. Hill of New York and Senator William F. Vilas of Wisconsin, who spoke for the Gold men; and culminated in the famous "Cross of Gold" speech by William Jennings Bryan, orator and ex-congressman from Nebraska. The opportunity to make the closing speech in the debate was the bit of luck Bryan needed, and for which he had prepared himself carefully if it came. That the opportunity came at all may truly have been luck, for one of the principal managers of the Silver faction stated in his reminiscences that Bryan was given the job simply because he was the only prominent Silver man who had not already been given an opportunity to speak, though other versions indicate that friendly forces may have pushed for Bryan at a critical moment.

The essential part of the monetary plank proposed by the platform committee read:

> We demand the free and unlimited coinage of both silver and gold at the present legal ratio of 16 to 1 without waiting for the aid or consent of any other nation.
> We demand that the standard silver dollar shall be a full legal tender, equally with gold, for all debts, public and private, and we favor such legislation as will prevent for the future the demonetization of any kind of legal-tender money by private contract.[7]

The Gold minority proposed:

> Until international co-operation among the leading nations in the coinage of silver can be secured we favor the rigid maintenance of the existing gold standard as essential to the preservation of our national credit, the redemption of our public pledges and the keeping inviolate of our country's honor.
> We insist that all our paper and silver currency shall be kept absolutely at a parity with gold. The Democratic party is the party of

[7] DNC, *Proceedings*, 1896, p. 192.

hard money, and is opposed to legal-tender paper money as a part of our permanent financial system, and we therefore favor the gradual retirement and cancellation of all United States notes and Treasury notes under such legislative provisions as will prevent undue contraction.[8]

The roll call vote on this clear-cut issue revealed the Silverites to have more than a two thirds majority in the convention. The Gold plank was rejected 626 to 303.

A second roll call was held upon a resolution proposed by Grover Cleveland's opponent of 1892, Senator Hill. This resolution stated:

> We commend the honesty, economy, courage and fidelity of the present Democratic National Administration.[9]

New York, leader of the fight against Cleveland's renomination in 1892, voted solidly in support of this commendation, but the resolution was defeated 564 to 357, with 9 votes not cast, the lines drawn being similar to preceding votes. This is one of the very few times in political history when a major political party has deliberately and openly repudiated its own administration.

The Gold delegates made additional attempts to soften the Silver plank, but all attempts were rejected by voice vote, following which the platform, as originally proposed, was passed 628 to 301.

The Presidential Nomination

The Gold delegations refused to enter a candidate, but so many favorite sons and minor candidates were presented by the Silverites and the middle-of-the-road groups that a Wisconsin delegate climbed upon his chair and said: "We will, with your permission, search for another straggler and get another candidate for this Convention."[10]

The speaker who nominated Bryan evidenced excellent judgment by restraining himself to a short, relatively matter-of-fact speech that made no attempt to compete with Bryan's oration of the previous day.

Only five candidates proved to have more than favorite son backing—Bryan; Senator Richard P. (Silver Dick) Bland of Missouri, the long-time champion of free silver; Robert E. Pattison, twice governor of Pennsylvania and possessor of an enviable record for administration and reform; Senator Joseph Blackburn of Kentucky, ex-Confederate general; and Horace Boies, former governor of Iowa. The first-ballot vote was spread thinly over a field of fourteen candidates, ranging from 235 for Bland, 137 for Bryan, 100 for Pattison, down to 1 for Hill. There were 178 votes not cast—representing the concerted abstention of the more bitter Gold men, headed by the entire New York and New Jersey delegations.

Despite the tremendous enthusiasm raised by Bryan's "Cross of Gold" speech, commitments made to other candidates— long before Bryan had been given serious consideration—had to be honored. Five ballots were therefore required to do what most observers believed would inevitably be done from the moment Bryan finished the peroration of his speech. On the second ballot Bryan increased his vote to 197, but Bland kept pace with 281, Blackburn remaining steady at 100. The two leaders continued to gain on the third ballot, Bland remaining out in front. On the fourth ballot, however, Bland lost 50 votes and Bryan took the lead with 280; on the fifth, Bryan won the nomination with 652 of the 930 votes authorized in the convention. He received practically all of the Silverite votes, but 162 stubborn delegates declined to vote, as they had throughout the balloting. Almost all of Pattison's strength, which came from eastern states where free silver held little appeal, stayed with him to the end, and Bryan received only 22 votes from the Northeast.

The Vice-Presidential Nomination

The convention adjourned immediately following the nomination, and reconvened at eight that evening. Apparently the intervening time had not been enough. A

[8] *Ibid.*, p. 237.
[9] *Ibid.*, p. 242.
[10] *Ibid.*, p. 296.

motion was entered to adjourn again until the following morning, since the convention had been so completely engrossed with the questions of platform and the selection of the head of the ticket that more time was needed to deliberate before proceeding with nomination of the vice-presidential candidate. On the roll call by which the motion was passed, the Gold delegates continued to abstain.

Bryan's intention to keep hands off the choice of his running mate doubtless was known to the convention when the roll was called for the nominating speeches. Accordingly, a wide field was offered, many states adding favorite sons to the more serious candidates. Sixteen were either nominated or received votes without benefit of a nominating speech.

On the roll call for the first ballot, the chairman of the Nebraska delegation announced:

Nebraska, grateful for the very high honor that has been conferred upon it, is prepared to accept the result of the combined wisdom of this Convention, and is not willing to take any part in this contest, and therefore requests to be excused from voting.[11]

The four leaders on the ballot were Joseph C. Sibley, ex-congressman from Pennsylvania; John R. McLean, Ohio editor and publisher; Arthur Sewall of Maine; and George F. Williams, ex-congressman from Massachusetts. Of the votes accredited in the convention, 258 were absent or not voting. Sibley led his closest competitor by a comfortable margin, 163 to 111. Bland received 62 votes, putting him in fifth place.

[11] *Ibid.*, p. 351.

The second ballot saw Bland move far in front, with 294 votes, as Sibley dropped behind McLean with 113 to the latter's 158. Sewall and Williams also dropped sharply. Between the second and third roll calls, a telegram from Sibley withdrew his name, but 50 votes nevertheless stayed with him. Bland led again, but with only 250 votes, followed closely by McLean with 210. Sewall regained most of his first-ballot strength.

After announcement of the third-ballot totals, Bland's name was withdrawn, and on the forth much of his strength went to Sewall, whose 261 votes pushed McLean's 296. All others were far below 100 votes. A withdrawal telegram from McLean then settled the issue, and Sewall was nominated on the fifth and final ballot, 251 votes abstaining. In actual fact, neither Sewall nor Bryan received a two thirds majority of the total convention, since the bolters numbered more than one third; each was nominated by two thirds of the votes present and voting.

Analysis of Key Votes

Delegates representing 178 votes abstained from voting on the first roll call for presidential nominations, and not a single one came from a delegation that had voted above average with the majority on the roll call for temporary chairman. The bulk of these bolters came from the northeastern states, but some represented split-offs from middle-western delegations. The correlation between this vote and Bryan's fifth ballot majority was a very high +.95.

Presidential Election, November 3, 1896

WILLIAM McKINLEY (R) : popular vote, 7,035,638; electoral vote, 271
WILLIAM JENNINGS BRYAN (D): popular vote, 6,467,946; electoral vote 176

1900

THE YEARS SINCE 1896 had been good ones for the Republican party. The election had not only placed McKinley in the White House but had also strongly reaffirmed the 1894 Republican control of both Houses of Congress. The "splendid little war" had been fought and won with relatively few American casualties, and the American flag now flew in far distant places. The general level of prosperity was high, and open factional problems within the party were at a relatively low ebb. As generally is the case, what was good for the party in power was bad for the party out of power, at least so far as its prospects for victory were concerned. The general prosperity, plus the large increase in the national supply of gold by the discoveries in Alaska, took much of the force out of the silver issue of 1896. There probably are few arguments more potent for the party in power than the "full dinner pail" when a substantial proportion of the voting public is satisfied that the pail really is full. The Republicans were ready to use this argument to the utmost, along with its accompanying slogan: "Let well enough alone."

TWELFTH REPUBLICAN CONVENTION

There was, of course, never any question as to the presidential nominee. Neither was there much concern over the party platform. Victory in war and prosperity were enough; underlying differences with the administration stand on any issues were not apt to be brought into the open in the convention under the circumstances. However, Vice President Hobart had died during his term, and the Vice Presidency was open. McKinley undoubtedly could have named whomever he chose, but for reasons best known to himself he not only declined to state a preference, but specifically instructed Hanna not to attempt to influence the choice.

Selection of candidates for the Vice Presidency—an office to which few men have openly aspired—has been peculiarly susceptible to negotiation by professional political leaders. Rarely has a candidate been able to generate enthusiasm among the rank and file; and even more rarely has genuine fervor attended the balloting for the nomination. There was no question of the enthusiasm of the rank and file for the vice-presidential nominee of this convention; his nomination nevertheless was brought about by agreement among the party professionals, who merely found their task eased by the spontaneous enthusiasm for Theodore Roosevelt.

The facts seem clear that Thomas C. Platt, the "Easy Boss" of New York State, considered Roosevelt as governor too independent of the organization, yet too popular to defeat for renomination. Platt's problem was one with which other bosses were sympathetic, and some of them joined him in a move to elevate Roosevelt to an office where he could do the least damage. Some of the cooperation Platt received was undoubtedly out of spite against Hanna, whose opposition to Roosevelt for the Vice Presidency was well known. In any event, the big-city bosses in this instance wanted the same thing that a large number of the delegates wanted, and Hanna could probably have done nothing about it even if his hands had not been tied by McKinley.

158

Philadelphia, Pennsylvania,
June 19, 20, 21, 1900

The convention call followed the form of 1896, with the exception that territories and the District of Columbia were specifically allowed two delegates each, and in an appended clause a recommendation was made that the territories of Arizona, Indian Territory, New Mexico, and Oklahoma each elect six delegates and six alternates, and Alaska four of each, and that these be admitted to the convention.

As chairman of the national committee, Mark Hanna opened the convention and proposed Senator Edward O. Wolcott of Colorado as the temporary chairman. Selection of a representative from the state that had led the silver bolt in the last convention was undoubtedly intended as a symbol of party unity, and Wolcott stressed this unity in his opening speech. In his outline of the accomplishments of the administration, he also, as "a Western man," lauded the fiscal policy of the administration which not only had "made stable and permanent our financial credit, at home and abroad," but was "utilizing more silver as money than ever before in our history." "The stern logic of events" had convinced the Silverites, and removed finally "any sort of difference between Republicans of the East and of the West, growing out of currency problems."

Convention Organization

After routine appointment of the standing committees, the convention adjourned until the next day. The second session opened with a tribute to the surviving members of the first Republican convention, thirteen of whom were presented to the convention. The recommendations of the credentials committee, which included settlement of contests in Alabama, Delaware, Louisiana, and Texas, were presented, and the previous question immediately moved by the chairman. This evidently was a precaution taken to preclude

unrestricted debate if any of the ousted delegations should decide to bring the contest before the convention. It proved unnecessary, for when the previous question was ordered and the chairman reserved his time, no one requested the floor on behalf of the contestees and the report was accepted without debate.

The committee on permanent organization presented Senator Henry Cabot Lodge of Massachusetts as permanent chairman. Lodge laid the groundwork for the two main themes upon which the campaign would be waged. On the question of the newly won dependencies, he frankly admitted that the nation's concerns with them were not entirely unselfish, and that profit from them was to be expected; on the other hand, he anticipated that under American control these undeveloped areas would be able to raise their standards of living and ultimately be able to govern themselves. Republican policy, he said, did not advocate the principle that the Constitution necessarily followed the flag; control of the new areas must be maintained for their protection, but this did not mean that they would ever become an integral part of the United States. As the second theme, he stressed the current level of prosperity, and warned that it might be destroyed if the Democrats were returned to power.

The chairman of the committee on rules and order of business reported that the rules proposed were the same as those of the previous convention, and that a suggestion to change the apportionment, bringing delegation strength more nearly in line with Republican voting strength, had been laid aside by the committee. The committee considered it the better and safer course "to leave any new or additional rules to be the subject of your action here today." The committee then had adjourned, but was subject to the call of the chairman, so that it could act upon any change the convention desired.

The reason for this unusual procedure became clear when Matthew S. Quay of

Pennsylvania proposed a complete new rule to govern apportionment. The rule, which was accompanied by illustrative tables to show its effect, allotted four delegates at large to each state and one additional delegate for each 10,000 votes or majority fraction thereof cast for Republican electors at the last preceding election. As the clerk was reading the accompanying statement, with its tables of comparative delegation strength under the two systems, Quay interrupted to say that the proposed rule was too radical to be dealt with quickly, and he proposed that it be laid over until the next day to permit delegates to study it before taking action.

Objection was taken to the delay, and immediate debate was urged. A Negro delegate proposed a substitute for Quay's substitute stating:

In any State wherein the right to vote is denied to any of the male inhabitants thereof on account of race, color, or previous condition of servitude, or wherein said right is in any way abridged for the same reason, representation in Congress should be reduced in the proportion which the whole number of male inhabitants so deprived of the right to vote shall bear to the whole number of male inhabitants twenty-one years of age in such State.[1]

This was ruled not germane to the report of the rules and order of business. After some parliamentary quibbling, the convention accepted all parts of the rules report except those affected by Quay's substitute, and laid the affected parts over until the next morning.

Immediately after the morning session opened, Quay withdrew his substitute and the original report was accepted in total. It seems generally to have been accepted at the time that Quay's purpose in advancing this substitute rule of apportionment and his tactic in holding over the discussion until the next day was to bring the southern delegations, which would lose heavily under Quay's scheme, into line with the plan to nominate Roosevelt for Vice President. These groups were much more under the influence of Mark Hanna than most

[1] RNC, *Proceedings,* 1900, p. 100.

other sections, but the threat to their future strength from as strong a source as Quay, followed by assurances—which he purportedly gave during the recess—that the threat would be withdrawn if they would agree to support Roosevelt, was sufficient to bring them around.

The Platform

The platform was frankly expansionist on international affairs, and pro-business on national affairs. It noted with pride the vindication of the party stand on gold, and renewed allegiance to the principle of the gold standard. In view of the general high level of prosperity, the document throughout generally favored maintenance or moderate extension of current policies rather than the sponsoring of new ones, though it did advocate building of an Isthmian Canal by the Government, and coupled this proposal with the need to find markets for farm surplus, especially in the Orient. A Department of Commerce and Industries headed by a secretary of Cabinet rank was proposed. McKinley's aggressive handling of the Samoan crisis was approved, annexation of the Hawaiian Islands and extension of sovereignty in the Philippines and other areas were advocated.

The Presidential Nomination

The business of the convention could easily have been completed on the previous day, for when the session adjourned after the debate on Quay's proposal, the time was only three in the afternoon. Apparently the bosses had found that the night was needed to complete the negotiations for Roosevelt's nomination. In any case, a full day was thus provided to make two unanimous nominations—and the orators made the most of it. President McKinley was presented by Senator Foraker of his home state, Ohio. The first seconding speech was by the soon-to-be running mate, Theodore Roosevelt, who had become the certain choice during the night's deliberations. When the orators had finished, the roll call was a mere formality, McKinley receiving 926 votes out of 926.

The Vice-Presidential Nomination

As soon as the cheering was over, the roll was called for the vice-presidential nomination. The honor of presenting Roosevelt's name was given to Iowa, probably in recognition of the withdrawal of its favorite son, Jonathan P. Dolliver, who would probably have been a worthy contender in an open fight. But the real speech in the series was a seconding speech by Chauncey M. Depew, now a senator from New York. Depew humorously outlined Roosevelt's career, from "the child of Fifth Avenue," "the child of the clubs," the "child of the exclusiveness of Harvard," to cowboy, Assistant Secretary of the Navy, and soldier. He brought down the house with a paragraph about Roosevelt in Cuba:

At Santiago, a modest voice was heard, exceedingly polite, addressing a militia regiment laying upon the ground, while the Spanish bullets were flying over them. This voice said: "Get to one side, gentlemen . . . that my men can get out." And when this polite man got his men out in the open where they could face the bayonet and face the bullet, there was a transformation, and the transformation was that the dude had become a cowboy, the cowboy had become a soldier, the soldier had become a hero, and rushing up the hill, pistol in hand, the polite man shouted to the militiamen lying down: "Give them hell, boys! Give them hell!"[2]

Roosevelt did not receive a unanimous ballot. The New York delegation reported 71 for Roosevelt, and 1 vote not cast. Roosevelt was a delegate at large from New York.

EIGHTEENTH DEMOCRATIC CONVENTION

For the Democrats, 1900 did not look like a good year. From most standpoints, the McKinley administration was highly successful, and there was no issue with which to attack it that had very much public appeal. In such a year, men of substantial

[2] *Ibid.*, p. 135.

stature seldom care to risk much in attempts to win a hollow convention victory, and in 1900 none tried—at least very hard. In any case, it is doubtful that anyone could have beaten Bryan if he had wanted to. Bryan had run a highly acceptable race in 1896. Although for 1900 his dominant issue was somewhat less interesting to the public than it had been in the previous election year, he nevertheless presented the most clearly defined alternative to McKinley that the party had.

Bryan now had a little more strength in the Northeast—although still weak there—than in 1896, but most of the conservative Democrats of that area were probably not too unhappy with McKinley. Certainly none of them could have presented a sufficiently clear-cut alternative to attract the independent vote in the Northeast, and, even more certainly, none could hope to compete with Bryan's drawing power in the West. So, because he had earned it by his previous campaign and by default of his potential competitors, it was Bryan all the way.

Kansas City, Missouri, July 4, 5, 6, 1900

Quite appropriately, the convention was held in the Middle West, and the temporary chairman was a citizen of the far West, Governor Charles S. Thomas of Colorado. In his acceptance, Governor Thomas insisted that recovery from the depression period of the Cleveland administration was not the result of careful planning or efficiency by the McKinley administration, but came about through the accident that new gold supplies found in Alaska produced an increase in the supply of money—as advocated by the Democratic platform of 1896. Thus, his somewhat labored argument concluded, the theory of bimetallism was justified and its "opponents stand confounded by the irresistible operation of a law they have denied." He admitted that if the enormous gold yields of the past few years were to continue, bimetallism would have lost its point, but "the production of gold and silver oscillates, one or the other always preponderating. The pendulum will again swing to the other extreme." Therefore he urged the nation to embrace the silver standard. Without naming Bryan, he outlined the qualifications the Democratic candidate should have—all presumably possessed by Bryan.

Convention Organization

Before appointing the various standing committees, the convention approved a resolution to read the Declaration of Independence. The preliminary statements of the resolution declared that the Republican party in its Philadelphia convention "did endorse an administration which had repudiated the Constitution and did renominate a president who has betrayed the principles of the Declaration." Since the Democratic party convention was composed of men who still believed in the Declaration, "as a reaffirmation of Democratic fealty to the fundamental principles of American liberty," the secretary of the convention should be directed to read the historic document. Immediately before the secretary began his task, a bust of Bryan, wrapped in a flag, was brought to the rostrum, setting off a prolonged demonstration. Following the reading, the "Star-Spangled Banner" and "America" were sung, after which the convention proceeded with the business of naming the membership of the committees.

A second session was held in the early afternoon of the same day, but when it was announced that the credentials committee was still engaged in its task the session adjourned. In the evening session, a brief one-paragraph report from the rules committee was approved. This adopted the rules of the last Democratic national convention, including the rules of the House of Representatives of the 53rd Congress, as the convention rules, so far as applicable, and set the order of business for the balance of the convention.

A majority report of the committee on credentials endorsed the temporary roll of the national committee except in the cases of Oklahoma, Indian Territory, and the District of Columbia, where the committee decided to admit both sets of contestants with a split vote. A minority report protested against this action in the case of Oklahoma, and protest was raised from the floor on the District of Columbia decision. The majority report was sustained.

The permanent chairman was selected from Tennessee, Congressman James D. Richardson. In his speech, recalling that the previous campaign had been fought on the issue "sixteen to one," he said that the "momentous issue this year is again sixteen to one, but the sixteen parts as to the one part in this campaign . . . are wholly different from those of 1896." He then detailed the "sixteen parts," each of which was a charge against the Republicans for broken promises. The one part was a man.

It is apparent, therefore, to all that in this supreme exigency of the Republic a demand goes forth, not for a faint-hearted declaration of platform platitudes, but for a man. Yes, a man who stands like a mighty rock in the desert.[3]

This man was William Jennings Bryan.

While waiting for the platform committee, the convention spent the morning session of the second day listening to a series of speeches. All endorsed Bryan, but differences on the platform were expressed. These ranged from the demand of former Texas Governor James S. Hogg that the convention vote down any evasion of a single issue included in the platform of 1896, to a plea from a Maryland delegate to recognize the requests of the minority members of the platform committee.

The Platform

The platform was anti-imperialistic. It held that the Constitution follows the flag, and that the consequences would be grave:

[3] DNC, *Proceedings*, 1900, p. 76.

We assert that no nation can long endure half republic and half empire; and we warn the American people that imperialism abroad will lead quickly and inevitably to despotism at home.[4]

It struck hard against private monopoly: "We pledge the Democratic party to an unceasing warfare in nation, State and city against private monopoly in every form." The platform of 1896 was reaffirmed, and the bimetallism plank was specifically mentioned. Direct election of senators was favored. The platform was adopted unanimously after an enthusiastic demonstration.

The Presidential Nomination

Following the nominating speech for Bryan by a Nebraska delegate, William D. Oldham, more than a dozen full-scale seconding speeches and many shorter ones were made. Of special interest was the speech of Senator David B. Hill of New York. Hill gracefully acknowledged Bryan's "impression upon the minds, and hearts and conscience of the American people," and agreed that "from the closing of the polls four years ago until this very hour there never was a possibility of any other nomination being made." However, Hill had difficulty with the platform, which did not meet his approval "in some respects," but which was "as a whole worthy of the vote of every man who claims to be a Democrat in this country. Those who do not entirely approve some portions can

well speak of others."[5] The long list of speeches was closed gracefully "by the lady delegate from Utah." The one and only ballot was unanimous for Bryan.

The Vice-Presidential Nomination

The second-place nomination was carried over until the morning of the third day. Placed in nomination were former Vice President Adlai E. Stevenson of Illinois, Charles A. Towne of Minnesota, Senator David B. Hill of New York, John Walter Smith of Maryland, Julian S. Carr of North Carolina, Abram W. Patrick of Ohio, and James Hamilton Lewis of Washington. Lewis and Hill both withdrew, Hill immediately after the speech in which he was nominated.

Despite Hill's withdrawal delegates from many states seconded his nomination, and on the roll call, he received 207 of the 936 votes in the convention before vote shifting began. At the end of the roll call, former Vice President Stevenson held 559½ and Towne 89½, the balance being scattered. The scene after the roll call was confused; many states sought recognition to change their votes, and others tried to move the nomination be made unanimous. The chairman refused to entertain a motion for a unanimous nomination before all states had an opportunity to record their changes, and had the roll called again to ensure equal opportunity. At the end of the vote changing, the vote was unanimous.

[4] *Ibid.*, p. 114.

[5] *Ibid.*, p. 133.

Presidential Election, November 6, 1900

WILLIAM McKINLEY (R) : popular vote, 7,219,530; electoral vote, 292
WILLIAM JENNINGS BRYAN (D) : popular vote, 6,358,071; electoral vote, 155

1904

THE SITUATION in 1904 was in general similar to that of 1900. The prosperity level was high. The nation was still in an expansionist mood—a mood both evidenced and furthered by general public acceptance of the somewhat high-handed proceedings by which the United States procured rights to build a canal through Panama. There was one great difference, however. When McKinley, who epitomized the conservative business philosophy, was assassinated in September 1901, Roosevelt, of whom many of the more important business interests were suspicious, succeeded to the Presidency. Although Roosevelt was certainly no Bryan, he was considered progressive enough to capture support from many of the more conservative members of the growing Progressive movement.

THIRTEENTH REPUBLICAN CONVENTION

The peculiarities of Roosevelt's nomination as McKinley's running mate, his progressive record in the past, and his apparent intent as President to continue along the lines of that record, made opposition to him from the more conservative elements a certainty. Hanna was known to have been vehemently opposed to "that damn cowboy" in 1900, and for many others he had been an expediency choice that they would never have accepted had real thought been given to the possibility that he might succeed McKinley. The historical fact that no President by succession from the Vice Presidency had ever been elected to a term in his own right undoubtedly encouraged further opposition.

However, at the same time Roosevelt was building opposition in conservative circles,

he was creating support among the general public, to whom he epitomized the spirit of the age. It would have taken a carefully planned campaign for even a strong man to have beaten Roosevelt, if it could have been done at all. Most early gossip indicated that Mark Hanna might be the man to try, but it is not certain that he seriously considered the idea. His death occurred in February 1904—shortly before the penultimate stage of preconvention activities. No equally strong man was available for a contest, and by the time the convention opened the outcome was no longer in doubt.

Chicago, Illinois,
June 21, 22, 23, 1904

Mark Hanna's duties as chairman of the national committee devolved upon Henry C. Payne of Wisconsin. The call allocated four delegates to Alaska and six to each of the other territories, including Hawaii, without the reservation stated in the 1900 call. In other respects, it was substantially the same as the 1900 call.

The recommendation of Secretary of War Elihu Root of New York for temporary chairman was unanimously accepted. His keynote speech was a long, well-organized recitation of Republican party history and accomplishments, particularly of the McKinley and Roosevelt administrations. These latter he skillfully wove into one story, minimizing the differences between the two leaders. He asked for a "renewed expression of popular confidence in the Republican party" because of the proven record of the candidates and the party in contributing to the growth and prosperity of the nation. This applied not

164

only to the party record in internal affairs, but also, he said, to international affairs.

All Americans who desire safe and conservative administration which shall avoid cause of quarrel, all who abhor war, all who long for the perfect sway of the principles of that religion which we all profess, should rejoice that under this Republican administration their country has attained a potent leadership among the nations in the cause of peace and international justice.[1]

Following Root's speech, the standing committees were appointed and the convention adjourned until the next day to permit the committees time to work.

Convention Organization

Over sixty seats in thirteen states had been contested before the national committee, and the action of the committee was approved by the credentials committee of the convention in all but two instances. In a district contest in Missouri, the national committee recommended that both sets of contestants be seated with the vote split; the convention committee decided for only one set. On the other hand, in the contest for the entire Louisiana delegation, in which the national committee had decided for one set of contestants, the convention committee decided to seat both sets, with half a vote for each delegate. The report of the credentials committee was accepted without debate.

The committee on permanent organization presented Joseph G. Cannon, Speaker of the House of Representatives, as the permanent chairman. Cannon, whose strong control of a sometimes unruly House was already legendary, found himself chairman of a convention whose sole function was to ratify decisions already made. The delegates were badly in need of amusement, and Cannon rose to the occasion. According to contemporary accounts, he carried to the rostrum an oversized gavel, so large that the handle was a broomstick. He followed this with a few minutes of light extemporaneous talk,

after telling the delegates he would have to read his regular speech since he had not been able to memorize it. By the time he was ready to launch into his main speech, the delegates were in the mood to laugh and cheer about anything. Cannon did not disappoint them. He gave a good partisan speech, filled with rhetorical questions and biting sarcasm; it was frequently punctuated by laughter and applause.

The report of the rules committee contained no major changes from previous rules, but one minor clause brought about a contest unique in national convention annals. The committee recommended that the Hawaiian delegation, which had been allotted six delegates in the call, be given only 2 votes. Other apportionment in the call was not changed. The unusual feature of the contest was that anyone outside the Hawaiian delegation bothered to give it any real attention, least of all engage in a full-scale debate and roll call vote, for the votes—whether 2 or 6—had little value in a convention in which there were no decisions to be made.

The fact that the substitute amendment was offered by Joseph B. Foraker, senator from Ohio and one of the major party leaders, suggests that the contest may have been staged deliberately for the education of the delegates. The debate was conducted on a rational plane, centering upon the question of whether representation of the territories generally should be based upon population. The potential danger of overrepresentation of these areas in doubtful nomination contests was suggested, since they could not back their choice with electoral support. The vote was taken on a substitute for the substitute, by which it was provided that Hawaii receive 6 votes in the current convention only, leaving the basic question to the national committee for recommendation and to future conventions for action. On a voice vote, Chairman Cannon declared the motion carried, but a roll call was demanded. The close result, 495 to 490, in favor of the motion, was perhaps a tribute to Cannon's experienced ear.

[1] RNC, *Proceedings*, 1904, p. 60.

The Platform

The platform was a reiteration of that of 1900, brought up to date in terms of developments since then. It was frankly expansionist, gold standard, and protectionist—and vindicated its position by comparing the current level of prosperity and production with the level during the Cleveland administration. The unanimous acceptance of the platform was followed by a curious incident that illustrated Theodore Roosevelt's sometimes arbitrary methods and also his inability to leave the convention entirely in the hands of his lieutenants; he wanted to interject a little drama of his own.

The chairman, after requesting permission from the convention, read a dispatch sent by Secretary of State John Hay to the American consul in Morocco: "We want either Perdicaris alive or Raisuli dead." Ion Perdicaris was a presumably naturalized American citizen who had been seized by a Moroccan chieftain, Raisuli. Roosevelt had already sent units of the fleet to the scene, and this show of force had resulted in arrangements for the release of Perdicaris. The dispatch was, therefore, completely unnecessary, and its publication could have jeopardized the negotiations. Subsequent evidence suggested that Perdicaris was not an American citizen and that Roosevelt had been informed of this fact before the telegram was sent. Nevertheless, the bulletin roused the convention to a demonstration, as Roosevelt intended it to do. Secretary Hay is said to have remarked in connection with the incident: "It is curious how a concise impropriety hits the public."

The Presidential Nomination

As in 1900, the convention moved too quickly, and it was necessary to adjourn early in the afternoon of the second day to meet the commitments made to the host city for a minimum of three days in return for the expenses contracted for by the local committee and local businessmen. (In this connection, the proceedings are silent on the amount pledged by Chicago for these expenses, but they were substantial. An abstract of the meeting of the national committee at which the choice of cities was made indicates that St. Louis offered a bonus of $40,000 over and above all convention expenses. Senator Boies Penrose of Pennsylvania declared that a group of Pittsburgh Republicans, waiting outside the meeting with the cash to pay for the convention, insisted, "If $100,000 is not enough, we will give $500,000, and that would be a small matter."[2])

When the convention reconvened, New York was given the honor of presenting Roosevelt's name. The speaker, Frank S. Black, strove to make a virtue of Roosevelt's impulsiveness.

He is not a conservative, if conservatism means waiting till it is too late. He is not wise, if wisdom is to count a thing a hundred times when once will do. There is no regret so keen, in man or country, as that which follows an opportunity unembraced. . . . He does not claim to be the Solomon of his time. There are many things he may not know, but this is sure, that above all things else he stands for progress, courage and fair play, which are the synonyms of the American name.[3]

Six seconding speeches followed, the most important being that of Senator Albert J. Beveridge of Indiana. The opposition, he said, "select their candidate for the people, and the people select our candidate for us." In this respect he compared Roosevelt with such figures as Washington, Jefferson, Jackson, and Lincoln.

During the roll call, an attempt was made to suspend the rules and declare the nomination unanimous. The attempt was denied, as it has been in every Republican convention. All 994 delegates voted for Roosevelt.

The Vice-Presidential Nomination

Alabama yielded to Iowa for the honor of presenting the hand-picked nominee for

[2] *Ibid.*, p. 38.
[3] *Ibid.*, pp. 146-147.

Vice President. Jonathan P. Dolliver, later to be one of the insurgent leaders in the fight against the conservative control of Congress, presented conservative Senator Charles W. Fairbanks of Indiana as the candidate. Dolliver must have been hard put to say much about Fairbanks, and he solved the problem by talking of him as little as possible. His speech consisted almost entirely of a eulogy of the party and of Roosevelt, followed by a brief outline of Fairbanks' career. The real symbolism of Fairbanks' selection, he said, was the transfer of party leadership from the older leaders to the new by selection of a young running mate (Fairbanks was 52) for the young and aggressive President.

Chauncey Depew, without a speech from whom no important Republican convocation of the period would have been complete, made the principal seconding speech, and evidently shared Dolliver's reticence about Fairbanks.

After a long eulogy on the party history and Roosevelt's accomplishments and ability, he gave a short dissertation on the importance of the Vice Presidency, to which, he said, not enough importance was ascribed. The Vice President should be of "presidential size." "Everybody knows that if the towering figure of Theodore Roosevelt had been out of this canvass one of the promising candidates before this convention for president of the United States would have been Charles W. Fairbanks." Accordingly, since Fairbanks was also a good lawyer, had made a national name as a senator, was dignified, had character, and possessed a "genius for public affairs," Depew seconded his nomination.

Although Fairbanks was nominated by acclamation, signs were evident that this would not have happened had the control over the convention been less rigid. The Illinois delegation declared that it had intended to vote for its favorite son, but accepted the judgment of the convention. Nebraska, Missouri, and Georgia made similar remarks before the motion for unanimous nomination could be put. Fairbanks, who was a delegate, was called

for, but it was announced that he had left the convention hall.

NINETEENTH DEMOCRATIC CONVENTION

In 1900, renomination of William Jennings Bryan had been a certainty; in 1904, following two Bryan defeats, it was almost as certain that the convention would turn to another. In addition to being stigmatized as the first major-party nominee to lose on two consecutive occasions, Bryan did not offer as clear an alternative against Theodore Roosevelt as he had against the more conservative William McKinley. Even his more ardent followers were hard put to justify a third attempt in the face of the solid opposition of the conservative wing of the party. In any case, Bryan made no serious effort to gain the nomination for himself; he did, however, do everything possible to retain his stature as leader of the progressive wing of the party.

According to many, the best Democratic strategy would be to run a true conservative who might siphon off many votes from the more conservative Republican groups who were highly suspicious of the "damn cowboy." Unfortunately for the strategy, the Democratic ranks of conservatives of adequate stature were thin. Grover Cleveland, who undoubtedly would have been the strongest candidate the party could have put up, was in his late sixties and refused to assume the burden. David B. Hill, though younger than Cleveland, was a casualty of the bitter factional fighting of New York politics, a fight from which Cleveland had mostly abstained after leaving the Presidency. Hill could probably not have obtained the full support of the New York delegation. A long gap existed between these two and the next group of practicing politicians—too great a gap. It was necessary for the party organization to look outside its own ranks.

The conservative Democrats did not quite have it all their own way. Publisher William Randolph Hearst, who had won election to the House of Representatives in

1903, attempted, with some success in the West, to rally the progressives about him. If he counted on Bryan to support him, he was soon disappointed. In any case, Bryan was not likely to help him gain a position that could jeopardize Bryan's own leadership of the progressives.

St. Louis, Missouri, July 6, 7, 8, 9, 1904

The national committee called upon the deep South for the temporary chairman— John Sharp Williams of Mississippi, minority leader in the House of Representatives, who set the keynote by attacking the "volcanic, eruptive, and reckless character" of "Rooseveltism"—a charge remarkably different from those customarily made against Republicans. In his long speech, Williams attacked the keynote address of his opposite number in the Republican convention, Elihu Root, who had woven a historical thread from Washington through Lincoln to McKinley and Roosevelt. The historical accuracy of much that Root had said was questioned, and the idea that Roosevelt fitted into this chain of Republican statesmen was especially ridiculed.

Convention Organization

The committee on rules reported at the opening of the morning session on the second day. The report was identical in content with that of 1900, including retention of the House rules of the 53rd Congress as the basic parliamentary guide. This was an intentional slap at the Republican-controlled Houses under the leadership of Joseph G. Cannon, for the 53rd was the last previous Congress in which the Democrats controlled a majority in the House.

An auxiliary report of the rules committee recommended that delegates from Puerto Rico be granted seats with full voting rights. An attempt to do the same for the Philippine Islands was denied on the grounds that recent court decisions had ruled that Puerto Rico was "a part of the territory of these United States," whereas it had been ruled that the Philippine Islands were not. The report relating to the Puerto Rico delegation was approved.

The chairman of the credentials committee stated flatly that the committee had been unable to check all of the many contests thoroughly, and could not do so short of many days' work. The committee endorsed most of the temporary roll as established by the national committee, and most of the report was accepted without discussion by the convention. However, separate action on some of the contests was demanded, the most important relating to the contest in Illinois. One group of delegates led by Roger Sullivan, the powerful Chicago boss, had been seated by the national committee and endorsed by the credentials committee. The contesting delegates were confirmed Bryan supporters. Bryan himself presented the minority report, although he was a member of the platform, not the credentials, committee.

Since both groups reportedly were supporting the same candidate, the nomination was not at issue; it was a question of factional control, and Bryan forced a test vote. Nearly 300 of the 1,000 votes in the convention were cast on Bryan's side, and these represented what probably was the core of strength on which Bryan could depend in regard to any issue. The fact that it was short of a one third veto strength may have been a factor that restrained Bryan from forcing other votes, although he showed other signs of not being in accord with convention decisions. Bryan's delegates were defeated 299 to 647, the 54 votes from Illinois not being cast.

Congressman Champ Clark of Missouri was elected permanent chairman. Paralleling the tactics of Williams in attacking the opening address of Republican Elihu Root, Clark attacked the Republican platform, clause by clause.

The Platform

The platform was of more interest for what it did not contain than for what it did. There was little in it that could not be found in Democratic platforms of the past. However, Bryan's energetic efforts prevented inclusion of a plank admitting that the bimetallism question was dead, and nothing whatever was said about the currency question. No minority report was filed, and the platform was accepted by voice vote.

The Presidential Nomination

Judge Alton B. Parker of New York was presented for the Presidency as "a man who puts against the strenuous sword play of a swaggering administration, a simple faith in all the perfect power of the Constitution." With respect to the question of why Parker had not outlined his policy for the convention, the speaker stated:

I tell you that he does not believe that policies should be dictated, but that the sovereignty of the party is in the untrammeled judgment and wisdom of its members; if you ask me what his policy will be, if elected, I tell you that it will be that policy which finds expression in the platform of his party.[4]

William Randolph Hearst was the second candidate to be presented. His speaker made a bald plea for Bryan's support:

Three times did he support Grover Cleveland, and twice him who yonder sits, and who, untouched by ephemeral obloquy, misrepresentation and slander, will bequeath to posterity a name as pure, a character as lofty and a fame as bright as any recorded in the annals of Democracy.[5]

Bryan's second major appearance before the convention occurred during the roll call for nominations. The nominations of Parker and Hearst were followed by those of Judge George Gray, by Delaware; General Nelson A. Miles, by Kansas; Francis M. Cockrell, Senate minority leader, by Missouri; Richard Olney, Cleveland's last Secretary of State, by Massachusetts. When Nebraska was called, Bryan yielded to Wisconsin, reserving the right to speak when Wisconsin's regular turn came. Wisconsin nominated Edward C. Wall, but not without some difficulty, for the long nomi-

nating speech contained charges that many of Parker's supporters had not supported the Democratic ticket with Bryan at the helm. Attempts were made to have the speaker ruled out of order on the basis that he was making an arraignment of a section of the party instead of a nominating speech, but the chairman refused to do so.

North Dakota nominated John Sharp Williams. After the remainder of the states had passed or made seconding speeches, Bryan took the rostrum. As he was to do again and again in the future, he asked and was granted suspension of the rules limiting the length of his speech. His main subject was the need for a nominee that the West could accept. Although he specifically seconded Cockrell, he mentioned several others who would be acceptable, including Hearst. Notably absent from this list was the name of Alton B. Parker. He charged that he himself had lost in the past because "some who had affiliated with the Democratic party thought my election would be injurious to the country, and they left the party and helped to elect my opponent." It was clear to everybody, especially in the light of the speech of the Wisconsin delegate, that the men indicated were those supporting Parker.

The effort was to no avail. Parker received 658 votes, 9 short of the necessary two thirds, on the first ballot; Idaho led the band wagon that built his final total to 679 votes and the nomination. Hearst retained 181 votes after the switching was completed, the balance being scattered among ten other candidates. The convention then adjourned.

When the convention reconvened, five names were presented for the vice-presidential nomination. During the roll call a telegram arrived from Parker that was to throw the convention into an uproar. Immediately following the completion of the roll call for nominations, a motion was made to adjourn the convention before voting, on the grounds that "for reasons which are obvious to all the delegates here, it seems to me we ought not to proceed to nominate a candidate for Vice President at

[4] DNC, *Proceedings*, 1904, pp. 163-164.
[5] *Ibid.*, p. 170.

this time." Evidently the reasons were not obvious to all the delegates, for some shouted: "Why?" Others wished to continue in any event, but a recess of an hour and a half finally was agreed to.

Even after the recess, the situation remained ambiguous and rumors were flying. It was generally known that the chairman of the New York delegation had received some kind of message from Parker, but its exact content was unknown to most of the delegates. The press had apparently published one version of the telegram: "The gold standard is established by law, and I cannot accept the nomination unless that plank is contained in the platform."[6]

For over an hour after reconvening, the delegates were kept waiting while the New York delegation wrestled with the propriety of disclosing the actual text of the message to the public. Finally, it was read:

I regard the gold standard as firmly and irrevocably established, and shall act accordingly if the action of the Convention to-day shall be ratified by the people. As the platform is silent on the subject, my view should be made known to the Convention, and if it is proved to be unsatisfactory to the majority, I request you to decline the nomination for me at once, so that another may be nominated before adjournment.[7]

In effect, Judge Parker added another plank to the platform by this telegram—a plank that not only would have been bitterly opposed by Bryan and his friends, but that was diametrically opposite to a plank abandoned by Bryan as a *quid pro quo* in the arduous negotiations of the platform committee. The Bryan people felt, with some justice, that the platform as accepted by the committee and the convention represented a reasonable, if precarious, balance

[6] *Ibid.*, p. 276.
[7] *Ibid.*, p. 277.

of the conflicting forces within the convention. The telegram completely upset this balance. Parker supporters quickly moved that a reply be dispatched to Parker:

The platform adopted by this Convention is silent upon the question of the monetary standard, because it is not regarded by us as a possible issue in this campaign, and only campaign issues are mentioned in the platform. Therefore, there is nothing in the views expressed by you in the telegram just received which would preclude a man entertaining them from accepting a nomination on said platform.

This touched off an acrimonious debate, with Bryan taking a leading role. Parker's defenders argued that everyone in the convention had known Parker's position on the gold question before he was nominated, which was probably true. Since this could not readily be admitted, however, Bryan and others stressed the fact that Parker had never openly taken a stand. Bryan himself stated that he had assumed Parker to be a Gold man, but that he had done so on the basis of Parker's silence on the issue. When finally the roll was called, the reply to Parker was approved 794 to 191, with 15 votes not cast.

The Vice-Presidential Nomination

Despite the late hour—after 1:00 a.m.—the vote was taken for the vice-presidential nominee. Henry G. Davis of West Virginia, 70-year-old former senator, led with 654 votes, Robert Williams of Illinois followed with 165. Judge George Turner, ex-senator from Washington, received 100, and W. A. Harris, ex-senator from Kansas, 58.

Davis was 13 votes short of two thirds, and the motion for a unanimous nomination was put immediately by a Kentucky delegate and passed. After the customary housekeeping motions, the convention adjourned sine die.

Presidential Election, November 8, 1904

THEODORE ROOSEVELT (R) : popular vote, 7,628,834; electoral vote, 336
ALTON B. PARKER (D): popular vote, 5,084,401; electoral vote, 140

1908

THE LANDSLIDE proportions of the Republican victory of 1904 left the interparty situation badly out of balance. The Democrats had not yet been able to heal the breach between the progressive and conservative wings of their party, and the struggle for control was intense. The similar schism within the Republican ranks was temporarily hidden from general view by the strength and popularity of Theodore Roosevelt; so long as he remained in power, few were strong enough to risk his open wrath. Even the sharp but short depression of 1907 failed to shake Roosevelt's hold; if anything, it may have helped him—since the Wall Street financiers, rather than Roosevelt, were blamed. Despite that short financial dip, the general prosperity of the country seemed upward in trend—especially in terms of industrial production. If farmers and other elements of the population were not getting their full share of the national prosperity, the voices that would speak for them were just beginning to talk loudly enough to be heard.

FOURTEENTH REPUBLICAN CONVENTION

In the first flush of victory on election night in 1904, Roosevelt had rashly proclaimed that "under no circumstances" would he be a candidate to succeed himself in 1908, and although he may have regretted this statement even before 1908 rolled around, he stood by it. However, his statement in no way precluded his influencing, if not dictating, the choice of his successor, and this he set about doing. As an expert and realistic politician, he left nothing to chance. Having decided upon the Secretary of War, William Howard Taft, as his successor, he assigned the First Assistant Postmaster General the full-time job of organizing the southern delegates for Taft, and in other ways provided for his certain nomination.

The opposition was split. At the time, Taft was believed by most to share Roosevelt's political philosophy and goals, and it is probably true that he did. Accordingly, those who thought Roosevelt too conservative felt the same way about Taft. A more influential group, including many of the financial leaders of the country and not a few members of Congress, felt that Roosevelt and Taft were too progressive for their liking. With their widely different reasons for opposition, there was little probability that these two groups could combine, and neither had a candidate of adequate stature who was willing to break openly with the administration. Accordingly, the opponents to Taft's succession resorted to a favorite son strategy in an attempt to stop the tide, though with no apparent plan of what they would do in the unlikely event that Taft were to be deadlocked.

Chicago, Illinois,
June 16, 17, 18, 19, 1908

The call to the convention contained the first major change since the form was stabilized in 1892. In addition to changes of order and the form of presentation, a substantive change provided for election of delegates by the new primary method being introduced in some states for the first time:

171

. . . delegates both from the State-at-large and their alternates and delegates from each Congressional district and their alternates, may be elected in conformity with the laws of the State in which the election occurs, provided, the State Committee or any such Congressional committee shall so direct; but provided further, that in no State shall an election be so held as to prevent the delegates from any Congressional district and their alternates being selected by the Republican electors of that district.[1]

Thus, while willing to move with the times, the Republican party made it clear that it did not intend to give up its long-established custom of preserving the autonomy of congressional districts.

The temporary chairman, Senator Julius Caesar Burrows of Michigan, although presented by the chairman of the national committee and approved by the convention, was almost certainly not the choice of Roosevelt. According to contemporary accounts, Roosevelt's choice was the historian, Senator Albert J. Beveridge of Indiana, or someone of similar progressive views. However, the conservatives were able to sidetrack Beveridge on the grounds that he came from the same state as a potential candidate, Vice President Fairbanks, and by adroit maneuvering managed to install their own choice.

Burrows, though conservative in politics, was not conservative with words. His keynote speech was one of the longest in convention records, and heavily laden with financial and production statistics and quotations from various speeches and reports.

The name of Roosevelt was mentioned only twice, the first time when Burrows quoted from a message to the Secretary of the Treasury, in which Roosevelt said: "I congratulate also those conservative and substantial business men, who, in this crisis, have acted with such wisdom and public spirit." The second mention was not particularly complimentary in the context; in speaking of the requirements for the candidates to be nominated by the convention, Burrows stated: "They must

have the patriotism and sagacity of a Lincoln, the tenacity of a Grant, the wisdom and moderation of a McKinley, and the courage of a Roosevelt."[2] Another barb, near the end of the speech, referred to Roosevelt, but not by name:

Yet nothing has added so much to his just fame as his persistent and irrevocable refusal to break the unwritten law of the Republic by accepting a nomination for a third term.[3]

Convention Organization

Just before the report of the credentials committee was received, delegates who had been present at the first convention of 1856 were called to the platform. Only three responded this time.

The reports of the credentials and permanent organization committees were accepted without debate, and Roosevelt's close personal friend, Henry Cabot Lodge, senator from Massachusetts, was selected permanent chairman. Lodge's acceptance speech outlined a moderate but positive progressive philosophy that, had it been followed by Taft and his administration, might have prevented the Armageddon to come.

Lodge struck out squarely against ill-gotten and misused wealth—though he defended wealth gained by legitimate means and used for responsible ends. He faced squarely the fact that the question of concentration of wealth, and the other rapidly increasing complexities of the period, called for courageous and drastic action. He foresaw that the solutions would have to be new solutions fitted to the new problems. He recognized the "ominous unrest" building up beneath the surface, and expressed sympathy for the "righteous demands" behind this unrest. The solution, he felt, would not be found in the direction of government ownership, as recommended by the opposition, for this would "tend directly to socialism and to all its attendant miseries and evils."

[1] RNC, *Proceedings*, 1908, p. 27.

[2] *Ibid.*, p. 45.
[3] *Ibid.*

Rather, he proposed an extension of the policy of using

> . . . government regulation and supervision for the control of corporations and combinations so that these great and necessary instruments of commerce and business may be preserved as useful servants and not destroyed because they threaten to become dangerous masters.[4]

If the "praise" extended to Roosevelt by the temporary chairman for refusing to break the third-term tradition was a reflection of fear on the part of the conservatives that Roosevelt might accept a spontaneous draft—and it probably was—Lodge removed it by emphatically taking him out of the running:

> Any one who attempts to use his name as a candidate for the presidency impugns both his sincerity and his good faith. . . . That man is no friend to Theodore Roosevelt and does not cherish his name and fame, who now, from any motive, seeks to urge him as a candidate for the great office which he has finally declined.[5]

While Lodge was speaking, some of the delegates apparently were searching the hall for more men who had attended the 1856 convention. Their efforts turned up one man who had voted for every Republican presidential candidate beginning with Frémont, and one who had been a delegate to the 1860 convention. These were duly invited to take seats on the platform.

The report of the committee on rules and order of business followed the previous rules, except that the change required by introduction of primary elections, as indicated in the call, was added. An amendment (substantially the same as the one offered by Matthew Quay in 1900) proposing to base the congressional district apportionment on the basis of one delegate for each 10,000 votes, was signed by delegates from fifteen states, including New York, Pennsylvania, Illinois, and Colorado. It was defeated by the relatively close vote of 506 to 471.[6] The southern delegations were joined by enough of the pro-Taft

northern strength to defeat the measure. According to contemporary reports, Roosevelt urged its defeat on the grounds that passage might upset the southern delegates so much that they might not carry through with their pledges for Taft. If he did so he probably regretted it four years later.

The Platform

The platform was presented on the morning of the third day. In large part, it consisted of a recitation of the tremendous strides made by the nation during the period since the Republican party was organized, and attributed most of this progress to the fact that the Republicans had controlled the administration throughout most of this period. On the more pressing problems of the day, it was cautious, in general advocating gradual extension of current principles and agencies rather than new programs. An extensive minority report was presented, signed only by the committee member from Wisconsin—a report that, despite its failure to be adopted in this convention, was remarkable for the number of recommendations that subsequently were adopted. Two of its more important planks recommended:

> The immediate enactment of a law authorizing the Interstate Commerce Commission to make an exact and complete inventory of all the physical property of every railroad company engaged in interstate commerce, to the end that such valuation be made the basis of just and reasonable railway rates.

> Immediate revision of the tariff by the imposition of such duties only, as will equal the difference between the cost of production at home and abroad. . . . [To provide a scientific basis for insuring this] we favor the early establishment of a permanent tariff commission, to be appointed by the President.[7]

With respect to trusts and combinations, the minority report urged that the promises of the platform of 1900 be carried out through enactment of adequate legislation and by administration enforcement of existing legislation. It also recommended

[4] *Ibid.*, p. 87.
[5] *Ibid.*, p. 88.
[6] See *Analysis of Key Votes.*

[7] RNC, *Proceedings*, 1908, pp. 126-127.

direct election of senators, enactment of a law requiring publication of campaign expenditures, creation of a Department of Labor, and establishment of an eight-hour day for all employees of the government or contractors doing work on behalf of the government.

Although only a fraction of the convention was willing to support these measures, several roll call votes were held in defeating them. The first vote was taken upon all sections of the minority report not reserved for separate votes—these were overwhelmingly defeated 952 to 28. The sections reserved for separate vote were the clause relating to publication of campaign contributions: defeated 880 to 94; physical evaluation of railroads: defeated 917 to 63; direct election of senators: defeated 866 to 114. The majority report was then adopted by voice vote.

The Presidential Nomination

The candidates presented to the convention were Speaker of the House Joseph G. (Uncle Joe) Cannon of Illinois; Vice President Charles W. Fairbanks of Indiana; Charles Evans Hughes, reform governor of New York; Secretary of War William Howard Taft; Senator Joseph B. Foraker of Ohio; Senator Philander C. Knox of Pennsylvania, formerly U.S. Attorney General; and finally the progressive former governor of Wisconsin, Senator Robert M. La Follette. If seconded at all, most of these were seconded by another member of the delegation making the nomination, or by a southen delegate. Only Cannon and Taft received seconds from more than one northern state, and in Cannon's case the speaker was the only member of his delegation who voted for him.

On the single roll call, Taft received 702 votes. Only three others received over 50 votes each: Cannon, 58, Hughes, 67, and Knox, 68, and in each case most of the votes came from their home states. A Hughes supporter led the parade for unanimity.

The Vice-Presidential Nomination

Although it was but six o'clock, the convention put off the vice-presidential proceedings until the next morning. The honor of nominating and seconding the selected candidate was given to states that had opposed the Taft nomination. New York nominated James S. Sherman, its congressman, and he was seconded by Joseph G. Cannon personally. Henry Cabot Lodge apparently took the opportunity of discharging a political debt by nominating Massachusetts Governor Curtis Guild, for it is unlikely that Guild was a serious choice either for Roosevelt or Lodge. New Jersey presented Franklin Murphy, its ex-governor. Guild and Murphy received 75 and 77 votes each; 11 votes went to two other minor candidates. Sherman received the balance—816.

Analysis of Key Votes

Over 95 per cent of the delegations voting higher than the convention average on the negative side of the roll call by which the proposed change of convention apportionment was defeated subsequently voted for Taft on the nominating ballot. The correlation between the votes was −.88. Much of this relationship is of course due to the fact that southern delegates were opposed to the apportionment change because it would affect their future convention power adversely, and most of them also were pledged to Taft as the administration candidate. However, the very high correlation indicates that many northern Taft delegates also voted on the negative side, and that almost all of the Taft opponents were on the affirmative side.

TWENTIETH DEMOCRATIC CONVENTION

The experiment of running a conservative Democrat in 1904 had proved a dismal failure; Parker was defeated by one of the largest margins in recent political history.

The defeat buried most of the remaining conservatives, and the generally low ebb of the Democratic tide gave little opportunity for new figures to rise—either conservative or liberal. The same low ebb undoubtedly encouraged genuine hopefuls to wait for a better opportunity. Whatever their reasons—whether they genuinely preferred Bryan or were merely willing to let him run a hopeless campaign—most delegates came to the 1908 convention prepared to vote for him.

Denver, Colorado,
July 7, 8, 9, 10, 1908

The temporary chairman, Theodore A. Bell of California, ridiculed the platform adopted in the Republican convention two weeks before by pointing out that the Republicans had enjoyed an overpowering majority in both houses of Congress, and accordingly could have proposed and adopted any legislation that it chose. Why, then, did the platform consist of statements of what "we will" do? Rather, he said, it should be the same list of planks prefaced by "we did not." He then proceeded to itemize the so-called neglected opportunities:

> We did not revise the tariff.
> We did not amend the anti-trust laws to secure greater effectiveness in prosecution of criminal monopolies.
> We did not admit into the Union the Territories of New Mexico and Arizona as separate States.[8]

He also recalled the refusal of the Republican convention to accept some of the Wisconsin minority proposals, and particularly charged that the party acknowledged its guilt in depending upon large sums "collected from the vast monopolies of the country and corruptly used in the conduct of its campaigns," when the convention defeated, by a 10-to-1 majority, the proposal to publish campaign contributions.

[8] DNC, *Proceedings*, 1908, pp. 8-9.

Convention Organization

The report of the rules committee remained the same as it had been for the previous two conventions, including retention of the rules of the House of Representatives for the 53rd Congress as the basic parliamentary guide. None of the other committees being ready to report during the first session of the second day, popular speakers were called for, and a remarkable demonstration occurred during one of the speeches. The blind senator from Oklahoma, Thomas P. Gore, celebrating the fact that this was the first convention in which Oklahoma participated as a full-fledged state, mentioned the name of Bryan. Immediately the delegates broke into an uproar, and it was an hour and twenty minutes before Gore could continue. At least one speaker believed that this demonstration affected the nominations, for he remarked:

> As to the Vice President, we have a number of names of distinguished men floating around on the air. But a good many of them—I think all of them—are candidates for President. At least they were until the demonstration of today.[9]

In its majority report, the committee on credentials approved most of the delegates seated on the temporary roll by the national committee, but reversed the ruling for delegates from one Ohio and five Pennsylvania districts. The Ohio contest was not protested on the floor of the convention, but a minority report was submitted in the Pennsylvania case. The seats at issue were all in the city of Philadelphia, and the question involved appears to have been whether or not Republicans, in cooperation with a faction of the Democratic party, had raided the Democratic primary.

The majority held that this was the case, and cited the sudden rise in one district from a Democratic primary vote averaging about 1,000 in the past to nearly 2,700 in the primary of 1908. The minority based its claim upon the fact that the dele-

[9] *Ibid.*, p. 47.

gates whom it supported had received a majority of the vote cast in the primary, and this contention was not denied. The additional claim by the majority that the delegates seated by the majority report were favorable to Bryan, as were those who had supported them in the primary, made it almost inevitable that a convention dominated by Bryan would approve their being seated. A roll call was demanded, and the minority report was defeated 604½ to 386½.[10] The majority report then carried by voice vote.

Congressman Henry D. Clayton of Alabama was elected permanent chairman, and took his place on the morning of the third day. He, too, stressed the inconsistency between what the Republican platform promised and what the Republican majority in Congress had done. "If thirty of them had joined the Democrats," he said, "many of these platform promises would already have been accomplished."

The Platform

Despite gratification of the chairman of the platform committee "with the most complete harmony among the members of the committee," the report was delayed considerably. Several speakers were heard during the afternoon of the third day, a recess was taken until evening, and four additional speakers were heard before the report finally was given. Some of the major points attacked were the increase of public officeholders; increased expenditures leading to a large deficit; the rigid control exercised by the Speaker of the House of Representatives; and the misuse of patronage, including "establishment of a dynasty," through "forced succession to the Presidency." Legislation was demanded:

. . . terminating the partnership which has existed between corporations of the country and the Republican party under the expressed or implied agreement that in return for the contribution of great sums of money where-

[10] See *Analysis of Key Votes.*

with to purchase elections, they should be allowed to continue substantially unmolested in their efforts to encroach upon the rights of the people.[11]

The Democratic party pledged itself to prohibit any corporation from contributing to a campaign fund. Planks on the tariff, private monopoly, railroad regulation, and others substantially followed previous platforms.

The Presidential Nomination

For a convention in which even a small minority of opposition existed, the words by which the permanent chairman introduced the speaker for Bryan's nomination were highly unusual, if not in bad taste. He said: "Gentlemen, I introduce to you a man who comes from the midway of the mighty American continent and whose message is significant of the fact that we are midway to the White House next November."[12]

In presenting Bryan, the nominating speaker said that every important civilization had faced crises in which its institutions and its very existence were threatened. For those that managed to survive, some "master mind" was "produced as it were by the conditions themselves, with capacity to direct aright the energies of the people." Such a condition faced the United States at the moment, and the "master mind" ready to meet the crisis was already available—William Jennings Bryan.

After more than an hour of demonstration, two long seconding speeches were given. Only after this did the convention approve a motion to limit additional seconding speeches to five minutes. Nearly every delegation seconded Bryan, some with a few words, but many with speeches. The chain was broken only by the nominating and seconding speeches for Minnesota's favorite son, Governor John A. Johnson, and the nomination of Judge George Gray, by Delaware. Of the 1,002

[11] DNC, *Proceedings,* 1908, p. 162.
[12] *Ibid.,* p. 176.

votes apportioned, 888½ were recorded for Bryan. Gray received 59½ and Johnson 46.

The Vice-Presidential Nomination

With the profusion of speeches for Bryan still in mind, a motion to restrict nominating speeches for Vice President to ten minutes, and seconding speeches to two in number and five minutes in length, passed without difficulty. Under these rules, John W. Kern of Indiana was nominated, followed by Charles A. Towne, one of the rare individuals who had held high political office in two states, and rarer than most of these because he had been first congressman and senator from Minnesota and then a congressman from New York, thus reversing the more common East to West pattern. Connecticut presented a prominent businessman, Archibald McNeil, as a favorite son; Georgia urged the selection of Clark Howell, Georgia citizen, "inasmuch as the South furnishes the votes for the Democratic party . . . we should have some recognition in this party."

Despite the limitation placed on seconding speeches, nearly every delegation seconded Kern with at least a few words. As in 1896, Nebraska asked to be passed during the regular roll. When the roll had been completed, and the inclination of the convention for Kern made clear, Nebraska asked to be called again to move his nomination by acclamation. The motion carried unanimously.

Analysis of Key Votes

Despite the fact that Bryan received nearly 90 per cent of the vote on the presidential nominating ballot, and that this almost certainly included considerable band-wagon vote, the relationship between this ballot and the vote by which the minority credentials report was defeated is clearly candidate-oriented. Of the total votes in the convention, only 113½ failed to go for Bryan; of these, all but 7 were from delegations supporting the minority or losing side of the issue. The correlation between the issue vote and the nominating ballot was +.89.

Presidential Election, November 3, 1908

WILLIAM HOWARD TAFT (R) : popular vote, 7,679,006; electoral vote, 321
WILLIAM JENNINGS BRYAN (D) : popular vote, 6,409,106; electoral vote, 162

1912

In the mid-term elections of 1910, the Democrats captured the House of Representatives for the first time since the Republican majority took it over in 1894, and also won many governorships. Hopes for winning the Presidency in 1912 soared. On the other hand, the Republicans found themselves unable to conceal the basic split within the party—a split that widened rapidly after ex-President Theodore Roosevelt's return from his trip to Africa and Europe in June 1910. By that time, Senator Nelson W. Aldrich, Speaker Joseph G. Cannon, and other conservatives had become President William Howard Taft's closest advisers, and the progressive elements in the party were in a state of near rebellion. Most of the Republican congressional losers in 1910 were conservatives: the public was in a progressive state of mind.

FIFTEENTH REPUBLICAN CONVENTION

Several incidents helped to develop and widen the breach between ex-President and President. To complicate matters further, Senator Robert M. La Follette of Wisconsin openly declared his presidential candidacy as a progressive Republican at an early date. As governor of Wisconsin from 1901 to 1906 and a leader of the progressive element in the Senate since 1906, La Follette had an impressive record, and at the outset apparently expected Roosevelt's cooperation. As the preconvention campaign progressed, however, La Follette increasingly suspected that Roosevelt was playing a waiting game and finally became convinced that the former President intended to appropriate for himself the fruits of La

Follette's campaign work. A physical and mental breakdown early in 1912 forced La Follette to reduce the pace of his campaign, and he entered the convention with little more than the Wisconsin vote pledged to him. He nevertheless had a substantial following among delegates from other states who sympathized with him, and who were willing to give him some support on issues other than the candidacy itself. His animosity to Roosevelt, manifested in complete refusal to cooperate in any way with the Roosevelt branch of the progressives, was an important factor in the convention.

Roosevelt officially threw his hat in the ring late in February 1912, and was immediately faced with the difficult problem of effectively opposing administration control of the delegation selection process in those areas where primaries had not yet been adopted, particularly in the South. In 1908, Taft had declared:

The South has been the section of rotton boroughs in the Republican national politics, and it would delight me if no southern state were permitted to have a vote in the National Convention except in proportion to its Republican vote. . . . But when a man is running for the presidency, and I believe that is what I am now doing, he cannot afford to ignore the tremendous influence, however undue, that the southern vote has, and he must take the best way he can honorably to secure it. In the past it has been secured too frequently by pure purchase. Of course I would never stoop to that method.[1]

The southern delegations, as well as most delegations where party machines were strong, were lined up solidly for Taft. Furthermore, some local and state conventions had been held before Roosevelt de-

[1] Henry F. Pringle, *The Life and Times of William Howard Taft* (1939), p. 347.

178

clared his candidacy. Others were scheduled for meetings too early for him to prepare adequately for them, with the result that Taft had a big lead in pledged delegates.

To overcome this lead, Roosevelt depended upon two principal strategies. The first, and more legitimate, was to exploit his very real popularity with the rank and file by entering the newly installed presidential primaries wherever he could. He picked up about three times as many votes in primaries as La Follette and Taft combined. In most states where the candidates met head on, Roosevelt won overwhelmingly. Taft received only 34 votes from primary states on the presidential ballot in the convention, La Follette 41, whereas 236 delegates from primary states either voted for Roosevelt or, in compliance with his request, abstained from voting. The total Roosevelt vote from the primary states amounted to only about 20 per cent of the total convention vote, however, and the additional votes he gained from non-primary states still left him substantially under a majority in the convention.

The second strategy was to confuse the issue by creating contests wherever possible —and it was not difficult to do so with at least a degree of justification in the southern states. According to Victor Rosewater, chairman of the national committee, whose testimony could be discounted as pro-Taft but who quotes from a pro-Roosevelt source, the Roosevelt contests were deliberately instigated at the early stages of the campaign for publicity purposes and to make the fight appear more even. Also, according to Rosewater, Roosevelt supporters when faced with defeat attempted to translate the spurious contestants into qualified delegates by seizing control of the convention organization; in support of this charge, he quotes the *Washington Times,* a pro-Roosevelt paper:

On the day when Roosevelt formally announced that he was a candidate something over a hundred delegates had actually been selected. When Senator Dixon took charge of

the campaign a tabulated showing of delegates selected to date would have looked hopelessly one-sided. Moreover, a number of southern states had called their conventions for early dates and there was no chance to develop the real Roosevelt strength in the great northern states till later. For psychological effect as a move in practical politics it was necessary for the Roosevelt people to start contests on these early Taft selections in order that a tabulation of delegate strength could be put out that would show Roosevelt holding a good hand. In the game, a table showing Taft 150, Roosevelt 19, contested none, would not be very much calculated to inspire confidence, whereas one showing Taft 23, Roosevelt 19, contested 127, looked very different. That is the whole story of the larger number of southern contests that were started early in the game. It was never expected that they would be taken very seriously. They served a useful purpose, and now the National Committee is deciding them in favor of Taft in most cases without real division.[2]

In preparing the preliminary roll call for the convention, Taft supporters held a clear majority of at least 37 out of 53 votes in the national committee. The committee's first act was to pass a rule that a roll call could be demanded only if twenty or more members demanded it—which in view of the numbers involved made it impossible for the minority to get even this satisfaction. More than two hundred contested seats were acted upon, and almost all decisions were made in Taft's favor. How many seats legitimately belonged to Roosevelt will never be known; he carried only seventy-two contests to the floor of the convention. A statement credited by Nicholas Murray Butler to Governor Herbert S. Hadley of Missouri, Roosevelt's floor manager in the early part of the convention, is revealing as to the authenticity of these contests:

During the course of the journey [in 1913] I said to the Governor: "It is all past now, but I should be very much interested to know how you arrived at the decision to make contests of 74 [sic] seats at the convention last June?" Governor Hadley smiled and said: "I will tell

[2] *Washington Times,* June 9, 1912, as cited by Victor Rosewater, *Backstage in 1912* (1932), pp. 64-65.

you. After the National Committee had heard the various contests and reached their conclusions, Borah, Frank Kellogg and I decided that in twenty-four cases we had been literally defrauded of our representation. We recognized that we had a very strong case in respect to other contests, but that there were debatable questions, every one of which, however, had been decided against us. There remained twenty-four contests in which we felt that we had been outraged and that injustice had plainly been done. So we three went to Colonel Roosevelt and told him this fact. We said we were going to contest these twenty-four seats on the floor of the convention. On hearing this statement, Colonel Roosevelt cried with great vehemence: 'Twenty-four seats! Twenty-four! What is the use of contesting twenty-four? You must contest seventy-four if you expect to get anywhere.' So we raised the number to seventy-four."[3]

Butler adds that this was confirmed by Murray Crane, a Taft leader, who admitted that, although all doubtful cases had been decided in favor of the Taft contestants, there were a few cases in which much was to be said for the other side.

By the time the opening day of the convention arrived, tempers were at white heat. The conservatives were concentrated behind Taft, and operated from a strong base with a majority of the national committee. The coterie of administration-controlled southern delegates was the core of what was to prove a slim majority of the convention. The Progressives, on the other hand, were split between Roosevelt and La Follette, and the dictum that the closer the kin the bitterer the fight was well borne out. Neither Roosevelt nor La Follette would give an inch to the other.

Chicago, Illinois,
June 18, 19, 20, 21, 22, 1912

The call for the convention differed from that of 1908 in three respects. First, a provision was inserted directing that all delegates or alternates participating in state or district conventions must be elected subsequent to the adoption of the call, which

[3] Nicholas Murray Butler, *Across the Busy Years* (1940), Vol. 1, p. 244.

was dated December 11, 1911. Second, a clause was added to the paragraph detailing the period in which delegates to the national convention must be elected (not less than thirty days after date of the call, and not less than thirty days before the convention). This clause permitted the time period to be suspended if state law directed otherwise. Finally, a new paragraph was added directing the secretary of the Republican national committee to send copies of the call to the member of the national committee for each state, with additional copies for the chairman and secretary of the state executive committee.

Convention Organization

In conventions where there is a fairly clear division of strength between two major candidates, and in which either of the candidates is in position for quick victory if favorite sons and waverers can be won over, it is characteristic for a battle for control of the convention machinery to develop quickly. The convention of 1912 was no exception, and immediately following the reading of the call Roosevelt's floor manager opened the attack.

The fundamental question was: Who is qualified to vote in the organization of the convention? Governor Hadley's approach was in the form of a motion to substitute an amended list of delegates for the list compiled by the national committee, but after long and heated debate his motion was ruled out of order by Chairman Rosewater on the grounds that the only business before the convention was the selection of a temporary chairman.

The attack was then continued from another source. A Wisconsin delegate, making it clear he was acting as an individual delegate and not as representative of the Wisconsin delegation, nominated Governor Francis McGovern of his state in opposition to the national committee's choice for temporary chairman, Elihu Root. Currently in the Senate, formerly Secretary of War under McKinley and

Secretary of State under Roosevelt, Root, though Roosevelt's friend, was too much of a party regular to follow his ex-chief in what Root believed to be a movement that would destroy the party. According to most commentators, the McGovern nomination was a last-ditch attempt by the Roosevelt people to effect a combination with the La Follette strength at least in organizing the convention.

Convention proceedings rarely make exciting reading, but the drama and excitement in this convention cannot be concealed by print. As speaker after speaker rose to support his choice for temporary chairman, few failed to be interrupted many times by such cries as: "Liar! Liar! Liar!" or "You stole your seat!" The last speaker was a Wisconsin delegate who declared that he was not backing any candidate for temporary chairman, since La Follette refused to enter into any combination or alliance. This statement effectively destroyed any hope on the part of the Roosevelt backers of defeating Root, and the resulting preliminary defeat was decisive. The fight dragged on for days, but there was no longer any doubt of the outcome.

In calling the roll for the election of temporary chairman, Victor Rosewater reverted to a precedent of 1884 and directed that the roll be called by individual name instead of by delegation. Subsequently, he defended his action thus:

I was, and am, convinced that this move saved the situation by its guaranty to every delegate, whose name was on the accredited list, of the right to cast his vote, holding him to responsibility for himself. It doubtless prolonged the balloting but it obviated the interminable squabbles over an unavoidable succession of polling the delegations if the roll were called by states and territories and the chairman of each delegation had announced the vote in bulk, in many cases, as would surely have happened, ignoring the delegates seated in adjudication of the contests and, in fact, making up his own roll for his own state. The inherent difficulties were not wholly removed, however, as was soon seen as the calling of the names proceeded.[4]

[4] Rosewater, *op. cit.*, p. 167.

The roll call was repeatedly interrupted by contestants protesting that individuals called had obtained their seats fradulently, that alternates were incorrectly called, and so on. Delegates allowed to vote in each case were those listed on the roster prepared by the national committee, whether their seats were contested or not. If all delegates whose seats were contested had been denied the right to vote on matters pertaining to organization of the convention, Roosevelt supporters would clearly have been able to control the organization. It is a moot question, however, what the outcome would have been if the "Fair Play" rule to be passed in the 1952 and 1956 Republican conventions had been in effect.[5]

The general level of the proceedings can best be described by such fragments of the repartee as these: "You are raping your own roll," and "You are a pack of thieves, that is what you are." When the roll was finally concluded, the count stood:

Root	558
McGovern	501
Lauder	12
Houser	1
Gronna	1
Not Voting	5

and the pattern of the convention was firmly set.[6]

Greeted with the cry "receiver of stolen goods," Root ascended the rostrum and began his keynote speech: "Ladies and gentlemen of the Convention. Believe that

[5] Under this rule, a contested delegate is allowed voting rights on convention organization only if seated on the temporary roll by two thirds or more of the national committee. The Taft followers had slightly better than a two thirds majority on most of the recorded votes taken by the committee on the credentials questions in 1912, but since only a simple majority was required it can be hypothesized that a few members of the majority may have been lukewarm for Taft or even anti-Taftites who were riding the band wagon. It can certainly be assumed that Roosevelt would have exerted every available pressure upon wavering committee members to build up the necessary one third veto power, and he would have needed only three or four additional votes in the committee to do it if the 1952-1956 rule had been available.

[6] See *Analysis of Key Votes*.

I appreciate this expression of confidence."

Following the keynote speech, temporary officers were elected and temporary rules adopted without incident, but upon motion to establish the committees Governor Hadley returned to the attack with a substitute motion to replace seventy-two delegates on the temporary roll of the convention. Apparently by agreement, he immediately yielded the floor in favor of a motion to adjourn, and the debate was carried over to the next session. Again, by agreement, debate was limited to one and one-half hours for each side, time to be controlled by the respective floor managers. It was moved to table Governor Hadley's motion, following which a substitute to the motion to table was offered as follows:

> I move as an amendment to Representative Watson's motion [to table] that the substitute of Governor Hadley be referred to the Committee on Credentials, and that no delegate whose right to a seat in this Convention is questioned by that motion have a right to vote on the selection of the members of the Committee on Credentials or on the report of the Committee.[7]

Motion was promptly made to table this substitute, and the actual roll call was taken on this motion to table. When the first state was called, Hadley asked if individuals whose seats were challenged were to be allowed to vote. Chairman Root replied: "The Chair will rule upon that question at the conclusion of the roll call." This made it quite clear that the final ruling would recognize the votes of the contested members on the temporary roll as presented by the national committee, since it was highly improbable that Root would have ruled in such a way as to reverse the results of the roll call. Immediately following the roll call, and before the results were announced, Root ruled that contested delegates could not vote on their own case, but could vote on all others—a slight concession, but one that did not affect the results.

Root defended his ruling with a lengthy

statement calling upon the precedents of the House of Representatives rules in similar cases. However, his principal point was that, if contested delegates were not to be allowed to vote at all in connection with the organization of a convention, it would be possible for a minority, by setting up enough contests, to secure control or even to prevent the organization of a convention:

> . . . any minority could secure control of a deliberative body by grouping a sufficient number of the opponents in one motion, and by thus disqualifying them turn the minority into a majority without any decision upon the merits of the motion. . . .

To hold that a member whose seat is contested may take no part in the proceedings of this body would lead to the conclusion that if every seat were contested, as it surely would be if such a rule were adopted, there could be no Convention at all, as nobody would be entitled to participate.[8]

The substitute was tabled by a vote of 567 to 507 with 4 votes not cast.

When, after considerable delay, the committee on credentials was able to report, there followed a long series of debates and roll call votes on various contests. Each was decided in the same way, the Taft delegations winning their seats, and most by about the same margin as the previous two votes. In all, four roll calls were held before the Roosevelt supporters decided that nothing could be gained by demanding further roll calls. The balance of the contests were settled by voice votes, although the debates were continued at length on each contest. From that point on, most of the Roosevelt people stopped voting, although they did not leave the convention. Henry J. Allen, of the Kansas delegation, made the position clear when he said:

> We do not bolt. We merely insist that you, not we, are making the record. And we refuse to be bound by it. We have pleaded with you ten days. We have fought with you five days for a square deal. We fight no more, we plead no longer. We shall sit in protest, and the people who sent us here shall judge us.[9]

[7] RNC, *Proceedings*, 1912, p. 144.

[8] *Ibid.*, p. 160.
[9] *Ibid.*, p. 335.

One aspect of the conflict carried over, however, since the rules committee had met simultaneously with the committee on credentials, and the minority report had already been prepared. The majority report retained approximately the rules as used in the 1908 convention with respect to convention procedure, although it proposed a new set of rules which were, in effect, a constitution for the national committee. The minority report also presented a complete set of rules, the major changes incorporated being: (1) a change in apportionment providing one delegate for each congressional district, plus one additional delegate for every 10,000 votes, or fraction thereof, cast for Republican electors in the previous election; (2) a provision that contested delegates could not vote on any matter pertaining to organization of the convention.

Both reports were tabled by voice vote, and the temporary rules continued in effect. Since the temporary rules were the rules of the 1908 convention, the result was substantially the same as if the majority report had been adopted.

The Platform

The platform contained a long eulogy of the Republican party and its leaders as the party under whose leadership the country had grown great. The party, for instance, believed in government by laws rather than men, laws which guaranteed every citizen full rights "to the freest possible development of his own powers and resources and to the control of his own justly acquired property, so far as those are compatible with the rights of others." The party was "opposed to special privilege and to monopoly" as evidenced by the Antitrust Act of 1890. The party clearly stood for the principle of the protective tariff, and warned that tariff for revenue only "would destroy many industries and throw millions of our people out of employment." Further steps should be taken to prohibit corporations from contributing

directly or indirectly to campaigns involving the presidential ticket or congressmen. The platform closed with an appeal to the electorate for support based upon the record of the last sixteen years under McKinley, Roosevelt, and Taft.

A complete minority platform was presented containing many of the planks proposed by the Wisconsin Progressives in 1908. The minority report was tabled by a voice vote, but the chairman of the committee on resolutions himself requested a roll call on the adoption of the majority report, apparently with the intent of learning what the minority tactics would be before the balloting for candidates. On the roll call, 343 were recorded as present and not voting, and 21 were absent, a voting pattern that persisted for the balance of the convention.

The Presidential Nomination

By this point, the convention really was over, and the selection of candidates anticlimactic. A newcomer to the national political scene, Senator Warren G. Harding of Ohio, nominated President Taft, and seconding speeches duly followed. Generally speaking, the Roosevelt men sat quietly, though when Harding said, ". . . except for the attack of disloyalty in our own ranks, inspired by pap rather than patriotism," there was disorder in the hall, according to the reporter. The only other candidate formally nominated was Robert La Follette. On the single ballot, despite Roosevelt's request that his followers abstain from voting, 107 voted for him, 349 were present but not voting, and 6 were absent. Taft received 556 votes, La Follette 41.

The Vice-Presidential Nomination

Vice President James S. Sherman was renominated by a short speech, and seconded even more briefly. A motion to renominate by acclamation was disregarded by the chairman, and a roll call was taken.

It was no competition; the second candidate received only 21 votes to Sherman's 595, but 352 were present and not voting, and the absentees rose to 72. Sherman thus became the first Vice President to be renominated to succeed himself since the convention system began. His nomination was accompanied by a somber note, however. Apparently in recognition of his physical condition, the convention, without fanfare, passed a resolution providing that the national committee be empowered to fill any vacancies on the ticket—the first such resolution to be passed by a Republican convention.

Sherman died the week before the election, but the committee did not act until after the election, when the entire matter had become academic. Perhaps in acknowledgment of that fact, the committee selected Nicholas Murray Butler of New York, president of Columbia University, to receive the 8 electoral votes for Vice President.

Analysis of Key Votes

As usual in a convention where lines are as clearly drawn and tempers at as high a pitch as in this one, all the roll call votes tend to correlate very high with the nominating ballots. The first roll call vote taken was the crucial one, for it clearly indicated the balance of power. The correlation with the nominating vote was +.91, as only 16 additional votes from the delegations high for Root joined the band-wagon move to Taft, and 13 votes from the low delegations that were recorded for Root refused to vote for Taft.

TWENTY-FIRST DEMOCRATIC CONVENTION

The Democratic gains in the 1910 elections had produced a rise in stature of the Democratic congressional leaders and an abundant crop of Democratic governors. Two congressional veterans, both of whom · first entered the House during Cleveland's

second term, were presidential candidates: Champ Clark of Missouri, who had become Speaker of the House in 1911, and Oscar W. Underwood, who had been minority floor leader for several years of Republican dominance and in 1911 became chairman of the powerful Ways and Means Committee.

The two governors among the major candidates presented backgrounds entirely different from each other. Woodrow Wilson, without previous political experience, was elected governor of New Jersey in 1910 directly from his position as president of Princeton University; Judson Harmon in the same election became governor of Ohio after many years in politics as mayor of a small Ohio town, as a judge, and for two years as United States Attorney General in the latter half of Cleveland's second term. Four other governors hovered in the background as potential favorite sons.

Delegates were being selected through Democratic primaries in several states for the first time, and Clark and Wilson met head-on in certain contests. Where the two met, Clark had the better of it, winning in California, Illinois, Maryland, and Massachusetts, and also in Nebraska where Harmon made it a three-way race. Wilson outran Clark in Oregon, South Dakota, and Wisconsin, and also won in New Jersey and Pennsylvania, where his opponents did not file. Harmon contested only in Nebraska, Ohio, and Maryland, his sole victory being in his home state. Except in Georgia, where he was unopposed, Underwood did not enter the primaries, contenting himself with seeking delegates in states where the convention system still obtained.

Including states where candidates ran unopposed, the delegates elected in the thirteen primaries provided the following first-ballot support to the major candidates: Clark 155; Wilson 178; Harmon 44; Underwood 28. Of Wilson's total, 10 votes came from North Dakota when the favorite son of that state withdrew and transferred his vote to Wilson in the convention.

The ideological orientation of the candidates was somewhat confused. Harmon was quite clearly conservative in outlook and backing, and Underwood, though not extreme in his own views, was backed principally by conservative southerners. Clark had developed a reputation as a progressive and a supporter of William Jennings Bryan, but in this campaign he sought conservative and organization support. Wilson, on the other hand, though once opposed to Bryan and supported in the early part of the campaign by conservatives, turned early in the campaign to an espousal of progressive principles, support of Bryan, and an attack on Wall Street. The preconvention campaign developed into a contest primarily of Wilson against the field, and, indeed, Wilson's supporters charged that the others divided the country between them in order to effect his defeat.

Although not an avowed candidate, William Jennings Bryan was an important factor in the preconvention activities. Despite his three defeats, his following was still large, and it was improbable that a winning coalition could be put together without receiving at least some help from Bryan supporters. He insisted that the nominee must be progressive and uncommitted to the Wall Street interests. Unequivocally opposed to Harmon and Underwood, he reserved judgment on Clark and Wilson, refusing to commit himself on either of them before the convention.

As a member of the Nebraska delegation, Bryan was committed by the primary to vote for Clark on the early ballots. Immediately before the convention met, he sent identical telegrams to Wilson, Clark, and other candidates requesting their support in opposing the selection of Judge Alton B. Parker of New York, the presidential nominee of 1904, as temporary chairman of the convention. He argued that selection of a conservative keynoter would jeopardize prospects for success in the election by characterizing the convention as under reactionary control. Clark hedged in his reply. Only Wilson proffered full support to Bryan's proposal.

Baltimore, Maryland,
June 25, 26, 27, 28, 29; July 1, 2, 1912

The brief convention call provided two delegates for every senator and representative in Congress for the states, and six delegates each for Alaska, the District of Columbia, the Philippines, Hawaii, and Puerto Rico. Provision was included for direct election of delegates in states with primary laws.

Convention Organization

As in the Republican convention of the same year, a dichotomy developed within the convention, although, unlike the Republican situation, the opposing forces were not clearly aligned behind two opposing candidates, and the two thirds rule made a deadlock easy to maintain. As a result the true alignment within the convention was not clearly understood by the general public or by the convention delegates. William Jennings Bryan did understand it, and adopted a strategy to clarify and dramatize the potential split.

As Bryan had foreseen, the conservatives and organization Democrats who controlled the national committee proposed Judge Parker as the temporary chairman. Bryan immediately opposed this by nominating Senator John W. Kern of Indiana, Bryan's running mate in 1908. Kern, apparently without consulting Bryan, did perhaps the one thing best calculated to further Bryan's goal: he rejected the candidacy, but first made a dramatic appeal to Parker to withdraw with him. By refusing to do so, Parker alienated those delegates who desired peace, and this reflected upon the conservative elements with whom Clark was known to be associated and by whom he was backed. When Parker failed to respond affirmatively, Kern nominated Bryan for the temporary chairmanship. Bryan was defeated on a roll call vote 579 to 508, with a few scattered votes for others.[10]

The victory was costly for Clark. Throughout the country, Bryan supporters, Wilson supporters, and others opposed to the conservatives began sending a deluge of telegrams to the delegates. Contemporary reports estimated more than 100,000 telegrams, some signed by many individuals, were received by the participants of the convention before it was over. Since most of these supported the progressive and liberal point of view, and many favored Wilson as the most acceptable exponent, Clark's cause was weakened. This was particularly true since Clark delegations had provided Parker with a large share of his total vote, which pointed to a substantial conservative wing within Clark's following, and identified quite accurately where this conservative strength was concentrated. To drive a wedge between the two elements within the Clark support became Bryan's— and even more importantly, Wilson's— problem. How well they succeeded is indicated by the fact that on the critical ballot for Wilson, the 45th, Wilson received proportionately about twice as much support from delegations that had supported Clark at his peak but had voted for Bryan for temporary chairman, than he did from Clark delegations that had voted for Parker.

The convention recessed after the vote on the temporary chairmanship; Parker ascended the rostrum when the convention reconvened. In his keynote speech, he took an unprecedented step in an attempt to reconcile Bryan: he urged every member of the resolutions committee to vote for Bryan as chairman of the committee. Bryan refused the job. Following Parker's speech, temporary rules were adopted, the customary committees were appointed without further incident, and the convention adjourned.

The convention met at noon the next day. Since no committee was ready to report, time was filled by a series of speeches. In the evening session, the committee on

rules and order of business reported. The rules adopted included "the rules of the last Democratic Convention, including the rules of the House of Representatives of the Sixty-second Congress so far as applicable." The only specific rule stated was a restriction of any speech in debate to thirty minutes, except by unanimous consent. However, the order of business proposed an important departure from the customary order—the platform committee report was placed after the selection of the candidates. In presenting this change, the chairman stated the action was taken at the request of the committee on resolutions, based upon a 41 to 11 vote in the latter committee. The unusual step undoubtedly reflected the reluctance of the committee to commit itself to a platform stand until it was known whether the candidate would be conservative or progressive.

Subsequent to adoption of the main report, a subsidiary report was presented by the majority of the committee:

It shall be the rule of this Convention that all State delegations which have been instructed by their respective State Democratic conventions, or by State Democratic Presidential preference primary, shall follow those instructions, so long as a majority of the delegates from such State are of the opinion that such instructions are applicable.[11]

To this report, a substitute report signed by delegates of nineteen states was offered:

Resolved, That in casting votes on a call of the States, the Chair shall recognize and enforce a unit rule enacted by a State convention, except in such States as have by mandatory statute provided for the nomination and election of delegates and alternates to national political conventions in Congressional districts, and have not subjected delegates so selected to the authority of the State committee or convention of the party, in which case no such rule shall be held to apply.[12]

The question at issue was whether state conventions could bind district delegates elected in local primaries, and was occasioned by a problem in Ohio, where Harmon had defeated Wilson in a statewide preference primary, though Wilson

[10] See Analysis of Key Votes.

[11] DNC, Proceedings, 1912, p. 59.
[12] Ibid., pp. 59-60.

won in several districts. In addition to district delegates, delegates were selected to attend a state convention for electing delegates at large; Harmon won a majority of the delegates to the state convention thus enabling his supporters to instruct the entire state delegation for Harmon. This would have tied the hands of the Wilson district delegates if honored by the convention.

After an extended debate, the Wilson forces won a first victory, when the minority report was accepted 565½ to 492⅓, with 36⅙ votes not cast. As a result, Wilson received 10 votes from Ohio on the first ballot. On the roll call leading to acceptance of the minority report, most delegations split their vote; Wilson supporters voted preponderantly for the minority, Harmon suporters against, Underwood supporters splitting, and Clark supporters tending to oppose. The split in the Underwood vote is significant, since it indicated that his supporters were not tied irrevocably to support of conservatives in conflict with the progressive Wilsonians as might have been suggested by the near-unanimous support of Underwood's committed strength for Parker on the previous roll call. The roll call also again indicated the affinity of many Clark supporters for conservatism.

Following the roll call, the committee on credentials submitted a report, but in view of the late hour and of the fact that a minority report also was to be presented the convention adjourned. The first action at the next session was the reading of the minority report. The question was over a contest for the entire South Dakota delegation, and specifically whether ten Wilson delegates or Clark delegates should be seated. Three tickets had been run in the primaries: a Wilson-Bryan Progressive Democracy; a Wilson-Bryan-Clark Democracy; and a Champ Clark for President.

The first ticket, which was pledged to Wilson, won a plurality but not a majority of the vote. The second ticket, despite the presence of three names in the title, apparently was committed to Clark. Clark supporters charged that the Champ Clark for President ticket, which was filed on the last day for filing, was an attempt by Wilson supporters to split the Clark vote; the use of Wilson's name on the other ticket comprised of individuals committed to Clark did not disturb the latter's friends. According to the minority speaker, the Wilson-Bryan Progressive Democracy ticket was certified to the convention by the proper state authority, but the secretary of the state Democratic party certified the Wilson-Bryan-Clark Democracy delegates on the basis that the combined vote of the latter and the Champ Clark for President ticket constituted a majority vote for delegates committed to Clark. The national committee, in acting on the case, held for the Wilson delegates, but this ruling was reversed by the majority of the committee on credentials. The majority could not have been large, for the minority report was signed by twenty-two names.

The convention reversed the committee on credentials, approving the minority report 639½ to 437, with 17½ not voting. The increased majority in favor of Wilson over the previous roll call attests the relative merit of his side of the case; even the anti-Wilson ninety-man delegation from New York voted for the minority report. After the roll call, the balance of the majority report was accepted by voice vote, except for a refusal to seat the Philippine Islands delegation on the grounds that a Supreme Court decision had established the Philippines as a territorial appendage and not a part of the United States.

The next order of business was the report of the committee on permanent organization, which was adopted without debate. Congressman Ollie James of Kentucky, who had been Clark's original choice for temporary chairman, was selected as the permanent chairman.

The Presidential Nomination

After James' acceptance speech, the convention recessed until the evening, at which time the scheduled order of business was to be the nomination of presidential candidates. This prospect proved to be illusory, however, for William Jennings Bryan threw a bombshell into the mechanism. On the grounds that he had a resolution "which I think ought to be acted upon before we begin the nominations," Bryan requested and received unanimous approval to present it. As originally presented the resolution read as follows:

> Resolved, That in this crisis in our party's career and in our country's history this convention sends greeting to the people of the United States, and assures them that the party of Jefferson and of Jackson is still the champion of popular government and equality before the law. As proof of our fidelity to the people, we hereby declare ourselves opposed to the nomination of any candidate for president who is the representative of or under obligation to J. Pierpont Morgan, Thomas F. Ryan, August Belmont, or any other member of the privilege-hunting and favor-seeking class.
> Be it further resolved, That we demand the withdrawal from this convention of any delegate or delegates constituting or representing the above-named interests.[13]

The wording of the first clause of the resolution made it difficult for most of the delegates to reject it, and Bryan withdrew the second clause when he saw that it might jeopardize passage of the first, since the opponents charged it violated state sovereignty. The resolution was then passed easily, 883 to 201½, with 3½ not voting. Once again, Bryan had dramatized the issue between the conservative and progressive elements.

Four major candidates (Underwood, Clark, Wilson, and Harmon) and two favorite sons (Governor Simeon E. Baldwin of Connecticut and Governor Thomas R. Marshall of Indiana) received nominating and seconding speeches. One other favorite son, Governor John Burke of North Dakota, submitted a letter releasing the delegates pledged to him, and the chairman of the North Dakota delegation announced for Wilson.

Balloting began immediately, with Clark out in front as predicted. With 1,088

[13] Ibid., p. 129.

votes in the convention, 726 votes were required for nomination under the two thirds rule. Clark had 440½, Wilson 324, Harmon 148, and Underwood 117½, with the balance scattered. With only 60 votes held by candidates other than the four leaders, no combination except the Clark-Wilson combination could reach a two thirds majority without including substantially all the votes from at least three of the major candidates. Any candidate or coalition with 363 or more votes firmly committed could deadlock the convention.

Clark had veto strength without combining with others, but Wilson needed (1) help from either Harmon or Underwood, or (2) substantially all of the scattered votes in order to exercise a veto. Harmon or Underwood could develop a veto situation only by combining with Wilson, since Clark did not need them, and their combined vote plus the scattered votes was less than one third of the convention. The convention was stalemated because Underwood and Wilson kept their forces intact, and the relatively early movement of Harmon delegates to Clark proved useless to the latter.

The regional characteristics of the support for the four major candidates were demonstrated on the first-ballot vote. From the Northeast, Wilson received a little over one third of the vote, Clark and Harmon each a little less than 30 per cent, with Underwood running a very poor fourth. In the South, Wilson and Underwood shared three quarters of the vote, most of the balance going to Clark, with Harmon receiving only a token vote; much of Clark's southern vote came from the border areas. The Middle West went over 50 per cent for Clark, 25 per cent for Wilson, and less than 15 per cent for Harmon despite his home base in Ohio. The West, though its vote was relatively small in total, was almost all Clark—85 per cent compared to Wilson's 15 per cent; Harmon received only one half vote from the section, and Underwood none.

For nine ballots, the vote of each of the four leaders remained remarkably steady, Clark gaining a scant dozen votes, Wilson less than 20, and Underwood 5. Harmon dropped to 127, and the scattered votes diminished. On the 10th ballot New York shifted its entire 90 votes from Harmon to Clark in a dramatic effort by Tammany Hall to start a band-wagon movement.

At this point, according to contemporary commentators, the Clark leaders made what may have been a disastrous mistake: they allowed a long demonstration to be staged by Clark delegates, who scented early victory. Thus Wilson and Underwood leaders had time to contact their delegates and to rally them for a firm stand. Had the 11th ballot been taken quickly, many delegates might have succumbed to the urge to get on the Clark band wagon, an urge always present in political conventions. It was quite obvious that the permanent chairman, Ollie James, thought the end was in sight when New York shifted from Harmon, for he announced the vote in what was, to say the least, a leading manner:

No candidate having received two-thirds of the votes cast, no nomination is made. Mr. Clark having received 11 more than a majority, is not the nominee until he receives two-thirds.[14]

James was quickly called to account by Congressman A. Mitchell Palmer, a Wilson floor leader, who raised the parliamentary inquiry as to the purpose of the chair in gratuitously announcing that one candidate had received a majority. The Wilson and Underwood lines not only held on the 11th ballot, but actually gained slightly, and Clark began a slow but steady decline. Even at his peak strength, however, Clark could not have accumulated the balance of the required two thirds majority without the votes of all candidates other than Wilson, or some part of the Wilson vote.

On the 10th ballot, Wilson's 350½ votes

14 *Ibid.*, p. 221.

plus Marshall's 30 from Indiana were enough to maintain the deadlock if all could be held—a not too remote probability, since most of Wilson's delegates had been with him from the beginning, had won their seats against bitter opposition of Clark supporters, and Marshall's well-controlled Indiana group could be depended upon. This may have been a determining factor in the decision of the Underwood leaders to maintain the fight. To have released his delegates might have resulted in loss of bargaining power without breaking the deadlock, particularly since some of the Underwood delegates would almost certainly have moved to Wilson, thus offsetting possible band-wagon losses elsewhere in Wilson's ranks.

In the course of the 14th ballot, Bryan played another card. During the polling of the Nebraska delegation, he asked for unanimous consent to explain his vote. Only through a magnanimous gesture of the Clark leader from Missouri was consent given him, but he was permitted to speak. The substance of his long explanation was that so long as the Tammany-controlled New York delegation voted for a candidate, as they were now doing for Clark, he, Bryan, would not vote for that candidate. He was followed by most of the Nebraska delegation in shifting his vote from Clark to Wilson.

The vote on this ballot was not otherwise significantly affected, however, and only minor changes occurred until Kansas swung 20 votes from Clark to Wilson on the 20th ballot. At this stage, Clark had 512, Wilson 388½, and Underwood 121½; from this point on, Wilson's vote exceeded the critical one third of the total convention. As the roll calls continued, Clark continued to lose steadily, if slowly, as Wilson gained. On the 28th ballot the Indiana delegation left its favorite son, Marshall, for Wilson. Wilson passed Clark on the 30th ballot, but it was not until after the 42nd that Clark dropped below one third.

Following the 42nd ballot, a motion to adjourn was passed 791½ to 296½. The motion had been proposed and seconded by Clark delegates, and was opposed by A. Mitchell Palmer, who, after failing in his efforts to have the motion postponed until two additional ballots should be taken, demanded a roll call. The motion for adjournment was undoubtedly intended to permit the anti-Wilson forces to gain time, but the vote was highly confused on both sides of the fight. Some Wilson delegates voted against it, but many did not. The hour was late, and it had been a long, hard day.

After the convention reconvened the next day, Wilson passed the majority mark, primarily due to the shift of 58 votes from Illinois—a shift engineered by the Chicago boss, Roger Sullivan. The Wilson trend continued. On the 44th ballot Underwood's total was 99, Wilson's 629—and for the first time Underwood could be said to be in the position to effect the nomination by releasing his vote to a major candidate. On the 46th and final ballot, when Alabama was called, Underwood's name was withdrawn and his delegates were released to vote as they wished.

The chairman of the Missouri delegation then released all Clark votes except those of Missouri, saying "So far as the Missouri delegation is concerned, under the peculiar circumstances that have surrounded this Convention and its proceedings, we shall vote for Speaker Clark until the last ballot is cast." He went on to assure the convention that Clark and his friends would support the ticket.

Other assurance of loyalty to Wilson followed, but 84 votes stayed with Champ Clark and 12 with Harmon even on the final ballot. The Missouri chairman was recognized after the ballot for a motion to make the nomination unanimous, following which the convention recessed to give time for a little thought to the question of the second part of the ticket.

The Platform

A few of the vice-presidential speeches had been made before the resolutions committee gave its report. The platform was a long document covering most of the major problems of the day. Much of it was reminiscent of the La Follette minority report to the Republican platform of 1908, as well as of Democratic platforms during the Bryan period. Trusts were assailed, and regulation of railroads was urged, including establishment of a uniform rate system based upon physical valuation. The national income tax proposal and the proposal for direct election of senators were hailed. Presidential primaries were advocated, and the party pledged itself to enactment of laws prohibiting corporations from contributing to campaign funds. A single six-year term for the president was favored. In general, it was a progressive platform, but not very different from preceding Democratic platforms.

The Vice-Presidential Nomination

The withdrawal of Underwood's name from the presidential balloting had been accompanied by the request that he not be considered for the Vice Presidency. The first vice-presidential nominating speech was made for Champ Clark, whose name was speedily withdrawn—with further protestations of support for the ticket. Governor John Burke of North Dakota was then presented, followed by several others, the speeches at one point being interrupted by the report of the committee on resolutions.

Nine candidates received votes on the first roll call. Thomas R. Marshall, whose Indiana delegation had played an important role during the presidential balloting, led with 389; John Burke was in second place with 304⅔, followed by Senator George E. Chamberlain of Oregon.

As a political regular, Marshall was undoubtedly the best offset to Wilson, a political newcomer. He also had the advantage of coming from a larger state than either of his two chief rivals. In any case, following the second ballot, when his vote climbed to 644½, a New Jersey delegate gave him Wilson's sign of approval by moving to make his nomination unanimous. The motion was seconded quickly by North Dakota and Oregon. Following the usual resolutions of thanks, the convention adjourned.

Analysis of Key Votes

The correlations between the Bryan-Parker vote for temporary chairman and the first nominating ballot clearly reveal the basic division in the convention. Wilson's first-ballot vote correlates −.74, indicating strong opposition on the part of his followers to Parker. Correlations for all the other candidates, including the combined minor candidates, are positive. The correlation coefficients are: Clark .07; Harmon .79; Underwood .90; other .99.

The important feature in this array is the Clark coefficient which, though positive, is not significant. Clark people, in other words, were about evenly divided on this vote, indicating a basic split among his followers between a liberal pro-Bryan and a conservative pro-Parker stand. It was probably to dramatize this split that Bryan made the fight in the first place, and each of his subsequent moves was directed at driving a wedge between the two groups of Clark supporters.

Bryan's (and Wilson's) success in these maneuvers is illustrated by examination of the 45th, or critical, ballot. Despite receiving 90 votes from New York that had been cast for Harmon on the first ballot, Clark lost 135 votes, almost all to Wilson. His total loss to Wilson, added to Wilson's first-ballot vote, put the latter over the 50 per cent mark, thus encouraging others to join the band wagon. The correlation be-

tween Parker's vote and Clark's 45th ballot vote was +.53, indicating that a major part of those who stayed with Clark had voted for Parker. By the same token, most of those who switched from Clark to Wilson voted for Bryan on the roll call for temporary chairman.

*   *   *

At the close of the Republican convention Theodore Roosevelt announced the formation of the Progressive (Bull Moose) party, and stated that its convention would be soon held. It was clearly understood that Roosevelt would be the nominee, and during the period before the convention met he acted in every respect as if he were already nominated.

The convention met in Chicago from August 5 to 7, with Senator Joseph M. Dixon of Montana presiding over the opening. Senator Albert J. Beveridge of Indiana was elected chairman and officiated throughout the meeting. All states except South Carolina were represented, but no territories. Women predominated in numbers among the delegates; veteran political reporters complained that few familiar faces were to be seen in the delegations—that this was a gathering of amateurs.

No roll call votes were taken, and to outward appearance complete harmony prevailed. Actually an undercurrent of protest existed—widely publicized in the press—which stemmed from Roosevelt's insistence that no southern Negro delegates be accepted: northern Negroes were welcome, but southern delegations must be made up of white men. He explained his position on the grounds of being opposed to the rotten boroughs of the South, and he described southern Negro delegates as uneducated and purchasable. During the convention it was obvious that the northern Negroes sided vehemently with their non-present southern brothers. They did not carry the fight to the convention floor, but their lack of enthusiasm for Roosevelt's nomination was noticeable.

Nominating speeches for Roosevelt and for Governor Hiram W. Johnson of California as his running mate were made while the platform committee was deliberating. Jane Addams, founder of Chicago's Hull House, was a seconder of the Roosevelt nomination—the first woman in this role in a major national convention.

The platform—termed "A Contract with the People"—made demands for tariff revision; stricter regulation of industrial combinations; national primaries for presidential candidates; the initiative, referendum, and recall; woman suffrage; prohibition of child labor; and minimum wage standards for working women.

Platform and nominees were accepted by acclamation and with great enthusiasm. The split within the Republican party thus became formal and complete.

Presidential Election, November 5, 1912

WOODROW WILSON (D) : popular vote, 6,286,214; electoral vote, 435
THEODORE ROOSEVELT (P) : popular vote, 4,126,020; electoral vote, 88
WILLIAM HOWARD TAFT (R) : popular vote, 3,483,922; electoral vote, 8

1916

DESPITE HIS SHORT political career, Woodrow Wilson had quickly assumed leadership of the party. Even Bryan became clearly subordinate, despite what may have been his early ambitions to act as a prime minister from his position of Secretary of State. By sheer force of leadership, Wilson coerced a sometimes reluctant Congress into carrying out the platform pledges. Only his own refusal to accept renomination could have prevented it from coming about—and he did not refuse.

During the year 1916, United States public opinion was gradually drawing toward acceptance of the probability of war against Germany, but few were ready to accept it. Accordingly, Democratic assertions that Wilson had kept the nation out of war, despite the fact that the neutrality was somewhat one-sided and strained, fell on responsive ears—perhaps the more responsive because their owners instinctively felt that things were too good to last.

Certainly the public mood would not allow the Republicans to make an outright demand for a war policy. Therefore they were unable to establish a clearly differentiated party policy on this, the dominant issue of the day.

SIXTEENTH REPUBLICAN CONVENTION

The Republicans had many problems. The schism of 1912 had committed nearly all the party leaders on one side or the other of the split, and many of the Progressives were still operating outside the Republican party. Wilson's victory in 1912 clearly demonstrated that Republican chances of victory were slim unless substantial elements of the bolting faction could be brought back into the main party; the problem was how to do it.

The Progressives could not be expected to join in support of a candidate who had been deeply involved in the 1912 Taft "steamroller." This eliminated such candidates as Elihu Root, convention chairman in 1912, Henry Cabot Lodge, and many more. On the other hand, the regular party members could not be expected to support with enthusiasm anyone who had bolted, which eliminated Theodore Roosevelt, Hiram W. Johnson, his running mate, and others. The needed compromise was a candidate who had remained in the regular Republican party, but who had not been seriously involved in the 1912 fight. Tempers being what they were in that year, about the only way a public figure could escape involvement was by being out of the country (as James Buchanan was in the hectic years preceding his nomination in 1856) or by holding an office that legitimately entitled him to avoid political commitment. In the American scheme of government, one office above all others fulfills the latter requirement: a Supreme Court justiceship. In 1916, the most eligible member of the Court was Charles Evans Hughes.

Before his appointment as a justice in 1910, Hughes had made a good record as a reform governor of New York. His reputation for integrity and intelligence was as high as that of any man in the nation. He was widely known among the general public, and fully acceptable as a man of presidential stature. However, his record of independence from the regular party organization during his tenure as governor of New York made him suspect to organization leaders. They would have preferred a candidate who had demonstrated greater willingness to cooperate, especially in patronage matters. Furthermore, the Progressive leader, Roosevelt, did not particularly like Hughes, whom he called "a Wilson in long whiskers."

Hughes considered it inappropriate for a member of the Supreme Court to be involved in a political battle, and therefore had adamantly refused, whenever his permission was required, to allow his name to be used in the primaries, although he could not prevent its use in Oregon. He did not refuse to accept the nomination if it should be tendered; he simply refused to run actively for it. As a result, the primaries and state conventions had produced a host of favorite sons, none very strong and none willing to cooperate with the others.

Regular organization leaders in the states were interested primarily in making sure that delegates to the convention were anti-Roosevelt; other than that, it made little difference whom they preferred. In obtaining the desired result, the party leaders produced a coalition whose strength was based on the negative principle of stopping a Roosevelt nomination. They ended up with no positive principle, and with no outstanding name about whom all could coalesce to stop Hughes. The wide distribution of strength just before the convention opened was indicated in a tabulation given by the *New York Times* on June 7, 1916, which reported committed strength as follows:

Hughes	224
Roosevelt	60
Root	82
Fairbanks	65
Weeks	54
Burton	70
Cummins	89
Others	339

Many of the bolting Progressives of 1912 had not yet returned to the parent party, either through their own choice or because the regular organizations had not permitted them to participate in the delegation selection process. A substantial number of these held a convention of their own in Chicago at the same time the regular Republican convention was meeting there. Although all had joined wholeheartedly with Roosevelt in 1912, by 1916 there were many shades of opinion as to what the future of the Progressive movement should be. Undoubtedly, some members genuinely hoped to keep the party alive; others hoped to strike a bargain with the regular organization, perhaps even to persuade the latter to accept Theodore Roosevelt once more as a candidate. Another group, and the one that prevailed, saw little hope for the Progressives, and were ready to return to the fold under almost any conditions. From the way things worked out, it appears that Roosevelt saw the logic of the latter position, whether he liked it or not. In any event, when the crucial moment came, he pursued a course most likely to destroy what remained of the Progressive party, leaving its members no place to go except into one or the other of the major parties.

Chicago, Illinois,
June 7, 8, 9, 10, 1916

Because Taft's victory in the convention of 1912 was so clearly based upon administration control of the southern delegations and the resulting furor was so widespread, the national committee took unprecedented action before issuing the call for the 1916 convention. A drastic new apportionment scheme was submitted to the state parties for ratification. This provided four delegates at large for each state, and two delegates for each representative at large in Congress; one delegate from each congressional district; and an additional delegate from each congressional district in which the vote for the Republican nominee for Congress in 1914, or for a Republican elector in 1908, was not less than 7,500.

The proposal was ratified by the requisite majority of state parties, and reduced the strength of the southern delegations considerably. For example, Alabama, which had twenty-eight delegates in 1912, received only sixteen in 1916; Georgia fell from twenty-four to seventeen, Texas from forty to twenty-six. In total, the eleven states of the former Confederacy lost 78 votes, more than one third of their 1912 strength.

Convention Organization

The first official act of the convention was the election of the temporary chairman, Senator Warren G. Harding of Ohio. Election of other temporary officers, and appointment of the committees followed without incident, and the convention adjourned until the following day, at which time the report of the credentials committee was accepted unanimously. Several contests involving southern delegations were acted upon, and the report stipulated that none of the three sets of contesting delegates from the District of Columbia be seated. By special resolution, full voting rights were given two delegates each from the territory of Hawaii, the Philippine Islands, and Puerto Rico.

The report of the committee on rules and order of business was accepted. In addition to confirming the change in apportionment given in the call, the rules empowered the national committee "to declare vacant the seat of any member who refuses to support the nominees of the Convention . . . and to fill such vacancies." This rule was obviously a further result of the storm of 1912.

The Platform

The platform accused the Democratic administration of failure to protect American rights at home and abroad, and pledged that a Republican administration would "unflinchingly maintain" these rights. Although it advocated "pacific

settlement of international disputes" and strict neutrality toward the belligerents in the European war, it was careful to add, "we must perform all our duties and insist upon all our rights as neutrals without fear and without favor." The regular army and navy and the reserves must be built up to ensure adequate defense of the nation.

The historic party stand for a protective tariff was reiterated, and creation of a tariff commission empowered to "gather and compile information for the use of Congress" advocated. Regulation of corporations and railroads was supported in principle, but the policies of the Democratic administration in this regard, it charged, "are within the sphere of private enterprise and in direct competition with its own citizens." Other planks insisted upon elimination of waste, development of the merchant marine aided by "liberal compensation for services actually rendered in carrying the mails," and extension of the Civil Service to cover more government workers.

As in most Republican conventions during the period, the Wisconsin delegation proposed a minority report as a substitute for the majority platform. Among other provisions, the report demanded a referendum before the declaration of war against any foreign power, denounced "Dollar Diplomacy," advocated women's suffrage, and recommended constitutional amendments providing for initiative, referendum, and recall. The speaker was interrupted frequently while reading the platform and during his short speech. The chairman of the platform committee refused to debate the issues, confining himself to the statement that the minority report was signed by only one member of the committee. The minority report was rejected and the majority accepted by voice vote.

The Presidential Nomination

Following adoption of the platform, a communication from the Progressive convention was read. This incorporated a resolution providing for a joint committee of the two conventions to consult upon future actions. The resolution was approved by voice vote, and Senator Reed Smoot of Utah, ex-Senator Murray Crane of Massachusetts, Senator William E. Borah of Idaho, Nicholas Murray Butler of New York, and ex-Congressman A. R. Johnson were appointed to the committee. Before adjournment, to permit the committee to meet, the members of the national committee were elected. Contests appeared in the Tennessee and Kentucky delegations, both of which were referred to the national committee for disposal.

The joint committee reported that, although representatives of both conventions believed the future welfare of the country to depend upon defeat of the Democratic incumbent, the Progressive members were adamant in believing Theodore Roosevelt to be the only desirable candidate. Chairman Harding authorized the committee to continue its conferences in the hope that a compromise might be reached. While the committee went about its labors, the convention proceeded to nominate candidates for the Presidency. Chairman Harding introduced a new procedure in connection with seconding speeches by announcing, on his own initiative, that no seconding speeches would be made until the full roll had been called for nominations.

Nominating speeches were made for Charles E. Hughes, Elihu Root, Senator John W. Weeks of Massachusetts, as well as for several favorite sons. The nomination of Theodore Roosevelt by Senator Albert B. Fall of New Mexico aroused the convention, and the speaker was alternately interrupted by hisses, catcalls, and applause. A forty-minute demonstration followed the speech—with more members in the gallery than delegates as participants if the official account of the proceedings can be accepted.

The preconvention estimate given by the *New York Times* proved a remarkably accurate prediction of the first-ballot re-

sults. Hughes led with 253½ votes, with none of the others near him; Weeks had 105 and Root 103, and most of the balance was spread evenly among five other candidates—among them, Roosevelt with 65 votes—receiving between 65 and 85 votes each. Nine others received at least 1 vote. A second ballot followed immediately. Hughes gained substantially, to 328½, but no other candidate exceeded 100; sixteen candidates, among them Warren G. Harding with 1 vote, received mention. As soon as the totals were announced, Senator Boies Penrose of Pennsylvania moved an adjournment until the next morning. A roll call was demanded by a Hughes delegate, but the motion passed 694½ to 286½, with six not voting.[1] The motion was recognized as a move by leaders of the "Old Guard" to gain time in the hope that agreement could be reached on a candidate other than Hughes.

According to all reports, there was a great deal of activity during the recess. The committee continued in its attempt to reach an agreement with the Progressives, but without success; favorite sons negotiated for each other's support, also without success. The regular convention members of the joint committee proposed Hughes as the compromise candidate to the Progressives, who agreed publicly to present his name to the Progressive convention—while privately stating that it would be unacceptable: it had to be Roosevelt or someone to whom Roosevelt agreed. Roosevelt refused to accept Hughes until his stand had been made clear on the issues of the day; Hughes refused to make his stand clear while he was a member of the Supreme Court, from which he would not resign until nominated. Here, so far, was a clear impasse.

Following the joint conference, the Progressive convention received a long communique from Roosevelt, in which, after a fervent avowal of his desire to see the two segments of the party rejoined, he recom-

[1] See *Analysis of Key Votes.*

mended Henry Cabot Lodge as the nominee of the Progressive convention.

Despite the long friendship between the two men, Roosevelt could scarcely have expected that Lodge, one of the arch-conservatives of the Senate, would be accepted as standard-bearer by the Progressives. Both conventions were temporarily taken aback; then each reacted in a different way. The Progressives broke away from their convention leaders who had been trying to find a compromise, and nominated Roosevelt by acclamation tinged with anger, thus placing the burden of determining the party's future squarely upon Roosevelt's shoulders. Roosevelt answered with an immediate statement that he would decline the nomination if Hughes could satisfy him on policy. A few weeks later, after conference with Hughes, he withdrew finally, and the Progressive party disintegrated.

In the meantime, the leaders in the regular convention—having already proposed Hughes to the Progressives as the compromise choice, and with none of the favorite son candidates able to form a winning coalition—found themselves with no acceptable alternative to Hughes. On the morning of the final day, after Roosevelt's letter recommending Lodge had been read, most of the favorite sons withdrew and the Roosevelt floor leader announced for Hughes. On the third roll call, Hughes received 949½ of the 987 votes in the convention, and his nomination was then declared unanimous.

Political commentators of the period advanced the theory that this was the result Roosevelt intended when he suggested Lodge as the candidate. Throughout the early part of the convention, Roosevelt apparently maintained a real hope that he might become the joint nominee of the conventions, but he had little taste for another three-way race with even less chance of victory than in 1912. Although he had little liking for Hughes, for reasons similar to those of the general mass of delegates in the regular convention, he found him less objectionable than the other candidates. However, part of his strategy, when he was still hopeful of winning, had been the statement that he could not accept Hughes until the latter clarified his views on basic issues; it was not very easy to withdraw the statement gracefully. The commentators theorize, therefore, that by proposing a candidate who was certain to be refused, Roosevelt tacitly approved the nomination of Hughes without actually saying so. The action of the Roosevelt floor leader further substantiates this theory.

The Vice-Presidential Nomination

The ticket was balanced with an organization regular from the Midwest—Charles W. Fairbanks of Indiana. Fairbanks, who had been Vice President under Roosevelt in the latter's second administration, won easily. He received 863 votes to his nearest competitor's 108.

Analysis of Key Votes

The decision to adjourn after the second ballot appears to have been supported mostly by delegations that had not yet decided to vote for Hughes and wished time to negotiate further, for more than twice as many second-ballot Hughes votes were supplied by delegations low on the issue than by delegations high on the issue, and the correlation between the adjournment vote and Hughes second ballot is +.58.

TWENTY-SECOND DEMOCRATIC CONVENTION

As Woodrow Wilson's first term neared its end, his position in the Democratic party and the nation was so strong that few cared or dared to oppose his renomination, despite the fact that the 1912 Democratic platform had included a plank advocating one term for the Presidency—a plank in which Wilson concurred. This did not mean that party members uniformly agreed with Wilson's policies, at home or abroad, but his general popularity was too great to be openly opposed. He was unopposed in the primaries, and received over 98 per cent of the total vote cast; a few scattered votes were cast for unpledged delegations. The Democrats had a strong leader.

There might have been some question about Vice President Thomas R. Marshall's renomination, for it was commonly known that he and Wilson did not always see eye to eye. But eventually Wilson gave him the accolade, and the ticket was kept intact.

St. Louis, Missouri, June 14, 15, 16, 1916

By the time the convention opened there was almost nothing for the delegates to decide. Not only were both positions on the ticket set, but it was certain the platform would be dictated by Wilson. Such conventions have been comparatively rare; when they do happen, they pose a twofold major problem for the convention managers: how to keep the delegates happy and enthusiastic, and how to create interest for the general public. To these ends, the managers generally introduce a flood of speakers, each of whom tries to catch the fancy of the delegates and arouse them from their torpor. They seldom succeed.

One speaker in 1916 did succeed beyond all expectations, although apparently only because he was sufficiently sensitive to crowd reactions to recognize an opportunity when he saw it. The speaker was Martin H. Glynn of New York, the temporary chairman, and the occasion came during his keynote speech. Basically, the speech was the standard recital of the glories of America and of the Democratic party.

However, in discussing the policy of neutrality advocated by the administration and the party, Glynn used the orator's trick of rhythmic repetition in naming Grant, Harrison, Lincoln, Pierce, Van Buren, Adams, Washington, Jefferson, and Cleveland, describing in each case an international problem which might have ended in war, and after each recital announcing dramatically: "But we didn't go to War!" By the time he was halfway through the list, the audience was happily anticipating each finale with the shout, "What did he do?" At each answer, the delegates cheered. Unfortunately for his reputation as an orator, Glynn made the mistake of continuing at length after this high point, which occurred in the middle of a very long speech, but the phrase "He kept us out of War," a more applicable translation of "But we didn't go to War," emerged from the convention as the major campaign slogan.

Convention Organization

After this moment of excitement, the convention proceeded with its business. Committees were appointed, and the reports, except that of the platform committee, were accepted with apparent unanimity. Senator Ollie M. James of Kentucky was elected permanent chairman.

The Presidential Nomination

Only one name was put in nomination for President—Woodrow Wilson. A motion to nominate by acclamation was opposed by only one delegate; Wilson was declared the nominee without a roll call by 1,092 to 1.

The Vice-Presidential Nomination

Vice President Marshall was renominated by acclamation, after one of the briefest nominating speeches on record.

The Platform

Following a recess, the platform was presented. An attempt was made by the committee chairman to move the previous question, thus limiting debate, but this was objected to by an excited delegate who wished to submit a plank favoring Irish independence. The proposed plank was read from the floor and referred, under the rules, to the platform committee. No action was taken. A minority report, submitted somewhat belatedly, offered a substitute to the plank favoring women's suffrage. The majority plank read:

We recommend the extension of the franchise to the women of the country by the States upon the same terms as to men.[2]

The minority substitute was a reminder of the traditional party policy.

[2] DNC, *Proceedings,* 1916, p. 128.

The Democratic party has always stood for the sovereignty of the several States in the control and regulation of elections. We reaffirm the historic position of our party in this regard, and favor continuance of that wise provision of the Federal Constitution which vests in the several States of the Union the power to prescribe the qualifications of their electors.[3]

A lengthy debate ensued, after which the minority plank was defeated 888½ to 181½, 22 votes not cast. The southern states supported the minority plank in higher proportion than other regions, but they were by no means unanimous. The platform was then accepted by voice vote, no opposition being recorded, and the convention adjourned.

[3] *Ibid.,* p. 134.

Presidential Election, November 7, 1916

WOODROW WILSON (D) : popular vote, 9,129,606; electoral vote, 277
CHARLES EVANS HUGHES (R) : popular vote, 8,538,221; electoral vote, 254

1920

THE DEMOCRATIC PARTY retained the Presidency in 1916, but the margin was close, and in 1918 control of Congress was lost. The Republican congressional majority provided the Republicans an opportunity to embarrass Wilson during the postwar adjustment period—an opportunity seized with relish. A bitter struggle developed between a group of Republican senators and the President on the question of United States participation in the League of Nations, and the struggle was made the more bitter by the personal antagonism between Senator Henry Cabot Lodge and Woodrow Wilson.

Wilson attempted to take his case to the country, and in that era before radio and television networks, this required a strenuous trip by rail, punctuated by frequent speaking engagements. Late in 1919, while on such a trip, Wilson suffered a stroke from which he never fully recovered, and which made it improbable he would be available for a third term even if it were offered. Nevertheless, Wilson did not rule himself out. He consistently refused to commit himself in any way on the nomination, and potential candidates were seriously handicapped in their attempts to conduct prenomination campaigns. Furthermore, opponents of Wilson and Wilsonian policies within the party, and there were many of these, were unable to speak freely without appearing to discredit their own party administration.

A new factor appeared in the conventions of 1920 for the first time on a significant scale. By the time the Republican convention opened, only one additional state ratification of the pending women's suffrage amendment was needed to ensure national participation of women as voters in the forthcoming election. Consequently, many delegations included women. Almost all of the western and midwestern delegations did, and about half of the southern. Very few women appeared in the northeastern delegations, however, except for New York's, although most of the states of the section had ratified the amendment.

SEVENTEENTH REPUBLICAN CONVENTION

Charles Evans Hughes, the near-victor of 1916 had definitely excluded himself from the 1920 race, and had little inclination to concern himself with party affairs. Theodore Roosevelt, who might once more have been a strong contender, had died in January 1919. No one else stood out in the party, and the field was wide open. Three candidates made extensive preconvention campaigns: Major General Leonard Wood of New Hampshire, Governor Frank Lowden of Illinois, and Senator Hiram Johnson of California.

General Wood was the front-runner. As a close friend and associate of Theodore Roosevelt, he had considerable appeal to many of Roosevelt's followers, and his long public career had made his name well known to the rank and file of delegates. He had also recently acquired a politically useful martyr's role: Wilson's refusal to permit him to accompany his division to France for active duty in the field had been widely publicized as a spiteful act designed to prevent Wood from increasing his stature as a potential presidential candidate. The Wood campaign was well financed—so well, in fact, as to become a later source of embarrassment. Preconvention reports of the day tended to agree that Wood was the popular choice.

Early in the campaign, however, he made a serious mistake, when he replaced his first campaign manager, John T. King, with William Cooper Procter. King, national committeeman from Connecticut, was an organization regular closely associated with Boies Penrose, political boss of Pennsylvania. He had attempted to build support for Wood among the regular organization leaders throughout the country, but soon ran into conflict with the amateur leaders of the Wood movement. When a choice had to be made, Wood released King and turned his management over to Procter.

Procter, though an eminently successful businessman and lavish in his contributions to the campaign, was politically inexperienced. It is doubtful that Wood, after releasing King, could have hoped for much support from regular organizations, but Procter made matters even worse when he attempted to displace some regular state organizations with Wood organizations. This, coupled with Wood's reputation for independence, made it certain that he would be the prime target for the organizational leaders. Boies Penrose is reported to have said: "We fellows here in the East aren't going to make the same mistake we made in 1900. We're going to put in a man who will listen."

Lacking a public figure of sufficient stature about whom to rally their forces, the organization leaders and the conservative wing apparently employed various strategies. In some cases, favorite sons were presented, among them, Warren G. Harding of Ohio and Calvin Coolidge of Massachusetts. In others, uninstructed delegations were selected, with care taken to include as many anti-Wood people as possible. As a third strategy, considerable support was given to Lowden, and it appeared for a while that he might receive the nomination—not so much because he was the real choice of the organization

people as because he was considered by them definitely superior to Wood, who must be stopped at all costs.

Lowden had several assets. He could finance his own campaign, and indeed had done so during the preconvention period. His record as governor of Illinois was a sound one. He had a background in both farming and business, made an excellent appearance, and had few political enemies outside his own state. His liabilities were outstanding too. His connection by marriage with the Pullman family made him suspect to many. He had been unable to win a single delegate against either Johnson or Wood in primaries outside his own state, and due to the opposition of Mayor William ("Big Bill") Thompson of Chicago, he won only part of the Illinois delegation. From the standpoint of the regular organization people, his wealth, for all its advantages, permitted him a degree of independence that could make him hard to control. Accordingly, although he entered the convention with nearly as many votes as Wood, a good number of them were loosely attached and could move easily to someone more favored by the organization leaders. He was a serious candidate in his own right, but he was also used as a stalking-horse.

Hiram Johnson had long been a national figure, and a controversial one. His record as a Progressive and particularly his bolt to become Roosevelt's running mate in the ill-starred "Bull Moose" campaign in 1912 did not endear him to the regulars. Of all the candidates, Johnson alone took a firm stand on the League of Nations: he unequivocally opposed it. This extreme stand assured him a core of loyal supporters, but made him an unlikely second choice for followers of other candidates. His attacks on Wood and Lowden regarding campaign funds killed any remaining possibility of getting second-choice support in those quarters.

Behind these three loomed several minor hopefuls, none of whom had more than nominal pledged strength. Three were to become better known: Warren G. Harding, Calvin Coolidge, and Herbert Hoover.

Stories are rife that Harding was the first choice of the organization leaders, but that they feared to put him forward too early. As early as December 1919, Henry Stimson, former Secretary of War, had warned Wood that Harding's candidacy was dangerous and was aimed at defeating Wood, and too many predictions of Harding's possible nomination can be found in periodicals of the early preconvention period to permit this theory to be disregarded. However, Harding's poor record in the primaries, even in Ohio where he received only part of the delegation, made him appear less of a threat, particularly in the eyes of the press.

What was not noted, or if noted, not given the attention it deserved, was the impressive sum of Harding's availability factors when compared to those of any other candidate. He came from a critical state more doubtful than that of any of his major competitors; his political record, though undistinguished, was unmarred. His openhanded good nature made him well liked by his associates—particularly his fellow senators. Not even the slightest blemish could be charged against his "regularity." The fact that he was a senator would ordinarily have appeared to be a liability, for no incumbent senator had been elected to, or even nominated for, the Presidency since the Civil War; James G. Blaine and Benjamin Harrison were both ex-senators.

Like Harrison, however, Harding had not figured prominently in the Senate debates or in the more submerged party conflicts. Furthermore, in the minds of many in 1920, the Senate was seen as the bulwark of conservatism and "normalcy" against the radicalism and experimentation of a too-aggressive President. In physical appearance, Harding was reminiscent of McKinley—an important factor in an era when, after the excitement of war, many people nostalgically yearned for a return to the quiet, stable existence epitomized by McKinley, and which Harding himself made articulate in his phrase: "a return to normalcy." Insufficiently noted, too, were the assiduous efforts of Harry M. Daugherty and other friends to avoid antagonizing anyone, and to procure second-choice or even third- or fourth-choice support wherever they could find it.

Calvin Coolidge was never really in the running for the presidential nomination. In the absence of a major candidate favored by the New England delegations, his name was a useful one to hide behind until a choice could be found. The votes he received on each ballot did, however, keep his name before the convention and no doubt contributed to his vice-presidential nomination.

Hoover failed to develop the strength that was really his. One of the best-known yet least controversial figures in the nation at the time, he might well have shown extensive strength had he put on a strong primary campaign. He had allowed his name to be entered in only one primary, however, and that was one in which his chances were small. In his adopted state of California, despite the tremendous and organized strength of Hiram Johnson, Hoover made a respectable showing with a hastily assembled nonprofessional organization. He could not, however, have expected organization support. As an important member of Wilson's administration, he had cooperated fully with the President, and in 1918 he gave support to Wilson's demand for a sympathetic Congress. As late as 1919 he was considered a threat for the Democratic nomination, until he issued a statement definitely committing himself to Republican ranks. Even so, he received many votes in Democratic primaries.

Republican party primary activity was much greater in 1920 than in 1912 or 1916, both in the number of candidates actively involved and in the total vote turnout. More than 3 million votes were cast in twenty states, and in many primaries three or more of the major candidates opposed each other.

Wood and Johnson waged the most widespread and intensive primary campaigns. For Johnson, this was the only means to develop strong convention support, since he could expect little help from regular party organizations. Wood's campaign apparently involved several mistakes in strategy; by entering many states against favorite sons, he antagonized the latter and made it more difficult to win their second-choice votes. He entered primaries in the home states of both Lowden and Harding, opposed West Virginia's favorite son, and, although he did not enter his name in Johnson's home state of California, he opposed him in such Progressive strongholds as Montana, Nebraska, Oregon, Michigan, and South Dakota.

Wood was able to win a mere 38 out of the 196 delegates involved, and a full delegation only in South Dakota—a small return for the money spent and the enmity incurred. His contests with Johnson were particularly unfortunate, since Wood's one hope of victory lay in obtaining the full support of the Progressive wing of the party. The fight between Johnson and Wood split the Progressives and paved the way for a conservative nomination. Lowden, as a more conservative candidate, had what was in many respects an easier game to play. Where Wood opposed Johnson, Lowden had nothing to lose and there was a possibility that a split of the Progressive vote might permit him to win a plurality. This nearly happened in South Dakota, but his showing was poor in other contests of similar character. He did not oppose other conservative candidates, such as Harding in Ohio.

Chicago, Illinois,
June 8, 9, 10, 11, 12, 1920

The call to the convention, signed by Will H. Hays, chairman of the national committee, was similar to that of 1916,

except that a full list of the apportionment for each state and territory was appended, thus leaving no question as to the number of delegates allotted each delegation.

Convention Organization

The organization of the convention proceeded smoothly. Henry Cabot Lodge, leader in the Senate fight against the League of Nations, was selected temporary chairman. The great task ahead, he said, was to control the restlessness bred by war and to return to a more normal (by which he meant more conservative) state of mind. The Democrats, and particularly President Wilson, were too deeply committed to radical (and un-American) ideas to be intrusted with the task of adjusting to peace, and "the only other organized political force strong enough to grapple with the encircling dangers is the Republican party."

Although the committee on credentials did not in all cases endorse the temporary roll submitted by the national committee, the report was accepted unanimously and no minority report was presented. One contestant announced that he had a minority report in his hand relating to his own case, but that he was "not going to be the one man to bring any minority report before this convention," and would therefore carry his fight back to his home.

The committee on permanent organization endorsed the temporary organization as the permanent one, and Senator Lodge remained in the chair. The committee on rules and order of business also had an easy time of it, and contented itself with presenting the 1916 rules.

The platform committee being not yet ready to report, the venerable Chauncey Depew, darling of many conventions in the past, was called upon by the delegates to speak. Depew did not disappoint his audience. He first denied the allegation that he was an old man by quoting from a letter he had received:

I heard your speech last night, and they tell me that you said you were past eighty-six. Well, all I have got to say is, from the mountains of Colorado, that you are either a miracle or a d--d liar.

He then took the delegates on a brief trip through time, with references to his conversations and experiences with such men as Lincoln, Seward, Chase, and Blaine.

Following this brush with the past, the convention next was reminded of the changes that were taking place in the present: a woman delegate pledged the newly powerful women's votes for the Republican candidate, and a little later the chairman said:

The Convention will kindly be in order for a few minutes while we endure one of the afflictions of being in public life—having our picture taken for the movies.[1]

The Platform

The convention convened on the morning of the third day only to find the resolutions committee still laboring with its problems. The major problem—which if not solved might lead to a party bolt—was to find a formula for the League of Nations plank that would be generally acceptable despite the widely divergent views held. The platform as finally submitted that afternoon provided this solution: that international association be agreed to in principle and that the covenant signed by the President in Paris, and also Wilson's intransigence in refusing to allow any amendments, be vigorously denounced. The first part of the proposal permitted those who favored the League, but with reservations, to interpret the plank as favoring the League if modified to suit their conditions; the second satisfied those who wanted the League under no conditions. As one newspaper wag put it, this clause in the platform permitted the Republicans to make two powerful arguments in the campaign:

[1] RNC, *Proceedings*, 1920, p. 81.

1. Elect Harding and keep us out of the League;
2. Elect Harding as the only chance to get us into the League.

The platform consisted in large part of condemnation of the administration and praise for the current Republican majority in Congress for holding "executive autocracy" as much within bounds as it did. On the important agricultural question it opposed price-fixing as a solution and proposed greater farmer representation among governmental officials and on commissions, and "the scientific study of agricultural prices and farm production costs . . . and uncensored publication of such reports." It recognized the justice of collective bargaining, but it also opposed strikes and lockouts as weapons in the conflict.

A minority report including about twenty planks was presented by a Wisconsin delegate. It demanded immediate conclusion of the peace negotiations and the resumption of normal international relations, but opposed the League of Nations and the treaty as then constituted. It opposed compulsory military service in time of peace and denounced profiteering. It advocated election of federal judges, proposed a constitutional amendment to provide for initiative, referendum, and recall, and proposed a bonus to servicemen sufficient to bring their compensation to the same level enjoyed by civilian workers during the period served.

The presentation of the minority report was interrupted frequently by the gallery and by the delegates; at one point, interference was so great that the chairman threatened to clear the galleries. The speaker attempted to get a roll call vote on the report, but was unable to get the seconding of a second delegation, as required by the rules. On the voice vote, the only apparent support came from the Wisconsin delegation, and the report was rejected. The majority report was then adopted by voice vote.

The Presidential Nomination

Nominations for presidential candidates were made on the fourth day. The three candidates who had waged nationwide campaigns were presented, followed by eight others whose campaigns had been more restricted, most of them being favorite sons. In addition Coleman du Pont of Delaware and Senator Robert M. La Follette of Wisconsin, although not nominated, nevertheless carried the full support of their own delegations into the balloting. With a total convention vote of 984, the required majority for nomination was 493.

On the first ballot Wood received 287½, Lowden 211½, and Johnson 133½—none even close to the required majority. The remaining 351½ votes were scattered among twelve others, with only Governor William Cameron Sproul, Pennsylvania's favorite son, Nicholas Murray Butler of New York, and Harding, in that order, receiving significant support. Fourteen states contributed to Harding's vote—a much broader base of support than that of any other minor candidate, and one from which Harding's managers were able to operate when the deadlock developed. (On the tenth and final ballot, Harding received 88 per cent of the total vote of these fourteen delegations before vote shifting, as compared to only 55 per cent of the vote from the other delegations.)

Wood, though the front-runner, could expect little second-choice support from Lowden's people, since most of these were affiliated with regular organizations antagonistic to Wood. He could expect even less from Johnson—and this was reciprocal because of the ill feeling engendered by Johnson's charges against Wood on campaign expenditures. Since these two shared the Roosevelt heritage and most of the non-organization vote, only by combining could they stop the organization forces. They would not or could not cooperate, however, and their opponents were therefore free to deal with them separately.

Lowden, around whom organization leaders might have coalesced, was badly injured by a last-minute announcement of irregularities in the handling of his campaign funds, subjecting him to the charge of buying delegates.

Throughout the balloting, none of the three leaders was able to poll as much as one third of the total vote or to get within striking distance of the magic number—493. Wood's highest total was 314½ on the fourth ballot, Lowden's was 311½ on the sixth and seventh, and Johnson's 148 on the third. Following the third ballot, a motion was made by a Johnson supporter to adjourn the convention until the next morning; this was defeated by a roll call vote, 701½ to 275½. Johnson supporters tended to support the adjournment, and were joined by La Follette's Wisconsin and Senator Miles Poindexter's Washington supporters, but by few others. However, following the fourth ballot, when Wood reached his peak vote, Chairman Lodge declared the convention adjourned until the next day, despite what most observers reported to be a close if not actually a negative response to a voice vote. Thus the stage was set for the night of the famous "smoke-filled room."

Many conflicting stories in explanation of Harding's nomination have been circulated, several of them becoming legends. Much has been made of Daugherty's statement months before the convention—that the decision would be made "at two o'clock in the morning in a smoke-filled room." Daugherty confessed during the convention that the statement had been a major blunder, for it jeopardized his careful strategy of building Harding as a "second choice." Much also has been made of the influence of Boss Boies Penrose, operating from his sickbed in Pennsylvania; of the senatorial cabal; of the activities of the "oil interests"; of the machinations of George Harvey, influential editor and publisher and erstwhile Democrat. It is quite probable that all of these factors had their effect, but, as has been pointed out by such close observers as Mark Sullivan and Harry New, the nomination can be explained upon much less colorful grounds.

Once it became clear that none of the three leaders could be nominated, it became certain at the same time that no one with a record for leadership or with a positive position on the major issues of the day could be nominated. The very characteristics that bound Wood's, Johnson's, and La Follette's delegates to their respective leaders made it improbable that their allegiance could be shifted to another possessing similar charismatic appeal—they would more readily accept a nonentity.

On the other hand, major leaders among the organization people were in an equally impossible situation—Lodge, for example, however much he might have desired the nomination, could have developed only limited support in the convention. The compromise man had to be a compromise in every sense of the term. In addition to the usual availability factors, the candidate's record needed to be not only clean, but preferably uncluttered by any strong statements of position on major issues.

Harding met this special requirement, as well as the customary requirements for availability, as fully as anyone in the convention. His record of complete regularity in his dealing with organizational leaders made it possible for them to accept him. It is true that little in Harding's background indicated capacity for administration or presidential leadership; on the other hand, nothing indicated that he couldn't do the job—and, as Daugherty always said, he did look like a President. These attributes made it possible for the conservative elements in the convention, including Lowden's supporters and most of the organization votes behind favorite sons, to move to Harding's column—enough to have effected his nomination, particularly since the Progressives were split. In addition, his well-known affability

and the lack of anything in his record that could raise antagonism encouraged many of the less-committed Wood and some Johnson delegates to join him when the direction of the movement became clear. It should be noted also that he had been next to the three leaders on most of the ballots. He was not "pulled out of the air," as Polk had been.

In the morning session following the Friday night adjournment, Harding began a slow but steady climb. According to some stories, the coterie of senators and organization leaders controlling the convention machinery preferred to give Wood, Lowden, and Johnson a chance to prove to themselves that they could not be nominated; thus bitterness and the probability of a bolt might be reduced. The safety margin between the highest figure reached by any of these candidates and the required majority makes this theory plausible, but it is also probable that the control of the leaders over the delegates was tenuous enough to necessitate the slow build-up. In addition, the organization leaders were less than unanimous on the Harding decision. As late as Saturday afternoon some of the regulars were reported still working for various others, among them Will Hays, national committee chairman, despite the fact that he was known only as a politician.

Whatever the reasons, Harding moved slowly. Closing at 61½ the day before, he received 78, 89, 105, and 133½ on the fifth to eighth ballots respectively. Following the eighth ballot, a recess was taken upon motion of Lowden's floor manager. What happened during the three-hour recess is obscured in contradictions. It appears certain, however, that Wood and Lowden attempted to join forces at last—in a meeting in a taxicab, where they tried to reach an agreement but were unable to do so. It is doubtful that Lowden could have delivered his delegates even had an agreement been reached.

On the ninth roll call, taken immediately after the session was reconvened, much of Lowden's vote moved to Harding, who jumped into first place with 374½ votes. Wood and Johnson also dropped on this ballot, which would almost certainly have been the last had Governor Sproul then released his big Pennsylvania delegation. On the tenth and final ballot, 181½ votes stayed with Wood and 80 with Johnson, but almost all of Lowden's vote moved to Harding. After the roll call, a few of Wood's remaining delegates shifted their vote to Harding; none of Johnson's made the gesture.

The Vice-Presidential Nomination

Considering the reputation of this convention as one of the most "managed" in history, the vice-presidential nominating proceedings are of particular interest. According to some accounts, Hiram Johnson was offered the nomination by the senatorial group. Although two senators on the same ticket would have been unusual, he fitted most of the generally accepted criteria of vice-presidential availability: he was the leader of an adamant faction of the party that needed to be placated, and he came from a different section of the country than the presidential nominee. It is conceivable also that many of the senators would have preferred to have him sitting in the chair of the Senate, where he could effectively be muzzled, rather than fighting in the arena. In any case, Johnson declined.

The reputed second choice of the cabal—Senator Irvine L. Lenroot of Wisconsin—was unusual from the standpoint of availability. Wisconsin was in the same section as Harding's Ohio, and therefore Lenroot had no geographical advantage, as Johnson did, to offset the hazard of running two senators on the ticket. Although originally a Progressive, Lenroot had moved in the direction of political regularity and conservatism, so that his selection would scarcely have placated the Progressive elements of the party, and, in view of the suspicion generally held by the original inhabitants for new arrivals, his choice would not have been too popular with the long-time conservatives.

Nevertheless, the fact remains that Lenroot was placed in nomination by a senator from Illinois and seconded by the chairman of the Kentucky delegation who, as Lowden's floor manager, had engineered the shift of Kentucky to Harding at the critical moment. This appears to substantiate the theory that Lenroot was the choice of those who built the Harding coalition; but other factors suggest another interpretation. In the first place, Harding's nomination was not accomplished until Saturday evening. Immediately after the nomination was made unanimous, nominations for vice-presidential candidates began. There was certainly no time for any extended consultation in the interim.

In view of the rather hectic maneuvering leading to the principal nomination, it is doubtful that more than cursory consideration could have been given the second place on the ticket until the first was settled. Senator Medill McCormick, of the *Chicago Tribune* family, and Alvin D. Hert of Kentucky, who nominated and seconded Lenroot, had been leaders of the Lowden movement before and during most of the convention, but both figured prominently in the transfer from Lowden to Harding. Chairman Lodge's immediate recognition of McCormick indicates he knew what the latter was going to do, but his act of leaving the chair following McCormick's speech for Lenroot can be interpreted as an indication of lack of interest in McCormick's success.

No one knew better than Lodge the unpredictability of delegates, particularly in this convention. Having paid a political debt to McCormick and Hert, he may well have wished to wash his hands of the matter. He was too good a politician not to have known how much groundwork had been laid by people in his own state for the nomination of Governor Calvin Coolidge, and despite his somewhat austere relations with the latter, may well have preferred him to Lenroot.

Shortly after Lodge left the chair a delegate from Oregon obtained recognition from the temporary chairman and, standing upon his chair in the middle of the auditorium, presented the name of Calvin Coolidge. A wild demonstration followed, apparently completely out of control of the convention managers. The length of the demonstration certainly should have given Lodge and other leaders time to return to their places before the balloting began —but they did not return until afterwards.

Coolidge received 674½ votes on the first ballot, a majority; Lenroot got but 146½. Detailed analysis of the vote corroborates the thesis that organization leaders did not exercise significant control over the delegations. Had they done so, and really wanted Lenroot, it would be expected that the delegations providing Harding's basic support, and accordingly being presumably most amenable to the organization leaders' control, would have supported Lenroot more solidly than delegations remaining in opposition to Harding up to the last. This was not the case, for Coolidge received approximately the same support from delegations favoring Harding above the average as he did from those voting below average for Harding on the ninth or critical ballot.

The action of Ohio is particularly significant. Had the word been passed that the organization leaders, and therefore Harding, desired a particular running mate, it seems beyond the scope of political probability that the instructions would have been disregarded, particularly by the majority of a delegation that had consistently supported Harding throughout the convention. Yet Ohio voted—giving Coolidge and two others 10 each, Lenroot and one other 9 each. An evenly spread vote over a wide field is the classic convention maneuver for fence-straddling. Harding and those responsible for his nomination may not have been in favor of Coolidge, but they certainly did not do much for Lenroot.

TWENTY-THIRD DEMOCRATIC CONVENTION

With Wilson's ambivalent attitude toward the nominations, it is not surprising that Democratic activity in the presidential primaries was very low, and that such activity as existed was generally of the favorite son variety. Only rarely did major candidates contest the primary ballots, and then the results were indecisive.

The two candidates with the nearest committed strength at convention time were William Gibbs McAdoo, formerly Wilson's Secretary of the Treasury, and Attorney General A. Mitchell Palmer. As Wilson's son-in-law, McAdoo was assumed by many to be the heir apparent, although Wilson did nothing to encourage this view; nevertheless, McAdoo became a focal point of opposition for all who opposed Wilson. On the other hand, his candidacy was weakened among Wilson supporters because of Wilson's failure to support it. McAdoo was also displeasing to the organization leaders, particularly in Tammany, owing to his reluctance to cooperate with them in patronage matters while he was Secretary of the Treasury.

Palmer was a highly controversial figure as the result of his zealous conduct of "Red-hunts." Such figures may attract intensely loyal followers, but they seldom have much second-choice support. Palmer was unable to develop much more strength than he held on the first ballot.

Two other candidates entered the convention with substantial blocks of pledged delegates. One of these, the 47-year-old governor of New York, Alfred E. Smith, was not yet the national figure he was to become. With 90 per cent of his convention vote concentrated in his own state, and the balance from northeastern states, he was little more than a strong favorite son. The other was James M. Cox, governor of Ohio. With the solid support of his state as a base, the rest of his support was well scattered, some coming from each section of the nation, although he was far behind the leaders in number of pledged delegates.

Cox's main advantage lay in his high availability qualifications. He came from the critical state of Ohio, even more critical since the nomination of Harding as the Republican candidate. His record as governor was good, as attested by his recent precedent-shattering third-term election. In 1918 he had been the only Democrat elected on the state ticket—a tribute to his vote-getting ability. Although a Wilson supporter, he had not been identified closely or personally with Wilson. Outside of a term in Congress from 1909 to 1913, he had not figured on the national scene, and had therefore few political enemies outside his own state.

On June 15 a special correspondent of the *New York Times* stated that Cox was the real favorite of Tammany Hall, of Thomas Taggart, organization leader of Indiana, and of other organizational leaders. On the second day of the convention, the same paper quoted the Wall Street betting odds as only 2½ to 1 against Cox, which compared very favorably with those against the favorite, McAdoo, quoted at to 1. Of the four leaders, Cox was the only one who could hope to be accepted as second choice by supporters of the other three, as well as by the supporters of some of the favorite sons who flooded the convention.

*San Francisco, California,
June 28, 29, 30; July 1, 2, 3, 5, 6, 1920*

The convention met pursuant to a brief call limited to the time and place of meeting, and to instructions as to the apportionment of delegates. The call specifically stated that "no State or Territory shall elect any number of delegates with their alternates in excess of the quota to which each State or Territory or District may be entitled under the basis of representation herein indicated." The basis of representation was given as two delegates and two

alternates for each senator and representative in Congress for the states, and six each for the territories and the District of Columbia.

The attempt to restrict the membership of the convention was completely unsuccessful, for the actual representation contained a greater number of delegates with variant fractional voting rights than any other in modern history. Georgia, Maryland, Nevada, South Carolina, Virginia, Washington, and the District of Columbia sent double their authorized delegates, with one half vote each; Iowa, Kentucky, and Missouri doubled their at large quota, and Iowa some of its district allotment as well; Missouri sent full-vote delegates at large, but split some of the district votes; Idaho divided all of its votes into one third votes. North Carolina and Texas really complicated the problem: some North Carolina delegates were given a full vote, some one half, and some two fifths, while Texas authorized one quarter votes for all at large delegates and one half vote for district delegates.

Convention Organization

Homer S. Cummings of Connecticut was selected temporary chairman, and the temporary organization of the convention proceeded without incident up to the report of the committee on credentials. Although the report was approved by voice vote, a protest was registered by the delegate from the fifth district of Missouri against the refusal to seat Senator James A. Reed as a delegate from the fifth district. This brief protest and the equally brief rebuttal by the secretary of the committee on credentials were the only open signs in the convention of a bitter battle waged in Missouri and in the June meeting of the national committee over this seat.

Senator Reed had been duly elected as a district delegate by the local convention, but the state convention refused to endorse him and directed the delegation from the district to name another delegate, which they refused to do. This unusual action by the Missouri state convention, and by the national committee in endorsing it, was taken to punish Senator Reed for his opposition to the policies of the administration and particularly for his opposition to the League of Nations. Bitter though the recriminations against Reed were at this time, they did not keep him from re-election to the Senate two years later or from prominent mention as a presidential candidate in subsequent national conventions.

The report of the committee on permanent organization and the main report of the committee on rules and order of business were approved without discussion. The latter report was restricted to adoption of the rules of the House of Representatives, regulations for restriction of debate, and the order of business. The committee proposed two separate resolutions, one limiting nominating speeches for President to twenty minutes and for Vice President to ten minutes, with seconding speeches to be restricted to three of five minutes each for President and two of five minutes each for Vice President. The second resolution specifically recognized the unit rule when adopted by a state convention, except where state statutes directed otherwise. Both resolutions were passed without a record vote.

Senator Flood of Virginia proposed a resolution restricting the number of delegates in future conventions to twice the membership of the Senate and the House of Representatives for the state delegations, and such representation as might be provided in the future for the non-state delegations. After some discussion the resolution was passed, following which two additional resolutions relating to the national committee were presented. The first authorized selection of a national committee consisting of one man and one woman from each state and territory. After a somewhat confused discussion, primarily parliamentary in nature, the resolution

was referred to the committee on resolutions. The second authorized selection of officers of the committee, and the appointment of a campaign committee and other subcommittees of the national committee as might be necessary. This resolution was passed after considerable parliamentary wrangling, and the first resolution was then withdrawn from the committee on resolutions and passed by the convention.

The order of business called for nominating speeches before the report of the committee on resolutions. Despite restrictions on length and number of seconding speeches, two sessions and more than nine hours were required to get through the roll of the states. When the flow of oratory finally came to a pause, the platform committee still was unable to report, and shortly after 1:00 p.m. on the fourth day the convention adjourned. In the evening session, with the committee still at its labors, nothing was accomplished except ratification of the national committee.

The Platform

On the morning of the fifth day the resolutions committee made its report. The platform began with praise for Woodrow Wilson and the achievements of his administration, both before the war and during it. The League of Nations was favored as "the surest, if not the only, practicable means of maintaining the permanent peace of the world." The President's courage in advocating the League was extolled, and in the same sentence the refusal of the Republican Senate to ratify the treaty "merely because it was the product of Democratic statesmanship" condemned. Alteration of the Senate rules was favored to "permit the prompt transaction of the nation's legislative business."

Throughout the long document, frustration of the administration by the "Republican Congress" was reiterated. It was charged that, because of the failure by Congress to cooperate, administration of the public debt, tax revision, and the program to effect greater economy in government were seriously handicapped. This contributed to the rising scale of the cost of living.

The traditional stand was taken on the principle of a tariff for revenue only, but the party agreed with the Republicans that a nonpartisan commission was needed to study tariff problems. Compulsory arbitration in labor disputes was opposed "as a method plausible in theory, but a failure in fact." Republican charges that the Wilson administration interfered with freedom of the press and of speech were denied.

William Jennings Bryan, in a minority report, proposed five additional planks or amendments to planks to the platform. His plank proposing complete endorsement of prohibition met with a counterproposal permitting manufacture of light wines and beer for home consumption only. His other proposals included recommendation that a national bulletin or newspaper be established; a rather obscurely worded proposal designed to prevent profiteering by eliminating middlemen and by requiring interstate corporations to disclose the difference between cost and selling prices; a statement opposing universal compulsory military training in time of peace; and a proposal for a constitutional amendment providing that treaties be ratified by majority instead of a two thirds vote of the Senate. Additional minority resolutions were offered, one expressing sympathy and support for Ireland, and another recommending party support for benefits to veterans.

After long debate, the convention finally voted on these amendments. The first vote was on Bryan's prohibition plank, which read as follows:

We heartily congratulate the Democratic party on its splendid leadership in the submission and ratification of the prohibition amendment to the Federal Constitution, and we pledge the body to the effective enforcement of the present enforcement law, honestly and in good faith, without any increase in the alcoholic content of permitted beverages, and with-

out any weakening of any other of its provisions.[2]

This was defeated, 929½ to 155½. A second roll call vote was taken on the amendment proposed by Bourke Cockran of New York, who stated when he proposed it, that he would not have done so had not Bryan submitted his resolution. This amendment read:

The validity of the Eighteenth Amendment to the Constitution has been sustained by the Supreme Court and any law enacted under its authority must be enforced. In the interest of personal liberty, and to conserve the rights of the states, we favor federal legislation under the Eighteenth Amendment, allowing the manufacture and sale, for home consumption only, of cider, light wines, and beer; reserving to the various states power to fix any alcoholic contents thereof lower than that fixed by Congress, as may be demanded by the opinion and conscience of each locality.[3]

This too was defeated, but by the lesser margin of 726½ to 356, and the platform was silent on the prohibition question.

A third roll call was taken on the Irish question:

Ireland. Mindful of the circumstances of the birth of our nation, we reiterate the principle that all governments derive their just powers from the consent of the governed. We will support the continuance of our long-established and lawful practice of according recognition without intervention in all cases where the people of a nation have, by the free vote of a people, set up a republic and chosen a government to which they yield willing obedience.[4]

The platform reiterated the principle of national self-determination as a chief objective and stated that, within the limitations of international comity and usage, "this Convention repeats the several previous expressions of the sympathy of the Democratic Party of the United States for the aspirations of Ireland for self-government." The amendment was defeated by 676 to 402½. All other amendments were lost by voice votes, and the platform was approved in its original form.

[2] DNC, *Proceedings*, 1920, p. 255.
[3] *Ibid.*, p. 258.
[4] *Ibid.*, p. 263.

The Presidential Nomination

The next order of business was the balloting for presidential nominee. The convention had been in continuous session for approximately nine hours, and an attempt was made to call a recess. However, since most of the delegates were anxious to get to the main business, the motion was withdrawn and two ballots were taken before finally adjourning after eleven hours of continuous session.

Twenty-four candidates received one or more votes on the first ballot, but only four received more than 100 votes: McAdoo 266, Palmer 256, Cox 134, and Smith 109. Ten others received between 20 and 42 votes each. The total convention strength was 1,094 with 729 needed for a victory. Although it was obvious that a choice was a long way off, the convention took the second ballot before adjourning. The field of twenty-four was reduced to eighteen, the principal gainers being McAdoo and Cox, who picked up 23 and 25 votes respectively. Palmer gained only 8 and Smith lost the same number.

At 9:45 a.m. on the sixth day of the convention, balloting began again—and continued until 5:40 p.m. when an adjournment until 8:00 p.m. was approved by a roll call vote 619 to 455. The adjournment was supported in general by the McAdoo and Palmer supporters, and opposed by Cox people. Fourteen ballots had been taken during the session. On the last of these, the 16th, the field was reduced to eight names.

The first-ballot leader, McAdoo, had gained steadily for several ballots, reached a peak of 386 votes on the 9th ballot, then fallen gradually to 337 on the 16th. Palmer's vote fluctuated within a narrow range near his first-ballot total until the 12th ballot, when he dropped sharply to 201, and finished the session at 164½. Cox gained slowly but steadily on the first six ballots and then jumped 100 votes to 295½ on the 7th, to take second place. Most of his gain on this ballot came from Smith, who dropped to 4 votes and subsequently disappeared entirely on the 10th ballot. Cox continued to gain, passed McAdoo on the 12th, and closed the session at 454½, more than 100 votes ahead of McAdoo.

The convention reconvened shortly after 8:00 p.m., and six ballots were taken before the midnight adjournment. Relatively little change occurred through the 20th ballot, after which a motion to adjourn was defeated by a roll call vote 638 to 437. The correlation with the nominating ballots on this roll call is not high, but in general the adjournment appears to have been supported by McAdoo delegates and opposed by those of Palmer and Cox. On the 21st ballot, immediately following defeat of the adjournment motion, McAdoo gained more than 50 votes, as Cox and Palmer dropped 30 and 34 respectively, their losses moving to McAdoo and John W. Davis. On the next, and the last, ballot of the night, Cox was still in the lead with 430, McAdoo second with 372½, and Palmer third with 166½.

The first session of the seventh day was a bad one for Cox, who found himself in second place with 377 votes—nearly 100 below his 15th-ballot peak. McAdoo had indifferent success, gaining first, and then losing, to finish with 399 votes. However, he was again in first place, and his vote throughout this session tended to exceed his previous totals. Palmer moved sharply during the session, and his 36th-ballot total nearly reached his previous high, recorded on the 7th ballot. It was the beginning of the end for him, however, for he dropped rapidly when the convention reconvened for the evening session.

After the 30th ballot, the following motion was proposed:

I move that the rules of this Convention be suspended and that on the next ballot the candidate receiving the lowest number of votes be dropped and that on each succeeding ballot the candidate receiving the lowest number of votes be dropped until there is a nomination.[5]

An oddity of this motion is that, although it was presented by Senator Pat Harrison of Mississippi, his delegation voted unanimously against it. Mississippi, after a complimentary vote to a favorite son on the first ballot, had consistently been giving 20 votes to Cox. The Cox delegates from New York voted for the motion, but the Ohio delegation passed, with the statement that Ohio would vote the same as Pennsylvania, Palmer's state. McAdoo delegates tended to split their votes on both sides of the issue in about the same ratio as the total convention vote. It would appear, from the confusion of the voting, that the motion was presented by Harrison without any clearance with the Cox managers, and that the vote was taken so quickly thereafter that there was no time to communicate or agree on a strategy.

Adoption of the motion would have been fatal to Palmer's chances, if the two leaders kept their ground, for the total number of votes held by minor candidates on the 30th ballot amounted only to 123; if all went to Palmer, he would still have been a poor third when the field was reduced to three. With this in mind, Ohio's willingness to vote as Pennsylvania did seems a generous offer, and was undoubtedly a bid for support from Palmer delegates if and when his candidacy were given up as a lost cause. As the one explanation in the entire performance that makes political sense, a possibility exists that Harrison's motion was made for this very purpose.

The nomination finally was made in the evening session of the seventh day. The first ballot taken, the 37th in the series, recorded a serious drop for Palmer and put a definite stop to his boom. Both of the leaders gained a little. On the 39th ballot most of Palmer's support outside of Pennsylvania melted away. A detailed analysis of the changes between the 38th and 39th ballots reveals that Cox and McAdoo received almost exactly the same share of the Palmer defection, but that McAdoo lost 25 votes to Cox, including 18 from the Indiana delegation that had voted for McAdoo almost solidly from the 29th ballot. This delegation, with 30 votes, quite obviously was trying to utilize its strength to the utmost in influencing the convention decision. For the first few ballots it had held back from the main fight by hiding behind a favorite son. Suddenly, on the 19th ballot, all 30 votes were given to Cox, though his losses on this ballot elsewhere weakened the effect of the move. On the 20th, 11 votes were transferred to McAdoo, and from the 29th through the 38th ballots, McAdoo received 29 Indiana votes. Then, with Palmer definitely dropping from the race, after the full Georgia delegation and scattered other votes had moved to McAdoo, eighteen members of the delegation, of which the Vice President of the United States was a member, transferred to Cox, and by doing so made him the leader once more at the end of the ballot.

After the 41st ballot, with the two leaders still less than 40 votes apart, one final attempt was made to delay the decision: the Oklahoma delegation, still voting consistently for a favorite son, moved to adjourn until the next day. The motion was defeated 406 to 637, with most of the support for the motion coming from the McAdoo delegates, and the negative vote from Cox delegates.[6]

Cox continued to gain steadily. On the 44th ballot he received 699 votes or 27 short of the required two thirds. A McAdoo delegate then moved that Cox be declared the unanimous nominee of the convention. The convention adjourned just before 2:00 a.m.

[5] Ibid., p. 380.

[6] See Analysis of Key Votes.

The Vice-Presidential Nomination

After the hectic proceedings on the previous days, the last session on the eighth day was anticlimatic. A series of complimentary resolutions opened the proceedings, and the nominating speeches followed. Five names were officially presented for nomination, and speeches were made for two others, but with the statement that they had requested their names not be officially presented.

Franklin D. Roosevelt, Assistant Secretary of the Navy, was then presented by a delegate from the District of Columbia. As a young, vigorous, and highly loyal member of Wilson's administration, Roosevelt symbolized a much closer tie with the administration and its record than Cox did. How much the convention sensed this is not certain, but after his presentation other names were withdrawn with appropriate oratorical flourish. Roosevelt was then nominated by acclamation. After a few additional complimentary resolutions, the convention adjourned.

Analysis of Key Votes

The platform votes early in the convention were all on items of relatively small importance. However, some of the votes on adjournment during the extensive balloting were important to the contest, and the one chosen for analysis is that following the 41st ballot. This clearly was defeated by pro-Cox people, for the correlation of the negative vote with his 39th ballot vote (the one on which he resumed the lead) is +.77. Correlation with the McAdoo vote is −.47, indicating some uncertainty among his followers. Correlation with the sum of the other vote is −.64. Following defeat of the adjournment by the Cox supporters, the Cox vote continued to increase as the supporters of lesser candidates began to climb on his band wagon.

Presidential Election, November 2, 1920

WARREN G. HARDING (R) : popular vote, 16,152,200; electoral vote, 404
JAMES M. COX (D) : popular vote, 9,147,353; electoral vote, 127

1924

HARDING'S DEATH, followed closely by disclosures of Teapot Dome and other scandals, appeared at first to provide the Democratic party a golden opportunity to recover from the landslide defeat of 1920. But the effect of the scandals was largely offset by the manner in which Calvin Coolidge, as President, met the problem. His measured but apparently emphatic attack upon the guilty parties, coupled with his own appearance of unswerving honesty, reassured most of the public. The all-important factor of the national economy also worked in his—and the Republicans'—favor; almost as if timed with his assumption of Harding's place, the economy began to boom and kept on booming. True, prosperity was not uniformly distributed: there were ominous clouds forming in the farm belt. But Republican strength in the affected areas had been so great for a generation that a fairly large splinter movement could be accommodated there without losing the electoral votes. The tremendous political realignment that occurred during the years 1924 and 1928 has only lately begun to be fully understood. If Coolidge recognized what was going on, and it is possible he did, he may well have quoted another advocate of the status quo: *Après nous le déluge.*

The Democrats approached 1924 as a divided party. Many scars remained from the unresolved battle for power in 1920. Deprived of the full impact of the scandals of Harding's administration as a rallying force, they carried the personal animosities of their leaders into the preconvention and convention campaign. In addition, the conflicts existing between urban, Catholic, foreign-born, and anti-prohibitionist on the one hand, and rural, Protestant, native-born, and prohibitionist on the other, affected the Democrats more than the Republicans. Unfortunately for the Democrats, the nation was in the period that so frequently follows major wars in which divisions such as these can be unusually explosive.

EIGHTEENTH REPUBLICAN CONVENTION

Within his own party, Coolidge quickly developed sufficient strength to make the more conservative potential candidates, who may have thought to oppose him, reconsider. He was opposed in the primaries only by Senators Hiram Johnson and Robert M. La Follette, both party mavericks. Johnson entered his name against Coolidge in most of the primaries, but was able to defeat him only in South Dakota; generally, Coolidge won by overwhelming majorities. La Follette contested only Wisconsin and North Dakota, placing second to Coolidge in a three-way race in the latter, and winning in his home state.

By the time the convention assembled, Coolidge was assured of nomination by an overwhelming majority. His massive convention majority concealed a serious party split, however—a split that evidenced itself in the confusion surrounding the vice-presidential nomination, and that subsequently resulted in a third-party ticket headed by Robert La Follette.

Cleveland, Ohio,
June 10, 11, 12, 1924

The call for the convention included an important change in the method of apportionment. In addition to four delegates at

215

large for each state in recognition of the senatorial representation in Congress, and two for each representative at large, three delegates at large were alloted each state casting its electoral vote, or a majority thereof, for the Republican nominee for President in the last preceding election. As in 1920, one delegate was provided for each congressional district, but 10,000 instead of 7,500 district votes for Republican electors or for the Republican nominee for Congress were required to be eligible for a second district delegate. The first of these changes was the origin of the bonus system, whereby states, regardless of size, were given the same additional representation for Republican victory—a provision adding materially to the strength of the smaller states relative to the larger ones.

Convention Organization

This convention was unusual in that almost all the excitement occurred after the presidential nomination—as in 1900 when Theodore Roosevelt was nominated for the Vice Presidency. Convention organization proceeded smoothly, and Congressman Theodore E. Burton of Ohio was selected as temporary chairman. Burton paid homage to the dead presidents from the host state, particularly those who had died in office, and welcomed the women delegates and alternates who for the first time appeared in large numbers—about 400 being present. He then launched into a comprehensive survey of the Republican and current administration record. In one of the more important passages, that pertaining to agriculture, he blamed the current problems on overproduction of certain staples coupled with lack of foreign markets and cheap labor competition from other nations. The past Congress and the party had done a great deal about the problem:

The Republican Party has shown its willingness to extend liberality to the last degree in the enactment of legislation which will aid the farmer, but it can not respond to impracticable theories or accept measures which will only aggravate the situation. Any artificial stimulus to prices which are depressed by irresistible causes can only postpone the evil day and add to the distress.[1]

Committees were appointed and their reports were accepted without serious difficulty. The credentials committee endorsed the decisions of the national committee, and recommended that those having temporary seats be given permanent ones. This the convention approved. A motion from the floor recommended that a contesting delegate for one of the two seats on the Puerto Rico delegation be added to the delegation, and the three delegates each be given two thirds of one vote. This being seconded by the chairman of the credentials committee, it was approved by unanimous vote.

Frank W. Mondell of Wyoming was chosen permanent chairman. His acceptance speech asserted:

Confidence in President Coolidge is the most important and outstanding fact in the political situation today. . . . Every serious fault of recent legislation and every failure, so far as there has been failure, to complete and round out a wholly satisfactory legislative program, is due to the fact that we have not in the Congress, and our leaders in the Congress have not had at their command a dependable Republican majority.[2]

The report of the committee on rules and order of business confirmed the apportionment adopted in the call, thus institutionalizing the bonus system, and proposed two additional changes in the rules. The first of these expanded the basis for demanding a roll call from a majority of the delegates of two states to a majority of the delegates from six states. This may have been done to control the Wisconsin Progressives and their allies, who had forced repeated roll call votes upon past conventions, although the Progressives could muster only a small fraction of the total convention vote. Certain other states, particularly the Dakotas, frequently were willing to back the insurgents—but it was

[1] RNC, *Proceedings*, 1924, p. 23.
[2] *Ibid.*, pp. 87-88.

rare that as many as five other states were willing to do so. (After the rule was adopted, roll call votes became very infrequent in Republican conventions, and only one has occurred to date in which the minority vote was as low as one quarter of the convention.)

The second change reflected the entrance of women into politics on a national scale. The rule authorizing formation of the national committee provided for equal representation of the two sexes, one man and one woman from each state and territory.

The Platform

The majority platform praised the Republican party for its record since coming into power in 1921, particularly with respect to economies and lowered taxes resulting from establishment of the Bureau of the Budget. Membership in the Permanent Court of International Justice was endorsed, but not membership in the League of Nations. Opposed generally to international political commitments, the platform agreed to cooperation in humanitarian efforts. It advocated extension of the kind of international armament limitation applied to capital naval vessels at the Washington Conference in 1922 to other forms of war-making equipment, including land forces. It "steadfastly refused to consider the cancellation of foreign debts." Most of the other planks endorsed the current policies of the administration, including that on agriculture.

The La Follette Progressives presented a full minority platform that launched an all-out attack on government and private monopoly. Punctuated by such words as crushed, tyrannical, and usurpation, the platform warned of the growing disparity between farm income and the dividends being reaped by industrialists. Public ownership of water power and of railroads was proposed. Excess profits taxes should be increased and taxes on lower incomes reduced. The proposed substitute platform was defeated without a record vote, only

the Wisconsin delegation and a few other scattered delegates supporting it.

The Presidential Nomination

There was never any question over the presidential nominee. The nominating speech, one of the longest in convention history, was divided into three major sections: The Man; The American; and The Human Being. Seconding speeches were restricted to five minutes each, but nothing was said about the number. Nine were made altogether. During the roll call, an attempt was made to dispense with the balance of the call, and to nominate by acclamation, but the chairman ruled the motion out of order.

At the end of the only ballot, Coolidge held 1,065 of 1,109 votes. Six delegates from North Dakota and twenty-eight from Wisconsin voted for La Follette; ten from South Dakota declared for Hiram Johnson. After the motion for a unanimous nomination was put, the chairman announced: "With the exception of a very few voices the nomination of Calvin Coolidge for President of the United States is made unanimous."[3]

The Vice-Presidential Nomination

Eight names were presented as candidates in the vice-presidential race, and several others received one or more votes. One of the recipients, former Governor Frank O. Lowden of Illinois, had repeatedly stated he did not want and would not accept the nomination, and this was clearly stated to the convention by the Illinois delegation. Nevertheless, 222 delegates voted for him on the first ballot, 50 more than for his nearest opponent; and the rest scattered their votes over a total of 16 candidates. On the second ballot Lowden's total votes increased to 413 on the roll call, immediately following which state standards began to wave as delegation chairmen tried

[3] *Ibid.*, p. 165.

to gain attention from the chair in order to shift their vote to Lowden. The first change, according to the proceedings, was that of Oklahoma, although the official reporter confessed uncertainty as to the accuracy of his record. After the rush to the band wagon had subsided, Lowden held a majority with 766 votes, his nearest rival being Theodore E. Burton, the temporary chairman of the convention.

If the official reporter was confused at this point, the convention soon became more so. Immediately following the motion to make the nomination unanimous, a letter from Lowden, who was not attending the convention, was read; in it he thanked the convention for the honor, but declined the nomination. This letter was undated, having been written beforehand to be held for the eventuality. An Associated Press dispatch was read reiterating his refusal to run, but it was obvious that this, too, antedated the actual ballot. Additional AP dispatches, carrying later date lines, were read, but the convention approved an adjournment to allow the permanent chairman to get in touch with Lowden and ask him the direct question.

Lowden's refusal proved unequivocal, and the convention proceeded to a third ballot, from which Charles G. Dawes of Illinois, author of the famous Dawes Plan for German reparations payment, emerged as the candidate. Dawes received 682½ votes of the total 1,109 in the convention. Secretary of Commerce Herbert Hoover, the only other above 100, received 234½. As in the case of Coolidge, a few Noes were heard when the motion for unanimity was put, and the chairman declared: "It is all but unanimous."

TWENTY-FOURTH DEMOCRATIC CONVENTION

The Democratic campaign began early and was hard fought, but not in the primaries. The two principal opponents were William Gibbs McAdoo of California, who had returned to his law practice in 1919,

and Governor Alfred E. Smith of New York. Smith did not enter a single primary; McAdoo entered several, but only one in which there was a contest—Ohio, against a favorite son. In that primary, he was soundly defeated by the 1920 candidate, James M. Cox, who avowedly entered the primary only to stop McAdoo. Cox declared he was not a candidate in 1924, but he was bitterly opposed to the Ku Klux Klan, which supported McAdoo. McAdoo gained a substantial block of delegates through the primaries; Smith depended entirely upon states where the convention system prevailed.

The two leaders, McAdoo and Smith, represented two sides of a deep ideological cleavage within the party. McAdoo drew heavily from elements of the population that were suspicious of all minorities—religious, racial, or cultural; Smith, as a Roman Catholic, was sympathetic to minorities. McAdoo, as a Dry, was a firm believer in the prohibition amendment; Smith, as a Wet, considered the amendment hypocritical and doomed to failure. McAdoo's strength was based upon the conservative rural areas; Smith drew heavily from the more liberal urban areas. In some respects, the two men were less important as personalities than as representatives of points of view, and the probability of compromise between them or their followers was slight. McAdoo was in the stronger position since he held over one third of the total convention vote pledged to him—a veto strength under the two thirds rule. Smith's committed strength was less than one third, but there were enough favorite sons who were strongly anti-McAdoo, though not necessarily pro-Smith, to preclude McAdoo's early victory, if not to ensure his eventual defeat.

Sixteen favorite sons or sectional candidates entered the convention, many of them with the actual purpose of helping to stop one of the major candidates, as, for example, Cox did in Ohio. The availability qualities of these candidates except for Cox, were extremely low—a factor that undoubtedly contributed to the outcome. Only two came from large states and both of these had passed their prime: Senator and former Governor Samuel M. Ralston of Indiana was 67; Woodbridge Ferris of Michigan was 71. Both, as it turned out, died within the next four years. The rest, aside from the southerners, were from small states in most cases and without a national reputation.

No southern candidate had achieved nomination to the Presidency or the Vice Presidency since the Civil War, and the high racial tensions in both North and South resulting from the mass migrations of Negroes to northern cities during the war and postwar periods, and the rejuvenation of the Ku Klux Klan, made it unlikely that this precedent would be broken in 1924. Candidates from the South, of whom there were a number, could be discounted on this basis, although they served to preserve voting strength for later transfer to an acceptable candidate.

John W. Davis of West Virginia, the ultimate winner, had certain negative availability factors. He was identified with New York "big business"; his home state was only moderate in size; except for 1912, West Virginia had returned Republican majorities in every presidential election since 1896. However, residence in West Virginia did not disqualify him as much as residence in the South or New England did some of the other candidates, particularly since he had New York connections as well. As Ambassador to Great Britain from 1918 to 1921, Davis became a national figure; however, upon his return to the United States he resumed his law practice in New York, and was involved only slightly in factional politics. He was considered a moderate liberal but was not committed to an anti-Klan position as deeply as Underwood or Smith. Since much of the schism within the convention centered about the Mason-Dixon Line, the very position of his home state became an advantage. Considering both negative and positive availability factors, Davis's total

was low as compromise candidates go, but it was as high as or higher than that of any other favorite son or sectional candidate.

New York City, June 24-July 9, 1924

This longest of all national nominating conventions—the only one to spread into a third week—opened quietly. The call stipulated the time and place of the meeting, and made the same provisions for apportionment as the call for the 1920 convention. It also included a provision that no state, territory, or district should elect any number of delegates with their alternates in excess of the quota to which such state, territory, or district might be entitled. However, with the stated purpose of providing for recognition of women, permission was included for each state to send eight half-vote delegates and eight alternates at large, with the recommendation that half be women. Slightly over half the states complied with this suggestion; about one quarter sent only full-vote delegates; most of the rest sent half-vote delegates for the at large votes and for part or all of the district votes. Texas split the at large votes six ways, and Oklahoma three. North Carolina sent half-vote delegates at large, but divided district votes in various ways, including one half, one third, and two fifths.

Convention Organization

The choice of the national committee for temporary chairman, Senator Pat Harrison of Mississippi, was ratified, and Harrison attempted to set the keynote for the convention in a resounding attack upon the Republican record, particularly stressing corruption. As he pointed out the comparative virtues of past Democratic administrations, his mention of Woodrow Wilson caused a twenty-minute interruption of his speech while delegates conducted the kind of demonstration usually reserved for nominated candidates.

Committees were appointed and reports on credentials and permanent organization were accepted by unanimous vote, without debate. Senator Thomas J. Walsh of Montana, fresh from his investigation of the Teapot Dome scandals, was named permanent chairman. The report on rules and order of business, also accepted without opposition, adopted the rules of the last convention, "including the two thirds rule for the nomination of candidates for the office of President and Vice President," and accepted the rules of the House of Representatives of the 65th Congress so far as applicable. Specific mention of the two thirds rule was the first indication of things to come. Most of the recent conventions had adopted the rule without such mention—by simply accepting the rules of the previous convention.

The Presidential Nomination

The order of business called for presentation of names for the presidential nomination before the report of the committee on platform and resolutions. Forty-three speakers presented and seconded sixteen candidates. McAdoo alone received twelve seconding speeches, some very long, in addition to the formal nominating speech. The last nominee was John W. Davis.

The rules committee had not included any regulation regarding the speeches, an oversight not repeated in future conventions. Many interruptions occurred and disorder prevailed; speakers were hissed and cheered, and demonstrations at the end of speeches were long—nearly an hour and a half for McAdoo, and probably even more than that when Franklin D. Roosevelt presented Al Smith as "The Happy Warrior."

Starting halfway through the third day's proceedings, the speeches dragged throughout the entire fourth day, whereupon the convention adjourned to rest before beginning the real battle. Late in the afternoon of the third day, a roll call was held

on the question of adjournment. The question was not whether to adjourn, but at what hour the convention should reassemble. The original motion stipulated 7:30 the same evening, and the vote was taken on an amendment to change the hour to 10:30 the next morning. At the conclusion of the roll call, several delegations changed their vote on the basis that they had not correctly understood what they were voting for, but the majority remained in favor of adjournment until the following morning.

The Platform

Meanwhile, one aspect of the battle was being fought out in the committee on platform and resolutions. Even with the time given by the unusually long nominating procedure (and it is possible that the innumerable speeches were allowed for this reason), the committee was not ready to report, and after a short session on the fifth day, another adjournment was taken.

Included in the prayer that opened the session on the sixth day was a request to the Almighty: "Help us to be brotherly and forbearing to one another, but dauntlessly resolute for the right." Throughout the balance of the convention, there was little to indicate that the delegates had heard the first of these phrases, but they apparently accepted the second, though they differed sharply on the definition of "right." Bitterness and lack of restraint were frequently evidenced in the debates. Even the ill and failing William Jennings Bryan, in this his last Democratic convention, was hissed and booed repeatedly, although much of what he had to say was unusually conciliatory.

Two minority planks were proposed after the reading of the committee report. The first plank involved the party stand on the League of Nations and the World Court. Although both majority and minority supported the League in principle, they differed in the way support should be presented in the platform. The majority report stated, after introductory discussion:

Therefore, we believe that, in the interest of permanent peace, and of the lifting of the great burdens of war from the backs of the people, and in order to establish a permanent foreign policy on these supreme questions, not subject to change with change of party Administrations, it is desirable, wise and necessary to lift this question out of party politics, and to that end to take the sense of the American people at a referendum election, advisory to the Government, to be held officially under Act of Congress, free from all other questions and candidacies, after ample time for full consideration and discussion throughout the Country, upon the question, in substance, as follows:

Shall the United States become a member of the League of Nations upon such reservations or amendments to the Covenent of the League as the President and the Senate of the United States may agree upon?

Immediately upon an affirmative vote we shall carry out such a mandate.[4]

The minority preferred that the mandate for the League be by vote of the people in the presidential and congressional elections, and wanted a clear statement that the Democratic party favored the Court and the League and would work toward participation if placed in power. However, the wording of the minority report does not say this with complete clarity.

We approve the proposal so repeatedly trifled with by the Republican Party that the United States directly adhere to the Permanent Court of International Justice established under the auspices of the League of Nations . . .

. . . There is no substitute for the League of Nations as an agency working for peace. . . . The Democratic Party favors membership in that cooperative agency upon conditions which will make it clear that we are not committed to use force and such further conditions as the President with the approval of the Senate may deem appropriate to make our cooperation effective in fact and consistent with our practice. Under a Democratic Administration the Government will endeavor to lift this great question above partisanship, and to reflect the best opinion of those who place the welfare of the Nation above partisanship. It will pursue a course which safeguards American interests and conforms to American traditions, aspira-

[4] DNC, *Proceedings*, 1924, p. 244.

tions and ideals. It will cooperate with civilization to banish war. The Democratic Party has a foreign policy.[5]

Debate was limited to one hour for each side on each of the platform questions. On the League question, the principal point made by the main speaker for the majority was that a referendum would constitute a clear mandate, whereas if the question were mixed with other issues in the election campaign, no one could tell whether there was a mandate on the particular question.

You know we are busy explaining all the while that the seven millions majority for Mr. Harding did not mean rejection of the League; but the great mass of people took it to be such because it was injected into the campaign by the candidates and by the platform.[6]

The minority objected to the proposed referendum on the grounds that there was no constitutional or legal provison for one, that too much time would elapse before it could be taken, and that even if overwhelmingly approved there was no assurance that an unfriendly administration would implement it. Only by making it the responsibility of the party, and winning the election with a clear promise in the platform, could League membership be expedited. To this, a majority speaker responded that it would be impossible, within the foreseeable future, for the party to gain two thirds of the Senate. Only by taking the issue out of politics, and gaining League support from independents and Republicans could the desired goal be accomplished. This a referendum could do.

Newton D. Baker, Wilson's Secretary of War, made a major and lengthy speech for the minority resolution. He combined a bitter logical attack with a highly emotional appeal that recalled the love the party bore for the recently deceased Wilson, and "the closed eyes of soldiers in American uniform who were dying and who whispered to me messages to bring to their mothers."

[5] *Ibid.*, p. 247.
[6] *Ibid.*, p. 250.

His appeal did not move Senator Key Pittman of Nevada, who in speaking for the majority plank said:

> The speaker who spoke before here, with his wild burst of oratory, with tears in his eyes and his broken-down, slobbering body across this rail, is trying to appeal to your sympathies, not to your judgment.[7]

Neither Baker's logic nor his emotional appeal affected the vote of a majority in the convention. The minority amendment was defeated 742½ to 353½.

The minority plank on religious liberty accepted the text of the majority plank, but proposed the following far-reaching addition:

> We condemn political secret societies of all kinds as opposed to the exercise of free government and contrary to the spirit of the Declaration of Independence and of the Constitution of the United States. We pledge the Democratic Party to oppose any effort on the part of the Ku Klux Klan or any organization to interfere with the religious liberty or political freedom of any citizen, or to limit the civic rights of any citizen or body of citizens because of religion, birthplace or racial origin.[8]

The reading of this was punctuated by cheers, jeers, and general disorder, particularly in the galleries. Debate centered primarily upon specific mention of the Ku Klux Klan. The majority argued that to name the Klan as an organization interfering with religious and political liberties was to condemn without trial an organization of a million citizens because some of them had broken the law. The minority claimed that the plank did not oppose the Klan itself, but only committed the party to oppose any effort on the part of the Klan to interfere with civil liberties. No one participating in the debate supported the Klan in so many words—or admitted to membership, although one speaker mentioned "343 members of the Klan who are members of this Convention." The minority plank was defeated by the closest vote in convention history, 543³⁄₂₀ to 542⁷⁄₂₀.[9]

[7] *Ibid.*, p. 274.
[8] *Ibid.*, p. 248.
[9] See *Analysis of Key Votes.*

The Presidential Nomination (continued)

The final vote on the platform was not completed until two o'clock on Sunday morning. The convention then recessed until Monday before beginning the task of selecting a presidential candidate.

On the first ballot on Monday morning, nineteen individuals received one or more votes, but only two received as much as 10 per cent of the total vote: McAdoo 431½, and Smith 241. A two thirds majority required 733 votes. Nine ballots were taken during the morning and afternoon session, with only small gains registered by the two leaders, McAdoo receiving 444.6 and Smith 278 votes on the ninth ballot. Davis, starting from a modest 31 votes on the first ballot, moved into third place with 63 on the last ballot before adjournment. Six more ballots were taken during the evening session of this sixth day, the convention adjourning shortly after midnight.

Balloting continued throughout the week, the 77th ballot being taken before the adjournment on Saturday, July 5. No candidate had been able to get close to the required two thirds, although late Friday, on the 69th ballot, McAdoo reached a peak total of 530, nearly 50 per cent of the total vote. Smith reached his peak vote, 368, on the 76th ballot, taken on Saturday. Davis gained steadily up to the 24th ballot, when he reached 129½, remaining above 120 for several ballots before his support began to fall off. On the 77th he retained only 76½ to McAdoo's 513 and Smith's 367.

During the 38th roll call, William Jennings Bryan had risen to explain his vote. Although the response to the chairman's request for unanimous consent was by no means unanimous, the chairman pretended to hear no objection and Bryan was allowed to speak. In 1912, when he had similarly risen to explain his vote, he had bitterly opposed the financial interests; in 1924 he opposed anyone on the Wet side of the prohibition issue—which meant he was particularly opposed to Smith. After naming several possibilities, some not in the balloting, he closed with a plea for McAdoo.

The vote for McAdoo on the 38th ballot —444—was almost the same as it had been on the 37th, but it began to increase rapidly immediately thereafter—it was 499 on the 39th and 506.4 on the 40th. Most of the increase came from the release of Oklahoma's favorite son vote, and from the Davis column. It seems improbable, however, that Bryan's speech had much effect upon the vote, although it nearly caused a riot in the convention. Toward the last of his remarks he could scarcely complete a sentence without being interrupted by hisses, boos, and attempts of delegates to gain the floor in order to get him off the platform.

Following the 66th ballot, a resolution was presented to suspend the rules so that the convention might adjourn and meet again in executive session. The resolution also proposed that the chair invite each candidate to address the convention either personally or by designated representative. As a change in rules, the resolution required a two thirds majority and was lost, although supported by a majority of the convention: 551 Yes, 538 No, with 9 not voting.

Immediately thereafter, Franklin D. Roosevelt moved to suspend the rules and to hear a speech from the governor of New York, the host state. Since that governor was an active candidate, the proposal received but scattered support outside Smith's own following, and lost 604½ to 473, 20½ not voting. Lest the defeat of this proposal suggest that McAdoo followers were afraid to have Smith heard, McAdoo immediately dispatched a letter suggesting that the convention reconsider the matter and by unanimous consent permit Smith to address the convention. But the temper of the delegates was such that unanimous consent to anything would probably have been impossible. Objection was made and sustained by the chair.

Immediately following the 73rd ballot,

another attempt was made to amend the rules. A resolution providing that the lowest candidate on each ballot be dropped until only five candidates remained, and to be effective for the current day only, was defeated 589½ to 496, 12½ not voting. A motion was then made to adjourn after the 75th roll call, and if no nomination were made, to adjourn to Kansas City on July 21; this received only 82.7 votes in support. Further attempts to break the deadlock by rule changes were presented at various times, but all were defeated without recourse to a roll call vote. However, at the end of the balloting on Saturday, July 5, a resolution was passed directing the representatives of the candidates to hold a conference over the week end.

A report signed by representatives of all candidates except McAdoo was reported to the convention at the Monday morning session. In this, the several candidates agreed to:

. . . release each and every delegate from any pledge, instruction or obligation of any nature whatsoever in so far as their candidacy for the Democratic nomination for President is concerned, as completely as if their names had been withdrawn from the Convention.[10]

McAdoo proposed, in addition to releasing all delegates, that the unit rule be abrogated, majority rule be substituted for the two thirds rule, and the lowest candidate be dropped on each successive ballot. However, a motion to suspend the rules and report the above proposals to the committee on rules was defeated, and the convention resumed balloting. Following the 82nd ballot, a resolution to release the delegates from all pledges was presented; this passed with a preponderant majority of 985 to 105, 8 not voting. In view of the fact that several previous rulings of the chair supported attempts by delegates to abandon their pledges, the resolution had little effect at this stage of the proceedings. Certainly, there was little change between the 82nd and 83rd ballots.

When the balloting was first resumed

[10] DNC, *Proceedings*, 1924, p. 782.

with the 78th, on Monday, July 7, McAdoo slipped a bit from his top vote and from then on, with the exception of a short rally just before the end, declined steadily. Most of his vote, for several ballots, went to Senator Ralston, who enjoyed rather a spectacular run beginning with the 84th ballot and continuing through the 93rd, when part of his strength returned to McAdoo. The rest scattered, with a substantial part going to Davis on the 94th and 95th ballots, at which point Davis reached a new peak. Smith's vote remained remarkably steady, varying less than 20 votes between the 78th and 100th ballots.

Following the 93rd ballot, Roosevelt announced that Smith was willing to withdraw his name if McAdoo would do likewise—an offer rejected by the McAdoo camp at that point. Immediately after the 99th ballot, however, a letter from McAdoo gave his friends and supporters permission "to take such action as, in their judgment, may best serve the interests of the party." He added that he would continue to fight "for the defeat of the reactionary and Wet elements in the party." He certainly was not releasing his supporters to vote for Smith, but this was the beginning of the end.

McAdoo's vote on the 100th ballot melted from 353½ to 190. The defaulters did not move immediately to Davis, nor did they concentrate on any one candidate; actually, both Davis and Smith lost slightly on this ballot. The several beneficiaries of the movement were favorite sons, whose strength temporarily returned to them, and minor candidates such as Senators Thomas J. Walsh and Joseph T. Robinson, who previously had received only token support.

Walsh was an interesting compromise candidate. He had headed the investigations of the Teapot Dome scandals, and was widely known throughout the country. According to all accounts, as permanent chairman, he handled the job of controlling the convention during the bitter debates on prohibition and the Ku Klux Klan firmly and fairly to all concerned.

However, as a Catholic and a Dry, he was committed to a definite stand upon both the volatile issues before the convention and could scarcely expect support either from Ku Klux Klan advocates, who considered that issue more important than prohibition, or from Wets, who were more interested in the question of prohibition than of civil rights. In addition, he had no organization working for him on the floor. Two late comers also received blocks of votes: Edwin T. Meredith, former Secretary of Agriculture, and Josephus Daniels, former Secretary of the Navy, both members of Wilson's cabinet. This wide distribution of the McAdoo vote may have been due to the delegates' desire to gain time to adjust to the McAdoo letter; a motion to adjourn was made immediately after the totals were announced.

A decision finally was reached on the fourteenth day of the convention. On the 101st ballot, Smith's vote broke to 121 and McAdoo's to a mere 52. Davis, Underwood, and Meredith became the top three. Walsh received the respectable total of 98 votes, and on the next ballot moved into third place. Both Davis and Underwood gained substantially on the 102nd ballot, but at the end of the 103rd Davis continued to increase, while Underwood dropped. At this point, Davis's total was 575, still considerably short of the two thirds mark. Following the roll call, however, Iowa withdrew the name of Meredith, transferred her vote to Davis, and the band wagon began to roll. As delegates clamored for attention, "frantic, persistent and continuous cries of 'Mr. Chairman,' 'Mr. Chairman,' 'Mr. Chairman,' [were heard] from many delegations."

After the changes were recorded, the rules were suspended and the nomination was declared unanimous. In a short speech urging the necessity of wise counsel in the selection of a running mate in view of recent experience [the death of Harding], Josephus Daniels moved an adjournment. At this point, a demonstration began for the nomination of Chairman Thomas J.

Walsh, and a motion placing him in nomination was presented. Walsh ruled this out of order. After thanking the convention for the honor, he called for the vote on the motion to adjourn and declared it carried. As an additional precautionary measure, Walsh turned the chair over to Congressman Alben W. Barkley of Kentucky for the next session and also presented a letter refusing to allow his name to be entered for the vice-presidential nomination.

The Vice-Presidential Nomination

Thirteen candidates, including one woman and Governor Charles W. Bryan of Nebraska, brother of William Jennings Bryan, were placed in nomination for the Vice Presidency. At the end of the roll call Bryan, with 238 votes, was second to George L. Berry of Tennessee, a labor union executive, with 263½. West Virginia split its 16 votes among eight candidates. Selection of a Tennessean, with a West Virginian in the first position, would have violated the time-honored geographical criterion of availability. Mayor John F. Hylan of New York City, with 110 votes, and Alvin Owsley of Texas, with 152, were the next strongest candidates. Davis's current residence in New York probably weakened Hylan's candidacy; in any case, the break to Bryan came from Hylan's support. Illinois, which had split its vote evenly between Hylan and Bryan, changed its vote to Bryan. New York followed suit immediately, and the band wagon was in full motion. The vote did not swing much beyond the required two thirds, however, and after the announcement of Bryan's vote was greeted with boos and hisses no attempt was made to make the nomination unanimous. After fourteen long and full days, the convention finally adjourned sine die.

Analysis of Key Votes

The pattern of relationship between the historic vote on the Ku Klux Klan issue during the platform fight and the first ballot for the nominations clearly presaged the area of potential coalition—and indicated also the probability that formation of the coalition would not be easy. All but one of Smith's first-ballot supporters voted for the minority plank for an almost perfect negative correlation.[11]

The correlation with McAdoo's first-ballot vote is +.63, indicating less consistency on the part of his supporters—and less intensity on the part of many of them in the way they viewed the issue. The other candidates' vote correlation was zero, indicating that they were supported equally by people on both sides of the issue.

Smith's total vote on the first ballot was less than 25 per cent of the total convention strength; McAdoo's was nearly 40 per cent. Smith's supporters, while reliable, owing to the intensity with which they viewed the issue, did not hold a veto power under the two thirds rule. McAdoo's supporters, on the other hand, although not as cohesive on the issue, were strong enough to exercise veto power if they could be held together. Conceivably, either Smith or McAdoo could draw considerable strength from the other candidates, but this would do Smith less good than McAdoo because of his smaller vote base. If a candidate could be found who satisfied McAdoo's followers and was also acceptable to supporters of the other candidates, a nominating coalition could be formed. This, in fact, is what happened.

The correlation between the Klan vote and the critical vote for Davis on the 103rd ballot before vote shifting is +.71. The correlation with Underwood's vote, containing much of the hard-core Smith support, is −.81, and with the other votes still outside either coalition the correlation was −.32. Thus, Davis's coalition on the critical ballot clearly is composed primarily of ex-McAdoo and other votes, and drawn

[11] Technically, calculation of tetrachoric r is not valid for distributions in which less than five cases occur in one of the cells, but with 240 of 241 of Smith's votes from delegations that voted higher than the convention average for the minority report, the relationship in this instance is clear.

mainly from those supporting the majority rather than the minority plank on the Klan.

* * *

With each major-party ticket headed by a conservative easterner, the farmers of the Middle West and West, who did not share in the general national prosperity, saw little hope for recognition of their problems—whichever party won. They were joined by labor elements and liberal intellectuals in an attempt to establish a new party dedicated to the improvement of the lot of the common man. In a convention held on July 4 at Cleveland, Ohio, these groups nominated Robert M. La Follette for President. La Follette symbolized the progressive group in the Republican party that had for many years fought to liberalize the party. Burton K. Wheeler, Democratic senator from Montana, was chosen as his running mate.

The platform of the new party was liberal in domestic policy and somewhat isolationist with respect to international relations. It favored extension of public ownership of railroads and important natural resources; a sharply graduated income tax; greater rights for labor in the bargaining process. It also suggested greater popular control of the judicial process and of presidential nominations and elections. In the international field, the party advocated reduction of armaments, a popular referendum for declaration of war, and the outlawing of war by legislative agreement.

Presidential Election, November 4, 1924

CALVIN COOLIDGE (R) : popular vote, 15,725,016; electoral vote, 382
JOHN W. DAVIS (D) : popular vote, 8,385,586; electoral vote, 136
ROBERT M. LA FOLLETTE (P) : popular vote, 4,822,856; electoral vote, 13

1928

AFTER THE DEBACLE of the 1924 convention, the Democrats went down to electoral college defeat with John W. Davis almost as completely as with Cox in 1920. The Progressives, with Robert M. La Follette, cut into the vote of both major parties, and the Democratic share of the total popular vote fell to a new low. The congressional defeat was less crushing, however, and in 1926 the Democratic minority attained somewhat respectable proportions, when substantial gains were registered in the mid-term elections. Nevertheless, in 1928, because prosperity seemed still on an upward spiral, the out-party was faced with the always difficult problem of finding an issue that would outweigh the general reluctance of the public to change helmsmen when the voyage was smooth.

Actually, a sharp eye could discover many eddies and whirlpools of discontent. But most of them seemed small, and the majority of people disliked to have their optimistic mood disturbed by the warning cries of the few prophets of doom who dared to point out the rocks ahead. On only one issue could the Democrats hope to attract wide support: the leading Republican candidate for the Presidency was a staunch prohibitionist; by taking a firm stand for repeal of the prohibition amendment, the Democrats would certainly find sympathizers among people of all walks of life. On nearly every other issue, they were forced to back the causes of minorities —minorities whose social standing was poor or even suspect in the eyes of the millions who were, or thought they were, benefiting from the orgy of speculation taking place with the benign approval of the party in power.

NINETEENTH REPUBLICAN CONVENTION

President Coolidge, despite his frequent altercations with Congress, could probably have been nominated for a second full term had he clearly stated he wanted to be. Except for the farm sector, most of the economy appeared prosperous, if not booming, and no party has rejected an incumbent desiring renomination under these conditions. However, in August 1927, he released to the press his famous, if somewhat ambiguous, statement: "I do not choose to run for President in 1928."

Although many of his friends, as well as others who preferred the known to the unknown, assumed that the statement meant that he might be amenable to a draft, a number of Republicans took it at its face value as his flat refusal to be a candidate. To these latter, the way was therefore cleared for open candidacy without fear of presidential reprisal. Only one of them, however, waged a really aggressive and nationwide preconvention campaign: Herbert Hoover of California, who first received consideration as a presidential possibility in 1920 and who had continued to develop in stature, particularly as Secretary of Commerce under Harding and Coolidge.

Coolidge consistently refused to amplify his first statement on the 1928 nomination, but the fact that he did not block the candidacy of a member of his official family seemed to indicate that he favored Hoover —or at the very least did not oppose him. Coolidge's tactics in restricting himself to the single cryptic phrase may have been designed (as William Allen White, "The Sage of Emporia," suggested they were) to leave the way open for a draft if it appeared that a candidate whom he disliked might be nominated—specifically Frank O. Lowden, Vice President Charles G. Dawes, or any other supporter of the McNary-Haugen bill. Such a nomination would, from Coolidge's viewpoint, be a repudiation of his administration. As an open supporter of Coolidge on the McNary-Haugen bill, Hoover was the only avowed candidate whose nomination would appear to be an endorsement of Coolidge's stand.

In any event, Hoover's campaign was widespread, vigorous, and backed by ample funds and an efficient campaign organization. The only other candidate operating much above the favorite son level was Frank O. Lowden, whose campaign, even so, was much less strenuous and heavily financed than the one he had waged in 1920. As a leading supporter of McNary-Haugenism, Lowden was anathema to Coolidge and suspect to the organization people and the financial interests of the eastern seaboard. His best potential source of support was the Middle West, but the fact that all but one of the favorite sons presented to the convention were from this area cut sharply into his strength by fragmenting the farm bloc vote.

Under the leadership of Andrew W. Mellon, Secretary of the Treasury, a small but influential group centered in New York and Pennsylvania kept hopes alive that Coolidge would be drafted. By convention time, however, these hopes had largely been dissipated by Hoover's success in accumulating pledged delegates. Backed by the solid support of his home state, and bolstered by the advantage generally enjoyed with southern delegates by an incumbent administration—an advantage held because of Coolidge's hands-off policy, Hoover also had considerable success in the primaries. Since Lowden's policy was not to enter a primary unless his appraisal of his chances was high, and since the other candidates, with the exception of Senator George W. Norris of Nebraska, did not enter primaries other than in their own states, Hoover was unopposed in many of the primaries he entered.

He was defeated by Senator James E. Watson by a narrow margin in the latter's home state, Indiana, and by West Virginia's favorite son, Senator Guy D. Goff. Lowden won in Illinois, but he did not make a clean sweep, and his victory was more than offset by Hoover's victories in Massachusetts and Ohio. The Ohio primary was unusual because the favorite son of that state, Senator Frank B. Willis, died less than a month before the primary, too late to take his name off the ballot. Even against Norris in Nebraska, Hoover won a number of delegates, although his name was not on the ballot. One other candidate, Senator Charles Curtis of Kansas, won a few votes in addition to a majority of his own state delegation, mostly in states where the convention system prevailed. On the day the convention opened, the *New York Times* estimated Hoover's committed strength at 600 votes, a majority of the convention, and by the second day the estimate was increased to 724.

Kansas City, Missouri, June 12, 13, 14, 15, 1928

The long and detailed convention call contained no significant changes from 1924. The system of apportionment remained the same; instructions on selection of delegates and on filing contests, as well as how the national committee should act on contests, were described in detail.

Convention Organization

In a little over two hours on the first day, the convention completed the preliminary amenities, including the keynote speech by Senator Simeon D. Fess of Ohio, the temporary chairman. Committees were appointed without incident. On the second day, a small storm erupted in connection with the credentials of the eighteen district members of the Texas delegation. The majority report, presented by the first

woman to be chairman of a major committee in a Republican convention, recommended that the names placed on the temporary roll by the national committee be
retained. The minority report recommended they be substituted by eighteen
others. The delegates on the temporary
roll were Hoover supporters. It can be assumed that some, at least, of the proposed
substitutes were Lowden people, for his
campaign manager fought for them before
the national committee and the vote on
the contest correlates very high with the
nomination roll call.

If any question existed that Hoover had
the strength to win, it was dissipated by the
results of this contest, and many waverers
decided to get on the band wagon. As an
example, although the minority report was
presented by a delegate from Delaware and
the Delaware delegation voted unanimously
in support, the same delegation subsequently voted for Hoover. According to
contemporary accounts, Delaware entered
the convention pledged to Coleman du
Pont, a favorite son, with Lowden as a
probable second choice. The minority report was defeated 659½ to 399½, 30 not
voting.[1]

The reports of the committees on permanent organization rules and order of business were approved without debate. Senator George H. Moses of New Hampshire
was selected as permanent chairman. He
congratulated the Republican party upon
its plenitude of presidential timber, and
as for the opposition—"We challenge them
to bring forth their strongest champion.
. . . And we care not whether his name be
Brown, Jones, Robinson or Smith."[2]

The report of the rules committee tightened up the requirements for delegates to
district and state conventions by stipulating
that such delegates must be legal and qualified voters of the districts which they represent. The authority of the national committee to decide contests for national
committeeman or committeewoman was

clearly granted. No state or territory was
to elect more delegates or alternates than
the call provided. With the exception of
these, and other minor clarifications of existing customs, the rules followed those of
1924.

The Platform

The platform endorsed "without qualification the record of the Coolidge administration."

The record of the United States Treasury
under Secretary Mellon stands unrivalled and
unsurpassed. . . . In 1921 the credit of our
government was at a low ebb. We were burdened with a huge public debt, a load of war
taxes, which exceeded anything in our national
life. . . . This critical situation was evidenced
by a serious disturbance in our own life which
made for unemployment.
Today all these major financial problems
have been solved.[3]

To prove the point, the record of lower
taxes and the reduction of public debt
were cited. The isolationist stand of the
administration was endorsed, though again
cooperation in humanitarian efforts was accepted. In general, other planks endorsed
the administration stand and, where perti-
nent, suggested further progress along the
same lines. The agricultural plank became
a matter for debate (discussed below).
The closing plank on home rule included
an indictment of all efforts to extend the
federal government into the fields of state
and local activities, even where encouraged
by the latter:

There is a real need for the people once more
to grasp the fundamental fact that under our
system of government they are expected to solve
many problems themselves through their municipal and State governments, and to combat
the tendency that is all too common to turn to
the Federal Government as the easiest and least
burdensome method of lightening their own
responsibilities.[4]

Senator Robert M. La Follette, Jr., who
had succeeded to his father's Senate seat in
1923, presented a complete substitute plat-

[1] See *Analysis of Key Votes.*
[2] RNC, *Proceedings*, 1928, p. 101.

[3] *Ibid.*, p. 115.
[4] *Ibid.*, p. 131.

form signed by delegates from eight states. His presentation was received with good humor, interspersed with such remarks as, "That's all right, Bob; we like you, if we are not with you." The main theme of the proposed substitute platform, as stated in the preamble, was opposition to "privilege in all its forms, whether it be the privilege of individuals, of class, of interest, or of section."[5]

It warned that "the plight of agriculture today is not solely the concern of the farmer and his family. . . . It menaces the stability of our economic, social, and political life." It called for stabilization of farm prices above the cost of production, and to this end favored enactment of the McNary-Haugen bill and its administration "by those in sympathy with its objects." It also advocated governmental development and operation of major electric power systems at Muscle Shoals, Boulder Dam, and other strategic points. The right of labor to bargain collectively was upheld, increased income taxes for the higher brackets was advocated, and liberalization of the Volstead Act "along the lines proposed by popular referendums in several states" was favored.

After La Follette's presentation a motion was made to substitute another minority plank on agriculture differing from both the majority and minority platforms. It was stated that this plank had been approved by the representatives of fifteen states.

The debate centered upon this plank, with the minority proponents doing most of the talking. Again, the majority was tolerant, and there were few interruptions during the speeches. At the end of the debate on the agriculture plank, Nicholas Murray Butler of New York presented a minority plank which, in effect, advocated repealing the Eighteenth Amendment, and leaving liquor regulation to the states. This was tabled by voice vote and without debate other than the remarks appended by Butler to the reading of the plank.

[5] *Ibid.*, p. 135.

A roll call was demanded upon an agricultural plank presented by Earl C. Smith of Illinois, which differed from both the majority plank and that proposed by La Follette.

. . . the Republican party pledges that the united efforts of the legislative and executive branches of government, so far as they are controlled by the party, will be devoted to the immediate enactment of legislation aimed to restore and maintain the purchasing power of farm products, and the complete economic equality of agriculture.

. . . it is of fundamental concern that a proper balance be maintained between . . . [agriculture and industry] in the future, and we pledge the party to the enactment in future tariffs of agricultural schedules commensurate with tariffs on industrial products.[6]

In effect, the plank attempted to advocate the basic principles of the McNary-Haugen bill without spelling them out completely or mentioning the bill by name. The minority platform presented by La Follette specifically mentioned the bill by name and advocated its espousal as a party platform. The agricultural plank in the majority report advocated establishment of a Federal Farm Board "clothed with necessary powers to promote the establishment of a farm marketing system of farmer-owned-and-controlled stabilization corporations or associations to prevent and control surpluses through orderly distribution."

Although favoring adequate tariff protection for commodities affected by foreign competition, the majority advocated, as a solution to the farm problem, improvement of the distribution system rather than any form of subsidy such as incorporated in the McNary-Haugen plan. The minority agricultural plank was beaten 807 to 277, with 5 votes not cast. (Of those who later voted for Hoover, before vote shifting, almost none had voted for the minority side of this question.) The convention then approved the majority platform in its original form by voice vote. No action

[6] *Ibid.*, p. 145.

is recorded in the proceedings on the substitute minority platform proposed by La Follette, but it is obvious it would have received little support in a convention dominated by Hoover.

The Presidential Nomination

When the nominating roll call commenced, Alabama yielded to California. Almost at the beginning of the nominating speech, the speaker mentioned Hoover's name and was interrupted by a long and noisy demonstration. When order finally was restored, the speech was completed, whereupon a second demonstration began. When order returned again, Arizona yielded to Illinois for the expected nomination of Lowden; instead, a letter was read announcing Lowden's withdrawal on the grounds that the platform did not "meet fully and fairly the agricultural problem." This was consistent with a statement made by Lowden in the course of the preconvention campaign. Other nominations followed: James E. Watson of Indiana; Charles Curtis of Kansas; Guy D. Goff of West Virginia; George W. Norris of Nebraska; and even Calvin Coolidge.

Lowden's withdrawal, coming as a surprise to some of his adherents, took the heart out of the opposition bent on "stopping Hoover," and the ballot undoubtedly reflected considerably more of a margin for Hoover than would have been the case if Lowden had stayed in the race. It is doubtful that Hoover could have been stopped, however, and this probably entered into Lowden's final decision. Many delegates who would have preferred to fight to the finish felt that Lowden had let them down. Political leaders who abandon their followers suddenly without giving them time to make other commitments and to save face seldom retain much political influence thereafter. Lowden was no exception.

On the only roll call, Hoover received 837 of the 1,089 votes in the convention, Lowden, despite his withdrawal, was second with 74, and Curtis third with 64.

The Vice-Presidential Nomination

Before the vice-presidential nominations, a minor dispute arose concerning the Georgia members of the national committee. The rules provided that all contests be submitted to the national committee with full power to act, but a Georgia delegate moved that the rule be suspended, and the Georgia delegation be polled to select the national committee members from the convention floor. A roll call was taken on a motion to table the resolution, and tabling won, 761 to 308 with 20 not voting. The correlation with the presidential ballot was low, indicating that the division was along lines other than the main division within the convention.

Three candidates other than Charles Curtis were presented to the convention, but all withdrew in his favor. Only a scattered few die-hard Progressives failed to vote for Curtis on the roll call; he received 1,052 of the 1,089 votes, and no negative vote was recorded on the motion to make the nomination unanimous.

Analysis of Key Votes

Despite the obvious band-wagon shift caused partly by Hoover's demonstrated strength and partly by the disorganization following Lowden's withdrawal, the correlation between the vote on the Texas credentials issue and Hoover's nominating ballot is +.87. This would indicate that almost all, if not all, delegates who voted with the majority on the credentials question voted for Hoover, and that they were joined in the Hoover vote by a substantial number who voted with the minority on credentials.

TWENTY-FIFTH DEMOCRATIC CONVENTION

During the years between the 1924 fiasco and the 1928 convention, Al Smith maintained and developed his leadership of the urban-wet-liberal section of the party.

William G. McAdoo not only failed to exercise equivalent leadership over the rural-dry-conservative elements but also issued a statement that he was not a candidate in 1928. No one took his place as leader of the anti-Smith forces.

Smith did all he could to placate the opposition, and this almost certainly explains the selection of a southern city as the convention site, which could not have occurred without Smith's approval. His campaign was well financed and well organized. He was opposed only by sectional candidates and favorite sons, and generally followed a policy of not entering his name in primaries where such candidates appeared. Accordingly, Atlee Pomerene of Ohio, Evans Woolen of Indiana, and Gilbert Hitchcock of Nebraska won the delegations of their respective states without serious contest. Smith entered his name everywhere else and won the complete delegation in most cases. Senator James A. Reed of Missouri salvaged 2 votes in Illinois and approximately one third of the West Virginia delegation, but of the 345 votes involved in the twelve states in which primaries were held, Smith received 233½ on the first ballot before vote switching. By the time the convention assembled few newspaper commentators saw any probability that Smith could be stopped.

Houston, Texas,
June 26, 27, 28, 29, 1928

The convention call again stipulated that "no state or territory shall elect any number of delegates with their alternates in excess of the quota to which such state or territory may be entitled," and the basis remained the same as in 1924. This provided two delegates and alternates for each United States senator and for each representative in Congress, with six each for the District of Columbia, Philippines, Hawaii, Puerto Rico, Alaska, and the Canal Zone, and two for the Virgin Islands. The call again provided the option of four delegates for each senator with the recommendation the additional delegates be women. As in

previous conventions, little attention was paid to the rule, for almost every combination of fractional votes was included—full votes, half votes, two thirds votes, quarter votes. The recommendation that women be included if the provision for half votes for the at large seats was adopted was also frequently disregarded, although most delegations included at least one woman alternate.

Convention Organization

In an unprecedentedly short opening session, nothing was done except to read the call and receive greetings from the mayor of Houston. At the opening of the second session, Claude G. Bowers of Indiana, well-known historian, was presented as temporary chairman. Bowers greeted the convention with a long oration, verging on brilliance at times, in which he enlarged upon the theme of the fundamental philosophies of the two parties. Basing the Democratic philosophy firmly upon that of Jefferson, he endeavored to drive a wedge between the two segments of the Republican party by showing the incompatibility of the Hamiltonian philosophy, to which he attributed that which was bad in the party, and the Lincolnesque philosophy, from which stemmed what little that was good.

The convention moved smoothly through the first phases of the organization procedure, but a minority report was presented in protest against the report of the committee on credentials. In presenting the minority report, the speaker stated that it was merely a protest, and he would not ask for debate or for a vote. The majority report was accepted by voice vote.

Reports on permanent organization and rules and order of business were accepted without debate. Senator Joseph T. Robinson of Arkansas was selected permanent chairman. The report of the committee on rules and order of business resumed the precedent, broken in 1924, of inserting the report of the committee on platform and resolutions between the presentation of the presidential candidates and the actual balloting, an indication that in this convention tensions were lower than in 1924. William Jennings Bryan, absent for the first time in thirty-two years, was memorialized in a long eulogy by Josephus Daniels, which was followed by resolutions honoring Bryan's services to the party and extending sympathy to his widow.

The Presidential Nomination

Pending the completion of the platform report, the presidential nominating speeches were ordered. Alfred E. Smith for the third time since 1920 was presented in nomination, and as in 1924 the nominating speech was made by Franklin D. Roosevelt. Nine other candidates were presented, most of whom received one or two seconding speeches. The outcome was clearly indicated, however, by the number and distribution of seconding speeches for Al Smith: one after another, approximately twenty delegates from all sections of the nation rose to second Smith.

The Platform

Immediately following the nominating speeches, a petition was presented, reputedly "represent[ing] a population of more than six and a quarter million and a voting personnel of not less than one million"; it was stated that the protest came from southern states. The protest was against the selection of any candidate in favor of repealing either the Eighteenth Amendment or the Volstead Act, or who was not fully committed to complete prohibition of the liquor traffic. No action was requested on the petition, nor was any action taken.

Following the reading of the report of the committee on platform and resolutions, the liquor question was again raised by delegates who desired the convention to take a positive stand, not only for full enforcement, but also for a statement of full approval of the prohibition amendment; a plank was proposed that charged the Republicans with failure to enforce the law, and pledged the Democratic party to "an honest effort to enforce the eighteenth amendment."

As further indication that everything was too well settled in advance to make a fight worth while, the speaker presenting the minority plank stated that he would not carry it to a poll, and the majority platform was adopted by a voice vote.

The Presidential Nomination (continued)

At the end of the roll call for the first balloting, Smith lacked 10 votes of the required two thirds. A number of delegates demanded recognition simultaneously, and the chair recognized Ohio. The transfer of 47 votes from Ohio's favorite son, Pomerene, put Smith well over the top, and other delegations changed their vote to build his total to 849⅔.

The Vice-Presidential Nomination

Although several candidates were presented for the vice-presidential nomination, none proved a serious threat to Senator Robinson, the convention chairman, who received 914⅙ votes on the first ballot; Senator Alben W. Barkley of Kentucky was his closest rival with 77. Robinson's total was raised to 1,035⅙ after various delegations shifted their vote. As a Dry, a Protestant, and a resident of a rural southern state, Robinson complemented Smith in every respect—thus providing the balance to the ticket deemed so important. He was the first nominee with residence in the South to appear on the ticket of a major party since the end of the Civil War.

Presidential Election, November 6, 1928

HERBERT C. HOOVER (R) : popular vote, 21,392,190; electoral vote, 444
ALFRED E. SMITH (D) : popular vote, 15,016,443; electoral vote, 87

1932

THE LANDSLIDE Republican victory of 1928 was followed within a year by the stock market crash of 1929, and the country soon found itself in the grip of one of the most severe depressions in history. The economic change was quickly reflected in political change, and in the mid-term elections of 1930 the Democratic party captured both houses of Congress, the first time they had won either since the Wilson era. As the depression deepened, personal financial reserves were depleted and suffering increased; demands for speedy and effective action became more pressing. The administration, however, could not, or at any rate did not, stop the downward spiral.

Early in the preconvention period, the chairman of the Democratic national committee added a section to his staff that, if not unprecedented, was certainly more strongly backed and more effective than anything of its kind had been in the past. With the new section working under the guidance of Charles Michelson, every act of President Hoover was examined and presented to the public in the worst light possible. Nothing the Republicans tried could quite counteract the steady flow from Michelson's pen.

TWENTIETH REPUBLICAN CONVENTION

Long before the convention opened, it was suggested by Arthur Krock of the *New York Times,* among others, that the Republicans were in a position where they must renominate a President whose administration was unpopular as a result of the depression, and that they were there-

fore faced with the problem of justifying his administration. Many Republicans believed that Herbert Hoover was doing the best that could be done under the circumstances, or at any rate, that no one else could do any better. Others felt that abandonment of Hoover would be an acknowledgment of party failure. Substantial elements of the party would have been willing to oppose his renomination openly if they had believed there were any reasonable prospects of making the opposition stick, but few actually did so. The strong men in the party who were seriously opposed to his candidacy reserved their fire, and subsequently either bolted, as in the cases of Senators George W. Norris, Hiram W. Johnson, and Robert M. La Follette, Jr., or withheld support, as in the cases of Frank O. Lowden and Senator William E. Borah.

Much of the open opposition that did develop centered around a curious campaign waged in the primaries by Joseph I. France, an ex-senator from Maryland. France entered most of the preferential primaries that were held in 1932, and appeared to score impressive victories in many of them. These victories were somewhat shadowy, however, for his generally was the only name on the ballot; with the exception of Oregon, where the presidential preference vote was binding on the delegates, his victories did not result in pledged support. France's real purpose, apparently, was to demonstrate the degree of opposition to Hoover that existed in the party, and to set the stage for a possible "draft" of Coolidge in the convention. In two states, North Dakota and Ohio, he was opposed by a quaint figure out of the past,

Jacob S. Coxey, the leader of "Coxey's Army" in its march on Washington, D. C., in 1894. In North Dakota, France defeated Coxey, but the latter received a substantial plurality over France in Ohio, Coxey's home state.

Hoover and his supporters, in the meantime, paid little attention to the popularity aspects of the delegate selection process. Instead, they spent their energies on the selection, through regular party organization processes, of delegates who reputedly could be depended upon to secure Hoover's renomination.

Chicago, Illinois,
June 14, 15, 16, 1932

As predicted by press commentators, Hoover and the administration record were the main themes of the convention. The convention was opened by the national committee chairman, Senator Simeon D. Fess of Ohio, who made a short patriotic speech that was followed by a massing of the colors by a color guard and the singing of the national anthem. Hoover was then honored by the Ohio Glee Club, singing "Our President."

Convention Organization

The themes were stressed by the keynote speaker and temporary chairman, Senator Lester J. Dickinson of Iowa, and appeared again in the speech of Congressman Bertrand H. Snell of New York, the permanent chairman, and as an important part of the platform itself. No controversy arose during the organization of the convention; reports of the committees on credentials, permanent rules, and permanent organization were accepted without debate or record vote.

The Platform

The platform was presented during the third session, and for the first time in the convention open dissension appeared. A long plank on the prohibition question began by reaffirming Republican party belief in strict obedience to and enforcement of the law. However, the plank continued, the Constitution provides ways for change in the basic laws of the land, but Article V limits the proposal of amendments to two methods: (1) by two thirds of both houses of Congress or (2) by a national constitutional convention called on application of the legislatures of two thirds of the states. Ratification of constitutional change also is restricted to two methods: (1) by the legislatures of three fourths of the states or (2) by conventions held in three fourths of the states. Accordingly, proposals to hold a national referendum on the question of repeal of the Eighteenth Amendment had no constitutional sanction. When first incorporated in the Constitution, the Eighteenth Amendment was supported and opposed by members of both parties. "It was not then and is not now a partisan political question." With respect to what should be done, the plank stated:

We do not favor a submission limited to the issue of retention or repeal, for the American nation never in its history has gone backward, and in this case the progress which has been thus far made must be preserved, while the evils must be eliminated.

We therefore believe that the people should have an opportunity to pass upon a proposed amendment the provision of which, while retaining in the Federal Government power to preserve the gains already made in dealing with the evils inherent in the liquor traffic, shall allow States to deal with the problem as their citizens may determine, but subject always to the power of the Federal Government to protect those States where prohibition may exist and safeguard our citizens everywhere from the return of the saloon and attendant abuses.

Such an amendment should be promptly submitted to the States by Congress, to be acted upon by State conventions called for that sole purpose in accordance with the provisions of Article V of the Constitution and adequately safeguarded so as to be truly representative.[1]

The reading of the plank was followed by a demonstration in which applause and

[1] RNC, *Proceedings*, 1932, pp. 120-121.

protest were more or less equally mixed. After the entire platform had been read a minority report was submitted that proposed that the section of the majority plank beginning with and following the words "We do not favor a submission limited to the issue of retention or repeal" be stricken out and the following inserted in its place:

We therefore recommend that the Congress of the United States immediately propose an amendment of the Federal Constitution repealing the 18th Amendment thereto, to be submitted in conventions of the people of the several States called for that sole purpose in accordance with the provision of Article V of the Constitution of the United States, and adequately safeguarded so as to be truly representative.

Should the 18th Amendment be repealed we pledge our best efforts toward the enactment of such measures in the several States as will actually promote temperance, effectively abolish the saloon whether open or concealed, and bring the liquor traffic itself under complete public supervision and control, with revenues properly drawn from legalized sources for the relief of the burdened taxpayers.[2]

The debate was long and repeatedly interrupted by the predominately pro-repeal galleries. Both sides agreed in general that something had to be done, but differed as to what it should be. The majority insisted that complete repeal and abandonment of all federal control would lead directly back to the conditions that inspired the amendment in the first place. The minority argued that federal control, as advocated in the majority plank, could and probably would lead to invasion of states rights. Other arguments related to the economic, social, and moral consequences of the two approaches, but the question of federal versus state control received the most attention.

Hoover was known to favor the majority proposal, and when the matter was finally put to a vote the minority substitute was defeated 690^{19}⁄$_{36}$ to 460⅚, with 3¾ not voting.[3] With the exception of Mississippi

and Kentucky, the southern delegations voted almost unanimously on the side of the question preferred by Hoover, and they more than provided the margin of victory. According to Turner Catledge of the *New York Times,* the Mississippi vote was explained by the leader of the delegation as a "pure fumble" due to a misunderstanding of the question. Following the defeat of the minority plank, the majority platform was accepted by voice vote, though by no means unanimously.

Aside from the prohibition issue, several other planks were of considerable interest, though there was no open dissension about them on the convention floor. The party stand on how to meet the depression was well expressed in two short statements, though many other paragraphs were included on the subject. The first of these asserted:

The people themselves, by their own courage, their own patient and resolute effort in the readjustments of their own affairs, can and will work out the cure. It is our task as a party, by leadership and wise determination of policy, to assist that recovery.[4]

It was neither the prerogative nor the duty of government, therefore, to intervene actively in the recovery process, but rather to assist efforts made by private individuals. The second passage stated:

Constructive plans for financial stabilization cannot be completely organized until our national, State and municipal governments not only balance their budgets but curtail their current expenses as well to a level which can be steadily and economically maintained for some years to come.

We urge prompt and drastic reduction of public expenditure and resistance to every appropriation not demonstrably necessary to the performance of government, national or local.[5]

---

[2] *Ibid.,* p. 127.

[3] The fractions, unusual in a Republican convention, were due primarily to the fact that many states had not redistricted, following changes in congressional apportionment resulting from the

census of 1930. Missouri, for example, had dropped from sixteen to thirteen seats in Congress, and this was reflected in the convention apportionment, the state being allotted thirty-three delegates instead of thirty-nine as in 1928. The problem was solved by allowing 1½ votes to each of the sixteen old congressional districts, or ¾ of a vote for each delegate and full votes for the delegates at large.

[4] RNC, *Proceedings,* 1932, p. 103.

[5] *Ibid.,* p. 106.

The way to beat the depression, in other words, was not pump priming but reduction of government spending.

An unusual plank for a national party platform vigorously attacked the members of the party who had not wholeheartedly supported the administration.

We believe that the majority of the Congressmen elected in the name of a party have the right and duty to determine the general policies of that party requiring Congressional action, and that Congressmen belonging to that party are, in general, bound to adhere to such policies. Any other course inevitably makes of Congress a body of detached delegates which, instead of representing the collective wisdom of our people, become the confused voices of a heterogeneous group of unrelated local prejudices.

We believe that the time has come when Senators and Representatives of the United States should be impressed with the inflexible truth that their first concern should be the welfare of the United States and the well-being of all its people, and that stubborn pride of individual opinion is not a virtue, but an obstacle to the orderly and successful achievement of the objects of representative government.

Only by cooperation can self-government succeed. Without it election under a party aegis becomes a false pretense.

We earnestly request that Republicans throughout the Union demand that their representatives in the Congress pledge themselves to these principles, to the end that the insidious influences of party disintegration may not undermine the very foundations of the Republic.[6]

The Presidential Nomination

The nominations began the next day with the presentation of Herbert Hoover by California, to whom Alabama had yielded. A lengthy demonstration followed. When order finally was restored, the roll of states was resumed, with no response until Oregon was reached. A member of the Oregon delegation that technically was pledged to Joseph I. France presented him to the convention in a speech filled with anti-Hoover implications such as the following:

Shall the people of these United States elect to the presidency, at this critical time, any man

[6] *Ibid.*, pp. 123-124.

who has lacked the candor and the courage to state boldly and clearly where he stands upon this [the Prohibition question] and every important issue of vital concern to the American people?

Immediately after the speech, France himself approached the platform and requested permission to address the convention. When asked for his credentials he was unable to show anything other than a badge, evidently obtained from one of the Oregon delegates. When he continued to insist upon his right to speak for Oregon, the chairman called upon the sergeant at arms to escort him out of the hall; the escorting was done with very little ceremony. According to the *New York Times* correspondent, France's plan was to obtain the rostrum, then resign in favor of Calvin Coolidge in the hope that the convention might be stampeded into a draft-Coolidge movement.

When order was restored after France's exit, nine seconding speeches for Hoover proceeded in orderly fashion. On the first ballot Hoover received nomination, with 1,126½ of the 1,154 votes in the convention. France received a total of 4 votes, most of the Oregon delegates realistically disregarding their instructions.

The Vice-Presidential Nomination

The renomination of Vice President Charles Curtis was not so easily accomplished. Many delegates were undoubtedly in a rebellious mood because of what appeared to them to be too-rigid control of the convention by President Hoover, who reportedly had a direct telephone line from his desk to the convention hall. Many other delegates may have believed that Hoover would not be much disturbed if Curtis were replaced.

Whatever the reason several active candidates received support, the two strongest competitors being Major General James G. Harbord of New York and Hanford MacNider of Iowa. General Harbord had served with distinction during the first World War, and was Deputy Chief of

Staff for a year before retiring in 1922 after thirty-three years of service. Mac-Nider also had a military background, rising from the ranks during the war to the rank of colonel; subsequently, he served as Assistant Secretary of War under Coolidge, and had recently been elected national commander of the American Legion.

At the end of the first roll call, Curtis lacked only a few votes for a majority, and this quickly was supplied by the transfer of Pennsylvania's 75 votes from its favorite son to Curtis. The vote then stood 634¼ for Curtis; MacNider had 182¾ and Harbord 161¾, the remaining votes being scattered among ten candidates. The nomination was then approved as unanimous.

TWENTY-SIXTH DEMOCRATIC CONVENTION

For the first time since 1916, Democratic leaders could hope realistically for success in the presidential campaign. As in 1910, after a long period of Republican dominance, the Democrats in 1930 won control of Congress and elected a group of new governors. Of the latter, Governor Franklin Delano Roosevelt of New York (first elected in 1928 and re-elected in 1930) stood far out from the field—not by virtue of having overturned a Republican administration, but because he had proved an even better vote-getter than his predecessor, Alfred E. Smith, who himself had reversed the heavy Republican tide in New York during the lean Democratic years of the early and middle twenties. Roosevelt, scion of an aristocratic family, entered New York state politics in 1911 by winning a seat in the assembly from a predominantly Republican district. Later, he served as Assistant Secretary of the Navy under Wilson, and in 1920 became the Democratic nominee for Vice President.

His career received a severe setback when he was attacked by poliomyelitis in 1921, but he had recovered enough of his health by 1928 to accept the nomination for governor of New York, although only after a great deal of persuasion by the presidential nominee of that year, Al Smith. In the election he ran far ahead of Smith in New York, winning where Smith lost, and in 1930 won again with an overwhelming majority. This marked him as presidential timber, especially in view of Smith's statement after his 1928 defeat that he would never again run for public office.

Backed by a number of enthusiastic followers, of whom one of the more important was James A. Farley, Roosevelt became an early front-runner. Farley, a New York businessman with a wide acquaintance throughout the country by virtue of his activities with fraternal organizations and the Democratic party, seeing the possibility of nominating Roosevelt, took advantage of a nationwide business tour to explore and to further the possibility. The tour having persuaded him that the nomination was possible, he thenceforward devoted his considerable energies to the task.

The late entrance of Smith into the race complicated the problem somewhat, particularly in New York, but the Roosevelt movement had gathered sufficient momentum by then to make it difficult for Smith to stop it. Most of the efforts for Roosevelt were made with delegations selected through convention methods, the South particularly being won almost solidly for him. Only rarely did he face Smith directly in a primary, and where he did the results were inconclusive. In the California primary—which was to prove critical—Roosevelt ran second and Smith third, to Speaker of the House John Nance Garner of Texas, who received the backing of Californian William G. McAdoo, long an opponent of Smith's.

By convention time, it appeared obvious to most observers that Roosevelt had a majority of the delegates pledged to him, but that he was considerably short of the required two thirds. It was also obvious that two important battles for control of the convention machinery were looming: the selection of the permanent chairmanship, and the perennial question of the two thirds rule.

Shortly before the convention opened, the national committee endorsed a recommendation by the subcommittee on arrangements that Jouett Shouse, chairman of the national executive committee, be made permanent chairman of the convention. In April 1932, Roosevelt had been approached regarding the acceptability of Shouse; he gave a somewhat ambiguous reply that appeared to endorse Shouse, but left room for other interpretation.

Whatever Roosevelt's intention was at that time, the fact that the wording of the resolution approved by Roosevelt and made by the committee on arrangements "commended" Shouse as permanent chairman, while it "recommended" Senator Alben W. Barkley of Kentucky as temporary chairman, suggests that Roosevelt may even then have foreseen the desirability of keeping the pro-Smith Shouse out of the chair. Certainly, the gathering bitterness between Smith and himself during the interim before the convention made control of the chairmanship important to Roosevelt.

Chicago, Illinois,
June 27, 28, 29, 30; July 1, 2, 1932

As in the case of the Republican convention, the apportionment of delegates was complicated by the new congressional apportionment arising out of the census of 1930, but the solution reached by the Democratic national committee, and incorporated in the call, differed from the Republican. Where the latter used the new congressional apportionment as the base, the Democratic call provided that states whose congressional representation remained the same, or were reduced by reapportionment, should receive the same number of seats as they held in 1928; states that received additional congressional seats through congressional reapportionment were apportioned convention seats in accordance with the new Congress. By this formula, states such as Missouri that lost three seats in Congress sent the same number of delegates as in 1928, and states such as California, with its rapidly growing population, received the benefit of growth.

Convention Organization

The convention got off to a good start with a rousing speech by Alben W. Barkley, the temporary chairman. Following the speech, committees were appointed, whereupon the convention adjourned until the next day.

Both major credentials contests involved pro-Roosevelt delegations, the loss of which would have been serious to his cause. From Louisiana, two delegations contested the seats of the delegation headed by Senator and former Governor Huey Long. Long's delegation, containing most of the high elected officers of the state, had been elected by the state central committee, then fully controlled by Long. It was seated on the temporary roll by a divided vote of the national committee after strong protests from the other two delegations.

The majority report of the credentials committee recommended approval of the decision by the national committee, but a minority report recommended substitution of the delegation headed by Frank J. Looney. This one included three ex-governors and several other prominent people, all of whom were trying to break the hold of the Long machine in Louisiana; it had been selected in a convention especially called for the purpose by four members of the state central committee and a group of parish chairmen.

There seems little question that the Long group represented the controlling faction in the state, but it also seems clear that the method by which they were selected precluded any real participation by the rank and file of the party, or by any factional leaders outside the Long organization. Long had announced for Roosevelt, and the 20 votes of the Louisiana delegation were a prize worth seeking. The third contesting delegation had little pretense of legitimacy and received scant attention from the convention. On the roll call, the minority report was defeated 638¾ to 514¼ in a vote that correlated closely with Roosevelt's critical vote.

The second major contest involved Minnesota. The minority claims were based upon two factors: (1) members of the state central committee were allowed to vote in the convention called for the purpose of selecting delegates to the national convention; (2) delegates from the largest county in the state were not allowed to participate. According to the majority supporters, members of the state central committee had been given votes in the convention of 1928, and the call issued in 1932, which included the same provisions, was not protested by the minority before the state convention. The county delegation was excluded only on the roll call for temporary chairman, and this was due to the fact that the delegation was contested. According to the majority, the vote on this roll call was 444 to 86, excluding the votes of the state central committee. Thus, even the 106 members of the committee plus 141 delegates from the county excluded could not have changed the decision.

After the election of the temporary chairman, the excluded delegation and some other members of the original convention withdrew and formed a rump convention. Aside from the merits of the case, the regular delegates were committed to Roosevelt and the rump convention delegates were unpledged. On a vote very similar to the Louisiana contest, the minority report was rejected 658¼ to 492¾. Delegations listed on the temporary roll for these two states were allowed to vote in both contests.

The two victories for Roosevelt on the credentials contests were quickly followed by another. The committee on permanent organization, disregarding the recommendation of the national committee, nominated Senator Thomas J. Walsh of Montana for permanent chairman. Walsh, the candidate of the Roosevelt people, was a shrewd choice. He was highly respected and generally liked, and his record in disclosing major scandals in the Republican administration made him a logical selection for opening a campaign that would consist largely of attacks upon Republican ineptitude and corruption. As chairman of the long and bitter 1924 convention, he had handled a difficult task so well that he narrowly escaped being drafted for the vice-presidential nomination by a spontaneous uprising of the delegates. There could be no question as to his ability in the chair. His opponent, Jouett Shouse, was, however, an almost equally difficult target to attack. Shouse had spearheaded the campaign against Hoover and the administration ever since his appointment in 1929 as chairman of the national executive committee and had done important work in developing the party organization.

The debate consisted of a curious series of speeches in which each speaker eulogized both Walsh and Shouse. The main point made by supporters of the minority report was that the national committee recommendation had been based upon clearance with party leaders, including Roosevelt, and that reversal of the recommendation was a repudiation of Shouse. The Roosevelt people, on the other hand, insisted that Roosevelt had merely *commended* Shouse for presentation to the convention, but had not *recommended* him.

This quibbling over words arose from the wording of the resolution as approved by the national committee after clearance with Roosevelt:

This committee commends to the Permanent Committee on Organization of the Democratic National Convention for consideration as Permanent Chairman of that convention the name of Jouett Shouse, of Kansas.[7]

[7] DNC, *Proceedings,* 1932, p. 507.

Roosevelt supporters further contended that the committee went beyond its prerogatives in recommending a permanent chairman. Although it was necessary for the committee to recommend the temporary officers, since the convention was not yet organized at the time of their selection, permanent officers should be selected by the regularly constituted committee of the convention. When the roll call vote was taken, the pattern of voting remained much the same—except that the Roosevelt majority was somewhat reduced—as on the two credentials contests: the motion to substitute Shouse for Walsh was defeated 626 to 528.[8]

The report of the committee on rules and order of business was approved by voice vote without opposition or debate, but an earlier sharp battle had occurred during the preconvention and convention organization period. The conflict centered about a proposed move by the Roosevelt people to abolish the century-old two thirds rule for the nomination, thus exploiting their majority in the convention. In developing their strategy, the Roosevelt managers evidently failed to recognize that an important part of their candidate's support lay in the South, and that southern delegates considered the rule to be of great importance for protection of their interests. So long as the rule prevailed, the southern delegates reasoned that no candidate whom they uniformly opposed could be forced upon them, since the South held approximately one third of the total convention strength and accordingly could exercise a veto.

When rumors of the proposed move reached the delegates, the volume of protest made it quickly obvious that southern delegates might bolt from Roosevelt if he persisted in pushing the rule change. Roosevelt quickly withdrew attempts to change the rule, and as a compromise a future recommendation was added to the report of the committee on rules.

[8] See *Analysis of Key Votes.*

We recommend to the next National Convention of the party that it shall consider the question of changing the two-thirds rule now required for the nomination of President and Vice-President of the United States so as to make the nomination by a majority vote of the delegates to the convention with a further declaration that the convention is to be the sole judge of its own rules.[9]

The Platform

Despite the fact that work was done on the platform by committee members appointed by the delegations prior to the opening of the convention, the difficulties in arriving at an agreement were so great that the platform committee was unable to report until the evening of the third day. The prohibition plank in the majority report was accompanied by a minority plank, and a debate lasting nearly five hours followed. The majority plank stated:

We advocate the repeal of the Eighteenth Amendment. To effect such repeal we demand that the Congress immediately propose a Constitutional Amendment to truly represent the conventions in the states called to act solely on that proposal; we urge the enactment of such measures by the several states as will effectively prevent the return of the saloon, and bring the liquor traffic into the open under complete supervision and control by the states.[10]

The minority proposed as a substitute:

. . . that the Congress immediately propose to truly representative conventions in the states, called to meet solely on the proposal, a repeal of the Eighteenth Amendment. In the event of repeal, we urge that the Democratic Party cooperate in the enactment of such measures as in the several states will actually promote temperance, effectively prevent return of the saloon and bring the liquor traffic under complete supervision and control by the states, and that the Federal Government effectively exercise its power to protect states against importation of liquors in violation of their laws.[11]

[9] DNC, *Proceedings*, 1932, p. 140.
[10] *Ibid., p.* 149.
[11] *Ibid.,* p. 150.

The principal argument made by the minority was that the prohibition question was not and should not be made a partisan question; accordingly, the Democratic party should not endorse one side of the issue. The minority agreed that something had to be done, and also approved the mechanism suggested in the majority plank for "representative conventions" to be called in the states to deal with the problem. But the minority did not believe that the party should prejudice the decision by an outright endorsement of repeal.

The supporters of the original plank contended that if a majority of the states, containing an even larger majority of the population, desired outright repeal, it would be hypocritical not to say so. The "noble experiment" was demonstrably a failure. Other arguments were advanced, such as the increase in employment the revived industry would bring, but the principal theme reiterated by many speakers was that it was the responsibility of the party to take a clear stand upon the issue. The ambiguous plank adopted by the Republican convention two weeks before was mentioned frequently.

Both avowed major candidates were known to favor the majority plank, and Alfred E. Smith took the unusual step of appearing in the convention to support outright repeal personally. The vote accordingly did not divide along lines of candidacy, and the minority plank was defeated by the overwhelming margin of 934¾ to 213¾, 5½ not voting.

Several other minority planks or substitutes were offered, but none created much interest and all except one were rejected by voice vote. A plank advocating "continuous responsibility of government for human welfare, especially for the protection of children" was adopted by a standing vote, no count being recorded, and with this amendment, the platform was adopted by voice vote.

The balance of the platform, which the chairman of the committee called "the shortest and one of the most impressive platforms ever adopted in a National Convention in the United States," differed only in a few clauses from the Republican platform of the same year. All the woes of the depression were blamed upon "the disastrous policies pursued by our government since the World War," and the only hope for prosperity lay in "a drastic change in governmental policies." However, the platform agreed that one of the best ways to accomplish this was to reduce governmental expenditures "to accomplish a saving of not less than twenty-five per cent in the cost of Federal Government," and called upon the states to do likewise. A balanced budget and a sound currency were urged. As in the past, the Democratic stand on the tariff called for revenue only, and thus differed from the Republican. It agreed with the Republicans that work days and work weeks should be shorter, and that cooperatives for farmers should be encouraged. It differed from the Republicans in its advocacy of unemployment and old age insurance under state laws, and of enactment of price-support laws for farm products. On the whole, there was little in the platform that had not appeared in previous Democratic platforms.

The Presidential Nomination

Immediately following adoption of the platform, the roll call began for nominations for the Presidency. Franklin D. Roosevelt's name was presented by an old friend, Judge John E. Mack, of Dutchess County, New York. In quiet fashion Judge Mack first paid homage to the other candidates soon to be presented as a "galaxy of men whose reputation for intelligence, probity and statesmanship is so well established as to make any of them . . . well fitted to hold the high office of the Presidency of the United States." He then made the case for his own candidate by a recitation of Roosevelt's achievements. Nomination of John Nance Garner and Alfred E. Smith followed before adjournment until the evening session.

During the evening session, the series of nominating and seconding speeches continued. Candidates included former Governor Harry F. Byrd of Virginia; Melvin A. Traylor, Chicago banker and Illinois' favorite son; Governor Albert C. Ritchie of Maryland; former Senator James A. Reed of Missouri, politically recovered from his isolation in the 1920 convention when he was refused a seat because of failure to support Wilson's policies; and Governor George White of Ohio. By this time it was nearly 3:00 a.m., and an attempt was made to adjourn the convention until later in the morning. The motion, made by the Texas delegation, was supported by many Smith supporters including those from New York, and opposed in the main by Roosevelt's people. It was defeated by a roll call vote, 863½ to 281½, and the speeches continued.

Although several seconding speeches followed the attempted adjournment, only one new candidate was presented—Governor William H. Murray of Oklahoma, popularly known as Alfalfa Bill. Finally, at nearly 4:30 a.m., the first roll call began. At the conclusion of the roll call, which was interrupted by the necessity for polling various delegations, New York among them, Roosevelt was in the lead with a majority. With a total convention strength of 1,154 votes, 769 were necessary for a two thirds majority. Roosevelt was a little over 100 votes short with 666¼; Smith received 201¾, and Garner 90¼. The balance of the vote was scattered among the favorite sons and others, including one whose potential strength far exceeded the vote he received. This was Newton D. Baker, Secretary of War under Wilson, considered by many as a possible dark horse if a deadlock developed.

Despite the hour, a second ballot followed. As on the first ballot, the tabulation was delayed by polling of delegations —Minnesota for the second time, and the big Ohio and Pennsylvania delegations. Roosevelt showed a slight gain, moving to 677¾, as Smith dropped slightly to

194¼ and Garner remained steady. Minor movement occurred among the favorite sons, the most interesting being the transfer of the Oklahoma vote from Murray to the state's famous cowboy humorist and philosopher, Will Rogers.

Another attempt was made to adjourn, this time by a Roosevelt delegate. When a Smith delegate objected, a roll call was demanded, the motion was withdrawn, and the third ballot began. Roosevelt again gained a little, Smith lost, and Garner gained a few votes. The respective totals were 682.79, 190¼, and 101¼, Garner's new votes coming from the Oklahoma delegation that still temporized, this time by splitting its 22 votes between Garner and Reed. No objection being raised to another motion to adjourn, the delegates dispersed at 9:15 a.m.

That evening, as the fourth roll call began, the first three states on the list voted as they had on the previous ballot, but when California was called, William Gibbs McAdoo rose to explain the vote of the delegation:

California came here to nominate a President of the United States. She did not come here to deadlock this convention or to engage in another disastrous contest like that of 1924.[12]

He further stated that he believed any candidate who came to the convention with more than a majority, and within reach of the necessary two thirds, deserved to be nominated. Therefore, without relinquishing in any way his love and respect for John Nance Garner, who, he said, agreed with his action, McAdoo announced California's 44 votes for Roosevelt.

During the demonstration that followed, McAdoo must have derived considerable satisfaction from this reversal of the 1924 convention—when he had held almost a majority but was stopped by the antipathy of Smith. With the assurance that Texas would follow the California lead, all but the most bitter anti-Roosevelt delegates climbed on the band wagon, and Roosevelt

[12] *Ibid.*, p. 325.

received 945 of the 1,154 votes. Smith held his third-ballot vote, and a few other delegates stayed with their minor candidates. In view of this remaining opposition, no motion was made to declare the nomination unanimous.

Very soon after the chairman declared Roosevelt the nominee, a telegram was received from Hyde Park, where Roosevelt had been following the proceedings by radio. He offered to come immediately to Chicago and accept the nomination in person, in preference to the archaic procedure of waiting for several weeks. The offer was accepted, and after performing some routine business the convention adjourned until the following afternoon.

The Vice-Presidential Nomination

Upon resumption of the proceedings, John Nance Garner was placed in nomination for the second place on the ticket by Congressman John McDuffie of Alabama, Democratic whip of the House. This apparently came as a surprise to no one, for Garner was seconded by forty delegations, the parade being interrupted only by presentation of the name of Matthew A. Tinley of Iowa, World War I general who was prominent in veterans associations. At the end of the speeches Tinley moved that the rules be suspended and Garner be declared the unanimous nominee.

Just as the motion was passed, word was received that the plane bearing the Roosevelt party was approaching Chicago. To fill the time, several routine resolutions were passed, most of which were in appreciation for the service of various party leaders. As the plane landed, the convention listened to the reception at the airport, following which another series of congratulatory resolutions and some business motions were passed.

In the course of his speech of acceptance, Roosevelt pledged himself to a "new deal" for the American people. Inconspicuous at the time, the words were subsequently picked up by reporters and cartoonists, and soon became the slogan for the Democratic campaign.

Analysis of Key Votes

The vote for permanent chairman was clearly Roosevelt against the field, for of the delegations voting above average for the minority report—or for Walsh—89 per cent subsequently voted for Roosevelt on the first ballot, and the correlation between the Walsh and first-ballot Roosevelt votes was +.90. Additional potential Roosevelt strength indicated that supporters of other candidates, including Smith delegations, were less solid on the vote for permanent chairman, the Smith first-ballot vote correlating −.76 and the combined vote of the others −.87. Most of Smith's delegates stayed with him on the nominating ballot, but the tendency for more of those who moved to come from delegations voting higher than average for Shouse is indicated by the rise of the correlation between Walsh's vote for permanent chairman and Smith's final ballot to −.79. Even after the band-wagon movement began, Roosevelt's final ballot correlation with Walsh's vote remained at a relatively high +.76.

Presidential Election, November 8, 1932

FRANKLIN D. ROOSEVELT (D) : popular vote, 27,821,857; electoral vote, 472
HERBERT C. HOOVER (R) : popular vote, 15,761,841; electoral vote, 59

1936

DEPRESSION STILL gripped the country as the 1936 presidential year drew near. For the first time in the national history the same depression had spanned two election years, and the adage that party overturn is most likely in a year when times are bad received an entirely new test. Two important factors operated in favor of the Democrats: first, the Republicans were still held responsible for the depression by a majority of the people, and second, millions of those who were in the worst economic plight believed that they owed most of what little they did have to the efforts of the Roosevelt administration.

Immediately on acceding to power in 1933 the administration had begun courageously attacking the many problems confronting the nation, and operated generally on the principle that it was better to act than to drift, even though much of the action was not carefully planned or coordinated. Many schemes proved unworkable, and were dropped. Others seemed workable, and were expanded, but some of these ran into trouble with the Supreme Court, which ruled them unconstitutional. The rulings began to appear shortly before the conventions, and the question of the relative positions under the Constitution of the judiciary, Congress, and the administration was much in the public mind.

TWENTY-FIRST REPUBLICAN CONVENTION

The proportions of the defeat suffered by President Herbert Hoover in 1932, plus the fact that millions still associated his name with the depression, made him an unlikely choice for renomination in 1936. Although many in the party believed Hoover was blamed for things that were not his fault and that he was the best man to lead the country out of the depression, these were more than counterbalanced by others who, for a variety of reasons, were vigorously opposed to his renomination. Hoover did not declare himself to be a candidate, but it seemed clear that he would accept the nomination if offered.

The rest of the field was limited. The elections of 1932 and the intervening years had removed a great many Republican governors and reduced the congressional leaders to a handful. Most of those surviving were from safe Republican states, and the availability of such candidates has always been considered low. The obvious need was for a candidate who could match the proven vote-getting ability of Franklin D. Roosevelt—and few Republicans could even pretend to do this in 1936.

The field of potential candidates was further limited by the virtual defection in 1932 of many in the more liberal wing of the party—Robert M. La Follette, Jr., George W. Norris, and others—and by the failure of such leaders as Senator William E. Borah to campaign for Hoover in that year. Borah made a preconvention effort to win the 1936 nomination, but few of the Old Guard were willing to forget the past; in any case, he was considered a poor alternative to Roosevelt. One candidate from outside the regular political circles, Frank Knox, Chicago newspaper publisher, tried to build support for his own nomination, but was unable to generate much enthusiasm; by convention time he was not considered a serious threat.

Among the governors, Styles Bridges of New Hampshire and Alfred M. Landon of Kansas seemed the most likely possibilities.

Bridges' residence was a handicap—New Hampshire was not only small but considered entirely "safe," and New England had not been a popular source of candidates since westward expansion moved the center of population across the Alleghenies. Landon's state, though small, was considered well-located geographically, and Landon had won his governorship against stiffer competition than Bridges had met—in fact, he would probably not have won it at all except for a split in the opposition vote. Furthermore, Bridges was considered ultra-conservative, while Landon's political philosophy and background was such that, by playing up one part or another, he could be presented as all things to all people.

Cleveland, Ohio,
June 9, 10, 11, 12, 1936

The convention was almost devoid of open conflict, and what little difference of opinion was expressed related to minor matters. Most of the printed pages of the proceedings are devoted to speeches attacking Roosevelt and the New Deal. The few high lights of the convention included the reception given Herbert Hoover when he addressed the delegates, and the nomination of Alfred M. Landon as the presidential candidate.

Convention Organization

Senator Frederick Steiwer of Oregon was elected temporary chairman immediately following the reading of the call, but he did not take the chair during the first session. Following his election, the regular committees were appointed; shortly after noon the convention adjourned.

In the evening session Senator Steiwer stated that the basic purpose of the convention was "to start the drive to put an American deal into the place now usurped by a self-styled 'New Deal.'" He attacked the administration on the one hand for not carrying out its platform pledges of 1932, and on the other for moving too far too fast with methods based upon unconsti-

tutional legislation. Whether by accident or design, Steiwer struck upon a rhetorical device that brought his audience into enthusiastic collaboration with him—a condition often sought but seldom achieved by political orators. In attacking the administration record, he repeatedly used the phrase "for three long years." Its rhythm caught the ear of the audience, and the delegates repeated it at the end of each of his series of rhetorical questions. The phrase was popular throughout the campaign.

The report of the credentials committee was accepted by voice vote and without debate, although the committee reversed the recommendation of the national committee on the seating of the South Carolina delegation. An attempt made to obtain a roll call vote on the election of permanent officers was unsuccessful because the motion lacked an adequate second. Congressman Bertrand H. Snell of New York was elected permanent chairman. The main burden of his speech was the failure of the Democratic administration to live up to its 1932 platform promises.

The rules committee report was accompanied by a minority report raising the only debate in the entire convention. The question involved the number of votes to be allowed the territorial and District of Columbia delegations. The majority report stipulated 6 votes each for Alaska, Hawaii, and the District of Columbia, and objection was raised that this gave these units strength equal to such states as Arizona, Nevada, New Mexico, and Wyoming. The minority report set the voting strength in question at 3 each; the convention accepted the minority report by voice vote, although the majority report had been accepted in the rules committee by a vote of 32 to 4.

The Platform

Preceding the report of the platform committee, ex-President Herbert Hoover took the rostrum to speak to the convention. The mammoth demonstration that greeted him held up the speech for nearly half an hour. When order was restored, he launched into an attack on the administration and its policies, calling them un-American and comparing the methods used and the goals sought to those of the rising dictatorships of Europe. When he finished, there was another demonstration, longer and louder than the first.

The platform began with the indictment of the New Deal in a series of terse statements, among them:

The powers of Congress have been usurped by the President.
The integrity and authority of the Supreme Court have been flouted.
The rights and liberties of American citizens have been violated.
It [the administration] has insisted on the passage of laws contrary to the Constitution.[1]

These and other wrongs the Republican party pledged itself to correct. However, the platform was by no means a completely laissez-faire document. Responsibilities of government for relief of the needy, for social security, and for laws affording protection to labor, among other such matters, were recognized, but the platform stressed that the major responsibility lay with the state governments rather than the national government. Other clauses demanded economy in government and a stable valuation of the dollar. A final clause sought to bind the nominees to the platform:

The acceptance of the nomination tendered by this Convention carries with it, as a matter of private honor and public faith, an undertaking by each candidate to be true to the principles and program herein set forth.[2]

The Presidential Nomination

Landon's was the only name placed in nomination for the Presidency, but on the roll call Borah received 19 votes from Wisconsin, despite his previous withdrawal. A telegram was received from Landon, just before the presentation of him as a candidate, in which he informed the convention that he approved the platform in "word

[1] RNC, *Proceedings*, 1936, pp. 136-137.
[2] *Ibid.*, p. 147.

and spirit." He wished, however, to make his stand clear on certain points.

The platform had asserted the belief that necessary legislation to protect women and children with respect to minimum hours, wages, and working conditions could be passed within the Constitution as it stood. Landon stated that he would, if this belief proved erroneous, advocate a constitutional change to accomplish the desired ends. On the currency plank, he wanted the delegates to understand that he interpreted sound currency as currency convertible to gold. On the civil service, his interpretation of the plank pledging the party to the restoration, improvement, and extension of the merit system was that all government workers below the rank of assistant secretaries of major departments and agencies, including the Post Office Department explicitly, should be included under civil service.

The Vice-Presidential Nomination

In addition to Frank Knox, former Governor Walter E. Edge of New Jersey, Governor Harry W. Nice of Maryland, and Arthur W. Little, who combined the professions of publisher and rancher, were nominated. All but Knox were withdrawn before the balloting. The convention then unanimously nominated a second westerner to the party ticket. Before the convention adjourned, both candidates had wired acceptance.

TWENTY-SEVENTH DEMOCRATIC CONVENTION

Roosevelt was so firmly in the saddle in 1936 that he had no need to concern himself with campaigning for renomination. Opposition within his own party was confined to minor sniping by disgruntled nonentities and by ultraconservatives; many of the latter had moved, or were in process of moving, into the Republican ranks. The President directed his campaign efforts against the Republican party, driving it more and more into a reactionary position and thus restricting its base of operations. By directing his basic appeal toward the "have-nots" at a time when most of the population felt itself to be in that category, he laid the groundwork for his spectacular victory in November.

Philadelphia, Pennsylvania,
June 23, 24, 25, 26, 27, 1936

Insofar as conventions can be typified, this was the most atypical of all Democratic conventions. No debates occurred; no roll call votes were taken; no vote was held on either the presidential or the vice-presidential nominations. Yet, in revoking the two thirds rule and substituting majority rule for nominations, the convention settled, at least for the time being, a controversy that had plagued Democratic conventions for a hundred years. But even this issue—and every other issue that might have stirred the smooth tenor of the assembly—was settled quietly in committee and in caucus.

Convention Organization

The convention was opened by the chairman of the national committee, James A. Farley of New York, who defined the main issue, "stripped of all camouflage," to be: "Shall we continue the New Deal . . . or shall the Government be turned back to the Old Dealers who wrecked it?" Aside from Farley's speech, little was done during the first session. The reading of the call and selection of temporary officers occurred in the evening session. Senator Alben W. Barkley of Kentucky was selected temporary chairman, and his keynote address was one of the high lights of the convention.

First stating that "ancient theories" were no longer adequate to meet the needs of the "moving, changing world in which we live," Barkley painted a stark word picture of conditions as they were when the new administration took office in 1933. These conditions, he claimed, were due to the fact that "for twelve long years the ancient doctrinaires of special privilege had stood at the pilot's wheel on our ship of state." (The phrase "twelve long years" was obviously a take-off on the "three long years" so popular in the Republican convention; Barkley used it several times in his speech.) He then contrasted Republican efforts to prevent and to alleviate the depression with the record of the New Deal. He castigated the Supreme Court for the recent decisions that struck at the roots of some of the New Deal program. It was a hard-hitting, fighting speech, and was followed by a fifteen-minute demonstration.

The convention was in no hurry to finish its business. Standing committees were not appointed until the afternoon of the second day, after which the chairman turned the rostrum over to Eddie Dowling, a well-known entertainer, who conducted a sort of variety show. One after another, he called upon those luminaries of the press, screen, and radio who were present, as well as some of the lesser political notables, all of whom obliged, according to their talents, with songs and anecdotes. Dowling himself entertained the delegates with several monologues.

In the meantime the committees were working. Something went wrong with the timing, however, for the credentials committee was not ready to report when the evening session opened, and Chairman Barkley was forced to admit that the plan called for completion not only of the credentials report but also of the report of the committee on permanent organization. Since radio time had been scheduled for an acceptance speech by the permanent chairman, Barkley announced that he would recognize Senator Joseph T. Robinson as a delegate from Arkansas and permit him to make his speech, even though he had not been elected. This was an unusually clear illustration of the difficulties, later compounded by television, so frequently encountered by convention managers in meshing the relatively uncontrollable pace of convention business to the rigid requirements of mass media schedules.

In addition to retreading much of the ground covered by Barkley's speech, Robinson taunted the Republicans with Landon's disagreement with parts of the Republican platform. His speech was much quieter in tone—at least in the printed version—than Barkley's, and he received a somewhat shorter ovation at the end.

The committee on credentials reported on the morning of the third day. The report endorsed all of the temporary roll except for Puerto Rico, the Canal Zone, and Minnesota, in which instances it recommended seating both sets of contestants with split votes. The report was adopted unanimously. The convention then ratified selection of Senator Robinson as permanent chairman, and confirmed the balance of the temporary officers as permanent officers. The rules committee still being in session—no doubt owing to difficulties over the two thirds rule—the convention adjourned until evening.

When the report of the rules committee was submitted in the evening session it contained only one important change—revocation of the two thirds requirement for nominating majorities. The clause read:

That all questions, including the question of nominations of candidates for President of the United States and Vice President of the United States, shall be determined by a majority vote of the delegates to the convention, and the rule heretofore existing in Democratic conventions requiring a two thirds vote in such cases is hereby specifically abrogated.[3]

The rules were read, quite appropriately, by Senator Bennett Champ Clark of Missouri, whose father, Champ Clark, had been one of the two candidates in Democratic convention history to be defeated for nomination by the two thirds rule after actually receiving a majority of the convention vote.

As partial recompense to the southern delegations who lost their veto power through this rule change, two instructing resolutions were appended to the report.

That the Democratic National Committee is hereby instructed to formulate and to recommend to the next National Convention a plan for improving the system by which delegates and alternates to Democratic National Conventions are apportioned.
And be it Further Resolved That in formulating this plan, the National Committee shall take into account the Democratic strength within each State, District of Columbia, and Territory, etc., in making said apportionment.[4]

The bonus system contemplated by these resolutions was expected to benefit the southern states, with their steady Democratic majorities, more than other sections, thus partially redressing some of the power lost by the change to majority rule. After a short speech by Clark in justification of the rule change, the report was adopted without debate and by voice vote. The adoption may have been of doubtful unanimity, however, for after the vote on the previous question and on the acceptance of the report itself, Chairman Robinson announced, "The 'Ayes' seem to have it."

The Platform

The most fundamental difference between the Democratic platform and the platform presented by the Republican convention was the emphasis in the former on solution of national problems by national government, as opposed to solution by state governments as advocated by the Republicans. Among the problems considered "national" were unemployment, agricultural relief, social security, labor relations, public housing, and rural electric power. In addition, the Democrats refused to accept the Republican concept of the infallibility of the Supreme Court as the final arbiter of constitutional questions. The Democratic position was that in the event the Court continued obstructionist tactics

[3] DNC, *Proceedings*, 1936, p. 189.

[4] *Ibid.*, p. 190.

against the trends and needs of the times, it would be necessary to

. . . seek such clarifying amendment as will assure to the legislatures of the several States and to the Congress of the United States, each within its proper jurisdiction, the power to enact those laws which the State and Federal legislatures, within their respective spheres, shall find necessary, in order adequately to regulate commerce, protect public health and safety and safeguard economic security. Thus we propose to maintain the letter and spirit of the Constitution.[5]

The Presidential Nomination

A full day was allocated to the presidential nomination, despite the fact that no contest whatsoever existed. Listening to the long parade of speakers, one or more from each and every delegation, was but part of the price the delegates had to pay the merchants of Philadelphia for their generosity in financing the convention. Judge John E. Mack was again entrusted

[5] *Ibid.*, p. 196.

with the formal presentation of his old friend, Franklin D. Roosevelt, and drew upon his personal knowledge of Roosevelt's career since boyhood. The speech, which was not excessively long, was made soon after the convention was called to order at 12:55 p.m. At 12:55 a.m., immediately after the demonstration that followed Roosevelt's nomination by acclamation, the convention adjourned until later in the morning.

The Vice-Presidential Nomination

In view of the lesser prominence of the Vice Presidency, it was fitting that less time was required to nominate Garner. The final session lasted almost exactly five hours, and part of the time was taken with complimentary and other closing resolutions. Nevertheless, seventeen delegates spoke for Garner, before the rules were suspended to nominate him by acclamation.

Presidential Election, November 3, 1936

FRANKLIN D. ROOSEVELT (D) : popular vote, 27,751,612; electoral vote, 523
ALFRED M. LANDON (R) : popular vote, 16,681,913; electoral vote, 8

1940

PERHAPS TO AN EVEN greater extent than in 1916, events outside the United States in 1940 loomed larger than internal affairs during the preconvention period. Within the country, the Roosevelt administration could point to a rising economic barometer, rising wages, and falling unemployment. Although much of this was due to external conditions that increased foreign trade and forced an ever-increasing build-up of national defenses, much also could be traced to policies and actions of the administration, some of which were based upon new economic principles that were bitterly opposed by many. Within the Democratic party, stresses had appeared—as the widely divergent groups constituting the record-breaking majority coalition in 1936 began to discover the true extent of their incompatability.

In 1938 the Republicans made substantial gains in Congress from the low ebb of 1936; in the same year the split within Democratic ranks was highlighted by Roosevelt's attempt to "purge" opposition within his own party by actively opposing nomination of opposition leaders in the Democratic primaries. He failed in his efforts, but by them had fostered deep resentment, particularly among southern conservatives.

Throughout the active period of preconvention activity, the major news items concerned the war in Europe, as it steadily increased in tempo. By the time of the Republican convention, the Low Countries, the Scandinavian countries, and France had fallen to the Nazis; Britain had withdrawn from the Continent in the dramatic but costly Dunkirk evacuation. By the time of the Democratic convention, the active

phase of the bombing of Britain was in progress. In considering presidential nominees, every citizen had to include the question as to which man would most effectively meet the international crisis.

TWENTY-SECOND REPUBLICAN CONVENTION

The Republican resurgence in 1938 brought several new figures to the fore to join the thin line of those left after the Democratic sweeps of 1932, 1934, and 1936. Of the new figures, Senator Robert A. Taft of Ohio, son of William Howard Taft, was the leading congressional member. His principal rival was the brilliant young district attorney of New York City, Thomas E. Dewey. Both were young, as presidential candidates go, Taft being just over 50 and Dewey 38. Among the older leaders, the 1936 candidate, Alfred M. Landon, had dropped sharply in the popularity polls following his defeat, and was not given significant consideration in 1940; the same was true of ex-President Herbert Hoover. In the early stages, Arthur H. Vandenberg, senator from Michigan since 1928, was the chief rival to Taft and Dewey, and at the age of 56 was young enough to have ambitions beyond the 1940 campaign. Some consideration also was given to Senator and Minority Leader Charles McNary of Oregon, though his boom never gathered much momentum.

The three leading contenders, in addition to sharing the qualities of ambition and relative youthfulness, were orthodox in their relations with their respective political organizations. Each unquestionably considered the other two the principal barriers to his own national leadership. Taft and Vandenberg were much closer together ideologically on the important international issues, each at the time being a leader of midwestern isolationists. Dewey, in keeping with the more internationalist viewpoint of his geographical section, was suspected of being himself an internationalist, although his public activities up to that time had not involved him in the question. The situation was ripe for a deadlock: chances of any two combining against the third were small, and favorite sons were encouraged to develop and hold their strength in the balance, with the hope that they either might become a compromise choice or could exercise decisive power at the right moment.

In the early public opinion polls Dewey took an early and substantial lead. In November 1938 he polled 33 per cent of the public choice, as measured by the Gallup Poll, Vandenberg and Taft receiving 18 per cent each. Throughout 1939, Dewey continued to maintain a substantial lead, sometimes receiving 50 per cent or more of the total poll. He reached his peak in the poll taken May 8, 1940, when he received 67 per cent, but a name not listed in previous polls—that of Wendell Willkie—received 3 per cent. This was the first reflection of what was to prove one of the most spectacular campaigns for nomination in the history of the United States.

Wendell Willkie, a native of a small Indiana town, had risen rapidly as a utilities lawyer, and had become president of the Commonwealth and Southern Corporation. In this position his opposition to federal intervention in the utilities field, particularly the Tennessee Valley Authority, had in the view of many informed people made him the outstanding proponent of free private enterprise; the number who knew of him, however, was a very small fraction of the total electorate. In addition to his personal charm, determination, and executive ability, however, Willkie was fortunate in having very good managers as well as ample funds, of his

own and from his associates, to provide for the kind of campaign that had to be waged.

His first appearance on a national scale was in the radio program "Information Please," on April 29, 1940; his first appearance in the Gallup Poll a little more than a week later was a reflection of his success on the program. Other personal appearances followed, and Willkie-for-President clubs began to spread rapidly throughout the nation. Everything conceivable was done to develop the idea that Willkie was the man of the hour and the pre-eminent choice of the people, and the swift rise of the Willkie index in the Gallup Poll, which was taken at approximately ten-day intervals from the time Willkie first appeared on it until immediately before the convention, both reflected and aided these efforts. On five successive polls, Willkie scored 3, 5, 10, 17, and 29 per cent; Dewey meanwhile dropped progressively, with 67, 62, 56, 52, and 47 per cent. As George H. Gallup himself has pointed out, only a relatively small part of the electorate follows the polls closely, and accordingly previous poll results do not necessarily have material effect on subsequent polls. The effect on party leaders and delegates, however, is another matter. These undoubtedly follow the polls much more closely than the general public, and it is logical to assume that the rapid rise of Willkie in the later preconvention period made it easier for Willkie supporters to persuade doubtful or uncommitted delegates.

Except in Nebraska and Wisconsin, major opponents did not meet in the primaries, but Dewey's success in those two states against Vandenberg boosted his stock considerably. Non-organizational candidates such as Willkie ordinarily wage strong primary campaigns, since primaries present an excellent opportunity to get the candidate's name before the public, but Willkie's campaign was started too late to make the method effective. In any case, only in New Jersey did he receive a significant vote, when a few more than 5 per cent of those expressing a preference wrote his name on the ballot; Dewey received almost all the rest of the New Jersey votes. Dewey also won the preferential vote without significant opposition in Illinois, Maryland, and Pennsylvania. Taft and McNary easily carried their own states of Ohio and Oregon, but entered no others. Favorite sons won the primaries in California and West Virginia.

Philadelphia, Pennsylvania,
June 24, 25, 26, 27, 28, 1940

The convention was called to order by John Hamilton of Kansas, chairman of the Republican national committee, and young Governor Harold E. Stassen of Minnesota was elected temporary chairman.

Convention Organization

The balance of the morning session was spent in appointing committees and other preliminary business. A short afternoon session was termed an "Americanism-Patriotism Session," and consisted of a series of speeches on this theme punctuated by patriotic songs and poems. Taking advantage of the convention location in Philadelphia, the Liberty Bell was tapped thirteen times—in commemoration of the original states—and the sound was carried on the radio broadcast of the convention: "the first time our Liberty Bell has ever been heard by the people of America from the Atlantic to the Pacific, the Mexican border to Canada."

Governor Stassen took the chair shortly after the opening of the evening session, and in his speech continued the patriotism theme. Reference was made to the rise of despotism in Europe, and the appalling lack of preparedness of the United States. He attributed this unpreparedness and other ills of the nation to "bungling" by the administration, and called for selection of a Republican candidate to lead the nation in a program designed "to make America strong and our way of life secure."

On the morning of the second day the committee on credentials report was accepted unanimously, as also was the report of the committee on permanent organization. For the first time in what was to prove a series, House Minority Leader Joseph W. Martin, Jr., of Massachusetts was named permanent chairman. Martin called for a crusade "to rescue our beloved America from the bog of failure and futility." He warned against destruction of the Constitution by "Fifth Columnists" and "Trojan Horses." He charged the Democratic party with encouraging sectional and class hatreds, with renunciation of traditions of Americanism, and with a "march toward one-man government."

The report of the rules committee increased the basis of eligibility for a bonus of three delegates at large to include election of a Republican senator at the last previous election, even if the state had failed to give its electoral vote to the Republican nominee. A slight modification of the rules for district delegates provided:

One District Delegate from each Congressional District casting one thousand votes or more for any Republican elector in the last preceding Presidential election or for the Republican nominee for Congress in the last preceding Congressional election.[1]

The provision for an additional district delegate for each district casting 10,000 votes for elector or congressman remained the same. By the new rule, districts failing to cast 1,000 Republican votes would receive no representation in the following convention.

The afternoon session of the second day was devoted to a long and methodical speech by Herbert Hoover, in which he systematically analyzed the problems which the Republican party and the nation faced. With "the whole world in confusion," seven stern tasks must at once be undertaken:

First. We must restore and revitalize liberty in America.
Second. We must restore and rebuild morals in government.

[1] RNC, *Proceedings*, 1940, pp. 103-104.

Third. We must restore decent life and living to one-third of our farmers and workers, who have been chronically submerged by the New Deal.

Fourth. We must restore competence to government.

Fifth. We must prepare this nation to defend the Western Hemisphere.

Sixth. We must develop and maintain foreign policies that keep us out of these wars unless we are attacked. We should facilitate all nations fighting for their freedom in procuring materiels and munitions, but subject to definite limitations which keep us out of war.

Seventh. We must recall our people from the flabbiness of the New Deal. We must re-establish stamina, character and ideals. We must regenerate hope and confidence in America.[2]

Each of these tasks he then discussed at length, showing how the Democratic administration had proved unable or unfit to cope with them. In a campaign developed about these issues, he said, "we Republicans would welcome Mr. Roosevelt as a candidate. For this battle must be fought out under the guns of debate. And that debate will be done best with the man who is responsible for it."[3]

The Platform

The long delay before the report of the committee on resolutions was ready indicated some difficulty in agreeing on the platform. Although no minority report was submitted, the committee member from Illinois stated that his delegation would have preferred a stronger stand in opposition to involvement in foreign war, but that the language included in the platform had been accepted on the understanding that it incorporated the spirit of this thought without explicitly saying it. The plank began with the statement "The Republican party is firmly opposed to involving this Nation in foreign war." It continued with a complaint that, although the current administration had spent billions of dollars,

[2] *Ibid.*, p. 117.
[3] *Ibid.*, p. 120.

. . . by the President's own admission we are still wholly unprepared to defend our country. . . . [The party pledged to] support all necessary and proper defense measures proposed by the Administration in its belated effort to make up for lost time; [but deplored] explosive utterances by the President directed at other governments which serve to imperil our peace; and [condemned] all executive acts and proceedings which might lead to war without the authorization of the Congress of the United States.[4]

However, no specific recommendations regarding national defense needs were mentioned.

The Presidential Nomination

Nominating speeches were limited to one of not more than a half hour, and seconding speeches to four, not to exceed five minutes each, for each candidate. As in 1936, the roll of states was first called and reservations made to establish the order of nominating speeches. Ten names were presented, most of them receiving three or four seconding speeches in addition to the main nomination speech. For nearly all of the candidates, an obvious attempt was made to show widespread strength by drawing upon different sections of the country for the speakers, though the purely favorite son candidacy of Governor Arthur H. James was indicated when his nominating speech and the three seconding speeches all came from the Pennsylvania delegation.

In addition to the principal candidates and Governor James, other nominees were Frank E. Gannett, New York newspaper publisher; Hanford MacNider of Iowa, Assistant Secretary of War under Coolidge, Minister to Canada under Hoover, and past commander of the American Legion; Senator and former Governor Styles Bridges of New Hampshire; and Governor Harlan J. Bushfield of North Dakota. All received votes on the first ballot. In addition Senator Arthur Capper was given the favorite son vote of his Kansas delegation; Chairman Joseph Martin received most of

[4] *Ibid.*, p. 142.

the Massachusetts vote, plus other scattering votes; and ex-President Hoover had 17 scattered votes from several delegations.

Dewey led the field by a substantial margin, with 360 out of the total of 1,000 votes in the convention. Taft had 189, Willkie 105, Vandenberg 76, and James—mostly from the Pennsylvania delegation—70. In many delegations, Willkie received only a token vote; for example, Massachusetts and Pennsylvania gave him 1 vote each. But the presence of even one avowed supporter and the accompanying assurance that Willkie would be represented in a majority of the caucuses was to prove important.

The number of candidates receiving votes on the second ballot remained the same as on the first; although Bushfield dropped out, one vote was cast for Fiorello H. La Guardia, mayor of New York City. Dewey remained in the lead, but dropped to 338; Willkie moved up to 171, Taft to 203. Minor changes occurred with the other candidates.

The field began to narrow on the third ballot, as the same trends among the primary candidates continued: Dewey dropped to 315 but still led, Willkie and Taft increased to 259 and 212. The most important developments during this ballot were the break of an additional 10 votes from the Pennsylvania delegation to Willkie, bringing his total from that important delegation to 15, and the transfer of most of the Massachusetts favorite son vote to Willkie's column.

On the fourth ballot, as Willkie took the lead with 306 votes, Taft followed with 254 and Dewey dropped to third place with 250. Willkie's gains on this ballot came from small scattered additions, but most of Taft's came from the isolationist wing of the Illinois delegation as that delegation began to break up, following satisfaction of its primary election commitment to Dewey.

At the end of the fifth ballot, the race essentially was narrowed to Taft, 377 votes, and Willkie, 429. Most of the balance were

scattered among Dewey, James, and Vandenberg, but no one of these had enough to nominate Willkie by transferring them in block. A sixth ballot accordingly was required, during which Vandenberg and McNary withdrew. The disposition of Vandenberg's vote was an illustration of what frequently happens when men with positive ideas and strong ambitions are concerned: Vandenberg's vote did not go to Taft, who ideologically was probably closer to Vandenberg—who as of 1940 was still an isolationist—than any of the other candidates was and certainly closer than Willkie; instead it moved almost en masse to Willkie. The action of the Michigan delegation was decisive; from that moment, delegates began to break away from Taft and move to Willkie, although up to the call of Michigan on the roll, Taft actually had been picking up additional votes. When the roll call was completed, Taft retained 318 votes and Willkie was safely nominated with 655. Following the balloting, all but two delegates, apparently absent, transferred their votes to Willkie, and the nomination was declared unanimous on motion of Governor John W. Bricker of Ohio. The convention then adjourned at approximately two o'clock in the morning, to reassemble twelve hours later for action on the second half of the ticket.

The Vice-Presidential Nomination

Two candidates were presented for the vice-presidential nomination: Congressman Dewey Short of Missouri and Senator Charles L. McNary of Oregon, minority floor leader. Both complemented Willkie in several respects: both had long records in Congress to offset Willkie's lack of experience in government; both were westerners, while Willkie was associated primarily in the public mind with the East, despite his midwestern birth; both were associated with farm policy, an offset to Willkie's financial and industrial connections. The principal difference between the two was that McNary had been long associated with liberal policies and had, in fact, supported some of the New Deal; Short was widely known as an uncompromising opponent of the New Deal and all that it stood for.

Willkie gave the nod to McNary, and this was made clear to the delegates when the seconding speeches for McNary were given by representatives of four states that had played critical roles in Willkie's nomination: Michigan, with Vandenberg himself delivering the speech, Massachusetts, represented by Senator Henry Cabot Lodge, Jr., Kansas, and Pennsylvania. On the single ballot, McNary was nominated with 890 votes, Short receiving 108 and Styles Bridges 2.

Immediately before the roll call the chairman announced that Willkie was expected momentarily. After the roll call the convention filled the interval with completion of routine business, including the customary complimentary motions, until Mr. and Mrs. Willkie arrived. In his short speech, Willkie pledged "a crusading, aggressive fighting campaign." Following the speech and its ovation, the convention adjourned.

TWENTY-EIGHTH DEMOCRATIC CONVENTION

The electoral votes had scarcely been counted in 1936 before speculation began as to Roosevelt's intentions for 1940. Many of those closest to him insist in their memoirs that he really preferred not to run again—that he would like to return to the relaxed atmosphere of Hyde Park where he could rest from the grueling labors of eight years as the nation's leader. It seems safe to assume that this desire was real, and that, had the nation and the world been in a relatively quiet condition, he would have retired both for personal reasons and because it was doubtful that the American public would willingly acquiesce in destruction of the tradition against a third term. The mounting crescendo of war in

Europe undoubtedly was the dominating factor in forcing Roosevelt to a decision to run and in inducing the American public to consent to a third term, but other factors were important. In common with most national leaders, Roosevelt was highly conscious of his place in history. As of the spring of 1940, he could not be sure that this place would be as high as he would like it to be. His New Deal program had been severely attacked, and in several instances set back. Some of the more prominent candidates for succession within his own party were opposed to, or soft on, his policies, and it was by no means certain that any of them could defeat a strong Republican candidate. Although the economic state of the nation was considerably stronger than in 1932, economic indexes were still relatively low, with unemployment still high.

Therefore, viewing the record of his two terms, Roosevelt may have been quite uncertain as to his place in the judgment of history. On the other hand, at that point to take active steps to obtain the nomination might prove disastrous; aside from other considerations, this surely would foster the fears of many that another term would result in dictatorship. A unanimous, or near-unanimous, draft by the party of a reluctant candidate would serve to allay the fears, and in general would place the candidate in a much stronger position than if the nomination appeared to be of his own seeking. Whether or not Roosevelt actually reasoned this way can probably never be determined accurately, but his strategy throughout the preconvention period was consistent with such reasoning. Despite constant pressure from the press and from potential candidates to declare his intentions, he never revealed them. Even those closest to him have published widely differing accounts as to when he finally made up his mind, one going so far as to state that the actual decision was not made until the day after the nomination in the convention, when it became clear that his preference for Henry A. Wallace as the second man on the ticket would be honored.

Roosevelt's tactics during the period were much more complicated than Coolidge's had been in somewhat similar circumstances in 1928. Although Roosevelt frequently stated that he wanted to retire and gave many indications that he actually planned to do so, he never explicitly stated that he would or would not run. At times he seemed to encourage one or another of his official family as a candidate, but always in words that left enough unsaid to preserve his own freedom of action. At one time or another, Harry Hopkins, Roosevelt's intimate friend and (1939-1940) Secretary of Commerce, Cordell Hull, Secretary of State, and Henry A. Wallace, Secretary of Agriculture, believed that Roosevelt considered him the heir apparent. Several men not so closely associated with the official family at the time also believed themselves encouraged to run. These included Paul V. McNutt, former governor of Indiana, whose transfer from his post as High Commissioner of the Philippine Islands to that of Federal Security Administrator was interpreted by many as a move to permit him to work toward his own nomination; Postmaster General James A. Farley, whose relations with Roosevelt had drifted far from the close entente of the 1932 and 1936 campaigns; and Vice President John Nance Garner, who for some time had been joined with the opposition to the New Deal.

As convention time approached, international events created increasing pressure upon Roosevelt, and more and more people, including party officials, were convinced that it was necessary to keep an experienced hand at the helm. Hopkins suffered a serious illness that effectively removed him from the running, if he was ever really in it. By convention time, only Hull, Farley, and Garner remained as possibly serious contenders. Hull would do nothing without Roosevelt's explicit approval, but Farley and Garner were sufficiently disgruntled to campaign openly.

The primaries proved to be no contest, though both Garner and Farley made efforts in some and Roosevelt took no active part. Wherever the Roosevelt name appeared, he received overwhelming majorities—except in New Hampshire, where his plurality was still more than double that of any other contestant, including Garner and Farley. West Virginia and Ohio named favorite sons in the primaries; in the convention, Ohio supported Roosevelt unanimously and West Virginia nearly so.

The public opinion polls gave equally decisive results: Roosevelt always held a substantial lead over any possible convention opponent. This lead increased to prohibitive proportions in the last polls before the convention, when Roosevelt received 92 per cent of the vote from Democratic party supporters.

Chicago, Illinois,
July 15, 16, 17, 18, 1940

James A. Farley, in his position as national committee chairman, called to order what James M. Burns dubbed "one of the most extraordinary conventions in history." Once again, several delegations were oversized, some doubling the quota for the at large delegates, others sending several delegates (ten from one North Carolina congressional district) to cast the 2 votes for a congressional district. Many states had not yet adjusted to the new apportionment resulting from the 1940 census, and sent the entire delegations on an at large basis. Aside from the fact that the convention was opened by one of the strongest contestants for the nomination, the preliminary proceedings were quite ordinary. Before turning over the gavel to the temporary chairman, Speaker of the House William B. Bankhead of Alabama, Farley made a discreet speech, in which he gave credit to the party workers for past successes and future prospects, and managed to praise the administration without mentioning the head of the administration by name.

Convention Organization

Committees were not appointed until the fourth session, held on the second day of the convention. It is clear that some, at least, of the committees had been functioning before being officially constituted, for the committee on permanent organization made its report almost immediately afterward. The majority leader of the Senate, Alben W. Barkley of Kentucky, was elected permanent chairman, and it was during a characteristic fighting speech by him that the first real excitement occurred. When he mentioned the name of Franklin D. Roosevelt, the audience began a lengthy demonstration, including a parade, that interrupted the speech for a considerable time. Finally able to finish his address, Barkley then read a message from Roosevelt "at the specific request and authorization of the President."

> The President has never had, and has not today, any desire or purpose to continue in the office of President, to be a candidate for that office, or to be nominated by the convention for that office.
>
> He wishes in all earnestness and sincerity to make it clear that all of the delegates to this convention are free to vote for any candidate.

According to some participants, this statement was followed by a moment of stunned silence as the delegates tried to digest its meaning. The silence was broken by a voice on the loud-speakers crying, "We want Roosevelt!" Pandemonium followed for an hour. The voice, later ascribed to a member of Mayor Edward J. Kelley's Chicago organization and called "the voice from the sewer," undoubtedly made easier the task of those who were trying to develop a genuine draft for Roosevelt; it probably did not actually change the result, however, for Roosevelt had a definite majority in the convention.

The Platform

The preamble to the platform expressed the need to strengthen Democracy against "social maladjustment within and the to-

talitarian greed without." To accomplish this, the Democratic party goal was threefold:

1. To strengthen democracy by defensive preparedness against aggression, whether by open attack or secret infiltration;

2. To strengthen democracy by increasing our economic efficiency; and

3. To strengthen democracy by improving the welfare of the people.[5]

Each of these three ideas served as a subtitle under which the ways and means by which the objective would be sought were itemized.

Under the first subtitle, the party pledged not to "participate in foreign wars, and we will not send our army, naval or air forces to fight in foreign lands outside of the Americas, except in case of attack."[6] But since weakness and unpreparedness invite aggression, "we must be so strong that no possible combination of powers would dare to attack us."

Economic efficiency was to be accomplished primarily by continuing and expanding programs already under way. Economic aid to farmers and preservation of "the ever-normal granary" were fundamental programs. Protective labor legislation should be passed and enforced. Monopoly in business should continue to be attacked, but "legitimate business" should be encouraged in every way possible.

Public welfare should be fostered by a continuing war upon unemployment, and relief of the unemployed should be federally controlled where it was federally financed. Social security benefits should be expanded and more and better health facilities provided, particularly in rural areas; public schools should be improved, and public low-cost housing projects expanded.

Following the report, an amendment was offered:

> We reaffirm the traditional position of the Democratic Party as adopted at our Party Convention in 1896, to wit:

[5] DNC, *Proceedings*, 1940, p. 153.
[6] *Ibid.*, p. 154.

"We declare it to be the unwritten law of this Republic established by the unbroken custom and usage of 150 years and sanctioned by the examples of the greatest" [cries of "no"] "and wisest of those who founded it and have maintained our government, that no man should be eligible for a third term of the Presidential office." [7]

The quoted portion of the resolution had been passed in 1896 as a gratuitous slap at Grover Cleveland, in circumstances where it was clear that he was not seeking renomination and in any case had only a small minority of the delegates in the convention favorable to him. The circumstances in 1940 were quite different; Roosevelt had not clearly taken himself from the race, and a substantial majority believed him to be the strongest candidate before the convention. The amendment was rejected, and the platform adopted without further debate.

The Presidential Nomination

Franklin Delano Roosevelt, James A. Farley, and John Nance Garner were formally nominated for the Presidency, and Maryland presented Senator Millard E. Tydings as its favorite son. As the roll call progressed, nearly every delegation declared in whole or in part for Roosevelt; Farley received only scattered seconds and Garner even fewer. Roosevelt was nominated on the first ballot, receiving 946$^{13}\!/_{30}$ votes. Farley's vote included not a single solid state delegation, although two non-state delegations were solid for him. Only these two non-state delegations and one state delegation failed to give at least part of its vote to Roosevelt. Texas went solid for Garner.

The Vice-Presidential Nomination

It has been pointed out by many commentators that the large Roosevelt majority included many delegates who were at best lukewarm to his renomination, but who

[7] *Ibid.,* pp. 164-165.

for a variety of reasons joined the majority. Some, of course, were counted in because they were a minority in a delegation governed by the unit rule; others moved of their own accord for various reasons of expediency. Under such conditions, people are usually eager for some way to demonstrate their feelings and their independence. The vice-presidential nomination provided the opportunity.

The convention took its time about getting down to this, its final business, however. The gestures leading to the *pro forma* unanimous nomination of the presidential candidate were not completed until after 1:30 a.m., and the convention then adjourned. When it reassembled in the afternoon of the fourth day, contrary to usual custom nothing was done immediately about the vice-presidential question.

One important piece of business was transacted, however. In 1936, as a *quid pro quo* for acceptance of majority rule instead of the historic two thirds rule, the southern delegates had been assured that a change in apportionment would be made that would reward states delivering electoral votes to Democratic candidates. Since the South was more constant in this respect than the other sections, the proposed change would tend to raise the proportionate strength of the southern delegations in future conventions, thus partially offsetting loss of veto power previously held by the section under the two thirds rule. The proposal presented to the rules committee was not satisfactory, and the original report of the committee was silent on the subject.

It was clear to all that the matter could not be left hanging, and the rules committee presented a subsidiary report in this session. After reviewing the instructions given the national committee in 1936, and acknowledging that the report submitted required further consideration, the national committee was instructed accordingly. In the interim, however, the following provisions were made:

Resolved, That pending such a study, such States as cast their electoral votes for the Democratic Presidential nominees for President and Vice President shall have two additional delegates-at-large to the Democratic National Convention.

WHEREAS the Democratic National Committee has recommended reduction in the number of regular delegates and alternates to National Conventions allotted to the District of Columbia, territories and insular possessions; and

WHEREAS it is to the direct interest of the National Democratic Party to maintain and encourage Democratic organization in those areas: Therefore be it

Resolved, That this Committee on Rules and Order of Business hereby recommends to the Democratic Convention of 1940 that the allotment of delegates and alternates of the District of Columbia, territories and insular possessions be maintained at their present numerical strength; and be it further

Resolved, That no further fractional distribution shall be permitted that will give any delegate to a Democratic National Convention less than one-half vote.[8]

The resolution was adopted by voice vote, and apportionment in 1944 was based upon this principle. The last part of the resolution pertaining to fractional votes was to prove as unsuccessful as similar resolutions had been in the past.

The balance of the brief afternoon session was devoted to clearing up the usual resolutions of appreciation, and so on. The vice-presidential nominating speeches finally began in the evening session. At the beginning, the proceedings were routine. William B. Bankhead, the temporary chairman, was nominated by his home state delegation, Alabama. Nominations of Jesse H. Jones of Texas, administrator of the Federal Loan Agency, Henry A. Wallace of Iowa, Secretary of Agriculture, Governor Alva B. Adams of California, and Paul V. McNutt of Indiana followed.

At this point, the tenor of the convention changed. McNutt requested recognition from the chair; when he mounted the rostrum a demonstration broke out, led by McNutt supporters trying to prevent his withdrawal. Apparently the galleries contributed substantially to the confusion, and charges subsequently were made that they

[8] *Ibid.,* pp. 200-201.

had been packed by McNutt supporters provided with forged tickets. When he could make himself heard, McNutt withdrew; in his brief speech, he stated, "[Franklin Delano Roosevelt] is my commander in chief. I follow his wishes, and I am here to support his choice for Vice President of the United States." Although he did not name Wallace, this was the first of what was to be the most remarkable series of signals given to rebellious delegates in any convention in history.

He was followed by Philip Murray, at that time vice president of the United Mine Workers, who surprised nobody when he seconded Wallace. A second signal was given by Congressman Sam Rayburn when he thanked the Texas delegation for honoring him with their endorsement for the vice-presidential nomination but declined the honor. He then seconded Wallace in a speech that indicated clearly he was doing it as a political duty rather than because he wanted to.

I come to second the nomination of another. Let me say that if I consulted my loyalty to friendship and my love, I would probably be seconding the nomination of [still] another, but under the circumstances I can do none other than follow what I believe to be the wish of our great leader.[9]

Other speakers indicated the same pressure. Senator Scott Lucas of Illinois, in withdrawing his name from nomination, said:

Had this been a free and open convention, I would not have hesitated but on last evening I saw here men and women, delegates and those in the gallery alike, cheer until they were hoarse for the great President of the United States, in insisting that he be drafted to run for a third term. And so, under these circumstances, it seems to me that if the President of the United States desires Henry Wallace as his running mate, that we should respect his request, because after all, Roosevelt is the individual who is going to carry the load.[10]

Despite the clear signals, protests continued in the form of additional nominees. Senator Prentiss M. Brown of Michigan

[9] *Ibid.,* p. 226.
[10] *Ibid.,* p. 235.

and Bascom Timmons, newspaper man from Texas, were nominated. Like Lucas, Brown withdrew his name, as also did Jesse Jones. In the brief but impassioned speech nominating Timmons, in effect Wallace was charged with being an apostate, and the speaker pleaded with Roosevelt to "nominate a fellow like Bascom Timmons or Jim Farley or another great Democrat in this convention."

The culminating signal was given by no less a person than Eleanor Roosevelt, who had been flown from Washington to help quiet the storm. Immediately following the last seconding speech, she was presented to the convention. Her mere appearance under the time and circumstances was enough. She made no obvious gesture in support of any candidate, though much could be, and probably was, read into such statements as these: "You will have to rise above considerations which are narrow and partisan. . . . This is no ordinary time, no time for thinking about anything except what we can best do for the country as a whole." Immediately after her speech, the roll call began.

The 1,100 votes in the convention were spread between thirteen candidates, but only three received a significant number: Wallace $626^{11}/_{30}$; Bankhead $329\frac{3}{5}$; and McNutt, despite his withdrawal and the fact that he had insisted that his own state of Indiana should not vote for him, $68\frac{4}{5}$. After the roll, several states had changed their vote in Wallace's favor and more were requesting recognition, when Senator John H. Bankhead of Alabama was recognized to thank his brother's supporters and to move suspension of the rules for the unanimous nomination of Wallace. As it turned out, nomination of William Bankhead would have complicated the election, for he died in September.

Presidential Election, November 5, 1940

FRANKLIN D. ROOSEVELT (D) : popular vote, 27,244,160; electoral vote, 449
WENDELL L. WILLKIE (R) : popular vote, 22,305,198; electoral vote, 82

1944

PREOCCUPATION WITH the war, its problems, and its conduct overshadowed all else between 1940 and 1944. At the time of the elections in 1942 the picture was dark; as under similar conditions in 1862, this was reflected in substantial gains by the party out of power. In both houses of Congress, the Republicans narrowed the gap, though in neither case were they able to capture control. In several states Democratic governors were supplanted by Republicans, the most important change occurring in New York, where Thomas E. Dewey won his first term.

In 1943 the war tide began to turn as the growing national military strength was increasingly exerted. Successively, North Africa, Sicily, and Italy were invaded. In the Pacific, the island-hopping campaign directed by Admiral Nimitz and General MacArthur rolled steadily forward. Around-the-clock bombing of Germany became the order of the day. With each military success, the Republicans found it more difficult and politically more dangerous to criticize the administration in the conduct of the war; by the same token, the Democrats found more to which they could point with pride, and their basic argument that the Nation should not change horses in the middle of the stream became more effective. The successful Allied landings on the shores of France barely two weeks before the Republican convention climaxed the trend.

TWENTY-THIRD REPUBLICAN CONVENTION

Wendell Willkie, although the official titular leader of the Republicans, found only a fragment of the party willing to accept his leadership. Following his defeat in 1940 he further alienated the isolationist segment of the party by endorsing Roosevelt's Lend-Lease policy, and by his continuing trend toward general support of Roosevelt's program. Meanwhile, other potential contestants found their positions influenced by events.

Harold E. Stassen won a second term as governor of Minnesota, and shortly thereafter resigned to enter the Navy. John W. Bricker proved his vote-getting ability by winning re-election as governor of Ohio. General Douglas MacArthur won tremendous publicity through his operations in the Pacific and was not yet the controversial figure he was to become. MacArthur and Stassen, however, were unable to press their own causes, and efforts of their supporters did not gain much headway against the energetic Dewey campaign. Against Bricker, Dewey appeared to have much greater public attraction, both in personality and in the breadth of the political spectrum to which he could appeal. Bricker was widely known as a conservative and an isolationist.

Relatively few primary contests were held, although one was so important to the outcome that it became the classic case of the negative potential of the primary system. Warren in California, and Bricker in Ohio, were unchallenged. MacArthur received most of the light preferential vote in Illinois, as Dewey did in New Jersey. The more important contests occurred in Wisconsin, Nebraska, Oregon, and South Dakota, but particularly in Wisconsin. Against the advice of his friends, and probably against his own better judgment, Willkie decided to risk everything in Wisconsin, where the odds against him were

262

perhaps greater than in any other state.

Whatever slight chance he may have had was further diminished by the late entrance of Stassen's name—a contingency that Willkie probably did not expect. In any case, despite a strenuous personal appeal to the voters of Wisconsin in which he pleaded for support in his campaign against isolationism and reaction, Willkie found himself running fourth to Dewey, MacArthur, and Stassen, none of whom had committed himself to a serious effort. Shortly thereafter, Willkie withdrew.

Chicago, Illinois, June 26, 27, 28, 1944

No contest of any kind riffled the surface of this abbreviated convention. Committees were appointed and their reports accepted without a recorded vote. In addition to the customary speeches by the temporary chairman, Governor Earl Warren of California, and the permanent chairman, Joe Martin of Massachusetts, minority leader of the House, major addresses were made by Herbert Hoover and Congresswoman Clare Boothe Luce of Connecticut. None of the speakers dealt with the conduct of the war by the administration; all four stressed the universal desire to get "the boys" home as quickly as possible, and the hope that peace, when it came, would be a lasting peace. Centralization of government, identified with the New Deal, was sharply attacked, and an effort was made to divide the pro-New Deal "minority" from the rank and file of the Democratic party and to invite the latter to join with Republicans in fighting New Dealers as common enemies. The concept of the "indispensable man" came under particularly heavy fire.

The Presidential Nomination

The presentation of Thomas E. Dewey for the Presidency was followed by a series of seconds by erstwhile rivals or their supporters, who at the same time announced withdrawals in favor of complete party harmony. Bricker, who led the parade, was given a particularly large ovation. No other candidates were presented, although one vote was cast for MacArthur. Dewey received all the rest.

The Vice-Presidential Nomination

The unanimous nomination of Bricker for Vice President followed. During the seconding speeches, Representative Charles A. Halleck of Indiana presented an unusual statement in which the Indiana delegation endorsed their first choice for Vice President, William L. Hutcheson, a labor leader, for Secretary of Labor, in view of the obvious fact that there would be no point in nominating him against Bricker.

TWENTY-NINTH DEMOCRATIC CONVENTION

So far as Roosevelt's renomination was concerned, no question existed at any time and he had no need to campaign for it. Polls taken of Democrats throughout the nation indicated an overwhelming preference for a fourth term. The improving war picture was a potent argument in the President's favor, and, with the two-term tradition already broken, the delicate negotiations of 1940 could be dispensed with. Shortly before the convention Roosevelt announced clearly that he would accept a renomination.

The skies were not entirely unclouded, however. The makings of a sizable revolt existed among those who opposed the New Deal, particularly in the South. The southern opposition had for some time protested the invasion of states rights considered by many to be inherent in some of the Rooseveltian domestic policies; recently it had a further grievance in the belief that the South had been cheated by institution of majority rule in the conventions without adequate compensation in apportionment. Helpless to stop Roosevelt, the southerners found a center on which they could focus much of their protest—the renomination of Vice President Henry A. Wallace.

Though the Republicans were handicapped by inability to attack the Democrats on issues connected with the war, the Democrats were under no compulsion to refrain from taking full credit for the increasing Allied successes in all theaters. By mid-July 1944, the war was by no means won, but France had been invaded, Cherbourg and Caen had been captured, and the American breakthrough at Saint-Lô was being exploited. In Italy, Rome finally had fallen after the long tie-up at Cassino. In the Pacific, the Marshall and Admiralty Islands had been seized, superfortresses had begun to bomb the Japanese home islands, and three days before the Democratic convention opened, American forces invaded the Marianas. In the meantime, on the home front, production had reached unparalleled heights and, with man power at a premium, forced unemployment was almost nonexistent. Under these conditions, the theme "Don't change horses in the middle of the stream" was a potent one, and was fully exploited throughout the convention. From the standpoint of public interest in the convention, the Democrats were fortunate also to have a genuine contest develop for the vice-presidential nomination.

Chicago, Illinois,
July 19, 20, 21, 1944

Despite the resolution in the 1940 convention recommending that the national committee produce a permanent plan of apportionment that "should take into account the Democratic strength within each State," the 1944 convention apportionment remained unchanged from that of 1940. In addition to double its electoral strength two bonus votes were added for each state that produced a popular majority for Roosevelt in 1940—which most of them did.

Convention Organization

The convention took its time about getting down to the business of organizing. Several speeches were heard, mostly from representatives of the host city of Chicago and the state of Illinois. One speaker, however, introduced a businesslike note amidst the welcoming oratory: the treasurer of the Democratic committee warned the delegates that, although the party momentarily was in the black, funds were needed immediately, and a minimum of $3 million would be required for the campaign. He urged his listeners to send their checks at once, and added the warning, "You must of course limit your enthusiasm to checks of $5,000 or less, under the Hatch Act."

Governor Robert S. Kerr of Oklahoma was selected temporary chairman. His acceptance speech was delayed until well into the second session, as speeches first were made by Robert E. Hannegan, chairman of the Democratic national committee, and by Mrs. Charles W. Tillett, director of the women's division. Hannegan warned that although "we are resolved that nothing that we do in this campaign shall interfere with a single man-hour of war work," this did not mean that they could fail to get out the maximum vote. Mrs. Tillett stressed the need for planning for the postwar period, so that returning veterans might be assured of adequate job opportunities.

Kerr charged that the nomination of Thomas E. Dewey by the Republicans indicated a return of the "Old Guard" to control of that party, and recited Republican voting records during the immediate prewar period in which congressmen from that party opposed defensive measures. The Republican party, he said, had no program today, except to oppose. A large part of his speech was a rebuttal of the Republican charges that Roosevelt was "a tired old man." "What would Churchill and Stalin and the Generalissimo [Chiang Kai-shek] and the other allied leaders think when they learned that he [Dewey] looked on them as just a group of 'tired old men'?"

The committee on permanent organization presented Senator Samuel D. Jackson of Indiana as the permanent chairman early in the first session on the second day. This was not an election which the nation could afford to muddle through, he said. "This is not nineteen hundred and twenty; it is not nineteen hundred and twenty-four; not nineteen hundred twenty-eight. . . . What the Presidency demands now, is not so much a bright young man, as a man of wisdom and experience, with depth and breadth of vision."

The committee on rules and order of business followed. The report recommended the rules of the 78th Congress as the parliamentary guide, restricted nominating speeches to twenty minutes and seconding speeches to four for each candidate presented, each not to exceed five minutes. In addition to other routine clauses, the committee added a special resolution in an attempt to clear up once and for all the bothersome question of apportionment.

BE IT RESOLVED, That this Committee reaffirms its recommendation heretofore made in the Democratic Convention of 1936 and the Democratic National Committee is again hereby instructed and authorized to formulate and adopt a plan for improving the system by which delegates and alternates to Democratic National Conventions are apportioned and that such action by said National Committee be taken not later than two years from and after this date.

AND BE IT FURTHER RESOLVED, That in formulating this plan the National Committee shall take into account the Democratic strength within each State, District of Columbia, and Territory, etc., in making said apportionment.[1]

This resolution was much stronger than any previously passed, and specifically directed the committee to act—whereas action

[1] DNC, *Proceedings*, 1944, pp. 62-63.

had been merely recommended before. In addition, the committee was authorized to *adopt* the results of its labors.

Immediately after adoption of the order of business, at the recommendation of the permanent chairman, the convention unanimously approved a change. The committees on credentials and platform were not ready to report, and the convention agreed to proceed with the nomination and seconding speeches, though not the actual balloting.

After the nominating speeches had been completed, the committee on credentials reported. The report approved all the seats on the temporary roll with the exception of Texas, in which contest it recommended seating both sets of delegates. This was protested by the Texas delegation seated on the temporary roll on the grounds that it was the "regular" delegation elected by the regular state convention; it proposed an amendment that its members alone be seated. The contesting delegates, admitting that they had been elected by a rump convention, charged that they left the regular convention because that convention insisted upon passing a series of resolutions declaring that the Texas electors would not be bound to support the nominees of the national convention unless certain demands were met. Neutral members of the credentials committee stated that they had arranged the compromise in the hope that the conflict could be resolved, and the chairman of the committee pleaded unsuccessfully with the "regulars" to withdraw their motion in the name of good sportsmanship. The amendment was defeated and the original report was accepted, both by voice vote.

The Platform

The opening sentence of the platform was short and clear: "The Democratic Party stands on its record in peace and war." The platform pledged to cooperate with the other allied nations

. . . in the establishment of an international organization based on the principle of the sovereign equality of all peace-loving states, open to membership of all such states, large and small, for the prevention of aggression and maintenance of international peace and security.[2]

The postwar program planks included such matters as price guarantees and crop insurance to farmers, and support for home ownership for family-sized farms. Compensation for workers during demobilization and benefits to ex-servicemen were assured. The platform closed with a paragraph of praise for President Roosevelt.

A minority report advocated an international air force as a minimum requirement to enforce peace between nations. It was defeated after the chairman of the platform committee pointed out that one of the platform planks on international relations pledged the party:

To make all necessary and effective agreements and arrangements through which the nations would maintain adequate forces to meet the needs of preventing war and of making impossible the preparation for war and which would have such forces available for joint action when necessary.[3]

The air force, he said, was included under the definition of "adequate" forces.

The Presidential Nomination

In a very real sense, Roosevelt had been nominated in nearly every speech in the convention, but his name was placed officially before the delegates by the Senate majority leader, Alben W. Barkley of Kentucky. Barkley ran the gamut of all the points brought out in the previous speeches. He extolled the party record, and the presidential record. Republicans were charged with having prevented the nation from being prepared for attack. To

[2] *Ibid.,* p. 93.
[3] *Ibid.*

the Republican charge that "those in charge of our government have grown old or tired in office," Barkley retorted that the Republican platform was the "Tired Old Platform," and that in any case Roosevelt had held high office for a shorter period than the leaders of any of the other major governments in the United Nations. The party had made mistakes, Barkley admitted, but "only through error can man or nation come to know the truth." The Democratic party, he said, had from its past experience evolved a comprehensive and practical program for solution of the postwar problems.

The seconding speakers, selected to show the scope of party representation, included a labor man, a southerner, a midwesterner, and so on. But the most unusual speaker was the Vice President, Henry Wallace. In an obvious attempt to identify himself with Roosevelt ideologically, Wallace described the President as the "greatest liberal in the history of the U. S.," asserting further that "Roosevelt is a greater liberal today than he has ever been."

As a protest of the conservatives, particularly the southerners, Senator Harry F. Byrd of Virginia was placed in nomination. Roosevelt received 1,086 of the 1,176 votes in the convention; of the remaining 90, Byrd received 89 and Farley 1.

The Vice-Presidential Nomination

Prior to the presidential nomination, a letter from Roosevelt regarding the Vice-Presidency had been read to the convention. He wished, the letter said, to clear up some of the rumors that were circulating by giving the convention his personal thoughts. After stating that, after years of association with Henry Wallace, he liked and respected him as a personal friend, he added:

For these reasons, I personally would vote for his renomination if I were a delegate to the Convention. At the same time, I do not wish to appear in any way as dictating to the Convention. Obviously the Convention must do the deciding. And it should—and I am sure it will—give consideration to the pros and cons of its choice.[4]

If Roosevelt intended this statement to be an endorsement of Wallace—and it is certainly subject to more than one interpretation—the convention evidently preferred to consider the pros and cons. The delegates had plenty of time to think, for an adjournment was called immediately after the presidential nomination, and the evening session was devoted primarily to a speech by Helen Gahagan Douglas and to a radio address by the President from the West Coast, where he was about to embark for Pearl Harbor to confer with Admiral Nimitz and General MacArthur. The vice-presidential nominations were not made until the next day.

Twelve names were officially placed in nomination, sixteen receiving votes on the first ballot. Under the majority rule in effect since 1936, 589 votes were required for nomination. Vice President Henry A. Wallace received 429½ on the first ballot. His only near competitor was Senator Harry S. Truman of Missouri, head of the Truman Committee of the Senate, in which capacity he was credited with saving millions of dollars by elimination of waste and duplication in the war effort. None of the other candidates exceeded 100 votes.

In view of the known—or at least suspected—deterioration of the President's health, the selection of a vice-presidential candidate was viewed with greater concern

[4] *Ibid.*, p. 63.

than is ordinarily the case. Wallace was a leading exponent of the New Deal philosophy, and his support came primarily from the more liberal wing. Truman, although not anti-New Deal, seemed more conservative, in the light of his past record, and accordingly more acceptable to those who were lukewarm or actively opposed to extension of New Deal principles. On the second ballot, the dichotomy became more clear, as many of the delegates who voted for minor candidates turned to Wallace or Truman, with Truman getting the better of it. The Wallace vote increased to 473, but Truman passed him with 477½, about 112 short of nomination.

The break came quickly. Even before conclusion of the roll call Alabama requested permission to change its vote, but was refused until the call had been completed. At that point, Senator John H. Bankhead of Alabama withdrew his name and transferred most of his delegation's vote to Truman. Paul McNutt's name next was withdrawn, most of the Indiana delegation then moving its vote to Truman. State after state followed, and when the changes were completed Wallace retained only 105 votes. Truman received 1,031. A few delegates, including the entire Tennessee contingent, refused to vote for either leader, and no vote for unanimous nomination is recorded. Chairman Jackson made the formal announcement that Harry S. Truman was the nominee, whereupon Truman thanked the convention in a brief statement. Shortly thereafter the convention adjourned.

Presidential Election, November 7, 1944

FRANKLIN D. ROOSEVELT (D) : popular vote, 25,602,505; electoral vote, 432
THOMAS E. DEWEY (R) : popular vote, 22,006,278; electoral vote, 99

1948

WITH THE DEATH OF Franklin D. Roosevelt in April 1945, the problems of finishing the war and meeting the complicated questions of postwar adjustment devolved upon Harry S. Truman. Relatively unknown at the outset, Truman enjoyed a honeymoon period, during which most factional conflict was temporarily subdued. This brief respite was probably due partly to shock at the loss of a great leader, and partly to uncertainty about the qualities and strength of his successor, but undoubtedly it also reflected genuine sympathy for the tremendous obstacles which Truman faced. As generally is the case in politics, the honeymoon was relatively short; the rifts began to appear when Truman's positive qualities and stands upon issues became better known. As his term progressed, Truman's views on many questions were seen to be fully as liberal as Roosevelt's, and his "Fair Deal" program aroused fear and ire among conservatives generally, but especially among the conservative southerners.

Reversion to conservatism was indicated by the sweeping Republican gains in the mid-term elections of 1946; for the first time in many years the Republican party could control both houses of Congress. As a result, the last two years of Truman's term were characterized by bitter conflict between Congress and the administration, a conflict highlighted by frequent administration vetoes of congressional acts and an unusually large number of cases in which Congress overrode the vetoes.

TWENTY-FOURTH REPUBLICAN CONVENTION

Thomas E. Dewey's relatively easy nomination in 1944 was not to be repeated. His long-term antagonist, Senator Robert A. Taft, had increased his stature considerably through his leadership in the Senate—particularly with Republicans again holding a majority there. By many, particularly the party regulars, he was seen as the actual and logical opponent to Truman in the oncoming election, just as he had been the administration's major antagonist in the present term.

Other possibilities included Harold E. Stassen, fresh from his service as an officer in the Navy, who had been able to get adequate financial support to mount an energetic campaign on a wide scale. Two war heroes, Douglas MacArthur and Dwight D. Eisenhower, received considerable attention, but the latter finally firmly refused to be a candidate. Among favorite sons, the popular California governor, Earl Warren, and Senator Arthur Vandenberg of Michigan were the most prominent.

Neither Taft nor Dewey, the front-runners, preferred the kind of campaigning the primaries required, but each was forced to depend upon it to some extent. As in 1944, when Dewey defeated Wendell Willkie in Wisconsin, the primaries proved once again that they could ensure defeat of a presidential hopeful but could not assure his selection. MacArthur ran poorly in Wisconsin and Nebraska, and the momentum of his campaign dropped sharply.

268

Stassen made the mistake of meeting Taft on the latter's home ground, Ohio, and also lost to an energetic campaign by Dewey in Oregon. Most of the Dewey and Taft delegations, however, were won through the time-honored party processes in states where no primaries were held.

Philadelphia, Pennsylvania, June 21, 22, 23, 24, 25, 1948

Throughout the years, the Republican party had consistently added more and more material to the convention call; it had become a long document explicitly detailing the actual apportionment and the methods for selecting delegates and handling contests during the preconvention period. Accordingly, after the preliminary paragraph stating the time, place, and purpose of the convention had been read, motion was made and approved that reading of the balance of the call be dispensed with, a procedure standardized in subsequent conventions. The delegates were greeted by the mayor of Philadelphia and the governor of Pennsylvania before proceeding with appointment of the standing committees.

Convention Organization

The early stages of the convention were unusual, for the call to order came from the chairman of the committee on arrangements, Walter S. Hallanan of West Virginia, who presided until the convention call had been read and the welcoming speeches delivered. At this point he released the gavel to the chairman of the national committee, Carroll Reece of Tennessee, who made a brief speech and continued in the chair while the standing committees were appointed.

The temporary chairman, Governor Dwight H. Green of Illinois, was elected after the committees were established, and did not take the chair until the evening session. In his acceptance speech, Governor Green regaled the delegates with highly partisan remarks. "The New Deal Party can have no real program," he said, "because it is no longer a real party. It mustered its majorities from a fantastic partnership of reaction and radicalism. For years, this strange alliance was held together by bosses, boodle, buncombe, and blarney. . . . That group of crackpots was never competent to hold responsible office. The lunatic fringe is neither competent to govern nor to let others govern."

The next speech was even more partisan. Congresswoman Clare Boothe Luce of Connecticut charged the Democratic party and the administration with nearly every fault, if not crime, in the book. The modern "New Deal" party, composed as it was of three major groups—the right, or Jim Crow wing; the left, or Moscow wing; and the center "run by the wampum and boodle boys"—kept itself in power by effective use of three formulas. The first was "Padding the Public Payroll," which Mrs. Luce said produced about 5 votes for each employee. The second was "Confusion and Crisis," by which issues were made or magnified out of proportion; the Democratic party, she declared, "cannot win elections except in the climate of crisis." The third formula was "arousing of extravagant hopes, or equally extravagant fears." She further charged the administration with virtually selling out to communism.

The reports of the committees were in each case approved without debate and by voice vote. The rules and order of business report contained important changes in apportionment. The District of Columbia and Hawaii were allotted six delegates at large for the next convention, and Puerto Rico three; in the 1948 apportionment, the District and Hawaii were represented by five and three delegates respectively, and Puerto Rico by two. The Virgin Islands, unrepresented in 1948, was given one seat for 1952. The representation of Alaska remained unchanged with three delegates. In addition, Alaska, the District of Columbia, and Hawaii would be allotted two additional delegates each should they elect a Republican delegate to Congress in the midterm election preceding the 1952 convention.

The bonus for Republican election success was raised from three to six for states electing Republican electors, a Republican governor, or a Republican senator in the last election for either of these offices preceding the 1952 convention. Provision also was made for an assistant chairman of the national committee, the post to be filled by a woman.

Once again the Speaker of the House, Joseph T. Martin, was named permanent chairman, but he did not make his acceptance speech until after the report of the credentials committee. Both Martin's speech and that of Herbert Hoover which followed continued the attack against communism within and without the country, and flayed the administration for encouraging its spread. However, as befitted positions of greater responsibility, their language was somewhat restrained; while they charged their opponents with fumbling and fuzzy-headedness, they did not press the charge of sinister motivation as strongly as Governor Green and Congresswoman Luce had done.

Contests were reported in four delegations, but in each case the committee on credentials upheld the recommendation of the national committee and this was approved by the convention. Subsequent to approval of the report, a resolution prepared by a subcommittee of the credentials committee was passed, stipulating that current provisions for deciding contests and appeals were inadequate, cumbersome, and unfair, and recommending that the national committee be authorized and instructed to revise and improve them. This action was of particular interest in view of the importance of credentials problems in the convention of 1952.

The Platform

The platform was presented as "the shortest Republican platform ever written," and there is no question that a serious attempt had been made to make the planks as short and concise as possible. The platform was further unusual in being almost entirely positive in tone—a presentation of a program rather than an attack upon the opposition. Having stated that "we will waste few words on the tragic lack of foresight and general inadequacy of those now in charge of the Executive Branch," it made only two specific accusations: the administration had used obstructionist tactics against the Republican-controlled Congress; the administration had contributed to the "present cruelly high prices" by its failure to use effectively the powers it possessed to combat inflation.

The stand for civil rights was strong. The party favored equal justice for all, regardless of race, creed, or color; abolition of racial segregation in the armed forces; abolition of the poll tax; a constitutional amendment providing equal rights for women; equal educational opportunity for all. Tolerance was not universal, however, for among the things classified as fundamental was "the routing out of communism wherever found."

On the international front, one plank seemed to provide an unusually large number of different interpretations, depending upon what one wished to read into it.

Our foreign policy is dedicated to preserving a free America in a free world of free men. This calls for strengthening the United Nations and primary recognition of America's self-interest in the liberty of other peoples. Prudently conserving our own resources, we shall cooperate on a self-help basis with other peace-loving nations.[1]

The Presidential Nomination

The roll was called for nominations in the evening session of the same day, and

[1] RNC, *Proceedings*, 1948, p. 188.

time was reserved by Pennsylvania, to make the nominating speech for Thomas E. Dewey; Ohio, for Robert A. Taft; California, for Earl Warren; Minnesota, for Harold E. Stassen; Connecticut, for Raymond E. Baldwin, favorite son; Michigan, for Arthur H. Vandenberg; and Wisconsin, for Douglas MacArthur, in that order. The first four states received their early positions on the list through courtesy of states with names early in the alphabet who yielded their positions. The rules permitted no more than four seconding speeches, and most candidates received this number. All seconding speeches for a candidate followed the nomination speech for that candidate. The speeches were not completed until 4:00 a.m., at which time the convention adjourned.

On the first ballot the next afternoon, twelve candidates received votes. The total voting strength of the convention was 1,094, with 548 a nominating majority. Dewey led with 434, followed by Taft with 224, and Stassen with 157. All other candidates were substantially below 100 votes each. Of the three leaders, Stassen had, on the whole, the least securely bound delegates, who were therefore the most likely to shift to another. Among the favorite son delegations, those for Vandenberg and Warren were probably the most stable and least likely to change; without them, Dewey would need most of the other favorite son vote, unless he received help from Stassen followers. Since both the Illinois and Tennessee favorite son vote was much more likely to go to Taft, help from the Stassen delegation was almost imperative if Dewey was to win.

On the second ballot, the instability of the Stassen vote and its tendency to consider Dewey as second choice were demonstrated. Although Stassen gained at several points from the melting of the favorite son vote, he lost in the aggregate, when several delegates from Iowa, Maryland, Nebraska, and South Dakota, among others, moved into the Dewey column. Stassen ended the

second ballot with 149 votes; Dewey had increased to 515 and Taft to 274, the latter's increase being largely from Illinois and Tennessee.

At this point, a motion to adjourn was made by the chairman of the Pennsylvania delegation—the delegation that had nominated Dewey but had then indicated a lack of solidarity by giving him only a little more than half its vote. The motion was seconded by the Warren-pledged California delegation and Taft's Ohio delegation. On a voice vote, the chairman was unable to determine the result, and asked if six states would second a request for a roll call. The necessary seconds were quickly found, but before the roll could be called a Dewey representative from New York informed the convention that New York did not object to an adjournment, and the convention recessed until evening.

Following the recess, the names of Taft, Warren, Stassen, Vandenberg, Baldwin, and MacArthur were withdrawn. Dewey received a unanimous vote on the roll call, though the call was delayed by a request from California that its delegation be polled. This request resulted from the California primary law by which delegates were pledged to a candidate until released by him. Time was not available for a caucus following receipt of a release from Warren, and the device of an open poll on the convention floor was adopted to ensure that every delegate had an opportunity to declare his vote.

Immediately following the nomination, Governor and Mrs. Dewey were escorted to the platform, where Dewey made an acceptance speech. An overnight adjournment was then taken.

The Vice-Presidential Nomination

On the roll call for vice-presidential nominations, Arizona reserved time to present the name of Harold E. Stassen and California yielded to New York. If any delegate had not been informed before, this was a clear indication that Governor Earl Warren of California was Dewey's choice for his running mate. No vote was taken. The chairman dealt with the matter by saying:

Is there objection to the waiving of the rule and making the Vice-Presidential nomination of Governor Warren by acclamation? The Chair hears none, and it is so declared.[2]

THIRTIETH DEMOCRATIC CONVENTION

By the fall of 1947, President Harry Truman had recovered much ground from his previous low point in the public estimation as measured by the polls in 1946. But in 1948, beginning with his State of the Union message in January, his popularity began a new slide. Everything he did seemed to go wrong. Villified not only by Republicans but by the more extreme conservatives and liberals in his own party, he was given little chance of re-election against a strong Republican candidate. Many within the Democratic party would have been glad to block him from the renomination, and some cherished notions of trying to do so, but as usual in the party in power, this proved to be a task that was not easy. The difficulty was compounded by the wide split within the opposition; there could be no candidate suitable alike to the liberals surrounding Henry Wallace and to the southern conservatives.

In any case, Truman entered the convention with strength to spare under majority rule, but there were many questions to be answered before he could depend upon the support of a united party. Wallace had already declared his intention to run on a third-party ticket, regardless of the results of the Democratic convention, and prospects were high that the southerners would also present a third-party ticket. It was likely that Truman could depend only on the support of the rank and file of the party organization throughout the nation—except in the South—and on his own firm

[2] *Ibid.*, p. 290.

belief that a majority of the inarticulate voters would stand by him in the end.

*Philadelphia, Pennsylvania,
July 12, 13, 14, 1948*

In accordance with a resolution passed in the convention of 1944, the national committee altered the system of apportionment for the convention of 1948. The new system provided an additional eight delegates, each with a half vote, for any state that had cast its electoral vote for the Democratic nominees for President and Vice President in the election of 1944. Voting strength otherwise remained the same, although it was specifically provided that all at large state delegates be elected on a half vote basis. Congressional districts, the territories, and the District of Columbia were instructed to send only full-vote delegates.

As usual in Democratic conventions, the latter rule was not followed; some congressional districts split the allotted two votes between three, four, six, and even seven delegates. With the exception of a few half votes, this did not complicate the voting in this convention, however, for, because of the unit rule, and also because of the structure of the division within the convention, most delegations voted solidly on each of the several ballots taken.

Convention Organization

Senator Alben W. Barkley of Kentucky was named temporary chairman and made his keynote speech during the evening session. He began by extolling the record of "the whipping boy" of every Republican convention since 1932, the New Deal. He continued with an attack on the 80th Congress, laying the groundwork for the subsequent appellation—the "Do-Nothing Congress." As in the Republican convention, the keynote speech was followed by a speech from a woman—in this case India Edwards, executive director of the women's division of the national committee. Both

Barkley and Mrs. Edwards followed the cue of their Republican counterparts by charging invidious motivation to the opposition. Republicans, and particularly the members of the 80th Congress, were the tools of vested interests; this explained the actions of the congressional majority—which in turn caused the increasing spiral of living costs. Mrs. Edwards illustrated the impact of rising costs upon the average budget of food by the graphic device of a shopping bag, from which she pulled various items, while comparing the prices with the prices of two years before. To illustrate the rise in clothing costs, a small girl was brought to the stage to have each of her garments described in terms of current price and what it had been before price controls were eliminated by the Republican majority in Congress.

Committees having been appointed in the evening session of the first day, the committee on credentials gave its report the next evening. The majority report recognized all delegates on the temporary roll. The minority report was unusual, since there was no contesting delegation; it concerned the series of resolutions by which the Mississippi state convention had bound the Mississippi delegation to withdraw from the national convention unless there were a positive plank in support of states rights. The resolutions also denied the delegates the power to bind the Democratic party of Mississippi to the support of any nominee who favored the civil rights program sponsored by President Truman, or who failed to denounce that program.

These resolutions were incorporated as a certified part of the credentials of the Mississippi delegates. The minority report recommended that the delegation not be seated in view of the limitations appended to its credentials. Following a brief debate, the minority report was rejected by a voice vote. A roll call was called for, but the chairman announced that the minority group had agreed not to demand a roll call, and the request was not pursued. Following adoption of the majority report by voice vote, however, the New York and California delegations requested they be recorded as having voted for the minority and against the majority report.

The request was granted, and subsequently the chairman announced that several additional states had also requested their votes be recorded in the same way. In this informal manner, 503 votes were recorded for the minority and against the majority report. Since several important northern states, including New Jersey and Massachusetts, that usually voted consistently with the states listed were not included in the list, it appears probable that the supporters of the minority report were indeed a majority of the convention, but that they had abstained from exercising their majority rights in the interests of harmony. At the same time, by recording their opposition informally for the record, a clear warning was given the southern delegates that strength was available if the latter forced the issue.

The southerners were willing to accept the challenge, for both rules and platform committee reports were accompanied by minority reports. In the case of rules, a minority report signed by "the State of Texas and six other states" stated that it was its purpose "to request and command the restoration of the two thirds nominating rule." Wright Morrow of Texas, in presenting the report, charged that the unit rule, in the absence of the two thirds rule, made it possible for a few large states easily to dominate the convention. Other proponents charged lack of good faith on the part of the northern majority for failure to keep the promise of a new allocation of representation to protect minority interests, which was made in 1936 in return for southern acquiescence in abolishing the two thirds rule. Supporters of majority rule pointed out past bitter experiences with the two thirds rule, particularly in the 1924 convention. The minority report was rejected and the majority report accepted by voice vote, with no record in the proceedings of a demand for a roll call.

A southerner, Sam Rayburn of Texas, Democratic leader in the House, was accepted as permanent chairman. He was immediately escorted to the chair to assume his duties. In his acceptance speech he mentioned the division within the Democratic party only obliquely—when he insisted that for sixteen years the Democratic party, and not the Republican party, had been the majority party in the land, despite the Republican congressional victory in 1946, "and for God's sake at this Convention let us act like it." He tried to point up divisions in the Republican ranks. "They do not pick a candidate like Senator Taft, who speaks their honest convictions in the Senate of the United States. . . . Instead, they use as 'front men' two affable State Governors who have led very sheltered lives." Dewey was charged with being a "me too" candidate, and Warren with being "so far out of the Republican Party that he was Democratic candidate for Governor in the Democratic State of California."

The Platform

The second southern move followed the reading of the platform. The proposed platform contained the following civil rights plank:

The Democratic party is responsible for the great civil rights gains made in recent years in eliminating unfair and illegal discrimination based on race, creed or color.
The Democratic Party commits itself to continuing its efforts to eradicate all racial, religious and economic discrimination.
We again state our belief that racial and religious minorities must have the right to live, the right to work, the right to vote, the full and equal protection of the laws, on a basis of equality with all citizens as guaranteed by the Constitution.
We again call upon the Congress to exert its full authority to the limit of its constitutional powers to assure and protect these rights.[3]

The southern minority attack was oblique rather than direct, and did not mention the civil rights section of the platform.

[3] DNC, *Proceedings*, 1948, p. 176.

Instead, three amendments were offered as additions to the platform, differing from each other in detail but all endorsing a strong states rights interpretation of the Constitution. By this strategy, it evidently was hoped that the battle could be fought on the more defensible field of constitutional interpretation of the relative powers of state and national governments, rather than on the risky ethical and moral grounds of the civil rights problem as such. If this were the southern hope, it was quickly frustrated by the proponents of a strong civil rights program.

The first minority report was presented by former Governor Dan Moody of Texas and was signed by fifteen members of the committee. The Moody resolution affirmed:

The Democratic Party stands for the principle that the Constitution contemplated and established a union of indestructible sovereign States and that under the Constitution the general Federal Government and the separate States have their separate fields of power and have permitted activities. Traditionally it has been and it remains a part of the faith of the Democratic Party that the Federal Government shall not encroach upon the reserved powers of the States by centralization of government or otherwise.
Within the reserved powers of the States, to be exercised subject to the limitations imposed by the Fourteenth and Fifteenth Amendments to the Constitution on the manner of their exercise, is the power to control and regulate local affairs and act in the exercise of police powers.[4]

It was requested that these resolutions be incorporated as the first two paragraphs of the section of the platform entitled "Our Domestic Policies."

The second minority report, a brief one, was signed by two Tennessee members of the platform committee.

The Democratic Party reaffirms its adherence to the fundamental principle of States Rights as reserved in the Federal Constitution, and pledges that it will oppose any attempt, by legislation or otherwise, to invade the exclusive jurisdiction of the States in their domestic affairs.[5]

[4] *Ibid.*, p. 179.
[5] *Ibid.*

The third minority report was presented by the Mississippi delegation, as a substitute for the Moody amendment, and was specific about the intent of its sponsors. After a brief preliminary, the proposal read:

And the party declares that the several states shall exercise, free from federal interference or encroachment by legislation, directive or otherwise, all the rights and powers reserved to them by the Constitution, among them being the power to provide by law for qualifications of electors, the conduct of elections, regulation of employment practices within the states, segregation within the states, and define crimes committed within their borders and prescribe penalties therefor, except such crimes which under the grant of power by the Constitution to the federal government may be defined by it.[6]

These three resolutions represented varying shades of willingness on the part of the southerners to compromise with the northern delegates, yet still carry out the mandate imposed upon most of the southern delegates by their constituencies. The Moody amendment restricted itself to broad statements of principle, without specifically mentioning the real problem, and without including a pledge. The Tennessee proposal added the concept that the Democratic party pledged itself to operate in accordance with these principles. The Mississippi report, representing the wing of the southern point of view that refused any form of compromise, specifically mentioned what everyone knew to be the real problem at issue.

The original planks in the civil rights section of the platform undoubtedly represented the limit of compromise to which a majority of the northerners were willing to go, and, if the southern delegates had not opened the attack, the more extreme northern delegates probably also would have gone along. However, when the southern amendments opened the door, the more extreme northern wing responded with a much stronger integration plank, and rubbed additional salt into the southern wounds by specifically endorsing President Truman's civil rights program. The plank

[6] *Ibid.*, p. 180.

was presented by Andrew J. Biemiller of Wisconsin, and co-sponsored by three others. It provided a substitute for the fourth of the four paragraphs in the original platform, to read as follows:

We highly commend President Harry Truman for his courageous stand on the issue of civil rights.

We call upon the Congress to support our President in guaranteeing these basic and fundamental American principles: The right of full and equal political participation, the right of equal opportunity of employment, the right of security of persons, and the right of equal treatment in the service and defense of our Nation.[7]

In the debate, the southerners talked about states rights and avoided the moral question. The northerners, led by Biemiller and Hubert Humphrey, mayor of Minneapolis, talked primarily about human rights and had relatively little to say about states rights.

The first roll call was taken on the Moody resolution, which was defeated by 925 to 309. Only five of the fifty-four delegations split their vote, and only 12 of the votes favoring the resolution came from states other than the eleven that once had formed the Confederacy. The other two southern resolutions were defeated by voice vote; a roll call was taken on the Biemiller amendment. Although the amendment passed by a comfortable margin, 651½ to 582½, the smaller margin of difference between the majority and minority, as compared to the previous roll call, was undoubtedly due in part to the reluctance of many northern delegates to take the extreme position postulated in the amendment, and to push the southern delegates too far.[8]

In view of the composition of the minority vote, it appears probable that the chronic fear of the small states—that they will be submerged by the larger states—was also a factor. All the delegates from the former Confederate states voted solidly against the amendment; they were joined,

[7] *Ibid.*, p. 181.
[8] See *Analysis of Key Votes.*

as might have been expected, by the border states of Delaware, Maryland, Kentucky, Missouri, and most of West Virginia, and, more surprisingly, by most of the small delegations regardless of section. The victory was won by a coalition of the large and moderate-sized northern states against the South and the small states. The complete platform, as amended, was accepted by voice vote, though the decision was by no means unanimous.

The Presidential Nomination

Following the adoption of the platform, the convention proceeded with less contentious matters: speeches, appointment of the new national committee, and various resolutions of appreciation. When finally these were completed the roll call for nominations for President began, whereupon the chairman of the first state on the list, Alabama, announced that thirteen members of his delegation were withdrawing from the convention in compliance with instructions from the state convention that they should do so if a civil rights plank such as had been adopted were included in the platform. He also announced that the Mississippi delegation was withdrawing.

One of the remaining members of the Alabama delegation then yielded to Georgia for the nomination of Senator Richard B. Russell of Georgia. The nomination of Harry S. Truman followed when Arizona yielded to Missouri for the purpose. Other candidates presented were Paul McNutt of Indiana and William Alexander Julian, favorite son of Ohio, who withdrew immediately.

Truman became the nominee on the first ballot with 926 votes; Russell had 266. Several delegations then shifted votes from minor candidates and Truman's final total was 947½, Russell finishing with 263. Enough Alabama delegates and alternates remained to cast the vote of that state for Russell, but Mississippi did not vote. All of Russell's votes came from the states that

had formed the Confederacy; of that group's votes, Truman received only the 13 of North Carolina.

The Vice-Presidential Nomination

The nominations for the Vice Presidency followed immediately. Senators Russell and Barkley were nominated. When Russell's home state was called, the chairman declared that Russell had been presented to the convention as presidential timber, but that he was in no sense of the word a candidate for the Vice Presidency. Most of the southern delegations passed, but the other delegations, almost without exception, seconded the nomination of Barkley. On motion of the governor of Kentucky the rules were suspended and Barkley declared the nominee. Evidently the response was not unanimous, for the chairman in making the announcement said:

> In the opinion of the Chair, two-thirds and more having voted in the affirmative, the Chair desires to declare Alben W. Barkley of Kentucky the Democratic nominee for Vice President of the United States.[9]

Analysis of Key Votes

The correlations of the Moody and Biemiller votes with Truman's nominating ballot are among the highest in convention history. The Moody correlation coefficient is +.99, and the somewhat lower coefficient of +.90 for the Biemiller substitute reflects the reluctance of some of the northern delegates to go quite that far in punishing the South, plus the flattening tendency of a second issue, states rights, which divided some Truman strength. The southerners had no such ambivalence; of the 304 votes among those delegations that voted higher than average for the Moody resolution, only 2 were cast for the Biemiller resolution.

It is probable (although it cannot be determined from the information available) that the 651½ votes cast for the Biemiller resolution more nearly represented the

[9] DNC, *Proceedings*, 1948, p. 297.

basic Truman strength in the convention than did the 926 he received on the nomination ballot, for the latter undoubtedly included considerable band-wagon vote. Under the two thirds rule, Truman might have fallen short of the required nominating majority on the first ballot, and conceivably could have been blocked from the nomination altogether. It is difficult to see, however, where a candidate suitable to both the southern conservatives and to the non-Truman northerners could have been found.

* * *

Immediately after the close of the Democratic convention, the more irascible of the anti-Truman southerners met in Birmingham, Alabama. They nominated Governor J. Strom Thurmond of South Carolina for the Presidency and Governor Fielding L. Wright of Mississippi for the Vice Presidency on a States' Rights ticket. The group, soon to become known as "Dixiecrats," hoped to capture enough electoral votes to hold the balance of power in the event that neither major candidate received a clear majority—a possibility somewhat enhanced by the existence of another new third-party group. Henry A. Wallace was the presidential nominee of the so-called Progressive party; how many Democratic votes might thereby be drawn off was still a question.

Presidential Election, November 2, 1948

HARRY S. TRUMAN (D) : popular vote, 24,104,836; electoral vote, 304
THOMAS E. DEWEY (R) : popular vote, 21,969,500; electoral vote, 189

1952

THE NOMINATION OF Franklin D. Roosevelt in 1932 had been accomplished largely through the support of southern delegations, and his running mate had been a southerner. This marriage of convenience ran into difficulties fairly early in his presidential career, and the subsequent years brought a gradual widening of the gap between Roosevelt and the conservative southerners, culminating in a substantial protest vote for Senator Harry F. Byrd of Virginia in the convention of 1944.

Roosevelt's tremendous success at the polls made the contest an unequal one. Furthermore, his near destruction of the Republican party in heavily urbanized areas of the North made it possible for the Democratic party to win a national election without the southern electoral vote, as each of his own elections proved. Thus, it was possible for him to force through the revocation of the historic two thirds rule in the 1936 convention. Thus, also, the southern protests were kept chiefly at the verbal level, and the southern states, despite their unhappiness, continued to return popular Democratic majorities.

Whatever the judgment of history may be, Harry S. Truman in 1948 was no Roosevelt, even in the eyes of the staunchest Truman supporters. In the eyes of the South, he appeared fully as objectionable as his predecessor, without the latter's strength. Accordingly, in 1948 the southern leaders did more than protest, and accepted a trial of strength. The bolting elements undoubtedly hoped to become the balance of power in an election in which the northern states split the vote. The attempt failed, partly because all of the southern states were not ready to cast

aside their historic allegiance to the Democratic party, and partly because Truman ran much better in the North than most people expected. But analyses of the results of the election gave strategists much to ponder.

For Republicans, the 1948 election results in the North provided a bitter lesson: substantial portions of the Roosevelt majorities had become institutionalized as Democratic party majorities. Somehow and somewhere a candidate must be found who could break the pattern, and either bring some of these voters back to the Grand Old Party, or attract new voters who would change the balance. On the brighter side of the ledger, the election returns in the South indicated that thousands of voters were willing to break their previous voting pattern, even if only for a third-party candidate; perhaps many of these protesting voters might be persuaded to vote for a Republican, if a candidate could be found who was attractive in his own right and unobjectionable to the South on the one issue of overriding importance to that section—civil rights. This possibility was all the more likely since three important southern states—Virginia, Texas and Florida—had not merely given a substantial protest vote to Russell, but had increased their total Republican vote to a point where it was a significant share of the total vote cast.

For Democratic strategists, the problem was different. On the bright side, the party had won the 1948 election. But the margin was only 37 electoral votes over the required 266. Of these, 29 were supplied by southern states in which Democratic victory was only a plurality; had the Russell and Dewey votes been combined on one candidate in these states the national margin of victory would have been thin indeed. Much would depend upon what the Republicans did in their 1952 convention, which met first. If the candidate seemed unlikely to improve Dewey's record in the South, it would be possible to nominate a northern liberal candidate in the hopes of duplicating the pattern of the Truman victory. But should the Republicans come up with a candidate who seemed likely to be attractive in the South, the demands of that section would have to be given serious consideration in the Democratic convention if the southern electoral votes were to be held.

To complicate the problem further, the Democrats were the party in power at the time when a highly unpopular war was being fought. Whatever the necessity for it and whatever the merits of its conduct, the Korean conflict was frustrating to the average man in the street, and accordingly unpopular. In effect, it had the same sort of impact that a serious depression would have had—and the administration is always blamed for situations creating unhappiness, whether it should be or not.

TWENTY-FIFTH REPUBLICAN CONVENTION

Following his defeat by Thomas E. Dewey in the 1948 convention, Robert A. Taft continued to increase in stature as "Mr. Republican." He made no secret of his presidential ambitions, and declared open candidacy early in the fall of 1951. His somewhat reserved personality restrained him from the "popularity contest" type of campaign required by the primaries, and he concentrated upon winning delegates through political negotiations with regular party organizations—a business which he understood very well. He quickly built up a substantial lead in committed delegates.

Two other 1948 contestants returned to the fray in 1952. Harold E. Stassen, whose ties with organization leaders outside his own state were tenuous, once again tried the primary road, but his financial backing was much more limited than in 1948. He was unable to win even the solid Minnesota delegation, and his support outside that state at convention time was negligible. As it turned out, the 19 votes committed to him in Minnesota were nevertheless an important factor in the convention decision. Governor Earl Warren of California was more successful, for he brought the solid California delegation to the convention with a firm commitment to him, as well as a scattering of votes from other states—though the commitments of the latter were much less firm.

Neither of these men, nor any other established political figure, was deemed satisfactory by the anti-Taft, internationalist, and relatively liberal wing of the party. Taft's acknowledged stature, the almost evangelical loyalty of his followers, and the big lead he had gained in the race for delegates made it improbable that any ordinary candidate could give him even a good race. In ordinary times, no one would have had the opportunity to create a public image other than through political activity that would have made him competitive with Taft from the standpoint of public appeal. The one political figure who might have been competitive— Thomas E. Dewey—having lost the last two elections, did not try. Instead, he led the search for an opposition candidate.

The search found its man in General Dwight D. Eisenhower. The war had produced many heroes, but for only two was their military popularity translated into political appeal. One of these, General Douglas MacArthur, never quite capitalized upon his potential, and in any case his close identification with the ideology of most of Taft's supporters made him unacceptable to Dewey and his group. General Eisenhower was another matter; on the whole, he had kept clear of political commitments, and the public had little knowledge of his political views, including his views on civil rights. He thus was the sort of candidate, not uncommon in American politics, whose record was a relatively clean slate upon which anything might subsequently be written. His Texas roots could be expected to soften southern resistance to a Republican candidate; his Kansas background could do the same in the Midwest where Taft's greatest delegation strength lay. As a solid, unassuming American who had risen from a humble background to a position where kings and heads of governments were his consorts, he provided the ideal prototype of the Horatio Alger ideal, still an important element of the American dream.

Eisenhower was slow to commit himself —he did not say no, but he did not say yes positively until late in the preconvention campaign. However, the fact that he allowed his name to be entered in the New Hampshire primary early in 1952 made it clear that he probably could be persuaded if the odds looked sufficiently good; an all-out campaign was then started, and Eisenhower himself finally joined the contest when he resigned his NATO command in early June.

The Taft people controlled the national committee, and accordingly had a big edge in setting the convention keynote and in settling any credentials fights that might occur. Eisenhower's relatively late entry made it necessary not only to capture uncommitted delegates, but wherever possible to cancel commitments already made to Taft.

Ironically, the best precedent for Eisenhower's situation involved another member of the Taft family, William Howard Taft. Theodore Roosevelt's late entry in the race of 1912 had brought him face to face with the heavy handicap of finding hundreds of delegates already committed by the effective work of Taft's organization. Roosevelt supporters did all they could to send legitimate, or at least plausible, contending delegations to the convention, but most of these were quickly disposed of as they ran the Taft-controlled

gantlet of the national committee and the credentials committee of the convention.

In 1952 as in 1912, contesting delegations represented the balance of power. Just before the convention opened, the Eisenhower managers began an aggressive publicity campaign charging irregularities in the selection of contested pro-Taft delegations. Charge and countercharge flew back and forth, as each side claimed the other was attempting to steal delegates and thus control the convention and the nomination. As a sort of capstone for the Eisenhower campaign, a substantial group of Republican governors attending the annual meeting of governors issued a "manifesto" laying the base for the so-called "Fair Play" rule that was to be the subject of the critical vote in the convention.

Chicago, Illinois, July 7, 8, 9, 10, 11, 1952

In his opening address, the chairman of the national committee, Guy George Gabrielson, assured the convention that "the only steam roller in this Amphitheatre will be the determined will of the majority of the 1,206 delegates." The names of the 1,206 delegates and the 1,206 alternates to be supplied by the national committee as certified on the temporary roll would make the decisions. Despite the intensity of the differences in opinions evidenced during the past few days, he stated that there could be no disunity after the convention had completed its work. He then read brief statements from the major candidates in which each pledged support for the nominee, whomever he might be.

After this speech, the opening paragraph of the call was read, and the balance dispensed with but incorporated in the proceedings. The temporary roll was presented, and the national committee recommendation for temporary chairman, Walter S. Hallanan of West Virginia, was approved, all without recorded incident. But with the presentation of what in most conventions was a routine motion to adopt the rules of the previous convention as the temporary rules, all pretense of harmony was dropped.

Convention Organization

Senator John W. Bricker of Ohio made the motion as follows:

That until the Permanent Organization is effected and permanent rules adopted, this convention be governed by the rules adopted by the National Convention of 1948.[1]

This resolution would have permitted contested delegates to vote on all contests other than their own; contested delegates from Louisiana and Texas, for example, could vote to seat pro-Taft delegates from Georgia.

Governor Arthur B. Langlie of Washington, representing the pro-Eisenhower group, rose immediately to propose the following substitute for the Bricker motion:

Resolved, That until the permanent organization is effected and the permanent rules adopted this Convention be governed by the rules of the National Convention of 1948; provided that no person on the temporary roll of the Convention and whose right to be seated as a delegate or alternate is being contested—except those placed on the temporary roll by the affirmative vote of at least two-thirds of the members of the National Committee—namely the 68 persons listed as delegates and the 68 persons listed as alternates in the list now handed to the Secretary of the Convention, the delegates and alternates listed include all the delegates and alternates listed on the temporary roll of Georgia, Louisiana except Districts 4 and 5, and all the delegates and alternates from Texas, shall be entitled to vote in the Convention or in any committee thereof until by vote of the Convention the contest as to such person has been finally decided and such person has been permanently seated, except that each such contest shall be determined separately and decided before the next such contest is taken up and that any person so seated shall forthwith be entitled to vote in the Convention or in any committee thereof to

the membership of which he has been designated.[2]

Congressman Clarence J. Brown of Ohio immediately demanded recognition and proposed the following amendment to the Langlie substitute:

I move, Mr. Chairman, to amend the Langlie substitute by changing the figures 68 as appear in line 9, striking out those figures and substituting in place thereof the figure 61, and further to delete from the accompanying list of delegates the seven delegates from the districts of Louisiana who were not under contest before the National Committee, and under this rule, in my opinion, and I believe in the opinion of almost every one, should not be under contest here.[3]

Brown's contention was that although the seven delegates had been contested, the contests were decided by the state committee of Louisiana in accordance with Rule 4, Section (b) of the 1948 convention rules, which read as follows:

All contests arising in any State electing District Delegates by District Conventions, shall be decided by its State Convention, or if the State Convention shall not meet prior to the National Convention, then by its State Committee; and only contests affecting delegates at large shall be presented to the National Committee.

By proposing his amendment, Brown sought to obtain a vote on the question as to whether the convention could adopt a rule which operated retroactively to deny seats assigned according to previously accepted procedure, and he charged that, if this were the case, it would be possible for anyone to offer an amendment to the rules and place the legality of every district delegate in peril.

Both sides called for "fair play"—but they defined it differently. The Taft supporters declared that changing rules in the middle of a contest transgressed the principle of fair play. Eisenhower supporters argued that it was against the rules of fair play to permit delegates whose credentials were in question to vote on ques-

[1] RNC, *Proceedings,* 1952, p. 26.

[2] *Ibid.,* p. 27.
[3] *Ibid.,* p. 29.

tions of credentials for other delegations in whose success or failure they had a common interest. They warned "that serious breaches of party rules and practices had been accomplished or had taken place in a number of states," and that the general public was well aware of this. "Nothing has happened that would give the people confidence that these issues have been resolved in justice and equity."

Although the pro-Taft speakers cited the precedent of twenty-four conventions, and repeated their plea against changing rules in the middle of a contest, it quickly became evident that they had abandoned hope of carrying Bricker's original motion, and Bricker himself proposed to accept Langlie's substitute if Langlie would accept Brown's amendment. The Taft side of the argument was closed by able expositions by Senator C. Wayland Brooks of Illinois and Charles I. Dawson of Kentucky, both of whom pointed to logical inconsistencies in the minority argument. For example, Dawson indicated the illogic of agreeing to allow contested delegates— against whom the original charge was that they had obtained their credentials by fraud—to vote before being seated by the convention, even if seated on the temporary roll by vote of the national committee.

Actually, once the Taft supporters agreed to accept the Langlie substitute if the Brown amendment were also accepted by their opponents, they indicated acceptance of defeat in the battle for control of the convention. Certainly the seven Louisiana votes involved in the Brown amendment could not swing the balance. If it were the hope that the Eisenhower supporters might lose support from the moderate and uncommitted delegates by seeming to be too greedy, it did not work out that way; the Brown amendment was defeated on a roll call, 658 to 548, and the Langlie substitute accepted by voice vote.[4]

Following the hectic first session, the evening session was devoted to speeches from party leaders. The keynote address was made by General Douglas MacArthur. Interspersed with frequent references to high governmental spending and high taxation, the speech denounced the Democratic administration for tampering with, if not trying to destroy, the Constitution. In his own field, MacArthur charged Democratic leadership with weakness and indecision, and with "discarding victory as the military objective and thereby condemning our forces to a stalemated struggle of attrition." By entering into the Korean armistice negotiations, "we again yielded to Communist intrigue," thus allowing the enemy time to reinforce his military capabilities.

On the second day it was announced that there would be a delay in the credentials committee report, and speakers were called upon. Senator Styles Bridges of New Hampshire stressed the need for party unity, and suggested a loyalty pledge to support the winner, as adopted by the convention of 1880. Throughout his speech, he carefully avoided appearance of bias. Congresswoman Marguerite S. Church was not so objective; her speech contained veiled hints that Taft should be the man. Among those responsible for the loss of American freedom were "really intelligent members of the public and even of our own party who are almost as culpable because they cannot see, or refuse to see, the disastrous end of our economy." The party must have unity, "but I warn you, it must be a unity based on principle— not on expediency; unity that dares attack and refuses to compromise."[5]

The second major speech of the convention was given by ex-President Herbert Hoover during the evening session of the second day. A large portion of his speech was devoted to the international problem, with heavy stress on the military side. He declared the attempts to build European defenses by building a large ground force of infantry units contributed by NATO

---

[4] See *Analysis of Key Votes.*

[5] RNC, *Proceedings,* 1952, pp. 87-88.

nations to be a failure, because these nations did not see the need nor have the will to put the plan into operation. And even if they did, the forces contemplated would not be enough against the hordes Russia could oppose to them. America's strength lay in her ability to develop newer and more powerful weapons, not bayonets. Hoover said that he did "not propose that we retreat into our shell like a turtle. I do propose the deadly reprisal strategy of a rattlesnake." [6]

The series of speeches was broken by the selection of the permanent officers, with Congressman Joseph W. Martin, Jr., of Massachusetts once again being named as permanent chairman; it was announced that his introductory speech would not be made until the following evening. The credentials committee was still in session, and speeches continued until the convention adjourned. The permanent chairman-elect was presented at the evening session of the third day for purposes of making his scheduled speech, but because the credentials committee was still not ready, he did not assume the gavel.

Martin's main theme was the charge that the Democratic leaders operated on the philosophy that the nation had passed the frontier stage and there were no new horizons to conquer. This, he said, was a defeatist philosophy and led to a defeatist attitude in the solution of problems. "Their fundamental solution for every problem has been more centralization of power in Government, more bureaucratic control, and the substitution of personal edict for law." This, he declared, was the same formula of defeatism which led the world into the Dark Ages. The great need of America was leaders who believed in the future of the nation, and who had the vision to see the vast new horizons opened by scientific development.

Following Martin's speech, the credentials committee reported. The majority report endorsed the temporary roll as presented by the national committee except

[6] *Ibid.*, p. 109.

for a part of the Louisiana delegation, and the delegation from Puerto Rico. The minority reports were presented in an unusual way. Instead of a single report or a series of reports following the majority report, the roll of contested states was called, the minority report presented, and acted upon individually. The Florida dispute was settled quickly when a pro-Eisenhower delegate seconded the motion of the majority and admitted that the merits of the case supported the "delegation which did not represent the candidate of our choice."

Georgia was another matter, and a full-scale debate took place. The contest involved two factions of long standing in Georgia. In this convention, the faction supported by the majority report was headed by Roy S. Foster, Sr., and that supported by the minority by Harry Summers and W. R. Tucker. In the conventions of 1944 and 1948, the same factions contested, and in each case the convention approved the Summers-Tucker delegates. The minority speakers stressed this fact. The minority also argued that the Summers-Tucker faction was the legitimate Republican party in Georgia; Tucker was the state chairman, and as such had been issued the call from the national committee. This faction also was the one that fulfilled the financial quota requirements for the state to the national committee. The Foster group "admittedly" never contributed money as a group.

In the debate, the minority argued fairly closely to the facts of the case; the majority relied more on appeals that reversal of the national committee and majority credentials committee decisions would discredit those bodies, and therefore the party that had selected them. The one aspect of the case itself stressed by the majority was a judgment of a Georgia judge, made shortly before the convention, declaring the Foster faction to be the legitimate party of Georgia. The minority declared the case to have been deliberately presented at a time when it would be impossible for an appeal to be acted upon, and that the decision had no validity until such appeal, which had been made, was acted upon.

When the debate ended, Eisenhower supporters took the opportunity to display once again the majority strength indicated by the previous vote on the Fair Play rule by demanding a roll call. As in the previous vote, the basic Eisenhower strength was backed by Minnesota and most of California, but the margin of victory was smaller. The minority report was adopted 607 to 531, with Georgia, Texas, and the contested part of the Louisiana delegation not voting.[7]

Following the Georgia case, the balance of the contests, including reversal of the Louisiana seating, were approved without difficulty until Texas was called. The Texas case was debated at length, but neither side called for a roll call, and the minority report substituting a predominately pro-Eisenhower delegation was approved by voice vote. The convention then adjourned.

At the next session—the temporary chairman still presiding—the report of the committee on rules and order of business was presented. The previous rules were followed except in a few cases, one of the more important being an elaboration of the system for handling contests, and including the principle of the Fair Play amendment requiring approval of two thirds of the national committee for voting rights of contested delegates to the next convention.

An unexpected protest was made to another proposed rule change. The new rule proposed that the national committee be augmented by adding the state chairmen from states recording Republican majorities. Since the rules committee was composed almost exclusively of men, the implications to women party members may not have been considered. The principal purpose of the proposed change was undoubtedly to reduce the influence of the relatively weak southern state parties on the committee, and protests were duly

lodged by southern delegates. However, it was a woman delegate who moved to strike out the new passages. She, and others who followed, argued that the new rules not only removed the stipulation of the previous rules that one of the members of the national committee be a woman, but that the proposed third member would invariably be a man, since women never held the post of state chairman. Her motion to strike out was defeated by voice vote, but a roll call was demanded upon the motion to adopt the original report. The rules were adopted 683 to 513, but the vote pattern did not conform to the pattern of the basic convention division on nominations. New York voted Aye, Pennsylvania No; Ohio split its vote evenly.[8]

The Platform

Shortly after approval of the rules committee report, the permanent chairman took his place. The first order of business was the report of the platform committee. The platform charged the Democratic party with fostering socialism and bureaucracy, and with weakening local self-government. It charged corruption and even treason in high places. Administration policies had led to loss of American prestige, and even worse, had contributed to making enemies among those who once were friends. To the sharply worded attacks was added a less well-defined proposed program. In general, the positive part of the platform advocated less government at the national level and greater local autonomy; less governmental control of business; a tougher anti-Communist line in national and international affairs; and reduction of governmental spending and taxation.

The Presidential Nomination

On the evening of the fourth day, the roll call for nominations began. Alabama yielded to Illinois for the purpose of nominating Taft, thus placing him first on the

[7] See *Analysis of Key Votes.*

[8] See *Analysis of Key Votes.*

list. The order of nomination for other candidates was: Warren, to be nominated by California; Eisenhower, by Maryland; Stassen, by Minnesota; and MacArthur, by Oklahoma.

Senator Everett M. Dirksen presented Taft as "Mr. Republican, Mr. Integrity, Mr. American." As the trustee of the Republican legacy deriving from Lincoln, Taft was contrasted sharply with those who had led and lost the last four elections. These, Dirksen said "were so preoccupied with the engaging task of dividing America into economic, social and minority groups that they forgot the American vote." This was the vote that Taft could call upon to win.

Governor Theodore McKeldin of Maryland stressed the identification of Eisenhower's name with victory, as well as his ability to work with people. Not only was he a man about whom all Republicans could unite, he was a man about whom all Americans and all non-Communists everywhere could unite.

The ballot was taken on the morning of the fifth day, and was punctuated by frequent requests for polling individual delegations. At the end of the call, Eisenhower had 595 votes, with 604 required for a majority. The deficit was supplied by transfer of the 19 Minnesota votes previously recorded for Stassen, and the bandwagon move began. When it was over, the count stood Eisenhower 845; Taft 280; Warren 77; and MacArthur 4. A joint motion for unanimous nomination from representatives of Taft and Warren followed.

The Vice-Presidential Nomination

The vice-presidential proceedings took place during the evening session following the presidential nomination. The session opened with a parade of candidates for Congress, during the course of which a resolution was offered to request legislatures of all states that did not currently have primaries to pass legislation to that effect. This was referred to the committee on resolutions without debate.

On the roll call to reserve time for nominations, only California responded, but following the call, Congresswoman Clare Boothe Luce of Connecticut obtained recognition. She announced that the women delegates had desired to nominate Senator Margaret Chase Smith of Maine, but due to the obvious agreement of the convention on one candidate, and in conformance with a request from her candidate, her name would not be put in nomination.

Senator Richard M. Nixon of California was nominated by William F. Knowland, fellow California senator, who presented him as a young man with great drive and determination, willing to work hard for other Republican candidates. Others stressed Nixon's potential appeal to young people and to the women of the country. By unanimous agreement, the calling of the roll was dispensed with, as the permanent chairman said:

> The delegate from Pennsylvania, Governor Fine, has made the motion, seconded by Senator Knowland of California, that the nomination be made by acclamation. Is there any objection?
> The Chair hears none, and declares Richard M. Nixon the Republican nominee for Vice President by acclamation.[9]

Both the presidential and vice-presidential nominees were presented to the convention during the closing session. Each pledged a hard fighting campaign. Eisenhower stated that he had held "helpful and heartwarming talks with Senator Taft, Governor Warren, and Governor Stassen." Nixon went to considerable lengths to express his admiration for Taft. Shortly thereafter, the convention adjourned.

Analysis of Key Votes

Correlations of the three roll call votes with Eisenhower's critical nominating ballot provide interesting comparisons. The correlation of his ballot with the vote on the Brown amendment in the temporary

[9] RNC, *Proceedings*, 1952, p. 421.

rules fight is +.74. Many delegates seated on the temporary roll voted on this roll call who subsequently did not vote on the Georgia rules committee owing to the results of the rules fight, and subsequently were replaced by pro-Eisenhower delegates on the roll call on permanent rules.

The correlation of +.74 is a high correlation generally, but not particularly high for a convention as sharply dichotomized as this one. The correlation was undoubtedly lowered by the moral overtones implicit in the "Fair Play" arguments stressed by the Eisenhower leaders, since many delegates undoubtedly felt pressure to vote with the Eisenhower people on this issue, although not ready to vote for Eisenhower himself.

The vote on the Georgia contest did not have these overtones, and was seen more clearly as a factional vote. This is indicated by the higher correlation of +.81—a correlation that would undoubtedly have been higher if the contested delegates had been allowed to vote.[10]

The vote on the permanent rules was complicated by two interests—the interest of women in maintaining parity on the national committee, and the interest of the southern delegations in keeping their current relative strength. The women's side of the question was non-factional and non-geographical, and accordingly the influence on the correlation would have been random; however, the southern delegations, even after settlement of the credentials contests in favor of Eisenhower delegates in some states, were largely for Taft. Accordingly, the influence of the southern vote on the correlation would tend to raise it. The combined influence of the two forces resulted in a correlation of +.32.

[10] Obviously most of these delegates would have voted against Eisenhower's side of the issue, and subsequently for Taft. Accordingly, in the calculation of tetrachoric r, d would have increased in number, the other factors remaining fairly constant. Thus, ad would increase, bc would be relatively unchanged, and the correlation would be raised approximately to +.85.

THIRTY-FIRST DEMOCRATIC CONVENTION

A special clause in the Twenty-second Amendment to the Constitution excepted President Truman, and accordingly he was legally eligible for a third term. In the spring of 1952, however, he made it clear that he would not run. Even before this declaration, Senator Estes Kefauver of Tennessee had begun an energetic campaign, with emphasis upon the primaries. Kefauver was in somewhat the same position with regular organizations as Stassen in the Republican party, and since he lacked organization support, he had to depend upon a campaign designed to exploit his dynamic personality. This campaign frequently led him into areas where he was less than welcome to the local leaders, and he soon became known as an anti-organization candidate. Nevertheless, he had considerable success and built up a moderately strong front-runner position by the time the convention opened. He was far below majority strength, however, and his second choice commitments were limited.

A clearly anti-administration candidate was Senator Richard Russell of Georgia, upon whom the southern conservatives pinned their hopes. Russell, as a sectional candidate, could hope for little help outside the South. But he served to concentrate southern strength and provided a focal point for negotiation with northern liberals. The need for such negotiation had been increased by the nomination of Eisenhower, for dissident southerners might find it much easier to vote for a man who had once been discussed seriously as a potential Democratic candidate than for "Mr. Republican," regardless of how close they might have felt ideologically to the latter.

Although Truman declared himself out of the picture as a candidate, he remained very much in it in regard to selecting a candidate to be his successor. But he refused to give clear endorsement to any one, although he appeared to be favorable to Vice President Alben Barkley in the immediate preconvention period. As a result of this apparent indecision, most of the convention delegates were split among favorite sons such as Averell Harriman of New York and Senator Robert S. Kerr of Oklahoma.

The difficulty of the organization leaders in the North, and Truman's own difficulty, stemmed from recognition that the Republicans might make heavy inroads in the South unless a candidate could be found to whom southerners would not object too strenuously, even though they might not embrace him enthusiastically. With such a candidate, it was hoped that the patterns of a lifetime would serve to hold the electoral vote of that section. On the other hand, the candidate would have to be reasonably attractive to northern liberals. This, of course, ruled out Russell. Kefauver, in the eyes of this group, not only was unacceptable but must be defeated at any cost. Leaders of the group, such as Harriman, would not serve the purpose, for the South could not accept them and a bolt might ensue as in 1948.

A man was needed whose record was good, but who was not publicly committed deeply to the divisive issue that threatened to split the party—the same need that had resulted in the nominations of Polk, Pierce, Buchanan, Garfield, Hughes, and Harding. Many of the northern leaders, and apparently Truman himself, found the best possibility in the same man—Adlai E. Stevenson of Illinois. Stevenson had held several posts in the national government, and was currently governor of Illinois. He was considered a liberal, but he had never offended the South. However, he expressed great reluctance, almost amounting to outright refusal, to be a candidate.

Regardless of Stevenson's real desires in the matter, his prospects for electoral support from the South, if he were nominated, would almost certainly have been destroyed if he had appeared to welcome support from prominent northern liberals, and most particularly from Truman. A great deal of work was done to promote his candidacy during the period of uncertainty. A poll taken of county and city chairmen shortly before the convention revealed a surprisingly large percentage who stated preference for Stevenson above all others. For so many of the minor party leaders to have agreed upon a man whom similar polls showed few of the general public even recognized, much less preferred as a candidate, seems scarcely possible without benefit of a fairly widespread, though quietly conducted, educational program.

Chicago, Illinois,
July 21, 22, 23, 24, 25, 26, 1952

In his address of welcome to the delegates soon after the opening of the convention, Adlai Stevenson ridiculed attempts of the Republicans in the same hall a short time before to label the twenty years of Democratic administration as a miserable failure. To provide a favorable contrast to the bitter Republican battle, he pleaded for an open but orderly convention. Although the delegates gave him and his words careful attention, his plea for decorum did not succeed in preventing explosion of the tensions existing among the delegates.

That Stevenson should have made the opening speech was somewhat unusual. Although, as governor of Illinois, he was the most logical public figure for the job, it is not usual for prominent candidates to take an active part in convention proceedings. Seymour and Garfield, of course, had done so, but both objected more or less strenuously when the moves started that resulted in their nominations, and neither of them had waged, nor had anyone waged for them, an open campaign prior to the convention. Bryan in 1896 was an outstanding exception, but Bryan's candidacy was primarily a one-man operation and, from the standpoint of the average delegate, he was much more of an unknown than Stevenson was in 1952. At the time of his speech, Stevenson still was disclaiming candidacy, and the fact that he was willing to speak could be interpreted as further evidence that he meant what he said; on the other hand, his speech, and the manner in which he was received by the delegates, made the prospects of his nomination more likely.

The next speaker was Senator Paul Douglas, also of Illinois, who gave a well-organized defense of administration policy and actions with respect to the Korean conflict—a defense punctuated with frequent citations of Republican inconsistencies and errors. Jacob Arvey, national committeeman, declared that the Republican convention had given "the impression of a free-for-all of town drunks."

The apportionment rules provided for two delegates, each with one full vote from each congressional district, and for half-vote delegates for the at large seats. As usual in Democratic conventions, however, several states sent oversized delegations, with the result that 90 delegates and 86 alternates in excess of the total allotted for the convention arrived in Chicago. Again, as usual, the oversized delegations were seated on the temporary roll by the national committee and subsequently accepted by the convention.

Convention Organization

Shortly after the election of Governor Paul A. Dever of Massachusetts as temporary chairman, the battle that had been under way in committees and caucus rooms was brought to the floor of the convention. Apparently as a conciliatory move, the chairmen of the delegations seated on the temporary roll of the convention for Texas and Mississippi stated that since their delegations were in contest, they would not vote on any matter pertaining to the seating contest. This act, and the stress on the words "fair play" was doubtless inspired by the experience of the Republican convention held in the same hall a short time before. If the announcements were intended to delay or soften the attack of the northern liberal group, they did not succeed, for they were immediately followed by a resolution presented by Senator Blair Moody of Michigan.

The Moody resolution provided, as an addendum to the customary resolution, that the rules of the previous convention be adopted as the temporary rules of the convention.

Resolved, That this Convention believes in the great American principle of majority rule. No delegate shall be seated unless he shall give assurance to the Credentials Committee that he will exert every honorable means available to him in any official capacity he may have, to provide that the nominees of this Convention for President and Vice President, through their names or those of electors pledged to them, appear on the election ballot under the heading, name or designation of the Democratic Party.

Such assurance shall be given by the Chairman of each delegation, and shall not be binding upon those delegates who shall so signify to the Credentials Committee prior to its report to this Convention.[11]

In the course of the debate, Senator Jonathan Daniels of North Carolina proposed a substitute for this resolution, intended to soften it while still including the main content:

Resolved: That it is the consensus of this Convention that the honorable course of every delegate who participates in its proceedings is to support the majority decisions of the Convention here and hereafter.[12]

Senator Daniels' presentation was verbal, and evidently not recognized by the chair as a formal motion, for a written version was later presented to the clerk by Senator Spessard L. Holland, of Florida, who indicated it was sponsored by eight members of the credentials subcommittee. The motion was rejected by voice vote, and the Moody resolution was adopted in the same manner. Requests for roll call votes were

[11] DNC, *Proceedings,* 1952, p. 55.
[12] *Ibid.,* p. 64.

demanded on both resolutions but denied by the chair. In the opinion of many observers and delegates, the two requests for a roll call were supported by substantially more than 20 per cent of the convention as required by the rules, and the arbitrary decisions by the chairman created considerable resentment.[13] No official protest was lodged, however, and the decisions of the chairman stood. The convention then proceeded with the less controversial work of appointing the standing committees.

The credentials committee was first to report. It endorsed all actions of the national committee, including seating of oversized delegations. In addition, the report incorporated the Moody resolution, but in deference to the fact that certain delegates were of the opinion that the resolution was in contravention of existing state laws or instructions from state organizations, the following clause was added: "That for this Convention, only, such assurance shall not be in contravention of the existing law of the State, nor of the previous instructions of the State Democratic governing bodies."[14] A list of the delegations that had or had not complied with the terms of the Moody resolution was appended. In only three cases did failure to comply appear to be intentional: Louisiana, South Carolina, and Virginia.

A minority report on the Texas question was backed by thirteen members of the committee. The contest was between the delegation selected by the regular convention, dominated by the factions in control of the party machinery, and a delegation selected by a rump convention admittedly of questionable legitimacy. From the standpoint of a majority of the convention the difficulty was that the more legitimate delegation was Dixiecrat in orientation, while the other delegation was willing to accept the Moody pledge without reserva-

tion. The minority report recommending that the rump delegates be seated was rejected, and the regular delegation was seated, but not without considerable protest from the northern liberal wing.

The report of the committee on rules and order of business included the Moody resolution, obviously with the intent that it would become part of the temporary rules of the next convention. With one other exception, the rules presented were similar to those of the past. The exception provided that all minority reports must be supported by no less than 10 per cent of the total membership of the committee involved. Before a vote was called, a delegate requested clarification on the question of further participation by the three states which had not accepted the Moody resolution. The chairman refused to make a general ruling, but stated that he would rule on a point of order directed at an act of participation by one of the delegates or delegations involved.

During the discussion an interruption occurred, when Senator Kefauver, accompanied by his father, entered the convention hall. Signs of preparation observed by those present suggest that the diversion may have been planned, possibly as an offset to the favorable reception given to Stevenson during his convention appearance. Shortly after the delegates were brought back to order, the report of the committee on rules and order of business was accepted without a record vote. Speaker of the House of Representatives Sam Rayburn was selected as permanent chairman of the convention, and assumed the chair on the evening of the third day.

The Platform

In its preamble, the platform pledged not to retreat one inch from the road traveled by the party under the leadership of Roosevelt and Truman. Rather, the same road should be traveled further—the Taft-Hartley Act should be repealed; agricultural price supports should be continued

---

[13] Paul T. David, Malcolm Moos, and Ralph M. Goldman, *Presidential Nominating Politics in 1952* (1954), Vol. 1, p. 127.
[14] DNC, *Proceedings*, 1952, p. 137.

and extended; public agencies should be preferred to private for development of electrical power systems. In the sensitive field of civil rights, the platform pledged to "continue our efforts to eradicate discrimination based on race, religion or national origin." This cannot be done by state and local governments alone, though the cooperation of these units is imperative; "it also requires Federal action." Georgia and Mississippi requested that they be recorded as having voted No on the report after the platform was approved by a voice vote.

The Presidential Nomination

Shortly after noon on the fourth day, the roll call for nominations for the Presidency began. Contrary to previous practice in Democratic conventions, all seconding speeches for a candidate followed the nominating speech (this had been customary for some time in Republican conventions). The procedure still differed slightly from Republican practice, since all speeches were in response to a single roll call, while recent Republican conventions first called the roll to permit delegations to reserve time for a nomination.

Senator Richard B. Russell of Georgia was presented by his home state, Alabama having yielded for the purpose. The nominations of Senator Estes Kefauver of Tennessee, Senator Robert S. Kerr of Oklahoma, Senator J. William Fulbright of Arkansas, Averell Harriman of New York, Oscar R. Ewing of Indiana, Senator Brien McMahon of Connecticut, Governor Adlai E. Stevenson of Illinois and Governor G. Mennen Williams of Michigan were duly made and seconded. The call of the states had then reached Louisiana, which yielded to Virginia. Governor John S. Battle of Virginia then raised the question of the status of the three delegations that had not complied with the requirements of the Moody resolution: Louisiana, South Carolina, and Virginia.

After some discussion, including statements of position by leaders of the states in question, Chairman Rayburn ruled that these states had not complied with the rules of the convention. A motion was then presented by a Maryland delegate,

> . . . in view of the statement made by Governor Battle, which is a substantial compliance of the spirit of the rule, that the delegations of Virginia and South Carolina be seated.[15]

A roll call was demanded—which turned out to be one of the most confused and certainly the most time-consuming in convention history. In view of the fact that it had long been obvious to all that the issue would arise, and in view of the stated position of the chairman that he would not rule finally until action was taken by one of the delegations in question, it should have been fairly clear at about what point the issue would arise. It is therefore difficult to understand why the confusion occurred. However, according to contemporary accounts, the hall was in considerable disorder, the session had been long, and many delegates were absent for lunch or other purposes.

Many states passed when first called, and were called again after the first roll was completed. While they were being called, states that had responded on the regular roll changed their votes. One of the major changes was recorded by the Illinois delegation, which had voted 15 Yes and 45 No on the original call, but shifted to 52 Yes and 8 No, accompanied by a statement of confidence in the governor of Virginia. Many delegations had to be called several times before they recorded their vote, and others had to be polled from the floor. Finally, however, the results were announced: 615 Yes, 529 No, and 86 delegates still not voting.[16]

The nominations then continued. Massachusetts nominated Paul A. Dever, its governor; Minnesota, Hubert H. Humphrey, its senator; and Missouri, the Vice President Alben W. Barkley. Once again

[15] *Ibid.*, p. 340.
[16] See *Analysis of Key Votes.*

the roll call was suspended to recognize Governor Battle of Virginia, who thanked the convention for its action on the Virginia resolution, and moved the admission of Louisiana and South Carolina. Attempts by the chairman to call a vote on this motion were interrupted by a motion to adjourn, upon which a roll call vote was demanded. The vote was taken on a motion to table and carried: 671 Yes, 534 No, with 25 not voting. The roll call then continued briefly, until the motion to admit the two states was renewed and passed by a voice vote. Attempts to get a roll call on this motion finally were dropped after the delegation chairmen from Louisiana and South Carolina explained their positions and the chairman of the credentials committee stated that he had received statements "practically identical" to the one from Virginia. The convention then adjourned for the night.

The balloting began shortly after the new session opened. As in the previous votes, the roll call was interrupted frequently by requests to poll individual delegations. The first ballot showed Kefauver leading with 340, Stevenson second with 273, followed by Russell 268, and Harriman 123½. Ten others received mention, only Kerr receiving more than 50 votes. The second ballot followed immediately.

All three front-runners on the first ballot moved up on the second, with Stevenson recording the biggest gain. Kefauver still led with 362½, Stevenson was second with 324½, Russell third with 294. Another recess was taken until evening. Harriman and Dever then withdrew in favor of Adlai Stevenson, who was nominated on the third and final ballot, with 617½ of the total 1,230. Kefauver retained 275½ votes and Russell 261; most of the remainder went to Barkley.

The convention spent the rest of the evening listening to President Harry Truman and its new nominee, Adlai Stevenson, both of whom pledged their utmost in the coming campaign.

The Vice-Presidential Nomination

At noon on the sixth day, the convention met for the last time. A number of resolutions thanking various people connected with the convention preceded the main order of business—the nomination of the vice-presidential candidate. Senator John J. Sparkman of Alabama was placed in nomination by Lister Hill, his fellow senator. Token nominations followed for Mrs. India Edwards, vice chairman of the national committee, and Judge Sara T. Hughes of Texas. Both immediately withdrew, and Sparkman was nominated by acclamation, Chairman Sam Rayburn stating that "in the opinion of the Chair, 99½ per cent of the delegates voted 'aye.'" Stevenson then introduced Senator Sparkman, who added his assurances of a hard-fought campaign, and the convention adjourned.

Analysis of Key Votes

The confused voting pattern of the roll call on the Virginia seating becomes considerably clearer when related to the first-ballot vote of the several candidates. Harriman voters, with a correlation coefficient of $-.76$, were strongly opposed; Russell supporters, with a coefficient of $+.80$, were equally in support. Between these extremes were: Kefauver, whose coefficient of $-.41$ indicated moderate opposition; Stevenson, with a support coefficient of $+.22$; and the combined vote of the lesser candidates indicating considerable ambivalence with the low coefficient of $+.11$.

Normally, it might be expected that the nominating coalition would be formed from the middle groups, who certainly had sufficient strength to nominate anyone upon whom they could agree. However, the fight between Kefauver and the organization leaders supporting Stevenson in the preconvention period had been too bitter to permit easy *rapprochement*. The combined vote of Stevenson and the lesser candidates aggregated only about 40 per cent of the total convention strength. Accordingly, the combination had to be made between a middle coalition and one of the extremes.

Southern leaders probably felt that they could not quickly leave Russell because of possible reactions back home—more time for face-saving was required. Harriman, on the other hand, was relatively a late comer in the field, and had not developed serious animosities against any of the candidates or their managers. However, his supporters could not accept Kefauver for more or less the same reasons that Stevenson could not. From their standpoint, Stevenson was the lesser of two evils, and also more apt to be a winner since he probably could retain southern support—especially in view of the fact that the insult to Virginia and the South, which would have been inherent in rejection of the Virginia delegates, was averted by Stevenson supporters, particularly those from Illinois.

Presidential Election, November 4, 1952

DWIGHT D. EISENHOWER (R) : popular vote, 33,936,252; electoral vote, 442
ADLAI E. STEVENSON (D) : popular vote, 27,314,992; electoral vote, 89

1956

THE HEAVY ELECTORAL college majority registered for the Republican presidential ticket in 1952 was not reflected in the congressional elections, for the party was able to win only a slim majority in the two houses of Congress. Even this lead disappeared in 1954, as Democrats took control of both branches—though the majority in the Senate resulted from the apostasy of Senator Wayne Morse of Oregon, who transferred from the Republican to the Democratic side of the aisle.

Part of the Democratic gain in the midterm elections undoubtedly reflected the moderate depression that struck the country in 1954, but by 1955 the economic barometer was rising rapidly, and continuation of the trend in 1956 transferred the economic issue from pro-Democratic to pro-Republican.

Throughout the quadrennium the protagonists of 1952, Dwight D. Eisenhower and Adlai Stevenson, remained the leading figures for renomination, although, for different reasons, there were moments of doubt that either would finally emerge as the convention choice. The doubt in the case of President Eisenhower arose from a heart attack he suffered in September 1955, and for several months thereafter whether he would or would not decide that he should accept a second term was perhaps the most discussed question in the country. Stevenson, on the other hand, found himself in an all-out fight for renomination against the tenacious Estes Kefauver, who challenged him in every primary he could. For a short time, it looked as if Kefauver would be able to knock Stevenson out of the running, even if he were unable to win the nomination for himself.

THIRTY-SECOND DEMOCRATIC CONVENTION

Adlai Stevenson opened the overt stage of the preconvention campaign with announcement of candidacy in November 1955. A month later, Estes Kefauver announced, and for several months the open battle lay between these two. Others were waiting in the background, but did not campaign as openly. The most important of these was Averell Harriman of New York who did not announce actual candidacy until June 1956, but whose intentions were fairly clear for many months before.

The four key primaries in the Stevenson-Kefauver battle were in Minnesota, Oregon, Florida, and California, and in the first of these, Kefauver scored a stunning victory by winning twenty-six of the thirty Minnesota delegates. Stevenson reacted quickly and began an intensive campaign in the remaining three states. The results were impressive: he led Kefauver by a wide margin in a write-in preference vote in Oregon; he won twenty-two of the twenty-eight Florida delegates; and he scored a landslide victory in California. This proved to be too much for Kefauver, who withdrew shortly before the convention and asked his supporters to vote for Stevenson.

Harriman delayed his major efforts until after the primaries were over. His candidacy was climaxed by the dramatic move of former President Harry S. Truman, who announced his support for Harriman in a press interview held just before the convention opened.

Chicago, Illinois,
August 13, 14, 15, 16, 17, 1956

The Eisenhower landslide in 1952 created apportionment problems for the Democratic national committee in preparing the convention call in 1956. Previous Democratic practice had based the bonus votes upon a state's success in winning presidential electoral votes only, and did not recognize party victories for senator and governor as the Republicans did. Since many of the states that did not qualify for bonus votes based upon the 1952 election were in the South, where sensitivity over proportionate strength had been acute since abolishment of the two thirds rule in 1936, the national committee changed the apportionment rules. The revised apportionment as stated in the call read:

The basis for the foregoing distribution of votes is the number of votes allotted to each State in the 1952 Democratic Convention plus four additional votes for those States which either:
(a) cast their electoral votes for the Democratic nominees for President and Vice President in the 1952 elections, or
(b) elected a Democratic Governor or United States Senator on or after November 4, 1952.[1]

All southern states qualified under these rules, as in fact did a majority of the northern states, and the result was a convention with 1,372 votes, the largest in history.

The call also recognized other problems, particularly those relating to party loyalty, concerning which the call stated:

Resolved, That it is the understanding that a State Democratic Party, in selecting and certifying delegates to the Democratic National Convention, thereby undertakes to assure that voters in the State will have the opportunity

to cast their election ballots for the Presidential and Vice-Presidential nominees selected by said Convention, and for electors pledged formally or in good conscience to the election of these Presidential and Vice Presidential nominees, under the Democratic Party label and designation.

Resolved, That it is understood that the Delegates to the Democratic National Convention, when certified by the State Democratic Parties, are bona fide Democrats who have the interests, welfare and success of the Democratic Party at heart, and will participate in the Convention in good faith, and therefore, no additional assurances shall be required of Delegates to the Democratic National Committee in the absence of credentials contest or challenge.

Resolved, That it is the duty of every member of the Democratic National Committee to declare affirmatively for the nominees of the Convention and that his or her failure to do so shall be cause for the Democratic National Committee, or its duly authorized subcommittee, to declare his or her seat vacant after notice and opportunity for hearing.[2]

The second resolution was obviously designed to prevent repetition of the situation leading to the Virginia seating fight in 1952. The third was intended to provide a mechanism to replace members of the national committee who jumped party lines, as many did to Eisenhower in 1952.

The convention opened with greetings from Mayor Richard J. Daley of Chicago, Senator Paul H. Douglas of Illinois, and others who lauded the host city and state and the Democratic party. Governor Frank G. Clement of Tennessee was named temporary chairman, but did not assume the chair during the first session. The balance of the session was devoted to speeches, among them one by the chairman of the Democratic senatorial campaign committee, George A. Smathers of Florida. Smathers stressed the need to win the congressional races, taunted the Republicans for placing more stress on a balanced budget rather than on the lives and liberties of the people, and claimed that, since the beginning of the century, Republican Congresses had passed only three good laws, two of them under the first Roosevelt, compared

[1] DNC, *Proceedings*, 1956, p. 5.

[2] *Ibid.*, p. 4.

with sixty-six good laws passed by Democratic Congresses.

The second session of the first day began with a short statement by the national committee chairman, Paul Butler, who declared that the party had recovered from its low ebb in 1952 and was stronger than ever. This was followed by a long documentary film showing high lights in the nation's history and narrated by Senator John F. Kennedy of Massachusetts. Immediately after Kennedy closed, Chairman Butler announced that one of the leading broadcasting companies had not carried the film in its televising of the convention, and made it clear which one by thanking the National and American Broadcasting companies for "keeping their commitments."

Governor Clement, in his speech accepting the temporary chairmanship, termed the Republican party a "party of privilege and pillage." President Eisenhower, he said, was merely a front for a party with no real leaders. Although he stated, "We are not going to engage in the 'smile and smear' technique," he used the term "hatchetman" in referring to Nixon in the next paragraph. After quoting a series of figures to show that corporation profits had increased more rapidly than profits for workers and farmers, he charged the Republican party with bad treatment of farmers, laborers, and small businessmen; with corruption in high places; with secrecy in government; with having a President who delegated his powers; with indecisive foreign policy; and so on.

Before the routine business of appointing committees was tackled, a light touch was added by introducing to the convention two young people who recently had won large sums of money in quiz contests. Through a series of leading questions, the Democratic party was shown to be the one preferred by these youngsters. Perhaps for contrast, their appearance was followed by that of Eleanor Roosevelt, one of the most venerated members of the Democratic party.

The morning session of the second day was devoted almost entirely to speeches from representatives of various groups and geographic areas. In the evening session Sam Rayburn assumed the chair as the permanent chairman. He, too, stressed the comparative record of the two parties, and charged Eisenhower with delegating his presidential duties.

The report of the committee on rules and order of business incorporated the resolutions in the convention call. The rules for polling delegations were changed to provide that a roll call could be demanded only by the majority of eight delegations. Delegations demanding a poll of the individual delegates would first be polled by a representative sent by the chairman to the delegation, this poll to be taken while the regular roll call continued. If, after this private poll, one third of the delegates demanded an open poll it would be granted.

The provision for filling vacancies on the ticket was changed to authorize each member of the national committee in voting for replacement of either nominee on the ticket (if this became necessary) to cast as many votes as his or her state delegation was authorized in the convention. Previous practice had allowed equal voting strength to each state regardless of size.

In an attempt to expedite the work of future conventions, a new rule directed the Democratic national committee to request state delegations to nominate members for the various convention committees at least seven days before the convention opening date, and directed that the members named be prepared to meet on the call of the chairman of the national committee. Per diem expenses for these members were authorized for time served before the opening of the convention.

Another new rule provided that delegates on the temporary roll of a convention were not to vote on their own credentials. Except for these additions, the rules of the 1952 convention were adopted.

The credentials committee dismissed the contestants for two delegations and approved the temporary roll as prepared by the national committee. The committee stated that the new resolutions included in the call had been most helpful in making the decisions.

The Platform

The method of presentation of the platform was an innovation. Each section was assigned to a different reader, including several candidates for Congress. (This of course was an effective way of providing these people with the benefit of television publicity for home consumption.) Among the eleven main sections of the text were planks on foreign policy and national defense, in which the President was charged with lack of leadership, as a result of which the nation's friends abroad were losing faith in the United States. In the section on domestic policy, Republican reaction after twenty years of progress under the Democrats was attacked and the Republican claims that "we are now more prosperous than ever before in peacetime" were declared to an illusion so far as "the American farmer, the small businessman, and the low-income worker" were concerned.

A minority report presented by a Minnesota member of the platform committee and signed by "14 per cent of the 108 members," moved a substitution for the fourth paragraph of the platform's civil rights section. (The substitute was exactly the same as the majority paragraph, except for the italicized sentence as shown below, which did not appear in the minority plank.)

Recent decisions of the Supreme Court of the United States relating to segregation in publically supported schools and elsewhere have brought consequences of vast importance to our nation as a whole, and especially to communities directly affected. *We pledge to carry out these decisions.* We reject all proposals for use of force to interfere with the orderly determination of these matters by the Courts.[3]

The third paragraph concerning civil rights in the majority report read:

[3] *Ibid.*, pp. 322-323.

We are proud of the record of the Democratic Party in securing equality of treatment and opportunity in the nation's armed forces, the Civil Service, and in all areas under Federal jurisdiction. The Democratic Party pledges itself to continue its efforts to eliminate illegal discriminations of all kinds, in relation to (1) full rights to vote, (2) full rights to engage in gainful occupations, (3) full rights to enjoy security of the person, and (4) full rights to education in all publicly supported institutions.[4]

To this, the minority report wished to add:

At the same time we favor Federal legislation effectively to secure these rights to everyone: the right to equal opportunity for employment; the right to security of person; the right to full and equal participation in this Nation's political life free from arbitrary restraints.

We also favor legislation to perfect existing Federal civil rights statutes, and to strengthen the administrative machinery for protection of civil rights.

The minority report was received with mingled boos and applause. The chairman called for a voice vote, despite the many standards waving for recognition to demand a record vote. Refusing to recognize anyone, he said: "Well now, just a moment. I have taken 'ayes' and 'noes' many times, and I think I can tell which one has the most. In the opinion of the Chair, the 'noes' have it, and the minority report is rejected." The majority report was then approved by a voice vote.

The Presidential Nomination

The nominating speeches began on the fourth day, with Senator Warren G. Magnuson of Washington the first to be named. He withdrew immediately, stating that he was not a delegate, but if he were, he would vote for Stevenson. Senator Kennedy appeared in a second featured role as the nominating speaker for Adlai Stevenson. The roster of Stevenson's five seconding speakers was impressive; two governors, one senator, and two congressmen, representing widely scattered states and a considerable aggregation of power.

The presentation of Senator Lyndon B.

[4] *Ibid.*, pp. 321-322.

Johnson followed in routine fashion, but the next nomination provided a platform for Governor Marvin Griffin of Georgia to protest the fact that Georgia had not been given recognition during the debate and vote on the minority platform report. In a brief speech, he charged that those "who last night would have crucified the people of the South will not be able to carry their States for the Democratic nominee in November 1956." He then named James C. Davis, Georgia congressman, as his candidate.

Averell Harriman was presented as the "best equipped man for the presidency," and was seconded by Harry Truman. Others nominated in this session were A. B. (Happy) Chandler, governor of Kentucky; John W. McCormack, chairman of the platform committee and leader in Congress from Massachusetts; John S. Battle, former governor of Virginia; Senator Stuart Symington of Missouri; and Governor George Bell Timmerman of South Carolina.

At the opening of the next session, McCormack released delegates pledged to him in the primary, without, however, indicating his personal choice of nominee. He also took the time to explain to Governor Griffin why he had not been recognized on the platform debate and vote.

On the roll call, Stevenson's vote passed the necessary majority with the announcement of most of Pennsylvania's vote in his column, and a demonstration parade began at once to form. The chairman broke it up by saying, "No parade now, please. We have got to proceed in order." At the end of the roll call he asked, "Does any State desire to change its vote?"

There was no response, but a motion was made by a Harriman supporter that the nomination be made unanimous, and it was so declared. Stevenson's share of the 1,372 votes in the convention was 905½. Harriman received 210, Johnson 80, and 176½ were scattered among six others.

The Vice-Presidential Nomination

Immediately after the presidential nomination, Adlai Stevenson took the platform and, borrowing a leaf from Bryan's 1896 book, declared that he would keep hands off the vice-presidential nominating proceedings. He stressed the increased importance of the second office, and declared his confidence that the convention would make a good choice.

Before recognizing any of the speakers for nominations, the chairman requested unanimous consent to limit each nominating speech to five minutes and seconding speeches to two of two minutes each. He also asked that no demonstrations be made. Names placed in nomination were: Senator Albert Gore of Tennessee, Senator Estes Kefauver of Tennessee, Senator John F. Kennedy of Massachusetts, Governor LeRoy Collins of Florida, Senator Hubert Humphrey of Minnesota, Mayor Robert F. Wagner of New York City, and Governor Luther H. Hodges of North Carolina.

Stevenson's unexpected announcement apparently caused confusion in some delegations, for a number of states, including the first on the roll call, Alabama, passed when first called, and others changed their votes before the totals were announced. Kefauver, with 483½ votes, was considerably short on the first ballot of the 687 required for a majority. He was followed by Kennedy with 304, Wagner 162½, and Humphrey 134½. Several others received nominal mention.

The second ballot was taken amidst wild confusion. Alabama passed again, and the important California delegation shortly followed suit, as did others. At the end of the regular roll, and before the passed states were recalled, the score stood: Kefauver 479½ and Kennedy 559, with 156 votes to be cast by the states that had passed—enough to put Kennedy over if all were cast in his favor. But these returns favored Kefauver slightly, and the count stood: Kefauver 552½, Kennedy 617½.

The convention hall was an absolute bedlam as standards waved and delegates shouted for recognition. Voices in this hall were of no importance, however, for recognition by the chairman could only be had through the microphones held by each delegation chairman, and which one should be heard first was the prerogative of the chair. The first to be recognized was Kentucky, which transferred 30 votes to Kennedy, bringing him to 647½, only 39 short of a majority. Chairman Rayburn then recognized Senator Gore, who withdrew in favor of Kefauver. Oklahoma, following the cue, transferred its 28 votes, previously given to Gore, to Kefauver. Minnesota added 16½ votes previously cast for Humphrey. Tennessee was again recognized, and Gore's failure to transfer the 32 votes of the delegation to Kefauver when he withdrew his name was rectified.

Kefauver had by this point closed the gap almost entirely, and during the flood that followed only a few scattering votes transferred to Kennedy—votes that less than covered his losses. Finally, the last to be recognized, the chairman of the Virgin Islands delegation, declared with refreshing frankness, "For the sake of expediency, the Virgin Islands decides to change their vote to Estes Kefauver." Kennedy was then recognized to move a unanimous nomination.

Although the work was finished, the convention was not yet over. In an evening session, the two who had carried the main load of directing the activities of the convention, John McCormack and Sam Rayburn, were given an opportunity to speak. They were followed, first by Harry Truman, who had failed in his outright effort to change the course of events, and by the two nominees, who pledged an all-out fight for election.

TWENTY-SIXTH REPUBLICAN CONVENTION

Two factors dominated the preconvention period for the Republican party—the question of President Eisenhower's health, and the question of the renomination of Vice President Nixon. The period of recovery following the President's heart attack in September 1955 was one of uncertainty: could he or would he accept a second term? Few were willing to gamble on the negative answer, although Senate minority leader William F. Knowland announced that he would run if the President decided not to do so. The question was settled for a while at the end of February 1956, when Eisenhower announced that he would accept the nomination. This was not to be the end of the matter, however, for in June 1956 the President suffered another serious illness, requiring an operation. But again he recovered rapidly, and within a month it was announced that he considered himself fit to assume another term of office.

The decision that had been made some months earlier—to hold the convention at an unprecedentedly late date—thus proved to have been a fateful one. What might have happened had the convention date been set for any time in the month of June provides food for a wealth of interesting, if fruitless, conjecture.

At no time in history had the physical fitness, with reference to the renomination of an incumbent President, been so much a matter of public discussion. Although at least equal question undoubtedly existed in the case of President Franklin D. Roosevelt in 1944, it received comparatively little public notice. Under the circumstances, the selection of a vice-presidential candidate assumed unusual importance. Considerable opposition existed within the party to Vice President Nixon, and this surely would have assumed greater proportions had it been encouraged by the President, who, however, refused to take a definite stand during early 1956. Nixon received a major boost in March when 22,000 voters wrote his name in on the ballots in the New Hampshire primary. Following this, the President stated that he "would be very happy to be on any political ticket" with Nixon.

Subsequent to the President's operation in June, Harold Stassen announced formation of a movement to nominate Governor Christian Herter of Massachusetts in Nixon's stead, giving as his reason that an Eisenhower-Herter ticket would run at least 6 per cent stronger than an Eisenhower-Nixon ticket, basing this statement upon a poll that he had taken.

Much of the impact of Stassen's surprise move was reduced when the chairman of the Republican national committee announced that Herter had agreed to nominate Nixon in the convention. By August 20, the Stassen headquarters was one of the quietest places in San Francisco; curious passers-by stared into the windows, but few ventured in. The last major decision had therefore been made before the convention opened, and the convention's function was to ratify these decisions formally and to create as much enthusiasm as possible among the delegates to stimulate them in the forthcoming campaign.

San Francisco California,
August 20, 21, 22, 23, 1956

The campaign-rally aspects of the convention were stressed from the beginning, since the deliberative aspects had so little current meaning. Time was filled by well-planned demonstrations and by innumerable speeches by party figures. If sometimes it got a little boring, there were always the attractions of San Francisco to lure the delegates, and frequently it was difficult to find enough alternates to fill the floor for the benefit of the television cameras.

Convention Organization

The temporary organization was completed quickly and smoothly, and Senator William F. Knowland of California was elected temporary chairman. He was not immediately installed, for the chairman of the national committee, Leonard Hall, continued in the chair throughout the first session. During this session, the usual committees were appointed and temporary rules were adopted. Then a long series of

speeches began, which were finally continued into the second session, so that it was some time before Senator Knowland finally was escorted to the chair. He made his acceptance speech, but the keynote was given by the governor of Washington, Arthur B. Langlie. Throughout all the speeches, the themes were (1) praise for the record of the administration and its leaders and (2) the superior qualifications of the Republican party to govern—all compared to the opposition.

The convention adjourned late in the afternoon of the first day, not to reconvene until 3:30 the next day, in order to allow the committees time for their deliberations and to time the more important convention business with the afternoon television hours throughout the nation—a difficult problem due to the time differential between the West and East Coasts. The first order of business in the third session was the report of the committee on credentials. Only one contest was acted upon—a contestant delegation from South Carolina—and the previous action of the national committee was upheld. Vacancies reported by several states in their delegations were filled, and the entire report adopted by voice vote without debate.

Unanimity continued as the committee on permanent organization reported. As in several conventions in the past, Congressman Joseph W. Martin, Jr., of Massachusetts, minority leader of the House, was named permanent chairman, but he did not take his seat until after the rules committee reported. The rules, including the "Fair Play" rule first written into the permanent rules in the 1952 convention, were adopted without debate and by voice vote.

Subsequent to the acceptance speech of the permanent chairman, a speech by Herbert Hoover and a curious display by some of the more prominent women of the party intervened before the report of the platform committee. This display might best be characterized as a verbal pageant, in which each woman presented a Republican word—employment, peace, unity, etc.—and made a few remarks tying the word to the

Republican record. When all the words had been presented, in proper arrangement, their first letters formed an acrostic. A group of Young Republicans carried placards, with the words on one side, and large initials on the other; at the appropriate moment, they reversed the placards, which had up to then been held with the words toward the audience, and turned the initial side to view, thus spelling REPUBLICAN WOMEN.

That this routine, with its unlikely combination of some of the elements of a young people's church pageant with the antics of college football cheering squads, and carried out by some of the most eminent women in America, was felt needed, illustrates forcibly the problem faced by convention managers when there is no real nominating contest to be the natural focus of attention.

The Platform

The platform was a long eulogy of the Republican record and of President Eisenhower. Since it had been released to the press and presented to the delegates some time before actual presentation to the convention, a motion was passed that it not be read. The platform was approved without open opposition, although a number of southerners objected to the strong civil rights section—some of them to the extent that they left the convenion and went home. These were few, however, and their leaving was so quiet that it passed unnoticed in the general air of unanimity prevailing in the convention.

Following acceptance of the platform, all members of the Cabinet, except John Foster Dulles, Secretary of State, who was represented by Herbert Hoover, Jr., Under Secretary of State, were called upon to speak. They were introduced by Sherman Adams, assistant to the President. The convention then adjourned until the following afternoon.

The Presidential Nomination

Aside from ratification of the new national committee, which was quickly accomplished, the remaining business of the convention was the selection of the nominees. This, however, was delayed by two additional speakers. The first was announced as an "independent," although he had served as a special assistant to the President. This obvious appeal to the "Independents for Eisenhower" was followed by a speech from Thomas E. Dewey, whose influence had been so great in Eisenhower's first nomination.

Finally, the roll was called to reserve time for nominations for the Presidency. Alabama yielded to Indiana to enable Congressman Charles A. Halleck, a stalwart representative of the so-called Taft wing of the party, to make the official nominating speech. Eight seconding speakers followed: a housewife, a football coach, a southerner, a farmer, an educator, a union laborer, a representative of a minority group, and finally Governor McKeldin of Maryland, who had nominated Eisenhower in 1952. All this was accompanied by demonstrations led by the well-organized Young Republicans. When the roll was called, every delegation cast its unanimous vote for President Dwight D. Eisenhower, as was expected.

The Vice-Presidential Nomination

Almost identical procedure was followed in the vice-presidential nomination. The abortive attempt by Harold Stassen had been fully squelched by this time, and Alabama yielded to Massachusetts to enable Stassen's erstwhile candidate, Christian Herter, governor of Massachusetts, to make the formal nominating speech—in accord with the arrangements made by Leonard Hall, chairman of the national committee, in countering Stassen.

During the calling of the roll, an amusing bit of by-play occurred when a delegate from Nebraska insisted that he wanted to nominate an undesignated candidate. When Chairman Martin insisted that the delegate name the potential nominee, he gave the name of "Joe Smith." Although it is not reported in the official proceedings, considerable delay was caused by this affair, largely because reporters and photographers quite understandably converged upon the Nebraska delegation in an effort to get what they could out of this surprise bit of newsworthy material in an otherwise unexciting convention. The chairman at last directed that the offending delegate leave the hall, with his press entourage—which he finally did.

Following Governor Herter's nominating speech, nine seconding speeches provided opportunity for recognition of as many social groups, geographical areas, and political factions: Citizens for Eisenhower and Nixon, the veterans of foreign wars, the Taft wing of the party, labor, the Far West, the East, the South, the Middle West, as well as the defeated and now overtly amenable Harold Stassen. On the roll call, all delegations except Nebraska cast a unanimous ballot for Richard Nixon, and the one abstention in the Nebraska delegation was changed at the end to make the nomination unanimous.

Although the business of the convention was officially completed except for the usual housekeeping resolutions and the resolutions of appreciation, the convention recessed until the next afternoon in order to prepare for the arrival of the President and the Vice President. Prior to recessing, a resolution of sympathy was extended to Vice President Nixon for the illness of his father, at whose bedside he then was.

During the final session, while the delegations were awaiting the appearance of the nominees, another of the many public displays of party figures was presented; one after another, the Republican candidates for major offices throughout the nation who were present were called to the stand. Each was presented there to receive the applause of the audience, and no less than fifty-nine made the long walk from the rear of the stage to the rostrum, where the television cameras relayed their faces for a brief moment to the television screens of their constituents.

When the nominees arrived, the Vice President made his acceptance speech first. The President's followed. The ubiquitous Young Republicans led the enthusiastic displays that accompanied each speech. As a climax to the demonstration for the President, hundreds of balloons were released. This provided great entertainment to the audience, and everyone joined happily in the game of exploding them. The game must have been less than amusing to the secret service men scattered throughout the hall, as the cheers of the thousands of people were punctuated by scores of sharp explosions resembling pistol shots. Gradually, the noise level dropped, the President and his party left the hall, and the convention adjourned.

Presidential Election, November 6, 1956

DWIGHT D. EISENHOWER (R) : popular vote, 35,590,472; electoral vote, 447
ADLAI E. STEVENSON (D) : popular vote, 26,029,752; electoral vote, 74

1960

DWIGHT D. EISENHOWER won two successive landslide victories in presidential elections, but more voters across the nation continued to identify themselves as Democrats than as Republicans throughout the 1950s. As the first presidential contest of the new decade loomed ahead, the Eisenhower magic was put to the test. The Twenty-second Amendment to the Constitution prohibited him from running for a third term. Could he transfer his own popularity to a successor?

Although Eisenhower himself was unbeatable at the polls, other Republicans were not. The Republicans gained control of Congress in 1952 but lost it in 1954 and failed to regain it in 1956. The 1958 election provided a historic Democratic sweep —an additional forty-nine seats in the House and seventeen in the Senate. Twenty-seven Democrats and only nine Republicans were elected as state governors in 1958.

The Democrats' best issue was economic. There was a recession in 1957–58, more serious than the earlier one of 1953–54, and the economy dipped significantly in October 1958, just in time for the election. Public opinion polls showed that blue-collar workers were concerned about unemployment. There were rumblings of discontent from the farmers. Meanwhile, after the Soviet Union orbited its *Sputnik* in October 1957, many voters began to fear that the United States had fallen behind the Russians in science, technology, education, and perhaps in missile capability. As effects of the Supreme Court's 1954 school desegregation decision became clear—dramatized by President Eisenhower's sending of federal troops to enforce school integration in Little Rock, Arkansas, in the autumn of 1957—both segregationists and integrationists had com-

plaints about the policies of the Republican administration in Washington. Public confidence dropped in the administration's ability to maintain prosperity at home and peace abroad. Many intellectuals and others were dissatisfied with the status quo and sought, in what became a Democratic slogan, to "get the country moving again."

Yet the fact remained that Eisenhower had been phenomenally successful in presidential races. He would be campaigning for his successor as the Republican nominee. For all their gains in 1958, the Democrats would have to wage a skillful battle to win back the allegiance of the "presidential Republicans" who had supported Eisenhower in 1952 and 1956.

THE DEMOCRATIC CONTEST

There was no lack of Democratic candidates seeking to lead their party's return to the White House. Adlai E. Stevenson was unwilling to conduct an overt campaign, but he evidently desired a third presidential nomination, and many Democrats thought he deserved an opportunity to run against someone other than Eisenhower. John F. Kennedy had emerged as a presidential contender when he came close to winning the vice-presidential nomination in 1956. Intelligent and attractive, he had defeated the popular incumbent Henry Cabot Lodge, Jr., in winning election to the Senate in 1952 and had rolled up an 800,000-plus plurality in being reelected in 1958; but some found him too young at forty-three and many feared that a Roman Catholic candidate in 1960 would lose badly, just as Al Smith had in 1928. The Senate majority leader, Lyndon B. Johnson of Texas, had achieved prominence and high marks for his leadership in the Democratically controlled Congress. Yet many believed that being a southerner was as much of a handicap for a presidential candidate as being a Catholic; and Johnson concentrated on Senate business rather than campaigning across the nation like other hopefuls. The effervescent Senator Hubert H. Humphrey of Minnesota had been a leader of the liberal faction of the party since his civil rights speech at the 1948 Democratic convention; but for some Democrats, he was *too* liberal. Senator Stuart Symington of Missouri had national experience dating back to the Truman administration, a solid record as a vote-getter, and considerable strength as "everyone's second choice." He could be nominated, however, only if the party failed to agree on a first choice.

The presidential primaries were the testing ground for the candidates. As he probably had to do to be nominated, Kennedy swept all those in which he ran—New Hampshire, Indiana, Maryland, Nebraska, Ohio, Oregon, West Virginia, and Wisconsin. His defeat of Hubert Humphrey by more than 80,000 votes in West Virginia demonstrated Kennedy's appeal in a heavily Protestant state and sufficed to persuade Humphrey to withdraw from the presidential race. Kennedy, who had been the most popular Democratic candidate since the first Gallup poll of the year was released on January 29, climbed steadily as he gained primary victories. In the poll of July 10, on the eve of the Democratic convention, he led as the preference of 41 percent of the rank-and-file Democrats surveyed; Stevenson had 25 percent, Johnson 16 percent, and Symington 7 percent, with 11 percent scattered. Kennedy appeared to have at least 600 of the 761 delegate votes necessary for nomination. The only question was whether any coalition could develop enough strength to stop him on the first ballot.

Los Angeles, California, July 11, 12, 13, 14, 15, 1960

The convention that opened in Los Angeles on July 11 was constituted differently from its predecessors. The Democratic National Committe had approved a formula for apportioning convention votes, stated in the official call to the convention, that was an almost wholly congressional system. Each state received 2½ votes for each of its U.S. senators and representatives (the total rounded upward if necessary to obtain a whole number), half a vote each for its two members of the Democratic National Committee, and more votes if needed to reach its 1956 convention vote total. In addition, the District of Columbia got 8 votes; Puerto Rico, 6; the Virgin Islands, 3; and Guam, 3. Party voting had been a major factor in the system for apportioning votes at the 1956 convention. The new apportionment formula was approved to prevent disproportionate strength in population terms for the southern states, which had been Adlai Stevenson's chief supporters in the 1956 election (and had elected numerous Democrats to Congress and the statehouses in 1956 and 1958). The 1960 apportionment formula was intended to be "fair" to the northern Democrats, who represented a majority of the party's usual presidential voters but who had been unable to carry their states against President Eisenhower. In all, the delegates at the 1960 convention cast a total of 1,521 votes.

The initial session of the 1,521 and their entourage was devoted to pomp, pageantry, and party unity. After the invocation, the presentation of the colors, the playing of the national anthem, the recitation of the pledge of allegiance to the flag, the taking of the official convention photograph, the reading of the convention call, and presentations of a Gideon Bible and a gavel, the official business began with approval of the temporary convention rules by voice vote. There were speeches of welcome by California officials. The major addresses of the evening were delivered by Democratic National Chairman Paul M. Butler, who accused the Republicans of "eight years of golfing and goofing," and the youthful senator from Idaho, Frank Church, who in an address ringing with Ciceronian figures of speech, chided the Republicans and promised that if elected the Democrats would do more to meet the nation's needs. In the only other important business transacted, the report of the convention rules committee calling for rules similar to those used at past conventions was approved without opposition in a voice vote. (Attempts to change the rules significantly had failed within the rules committee, and no one sought to take the issue to the floor.)

At the second session of the convention the cloak of party unity began to show signs of strain. The initial presentations from the podium were noncontroversial. These proceedings commanded less than full attention from those in the hall, most of whom were concerned with more urgent matters. There was so much disorder that permanent chairman LeRoy Collins, the governor of Florida, nearly broke off delivery of his own speech to the convention; only a hastily penned note from the national chairman, telling him that the speech was projecting well on national television, persuaded Collins to continue. When he had concluded, the convention routinely approved the report of its credentials committee, which in the single seating contest had divided Puerto Rico's six votes between two contending factions.

The Platform

The major business of the evening was the party platform. Democratic National Chairman Paul Butler and platform committee chairman Chester Bowles, U.S. representative and former governor of Connecticut, had been determined to draft a "liberal" platform that would appeal to a wide consensus. On the whole, they succeeded. By several key votes in committee, party conservatives were defeated roughly two to one and planks were approved that recommended elimination of national quotas for immigration, farm price supports at 90 percent of parity, repudiation of "right to work" laws that were anathema to organized labor, and a strong civil rights program.

The civil rights plank called for empowering the U.S. attorney general to file civil injunction suits to prevent racial discrimination; establishing a Fair Employment Practices Commission; making the Civil Rights Commission a permanent agency; ending discriminatory practices in federal activities; and desegregating all schools by 1963, the centennial year of the Emancipation Proclamation. A group of southerners, led by Georgia delegation chairman James H. Gray and Senator Sam J. Ervin, Jr., of North Carolina, filed a minority report calling for deletion of the civil rights plank, which they said rewarded "the loyalty of the people of the South to their party . . . with scolding and derision." They argued that the plank, which had been strengthened in committee, violated states' rights under the Tenth Amendment by favoring "ever-enlarging big government control, which always corrupts and always dehumanizes." The Virginia delegation also presented a minority statement urging rapid repayment of the national debt.

In the floor debate, each side was allotted five minutes to discuss the national debt issue and thirty minutes for the civil rights plank. Both minority reports were then voted down in voice votes. Thus the southerners had their say (on prime-time television) and the party majority worked its will with minimum rancor between the factions.

Presidential Nomination

Convention suspense reached its high point in the presidential balloting at the third session. The central drama at the 1960 Democratic gathering concerned whether the stop-Kennedy movement could prevent him from getting approximately 150 additional votes which he needed to win on the first ballot. If a coalition could stop him, the other candidates hoped, the Kennedy strength would begin to erode and someone else could be nominated. But theirs was the strategy of desperation. As one veteran reporter put it: "Whenever I hear about a stop-X movement at a convention, I know that X is about to be nominated."

Besides Kennedy the candidate with the most open support at the convention was Adlai Stevenson. Humphrey had lost in the primaries. Johnson had deliberately avoided the primaries and lacked real support outside the congressional leaders and some southern delegations. Symington's strategy was to get second-round commitments, and his wide acceptability within the party made him a likely prospect in the event the front-running Kennedy lost.

Though many Democratic politicians considered their strength more apparent than real, or their sympathies more anti-Kennedy than pro-Stevenson, the avowed partisans of the former governor of Illinois were numerous in California, the scene of the convention. They marched around the hall, packed the galleries, and broke loose in a wild demonstration when he appeared on the convention floor shortly before the platform debate. The following day in one of the most eloquent nominating speeches ever delivered, Senator Eugene J. McCarthy of Minnesota urged: "Do not reject this man who has made us all proud to be called Democrats. Do not leave this prophet without honor in his own party." The ovation for McCarthy's speech was tremendous and prolonged. Eventually officials shut off the lights in the hall to quiet the Stevenson enthusiasts and allow the convention to continue.

The names of nine candidates for president were placed in nomination: Kennedy, Johnson, Stevenson, Symington, Senator George A. Smathers of Florida, Governor Herschel D. Loveless of Iowa, Governor George Docking of Kansas, Governor Robert B. Meyner of New Jersey, and Governor Ross R. Barnett of Mississippi. As the balloting proceeded, Kennedy's expected strength held firm. Leaders of several crucial states—notably Mayor Richard J. Daley of Chicago—delivered most of their delegations to Kennedy. The California delegation, in revolt against an attempt by their governor, Edmund G. (Pat) Brown, to do the same, divided about evenly between Kennedy and Stevenson. But by the time the alphabetical roll call reached Wyoming, Kennedy was on the brink of victory. The state unanimously cast its 15 votes for the senator from Massachusetts and clinched his nomination. When the roll call had been completed amid a demonstration by jubilant Kennedy supporters, the nominee

had 806 votes to 409 for Johnson, 86 for Symington, 79½ for Stevenson, and 140½ for the favorite sons. The nomination was made unanimous by voice vote. The cheers continued until Kennedy appeared on the podium to acknowledge them briefly.

Vice-Presidential Choice

Easily the most controversial decision of the convention was Kennedy's endorsement of Lyndon Johnson as the party's vice-presidential nominee. It was a logical choice; Johnson was particularly strong in the South, where Kennedy was not. Yet for precisely the same reason Johnson was unpopular with the liberal-labor wing of the party. The true story of Kennedy's negotiations with Johnson will probably never be established; there are many differing reports from highly partisan witnesses. Some claim that Kennedy never thought that Johnson would accept the nomination and offered it only as a gesture; others say that Johnson did not want the job but agreed for reasons of patriotism and party loyalty. In any event, Johnson was Kennedy's choice, and the decision was announced at an afternoon press conference.

Lyndon Johnson was nominated by Governor David L. Lawrence of Pennsylvania and seconded by an array of Democratic notables—Senator Henry M. Jackson of Washington (a vice-presidential contender), Representative William L. Dawson of Illinois (senior black elected official in the country), Governors George Docking of Kansas and J. Lindsay Almond of Virginia, and Representatives Chet Holifield of California and Stewart L. Udall of Arizona. Midway through the roll call, House Majority Leader John W. McCormack of Massachusetts moved that Johnson's nomination be made unanimous; in a voice vote, it was.

In his acceptance speech, Johnson said that he could not reject his party's call to service and went on to predict a Democratic victory and "a new era." Rephrasing his own campaign slogan, Johnson declared: "The Democratic party is going all the way with J.F.K. and L.B.J., and I am proud to be on the bandwagon."

The final convention session, held for a crowd of 80,000 in the Los Angeles Coliseum, was a performance with many party leaders in cameo roles and John F. Kennedy as the star. There were brief remarks by House Speaker Sam Rayburn of Texas; a message from former President Harry S. Truman; and short speeches by Hubert Humphrey, Michigan Governor (and labor favorite) G. Mennen Williams, California Representative (and president's son) James Roosevelt, Stuart Symington, Lyndon Johnson, and Adlai Stevenson.

John Kennedy's acceptance speech began with compliments to his opponents in the race for the nomination: "I feel a lot safer now that they are on my side again." Of his Catholic faith, he said that he would "reject any kind of religious pressure or obligation that might directly or indirectly interfere with my conduct of the presidency in the national interest." Throughout the address, he emphasized the need for new national leadership; for the first time he struck a campaign theme—the New Frontier.

I stand tonight facing west on what was once the last frontier. . . .
Today some would say . . . that there is no longer an American frontier. But . . . we stand today on the edge of a new frontier—the frontier of the 1960s. . . .
The new frontier of which I speak is not a set of promises—it is a set of challenges. It sums up not what I intend to offer the American people, but what I intend to ask of them. . . .
Beyond that frontier are uncharted areas of science and space, unsolved problems of peace and war, unconquered pockets of ignorance and prejudice, unanswered questions of poverty and surplus.
I believe the times demand invention, innovation, imagination, decision. I am asking each of you to be new pioneers on that New Frontier.

THE REPUBLICAN CONTEST

Although he was a president of the United States who enjoyed enormous popularity and prestige, Dwight D. Eisenhower chose not to openly name a successor as the presidential nominee of the Republican convention. Richard Nixon had twice been his running mate in presidential elections, but Eisenhower's attitude toward Nixon often seemed ambivalent at best. Others aimed for the White House. Chief among them was Nelson A. Rockefeller, elected governor of New York in 1958 after serving in the Eisenhower administration. Others "mentioned" as possible Republican candidates included United Nations Ambassador Henry Cabot Lodge, Jr., former senator from Massachusetts; Senator Barry M. Goldwater of Arizona; and several cabinet officers.

But nothing ever really disturbed Nixon's position as the front-runner after his re-nomination for the vice-presidency in 1956. In early January 1960 he let it be known publicly that he would seek the presidential nomination and run in the primaries. He drew no active opposition in those contests and rolled up large majorities. He was the choice of most state party leaders. He was far and away the leader in all the 1960 Gallup polls of Republican preferences. The poll published the day before the national convention opened gave Nixon 75 percent of the Republicans surveyed; his nearest rival, Rockefeller, had 12 percent.

Rockefeller nonetheless sought to leave his mark on the convention. He had announced in late 1959 that he would *not* run for the presidency, but he retained his campaign staff, concentrated on policy issues, and hoped for a convention draft. After Nixon's victories in the primaries, Rockefeller realized that his own maximum leverage was in the issues; accordingly, on June 8 he issued a call for "leadership of clear purpose, candidly proclaimed," accompanied by a nine-point policy program that was sharply critical of administration efforts both domestically and abroad. The major battleground between the vice-president and the New York governor would be the party platform.

Struggle over the Platform

The platform committee hearings began the week after Rockefeller's announcement and a week before the full convention opened. The platform panel was chaired by Charles H. Percy, a corporation president whom President Eisenhower had chosen to head the Committee on Program and Progress, a Republican organization that had worked through 1959 and 1960 to develop a statement of "modern Republicanism" aimed at broad popular appeal and sent to every 1960 convention delegate. The draft platform that Percy distributed to members of the 1960 convention panel had been written in the White House along "modern Republican" lines; the President, the vice-president, and other party leaders had privately pronounced it generally acceptable.

After a public plenary session that heard from Governor Rockefeller, Senator Goldwater, and others, the platform committee divided into subcommittees specializing in particular policy areas. As they got down to the business of drafting platform planks, conflict became apparent between those who sought primarily to praise the record of the Eisenhower administration and the Rockefeller supporters who wanted to urge that the government do more, particularly on defense and civil rights programs.

The necessary compromise was negotiated at the party summit. Vice-President Nixon, realizing the jeopardy to his campaign of a convention floor fight on the platform and the possibility of the New York governor's sitting out the election, went to Rockefeller's Manhattan apartment. There they worked out the "compact of Fifth Avenue," in which Nixon agreed to most of Rockefeller's proposed changes in national security programs, government organization, civil rights policy, the economic growth rate, and the provision of medical care for the elderly. Once the agreement with Rockefeller had been reached, Nixon had to conciliate the confused delegates, the angry platform committee, and a reportedly furious President. Eventually the Rockefeller forces agreed to new compromise language on national defense written by the presidential staff; rebellious platform committee members were called in by Nixon and told that the statement on civil rights reflected his own views, which he was prepared to defend if necessary on the conven-

tion floor; and after an initial rebuff in the civil rights subcommittee, the Nixon-Rockefeller forces narrowly succeeded in getting their proposals adopted by the platform committee.

Chicago, Illinois, July 25, 26, 27, 28, 1960

The formalities and appeals of the first convention session did nothing to inflame the passions aroused during the platform debate. The major address of the evening was made by Republican National Chairman Thruston B. Morton, senator from Kentucky.

The second session built a partisan crescendo. Illinois Senate candidate Samuel W. Witwer delivered an address about Lincoln's nomination in Chicago a hundred years earlier. Illinois Congressman Leslie H. Arends and actors Lloyd Nolan and Efrem Zimbalist, Jr., read excerpts from Lincoln speeches. Chairman Morton introduced former President Herbert C. Hoover to the crowd, which responded with a four-minute demonstration. Ned Cushing, president of the Young Republican National Federation, presented Hoover with a gold badge. The convention reached a high point for conservative delegates in a speech by Senator Barry Goldwater, chairman of the Republican Senatorial Campaign Committee, who said Republicans believe "that man has a soul as well as a stomach." And finally Minnesota Representative Walter H. Judd delivered a keynote address that was a partisan classic, stating what the Republicans had done right and, particularly, what the Democrats had done wrong. He asked his audience: "Was it the Republicans who recognized the Soviet Union in 1933 . . . who . . . agreed to give the Russians a free hand in the Balkans . . . who agreed to the communist take-over of 100,000,000 free people in eastern Europe who are not Russian . . . that divided Korea and gave North Korea to the Communists?" To each rhetorical question the crowd shouted, "No!" It gave Judd a standing ovation for his speech.

The next evening the convention moved

briskly through its business and heard remarks by representatives of various party groups culminating in a presidential address. Reports of the convention committees on credentials, rules, and permanent organization were each adopted by voice vote. In a "tribute to Ike" came a collection of "representative Americans": Senator Hiram L. Fong of the new state of Hawaii, a recent high school graduate, the governor of Montana, a former Marine sergeant, a steelworker's wife, and a Negro White House assistant. Illinois Senator Everett M. Dirksen, the Senate minority leader, spoke about Lincoln and then introduced President Eisenhower. Not surprisingly, the President stressed the achievements of his administration, adding that he had "difficulty in restraining my feelings of indignation" at "pessimists" who criticized its military capability. He said that if "the facts" were communicated effectively to the voters, "the next President of the United States will be a Republican." The crowd responded to him with cheers of "We want Ike!"

The two major decisions of the convention—the presidential nomination and adoption of the party platform—came at a single convention session lasting only a little more than four hours. The platform came first. There was no minority report; and after all the preceding political furor, the platform was agreed to officially by voice vote.

Presidential Nomination

The presidential nomination was similarly formal. After the platform conflict had been settled in committee, Nelson Rockefeller told the New York delegation that he did not want his name to be placed in nomination. Thus only two names were proposed: Nixon and Barry Goldwater. Governor Mark O. Hatfield of Oregon nominated Nixon in a brief speech that was followed by a lengthy demonstration and eight seconding speeches. Governor Paul Fannin of Arizona nominated Goldwater, who also received an extended ovation. However, Goldwater appeared on the podium and

asked that his name be withdrawn and that those supporting him close ranks behind Nixon. He added: "Let's grow up, conservatives! If we want to take this party back, and I think we can some day, let's get to work." When the roll was called, Nixon received every convention vote except ten from Louisiana that went to Goldwater. The chairman of the Louisiana delegation promptly moved that the nomination be made unanimous, and in a voice vote it was.

The last session featured the vice-presidential nomination and the candidates' acceptance speeches. Nelson Rockefeller was an obvious choice just as Lyndon Johnson had been; but Rockefeller had consistently said that he was not a candidate for the job, and Richard Nixon took him at his word. Thus Nixon had tentatively decided before the convention to name Henry Cabot Lodge, hoping to stress during the campaign greater Republican experience in foreign policy. Shortly after his own nomination by the convention, Nixon called together thirty-six Republican leaders to discuss the vice-presidential selection. They talked for several hours. Most of the leaders agreed that Lodge was the best candidate, though others preferred a midwesterner or someone identified with the conservative faction of the party. However, once Nixon's decision was made known, Lodge was the only candidate proposed. He received all the convention votes except that of a Goldwater supporter in the Texas delegation who first abstained and then changed his vote at the end of the roll call to make Lodge's nomination unanimous.

Accepting the vice-presidential nomination, Lodge emphasized foreign affairs. In addition to stressing the accomplishments of the last eight Republican years, he pointed to his running mate's long-standing concern with foreign policy. "There is no man in America," Lodge told the convention, "who could represent us in the turmoil of world politics . . . as Richard Nixon would do."

In his acceptance speech, Nixon praised the Eisenhower administration as having "the best eight-year record of any administration in the history of this country." He pledged to take his campaign to every state in the union. He said that the United States was in a "race for survival" with the communist nations and that the quality of presidential leadership and commitment by citizens to prevail would have much to do with the outcome of the struggle. He called for rededication to the American ideal of freedom as "a battle cry for a grand offensive to win the minds and the hearts and the souls of men." He said that "our primary aim must be not to help government, but to help people—to help people attain the life they deserve."

Presidential election, November 8, 1960

JOHN F. KENNEDY (D): popular vote, 34,227,096; electoral vote, 303
RICHARD M. NIXON (R): popular vote, 34,108,546; electoral vote, 219
Fifteen other electors from Alabama, Mississippi, and Oklahoma voted for Senator Harry
F. Byrd of Virginia in the electoral college.

1964

Since he had won the presidency by only the narrowest of margins, many politicians thought John F. Kennedy would be vulnerable in 1964. Then came his assassination in November 1963, and Lyndon B. Johnson as Kennedy's successor received a great rush of immediate and persistent national support. Johnson was not merely assured of the Democratic nomination; he also led each of the various Republican candidates in every Gallup poll taken from January 1964 up to the election in November.

THE REPUBLICAN CONTEST

The story of Republican presidential hopefuls in 1964 is a tale of fits and starts. Former President Eisenhower, who had the prestige and popularity to influence the nomination perhaps decisively, chose not to do so. Richard M. Nixon as the party's 1960 nominee was initially in a good strategic position to seek another nomination; but after he lost decisively the race for governor of California in 1962 he was tagged a "loser," an epithet that politicians find it difficult to overcome. Nelson A. Rockefeller, handily reelected as governor of New York in 1962, became a rallying point for many who considered themselves Republican progressives. Nixon's running mate in 1960, Henry Cabot Lodge, Jr., became in 1963 U.S. ambassador to Vietnam; he was widely known and respected, although the memory of his supposed slights in past campaigns still rankled with some GOP politicians. Two Republican governors elected in 1962 were considered presidential possibilities: William W. Scranton of Pennsylvania and

George W. Romney of Michigan. And there was Senator Barry M. Goldwater of Arizona, lion of the new American Right and long a faithful worker for party candidates as chairman of the Republican Senatorial Campaign Committee.

The record of the primaries and the public opinion polls shows a divided Republican party in 1964. National popular support for the various candidates fluctuated wildly, at least partly in belated response to recent events. During the first three months of the year, the leading candidate in Gallup surveys of Republican voters was Richard Nixon, probably the party's best-known presidential prospect and its previous nominee. The New Hampshire primary on March 10 brought an unexpected write-in victory for Henry Cabot Lodge; Lodge led in the national Gallup surveys of April, May, and June. On April 14 Goldwater won the Illinois primary with 62 percent of the vote; but the only other candidate on the ballot was Senator Margaret Chase Smith of Maine. On April 28 came the all-write-in Pennsylvania primary, in which 58.3 percent of the vote was won by the state's governor, William Scranton. In May Goldwater won the Indiana primary, where his most serious opponent was Harold E. Stassen, the former governor of Minnesota; and he won the nonbinding Texas primary with 74.5 percent of the vote against Rockefeller, Stassen, Smith, and various write-in candidates. The chief confrontation that month, however, came in Oregon, where all the major candidates' names were on the ballot. Rockefeller won with 33 percent of the vote—more than five percentage points ahead of Lodge, who came in second.

The winner-take-all California primary on June 2 was the ultimate test. Nationally, none of the candidates had led consistently or developed steadily increasing momentum in popular strength. But the Goldwater organization had concentrated less on gathering popular support than on winning delegates, and it had been extremely successful in its appointed task. If the Arizona senator defeated Nelson Rockefeller in California, the Goldwater strategists would not only clinch enough delegate vote commitments for victory on the first ballot but also gain the demonstrated popular support needed to give their campaign against the Democrats a good start at the Republican convention. If Goldwater lost, he would be without a victory in a major primary. At the same time, California was the last-chance primary for the forces seeking to block Goldwater; thus Lodge and Scranton endorsed Rockefeller's efforts in the golden state. Harris polls showed the volatile California voters shifting from one candidate to the other almost daily. In the end, Goldwater's delegate slate defeated Rockefeller's with 51.4 percent of the vote in the two-way race. Many observers concluded that the decisive factor was the birth, three days before the primary, of Nelson A. Rockefeller, Jr.; both his mother and his father had been divorced from other spouses before their own marriage a year earlier, and Mrs. Rockefeller's legal settlement involved giving custody of the four children from her first marriage to their father. Birth of the new baby served to remind California voters of this melancholy situation.

Whatever the reason for Goldwater's victory in California, it left him in a commanding position—in terms of convention delegate votes. On the day before the national convention began, his campaign organization announced that he had 739 votes, comfortably more than the 655 needed to win the presidential nomination. The same day, the Gallup organization released a national survey of Republican voters showing that in a two-man contest, William Scranton was the choice of 60 percent and Goldwater the choice of 34 percent, with the remainder undecided. Scranton had announced his own last-minute campaign for the GOP presidential nomination exactly one month before the poll was released.

San Francisco, California,
July 13, 14, 15, 16, 1964

The convention opening was preceded by some bitter infighting. On July 8, the Republican National Committee voted on various proposed changes in the convention rules. It rejected, 59–41, an attempt by some Goldwater supporters to eliminate a newly drafted rule banning the unit rule in convention voting. Some of the Goldwater people feared that others pledged to but unenthusiastic about their candidate might interpret the new rule as freeing them from their commitment. The national committee also defeated, 70–30, a proposal sponsored by its Arizona members to make each national committeeman and committeewoman automatically a convention delegate, beginning in 1968. The platform committee overwhelmingly rejected amendments sponsored by Scranton supporters dealing with civil rights, political extremism, civilian control over nuclear weapons, and immigration laws. The credentials committee tabled a motion to ban the seating of any delegates or alternates selected by procedures that involved racial discrimination. And party unity was not enhanced when an angry Goldwater returned to Scranton a letter "signed" by the Pennsylvania governor that accused Goldwater of "nuclear irresponsibility" and "absurd and dangerous positions that would be soundly repudiated by the American people in November." (Scranton later said the letter had been sent by his staff without his knowledge, but that he would stand by its contents.)

Such rancor was only latent at the first official convention session on the morning of July 13. It featured the parade of party leaders and symbolic spokesmen for various groups that are typical of such occasions. The only overt controversy came when Maryland delegate Newton I. Steers, a

Scranton supporter, offered a substitute resolution on the temporary rules that would have barred the seating of any delegate or alternate selected under any racially discriminatory procedures. As in the credentials committee, the proposal was defeated.

The second session of the convention, which took place that evening, was distinguished by the keynote speech of Governor Mark O. Hatfield of Oregon, who opposed Goldwater's nomination. The speeches and presentations that preceded Hatfield's were aimed at Republican unity. Republican National Chairman William E. Miller, a congressman from upstate New York, promised "a fair convention" and predicted victory in 1964. Senate Minority Leader Everett M. Dirksen of Illinois read a message from former President Herbert C. Hoover, whom Dirksen called "a Grand Old Person in the Grand Old Party." In a presentation entitled "Call to Greatness," actors Victor Jory and Lloyd Nolan read words of famous American patriots (and the Israeli patriot, David Ben Gurion) to a musical accompaniment of "America, the Beautiful."

Mark Hatfield's keynote speech began in a similar vein. In a manner reminiscent of Walter H. Judd at the 1960 convention, Hatfield asked the kind of rhetorical questions that stir a partisan crowd: "Was it a Republican Administration that presided over the fiasco at the Bay of Pigs? Was it a Republican Administration that neutralized Laos and so initiated the chain of events that threatens freedom throughout all of Southeast Asia? And . . . was it a Republican Administration that ignored the problem in Cuba until it erupted into rioting and bloodshed? Was it a Republican Administration in power when the Berlin Wall was built?" But Hatfield further defined the Republican creed to exclude some of the extremist groups that the platform committee and many Goldwater supporters had been unwilling to condemn: "Our [the Republican] faith challenges any who would destroy freedom, whether they wrap themselves in a false cloak of patriotism or an equally false cloak of religion. There are bigots in this nation who spew forth their venom of hate. They parade under hundreds of labels, including the Communist Party, the Ku Klux Klan and the John Birch Society. They must be overcome." There were cheers from those who agreed, but the Goldwater forces, although opposed to the condemnation of extremism, did not respond in kind.

At the session on the following day, however, the passions could not be contained. Senator Hiram L. Fong of Hawaii, speaking on behalf of the nine incumbent Republican senators up for reelection in 1964, named each in turn; the last was Barry Goldwater, and mentioning him for the first time from the podium at the convention set off loud cheers and applause. He was followed by permanent chairman Thruston B. Morton, senator from Kentucky, who in an avowedly partisan speech "lay it on the line—I mean the dirty linen" (of the Democrats). Former President Eisenhower offered a tribute to Republicanism, attacked the Democrats, condemned "radicals of any kind," called for Republican unity, and received his most enthusiastic applause when he said: "Let us particularly scorn the divisive efforts of those outside our family, including sensation-seeking columnists and commentators. Because, my friends, I assure you that these are people who couldn't care less about the good of our party." Later, speaking of the need for better local government, Eisenhower received additional cheers when he said: "And let us not be guilty of maudlin sympathy for the criminal who, roaming the streets with switchblade knife and illegal firearm, seeking a helpless prey, suddenly becomes, upon apprehension, a poor, underprivileged person who counts upon the compassion of our society and the laxness or weaknesses of too many courts to forgive his offense."

Platform

The major business of the evening was adoption of the party platform. Committee chairman Melvin R. Laird, congressman from Wisconsin, presided over the reading of the entire 9,000-word document, which required two hours. This process was intended to discourage television viewers from watching the intraparty battle that ensued. The first amendment to the platform committee report was offered (at 1 A.M. on the East Coast) by Senator Hugh Scott of Pennsylvania, Scranton's floor manager. It specifically condemned the Communist party, the Ku Klux Klan, and the John Birch Society as extremist groups seeking to "infiltrate" or "attach themselves" to the Republicans. When Governor Rockefeller attempted to speak in support of the Scott amendment, he was interrupted by catcalls, boos, cheers, and "We want Barry" from the galleries. Ultimately the amendment was defeated in a standing vote. Governor Romney, through Michigan delegate Richard C. Van Dusen, then offered an amendment repudiating "irresponsible individuals and extremist groups" but mentioning none by name. His amendment also lost in a standing vote. Next Senator Scott proposed an amendment intended to strengthen the civil rights section of the platform with numerous specific recommendations; in a roll call vote, the amendment was defeated, 897–409. Another Scott amendment, affirming the principle of exclusive presidential control over the use of nuclear weapons, lost in a standing vote. A second amendment on civil rights, again sponsored by Governor Romney through delegate Van Dusen and calling simply for elimination of "discrimination on the basis of race, religion, color, or national origin in education, housing, employment opportunities and access to public accommodations," was defeated in a voice vote. The platform as approved by the committee was then adopted by the convention in a voice vote, and the convention adjourned at 12:36 A.M. Pacific time—as much as three hours later in the rest of the country.

Presidential Nomination

The presidential nominating session of the convention began in the afternoon and lasted through the evening. Seven names were offered for the presidency: Goldwater, Rockefeller, Scranton, Romney, Smith, Fong, and Judd. Senator Dirksen nominated "the grandson of a peddler," Goldwater, whom he called a man of courage, conscience, and "the right vision." His speech was followed by a thunderous ovation and a demonstration lasting more than half an hour. Rockefeller was nominated by Senator Kenneth B. Keating of New York, who set off a demonstration nearly as lengthy as the one for Goldwater. Favorite son Fong was nominated by state senator Toshio Ansai of Hawaii. Senator George D. Aiken of Vermont nominated his New England neighbor, Margaret Chase Smith, saying that if she were president the government would be "headed by the best qualified person you ever voted for." In a more somber vein, Johns Hopkins University president Milton S. Eisenhower, brother of the former President, punctuated his speech nominating Scranton with phrases like the "endless struggle for universal freedom" and "these perilous days" and noted that "the fate of the Whig Party a hundred years ago testifies to the futility of opposing only for the sake for opposing." Michigan Congressman Gerald R. Ford nominated "Michigan's leading citizen," Romney; Minnesota state chairman Robert A. Forsythe nominated Judd. Professor J. Duane Squires of New Hampshire nominated Lodge, but immediately thereafter the convention chairman read a message from the ambassador requesting that his name be withdrawn and adding that he was supporting Scranton.

By the time of the presidential roll call vote, its outcome was not in doubt. Goldwater achieved the necessary majority with the votes of South Carolina. The totals before states began switching votes were: Goldwater, 883; Scranton, 214; Rockefeller, 114; Romney, 41; Smith, 27; Judd, 22; Fong, 5; Lodge, 2. Scranton moved that the nomination be made unanimous, and Romney seconded his motion; it was approved in a voice vote with some audible nays.

Vice-Presidential Choice

The intention of the Goldwater faction of the party to cede little to its erstwhile opponents was made manifest at the last convention session. William E. Miller, Goldwater's choice, a northeastern Catholic and an intrepid debater, was selected as the vice-presidential nominee and ratified in a vote that was unanimous except for three abstentions. Charles H. Percy, the GOP candidate for governor of Illinois, introduced Miller in a speech that was longer than Miller's acceptance of the nomination. Goldwater was introduced by Richard Nixon, who made an urgent plea for party unity. "Before this convention we were Goldwater Republicans, Rockefeller Republicans, Scranton Republicans, Lodge Republicans, but now that this convention has met and made its decision, we are Republicans, period, working for Barry Goldwater for President of the United States."

Goldwater, however, emphasized not unity but "the cause of Republicanism": freedom. He drew cheers and applause from the crowd in the hall but just the reverse from "moderate" Republicans by saying:

Today . . . the task of preserving and enlarging freedom at home and of safeguarding it from the forces of tyranny abroad is great enough to challenge all our resources and to refire all our strength. Anyone who joins us in all sincerity, we welcome. Those who do not care for our cause, we don't expect to enter our ranks in any case. And let our Republicanism, so focused and so dedicated, not be made fuzzy and futile by unthinking and stupid labels.

I would remind you that extremism in the defense of liberty is no vice. And let me remind you also that moderation in the pursuit of justice is no virtue.

THE DEMOCRATIC CONTEST

"Let us continue," Lyndon Johnson urged Congress shortly after his predecessor's assassination; and throughout 1964 he carried on at an increasingly accelerated pace. To the great popular and political support that he had for essentially emotional reasons he added his own bargaining skills to produce a series of legislative triumphs, including passage of Kennedy's civil rights and tax bills and an Economic Opportunity Act to realize the dead President's idea for an antipoverty program. These successes in turn augmented his prestige and popularity. Only a monumental disaster could have precluded his nomination as his party's presidential candidate in 1964; and the Democratic convention in all major respects was what he chose to make it.

The one sour note for Johnson came in the primaries. His sponsorship of civil rights measures had provoked the protest candidacy of Alabama's Governor George C. Wallace, a last-ditch segregationist who had done all he could to prevent racial integration of the schools in his state. There were write-in campaigns for Wallace in several Democratic primaries in 1964. He did best where his name was actually on the ballot —in Indiana, where he received 29.8 percent of the vote running against Governor Matthew E. Welsh, President Johnson's stand-in; in Wisconsin, where he won 33.8 percent against Governor John B. Reynolds; and in Maryland, where he got 42.8 percent of the vote against another substitute for the President, Senator Daniel B. Brewster. But Wallace realized that he could make no real headway in his own party in 1964. He toyed briefly with the idea of an independent candidacy and then rejected that as well. Between the Republican and the Democratic conventions he dropped out of the race.

Meanwhile, as planning for the convention began, the Democratic National Committee in January 1964 approved a new plan for apportioning delegate votes among the states. The system used in 1960 had awarded nearly all the votes in proportion to a state's representation in Congress. The new plan served to reward the states, particularly the most populous states, that had supported the Kennedy-Johnson ticket. Its formula apportioned votes to the states as follows: 3 votes for each electoral vote (that is, for each U.S. senator and congressman); 1 additional vote for every 100,000 popular votes or major fraction thereof cast for the national Democratic ticket in 1960; 10 bonus votes for each state carried by that ticket; and a personal vote for each member of the Democratic National Committee. Every state was assured of as many votes and delegates as it had had at the 1960 convention. In addition, the District of Columbia was awarded 16 votes, Puerto Rico, 8, the Canal Zone and the Virgin Islands, 5 each, and Guam, 3 (Guam was being granted representation for the first time at a Democratic national convention). In all, the new apportionment formula served to increase the number of Democratic convention votes from 1,521 in 1960 to 2,316 in 1964—a 52 percent increase. Each delegation was also allotted as many alternates as delegates, less its 2 personal votes for members of the national committee. This brought the total number of official convention participants to well over 5,000 people.

Atlantic City, New Jersey,
August 24, 25, 26, 27, 1964

The celebration of Lyndon Johnson's presidency began with an efficient opening session. In voice votes, the temporary rules and officers, the permanent convention rules, and the credentials committee report minus one section were readily approved. The outstanding credentials issue concerned Mississippi, and it proved to be the one really lively dispute of an otherwise routine convention. There was considerable political gossip about the identity of the vice-presidential nominee; Minnesota Senator Hubert H. Humphrey was the heavy favorite.

Mississippi Credentials

The Mississippi seating dispute dominated the second day of the convention, overshadowing approval of a party platform that was Lyndon Johnson's own. In accordance with its own rules and state law, the regular Mississippi state party had selected an all-white delegation. The integrated Mississippi Freedom Democrats sent another full delegation to challenge it. Their counsel, Joseph L. Rauh, Jr., said to the credentials committee: "I will tell you a tale of terror"; and he did. A national television audience heard Fannie Lou Hamer, a sharecropper's wife, describe the physical violence and economic reprisals suffered by her and other blacks when they sought to register, let alone vote, in Mississippi. The Freedom Democrats also pointed out that the Mississippi regulars had not been loyal to the national party in the past, running unpledged electors in 1960 who voted against the Kennedy-Johnson ticket. Yet the regular delegation had been selected without violating any existing national party rule. The law was on their side; but the Freedom Democrats had the moral case and probably national political advantage as well.

Lyndon Johnson delegated to Hubert Humphrey the masterminding of a settlement: the Mississippi regulars would be seated provided they signed a pledge to support the national ticket and made an effort to get their state's presidential electors to vote for it; a new national party rule prohibiting discrimination would be enforced in 1968; a special Democratic National Committee panel would be established to monitor it; two of the Freedom Democrats, Dr. Aaron Henry and the Reverend Edward King, would be seated in 1964 as "delegates-at-large to the whole convention"; and the remaining Freedom Democrats would be treated as honored guests. The Freedom Democrats formally rejected the offer; all but four of the regulars refused to sign the oath and walked out of the convention; but the convention itself ratified the compromise in a voice vote.

Earlier, the credentials committee had resolved a challenge to the loyalty of the regular delegation from Alabama—a state where six of the presidential electors had voted against Kennedy in 1960 and an entire slate of "unpledged" (anti-Johnson) electors had been chosen in the 1964 primary—by requiring its delegates to sign a personal loyalty oath before they were seated. The convention had adopted that recommendation at its first session. Eleven of the Alabamians signed the oath; the others left the convention.

With the credentials problem solved, the convention moved rapidly through the necessary business required to rally behind the President. Like all the other motions at this convention, the platform committee report—which specifically condemned the extremism of the Communist party, the John Birch Society, and the Ku Klux Klan —was adopted by voice vote.

Nominations

On the third day came the nominations. Johnson's nominating speech was made by Governor John B. Connally of Texas, who had become nationally known when he was wounded by President Kennedy's assassin.

After he had been officially chosen by acclamation, Johnson appeared before the convention and announced what he had already told reporters—that his preference for a running mate was Hubert Humphrey. The President had weighed the vice-presidential matter almost from the moment he assumed office. Seeking to be President in his own right, he had rejected the politically most logical choice, John Kennedy's brother Robert, the attorney general. He did so in a public announcement on July 30, nearly a month before the convention. He said that he had "reached the conclusion that it would be inadvisable for me to recommend to the convention any member of my Cabinet or any of those who meet regularly with the Cabinet"—meaning by the latter United Nations Ambassador Adlai E. Stevenson and Peace Corps/Office of Economic Opportunity director R. Sargent Shriver, a Kennedy brother-in-law. The mass elimination led Robert Kennedy to quip: "I'm sorry I took so many nice fellows over the side with me." After a time it was evident that Johnson's consideration had narrowed to the two Minnesota senators, Humphrey and Eugene J. McCarthy.

By the day of the nomination McCarthy realized that the choice of Humphrey had in effect been made, and he released to the press a telegram to the President removing his name from consideration. Johnson tried to maintain the suspense by calling Humphrey to the White House along with Connecticut's Senator Thomas J. Dodd; but it was Humphrey who was offered the job, with the specific understanding that he must be completely loyal to Johnson. At the convention, Humphrey was nominated by McCarthy. After an unsuccessful attempt by an Alabama delegate to nominate Governor Carl E. Sanders of Georgia, who withdrew his name, Humphrey's nomination was made unanimous by voice vote.

The final day of the convention was marked by a great show of affection for both Johnson and the Kennedys. In the afternoon, Jacqueline Kennedy, the President's widow, greeted several thousand delegates, alternates, and others at a reception sponsored by Undersecretary of State W. Averell Harriman. In the evening, the convention saw a film about President Johnson, "The Road to Leadership." It then heard a tribute to President Kennedy (postponed from the first day lest it spark a movement to draft Robert Kennedy for vice-president). Met with a tremendous ovation, the attorney general introduced a film about his brother's presidency entitled "A Thousand Days." Many wept.

Hubert Humphrey gave a rousing acceptance speech in which he referred to Goldwater as "the temporary spokesman of the Republican party" who was "not only out of tune with the great majority of his countrymen" but also "out of step with his own party." The convention crowd cheered as he ticked off a list of major bills for which most Senate Democrats and Republicans had voted, "but not Senator Goldwater!"

Johnson in accepting his nomination called for a broad popular mandate "not to preside over a finished program, not just to keep things going [but] . . . to begin." He said: "The needs of all cannot be met by a business party, or a labor party; not by a war party or a peace party; not by a Southern party or a Northern party. Our deeds will meet our needs only if we are served by a party which serves all our people." He urged his audience to join him in an effort "to build a great society" that would give "every American the fullest life which he can hope for."

Presidential election, November 3, 1964

LYNDON B. JOHNSON (D): popular vote, 43,129,484; electoral vote, 486
BARRY M. GOLDWATER (R): popular vote, 27,178,188; electoral vote, 52

1968

THE VOLATILITY OF POLITICS was never better illustrated than in 1968. First came the reversal of Lyndon B. Johnson's fortunes after 1964. Elected by the greatest popular margin of any president up to that time, Johnson left the White House four years later the victim of what was called "the breaking of the president."

The chipping away of Johnson's huge "consensus" initially took the political form of two separate movements—one led by former Governor George C. Wallace of Alabama and one headed by Senator Eugene J. McCarthy of Minnesota. Stressing quite different issues, each considered himself the candidate of people whose interests were being ignored.

Increasing U.S. engagement in the Vietnam war had met growing resistance, particularly among young people (potential soldiers), intellectuals, and advocates of more government spending for domestic social welfare programs than for weapons. Student demonstrations against the war became increasingly virulent. Some rejected electoral politics for the politics of the streets. Others took a more conventional approach; a group led by the liberal activist Allard K. Lowenstein sought a "peace" candidate to run against the President in the Democratic primaries. After their overtures had been rejected by several prominent "doves" on the war, including Senators Robert F. Kennedy of New York and George S. McGovern of South Dakota, they were able to persuade McCarthy to run in New Hampshire. While Johnson's name was not on the ballot, a vigorous write-in campaign was carried on for him with the help of nearly all leading New Hampshire Democrats, including Governor John W.

King and Senator Thomas J. McIntyre. Thousands of college students campaigned for McCarthy. In the end, Johnson won 50 percent of the Democratic vote, but McCarthy's showing of 42 percent was regarded as reflecting a powerful protest against the President's Vietnam policy, the one issue McCarthy had stressed. (New Hampshire was a traditionally conservative state, "hawkish" on the war. Later surveys showed that, while McCarthy voters were repudiating Johnson, more did so from the "hawk" than from the "dove" perspective.) Four days after the primary, Robert Kennedy announced that he would be a candidate for president; two weeks later, Lyndon Johnson announced that he would not.

Meanwhile, George Wallace was attacking the administration on its right flank. Although he had made his national political name as a segregationist, Wallace insisted in 1968 that his principal concern was "law and order," not racial integration. The phrase struck a responsive chord in many alarmed by disorders on college campuses and upheavals in black slums, beginning with the Watts, California, riot of 1965. Wallace said that, whereas there was not "a dime's worth of difference" between the Republicans and the Democrats, he and his new American Independent party (AIP) stood for "the little man" against unwarranted intrusions of "anarchists"—and of the federal government. With only a remote chance of winning the presidential election, Wallace aimed at carrying the electoral votes of enough states, principally in the South, to gain the balance of power in the electoral college. The Wallace electors signed affadavits pledging to support Wallace "or whomsoever he may direct"—

whichever major party candidate would concede the most to Wallace. Wallace drew large crowds that lustily cheered his familiar assertions that he was "sick and tired" of the "pointy-headed bureaucrats" in Washington telling him "when to get up in the morning and when to go to bed at night," and that if a nonviolent demonstrator lay down in front of his car, "that would be the last thing he would ever lay down in front of."

THE REPUBLICAN CONTEST

The leading early contender for the presidential nomination was Governor George W. Romney of Michigan, who had been re-elected in 1964 (despite an anti-Goldwater landslide in his state) and 1966, who led Lyndon Johnson in trial heats from late 1966 through the spring of 1967, and who was the choice of Nelson A. Rockefeller and other Republican governors. But disaster came when Romney told a television interviewer that he had undergone "brainwashing" by generals and diplomats in Vietnam. The press pounced on the phrase; the administration defended its generals and diplomats; and Romney was unable to take back the words that had made him appear incompetent. Private polls in New Hampshire told him he had no chance. On the last day of February 1968, he dropped out of the race for president.

That left the field to others. Richard M. Nixon had rebounded from his earlier defeats to campaign widely for Republican candidates in 1966 and serve as the party's spokesman in an election-eve telecast. In 1968, he was the consistent front-runner among Republicans polled about their presidential preferences. Apparently with little stomach for another contest with Nixon, Nelson Rockefeller at first said he would not run but finally moved into the race when it was clear that Romney was out of it. At the opposite end of the party spectrum was California's governor, Ronald Reagan, elected in 1966 with a plurality of

nearly a million votes. Initially shaken by a morals scandal in his administration, Reagan did not actively seek the presidential nomination, but by the spring of 1968 he had a staff that was quietly seeking convention delegate commitments. Former Governor of Minnesota Harold E. Stassen announced his candidacy in November 1967 but generated little support.

Nixon contested every presidential primary without a favorite-son candidate and won all in which his name was on the ballot. Rockefeller won a narrow write-in victory in Massachusetts over Governor John A. Volpe. A Reagan slate carried California. The day before the national convention opened, a United Press International delegate poll indicated that Nixon had 656 of the 667 votes needed to win the presidential nomination on the first ballot.

Miami Beach, Florida,
August 5, 6, 7, 8, 1968

A routine morning business session opened the convention. The major event of the day was not part of the formal program: Governor Reagan's announcement that he was a candidate for president. Some delegate-counters found Reagan gains, but Barry Goldwater told CBS News that he thought Nixon had the nomination "in the bag."

The evening convention session featured several major speakers. Speaking by telephone from Walter Reed Hospital, where he was recovering from a heart attack, former President Eisenhower stressed the need to resist "expansionist tyranny" abroad; he received cheers to the tune of "The Caissons Go Rolling Along" played by the orchestra. The temporary convention chairman, Senator Edward W. Brooke from Massachusetts, called for rejection of racial separatism by both blacks and whites. Barry Goldwater, a candidate for reelection to the Senate, was met with a standing ovation and chants of "We want Barry!" Saying "We are not here to bemoan the past," Goldwater emphasized that although Republicanism was based on faith in freedom for individual initiative this did not mean racial hatred, which he called "wrong, dead wrong . . . ugly . . . vicious . . . sick . . . warped, and wrong, wrong, wrong." Delivering the keynote speech, Governor Daniel J. Evans of Washington termed the United States "an uneasy nation" that was "frustrated by a war on the mainland of Asia" and "even more burdened . . . by the crisis of the main streets of America."

At the third session the convention disposed of all its major business except for the nominations. Although the reports of the convention committees on credentials, rules, permanent organization, and resolutions were approved by voice votes with little or no open opposition, the show of unity in several instances concealed considerable dissent.

Credentials

The credentials report involved a controversial decision to seat Iowa Representative H. R. Gross as a delegate-at-large rather than Joy Rohm, head of the Iowa Republican Workshop, who had originally been appointed and then removed—she said, by improper procedures—by the state convention. The credentials committee had also refused on procedural grounds to entertain any motion from District of Columbia committee member Barrington D. Parker about the absence of blacks from the Florida and Louisiana delegations. The losers in these contests felt that party conservatives had railroaded the decisions through the committee.

Rules

The rules committee (and the convention) approved a new rule specifically forbidding discrimination in delegate selection on grounds of race, religion, color, or national origin. The panel also disapproved a Republican National Committee recommendation that each of its members be automatically made delegates-at-large to subsequent national conventions: the rules group did agree, however, to make all state chairmen members of the national com-

mittee. The new Republican party in Guam was given two national committee seats and three delegates at the 1972 convention. Another proposed rules change, which would have added a convention seat for each Republican congressman, was voted down in committee.

Additional rules aimed at a more orderly and efficient convention had been recommended by the Committee on Convention Reforms established at former President Eisenhower's behest. Those rules adopted by the convention included limiting speeches for presidential and vice-presidential candidates to twenty-five and twenty minutes, respectively; giving specific authority to the national committee to govern the party between conventions; changing the deadlines for filing credentials challenges; and providing mandatory appointment of a pre-convention rules committee.

The Platform

As in 1960, Richard Nixon joined forces with Nelson Rockefeller to get a platform that party conservatives considered more "liberal" than they would have liked. The 1968 platform was at least several steps away from, if not a reversal of, the 1964 document, particularly in its approach toward Soviet, Chinese, and Vietnamese communism. Where the 1964 platform had talked of inevitable conflict between "freedom" and "slavery," the 1968 version spoke of a negotiated settlement in Vietnam and nonstrategic trade with Eastern Europe. The Vietnam plank, which called for giving the South Vietnamese principal responsibility for their own defense, replaced a much more hawkish draft prepared by the foreign policy and national security subcommittee. In the domestic sector, the 1968 platform pledged "a peaceful, reunified America" that would include better-run government and efforts at all public levels and in the private sector to provide jobs, housing, and urban and rural redevelopment. The platform said flatly: *"We will not tolerate violence!"*

Any dissent over the report was smoothed

over during its presentation. The committee chairman—the rococo Senate minority leader, Everett M. Dirksen of Illinois—took issue with the view of "cerebrating pessimists" about America. "No, fellow citizens," Dirksen said, "we're not sick. We're not even indisposed. We're just mismanaged." George Romney was recognized to say that he regretted the absence of a pledge to reform the collective bargaining laws, but "it's unwise to open up the platform to amendments at this time." With no amendments, the report was adopted.

The Presidential Nomination

The convention's presidential nominating session provided few surprises but a plethora of speeches; it lasted nine hours. Twelve names were put forward. Former United States Treasurer Ivy Baker Priest Stevens nominated Ronald Reagan, whom she termed "the man to lead us out of the storms and upward to the stars." Governor Walter J. Hickel of Alaska was nominated by that state's congressman, Howard W. Pollock, but withdrew in favor of Nixon. An Arkansas delegate nominated the state's governor, Winthrop Rockefeller (brother of Nelson). Senator Robert P. Griffin of Michigan nominated Governor Romney, who, he said, "epitomizes . . . the American ideal." Wyoming Senator Clifford P. Hansen offered the name of his colleague, Senator Frank Carlson of Kansas. The Hawaii Republican chairman nominated Senator Hiram L. Fong as a favorite son. To roars of "We want Rocky!" Governor Raymond P. Shafer of Pennsylvania put in nomination "the man for our time," Nelson Rockefeller. Governor Spiro T. Agnew of Maryland nominated Nixon, "a man whose time has come," and set off a twenty-five-minute demonstration. J. Robert Stassen, a Minnesota delegate, nominated his uncle Harold. Former Treasury Secretary C. Douglas Dillon nominated Senator Clifford P. Case of New Jersey. The Ohio favorite son, Governor James A. Rhodes, was recommended by the chancellor of the State Board of Regents. Representative Albert W. Watson of South Carolina offered the name of Senator J. Strom Thurmond, who withdrew in favor of "that world statesman and that great American, Richard M. Nixon."

Before the delegations began switching votes, Nixon had 692 votes, with 667 needed for nomination. Nelson Rockefeller, his nearest rival, had 277. The Nixon nomination was made unanimous in a voice vote.

The Vice-Presidential Choice

With Nixon's nomination a virtual certainty, there had been much speculation about the second place on the ticket. Even as the presidential balloting took place, messengers delivered notes from Nixon to party leaders, calling them to meet with him to discuss the vice-presidency. In all, four such meetings, including more than a hundred people, were held. The sessions yielded no obvious consensus choice. Nelson Rockefeller said he would not take the job, and he was not consulted; Ronald Reagan was unacceptable to leaders in northern industrial states. New York City's Mayor John V. Lindsay was anathema to conservatives. Nixon himself reportedly wanted California's lieutenant governor, Robert H. Finch, but he was unwilling to run. The two most widely acceptable men, John Volpe and Spiro Agnew, were both governors. Nixon chose Agnew.

As the candidate himself disarmingly pointed out at a news conference, "The name of Spiro Agnew is not a household name." Elected to the statehouse at Annapolis in 1966, Agnew's highest elective office before that had been as county executive of Baltimore County. He was the first Marylander to run for national office since Joshua T. Levering was the presidential candidate of the Prohibition party in 1896. Agnew's wide acceptability was based not only on his position as a border state governor but also on the fact that, while elected as a "liberal" on race relations, he had come down hard in 1968 on Baltimore's black leaders after disturbances in the city's Negro slums.

Opposition to Agnew developed among black Republicans and many GOP liberals. As an alternative, they sought to nominate John Lindsay, but the mayor chose to second Agnew's nomination. The anti-Agnew forces then turned to George Romney. Agnew was nominated by Maryland Congressman Rogers C. B. Morton, who said Agnew "has governed superbly at a level of government closest to the people" and "will help America reach for a new greatness." Agnew received 1,119 votes to Romney's 186 and a scattering for others who had not been formally nominated. Romney moved that the nomination be made unanimous, and the convention complied.

Agnew began his acceptance speech by saying: "I stand here with a deep sense of the improbability of the moment." Of his convictions, he said that "racial discrimination, unfair and unequal education and unequal job opportunities must be eliminated no matter whom that displeases." He added: "And I believe quite compatibly the observation that anarchy, rioting, or even civil disobedience has no constructive purpose in a constitutional republic."

Accepting the presidential nomination, Nixon recalled his selection sixteen years before as Eisenhower's running mate and saluted the former President, who had suffered another heart attack after his speech to the convention earlier in the week. Nixon told his audience: "Let's win this one for Ike!" He pledged "to bring an honorable end to the war in Vietnam" and "a policy to prevent more Vietnams." He addressed "the leaders of the communist world," saying, "After an era of confrontation, the time has come for an era of negotiation." On the law-and-order issue, he said that "the first civil right of every American is to be free from domestic violence." He also called for building "bridges to human dignity across that gulf that separates black America from white America." He spoke of his own success in life and those who had aided him along the way and concluded: "You can see why I believe so

deeply in the American dream. For most of us the American Revolution has been won; the American dream has come true. And what I ask you to do tonight is to help me make that dream come true for millions to whom it's an impossible dream today."

THE DEMOCRATIC CONTEST

With President Johnson out of the race, there remained three major candidates: McCarthy, Kennedy, and the administration's heir apparent, Vice-President Hubert H. Humphrey. Humphrey delayed the announcement of his candidacy until after the filing dates for all the presidential primaries; this left McCarthy and Kennedy to fight each other while the Humphrey forces lined up delegates elsewhere. Johnson endorsed no one.

Unsurprisingly, the primaries were not conclusive. McCarthy won in Wisconsin, where Johnson's was the only other name on the ballot, and in Pennsylvania and Massachusetts, where McCarthy was the sole Democratic candidate listed. Then Kennedy captured Indiana, defeating the administration's stand-in, Governor Roger D. Branigin, and a badly trailing McCarthy. In the District of Columbia a Kennedy delegate slate (originally a Kennedy-McCarthy fusion slate that the McCarthy group subsequently disavowed) beat a pro-Humphrey slate. In Nebraska Kennedy roundly defeated McCarthy and Johnson. A favorite-son slate pledged to Senator George A. Smathers won over a McCarthy slate and a "no preference" slate in Florida. McCarthy came back in Oregon to triumph over Kennedy and Johnson. In the most important prize strategically, the winner-take-all California primary, the Kennedy slate narrowly beat a McCarthy slate and a no-preference slate. Then, in his hour of triumph Kennedy was assassinated. The ensuing shock eclipsed the other two primaries held the same day and the final one a week later. In them, Kennedy's slate beat Johnson's and McCarthy's in South Dakota, and McCarthy finished first in all write-in contests in New Jersey and Illinois. On August 10, George McGovern entered the presidential race, primarily as the candidate of Kennedy supporters who preferred the South Dakotan to McCarthy or Humphrey.

By the time the national convention opened, Humphrey was the clear frontrunner. Most party leaders were on his side; he led McCarthy in the polls; and he was far ahead in delegates. On the day before the convention, United Press International reported that Humphrey had 1,098 of the 1,311 votes needed for a first-ballot nomination, with an additional 516 votes committed to favorite sons, many of whom preferred Humphrey. The only real threat was the rumor of a convention draft of Robert Kennedy's brother, Senator Edward M. Kennedy of Massachusetts.

Chicago, Illinois, August 26, 27, 28, 29, 1968

In his welcoming address, Richard J. Daley asserted that "as long as I am mayor of this town, there will be law and order in Chicago." Several thousand antiwar demonstrators had arrived for the convention, and Chicago's 11,900 police were supplemented by 7,500 Army regulars, 7,500 Illinois National Guardsmen, and 1,000 FBI and Secret Service agents. Yet Daley distinguished between "the extremists on the left and the right who seek to destroy instead of to build" and "those who come conscientiously because they know at this political gathering there is hope and opportunity."

Democratic National Chairman John M. Bailey told the delegates that 94 percent of the 1964 Democratic platform had been passed into law, "a new record for any party." He added that "this party is America."

Adopting a different tone, keynote speaker Daniel K. Inouye, senator from Hawaii, said: "I do not view this occasion as one for flamboyance." He cited student rebellions, increased crime, urban riots, and political assassinations but disputed the contention that the Vietnam war was responsible for "all our ills and agonies."

Inouye, who lost an arm fighting in World War II, said, "I believe that all wars are immoral," but suggested that until evil men "renounced the use of force" it would have to be resisted in kind.

Temporary Rules

The first real business was adoption of the temporary rules. The committee report recommended establishment of a party commission to codify the Democratic convention rules, which had never existed in written form. Also included in the committee report was a ban on the unit rule, under which the votes of all members of a delegation were cast as the majority preferred. A Texas delegate presented a minority report suggesting that the unit rule be abandoned beginning with the 1972 rather than the 1968 convention. His report, and the unit rule, were rejected by voice vote.

Next, California Assembly Speaker Jesse M. Unruh moved that votes on the record seventeen credentials contests be postponed until the following session, as originally scheduled. The Unruh motion was defeated, 1,691½–832. The committee report was approved by voice vote.

Credentials Disputes

By the time Senator Inouye introduced the credentials committee chairman, Governor Richard J. Hughes of New Jersey, it was after 11 P.M. Hughes began with Mississippi, where the Loyal Democrats, descendants of the 1964 Freedom Democrats, were challenging the regular state delegation on grounds that blacks had been systematically excluded from participation in delegate selection. The Equal Rights Committee of the Democratic National Committee had supported their contention; and presidential candidates Humphrey, McCarthy, and McGovern had urged that the loyalists be seated. In a voice vote, the convention complied. It also voted similarly to accept the credentials committee's recommendations that the regular Washington, Pennsylvania, Minnesota, and Connecticut delegations be seated, despite procedural challenges from the McCarthy forces. (None of these challenges obtained sufficient support in the credentials committee to cause a minority report to be written.)

Ironically, the first major credentials contest came in Lyndon Johnson's Texas. The challengers argued that imposition of the unit rule at the state and local level had served to exclude Negroes and Mexican-Americans from full participation in delegate selection. The spokesman for the regulars responded, "If you boil down every allegation submitted by the challengers . . . it amounts to no more than an allegation that . . . they got beat badly, they are unhappy about it, and they want to complain." The challengers' minority report was rejected, 1,368–955.

For Georgia, the credentials committee recommended that the convention divide the votes equally between the state party regulars and the Loyal National Democrats, the challenging group led by black state representative Julian Bond. The latter charged that blacks had been systematically discriminated against in delegate selection; the delegates had been picked by Governor Lester G. Maddox and the state party's executive committee chairman, James H. Gray, both of whom had worked for Barry Goldwater in 1964. Under the committee compromise, no Georgia delegate was to be seated without signing a pledge that he or she was a bona fide Democrat who would not support any presidential ticket in 1968 other than that of the Democratic National Convention and who would "take all necessary steps" to get that ticket on the Georgia ballot in November. There was a minority report on behalf of the Bond group, sponsored by borough president Herman Badillo of the Bronx; it called for throwing out the regulars and replacing them with the Loyal National Democrats. The regulars responded with their own minority report, calling for just the reverse. Badillo's minority report was rejected, 1,413–1,041½. Because of the hour—2:45 A.M.—the session adjourned.

That evening, the regulars' minority report was defeated and the credentials committee report approved in voice votes. James Gray walked out of the convention saying that he would not support its nominees, whoever they were. Some Georgia regulars attempted to take the state's standard from the convention floor; one was led away by a security guard, and when Dan Rather of CBS News tried to interview him, Rather was thrown to the ground and, he reported, kicked in the stomach by a guard.

The next credentials contest concerned Alabama, where there was a three-way split among the regulars, the integrated Alabama Independent Democratic party (AIDP), and the predominantly black National Democratic party of Alabama (NDPA). The AIDP had been formed expressly to run a slate of presidential electors loyal to the national party against George Wallace, whose slate of electors had won the right to use the party emblem in the state's Democratic primary. The credentials committee report recommended that the regulars be required to sign a loyalty pledge; those who refused would be replaced by loyal alternates or members of the AIDP delegation. In retaliation, Robert S. Vance, the state chairman, filed a challenge to all the McCarthy delegates at the convention, saying that *they* should be required to sign an oath pledging to support the party nominees. The convention rejected the Vance challenge in a voice vote. The NDPA, supported by the McCarthy forces, filed a minority report aimed at replacing the entire Alabama delegation with its own representatives; it lost, 801½–1,525. The committee report on Alabama was approved by voice vote.

The assembled delegates by voice vote rapidly disallowed a challenge in Wisconsin, where three McCarthy delegates had been accused of not being bona fide Democrats. Next came consideration of a minority report on North Carolina, which contended that blacks were underrepresented in that delegation because of "an overt attempt to exclude" them. In voice votes, the convention rejected the minority report and approved the committee recommendations. In two more swift decisions, the convention by voice vote approved the committee recommendation about challenges in Louisiana and Tennessee concerning the appropriate number of blacks in the delegations and related "fair representation" issues. At the committee's urging, the convention agreed in voice votes to seat the regular (Humphrey) delegates from Michigan and Indiana over McCarthy-camp protests of unfair procedures.

Although most procedural challenges were disallowed, the credentials committee recommended and the convention approved a broad study of the delegate selection process for the Democratic National Committee and the 1972 convention. Setting forth its purposes, credentials committee chairman Hughes said that the timeliness of delegate selection, the extent of popular participation, and the unit rule would all be examined. His resolution, adopted by the convention along with the full committee report, provided specific language to be added to the 1972 convention call expressing the "understanding" that the state parties would ensure that "all Democrats . . . will have meaningful and timely opportunities to participate fully in the election or selection" of delegates and alternates.

Convention Rules

What would ordinarily have been a routine motion by the chairman of the rules committee to make the temporary rules of the convention its permanent rules as well resulted in one of the major votes of the 1968 convention. A minority report was filed by delegate Joseph S. Crangle of New York to abolish the unit rule in every stage of the 1972 delegate selection process and to require that "all feasible efforts have been made to assure that delegates are elected through party primary, convention, or committee procedures open to public participation within the calendar year of the national convention." Rules committee chairman Samuel H. Shapiro, the governor

of Illinois, said that the idea of abolishing the unit rule altogether should be referred to the study committee that would report to the 1972 convention. But the minority report was approved, 1,350–1,206.

A second minority report on rules, sponsored by James B. Hunt, Jr., of North Carolina, called for addition of each Democratic state chairman and each state's Young Democrats president to the national committee membership. It lost, 1,349¼–1,125¾.

The Platform

Bad omens marked the start of platform deliberations. The hour was late (after midnight); the delegates were restless; rumors about Edward Kennedy's candidacy abounded; there were reports of clashes between antiwar demonstrators and the Chicago police. Platform committee chairman Hale Boggs, congressman from Louisiana and House majority whip, began the debate. At 1:04 A.M. the Wisconsin delegation began waving its standard, seeking recognition; others did likewise. When Boggs called on California Congressman Phillip Burton to present the minority report on Vietnam, he was drowned out by commotion. Permanent chairman Carl Albert, congressman from Oklahoma and House majority leader, recognized Donald O. Peterson, chairman of the Wisconsin delegation, who moved adjournment until 4:00 that afternoon because "I think every delegate in this hall wants to go home and go to bed." Albert replied that adjournment was "not a recognizable motion." There were loud boos, clapping in unison, and chants of "Let's go home." Albert recognized Mayor Daley, who threatened to clear the balconies, implying that the disorder was not coming from the delegates. More loud boos. Unable to restore order, Albert again recognized Daley, who moved adjournment until noon; the delegates readily agreed.

Tempers had cooled by the following session. Only after putative engineers of party unity had failed to write a compromise statement acceptable to the administration, Humphrey, and the party doves did the platform debate take place. The doves wanted an immediate end to the bombing of North Vietnam and U.S. offensive search-and-destroy missions, plus a negotiated withdrawal of enemy troops and a negotiated coalition government that would include the Communists. The platform committee statement favored a bombing halt only if it "would not endanger the lives of our troops in the field"; did not recommend an end to search-and-destroy missions; called for troop withdrawal after the war; and endorsed internationally supervised free elections in South Vietnam. The platform committee plank sought "an honorable and lasting settlement which respects the rights of all the people of Vietnam"; the minority plank sought "a swift conclusion" to the war to save lives and resources.

The floor debate on Vietnam juxtaposed the pros and cons. Speaking for the committee report, Senator Edmund S. Muskie of Maine called the difference between the two positions "negligible," but termed the committee position more prudent because it protected U.S. troops, safeguarded free elections, and allowed the South Vietnamese to vote to decide their own destiny. Congressman Phillip Burton deplored the waste of the war and what he termed the increasing use of violence to solve human problems. Senator Gale W. McGee of Wyoming responded that if South Vietnam lost its struggle there would be dire consequences from Laos to Korea "and all that that portends." New York senatorial candidate Paul O'Dwyer urged that the delegates respond to the voters in the presidential primaries who, he said, had repudiated the war. Reversing that theory, Missouri Governor Warren E. Hearnes addressed himself to the voters who were following the debate by radio or television and told them that the minority report would "jeopardize the lives of the servicemen in Vietnam." Kenneth P. O'Donnell, a Massachusetts delegate, invoked his association with the Kennedys and said that the domestic programs of the

platform could not be adopted while the United States continued "a foreign adventure . . . that is costing $30 billion a year." Geri Joseph, Democratic national committeewoman from Minnesota, said that only the majority report would safeguard the right of self-determination for the South Vietnamese. Ohio senatorial nominee John J. Gilligan, who had labored long and unsuccessfully for a compromise plank, pointed out the ironies of the war ("We went to Vietnam to help, but now we remain to destroy") and said that only the Democratic party could reorder national priorities to spend U.S. resources on domestic needs instead of Vietnam.

Compared to the shouting over adjournment earlier, the initial audience response to the Vietnam debate was subdued; but as the speeches continued, passions emerged. There were prolonged cheers when former Senator Pierre Salinger of California said that if Robert Kennedy "were alive today he would be on this platform speaking for this minority plank." And Congressman Wayne L. Hays of Ohio got a loud mixed response for calling the antiwar demonstrators in Chicago "a minority who would substitute anarchism for ambition . . . beards for brains, license for liberty." Hays evidently set off a "stop the war" chant in the California delegation and the galleries; despite appeals for order, the chant continued sporadically; antiwar signs also appeared on the floor. Ultimately the minority Vietnam plank lost 1,041¼–1,567¾. The entire platform was then adopted by voice vote.

The Presidential Nomination

At the nominating session, Chairman Carl Albert read two telegrams, one from Lyndon Johnson and one from Edward Kennedy, each saying that he did not choose to be nominated for president. As the names were called of the five candidates who did choose to be nominated, violence erupted in downtown Chicago. Police and national guardsmen with nightsticks and rifle butts battled thousands of antiwar demonstrators, most of them young and many taunting the police. So much tear gas was used to disperse the crowd that it wafted its way into Hubert Humphrey's campaign suite. The news blackened the mood of the already surly convention.

Convention business continued inexorably. The North Carolina delegation nominated its "distinguished and beloved governor," Dan K. Moore. Quoting President Kennedy, who said that "those who would make peaceful revolution impossible make violent revolution inevitable," Governor Harold E. Hughes of Iowa recommended Eugene McCarthy, whom he called "an evangelist of reason." Great cheers greeted Mayor Joseph L. Alioto when he began by saying, "I came here from San Francisco to talk to you about Hubert H. Humphrey." He termed his candidate "the articulate exponent of the aspirations of the human heart," the champion of civil rights, the Peace Corps, Food for Peace, nuclear disarmament, and Medicare.

As Humphrey, McCarthy, and McGovern separately watched demonstrators and police outside the Conrad Hilton Hotel, television similarly shifted its attention. The National Broadcasting Company broke away from the podium to the violence. When the convention roll call reached Colorado, its chairman raised a point of information, asking, "Is there any rule under which Mayor Daley can be compelled to suspend the police state being perpetrated this minute?" Chairman Albert responded that the question was out of order during a roll call. When Connecticut's Senator Abraham A. Ribicoff made the next nomination, he said, almost casually, that "with George McGovern as president of the United States we wouldn't have to have gestapo tactics in the streets of Chicago." Mayor Daley leapt from his seat and shouted angrily at Ribicoff. The roll call for nominations continued. District of Columbia national committeeman Channing E. Phillips, the first black ever nominated for the presidency at a national convention, was recommended by D.C. delegate Philip M. Stern. When New Hampshire was

reached in the roll call, it moved that the convention be recessed in protest against the Chicago police; this was ignored. When Wisconsin was reached, its chairman said, "Most delegates to this convention do not know that thousands of young people are being beaten in the streets of Chicago." He requested a suspension of the rules to allow a two weeks' adjournment and relocation of the convention in a different city; he was summarily ruled out of order. Chairman Albert later said that motions to suspend the rules were out of order during a roll call.

When the results were announced, Humphrey had 1,761¾ votes, McCarthy, 601, McGovern 146½, Phillips 67½, and others 47¾. On the motion of an Illinois delegate, Humphrey's nomination was made unanimous. Chairman Albert did not ask for the nays on that motion, calling instead for the benediction.

The Vice-Presidential Choice

Edward M. Kennedy had declined to run, and Eugene McCarthy was uninterested. Among the names most seriously discussed by Humphrey and his advisers were Governor Richard J. Hughes of New Jersey, Senator Edmund S. Muskie of Maine, Senator Fred R. Harris of Oklahoma, and one off-beat possibility—Cyrus R. Vance, a former deputy defense secretary, who was negotiating with the North Vietnamese in Paris. Southerners were unwilling to accept Hughes; politicians tended to dismiss Vance; Harris at thirty-seven had slight national experience, almost none of it in foreign affairs. Muskie had brought about a Democratic renaissance in Republican Maine and was respected in the Senate, where he had served for ten years. And so, as the loquacious Humphrey put it: "I went for the quiet man."

The passions of earlier sessions also marked the one that nominated Muskie. It began with a filmed tribute to Robert Kennedy, introduced by a tape-recorded statement by his brother Edward. Greatly moved by the evocation of the second slain Kennedy, participants in the convention hall responded with a standing ovation lasting nearly twenty minutes and the singing of "The Battle Hymn of the Republic." Only a previously unscheduled tribute to Martin Luther King, Jr., assassinated civil rights leader, was able to restore decorum. Fred Harris nominated Muskie, whom he termed "an extraordinary man" and "the single most effective senator" in the field of intergovernmental relations. Wisconsin delegate Ted Warshafsky nominated Julian Bond: "It may be a symbolic nomination tonight but it may not be symbolic for years hence." At twenty-eight, Bond was too young to run for vice-president; he withdrew his name. After all the states had been called once, Muskie had 1,942½ votes (a majority), Bond 48½, others 26¾. Several states that had passed initially never got the customary second opportunity to cast their votes. Mayor Daley, who received 3½ votes in the Alabama delegation and thus drew mixed cheers and boos, successfully moved for suspension of the rules and a unanimous vote for Muskie.

With some order restored by a prayer for God's blessing on Humphrey, Muskie, and those who disagreed with them, the senator from Maine mounted the podium to give his acceptance speech. He relieved the tension a bit with a Down East joke about his mother, who told a reporter that she would vote for her son "if no one offers anyone better." He went on to make a plea for party and national unity based on neigh-borliness, tolerance of others, and "the self-discipline of free citizens in an enlightened and civilized society without which it cannot survive."

The extraordinarily difficult situation of Hubert Humphrey was reflected in his speech. He deplored both the "violence" and the "personal injuries" in Chicago. He quoted St. Francis of Assisi ("Where there is hatred, let me sow love") and added, "May America tonight resolve that never, never again shall we see what we have seen." He urged his audience to see the creative possibilities in national challenges and "frank, hard debate." He pointed out that "this convention has literally laid the foundations of a new Democratic party structure in America." He invoked the litany of great Democratic leaders, beginning with Franklin D. Roosevelt and continuing gamely through Lyndon Johnson. Humphrey continued: "President Johnson has accomplished more of the unfinished business of America than any of his modern predecessors. . . . I say 'Thank you, thank you, Mr. President.' " Humphrey called for "a new day" that would require peace in Vietnam, peace in the cities, and national unity. He said that as president he would "do everything within my power . . . to aid the negotiations and to bring a prompt end to this war" in Southeast Asia. He spoke graciously of McCarthy (who had refused to sit on the podium as Humphrey spoke, preferring to preserve his strategic options) and McGovern (who was there). Humphrey called for their help and that of the young.

Presidential election, November 5, 1968

RICHARD M. NIXON (R): popular vote, 31,785,480; electoral vote, 301
HUBERT H. HUMPHREY (D): popular vote, 31,275,166; electoral vote, 191
GEORGE C. WALLACE (AIP): popular vote, 9,906,473; electoral vote, 46
One Republican elector in North Carolina voted for Wallace in the electoral college.

1972

RICHARD M. NIXON'S most urgent objective after his narrow victory in 1968 was to broaden his political base. His Democratic opponents sought to reunite the party coalition that George C. Wallace had sundered. The effects of these attempted regroupings were mixed. Nixon succeeded in getting about three-quarters of his legislative program (much of it routine) through the Democratic Congress, but he lost major battles over the Supreme Court nominations of Clement F. Haynsworth, Jr., and G. Harrold Carswell, the effort to develop a supersonic transport plane, his government reorganization scheme, his welfare reform bill, and (initially) his proposal for sharing federal revenue with state and local governments. Despite vigorous campaigning by the President and Vice-President in the 1970 congressional elections, their party suffered a net loss. Although the Republicans picked up three Senate seats, they lost twelve in the House and eleven governorships.

THE DEMOCRATIC CONTEST

Yet the Democrats were divided. At least a score seriously considered a race for the presidency. Hubert H. Humphrey had come tantalizingly close to winning in 1968; only someone unacquainted with Humphrey could imagine that he would not try again. Edmund S. Muskie had enjoyed favorable national prominence in 1968 and served as the party's spokesman in a 1970 election-eve broadcast that was considered successful. Edward M. Kennedy was the candidate of many who had admired his brothers, but

his reputation was damaged by the accidental drowning of a young woman in the car that Kennedy was driving when it plunged into a tidal pond on Chappaquiddick Island, Massachusetts. In addition, there was the antiwar senator from South Dakota, George S. McGovern, who announced his candidacy in January 1971; George C. Wallace, who was again elected governor of Alabama in 1970; Mayor John V. Lindsay of New York City, who switched from the Republican party in August 1971; and Senators Henry M. Jackson of Washington, Birch E. Bayh of Indiana, Harold E. Hughes of Iowa, Fred R. Harris of Oklahoma, Vance Hartke of Indiana, and William Proxmire of Wisconsin, and Representatives Wilbur D. Mills of Arkansas, Shirley Chisholm of New York, William R. Anderson of Tennessee, and Patsy T. Mink of Hawaii. Others campaigning actively included former Senator Eugene J. McCarthy of Minnesota, former Governor of North Carolina Terry Sanford, Mayor of Los Angeles Sam Yorty, and Lieutenant Governor Lester G. Maddox of Georgia.

The strength of the candidates fluctuated dramatically between 1968 and 1972. According to the Harris poll, Nixon's popularity swung from its early crest (a 62 percent favorable score in June 1969) to a low of 47 percent favorable in November 1970 and a still lower 41 percent favorable in March 1971; it then climbed almost steadily to a 59 percent favorable rating by August 1972, the month of the Republican national convention. Except for his low period, Nixon consistently led all potential Democratic challengers in trial heat surveys. At the times of greatest Nixon vulnerability,

Muskie alone led in three-way races with George Wallace; and Muskie had pulled even again in the Harris poll of January 1972.

Initially, Humphrey, Muskie, and Kennedy were most popular with Democratic voters and county chairmen. None consistently led the others. During the primary season, however, George McGovern, first choice of only 3 percent of the Democratic voters in January 1972, came from behind in the Gallup poll to lead all other candidates as the first choice of 30 percent of Democratic voters. His understanding of the new party rules and his showing in the primaries brought him that far.

The McGovern-Fraser Commission

By authority of the 1968 convention, Democratic National Chairman Fred Harris in February 1969 appointed a Commission on Party Structure and Delegate Selection and a Commission on Rules. The latter panel, chaired by Michigan Representative James G. O'Hara, drafted the first rules ever written for Democratic convention procedure. The delegate-selection panel, headed first by George McGovern and subsequently by Representative Donald M. Fraser of Minnesota, had profound influence before the national convention.

The eighteen guidelines of the McGovern-Fraser Commission were approved in November 1969 and published in April 1970. McGovern resigned as chairman before announcing his presidential candidacy. In February 1971 the Democratic National Committee voted to include the guidelines in the official call to the national convention, thus making compliance a precondition for seating state delegations.

The guidelines established procedural safeguards designed to open up delegate selection to all interested Democrats. The guidelines *banned* proxy voting, the unit rule, mandatory assessments of national convention delegates, ex officio delegates, and the selection of more than 10 percent of any delegation by party committee. They *required* that the state parties limit each delegate's fees to a total of $10 and any peti-

tion signatures to 1 percent of the state's Democratic voters; hold all meetings in easily accessible public places on uniform dates; provide adequate public notice of all meetings involving delegate selection; add the national committee's antidiscrimination rules to their own; include minority group members, women, and the young in convention delegations "in reasonable relationship" to their share of the state's population; allow everyone eighteen or older to participate in party affairs; select alternates in the same way as delegates; carry out delegate selection during the calendar year of the convention; in convention states, choose at least 75 percent of the delegates at the congressional district level or below and apportion conventions on the bases of population and party voting; and establish full, public procedures for challenging delegate slates. The guidelines *recommended* eliminating all costs and fees in delegate selection, studying ways to ease financial strain on would-be delegates, removing all restrictive registration and voting procedures, providing easy access and frequent opportunity for non-Democrats to become party members, ending entirely the appointment of delegates, and providing fair representation for candidate factions.

For state and local leaders accustomed to wide discretion within their own fiefdoms, the guidelines were less than entirely welcome. But the commission staff explained how to comply and stated that noncompliance would mean exclusion from the 1972 convention. By July 10, forty-five delegations were in full compliance and the remainder in substantial compliance.

The Democratic Primaries

The guidelines unexpectedly brought many more presidential primaries. In 1968, fifteen states and the District of Columbia, accounting for 41 percent of the delegates, had held primaries; in 1972, twenty-two states and the District had primaries to select nearly two-thirds of the Democratic delegates. A primary was thought to ensure compliance with the guidelines without major change in other accustomed procedures. Also, some state leaders anticipated publicity and economic advantages for their states.

When the race officially began with the New Hampshire primary March 7, it was widely assumed that Edmund Muskie would handily win the nomination and very possibly the general election. But while Muskie captured 46.4 percent of the New Hampshire vote to McGovern's 37.2 in a five-man race (plus write-ins), the senator from Maine had been unable to muster a majority in his native New England. Worse, he had made an emotional speech in a snowstorm outside the offices of a newspaper publisher who had attacked "Moscow Muskie"—and Muskie's wife. This "crying" incident, nationally televised, left the impression that Muskie was unable to control his feelings under pressure.

The following Tuesday Muskie suffered a worse blow in the Florida primary, which George Wallace carried with 41.6 percent of the vote. A poor second was Hubert Humphrey, with 18.6 percent; Henry Jackson got 13.5 percent; Muskie could do no better than fourth with 8.9 percent. McGovern, who had chosen to write off the state to Wallace and concentrate his efforts in more favorable places, got 6.1 percent.

A week later Muskie did better in Illinois, defeating Eugene McCarthy with 63 percent of the vote in a two-man personality contest. Convention delegates were selected separately; Muskie won 59, McGovern 14; and most of the additional 87 uncommitted delegates were controlled by Chicago's Mayor Richard J. Daley.

April brought the turning point of the campaign. In his initial victory McGovern won the Wisconsin primary on April 4 with a scant 29.6 percent; Wallace got 22.1 percent; Humphrey, 20.7 percent; Muskie was fourth again with 10.3 percent. John Lindsay, McGovern's principal rival for the party's left, finished sixth and dropped out of the race. For the next three weeks, Muskie waged a desperate battle on two fronts—against Humphrey in Pennsylvania and McGovern in Massachusetts, with both contests on the same day. The senator from

Maine divided his efforts; his two colleagues concentrated on where they thought they would do best. Humphrey won in Pennsylvania with 35.1 percent of the vote; McGovern won Massachusetts with 52.7 percent; Muskie got just over 20 percent in each state and abandoned his primary campaign.

During the next phase of the race, it was Humphrey, Wallace, and McGovern. On May 2 Humphrey beat each of his opponents in a different primary—McGovern in Ohio (by two percentage points) and Wallace in Indiana (by five points). After Ohio, Henry Jackson ceased active campaigning. Also on May 2, a delegate slate pledged to Walter E. Fauntroy, the District of Columbia's nonvoting congressional representative, was elected. On May 4 Wallace swept the Tennessee primary with 68 percent of the vote; on May 6 he beat Terry Sanford in the latter's own state, North Carolina. On May 9 Humphrey beat Wallace in West Virginia, 67 percent to 33 percent, and McGovern beat them both in Nebraska with 40.7 percent of the vote. One week later Wallace scored his greatest triumph in winning two northern primaries—Michigan with 51.0 percent of the vote and Maryland with 39.1.

But violence intervened. On the day before his two election victories in Michigan and Maryland, George Wallace was shot at point blank range in Laurel, Maryland, and the lower half of his body was paralyzed, evidently permanently.

Everyone deplored the violence, but the show went on. After the Wallace shooting, the momentum was with McGovern. He won the seven remaining primaries—Oregon, Rhode Island, New Jersey, New Mexico, South Dakota, winner-take-all California, and New York. Although he was the first choice of only 30 percent of the nation's Democrats, by the time of the convention McGovern had enough votes to anticipate a first-ballot victory. But he would have to regain 151 of his 271 California delegates, whom the convention's credentials committee—acting in what it argued was the spirit of the McGovern-Fraser guidelines—had voted to take away.

Miami Beach, Florida, July 10, 11, 12, 13, 1972

The credentials decisions came at the first session, but by then the tone of the convention had already been set. The convention *looked* different from its predecessors. Prodded by lawsuits urging that the "one person, one vote" doctrine be applied to party conventions, the national committee had reapportioned the convention. Its 3,016 votes (the most ever) were distributed among the states and the District of Columbia on the basis of electoral college votes and share of the Democratic presidential vote in the past three elections, with 16 additional votes for the unenfranchised Canal Zone, Guam, Puerto Rico, and Virgin Islands. Delegations with fewer than 20 votes were permitted up to 20 delegates. Convention committees were also expanded to 150 members, apportioned according to each delegation's size. And the faces were different. Fully 85 percent had never before been national convention delegates. The McGovern-Fraser Commission's recommendation about "reasonable representation" led to a convention that was 15 percent black (three times the 1968 percentage), 40 percent female (also tripled), and 21 percent younger than thirty (quadrupled).

The 1972 convention also *sounded* different. "We have come here to a great playground," Democratic National Chairman Lawrence F. O'Brien told his fellow Democrats at Miami Beach, "but . . . we have not come here to play. We have come to work." Citing national problems—Vietnam, crime, the economy—O'Brien cautioned against saying "that the Democratic party has all of the answers" because "it wouldn't be true" and "nobody would believe it." The financial news was also unusual: it was good. Party treasurer Robert S. Strauss and John Young Brown, Jr., sponsor of a Democratic telethon held the previous night, reported that all the convention expenses had been paid and the telethon had yielded about $3 million net.

Credentials Challenges

The presidential nomination hinged on the outcome of the credentials disputes. A record twenty-three challenges from fifteen states were settled on the convention floor; the credentials committee had considered eighty-two challenges from thirty-one delegations.

The most important contest was California, where the fate of the largest bloc of delegates—who would all vote either for or against McGovern—was decided. California law gave all the state's delegates to McGovern as the winner of the primary. The Democratic National Committee had instructed the California party that the law was in compliance with the McGovern-Fraser guidelines. After the primary, supporters of Hubert Humphrey challenged the delegation, arguing that its votes should be split among all the candidates according to their showing. The credentials committee's hearing examiner ruled in favor of McGovern. The committee ruled in favor of Humphrey. McGovern took the issue to court. A district court upheld the committee, but the court of appeals reversed that ruling and ordered that McGovern be given back the 151 disputed delegates. The Supreme Court on July 7 stayed the order but declined to rule on the merits of the case, implying that the convention itself should decide. Muskie then called for all the presidential candidates to meet to settle the dispute; but McGovern declined, finding "little to be gained by going into a closed room with six anti-McGovern candidates."

Maneuvering over the California prize determined the outcome of the major challenge considered first by the convention. In South Carolina, the National Women's Political Caucus, with the avowed support of McGovern, sought to increase the number of women delegates from seven to sixteen. Ordinarily, that effort would have needed 1,509 votes for a majority of the 3,016 total. But Lawrence O'Brien had ruled the day before the opening of the convention that a sufficient majority would consist of one more than half the delegates eligible to vote—that is, the delegates whose own credentials were not being challenged. For the South Carolina challenge this amounted to 1,497 votes. Hence the McGovern tacticians sought either to win by 1,509 or more votes or to lose with less than 1,497; in either case, a challenge to the O'Brien ruling about majorities would have been moot. As the roll call progressed, the McGovern camp decided that it was safer to lose. The final vote was 1,555.75 to 1,429.05 against the challenge. Some of McGovern's women supporters were irate, and some of his opponents thought that his strength had proved evanescent.

Next came consideration of relatively minor challenges. In Alabama, a minority report calling for seating the predominantly black National Democratic party of Alabama instead of the party regulars was defeated by voice vote. A second compromise minority report that would have divided the state's votes between the two delegations also lost by voice vote. The Georgia minority report proposed to seat forty regular delegates plus certain challengers, essentially giving added voting strength to the regulars. The minority report was rejected. A second minority report backed by the regulars was withdrawn.

California came next. State Assemblyman Willie L. Brown, Jr., cochairman of the California McGovern delegation, brought the delegates to their feet when he shouted: "I deserve nothing less. Give me back my delegation." Arizona's Robert Began argued that proportional distribution of the contested delegates would mean more representation for Chicanos; Humphrey's California supporter Doris Davis said that party reformers were "hypocrites" if they voted to endorse a winner-take-all primary. Ultimately, the McGovern challenge was upheld, 1,618.28–1,238.22. Immediately after the vote, Norman Bie, Jr., a Wallace supporter in the Florida delegation, argued that the 120 McGovern delegates in California should not have been allowed to vote

on the challenge since all the state's delegates had been contested. If Bie's assertion had been upheld, it might have been enough to overturn O'Brien's ruling about what constituted a majority in credentials contests. But O'Brien responded that only the delegates who had been directly challenged were not permitted to vote; regardless of what happened to the other 151 California votes, O'Brien contended, McGovern clearly deserved the 120. Bie moved that the O'Brien ruling be overturned. His appeal lost, 1,162.23–1,689.52. The McGovern organization clearly had a working majority on the convention floor.

The next order of business concerned the Illinois controversy. After two quick voice votes rejecting challenges that would have replaced insurgent delegates in five congressional districts with party regulars whom the credentials committee had unseated, the convention moved to the major issue. The credentials committee had voted to unseat Mayor Daley and fifty-eight other Cook County delegates because their slate, although elected in a primary, had been organized in violation of several McGovern-Fraser guidelines, particularly in underrepresenting minority groups. The Daley forces sued their challengers, led by Alderman William Singer and black organizer Jesse Jackson. The district court ruled that the guidelines could not supersede the Illinois law governing primaries, which did not incorporate the McGovern-Fraser Commission guidelines, but the court of appeals reversed, finding no constitutional reason for overriding the credentials committee's decision to unseat the Daley group. Understanding the mayor's strategic importance, the McGovern forces and others tried for weeks to work out a compromise. Their efforts were unsuccessful. On the convention floor, a motion to adjourn, backed by McGovern supporters who hoped that Daley could be persuaded to compromise, was defeated by voice vote. Frank B. Morrison, a McGovern supporter and former governor of Nebraska, then moved to suspend the rules to seat both delegations and divide the Illinois vote; the insurgents had agreed to accept this solution. The compromise lost, 1,411.05–1,483.08. The convention then rejected the Daley challenge, 1,371.55–1,486.05.

At 4:45 A.M. credentials committee chairman Patricia Roberts Harris announced that challenges in Michigan, Washington, Rhode Island, Texas, Connecticut, and Oklahoma had been withdrawn. The credentials committee report was approved by voice vote and the first 1972 convention session adjourned at 4:53 A.M.

Any lingering uncertainty about McGovern's nomination ended the following afternoon when Hubert Humphrey released his delegates and Edmund Muskie withdrew and endorsed the South Dakotan. The second session, beginning that evening, featured adoption of the rules and the platform, plus a keynote address by Governor Reubin Askew of Florida.

Rules

A more permanent solution to the California situation was provided in the rules committee report. In a key provision, it resolved that the call for the 1976 convention should include requirements that delegates be selected "in a manner which fairly reflects the division of preferences expressed by those who participate in the presidential nominating process." That meant the abolition of the winner-take-all primary. Henceforth each delegation would be divided according to the candidate preferences in its constituency. The committee report was approved by voice vote after the rejection of a minority statement intended to make it easier for non-Democrats to join the party and take part in delegate selection.

The Platform

In the climax of the convention's platform deliberations, George Wallace was wheeled to the podium to speak for the substitute opening statement and other minority planks that he endorsed. Delivered firmly but without his quondam fervor, Wallace's remarks won cheers from his

partisans and mostly polite silence from others. He generated the loudest response when he denounced "the senseless, asinine busing of school children to achieve racial balance." The convention responded with a series of voice votes disapproving his eight minority planks, which called for a new platform introduction, a constitutional amendment against busing, tax reform, imposition of the death penalty "as a deterrent to crime," reduction of foreign aid, voter referenda on federal judges and Senate reconfirmation of Supreme Court justices, a constitutional amendment to permit prayers in public schools, and a proposal supporting the "right of the people to keep and bear arms" for noncriminal use.

Having disposed of the Wallace recommendations, the convention anticlimactically turned to other minority planks. In voice votes, it rejected two other minority reports that would have changed the platform introduction, which emphasized popular skepticism about government, including some of the recent Democratic past. Next the convention moved to a minority report supported by Senator Fred Harris, whose slogan was "Take the rich off welfare." His proposal called for repeal of the existing personal income tax laws and their replacement with a system taxing all income at uniform rates, with no "loopholes." The Harris measure lost in a close voice vote; Yvonne Brathwaite Burke, a California assemblywoman serving as the convention's presiding officer, called for a second vote with the same result. By the time supporters of the Harris minority report were able to request a roll call, she had moved to the next item of business and ruled their motion out of order as too late. On a proposal sponsored by the National Welfare Rights Organization that endorsed a government-guaranteed annual income of $6,500 for a family of four, the convention rejected the measure, 1,852.86–999.34. By voice vote, it disapproved a minority report that would have returned all rents to the level prevailing before the Nixon administration established limited rent control in August 1971. At 2:59 A.M., the delegates turned down a motion to adjourn and proceeded to the only other roll call of the session—on a minority report that read: "In matters relating to human reproduction, each person's right to privacy, freedom of choice and individual conscience should be fully respected, consistent with relevant Supreme Court decisions." Generally described as the "abortion plank"—though that was a simplification—the minority report lost, 1,572.80–1,101.37. A motion to adjourn was shouted down and the convention moved on to reject by voice vote a minority plank urging the repeal of all laws against homosexuality. The convention considered five more minority reports, rejecting three and adopting two in voice votes. Those approved were a proposal that American Indians be given priority in the distribution of surplus public lands and a plank endorsing a U.S. military force in the Mediterranean to protect Israel from the Soviet Union. Rejected were measures that required all landlords to repair substandard housing, that accepted busing only when it could be shown to improve educational standards, and that asked that withdrawal of U.S. troops from Southeast Asia coincide with the release there of American prisoners of war.

Presidential Nomination

By the third session, George McGovern was regarded as the party's de facto presidential candidate. When the presidential roll was called, five names were placed in nomination. State Senator Bob Wilson of Alabama nominated the wounded governor as his supporters waved placards reading 'Send Them a Message." Hodding Carter III, editor of the Greenville, Mississippi, *Delta Democrat Times,* nominated former Governor Terry Sanford. As in 1968, McGovern was nominated by Senator Abraham A. Ribicoff of Connecticut, who called the South Dakotan's volunteers "the finest political organization in the history of American politics." Ribicoff urged party unity, saying that Democrats should concentrate on the contest with Richard Nixon. Shirley Chisholm was nominated by Bronx

borough president Percy E. Sutton. Governor Jimmy Carter of Georgia put Henry Jackson's name in nomination. In accordance with the new convention rules, the speeches were relatively short and no demonstrations were permitted—only applause, cheers, and placards, modest by the standards of bygone days.

Illinois, the twenty-second delegation called in the order of states scrambled by lot under the new rules to ensure fairness, gave McGovern the majority of convention votes. He captured the nomination with 1,864.95 to 485.65 for Jackson, 377.50 for Wallace, 101.45 for Chisholm, 69.50 for Sanford, and 116.95 votes scattered among other candidates. Shirley Chisholm came to the podium to pledge her support. Henry Jackson sent a congratulatory telegram; Hubert Humphrey telephoned McGovern. There was no motion to make the nomination unanimous.

The Vice-Presidential Choice

Edward Kennedy was McGovern's preference—and the preference of most Democratic leaders—for the vice-presidential nomination, but Kennedy consistently declined. The customary rumors about possible candidates abounded. McGovern's list reportedly consisted of fifty-five names, among them United Auto Workers president Leonard Woodcock, Theodore M. Hesburgh, the president of Notre Dame University, and CBS television anchorman Walter Cronkite. The new party rules required nominating petitions for vice-president with a 4 o'clock filing deadline; minutes before that, McGovern's choice of Senator Thomas F. Eagleton of Missouri was announced.

Eagleton later said that when McGovern asked him to run he responded: "Well, George, before you change your mind, I accept." Among his presumed assets were his Roman Catholic faith, close ties with organized labor, representation of a populous marginal state, and relatively youthful age of forty-two. An early supporter of Muskie's presidential candidacy, Eagleton had urged the senator from Maine to endorse McGovern before the national convention.

The choice of Eagleton was ratified by the convention that evening, but not in routine fashion. The decision was postponed by a roll call vote on a resolution concerning the proposed party charter. The first name offered was that of former Governor Endicott Peabody of Massachusetts, who in an unprecedented way had campaigned for the job, winning the nation's only vice-presidential primary in New Hampshire and buttonholing delegates elsewhere. Eagleton's nomination by Newark's Mayor Kenneth A. Gibson was next. Senator Mike Gravel of Alaska, who also had sought the vice-presidency actively, seconded his own nomination in an impassioned speech. Women's movement leader Gloria Steinem nominated Frances T. Farenthold, a McGovern supporter and state legislator who that year had run for governor of Texas. Withdrawing in favor of Eagleton, Hodding Carter III pleaded with party leaders not to abandon the South to the Republicans. Stanley N. Arnold, a New York City advertising man, was nominated. New Jersey Representative Peter W. Rodino, Jr., was nominated. Black newsman Clay Smothers from Texas delivered his own nominating speech.

In the lengthy roll call, Eagleton won with 1,741.81 votes to 404.04 for Farenthold, 225.38 for Gravel, 107.26 for Peabody, 74 for Smothers, and 463.49 for others. Among the more than sixty "others" were George McGovern's wife, Eleanor; CBS newsman Roger Mudd; antiwar priests Daniel and Philip Berrigan; and Martha Mitchell, outspoken wife of the head of the Committee to Re-elect the President and former attorney general. When at length it was clear that Eagleton had a majority, the roll call was suspended and he was nominated by acclamation on the motion of Frances Farenthold.

Party Charter

The earlier vote on the proposed national party charter was an outgrowth of the McGovern-Fraser and O'Hara Commissions.

Many congressional Democrats felt threatened by the national party superstructure that would be built: a midterm national policy conference with delegates selected at the grass-roots level, seven regional policy conferences to meet in odd-numbered years, an enlarged and strengthened Democratic National Committee with a national executive committee made up of party leaders including but not limited to congressional leaders, and a new dues-paying party membership category.

The convention rules committee approved a compromise resolution calling for a commission to recommend a party charter to the 1974 midterm conference. The compromise also included enlarging the Democratic National Committee to 303 members with a voting strength of 234, 147 votes to be apportioned on the basis of the representation of each state, the District of Columbia, and Puerto Rico on committees at the 1972 convention; plus 52 votes for the state chairman and highest-ranking Democrat of the opposite sex in each state, the District, and Puerto Rico; 4 members each from Guam, the Virgin Islands, and the Canal Zone, each delegation with a single vote; one vote apiece for 3 representatives of the Democratic Governors' Conference; the highest-ranking Democrat and one other member selected by the Democratic caucus in each house of Congress; and up to 25 more members, with a total of 25 votes, to ensure balanced representation of all Democratic voters.

The Massachusetts delegation, which had favored the original party charter, insisted on a roll call. The New York delegation, angered that it was not allowed suspension of the rules to make a proposal allowing it to pick eight of its state's new national committee members (instead of four under the compromise), stalked off the floor. At length the vote was tallied without New York, and the compromise party charter measure was adopted, 2,418.45–195.10.

Because of the preceding, the party's nominees did not make their acceptance speeches until well after 2 A.M. Eagleton attacked the Republicans: "From the people who promised to bring us together . . . we have gotten deception and more distrust." He urged his fellow Democrats to act so that future historians would say: "1972 was the year, not when America lost its way, but the year when America found its conscience." McGovern was introduced by Edward Kennedy, whose short, partisan speech brought cheers.

McGovern's rhetoric was evangelistic. "Let our opponents stand on the status quo while we seek to refresh the American spirit," he told the delegates. Outlining once more his plan to end the U.S. involvement in Vietnam, McGovern added: "Let us resolve that never again will we send the precious young blood of this country to die trying to prop up a corrupt military dictatorship abroad." In phrases borrowed from John and Robert Kennedy, Martin Luther King, Jr., and folk singer Woody Guthrie, McGovern said that he and Eagleton would "call America home to the ideals that nourished us from the very beginning."

From secrecy and deception in high places, come home, America. From military spending . . . come home, America. From the entrenchment of special privilege and tax favoritism; from the waste of idle lands to the joy of useful labor; from the prejudice based on race and sex; from the loneliness of the aging poor and the despair of the neglected sick—come home, America.

Come home to the affirmation that we have a dream; come home to the conviction that we can move our country forward.

Come home to the belief that we can seek a newer world, and let us be joyful in that homecoming, for this land is your land; this land is my land—from California to the New York Island, from the redwood forest to the Gulfstream waters—this land was made for you and me.

And then, shortly after 3 A.M., the audience cheered as McGovern joined hands with Eagleton, Humphrey, Muskie, Jackson, Chisholm, and Sanford.

The Vice-Presidency Revisited

This image of unity was soon shattered. On July 25, McGovern and Eagleton held joint news conference at which the vice-presidential nominee anounced that between 1960 and 1966 he had been hospitalized three times for "nervous exhaustion and fatigue" and had undergone psychiatric treatment, including electric shock therapy. Eagleton added that he had been pronounced completely fit after a thorough checkup the preceding week.

At the news conference, George McGovern said, "There is no one sounder in body, mind, and spirit than Tom Eagleton." Asked during a subsequent television interview whether he had made "an irrevocable decision" to keep Eagleton on the presidential ticket, McGovern responded, "Absolutely."

National furor ensued. Reporters speculated that McGovern might reconsider his decision. McGovern angrily reiterated that he was "1,000 percent for Tom Eagleton" and had "no intention of dropping him from the ticket." Many party leaders and several influential newspapers called for Eagleton's withdrawal, arguing that his case was providing "cruel diversionary conflicts," as the New York *Post* put it, that overshadowed the real issues of the election. Opinion polls indicated popular sympathy for Eagleton.

Eagleton vowed to educate the public about mental health, but it became clear that his running mate disagreed. When Democratic National Chairman Jean Westwood publicly called for Eagleton to do "the noble thing" and step down, it was understood to be McGovern's wish. On July 31, at another joint press conference, Eagleton bowed out of the race. McGovern explained his original hope that the health issue would fade and his later conclusion that it would instead eclipse important issues.

On August 8 the Democratic National Committee, at McGovern's recommendation, nominated R. Sargent Shriver to replace Eagleton. He received 2,936 votes; Missouri's Governor Warren E. Hearnes cast his state's votes for Eagleton, and 4 Oregon votes went to former Senator Wayne Morse. After Eagleton's resignation, McGovern's offer of the vice-presidential nomination had reportedly been refused by Edward Kennedy, Abraham Ribicoff, Gaylord Nelson, Reubin Askew, Hubert Humphrey, and Edmund Muskie.

THE REPUBLICAN CONTEST

Richard Nixon's popularity within his own party ensured his renomination. In the polls, he consistently trounced all Republican comers. In the primaries, he did the same to antiwar Congressman Paul N. McCloskey of California and conservative Congressman John M. Ashbrook of Ohio. McCloskey's best showing was 20.2 percent of the vote in New Hampshire. Ashbrook peaked in the California primary, where he got 9.9 percent.

Lacking other suspense, political speculation centered on whether Spiro T. Agnew would be kept on the ticket. Some observers thought that Nixon might prefer a national unity ticket with erstwhile Democrat John B. Connally, whom he had made secretary of the treasury in 1971, as his running mate. And some Republican moderates found Agnew, who had often criticized "radical liberals" and the news media that publicized them, too conservative. Shortly after the Democratic convention, however, the White House press secretary told reporters that the decision had been made to keep Agnew.

A New Convention Site

As with Sherlock Holmes's dog that did not bark, one salient fact about the 1972 Republican national convention concerned something that failed to happen: the convention did not meet in San Diego, California, as originally planned. The California city was President Nixon's personal choice and the White House staff persuaded the reluctant city council to place a last-minute bid of $1.5 million with the Republican site-selection committee.

Difficulties began when a group of San Diego citizens led by Virginia W. Taylor, a candidate for mayor and a member of the Republican county central committee, sought a preliminary injunction to prevent the city council from spending tax revenues on the convention. While the injunction was denied, the resulting publicity included the disclosure that the Sheraton Hotel subsidiary of the International Telephone and Telegraph Corporation (ITT) had underwritten several hundred thousand dollars (the exact figure was hotly debated) in needed local contributions for the convention bid. In July 1971—the same month that the convention site was announced—the Justice Department had agreed to settle an antitrust case against ITT out of court.

Still worse to Republican convention planners was San Diego's failure to provide promised facilities on schedule. By April 1972 the planned remodeling of the convention hall had not yet begun. Republican officials began negotiating with Miami Beach as an alternate site. On May 5 the Republican National Committee unanimously approved a $350,000 bid from the Florida city where Richard Nixon had been nominated in 1968. It was the first time since 1952 that both national party conventions had met in the same place. The television networks estimated that as a group they had saved $3 million by not having to move their equipment.

Miami Beach, Florida, August 21, 22, 23, 1972

That there was little controversy at the Republican convention made for five brisk sessions (some found them contrived) over three days; the only major battle concerned the party rules. Before the first plenary session, the national committee and the convention rules committee deliberated on a formula for apportioning the convention votes and new regulations for selecting delegates in 1976 and beyond. Stakes were high, since both decisions might affect the 1976 presidential nomination.

Apportionment of Future Convention Votes

The Republicans wrote new apportionment rules because the federal district court required it. In November 1971 the Ripon Society, an organization of Republican intellectuals, had sued the Republican National Committee on the grounds that its apportionment formula discriminated against the more populous states, giving them fewer votes than their number of Republican voters deserved. The following April the court ruled in favor of the Ripon Society and issued an injunction (later stayed by Supreme Court Justice William H. Rehnquist) against the GOP practice of giving six bonus votes to every state that went Republican for president, governor, senator, or a majority of its delegation to the House of Representatives, without regard for the state's popular or electoral vote for president.

Although nineteen apportionment plans were proposed, only two were seriously considered in committee. The two differed essentially in the bases for bonus votes. A plan proposed by Senator John G. Tower of Texas and Congressman Jack F. Kemp of New York with White House backing provided that every state going Republican in 1972 would receive 4½ votes plus additional votes equal to 60 percent of its electoral vote (rounded to the highest whole number). Under the major alternative plan, bonus votes would be awarded to states going Republican for the House, the Senate, and the statehouse as well as for president. The Tower-Kemp plan was generally believed to benefit small states, which more often have gone Republican for president, whereas the other plan was considered to serve the interests of the more populous states that sometimes have elected other GOP candidates while failing to support the party's presidential nominee. Since Vice-President Agnew was seen as more popular in the smaller, frequently more conservative states, the Tower-Kemp plan was considered a boost for his candidacy in 1976. Some observers noted, however, that if President Nixon carried the populous states in a landslide victory in 1972, they would gain more bonus votes under the Tower-Kemp formula.

After discussions that ran nearly as late as a Democratic convention session, the preconvention subcommittee on membership in the next national convention voted 6–5 to approve the plan benefiting the populous states. The following day, however, the Republican National Committee's preconvention rules committee approved the Tower-Kemp plan, 31–16. The Republican National Committee ratified that action by voice vote, although its general counsel warned that the Tower-Kemp plan might not survive judicial scrutiny.

The rules committee at the convention reached a compromise, consisting in essence of the Tower-Kemp plan plus extra delegates for states that elected GOP governors, senators, or a House delegation majority. In all, the rules committee plan provided for: six delegates at large for each state; three delegates for each House district; fourteen votes at large for the District of Columbia, eight for Puerto Rico, and four each for Guam and the Virgin Islands; for each state going Republican for president in the previous election, four and a half delegates plus 60 percent of the state's electoral vote total, rounded upward if necessary; one delegate for each GOP senator elected; a maximum of one delegate for states going Republican for governor; and one delegate for states electing a House delegation at least half Republican. The District of Columbia would get a nine-vote bonus for going Republican for president. Each delegate would have one full vote; thus the convention size would increase from 1,348 in 1972 to roughly 2,000 in 1976. Every state was assured of at least as many votes as it had at the 1972 convention. A concluding proviso stated that if the new formula was declared legally invalid, the Republican National Committee—with each delegation casting as many votes as at the 1972 convention—would write a new formula.

DO Committee Recommendations on Rules

The 1968 GOP convention had voted approval of a new party rule against discrimination based on race, religion, color, or national origin in the delegate selection; it also had approved a rule calling on the national committee to establish a group to make recommendations to the 1972 convention about implementation of the anti-bias rule. The result was the Delegates and Organizations (DO) Committee, which was headed by Rosemary Ginn, the national committeewoman from Missouri. The DO Comittee report urged some procedural changes: use of Robert's Rules of Order Revised, rather than the less commonly understood rules of the House of Representatives, as the parliamentary rules of the convention; shortening time for nominating and seconding speeches, especially for favorite sons; and beginning roll calls with a state chosen by lot, so that the same delegations would not always be first and last. In July 1971, the DO Committee offered ten more substantive recommendations to the national committee, calling for: wide participation through open meetings held at various sites; electing alternates in the same manner as delegates; bans on mandatory assessments of convention participants, proxy voting, and ex officio delegates; doubling the size of convention committees to encompass a new requirement for one person under twenty-five years old and one member of "a minority ethnic group," as well as one man and one woman, from each delegation; an "endeavor" by each delegation to have an equal number of women and men; representation of persons under twenty-five "in numerical equity to their voting strength" in each delegation; and an effort by the national committee to publicize delegate selection procedures widely.

While there was broad agreement that the Republican party should be, in President Nixon's words, "the party of the open door," there was an equivalent GOP consensus that *quotas* for the representation of various groups were undesirable. Many opposed what New York's Senator James L. Buckley called an attempt to "McGovernize the Republican party." They noted that singling out women, young people, and minority groups might arouse hostility

among other voting blocs. In the rules committee, all the major DO Committee recommendations were accepted except those urging separate locations for state and district conventions and requiring representation for the young and minority group members. The committee approved the recommendation about equal representation of the sexes and urged the party to "take positive action to achieve the broadest possible participation by women, young people, minority and heritage groups and senior citizens in the delegate selection process."

On procedural rules, the convention rules committee agreed to switch to Robert's Rules of Order in 1976 but did not follow the other suggestions of the DO Committee. The rules panel did vote to ban favorite-son nominations by requiring that presidential candidates demonstrate majority strength in at least three delegations; limit each candidate's time for nominating and seconding speeches to fifteen minutes; and spell out new arrangements for the GOP national committee, its officers, and its executive committee. In addition, the national chairman was instructed to establish a panel to monitor the new delegate selection rules.

"Ours will be a prime-time convention," said Republican National Chairman Robert Dole, senator from Kansas. "It will be short, compact, and concise." It was. In the afternoon session on August 21 the usual speeches each lasted less than ten minutes.

Equally smooth was the evening session. In an outright appeal to Democrats unhappy with Senator McGovern, a tribute to former Presidents Harry S. Truman and Lyndon B. Johnson was offered by national chairman Dole. Senate minority leader Hugh Scott of Pennsylvania introduced the party's 1936 nominee for president, Alfred M. Landon. The permanent convention chairman, California's Governor Ronald Reagan, gave a rousing Republican speech sharply criticizing McGovern's programs. He also taunted the opposition on the Eagleton affair, saying that to find a running mate McGovern had to "run through the yellow pages and call central casting." His phrases reflected the professional quality of the GOP production.

Instead of one thirty-minute keynote speech, the Republicans broke precedent and had three addresses of ten minutes each. In them, Senator Edward W. Brooke of Massachusetts said that "this President has actually done more to establish a lasting world peace than . . . any national leader in our lifetime." Of the domestic situation, Brooke added: "The politics of empty promise has been replaced by quiet determination to deliver." The mayor of Indianapolis, Richard G. Lugar, often called President Nixon's favorite mayor, indirectly attacked McGovern's programs and said that he threatened "radical change" and "must be defeated resoundingly to prevent unparalleled disaster at home and abroad." Anne L. Armstrong, Republican national co-chairman, spoke as a former Democrat, urging members of that party to "come in and join us." At the close of her speech Transportation Secretary John A. Volpe, a delegate from Massachusetts, offered a resolution, passed by voice vote, inviting all Democrats to join the Nixon campaign. Arizona's Senator Barry M. Goldwater turned the tables on past critics of his "extremism" by attacking Senator McGovern on the same grounds. "Reject once and for all any isolationist threat to our freedom which is incorporated in the socialistic promises of McGovern," the 1964 Republican nominee told his audience.

Credentials

At the next session, the following day, there was less rhetoric and more action. By voice vote, the convention approved the credentials committee report. The few seating controversies that arose had been settled in committee. In New Mexico, Congressman Paul McCloskey was entitled by state law to one convention vote. To cast it, the state convention selected a Nixon supporter who was instructed to vote for McCloskey. The congressman sought to name his own delegate so that he could at least have his views expressed on the floor, but the credentials committee upheld the state convention action. The credentials committee also rejected challenges alleging underrepresentation of blacks in the District of Columbia and Virginia delegations.

Platform

With little controversy, the Nixon administration's policies were endorsed. The platform differed significantly in content from its Democratic counterpart. The Republicans endorsed the Nixon Vietnam policy, opposed school busing for racial integration, supported voluntary school prayer, and opposed amnesty for war resisters—all in direct contrast to Democratic planks.

The platform draft approved by the convention differed little from the original White House proposals. In committee, sections opposing economic discrimination against women were strengthened and a provision endorsing certain day-care programs for working mothers was approved. On the floor, two amendments were offered. A pledge to prohibit federal deficit spending was defeated by voice vote. Then, with the consent of the platform committee chairman, Representative John J. Rhodes of Arizona, an amendment advocating self-determination for American Indians was approved in a voice vote. The amended committee report also passed by voice vote.

Rules

The convention's most controversial issue, the rules committee report, called for numerous changes, most of them minor, in the party's official rules for the 1976 convention. There was no floor debate about the new rules of procedure or delegate selection. By voice vote, the convention approved an amendment, sponsored by Mayor Edward Bivens, Jr., of Inkster, Michigan, and endorsed by the rules committee chairman, former Congressman William C. Cramer from Florida, which added a representative of black GOP organizations to the

Republican National Committee's executive committee.

The major debate came on a delegate apportionment amendment sponsored by Representative William A. Steiger of Wisconsin. Like the rules committee formula, the Steiger proposal called for six delegates for each state and two for each congressional district. In rewarding party voting, however, the Steiger amendment was very different, providing one delegate to each congressional district that was carried by the GOP candidate for president, governor, senator, or representative in any election between one convention and the call for the next. In addition, the Steiger formula provided for four hundred delegates to be divided among the states in proportion to their share of the party's presidential vote in the last election, plus a further bonus to each state supporting the last presidential ticket: delegates amounting to 60 percent of the state's electoral votes.

Steiger contended that the rules committee formula, which granted only one vote to a state for going Republican for the Senate, House, or governorship, would not help build a strong party. "No President, whether he is Republican or Democrat, can sustain himself successfully without control of Congress and the statehouses," Steiger declared. Steiger's supporters argued that acceptance of the committee formula would mean that the courts would decide the apportionment formula for the next Republican convention. New York State Assembly Speaker Perry B. Duryea pointed out that under the committee formula some delegates in 1976 would represent as many as 25,500 people and others as few as 2,350 people.

In opposing the Steiger amendment, rules committee chairman Cramer stressed that his panel had adopted its formula after careful and open deliberation. Republican national committeeman Tom Stagg from Louisiana said that the committee formula balanced the interests of all states and did not "permit a group of larger states to dominate our national convention." The final speaker, Ronald Reagan, said: "To

make a snap judgment on this floor at this hour on a plan that not many of us have seen before makes it look too much like the [Democratic] convention that just took place in July." The Steiger amendment was defeated, 910–434. Another amendment on apportionment, offered by a Maryland delegate to protect the "grass roots input"— particularly by the GOP state central committees—was shouted down. By voice vote, the committee report was approved.

Presidential Nominating Session

The session that renominated Richard Nixon was a model of unity. Governor of New York Nelson A. Rockefeller nominated his one-time antagonist, saying: "We need this man of action, this man of accomplishment, this man of courage. We need this man of faith in America." Listing the administration's accomplishments, Rockefeller said that Nixon had brought the nation "to the threshold of a generation of peace" and had "renewed confidence" in a country plagued four years earlier with violence, inflation, riots, and internal division. Eleven people seconded Nixon's nomination, including former Secretary of the Interior Walter J. Hickel, who had been fired because of his disagreements with the President; John McCarrell, president of a United Auto Workers local in Pittsburgh; Mary Ann Maier, wife of the Democratic mayor of Milwaukee; John O'Neill, a Vietnam veteran; conservative Senator James L. Buckley of New York; former astronaut Frank Borman; and representatives of southerners, blacks, Chicanos, and other ethnic groups, and of the young. In the roll call vote, Nixon received 1,347 of the convention's 1,348 votes, the exception being the New Mexico vote for McCloskey.

Final Session

The mood of unity was sustained through the last evening. Spiro Agnew's was the only name put in nomination for the vice-presidency. He was nominated by his fellow Marylander, Secretary of the Interior Rogers C. B. Morton. The only surprise in the roll call that gave Agnew 1,345 of the 1,348 total votes came when an Oregon delegate cast a vote for NBC television commentator David Brinkley. Wayne Whitehead, the maverick delegate, worked for NBC and wanted to offset the votes at the Democratic convention for Roger Mudd of CBS. The two remaining votes not cast for Agnew were abstentions.

In his acceptance speech, Agnew played a consciously penultimate role. As he said, "A vice president lives in flickering strobe lights that alternately illuminate or shadow his unwritten duties." Instead of stressing his own activities, Agnew emphasized the merits of the Nixon administration, particularly as contrasted with the Democratic alternative. He asked: "Do we turn our country over to the piecemeal, inconsistent and illusory policies of George McGovern? Or do we entrust the future of this nation to the sound, tested leadership of Richard Nixon?" Then, as the crowd cheered, Agnew introduced the man whom it chose.

Richard Nixon invited his audience "to join us as members of a new American majority bound together by our common ideals," which he then proceeded to define. "The choice in this election," Nixon said, "is between change that works and change that won't work." He added that while many critics emphasized its failings, "I believe in the American system." His travels abroad, he said, had persuaded him that "we have more freedom, more opportunity, more prosperity than any people in the world." Indeed, he said, "the people on welfare in America would be rich in most of the nations of the world today." Conceding that there was room for improvement, Nixon noted that "taxes are still too high," inflation could be reduced, and there should be "a job for every American who wants

to work, without war and without inflation." But he said that the Democrats' policies to that end would bring "a net increase in the budget of $144 billion" and "an increase of 50 percent in what the taxpayers of America pay" as well as adding "82 million people to the welfare rolls."

In the second half of his speech, Nixon turned to foreign policy. Echoing Thomas Jefferson, he declared: "We are not Republicans, we are not Democrats, we are Americans first, last, and always." He pledged to uphold the "proud bipartisan tradition" of Franklin Roosevelt, Harry Truman, Dwight Eisenhower, John Kennedy, and Lyndon Johnson—"total opposition to isolation for America," "the responsibilities of leadership in the world," and "the conviction that the United States should have a defense second to none." With some pride, Nixon recalled his pledge four years earlier to end the Vietnam war honorably and noted that his administration had brought home more than 500,000 troops, ended the U.S. ground combat role, reduced casualties "by 98 percent," and sought a negotiated settlement. He emphasized, however, three conditions for such an agreement. First, "we will never abandon our prisoners of war." Moreover, "we will not join our enemies in imposing a communist government" in South Vietnam. Finally, "we will never stain the honor of the United States." In concluding, Nixon stressed his journeys abroad and other efforts to reach détentes with the Soviet Union and the Chinese. He told the story of a small girl named Tanya who had experienced the suffering the Russians endured in World War II and declared: "Let us build a peace that our children and all the children of the world can enjoy for generations to come."

Presidential election, November 7, 1972

RICHARD M. NIXON (R): popular vote, 47,042,943; electoral vote, 521
GEORGE S. MCGOVERN (D): popular vote, 29,071,629; electoral vote, 17
A Republican elector in Virginia cast his vote for the Libertarian party candidate, John Hospers.

APPENDIXES

A. Nominees of the Major Parties

PRESIDENTIAL AND VICE-PRESIDENTIAL NOMINEES, 1832-1972[a]

	Democratic		National Republican, Whig, Republican	
Year	Presidential candidate	Vice-presidential candidate	Presidential candidate	Vice-presidential candidate
1832	Andrew Jackson*	Martin Van Buren	Henry Clay	John Sergeant
1836	Martin Van Buren*	Richard M. Johnson	(no convention)	
1840	Martin Van Buren	(no nominee)	William Henry Harrison*	John Tyler
1844	James K. Polk*	Silas Wright[b] George M. Dallas[c]	Henry Clay	Theodore Frelinghuysen
1848	Lewis Cass	William O. Butler	Zachary Taylor*	Millard Fillmore
1852	Franklin Pierce*	William R. King	Winfield Scott	William A. Graham
1856	James Buchanan*	John C. Breckinridge	John C. Frémont	William L. Dayton
1860	Stephen A. Douglas	Benjamin Fitzpatrick[b] Herschel V. Johnson[d]	Abraham Lincoln*	Hannibal Hamlin
1864	George B. McClellan	George H. Pendleton	Abraham Lincoln*	Andrew Johnson
1868	Horatio Seymour	Francis P. Blair, Jr.	Ulysses S. Grant*	Schuyler Colfax
1872	Horace Greeley	B. Gratz Brown	Ulysses S. Grant*	Henry Wilson
1876	Samuel J. Tilden	Thomas A. Hendricks	Rutherford B. Hayes*	William A. Wheeler
1880	Winfield Scott Hancock	William H. English	James A. Garfield*	Chester A. Arthur
1884	Grover Cleveland*	Thomas A. Hendricks	James G. Blaine	John A. Logan
1888	Grover Cleveland	Allen G. Thurman	Benjamin Harrison*	Levi P. Morton
1892	Grover Cleveland*	Adlai E. Stevenson	Benjamin Harrison	Whitelaw Reid
1896	William Jennings Bryan	Arthur Sewall	William McKinley*	Garret A. Hobart
1900	William Jennings Bryan	Adlai E. Stevenson	William McKinley*	Theodore Roosevelt
1904	Alton B. Parker	Henry G. Davis	Theodore Roosevelt*	Charles W. Fairbanks
1908	William Jennings Bryan	John W. Kern	William Howard Taft*	James S. Sherman
1912	Woodrow Wilson*	Thomas R. Marshall	William Howard Taft	James S. Sherman[e] Nicholas Murray Butler[f]
1916	Woodrow Wilson*	Thomas R. Marshall	Charles Evans Hughes	Charles W. Fairbanks
1920	James M. Cox	Franklin D. Roosevelt	Warren G. Harding*	Calvin Coolidge
1924	John W. Davis	Charles W. Bryan	Calvin Coolidge*	Frank O. Lowden[b] Charles G. Dawes[c]
1928	Alfred E. Smith	Joseph T. Robinson	Herbert Hoover*	Charles Curtis
1932	Franklin D. Roosevelt*	John N. Garner	Herbert Hoover	Charles Curtis
1936	Franklin D. Roosevelt*	John N. Garner	Alfred M. Landon	Frank Knox
1940	Franklin D. Roosevelt*	Henry A. Wallace	Wendell L. Willkie	Charles L. McNary
1944	Franklin D. Roosevelt*	Harry S. Truman	Thomas E. Dewey	John W. Bricker
1948	Harry S. Truman*	Alben W. Barkley	Thomas E. Dewey	Earl Warren
1952	Adlai E. Stevenson	John J. Sparkman	Dwight D. Eisenhower*	Richard M. Nixon
1956	Adlai E. Stevenson	Estes Kefauver	Dwight D. Eisenhower*	Richard M. Nixon
1960	John F. Kennedy*	Lyndon B. Johnson	Richard M. Nixon	Henry Cabot Lodge, Jr.
1964	Lyndon B. Johnson*	Hubert H. Humphrey	Barry M. Goldwater	William E. Miller
1968	Hubert H. Humphrey	Edmund S. Muskie	Richard M. Nixon*	Spiro T. Agnew
1972	George S. McGovern	Thomas F. Eagleton[g] R. Sargent Shriver[d]	Richard M. Nixon*	Spiro T. Agnew

a. Winning party candidate is indicated by asterisk (*). William Henry Harrison and Zachary Taylor were Whig winners; the first nominee of the new Republican party was John C. Frémont.
b. Nominated but refused.   c. Named by convention.   d. Named by Democratic National Committee.
e. Died October 30, 1912.   f. Named by Republican National Committee.
g. Nominated by convention but resigned from ticket.

B. Convention Officers

Year	Chairman, National Committee	Temporary chairman	Permanent chairman
1832	No committee	Robert Lucas, Ohio	Robert Lucas, Ohio
1836	No committee	Andrew Stevenson, Va.	Andrew Stevenson, Va.
1840	No committee	Isaac Hill, N.H.	William Carroll, Tenn.
1844	No committee	Hendrick B. Wright, Pa.	Hendrick B. Wright, Pa.
1848	B. F. Hallet, Mass.	J. S. Bryce, La.	Andrew Stevenson, Va.
1852	Robert McLane, Md.	Gen. Romulus M. Saunders, N.C.	John W. Davis, Ind.
1856	David A. Smalley, Va.	Samuel Medary, Ohio	John E. Ward, Ga.
1860	August Belmont, N.Y.	Francis B. Flournoy, Ark.	Caleb Cushing, Mass.
1864	August Belmont, N.Y.	William Bigler, Pa.	Horatio Seymour, N.Y.
1868	August Belmont, N.Y.	Henry L. Palmer, Wis.	Horatio Seymour, N.Y.
1872	Augustus Schell, N.Y.	Thomas Jefferson Randolph, Va.	James R. Doolittle, Wis.
1876	William H. Barnum, Conn.	Henry M. Watterson, Ky.	Gen. John A. McClernand, Ill.
1880	William H. Barnum, Conn.	George Hoadly, Ohio	John W. Stevenson, Ky.
1884	William H. Barnum, Conn.	Richard D. Hubbard, Tex.	William F. Vilas, Wis.
1888	William H. Barnum, Conn.	Stephen M. White, Calif.	Patrick A. Collins, Mass.
1892	C. S. Brice, Ohio	William C. Owens, Ky.	William L. Wilson, W.Va.
1896	William F. Harrity, Pa.	John W. Daniel, Va.	Stephen M. White, Calif.
1900	James K. Jones, Ark.	Charles S. Thomas, Colo.	James D. Richardson, Tenn.
1904	James K. Jones, Ark.	John Sharp Williams, Miss.	Champ Clark, Mo.
1908	Thomas Taggart, Ind.	Theodore A. Bell, Calif.	Henry D. Clayton, Ala.
1912	Norman E. Mack, N.Y.	Alton B. Parker, N.Y.	Ollie M. James, Ky.
1916	William F. McCombs, N.Y.	Martin H. Glynn, N.Y.	Ollie M. James, Ky.
1920	Vance C. McCormick, Pa.	Homer Cummings, Conn.	Joseph T. Robinson, Ark.
1924	Cordell Hull, Tenn.	Pat Harrison, Miss.	Thomas J. Walsh, Mont.
1928	Clem Shaver, W.Va.	Claude G. Bowers, Ind.	Joseph T. Robinson, Ark.
1932	John J. Raskob, Md.	Alben W. Barkley, Ky.	Thomas J. Walsh, Mont.
1936	James A. Farley, N.Y.	Alben W. Barkley, Ky.	Joseph T. Robinson, Ark.
1940	James A. Farley, N.Y.	William B. Bankhead, Ala.	Alben W. Barkley, Ky.
1944	Robert E. Hannegan, Mo.	Robert S. Kerr, Okla.	Samuel D. Jackson, Ind.
1948	J. Howard McGrath, R.I.	Alben W. Barkley, Ky.	Sam Rayburn, Tex.
1952	Frank E. McKinney, Ind.	Paul A. Dever, Mass.	Sam Rayburn, Tex.
1956	Paul M. Butler, Ind.	Frank G. Clement, Tenn.	Sam Rayburn, Tex.
1960	Paul M. Butler, Ind.	Frank Church, Idaho	LeRoy Collins, Fla.
1964	John M. Bailey, Conn.	John O. Pastore, R.I.	John W. McCormack, Mass.
1968	John M. Bailey, Conn.	Daniel K. Inouye, Hawaii	Carl B. Albert, Okla.
1972	Lawrence F. O'Brien, Mass.	None[a]	Lawrence F. O'Brien, Mass.

a. Position eliminated under new rules.

REPUBLICAN NATIONAL CONVENTIONS[a]

Year	Chairman, National Committee	Temporary chairman	Permanent chairman
1832	No committee	Abner Lacock, Pa.	James Barbour, Va.
1840	No committee	Isaac C. Bates, Mass.	James Barbour, Va.
1844	No committee	Arthur S. Hopkins, Ala.	Ambrose Spencer, N.Y.
1848	No committee	John A. Collier, N.Y.	John M. Morehead, N.C.
1852	No committee	George C. Evans, Maine	John G. Chapman, Md.
1856	Edwin D. Morgan, N.Y.	Robert Emmet, N.Y.	Henry S. Lane, Ind.
1860	Edwin D. Morgan, N.Y.	David Wilmot, Pa.	George Ashmun, Mass.
1864	Edwin D. Morgan, N.Y.	Robert J. Breckinridge, Ky.	William Dennison, Ohio
1868	Marcus L. Ward, N.J.	Carl Schurz, Mo.	Joseph R. Hawley, Conn.
1872	William Claflin, Mass.	Morton McMichael, Pa.	Thomas Settle, N.C.
1876	Edwin D. Morgan, N.Y.	Theodore M. Pomeroy, N.Y.	Edward McPherson, Pa.
1880	J. Donald Cameron, Pa.	George F. Hoar, Mass.	George F. Hoar, Mass.
1884	Dwight M. Sabin, Minn.	John R. Lynch, Miss.	John B. Henderson, Mo.
1888	B. F. Jones, Pa.	John M. Thurston, Nebr.	Morris M. Estee, Calif.
1892	James S. Clarkson, Iowa	J. Sloat Fassett, N.Y.	William McKinley, Jr., Ohio
1896	Thomas H. Carter, Mont.	Charles W. Fairbanks, Ind.	John M. Thurston, Nebr.
1900	Marcus A. Hanna, Ohio	Edward O. Wolcott, Colo.	Henry Cabot Lodge, Mass.
1904	Henry C. Payne, Wis.	Elihu Root, N.Y.	Joseph G. Cannon, Ill.
1908	Harry S. New, Ind.	Julius C. Burrows, Mich.	Henry Cabot Lodge, Mass.
1912	Victor Rosewater, Nebr.	Elihu Root, N.Y.	Elihu Root, N.Y.
1916	Charles D. Hilles, N.Y.	Warren G. Harding, Ohio	Warren G. Harding, Ohio
1920	Will H. Hays, Ind.	Henry Cabot Lodge, Mass.	Henry Cabot Lodge, Mass.
1924	John T. Adams, Iowa	Theodore E. Burton, Ohio	Frank W. Mondell, Wyo.
1928	William M. Butler, Mass.	Simeon D. Fess, Ohio	George H. Moses, N.H.
1932	Simeon D. Fess, Ohio	L. J. Dickinson, Iowa	Bertrand H. Snell, N.Y.
1936	Henry P. Fletcher, Pa.	Frederick Steiwer, Oreg.	Bertrand H. Snell, N.Y.
1940	John Hamilton, Kans.	Harold E. Stassen, Minn.	Joseph W. Martin, Jr., Mass.
1944	Harrison E. Spangler, Iowa	Earl Warren, Calif.	Joseph W. Martin, Jr., Mass.
1948	Carroll Reece, Tenn.	Dwight H. Green, Ill.	Joseph W. Martin, Jr., Mass.
1952	Guy George Gabrielson, N.J.	Walter S. Hallanan, W.Va.	Joseph W. Martin, Jr., Mass.
1956	Leonard W. Hall, N.Y.	William F. Knowland, Calif.	Joseph W. Martin, Jr., Mass.
1960	Thruston B. Morton, Ky.	Cecil H. Underwood, W.Va.	Charles A. Halleck, Ind.
1964	William E. Miller, N.Y.	Mark O. Hatfield, Oreg.	Thruston B. Morton, Ky.
1968	Ray C. Bliss, Ohio	Edward W. Brooke, Mass.	Gerald R. Ford, Mich.
1972	Robert Dole, Kans.	Ronald Reagan, Calif.	Gerald R. Ford, Mich.

a. Includes National Republican (1832) and Whig (1840-1852); no convention in 1836.

C. The Voting Records

THE VOTING TABLES that follow are arranged in chronological order within each convention of each party. For all conventions in which there were ten or less ballots for the presidential nomination, all roll call votes are given for which state-by-state figures were available. For some of the earliest conventions, no state-by-state figures were listed; for others, the listings frequently contained discrepancies. Wherever the discrepancy was obvious and the correct figure could be clearly derived, the record has been printed in corrected form. When the added totals of detailed figures listed differ from the sums as printed in the proceedings, both totals are given. (It will be noted that these discrepancies are not limited to the earliest conventions.)

For the conventions in which more than ten nominating ballots were taken, sampling is used. In general, for the long-ballot conventions, every fifth ballot has been listed (every tenth ballot in the long 1924 Democratic convention), but this was not rigidly adhered to if an intervening ballot reflected greater vote movement. All ballots on which major shifts occurred are listed. As the culminating ballot is approached, the frequency of ballots listed is increased, in order to permit more careful study of the formation of the final nominating coalition.

Except for the 1860 Democratic convention, all nonnominating roll call votes are listed where state-by-state records were available. The Democrats' 1860 roll calls were so numerous, many being unanimous or near-unanimous and many others reflecting almost identical voting patterns, that it seemed adequate to include only a representative sample of the more important votes.

	1832 DEMOCRATIC				1835 DEMOCRATIC										1840 DEMOCRATIC	
	Votes	Vice-Presidential First Ballot			Votes	Formation of Electoral Tickets			Reconsider Electoral Tickets Resolution			Pres Van Buren	Vice-Pres First Ballot		Pres.	Vice-Pres.
Delegation	Votes	Van Buren	Johnson	Barbour	Votes	Yea	Nay	Not Voting	Yea	Nay	Not Voting	Van Buren	Johnson	Rives	Pres.	Vice-Pres.
Alabama	7	1	...	6	...	...	...	...	...	...	...	...	...	...		
Arizona	...	...	...	...	...	...	...	...	...	...	...	...	...	...		
Arkansas	...	...	...	...	...	...	...	...	...	...	...	...	...	...		
California	...	...	...	...	...	...	...	...	...	...	...	...	...	...		
Colorado	...	...	...	...	...	...	...	...	...	...	...	...	...	...		
Connecticut	8	8	...	...	8	8	...	...	...	8	...	8	8	...		
Delaware	3	3	...	...	3	3	...	...	...	3	...	3	3	...		
Florida	...	...	...	...	...	...	...	...	...	...	...	...	...	...		
Georgia	11	11	...	...	11	...	11	...	11	...	...	11	...	11		
Idaho	...	...	...	...	...	...	...	...	...	...	...	...	...	...		
Illinois	4	2	2	...	...	...	...	...	...	...	...	...	...	...		
Indiana	9	...	9	...	9	9	...	...	...	9	...	9	9	...		
Iowa	...	...	...	...	...	...	...	...	...	...	...	...	...	...		
Kansas	...	...	...	...	...	...	...	...	...	...	...	...	...	...		
Kentucky	15	...	15	...	15	15	...	...	...	15	...	15	15	...		
Louisiana	5	5	...	...	5	5	...	...	5	...	...	5	5	...		
Maine	10	10	...	...	10	...	10	...	10	...	...	10	...	10		
Maryland	10	7	...	3	10	...	10	...	10	...	...	10	...	10		
Massachusetts	14	14	...	...	14	14	...	...	...	14	...	14	4	10		
Michigan	...	...	...	...	...	...	...	...	...	...	...	...	...	...		
Minnesota	...	...	...	...	...	...	...	...	...	...	...	...	...	...		
Mississippi	4	4	...	...	4	...	4	...	...	4	...	4	4	...		
Missouri	...	...	...	...	4	...	...	4	4	...	...	4	4	...		
Montana	...	...	...	...	...	...	...	...	...	...	...	...	...	...		
Nebraska	...	...	...	...	...	...	...	...	...	...	...	...	...	...		
Nevada	...	...	...	...	...	...	...	...	...	...	...	...	...	...		
New Hampshire	7	7	...	...	7	7	...	...	...	7	...	7	7	...		
New Jersey	8	8	...	...	8	8	...	...	...	8	...	8	...	8		
New Mexico	...	...	...	...	...	...	...	...	...	...	...	...	...	...		
New York	42	42	...	...	42	42	...	...	...	42	...	42	42	...		
North Carolina	15	9	...	6	15	...	15	...	15	...	...	15	...	15		
North Dakota	...	...	...	...	...	...	...	...	...	...	...	...	...	...		
Ohio	21	21	...	...	21	21	...	...	...	21	...	21	21	...		
Oklahoma	...	...	...	...	...	...	...	...	...	...	...	...	...	...		
Oregon	...	...	...	...	...	...	...	...	...	...	...	...	...	...		
Pennsylvania	30	30	...	...	30	...	...	30	...	...	30	30	30	...		
Rhode Island	4	4	...	...	4	...	4	...	4	...	...	4	4	...		
South Carolina	11	...	...	11	...	...	...	...	...	...	...	...	...	...		
South Dakota	...	...	...	...	...	...	...	...	...	...	...	...	...	...		
Tennessee	15	15	...	...	15	15	...	...	15	...	...	15	15	...		
Texas	...	...	...	...	...	...	...	...	...	...	...	...	...	...		
Utah	...	...	...	...	...	...	...	...	...	...	...	...	...	...		
Vermont	7	7	...	...	7	7	...	...	...	7	...	7	7	...		
Virginia	23	...	...	23	23	...	23	...	...	...	23	23	...	23		
Washington	...	...	...	...	...	...	...	...	...	...	...	...	...	...		
West Virginia	...	...	...	...	...	...	...	...	...	...	...	...	...	...		
Wisconsin	...	...	...	...	...	...	...	...	...	...	...	...	...	...		
Wyoming	...	...	...	...	...	...	...	...	...	...	...	...	...	...		
Alaska	...	...	...	...	...	...	...	...	...	...	...	...	...	...		
Canal Zone	...	...	...	...	...	...	...	...	...	...	...	...	...	...		
District of Columbia	...	...	...	...	...	...	...	...	...	...	...	...	...	...		
Hawaii	...	...	...	...	...	...	...	...	...	...	...	...	...	...		
Philippine Islands	...	...	...	...	...	...	...	...	...	...	...	...	...	...		
Puerto Rico	...	...	...	...	...	...	...	...	...	...	...	...	...	...		
Virgin Islands	...	...	...	...	...	...	...	...	...	...	...	...	...	...		
Total	283	208	26	49	265	154	77	34	70	142	53	265	178	87	Van Buren by Acclamation	No Vice-Presidential Nominee

Source: Proceedings of a Convention of Republican Delegates from the Several States in the Union, for the Purpose of Nominating a Candidate for the Office of Vice-President of the United States, 1832, also in Baltimore *Republican*, May 23, 1832.

Source: Votes on Resolutions from Baltimore *Republican*, May 25, 1835, (Presidential ballot) *Niles' Register*, 1835.

1844 DEMOCRATIC

Presidential

Delegation	Votes	Amendment Ratifying Two-Thirds Rule		First Ballot			Second Ballot			Third Ballot			Fourth Ballot			Fifth Ballot		
		Yea	Nay	Van Buren	Cass	Other	Van Buren	Cass	Other	Van Buren	Cass	Other	Van Buren	Cass	Other	Van Buren	Cass	Other
Alabama	9	9	...	1	8	...	1	8	...	1	8	...	1	8	...	1	8	...
Arizona	...	...	...	...	...	...	...	...	...	...	...	...	...	...	...	...	...	...
Arkansas	3	3	...	...	...	3	...	...	3	...	...	3	...	...	3	...	...	3
California	...	...	...	...	...	...	...	...	...	...	...	...	...	...	...	...	...	...
Colorado	...	...	...	...	...	...	...	...	...	...	...	...	...	...	...	...	...	...
Connecticut	6	3	3	6	...	...	...	...	6	...	...	6	...	...	6	...	...	6
Delaware	3	3	...	...	3	...	...	3	...	...	3	...	...	3	...	...	3	...
Florida	...	...	...	...	...	...	...	...	...	...	...	...	...	...	...	...	...	...
Georgia	10	10	...	...	9	1	...	9	1	...	8	2	...	9	1	...	9	1
Idaho	...	...	...	...	...	...	...	...	...	...	...	...	...	...	...	...	...	...
Illinois	9	9	...	5	2	2	2	2	5	2	2	5	2	2	5	2	4	3
Indiana	12	12	...	3	9	...	3	9	...	3	9	...	3	9	...	1	11	...
Iowa	...	...	...	...	...	...	...	...	...	...	...	...	...	...	...	...	...	...
Kansas	...	...	...	...	...	...	...	...	...	...	...	...	...	...	...	...	...	...
Kentucky	12	12	...	...	...	12	...	...	12	...	...	12	...	...	12	...	...	12
Louisiana	6	6	...	...	...	6	...	...	6	...	...	6	...	...	6	...	...	6
Maine	9	...	9	8	...	1	8	1	...	8	1	...	8	1	...	8	1	...
Maryland	8	6	2	2	4	2	2	5	1	2	6	...	2	6	...	2	6	...
Massachusetts	12	5	7	8	1	3	7	3	2	7	3	2	7	3	2	7	3	2
Michigan	5	5	...	1	4	...	1	4	...	...	5	...	...	5	...	...	5	...
Minnesota	...	...	...	...	...	...	...	...	...	...	...	...	...	...	...	...	...	...
Mississippi	6	6	...	...	6	...	...	6	...	...	6	...	...	6	...	...	6	...
Missouri	7	...	7	7	...	...	7	...	...	7	...	...	7	...	...	7	...	...
Montana	...	...	...	...	...	...	...	...	...	...	...	...	...	...	...	...	...	...
Nebraska	...	...	...	...	...	...	...	...	...	...	...	...	...	...	...	...	...	...
Nevada	...	...	...	...	...	...	...	...	...	...	...	...	...	...	...	...	...	...
New Hampshire	6	...	6	6	...	...	6	...	...	3	...	3	2	...	4	2	...	4
New Jersey	7	7	...	3	2	2	2	2	3	1	4	2	1	4	2	...	4	3
New Mexico	...	...	...	...	...	...	...	...	...	...	...	...	...	...	...	...	...	...
New York	36	...	38	36	...	...	36	...	...	36	...	...	36	...	...	36	...	...
North Carolina	11	5	5	2	4	5	...	5	6	...	...	11	...	11	...	...	7	4
North Dakota	...	...	...	...	...	...	...	...	...	...	...	...	...	...	...	...	...	...
Ohio	23	...	23	23	...	...	23	...	...	23	...	...	22	1	...	20	3	...
Oklahoma	...	...	...	...	...	...	...	...	...	...	...	...	...	...	...	...	...	...
Oregon	...	...	...	...	...	...	...	...	...	...	...	...	...	...	...	...	...	...
Pennsylvania	26	12	13	26	...	...	26	...	...	26	...	...	18	...	8	16	...	10
Rhode Island	4	2	2	4	...	...	3	1	...	2	1	1	2	1	1	1	1	2
South Carolina	...	...	...	...	...	...	...	...	...	...	...	...	...	...	...	...	...	...
South Dakota	...	...	...	...	...	...	...	...	...	...	...	...	...	...	...	...	...	...
Tennessee	13	13	...	...	...	13	...	...	13	...	...	13	...	...	13	...	...	13
Texas	...	...	...	...	...	...	...	...	...	...	...	...	...	...	...	...	...	...
Utah	...	...	...	...	...	...	...	...	...	...	...	...	...	...	...	...	...	...
Vermont	6	3	3	5	1	...	...	...	6	...	...	6	...	...	6	...	...	6
Virginia	17	17	...	...	17	...	...	17	...	...	17	...	...	17	...	...	17	...
Washington	...	...	...	...	...	...	...	...	...	...	...	...	...	...	...	...	...	...
West Virginia	...	...	...	...	...	...	...	...	...	...	...	...	...	...	...	...	...	...
Wisconsin	...	...	...	...	...	...	...	...	...	...	...	...	...	...	...	...	...	..
Wyoming	...	...	...	...	...	...	...	...	...	...	...	...	...	...	...	...	...	..
Alaska	...	...	...	...	...	...	...	...	...	...	...	...	...	...	...	...	...	...
Canal Zone	...	...	...	...	...	...	...	...	...	...	...	...	...	...	...	...	...	...
District of Columbia	...	...	...	...	...	...	...	...	...	...	...	...	...	...	...	...	...	...
Hawaii	...	...	...	...	...	...	...	...	...	...	...	...	...	...	...	...	...	...
Philippine Islands	...	...	...	...	...	...	...	...	...	...	...	...	...	...	...	...	...	...
Puerto Rico	...	...	...	...	...	...	...	...	...	...	...	...	...	...	...	...	...	...
Virgin Islands	...	...	...	...	...	...	...	...	...	...	...	...	...	...	...	...	...	...
Total	266	148	118	146	83	37[a]	127	94	45[b]	121	92	53[c]	111	105	50[d]	103	107	56[e]

Source: *Niles' Register, 1844.*
Amendment ratifying two-thirds rule, p. 212.
Presidential. First ballot, p. 213.
a/ Other candidates: Richard M. Johnson, 24; John C. Calhoun, 6; James Buchanan, 4; Levi Woodbury, 2; Commodore Stewart, 1.
Second ballot, p. 214.
b/ Other candidates: Johnson, 33; Buchanan, 9; Stewart, 1; Woodbury, 1; Calhoun, 1.
Third ballot, p. 214.
c/ Other candidates: Johnson, 38; Buchanan, 11; Woodbury, 2; Calhoun, 2.
Fourth ballot, p. 215.
d/ Other candidates: Johnson, 32; Buchanan, 17; not voting, 1.
Fifth ballot, p. 215.
e/ Other candidates: Johnson, 29; Buchanan, 26; not voting, 1.

		1844 DEMOCRATIC														Vice-Pres.	
		Presidential														First Ballot	
		Sixth Ballot			Seventh Ballot			Eighth Ballot				Ninth Ballot (before shift)			Ninth (after)		
Delegation	Votes	Van Buren	Cass	Other	Van Buren	Cass	Other	Van Buren	Cass	Polk	Other	Polk	Cass	Other	Polk	Wright	Woodbury
Alabama	9	1	8	...	1	8	...	...	...	9	...	9	...	...	9	9	...
Arizona	...	...	...	...	...	...	...	...	...	...	...	...	...	...	...	...	...
Arkansas	3	...	...	3	...	...	3	...	3	...	...	3	...	...	3	3	...
California	...	...	...	...	...	...	...	...	...	...	...	...	...	...	...	...	...
Colorado	...	...	...	...	...	...	...	...	...	...	...	...	...	...	...	...	...
Connecticut	6	...	6	...	...	6	...	...	6	...	...	6	...	...	6	6	...
Delaware	3	...	3	...	...	3	...	...	3	...	...	3	...	...	3	3	...
Florida	...	...	...	...	...	...	...	...	...	...	...	...	...	...	...	...	...
Georgia	10	...	9	1	...	9	1	...	9	...	1	9	...	1	10	2	8
Idaho	...	...	...	...	...	...	...	...	...	...	...	...	...	...	...	...	...
Illinois	9	...	5	4	1	5	3	1	8	...	...	9	...	...	9	9	...
Indiana	12	1	11	...	1	11	...	1	11	...	...	12	...	...	12	12	...
Iowa	...	...	...	...	...	...	...	...	...	...	...	...	...	...	...	...	...
Kansas	...	...	...	...	...	...	...	...	...	...	...	...	...	...	...	...	...
Kentucky	12	...	...	12	...	...	12	...	12	...	...	12	...	...	12	12	...
Louisiana	6	...	...	6	...	...	6	...	...	6	...	6	...	...	6	6	...
Maine	9	8	1	...	8	1	...	8	1	...	...	7	1	1	9	9	...
Maryland	8	2	6	...	...	8	...	1	6	1	...	7	1	...	8	8	...
Massachusetts	12	6	4	2	6	5	1	...	5	7	...	10	2	...	12	12	...
Michigan	5	...	5	...	...	5	...	...	5	...	...	...	5	...	5	5	...
Minnesota	...	...	...	...	...	...	...	...	...	...	...	...	...	...	...	...	...
Mississippi	6	...	6	...	...	6	...	...	6	...	...	6	...	...	6	6	...
Missouri	7	7	...	...	7	...	...	7	...	...	...	7	...	...	7	7	...
Montana	...	...	...	...	...	...	...	...	...	...	...	...	...	...	...	...	...
Nebraska	...	...	...	...	...	...	...	...	...	...	...	...	...	...	...	...	...
Nevada	...	...	...	...	...	...	...	...	...	...	...	...	...	...	...	...	...
New Hampshire	6	2	...	4	3	...	3	...	...	6	...	6	...	...	6	6	...
New Jersey	7	...	5	2	...	5	2	1	5	...	1	2	5	...	7	7	...
New Mexico	...	...	...	...	...	...	...	...	...	...	...	...	...	...	...	...	...
New York	36	36	...	...	36	...	...	36	...	...	...	35	...	1	36	36	...
North Carolina	11	...	7	4	2	7	2	2	8	...	1	11	...	...	11	11	...
North Dakota	...	...	...	...	...	...	...	...	...	...	...	...	...	...	...	...	...
Ohio	23	20	3	...	20	3	...	21	2	...	...	18	2	3	23	23	...
Oklahoma	...	...	...	...	...	...	...	...	...	...	...	...	...	...	...	...	...
Oregon	...	...	...	...	...	...	...	...	...	...	...	...	...	...	...	...	...
Pennsylvania	26	17	...	9	12	4	10	22	1	2	1	19	7	...	26	26	...
Rhode Island	4	1	1	2	2	1	1	4	...	...	...	4	...	...	4	4	...
South Carolina	...	...	...	...	...	...	...	...	...	...	...	...	...	...	...	...	...
South Dakota	...	...	...	...	...	...	...	...	...	...	...	...	...	...	...	...	...
Tennessee	13	...	13	...	...	13	...	...	...	13	...	13	...	...	13	13	...
Texas	...	...	...	...	...	...	...	...	...	...	...	...	...	...	...	...	...
Utah	...	...	...	...	...	...	...	...	...	...	...	...	...	...	...	...	...
Vermont	6	...	6	...	...	6	...	...	6	...	...	...	6	...	6	6	...
Virginia	17	...	17	...	...	17	...	...	17	...	...	17	...	...	17	17	...
Washington	...	...	...	...	...	...	...	...	...	...	...	...	...	...	...	...	...
West Virginia	...	...	...	...	...	...	...	...	...	...	...	...	...	...	...	...	...
Wisconsin	...	...	...	...	...	...	...	...	...	...	...	...	...	...	...	...	...
Wyoming	...	...	...	...	...	...	...	...	...	...	...	...	...	...	...	...	...
Alaska	...	...	...	...	...	...	...	...	...	...	...	...	...	...	...	...	...
Canal Zone	...	...	...	...	...	...	...	...	...	...	...	...	...	...	...	...	...
District of Columbia	...	...	...	...	...	...	...	...	...	...	...	...	...	...	...	...	...
Hawaii	...	...	...	...	...	...	...	...	...	...	...	...	...	...	...	...	...
Philippine Islands	...	...	...	...	...	...	...	...	...	...	...	...	...	...	...	...	...
Puerto Rico	...	...	...	...	...	...	...	...	...	...	...	...	...	...	...	...	...
Virgin Islands	...	...	...	...	...	...	...	...	...	...	...	...	...	...	...	...	...
Total	266	101	116	49[a]	99	123	44[b]	104	114	44	4[c]	231	29	6[d]	266	258	8

Source: *Niles' Register, 1844.*
Sixth ballot, p. 216.
a/ Other candidates: Buchanan, 25; Johnson, 23; not voting, 1.
Seventh ballot, p. 216.
b/ Other candidates: Buchanan, 22; Johnson, 21; not voting, 1.
Eighth ballot, p. 217.
c/ Not voting, 4.
Ninth ballot (before shift), p. 217.
d/ Not voting, 6.
Ninth ballot (after shift), p. 217.
Vice-Presidential. First ballot, p. 218.

	1844 DEMOCRATIC								1848 DEMOCRATIC									
	Vice-Presidential									Table Two-Thirds Rule			Adoption of Two-Thirds Rule			Previous Question, New York Credentials		
		Second Ballot				Third Ballot												
Delegation	Votes	Fairfield	Woodbury	Cass	Other	Fairfield	Dallas	Other	Votes	Yea	Nay	Not Voting	Yea	Nay	Not Voting	Yea	Nay	Not Voting
Alabama	9	...	...	9	...	...	9	...	9	...	9	...	9	...	...	8	1	...
Arizona	...	...	...	...	...	...	...	...	...	...	...	...	...	...	...	...	...	...
Arkansas	3	...	3	...	...	...	3	...	3	3	...	...	3	...	...	3	...	...
California	...	...	...	...	...	...	...	...	...	...	...	...	...	...	...	...	...	...
Colorado	...	...	...	...	...	...	...	...	...	...	...	...	...	...	...	...	...	...
Connecticut	6	...	...	...	6	...	6	...	6	...	6	...	6	...	...	...	6	...
Delaware	3	...	...	...	3	...	3	...	3	3	...	...	2	1	...	3	...	...
Florida	...	...	...	...	...	...	...	...	3	...	3	...	3	...	...	3	...	...
Georgia	10	...	10	...	...	...	10	...	10	...	10	...	10	...	...	10	...	...
Idaho	...	...	...	...	...	...	...	...	...	...	...	...	...	...	...	...	...	...
Illinois	9	11	...	...	...	...	9	...	9	9	...	...	9	...	...	9	...	...
Indiana	12	11	...	...	1	...	12	...	12	12	...	...	3	9	...	12	...	...
Iowa	...	...	...	...	...	...	...	...	4	...	4	...	4	...	...	4	...	...
Kansas	...	...	...	...	...	...	...	...	...	...	...	...	...	...	...	...	...	...
Kentucky	12	12	...	...	...	...	12	...	12	4	8	...	12	...	...	2	10	...
Louisiana	6	...	6	...	...	...	6	...	6	6	...	...	6	...	...	6	...	...
Maine	9	9	...	...	...	9	...	...	9	...	9	...	9	...	...	8	1	...
Maryland	8	...	8	...	...	...	8	...	8	8	...	...	7	1	...	8	...	...
Massachusetts	12	12	...	...	...	11	1	...	12	4	8	...	10	2	...	...	12	...
Michigan	5	...	...	...	5	...	5	...	5	5	...	...	5	...	...	5	...	...
Minnesota	...	...	...	...	...	...	...	...	...	...	...	...	...	...	...	...	...	...
Mississippi	6	...	...	...	6	...	...	...	6	6	...	...	6	...	...	6	...	...
Missouri	7	7	...	...	...	...	7	...	7	6	1	...	1	6	...	6	1	...
Montana	...	...	...	...	...	...	...	...	...	...	...	...	...	...	...	...	...	...
Nebraska	...	...	...	...	...	...	...	...	...	...	...	...	...	...	...	...	...	...
Nevada	...	...	...	...	...	...	...	...	...	...	...	...	...	...	...	...	...	...
New Hampshire	6	...	6	...	...	...	...	6	6	...	6	...	6	...	...	...	6	...
New Jersey	7	...	...	...	7	...	7	...	7	...	7	...	7	...	...	...	7	...
New Mexico	...	...	...	...	...	...	...	...	...	...	...	...	...	...	...	...	...	...
New York	36	36	...	...	...	...	36	...	36	...	...	36	...	...	36	...	...	36
North Carolina	11	...	11	...	...	...	11	...	11	...	11	...	11	...	...	11	...	...
North Dakota	...	...	...	...	...	...	...	...	...	...	...	...	...	...	...	...	...	...
Ohio	23	...	...	...	23	...	23	...	23	23	...	...	...	23	...	23	...	...
Oklahoma	...	...	...	...	...	...	...	...	...	...	...	...	...	...	...	...	...	...
Oregon	...	...	...	...	...	...	...	...	...	...	...	...	...	...	...	...	...	...
Pennsylvania	26	...	...	...	26	...	26	...	26	...	26	...	...	26	...	26	...	...
Rhode Island	4	4	...	...	...	4	...	...	4	...	4	...	3	1	...	4	...	...
South Carolina	...	...	...	...	...	...	...	...	9	...	9	...	9	...	...	9	...	...
South Dakota	...	...	...	...	...	...	...	...	...	...	...	...	...	...	...	...	...	...
Tennessee	13	...	...	13	...	...	13	...	13	7	6	...	13	...	...	4	7	2
Texas	...	...	...	...	...	...	...	...	4	...	4	...	4	...	...	4	...	...
Utah	...	...	...	...	...	...	...	...	...	...	...	...	...	...	...	...	...	...
Vermont	6	5	...	...	1	6	...	...	6	4	2	...	1	5	...	6	...	...
Virginia	17	...	...	17	...	...	17	...	17	17	...	...	17	...	...	17	...	...
Washington	...	...	...	...	...	...	...	...	...	...	...	...	...	...	...	...	...	...
West Virginia	...	...	...	...	...	...	...	...	...	...	...	...	...	...	...	...	...	...
Wisconsin	...	...	...	...	...	...	...	...	4	4	...	...	...	4	...	4	...	...
Wyoming	...	...	...	...	...	...	...	...	...	...	...	...	...	...	...	...	...	...
Alaska	...	...	...	...	...	...	...	...	...	...	...	...	...	...	...	...	...	...
Canal Zone	...	...	...	...	...	...	...	...	...	...	...	...	...	...	...	...	...	...
District of Columbia	...	...	...	...	...	...	...	...	...	...	...	...	...	...	...	...	...	...
Hawaii	...	...	...	...	...	...	...	...	...	...	...	...	...	...	...	...	...	...
Philippine Islands	...	...	...	...	...	...	...	...	...	...	...	...	...	...	...	...	...	...
Puerto Rico	...	...	...	...	...	...	...	...	...	...	...	...	...	...	...	...	...	...
Virgin Islands	...	...	...	...	...	...	...	...	...	...	...	...	...	...	...	...	...	...
Total	266	107	44	39	78a	30	230b	6c	290	121	133	36	176	78	36	201	51	38

Source: *Niles' Register, 1844.*
Second ballot, p. 218.
a/ Other candidates: Richard M. Johnson, 26; Commodore Stewart, 23; George M. Dallas, 13; William L. Marcy, 5; not voting, 11.
Third ballot, p. 218.
b/ Sum of column; proceedings record 220.
c/ Other candidates: Woodbury, 6.

Source: *Niles' Register, 1848.*
Table two-thirds rule, p. 75.
Adoption of two-thirds rule, p. 76.
Previous question, New York credentials, p. 326.

1848 DEMOCRATIC

Delegation	Votes	Amendment to Amendment, New York Credentials			Amendment to Resolution, New York Credentials			Resolution, New York Credentials			Table Revision of Previous Motion, N. Y. Credentials			Presidential First Ballot			
		Yea	Nay	Not Voting	Yea	Nay	Not Voting	Yea	Nay	Not Voting	Yea	Nay	Not Voting	Cass	Buchanan	Woodbury	Other
Alabama	9	...	9	...	...	9	...	...	9	...	9	...	...	...	4	5	...
Arizona	...	...	...	...	...	...	...	...	...	...	...	...	...	...	...	...	...
Arkansas	3	...	3	...	...	3	...	...	3	...	...	3	...	3	...	...	...
California	...	...	...	...	...	...	...	...	...	...	...	...	...	...	...	...	...
Colorado	...	...	...	...	...	...	...	...	...	...	...	...	...	...	...	...	...
Connecticut	6	6	...	...	6	...	...	2	...	4	6	...	...	...	...	6	...
Delaware	3	1	2	...	1	2	...	1	2	...	1	2	...	3	...	...	3
Florida	3	...	3	...	...	3	...	...	3	...	...	3	...	...	...	...	3
Georgia	10	...	10	...	...	10	...	...	10	...	3	7	...	...	2	5	3
Idaho	...	...	...	...	...	...	...	...	...	...	...	...	...	...	...	...	...
Illinois	9	9	...	...	9	...	...	9	...	...	9	...	...	9	...	...	...
Indiana	12	7	5	...	9	2	1	...	12	...	10	1	1	12	...	...	...
Iowa	4	4	...	...	4	...	...	4	...	...	4	...	...	1	3	...	...
Kansas	...	...	2	...	...	2	...	...	2	...	11	1	...	7	1	1	3
Kentucky	12	10	2	...	10	2	...	10	2	...	11	1	...	7	1	1	3
Louisiana	6	...	6	...	...	6	...	...	6	...	...	6	...	6	...	...	...
Maine	9	9	...	...	9	...	...	9	...	...	9	...	...	...	...	9	...
Maryland	8	2	5	1	3	5	...	3	5	...	8	...	...	6	...	2	...
Massachusetts	12	11	1	...	9	2	1	10	2	...	12	...	...	...	...	12	...
Michigan	5	...	5	...	...	5	...	...	5	...	1	4	...	5	...	...	...
Minnesota	...	...	...	...	...	...	...	...	...	...	...	...	...	...	...	...	...
Mississippi	6	...	6	...	...	6	...	...	6	...	...	6	...	6	...	...	...
Missouri	7	1	4	2	1	5	1	2	4	1	2	4	1	7	...	...	...
Montana	...	...	...	...	...	...	...	...	...	...	...	...	...	...	...	...	...
Nebraska	...	...	...	...	...	...	...	...	...	...	...	...	...	...	...	...	...
Nevada	...	...	...	...	...	...	...	...	...	...	...	...	...	...	...	...	...
New Hampshire	6	6	...	...	6	...	...	6	...	...	6	...	...	...	...	6	...
New Jersey	7	7	...	...	7	...	...	7	...	...	7	...	...	...	7	...	...
New Mexico	...	...	...	...	...	...	...	...	...	...	...	...	...	...	...	...	...
New York	36	...	...	36	...	...	36	...	...	36	...	...	36	...	...	...	36
North Carolina	11	...	11	...	...	11	...	...	11	...	...	11	...	...	10	1	...
North Dakota	...	...	...	...	...	...	...	...	...	...	...	...	...	...	...	...	...
Ohio	23	14	9	...	10	12	1	10	...	13	12	11	...	23	...	...	...
Oklahoma	...	...	...	...	...	...	...	...	...	...	...	...	...	...	...	...	...
Oregon	...	...	...	...	...	...	...	...	...	...	...	...	...	...	...	...	...
Pennsylvania	26	19	7	...	26	...	...	26	...	...	26	...	...	...	26	...	...
Rhode Island	4	2	2	...	2	2	...	2	2	...	2	2	...	1	...	3	...
South Carolina	9	...	9	...	...	9	...	...	9	...	...	9	...	...	...	...	9
South Dakota	...	...	...	...	...	...	...	...	...	...	...	...	...	...	...	...	...
Tennessee	13	9	4	...	9	4	...	9	4	...	9	4	...	7	2	1	3
Texas	4	4	...	...	4	...	...	4	...	...	4	...	...	4	...	...	...
Utah	...	...	...	...	...	...	...	...	...	...	...	...	...	...	...	...	...
Vermont	6	5	1	...	5	1	...	6	...	...	6	...	...	4	...	2	...
Virginia	17	...	17	...	...	17	...	...	17	...	...	17	...	17	...	...	...
Washington	...	...	...	...	...	...	...	...	...	...	...	...	...	...	...	...	...
West Virginia	...	...	...	...	...	...	...	...	...	...	...	...	...	...	...	...	...
Wisconsin	4	...	4	...	...	4	...	...	4	...	...	4	...	4	...	...	...
Wyoming	...	...	...	...	...	...	...	...	...	...	...	...	...	...	...	...	...
Alaska	...	...	...	...	...	...	...	...	...	...	...	...	...	...	...	...	...
Canal Zone	...	...	...	...	...	...	...	...	...	...	...	...	...	...	...	...	...
District of Columbia	...	...	...	...	...	...	...	...	...	...	...	...	...	...	...	...	...
Hawaii	...	...	...	...	...	...	...	...	...	...	...	...	...	...	...	...	...
Philippine Islands	...	...	...	...	...	...	...	...	...	...	...	...	...	...	...	...	...
Puerto Rico	...	...	...	...	...	...	...	...	...	...	...	...	...	...	...	...	...
Virgin Islands	...	...	...	...	...	...	...	...	...	...	...	...	...	...	...	...	...
Total	290	126	125	39	130	120	40	120[a]	116	54	157	95	38	125	55	53	57[b]

Source: *Niles' Register, 1848.*

Amendment to amendment, New York credentials, p. 326.
Amendment to resolution, New York credentials, p. 326.
Resolution, New York credentials, p. 326.
a/ Sum of column; proceedings record 129.
Table revision of previous motion, New York credentials, p. 326.
Presidential. First ballot, p. 327.
b/ Other candidates: John C. Calhoun, 9; W. J. Worth, 6; George M. Dallas, 3; not voting, 39.

1848 DEMOCRATIC

Presidential — Vice-Presidential

Delegation	Votes	Second Ballot				Third Ballot				Fourth Ballot				First Ballot		
		Cass	Buchanan	Wood	Other	Cass	Buchanan	Woodbury	Other	Cass	Buchanan	Woodbury	Other	Butler	Quitman	Other
Alabama	9	...	4	5	...	...	4	5	...	...	4	5	...	...	...	9
Arizona	...	...	...	...	...	...	...	...	...	...	...	...	...	...	...	...
Arkansas	3	3	...	...	...	3	...	...	...	3	...	...	...	...	3	...
California	...	...	...	...	...	...	...	...	...	...	...	...	...	...	...	...
Colorado	...	...	...	...	...	...	...	...	...	...	...	...	...	...	...	...
Connecticut	6	...	...	6	...	...	...	6	...	...	...	6	...	6	...	...
Delaware	3	3	...	...	...	3	...	...	...	3	...	...	...	3	...	...
Florida	3	...	...	...	3	...	...	3	...	...	...	3	...	3	...	...
Georgia	10	4	1	2	3	8	...	2	...	10	...	...	...	2	4	4
Idaho	...	...	...	...	...	...	...	...	...	...	...	...	...	...	...	...
Illinois	9	9	...	...	...	9	...	...	...	9	...	...	...	...	9	...
Indiana	12	12	...	...	...	12	...	...	...	12	...	...	...	5	3	4
Iowa	4	1	3	...	...	4	...	...	...	4	...	...	...	4	...	...
Kansas	...	...	...	...	...	...	...	...	...	...	...	...	...	...	...	...
Kentucky	12	8	1	1	2	8	1	1	2	8	1	1	2	12	...	...
Louisiana	6	6	...	...	...	6	...	...	...	6	...	...	...	...	6	...
Maine	9	...	...	9	...	...	...	9	...	...	...	9	...	9	...	...
Maryland	8	6	...	2	...	6	...	2	...	6	...	2	...	4	1	3
Massachusetts	12	3	...	9	...	5	...	7	...	8	...	4	...	7	5	...
Michigan	5	5	...	...	...	5	...	...	...	5	...	...	...	3	1	1
Minnesota	...	...	...	...	...	...	...	...	...	...	...	...	...	...	...	...
Mississippi	6	6	...	...	...	6	...	...	...	6	...	...	...	...	6	...
Missouri	7	7	...	...	...	7	...	...	...	7	...	...	...	7	...	...
Montana	...	...	...	...	...	...	...	...	...	...	...	...	...	...	...	...
Nebraska	...	...	...	...	...	...	...	...	...	...	...	...	...	...	...	...
Nevada	...	...	...	...	...	...	...	...	...	...	...	...	...	...	...	...
New Hampshire	6	...	...	6	...	...	...	6	...	...	...	6	...	6	...	...
New Jersey	7	...	7	...	...	...	6	...	1	7	...	...	...	...	7	...
New Mexico	...	...	...	...	...	...	...	...	...	...	...	...	...	...	...	...
New York	36	...	...	...	36	...	...	36	...	...	...	36	...	...	...	36
North Carolina	11	...	10	1	...	11	...	...	...	11	...	...	...	...	...	11
North Dakota	...	...	...	...	...	...	...	...	...	...	...	...	...	...	...	...
Ohio	23	23	...	...	...	23	...	...	...	23	...	...	...	12	10	1
Oklahoma	...	...	...	...	...	...	...	...	...	...	...	...	...	...	...	...
Oregon	...	...	...	...	...	...	...	...	...	...	...	...	...	...	...	...
Pennsylvania	26	...	26	...	...	...	26	...	...	...	26	...	...	10	2	14
Rhode Island	4	1	...	3	...	4	...	...	...	4	...	...	...	3	...	1
South Carolina	9	...	...	9	...	...	...	9	...	9	...	...	...	...	9	...
South Dakota	...	...	...	...	...	...	...	...	...	...	...	...	...	...	...	...
Tennessee	13	7	2	1	3	7	2	1	3	7	2	2	2	13	...	...
Texas	4	4	...	...	...	4	...	...	...	4	...	...	...	...	4	...
Utah	...	...	...	...	...	...	...	...	...	...	...	...	...	...	...	...
Vermont	6	4	...	2	...	4	...	2	...	6	...	...	...	6	...	...
Virginia	17	17	...	...	...	17	...	...	...	17	...	...	...	...	...	17
Washington	...	...	...	...	...	...	...	...	...	...	...	...	...	...	...	...
West Virginia	...	...	...	...	...	...	...	...	...	...	...	...	...	...	...	...
Wisconsin	4	4	...	...	...	4	...	...	...	4	...	...	...	...	4	...
Wyoming	...	...	...	...	...	...	...	...	...	...	...	...	...	...	...	...
Alaska	...	...	...	...	...	...	...	...	...	...	...	...	...	...	...	...
Canal Zone	...	...	...	...	...	...	...	...	...	...	...	...	...	...	...	...
District of Columbia	...	...	...	...	...	...	...	...	...	...	...	...	...	...	...	...
Hawaii	...	...	...	...	...	...	...	...	...	...	...	...	...	...	...	...
Philippine Islands	...	...	...	...	...	...	...	...	...	...	...	...	...	...	...	...
Puerto Rico	...	...	...	...	...	...	...	...	...	...	...	...	...	...	...	...
Virgin Islands	...	...	...	...	...	...	...	...	...	...	...	...	...	...	...	...
Total	290	133	54	56	47[a]	156	39	53	42[b]	179	33	38	40[c]	114	74[d]	102[e]

Source: *Niles' Register, 1848.*

Second ballot, p. 327.
a/ Other candidates: Worth, 6; Dallas, 3; not voting, 38.
Third ballot, p. 328.
b/ Other candidates: Worth, 5; not voting, 37.
Fourth ballot, p. 328.
c/ Other candidates: William O. Butler, 4; Worth, 1; not voting, 35.
Vice-Presidential. First ballot, p. 329.
d/ Sum of column is 70, but with inclusion of Wisconsin, total is 74.
e/ Other candidates: William R. King, 26; John Y. Mason, 24; James J. McKay, 13; Jefferson Davis, 1; not voting, 38.

		1848 DEMOCRATIC								
Delegation	Votes	Vice-Presidential				Minority Plank on Slavery			Adoption of Platform	
		Second Ballot (before shift)			Second Ballot (after)					
		Butler	Quitman	Other	Butler	Yea	Nay	Not Voting	Yea	Not Voting
Alabama	9	...	2	7	9	9	...	...	7	2
Arizona	...	...	...	...	...	...	...	...	...	...
Arkansas	3	...	3	...	3	3	...	...	3	...
California	...	...	...	...	...	...	...	...	...	...
Colorado	...	...	...	...	...	...	...	...	...	...
Connecticut	6	6	...	...	6	...	6	...	6	...
Delaware	3	3	...	...	3	...	3	...	3	...
Florida	3	...	2	1	3	3	...	...	...	3
Georgia	10	10	...	...	10	9	...	1	10	...
Idaho	...	...	...	...	...	...	...	...	...	...
Illinois	9	9	...	...	9	...	9	...	9	...
Indiana	12	12	...	...	12	...	12	...	10	2
Iowa	4	4	...	...	4	...	4	...	4	...
Kansas	...	...	...	...	...	...	...	...	...	...
Kentucky	12	12	...	...	12	1	11	...	12	...
Louisiana	6	...	6	...	6	...	6	...	6	...
Maine	9	9	...	...	9	...	9	...	9	...
Maryland	8	8	...	...	8	1	6	1	8	...
Massachusetts	12	12	...	...	12	...	12	...	12	...
Michigan	5	2	3	...	5	...	5	...	5	...
Minnesota	...	...	...	...	...	...	...	...	...	...
Mississippi	6	...	6	...	6	...	6	...	6	...
Missouri	7	7	...	...	7	...	7	...	7	...
Montana	...	...	...	...	...	...	...	...	...	...
Nebraska	...	...	...	...	...	...	...	...	...	...
Nevada	...	...	...	...	...	...	...	...	...	...
New Hampshire	6	6	...	...	6	...	6	...	6	...
New Jersey	7	...	7	...	7	...	7	...	7	...
New Mexico	...	...	...	...	...	...	...	...	...	...
New York	36	...	...	36	36	...	...	36	...	36
North Carolina	11	...	...	11	11	...	11	...	11	...
North Dakota	...	...	...	...	...	...	...	...	...	...
Ohio	23	11	11	1	23	...	23	...	23	...
Oklahoma	...	...	...	...	...	...	...	...	...	...
Oregon	...	...	...	...	...	...	...	...	...	...
Pennsylvania	26	16	7	3	26	...	26	...	26	...
Rhode Island	4	4	...	...	4	...	4	...	4	...
South Carolina	9	...	9	...	9	9	...	...	9	...
South Dakota	...	...	...	...	...	...	...	...	...	...
Tennessee	13	13	...	...	13	1	12	...	13	...
Texas	4	2	2	...	4	...	4	...	4	...
Utah	...	...	...	...	...	...	...	...	...	...
Vermont	6	6	...	...	6	...	6	...	6	...
Virginia	17	17	...	...	17	...	17	...	17	...
Washington	...	...	...	...	...	...	...	...	...	...
West Virginia	...	...	...	...	...	...	...	...	...	...
Wisconsin	4	...	4	...	4	...	4	...	4	...
Wyoming	...	...	...	...	...	...	...	...	...	...
Alaska	...	...	...	...	...	...	...	...	...	...
Canal Zone	...	...	...	...	...	...	...	...	...	...
District of Columbia	...	...	...	...	...	...	...	...	...	...
Hawaii	...	...	...	...	...	...	...	...	...	...
Philippine Islands	...	...	...	...	...	...	...	...	...	...
Puerto Rico	...	...	...	...	...	...	...	...	...	...
Virgin Islands	...	...	...	...	...	...	...	...	...	...
Total	290	169	62	59a	290	36	216	38	247b	43

Source: *Niles' Register, 1848.*

Second ballot (before shift), p. 329.

a/ Other candidates: McKay, 11; King, 8; Mason, 3; not voting, 37.

Second ballot (after shift), p. 329.

Minority plank on slavery, p. 349.

Adoption of platform, p. 349.

b/ Sum of column; proceedings record 249.

Delegation	Votes	Table Reconsideration of Two-Thirds Rule			Table Order of Business			Majority Report, Massachusetts Credentials			Presidential First Ballot		
		Yea	Nay	Not Voting	Yea	Nay	Not Voting	Yea	Nay	Not Voting	Cass	Buchanan	Other
Alabama	9	9	...	...	...	9	...	9	...	...	...	9	...
Arizona	...	...	...	...	...	...	...	...	...	...	...	...	...
Arkansas	4	4	...	...	...	4	...	4	...	...	...	4	...
California	4	4	...	...	...	4	...	4	...	...	...	...	4
Colorado	...	...	...	...	...	...	...	...	...	...	...	...	...
Connecticut	6	6	...	...	6	...	...	3	3	...	2	2	2
Delaware	3	3	...	...	3	...	...	3	...	...	3	...	...
Florida	3	3	...	...	3	...	...	3	...	...	...	...	3
Georgia	10	10	...	...	...	...	10	10	...	...	...	10	...
Idaho	...	...	...	...	...	...	...	...	...	...	...	...	...
Illinois	11	11	...	...	12	...	...	4	7	...	...	...	11
Indiana	13	13	...	...	...	13	...	13	...	...	...	...	13
Iowa	4	4	...	...	4	...	...	...	4	...	2	...	2
Kansas	...	...	...	...	...	...	...	...	...	...	...	...	...
Kentucky	12	12	...	...	...	12	...	12	...	...	12	...	...
Louisiana	6	6	...	...	6	...	...	6	...	...	6	...	...
Maine	8	8	...	...	8	...	...	6	2	...	5	3	...
Maryland	8	8	...	...	8	...	...	8	...	...	8	...	...
Massachusetts	13	13	...	...	13	...	...	7	5	1	9	...	4
Michigan	6	6	...	...	6	...	...	6	...	...	6	...	...
Minnesota	...	...	...	...	...	...	...	...	...	...	...	...	...
Mississippi	7	7	...	...	7	...	...	7	...	...	...	7	...
Missouri	9	9	...	...	...	9	...	9	...	...	9	...	...
Montana	...	...	...	...	...	...	...	...	...	...	...	...	...
Nebraska	...	...	...	...	...	...	...	...	...	...	...	...	...
Nevada	...	...	...	...	...	...	...	...	...	...	...	...	...
New Hampshire	5	5	...	...	5	...	...	5	...	...	4	...	1
New Jersey	7	7	...	...	7	...	...	...	7	...	7	...	...
New Mexico	...	...	...	...	...	...	...	...	...	...	...	...	...
New York	35	31	3	1	24	11	...	15	20	...	11	...	24
North Carolina	10	10	...	...	...	10	...	10	...	...	...	10	...
North Dakota	...	...	...	...	...	...	...	...	...	...	...	...	...
Ohio	23	7	10	6	17	5	1	...	23	...	16	...	7
Oklahoma	...	...	...	...	...	...	...	...	...	...	...	...	...
Oregon	...	...	...	...	...	...	...	...	...	...	...	...	...
Pennsylvania	27	27	...	...	...	27	...	14	13	...	...	27	...
Rhode Island	4	4	...	...	4	...	...	...	4	...	3	...	1
South Carolina	...	...	...	...	...	...	...	...	...	...	...	...	...
South Dakota	...	...	...	...	...	...	...	...	...	...	...	...	...
Tennessee	12	12	...	...	12	...	...	12	...	...	6	6	...
Texas	4	4	...	...	...	4	...	4	...	...	...	...	4
Utah	...	...	...	...	...	...	...	...	...	...	...	...	...
Vermont	5	6	...	...	6	...	...	6	...	...	5	...	1
Virginia	15	15	...	...	...	15	...	15	...	...	...	15	...
Washington	...	...	...	...	...	...	...	...	...	...	...	...	...
West Virginia	...	...	...	...	...	...	...	...	...	...	...	...	...
Wisconsin	5	5	...	...	5	...	...	...	5	...	2	...	3
Wyoming	...	...	...	...	...	...	...	...	...	...	...	...	...
Alaska	...	...	...	...	...	...	...	...	...	...	...	...	...
Canal Zone	...	...	...	...	...	...	...	...	...	...	...	...	...
District of Columbia	...	...	...	...	...	...	...	...	...	...	...	...	...
Hawaii	...	...	...	...	...	...	...	...	...	...	...	...	...
Philippine Islands	...	...	...	...	...	...	...	...	...	...	...	...	...
Puerto Rico	...	...	...	...	...	...	...	...	...	...	...	...	...
Virgin Islands	...	...	...	...	...	...	...	...	...	...	...	...	...
Total	288[a]	269	13	7	156[b]	123[c]	11	195[d]	93[e]	1	116	93	79[f]

Source: *Official Proceedings, 1852.*

a/ 289 for first four roll-call votes; 288 thereafter.
Table reconsideration of two-thirds rule, p. 8.
Table order of business, p. 12.
b/ Sum of column; proceedings record 155.
c̄/ Sum of column; proceedings record 111.
Majority report, Massachusetts credentials, p. 28.
d/ Sum of column; proceedings record 194.
ē/ Sum of column; proceedings record 83.
Presidential. First ballot, pp. 28-9.
f/ Other candidates: William L. Marcy, 27; Stephen A. Douglas, 20; Joseph Lane, 13; Samuel Houston, 8; J. B. Weller, 4; Henry Dodge, 3; William O. Butler, 2; Daniel S. Dickinson, 1; not voting, 1.

Delegation	Votes	1852 DEMOCRATIC — Presidential															
		Fifth Ballot				Tenth Ballot				Fifteenth Ballot				Twentieth Ballot			
		Cass	Buchanan	Douglas	Other	Cass	Buchanan	Douglas	Other	Cass	Buchanan	Douglas	Other	Buchanan	Cass	Douglas	Other
Alabama	9	...	9	...	...	...	9	...	...	...	9	...	...	9	...	...	...
Arizona	...	...	...	...	...	...	...	...	...	...	...	...	...	...	...	...	...
Arkansas	4	...	..	4	...	...	..	4	...	...	...	4	...	...	...	4	...
California	4	...	1	3	...	...	1	3	...	...	1	3	...	1	...	3	...
Colorado	...	...	...	...	...	...	...	...	...	...	...	...	...	...	...	...	...
Connecticut	6	2	2	1	1	2	2	1	1	2	2	1	1	2	2	1	1
Delaware	3	3	...	...	...	3	...	...	...	3	...	...	...	...	3	...	...
Florida	3	...	...	2	1	...	...	2	1	...	...	3	...	...	...	2	1
Georgia	10	...	10	...	...	...	10	...	...	...	10	...	...	10	...	...	...
Idaho	...	...	...	...	...	...	...	...	...	...	...	...	...	...	...	...	...
Illinois	11	...	...	11	...	...	...	11	...	...	...	11	...	...	...	11	...
Indiana	13	...	...	...	13	...	...	...	13	...	...	...	13	...	...	...	13
Iowa	4	2	...	2	...	2	...	2	...	2	...	2	...	...	1	3	...
Kansas	...	...	...	...	...	...	...	...	...	...	...	...	...	...	...	...	...
Kentucky	12	12	...	...	...	12	...	...	...	12	...	...	...	...	12	...	...
Louisiana	6	6	...	...	...	6	...	...	...	6	...	...	...	...	6	...	...
Maine	8	5	3	...	...	5	3	...	...	4	4	...	...	1	4	3	...
Maryland	8	8	...	...	...	8	...	...	...	8	...	...	...	...	8	...	...
Massachusetts	13	9	...	1	3	8	...	1	4	8	...	1	4	...	1	7	5
Michigan	6	6	...	...	...	6	...	...	...	6	...	...	...	...	6	...	...
Minnesota	...	...	...	...	...	...	...	...	...	...	...	...	...	...	...	...	...
Mississippi	7	...	7	...	...	...	7	...	...	...	7	...	...	7	...	...	...
Missouri	9	9	...	...	...	9	...	...	...	...	...	9	...	...	...	9	...
Montana	...	...	...	...	...	...	...	...	...	...	...	...	...	...	...	...	...
Nebraska	...	...	...	...	...	...	...	...	...	...	...	...	...	...	...	...	...
Nevada	...	...	...	...	...	...	...	...	...	...	...	...	...	...	...	...	...
New Hampshire	5	4	1	...	...	4	...	1	...	4	...	1	...	...	5	...	...
New Jersey	7	7	...	...	...	7	...	...	...	7	...	...	...	...	7	...	...
New Mexico	...	...	...	...	...	...	...	...	...	...	...	...	...	...	...	...	...
New York	35	13	...	...	22	12	...	...	23	12	...	...	23	...	12	...	23
North Carolina	10	...	10	...	...	...	9	1	...	...	9	1	...	9	...	1	...
North Dakota	...	...	...	...	...	...	...	...	...	...	...	...	...	...	...	...	...
Ohio	23	18	...	3	2	17	...	3	3	14	...	5	4	...	13	6	4
Oklahoma	...	...	...	...	...	...	...	...	...	...	...	...	...	...	...	...	...
Oregon	...	...	...	...	...	...	...	...	...	...	...	...	...	...	...	...	...
Pennsylvania	27	...	27	...	...	...	27	...	...	...	27	...	...	27	...	...	...
Rhode Island	4	3	...	...	1	3	...	...	1	3	...	...	1	...	...	4	...
South Carolina	...	...	...	...	...	...	...	...	...	...	...	...	...	...	...	...	...
South Dakota	...	...	...	...	...	...	...	...	...	...	...	...	...	...	...	...	...
Tennessee	12	6	4	1	1	4	3	4	1	5	3	4	...	4	5	3	...
Texas	4	...	...	...	4	...	...	...	4	...	...	...	4	...	...	...	4
Utah	...	...	...	...	...	...	...	...	...	...	...	...	...	...	...	...	...
Vermont	5	...	...	5	...	...	...	5	...	...	...	5	...	...	...	5	...
Virginia	15	...	15	...	...	...	15	...	...	...	15	...	...	15	...	...	...
Washington	...	...	...	...	...	...	...	...	...	...	...	...	...	...	...	...	...
West Virginia	...	...	...	...	...	...	...	...	...	...	...	...	...	...	...	...	...
Wisconsin	5	2	...	...	3	3	...	2	...	3	...	2	...	...	3	2	...
Wyoming	...	...	...	...	...	...	...	...	...	...	...	...	...	...	...	...	...
Alaska	...	...	...	...	...	...	...	...	...	...	...	...	...	...	...	...	...
Canal Zone	...	...	...	...	...	...	...	...	...	...	...	...	...	...	...	...	...
District of Columbia	...	...	...	...	...	...	...	...	...	...	...	...	...	...	...	...	...
Hawaii	...	...	...	...	...	...	...	...	...	...	...	...	...	...	...	...	...
Philippine Islands	...	...	...	...	...	...	...	...	...	...	...	...	...	...	...	...	...
Puerto Rico	...	...	...	...	...	...	...	...	...	...	...	...	...	...	...	...	...
Virgin Islands	...	...	...	...	...	...	...	...	...	...	...	...	...	...	...	...	...
Total	288	115	89	33[a]	51[b]	111	86	40	51[c]	99	87	52[d]	50[e]	92	81	64	51[f]

Source: *Official Proceedings, 1852.*

Fifth ballot, pp. 30-1.

a/ Sum of column; proceedings record 34.

b/ Other candidates: Marcy, 25; Lane, 13; Houston, 8; Dodge, 3; Dickinson, 1; Butler, 1.

Tenth ballot, p. 35.

c/ Other candidates: Marcy, 27; Lane, 14; Houston, 8; Butler, 1; Dickinson, 1.

Fifteenth ballot, p. 37.

d/ Sum of column; proceedings record 51.

e/ Other candidates: Marcy, 26; Lane, 13; Houston, 10; Butler, 1; Dickinson, 1.

Twentieth ballot, p. 41.

f/ Other candidates: Marcy, 26; Lane, 13; Houston, 10; Butler, 1; Dickinson, 1.

1852 DEMOCRATIC — Presidential

| | | Twenty-fifth Ballot | | | | Thirtieth Ballot | | | | Thirty-second Ballot | | | | Thirty-fifth Ballot | | | | |
Delegation	Votes	Buchanan	Douglas	Cass	Other	Douglas	Buchanan	Cass	Other	Cass	Douglas	Buchanan	Other	Cass	Douglas	Marcy	Buchanan	Other
Alabama	9	9	...	...	...	...	9	...	...	...	...	9	...	...	...	...	9	...
Arizona	..	...	...	...	...	...	...	...	...	...	...	...	...	...	...	...	...	...
Arkansas	4	...	4	...	...	4	...	...	...	...	4	...	...	...	4	...	...	...
California	4	1	3	...	...	3	1	...	...	...	3	1	...	2	1	...	1	...
Colorado	..	...	...	...	...	...	...	...	...	...	...	...	...	...	...	...	...	...
Connecticut	6	5	...	1	...	6	...	...	...	3	3	...	...	3	3	...	...	...
Delaware	3	...	...	...	3	...	...	...	3	3	...	...	...	3	...	...	...	...
Florida	3	...	2	...	1	2	...	...	1	...	2	...	1	...	2	...	...	1
Georgia	10	10	...	...	...	...	10	...	...	...	...	10	...	...	10	...	...	...
Idaho	..	...	...	...	...	...	...	...	...	...	...	...	...	...	...	...	...	...
Illinois	11	...	11	...	...	11	...	...	...	...	11	...	...	...	11	...	...	...
Indiana	13	...	...	...	13	...	...	...	13	13	...	...	...	13	...	...	...	...
Iowa	4	...	4	...	...	4	...	...	...	...	4	...	...	2	2	...	...	...
Kansas	..	...	...	...	...	...	...	...	...	...	...	...	...	...	...	...	...	...
Kentucky	12	...	...	...	12	...	...	...	12	12	...	...	...	12	...	...	...	...
Louisiana	6	...	6	...	...	6	...	...	...	...	6	...	...	6	...	...	...	...
Maine	8	5	3	...	...	5	2	...	1	1	5	2	...	2	5	...	1	...
Maryland	8	1	1	1	5	...	...	8	...	8	...	...	...	8	...	...	...	...
Massachusetts	13	...	7	1	5	7	...	1	5	5	3	...	5	7	1	5	...	...
Michigan	6	...	...	6	...	...	...	6	...	6	...	...	...	6	...	...	...	...
Minnesota	..	...	...	...	...	...	...	...	...	...	...	...	...	...	...	...	...	...
Mississippi	7	7	...	...	...	...	7	...	...	...	7	...	...	...	...	7	...	...
Missouri	9	...	9	...	...	9	...	...	...	...	9	...	...	9	...	...	...	...
Montana	..	...	...	...	...	...	...	...	...	...	...	...	...	...	...	...	...	...
Nebraska	..	...	...	...	...	...	...	...	...	...	...	...	...	...	...	...	...	...
Nevada	..	...	...	...	...	...	...	...	...	...	...	...	...	...	...	...	...	...
New Hampshire	5	2	...	...	3	...	2	...	3	5	...	...	...	5	...	...	...	...
New Jersey	7	7	...	...	...	...	7	...	...	7	...	...	...	7	...	...	...	...
New Mexico	..	...	...	...	...	...	...	...	...	...	...	...	...	...	...	...	...	...
New York	35	...	...	12	23	1	...	11	23	11	1	...	23	12	1	22	...	...
North Carolina	10	8	2	...	...	4	6	...	...	...	...	10	...	...	...	10	...	...
North Dakota	..	...	...	...	...	...	...	...	...	...	...	...	...	...	...	...	...	...
Ohio	23	...	6	13	4	9	...	7	7	14	6	...	3	18	3	...	...	2
Oklahoma	..	...	...	...	...	...	...	...	...	...	...	...	...	...	...	...	...	...
Oregon	..	...	...	...	...	...	...	...	...	...	...	...	...	...	...	...	...	...
Pennsylvania	27	27	...	...	...	...	27	...	...	...	...	27	...	...	...	...	27	...
Rhode Island	4	...	4	...	...	4	...	...	...	...	4	...	...	4	...	...	...	...
South Carolina	..	...	...	...	...	...	...	...	...	...	...	...	...	...	...	...	...	...
South Dakota	..	...	...	...	...	...	...	...	...	...	...	...	...	...	...	...	...	...
Tennessee	12	4	7	...	1	7	5	...	...	10	2	...	...	9	2	...	1	...
Texas	4	...	...	...	4	...	...	...	4	...	...	...	4	...	...	...	...	4
Utah	..	...	...	...	...	...	...	...	...	...	...	...	...	...	...	...	...	...
Vermont	5	...	5	...	...	5	...	...	...	...	5	...	...	...	5	...	...	...
Virginia	15	15	...	...	...	...	15	...	...	...	...	15	...	...	...	...	...	15
Washington	..	...	...	...	...	...	...	...	...	...	...	...	...	...	...	...	...	...
West Virginia	..	...	...	...	...	...	...	...	...	...	...	...	...	...	...	...	...	...
Wisconsin	5	...	5	...	...	5	...	...	...	...	5	...	...	3	2	...	...	...
Wyoming	..	...	...	...	...	...	...	...	...	...	...	...	...	...	...	...	...	...
Alaska	..	...	...	...	...	...	...	...	...	...	...	...	...	...	...	...	...	...
Canal Zone	..	...	...	...	...	...	...	...	...	...	...	...	...	...	...	...	...	...
District of Columbia	..	...	...	...	...	...	...	...	...	...	...	...	...	...	...	...	...	...
Hawaii	..	...	...	...	...	...	...	...	...	...	...	...	...	...	...	...	...	...
Philippine Islands	..	...	...	...	...	...	...	...	...	...	...	...	...	...	...	...	...	...
Puerto Rico	..	...	...	...	...	...	...	...	...	...	...	...	...	...	...	...	...	...
Virgin Islands	..	...	...	...	...	...	...	...	...	...	...	...	...	...	...	...	...	...
Total	288	101	79	34	74a	92	91	33	72b	98	80	74	36c	131	52	44	39	22d

Source: *Official Proceedings, 1852*.

Twenty-fifth ballot, p. 43.

a/ Other candidates: Marcy, 26; Butler, 24; Lane, 13; Houston, 10; Dickinson, 1.

Thirtieth ballot, p. 45.

b/ Other candidates: Marcy, 26; Butler, 20; Lane, 13; Houston, 12; Dickinson, 1.

Thirty-second ballot, p. 46.

c/ Other candidates: Marcy, 26; Houston, 8; Butler, 1; Dickinson, 1.

Thirty-fifth ballot, p. 51.

d/ Other candidates: Franklin Pierce, 15; Houston, 5; Butler, 1; Dickinson, 1.

1852 DEMOCRATIC — Presidential

Delegation	Votes	Fortieth Ballot					Forty-fifth Ballot					Forty-sixth Ballot				
		Cass	Marcy	Douglas	Pierce	Other	Marcy	Cass	Douglas	Pierce	Other	Marcy	Cass	Pierce	Douglas	Other
Alabama	9	...	9	...	...	...	9	...	...	...	...	9	...	...	...	...
Arizona	...	...	...	...	...	...	...	...	...	...	...	...	...	...	...	...
Arkansas	4	...	...	4	...	...	...	...	4	...	...	...	...	...	4	...
California	4	4	...	...	...	...	...	4	...	...	...	...	4	...	...	...
Colorado	...	...	...	...	...	...	...	...	...	...	...	...	...	...	...	...
Connecticut	6	...	6	...	...	...	6	...	...	...	...	6	...	...	...	...
Delaware	3	3	...	...	...	...	...	3	...	...	...	...	3	...	...	...
Florida	3	...	...	2	...	1	...	...	2	...	1	...	...	...	2	1
Georgia	10	...	10	...	...	...	10	...	...	...	...	10	...	...	...	...
Idaho	...	...	...	...	...	...	...	...	...	...	...	...	...	...	...	...
Illinois	11	...	...	11	...	...	...	...	11	...	...	...	...	...	11	...
Indiana	13	13	...	...	...	...	...	13	...	...	...	...	13	...	...	...
Iowa	4	2	...	2	...	...	...	2	2	...	...	...	2	...	2	...
Kansas	...	...	...	...	...	...	...	...	...	...	...	...	...	...	...	...
Kentucky	12	12	...	...	...	...	...	12	...	...	...	...	...	12	...	...
Louisiana	6	6	...	...	...	...	...	6	...	...	...	...	6	...	...	...
Maine	8	...	...	...	8	...	...	...	...	8	...	...	...	8	...	...
Maryland	8	8	...	...	...	...	...	8	...	...	...	...	3	3	...	2
Massachusetts	13	...	11	1	1	...	11	...	1	1	...	11	...	1	1	...
Michigan	6	6	...	...	...	...	...	6	...	...	...	...	6	...	...	...
Minnesota	...	...	...	...	...	...	...	...	...	...	...	...	...	...	...	...
Mississippi	7	...	7	...	...	...	7	...	...	...	...	7	...	...	...	...
Missouri	9	9	...	...	...	...	...	9	...	...	...	...	9	...	...	...
Montana	...	...	...	...	...	...	...	...	...	...	...	...	...	...	...	...
Nebraska	...	...	...	...	...	...	...	...	...	...	...	...	...	...	...	...
Nevada	...	...	...	...	...	...	...	...	...	...	...	...	...	...	...	...
New Hampshire	5	...	...	...	5	...	...	...	...	5	...	...	...	5	...	...
New Jersey	7	...	7	...	...	...	7	...	...	...	...	7	...	...	...	...
New Mexico	...	...	...	...	...	...	...	...	...	...	...	...	...	...	...	...
New York	35	10	24	1	...	...	24	10	1	...	...	25	9	...	1	...
North Carolina	10	...	10	...	...	...	10	...	...	...	...	10	...	...	...	...
North Dakota	...	...	...	...	...	...	...	...	...	...	...	...	...	...	...	...
Ohio	23	18	...	3	...	2	...	18	3	...	2	...	18	...	3	2
Oklahoma	...	...	...	...	...	...	...	...	...	...	...	...	...	...	...	...
Oregon	...	...	...	...	...	...	...	...	...	...	...	...	...	...	...	...
Pennsylvania	27	...	...	...	...	27	...	...	...	...	27	...	...	...	...	27
Rhode Island	4	4	...	...	...	...	2	2	...	...	...	2	2	...	...	...
South Carolina	...	...	...	...	...	...	...	...	...	...	...	...	...	...	...	...
South Dakota	...	...	...	...	...	...	...	...	...	...	...	...	...	...	...	...
Tennessee	12	9	1	2	...	...	11	...	1	...	...	10	...	...	1	1
Texas	4	...	...	...	...	4	...	...	...	...	4	...	...	...	...	4
Utah	...	...	...	...	...	...	...	...	...	...	...	...	...	...	...	...
Vermont	5	...	...	5	...	...	...	...	5	...	...	...	...	...	5	...
Virginia	15	...	...	...	15	...	...	...	...	15	...	...	...	15	...	...
Washington	...	...	...	...	...	...	...	...	...	...	...	...	...	...	...	...
West Virginia	...	...	...	...	...	...	...	...	...	...	...	...	...	...	...	...
Wisconsin	5	3	...	2	...	...	...	3	2	...	...	...	3	...	2	...
Wyoming	...	...	...	...	...	...	...	...	...	...	...	...	...	...	...	...
Alaska	...	...	...	...	...	...	...	...	...	...	...	...	...	...	...	...
Canal Zone	...	...	...	...	...	...	...	...	...	...	...	...	...	...	...	...
District of Columbia	...	...	...	...	...	...	...	...	...	...	...	...	...	...	...	...
Hawaii	...	...	...	...	...	...	...	...	...	...	...	...	...	...	...	...
Philippine Islands	...	...	...	...	...	...	...	...	...	...	...	...	...	...	...	...
Puerto Rico	...	...	...	...	...	...	...	...	...	...	...	...	...	...	...	...
Virgin Islands	...	...	...	...	...	...	...	...	...	...	...	...	...	...	...	...
Total	288	107	85	33	29	34[a]	97	96	32	29	34[b]	97[c]	78	44	32	37[d]

Source: *Official Proceedings, 1852*.

Fortieth ballot, p. 53.

[a] Other candidates: Buchanan, 27; Houston, 5; Butler, 1; Dickinson, 1.

Forty-fifth ballot, p. 55.

[b] Other candidates: Buchanan, 27; Houston, 5; Butler, 1; Dickinson, 1.

Forty-sixth ballot, pp. 55-6.

[c] Sum of column; proceedings record 98.

[d] Other candidates: Buchanan, 28; Houston, 5; Butler, 1; Dickinson, 1; William R. King, 1; not voting, 1.

		1852 DEMOCRATIC														
		Presidential							Vice-Presidential						Table Resolution on Delegate Apportionment	
		Forty-eighth Ballot					49th Ballot		First Ballot				Second Ballot			
Delegation	Votes	Marcy	Cass	Pierce	Douglas	Other	Pierce	Other	King	Downs	Weller	Other	King	Other	Yea	Nay
Alabama	9	9	...	...	...	...	9	...	9	...	...	...	9	...	...	9
Arizona	...	...	...	...	...	...	...	...	...	...	...	...	...	...	...	...
Arkansas	4	...	...	...	4	...	4	...	...	...	...	4	4	...	4	...
California	4	...	4	...	...	...	4	...	...	...	4	...	4	...	4	...
Colorado	...	...	...	...	...	...	...	...	...	...	...	...	...	...	...	...
Connecticut	6	6	...	...	...	...	6	...	6	...	...	...	6	...	...	6
Delaware	3	...	3	...	...	...	3	...	...	...	...	3	3	...	...	3
Florida	3	...	...	...	2	1	3	...	3	...	...	...	3	...	3	...
Georgia	10	10	...	...	...	...	10	...	10	...	...	...	10	...	10	...
Idaho	...	...	...	...	...	...	...	...	...	...	...	...	...	...	...	...
Illinois	11	...	...	...	11	...	11	...	...	...	...	11	...	11	...	11
Indiana	13	...	13	...	...	...	13	...	...	13	...	...	13	...	...	13
Iowa	4	...	2	...	2	...	4	...	...	...	...	4	4	...	...	4
Kansas	...	...	...	...	...	...	...	...	...	...	...	...	...	...	...	...
Kentucky	12	...	...	12	...	...	12	...	...	...	...	12	12	...	12	...
Louisiana	6	...	6	...	...	...	6	...	...	6	...	...	6	...	6	...
Maine	8	...	...	8	...	...	8	...	8	...	...	...	8	...	7	1
Maryland	8	1	1	5	...	1	5	3	8	...	...	...	8	...	...	8
Massachusetts	13	6	...	6	1	...	13	...	...	...	...	13	13	...	...	13
Michigan	6	...	6	...	...	...	6	...	...	6	...	...	6	...	...	6
Minnesota	...	...	...	...	...	...	...	...	...	...	...	...	...	...	...	...
Mississippi	7	7	...	...	...	...	7	...	7	...	...	...	7	...	7	...
Missouri	9	...	9	...	...	...	9	...	...	...	...	9	9	...	9	...
Montana	...	...	...	...	...	...	...	...	...	...	...	...	...	...	...	...
Nebraska	...	...	...	...	...	...	...	...	...	...	...	...	...	...	...	...
Nevada	...	...	...	...	...	...	...	...	...	...	...	...	...	...	...	...
New Hampshire	5	...	...	5	...	...	5	...	3	...	...	2	5	...	5	...
New Jersey	7	7	...	...	...	...	7	...	7	...	...	...	7	...	...	7
New Mexico	...	...	...	...	...	...	...	...	...	...	...	...	...	...	...	...
New York	35	24	10	...	1	...	35	...	18	1	1	15	35	...	...	35
North Carolina	10	10	...	...	...	...	10	...	...	...	...	10	10	...	10	...
North Dakota	...	...	...	...	...	...	...	...	...	...	...	...	...	...	...	...
Ohio	23	...	15	...	4	4	17	6	...	...	23	...	23	...	...	23
Oklahoma	...	...	...	...	...	...	...	...	...	...	...	...	...	...	...	...
Oregon	...	...	...	...	...	...	...	...	...	...	...	...	...	...	...	...
Pennsylvania	27	...	...	...	...	27	27	...	27	...	...	...	27	...	27	...
Rhode Island	4	...	...	4	...	...	4	...	4	...	...	...	4	...	...	4
South Carolina	...	...	...	...	...	...	...	...	...	...	...	...	...	...	...	...
South Dakota	...	...	...	...	...	...	...	...	...	...	...	...	...	...	...	...
Tennessee	12	9	...	...	1	2	12	...	...	...	...	12	12	...	12	...
Texas	4	...	...	...	...	4	4	...	...	4	...	...	4	...	...	4
Utah	...	...	...	...	...	...	...	...	...	...	...	...	...	...	...	...
Vermont	5	...	...	...	5	...	5	...	...	...	...	5	5	...	5	...
Virginia	15	...	...	15	...	...	15	...	15	...	...	...	15	...	15	...
Washington	...	...	...	...	...	...	...	...	...	...	...	...	...	...	...	...
West Virginia	...	...	...	...	...	...	...	...	...	...	...	...	...	...	...	...
Wisconsin	5	...	3	...	2	...	5	...	...	...	...	5	5	...	...	5
Wyoming	...	...	...	...	...	...	...	...	...	...	...	...	...	...	...	...
Alaska	...	...	...	...	...	...	...	...	...	...	...	...	...	...	...	...
Canal Zone	...	...	...	...	...	...	...	...	...	...	...	...	...	...	...	...
District of Columbia	...	...	...	...	...	...	...	...	...	...	...	...	...	...	...	...
Hawaii	...	...	...	...	...	...	...	...	...	...	...	...	...	...	...	...
Philippine Islands	...	...	...	...	...	...	...	...	...	...	...	...	...	...	...	...
Puerto Rico	...	...	...	...	...	...	...	...	...	...	...	...	...	...	...	...
Virgin Islands	...	...	...	...	...	...	...	...	...	...	...	...	...	...	...	...
Total	288	89	72	55	33	39[a]	279[b]	9[c]	125	30	28	105[d]	277	11[e]	136	152

Source: *Official Proceedings, 1852.*

Forty-eighth ballot, pp. 56-7.

a/ Other candidates: Buchanan, 28; Houston, 6; Linn Boyd, 2; Butler, 1; R. J. Ingersoll, 1; Dickinson, 1.

Forty-ninth ballot, p. 64.

b/ Sum of column; proceedings record 283.

c/ Other candidates: Cass, 2; Douglas, 2; Butler, 1; Houston, 1; not voting, 3.

Vice-Presidential. First ballot, p. 66.

d/ Other candidates: Gideon J. Pillow, 25; David R. Atchison, 25; Robert Strange, 23; William O. Butler, 13; Thomas J. Rusk, 13; Jefferson Davis, 2; Howell Cobb, 2; not voting, 2.

Second ballot, pp. 66-7.

e/ Other candidates: Davis, 11.

Table resolution on delegate apportionment, p. 70.

Delegation	1852 DEMOCRATIC Votes	Adoption of Report on Next Convention Yea	Nay	Not Voting	1856 DEMOCRATIC Votes	Table Appointment of Resolutions Committee Yea	Nay	Not Voting	Table Motion on Gallery Seats Yea	Nay	Not Voting	Table Issuing of Gallery Tickets Yea	Nay	Not Voting	Adoption of Domestic Policy Platform Yea	Not Voting
Alabama	9	...	9	...	9	...	9	...	...	9	...	...	9	...	9	...
Arizona	...	...	...	...	...	...	...	...	...	...	...	...	...	...	...	...
Arkansas	4	...	...	4	4	4	...	...	4	...	...	...	4	...	4	...
California	4	4	...	...	4	...	4	...	4	...	...	4	...	...	4	...
Colorado	...	...	...	...	...	...	...	...	...	...	...	...	...	...	...	...
Connecticut	6	...	...	6	6	6	...	...	6	...	...	6	...	...	6	...
Delaware	3	3	...	...	3	3	...	...	3	...	...	3	...	...	3	...
Florida	3	...	3	...	3	...	3	...	...	3	...	...	3	...	3	...
Georgia	10	...	10	...	10	...	10	...	6	4	...	6	4	...	10	...
Idaho	...	...	...	...	...	...	...	...	...	...	...	...	...	...	...	...
Illinois	11	13	...	...	11	...	11	...	11	...	...	11	...	...	11	...
Indiana	13	13	...	...	13	...	13	...	13	...	...	...	13	...	13	...
Iowa	4	4	...	...	4	4	...	...	4	...	...	4	...	...	4	...
Kansas	...	...	...	...	...	...	...	...	...	...	...	...	...	...	...	...
Kentucky	12	12	...	...	12	...	12	...	...	12	...	...	12	...	12	...
Louisiana	6	...	6	...	6	...	6	...	6	...	...	6	...	...	6	...
Maine	8	8	...	...	8	...	8	...	...	8	...	...	8	...	8	...
Maryland	8	...	8	...	8	8	...	...	...	8	...	...	8	...	8	...
Massachusetts	13	13	...	...	13	...	13	...	13	...	...	13	...	...	13	...
Michigan	6	3	...	3	6	6	...	...	6	...	...	6	...	...	6	...
Minnesota	...	...	...	...	...	...	...	...	...	...	...	...	...	...	...	...
Mississippi	7	...	7	...	7	7	...	...	...	7	...	...	7	...	7	...
Missouri	9	9	...	...	9	...	9	...	...	9	...	9	...	...	9	...
Montana	...	...	...	...	...	...	...	...	...	...	...	...	...	...	...	...
Nebraska	...	...	...	...	...	...	...	...	...	...	...	...	...	...	...	...
Nevada	...	...	...	...	...	...	...	...	...	...	...	...	...	...	...	...
New Hampshire	5	5	...	...	5	...	5	...	...	5	...	5	...	...	5	...
New Jersey	7	7	...	...	7	7	...	...	7	...	...	7	...	...	7	...
New Mexico	...	...	...	...	...	...	...	...	...	...	...	...	...	...	...	...
New York	35	36	...	...	35	...	...	35	...	...	35	...	...	35	...	35
North Carolina	10	...	10	...	10	...	10	...	10	...	...	11	...	...	10	...
North Dakota	...	...	...	...	...	...	...	...	...	...	...	...	...	...	...	...
Ohio	23	24	...	...	23	...	23	...	12	12	...	...	24	...	23	...
Oklahoma	...	...	...	...	...	...	...	...	...	...	...	...	...	...	...	...
Oregon	...	...	...	...	...	...	...	...	...	...	...	...	...	...	...	...
Pennsylvania	27	27	...	...	27	27	...	...	21	6	...	27	...	...	27	...
Rhode Island	4	...	...	4	4	...	3	1	4	...	...	4	...	...	4	...
South Carolina	...	...	...	...	8	8	...	...	8	...	...	8	...	...	8	...
South Dakota	...	...	...	...	...	...	...	...	...	...	...	...	...	...	...	...
Tennessee	12	...	...	12	12	...	12	...	12	...	...	...	12	...	12	...
Texas	4	4	...	...	4	4	...	...	4	...	...	4	...	...	4	...
Utah	...	...	...	...	...	...	...	...	...	...	...	...	...	...	...	...
Vermont	5	5	...	...	5	...	5	...	...	5	...	...	5	...	5	...
Virginia	15	...	15	...	15	...	15	...	...	15	...	...	15	...	15	...
Washington	...	...	...	...	...	...	...	...	...	...	...	...	...	...	...	...
West Virginia	...	...	...	...	...	...	...	...	...	...	...	...	...	...	...	...
Wisconsin	5	5	...	...	5	5	...	...	5	...	...	2	2	1	5	...
Wyoming	...	...	...	...	...	...	...	...	...	...	...	...	...	...	...	...
Alaska	...	...	...	...	...	...	...	...	...	...	...	...	...	...	...	...
Canal Zone	...	...	...	...	...	...	...	...	...	...	...	...	...	...	...	...
District of Columbia	...	...	...	...	...	...	...	...	...	...	...	...	...	...	...	...
Hawaii	...	...	...	...	...	...	...	...	...	...	...	...	...	...	...	...
Philippine Islands	...	...	...	...	...	...	...	...	...	...	...	...	...	...	...	...
Puerto Rico	...	...	...	...	...	...	...	...	...	...	...	...	...	...	...	...
Virgin Islands	...	...	...	...	...	...	...	...	...	...	...	...	...	...	...	...
Total	288	195	68	29	296	89[a]	171[b]	36	159	103	35	136	126	36	261	35

Source: *Official Proceedings, 1852.*
Adoption of report on next convention, p. 70.

Source: *Official Proceedings, 1856.*
Table appointment of resolutions committee, p. 14.
a/ Sum of column; proceedings record 84.
b/ Sum of column; proceedings record 177.
Table motion on gallery seats, p. 19.
Table issuing of gallery tickets, p. 19.
Adoption of domestic policy platform, p. 28.

Delegation	Votes	Free Trade Plank			Monroe Doctrine Plank			Transcontinental Railway Plank			Central America Plank			Gulf of Mexico Plank		
		Yea	Nay	Not Voting	Yea	Nay	Not Voting	Yea	Nay	Not Voting	Yea	Nay	Not Voting	Yea	Nay	Not Voting
Alabama	9	...	...	9	9	...	...	9	...	...	9	...	...	9	...	...
Arizona	...	...	...	...	...	...	...	...	...	...	...	...	...	...	...	...
Arkansas	4	4	...	...	4	...	...	4	...	...	4	...	...	4	...	...
California	4	...	...	4	4	...	...	4	...	...	4	...	...	4	...	...
Colorado	...	...	...	...	...	...	...	...	...	...	...	...	...	...	...	...
Connecticut	6	1	5	...	6	...	...	4	2	...	4	2	...	4	2	...
Delaware	3	...	3	...	...	3	...	...	3	...	...	3	...	...	4	...
Florida	3	3	...	...	3	...	...	3	...	...	3	...	...	3	...	...
Georgia	10	...	10	...	6	4	...	10	...	...	10	...	...	10	...	...
Idaho	...	...	...	...	...	...	...	...	...	...	...	...	...	...	...	...
Illinois	11	11	...	...	11	...	...	11	...	...	11	...	...	11	...	...
Indiana	13	13	...	...	13	...	...	13	...	...	13	...	...	13	...	...
Iowa	4	4	...	...	4	...	...	4	...	...	4	...	...	4	...	...
Kansas	...	...	...	...	...	...	...	...	...	...	...	...	...	...	...	...
Kentucky	12	12	...	...	12	...	...	...	12	...	...	12	...	12	...	...
Louisiana	6	6	...	...	6	...	...	6	...	...	6	...	...	6	...	...
Maine	8	8	...	...	8	...	...	7	1	...	8	...	...	7	1	...
Maryland	8	...	6	2	...	8	...	...	6	2	...	6	2	...	8	...
Massachusetts	13	13	...	...	12	1	...	13	...	...	13	...	...	11	2	...
Michigan	6	6	...	...	6	...	...	6	...	...	6	...	...	6	...	...
Minnesota	...	...	...	...	...	...	...	...	...	...	...	...	...	...	...	...
Mississippi	7	...	...	7	7	...	...	7	...	...	7	...	...	7	...	...
Missouri	9	9	...	...	9	...	...	9	...	...	9	...	...	9	...	...
Montana	...	...	...	...	...	...	...	...	...	...	...	...	...	...	...	...
Nebraska	...	...	...	...	...	...	...	...	...	...	...	...	...	...	...	...
Nevada	...	...	...	...	...	...	...	...	...	...	...	...	...	...	...	...
New Hampshire	5	5	...	...	5	...	...	5	...	...	5	...	...	5	...	...
New Jersey	7	7	...	...	7	...	...	7	...	...	7	...	...	7	...	...
New Mexico	...	...	...	...	...	...	...	...	...	...	...	...	...	...	...	...
New York	35	...	...	35	...	...	35	...	...	35	...	...	35	...	...	35
North Carolina	10	10	...	...	10	...	...	10	...	...	9	1	...	9	1	...
North Dakota	...	...	...	...	...	...	...	...	...	...	...	...	...	...	...	...
Ohio	23	23	...	...	23	...	...	23	...	...	23	...	...	23	...	...
Oklahoma	...	...	...	...	...	...	...	...	...	...	...	...	...	...	...	...
Oregon	...	...	...	...	...	...	...	...	...	...	...	...	...	...	...	...
Pennsylvania	27	27	...	...	27	...	...	27	...	...	27	...	...	27	...	...
Rhode Island	4	...	4	...	...	4	...	...	4	...	...	4	...	...	4	...
South Carolina	8	8	...	...	8	...	...	...	8	...	...	8	...	...	8	...
South Dakota	...	...	...	...	...	...	...	...	...	...	...	...	...	...	...	...
Tennessee	12	11	1	...	11	1	...	7	5	...	10	2	...	9	3	...
Texas	4	4	...	...	4	...	...	4	...	...	4	...	...	4	...	...
Utah	...	...	...	...	...	...	...	...	...	...	...	...	...	...	...	...
Vermont	5	5	...	...	5	...	...	5	...	...	5	...	...	5	...	...
Virginia	15	15	...	...	15	...	...	...	15	...	15	...	...	15	...	...
Washington	...	...	...	...	...	...	...	...	...	...	...	...	...	...	...	...
West Virginia	...	...	...	...	...	...	...	...	...	...	...	...	...	...	...	...
Wisconsin	5	5	...	...	5	...	...	5	...	...	5	...	...	5	...	...
Wyoming	...	...	...	...	...	...	...	...	...	...	...	...	...	...	...	...
Alaska	...	...	...	...	...	...	...	...	...	...	...	...	...	...	...	...
Canal Zone	...	...	...	...	...	...	...	...	...	...	...	...	...	...	...	...
District of Columbia	...	...	...	...	...	...	...	...	...	...	...	...	...	...	...	...
Hawaii	...	...	...	...	...	...	...	...	...	...	...	...	...	...	...	...
Philippine Islands	...	...	...	...	...	...	...	...	...	...	...	...	...	...	...	...
Puerto Rico	...	...	...	...	...	...	...	...	...	...	...	...	...	...	...	...
Virgin Islands	...	...	...	...	...	...	...	...	...	...	...	...	...	...	...	...
Total	296	210[a]	29	57	240[b]	21	35	203[c]	56	37	221	38	37	229	33	35

Source: *Official Proceedings, 1856.*
Free trade plank, p. 30.
a/ Sum of column; proceedings record 230.
Monroe Doctrine plank, p. 30.
b/ Sum of column; proceedings record 239.
Transcontinental railway plank, p. 31.
c/ Sum of column; proceedings record 180.
Central America plank, p. 31.
Gulf of Mexico plank, p. 31.

1856 DEMOCRATIC

Delegation	Votes	Table Transcontinental Roads Plank			Table Reconsideration of Previous Resolutions			Motion to Suspend Rules			Table New York Delegation Question			Minority Report on Credentials			Motion to Reconsider Railway Plank	
		Yea	Nay	Not Voting	Yea	Nay	Not Voting	Yea	Nay	Not Voting	Yea	Nay	Not Voting	Yea	Nay	Not Voting	Yea	Nay
Alabama	9	9	...	...	...	9	...	...	9	...	...	9	...	...	9	...	...	9
Arizona	...	...	...	...	...	...	...	...	...	...	...	...	...	...	...	...	...	...
Arkansas	4	...	4	...	4	...	...	4	...	...	3	1	...	2	2	...	...	4
California	4	...	4	...	4	...	...	...	4	...	...	4	...	4	...	...	...	4
Colorado	...	...	...	...	...	...	...	...	...	...	...	...	...	...	...	...	...	...
Connecticut	6	6	...	...	...	6	...	...	6	...	...	6	...	6	...	...	...	6
Delaware	3	3	...	...	...	3	...	3	...	...	...	3	...	3	...	...	...	3
Florida	3	3	...	...	3	...	...	3	...	...	...	3	...	...	3	...	...	3
Georgia	10	6	4	...	...	9	1	...	10	...	...	10	...	4	6	...	1	9
Idaho	...	...	...	...	...	...	...	...	...	...	...	...	...	...	...	...	...	...
Illinois	11	...	11	...	11	...	...	...	11	...	...	11	...	...	11	...	11	...
Indiana	13	...	13	...	13	...	...	...	13	...	13	...	...	13	...	...	...	13
Iowa	4	...	4	...	4	...	...	...	4	...	...	4	...	...	4	...	4	...
Kansas	...	...	...	...	...	...	...	...	...	...	...	...	...	...	...	...	...	...
Kentucky	12	8	4	...	...	12	...	12	...	...	7	...	...	6	5	1	...	12
Louisiana	6	...	6	...	6	...	...	...	6	...	6	...	...	...	6	...	6	...
Maine	8	1	7	...	8	...	...	...	8	...	...	8	...	6	2	...	1	7
Maryland	8	...	6	2	1	7	...	7	1	...	...	8	...	6	2	...	8	...
Massachusetts	13	17	12	...	5	4	4	...	13	...	2	11	...	3	10	...	11	2
Michigan	6	...	6	...	6	...	...	...	6	...	...	6	...	...	6	...	6	...
Minnesota	...	...	...	...	...	...	...	...	...	...	...	...	...	...	...	...	...	...
Mississippi	7	7	...	...	7	...	...	...	7	...	...	7	...	...	7	...	...	7
Missouri	9	...	9	...	9	...	...	...	9	...	...	9	...	6	3	...	9	...
Montana	...	...	...	...	...	...	...	...	...	...	...	...	...	...	...	...	...	...
Nebraska	...	...	...	...	...	...	...	...	...	...	...	...	...	...	...	...	...	...
Nevada	...	...	...	...	...	...	...	...	...	...	...	...	...	...	...	...	...	...
New Hampshire	5	4	1	...	5	...	...	...	5	...	...	5	...	...	5	...	...	5
New Jersey	7	7	...	...	7	...	...	...	7	...	4	3	...	6	1	...	...	7
New Mexico	...	...	...	...	...	...	...	...	...	...	...	...	...	...	...	...	...	...
New York	35	...	...	35	...	...	35	...	...	35	...	...	35	...	...	35	35	...
North Carolina	10	10	...	...	10	...	...	...	10	...	...	10	...	...	10	...	...	10
North Dakota	...	...	...	...	...	...	...	...	...	...	...	...	...	...	...	...	...	...
Ohio	23	16	6	1	23	...	...	...	23	...	1	22	...	10	13	...	6	17
Oklahoma	...	...	...	...	...	...	...	...	...	...	...	...	...	...	...	...	...	...
Oregon	...	...	...	...	...	...	...	...	...	...	...	...	...	...	...	...	...	...
Pennsylvania	27	27	...	...	27	...	...	...	27	...	...	27	...	27	...	...	...	27
Rhode Island	4	4	...	...	...	4	...	...	4	...	...	4	...	1	3	...	...	4
South Carolina	8	8	...	...	...	8	...	8	...	...	8	...	...	...	8	...	...	8
South Dakota	...	...	...	...	...	...	...	...	...	...	...	...	...	...	...	...	...	...
Tennessee	12	3	9	...	10	2	...	9	3	...	...	5	7	10	2	...	5	7
Texas	4	...	4	...	4	...	...	4	...	...	...	4	...	3	...	1	4	...
Utah	...	...	...	...	...	...	...	...	...	...	...	...	...	...	...	...	...	...
Vermont	5	...	5	...	5	...	...	...	5	...	...	5	...	...	5	...	5	...
Virginia	15	15	...	...	...	15	...	15	...	...	...	15	...	15	...	...	...	15
Washington	...	...	...	...	...	...	...	...	...	...	...	...	...	...	...	...	...	...
West Virginia	...	...	...	...	...	...	...	...	...	...	...	...	...	...	...	...	...	...
Wisconsin	5	...	5	...	5	...	...	...	5	...	...	5	...	5	...	...	5	...
Wyoming	...	...	...	...	...	...	...	...	...	...	...	...	...	...	...	...	...	...
Alaska	...	...	...	...	...	...	...	...	...	...	...	...	...	...	...	...	...	...
Canal Zone	...	...	...	...	...	...	...	...	...	...	...	...	...	...	...	...	...	...
District of Columbia	...	...	...	...	...	...	...	...	...	...	...	...	...	...	...	...	...	...
Hawaii	...	...	...	...	...	...	...	...	...	...	...	...	...	...	...	...	...	...
Philippine Islands	...	...	...	...	...	...	...	...	...	...	...	...	...	...	...	...	...	...
Puerto Rico	...	...	...	...	...	...	...	...	...	...	...	...	...	...	...	...	...	...
Virgin Islands	...	...	...	...	...	...	...	...	...	...	...	...	...	...	...	...	...	...
Total	296	154	120	38	177[a]	79	40	74	187[b]	35	44	217	42	136[c]	123	37	121	175

Source: *Official Proceedings, 1856.*
Table transcontinental roads plank, p. 31.
Table reconsideration of previous resolutions, p. 32.
a/ Sum of column; proceedings record 171.
Motion to suspend rules, p. 32.
b/ Sum of column; proceedings record 171.
Table New York delegation question, p. 35.
Minority report on credentials, p. 36.
c/ Sum of column; proceedings record 137.
Motion to reconsider railway plank, p. 38.

Source: *Official Proceedings, 1856.*

1856 DEMOCRATIC — Presidential

		First Ballot				Fifth Ballot				Tenth Ballot				Motion to Adjourn		Motion to Adjourn	
Delegation	Votes	Buchanan	Pierce	Douglas	Other	Buchanan	Pierce	Douglas	Other	Buchanan	Pierce	Douglas	Other	Yea	Nay	Yea	Nay
Alabama	9	...	9	...	...	...	9	...	...	...	9	...	...	9	...	9	...
Arizona	...	...	...	...	...	...	4	...	...	...	...	4	...	4	...	4	...
Arkansas	4	...	4	...	...	...	4	...	...	...	...	4	...	4	...	4	...
California	4	...	...	...	4	...	...	...	4	...	...	...	4	4	...	4	...
Colorado	...	...	...	...	...	...	...	...	...	...	...	...	...	...	...	...	...
Connecticut	6	6	...	...	...	6	...	...	...	6	...	...	...	...	6	...	6
Delaware	3	3	...	...	...	3	...	...	...	3	...	...	...	...	3	5	...
Florida	3	...	3	...	...	...	3	...	...	...	3	...	...	3	...	3	...
Georgia	10	...	10	...	...	...	10	...	...	3	...	7	...	10	...	9	1
Idaho	...	...	...	...	...	...	...	...	...	...	...	...	...	...	...	...	...
Illinois	11	...	...	11	...	...	...	11	...	...	...	11	...	11	...	11	...
Indiana	13	13	...	...	...	13	...	...	...	13	...	...	...	...	13	13	...
Iowa	4	...	...	4	...	2	...	2	...	2	...	2	...	2	2	4	...
Kansas	...	...	...	...	...	...	...	...	...	...	...	...	...	...	...	...	...
Kentucky	12	4	5	3	...	3½	4½	4	...	4½	...	7½	...	5	7	12	...
Louisiana	6	6	...	...	...	6	...	...	...	6	...	...	...	...	6	6	...
Maine	8	5	3	...	...	5	3	...	...	6	2	...	...	...	8	1	7
Maryland	8	6	2	...	...	6	2	...	...	7	1	...	...	...	8	...	8
Massachusetts	13	4	9	...	...	5	8	...	...	6	7	...	...	...	13	8	5
Michigan	6	6	...	...	...	6	...	...	...	6	...	...	...	...	6	...	6
Minnesota	...	...	...	...	...	...	...	...	...	...	...	...	...	...	...	...	...
Mississippi	7	...	7	...	...	...	7	...	...	...	7	...	...	7	...	7	...
Missouri	9	...	...	9	...	...	...	9	...	...	...	9	...	9	...	9	...
Montana	...	...	...	...	...	...	...	...	...	...	...	...	...	...	...	...	...
Nebraska	...	...	...	...	...	...	...	...	...	...	...	...	...	...	...	...	...
Nevada	...	...	...	...	...	...	...	...	...	...	...	...	...	...	...	...	...
New Hampshire	5	...	5	...	...	...	5	...	...	...	5	...	...	5	...	5	...
New Jersey	7	7	...	...	...	7	...	...	...	7	...	...	...	...	7	7	...
New Mexico	...	...	...	...	...	...	...	...	...	...	...	...	...	...	...	...	...
New York	35	17	18	...	...	17	18	...	...	18	17	...	...	17	18	17	18
North Carolina	10	...	10	...	...	...	10	...	...	...	10	...	...	5	5	10	...
North Dakota	...	...	...	...	...	...	...	...	...	...	...	...	...	...	...	...	...
Ohio	23	13½	4½	4	1	13½	3	5	1½	13	3½	5	1½	8	15	15	8
Oklahoma	...	...	...	...	...	...	...	...	...	...	...	...	...	...	...	...	...
Oregon	...	...	...	...	...	...	...	...	...	...	...	...	...	...	...	...	...
Pennsylvania	27	27	...	...	...	27	...	...	...	27	...	...	...	...	27	27	...
Rhode Island	4	...	4	...	...	...	4	...	...	...	4	...	...	4	...	4	...
South Carolina	8	...	8	...	...	...	8	...	...	...	8	...	...	8	...	8	...
South Dakota	...	...	...	...	...	...	...	...	...	...	...	...	...	...	...	...	...
Tennessee	12	...	12	...	...	...	12	...	...	...	...	12	...	12	...	6	6
Texas	4	...	4	...	...	...	4	...	...	...	...	4	...	4	...	4	...
Utah	...	...	...	...	...	...	...	...	...	...	...	...	...	...	...	...	...
Vermont	5	...	5	...	...	...	5	...	...	...	...	5	...	5	...	5	...
Virginia	15	15	...	...	...	15	...	...	...	15	...	...	...	...	15	15	...
Washington	...	...	...	...	...	...	...	...	...	...	...	...	...	...	...	...	...
West Virginia	...	...	...	...	...	...	...	...	...	...	...	...	...	...	...	...	...
Wisconsin	5	3	...	2	...	5	...	...	...	5	...	...	...	...	5	5	...
Wyoming	...	...	...	...	...	...	...	...	...	...	...	...	...	...	...	...	...
Alaska	...	...	...	...	...	...	...	...	...	...	...	...	...	...	...	...	...
Canal Zone	...	...	...	...	...	...	...	...	...	...	...	...	...	...	...	...	...
District of Columbia	...	...	...	...	...	...	...	...	...	...	...	...	...	...	...	...	...
Hawaii	...	...	...	...	...	...	...	...	...	...	...	...	...	...	...	...	...
Philippine Islands	...	...	...	...	...	...	...	...	...	...	...	...	...	...	...	...	...
Puerto Rico	...	...	...	...	...	...	...	...	...	...	...	...	...	...	...	...	...
Virgin Islands	...	...	...	...	...	...	...	...	...	...	...	...	...	...	...	...	...
Total	296	135½	122½	33	5[a]	140	119½	31	5½[b]	147½	80½	62½	5½[c]	132	164	233[d]	65

Source: *Official Proceedings, 1856.*

Presidential. First ballot, p. 39.
a/ Other candidates: Lewis Cass, 5.
Fifth ballot, p. 40.
b/ Other candidates: Cass, 5½.
Tenth ballot, p. 41.
c/ Other candidates: Cass, 5½.
Motion to adjourn, p. 42.
Motion to adjourn, p. 43.
d/ Sum of column; proceedings record 231.

		1856 DEMOCRATIC													
		Presidential						17th Ballot	Table Resolution on Railway		Motion to Suspend Rules		Transcontinental Railway		
		Fifteenth Ballot			Sixteenth Ballot										
Delegation	Votes	Buchanan	Douglas	Other	Buchanan	Douglas	Other	Buchanan	Yea	Nay	Yea	Nay	Yea	Nay	Not Voting
Alabama	9	...	9	...	...	9	...	9	...	9	9	...	9	...	...
Arizona	...	...	...	...	...	...	...	...	...	...	...	...	...	...	...
Arkansas	4	...	4	...	...	4	...	4	...	4	4	...	4	...	...
California	4	...	...	4	...	...	4	4	...	4	4	...	4	...	...
Colorado	...	...	...	...	...	...	...	...	...	...	...	...	...	...	...
Connecticut	6	6	...	...	6	...	...	6	4	2	3	3	3	3	...
Delaware	3	3	...	...	3	...	...	3	1	2	2	1	1	1	1
Florida	3	...	3	...	...	3	...	3	3	...	...	3	...	3	...
Georgia	10	3	7	...	3	7	...	10	7	3	3	7	6	4	...
Idaho	...	...	...	...	...	...	...	...	...	...	...	...	...	...	...
Illinois	11	...	11	...	...	11	...	11	...	11	11	...	11	...	...
Indiana	13	13	...	...	13	...	...	13	...	13	13	...	13	...	...
Iowa	4	2	2	...	2	2	...	4	...	4	4	...	4	...	...
Kansas	...	...	...	...	...	...	...	...	...	...	...	...	...	...	...
Kentucky	12	4	7	1	...	12	...	12	...	12	12	...	12	...	...
Louisiana	6	6	...	...	6	...	...	6	...	6	6	...	6	...	...
Maine	8	7	...	1	8	...	...	8	...	8	8	...	8	...	...
Maryland	8	8	...	...	8	...	...	8	...	8	8	...	8	...	...
Massachusetts	13	10	3	...	10	3	...	13	1	12	11	2	11	2	...
Michigan	6	6	...	...	6	...	...	6	...	6	6	...	6	...	...
Minnesota	...	...	...	...	...	...	...	...	...	...	...	...	...	...	...
Mississippi	7	...	7	...	...	7	...	7	7	...	7	...	7	...	...
Missouri	9	...	9	...	...	9	...	9	...	9	9	...	9	...	...
Montana	...	...	...	...	...	...	...	...	...	...	...	...	...	...	...
Nebraska	...	...	...	...	...	...	...	...	...	...	...	...	...	...	...
Nevada	...	...	...	...	...	...	...	...	...	...	...	...	...	...	...
New Hampshire	5	...	5	...	...	5	...	5	4	1	1	4	1	4	...
New Jersey	7	7	...	...	7	...	...	7	7	...	...	7	...	7	...
New Mexico	...	...	...	...	...	...	...	...	...	...	...	...	...	...	...
New York	35	17	18	...	18	17	...	35	...	35	35	...	35	...	...
North Carolina	10	...	10	...	...	10	...	10	10	...	...	10	...	10	...
North Dakota	...	...	...	...	...	...	...	...	...	...	...	...	...	...	...
Ohio	23	13½	6½	3	15	6	2	23	6	17	19	4	14	6	3
Oklahoma	...	...	...	...	...	...	...	...	...	...	...	...	...	...	...
Oregon	...	...	...	...	...	...	...	...	...	...	...	...	...	...	...
Pennsylvania	27	27	...	...	27	...	...	27	...	27	6	21	6	21	...
Rhode Island	4	4	...	...	4	...	...	4	2	2	2	2	2	2	...
South Carolina	8	...	8	...	...	8	...	8	8	...	...	8	...	8	...
South Dakota	...	...	...	...	...	...	...	...	...	...	...	...	...	...	...
Tennessee	12	12	...	...	12	...	...	12	1	11	11	1	11	1	...
Texas	4	...	4	...	...	4	...	4	...	4	4	...	4	...	...
Utah	...	...	...	...	...	...	...	...	...	...	...	...	...	...	...
Vermont	5	...	5	...	...	5	...	5	...	5	5	...	5	...	...
Virginia	15	15	...	...	15	...	...	15	15	...	...	15	...	15	...
Washington	...	...	...	...	...	...	...	...	...	...	...	...	...	...	...
West Virginia	...	...	...	...	...	...	...	...	...	...	...	...	...	...	...
Wisconsin	5	5	...	...	5	...	...	5	...	5	5	...	5	...	...
Wyoming	...	...	...	...	...	...	...	...	...	...	...	...	...	...	...
Alaska	...	...	...	...	...	...	...	...	...	...	...	...	...	...	...
Canal Zone	...	...	...	...	...	...	...	...	...	...	...	...	...	...	...
District of Columbia	...	...	...	...	...	...	...	...	...	...	...	...	...	...	...
Hawaii	...	...	...	...	...	...	...	...	...	...	...	...	...	...	...
Philippine Islands	...	...	...	...	...	...	...	...	...	...	...	...	...	...	...
Puerto Rico	...	...	...	...	...	...	...	...	...	...	...	...	...	...	...
Virgin Islands	...	...	...	...	...	...	...	...	...	...	...	...	...	...	...
Total	296	168½	118½	9[a]	168	122	6[b]	296	76[c]	220	208	88	205	87	4

Source: *Official Proceedings, 1856.*
Fifteenth ballot, p. 45.
a/ Other candidates: Cass, 4½; Pierce, 3½; not voting, 1.
Sixteenth ballot, p. 45.
b/ Other candidates: Cass, 6.
Seventeenth ballot, p. 58.
Table resolution on railway, p. 61.
c/ Sum of column; proceedings record 74.
Motion to suspend rules, p. 62.
Transcontinental railway, p. 62.

1856 DEMOCRATIC / 1860 DEMOCRATIC

Delegation	1856 Votes	Quitman	Boyd	Brown	Johnson	Breckinridge	Bayard	Other	2nd Ballot Breckinridge	1860 Votes	Prev. Q. Yea	Prev. Q. Nay	Table Bar Yea	Table Bar Nay	Strike Yea	Strike Nay	Strike Not Voting
Alabama	9							9	9	9		9		9	9		
Arizona										4		4		4	½	3½	
Arkansas	4	4								4	4			4	2½	1½	
California	4			4						4	2	2		4	2½	1½	
Colorado																	
Connecticut	6				6					6	6		6		6		
Delaware	3					3				3	3		3		1½	1½	
Florida	3							3	3	3	3		3		3		
Georgia	10				10					10	10			10	10		
Idaho																	
Illinois	11	11								11	11		11			11	
Indiana	13		13							13	13		13			13	
Iowa	4					4				4	4		4			4	
Kansas																	
Kentucky	12		12							12	12		12			12	
Louisiana	6					6				6		6	6		6		
Maine	8					8				8	8		8		3½	4½	
Maryland	8						8			8	7	1	8		3½	4½	
Massachusetts	13	1		6	1		1	4		13	13		13		6	5½	1½
Michigan	6			6						6	6		6			6	
Minnesota										4	4		4			4	
Mississippi	7	7								7		7		7	7		
Missouri	9							9		9	9		9		3	7	
Montana																	
Nebraska																	
Nevada																	
New Hampshire	5					5				5	5		5			5	
New Jersey	7		2				5			7	7		7			7	
New Mexico																	
New York	35	17					18			35	35		35			35	
North Carolina	10							10	10	10	10		10		7	3	
North Dakota																	
Ohio	23	8	6		2	7				23	23		23			23	
Oklahoma																	
Oregon										3	3		3		3		
Pennsylvania	27							27	27	27	27		27		14	10½	2½
Rhode Island	4				4					4	4		4		4		
South Carolina	8	8								8	8		8		8		
South Dakota																	
Tennessee	12			12						12	12		12			12	
Texas	4	3		1						4		4		4	4		
Utah																	
Vermont	5				5					5	5		5			5	
Virginia	15					15				15	15		15		15		
Washington																	
West Virginia																	
Wisconsin	5							5	5	5	5		5			5	
Wyoming																	
Alaska																	
Canal Zone																	
District of Columbia																	
Hawaii																	
Philippine Islands																	
Puerto Rico																	
Virgin Islands																	
Total	**296**	**59**	**33**	**29**	**31**	**50ᵃ**	**31**	**63ᵇ**	**296**	**303**	**255ᶜ**	**48**	**259**	**44**	**103ᵈ**	**197**	**4**

Source: *Official Proceedings, 1856.*
Vice-Presidential. First ballot, pp. 65-6.
a/ Sum of column; proceedings record 51.
b/ Other candidates: Benjamin F. Butler, 27; James C. Dobbin, 13; Benjamin Fitzpatrick, 11; Thomas J. Rusk, 7; Trusten Polk, 5.
Second ballot, p. 67.

Source: *Official Proceedings, 1860.*
Previous question, formation of committees, p. 8.
c/ Sum of column; proceedings record 257.
Table bar to New York, Illinois voting, p. 8.
Striking of unit rule modification, p. 20.
d/ Sum of column; proceedings record 103½.

		Table Order of Business		Limitation of Speaking Time		Minority Report, New York Credentials			Motion to Adjourn			Recommit Platform		Table Instructions on Platform		
Delegation	Votes	Yea	Nay	Yea	Nay	Yea	Nay	Not Voting	Yea	Nay	Not Voting	Yea	Nay	Yea	Nay	Not Voting
Alabama	9	...	9	...	9	9	...	...	9	...	...	9	...	9	...	...
Arizona	...	...	...	...	...	...	...	...	...	...	...	...	...	...	...	...
Arkansas	4	...	4	...	4	3	1	...	4	...	...	4	...	4	...	...
California	4	...	4	4	...	3½	½	...	4	...	...	4	...	3½	½	...
Colorado	...	...	...	...	...	...	...	...	...	...	...	...	...	...	...	...
Connecticut	6	2	4	1	5	...	6	...	1	5	...	1½	4½	5	1	...
Delaware	3	...	3	3	...	...	3	...	3	...	...	3	...	3	...	...
Florida	3	...	3	...	3	...	3	...	3	...	...	3	...	3	...	...
Georgia	10	...	10	...	10	10	...	...	10	...	...	10	...	10	...	...
Idaho	...	...	...	...	...	...	...	...	...	...	...	...	...	...	...	...
Illinois	11	...	11	11	...	...	11	...	5	6	...	...	11	11	...	...
Indiana	13	...	13	13	...	...	13	...	...	13	...	...	13	13	...	...
Iowa	4	...	4	4	...	...	4	...	...	4	...	...	4	4	...	...
Kansas	...	...	...	...	...	...	...	...	...	...	...	...	...	...	...	...
Kentucky	12	...	12	11	1	...	12	...	12	...	...	12	...	5	7	...
Louisiana	6	...	6	...	6	...	6	...	6	...	...	6	...	6	...	...
Maine	8	8	...	8	...	...	8	...	8	...	...	3	5	8	...	...
Maryland	8	5½	2½	...	8	...	8	...	8	...	...	5½	2½	5½	2½	...
Massachusetts	13	...	13	...	13	...	13	...	7	5½	½	8	5	12½	½	...
Michigan	6	...	6	6	...	...	6	...	...	6	...	...	6	6	...	...
Minnesota	4	...	4	...	4	...	4	...	1½	2½	...	1	3	4	...	...
Mississippi	7	...	7	...	7	7	...	...	7	...	...	7	...	7	...	...
Missouri	9	...	9	9	...	1	8	...	3	6	...	5	4	4	5	...
Montana	...	...	...	...	...	...	...	...	...	...	...	...	...	...	...	...
Nebraska	...	...	...	...	...	...	...	...	...	...	...	...	...	...	...	...
Nevada	...	...	...	...	...	...	...	...	...	...	...	...	...	...	...	...
New Hampshire	5	...	5	...	5	...	5	...	...	5	...	...	5	5	...	...
New Jersey	7	...	7	7	...	...	7	...	7	...	...	4	3	...	7	...
New Mexico	...	...	...	...	...	...	...	...	...	...	...	...	...	...	...	...
New York	35	...	35	...	35	...	...	35	...	35	...	...	35	35	...	...
North Carolina	10	...	10	...	10	5	4	1	10	...	...	10	...	10	...	...
North Dakota	...	...	...	...	...	...	...	...	...	...	...	...	...	...	...	...
Ohio	23	...	23	...	23	...	23	...	...	23	...	...	23	23	...	...
Oklahoma	...	...	...	...	...	...	...	...	...	...	...	...	...	...	...	...
Oregon	3	...	3	...	3	...	3	...	3	...	...	3	...	...	3	...
Pennsylvania	27	17	10	27	...	...	27	...	8	19	...	16	11	8	15	4
Rhode Island	4	...	4	...	4	...	4	...	...	4	...	...	4	4	...	...
South Carolina	8	...	8	...	8	...	8	...	8	...	...	8	...	8	...	...
South Dakota	...	...	...	...	...	...	...	...	...	...	...	...	...	...	...	...
Tennessee	12	...	12	12	...	9	3	...	12	...	...	11	1	...	11	1
Texas	4	...	4	...	4	4	...	...	4	...	...	4	...	4	...	...
Utah	...	...	...	...	...	...	...	...	...	...	...	...	...	...	...	...
Vermont	5	...	5	...	5	...	5	...	...	5	...	...	...	...	...	...
Virginia	15	...	15	...	15	3½	10	1½	15	...	...	14	1	15	...	...
Washington	...	...	...	...	...	...	...	...	...	...	...	...	...	...	...	...
West Virginia	...	...	...	...	...	...	...	...	...	...	...	...	...	...	...	...
Wisconsin	5	...	5	5	...	...	5	...	...	5	...	...	5	5	...	...
Wyoming	...	...	...	...	...	...	...	...	...	...	...	...	...	...	...	...
Alaska	...	...	...	...	...	...	...	...	...	...	...	...	...	...	...	...
Canal Zone	...	...	...	...	...	...	...	...	...	...	...	...	...	...	...	...
District of Columbia	...	...	...	...	...	...	...	...	...	...	...	...	...	...	...	...
Hawaii	...	...	...	...	...	...	...	...	...	...	...	...	...	...	...	...
Philippine Islands	...	...	...	...	...	...	...	...	...	...	...	...	...	...	...	...
Puerto Rico	...	...	...	...	...	...	...	...	...	...	...	...	...	...	...	...
Virgin Islands	...	...	...	...	...	...	...	...	...	...	...	...	...	...	...	...
Total	303	32½	270½	121	182	55	210½	37½	158½	144	½	152	151	245½[a]	52½[b]	5

Source: *Official Proceedings, 1860.*
Table order of business, p. 20.
Limitation of speaking time, p. 22.
Minority report, New York credentials, p. 25.
Motion to adjourn, p. 41.
Recommit platform, p. 44.
Table instructions on platform, p. 45.
a/ Sum of column; proceedings record 242½.
b/ Sum of column; proceedings record 56½.

	1860 DEMOCRATIC															
		Motion to Adjourn			Motion to Adjourn			Table Consideration of Platform		Motion to Adjourn			Main Question on Platform		Butler Amendment to Platform	
Delegation	Votes	Yea	Nay	Not Voting	Yea	Nay	Not Voting	Yea	Nay	Yea	Nay	Not Voting	Yea	Nay	Yea	Nay
Alabama	9	9	...	...	9	...	...	...	9	9	...	...	9	...	...	9
Arizona	...	...	...	...	...	...	...	...	...	...	...	...	...	...	...	...
Arkansas	4	4	...	...	4	...	...	...	4	4	...	...	4	...	...	4
California	4	4	...	...	4	...	...	...	4	4	...	...	4	...	...	4
Colorado	...	...	...	...	...	...	...	...	...	...	...	...	...	...	...	...
Connecticut	6	1	5	...	...	6	...	...	6	1½	4½	...	6	...	2½	3½
Delaware	3	3	...	...	3	...	...	...	3	3	...	...	3	...	3	...
Florida	3	3	...	...	3	...	...	3	...	3	...	...	3	...	...	3
Georgia	10	10	...	...	10	...	...	10	...	10	...	...	...	10	10	...
Idaho	...	...	...	...	...	...	...	...	...	...	...	...	...	...	...	...
Illinois	11	...	11	...	...	11	...	...	11	...	11	...	11	...	...	11
Indiana	13	...	13	...	...	13	...	...	13	...	13	...	13	...	...	13
Iowa	4	...	4	...	...	4	...	...	4	...	4	...	4	...	...	4
Kansas	...	...	...	...	...	...	...	...	...	...	...	...	...	...	...	...
Kentucky	12	6	6	...	7½	1½	3	...	12	11½	½	...	10	2	9	3
Louisiana	6	6	...	...	6	...	...	...	6	6	...	...	6	...	...	6
Maine	8	...	8	...	...	8	...	...	8	...	8	...	8	...	3	5
Maryland	8	5	3	...	5½	2½	...	...	8	5½	2½	...	8	...	5½	2½
Massachusetts	13	6½	6½	...	5	7½	½	4½	8½	5½	7	½	13	...	8	5
Michigan	6	...	6	...	...	6	...	...	6	...	6	...	6	...	...	6
Minnesota	4	...	4	...	...	4	...	...	4	1	3	...	4	...	1½	2½
Mississippi	7	7	...	...	7	...	...	...	7	7	...	...	7	...	...	7
Missouri	9	...	9	...	...	9	...	...	9	4	5	...	5	4	4½	4½
Montana	...	...	...	...	...	...	...	...	...	...	...	...	...	...	...	...
Nebraska	...	...	...	...	...	...	...	...	...	...	...	...	...	...	...	...
Nevada	...	...	...	...	...	...	...	...	...	...	...	...	...	...	...	...
New Hampshire	5	...	5	...	...	5	...	...	5	...	5	...	5	...	...	5
New Jersey	7	4	...	3	7	...	...	...	7	4	3	...	7	...	5	2
New Mexico	...	...	...	...	...	...	...	...	...	...	...	...	...	...	...	...
New York	35	...	35	...	...	35	...	...	35	...	35	...	35	...	...	35
North Carolina	10	...	10	...	10	...	...	...	10	10	...	...	10	...	10	...
North Dakota	...	...	...	...	...	...	...	...	...	...	...	...	...	...	...	...
Ohio	23	...	23	...	...	23	...	...	23	...	23	...	23	...	...	23
Oklahoma	...	...	...	...	...	...	...	...	...	...	...	...	...	...	...	...
Oregon	3	3	...	...	3	...	...	...	3	3	...	...	3	...	3	...
Pennsylvania	27	14	11	2	13	11	3	3	24	14	13	...	27	...	16½	10½
Rhode Island	4	...	4	...	...	4	...	...	4	...	4	...	4	...	...	4
South Carolina	8	8	...	...	...	8	...	...	8	8	...	...	...	8	...	8
South Dakota	...	...	...	...	...	...	...	...	...	...	...	...	...	...	...	...
Tennessee	12	...	12	...	12	...	...	...	12	12	...	...	5	7	11	1
Texas	4	4	...	...	4	...	...	...	4	4	...	...	4	...	...	4
Utah	...	...	...	...	...	...	...	...	...	...	...	...	...	...	...	...
Vermont	5	...	5	...	...	5	...	...	5	...	5	...	5	...	...	5
Virginia	15	...	15	...	14	1	...	...	15	...	15	...	15	...	12½	2½
Washington	...	...	...	...	...	...	...	...	...	...	...	...	...	...	...	...
West Virginia	...	...	...	...	...	...	...	...	...	...	...	...	...	...	...	...
Wisconsin	5	...	5	...	...	5	...	...	5	...	5	...	5	...	...	5
Wyoming	...	...	...	...	...	...	...	...	...	...	...	...	...	...	...	...
Alaska	...	...	...	...	...	...	...	...	...	...	...	...	...	...	...	...
Canal Zone	...	...	...	...	...	...	...	...	...	...	...	...	...	...	...	...
District of Columbia	...	...	...	...	...	...	...	...	...	...	...	...	...	...	...	...
Hawaii	...	...	...	...	...	...	...	...	...	...	...	...	...	...	...	...
Philippine Islands	...	...	...	...	...	...	...	...	...	...	...	...	...	...	...	...
Puerto Rico	...	...	...	...	...	...	...	...	...	...	...	...	...	...	...	...
Virgin Islands	...	...	...	...	...	...	...	...	...	...	...	...	...	...	...	...
Total	303	97½[a]	200½[b]	5	127[c]	169½[d]	6½	20½	282½[e]	130[f]	172½[g]	½	272	31	105	198

Source: *Official Proceedings, 1860.*
Motion to adjourn, p. 48.
a/ Sum of column; proceedings record 97.
b/ Sum of column; proceedings record 205½.
Motion to adjourn, p. 49.
c/ Sum of column; proceedings record 139.
d/ Sum of column; proceedings record 169.
Table consideration of platform, p. 49.
e/ Sum of column; proceedings record 283½.
Motion to adjourn, p. 49.
f/ Sum of column; proceedings record 126.
g/ Sum of column; proceedings record 178.
Main question on platform, p. 49.
Butler amendment to platform, p. 50.

1860 DEMOCRATIC

Delegation	Votes	Table Appeal from Chair, New Jersey Unit Rule			Sustain Decision of Chair, N. J. Unit Rule			Minority Report on Platform		Reaffirmation of 1856 Platform			Table Remaining Resolutions			Support of Supreme Court Decisions		
		Yea	Nay	Not Voting	Yea	Nay	Not Voting	Yea	Nay	Yea	Nay	Not Voting	Yea	Nay	Not Voting	Yea	Nay	Not Voting
Alabama	9	9	...	...	9	...	...	...	9	...	9	...	...	...	9	...	...	9
Arizona	...	...	...	...	...	...	...	...	...	...	...	...	...	...	...	...	...	...
Arkansas	4	3	1	...	3	1	...	...	4	...	4	...	...	1	3	...	...	4
California	4	4	...	...	4	...	...	...	4	½	3½	...	...	4	...	...	4	...
Colorado	...	...	...	...	...	...	...	...	...	...	...	...	...	...	...	...	...	...
Connecticut	6	2½	3½	...	2½	3½	...	6	...	6	...	...	2	4	...	6	...	...
Delaware	3	3	...	...	3	...	...	...	3	2	1	...	2	1	...	2	...	1
Florida	3	3	...	...	3	...	...	...	3	...	3	...	...	3	...	...	...	3
Georgia	10	10	...	...	10	...	...	...	10	...	10	...	...	10	...	...	...	10
Idaho	...	...	...	...	...	...	...	...	...	...	...	...	...	...	...	...	...	...
Illinois	11	...	11	...	...	11	...	11	...	11	...	...	...	11	...	...	11	...
Indiana	13	...	13	...	...	13	...	13	...	13	...	...	...	13	...	...	13	...
Iowa	4	...	4	...	...	4	...	4	...	4	...	...	...	4	...	...	4	...
Kansas	...	...	...	...	...	...	...	...	...	...	...	...	...	...	...	...	...	...
Kentucky	12	10	2	...	10½	1½	...	2½	9½	12	...	...	7½	4½	...	4	8	...
Louisiana	6	6	...	...	6	...	...	...	6	...	6	...	...	6	...	...	...	6
Maine	8	3	5	...	3	5	...	8	...	...	8	...	...	8	...	...	8	...
Maryland	8	5	3	...	5	3	...	3½	4½	5	3	...	...	8	...	...	8	...
Massachusetts	13	9	4	...	7½	5½	...	7	6	13	...	...	8½	4½	...	...	13	...
Michigan	6	...	6	...	...	6	...	6	...	6	...	...	...	6	...	...	6	...
Minnesota	4	...	4	...	...	4	...	4	...	4	...	...	1	3	...	...	4	...
Mississippi	7	7	...	...	7	...	...	...	7	...	7	...	...	...	7	...	...	7
Missouri	9	4½	4½	...	4½	4½	...	4	5	7½	1½	...	...	9	...	4	5	...
Montana	...	...	...	...	...	...	...	...	...	...	...	...	...	...	...	...	...	...
Nebraska	...	...	...	...	...	...	...	...	...	...	...	...	...	...	...	...	...	...
Nevada	...	...	...	...	...	...	...	...	...	...	...	...	...	...	...	...	...	...
New Hampshire	5	...	5	...	...	5	...	5	...	5	...	...	...	5	...	1	4	...
New Jersey	7	...	...	7	...	...	7	5	2	7	...	...	5	2	...	...	7	...
New Mexico	...	...	...	...	...	...	...	...	...	...	...	...	...	...	...	...	...	...
New York	35	...	35	...	...	35	...	35	...	35	...	...	...	35	...	...	35	...
North Carolina	10	10	...	...	10	...	...	...	10	10	...	...	9	1	...	...	10	...
North Dakota	...	...	...	...	...	...	...	...	...	...	...	...	...	...	...	...	...	...
Ohio	23	...	23	...	...	23	...	23	...	23	...	...	...	23	...	...	23	...
Oklahoma	...	...	...	...	...	...	...	...	...	...	...	...	...	...	...	...	...	...
Oregon	3	3	...	...	3	...	...	...	3	...	3	...	...	3	...	...	3	...
Pennsylvania	27	17	10	...	17	10	...	12	15	27	...	...	16½	10½	...	8	19	...
Rhode Island	4	...	4	...	...	4	...	4	...	4	...	...	...	4	...	4	...	...
South Carolina	8	8	...	...	8	...	...	...	8	...	8	...	8	...	...	4	...	...
South Dakota	...	...	...	...	...	...	...	...	...	...	...	...	...	...	...	...	...	...
Tennessee	12	11	1	...	11	1	...	1	11	10½	1	½	10½	1½	...	...	12	...
Texas	4	4	...	...	4	...	...	...	4	...	4	...	...	...	4	...	...	4
Utah	...	...	...	...	...	...	...	...	...	...	...	...	...	...	...	...	...	...
Vermont	5	...	5	...	...	5	...	5	...	5	...	...	...	5	...	...	5	...
Virginia	15	14	1	...	14	1	...	1	14	14	1	...	11	4	...	...	15	...
Washington	...	...	...	...	...	...	...	...	...	...	...	...	...	...	...	...	...	...
West Virginia	...	...	...	...	...	...	...	...	...	...	...	...	...	...	...	...	...	...
Wisconsin	5	...	5	...	...	5	...	5	...	5	...	...	...	5	...	...	5	...
Wyoming	...	...	...	...	...	...	...	...	...	...	...	...	...	...	...	...	...	...
Alaska	...	...	...	...	...	...	...	...	...	...	...	...	...	...	...	...	...	...
Canal Zone	...	...	...	...	...	...	...	...	...	...	...	...	...	...	...	...	...	...
District of Columbia	...	...	...	...	...	...	...	...	...	...	...	...	...	...	...	...	...	...
Hawaii	...	...	...	...	...	...	...	...	...	...	...	...	...	...	...	...	...	...
Philippine Islands	...	...	...	...	...	...	...	...	...	...	...	...	...	...	...	...	...	...
Puerto Rico	...	...	...	...	...	...	...	...	...	...	...	...	...	...	...	...	...	...
Virgin Islands	...	...	...	...	...	...	...	...	...	...	...	...	...	...	...	...	...	...
Total	303	146	150	7	145	151	7	165	138	237½	65	½	81	199[a]	23	21	238	44

Source: *Official Proceedings, 1860.*
Table appeal from chair, New Jersey unit rule, p. 51.
Sustain decision of chair, New Jersey unit rule, p. 51.
Minority report on platform, p. 52.
Reaffirmation of 1856 platform, p. 53.
Table remaining resolutions, p. 53.
a/ Sum of column; proceedings record 188.
Support of Supreme Court decisions, p. 54.

		1860 DEMOCRATIC														
		Transcontinental Railway Plank			Motion to Adjourn			Main Question, Order of Business			Table Motion on Two-Thirds Rule			Sustain Chair on Two-Thirds Rule		
Delegation	Votes	Yea	Nay	Not Voting	Yea	Nay	Not Voting	Yea	Nay	Not Voting	Yea	Nay	Not Voting	Yea	Nay	Not Voting
Alabama	9	...	...	9	...	...	9	...	...	9	...	...	9	...	...	9
Arizona	...	...	...	...	...	...	...	...	...	...	...	...	...	...	...	...
Arkansas	4	4	...	...	...	1	3	1	...	3	...	1	3	...	...	4
California	4	4	...	...	3	1	...	...	4	...	...	4	...	4	...	...
Colorado	...	...	...	...	...	...	...	...	...	...	...	...	...	...	...	...
Connecticut	6	6	...	...	2	4	...	3	2	1	3½	2½	...	2½	3	½
Delaware	3	...	2	1	2	...	1	...	2	1	...	2	1	2	...	1
Florida	3	...	...	3	...	...	3	...	...	3	...	...	3	...	...	3
Georgia	10	10	...	...	...	...	10	...	...	10	...	...	10	...	...	10
Idaho	...	...	...	...	...	...	...	...	...	...	...	...	...	...	...	...
Illinois	11	11	...	...	...	11	...	11	...	...	11	...	...	...	11	...
Indiana	13	13	...	...	...	13	...	13	...	...	13	...	...	...	13	...
Iowa	4	4	...	...	...	4	...	4	...	...	4	...	...	...	4	...
Kansas	...	...	...	...	...	...	...	...	...	...	...	...	...	...	...	...
Kentucky	12	12	...	...	11½	½	...	...	12	...	...	12	...	11½	½	...
Louisiana	6	...	...	6	...	...	6	...	...	6	...	...	6	...	...	6
Maine	8	8	...	...	2	6	...	5	3	...	5	3	...	3	5	...
Maryland	8	7	1	...	4	4	...	3	5	...	2	6	...	6	2	...
Massachusetts	13	12½	...	½	8	5	...	6	7	...	4½	8½	...	5½	3½	4
Michigan	6	6	...	...	...	6	...	6	...	...	6	...	...	...	6	...
Minnesota	4	4	...	...	1½	2½	...	2½	1½	...	2½	1½	...	1	2½	½
Mississippi	7	...	...	7	...	...	7	...	...	7	...	...	7	...	...	7
Missouri	9	9	...	...	4½	4½	...	4½	4½	...	4½	4½	...	4½	4½	...
Montana	...	...	...	...	...	...	...	...	...	...	...	...	...	...	...	...
Nebraska	...	...	...	...	...	...	...	...	...	...	...	...	...	...	...	...
Nevada	...	...	...	...	...	...	...	...	...	...	...	...	...	...	...	...
New Hampshire	5	5	...	...	...	5	...	5	...	...	5	...	...	1	4	...
New Jersey	7	7	...	...	5	2	...	7	...	...	1½	5½	...	5½	1½	...
New Mexico	...	...	...	...	...	...	...	...	...	...	...	...	...	...	...	...
New York	35	35	...	...	...	35	...	35	...	...	...	35	...	35	...	...
North Carolina	10	...	10	...	8½	1½	...	...	10	...	...	10	...	10	...	...
North Dakota	...	...	...	...	...	...	...	...	...	...	...	...	...	...	...	...
Ohio	23	23	...	...	...	23	...	23	...	...	23	...	...	...	23	...
Oklahoma	...	...	...	...	...	...	...	...	...	...	...	...	...	...	...	...
Oregon	3	3	...	...	3	...	...	...	3	...	...	3	...	3	...	...
Pennsylvania	27	27	...	...	12	13	2	10½	16½	...	10	16½	½	17½	9½	...
Rhode Island	4	4	...	...	...	4	...	...	4	...	4	...	...	...	4	...
South Carolina	8	8	...	...	1	...	7	...	...	8	...	...	8	1	...	7
South Dakota	...	...	...	...	...	...	...	...	...	...	...	...	...	...	...	...
Tennessee	12	8½	3½	...	9	3	...	1	11	...	1	11	...	11	1	...
Texas	4	...	...	4	...	...	4	...	...	4	...	...	4	...	...	4
Utah	...	...	...	...	...	...	...	...	...	...	...	...	...	...	...	...
Vermont	5	5	...	...	...	5	...	5	...	...	5	...	...	...	5	...
Virginia	15	11	4	...	15	...	...	...	15	...	...	15	...	15	...	...
Washington	...	...	...	...	...	...	...	...	...	...	...	...	...	...	...	...
West Virginia	...	...	...	...	...	...	...	...	...	...	...	...	...	...	...	...
Wisconsin	5	5	...	...	...	5	...	5	...	...	5	...	...	...	5	...
Wyoming	...	...	...	...	...	...	...	...	...	...	...	...	...	...	...	...
Alaska	...	...	...	...	...	...	...	...	...	...	...	...	...	...	...	...
Canal Zone	...	...	...	...	...	...	...	...	...	...	...	...	...	...	...	...
District of Columbia	...	...	...	...	...	...	...	...	...	...	...	...	...	...	...	...
Hawaii	...	...	...	...	...	...	...	...	...	...	...	...	...	...	...	...
Philippine Islands	...	...	...	...	...	...	...	...	...	...	...	...	...	...	...	...
Puerto Rico	...	...	...	...	...	...	...	...	...	...	...	...	...	...	...	...
Virgin Islands	...	...	...	...	...	...	...	...	...	...	...	...	...	...	...	...
Total	303	252	20½	30½	92	159	52	150½[a]	100½[b]	52	110½[c]	141	51½	139[d]	108	56

Source: *Official Proceedings, 1860.*
Transcontinental railway plank, p. 54.
Motion to adjourn, p. 69.
Main question, order of business, p. 71.
a/ Sum of column; proceedings record 149.
b/ Sum of column; proceedings record 102.
Table motion on two-thirds rule, p. 71.
c/ Sum of column; proceedings record 111½.
Sustain chair on two-thirds rule, p. 73.
d/ Sum of column; proceedings record 144.

		1860 DEMOCRATIC														
		Main Question on Two-Thirds Rule			Presidential											
					First Ballot				Tenth Ballot				Twentieth Ballot			
Delegation	Votes	Yea	Nay	Not Voting	Douglas	Hunter	Guthrie	Other	Douglas	Guthrie	Hunter	Other	Douglas	Guthrie	Hunter	Other
Alabama	9	...	...	9	...	...	...	9	...	...	...	9	...	...	...	9
Arizona	...	...	...	...	...	...	...	...	...	...	...	...	...	...	...	...
Arkansas	4	...	1	3	...	1	...	3	...	...	1	3	...	...	...	4
California	4	4	...	...	...	...	...	4	...	...	...	4	...	...	...	4
Colorado	...	...	...	...	...	...	...	...	...	...	...	...	...	...	...	...
Connecticut	6	2½	3½	...	3½	...	...	2½	3½	2½	...	...	3½	2½	...	...
Delaware	3	2	...	1	...	2	...	1	...	...	2	1	...	...	2	1
Florida	3	...	...	3	...	...	...	3	...	...	...	3	...	...	...	3
Georgia	10	...	...	10	...	...	...	10	...	...	...	10	...	...	...	10
Idaho	...	...	...	...	...	...	...	...	...	...	...	...	...	...	...	...
Illinois	11	...	11	...	11	...	...	...	11	...	...	...	11	...	...	...
Indiana	13	...	13	...	13	...	...	...	13	...	...	...	13	...	...	...
Iowa	4	...	4	...	4	...	...	...	4	...	...	...	4	...	...	...
Kansas	...	...	...	...	...	...	...	...	...	...	...	...	...	...	...	...
Kentucky	12	11	1	...	...	...	12	...	...	12	...	...	...	12	...	...
Louisiana	6	...	...	6	...	...	...	6	...	...	...	6	...	...	...	6
Maine	8	3	5	...	5	...	3	...	5	3	...	...	5	3	...	...
Maryland	8	6	2	...	2	5	...	1	3½	½	4	...	3½	½	4	...
Massachusetts	13	8½	4½	...	5½	6	...	1½	7	...	4½	1½	7	2½	2½	1
Michigan	6	...	6	...	6	...	...	...	6	...	...	...	6	...	...	...
Minnesota	4	1½	2½	...	4	...	...	...	3	...	...	1	3	...	...	1
Mississippi	7	...	...	7	...	...	...	7	...	...	...	7	...	...	...	7
Missouri	9	4½	4½	...	4½	...	4½	...	4½	4½	...	...	4½	4½	...	...
Montana	...	...	...	...	...	...	...	...	...	...	...	...	...	...	...	...
Nebraska	...	...	...	...	...	...	...	...	...	...	...	...	...	...	...	...
Nevada	...	...	...	...	...	...	...	...	...	...	...	...	...	...	...	...
New Hampshire	5	...	5	...	5	...	...	...	5	...	...	...	5	...	...	...
New Jersey	7	5½	1½	...	...	...	7	...	1½	5½	...	...	2	4½	...	½
New Mexico	...	...	...	...	...	...	...	...	...	...	...	...	...	...	...	...
New York	35	35	...	...	35	...	...	...	35	...	...	...	35	...	...	...
North Carolina	10	10	...	...	1	9	...	...	1	...	9	...	...	...	...	10
North Dakota	...	...	...	...	...	...	...	...	...	...	...	...	...	...	...	...
Ohio	23	...	23	...	23	...	...	...	23	...	...	...	23	...	...	...
Oklahoma	...	...	...	...	...	...	...	...	...	...	...	...	...	...	...	...
Oregon	3	3	...	...	...	...	...	3	...	...	...	3	...	...	...	3
Pennsylvania	27	17½	9½	...	9	3	9	6	9½	11½	3½	2½	9½	12½	2½	2½
Rhode Island	4	...	4	...	4	...	...	...	4	...	...	...	4	...	...	...
South Carolina	8	1	...	7	...	1	...	7	...	...	...	8	...	...	...	8
South Dakota	...	...	...	...	...	...	...	...	...	...	...	...	...	...	...	...
Tennessee	12	11	1	...	...	...	...	12	1	...	...	11	1	...	...	11
Texas	4	...	...	4	...	...	...	4	...	...	...	4	...	...	...	4
Utah	...	...	...	...	...	...	...	...	...	...	...	...	...	...	...	...
Vermont	5	...	5	...	5	...	...	...	5	...	...	...	5	...	...	...
Virginia	15	15	...	...	...	15	...	...	...	...	15	...	...	...	15	...
Washington	...	...	...	...	...	...	...	...	...	...	...	...	...	...	...	...
West Virginia	...	...	...	...	...	...	...	...	...	...	...	...	...	...	...	...
Wisconsin	5	...	5	...	5	...	...	...	5	...	...	...	5	...	...	...
Wyoming	...	...	...	...	...	...	...	...	...	...	...	...	...	...	...	...
Alaska	...	...	...	...	...	...	...	...	...	...	...	...	...	...	...	...
Canal Zone	...	...	...	...	...	...	...	...	...	...	...	...	...	...	...	...
District of Columbia	...	...	...	...	...	...	...	...	...	...	...	...	...	...	...	...
Hawaii	...	...	...	...	...	...	...	...	...	...	...	...	...	...	...	...
Philippine Islands	...	...	...	...	...	...	...	...	...	...	...	...	...	...	...	...
Puerto Rico	...	...	...	...	...	...	...	...	...	...	...	...	...	...	...	...
Virgin Islands	...	...	...	...	...	...	...	...	...	...	...	...	...	...	...	...
Total	303	141	112	50	145½	42	35½[a]	80[b]	150½	39½	39	74[c]	150	42	26	85[d]

Source: *Official Proceedings, 1860.*

Main question on two-thirds rule, p. 74.

Presidential. First ballot, p. 74.

a/ Sum of column; proceedings record 35.

b/ Other candidates: Andrew Johnson, 12; Daniel S. Dickinson, 7; Joseph Lane, 6; Isaac Toucey, 2½; Jefferson Davis, 1½; James A. Pearce, 1; not voting, 50.

Tenth ballot, p. 77.

c/ Other candidates: Johnson, 12; Lane, 5½; Dickinson, 4; Davis, 1½; not voting, 51.

Twentieth ballot, p. 79.

d/ Other candidates: Lane, 20½; Johnson, 12; Davis, 1; Dickinson, ½; not voting, 51.

Delegation	Votes	1860 DEMOCRATIC — Presidential — Thirtieth Ballot: Douglas	Guthrie	Hunter	Other	Fortieth Ballot: Douglas	Guthrie	Other	Fiftieth Ballot: Douglas	Guthrie	Other	Fifty-seventh Ballot: Douglas	Guthrie	Other	Table Order of Business: Yea	Nay	Not Voting
Alabama	9	...	...	...	9	...	...	9	...	...	9	...	...	9	...	...	9
Arizona	...	...	...	...	...	...	...	...	...	...	...	...	...	...	...	...	...
Arkansas	4	...	...	...	4	...	...	4	...	...	4	...	...	4	1	...	3
California	4	...	...	...	4	...	...	4	...	...	4	...	...	4	...	4	...
Colorado	...	...	...	...	...	...	...	...	...	...	...	...	...	...	...	...	...
Connecticut	6	3½	2½	...	...	3½	2½	...	3½	2½	...	3½	2½	...	6	...	...
Delaware	3	...	...	2	1	...	...	3	...	...	3	...	...	3	...	...	3
Florida	3	...	...	...	3	...	...	3	...	...	3	...	...	3	...	...	3
Georgia	10	...	...	...	10	...	...	10	...	...	10	...	...	10	...	...	10
Idaho	...	...	...	...	...	...	...	...	...	...	...	...	...	...	...	...	...
Illinois	11	11	...	...	...	11	...	...	11	...	...	11	...	...	11	...	...
Indiana	13	13	...	...	...	13	...	...	13	...	...	13	...	...	13	...	...
Iowa	4	4	...	...	...	4	...	...	4	...	...	4	...	...	4	...	...
Kansas	...	...	...	...	...	...	...	...	...	...	...	...	...	...	...	...	...
Kentucky	12	...	12	...	...	...	12	...	...	12	...	...	12	...	...	12	...
Louisiana	6	...	...	...	6	...	...	6	...	...	6	...	...	6	...	...	6
Maine	8	5	3	...	...	5	3	...	5	3	...	5	3	...	5	3	...
Maryland	8	4	...	4	...	4	4	...	4	4	...	4	4	...	4	4	...
Massachusetts	13	7	2½	2½	1	6	7	...	6	6	1	6	6	1	7½	5½	...
Michigan	6	6	...	...	...	6	...	...	6	...	...	6	...	...	6	...	...
Minnesota	4	3	...	...	1	3	...	1	3	...	1	3	...	1	3	1	...
Mississippi	7	...	...	...	7	...	...	7	...	...	7	...	...	7	...	...	7
Missouri	9	4½	4½	...	...	4½	4½	...	4½	4½	...	4½	4½	...	4½	4½	...
Montana	...	...	...	...	...	...	...	...	...	...	...	...	...	...	...	...	...
Nebraska	...	...	...	...	...	...	...	...	...	...	...	...	...	...	...	...	...
Nevada	...	...	...	...	...	...	...	...	...	...	...	...	...	...	...	...	...
New Hampshire	5	5	...	...	...	5	...	...	5	...	...	5	...	...	5	...	...
New Jersey	7	2	4½	...	½	2	5	...	2	5	...	2	5	...	7	...	...
New Mexico	...	...	...	...	...	...	...	...	...	...	...	...	...	...	...	...	...
New York	35	35	...	...	...	35	...	...	35	...	...	35	...	...	35	...	...
North Carolina	10	...	...	...	10	1	...	9	1	...	9	1	...	9	4	6	...
North Dakota	...	...	...	...	...	...	...	...	...	...	...	...	...	...	...	...	...
Ohio	23	23	...	...	...	23	...	...	23	...	...	23	...	...	23	...	...
Oklahoma	...	...	...	...	...	...	...	...	...	...	...	...	...	...	...	...	...
Oregon	3	...	...	...	3	...	...	3	...	...	3	...	...	3	...	3	...
Pennsylvania	27	9½	15	2½	...	9½	17½	...	9½	17½	...	9½	17½	...	27	...	...
Rhode Island	4	4	...	...	...	4	...	...	4	...	...	4	...	...	4	...	...
South Carolina	8	...	...	...	8	...	...	8	...	...	8	...	...	8	...	...	8
South Dakota	...	...	...	...	...	...	...	...	...	...	...	...	...	...	...	...	...
Tennessee	12	1	1	...	10	1	11	...	1	11	...	1	11	...	4½	7½	...
Texas	4	...	...	...	4	...	...	4	...	...	4	...	...	4	...	...	4
Utah	...	...	...	...	...	...	...	...	...	...	...	...	...	...	...	...	...
Vermont	5	5	...	...	...	5	...	...	5	...	...	5	...	...	5	...	...
Virginia	15	1	...	14	...	1	...	14	1	...	14	1	...	14	14½	½	...
Washington	...	...	...	...	...	...	...	...	...	...	...	...	...	...	...	...	...
West Virginia	...	...	...	...	...	...	...	...	...	...	...	...	...	...	...	...	...
Wisconsin	5	5	...	...	...	5	...	...	5	...	...	5	...	...	5	...	...
Wyoming	...	...	...	...	...	...	...	...	...	...	...	...	...	...	...	...	...
Alaska	...	...	...	...	...	...	...	...	...	...	...	...	...	...	...	...	...
Canal Zone	...	...	...	...	...	...	...	...	...	...	...	...	...	...	...	...	...
District of Columbia	...	...	...	...	...	...	...	...	...	...	...	...	...	...	...	...	...
Hawaii	...	...	...	...	...	...	...	...	...	...	...	...	...	...	...	...	...
Philippine Islands	...	...	...	...	...	...	...	...	...	...	...	...	...	...	...	...	...
Puerto Rico	...	...	...	...	...	...	...	...	...	...	...	...	...	...	...	...	...
Virgin Islands	...	...	...	...	...	...	...	...	...	...	...	...	...	...	...	...	...
Total	303	151½	45	25	81½ [a]	151½	66½	85 [b]	151½	65½	86 [c]	151½	65½	86 [d]	199	51	53

Source: *Official Proceedings, 1860.*
Thirtieth ballot, p. 82.
a/ Other candidates: Dickinson, 13; Johnson, 11; Lane, 5½; Davis, 1; not voting, 51.
Fortieth ballot, p. 85.
b/ Other candidates: Hunter, 16; Lane, 12½; Dickinson, 5½; not voting, 51.
Fiftieth ballot, p. 87.
c/ Other candidates: Hunter, 16; Lane, 14; Dickinson, 4; Davis, 1; not voting, 51.
Fifty-seventh ballot, p. 88.
d/ Other candidates: Hunter, 16; Lane, 14; Dickinson, 4; Davis, 1; not voting, 51.
Table order of business, p. 89.

	1860 DEMOCRATIC															
		Motion to Adjourn to Baltimore			Motion to Recess *			Previous Question on Credentials			Motion to Adjourn, 2nd Day			Motion to Adjourn, 4th Day		
Delegation	Votes	Yea	Nay	Not Voting	Yea	Nay	Not Voting	Yea	Nay	Not Voting	Yea	Nay	Not Voting	Yea	Nay	Not Voting
Alabama	9	...	...	9	...	...	9	...	...	9	...	...	9	...	...	9
Arizona	...	...	...	...	...	...	...	...	...	...	...	...	...	...	...	...
Arkansas	4	1	...	3	...	1	3	...	1	3	1	...	3	...	...	4
California	4	...	4	...	4	...	...	...	4	...	4	...	...	4	...	...
Colorado	...	...	...	...	...	...	...	...	...	...	...	...	...	...	...	...
Connecticut	6	6	...	...	1	5	...	3½	2	½	2½	3½	...	2	4	...
Delaware	3	...	...	3	2	...	1	...	2	1	2	...	1	2	...	1
Florida	3	...	...	3	...	...	3	...	...	3	...	...	3	...	...	3
Georgia	10	...	...	10	...	...	10	...	...	10	...	...	10	...	...	10
Idaho	...	...	...	...	...	...	...	...	...	...	...	...	...	...	...	...
Illinois	11	11	...	...	...	11	...	11	...	...	...	11	...	11	...	...
Indiana	13	13	...	...	...	13	...	13	...	...	...	13	...	13	...	...
Iowa	4	4	...	...	...	4	...	4	...	...	...	...	4	4	...	...
Kansas	...	...	...	...	...	...	...	...	...	...	...	...	...	...	...	...
Kentucky	12	...	12	...	3	9	...	1½	10½	...	12	...	...	12	...	...
Louisiana	6	...	...	6	...	...	6	...	...	6	...	...	6	...	...	6
Maine	8	5	3	...	1½	6½	...	6	2	...	8	...	...	8	...	...
Maryland	8	5	3	...	6	2	...	2	6	...	8	...	...	4	4	...
Massachusetts	13	10	3	...	...	13	...	4½	4½	4	13	...	...	4½	8	½
Michigan	6	6	...	...	...	6	...	6	...	...	6	...	...	6	...	...
Minnesota	4	3½	½	...	1½	2½	...	2½	1½	...	4	...	...	4	...	...
Mississippi	7	...	...	7	...	...	7	...	...	7	...	...	7	...	...	7
Missouri	9	6	3	...	6½	2½	...	2½	6½	...	3	6	...	6	3	...
Montana	...	...	...	...	...	...	...	...	...	...	...	...	...	...	...	...
Nebraska	...	...	...	...	...	...	...	...	...	...	...	...	...	...	...	...
Nevada	...	...	...	...	...	...	...	...	...	...	...	...	...	...	...	...
New Hampshire	5	5	...	...	½	4½	...	5	...	...	5	...	...	½	4½	...
New Jersey	7	2	5	...	5	2	...	2½	4½	...	7	...	...	4	3	...
New Mexico	...	...	...	...	...	...	...	...	...	...	...	...	...	...	...	...
New York	35	35	...	...	...	35	...	...	35	...	35	...	...	...	...	35
North Carolina	10	...	10	...	10	...	...	...	10	...	10	...	...	7½	2½	...
North Dakota	...	...	...	...	...	...	...	...	...	...	...	...	...	...	...	...
Ohio	23	23	...	...	...	23	...	23	...	...	...	23	...	23	...	...
Oklahoma	...	...	...	...	...	...	...	...	...	...	...	...	...	...	...	...
Oregon	3	...	3	...	3	...	...	...	3	...	3	...	...	3	...	...
Pennsylvania	27	23½	3½	...	6	21	...	9½	16½	1	26	1	...	15	11	1
Rhode Island	4	4	...	...	...	4	...	...	4	...	4	...	...	4	...	...
South Carolina	8	...	...	8	...	...	8	...	...	8	...	...	8	...	...	8
South Dakota	...	...	...	...	...	...	...	...	...	...	...	...	...	...	...	...
Tennessee	12	7	5	...	8½	3½	...	3	8	1	12	...	...	5	7	...
Texas	4	...	...	4	...	...	4	...	...	4	...	...	4	...	...	4
Utah	...	...	...	...	...	...	...	...	...	...	...	...	...	...	...	...
Vermont	5	5	...	...	...	5	...	4½	½	...	5	...	...	...	...	5
Virginia	15	14½	½	...	15	...	...	...	15	...	15	...	...	14	1	...
Washington	...	...	...	...	...	...	...	...	...	...	...	...	...	...	...	...
West Virginia	...	...	...	...	...	...	...	...	...	...	...	...	...	...	...	...
Wisconsin	5	5	...	...	...	5	...	5	...	...	...	...	5	5	...	...
Wyoming	...	...	...	...	...	...	...	...	...	...	...	...	...	...	...	...
Alaska	...	...	...	...	...	...	...	...	...	...	...	...	...	...	...	...
Canal Zone	...	...	...	...	...	...	...	...	...	...	...	...	...	...	...	...
District of Columbia	...	...	...	...	...	...	...	...	...	...	...	...	...	...	...	...
Hawaii	...	...	...	...	...	...	...	...	...	...	...	...	...	...	...	...
Philippine Islands	...	...	...	...	...	...	...	...	...	...	...	...	...	...	...	...
Puerto Rico	...	...	...	...	...	...	...	...	...	...	...	...	...	...	...	...
Virgin Islands	...	...	...	...	...	...	...	...	...	...	...	...	...	...	...	...
Total	303	194½	55½[a]	53	73½	178½	51	109[b]	136½[c]	57½	185½	57½[d]	60	161½	48	93½

Source: *Official Proceedings, 1860.*
Motion to adjourn to Baltimore, p. 90.
a/ Sum of column; proceedings record 55.
Motion to recess, p. 101.
Previous question on credentials, p. 101.
b/ Sum of column; proceedings record 107½.
c/ Sum of column; proceedings record 140½.
Motion to adjourn, 2nd day, p. 107.
d/ Sum of column; proceedings record 66½.
Motion to adjourn, 4th day, p. 125.

* Last ballot in Charleston Convention. All votes that follow were taken in the Baltimore Convention.

Delegation	Votes	Minority Report on Credentials			Majority Report, Louisiana Contest			Majority Report, Arkansas Contest(1)			Majority Report, Arkansas Contest(2)			Majority Report, Massachusetts Contest		
		Yea	Nay	Not Voting	Yea	Nay	Not Voting	Yea	Nay	Not Voting	Yea	Nay	Not Voting	Yea	Nay	Not Voting
Alabama	9	...	...	9	...	...	9	...	...	9	...	...	9	...	...	9
Arizona	...	...	...	...	...	...	...	...	...	...	...	...	...	...	...	...
Arkansas	4	½	½	3	½	½	3	...	...	4	...	...	4	...	1	3
California	4	4	...	...	...	4	...	...	4	...	...	4	...	...	4	...
Colorado	...	...	...	...	...	...	...	...	...	...	...	...	...	...	...	...
Connecticut	6	2½	3½	...	3½	2½	...	6	...	...	3½	2½	...	3½	2½	...
Delaware	3	2	...	1	...	2	1	2	...	1	...	2	1	...	2	1
Florida	3	...	...	3	...	...	3	...	...	3	...	...	3	...	...	3
Georgia	10	...	...	10	...	...	10	...	...	10	...	...	10	...	...	10
Idaho	...	...	...	...	...	...	...	...	...	...	...	...	...	...	...	...
Illinois	11	...	11	...	11	...	...	11	...	...	11	...	...	11	...	...
Indiana	13	...	13	...	13	...	...	13	...	...	13	...	...	13	...	...
Iowa	4	...	4	...	4	...	...	3½	½	...	4	...	...	3½	1½	...
Kansas	...	...	...	...	...	...	...	...	...	...	...	...	...	...	...	...
Kentucky	12	10	2	...	2	10	...	...	12	...	2	10	...	...	12	...
Louisiana	6	...	...	6	...	...	6	...	...	6	...	...	6	...	...	6
Maine	8	2½	5½	...	5½	2½	...	5½	2½	...	5½	2½	...	5½	2½	...
Maryland	8	5½	2	½	2½	5½	...	2½	5½	...	2	6	...	2½	5½	...
Massachusetts	13	8	5	...	5	8	...	13	...	...	5	8	...	3	8½	1½
Michigan	6	...	6	...	6	...	...	6	...	...	6	...	...	6	...	...
Minnesota	4	1½	2½	...	2½	1½	...	4	...	...	2½	1½	...	2½	1½	...
Mississippi	7	...	...	7	...	...	7	...	...	7	...	...	7	...	...	7
Missouri	9	5	4	...	4	5	...	9	...	...	4	5	...	4	5	...
Montana	...	...	...	...	...	...	...	...	...	...	...	...	...	...	...	...
Nebraska	...	...	...	...	...	...	...	...	...	...	...	...	...	...	...	...
Nevada	...	...	...	...	...	...	...	...	...	...	...	...	...	...	...	...
New Hampshire	5	½	4½	...	4	½	½	5	...	...	5	...	...	2½	2½	...
New Jersey	7	4	3	...	2½	4½	...	7	...	...	2½	4½	...	1½	4½	1
New Mexico	...	...	...	...	...	...	...	...	...	...	...	...	...	...	...	...
New York	35	...	35	...	35	...	...	35	...	...	35	...	...	35	...	...
North Carolina	10	9	1	...	2	8	...	1	9	...	1	9	...	...	10	...
North Dakota	...	...	...	...	...	...	...	...	...	...	...	...	...	...	...	...
Ohio	23	...	23	...	23	...	...	23	...	...	23	...	...	23	...	...
Oklahoma	...	...	...	...	...	...	...	...	...	...	...	...	...	...	...	...
Oregon	3	3	...	...	...	3	...	...	3	...	...	3	...	...	3	...
Pennsylvania	27	17	10	...	10	17	...	10	17	...	10	17	...	9½	17½	...
Rhode Island	4	...	4	...	4	...	...	4	...	...	4	...	...	4	...	...
South Carolina	8	...	...	8	...	...	8	...	...	8	...	...	8	...	...	8
South Dakota	...	...	...	...	...	...	...	...	...	...	...	...	...	...	...	...
Tennessee	12	10	1	1	2	10	...	11½	½	...	½	11	½	...	12	...
Texas	4	...	...	4	...	...	4	...	...	4	...	...	4	...	...	4
Utah	...	...	...	...	...	...	...	...	...	...	...	...	...	...	...	...
Vermont	5	1½	3½	...	4½	½	...	5	...	...	4½	½	...	3	2	...
Virginia	15	14	1	...	1	13	1	...	15	...	1	14	...	...	15	...
Washington	...	...	...	...	...	...	...	...	...	...	...	...	...	...	...	...
West Virginia	...	...	...	...	...	...	...	...	...	...	...	...	...	...	...	...
Wisconsin	5	...	5	...	5	...	...	5	...	...	5	...	...	5	...	...
Wyoming	...	...	...	...	...	...	...	...	...	...	...	...	...	...	...	...
Alaska	...	...	...	...	...	...	...	...	...	...	...	...	...	...	...	...
Canal Zone	...	...	...	...	...	...	...	...	...	...	...	...	...	...	...	...
District of Columbia	...	...	...	...	...	...	...	...	...	...	...	...	...	...	...	...
Hawaii	...	...	...	...	...	...	...	...	...	...	...	...	...	...	...	...
Philippine Islands	...	...	...	...	...	...	...	...	...	...	...	...	...	...	...	...
Puerto Rico	...	...	...	...	...	...	...	...	...	...	...	...	...	...	...	...
Virgin Islands	...	...	...	...	...	...	...	...	...	...	...	...	...	...	...	...
Total	303	100½	150	52½	152½[a]	98	52½	182	69	52	150	100½	52½	138	112½	53½

Source: *Official Proceedings, 1860.*

Minority report on credentials, p. 133.
Majority report, Louisiana contest, p. 134.
a/ Sum of column; proceedings record 153.
Majority report, Arkansas contest (1), p. 135.
Majority report, Arkansas contest (2), p. 135.
Majority report, Massachusetts contest, p. 136.

1860 DEMOCRATIC

Delegation	Votes	Majority Report, Missouri Contest			Majority Report, Alabama Contest			Majority Report, Georgia Contest			Table Reconsideration of Min. Rept. on Credentials			Reconsideration of Minority Report on Credentials		
		Yea	Nay	Not Voting	Yea	Nay	Not Voting	Yea	Nay	Not Voting	Yea	Nay	Not Voting	Yea	Nay	Not Voting
Alabama	9	...	...	9	...	...	9	...	...	9	...	...	9	...	...	9
Arizona	...															
Arkansas	4	½	½	3	½	½	3	½	½	3	½	½	3	½	½	3
California	4	...	4	...	...	4	...	...	4	...	...	4	...	4	...	...
Colorado	...															
Connecticut	6	3½	2½	...	3½	2½	...	3½	2½	...	3½	2½	...	2½	3½	...
Delaware	3	...	2	1	...	2	1	...	2	1	...	2	1	2	...	1
Florida	3	...	...	3	...	...	3	...	...	3	...	...	3	...	...	3
Georgia	10	...	...	10	...	...	10	...	...	10	...	...	10	...	...	10
Idaho	...															
Illinois	11	11	...	...	11	...	...	11	...	...	11	...	...	...	11	...
Indiana	13	13	...	...	13	...	...	13	...	...	13	...	...	...	13	...
Iowa	4	3½	½	...	4	...	...	4	...	...	4	...	...	...	4	...
Kansas	...															
Kentucky	12	...	12	...	1½	10½	...	...	11½	½	2	10	...	10	2	...
Louisiana	6	...	...	6	...	...	6	...	...	6	...	...	6	...	...	6
Maine	8	5½	2½	...	5½	2½	...	4	4	...	5½	2½	...	2½	5½	...
Maryland	8	2½	5½	...	2	6	...	2	6	...	2	6	...	6	2	...
Massachusetts	13	5	8	...	5	8	...	5	8	...	5	8	...	8	5	...
Michigan	6	6	...	...	6	...	...	6	...	...	6	...	...	...	6	...
Minnesota	4	2½	1½	...	2½	1½	...	2½	1½	...	2½	1½	...	1½	2½	...
Mississippi	7	...	...	7	...	...	7	...	...	7	...	...	7	...	...	7
Missouri	9	1½	6	1½	4	5	...	4	5	...	4½	4½	...	4½	4½	...
Montana	...															
Nebraska	...															
Nevada	...															
New Hampshire	5	2½	2½	...	2½	2	½	2	3	...	3	2	...	2	3	...
New Jersey	7	1½	5½	...	3	4	...	2	5	...	3½	3½	...	4½	2½	...
New Mexico	...															
New York	35	35	...	...	35	...	...	...	35	...	...	35	...	...	35	...
North Carolina	10	...	10	...	1½	8	½	1	9	...	1	9	...	9	1	...
North Dakota	...															
Ohio	23	23	...	...	23	...	...	23	...	...	23	...	...	...	23	...
Oklahoma	...															
Oregon	3	...	3	...	...	3	...	...	3	...	...	3	...	3	...	...
Pennsylvania	27	10	17	...	10	17	...	9½	17½	...	10	17	...	17	10	...
Rhode Island	4	4	...	...	4	...	...	4	...	...	4	...	...	...	4	...
South Carolina	8	...	...	8	...	...	8	...	...	8	...	...	8	...	...	8
South Dakota	...															
Tennessee	12	...	12	...	2	10	...	...	12	...	...	12	...	10	2	...
Texas	4	...	...	4	...	...	4	...	...	4	...	...	4	...	...	4
Utah	...															
Vermont	5	3	2	...	4½	½	...	3½	1½	...	4½	½	...	1	4	...
Virginia	15	...	15	...	½	14½	...	1	14	...	...	15	...	15	...	...
Washington	...															
West Virginia	...															
Wisconsin	5	5	...	...	5	...	...	5	...	...	5	...	...	...	5	...
Wyoming	...															
Alaska	...															
Canal Zone	...															
District of Columbia	...															
Hawaii	...															
Philippine Islands	...															
Puerto Rico	...															
Virgin Islands	...															
Total	303	138½	112	52½	149½[a]	101½	52	106½	145	51½	113½	138½	51	103[b]	149[c]	51

Source: *Official Proceedings, 1860.*
Majority report, Missouri contest, p. 136.
Majority report, Alabama contest, p. 137.
a/ Sum of column; proceedings record 148½.
Majority report, Georgia contest, p. 140.
Table reconsideration of minority report on credentials, p. 142.
Reconsideration of minority report on credentials, p. 143.
b/ Sum of column; proceedings record 113.
c/ Sum of column; proceedings record 139.

| | | 1860 DEMOCRATIC | | | | | | | | | 1864 DEMOCRATIC | | | | | |
| | | Reconsider Louisiana Credentials | | | Presidential First Ballot | | Second Ballot | | Vice-Pres. First Ballot | | | Presidential First Ballot (before shift) | | | First Ballot (after shift) | |
Delegation	Votes	Yea	Nay	Not Voting	Douglas	Other	Douglas	Other	Fitz-patrick	Other	Votes	McClellan	Seymour	Other	McClellan	Seymour
Alabama	9	...	...	9	9	...	9	...	9	...	...	...	...	...	...	...
Arizona	...	...	...	...	...	...	...	...	...	...	...	...	...	...	...	...
Arkansas	4	½	½	3	1	3	1½	2½	4	...	...	...	...	...	...	...
California	4	...	4	...	...	4	...	4	...	4	5	2½	2½	...	5	...
Colorado	...	...	...	...	...	...	...	...	...	...	...	...	...	...	...	...
Connecticut	6	3½	2½	...	3½	2½	3½	2½	6	...	6	5½	...	½	6	...
Delaware	3	...	2	1	...	3	...	3	...	3	3	...	3	...	...	3
Florida	3	...	...	3	...	3	...	3	...	3	...	...	...	...	...	...
Georgia	10	...	...	10	...	10	...	10	...	10	...	...	...	...	...	...
Idaho	...	...	...	...	...	...	...	...	...	...	...	...	...	...	...	...
Illinois	11	11	...	...	11	...	11	...	11	...	16	16	...	...	16	...
Indiana	13	13	...	...	13	...	13	...	13	...	13	9½	3½	...	9½	3½
Iowa	4	4	...	...	4	...	4	...	4	...	8	3	...	5	8	...
Kansas	...	...	...	...	...	...	...	...	...	...	3	3	...	...	3	...
Kentucky	12	2	10	...	...	12	3	9	4½	7½	11	5½	5½	...	11	...
Louisiana	6	...	...	6	6	...	6	...	6	...	...	...	...	...	...	...
Maine	8	5½	2½	...	5½	2½	7	1	7	1	7	4	3	...	7	...
Maryland	8	2	6	...	2½	5½	2½	5½	3	5	7	...	7	...	...	7
Massachusetts	13	5	8	...	10	...	10	3	10	3	12	11½	...	½	12	...
Michigan	6	6	...	...	6	...	6	...	6	...	8	6½	...	1½	8	...
Minnesota	4	2½	1½	...	2½	1½	4	...	4	...	4	4	...	...	4	...
Mississippi	7	...	...	7	...	7	...	7	...	7	...	...	...	...	...	...
Missouri	9	4½	4½	...	4½	4½	4½	4½	6	3	11	6½	...	4½	7	4
Montana	...	...	...	...	...	...	...	...	...	...	...	...	...	...	...	...
Nebraska	...	...	...	...	...	...	...	...	...	...	...	...	...	...	...	...
Nevada	...	...	...	...	...	...	...	...	...	...	...	...	...	...	...	...
New Hampshire	5	4½	½	...	5	...	5	...	5	...	5	5	...	...	5	...
New Jersey	7	2½	4½	...	2½	4½	2½	4½	7	...	7	7	...	...	7	...
New Mexico	...	...	...	...	...	...	...	...	...	...	...	...	...	...	...	...
New York	35	35	...	...	35	...	35	...	35	...	33	33	...	...	33	...
North Carolina	10	1	8½	½	1	9	1	9	1	9	...	...	...	...	...	...
North Dakota	...	...	...	...	...	...	...	...	...	...	...	...	...	...	...	...
Ohio	23	23	...	...	23	...	23	...	23	...	21	8½	10½	2	15	6
Oklahoma	...	...	...	...	...	...	...	...	...	...	...	...	...	...	...	...
Oregon	3	...	3	...	...	3	...	3	...	3	3	2	1	...	3	...
Pennsylvania	27	10	17	...	10	17	19	8	14	13	26	26	...	...	26	...
Rhode Island	4	4	...	...	4	...	4	...	4	...	4	4	...	...	4	...
South Carolina	8	...	...	8	...	8	...	8	...	8	...	...	...	...	...	...
South Dakota	...	...	...	...	...	...	...	...	...	...	...	...	...	...	...	...
Tennessee	12	2	10	...	3	9	3	9	3	9	...	...	...	...	...	...
Texas	4	...	...	4	...	4	...	4	...	4	...	...	...	...	...	...
Utah	...	...	...	...	...	...	...	...	...	...	...	...	...	...	...	...
Vermont	5	4½	½	...	5	...	5	...	5	...	5	4	1	...	5	...
Virginia	15	...	15	...	1½	13½	3	12	3	12	...	...	...	...	...	...
Washington	...	...	...	...	...	...	...	...	...	...	...	...	...	...	...	...
West Virginia	...	...	...	...	...	...	...	...	...	...	...	...	...	...	...	...
Wisconsin	5	5	...	...	5	...	5	...	5	...	8	7	1	...	8	...
Wyoming	...	...	...	...	...	...	...	...	...	...	...	...	...	...	...	...
Alaska	...	...	...	...	...	...	...	...	...	...	...	...	...	...	...	...
Canal Zone	...	...	...	...	...	...	...	...	...	...	...	...	...	...	...	...
District of Columbia	...	...	...	...	...	...	...	...	...	...	...	...	...	...	...	...
Hawaii	...	...	...	...	...	...	...	...	...	...	...	...	...	...	...	...
Philippine Islands	...	...	...	...	...	...	...	...	...	...	...	...	...	...	...	...
Puerto Rico	...	...	...	...	...	...	...	...	...	...	...	...	...	...	...	...
Virgin Islands	...	...	...	...	...	...	...	...	...	...	...	...	...	...	...	...
Total	303	151[a]	100½[b]	51½	173½	129½[c]	190½[d]	112½[e]	198½	104½[f]	226	174	38	14[g]	202½	23½[h]

Source: *Official Proceedings, 1860.*
Reconsider Louisiana credentials, p. 143.
a/ Sum of column; proceedings record 150½.
b/ Sum of column; proceedings record 99.
Presidential. First ballot, p. 163.
c/ Other candidates: James Guthrie, 9; John C. Breckinridge, 5; Thomas S. Bocock, 1; Horatio Seymour, 1; Henry A. Wise, ½; Daniel S. Dickinson, ½; not voting, 112½.
Second ballot, p. 168.
d/ Sum of column; proceedings record 181½.
e/ Other candidates: Breckinridge, 7½; Guthrie, 5½; not voting, 99½.
Vice-Presidential. First ballot, p. 173.
f/ Blank, 1; not voting, 103½.

Source: *Official Proceedings, 1864.*
Presidential. First ballot (before shift), p. 43.
g/ Other candidates: Horatio Seymour, 12; Charles O'Connor, ½; blank, 1½.
First ballot (after shift), p. 46.
h/ Sum of column; proceedings record 28½.

	1864 DEMOCRATIC							1868 DEMOCRATIC									
		Vice-Presidential							Order of Business			Table Reconsideration of Order of Business			Reconsider Order of Business		
		First Ballot (before shift)					First (after)										
Delegation	Votes	Pendleton	Cass	Guthrie	Powell	Other	Pendleton	Votes	Yea	Nay	Not Voting	Yea	Nay	Not Voting	Yea	Nay	Not Voting
Alabama	...	...	...	...	...	...	...	8	8	...	...	8	...	...	...	8	...
Arizona	...	...	...	...	...	...	...	...	...	...	...	...	...	...	...	...	...
Arkansas	...	...	...	...	...	...	...	5	5	...	...	5	...	...	...	5	...
California	5	...	...	...	5	...	5	5	5	...	...	5	...	...	...	5	...
Colorado	...	...	...	...	...	...	...	...	...	...	...	...	...	...	...	...	...
Connecticut	6	...	...	...	6	...	6	6	6	...	...	...	6	...	6	...	...
Delaware	3	...	...	...	3	...	3	3	3	...	...	3	...	...	1	...	2
Florida	...	...	...	...	...	...	...	3	3	...	...	3	...	...	...	3	...
Georgia	...	...	...	...	...	...	...	9	9	...	...	9	...	...	1	...	8
Idaho	...	...	...	...	...	...	...	...	...	...	...	...	...	...	...	...	...
Illinois	16	...	...	...	...	16	16	16	...	16	...	...	16	...	16	...	...
Indiana	13	...	...	...	...	13	13	13	13	...	...	13	...	...	13	...	...
Iowa	8	...	...	...	...	8	8	8	8	...	...	...	8	...	3½	...	4½
Kansas	3	1½	...	...	1½	...	3	3	3	...	...	1½	1½	...	1½	...	1½
Kentucky	11	...	...	5½	5½	...	11	11	...	11	...	...	11	...	11	...	...
Louisiana	...	...	...	...	...	...	...	7	7	...	...	...	7	...	...	7	...
Maine	7	4	...	3	...	...	7	7	...	...	7	3	3½	½	3	...	4
Maryland	7	...	...	...	7	...	7	7	...	7	...	½	6½	...	6½	...	½
Massachusetts	12	2½	...	9½	...	...	12	12	12	...	...	12	...	...	...	12	...
Michigan	8	6½	...	1½	...	...	8	8	8	...	...	8	...	...	...	8	...
Minnesota	4	1½	...	2½	...	...	4	4	4	...	...	4	...	...	1½	2	½
Mississippi	...	...	...	...	...	...	...	7	4	...	3	7	...	...	...	7	...
Missouri	11	1	...	...	1	9	11	11	10	1	...	7½	3½	...	5½	5½	...
Montana	...	...	...	...	...	...	...	...	...	...	...	...	...	...	...	...	...
Nebraska	...	...	...	...	...	...	...	3	...	3	...	...	3	...	...	...	3
Nevada	...	...	...	...	...	...	...	3	3	...	...	3	...	...	...	3	...
New Hampshire	5	2	...	2	...	1	5	5	...	5	...	...	5	...	5	...	...
New Jersey	7	7	...	...	...	...	7	7	7	...	...	5½	1½	...	2½	4½	...
New Mexico	...	...	...	...	...	...	...	...	...	...	...	...	...	...	...	...	...
New York	33	...	...	33	...	...	33	33	...	...	33	...	33	...	33	...	...
North Carolina	...	...	...	...	...	...	...	9	4½	4½	...	3	6	...	6	3	...
North Dakota	...	...	...	...	...	...	...	...	...	...	...	...	...	...	...	...	...
Ohio	21	21	...	...	...	...	21	21	21	...	...	...	21	...	21	...	...
Oklahoma	...	...	...	...	...	...	...	...	...	...	...	...	...	...	...	...	...
Oregon	3	...	...	...	3	...	3	3	3	...	...	2	1	...	1	...	2
Pennsylvania	26	...	26	...	...	...	26	26	...	26	...	...	26	...	26	...	...
Rhode Island	4	...	...	4	...	...	4	4	4	...	...	4	...	...	...	4	...
South Carolina	...	...	...	...	...	...	...	6	6	...	...	6	...	...	...	6	...
South Dakota	...	...	...	...	...	...	...	...	...	...	...	...	...	...	...	...	...
Tennessee	...	...	...	...	...	...	...	10	10	...	...	10	...	...	...	10	...
Texas	...	...	...	...	...	...	...	6	...	6	...	6	...	...	...	6	...
Utah	...	...	...	...	...	...	...	...	...	...	...	...	...	...	...	...	...
Vermont	5	...	...	4½	½	...	5	5	4	1	...	5	...	...	...	5	...
Virginia	...	...	...	...	...	...	...	10	...	10	...	...	10	...	...	10	...
Washington	...	...	...	...	...	...	...	...	...	...	...	...	...	...	...	...	...
West Virginia	...	...	...	...	...	...	...	5	5	...	...	2½	2½	...	2½	2½	...
Wisconsin	8	8	...	...	...	...	8	8	8	...	...	8	...	...	...	8	...
Wyoming	...	...	...	...	...	...	...	...	...	...	...	...	...	...	...	...	...
Alaska	...	...	...	...	...	...	...	...	...	...	...	...	...	...	...	...	...
Canal Zone	...	...	...	...	...	...	...	...	...	...	...	...	...	...	...	...	...
District of Columbia	...	...	...	...	...	...	...	...	...	...	...	...	...	...	...	...	...
Hawaii	...	...	...	...	...	...	...	...	...	...	...	...	...	...	...	...	...
Philippine Islands	...	...	...	...	...	...	...	...	...	...	...	...	...	...	...	...	...
Puerto Rico	...	...	...	...	...	...	...	...	...	...	...	...	...	...	...	...	...
Virgin Islands	...	...	...	...	...	...	...	...	...	...	...	...	...	...	...	...	...
Total	226	55[a]	26	65½	32½	47[b]	226	317	183½[c]	90½	43	143[d]	172	½	166½[e]	124½[f]	26

Source: *Official Proceedings, 1864.*

Vice-Presidential. First ballot (before shift), p. 55.

a/ Sum of column; proceedings record 55½.

b/ Other candidates: John D. Caton, 16; Daniel W. Voorhees, 13; Augustus C. Dodge, 9; J. S. Phelps, 8; blank, ½.

First ballot (after shift), p. 55.

Source: *Official Proceedings, 1868.*

Order of business, p. 43.

c/ Sum of column; proceedings record 189½.

Table reconsideration of order of business, p. 51.

d/ Sum of column; proceedings record 142.

Reconsider order of business, p. 52.

e/ Sum of column; proceedings record 179½.

f/ Sum of column; proceedings record 137.

Delegation	1868 DEMOCRATIC																
		Motion to Adjourn			Presidential: First Ballot					Presidential: Fifth Ballot				Motion to Recess		Motion to Adjourn	
	Votes	Yea	Nay	Not Voting	Pendleton	Hancock	Church	Johnson	Other	Hancock	Pendleton	Church	Other	Yea	Nay	Yea	Nay
Alabama	8	8	...	...	...	...	...	8	...	...	...	...	8	...	8	8	...
Arizona	...	...	...	...	...	...	...	...	...	...	...	...	...	...	...	...	...
Arkansas	5	5	...	...	...	...	...	...	5	...	3	...	2	...	5	5	...
California	5	5	...	...	2	...	...	...	3	...	1	...	4	...	5	5	...
Colorado	...	...	...	...	...	...	...	...	...	...	...	...	...	...	...	...	...
Connecticut	6	...	6	...	...	...	...	...	6	...	...	...	6	...	6	6	...
Delaware	3	3	...	...	3	...	...	...	...	...	3	...	...	1	2	2	1
Florida	3	3	...	...	...	...	...	3	...	...	...	...	3	...	3	3	...
Georgia	9	8	1	...	...	...	...	9	...	...	...	...	9	9	...	...	9
Idaho	...	...	...	...	...	...	...	...	...	...	...	...	...	...	...	...	...
Illinois	16	16	...	...	16	...	...	...	...	...	16	...	...	...	16	16	...
Indiana	13	...	13	...	13	...	...	...	...	...	13	...	...	...	13	13	...
Iowa	8	6½	1½	...	8	...	...	...	...	...	8	...	...	8	...	...	8
Kansas	3	3	...	...	2	...	...	...	1	...	2	...	1	...	3	3	...
Kentucky	11	...	11	...	11	...	...	...	...	...	11	...	...	...	11	11	...
Louisiana	7	7	...	...	...	7	...	...	...	7	...	...	...	...	7	7	...
Maine	7	4	2½	½	1½	4½	...	1	...	4½	1½	...	1	...	7	7	...
Maryland	7	...	7	...	4½	...	...	2½	...	...	5	...	2	...	7	7	...
Massachusetts	12	12	...	...	1	11	...	...	...	11	1	...	...	...	12	12	...
Michigan	8	8	...	...	...	...	...	...	8	...	...	...	8	...	8	8	...
Minnesota	4	4	...	...	4	...	...	...	...	...	4	...	...	...	4	4	...
Mississippi	7	7	...	...	...	7	...	...	...	7	...	...	...	7	...	...	7
Missouri	11	6½	3	1½	5	2	1	½	2½	2	5½	...	3½	...	11	11	...
Montana	...	...	...	...	...	...	...	...	...	...	...	...	...	...	...	...	...
Nebraska	3	...	3	...	3	...	...	...	...	...	3	...	...	...	3	3	...
Nevada	3	3	...	...	...	...	...	...	3	...	...	...	3	3	...	...	3
New Hampshire	5	2	3	...	2	2	...	...	1	3	1½	...	½	5	...	...	5
New Jersey	7	4½	2½	...	...	...	...	...	7	...	...	...	7	7	...	...	7
New Mexico	...	...	...	...	...	...	...	...	...	...	...	...	...	...	...	...	...
New York	33	33	...	...	...	...	33	...	...	...	...	33	...	...	33	33	...
North Carolina	9	6	3	...	...	...	...	9	...	5½	2½	...	1	9	...	...	9
North Dakota	...	...	...	...	...	...	...	...	...	...	...	...	...	...	...	...	...
Ohio	21	...	21	...	21	...	...	...	...	...	21	...	...	...	21	21	...
Oklahoma	...	...	...	...	...	...	...	...	...	...	...	...	...	...	...	...	...
Oregon	3	3	...	...	3	...	...	...	...	...	3	...	...	...	3	3	...
Pennsylvania	26	...	26	...	...	...	...	...	26	...	...	...	26	26	...	...	26
Rhode Island	4	4	...	...	...	...	...	...	4	...	...	...	4	4	...	...	4
South Carolina	6	6	...	...	...	...	...	6	...	...	2	...	4	...	6	6	...
South Dakota	...	...	...	...	...	...	...	...	...	...	...	...	...	...	...	...	...
Tennessee	10	10	...	...	...	...	...	10	...	...	...	...	10	...	10	10	...
Texas	6	6	...	...	...	...	...	6	...	6	...	...	...	...	6	6	...
Utah	...	...	...	...	...	...	...	...	...	...	...	...	...	...	...	...	...
Vermont	5	5	...	...	...	...	...	...	5	...	...	...	5	5	...	...	5
Virginia	10	10	...	...	...	...	...	10	...	...	10	...	...	10	...	...	10
Washington	...	...	...	...	...	...	...	...	...	...	...	...	...	...	...	...	...
West Virginia	5	2½	2½	...	5	...	...	...	...	...	5	...	...	5	...	...	5
Wisconsin	8	8	...	...	...	...	...	...	8	...	...	...	8	...	8	8	...
Wyoming	...	...	...	...	...	...	...	...	...	...	...	...	...	...	...	...	...
Alaska	...	...	...	...	...	...	...	...	...	...	...	...	...	...	...	...	...
Canal Zone	...	...	...	...	...	...	...	...	...	...	...	...	...	...	...	...	...
District of Columbia	...	...	...	...	...	...	...	...	...	...	...	...	...	...	...	...	...
Hawaii	...	...	...	...	...	...	...	...	...	...	...	...	...	...	...	...	...
Philippine Islands	...	...	...	...	...	...	...	...	...	...	...	...	...	...	...	...	...
Puerto Rico	...	...	...	...	...	...	...	...	...	...	...	...	...	...	...	...	...
Virgin Islands	...	...	...	...	...	...	...	...	...	...	...	...	...	...	...	...	...
Total	317	209	106	2	105	33½	34	65	79½[a]	46	122	33	116[b]	99	218	218	99

Source: *Official Proceedings, 1868.*
Motion to adjourn, p. 54.
Presidential. First ballot, p. 77.
a/ Other candidates: James E. English, 16; Joel Parker, 13; Asa Packer, 26; James R. Doolittle, 13; Thomas A. Hendricks, 2½; Frank P. Blair, ½; Reverdy Johnson, 8½.
Fifth ballot, p. 98.
b/ Other candidates: English, 7; Parker, 13; Packer, 27; Andrew Johnson, 24; Doolittle, 15; Hendricks, 19½; Blair, 9½; J. Q. Adams, 1.
Motion to recess, p. 102.
Motion to adjourn, p. 103.

		1868 DEMOCRATIC																
		Presidential																
		Seventh Ballot					Tenth Ballot				Fifteenth Ballot				Sixteenth Ballot			
Delegation	Votes	Hancock	Pendleton	Church	Hendricks	Other	Hancock	Pendleton	Hendricks	Other	Hancock	Pendleton	Hendricks	Other	Hancock	Pendleton	Hendricks	Other
Alabama	8	...	8	...	...	...	...	8	...	...	...	8	...	...	...	8	...	...
Arizona	...	...	...	...	...	...	...	...	...	...	...	...	...	...	...	...	...	...
Arkansas	5	...	...	...	5	...	...	...	5	...	...	...	5	...	5	...	...	...
California	5	1½	3	...	½	...	1½	3½	...	...	...	3	1½	½	...	3	1½	½
Colorado	...	...	...	...	...	...	...	...	...	...	...	...	...	...	...	...	...	...
Connecticut	6	...	...	...	...	6	...	3	3	...	3	3	...	...	3	3	...	...
Delaware	3	...	3	...	...	...	...	3	...	...	...	3	...	...	...	3	...	...
Florida	3	...	...	...	3	...	...	...	3	...	...	...	3	...	...	1	2	...
Georgia	9	...	8	...	1	...	...	8	1	...	...	7	2	...	6½	2½	...	...
Idaho	...	...	...	...	...	...	...	...	...	...	...	...	...	...	...	...	...	...
Illinois	16	...	16	...	...	...	...	16	...	...	...	16	...	...	...	16	...	...
Indiana	13	...	3½	...	9½	...	...	3	9½	½	...	3	9½	½	...	3	9½	½
Iowa	8	...	8	...	...	...	...	8	...	...	...	8	...	...	...	8	...	...
Kansas	3	...	2	...	½	½	...	2	½	½	...	½	2½	...	1	...	2	...
Kentucky	11	...	11	...	...	...	...	11	...	...	...	11	...	...	...	11	...	...
Louisiana	7	7	...	...	...	...	...	7	...	...	...	7	...	...	7	...	...	...
Maine	7	4½	1½	...	1	...	4½	1½	1	...	4½	1½	1	...	4½	1½	1	...
Maryland	7	...	6½	...	½	...	...	4½	2½	...	...	4½	2½	...	5½	1	½	...
Massachusetts	12	11	1	...	...	...	11	1	...	...	11	1	...	...	11	1	...	...
Michigan	8	...	...	...	8	...	...	...	8	...	...	...	8	...	...	...	8	...
Minnesota	4	...	4	...	...	...	...	4	...	...	...	4	...	...	...	4	...	...
Mississippi	7	...	7	...	...	...	...	7	...	...	...	7	...	...	7	...	...	...
Missouri	11	½	4	...	5	1½	1½	4	5	½	1	5	5	...	3	5	3	...
Montana	...	...	...	...	...	...	...	...	...	...	...	...	...	...	...	...	...	...
Nebraska	3	...	3	...	...	...	...	3	...	...	...	...	3	...	...	...	3	...
Nevada	3	...	3	...	...	...	...	3	...	...	...	3	...	...	...	3	...	...
New Hampshire	5	3	1½	...	½	...	3	1½	½	...	3	1½	½	...	3	1½	½	...
New Jersey	7	...	...	...	...	7	...	...	...	7	...	...	...	7	...	...	...	7
New Mexico	...	...	...	...	...	...	...	...	...	...	...	...	...	...	...	...	...	...
New York	33	...	...	33	...	...	...	...	33	...	...	...	33	...	...	...	33	...
North Carolina	9	9	...	...	...	...	...	2½	5½	1	9	...	...	...	9	...	...	...
North Dakota	...	...	...	...	...	...	...	...	...	...	...	...	...	...	...	...	...	...
Ohio	21	...	21	...	...	...	...	21	...	...	...	21	...	...	...	21	...	...
Oklahoma	...	...	...	...	...	...	...	...	...	...	...	...	...	...	...	...	...	...
Oregon	3	...	3	...	...	...	...	3	...	...	...	3	...	...	...	3	...	...
Pennsylvania	26	...	...	...	...	26	...	...	...	26	26	...	...	...	26	...	...	...
Rhode Island	4	...	...	...	...	4	...	...	...	4	...	...	...	4	...	...	...	4
South Carolina	6	...	...	...	...	6	6	...	...	...	6	...	...	...	6	...	...	...
South Dakota	...	...	...	...	...	...	...	...	...	...	...	...	...	...	...	...	...	...
Tennessee	10	...	4½	...	...	5½	...	4½	...	5½	...	4½	...	5½	...	4½	...	5½
Texas	6	6	...	...	...	...	6	...	...	...	6	...	...	...	6	...	...	...
Utah	...	...	...	...	...	...	...	...	...	...	...	...	...	...	...	...	...	...
Vermont	5	...	...	...	5	...	...	...	5	...	...	...	5	...	...	...	5	...
Virginia	10	...	10	...	...	...	½	9½	...	...	10	...	...	...	10	...	...	...
Washington	...	...	...	...	...	...	...	...	...	...	...	...	...	...	...	...	...	...
West Virginia	5	...	5	...	...	...	...	5	...	...	...	4	1	...	...	3½	1½	...
Wisconsin	8	...	...	...	...	8	...	...	...	8	...	...	...	8	...	...	...	8
Wyoming	...	...	...	...	...	...	...	...	...	...	...	...	...	...	...	...	...	...
Alaska	...	...	...	...	...	...	...	...	...	...	...	...	...	...	...	...	...	...
Canal Zone	...	...	...	...	...	...	...	...	...	...	...	...	...	...	...	...	...	...
District of Columbia	...	...	...	...	...	...	...	...	...	...	...	...	...	...	...	...	...	...
Hawaii	...	...	...	...	...	...	...	...	...	...	...	...	...	...	...	...	...	...
Philippine Islands	...	...	...	...	...	...	...	...	...	...	...	...	...	...	...	...	...	...
Puerto Rico	...	...	...	...	...	...	...	...	...	...	...	...	...	...	...	...	...	...
Virgin Islands	...	...	...	...	...	...	...	...	...	...	...	...	...	...	...	...	...	...
Total	317	42½	137½	33	39½	64½[a]	34	147½	82½	53[b]	79½	129½	82½	25½[c]	113½	107½	70½	25½[d]

Source: *Official Proceedings, 1868.*

Seventh ballot, p. 108.

a/ Other candidates: English, 6; Parker, 7; Packer, 26; Johnson, 12½; Doolittle, 12; Blair, ½.

Tenth ballot, p. 116.

b/ Other candidates: Parker, 7; Packer, 27½; Johnson, 6; Blair, ½; Doolittle, 12.

Fifteenth ballot, p. 129.

c/ Other candidates: Parker, 7; Johnson, 5½; Doolittle, 12; not voting, 1.

Sixteenth ballot, p. 131.

d/ Other candidates: Parker, 7; Johnson, 5½; Doolittle, 12; not voting, 1.

Delegation	1868 DEMOCRATIC														1872 DEMOCRATIC		
		Motion to Adjourn		Presidential									V.-P.		Previous Question on Platform		
				Twentieth Ballot			21st Ballot			22nd Ballot (before)			22nd (after)	First Ballot			
	Votes	Yea	Nay	Hancock	Hendricks	Other	Hancock	Hendricks	Other	Hancock	Hendricks	Other	Seymour	Blair	Votes	Yea	Nay
Alabama	8	...	8	8	...	...	8	...	...	8	...	...	8	8	20	10	10
Arizona	...	...	...	...	...	...	...	...	...	...	...	...	...	...	...	...	...
Arkansas	5	5	...	1	4	...	...	5	...	...	5	...	5	5	12	12	...
California	5	5	...	½	1½	3	...	1	4	...	5	...	5	5	12	11	1
Colorado	...	...	...	...	...	...	...	...	...	...	...	...	...	...	...	...	...
Connecticut	6	...	6	...	...	6	...	...	6	...	...	6	6	6	12	12	...
Delaware	3	1½	1½	3	...	...	3	...	...	3	...	...	3	3	6	...	6
Florida	3	...	3	...	3	...	...	3	...	...	3	...	3	3	8	6	2
Georgia	9	...	9	9	...	...	9	...	...	9	...	...	9	9	22	1	21
Idaho	...	...	...	...	...	...	...	...	...	...	...	...	...	...	...	...	...
Illinois	16	...	16	...	16	...	...	16	...	...	16	...	16	16	42	42	...
Indiana	13	13	...	...	13	...	...	13	...	...	13	...	13	13	30	30	...
Iowa	8	8	...	...	8	...	...	8	...	...	8	...	8	8	22	22	...
Kansas	3	...	3	1	2	...	1	2	...	1	2	...	3	3	10	10	...
Kentucky	11	11	...	3½	5	2½	3½	7	½	...	...	11	11	11	24	24	...
Louisiana	7	...	7	7	...	...	7	...	...	7	...	...	7	7	16	6	10
Maine	7	2	5	4½	2½	...	4½	2½	...	4½	2½	...	7	7	14	14	...
Maryland	7	...	7	3	1	3	6	1	...	6	1	...	7	7	16	14	2
Massachusetts	12	...	12	11	...	1	6	2	4	...	...	12	12	12	26	26	...
Michigan	8	8	...	...	8	...	...	8	...	...	8	...	8	8	22	22	...
Minnesota	4	...	4	½	3½	...	½	3½	...	...	4	...	4	4	10	10	...
Mississippi	7	...	7	7	...	...	7	...	...	7	...	...	7	7	16	...	16
Missouri	11	...	11	1	...	10	6	4	1	2	8	1	11	11	30	26	4
Montana	...	...	...	...	...	...	...	...	...	...	...	...	...	...	...	...	...
Nebraska	3	3	...	...	3	...	...	3	...	...	3	...	3	3	6	6	...
Nevada	3	3	...	...	...	3	...	...	3	...	...	3	3	3	6	...	6
New Hampshire	5	...	5	4½	...	½	4½	...	½	4½	...	½	5	5	10	10	...
New Jersey	7	...	7	...	7	...	...	7	...	...	7	...	7	7	18	...	18
New Mexico	...	...	...	...	...	...	...	...	...	...	...	...	...	...	...	...	...
New York	33	33	...	...	33	...	...	33	...	...	33	...	33	33	70	70	...
North Carolina	9	...	9	9	...	...	8	1	...	...	9	...	9	9	20	20	...
North Dakota	...	...	...	...	...	...	...	...	...	...	...	...	...	...	...	...	...
Ohio	21	21	...	11	...	10	11	...	10	...	...	21	21	21	44	44	...
Oklahoma	...	...	...	...	...	...	...	...	...	...	...	...	...	...	...	...	...
Oregon	3	3	...	...	...	3	...	...	3	...	...	3	3	3	6	...	6
Pennsylvania	26	...	26	26	...	...	26	...	...	26	...	...	26	26	58	37	21
Rhode Island	4	4	...	...	...	4	...	...	4	...	...	4	4	4	8	8	...
South Carolina	6	...	6	6	...	...	6	...	...	6	...	...	6	6	14	3	11
South Dakota	...	...	...	...	...	...	...	...	...	...	...	...	...	...	...	...	...
Tennessee	10	...	10	10	...	...	2½	1½	6	3½	1½	5	10	10	24	24	...
Texas	6	...	6	6	...	...	6	...	...	6	...	...	6	6	16	16	...
Utah	...	...	...	...	...	...	...	...	...	...	...	...	...	...	...	...	...
Vermont	5	4	1	...	5	...	...	5	...	...	5	...	5	5	10	10	...
Virginia	10	10	...	10	...	...	10	...	...	10	...	...	10	10	22	...	22
Washington	...	...	...	...	...	...	...	...	...	...	...	...	...	...	...	...	...
West Virginia	5	...	5	...	5	...	...	5	...	...	5	...	5	5	10	8	2
Wisconsin	8	8	...	...	...	8	...	...	8	...	...	8	8	8	20	20	...
Wyoming	...	...	...	...	...	...	...	...	...	...	...	...	...	...	...	...	...
Alaska	...	...	...	...	...	...	...	...	...	...	...	...	...	...	...	...	...
Canal Zone	...	...	...	...	...	...	...	...	...	...	...	...	...	...	...	...	...
District of Columbia	...	...	...	...	...	...	...	...	...	...	...	...	...	...	...	...	...
Hawaii	...	...	...	...	...	...	...	...	...	...	...	...	...	...	...	...	...
Philippine Islands	...	...	...	...	...	...	...	...	...	...	...	...	...	...	...	...	...
Puerto Rico	...	...	...	...	...	...	...	...	...	...	...	...	...	...	...	...	...
Virgin Islands	...	...	...	...	...	...	...	...	...	...	...	...	...	...	...	...	...
Total	317	142½	174½	142½	121	53½[a]	135½	132	49½[b]	103½	145½	68[c]	317	317	732	574	158

Source: *Official Proceedings, 1868.*
Motion to adjourn, p. 135.
Twentieth ballot, p. 149.
a/ Other candidates: English, 16; Doolittle, 12; Blair, 13; Stephen J. Field, 9; Thomas H. Seymour, 2; not voting, 2.
Twenty-first ballot, p. 151.
b/ Other candidates: Doolittle, 12; English, 19; Johnson, 5; Field, 8; Chase, 4; George B. McClellan, ½; John T. Hoffman, ½.
Twenty-second ballot (before shift), p. 160.
c/ Other candidates: Horatio Seymour, 22; English, 7; Doolittle, 4; Johnson, 4; not voting, 31.
Twenty-second ballot (after shift), p. 161.
Vice-Presidential. First ballot, p. 170.

Source: *Official Proceedings, 1872.*
Previous question on platform, p. 44.

| | 1872 DEMOCRATIC | | | | | | | 1876 DEMOCRATIC | | | | | | | | | |
| | | Adoption of Platform | | Pres. First Ballot | | Vice-Pres. First Ballot | | | Minority Financial Plank | | | Majority Report on Resolutions | | | Presidential First Ballot | | | |
Delegation	Votes	Yea	Nay	Greeley	Other	Brown	Other	Votes	Yea	Nay	Not Voting	Yea	Nay	Not Voting	Tilden	Hendricks	Hancock	Other
Alabama	20	20	...	20	...	20	...	20	...	20	...	20	...	...	13	5	2	...
Arizona	...	...	...	...	...	...	...	...	...	...	...	...	...	...	...	...	...	...
Arkansas	12	12	...	12	...	12	...	12	...	12	...	12	...	...	12	...	...	...
California	12	12	...	12	...	12	...	12	...	12	...	12	...	...	12	...	...	...
Colorado	...	...	...	...	...	...	...	6	...	6	...	6	...	...	...	6	...	...
Connecticut	12	12	...	12	...	12	...	12	...	12	...	12	...	...	12	...	...	...
Delaware	6	...	6	...	6	...	6	6	...	6	...	6	...	...	...	...	...	6
Florida	8	6	2	6	2	6	2	8	...	8	...	8	...	...	8	...	...	...
Georgia	22	3	19	18	4	22	...	22	...	22	...	22	...	...	5	...	1	16
Idaho	...	...	...	...	...	...	...	...	...	...	...	...	...	...	...	...	...	...
Illinois	42	42	...	42	...	42	...	42	18	22	2	39	3	...	19	23	...	...
Indiana	30	30	...	30	...	30	...	30	30	...	...	...	30	...	...	30	...	...
Iowa	22	22	...	22	...	22	...	22	5	17	...	18	4	...	14	6	2	...
Kansas	10	10	...	10	...	10	...	10	10	...	...	4	6	...	...	10	...	...
Kentucky	24	24	...	24	...	24	...	24	24	...	...	24	...	...	24	...	...	...
Louisiana	16	16	...	16	...	16	...	16	...	16	...	16	...	...	9	...	5	2
Maine	14	14	...	14	...	14	...	14	...	14	...	14	...	...	14	...	...	...
Maryland	16	16	...	16	...	16	...	16	...	16	...	16	...	...	11	3	...	2
Massachusetts	26	26	...	26	...	26	...	26	...	26	...	26	...	...	26	...	...	...
Michigan	22	22	...	22	...	22	...	22	5	17	...	21	1	...	14	8	...	...
Minnesota	10	10	...	10	...	10	...	10	...	10	...	10	...	...	10	...	...	...
Mississippi	16	7	9	16	...	16	...	16	...	16	...	16	...	...	16	...	...	...
Missouri	30	28	2	30	...	30	...	30	9	20	1	21	8	1	...	14	...	16
Montana	...	...	...	...	...	...	...	...	...	...	...	...	...	...	...	...	...	...
Nebraska	6	6	...	6	...	6	...	6	...	6	...	6	...	...	6	...	...	...
Nevada	6	6	...	6	...	6	...	6	...	6	...	6	...	...	3	3	...	...
New Hampshire	10	10	...	10	...	10	...	10	...	10	...	10	...	...	10	...	...	...
New Jersey	18	9	9	9	9	9	9	18	...	18	...	18	...	...	...	...	...	18
New Mexico	...	...	...	...	...	...	...	...	...	...	...	...	...	...	...	...	...	...
New York	70	70	...	70	...	70	...	70	...	70	...	70	...	...	70	...	...	...
North Carolina	20	20	...	20	...	20	...	20	...	20	...	20	...	...	9	4	5	2
North Dakota	...	...	...	...	...	...	...	...	...	...	...	...	...	...	...	...	...	...
Ohio	44	44	...	44	...	44	...	44	25	18	1	21	20	3	...	...	...	44
Oklahoma	...	...	...	...	...	...	...	...	...	...	...	...	...	...	...	...	...	...
Oregon	6	...	6	6	...	6	...	6	...	6	...	6	...	...	6	...	...	...
Pennsylvania	58	51	7	35	23	58	...	58	58	...	...	58	...	...	...	...	58	...
Rhode Island	8	8	...	8	...	8	...	8	...	8	...	8	...	...	8	...	...	...
South Carolina	14	14	...	14	...	14	...	14	...	14	...	14	...	...	14	...	...	...
South Dakota	...	...	...	...	...	...	...	...	...	...	...	...	...	...	...	...	...	...
Tennessee	24	24	...	24	...	24	...	24	24	...	...	24	...	...	...	24	...	...
Texas	16	16	...	16	...	16	...	16	...	16	...	16	...	...	$10\frac{1}{2}$	$2\frac{1}{2}$	2	1
Utah	...	...	...	...	...	...	...	...	...	...	...	...	...	...	...	...	...	...
Vermont	10	10	...	10	...	10	...	10	10	...	...	10	...	...	10	...	...	...
Virginia	22	22	...	22	...	22	...	22	1	21	...	21	1	...	17	1	...	4
Washington	...	...	...	...	...	...	...	...	...	...	...	...	...	...	...	...	...	...
West Virginia	10	8	2	8	2	8	2	10	10	...	...	...	10	...	...	...	...	10
Wisconsin	20	20	...	20	...	20	...	20	...	20	...	20	...	...	19	1	...	...
Wyoming	...	...	...	...	...	...	...	...	...	...	...	...	...	...	...	...	...	...
Alaska	...	...	...	...	...	...	...	...	...	...	...	...	...	...	...	...	...	...
Canal Zone	...	...	...	...	...	...	...	...	...	...	...	...	...	...	...	...	...	...
District of Columbia	...	...	...	...	...	...	...	...	...	...	...	...	...	...	...	...	...	...
Hawaii	...	...	...	...	...	...	...	...	...	...	...	...	...	...	...	...	...	...
Philippine Islands	...	...	...	...	...	...	...	...	...	...	...	...	...	...	...	...	...	...
Puerto Rico	...	...	...	...	...	...	...	...	...	...	...	...	...	...	...	...	...	...
Virgin Islands	...	...	...	...	...	...	...	...	...	...	...	...	...	...	...	...	...	...
Total	732	671a	62	686	46b	713	19c	738	229d	505e	4	651	83	4	$401\frac{1}{2}$f	$140\frac{1}{2}$	75	121g

Source: *Official Proceedings, 1872.*

Adoption of platform, p. 53.
a/ Sum of column; proceedings record 670.
Presidential. First ballot, p. 65.
b/ Other candidates: Thomas F. Bayard, 15; Jeremiah
S. Black, 21; William S. Groesbeck, 2; blank, 8.
Vice-Presidential. First ballot, p. 71.
c/ Other candidates: John W. Stevenson, 6; blank, 13.

Source: *Official Proceedings, 1876.*

Minority financial plank, p. 115.
d/ Sum of column; proceedings record 219.
e/ Sum of column; proceedings record 515.
Majority report on resolutions, p. 117.
Presidential. First ballot, p. 144.
f/ Sum of column; proceedings record $404\frac{1}{2}$.
g/ Other candidates: William Allen, 54; Allen G. Thurman, 3; Thomas F. Bayard, 33; Joel Parker, 18; James O. Broadhead, 16.

| | 1876 DEMOCRATIC | | | | | | | | 1880 DEMOCRATIC | | | | | | | | | |
| | Presidential Second Ballot | | | Vice-Pres. First Ballot | | Table Suspension of Two-Thirds Rule | | | Previous Question, Credentials | | | Minority Report, New York Credentials | | | Motion to Adjourn | | |
Delegation	Votes	Tilden	Hendricks	Other	Hendricks	Other	Yea	Nay	Votes	Yea	Nay	Not Voting	Yea	Nay	Not Voting	Yea	Nay	Not Voting
Alabama	20	20	...	...	20	...	20	...	20	5	15	...	11	8	1	6	14	...
Arizona	...	...	...	...	...	...	...	...	...	...	...	...	...	...	...	...	...	...
Arkansas	12	12	...	...	12	...	...	12	12	12	...	...	12	...	...	...	12	...
California	12	12	...	...	12	...	12	...	12	7	5	...	2	10	...	3	9	...
Colorado	6	6	...	...	6	...	...	6	6	4	2	.	3	3	...	6	...	...
Connecticut	12	12	...	...	12	...	...	12	12	12	...	...	...	12	...	12	...	...
Delaware	6	6	...	...	6	...	...	6	6	6	...	...	1	5	...	6	...	...
Florida	8	8	...	...	8	...	8	...	8	2	6	...	5	3	...	8	...	...
Georgia	22	22	...	...	22	...	22	...	22	17	5	...	9	13	...	5	11	6
Idaho	...	...	...	...	...	...	...	...	...	...	...	...	...	...	...	...	...	...
Illinois	42	26	16	...	42	...	16	26	42	16	24	2	26	16	...	...	42	...
Indiana	30	...	30	...	30	...	30	...	30	30	...	...	...	30	...	30	...	...
Iowa	22	22	...	...	22	...	7	15	22	19	3	...	...	22	...	10	11	1
Kansas	10	2	8	...	10	...	9	1	10	...	10	...	10	...	...	...	10	...
Kentucky	24	24	...	...	24	...	24	...	24	21	3	...	...	24	...	...	24	...
Louisiana	16	16	...	...	16	...	...	16	16	...	16	...	...	16	...	...	16	...
Maine	14	14	...	...	14	...	...	14	14	14	...	...	6	8	...	3	11	...
Maryland	16	14	2	...	16	...	...	16	16	...	16	...	12	4	...	...	16	...
Massachusetts	26	26	...	...	26	...	...	26	26	14	10	2	9½	15	1½	9½	11½	5
Michigan	22	19	3	...	22	...	...	22	22	17	5	...	2	20	...	12	3	7
Minnesota	10	10	...	...	10	...	...	10	10	...	10	...	...	10	...	...	10	...
Mississippi	16	16	...	...	16	...	...	16	16	10	6	...	4	12	...	...	16	...
Missouri	30	30	...	...	30	...	17	13	30	20	10	...	11	19	...	...	30	...
Montana	...	...	...	...	...	...	...	...	...	...	...	...	...	...	...	...	...	...
Nebraska	6	6	...	...	6	...	...	6	6	6	...	...	...	6	...	6	...	...
Nevada	6	4	...	2	6	...	5	1	6	6	...	...	...	6	...	6	...	...
New Hampshire	10	10	...	...	10	...	1	9	10	10	...	...	1	9	...	6	4	...
New Jersey	18	18	...	...	18	...	18	...	18	...	10	8	12	6	...	17	1	...
New Mexico	...	...	...	...	...	...	...	...	...	...	...	...	...	...	...	...	...	...
New York	70	70	...	...	70	...	...	70	70	...	...	70	...	...	70	70	...	...
North Carolina	20	20	...	...	20	...	20	...	20	6	14	...	...	20	...	2	18	...
North Dakota	...	...	...	...	...	...	...	...	...	...	...	...	...	...	...	...	...	...
Ohio	44	...	...	44	36	8	44	...	44	25	19	...	17	27	...	44	...	...
Oklahoma	...	...	...	...	...	...	...	...	...	...	...	...	...	...	...	...	...	...
Oregon	6	6	...	...	6	...	2	4	6	6	...	...	...	6	...	...	6	...
Pennsylvania	58	...	...	58	58	...	58	...	58	38	12	8	10	47	1	24	29	5
Rhode Island	8	8	...	...	8	...	...	8	8	8	...	...	2	6	...	1	7	...
South Carolina	14	14	...	...	14	...	...	14	14	...	14	...	5	9	...	...	14	...
South Dakota	...	...	...	...	...	...	...	...	...	...	...	...	...	...	...	...	...	...
Tennessee	24	...	24	...	24	...	24	...	24	2	22	...	11	12	1	6	17	1
Texas	16	16	...	...	16	...	2	14	16	...	16	...	13	3	...	5	11	...
Utah	...	...	...	...	...	...	...	...	...	...	...	...	...	...	...	...	...	...
Vermont	10	10	...	...	10	...	...	10	10	8	2	...	3	7	...	...	10	...
Virginia	22	17	1	4	22	...	...	22	22	4	18	...	4	18	...	...	22	...
Washington	...	...	...	...	...	...	...	...	...	...	...	...	...	...	...	...	...	...
West Virginia	10	...	...	10	10	...	10	...	10	5	4	1	4	5	1	2	8	...
Wisconsin	20	19	1	...	20	...	10	10	20	...	20	...	...	20	...	18	2	...
Wyoming	...	...	...	...	...	...	...	...	...	...	...	...	...	...	...	...	...	...
Alaska	...	...	...	...	...	...	...	...	...	...	...	...	...	...	...	...	...	...
Canal Zone	...	...	...	...	...	...	...	...	...	...	...	...	...	...	...	...	...	...
District of Columbia	...	...	...	...	...	...	...	...	...	...	...	...	...	...	...	...	...	...
Hawaii	...	...	...	...	...	...	...	...	...	...	...	...	...	...	...	...	...	...
Philippine Islands	...	...	...	...	...	...	...	...	...	...	...	...	...	...	...	...	...	...
Puerto Rico	...	...	...	...	...	...	...	...	...	...	...	...	...	...	...	...	...	...
Virgin Islands	...	...	...	...	...	...	...	...	...	...	...	...	...	...	...	...	...	...
Total	738	535	85	118a	730	8b	359	379	738	350c	297	91	205½	457	75½	317½	395½	25

Source: *Official Proceedings, 1876.*
Second ballot, p. 146.
a/ Other candidates: Allen, 54; Bayard, 4; Hancock, 58; Thurman, 2.
Vice-Presidential. First ballot, pp. 158-9.
b/ Blank, 8.
Table suspension of two-thirds rule, p. 167.

Source: *Official Proceedings, 1880.*
Previous question, credentials, p. 29.
Minority report, New York credentials, p. 50.
Motion to adjourn, p. 98.

Delegation	Votes	Bayard	Hancock	Payne	Other	Hancock	Bayard	Randall	Other	Hancock	Other	Votes	Yea	Nay	Not Voting	Yea	Nay	Not Voting
			First Ballot				Second Ballot (before shift)			Second (after shift)			Amend Rules on Polling of Delegations			Table Motion for Nominations		
							1880 DEMOCRATIC — Presidential								**1884 DEMOCRATIC**		
Alabama	20	7	7	...	6	11	5	...	4	20	...	20	15	5	...	1	19	...
Arizona	...	...	...	...	...	...	...	...	...	...	...	2	...	...	2	...	2	...
Arkansas	12	...	...	...	12	...	...	...	12	12	...	14	...	14	...	...	14	...
California	12	...	...	...	12	5	...	...	7	12	...	16	16	...	...	15	1	...
Colorado	6	...	...	...	6	...	...	...	6	6	...	6	4	2	...	6	...	...
Connecticut	12	4	...	2	6	...	1	...	11	12	...	12	2	10	...	...	12	...
Delaware	6	6	...	...	...	...	6	...	...	6	...	6	6	...	...	6	...	...
Florida	8	8	...	...	...	...	8	...	...	8	...	8	2	6	...	...	8	...
Georgia	22	5	8	...	9	7	5	...	10	22	...	24	12	12	...	8	16	...
Idaho	...	...	...	...	...	...	...	...	...	...	...	2	...	...	2	...	2	...
Illinois	42	...	...	...	42	42	...	...	...	42	...	44	22	22	...	17	26	1
Indiana	30	...	...	...	30	...	...	...	30	...	30	30	30	...	...	30	...	...
Iowa	22	3	7	2	10	9	1	12	...	21	1	26	6	20	...	...	26	...
Kansas	10	...	...	...	10	10	...	...	...	10	...	18	3	15	...	5	13	...
Kentucky	24	6	1	...	17	8	7	...	9	24	...	26	20	6	...	24	2	...
Louisiana	16	...	16	...	...	16	...	...	...	16	...	16	...	16	...	...	16	...
Maine	14	...	14	...	...	14	...	...	...	14	...	12	2	10	...	3	8	1
Maryland	16	16	...	...	...	...	16	...	...	14	2	16	...	16	...	...	16	...
Massachusetts	26	11½	6	...	8½	11	7	3½	4½	26	...	28	21	7	...	6	13	9
Michigan	22	2	5	1	14	14	4	1	3	22	...	26	12	12	2	...	26	...
Minnesota	10	...	10	...	...	10	...	...	...	10	...	14	...	14	...	14	...	...
Mississippi	16	8	5	...	3	6	8	...	2	16	...	18	18	...	...	11	7	...
Missouri	30	4	12	...	14	28	2	...	...	30	...	32	8	24	...	7	25	...
Montana	...	...	...	...	...	...	...	...	...	...	...	2	...	...	2	...	2	...
Nebraska	6	...	...	6	...	...	...	6	...	6	...	10	5	5	...	1	8	1
Nevada	6	...	...	...	6	...	...	1	5	6	...	6	6	...	...	6	...	...
New Hampshire	10	3	4	...	3	5	...	5	...	10	...	8	...	8	...	...	8	...
New Jersey	18	10	...	...	8	7	4	4	3	18	...	18	14	4	...	14	4	...
New Mexico	...	...	...	...	...	...	...	...	...	...	...	2	...	...	2	...	2	...
New York	70	...	...	70	...	...	70	...	70	70	...	72	...	72	...	...	72	...
North Carolina	20	7	9	...	4	20	...	...	...	20	...	22	10	12	...	...	22	...
North Dakota	...	...	...	...	...	...	...	...	...	...	...	*2	...	...	2	2	...	...
Ohio	44	...	...	...	44	...	...	...	44	44	...	46	25	21	...	19	24	3
Oklahoma	...	...	...	...	...	...	...	...	...	...	...	...	...	...	...	...	...	...
Oregon	6	...	...	...	6	...	...	...	6	6	...	6	...	6	...	5	1	...
Pennsylvania	58	7	28	...	23	32	...	25	1	58	...	60	21	39	...	24	35	1
Rhode Island	8	2	2	...	4	6	...	1	1	8	...	8	...	8	...	1	7	...
South Carolina	14	14	...	...	...	...	14	...	...	14	...	18	3	14	1	11	7	...
South Dakota	...	...	...	...	...	...	...	...	...	...	...	*	...	...	...	...	...	...
Tennessee	24	9	11	...	4	14	8	...	2	24	...	24	17	7	...	23	1	...
Texas	16	5	9	...	2	11	5	...	...	16	...	26	12	10	4	14	12	...
Utah	...	...	...	...	...	...	...	...	...	...	...	2	...	...	2	2	...	...
Vermont	10	...	10	...	...	10	...	...	...	10	...	8	...	8	...	...	8	...
Virginia	22	10	3	...	9	7	8	...	7	22	...	24	6	18	...	...	24	...
Washington	...	...	...	...	...	...	...	...	...	...	...	2	...	...	2	...	2	...
West Virginia	10	...	3	...	7	7	1	...	2	10	...	12	9	3	...	2	10	...
Wisconsin	20	6	1	...	13	10	2	...	8	20	...	22	5	17	...	2	20	...
Wyoming	...	...	...	...	...	...	...	...	...	...	...	2	...	...	2	2	...	...
Alaska	...	...	...	...	...	...	...	...	...	...	...	...	...	...	...	...	...	...
Canal Zone	...	...	...	...	...	...	...	...	...	...	...	...	...	...	...	...	...	...
District of Columbia	...	...	...	...	...	...	...	...	...	...	...	2	...	...	2	2	...	...
Hawaii	...	...	...	...	...	...	...	...	...	...	...	...	...	...	...	...	...	...
Philippine Islands	...	...	...	...	...	...	...	...	...	...	...	...	...	...	...	...	...	...
Puerto Rico	...	...	...	...	...	...	...	...	...	...	...	...	...	...	...	...	...	...
Virgin Islands	...	...	...	...	...	...	...	...	...	...	...	...	...	...	...	...	...	...
Total	738	153½	171	81	332½[a]	320	112	128½	177½[b]	705	33[c]	820	332	463	25	281	523	16

Source: *Official Proceedings, 1880.*
Presidential. First ballot, p. 99.
  a/ Other candidates: Allen G. Thurman, 68½; Stephen J. Field, 65; William R. Morrison, 62; Thomas A. Hendricks, 49½; Samuel J. Tilden, 38; Horatio Seymour, 8; W. A. H. Loveland, 5; Samuel J. Randall, 6; Thomas Ewing, 10; Joseph E. McDonald, 3; George B. McClellan, 2; Joel Parker, 1; Jeremiah Black, 1; Hugh J. Jewett, 1; James E. English, 1; Lothrop, 1; not voting, 10½.
  Second ballot (before shift), pp. 108-10.
  b/ Other candidates: Hendricks, 31; English, 19; Tilden, 6; Thurman, 50; Parker, 2; Field, 65½; Jewett, 1; not voting, 3.
  Second ballot (after shift), p. 114.
  c/ Other candidates: Hendricks, 30; Bayard, 2; Tilden, 1.

Source: *Official Proceedings, 1884.*
Amend rules on polling of delegations, p. 39.
Table motion for nominations, p. 92.

* Dakota Territory, 2 votes.

Delegation	Votes	Minority Tariff Plank			Motion to Recess			Presidential First Ballot				Motion to Adjourn			Presidential Second Ballot (before shift)			
		Yea	Nay	Not Voting	Yea	Nay	Not Voting	Cleveland	Bayard	Thurman	Other	Yea	Nay	Not Voting	Cleveland	Bayard	Hendricks	Other
Alabama	20	...	20	...	12	7	1	4	14	1	1	17	3	...	5	14	...	1
Arizona	2	...	2	...	...	2	...	2	...	...	...	...	2	...	2	...	...	...
Arkansas	14	5	9	...	...	14	...	14	...	...	...	...	14	...	14	...	...	...
California	16	12	4	...	16	...	...	...	...	16	...	16	...	...	...	...	...	16
Colorado	6	...	6	...	...	6	...	...	...	1	5	4	2	...	...	...	...	6
Connecticut	12	...	12	...	...	12	...	12	...	...	...	...	12	...	12	...	...	...
Delaware	6	...	6	...	5	1	...	...	6	...	...	6	...	...	...	6	...	...
Florida	8	...	8	...	...	8	...	8	...	...	...	...	8	...	6	2	...	...
Georgia	24	...	24	...	7	17	...	10	12	...	2	13	11	...	14	10	...	...
Idaho	2	...	2	...	...	2	...	2	...	...	...	...	2	...	2	...	...	...
Illinois	44	7	37	...	2	42	...	28	2	1	13	21	17	6	38	3	1	2
Indiana	30	8	22	...	...	30	...	...	...	...	30	30	...	...	...	...	30	...
Iowa	26	...	26	...	2	24	...	23	1	1	1	1	25	...	22	...	4	...
Kansas	18	...	18	...	...	18	...	11	5	2	...	6	12	...	12	4	...	2
Kentucky	26	...	26	...	...	26	...	...	...	...	26	20	6	...	3	7	15	1
Louisiana	16	...	16	...	...	16	...	13	1	1	1	...	16	...	15	...	...	1
Maine	12	...	12	...	...	12	...	12	...	...	...	...	12	...	12	...	...	...
Maryland	16	...	16	...	...	16	...	6	10	...	...	1	15	...	10	6	...	...
Massachusetts	28	20½	6½	1	17½	10½	...	5	21	2	...	17	11	...	8	7½	12½	...
Michigan	26	12	14	...	10	16	...	14	1	11	...	22	4	...	13	...	13	...
Minnesota	14	...	14	...	...	14	...	14	...	...	...	...	14	...	14	...	...	...
Mississippi	18	...	18	...	17	1	...	1	15	1	1	17	1	...	2	14	2	...
Missouri	32	...	32	...	9	23	...	15	10	3	4	26	6	...	21	5	6	...
Montana	2	...	2	...	...	2	...	2	...	...	...	...	2	...	2	...	...	...
Nebraska	10	...	10	...	2	8	...	8	1	1	...	3	7	...	9	1	...	...
Nevada	6	2	4	...	5	1	...	...	...	6	...	6	...	...	...	...	5	1
New Hampshire	8	1	7	...	...	8	...	8	...	...	...	...	...	...	8	...	...	...
New Jersey	18	11	7	...	14	4	...	4	3	...	11	11	7	...	5	2	11	...
New Mexico	2	...	2	...	...	2	...	2	...	...	...	2	...	...	1	...	...	1
New York	72	...	72	...	...	72	...	72	...	...	...	...	72	...	72	...	...	...
North Carolina	22	...	22	...	...	22	...	...	22	...	...	16	6	...	...	22	...	...
North Dakota	*2	...	2	...	...	2	...	2	...	...	...	...	2	...	...	2	...	...
Ohio	46	4	42	...	1	45	...	21	...	23	2	21	24	1	21	...	1	24
Oklahoma	...	...	...	...	...	...	...	...	...	...	...	...	...	...	...	...	...	...
Oregon	6	...	6	...	4	2	...	2	4	...	...	4	2	...	2	2	2	...
Pennsylvania	60	11	48	1	34	26	...	5	...	...	55	47	13	...	42	2	11	5
Rhode Island	8	...	8	...	...	8	...	6	2	...	...	1	7	...	6	2	...	...
South Carolina	18	...	18	...	9	9	...	8	10	...	...	18	...	...	8	9	1	...
South Dakota	*	...	...	...	...	...	...	...	...	...	...	...	...	...	...	...	...	...
Tennessee	24	...	24	...	15	9	...	2	8	9	5	19	5	...	2	10	1	11
Texas	26	2	24	...	1	25	...	11	10	4	1	18	8	...	12	12	1	1
Utah	2	1	1	...	2	...	...	...	...	...	2	...	2	...	1	...	1	...
Vermont	8	...	8	...	...	8	...	8	...	...	...	...	8	...	8	...	...	...
Virginia	24	...	24	...	6	18	...	13	9	1	1	10	14	...	13	8	2	1
Washington	2	...	2	...	...	2	...	1	...	...	1	...	2	...	2	...	...	...
West Virginia	12	...	12	...	...	12	...	7	2	2	1	3	9	...	6	3	...	3
Wisconsin	22	...	22	...	...	22	...	12	1	2	7	3	19	...	20	...	2	...
Wyoming	2	...	2	...	...	2	...	2	...	...	...	...	2	...	2	...	...	...
Alaska	...	...	...	...	...	...	...	...	...	...	...	...	...	...	...	...	...	...
Canal Zone	...	...	...	...	...	...	...	...	...	...	...	...	...	...	...	...	...	...
District of Columbia	2	...	2	...	...	2	...	2	...	...	...	2	...	...	...	...	2	...
Hawaii	...	...	...	...	...	...	...	...	...	...	...	...	...	...	...	...	...	...
Philippine Islands	...	...	...	...	...	...	...	...	...	...	...	...	...	...	...	...	...	...
Puerto Rico	...	...	...	...	...	...	...	...	...	...	...	...	...	...	...	...	...	...
Virgin Islands	...	...	...	...	...	...	...	...	...	...	...	...	...	...	...	...	...	...
Total	820	96½	721½	2	190½	628½	1	392	170	88	170[a]	401	412	7	475	151½	123½	70[b]

Source: *Official Proceedings, 1884.*
Minority tariff plank, p. 218.
Motion to recess, p. 224.
Presidential. First ballot, p. 227.
 a/ Other candidates: Joseph E. McDonald, 56; Samuel J. Randall, 78; John G. Carlisle, 27; George Hoadly, 3; Thomas A. Hendricks, 1; Samuel J. Tilden, 1; Roswell P. Flower, 4.
Motion to adjourn, p. 229.
Second ballot (before shift), p. 241.
 b/ Other candidates: Thurman, 60; Randall, 5; McDonald, 2; Tilden, 2; not voting, 1.

* Dakota Territory, 2 votes.

Delegation	1884 DEMOCRATIC Votes	Presidential Second Ballot (after shift) Cleveland	Bayard	Other	Vice-Pres. First Ballot Hendricks	Other	1888 DEMOCRATIC Votes	Motion to Adjourn Yea	Nay	Not Voting	Vice-Presidential First Ballot Thurman	Gray	Other	1892 DEMOCRATIC Votes	Amendment to Majority Tariff Plank Yea	Nay	Not Voting
Alabama	20	5	14	1	20	...	20	5	15	...	15	4	1	22	12	10	...
Arizona	2	2	...	...	2	...	2	2	...	...	2	...	...	6	6	...	...
Arkansas	14	14	...	...	14	...	14	...	14	...	14	...	...	16	...	16	...
California	16	16	...	...	16	...	16	...	16	...	16	...	...	18	...	18	...
Colorado	6	6	...	...	6	...	6	6	...	...	...	...	6	8	8	...	...
Connecticut	12	12	...	...	12	...	12	...	12	...	12	...	...	12	...	12	...
Delaware	6	...	6	...	6	...	6	...	6	...	3	3	...	6	...	6	...
Florida	8	8	...	...	8	...	8	8	...	...	8	...	...	8	3	5	...
Georgia	24	22	2	...	24	...	24	24	...	...	7	17	...	26	22	4	...
Idaho	2	2	...	...	2	...	2	...	2	...	2	...	...	6	6	...	...
Illinois	44	43	...	1	40	4	44	2	42	...	10	17	17	48	48	...	...
Indiana	30	30	...	...	30	...	30	...	30	...	...	30	...	30	15	15	...
Iowa	26	26	...	...	26	...	26	15	10	1	26	...	...	26	26	...	...
Kansas	18	17	1	...	18	...	18	18	...	...	14	2	2	20	...	20	...
Kentucky	26	4	21	1	26	...	26	10	16	...	8	17	1	26	26	...	...
Louisiana	16	15	...	1	16	...	16	...	16	...	16	...	...	16	8	8	...
Maine	12	12	...	...	12	...	12	...	12	...	12	...	...	12	...	12	...
Maryland	16	16	...	...	16	...	16	...	16	...	16	...	...	16	7	9	...
Massachusetts	28	8	7½	12½	28	...	28	22	6	...	19	7	2	30	26	4	...
Michigan	26	23	...	3	26	...	26	13	13	...	23	...	3	28	28	...	...
Minnesota	14	14	...	...	14	...	14	...	14	...	13	1	...	18	...	18	...
Mississippi	18	2	14	2	18	...	18	...	18	...	18	...	...	18	11	6	1
Missouri	32	32	...	...	32	...	32	...	32	...	28	...	4	34	34	...	...
Montana	2	2	...	...	2	...	2	...	2	...	2	...	...	6	6	...	...
Nebraska	10	9	1	...	10	...	10	...	10	...	8	2	...	16	16	...	...
Nevada	6	...	...	6	6	...	6	...	6	...	6	...	...	6	6	...	...
New Hampshire	8	8	...	...	8	...	8	8	...	...	8	...	...	8	...	8	...
New Jersey	18	5	2	11	18	...	18	18	...	...	18	...	...	20	...	20	...
New Mexico	2	2	...	...	2	...	2	...	2	...	2	...	...	6	5	1	...
New York	72	72	...	...	72	...	72	72	...	...	72	...	...	72	72	...	...
North Carolina	22	22	...	...	22	...	22	...	22	...	22	...	...	22	17	5	...
North Dakota	*2	2	...	...	2	...	*2	2	...	...	2	...	...	6	6	...	...
Ohio	46	46	...	...	46	...	46	...	46	...	45	1	...	*4	4	...	...
Oklahoma	...	...	...	...	...	...	...	...	...	...	...	...	...	8	1	7	...
Oregon	6	6	...	...	6	...	6	6	...	...	6	...	...	8	7	1	...
Pennsylvania	60	42	2	16	60	...	60	59	1	...	60	...	...	64	...	64	...
Rhode Island	8	7	1	...	8	...	8	8	...	...	8	...	...	8	...	8	...
South Carolina	18	10	8	...	18	...	18	3	15	...	18	...	...	18	18	...	...
South Dakota	*	...	...	...	*	...	*	...	...	...	...	...	...	8	1	7	...
Tennessee	24	24	...	...	24	...	24	24	...	...	24	...	...	24	5	18	1
Texas	26	26	...	...	26	...	26	26	...	...	26	...	...	30	30	...	...
Utah	2	2	...	...	2	...	2	...	2	...	2	...	...	2	2	...	...
Vermont	8	8	...	...	8	...	8	8	...	...	8	...	...	8	...	8	...
Virginia	24	23	...	1	24	...	24	10	14	...	24	...	...	24	11	11	2
Washington	2	2	...	...	2	...	2	...	...	2	2	...	...	8	8	...	...
West Virginia	12	10	2	...	12	...	12	3	9	...	11	...	1	12	12	...	...
Wisconsin	22	22	...	...	22	...	22	13	9	...	22	...	...	24	...	24	...
Wyoming	2	2	...	...	2	...	2	...	2	...	2	...	...	6	6	...	...
Alaska	...	...	...	...	...	...	2	...	...	2	2	...	...	2	...	2	...
Canal Zone	...	...	...	...	...	...	...	...	...	...	...	...	...	...	...	...	...
District of Columbia	2	2	...	...	2	...	2	2	...	...	2	...	...	2	...	2	...
Hawaii	...	...	...	...	...	...	...	...	...	...	...	...	...	...	...	...	...
Philippine Islands	...	...	...	...	...	...	...	...	...	...	...	...	...	...	...	...	...
Puerto Rico	...	...	...	...	...	...	...	...	...	...	...	...	...	...	...	...	...
Virgin Islands	...	...	...	...	...	...	...	...	...	...	...	...	...	...	...	...	...
Total	820	683	81½	55½[a]	816	4[b]	822	387	430	5	684	101	37[c]	910	564	342	4

Source: *Official Proceedings, 1884.*
Second ballot (after shift), p. 247.
a/ Other candidates: Hendricks, 45½; Thurman, 4; Randall, 4; McDonald, 2.
Vice-Presidential. First ballot, p. 267.
b/ Not voting, 4.

Source: *Official Proceedings, 1888.*
* Dakota Territory, 2 votes.
Motion to adjourn, p. 90.
Vice-Presidential. First ballot, p. 129.
c/ Other candidates: John C. Black, 36; not voting, 1.

Source: *Official Proceedings, 1892.*
* Including Indian Territory, 2 votes.
Amendment to majority tariff plank, p. 92.

* Dakota Territory, 2 votes.

		1892 DEMOCRATIC										1896 DEMOCRATIC			
		Presidential				Vice-Presidential						Temporary Chairman; Daniel for Hill			
		First Ballot				First Ballot			Revised Ballot						
Delegation	Votes	Cleveland	Boies	Hill	Other	Gray	Stevenson	Other	Gray	Stevenson	Other	Convention Strength	Yea	Nay	Not Voting
Alabama	22	14	1	2	5	...	...	22	...	...	22	22	22	...	...
Arizona	6	5	...	...	1	1	5	...	1	5	...	2	2	...	...
Arkansas	16	16	...	...	...	16	...	...	16	...	...	16	16	...	...
California	18	18	...	...	...	9	9	...	9	9	...	18	18	...	...
Colorado	8	...	5	3	...	...	8	...	...	8	...	8	8	...	...
Connecticut	12	12	...	...	...	12	...	...	12	...	...	12	12	...	...
Delaware	6	6	...	...	...	...	...	6	...	...	6	6	...	6	...
Florida	8	5	...	...	3	2	6	...	2	6	...	8	4	4	...
Georgia	26	17	...	5	4	9	7	10	...	26	...	26	26	...	...
Idaho	6	...	6	...	...	6	...	...	6	...	...	6	6	...	...
Illinois	48	48	...	...	...	...	48	...	...	48	...	48	48	...	...
Indiana	30	30	...	...	...	30	...	...	30	...	...	30	30	...	...
Iowa	26	...	26	...	...	...	...	26	...	26	...	26	26	...	...
Kansas	20	20	...	...	...	20	...	...	20	...	...	20	20	...	...
Kentucky	26	18	2	...	6	12	12	2	...	26	...	26	26	...	...
Louisiana	16	3	11	1	1	...	16	...	...	16	...	16	16	...	...
Maine	12	9	...	1	2	4	7	1	4	7	1	12	2	10	...
Maryland	16	6	...	...	10	12	4	...	12	4	...	16	4	12	...
Massachusetts	30	24	1	4	1	5	20	5	...	30	...	30	...	30	...
Michigan	28	28	...	...	...	...	...	28	...	...	28	28	...	28	...
Minnesota	18	18	...	...	...	18	...	...	...	18	...	18	7	11	...
Mississippi	18	8	3	3	4	9	8	1	9	8	1	18	18	...	...
Missouri	34	34	...	...	...	10	16	8	...	34	...	34	34	...	...
Montana	6	...	6	...	...	...	...	6	...	6	...	6	6	...	...
Nebraska	16	15	...	...	1	5	6	5	...	15	...	16	...	16	...
Nevada	6	...	4	...	2	6	...	...	1	5	...	6	6	...	...
New Hampshire	8	8	...	...	...	...	8	...	...	8	...	8	...	8	...
New Jersey	20	20	...	...	...	19	1	...	19	1	...	20	...	20	...
New Mexico	6	4	1	1	...	5	1	...	5	1	...	2	2	...	...
New York	72	...	...	72	...	...	72	...	...	72	...	72	...	71	1
North Carolina	22	3a	1	...	17b	...	22	...	...	22	...	22	22	...	...
North Dakota	6	6	...	...	...	6	...	...	6	...	...	6	6	...	...
Ohio	46	14	16	6	10	4	38	4	...	46	...	46	46	...	...
Oklahoma	4*	4	...	...	...	2	2	...	2	2	...	*4	4	...	...
Oregon	8	8	...	...	...	8	...	...	...	8	...	8	8	...	...
Pennsylvania	64	64	...	...	...	64	...	...	...	64	...	64	...	64	...
Rhode Island	8	8	...	...	...	8	...	...	8	...	...	8	...	8	...
South Carolina	18	2	13	3	...	...	18	...	...	18	...	18	18	...	...
South Dakota	8	7	1	...	...	2	4	2	2	4	2	8	...	8	...
Tennessee	24	24	...	...	...	14	8	2	...	24	...	24	24	...	...
Texas	30	23	6	1	...	4	26	...	...	30	...	30	30	...	...
Utah	2	2	...	...	...	1	...	1	1	...	1	6	6	...	...
Vermont	8	8	...	...	...	8	...	...	8	...	...	8	...	8	...
Virginia	24	12	...	11	1	...	24	...	...	24	...	24	23	1	...
Washington	8	8	...	...	...	8	...	...	8	...	...	8	5	3	...
West Virginia	12	7	...	1	4	4	4	4	4	4	4	12	9	3	...
Wisconsin	24	24	...	...	...	...	...	24	...	24	...	24	...	24	...
Wyoming	6	3	...	...	3	...	...	6	...	...	6	6	6	...	...
Alaska	2	2	...	...	...	...	1	1	...	1	1	2	...	2	...
Canal Zone	...	...	...	...	...	...	...	...	...	...	...	...	...	...	...
District of Columbia	2	2	...	...	...	...	1	1	...	1	1	...	2	...	...
Hawaii	...	...	...	...	...	...	...	...	...	...	...	...	...	...	...
Philippine Islands	...	...	...	...	...	...	...	...	...	...	...	...	...	...	...
Puerto Rico	...	...	...	...	...	...	...	...	...	...	...	...	...	...	...
Virgin Islands	...	...	...	...	...	...	...	...	...	...	...	...	...	...	...
Total	910	617c	103	114	75d	343	402	165e	185	652	73f	906	556	349	1

Source: *Official Proceedings, 1892.*
Presidential. First ballot, p. 158.
a/ . Add one-third.
b/ . Add two-thirds.
c/ . Add one-third.
d/ . Other candidates: Arthur P. Gorman, 36½; John G. Carlisle, 14; Adlai E. Stevenson, 16 and two-thirds; James E. Campbell, 2; William R. Morrison, 3; William E. Russell, 1; William C. Whitney, 1; Robert E. Pattison, 1; not voting, ½.
Vice-Presidential. First ballot, p. 177.
e/ Other candidates: Allen B. Morse, 86; John L. Mitchell, 45; Henry Watterson, 26; Bourke Cockran, 5; Lambert Tree, 1; Horace Boies, 1; not voting, 1.
Revised ballot, p. 178.
f/ Other candidates: Morse, 62; Mitchell, 10; not voting, 1.

Source: *Official Proceedings, 1896.*
Temporary Chairman; Daniel for Hill, p. 97.

* Including Indian Territory, 2 votes.

* Including Indian Territory, 6 votes.

1896 DEMOCRATIC

Delegation	Votes	Minority Report, Michigan Credentials			Substitute Financial Plank			Commendation of Cleveland Administration			Adoption of Platform			Presidential First Ballot			
		Yea	Nay	Not Voting	Yea	Nay	Not Voting	Yea	Nay	Not Voting	Yea	Nay	Not Voting	Bryan	Bland	Pattison	Other
Alabama	22	...	22	...	...	22	...	...	22	...	22	...	...	...	...	...	22
Arizona	6	...	6	...	...	6	...	...	6	...	6	...	...	...	6	...	...
Arkansas	16	...	16	...	...	16	...	...	16	...	16	...	...	...	16	...	...
California	18	11	6	1	...	18	...	11	3	4	18	...	...	4	...	...	14
Colorado	8	4	4	...	...	8	...	...	8	...	8	...	...	...	...	...	8
Connecticut	12	12	...	...	12	...	...	12	...	...	...	12	...	1	...	3	12
Delaware	6	6	...	...	5	1	...	5	1	...	1	5	...	1	...	3	2
Florida	8	8	...	...	3	5	...	7	1	...	5	3	...	1	2	1	4
Georgia	26	...	26	...	...	26	...	...	26	...	26	...	...	26	...	...	...
Idaho	6	...	6	...	...	6	...	...	6	...	6	...	...	...	6	...	...
Illinois	48	...	48	...	...	48	...	...	48	...	48	...	...	...	48	...	...
Indiana	30	8	22	...	...	30	...	...	30	...	30	...	...	...	...	...	30
Iowa	26	...	26	...	...	26	...	...	26	...	26	...	...	...	...	...	26
Kansas	20	...	20	...	...	20	...	...	20	...	20	...	...	...	20	...	...
Kentucky	26	...	26	...	...	26	...	...	26	...	26	...	...	...	...	...	26
Louisiana	16	...	16	...	...	16	...	...	16	...	16	...	...	16	...	...	...
Maine	12	10	...	2	10	2	...	11	1	...	2	10	...	2	2	5	3
Maryland	16	15	1	...	12	4	...	16	...	...	4	12	...	4	...	11	1
Massachusetts	30	27	3	...	27	3	...	28	1	1	3	27	...	1	2	3	24
Michigan	28	28	...	...	...	28	...	28	...	...	28	...	...	9	4	...	15
Minnesota	18	13	4	1	11	6	1	17	1	...	6	11	1	2	...	2	14
Mississippi	18	...	18	...	...	18	...	...	18	...	18	...	...	18	...	...	...
Missouri	34	...	34	...	...	34	...	...	34	...	34	...	...	...	34	...	...
Montana	6	...	6	...	...	6	...	...	4	2	6	...	...	...	4	...	2
Nebraska	16	...	16	...	...	16	...	...	16	...	16	...	...	16	...	...	...
Nevada	6	...	6	...	...	6	...	...	6	...	6	...	...	...	...	...	6
New Hampshire	8	8	...	...	8	...	...	8	...	...	...	8	...	...	...	1	7
New Jersey	20	20	...	...	20	...	...	20	...	...	...	20	...	...	...	...	20
New Mexico	6	...	6	...	...	6	...	...	6	...	6	...	...	...	6	...	...
New York	72	72	...	...	72	...	...	72	...	...	...	72	...	...	...	...	72
North Carolina	22	1	21	...	...	22	...	...	22	...	22	...	...	22	...	...	...
North Dakota	6	...	6	...	...	6	...	...	5	1	6	...	...	...	...	...	6
Ohio	46	...	46	...	...	46	...	...	46	...	46	...	...	...	...	...	46
Oklahoma	12	...	12	...	...	12	...	...	12	...	12	...	...	...	12	...	...
Oregon	8	...	8	...	...	8	...	...	8	...	8	...	...	...	...	...	8
Pennsylvania	64	64	...	...	64	...	...	64	...	...	...	64	...	...	...	64	...
Rhode Island	8	8	...	...	8	...	...	8	...	...	...	8	...	...	...	6	2
South Carolina	18	...	18	...	...	18	...	...	18	...	18	...	...	...	...	...	18
South Dakota	8	8	...	...	8	...	...	8	...	...	...	8	...	6	...	1	1
Tennessee	24	...	24	...	...	24	...	...	24	...	24	...	...	...	24	...	...
Texas	30	...	30	...	...	30	...	...	30	...	30	...	...	...	30	...	...
Utah	6	...	6	...	...	6	...	...	6	...	6	...	...	...	6	...	...
Vermont	8	8	...	...	8	...	...	8	...	...	...	8	...	4	...	...	4
Virginia	24	...	24	...	...	24	...	...	24	...	24	...	...	1	7	...	24
Washington	8	4	4	...	3	5	...	3	5	...	5	3	...	1	7	...	...
West Virginia	12	2	10	...	...	12	...	...	11	1	12	...	...	...	...	...	12
Wisconsin	24	24	...	...	24	...	...	24	...	...	...	24	...	4	...	...	20
Wyoming	6	...	6	...	...	6	...	...	6	...	6	...	...	...	...	...	6
Alaska	6	6	...	...	6	...	...	6	...	...	...	6	...	...	6	...	...
Canal Zone	...	...	...	...	...	...	...	...	...	...	...	...	...	...	...	...	...
District of Columbia	6	1	5	...	2	4	...	1	5	...	6	...	...	...	...	...	6
Hawaii	...	...	...	...	...	...	...	...	...	...	...	...	...	...	...	...	...
Philippine Islands	...	...	...	...	...	...	...	...	...	...	...	...	...	...	...	...	...
Puerto Rico	...	...	...	...	...	...	...	...	...	...	...	...	...	...	...	...	...
Virgin Islands	...	...	...	...	...	...	...	...	...	...	...	...	...	...	...	...	...
Total	930	368	558	4	303	626	1	357	564	9	622[a]	307[b]	1	137	235	97	461[c]

Source: *Official Proceedings, 1896.*
Minority report, Michigan credentials, pp. 162-6.
Substitute financial plank, pp. 238-41.
Commendation of Cleveland Administration, pp. 242-7.
Adoption of platform, p. 249.
a/ Sum of column; proceedings record 628.
b/ Sum of column; proceedings record 301.
Presidential. First ballot, p. 311.
c/ Other candidates: Horace Boies, 67; Claude Matthews, 37; John R. McLean, 54; Joseph S. C. Blackburn, 82; Adlai F. Stevenson, 6; Henry M. Teller, 8; William E. Russell, 2; Benjamin R. Tillman, 17; James E. Campbell, 1; Sylvester Pennoyer, 8; David B. Hill, 1; not voting, 178.

* Including Indian Territory, 6 votes.

1896 DEMOCRATIC

Presidential

Delegation	Votes	Second Ballot				Third Ballot				Fourth Ballot				Fifth Ballot		
		Bryan	Bland	Pattison	Other	Bryan	Bland	Pattison	Other	Bryan	Bland	Pattison	Other	Bryan	Pattison	Other
Alabama	22	...	22	...	...	...	22	...	...	22	...	...	...	22	...	...
Arizona	6	...	6	...	...	...	6	...	...	...	6	...	...	6	...	...
Arkansas	16	...	16	...	...	...	16	...	...	...	16	...	...	16	...	...
California	18	14	2	...	2	13	2	...	3	12	2	...	4	18	...	...
Colorado	8	...	...	...	8	8	...	...	...	8	...	...	...	8	...	...
Connecticut	12	...	...	2	10	...	...	2	10	...	...	2	10	...	2	10
Delaware	6	1	...	3	2	1	...	3	2	1	...	3	2	1	3	2
Florida	8	2	1	1	4	5	...	...	3	5	...	...	3	8	...	...
Georgia	26	26	...	...	...	26	...	...	...	26	...	...	...	26	...	...
Idaho	6	...	6	...	...	...	6	...	...	6	...	...	...	6	...	...
Illinois	48	...	48	...	...	...	48	...	...	...	48	...	...	48	...	...
Indiana	30	...	...	...	30	...	...	...	30	...	...	...	30	30	...	...
Iowa	26	...	...	...	26	...	...	...	26	...	...	...	26	26	...	...
Kansas	20	...	20	...	...	...	20	...	...	20	...	...	...	20	...	...
Kentucky	26	...	...	...	26	...	...	...	26	...	...	...	26	26	...	...
Louisiana	16	16	...	...	...	16	...	...	...	16	...	...	...	16	...	...
Maine	12	2	2	5	3	2	2	5	3	2	2	5	3	4	4	4
Maryland	16	4	...	11	1	5	...	10	1	5	...	10	1	5	10	1
Massachusetts	30	1	2	3	24	1	2	3	24	1	2	3	24	6	3	21
Michigan	28	28	...	...	...	28	...	...	...	28	...	...	...	28	...	...
Minnesota	18	4	...	1	13	9	1	...	8	10	1	...	7	11	...	7
Mississippi	18	18	...	...	...	18	...	...	...	18	...	...	...	18	...	...
Missouri	34	...	34	...	...	...	34	...	...	...	34	...	...	34	...	...
Montana	6	...	6	...	...	...	6	...	...	...	6	...	...	6	...	...
Nebraska	16	16	...	...	...	16	...	...	...	16	...	...	...	16	...	...
Nevada	6	...	...	...	6	...	...	...	6	6	...	...	...	6	...	...
New Hampshire	8	...	...	1	7	...	...	1	7	...	...	1	7	...	1	7
New Jersey	20	...	...	2	18	...	...	2	18	...	...	2	18	...	2	18
New Mexico	6	...	6	...	...	...	6	...	...	...	6	...	...	6	...	...
New York	72	...	...	...	72	...	...	...	72	...	...	...	72	...	...	72
North Carolina	22	22	...	...	...	22	...	...	...	22	...	...	...	22	...	...
North Dakota	6	...	...	...	6	...	...	...	6	...	...	...	6	4	...	2
Ohio	46	...	...	...	46	...	...	...	46	...	...	...	46	46	...	...
Oklahoma	*12	...	12	...	...	...	12	...	...	...	12	...	...	12	...	...
Oregon	8	...	...	...	8	5	2	...	1	8	...	...	...	8	...	...
Pennsylvania	64	...	...	64	...	...	...	64	...	...	...	64	...	...	64	...
Rhode Island	8	...	...	6	2	...	...	6	2	...	...	6	2	...	6	2
South Carolina	18	18	...	...	...	18	...	...	...	18	...	...	...	18	...	...
South Dakota	8	7	...	1	...	7	...	1	...	7	...	1	...	8	...	...
Tennessee	24	...	24	...	...	...	24	...	...	...	24	...	...	24	...	...
Texas	30	...	30	...	...	...	30	...	...	...	30	...	...	30	...	...
Utah	6	...	6	...	...	...	6	...	...	...	6	...	...	6	...	...
Vermont	8	4	...	...	4	4	...	...	4	4	...	...	4	4	...	4
Virginia	24	...	24	...	...	...	24	...	...	...	24	...	...	24	...	...
Washington	8	1	7	...	...	1	7	...	...	2	6	...	...	4	...	4
West Virginia	12	...	...	...	12	1	7	...	4	1	10	...	1	2	...	10
Wisconsin	24	4	...	...	20	3	2	...	19	5	...	...	19	5	...	19
Wyoming	6	6	...	...	...	6	...	...	...	6	...	...	...	6	...	...
Alaska	6	...	6	...	...	...	6	...	...	...	6	...	...	6	...	...
Canal Zone	...	...	...	...	...	...	...	...	...	...	...	...	...	...	...	...
District of Columbia	6	3	1	...	2	4	...	...	2	5	...	...	1	6	...	...
Hawaii	...	...	...	...	...	...	...	...	...	...	...	...	...	...	...	...
Philippine Islands	...	...	...	...	...	...	...	...	...	...	...	...	...	...	...	...
Puerto Rico	...	...	...	...	...	...	...	...	...	...	...	...	...	...	...	...
Virgin Islands	...	...	...	...	...	...	...	...	...	...	...	...	...	...	...	...
Total	930	197	281	100	352a	219	291	97	323b	280	241	97	312c	652	95	183d

Source: *Official Proceedings, 1896.*
Second ballot, p. 316.
a/ Other candidates: Boies, 37; Blackburn, 41; McLean, 53; Matthews, 34; Pennoyer, 8; Teller, 8; Stevenson, 10; Hill, 1; not voting, 160.
Third ballot, p. 319.
b/ Other candidates: Boies, 36; Matthews, 34; McLean, 54; Blackburn, 27; Stevenson, 9; Hill, 1; not voting, 162.
Fourth ballot, p. 321.
c/ Other candidates: Boies, 33; Matthews, 36; Blackburn, 27; McLean, 46; Stevenson, 8; Hill, 1; not voting, 161.
Fifth ballot, p. 327.
d/ Other candidates: Bland, 11; Stevenson, 8; Hill, 1; David Turpie, 1; not voting, 162.

* Including Indian Territory, 6 votes.

Delegation	Votes	Motion to Adjourn			Vice-Presidential First Ballot				Second Ballot				Third Ballot			
		Yea	Nay	Not Voting	Sibley	McLean	Sewall	Other	Sibley	McLean	Bland	Other	McLean	Sewall	Bland	Other
Alabama	22	22	...	...	...	...	4	18	...	...	22	...	...	...	22	...
Arizona	6	6	...	...	...	...	...	6	...	...	6	...	...	...	6	...
Arkansas	16	16	...	...	...	...	16	...	...	...	16	...	...	16	...	...
California	18	18	...	...	...	...	10	8	...	...	18	...	...	18	...	...
Colorado	8	8	...	...	...	...	4	4	...	8	...	...	...	8	...	...
Connecticut	12	...	12	...	...	...	...	12	...	...	...	12	...	...	...	12
Delaware	6	1	3	2	1	...	...	5	...	...	1	5	...	1	...	5
Florida	8	8	...	...	...	...	8	...	...	...	8	...	...	8	...	...
Georgia	26	26	...	...	...	...	...	26	...	...	26	...	...	...	26	...
Idaho	6	6	...	...	...	...	...	6	...	...	6	...	...	...	6	...
Illinois	48	48	...	...	48	...	...	...	48	...	...	...	...	...	...	48
Indiana	30	...	30	...	2	15	...	13	...	15	15	...	30	...	...	...
Iowa	26	26	...	...	14	...	...	12	26	...	...	...	26	...	...	...
Kansas	20	20	...	...	...	...	...	20	...	...	20	...	...	...	20	...
Kentucky	26	26	...	...	21	...	4	1	1	16	2	7	16	7	3	...
Louisiana	16	16	...	...	...	...	...	16	...	16	...	...	16	...	...	...
Maine	12	12	...	...	...	...	12	...	...	...	...	12	...	12	...	...
Maryland	16	...	16	...	...	5	...	11	...	5	...	11	5	...	...	11
Massachusetts	30	...	27	3	...	...	...	30	...	...	...	30	...	...	...	30
Michigan	28	28	...	...	28	...	...	...	...	28	...	...	28	...	...	...
Minnesota	18	18	...	...	10	...	2	6	4	6	...	8	5	...	3	10
Mississippi	18	11	...	7	...	...	18	...	...	18	...	...	18	...	...	...
Missouri	34	24	...	10	6	...	10	18	5	...	...	29	...	...	34	...
Montana	6	6	...	...	...	...	6	...	...	...	6	...	...	...	6	...
Nebraska	16	16	...	...	...	...	...	16	...	...	16	...	...	...	...	16
Nevada	6	6	...	...	...	6	...	...	...	...	6	...	6	...	...	...
New Hampshire	8	...	...	8	...	...	...	8	...	...	...	8	...	...	...	8
New Jersey	20	...	...	20	...	...	...	20	...	...	...	20	...	...	...	20
New Mexico	6	6	...	...	...	...	...	6	...	...	6	...	...	...	6	...
New York	72	...	...	72	...	...	...	72	...	...	...	72	...	...	...	72
North Carolina	22	22	...	...	...	...	...	22	...	...	...	22	...	...	...	22
North Dakota	6	6	...	...	...	...	6	...	...	...	...	6	...	6	...	...
Ohio	46	46	...	...	...	46	...	...	...	46	...	...	46	...	...	...
Oklahoma	*12	6	...	6	10	1	...	1	...	...	12	...	...	12	...	...
Oregon	8	8	...	...	8	...	...	...	4	...	4	...	...	...	8	...
Pennsylvania	64	...	64	...	7	...	...	57	5	...	2	57	3	4	...	57
Rhode Island	8	...	6	2	...	...	...	8	...	...	...	8	...	...	...	8
South Carolina	18	18	...	...	18	...	...	...	18	...	...	...	...	...	18	...
South Dakota	8	8	...	...	...	...	...	8	...	...	...	8	...	...	...	8
Tennessee	24	24	...	...	7	...	...	17	...	...	24	...	...	...	24	...
Texas	30	30	...	...	...	...	...	30	...	...	30	...	...	...	30	...
Utah	6	6	...	...	...	...	...	6	...	...	6	...	...	...	...	6
Vermont	8	...	8	...	...	4	...	4	...	...	4	4	...	...	4	4
Virginia	24	24	...	...	...	...	...	24	...	...	24	...	...	...	24	...
Washington	8	8	...	...	...	...	...	8	...	...	3	5	...	4	4	...
West Virginia	12	10	2	...	...	...	...	12	...	...	12	...	5	...	1	6
Wisconsin	24	24	...	...	5	...	...	19	2	...	3	19	...	1	4	19
Wyoming	6	6	...	...	6	...	...	...	...	...	6	...	...	...	6	...
Alaska	6	...	...	6	...	...	...	6	...	...	...	6	...	...	...	6
Canal Zone	...	...	...	...	...	...	...	...	...	...	...	...	...	...	...	...
District of Columbia	6	...	...	6	...	6	...	...	...	...	6	...	6	...	...	...
Hawaii	...	...	...	...	...	...	...	...	...	...	...	...	...	...	...	...
Philippine Islands	...	...	...	...	...	...	...	...	...	...	...	...	...	...	...	...
Puerto Rico	...	...	...	...	...	...	...	...	...	...	...	...	...	...	...	...
Virgin Islands	...	...	...	...	...	...	...	...	...	...	...	...	...	...	...	...
Total	930	620a	168	142	163	111	100	556b	113	158	294	365c	210	97	255	368d

Source: *Official Proceedings, 1896.*

Motion to adjourn, pp. 331-3.
a/ Sum of column; result not announced.
Vice-Presidential. First ballot, p. 371.
b/ Other candidates: George F. Williams, 76; Richard P. Bland, 62; Walter Clark, 50; John R. Williams, 22; William F. Harrity, 21; Horace Boies, 20; Joseph S. C. Blackburn, 20; John W. Daniel, 11; James H. Lewis, 11; Henry M. Teller, 1; Stephen M. White, 1; George W. Fithian, 1; not voting, 260.
Second ballot, p. 372.
c/ Other candidates: Sewall, 37; George F. Williams, 16; Clark, 22; John R. Williams, 13; Harrity, 21; Daniel, 1; Robert E. Pattison, 1; not voting, 255.
Third ballot, p. 373.
d/ Other candidates: Sibley, 50; George F. Williams, 15; Clark, 22; Harrity, 19; Daniel, 6; Pattison, 1; not voting, 255.

* Including Indian Territory, 6 votes.

1896 DEMOCRATIC — Vice-Presidential (Fourth Ballot: Votes, McLean, Sewall, Other; Fifth Ballot: Sewall, Other). **1900 DEMOCRATIC** — Pres. First Ballot (Votes, Bryan); Vice-Presidential First Ballot before shift (Stevenson, Hill, Other); First after shift (Stevenson). **1904 DEMOCRATIC** — Minority Report, Illinois Credentials (Votes, Yea, Nay, Not Voting).

Delegation	Votes	McLean	Sewall	Other	Sewall	Other	Votes	Bryan	Stevenson	Hill	Other	Stevenson	Votes	Yea	Nay	Not Voting
Alabama	22	...	22	...	22	...	22	22	3	19	...	22	22	...	22	...
Arizona	6	...	6	...	6	...	6	6	5	...	1	6	6	6	...	...
Arkansas	16	...	16	...	16	...	16	16	11	...	5	16	18	...	18	...
California	18	2	16	...	16	2	18	18	15	...	3	18	20	20	...	...
Colorado	8	...	8	...	8	...	8	8	8	...	...	8	10	2	8	...
Connecticut	12	...	...	12	...	12	12	12	9	...	3	12	14	...	14	...
Delaware	6	...	1	5	1	5	6	6	4	2	...	6	6	3	3	...
Florida	8	...	8	...	8	...	8	8	4	4	...	8	10	4	6	...
Georgia	26	26	...	...	26	...	26	26	26	...	...	26	26	...	26	...
Idaho	6	...	6	...	6	...	6	6	...	3	3	6	6	3	3	...
Illinois	48	48	...	...	48	...	48	48	48	...	...	48	54	...	...	54
Indiana	30	30	...	...	30	...	30	30	28	...	2	30	30	...	30	...
Iowa	26	26	...	...	26	...	26	26	26	...	...	26	26	26	...	...
Kansas	20	...	20	...	20	...	20	20	20	...	...	20	20	13	7	...
Kentucky	26	16	10	...	26	...	26	26	26	...	...	26	26	26	...	...
Louisiana	16	16	...	...	16	...	16	16	...	16	...	16	18	...	18	...
Maine	12	...	12	...	12	...	12	12	10	...	2	12	12	6	6	...
Maryland	16	9	...	7	9	7	16	16	...	16	...	16	16	...	16	...
Massachusetts	30	...	...	30	...	30	30	30	6	13	11	30	32	...	32	...
Michigan	28	28	...	...	28	...	28	28	23	...	5	28	28	...	28	...
Minnesota	18	11	...	7	11	7	18	18	...	...	18	18	22	12	10	...
Mississippi	18	18	...	...	18	...	18	18	18	...	...	18	20	20	...	...
Missouri	34	...	34	...	34	...	34	34	23	6	5	34	36	36	...	...
Montana	6	2	4	...	6	...	6	6	2	3	1	6	6	...	6	...
Nebraska	16	...	...	16	16	...	16	16	6	...	10	16	16	16	...	...
Nevada	6	6	...	...	6	...	6	6	...	4	2	6	6	3	3	...
New Hampshire	8	...	...	8	...	8	8	8	8	...	...	8	8	...	8	...
New Jersey	20	...	...	20	...	20	20	20	...	20	...	20	24	...	24	...
New Mexico	6	...	6	...	6	...	6	6	5	...	1	6	6	3	3	...
New York	72	...	...	72	...	72	72	72	...	72	...	72	78	...	78	...
North Carolina	22	...	...	22	...	22	22	22	...	...	22	22	24	...	24	...
North Dakota	6	...	6	...	6	...	6	6	...	6	...	6	8	8	...	...
Ohio	46	46	...	...	46	...	46	46	...	...	46	46	46	21	25	...
Oklahoma	*12	...	12	...	12	...	*12	12	9½	...	2½	12	*12	4	8	...
Oregon	8	...	8	...	8	...	8	8	5	2	1	8	8	4	4	...
Pennsylvania	64	4	3	57	5	59	64	64	64	...	...	64	68	...	68	...
Rhode Island	8	...	...	8	...	8	8	8	8	...	...	8	8	6	2	...
South Carolina	18	...	18	...	18	...	18	18	18	...	...	18	18	18	...	...
South Dakota	8	...	8	...	8	...	8	8	2	...	6	8	8	8	...	...
Tennessee	24	...	24	...	24	...	24	24	...	24	...	24	24	...	24	...
Texas	30	...	30	...	30	...	30	30	30	...	...	30	36	...	36	...
Utah	6	...	6	...	6	...	6	6	6	...	...	6	6	...	6	...
Vermont	8	4	...	4	...	4	8	8	8	...	...	8	8	...	8	...
Virginia	24	...	...	24	24	...	24	24	24	...	...	24	24	...	24	...
Washington	8	...	8	...	8	...	8	8	...	...	8	8	10	10	...	...
West Virginia	12	...	...	12	12	...	12	12	12	...	...	12	14	3	11	...
Wisconsin	24	...	5	19	4	20	24	24	21	...	3	24	26	26	...	...
Wyoming	6	...	6	...	6	...	6	6	6	...	...	6	6	6	...	...
Alaska	6	...	...	6	...	6	6	6	6	...	...	6	6	...	6	...
Canal Zone	...	...	...	...	...	...	...	...	...	...	...	...	...	...	...	...
District of Columbia	6	6	...	...	...	6	...	...	6	6	...	6	6	...	6	...
Hawaii	...	...	...	...	...	...	6	6	...	6	...	6	6	2	4	...
Philippine Islands	...	...	...	...	...	...	...	...	...	...	...	...	...	...	...	...
Puerto Rico	...	...	...	...	...	...	...	...	...	...	...	...	6	4	2	...
Virgin Islands	...	...	...	...	...	...	...	...	...	...	...	...	...	...	...	...
Total	930	298	261	371[a]	602[b]	328[c]	936	936	559½	200	176½[d]	936	1000	299	647	54

Source: *Official Proceedings, 1896.*
Fourth ballot, p. 374.
a/ Other candidates: George F. Williams, 9; Clark, 46; Harrity, 11; Daniel, 54; Pattison, 1; not voting, 250.
Fifth ballot, p. 375.
b/ Sum of column; proceedings record 568.
c/ Other candidates: McLean, 32; George F. Williams, 9; Clark, 22; Harrity, 31; Daniel, 36; Pattison, 1; not voting, 251.

Source: *Official Proceedings, 1900.*
Presidential. First ballot, p. 150.
Vice-Presidential. First ballot (before shift), pp. 182-3.
d/ Other candidates: John W. Smith, 16; Julian S. Carr 23; Abram W. Patrick, 46; James Hogg, 1; Elliott Danforth 1.
First ballot (after shift), pp. 185-6.

Source: *Official Proceedings, 1904.*
Minority report, Illinois credentials, pp. 121-2.

* Including Indian Territory, 6 votes.

	1904 DEMOCRATIC														1908 DEMOCRATIC			
		Presidential						Sending of Telegram to Parker			Vice-Presidential First Ballot					Minority Report, Pennsylvania Credentials		
		First Ballot (before shift)			First Ballot (after shift)													
Delegation	Votes	Parker	Hearst	Other	Parker	Hearst	Other	Yea	Nay	Not Voting	Davis	Williams	Turner	Other	Votes	Yea	Nay	Not Voting
Alabama	22	22	...	...	22	...	...	22	...	...	22	...	...	...	22	...	22	...
Arizona	6	...	6	...	...	6	...	...	6	...	...	...	6	...	6	...	6	...
Arkansas	18	18	...	...	18	...	...	18	...	...	18	...	...	...	18	...	18	...
California	20	...	20	...	...	20	...	16	4	...	20	...	...	...	20	6	12	2
Colorado	10	4	5	1	4	5	1	4	6	...	...	3	7	...	10	9	1	...
Connecticut	14	14	...	...	14	...	...	14	...	...	14	...	...	...	14	3	10	1
Delaware	6	...	...	6	...	...	6	6	...	...	3	...	3	...	6	6	...	...
Florida	10	6	4	..,	6	4	...	6	4	...	10	...	...	...	10	...	10	...
Georgia	26	26	...	...	26	...	...	26	...	...	26	...	...	...	26	26	...	...
Idaho	6	...	6	...	6	...	...	...	6	...	...	...	6	...	6	2	4	...
Illinois	54	...	54	...	...	54	...	54	...	...	...	54	...	...	54	54	...	...
Indiana	30	30	...	...	30	...	...	30	...	...	...	30	...	...	30	...	30	...
Iowa	26	...	26	...	...	26	...	...	26	...	10	...	...	16	26	2	24	...
Kansas	20	7	10	3	7	10	3	...	20	...	...	...	...	20	20	...	20	...
Kentucky	26	26	...	...	26	...	...	26	...	...	26	...	...	...	26	...	26	...
Louisiana	18	18	...	...	18	...	...	18	...	...	18	...	...	...	18	18	...	...
Maine	12	7	1	4	7	1	4	7	2	3	9	...	...	3	12	11	1	...
Maryland	16	16	...	...	16	...	...	16	...	...	16	...	...	...	16	12	4	...
Massachusetts	32	...	...	32	...	...	32	32	...	...	32	...	...	...	32	9	22	1
Michigan	28	28	...	...	28	...	...	28	...	...	28	...	...	...	28	...	28	...
Minnesota	22	9	9	4	9	9	4	9	13	...	...	...	22	...	22	22	...	...
Mississippi	20	20	...	...	20	...	...	20	...	...	...	20	...	...	20	...	20	...
Missouri	36	...	...	36	...	...	36	...	36	...	...	...	...	36	36	5	31	...
Montana	6	6	...	...	6	...	...	...	6	...	...	...	6	...	6	...	6	...
Nebraska	16	...	4	12	...	4	12	...	16	...	16	...	...	...	16	...	16	...
Nevada	6	...	6	...	2	4	...	2	4	...	...	...	6	...	6	...	6	...
New Hampshire	8	8	...	...	8	...	...	8	...	...	8	...	...	...	8	2	6	...
New Jersey	24	24	...	...	24	...	...	24	...	...	24	...	...	...	24	24	...	...
New Mexico	6	...	6	...	...	6	...	6	...	...	...	...	6	...	6	...	6	...
New York	78	78	...	...	78	...	...	78	...	...	78	...	...	...	78	78	...	...
North Carolina	24	24	...	...	24	...	...	24	...	...	...	24	...	...	24	2	22	...
North Dakota	8	...	...	8	...	...	8	...	8	...	8	...	...	...	8	...	8	...
Ohio	46	46	...	...	46	...	...	31	6	9	46	...	...	...	46	4	41	1
Oklahoma	*12	7	3	2	7	3	2	7	5	...	...	8	2	2	14	...	14	...
Oregon	8	4	2	2	4	2	2	4	4	...	...	...	8	...	8	...	8	...
Pennsylvania	68	68	...	...	68	...	...	68	...	...	68	...	...	...	68	36½	27½	4
Rhode Island	8	2	6	...	2	6	...	2	5	1	8	...	...	...	8	5	3	...
South Carolina	18	18	...	...	18	...	...	18	...	...	...	18	...	...	18	4	12	2
South Dakota	8	...	8	...	...	8	...	...	8	...	8	...	...	...	8	...	8	...
Tennessee	24	24	...	...	24	...	...	24	...	...	24	...	...	...	24	12	12	...
Texas	36	36	...	...	36	...	...	36	...	...	36	...	...	...	36	...	36	...
Utah	6	6	...	...	6	...	...	6	...	...	...	...	6	...	6	...	6	...
Vermont	8	8	...	...	8	...	...	8	...	...	8	...	...	...	8	3	5	...
Virginia	24	24	...	...	24	...	...	24	...	...	24	...	...	...	24	22	2	...
Washington	10	...	10	...	10	...	...	10	...	...	...	...	10	...	10	...	10	...
West Virginia	14	10	2	2	13	1	...	14	...	...	14	...	...	...	14	3	11	...
Wisconsin	26	...	...	26	...	...	26	26	...	...	26	...	...	...	26	...	26	...
Wyoming	6	...	6	...	...	6	...	2	2	2	6	...	...	...	6	...	6	...
Alaska	6	6	...	...	6	...	...	6	...	...	...	...	6	...	6	...	6	...
Canal Zone	...	...	...	...	...	...	...	...	...	...	...	...	...	...	...	...	...	...
District of Columbia	6	6	...	...	6	...	...	6	...	...	6	...	...	...	...	...	6	...
Hawaii	6	...	6	...	...	6	...	2	4	...	...	...	6	...	6	...	6	...
Philippine Islands	...	...	...	...	...	...	...	6	...	...	...	...	...	...	...	...	...	...
Puerto Rico	6	2	...	4	2	...	4	6	...	...	2	...	...	4	6	...	6	...
Virgin Islands	...	...	...	...	...	...	...	...	...	...	...	...	...	...	...	...	...	...
Total	1000	658	200	142ᵃ	679	181	140ᵇ	794	191	15	654	165	100	81ᶜ	1002	386½	604½	11

Source: *Official Proceedings, 1904.*
Presidential. First ballot (before shift), p. 250.
  a/ Other candidates: George Gray, 12; Nelson A. Miles, 3; Francis M. Cockrell, 42; Richard Olney, 38; Edward C. Wall, 27; George B. McClellan, 3; Charles A. Towne, 2; Robert E. Pattison, 4; John S. Williams, 8; Bird S. Coler, 1; Arthur P. Gorman, 2.
  First ballot (after shift), p. 250.
  b/ Other candidates: Gray, 12; Miles, 3; Cockrell, 42; Olney, 38; Wall, 27; McClellan, 3; Towne, 2; Pattison, 4; Williams, 8; Coler, 1.
  Sending of telegram to Parker, pp. 317-8.
  Vice-Presidential. First ballot, pp. 320-1.
  c/ Other candidates: William A. Harris, 58; not voting, 23.

Source: *Official Proceedings, 1908.*
Minority report, Pennsylvania credentials, pp. 120-2.

* Including Indian Territory, 6 votes.

	1908 DEMOCRATIC Presidential First Ballot			1912 DEMOCRATIC Temporary Chairman				Minority Report on Unit Rule			Minority Report, South Dakota Credentials			Anti-Morgan Candidate Resolution		
Delegation	Votes	Bryan	Other	Votes	Bryan	Parker	Other	Yea	Nay	Not Voting	Yea	Nay	Not Voting	Yea	Nay	Not Voting
Alabama	22	22	...	24	1½	22½	...	9½	14½	...	14	10	...	24	...	...
Arizona	6	6	...	6	4	2	...	2	3	1	...	6	...	5	1	...
Arkansas	18	18	...	18	...	18	...	...	18	...	...	18	...	18	...	...
California	20	20	...	26	7	18	1	5	21	...	...	26	...	15	11	...
Colorado	10	10	...	12	6	6	...	7	5	...	1	11	...	7	5	...
Connecticut	14	9	5	14	2	12	...	3	10	1	1	13	...	12	2	...
Delaware	6	...	6.	6	6	...	...	6	...	...	6	...	...	6	...	...
Florida	10	10	...	12	1	11	...	6	6	...	2	10	...	7	5	...
Georgia	26	4	22	28	...	28	...	...	28	...	...	28	...	...	28	...
Idaho	6	6	...	8	8	...	...	8	...	...	8	...	...	8	...	...
Illinois	54	54	...	58	...	58	...	...	58	...	58	...	...	58	...	...
Indiana	30	30	...	30	8	21	1	15	13	2	11	19	...	27	2	1
Iowa	26	26	...	26	13	13	...	12	11	3	11½	14½	...	24½	1½	...
Kansas	20	20	...	20	20	...	...	20	...	...	20	...	...	20	...	...
Kentucky	26	26	...	26	7½	17½	1	3½	21b	c	...	26	...	3½	22½	...
Louisiana	18	18	...	20	10	10	...	14	6	...	13	7	...	11	9	...
Maine	12	10	2	12	1	11	...	7	2	3	11	1	...	...	12	...
Maryland	16	7	9	16	1½	14½	...	3½	12½	...	½	15½	...	3	12½	½
Massachusetts	32	32	...	36	18	15	3	25	6	5	7	29	...	33	3	...
Michigan	28	28	...	30	9	21	...	8	20	2	11	19	...	9	21	...
Minnesota	22	...	22	24	24	...	...	24	...	...	24	...	...	24	...	...
Mississippi	20	20	...	20	...	20	...	20	...	...	...	20	...	20	...	...
Missouri	36	36	...	36	14	22	...	7	29	...	...	36	...	34	2	...
Montana	6	6	...	8	7	1	...	8	...	...	8	...	...	8	...	...
Nebraska	16	16	...	16	13	3	...	16	...	...	14	2	...	16	...	...
Nevada	6	6	...	6	6	...	...	6	...	...	2	3	1	6	...	...
New Hampshire	8	7	1	8	5	3	...	8	...	...	6	2	...	7	1	...
New Jersey	24	...	24	28	24	4	...	24	4	...	24	4	...	24	4	...
New Mexico	6	6	...	8	8	...	...	4	4	...	...	7	1	8	...	...
New York	78	78	...	90	...	90	...	...	90	...	90	...	...	90	...	...
North Carolina	24	24	...	24	9	15	...	20	4	...	20	4	...	21	3	...
North Dakota	8	8	...	10	10	...	...	10	...	...	10	...	...	10	...	...
Ohio	46	46	...	48	19	29	...	20½	25	2½	18	28	2	30	17½	½
Oklahoma	14	14	...	20	20	...	...	10	10	...	10	10	...	20	...	...
Oregon	8	8	...	10	9	1	...	9	1	...	10	...	...	9	1	...
Pennsylvania	68	49½	18½	76	67	9	...	65	11	...	71	5	...	60	16	...
Rhode Island	8	5	3	10	...	10	...	2	8	...	...	10	...	10	...	...
South Carolina	18	18	...	18	18	...	...	18	...	...	18	...	...	18	...	...
South Dakota	8	8	...	10	10	...	...	10	...	...	...	...	10	10	...	...
Tennessee	24	24	...	24	7	17	...	7	17	...	10	14	...	11	13	...
Texas	36	36	...	40	40	...	...	40	...	...	40	...	...	40	...	...
Utah	6	6	...	8	4	4	...	8	...	...	8	...	...	4½	3½	...
Vermont	8	7	1	8	...	8	...	3	4	1	8	...	...	8	...	...
Virginia	24	24	...	24	10	14	...	14	3	7	24	...	...	23½	...	½
Washington	10	10	...	14	14	...	...	7	7	...	...	14	...	14	...	...
West Virginia	14	14	...	16	4½	10½	1	3½	10½	2	3½	10	2½	13	3	...
Wisconsin	26	26	...	26	26	...	...	26	...	...	19	6	1	26	...	...
Wyoming	6	6	...	6	6	...	...	6	...	...	3	3	...	3	3	...
Alaska	6	6	...	6	2	4	...	...	6	...	2	4	...	6	...	...
Canal Zone	...			...												
District of Columbia	6	6	...	6	...	6	...	...	...	6	6	...	...	6	...	...
Hawaii	6	6	...	6	2	4	...	3	2	1	6	...	...	6	...	...
Philippine Islands	...			6	2	4	...	6	...	...	6	...	...	...	...	6
Puerto Rico	6	6	...	6	4	2	...	6	...	...	4	2	...	6	...	...
Virgin Islands	...															
Total	1002	888½	113½ a	1094	508	579	7d	565½	491e	37f	639½	437	17½	883	202½	8½

Source: *Official Proceedings, 1908.*
Presidential. First ballot, pp. 246-7.
a/ Other candidates: John A. Johnson, 46; George Gray, 59½; not voting, 8.

Source: *Official Proceedings, 1912.*
Temporary chairman, pp. 17-9.
d/ Other candidates: James A. O'Gorman, 4; John W. Kern, 1; not voting, 2.
Minority report on unit rule, pp. 76-7.
b/ Add five-sixths.
c/ Add one-sixth.
e/ Sum of column, 491 and one-third; proceedings record 492 and one-third.
f/ Add two-thirds.
Minority report, South Dakota credentials, pp. 93-4.
Anti-Morgan candidate resolution, pp. 137-8.

1912 DEMOCRATIC — Presidential

Delegation	Votes	First Ballot					Fifth Ballot					Tenth Ballot			
		Clark	Wilson	Harmon	Underwood	Other	Clark	Wilson	Harmon	Underwood	Other	Clark	Wilson	Underwood	Other
Alabama	24	...	...	...	24	...	...	...	...	24	...	...	...	24	...
Arizona	6	6	...	...	...	...	6	...	...	...	...	6	...	...	...
Arkansas	18	18	...	...	...	...	18	...	...	...	...	18	...	...	...
California	26	26	...	...	...	...	26	...	...	...	...	26	...	...	...
Colorado	12	12	...	...	...	...	12	...	...	...	...	12	...	...	...
Connecticut	14	...	...	...	...	14	4	1	...	9	...	7	...	7	...
Delaware	6	...	6	...	...	...	...	6	...	...	...	...	6	...	...
Florida	12	...	...	...	12	...	...	...	...	12	...	...	...	12	...
Georgia	28	...	...	...	28	...	...	...	...	28	...	...	...	28	...
Idaho	8	8	...	...	...	...	8	...	...	...	...	8	...	...	...
Illinois	58	58	...	...	...	...	58	...	...	...	...	58	...	...	...
Indiana	30	...	...	...	...	30	...	...	...	...	30	...	...	...	30
Iowa	26	26	...	...	...	...	26	...	...	...	...	26	...	...	...
Kansas	20	20	...	...	...	...	20	...	...	...	...	20	...	...	...
Kentucky	26	26	...	...	...	...	26	...	...	...	...	26	...	...	...
Louisiana	20	11	9	...	...	...	10	10	...	...	...	10	10	...	...
Maine	12	1	9	...	2	...	1	11	...	...	...	1	11	...	...
Maryland	16	16	...	...	...	...	16	...	...	...	...	16	...	...	...
Massachusetts	36	36	...	...	...	...	33	1	...	2	...	33	1	2	...
Michigan	30	12	10	7	...	1	15	11	2	...	2	18	9	...	3
Minnesota	24	...	24	...	...	...	...	24	...	...	...	...	24	...	...
Mississippi	20	...	...	...	20	...	...	...	...	20	...	...	...	20	...
Missouri	36	36	...	...	...	...	36	...	...	...	...	36	...	...	...
Montana	8	8	...	...	...	...	8	...	...	...	...	8	...	...	...
Nebraska	16	12	...	4	...	...	12	3	1	...	...	13	3	...	...
Nevada	6	6	...	...	...	...	6	...	...	...	...	6	...	...	...
New Hampshire	8	8	...	...	...	...	5	3	...	...	...	5	3	...	...
New Jersey	28	2	24	...	2	...	4	24	...	...	...	4	24	...	...
New Mexico	8	8	...	...	...	...	8	...	...	...	...	8	...	...	...
New York	90	...	...	90	...	...	...	...	90	...	...	90	...	...	...
North Carolina	24	...	16½	½	7	...	...	17	...	7	...	...	18	6	...
North Dakota	10	...	10	...	...	...	...	10	...	...	...	...	10	...	...
Ohio	48	1	10	35	...	1	1	12	34	...	1	6	11	...	31
Oklahoma	20	10	10	...	...	...	10	10	...	...	...	10	10	...	...
Oregon	10	...	10	...	...	...	...	10	...	...	...	...	10	...	...
Pennsylvania	76	...	71	5	...	...	...	73	3	...	...	5	71	...	...
Rhode Island	10	10	...	...	...	...	10	...	...	...	...	10	...	...	...
South Carolina	18	...	18	...	...	...	...	18	...	...	...	...	18	...	...
South Dakota	10	...	10	...	...	...	...	10	...	...	...	...	10	...	...
Tennessee	24	6	6	6	6	...	5	5	11½	2½	...	13	7½	3½	...
Texas	40	...	40	...	...	...	...	40	...	...	...	...	40	...	...
Utah	8	1½	6	...	½	...	1½	6½	...	...	...	1½	6½	...	...
Vermont	8	...	...	...	...	8	...	...	...	...	8	...	...	...	8
Virginia	24	...	9½	...	14½	...	½	9½	...	14	...	½	9½	14	...
Washington	14	14	...	...	...	...	14	...	...	...	...	14	...	...	...
West Virginia	16	16	...	...	...	...	16	...	...	...	...	16	...	...	...
Wisconsin	26	6	19	...	...	1	6	20	...	...	...	6	20	...	...
Wyoming	6	6	...	...	...	...	6	...	...	...	...	6	...	...	...
Alaska	6	4	...	...	...	2	4	2	...	...	...	3	3	...	...
Canal Zone	...	...	...	...	...	...	...	...	...	...	...	...	...	...	...
District of Columbia	6	6	...	...	...	...	6	...	...	...	...	6	...	...	...
Hawaii	6	2	3	...	1	...	2	3	...	1	...	2	3	1	...
Philippine Islands	6	...	...	...	...	6	...	...	...	...	6	...	...	...	6
Puerto Rico	6	2	3	...	1	...	3	3	...	...	...	2	4	...	...
Virgin Islands	...	...	...	...	...	...	...	...	...	...	...	...	...	...	...
Total	1094	440½	324	148	117½	64[a]	443	351	141½	119½	39[b]	556	350½	117½	70[c]

Source: *Official Proceedings, 1912.*
Presidential. First ballot, pp. 196-8.
a/ Other candidates: Simeon E. Baldwin, 22; Thomas R. Marshall, 31; William J. Bryan, 1; William Sulzer, 2; not voting, 8.
Fifth ballot, pp. 210-1.
b/ Other candidates: Marshall, 31; Kern, 2; not voting, 6.
Tenth ballot, pp. 220-1.
c/ Other candidates: Harmon, 31; Marshall, 31; Kern, 1; Bryan, 1; not voting, 6.

1912 DEMOCRATIC

Delegation	Votes	Fifteenth Ballot Clark	Wilson	Underwood	Other	Twentieth Ballot Clark	Wilson	Underwood	Other	Motion to Recess Yea	Nay	Not Voting	Twenty-fifth Ballot Clark	Wilson	Underwood	Other
Alabama	24	...	...	24	...	...	...	24	...	24	...	...	...	...	24	...
Arizona	6	5	1	...	...	2	1	...	3	6	...	...	2	1	...	3
Arkansas	18	18	...	...	...	18	...	...	...	18	...	...	18	...	...	...
California	26	26	...	...	...	26	...	...	...	26	...	...	26	...	...	...
Colorado	12	12	...	...	...	12	...	...	...	12	...	...	12	...	...	...
Connecticut	14	7	1	6	...	3	1	10	...	11	3	...	5	2	7	...
Delaware	6	...	6	...	...	...	6	...	...	...	6	...	...	6	...	...
Florida	12	...	...	12	...	...	...	12	...	12	...	...	...	...	12	...
Georgia	28	...	...	28	...	...	...	28	...	28	...	...	...	...	28	...
Idaho	8	8	...	...	...	2	6	...	...	...	8	...	...	8	...	...
Illinois	58	58	...	...	...	58	...	...	...	58	...	...	58	...	...	...
Indiana	30	...	...	...	30	...	...	...	30	...	30	...	...	...	...	30
Iowa	26	26	...	...	...	26	...	...	...	13	13	...	26	...	...	...
Kansas	20	20	...	...	...	...	20	...	...	...	20	...	...	20	...	...
Kentucky	26	26	...	...	...	26	...	...	...	26	...	...	26	...	...	...
Louisiana	20	10	10	...	...	9	10	...	1	10	10	...	7	12	...	1
Maine	12	4	8	...	...	1	8	3	...	...	11	1	1	8	3	...
Maryland	16	16	...	...	...	16	...	...	...	10	6	...	16	...	...	...
Massachusetts	36	33	1	2	...	32	1	2	1	...	36	...	...	2	...	34
Michigan	30	18	12	...	...	19	11	...	...	20	10	...	18	12	...	...
Minnesota	24	...	24	...	...	...	24	...	...	...	24	...	...	24	...	...
Mississippi	20	...	...	20	...	...	...	20	...	...	20	...	...	...	20	...
Missouri	36	36	...	...	...	36	...	...	...	36	...	...	36	...	...	...
Montana	8	2	6	...	...	2	6	...	...	...	8	...	1	7	...	...
Nebraska	16	4	12	...	...	2	13	...	1	1	15	...	2	14	...	...
Nevada	6	6	...	...	...	6	...	...	...	6	...	...	6	...	...	...
New Hampshire	8	5	3	...	...	5	3	...	...	...	...	...	4	4	...	...
New Jersey	28	4	24	...	...	4	24	...	...	4	24	...	4	24	...	...
New Mexico	8	8	...	...	...	8	...	...	...	8	...	...	8	...	...	...
New York	90	90	...	...	...	90	...	...	...	90	...	...	90	...	...	...
North Carolina	24	1½	18	4½	...	...	17	7	...	...	24	...	...	24	...	...
North Dakota	10	...	10	...	...	...	10	...	...	...	10	...	...	10	...	...
Ohio	48	2	14	...	32	2	17	...	29	29	19	...	...	19	...	29
Oklahoma	20	10	10	...	...	10	10	...	...	10	10	...	10	10	...	...
Oregon	10	2	8	...	...	2	8	...	...	5	1	4	1	9	...	...
Pennsylvania	76	5	71	...	...	5	71	...	...	5	71	...	5	71	...	...
Rhode Island	10	10	...	...	...	10	...	...	...	9	1	...	10	...	...	...
South Carolina	18	...	18	...	...	...	18	...	...	...	18	...	...	18	...	...
South Dakota	10	...	10	...	...	...	10	...	...	...	10	...	...	10	...	...
Tennessee	24	14½	8	1½	...	14	7½	2½	...	9	15	...	14	8½	1½	...
Texas	40	...	40	...	...	...	40	...	...	...	40	...	...	40	...	...
Utah	8	1½	6½	...	...	1½	6½	...	...	...	8	...	1½	6½	...	...
Vermont	8	1	7	...	...	2	6	...	...	...	8	...	...	...	...	8
Virginia	24	3	9½	11½	...	3	9	12	...	...	24	...	3	9½	11½	...
Washington	14	14	...	...	...	14	...	...	...	14	...	...	14	...	...	...
West Virginia	16	16	...	...	...	16	...	...	...	9½	2½	4	16	...	...	...
Wisconsin	26	6	19	...	1	6	19	...	1	7	19	...	6	19	...	1
Wyoming	6	6	...	...	...	6	...	...	...	6	...	...	6	...	...	...
Alaska	6	6	...	...	...	6	...	...	...	...	6	...	6	...	...	...
Canal Zone	...	...	...	...	...	...	...	...	...	...	...	...	...	...	...	...
District of Columbia	6	6	...	...	...	6	...	...	...	6	...	...	6	...	...	...
Hawaii	6	4	1	1	...	4	1	1	...	3	3	...	3	2	1	...
Philippine Islands	6	...	...	...	6	...	...	...	6	...	...	6	...	...	...	6
Puerto Rico	6	1½	4½	...	...	1½	4½	...	...	...	4	2	1½	4½	...	...
Virgin Islands	...	...	...	...	...	...	...	...	...	...	...	...	...	...	...	...
Total	1094	552	362½	110½	69a	512	388½	121½	72b	531½	545½	17	469	405	108	112c

Source: *Official Proceedings, 1912.*
Fifteenth ballot, pp. 243-4.
a/ Other candidates: Marshall, 30; Harmon, 29; Bryan, 2; Kern, 2; not voting, 6.
Twentieth ballot, pp. 255-6.
b/ Other candidates: Marshall, 30; Harmon, 29; Bryan, 1; Eugene N. Foss, 2; Ollie M. James, 3; Kern, 1; not voting, 6.
Motion to recess, pp. 261-2.
Twenty-fifth ballot, pp. 271-2.
c/ Other candidates: Marshall, 30; Harmon, 29; Foss, 43; James, 3; Bryan, 1; not voting, 6.

Delegation	Votes	Thirtieth Ballot				Thirty-fifth Ballot				Fortieth Ballot				Motion to Adjourn		
		Clark	Wilson	Underwood	Other	Clark	Wilson	Underwood	Other	Clark	Wilson	Underwood	Other	Yea	Nay	Not Voting
Alabama	24	...	...	24	...	...	...	24	...	...	...	24	...	24	...	...
Arizona	6	4	2	...	...	3	2	1	...	...	4	2	...	...	6	...	...
Arkansas	18	18	...	...	...	18	...	...	...	18	...	...	...	18	...	...
California	26	26	...	...	...	26	...	...	...	26	...	...	...	26	...	...
Colorado	12	12	...	...	...	12	...	...	...	11	1	...	...	12	...	...
Connecticut	14	7	3	4	...	7	3	4	...	3	3	8	...	14	...	...
Delaware	6	...	6	...	...	...	6	...	...	...	6	...	...	6	...	...
Florida	12	...	...	12	...	...	...	12	...	...	2	10	...	10	2	...
Georgia	28	...	...	28	...	...	...	28	...	...	...	28	...	28	...	...
Idaho	8	2½	5½	...	...	2½	5½	...	...	2½	5½	...	...	8	...	...
Illinois	58	58	...	...	...	58	...	...	...	58	...	...	...	58	...	...
Indiana	30	1	28	...	1	1	28	...	1	1	28	...	1	30	...	...
Iowa	26	12	14	...	...	12	14	...	...	11	15	...	...	18½	7½	...
Kansas	20	...	20	...	...	...	20	...	...	...	20	...	...	...	20	...
Kentucky	26	26	...	...	...	26	...	...	...	26	...	...	...	26	...	...
Louisiana	20	7	12	...	1	7	12	...	1	7	12	...	1	20	...	...
Maine	12	1	9	2	...	1	11	...	...	1	11	...	...	12	...	...
Maryland	16	11	4½	...	½	10	5	½	½	10	5	½	½	16	...	...
Massachusetts	36	...	7	...	29	...	9	...	27	...	9	...	27	36	...	...
Michigan	30	18	12	...	...	3	27	...	...	4	26	...	...	30	...	...
Minnesota	24	...	24	...	...	...	24	...	...	...	24	...	...	...	24	...
Mississippi	20	...	...	20	...	...	...	20	...	...	...	20	...	20	...	...
Missouri	36	36	...	...	...	36	...	...	...	36	...	...	...	36	...	...
Montana	8	2	6	...	...	1	7	...	...	1	7	...	...	8	...	...
Nebraska	16	3	13	...	...	3	13	...	...	3	13	...	...	16	...	...
Nevada	6	6	...	...	...	6	...	...	...	6	...	...	...	6	...	...
New Hampshire	8	3	5	...	...	3	5	...	...	3	5	...	...	3	5	...
New Jersey	28	4	24	...	...	4	24	...	...	4	24	...	...	4	24	...
New Mexico	8	8	...	...	...	8	...	...	...	8	...	...	...	8	...	...
New York	90	90	...	...	...	90	...	...	...	90	...	...	...	90	...	...
North Carolina	24	...	17½	6½	...	...	18	6	...	...	20	4	...	6	18	...
North Dakota	10	...	10	...	...	...	10	...	...	...	10	...	...	...	10	...
Ohio	48	...	19	10	19	...	19	...	29	...	20	...	28	48	...	...
Oklahoma	20	10	10	...	...	10	10	...	...	10	10	...	...	10	10	...
Oregon	10	...	10	...	...	...	10	...	...	...	10	...	...	10	...	...
Pennsylvania	76	4	72	...	...	2	74	...	...	2	74	...	...	...	76	...
Rhode Island	10	10	...	...	...	10	...	...	...	10	...	...	...	10	...	...
South Carolina	18	...	18	...	...	...	18	...	...	...	18	...	...	...	18	...
South Dakota	10	...	10	...	...	...	10	...	...	...	10	...	...	10	...	...
Tennessee	24	13½	8	2½	...	13½	8	2½	...	8	8	8	...	24	...	...
Texas	40	...	40	...	...	...	40	...	...	...	40	...	...	...	40	...
Utah	8	1½	6½	...	...	1½	6½	...	...	1½	6½	...	...	8	...	...
Vermont	8	...	8	...	...	...	8	...	...	...	8	...	...	8	...	...
Virginia	24	3	9½	11½	...	12	10	2	...	12	10	2	...	14	10	...
Washington	14	14	...	...	...	14	...	...	...	14	...	...	...	14	...	...
West Virginia	16	16	...	...	...	16	...	...	...	16	...	...	...	16	...	...
Wisconsin	26	6	19	...	1	6	20	...	...	5	21	...	...	...	26	...
Wyoming	6	6	...	...	...	...	6	...	...	...	6	...	...	...	6	...
Alaska	6	6	...	...	...	2	4	...	...	2	4	...	...	6	...	...
Canal Zone	...	...	...	...	...	...	...	...	...	...	...	...	...	...	...	...
District of Columbia	6	6	...	...	...	6	...	...	...	6	...	...	...	6	...	...
Hawaii	6	2	3	1	...	2	3	1	...	2	3	1	...	6	...	...
Philippine Islands	6	...	...	...	6	...	...	...	6	...	...	...	6	...	...	6
Puerto Rico	6	1½	4½	...	...	1	4½	½	...	1	4½	½	...	6	...	...
Virgin Islands	...	...	...	...	...	...	...	...	...	...	...	...	...	...	...	...
Total	1094	455	460	121½	57½a	433½	494½	101½	64½b	423	501½	106	63½c	791½	296½	6

Source: *Official Proceedings, 1912.*
Thirtieth ballot, pp. 301-2.
a/ Other candidates: Foss, 30; Harmon, 19; Kern, 2;
not voting, ½.
Thirty-fifth ballot, pp. 313-4.
b/ Other candidates: Foss, 28; Harmon, 29; Kern, 1;
not voting, ½.
Fortieth ballot, pp. 324-6.
c/ Other candidates: Harmon, 28; Foss, 28; Kern, 1;
not voting, ½.
Motion to adjourn, p. 331.

1912 DEMOCRATIC

Delegation	Votes	Forty-third Ballot (Presidential)			Forty-fifth Ballot			46th Ballot		First Ballot (Vice-Presidential)				Second Ballot		
		Clark	Wilson	Other	Clark	Wilson	Other	Wilson	Other	Burke	Marshall	Chamberlain	Other	Burke	Marshall	Other
Alabama	24	...	...	24	...	...	24	24	...	...	16	6	2	4	20	...
Arizona	6	3	2	1	3	3	...	6	...	...	5	1	...	...	5	1
Arkansas	18	18	...	...	18	...	...	18	...	...	...	...	18	...	18	...
California	26	26	...	...	26	...	...	2	24	...	...	26	...	26	...	...
Colorado	12	11	1	...	2	10	...	12	...	12	...	...	...	12	...	...
Connecticut	14	1	5	8	2	5	7	14	...	14	...	...	...	14	...	...
Delaware	6	...	6	...	...	6	...	6	...	...	5	1	...	...	5	1
Florida	12	...	2	10	...	3	9	7	5	3	3	...	6	5	5	2
Georgia	28	...	...	28	...	...	28	28	...	...	28	...	...	...	28	...
Idaho	8	1	7	...	1½	6½	...	8	...	8	...	...	...	8	...	...
Illinois	58	...	58	...	...	58	...	58	...	...	...	...	58	...	58	...
Indiana	30	1	28	1	...	30	...	30	...	1	29	...	...	...	30	...
Iowa	26	11½	14½	...	9	17	...	26	...	...	...	...	26	18	8	...
Kansas	20	...	20	...	...	20	...	20	...	20	...	...	...	20	...	...
Kentucky	26	26	...	...	26	...	...	26	...	3d	12	...	10e	3d	12	10e
Louisiana	20	6	14	...	5	15	...	18	2	2	18	...	...	2	18	...
Maine	12	1	11	...	1	11	...	12	...	...	...	12	...	...	12	...
Maryland	16	9	5½	1½	8½	7	...½	16	...	...	...	...	16	...	15½	...½
Massachusetts	36	...	9	27	...	9	27	36	...	9	9	9	9	3	33	...
Michigan	30	2	28	...	2	28	...	30	...	...	30	...	...	...	30	...
Minnesota	24	...	24	...	...	24	...	24	...	24	...	...	...	24	...	...
Mississippi	20	...	...	20	...	...	20	20	...	...	...	20	...	...	20	...
Missouri	36	36	...	...	36	...	...	...	36	...	...	...	36	...	36	...
Montana	8	1	7	...	1	7	...	8	...	7	...	1	...	6	2	...
Nebraska	16	3	13	...	3	13	...	16	...	8	...	7	1	15	...	1
Nevada	6	6	...	...	6	...	...	...	6	...	6	...	...	...	6	...
New Hampshire	8	3	5	...	3	5	...	8	...	...	8	...	...	3	5	...
New Jersey	28	4	24	...	4	24	...	24	4	8	8	8	4	12	12	4
New Mexico	8	8	...	...	8	...	...	8	...	...	...	8	...	8	...	...
New York	90	90	...	...	90	...	...	90	...	...	...	90	...	...	...	90
North Carolina	24	...	22	2	...	22	2	24	...	9	11	...	4	9	15	...
North Dakota	10	...	10	...	...	10	...	10	...	10	...	...	...	10	...	...
Ohio	48	...	20	28	...	23	25	33	15	33	3	9	3	48	...	...
Oklahoma	20	10	10	...	10	10	...	20	...	10	10	...	...	10	10	...
Oregon	10	...	10	...	...	10	...	10	...	...	...	10	...	9	1	...
Pennsylvania	76	2	74	...	...	76	...	76	...	16	21	3	36	19	27	30
Rhode Island	10	10	...	...	...	10	...	10	...	10	...	...	...	10	...	...
South Carolina	18	...	18	...	...	18	...	18	...	18	...	...	...	...	18	...
South Dakota	10	...	10	...	...	10	...	10	...	10	...	...	...	10	...	...
Tennessee	24	10	8	6	8	10	6	24	...	...	24	...	...	...	24	...
Texas	40	...	40	...	...	40	...	40	...	40	...	...	...	40	...	...
Utah	8	1½	6½	...	...	8	...	8	...	1	2	3	2	6	2	...
Vermont	8	...	8	...	...	8	...	8	...	...	8	...	...	...	8	...
Virginia	24	...	24	...	...	24	...	24	...	...	24	...	...	...	24	...
Washington	14	14	...	...	14	...	...	14	...	...	...	...	14	14	...	...
West Virginia	16	...	16	...	...	16	...	16	...	5	10	1	...	...	15	1
Wisconsin	26	4	22	...	...	26	...	26	...	18	2	6	...	18	2	6
Wyoming	6	...	6	...	...	6	...	6	...	...	...	...	6	...	6	...
Alaska	6	1	5	...	...	6	...	6	...	...	...	6	...	3	3	...
Canal Zone	...	...	...	...	...	...	...	...	...	...	...	...	...	...	...	...
District of Columbia	6	6	...	...	6	...	...	...	6	...	6	...	...	...	6	...
Hawaii	6	2	4	...	2	4	...	6	...	...	...	6	...	6	...	...
Philippine Islands	6	...	...	6	...	...	6	6	...	...	...	...	6	...	...	6
Puerto Rico	6	1	4½	½	1	4½	½	6	...	5	1	...	...	1	5	...
Virgin Islands	...	...	...	...	...	...	...	...	...	...	...	...	...	...	...	...
Total	1094	329	602	163a	306	633	155b	990	104c	304f	389	157	243g	386h	644½	63i

Source: *Official Proceedings, 1912.*

Forty-third ballot, pp. 337-8.

a/ Other candidates: Underwood, 98½; Harmon, 28; Foss, 27; Bryan, 1; Kern, 1; not voting, 7½.

Forty-fifth ballot, pp. 344-5.

b/ Other candidates: Underwood, 97; Foss, 27; Harmon, 25; not voting, 6.

Forty-sixth ballot, pp. 351-2.

c/ Other candidates: Clark, 84; Harmon, 12; not voting, 8.

Vice-Presidential. First ballot, pp. 384-5.

d/ Add two-thirds.

e/ Add one-third.

f/ Add two-thirds.

g/ Other candidates: Elmore W. Hurst, 78; James H. Preston, 58; Martin J. Wade, 26; William F. McCombs, 18; John E. Osborne, 8; William Sulzer, 3; not voting, 46 and one-third.

Second ballot, pp. 387-8.

h/ Add one-third.

i/ Other candidates: Chamberlain, 12½; not voting, 44 and two-thirds.

Recapitulation of Presidential Ballots

Ballot	Wilson	Clark	Underwood	Harmon	Baldwin	Marshall	Bryan	Kern	Foss	Sulzer	James	Gaynor	Lewis
1	324	440½	117½	148	22	31	1	...	...	2	...	...	...
2	339a	446½	111b	141	14	31	2	...	...	2	...	...	...
3	345	441	114½	140½	14	31	1	1	...	...	...	...	...
4	349½	443	112	136½	14	31	...	2	...	...	...	...	...
5	351	443	119½	141½	...	31	...	2	...	...	...	...	...
6	354	445	121	135	...	31	1	1	...	...	...	...	...
7	352½	449½	123½	129½	...	31	1	1	...	...	...	...	...
8	351½	448½	123	130	...	31	1	1	...	...	1	1	...
9	352½	452	122½	127	...	31	1	1	...	...	...	1	...
10	350½	556	117½	31	...	31	1	1	...	...	...	...	...
11	354½	554	118½	29	...	30	1	1	...	...	...	...	...
12	354	547½	123	29	...	30	1	1	...	...	...	...	...
13	356	554½	115½	29	...	30	1	...	2	...	...	...	...
14	361	553	111	29	...	30	2	2	...	...	...	...	...
15	362½	552	110½	29	...	30	2	2	...	...	...	...	...
16	362½	551	112½	29	...	30	1	2	...	...	...	...	...
17	362½	545	112½	29	...	30	1	4½	...	...	...	...	...
18	361	535	125	29	...	30	1	3½	...	...	...	...	...
19	358	532	130	29	...	30	7	1	1	...	...	...	...
20	388½	512	121½	29	...	30	1	1	2	...	3	...	...
21	395½	508	118½	29	...	30	1	1	5	...	...	...	...
22	396½	500½	115	...	...	30	1	1	43	...	...	1	...
23	399	497½	114½	...	...	30	1	...	45	...	...	1	...
24	402½	496	115½	...	...	30	1	...	43	...	...	...	...
25	405	469	108	29	...	30	1	...	43	...	3	...	...
26	407½	463½	112½	29	...	30	1	...	43	...	...	...	...
27	406½	469	112	29	...	30	1	...	38	...	...	...	...
28	437½	468½	112½	29	...	...	1	1	38	...	...	...	...
29	436	468½	112	29	...	...	...	4	38	...	...	...	...
30	460	455	121½	19	...	...	...	2	30	...	...	...	...
31	475½	446½	116½	17	...	...	...	2	30	...	...	...	...
32	477½	446½	119½	14	...	...	...	2	28	...	...	...	...
33	477½	447½	103½	29	...	...	...	2	28	...	...	...	...
34	479½	447½	101½	29	...	...	...	2	28	...	...	...	...
35	494½	433½	101½	29	...	...	...	1	28	...	...	...	...
36	496½	434½	98½	29	...	...	...	1	28	...	...	...	...
37	496½	432½	100½	29	...	...	...	1	28	...	...	...	...
38	498½	425	106	29	...	...	...	1	28	...	...	...	...
39	501½	422	106	29	...	...	...	1	28	...	...	...	...
40	501½	423	106	28	...	...	...	1	28	...	...	...	...
41	499½	424	106	27	...	...	1	1	28	...	...	1	...
42	494	430	104	27	...	...	½	1	28	...	1	1	1
43	602	329	98½	28	...	...	1	1	27	...	...	...	...
44	629	306	99	27	...	...	...	...	27	...	...	...	...
45	633	306	97	25	...	...	...	...	27	...	...	...	...
46	990	84	...	12	...	...	...	...	...	...	...	...	...

a Add three-fourths.
b Add one-fourth.

Delegation	1916 DEMOCRATIC				1920 DEMOCRATIC									
	Votes	Minority Plank on Woman Suffrage			Votes	Bryan Plank on Prohibition			Cochran Plank on Prohibition			Minority Plank on Ireland		
		Yea	Nay	Not Voting		Yea	Nay	Not Voting	Yea	Nay	Not Voting	Yea	Nay	Not Voting
Alabama	24	1	23	...	24	8	16	...	...	24	...	...	24	...
Arizona	6	...	6	...	6	...	6	...	2	4	...	2	4	...
Arkansas	18	...	18	...	18	...	18	...	...	18	...	...	18	...
California	26	...	26	...	26	7	18	1	5	21	...	5	18	3
Colorado	12	...	12	...	12	...	12	...	...	12	...	...	12	...
Connecticut	14	1	13	...	14	...	14	...	13	1	...	12	2	...
Delaware	6	...	6	...	6	...	6	...	...	6	...	...	6	...
Florida	12	4	8	...	12	...	12	...	1	11	...	2	10	...
Georgia	28	23½	4½	...	28	...	28	...	...	28	...	...	28	...
Idaho	8	...	8	...	8	8	...	...	...	8	...	...	8	...
Illinois	58	1	57	...	58	5	53	...	37	21	...	46	12	...
Indiana	30	24	6	...	30	...	30	...	4	26	...	6	24	...
Iowa	26	...	26	...	26	5	20	1	3	16½	6½	1	25	...
Kansas	20	...	20	...	20	20	...	...	...	20	...	...	20	...
Kentucky	26	...	26	...	26	2	24	...	1	25	...	2	24	...
Louisiana	20	8	12	...	20	...	20	...	1	19	...	2	18	...
Maine	12	...	6	6	12	...	12	...	1	11	...	5	7	...
Maryland	16	16	...	...	16	...	16	...	15½	½	...	8	8	...
Massachusetts	36	6	30	...	36	2	34	...	33	3	...	36	...	...
Michigan	30	...	30	...	30	7	20	3	2	26	2	3	26	1
Minnesota	24	9	15	...	24	5	18	1	3	20	1	9	13	2
Mississippi	20	...	20	...	20	...	20	...	...	20	...	...	20	...
Missouri	36	4	24	3	36	9½	25½	1	9½	23½	3	19½	17½	...
Montana	8	...	8	...	8	3	5	...	3	5	...	3	5	...
Nebraska	16	...	16	...	16	10	6	...	3	13	...	3	13	...
Nevada	6	...	6	...	6	...	6	...	...	6	...	...	6	...
New Hampshire	8	1	7	...	8	1	7	...	...	8	...	2	6	...
New Jersey	28	10	11	7	28	...	28	...	28	...	...	28	...	...
New Mexico	6	...	6	...	6	...	6	...	...	6	...	...	6	...
New York	90	...	90	...	90	3	87	...	78	12	...	80	10	...
North Carolina	24	11	13	...	24	...	24	...	...	24	...	...	24	...
North Dakota	10	...	10	...	10	5	5	...	...	10	...	1	9	...
Ohio	48	20	28	...	48	2	46	...	28	20	...	31	17	...
Oklahoma	20	...	20	...	20	20	...	...	...	20	...	2	18	...
Oregon	10	...	10	...	10	2	8	...	1	9	...	...	10	...
Pennsylvania	76	...	76	...	76	7	67	2	44	32	...	50	26	...
Rhode Island	10	1	9	...	10	...	10	...	7	3	...	9	1	...
South Carolina	18	...	18	...	18	...	18	...	...	18	...	...	18	...
South Dakota	10	...	10	...	10	4	6	...	2	8	...	1	9	...
Tennessee	24	...	24	...	24	...	24	...	...	24	...	...	24	...
Texas	40	32	8	...	40	...	40	...	...	40	...	...	40	...
Utah	8	...	8	...	8	2	6	...	...	8	...	1	7	...
Vermont	8	...	8	...	8	...	8	...	7	1	...	4	4	...
Virginia	24	...	24	...	24	1½	22½	...	1	23	...	5	7	12
Washington	14	...	14	...	14	8½	5½	...	...	14	...	2½	11	½
West Virginia	16	8	8	...	16	2	14	...	3	13	...	5	11	...
Wisconsin	26	...	26	...	26	4	22	...	7	19	...	9	17	...
Wyoming	6	...	6	...	6	...	6	...	...	6	...	...	6	...
Alaska	6	...	6	...	6	2	4	...	4	2	...	2	4	...
Canal Zone	...	...	...	...	2	...	2	...	...	2	...	...	2	...
District of Columbia	6	...	6	...	6	...	6	...	3	2	1	5½	½	...
Hawaii	6	...	6	...	6	...	6	...	6	...	...	...	6	...
Philippine Islands	6	1	4	1	6	...	6	...	...	6	...	...	6	...
Puerto Rico	6	...	6	...	6	...	6	...	...	6	...	...	6	...
Virgin Islands	...	...	...	...	...	...	...	...	...	...	...	...	...	...
Total	1092	181½	888½	22	1094	155½	929½	9	356	724½ a	13½	402½	674 b	18½

Source: *Official Proceedings, 1916.*
Minority Plank on Woman Suffrage, pp. 146-7.

Source: *Official Proceedings, 1920.*
Bryan Plank on Prohibition, pp. 256-7.
Cochran Plank on Prohibition, pp. 259-60.
a/ Sum of column; proceedings record 726½.
Minority Plank on Ireland, pp. 264-5.
b/ Sum of column; proceedings record 676.

Delegation	Votes	First Ballot McAdoo	Cox	Palmer	Smith	Other	Fifth Ballot McAdoo	Cox	Palmer	Other	Seventh Ballot McAdoo	Cox	Palmer	Other	Twelfth Ballot McAdoo	Cox	Palmer	Other
Alabama	24	9	3	6	2	4	12	3	4	5	12	3	4	5	11	3	5	5
Arizona	6	4	1	...	...	1	4	2	...	...	3½	1½	...	1	3	3	...	...
Arkansas	18	3	7	2	...	6	4	11	2	1	4	11	3	...	3	13	2	...
California	26	10	4	3	1	8	16	5	1	4	16	6	1	3	16	7	1	2
Colorado	12	3	...	8	...	1	3	...	8	1	3	...	8	1	3	3	5	1
Connecticut	14	...	...	...	...	14	...	...	...	14	...	...	...	14	1	1	10	2
Delaware	6	4	...	...	...	2	4	1	...	1	4	1	...	1	4	1	...	1
Florida	12	1	...	8	...	3	3	...	7	2	3	2	6	1	3	4	5	...
Georgia	28	...	...	28	...	...	...	...	28	...	...	...	28	...	...	...	28	...
Idaho	8	8	...	...	...	...	8	...	...	...	8	...	...	...	8	...	...	...
Illinois	58	9	9	35	5	...	14	12	32	...	14	12	32	...	14	44	...	...
Indiana	30	...	...	...	...	30	...	4	...	26	2	17	...	11	4	19	1	6
Iowa	26	...	...	...	...	26	...	...	...	26	...	...	26	...	...	...	26	...
Kansas	20	20	...	...	...	...	20	...	...	...	20	...	...	...	20	...	...	...
Kentucky	26	3	23	...	...	...	3	23	...	...	3	23	...	...	3	23	...	...
Louisiana	20	5	2	2	...	11	5	6	1	8	5	8	...	7	5	12	...	3
Maine	12	5	...	5	...	2	6	...	6	...	6	...	6	...	5	...	6	1
Maryland	16	5½	5½	...	...	5	5½	8½	...	2	5½	8½	...	2	5½	8½	...	2
Massachusetts	36	4	4	17	7	4	11	5	16	4	9	5	16	6	3	12	18	3
Michigan	30	15	...	12	...	3	15	1	11	3	16	1	11	2	16	2	11	1
Minnesota	24	10	2	7	...	5	15	2	5	2	15	3	5	1	15	6	2	1
Mississippi	20	...	...	...	...	20	...	20	...	...	...	20	...	...	...	20	...	...
Missouri	36	15½	2½	10	...	8	18½	5½	6	6	18	4½	9½	4	18½	8½	5	4
Montana	8	1	...	...	...	7	8	...	...	...	8	...	...	...	4	4	...	...
Nebraska	16	...	...	...	...	16	2	...	...	14	6	...	...	10	7	...	...	9
Nevada	6	...	6	...	...	...	6	...	...	...	6	...	...	...	6	...	...	...
New Hampshire	8	4	...	1	...	3	4	1	2	1	4	1	2	1	4	2	2	...
New Jersey	28	...	...	...	...	28	...	...	...	28	3	25	...	...	3	25	...	...
New Mexico	6	2	...	1	...	3	5	...	1	...	6	...	...	...	6	...	...	...
New York	90	...	...	...	90	...	...	...	...	90	16	68	2	4	17	72	...	1
North Carolina	24	...	...	...	...	24	24	...	...	...	24	...	...	...	24	...	...	...
North Dakota	10	6	1	2	...	1	8	1	1	...	7	2	1	...	7	2	1	...
Ohio	48	...	48	...	...	...	...	48	...	...	...	48	...	...	...	48	...	...
Oklahoma	20	...	...	...	...	20	...	...	...	20	...	...	...	20	...	...	...	20
Oregon	10	10	...	...	...	...	10	...	...	...	10	...	...	...	10	...	...	...
Pennsylvania	76	2	...	73	...	1	2	...	74	...	2	1	73	...	2	1	73	...
Rhode Island	10	2	...	5	2	1	1	2	4	3	1	2	4	3	1	5	3	1
South Carolina	18	18	...	...	...	...	18	...	...	...	18	...	...	...	18	...	...	...
South Dakota	10	...	...	...	...	10	...	...	10	...	4	...	6	...	4	1	4	1
Tennessee	24	2	8	9	...	5	4	9	6	5	4	10	5	5	5	10	4	5
Texas	40	40	...	...	...	...	40	...	...	...	40	...	...	...	40	...	...	...
Utah	8	8	...	...	...	...	8	...	...	...	8	...	...	...	8	...	...	...
Vermont	8	4	2	1	1	...	4	2	2	...	4	2	2	...	4	3	1	...
Virginia	24	...	...	...	...	24	...	...	...	24	...	...	...	24	...	...	...	24
Washington	14	10	...	...	...	4	11	1	...	2	11	1	...	2	9½	4	...	½
West Virginia	16	...	...	...	...	16	...	...	...	16	...	...	...	16	...	...	...	16
Wisconsin	26	11	5	3	1	6	19	7	...	...	19	7	...	...	19	7	...	...
Wyoming	6	6	...	...	...	...	6	...	...	...	6	...	...	...	6	...	...	...
Alaska	6	2	1	3	...	...	2	1	3	...	2	1	3	...	2	1	3	...
Canal Zone	2	1	...	1	...	...	1	...	1	...	1	...	1	...	1	...	1	...
District of Columbia	6	...	...	6	...	...	...	...	6	...	...	...	6	...	...	...	6	...
Hawaii	6	2	...	4	...	...	2	...	4	...	2	...	4	...	2	2	2	...
Philippine Islands	6	...	...	...	...	6	4	...	1	1	4	1	1	...	4	1	...	1
Puerto Rico	6	1	...	2	...	3	1	...	2	3	1	...	2	3	1	...	2	3
Virgin Islands	...																	
Total	1094	266	134	254a	109	331b	357	181	244	312c	384	295½	267½	147d	375½	404	201	113½e

Source: *Official Proceedings, 1920.*
Presidential Ballots. First, pp. 267-9.
a/ Sum of column; proceedings record 256.
b/ Other candidates: Homer S. Gerard, 25; James W. Gerard, 21; Robert L. Owen, 33; Gilbert M. Hitchcock, 18; Edwin T. Meredith, 27; Edward I. Edwards, 42; John W. Davis, 32; Carter Glass, 26½; Furnifold M. Simmons, 24; Francis B. Harrison, 6; John S. Williams, 20; Thomas R. Marshall, 37; Champ Clark, 9; Oscar W. Underwood, ½; William R. Hearst, 1; William J. Bryan, 1; Bainbridge Colby, 1; Josephus Daniels, 1; Wood, 4.
Fifth ballot, pp. 287-9.
c/ Other candidates: Cummings, 21; Owen, 34; Hitchcock, 5; Meredith, 27; Smith, 95; Edwards, 31; Davis, 29; Glass, 27; Marshall, 29; Clark, 9; not voting, 14.
Seventh ballot, pp. 295-7.
d/ Other candidates: Cummings, 19; Owen, 35; Smith, 4; Edwards, 2; Davis, 33; Glass, 27; Marshall, 14; Clark, 8; not voting, 6.

Twelfth ballot, pp. 315-7.
e/ Other candidates: Cummings, 8; Owen, 34; Davis, 31½; Glass, 25; Marshall, 7; Clark, 4; Gerard, 1; not voting, 20.

Delegation	Votes	Presidential Fifteenth Ballot				Motion to Recess			Presidential Twentieth Ballot				Motion to Adjourn		
		McAdoo	Cox	Palmer	Other	Yea	Nay	Not Voting	McAdoo	Cox	Palmer	Other	Yea	Nay	Not Voting
Alabama	24	10	9	...	5	3	17	4	8	10	...	6	...	24	...
Arizona	6	1	5	...	...	6	...	...	1	2	...	3	3	3	...
Arkansas	18	1	15	2	...	1	17	...	1	15	2	...	...	18	...
California	26	17	7	...	2	20	2	4	11	11	...	4	...	26	...
Colorado	12	3	8	...	1	12	...	...	3	4	3	2	...	12	...
Connecticut	14	...	...	...	14	12	1	1	...	6	4	4	6	8	...
Delaware	6	2	4	...	...	6	...	...	4	2	...	...	1	5	...
Florida	12	3	9	...	...	12	...	...	3	9	...	...	1	11	...
Georgia	28	...	...	28	...	28	...	...	...	...	28	...	28	...	...
Idaho	8	8	...	...	...	8	...	...	8	...	...	...	...	8	...
Illinois	58	14	42	2	...	10	48	...	14	40	2	2	30	28	...
Indiana	30	...	30	...	...	...	30	...	11	19	...	...	...	30	...
Iowa	26	...	26	...	...	...	26	...	...	26	...	...	...	26	...
Kansas	20	20	...	...	...	20	...	...	20	...	...	...	20	...	...
Kentucky	26	3	23	...	...	8	16	2	3	21	...	2	10	14	2
Louisiana	20	4	14	...	2	3	17	...	1	19	...	...	...	20	...
Maine	12	6	...	6	...	12	...	...	5	...	6	1	6	6	...
Maryland	16	5½	8½	...	2	7	7	2	5½	8½	...	2	8	8	...
Massachusetts	36	...	14	19	3	21	14	1	...	14	18	4	22	13	1
Michigan	30	15	4	10	1	26	3	1	15	6	8	1	23	6	1
Minnesota	24	14	5	4	1	20	3	1	14	5	4	1	9	11	4
Mississippi	20	...	20	...	...	...	20	...	...	20	...	...	...	20	...
Missouri	36	19½	13½	...	3	24	9	3	17	6	7	6	29	6	1
Montana	8	4	4	...	...	...	8	...	4	4	...	...	...	8	...
Nebraska	16	6	1	...	9	12	4	...	2	5	...	9	...	16	...
Nevada	6	...	6	...	...	6	...	...	...	6	...	...	...	6	...
New Hampshire	8	4	2	2	...	6	2	...	5	2	1	...	...	8	...
New Jersey	28	...	28	...	...	...	28	...	...	28	...	...	...	28	...
New Mexico	6	6	...	...	...	6	...	...	6	...	...	...	...	6	...
New York	90	17	73	...	...	14	76	...	16	73	...	1	13	77	...
North Carolina	24	24	...	...	...	24	...	...	24	...	...	...	24	...	...
North Dakota	10	6	3	1	...	10	...	...	6	2	1	1	10	...	...
Ohio	48	...	48	...	...	...	48	...	...	48	...	...	...	48	...
Oklahoma	20	...	...	...	20	20	...	...	...	...	...	20	20	...	...
Oregon	10	10	...	...	...	10	...	...	10	...	...	...	9	1	...
Pennsylvania	76	2	1	73	...	76	...	...	2	...	74	...	75	1	...
Rhode Island	10	...	6	3	1	4	5	1	1	5	3	1	1	9	...
South Carolina	18	18	...	...	...	18	...	...	18	...	...	...	18	...	...
South Dakota	10	4	5	1	...	10	...	...	6	2	1	1	...	10	...
Tennessee	24	4	12	3	5	24	...	...	10	8	2	4	...	24	...
Texas	40	40	...	...	...	40	...	...	40	...	...	...	40	...	...
Utah	8	8	...	...	...	5	3	...	8	...	...	...	...	8	...
Vermont	8	4	3	1	...	1	7	...	...	7	1	...	1	7	...
Virginia	24	...	...	...	24	20	4	...	...	...	...	24	20	4	...
Washington	14	7½	5½	...	1	6	8	...	7	6	...	1	2	12	...
West Virginia	16	...	...	...	16	...	16	...	...	...	...	16	...	16	...
Wisconsin	26	19	7	...	...	16	10	...	16	10	...	...	2	24	...
Wyoming	6	6	...	...	...	6	...	...	6	...	...	...	6	...	...
Alaska	6	2	1	3	...	6	...	...	2	1	3	...	...	6	...
Canal Zone	2	1	...	1	...	2	...	...	1	...	1	...	...	2	...
District of Columbia	6	...	...	6	...	6	...	...	...	...	6	...	6	...	...
Hawaii	6	1	5	...	...	6	...	...	1	5	...	...	...	6	...
Philippine Islands	6	4	1	...	1	6	...	...	4	1	1	...	2	4	...
Puerto Rico	6	1	...	2	3	...	6	...	1	...	2	3	2	4	...
Virgin Islands	...	...	...	...	...	...	...	...	...	...	...	...	...	...	...
Total	1094	344½	468½	167	114[a]	619	455	20	340½	456½	178	119[b]	447	638	9

Source: *Official Proceedings, 1920.*
Fifteenth ballot, pp. 328-30.
a/ Other candidates: Cummings, 19; Owen, 31; Davis, 32; Glass, 25; Clark, 4; not voting, 4.
Motion to recess, pp. 337-8.
Twentieth ballot, pp. 346-8.
b/ Other candidates: Cummings, 10; Owen, 41; Davis, 36; Glass, 26; Clark, 2; Gerard, 1; not voting, 3.
Motion to adjourn, pp. 349-50.

		1920 DEMOCRATIC														
		Presidential								Motion to Eliminate Lowest Candidate			Presidential			
		Twenty-fifth Ballot				Thirtieth Ballot							Thirty-fifth Ballot			
Delegation	Votes	McAdoo	Cox	Palmer	Other	McAdoo	Cox	Palmer	Other	Yea	Nay	Not Voting	McAdoo	Cox	Palmer	Other
Alabama	24	8	3	...	13	12	7	...	5	2	22	...	10	5	4	5
Arizona	6	3	3	...	...	3	2	...	1	...	6	...	3	2	...	1
Arkansas	18	2	15	1	...	3	14	1	...	18	...	...	3	14	1	...
California	26	10	14	1	1	10	13	1	2	...	26	...	15	9	2	...
Colorado	12	5	6	...	1	5	6	...	1	...	12	...	5	6	...	1
Connecticut	14	1	6	5	2	1	6	4	3	...	14	...	1	6	5	2
Delaware	6	2	4	...	...	4	2	...	...	...	6	...	4	2	...	...
Florida	12	3	9	...	...	3	9	...	...	1	11	...	3	9	...	...
Georgia	28	...	...	28	...	...	...	28	...	...	28	...	...	...	28	...
Idaho	8	8	...	...	...	8	...	...	...	...	8	...	8	...	...	...
Illinois	58	22	35	1	...	21	36	1	...	30	28	...	19	33	6	...
Indiana	30	11	19	...	...	29	...	...	1	12	18	...	29	1	...	...
Iowa	26	...	26	...	...	...	26	...	...	...	26	...	...	26	...	...
Kansas	20	20	...	...	...	20	...	...	...	...	20	...	20	...	...	...
Kentucky	26	5	20	...	1	5	20	...	1	8	12½	5½	8	16	1	1
Louisiana	20	2	13	...	5	4	14	...	2	11	6	3	7	12	...	1
Maine	12	6	...	5	1	7	...	5	...	3	9	...	7	...	5	...
Maryland	16	5½	8½	...	2	5½	8½	...	2	1	15	...	5½	8½	...	2
Massachusetts	36	1	13	19	3	2	15	16	3	12	24	...	2	13	18	3
Michigan	30	13	7	10	...	15	6	9	...	4	23	3	16	5	9	...
Minnesota	24	14	4	4	2	14	4	4	2	2	21	1	14	4	4	2
Mississippi	20	...	20	...	...	...	20	...	...	...	20	...	...	20	...	...
Missouri	36	18	7	5	6	18	6	5	7	29	6	1	16½	4	10½	5
Montana	8	8	...	...	...	8	...	...	...	8	...	...	8	...	...	...
Nebraska	16	7	...	...	9	7	...	...	9	1	15	...	7	...	...	9
Nevada	6	...	6	...	...	...	6	...	...	...	6	...	...	6	...	...
New Hampshire	8	5	2	1	...	5	2	1	...	...	5	3	5	2	1	...
New Jersey	28	...	28	...	...	...	28	...	...	28	...	...	...	28	...	...
New Mexico	6	5	...	...	1	6	...	...	...	...	6	...	6	...	...	...
New York	90	20	70	...	...	20	70	...	...	70	20	...	20	70	...	...
North Carolina	24	24	...	...	...	24	...	...	...	1	23	...	24	...	...	...
North Dakota	10	8	2	...	...	8	2	...	...	...	10	...	9	1	...	...
Ohio	48	...	48	...	...	...	48	...	...	...	48	...	...	48	...	...
Oklahoma	20	...	...	...	20	...	...	...	20	...	20	...	...	...	...	20
Oregon	10	10	...	...	...	10	...	...	...	2	8	...	10	...	...	...
Pennsylvania	76	2	1	73	...	2	1	73	...	...	76	...	2	1	73	...
Rhode Island	10	...	4	3	3	3	4	3	...	...	10	...	...	3	3	4
South Carolina	18	18	...	...	...	18	...	...	...	...	18	...	18	...	...	...
South Dakota	10	6	4	...	...	6	4	...	...	...	10	...	5	2	...	3
Tennessee	24	...	...	...	24	...	...	...	24	...	24	...	...	...	24	...
Texas	40	40	...	...	...	40	...	...	...	...	40	...	40	...	...	...
Utah	8	8	...	...	...	8	...	...	...	...	8	...	8	...	...	...
Vermont	8	1	6	1	...	1	6	1	...	2	6	...	3	3	2	...
Virginia	24	...	...	...	24	...	...	...	24	...	24	...	2	2	12	8
Washington	14	8	5½	...	½	14	...	...	...	7	6	1	12	...	1½	½
West Virginia	16	...	...	...	16	...	...	...	16	...	16	...	...	...	...	16
Wisconsin	26	19	7	...	...	19	7	...	...	5	21	...	19	7	...	...
Wyoming	6	6	...	...	...	6	...	...	...	...	6	...	6	...	...	...
Alaska	6	2	1	3	...	2	1	3	...	6	...	...	2	1	3	...
Canal Zone	2	1	...	1	...	1	...	1	...	...	2	...	1	...	1	...
District of Columbia	6	...	...	6	...	...	...	6	...	...	6	...	...	...	6	...
Hawaii	6	1	5	...	...	1	5	...	...	1	5	...	1	5	...	...
Philippine Islands	6	4	2	...	...	3	2	1	...	...	6	...	3	2	...	1
Puerto Rico	6	2	...	2	2	2	...	2	2	...	6	...	2	...	2	2
Virgin Islands	...	...	...	...	...	...	...	...	...	...	...	...	...	...	...	...
Total	1094	364½	424	169	136½a	403½	400½	165	125b	264c	812½d	17½	409	376½	222	86½e

Source: *Official Proceedings, 1920.*
Twenty-fifth ballot, pp. 362-4.
a/ Other candidates: Cummings, 4; Owen, 34; Davis, 58½; Glass, 25; Clark, 2; Underwood, 9; John J. Pershing, 1; not voting, 3.
Thirtieth ballot, pp. 379-80.
b/ Other candidates: Cummings, 4; Owen, 33; Davis, 58; Glass, 24; Clark, 2; Underwood, 2; not voting, 2.
Motion to eliminate lowest candidate, pp. 382-3.
c/ Sum of column; proceedings record 256.
d/ Sum of column; proceedings record 820½.
Thirty-fifth ballot, pp. 395-6.
e/ Other candidates: Davis, 33; Owen, 38½; Cummings, 3; Glass, 5; Clark, 2; not voting, 5.

		1920 DEMOCRATIC														
		Presidential 39th Ballot			Motion to Adjourn			Presidential 42nd Ballot			43rd Ballot			44th Ballot		
Delegation	Votes	McAdoo	Cox	Other	Yea	Nay	Not Voting	McAdoo	Cox	Other	McAdoo	Cox	Other	McAdoo	Cox	Other
Alabama	24	8	...	16	6	11	7	8	15	1	10	11	3	8	13	3
Arizona	6	4	2	...	6	...	...	2½	3½	...	2½	3½	...	2½	3½	...
Arkansas	18	4	14	...	...	18	...	3	15	...	3	15	...	...	18	...
California	26	14	12	...	20	6	...	14	12	...	14	12	...	13	13	...
Colorado	12	4	7	1	...	12	...	4	7	1	4	7	1	3	9	...
Connecticut	14	3	10	1	1	13	...	2	11	1	2	11	1	2	12	...
Delaware	6	4	2	...	5	1	...	4	2	...	4	2	...	3	3	...
Florida	12	3	9	...	...	12	...	3	9	...	3	9	...	...	12	...
Georgia	28	28	...	...	...	28	...	...	28	...	...	28	...	...	28	...
Idaho	8	8	...	...	8	...	...	8	...	...	8	...	...	8	...	...
Illinois	58	18	38	2	...	58	...	17	40	1	17	40	1	13	44	1
Indiana	30	11	19	...	...	30	...	11	19	...	10	20	...	...	30	...
Iowa	26	...	26	...	...	26	...	...	26	...	...	26	...	...	26	...
Kansas	20	20	...	...	20	...	...	20	...	...	20	...	...	20	...	...
Kentucky	26	5	20	1	10	16	...	4	22	...	3	23	...	...	26	...
Louisiana	20	7	12	1	5	9	6	6	13	1	...	20	...	...	20	...
Maine	12	12	...	...	6	5	1	12	...	...	12	...	...	5	5	2
Maryland	16	5½	8½	2	...	16	...	3½	8½	4	5½	8½	2	...	13½	2½
Massachusetts	36	1	33	2	1	35	...	2	30	4	2	30	4	...	35	1
Michigan	30	14	12	4	25	5	...	14	16	...	14	16	...	...	...	30
Minnesota	24	16	7	1	3	16	5	17	6	1	15	8	1	15	8	1
Mississippi	20	...	20	...	...	20	...	...	20	...	...	20	...	...	20	...
Missouri	36	20½	11½	4	22	13	1	20½	11½	4	19½	12½	4	17	18	1
Montana	8	8	...	...	8	...	...	6	2	...	5	3	...	2	6	...
Nebraska	16	7	...	9	10	6	...	7	...	9	3	4	9	2	5	9
Nevada	6	...	6	...	...	6	...	...	6	...	...	6	...	...	6	...
New Hampshire	8	5	2	1	...	5	3	6	2	...	6	2	...	6	2	...
New Jersey	28	...	28	...	...	28	...	...	28	...	...	28	...	...	28	...
New Mexico	6	6	...	...	6	...	...	6	...	...	6	...	...	6	...	...
New York	90	20	70	...	20	70	...	20	70	...	20	70	...	20	70	...
North Carolina	24	24	...	...	24	...	...	24	...	...	23	...	1	24	...	...
North Dakota	10	9	1	...	7	1	2	8	2	...	8	2	...	4	2	4
Ohio	48	...	48	...	...	48	...	...	48	...	...	48	...	...	48	...
Oklahoma	20	...	...	20	20	...	...	...	...	20	...	...	20	...	...	20
Oregon	10	10	...	...	10	...	...	10	...	...	10	...	...	10	...	...
Pennsylvania	76	2	1	73	48	18	10	49	14	13	47	17	12	4	68	4
Rhode Island	10	1	7	2	...	10	...	1	8	1	1	9	...	1	9	...
South Carolina	18	18	...	...	18	...	...	18	...	...	18	...	...	18	...	...
South Dakota	10	6	3	1	4	4	2	3	5	2	3	5	2	3	5	2
Tennessee	24	...	...	24	9	12	3	...	...	24	...	...	24	...	...	24
Texas	40	40	...	...	40	...	...	40	...	...	40	...	...	40	...	...
Utah	8	8	...	...	...	8	...	8	...	...	8	...	...	7	1	...
Vermont	8	4	4	...	1	7	...	4	4	...	4	4	...	...	8	...
Virginia	24	10	11	3	6	18	...	...	...	24	4	10½	9½	2½	18½	3
Washington	14	11	2½	½	6	8	...	5½	8	½	6½	7	½	...	13	1
West Virginia	16	...	...	16	1	15	...	...	...	16	...	...	16	...	...	16
Wisconsin	26	19	7	...	7	8	11	17	9	...	19	7	...	3	23	...
Wyoming	6	6	...	...	6	...	...	6	...	...	3	3	...	3	3	...
Alaska	6	4	2	...	6	...	...	2	4	...	2	4	...	...	6	...
Canal Zone	2	2	...	...	2	...	...	2	...	...	2	...	...	2	...	...
District of Columbia	6	...	6	...	...	6	...	...	6	...	...	6	...	...	6	...
Hawaii	6	1	5	...	...	6	...	1	5	...	1	5	...	...	6	...
Philippine Islands	6	3	2	1	6	...	...	3	2	1	3	2	1	2	4	...
Puerto Rico	6	6	...	...	3	3	...	3	3	...	1	3	2	1	5	...
Virgin Islands	...	...	...	...	...	...	...	...	...	...	...	...	...	...	...	...
Total	1094	440	468½	185½[a]	406	637	51	425[b]	540½	128½[c]	412	568	114[d]	270	699½	124½[e]

Source: *Official Proceedings, 1920.*
Thirty-ninth ballot, pp. 406-7.
a/ Other candidates: Palmer, 74; Davis, 71½; Owen, 32; Cummings, 2; Clark, 2; Colby, 1; not voting, 3.
Motion to adjourn, pp. 412-3.
Forty-second ballot, pp. 414-5.
b/ Sum of column; proceedings record 427.
c/ Other candidates: Palmer, 8; Davis, 49½; Owen, 34; Cummings, 3; Glass, 24; Clark, 2; Colby, 1; not voting, 6.
Forty-third ballot, pp. 416-7.
d/ Other candidates: Palmer, 7; Davis, 57½; Owen, 34; Cummings, 2; Glass, 5½; Clark, 2; Colby, 1; not voting, 5.
Forty-fourth ballot, pp. 418-9.
e/ Other candidates: Palmer, 1; Davis, 52; Owen, 34; Glass, 1½; Colby, 1; not voting, 36.

1920 DEMOCRATIC

Recapitulation of Presidential Ballots

Ballot	Cox	McAdoo	Palmer	Smith	Cummings	Gerard	Owen	Hitchcock	Meredith	Edwards	Davis	Glass	Marshall	Clark	Other
1	134	266	256	109	25	21	33	18	27	42	32	26½	37	9	58½
2	159	289	264	101	27	12	29	16	26	34	31½	25½	36	6	34
3	177	323½	251½	92	26	11	22	16	26	32½	28½	27	36	7	8
4	178	335	254	96	24	2	32	5	28	31	31	27	34	8	1
5	181	357	244	95	21	...	34	5	27	31	29	27	29	9	2
6	195	368½	265½	98	20	...	36	...	...	30	29	27	13	7	1
7	295½	384	267½	4	19	...	35	...	...	2	33	27	14	8	...
8	315	380	262	2	18	1	36	...	...	...	32	27	12	6	...
9	321½	386	257	1	18	1	37	...	...	...	32	25	7	5	...
10	321	385	257	....	19	2	37	...	...	...	34	25	7	4	...
11	332	380	255	....	19	1	35	...	...	...	33	25	7	4	...
12	404	375½	201	....	8	1	34	...	...	...	31½	25	7	4	...
13	428½	363½	193½	....	7	...	32	...	...	...	29½	25	7	4	...
14	443½	355½	182	....	7	...	34	...	...	...	33	25	7	4	...
15	468½	344½	167	....	19	...	31	...	...	...	32	25	...	4	...
16	454½	337	164½	....	20	...	34	...	...	...	52	25	...	4	...
17	442	332	176	....	19	...	36	...	...	...	57	27	...	2	...
18	458	330½	174½	....	19	...	38	...	...	...	42	26	...	2	...
19	468	327½	179½	....	19	1	37	...	...	...	31	26	...	2	...
20	456½	340½	178	....	10	1	41	...	...	...	36	26	...	2	...
21	426½	395½	144	....	7	...	36	...	...	...	54	26	...	2	...
22	430	372½	166½	....	6	...	35	...	...	...	52	25	...	2	2
23	425	364½	181½	....	5	...	34	...	...	...	50½	25	...	2	2
24	429	364½	177	....	5	...	33	...	...	...	54½	25	...	2	1
25	424	364½	169	....	4	...	34	...	...	...	58½	25	...	2	10
26	424½	371	167	....	3	...	33	...	...	...	55½	25	...	3	10
27	423½	371½	166½	....	3	...	34	...	...	...	60½	25	1	2	5
28	423	368½	165½	....	4	...	35½	...	...	...	62½	24	...	2	7
29	404½	394½	166	....	4	...	33	...	...	...	63	24	...	2	1
30	400½	403½	165	....	4	...	33	...	...	...	58	24	...	2	...
31	391½	415½	174	....	3	...	34	...	...	...	57½	12½	1	2	1
32	391	421	176	....	3	...	34	...	...	...	55½	9½	...	2	...
33	380½	421	180	....	3	...	34	...	...	...	56	13	...	2½	...
34	379½	420½	184	....	3	...	37	...	...	...	54	7½	...	2½	1
35	376½	409	222	....	3	...	38½	...	...	...	33	5	...	2	...
36	377	399	241	....	3	...	36	...	...	...	28	4	...	2	1
37	386	405	202½	....	3	...	33	...	...	...	50½	1	...	2	8
38	383½	405½	211	....	4	...	33	...	...	...	50	1	...	3	...
39	468½	440	74	....	2	...	32	...	...	...	71½	...	...	2	1
40	490	467	19	....	2	...	33	...	...	...	76	...	...	2	1
41	497½	460	12	....	2	...	35	...	...	...	55½	24	...	2	1
42	540½	427	8	....	3	...	34	...	...	...	49½	24	...	2	1
43	568	412	7	....	2	...	34	...	...	...	57½	5½	...	2	1
44	699½	270	1	....	...	...	34	...	...	...	52	1½	...	...	1

Other Candidates

Ballot	
1	Simmons 24, Williams 20, Harrison 6, Wood 4, Hearst 1, Bryan 1, Colby 1, Daniels 1, Underwood ½.
2	Simmons 25, Harrison 7, Bryan 1, Daniels 1.
3	Harrison 6, Bryan 1, Daniels 1.
4	Bryan 1.
5	Colby 2.
6	Colby 1.
22	Wilson 2.
23	Cobb 1½, Lardner ½.
24	Underwood 1.
25	Underwood 9, Pershing 1.
26	Underwood 9, Jones 1.
27	Underwood 4, Robinson 1.
28	Underwood 6, Hines 1.
29	Underwood 1.
30	Underwood 2.
31	Daniels 1.
34	Mrs. Clay 1.
36	Mrs. Stewart 1.
37	Mrs. Adams 1, Bonniwell 1, Lewis 6.
39	Colby 1.
40	Colby 1.
41	Colby 1.
42	Colby 1.
43	Colby 1.
44	Colby 1.

1924 DEMOCRATIC

Delegation	Votes	Motion to Adjourn (before changes)			Motion to Adjourn (after changes)			Minority Plank on League of Nations			Minority Plank on Ku Klux Klan			Presidential First Ballot		
		Yea	Nay	Not Voting	Yea	Nay	Not Voting	Yea	Nay	Not Voting	Yea	Nay	Not Voting	McAdoo	Smith	Other
Alabama	24	24	...	...	24	...	...	12½	11½	...	24	...	...	...	...	24
Arizona	6	6	...	...	1½	1	3½	1½	4½	...	1	5	...	4½	...	1½
Arkansas	18	18	...	...	18	...	...	3	15	...	...	18	...	...	...	18
California	26	...	26	...	...	26	...	4	22	...	7	19	...	26	...	...
Colorado	12	12	...	...	12	...	...	9½	2½	...	6	6	...	...	...	12
Connecticut	14	6	8	...	6	8	...	5	9	...	13	1	...	...	6	8
Delaware	6	6	...	...	6	...	...	6	...	...	6	...	...	...	...	6
Florida	12	...	12	...	...	12	...	5	7	...	1	11	...	12	...	...
Georgia	28	...	28	...	...	28	...	...	28	...	1	19½	7½	28	...	...
Idaho	8	8	...	...	...	8	...	8	...	...	...	8	...	8	...	...
Illinois	58	58	...	...	58	...	...	10	48	...	45	13	...	12	15	31
Indiana	30	10	20	...	10	20	...	...	30	...	5	25	...	...	...	30
Iowa	26	...	26	...	...	26	...	...	26	...	13½	12½	...	26	...	...
Kansas	20	...	20	...	...	20	...	...	20	...	...	20	...	...	...	20
Kentucky	26	...	26	...	...	26	...	9½	16½	...	9½	16½	...	26	...	...
Louisiana	20	...	20	...	...	20	...	...	20	...	...	20	...	...	...	20
Maine	12	...	12	...	3	6	3	11	1	...	8	4	...	2	3½	6½
Maryland	16	16	...	...	16	...	...	...	16	...	16	...	...	...	...	16
Massachusetts	36	35½	...	½	35½	...	½	8	28	...	35½	...	½	1½	33	1½
Michigan	30	30	...	...	30	...	...	6	24	...	12½	16½	1	...	...	30
Minnesota	24	24	...	...	24	...	...	10	14	...	17	7	...	5	10	9
Mississippi	20	...	20	...	...	20	...	...	20	...	...	20	...	...	...	20
Missouri	36	...	36	...	...	36	...	2	34	...	10½	25½	...	36	...	...
Montana	8	...	8	...	...	8	...	...	8	...	1	7	...	7	1	...
Nebraska	16	12	4	...	12	4	...	...	16	...	3	13	...	1	...	15
Nevada	6	...	6	...	...	6	...	...	6	...	...	6	...	6	...	...
New Hampshire	8	1	7	...	1	7	...	8	...	...	2½	5½	...	...	...	8
New Jersey	28	28	...	...	28	...	...	...	28	...	28	...	...	...	...	28
New Mexico	6	...	6	...	...	6	...	...	6	...	1	5	...	6	...	...
New York	90	90	...	...	90	...	...	35	55	...	90	...	...	...	90	...
North Carolina	24	...	24	...	...	24	...	6	18	...	3[a]	20[b]	...	24	...	...
North Dakota	10	10	...	...	...	10	...	1	9	...	10	...	...	10	...	...
Ohio	48	48	...	...	47	1	...	48	...	...	32½	15½	...	...	...	48
Oklahoma	20	...	20	...	...	20	...	...	20	...	...	20	...	20	...	...
Oregon	10	...	10	...	...	10	...	1	9	...	...	10	...	10	...	...
Pennsylvania	76	40	20½	15½	40	20½	15½	52	22	2	49½	24½	2	25½	35½	15
Rhode Island	10	10	...	...	10	...	...	...	10	...	10	...	...	...	10	...
South Carolina	18	...	18	...	...	18	...	18	...	...	...	18	...	18	...	...
South Dakota	10	...	10	...	...	10	...	...	10	...	6	4	...	10	...	...
Tennessee	24	...	24	...	...	24	...	15	9.	...	3	21	...	24	...	...
Texas	40	...	40	...	...	40	...	...	40	...	...	40	...	40	...	...
Utah	8	...	8	...	...	8	...	5½	2½	...	4	4	...	8	...	...
Vermont	8	8	...	...	...	8	...	2	6	...	8	...	...	1	7	...
Virginia	24	24	...	...	24	...	...	24	...	...	2½	21½	...	24	...	...
Washington	14	...	14	...	...	14	...	...	14	...	...	14	...	14	...	...
West Virginia	16	16	...	...	16	...	...	16	...	...	7	9	...	...	...	16
Wisconsin	26	25	1	...	25	1	...	4	22	...	25	1	...	3	23	...
Wyoming	6	...	6	...	...	6	...	3	3	...	2	4	...	...	...	6
Alaska	6	2	...	4	2	...	4	1	5	...	6	...	...	1	3	2
Canal Zone	6	...	6	...	...	6	...	...	6	...	2	4	...	6	...	...
District of Columbia	6	...	6	...	...	6	...	...	6	...	6	...	...	6	...	...
Hawaii	6	...	6	...	...	6	...	...	6	...	4	2	...	1	1	4
Philippine Islands	6	6	...	...	6	...	...	2	4	...	2	2	2	3	3	...
Puerto Rico	6	6	...	...	6	...	...	1	5	...	2	4	...	...	...	6
Virgin Islands	...	...	...	...	...	...	...	...	...	...	...	...	...	...	...	...
Total	1098	579½	499	19½	559	513	26	353½	742½	2	542[c]	543[d]	12½	431½	241	425½[e]

Source: *Official Proceedings, 1924.*
Motion to adjourn (before changes), pp. 157-60.
Motion to adjourn (after changes), pp. 163-4.
Minority plank on League of Nations, pp. 277-8.
Minority plank on Ku Klux Klan, pp. 309-10.
a/ Add seventeen-twentieths.
b/ Add three-twentieths.
c/ Add seven-twentieths.
d/ Add three-twentieths.
Presidential Ballots. First, pp. 338-40.
e/ Other candidates: Oscar W. Underwood, 42½; Joseph T. Robinson, 21; Willard Saulsbury, 7; Samuel M, Ralston, 30; Jonathan M. Davis, 20; Albert C. Ritchie, 22½; Woodbridge N. Ferris, 30; James M. Cox, 59; Charles W. Bryan, 18; Fred H. Brown, 17; George S. Silzer, 38; Carter Glass, 25; John W. Davis, 31; William E. Sweet, 12; Patrick Harrison, 43½; Houston Thompson, 1; John B. Kendrick, 6.

		1924 DEMOCRATIC																
		Presidential																
		Tenth Ballot			Twentieth Ballot				Thirtieth Ballot				Thirty-ninth Ballot			Fiftieth Ballot		
Delegation	Votes	McAdoo	Smith	Other	McAdoo	Smith	Davis	Other	McAdoo	Smith	Davis	Other	McAdoo	Smith	Other	McAdoo	Smith	Other
Alabama	24	...	...	24	...	...	...	24	...	...	...	24	...	...	24	...	...	24
Arizona	6	3½	...	2½	3½	...	1	1½	3½	...	1	1½	3½	...	2½	3½	...	2½
Arkansas	18	...	...	18	...	...	...	18	...	...	...	18	...	...	18	...	...	18
California	26	26	...	...	26	...	...	...	26	...	...	...	26	...	...	26	...	...
Colorado	12	4½	2	5½	4	3	4	1	5	3½	2½	1	3½	3½	5	4	3	5
Connecticut	14	2[a]	10½	1[b]	2	12	...	...	2	12	...	...	2	12	...	4	10	...
Delaware	6	...	...	6	...	...	...	6	...	...	...	6	...	...	6	...	...	6
Florida	12	12	...	...	11	1	...	...	10	1	...	1	10	1	1	10	1	1
Georgia	28	28	...	...	28	...	...	...	28	...	...	...	28	...	...	28	...	...
Idaho	8	8	...	...	8	...	...	...	8	...	...	...	8	...	...	8	...	...
Illinois	58	13	18	27	13	18	4	23	13	20	4	21	13	20	25	13	20	25
Indiana	30	...	...	30	...	...	...	30	...	...	...	30	...	...	30	...	...	30
Iowa	26	26	...	...	26	...	...	...	26	...	...	...	26	...	...	26	...	...
Kansas	20	20	...	...	20	...	...	...	20	...	...	...	20	...	...	20	...	...
Kentucky	26	26	...	...	26	...	...	...	26	...	...	...	26	...	...	26	...	...
Louisiana	20	...	...	20	...	...	20	...	...	...	20	...	...	...	20	...	...	20
Maine	12	2	4½	5½	2	4½	...	5½	2	4½	...	5½	2	4½	5½	2½	4½	5
Maryland	16	...	...	16	...	...	...	16	...	...	...	16	...	...	16	...	...	16
Massachusetts	36	2½	33	½	2½	33	...	½	2½	33	...	½	2½	33½	...	2½	33½	...
Michigan	30	12½	5	12½	11½	10½	5	3	11	11	7	1	15	11	4	15	15	...
Minnesota	24	5	13	6	5	15	2	2	5	15	2	2	6	15	3	6	15	3
Mississippi	20	...	...	20	...	...	20	...	...	...	20	...	20	...	...	...	...	20
Missouri	36	36	...	...	...	...	36	...	...	...	36	...	36	...	...	36	...	...
Montana	8	7	1	...	7	1	...	...	7	1	...	...	7	1	...	7	1	...
Nebraska	16	4	3	9	5	1	...	10	12	3	...	1	12	3	1	13	3	...
Nevada	6	6	...	...	6	...	...	...	6	...	...	...	6	...	...	6	...	...
New Hampshire	8	...	...	8	1	1	...	6	3	3½	...	1½	4	4	...	4½	3½	...
New Jersey	28	...	28	...	...	28	...	...	...	28	...	...	...	28	...	...	28	...
New Mexico	6	6	...	...	6	...	...	...	6	...	...	...	6	...	...	6	...	...
New York	90	...	90	...	...	90	...	...	...	90	...	...	2	88	...	2	88	...
North Carolina	24	24	...	...	24	...	...	...	20	1	3	...	20	...	4	17	...	7
North Dakota	10	5	4	1	5	4	1	...	5	5	...	...	5	5	...	5	5	...
Ohio	48	...	...	48	...	...	...	48	...	...	...	48	...	...	48	...	...	48
Oklahoma	20	20	...	...	20	...	...	...	...	...	...	20	20	...	...	...	...	20
Oregon	10	10	...	...	10	...	...	...	10	...	...	...	10	...	...	10	...	...
Pennsylvania	76	25½	37½	13	25½	38½	5	7	25½	38½	6	6	25½	38½	12	25½	38½	12
Rhode Island	10	...	10	...	...	10	...	...	...	10	...	...	...	10	...	...	10	...
South Carolina	18	18	...	...	18	...	...	...	18	...	...	...	18	...	...	18	...	...
South Dakota	10	10	...	...	9	...	...	1	9	...	...	1	9	...	1	9	...	1
Tennessee	24	24	...	...	24	...	...	...	24	...	...	...	24	...	...	24	...	...
Texas	40	40	...	...	40	...	...	...	40	...	...	...	40	...	...	40	...	...
Utah	8	8	...	...	8	...	...	...	8	...	...	...	8	...	...	8	...	...
Vermont	8	1	7	...	1	7	...	...	1	7	...	...	...	7	1	1	7	...
Virginia	24	...	...	24	...	...	...	24	...	...	...	24	...	...	24	...	...	24
Washington	14	14	...	...	14	...	...	...	14	...	...	...	14	...	...	14	...	...
West Virginia	16	...	...	16	...	...	16	...	...	...	16	...	...	...	16	...	...	16
Wisconsin	26	3	23	...	3	23	...	...	3	23	...	...	3	23	...	3	23	...
Wyoming	6	2	3	1	...	...	...	6	...	5	1	...	1	4½	½	1	4½	½
Alaska	6	1	3	2	1	3	...	2	...	4	...	2	1	3	2	1	3	2
Canal Zone	6	6	...	...	6	...	...	...	6	...	...	...	6	...	...	6	...	...
District of Columbia	6	6	...	...	6	...	...	...	6	...	...	...	6	...	...	6	...	...
Hawaii	6	1	1	4	1	1	3	1	1	1	3	1	1	1	4	1	1	4
Philippine Islands	6	3	3	...	3	3	...	...	3	3	...	...	3	3	...	3	3	...
Puerto Rico	6	...	...	6	...	...	5	1	5	...	...	1	...	1	5	...	...	6
Virgin Islands	...	...	...	...	...	...	...	...	...	...	...	...	...	...	...	...	...	...
Total	1098	471[c]	299½	326[d]	432	307½	122	236½[e]	420½[f]	323	121½[g]	233[h]	499	320½	278½[i]	461½	320½	316[j]

Source: *Official Proceedings, 1924.*
Tenth ballot, pp. 386-8.
a/ Add one-tenth.
b/ Add nine-tenths.
c/ Add three-fifths.
d/ Other candidates: Underwood, 43 and nine-tenths; Robinson, 20; Saulsbury, 6; Ralston, 30½; Jonathan M. Davis, 12; Ritchie, 17½; Cox, 60; Bryan, 12; Brown, 8; Glass, 25; John W. Davis, 57½; Harrison, 31½; Thompson, 1; Thomas J. Walsh, 1; Newton D. Baker, 1.
Twentieth ballot, pp. 435-7.
e/ Other candidates: Ralston, 30; Underwood, 45½; Robinson, 21; William E. Dever, ½; Baker, 1; Glass, 25; Ritchie, 17½; Cox, 60; Bryan, 11; Gilbert M. Hitchcock, 1; Saulsbury, 6; Walsh, 8; Jonathan M. Davis, 10.

Thirtieth ballot, pp. 488-90.
f/ Sum of column; proceedings record 415½.
g/ Sum of column; proceedings record 126½.
h/ Other candidates: Ralston, 33; Underwood, 39½; Robinson, 23; Glass, 24; Cox, 57; Ritchie, 17½; Saulsbury, 6; Walsh, 1½; Jonathan M. Davis, 6; Robert L. Owen, 25.
Thirty-ninth ballot, pp. 540-2.
i/ Other candidates: Underwood, 38½; Robinson, 23; John W. Davis, 71; Ralston, 32; Ritchie, 18½; Cox, 55; Glass, 25; Jonathan M. Davis, 3; Saulsbury, 6; Owen, 4; Walsh, 1; J. Holmes Jackson, 1; not voting, ½.
Fiftieth ballot, pp. 590-2.
j/ Other candidates: John W. Davis, 64; Ralston, 58; Underwood, 42½; Robinson, 44; Glass, 24; Cox, 54; Ritchie, 16½; Saulsbury, 6; Walsh, 1; Jonathan M. Davis, 2; Owen, 4.

1924 DEMOCRATIC

Delegation	Votes	Presidential Sixtieth Ballot			Executive Session, Addresses by Candidates			Motion to Allow Address by Smith			Presidential Seventieth Ballot			Motion to Cut List of Candidates to Five		
		McAdoo	Smith	Other	Yea	Nay	Not Voting	Yea	Nay	Not Voting	McAdoo	Smith	Other	Yea	Nay	Not Voting
Alabama	24	...	...	24	24	...	...	24	...	...	...	...	24	...	24	...
Arizona	6	3½	...	2½	4	2	...	3	3	...	3½	...	2½	3½	2½	...
Arkansas	18	...	...	18	...	18	...	18	...	...	...	...	18	...	18	...
California	26	26	...	...	1	25	...	...	26	...	26	...	...	26	...	...
Colorado	12	3½	3	5½	10	2	...	5½	4	2½	2½	3	6½	6	5	1
Connecticut	14	4	10	...	11	3	...	14	...	...	2	11	1	6	8	...
Delaware	6	...	...	6	...	6	...	...	6	...	...	...	6	...	6	...
Florida	12	10	1	1	3	9	...	2	10	...	10	1	1	9	3	...
Georgia	28	28	...	...	...	28	...	...	28	...	28	...	...	28	...	...
Idaho	8	8	...	...	...	8	...	...	8	...	8	...	...	8	...	...
Illinois	58	13	20	25	52	6	...	46	12	...	14	30	14	15	43	...
Indiana	30	...	...	30	13	17	...	20	10	...	20	10	...	15	15	...
Iowa	26	26	...	...	...	26	...	...	26	...	26	...	...	26	...	...
Kansas	20	20	...	...	...	20	...	...	20	...	20	...	...	20	...	...
Kentucky	26	26	...	...	...	26	...	2	21	3	26	...	...	26	...	...
Louisiana	20	...	...	20	20	...	...	20	...	...	...	...	20	...	20	...
Maine	12	2½	4½	5	3	5	4	5	7	...	2½	4½	5	...	12	...
Maryland	16	...	...	16	16	...	...	16	...	...	...	...	16	...	16	...
Massachusetts	36	2½	33½	...	34½	1½	...	35½	½	...	2½	33½	...	2	34	...
Michigan	30	5	25	...	30	...	...	13	11	6	25	5	...	8	22	...
Minnesota	24	6	15	3	16	7	1	18	5	1	6	15	3	8	15	1
Mississippi	20	20	...	...	...	20	...	20	...	...	20	...	...	20	...	...
Missouri	36	36	...	...	...	36	...	...	36	...	36	...	...	36	...	...
Montana	8	7	1	...	1	7	...	2	6	...	7	1	...	8	...	...
Nebraska	16	11	3	2	3	13	...	5	11	...	10	3	3	5	9	2
Nevada	6	6	...	...	...	6	...	...	6	...	6	...	...	6	...	...
New Hampshire	8	4½	3½	...	3½	4½	...	5½	2½	...	4½	3½	...	½	7½	...
New Jersey	28	...	28	...	28	...	...	28	...	...	...	28	...	...	28	...
New Mexico	6	6	...	...	...	6	...	2	4	...	6	...	...	6	...	...
New York	90	2	88	...	90	...	...	90	...	...	2	88	...	...	90	...
North Carolina	24	19	...	5	6	18	...	10	14	...	18½	...	5½	12	12	...
North Dakota	10	5	5	...	5	5	...	5	4	1	5	5	...	5	5	...
Ohio	48	...	...	48	38	10	...	37	4	7	...	...	48	...	48	...
Oklahoma	20	...	...	20	...	20	...	...	20	...	20	...	...	20	...	...
Oregon	10	10	...	...	...	10	...	...	10	...	10	...	...	10	...	...
Pennsylvania	76	25½	38½	12	47	25	4	60	16	...	25½	39½	11	24	43½	8½
Rhode Island	10	...	10	...	10	...	...	10	...	...	...	10	...	...	10	...
South Carolina	18	18	...	...	...	18	...	...	18	...	18	...	...	18	...	...
South Dakota	10	9	...	1	...	10	...	...	10	...	10	...	...	...	...	...
Tennessee	24	24	...	...	4	20	...	5	19	...	24	...	...	18	6	...
Texas	40	40	...	...	...	40	...	...	40	...	40	...	...	40	...	...
Utah	8	8	...	...	...	8	...	...	8	...	8	...	...	8	...	...
Vermont	8	1	7	...	8	...	...	8	...	...	1	7	...	...	8	...
Virginia	24	...	...	24	24	...	...	14	10	...	...	...	24	...	24	...
Washington	14	14	...	...	...	14	...	...	14	...	14	...	...	14	...	...
West Virginia	16	...	...	16	15	1	...	8	8	...	...	...	16	7	9	...
Wisconsin	26	3	23	...	25	1	...	25	1	...	3	23	...	1	25	...
Wyoming	6	½	4½	1	6	...	...	...	6	...	2	4	...	6	...	...
Alaska	6	1	3	2	6	...	...	6	...	...	1	5	...	...	6	...
Canal Zone	6	6	...	...	3	3	...	3	3	...	6	...	...	3	3	...
District of Columbia	6	6	...	...	...	6	...	6	...	...	6	...	...	6	...	...
Hawaii	6	1	1	4	6	...	...	6	...	...	1	1	4	3	3	...
Philippine Islands	6	2	2	2	3	3	...	3	3	...	2	2	2	3	3	...
Puerto Rico	6	...	1	5	6	...	...	4	2	...	...	1	5	3	3	...
Virgin Islands	...	...	...	...	...	...	...	...	...	...	...	...	...	...	...	...
Total	1098	469½	330½	298ᵃ	551	538	9	604½	473	20½	528½	334	235½ᵇ	496	589½	12½

Source: *Official Proceedings, 1924.*
Sixtieth ballot, pp. 642-4.
a/ Other candidates: John W. Davis, 60; Ralston, 42½; Underwood, 42; Robinson, 23; Glass, 25; Cox, 54; Ritchie, 16½; Walsh, 3; Saulsbury, 6; Owen, 24; Bryan, 2.
Executive session, addresses by candidates, p. 681.
Motion to allow address by Smith, pp. 687-8.
Seventieth ballot, pp. 721-3.
b/ Other candidates: John W. Davis, 67; Underwood, 37½; Robinson, 21; Glass, 25; Ritchie, 16½; Saulsbury, 6; Owen, 2; Bryan, 3; Baker, 56.
Motion to cut list of candidates to five, pp. 748-9.

Delegation	Votes	Motion to Adjourn to Kansas City — Yea	Nay	Not Voting	Presidential Eightieth Ballot — McAdoo	Smith	Other	Motion to Release Pledged Delegates — Yea	Nay	Not Voting	Presidential 87th Ballot — McAdoo	Smith	Other	Presidential Ninetieth Ballot — McAdoo	Smith	Ralston	Other
Alabama	24	...	24	...	...	...	24	24	...	...	...	...	24	...	...	...	24
Arizona	6	3½	2½	...	3½	...	2½	5	1	...	3½	...	2½	3½	...	...	2½
Arkansas	18	...	18	...	...	...	18	18	...	...	...	...	18	...	...	...	18
California	26	7	19	...	26	...	...	26	...	...	26	...	...	26	...	...	...
Colorado	12	5	6	1	3	3	6	10	...	2	3	3	6	1	3	½	7½
Connecticut	14	[a]	13[b]	...	2	12	...	13	1	...	2	12	...	2	12	...	...
Delaware	6	...	6	...	...	...	6	6	...	...	...	...	6	...	...	...	6
Florida	12	2	10	...	10	1	1	7	4	1	10	1	1	9	...	3	...
Georgia	28	...	28	...	28	...	...	...	28	...	28	...	...	28	...	...	...
Idaho	8	...	8	...	8	...	...	...	8	...	8	...	...	8	...	...	...
Illinois	58	...	58	...	15	35	8	44	14	...	13	35	10	12	36	6	4
Indiana	30	...	30	...	20	10	...	30	...	...	...	...	30	...	...	30	...
Iowa	26	...	26	...	26	...	...	26	...	...	...	...	26	...	...	...	26
Kansas	20	...	20	...	20	...	...	20	...	...	...	...	20	...	...	...	20
Kentucky	26	...	26	...	26	...	...	26	...	...	26	...	...	26	...	...	...
Louisiana	20	...	20	...	...	...	20	20	...	...	...	...	20	...	...	...	20
Maine	12	...	12	...	2	4½	5½	12	...	...	2	4½	5½	1½	4½	...	6
Maryland	16	...	16	...	...	...	16	16	...	...	...	...	16	...	...	...	16
Massachusetts	36	...	36	...	2½	33½	...	36	...	...	2½	33½	...	2½	33½	...	...
Michigan	30	...	30	...	1½	9	19½	29	1	...	1	10	19	...	10	20	...
Minnesota	24	3	20	1	6	15	3	21	...	3	6	15	3	6	15	...	3
Mississippi	20	...	20	...	20	...	...	20	...	...	...	...	20	...	...	20	...
Missouri	36	7½	28½	...	...	...	36	36	...	...	...	...	36	...	...	36	...
Montana	8	2	6	...	7	1	...	6	2	...	7	1	...	7	1	...	...
Nebraska	16	2	11	3	8	3	5	8	6	2	6	3	7	1	...	...	15
Nevada	6	...	6	...	6	...	...	6	...	...	...	...	6	...	...	6	...
New Hampshire	8	½	7½	...	2½	2½	3	8	...	...	½	2½	5	3	3½	...	1½
New Jersey	28	...	28	...	...	28	...	28	...	...	...	28	...	...	28	...	...
New Mexico	6	...	6	...	6	...	...	6	...	...	6	...	...	6	...	...	...
New York	90	...	90	...	2	88	...	90	...	...	2	88	...	2	88	...	...
North Carolina	24	4	20	...	13	...	11	24	...	...	12½	...	11½	3	5	...	21
North Dakota	10	2	8	...	5	5	...	5	5	...	5	...	...	5	5	...	...
Ohio	48	...	48	...	...	21½	26½	48	...	...	...	24½	23½	...	20½	17	10½
Oklahoma	20	...	20	...	20	...	...	20	...	...	...	...	20	...	...	20	...
Oregon	10	...	10	...	10	...	...	10	...	...	10	...	...	10	...	...	...
Pennsylvania	76	18½	54½	3	25½	39½	11	71	5	...	25½	39½	11	25½	39½	...	11
Rhode Island	10	...	10	...	...	10	...	10	...	...	...	10	...	...	10	...	...
South Carolina	18	18	...	...	18	...	...	...	18	...	18	...	...	18	...	...	...
South Dakota	10	1	9	...	9	...	1	9	1	...	9	...	1	9	...	...	1
Tennessee	24	1	23	...	24	...	...	24	...	...	24	...	...	24	...	...	...
Texas	40	...	40	...	40	...	...	40	...	...	40	...	...	40	...	...	...
Utah	8	...	8	...	8	...	...	...	8	...	8	...	...	8	...	...	...
Vermont	8	...	8	...	1	7	...	8	...	...	...	7	1	...	8	...	...
Virginia	24	1	23	...	...	...	24	24	...	...	...	...	24	...	...	...	24
Washington	14	...	14	...	14	...	...	14	...	...	14	...	...	14	...	...	...
West Virginia	16	...	16	...	1	...	15	13	3	...	1	...	15	1	...	1	15
Wisconsin	26	...	26	...	1	23	2	26	...	...	1	23	2	1	23	...	2
Wyoming	6	...	6	...	...	3	3	6	...	...	3	3	...	...	3	...	3
Alaska	6	...	6	...	1	5	...	6	...	...	1	5	...	...	5	...	1
Canal Zone	6	...	6	...	3	3	...	6	...	...	3	3	...	3	3	...	...
District of Columbia	6	...	6	...	6	...	...	6	...	...	6	...	...	6	...	...	...
Hawaii	6	...	6	...	1	1	4	6	...	...	1	2	3	1	...	...	5
Philippine Islands	6	3	3	...	3	3	...	6	...	...	2	2	2	2	2	...	2
Puerto Rico	6	1	5	...	...	1	5	6	...	...	...	1	5	...	1	...	5
Virgin Islands	...	...	...	...	...	...	...	...	...	...	...	...	...	...	...	...	...
Total	1098	82[c]	1007[d]	8	454½	367½	276[e]	985	105	8	336½	361½	400[f]	314	354½	159½	270[g]

Source: *Official Proceedings*, 1924.
Motion to adjourn to Kansas City, pp. 754-5.
a/ Add seven-tenths.
b/ Add three-tenths.
c/ Add seven-tenths.
d/ Add three-tenths.
Eightieth ballot, pp. 803-5.
e/ Other candidates: Underwood, 46½; Robinson, 29½; John W. Davis, 73½; Ferris, 17½; Ritchie, 16½; Ralston, 5; Glass, 68; Saulsbury, 6; Walsh, 4; Bryan, 4½; Josephus Daniels, 1; Owen, 1; Franklin D. Roosevelt, 1.
Motion to release pledged delegates, pp. 816-7.
Eighty-seventh ballot, pp. 843-5.
f/ Other candidates: Underwood, 38; Robinson, 20½; John W. Davis, 66½; Glass, 71; Ralston, 93; Ritchie, 23; Saulsbury, 6; Walsh, 4; Bryan, 7; Edwin T. Meredith, 26; Cox ½; Owen, 20; Mrs. Belle Miller, 1; Jonathan M. Davis, 20; Roosevelt, 1; not voting, 2½.

Ninetieth ballot, pp. 864-6.
g/ Other candidates: Underwood, 42½; Robinson, 20; John W. Davis, 65½; Glass, 30½; Ritchie, 16½; Saulsbury, 6; Walsh, 5; Bryan, 15; Jonathan M. Davis, 22; Daniels, 19; Meredith, 26; not voting, 2.

<table>
<tr><th rowspan="4">Delegation</th><th rowspan="4">Votes</th><th colspan="11">1924 DEMOCRATIC</th><th colspan="3" rowspan="2">Motion to Adjourn to 2 P.M.</th></tr>
</table>

Delegation	Votes	94th Ballot McAdoo	Smith	Other	95th Ballot McAdoo	Smith	Davis	Other	99th Ballot McAdoo	Smith	Davis	Other	Yea	Nay	Not Voting
Alabama	24	...	...	24	...	...	...	24	...	...	...	24	...	24	...
Arizona	6	2½	...	3½	3½	...	...	2½	3	...	...	3	...	6	...
Arkansas	18	...	...	18	...	...	...	18	...	...	...	18	...	18	...
California	26	26	...	...	26	...	...	...	26	...	...	...	...	26	...
Colorado	12	1½	3	7½	2	3	3	4	2½	2½	3	4	3	7	2
Connecticut	14	2	12	...	2	12	...	...	2	12	...	...	14	...	...
Delaware	6	..	...	6	...	...	...	6	...	...	...	6	6	...	...
Florida	12	9	1	2	9	1	...	2	9	...	3	...	5	6	1
Georgia	28	28	...	...	28	...	...	...	28	...	...	...	...	28	...
Idaho	8	8	...	...	8	...	...	...	8	...	...	...	...	8	...
Illinois	58	12	35	11	12	35	4	7	11	35	7	5	46	12	...
Indiana	30	25	5	...	25	5	...	...	6	...	10	14	15	15	...
Iowa	26	...	...	26	...	...	...	26	...	...	...	26	...	26	...
Kansas	20	...	...	20	20	...	...	...	...	...	20	...	...	20	...
Kentucky	26	26	...	...	26	...	...	...	26	...	...	...	...	26	...
Louisiana	20	...	...	20	...	...	20	...	...	...	20	...	...	20	...
Maine	12	1	5	6	1	5	1	5	1	5	1	5	10	2	...
Maryland	16	...	...	16	...	...	...	16	...	...	...	16	...	16	...
Massachusetts	36	2½	33½	...	2½	33½	...	...	2½	33½	...	...	13	11½	11½
Michigan	30	4	10	16	1	10	19	...	...	10	20	...	15	15	...
Minnesota	24	6	15	3	6	15	1	2	6	15	1	2	4	20	...
Mississippi	20	20	...	...	20	...	...	...	20	...	...	...	...	20	...
Missouri	36	...	...	36	...	...	36	...	...	...	36	...	...	36	...
Montana	8	7	1	...	7	1	...	...	7	1	...	...	2	6	...
Nebraska	16	4	2	10	3	3	...	10	3	3	1	9	2	12	2
Nevada	6	6	...	...	6	...	...	...	6	...	...	...	...	6	...
New Hampshire	8	...	4½	3½	½	4½	3	...	½	2½	4	1	½	7½	...
New Jersey	28	...	28	...	...	28	...	...	...	28	...	...	28	...	...
New Mexico	6	6	...	...	6	...	...	...	6	...	...	...	...	6	...
New York	90	2	88	...	2	88	...	...	2	88	...	...	90	...	...
North Carolina	24	8	...	16	11½	...	11[a]	1[b]	10½	...	11	2½	...	24	...
North Dakota	10	5	5	...	5	5	...	...	5	5	...	...	...	10	...
Ohio	48	...	20	28	...	20	10	18	...	15	20	13	38	10	...
Oklahoma	20	20	...	...	20	...	...	...	...	...	20	...	20	...	...
Oregon	10	10	...	...	10	...	...	...	10	...	...	...	...	10	...
Pennsylvania	76	25½	39½	11	25½	40½	5	5	25½	40½	5	5	70	6	...
Rhode Island	10	...	10	...	...	10	...	...	...	10	...	...	...	10	...
South Carolina	18	18	...	...	18	...	...	...	18	...	...	...	18	...	...
South Dakota	10	9	...	1	10	...	...	...	9	...	...	1	...	10	...
Tennessee	24	24	...	...	24	...	...	...	24	...	...	...	...	24	...
Texas	40	40	...	...	40	...	...	...	40	...	...	...	...	40	...
Utah	8	8	...	...	8	...	...	...	8	...	...	...	...	8	...
Vermont	8	...	8	...	...	8	...	...	...	8	...	...	...	8	...
Virginia	24	...	...	24	...	...	...	24	...	...	...	24	...	24	...
Washington	14	14	...	...	14	...	...	...	14	...	...	...	...	14	...
West Virginia	16	1	...	15	1	...	15	...	1	...	15	...	...	16	...
Wisconsin	26	1	23	2	1	23	...	2	1	23	...	2	24	2	...
Wyoming	6	...	3	3	...	3	3	...	...	3	3	...	...	6	...
Alaska	6	...	6	...	...	6	...	...	...	6	...	...	6	...	...
Canal Zone	6	3	3	...	3	3	...	...	3	3	...	...	4	2	...
District of Columbia	6	6	...	...	6	...	...	...	6	...	...	...	6	...	...
Hawaii	6	1	...	5	1	1	3	1	1	1	3	1	...	6	...
Philippine Islands	6	3	3	...	3	3	...	...	2	2	2	...	4	2	...
Puerto Rico	6	...	1	5	...	1	5	...	...	1	5	...	1	5	...
Virgin Islands	...	...	...	...	...	...	...	...	...	...	...	...	...	...	...
Total	1098	395	364½	338½[c]	417½	367½	139[d]	173[e]	353½	353	210	181½[f]	460½	621	16½

Source: *Official Proceedings, 1924.*
Ninety-fourth ballot, pp. 889-91.
c/ Other candidates: John W. Davis, 81 and three-fourths; Underwood, 46 and one-fourth; Ralston, 37; Robinson, 37; Glass, 37; Bryan, 9; Walsh, 4; Ritchie, 16½; Jonathan M. Davis, 20; Royal S. Copeland, 17; Meredith, 26; Homer S. Cummings, 1; Roosevelt, 2; Calvin Stewart, 1; not voting, 3.
Ninety-fifth ballot, pp. 898-900.
a/ Add one-fourth.
b/ Add three-fourths.
d/ Add one-fourth.
e/ Other candidates: Underwood, 44 and one-fourth; Glass, 34; Robinson, 31; Meredith, 26; Ritchie, 20½; Bryan, 9; Walsh, 2; Roosevelt, 2; Copeland, 2; not voting, 3.
Ninety-ninth ballot, pp. 931-33.
f/ Other candidates: Underwood, 39½; Robinson, 25; Glass, 38; Walsh, 4; Bryan, 5; Saulsbury, 6; Ritchie, 17½; Thomas R. Marshall, 2; Meredith, 37; Owen, 3; George L. Berry, 1; not voting, 3½.
Motion to adjourn to 2 P. M., pp. 937-8.

1924 DEMOCRATIC

Presidential

Delegation	Votes	One Hundredth Ballot				101st Ballot					102nd Ballot				103rd Ballot (before shift)		
		McAdoo	Smith	Davis	Other	Underwood	Smith	Davis	Meredith	Other	Underwood	Davis	Walsh	Other	Underwood	Davis	Other
Alabama	24	...	...	...	24	24	...	...	...	3	24	...	...	3	24	...	...
Arizona	6	3	...	...	3	3	...	...	...	18	3	...	...	18	3	...	3
Arkansas	18	...	...	...	18	...	...	1	...	18	...	...	26	...	2	...	18
California	26	$16\frac{1}{2}$	...	$3\frac{1}{2}$	$1\frac{1}{2}$	$6\frac{1}{2}$	1	3	$2\frac{1}{2}$	3	22	$6\frac{1}{2}$	$1\frac{1}{2}$	...	2	2	22
Colorado	12	...	...	...	...	...	...	...	1	$4\frac{1}{2}$	...	...	...	4	5	3	4
Connecticut	14	2	12	...	...	11	...	1	...	2	11	...	3	...	11	...	3
Delaware	6	...	...	...	6	...	...	6	...	...	...	...	...	6	6	...	...
Florida	12	9	...	3	...	...	...	3	...	9	...	...	5	4	3	...	6	6
Georgia	28	28	...	...	...	...	...	5	12	11	1	13	...	14	...	27	1
Idaho	8	...	...	...	8	...	...	...	...	8	...	...	8	...	...	8	...
Illinois	58	...	35	6	17	20	...	4	13	21	20	3	13	22	19	19	20
Indiana	30	...	...	14	16	3	...	10	6	11	10	10	...	10	5	25	...
Iowa	26	...	...	...	26	...	...	...	26	...	...	...	...	26	...	...	26
Kansas	20	...	...	20	...	...	...	20	...	...	...	...	20	...	...	20	...
Kentucky	26	12	...	$8\frac{1}{2}$	$5\frac{1}{2}$	1	1	9	...	$14\frac{1}{2}$	1	9	$6\frac{1}{2}$	$9\frac{1}{2}$	1	$22\frac{1}{2}$	$2\frac{1}{2}$
Louisiana	20	...	...	20	...	...	...	20	...	...	...	20	...	...	...	20	...
Maine	12	1	2	8	1	5	...	6	...	1	8	4	...	...	10	2	...
Maryland	16	...	...	...	16	...	...	16	...	...	...	16	...	...	...	16	...
Massachusetts	36	$2\frac{1}{2}$	$33\frac{1}{2}$	...	...	...	33	...	...	3	8	$\frac{1}{2}$	2	$25\frac{1}{2}$	$23\frac{1}{2}$	2	$10\frac{1}{2}$
Michigan	30	...	10	15	5	10	...	12	1	7	14	16	...	...	...	$29\frac{1}{2}$	$\frac{1}{2}$
Minnesota	24	6	15	1	2	...	15	1	...	8	14	2	1	7	16	3	5
Mississippi	20	...	...	...	20	...	...	20	...	...	...	20	...	...	...	20	...
Missouri	36	...	...	36	...	...	...	36	...	...	...	36	...	...	...	36	...
Montana	8	1	...	...	7	...	...	...	...	8	...	...	8	...	...	...	8
Nebraska	16	...	2	...	14	...	1	...	...	11	4	2	...	4	10	2	1	13
Nevada	6	...	6	...	...	...	...	...	...	6	...	...	6	...	...	6	...
New Hampshire	8	...	1	2	5	...	1	1	$1\frac{1}{2}$	$4\frac{1}{2}$	...	$3\frac{1}{2}$	$4\frac{1}{2}$	...	...	$3\frac{1}{2}$	$4\frac{1}{2}$
New Jersey	28	...	28	...	...	16	...	...	...	12	16	2	...	10	16	1	11
New Mexico	6	6	...	...	...	...	$1\frac{1}{2}$	1	1	$2\frac{1}{2}$	...	$2\frac{1}{2}$	...	$3\frac{1}{2}$	...	2	4
New York	90	2	88	...	...	$86\frac{1}{2}$	...	...	...	$3\frac{1}{2}$	84	1	1	4	44	4	42
North Carolina	24	...	...	...	24	1	...	20	...	2	...	23	...	1	$5\frac{1}{2}$	$17\frac{1}{2}$	...
North Dakota	10	3	5	...	2	...	5	...	1	4	5	...	5	...	...	...	10
Ohio	48	...	15	23	10	5	10	23	5	5	7	25	...	16	4	41	3
Oklahoma	20	...	...	...	20	...	...	...	...	20	...	20	...	...	...	20	...
Oregon	10	10	...	...	...	1	...	2	1	6	1	2	...	7	1	5	4
Pennsylvania	76	$17\frac{1}{2}$	$39\frac{1}{2}$	9	10	6	$36\frac{1}{2}$	$19\frac{1}{2}$	1	13	$32\frac{1}{2}$	$29\frac{1}{2}$	4	10	$31\frac{1}{2}$	$37\frac{1}{2}$	7
Rhode Island	10	...	10	...	...	10	...	...	...	...	10	...	...	...	...	10	...
South Carolina	18	18	...	...	...	...	...	18	...	...	...	18	...	...	...	18	...
South Dakota	10	...	...	...	10	...	...	...	...	10	2	...	...	8	2	...	8
Tennessee	24	6	...	8	10	1	...	15	...	8	...	19	...	5	...	19	5
Texas	40	40	...	...	...	...	...	...	40	...	...	40	...	...	...	40	...
Utah	8	...	...	4	4	...	...	...	...	8	...	4	4	...	...	8	...
Vermont	8	...	8	...	...	4	...	4	...	...	4	4	...	...	...	8	...
Virginia	24	...	...	...	24	...	...	12	...	12	...	12	...	12	...	12	12
Washington	14	...	...	...	14	...	...	...	...	14	...	...	14	...	14	...	...
West Virginia	16	...	...	16	...	...	...	16	...	...	16	...	...	...	16	...	...
Wisconsin	26	...	22	...	4	8	9	...	1	8	11	...	9	6	8	1	17
Wyoming	6	...	3	$\frac{1}{2}$	$2\frac{1}{2}$	...	3	3	...	...	...	6	...	...	...	6	...
Alaska	6	...	6	...	...	6	...	...	...	...	6	...	...	...	2	4	...
Canal Zone	6	3	3	...	...	...	...	1	3	2	3	3	...	...	...	6	...
District of Columbia	6	...	...	...	6	...	...	...	...	6	6	...	...	...	6	...	...
Hawaii	6	1	1	3	1	1	1	4	...	...	1	4	...	1	1	4	1
Philippine Islands	6	2	2	...	2	5	...	...	1	...	5	...	...	1	1	4	1
Puerto Rico	6	...	1	...	5	1	...	5	...	...	1	5	...	...	1	5	...
Virgin Islands	...	...	...	...	...	...	...	...	...	...	...	...	...	...	...	...	...
Total	1098	190	$351\frac{1}{2}$	$203\frac{1}{2}$	353[a]	$229\frac{1}{2}$	121	316	130	$301\frac{1}{2}$[b]	317	$415\frac{1}{2}$	123	$242\frac{1}{2}$[c]	$250\frac{1}{2}$	$575\frac{1}{2}$	272[d]

Source: *Official Proceedings*, 1924.
One hundredth ballot, pp. 941-3.
a/ Other candidates: Underwood, $41\frac{1}{2}$; Robinson, 46; Bryan, 2; Saulsbury, 6; Walsh, $52\frac{1}{2}$; Owen, 20; Ritchie, $17\frac{1}{2}$; Meredith, $75\frac{1}{2}$; David F. Houston, 9; Glass, 35; Daniels, 24; Baker, 4; Berry, 1; James W. Gerard, 10; not voting, 9.
One hundred and first ballot, pp. 950-2.
b/ Other candidates: Robinson, $22\frac{1}{2}$; McAdoo, 52; Walsh, 98; Ritchie, $\frac{1}{2}$; Berry, 1; A. A. Murphree, 4; Houston, 9; Owen, 23; Cummings, 9; Glass, 59; Gerard, 16; Baker, 1; Daniels, 1; Cordell Hull, 2; not voting, $3\frac{1}{2}$.
One hundred and second ballot, pp. 958-60.
c/ Other candidates: Robinson, 21; McAdoo, 21; Smith, 44; Thompson, 1; Ritchie, $\frac{1}{2}$; Bryan, 1; Gerard, 7; Glass, 67; Daniels, 2; Berry $1\frac{1}{2}$; Meredith, $66\frac{1}{2}$; Henry T. Allen, 1; Hull, 1; not voting, 8.
One hundred and third ballot (before shift), pp. 963-8.
d/ Other candidates: McAdoo, $14\frac{1}{2}$; Robinson, 21; Meredith, $42\frac{1}{2}$; Glass, 79; Hull, 1; Smith, $10\frac{1}{2}$; Daniels, 1; Gerard, 8; Thompson, 1; Walsh, $84\frac{1}{2}$; not voting, 9.

1924 DEMOCRATIC

Recapitulation of Presidential Ballots

Ballot	J. W. Davis	McAdoo	Smith	Underwood	Robinson	Saulsbury	Ralston	J. M. Davis	Ritchie	Cox	Ferris	Silzer	Glass	Harrison	Owen	Bryan	Walsh	Other
1	31	431½	241	42½	21	7	30	20	22½	59	30	38	25	43½	...	18	...	36
2	32	431	251½	42	41	6	30	23	21½	61	30	30	25	23½	...	18	1	31
3	34	437	255½	42	41	6	30	20	22½	60	30	28	29	23½	...	19	1	19
4	34	443a	260	41½	19	6	30	29	21½	59	30	28	45	20½	...	19	1	10e
5	34½	443b	261	41½	19	6	30	28	42e	59	30	28	25	20½	...	19	1	9½
6	55½	443b	261½	42½	19	6	30	27	22e	59	30	28	25	20½	...	18	1	9
7	55	442a	261½	42½	19	6	30	30	20e	59	30	28	25	20½	...	18	1	9
8	57	444a	273½	48	21	6	30	29	19e	60	6½	28	26	20½	...	16	1	11
9	63	444a	278	45½	21	6	30½	32d	17½	60	...	28	25	20½	...	15	1	10
10	57½	471a	299½	43e	20	6	30½	12	17½	60	...	...	25	31½	...	12	1	10
11	59	476c	303f	42½	20	6	32½	11	17½	60	...	...	25½	20½	...	11	1	12
12	60	478½	301	41½	19	6	31½	13½	17½	60	...	...	26	21½	...	11	1	10
13	64½	477	303½	40½	19	6	31½	11	17½	60	...	...	25	20½	...	10	1	11
14	64½	475½	306½	40½	19	6	31	11	17½	60	...	...	24	20½	...	11	1	10
15	61	479	305½	39½	20	6	31	11	17½	60	...	...	25	20½	...	11	1	10
16	63	478	305½	41½	46	6	31	11	17½	60	...	...	25	...	...	11	1	1½
17	64	471½	312½	42	28	6	30	10	17½	60	...	...	44	...	...	11	1	½
18	66	470½	312½	39½	22	6	30	10	18½	60	...	...	30	...	...	11	2	20
19	84½	474	311½	39½	22	6	31	9	17½	60	...	...	30	...	...	10	2	1
20	122	432	307½	45½	21	6	30	10	17½	60	...	...	25	...	...	11	8	2½
21	125	439	307½	45½	22	12	30	5	17½	60	...	...	24	...	...	...	8	1½
22	123½	438½	307½	45½	22	12	32	5	17½	60	...	...	25	...	...	...	8½	...
23	129½	438½	308	39½	23	6	32	5	17½	60	...	...	30	...	...	...	8	...
24	129½	438½	308	39½	22	6	33	5	17½	60	...	...	29	...	...	...	9	1
25	126	436½	308½	39½	23	6	31	5	17½	59	...	...	29	...	...	...	16	...
26	125	415½	311½	39½	23	6	32	5	17½	59	...	...	29	...	20	...	14	...
27	128½	413	316½	39½	23	6	32	6	18½	59	...	...	29	...	20	...	7	...
28	126	412	316½	39½	24	6	34	6	18	59	...	...	25	...	24	...	7	1
29	124½	415	321	39½	23	6	34	6	17½	59	...	...	25	...	24	...	1½	2
30	126½	415½	323½	39½	23	6	33	6	17½	57	...	...	24	...	25	...	1½	...
31	127½	415½	322½	39½	24	6	32	6	16½	57	...	...	24	...	25	...	2½	...
32	128	415½	322	39½	24	6	32	6	16½	57	...	...	24	...	24	...	3½	...
33	121	404½	310½	39½	23	6	32	6	16½	57	30	...	24	...	25	...	2½	½
34	107½	445	311	39½	24	6	31	3	16½	54	30	...	24	...	5	...	1½	...
35	107	439	323½	39½	24	6	33	3	16½	50	...	...	29	...	25	...	½	1
36	106½	429	323	39½	24	6	33½	3	16½	55	...	...	24	...	25	...	½	2
37	107	444½	321	39½	24	6	32	3	17½	55	...	...	24	...	24	...	½	...
38	105	444	321	39½	24	6	32	4	17½	55	...	...	24	...	24	...	1½	...
39	71	499	320½	38½	23	6	32	3	18½	55	...	...	25	...	4	...	1	1
40	70	506d	315b	41½	24	6	31	3	17½	55	...	...	24	...	4	...	...	...
41	70	504e	317a	39½	24	6	30	3	17½	55	...	...	24	...	4	...	...	2
42	67	503d	318a	39½	23	6	30	3	17½	56	...	...	28½	...	4	...	...	1
43	71	483d	319b	40	44	6	31	3	17½	54	...	...	24	...	4	...	1	...
44	71	484d	319b	39	44	6	31	2	17½	54	...	...	24	...	4	...	1	1
45	73	483d	319b	38	44	6	31	3	17½	54	...	...	24	...	4	...	1	...
46	71	486e	319b	37½	44	6	31	3	16½	54	...	...	24	...	4	...	1	...
47	70½	484d	320b	38½	45	6	31	3	16½	54	...	...	24	...	4	...	1	...
48	70½	483½	321	38½	44	6	31	3	16½	54	...	...	25	...	4	...	1	...
49	63½	462½	320½	42	45	6	57	2	16½	53	...	...	25	...	4	...	1	...
50	64	461½	320½	42½	44	6	58	2	16½	54	...	...	24	...	4	...	1	...

a Add three-fifths
b Add one-tenth.
c Add three-tenths.
d Add two-fifths.
e Add nine-tenths.
f Add one-fifth.

Other Candidates

Ballot

1 Brown 17, Sweet 12, Kendrick 6, Thompson 1.
2 Brown 12½, Sweet 12, Kendrick 6, Thompson 1.
3 Brown 12½, Kendrick 6, Thompson 1.
4 Brown 9e, Thompson 1.
5 Brown 8½, Thompson 1.
6 Brown 8, Thompson 1.
7 Brown 8, Thompson 1.
8 Brown 9, Thompson 1, W. J. Bryan 1.
9 Brown 8, Thompson 1, W. J. Bryan 1.
10 Brown 8, Thompson 1, Baker 1.
11 Brown 9, Thompson 1, Baker 1, Berry 1.
12 Brown 9, Thompson 1.
13 Brown 9, Baker 1, Krebs 1.
14 Brown 9, Baker 1.
15 Brown 9, Baker 1.
16 Brown 1, Copeland ½.
17 Copeland ½.
18 Hull 20.
19 Copeland 1.
20 Baker 1, Hitchcock 1, Dever ½.
21 Baker 1, Mrs. Miller ½.
24 Pomerene 1.

Ballot

28 Daniels 1.
29 Daniels 1, Martin 1.
33 Gaston ½.
35 Gerard 1.
36 Gerard 1, Doheny 1.
39 Jackson 1.
41 Cummings 1, Spellacy 1.
42 Spellacy 1.
44 Edwards 1.

1924 DEMOCRATIC

Recapitulation of Presidential Ballots

Ballot	J. W. Davis	McAdoo	Smith	Underwood	Robinson	Saulsbury	Ralston	J. M. Davis	Ritchie	Cox	Ferris	Glass	Owen	Bryan	Walsh	Baker	Meredith	Other
51	67½	442½	328	43	43	6	63	2	16½	55	...	25	4	...	2½	...	...	...
52	59	413½	320½	38½	42	6	93	...	16½	54	...	24	4	6	1	...	...	20
53	63	423½	320½	42½	43	6	94	...	16½	54	...	25	4	6	...	...	...	...
54	62	427	320½	40	43	6	92	...	17½	54	...	24	3	7	1	...	...	1
55	62½	426½	320½	40	43	6	97	...	16½	54	...	24	4	3	1	...	...	...
56	58½	430	320½	39½	43	6	97	...	16½	54	...	25	4	3	1	...	...	...
57	58½	430	320½	39½	43	6	97	...	16½	54	...	25	4	3	1	...	...	...
58	40½	495	331½	38	23	6	40½	...	16½	54	...	25	4	3	1	...	...	20
59	60	473½	331½	40	23	6	42½	...	16½	54	...	25	24	2	...	...	...	...
60	60	469½	330½	42	23	6	42½	...	16½	54	...	25	24	2	3	...	...	...
61	60	469½	335½	42	23	6	37½	...	16½	54	...	25	24	2	3	...	...	...
62	60½	469	338½	40	23	6	38½	...	16½	49	...	26	24	4	3	...	...	...
63	62	446½	315½	39½	23	6	56	...	16½	49	28	25	24	4	3	...	...	...
64	61½	488½	325	39½	24	6	1	...	16½	54	24½	25	24	3	3	...	...	2½
65	71½	492	336½	40	23	6	...	...	16½	1	6½	25	24	3	3	48	...	2
66	74½	495	338½	39½	21	6	...	...	16½	...	...	25	22	2	3	55	...	...
67	75½	490	336½	46½	21	6	...	...	16½	...	...	25	22	3	2	54	...	...
68	72½	488½	336½	46½	21	6	...	...	16½	...	...	26	22	3	1	57	...	1½
69	64	530	335	38	21	6	...	...	16½	...	...	25	2	2	...	56	...	2½
70	67	528½	334	37½	21	6	...	...	16½	...	...	25	2	3	...	56	...	...
71	67	528½	334½	37½	21	6	...	...	16½	...	...	25	2	2	1	56	...	...
72	65	527½	334	37½	21	6	...	...	16½	...	...	25	2	2	2	57½	...	...
73	66	528	335	38½	21	6	...	...	16½	...	...	25	2	3	2	54	...	...
74	78½	510	364	47	23	7	3½	...	18½	1	...	28	2	4	4½	5	...	1
75	78½	513	366	46½	25	6	4½	...	16½	1	...	28	4	4	2	2	...	...
76	75½	513	368	47½	25	6	4½	...	16½	1	...	29	4	4	2	1	...	...
77	76½	513	367	47½	24	6	6½	...	16½	1	...	27	4	4	2	1	...	1
78	73½	511	363½	49	22½	6	5	...	16½	...	17	21	...	3	6	...	...	2
79	71	507½	366½	50	28½	6	4	...	16½	...	18	17	...	3	6	...	...	2
80	73½	454½	367½	46½	29½	6	5	...	16½	...	17½	68	1	4½	4	...	...	2
81	70½	432	365	48	29½	6	4	...	16½	...	16	73	21	4½	7	...	...	3
82	71	413½	366	49	28½	6	24	...	16½	...	12	78	21	4½	4	...	...	2
83	72½	418	368	48½	27½	6	24	...	16½	...	7½	76	20	5½	4	...	...	2
84	66	388½	365	40½	25	6	86	...	16½	...	...	72½	20	6½	1½	...	...	2
85	68	380½	363	40½	27½	6	87	...	16½	...	...	67½	20	9½	3	6	...	1
86	65½	353½	360	38	25	6	92	...	23½	...	...	72½	20	7	5	...	26	2
87	66½	336½	361½	38	20½	6	93	20	23	½	...	71	20	7	4	...	26	2
88	59½	315½	362	39	23	6	98	20	22½	...	...	66½	20	9	5	...	26	24
89	64½	318½	357	41	20½	6	100½	20	22½	...	...	66½	20	9	3½	...	26	20½
90	65½	314	354½	42½	20	6	159½	22	16½	...	...	30½	...	15	5	...	26	19
91	66½	318	355½	46½	20	6	187½	4	16½	...	...	28½	...	8	4½	...	26	8½
92	69½	310	355½	45d	20	6	196c	...	16½	...	...	26½	...	8	4½	...	26	11½
93	68	314	355½	44c	19	6	196d	...	16½	...	...	27	...	8	4½	2	26	8½
94	81c	395	364½	46d	37	...	37	20	16½	...	...	37	...	9	4	...	26	21
95	139d	417½	367½	44d	31	...	...	...	20½	...	...	34	...	9	2	...	26	4
96	171½	421	359½	38½	32	...	...	...	21½	...	...	39	...	7	4	...	...	1
97	183d	415½	359½	37d	22	6	...	...	19½	...	...	39	1	6	4	...	...	2
98	194c	406½	354	38d	25	6	...	...	18½	...	...	36	1	5	6	...	...	3
99	210	353½	353	39½	25	6	...	...	17½	...	...	38	3	5	4	...	37	3
100	203½	190	351½	41½	46	6	...	...	17½	...	...	35	20	2	52½	4	75½	44
101	316	52	121	229½	22½	...	...	...	½	...	...	59	23	...	98	1	130	41
102	415½	21	44	317	21	...	...	...	½	...	...	67	...	1	123	...	66½	13½
103a	575½	14½	10½	250½	21	...	...	...	...	...	...	79	...	...	84½	...	42½	11
103b	844	11½	7½	102½	20	...	...	...	...	...	...	23	...	...	58	...	15½	8

a Before changes.
b After changes.
c Add three-fourths.
d Add one-fourth.

Other Candidates

Ballot	
52	Battle 20.
54	Roosevelt 1.
58	Behrman 20.
64	Walsh (David I.) 2½.
65	Wheeler 2.
68	Rogers 1, Coolidge ½.
69	Daniels 2½.
74	Kevin 1.
77	Roosevelt 1.
78	Roosevelt 1, Gerard 1.
79	Roosevelt 1, Gerard 1.
80	Roosevelt 1, Daniels 1.
81	Roosevelt 1, Daniels 1, Barnett 1.
82	Roosevelt 1, Daniels 1.
83	Roosevelt 1, Wheeler 1.
84	Roosevelt 1, Coyne 1.
85	Roosevelt 1.
86	Roosevelt 1, Maloney 1.
87	Roosevelt 1, Mrs. Miller 1.
88	Daniels 23, Roosevelt 1.
89	Daniels 19½, Roosevelt 1.
90	Daniels 19.
91	Cummings 8½.
92	Cummings 8½, Houston 2, Callahan 1.
93	Cummings 8½.
94	Copeland 17, Roosevelt 2, Cummings 1, Stewart 1.
95	Copeland 2, Roosevelt 2.
96	Roosevelt 1.
97	Marshall 2.
98	Marshall 3.
99	Marshall 2, Berry 1.
100	Daniels 24, Gerard 10, Houston 9, Berry 1.
101	Gerard 16, Houston 9, Cummings 9, Murphree 4, Hull 2, Daniels 1.
102	Gerard 7, Daniels 2, Berry 1½, Thompson 1, Allen 1, Hull 1.
103a	Gerard 8, Daniels 1, Thompson 1, Hull 1.
103b	Gerard 7, Hull 1.

Table spanning: **1924 DEMOCRATIC** — Presidential: 103rd Ballot (after shift) [Votes, Underwood, Davis, Other]; Vice-Presidential: First Ballot (before shift) [Bryan, Berry, Hylan, Owsley, Other]; First Ballot (after shift) [Bryan, Berry, Other]. **1928 DEMOCRATIC** — Presidential: First Ballot (before shift) [Votes, Smith, Other]; First Ballot (after shift) [Smith, Other].

Delegation	Votes	Underwood	Davis	Other	Bryan	Berry	Hylan	Owsley	Other	Bryan	Berry	Other	Votes	Smith	Other	Smith	Other
Alabama	24	...	24	...	4	...	...	4	16	24	...	...	24	1	23	1	23
Arizona	6	3	...	3	...	1	...	...	5	5	1	...	6	6	...	6	...
Arkansas	18	...	...	18	2	2	...	8	6	18	...	...	17	17	1	17	1
California	26	...	26	...	24	2	...	...	...	24	2	...	26	26	...	26	...
Colorado	12	5	3	4	...	12	...	...	...	6	6	...	12	12	...	12	...
Connecticut	14	...	14	...	1	2	2	...	9	14	...	...	14	14	...	14	...
Delaware	6	6	...	...	3	...	...	3	...	3	...	3	6	6	...	6	...
Florida	12	...	6	6	6	...	...	...	6	12	...	...	12	...	12	...	12
Georgia	28	...	27	1	16	10	...	1	1	16	10	2	28	...	28	...	28
Idaho	8	...	8	...	...	8	...	...	...	...	8	...	8	8	...	8	...
Illinois	58	...	58	...	29	...	29	...	...	58	...	...	58	56	2	56	2
Indiana	30	5	25	...	14	4	...	7	5	14	...	12	30	...	30	25	5
Iowa	26	...	26	...	...	...	26	...	...	...	26	...	26	26	...	26	...
Kansas	20	...	20	...	...	...	...	...	20	20	...	...	20	...	20	11½	8½
Kentucky	26	...	26	...	...	...	...	...	26	26	...	...	26	26	...	26	...
Louisiana	20	...	20	...	...	20	...	...	...	...	20	...	20	20	...	20	...
Maine	12	10	2	...	1	3	...	...	8	1	3	8	12	12	...	12	...
Maryland	16	...	16	...	...	...	...	...	16	16	...	...	16	16	...	16	...
Massachusetts	36	23½	2	10½	...	25	5	...	6	...	36	...	36	36	...	36	...
Michigan	30	...	29½	½	...	...	...	29	1	30	...	...	30	30	...	30	...
Minnesota	24	16	3	5	...	...	...	...	24	20	...	4	24	24	...	24	...
Mississippi	20	...	20	...	...	...	...	20	...	20	...	...	20	...	20	9½	10½
Missouri	36	...	36	...	...	1	...	...	35	28	...	8	36	...	36	...	36
Montana	8	...	...	8	7	1	...	...	...	7	1	...	8	8	...	8	...
Nebraska	16	2	1	13	16	...	...	...	...	16	...	...	16	...	16	12	4
Nevada	6	...	6	...	6	...	...	...	...	6	...	...	6	6	...	6	...
New Hampshire	8	...	3½	4½	...	5½	...	2	½	...	8	...	8	8	...	8	...
New Jersey	28	16	1	11	...	...	28	...	...	27	1	...	28	28	...	28	...
New Mexico	6	...	2	4	...	3	...	...	3	...	...	6	6	6	...	6	...
New York	90	...	60	30	10	5	40	...	35	90	...	...	90	90	...	90	...
North Carolina	24	...	24	...	12	...	...	8	4	24	...	...	24	4[a]	19[b]	4[a]	19[b]
North Dakota	10	...	...	10	...	10	...	...	...	...	10	...	10	10	...	10	...
Ohio	48	1	46	1	1	40	...	...	7	24	...	24	48	1	47	45	3
Oklahoma	20	...	20	...	...	...	...	20	...	20	...	...	20	10	10	10	10
Oregon	10	1	5	4	...	10	...	...	...	...	10	...	10	10	...	10	...
Pennsylvania	76	...	76	...	38	5	5	5	23	38	5	33	76	70½	5½	70½	5½
Rhode Island	10	...	10	...	...	...	...	...	10	...	...	10	10	10	...	10	...
South Carolina	18	...	18	...	...	...	...	...	...	...	...	18	18	...	18	...	18
South Dakota	10	2	...	8	...	...	...	...	10	...	...	10	10	10	...	10	...
Tennessee	24	...	19	5	...	24	...	...	...	...	...	24	24	...	24	23	1
Texas	40	...	40	...	...	...	...	40	...	40	...	...	40	40	...	40	...
Utah	8	...	8	...	8	...	...	...	...	8	...	...	8	8	...	8	...
Vermont	8	...	8	...	...	...	...	...	8	...	8	...	8	8	...	8	...
Virginia	24	...	24	...	20	...	...	2	2	24	...	...	24	6	18	6	18
Washington	14	...	14	...	...	...	14	...	...	14	...	...	14	14	...	14	...
West Virginia	16	...	16	...	2	3	...	3	8	16	...	...	16	10½	5½	10½	5½
Wisconsin	26	1	22	3	1	23	...	...	2	1	23	2	26	26	...	26	...
Wyoming	6	...	6	...	6	...	...	...	...	6	...	...	6	6	...	6	...
Alaska	6	2	4	...	...	...	...	...	...	...	...	6	6	6	...	6	...
Canal Zone	6	...	6	...	...	...	...	...	6	...	6	...	6	6	...	6	...
District of Columbia	6	6	...	...	3	...	...	...	3	...	...	...	6	6	...	6	...
Hawaii	6	1	4	1	6	...	...	...	...	...	...	...	6	6	...	6	...
Philippine Islands	6	1	4	1	...	4	1	...	1	...	4	2	6	6	...	6	...
Puerto Rico	6	1	5	...	2	...	...	...	4	...	...	...	6	6	...	6	...
Virgin Islands	...												2	2	...	2	...
Total	1098	102½	844	151½[c]	238	263½	110	152	334½[d]	740	208	150[e]	1100	724[f]	375[g]	849[h]	250[i]

Source: *Official Proceedings, 1924.*
One hundred and third ballot (after shift), pp. 969-71.
c/ Other candidates: Robinson, 20; McAdoo, 11½; Smith, 7½; Walsh, 58; Meredith, 15½; Glass, 23; Gerard, 7; Hull, 1; not voting, 8.
Vice-Presidential Ballots. First (before shift), pp. 1026-8.
d/ Other candidates: John C. Greenway, 32; George S. Silzer, 12; Mrs. Margaret Chadbourne, 2; William S. Flynn, 21; Mrs. Martha Bird, 1; Bennett C. Clark, 24; Richard E. Enright, 5; Jonathan M. Davis, 56½; William J. Fields, 26; Andrew C. Erwin, 1; Mrs. LeRoy Springs, 44; Brand Whitlock, 1; John Farrell, 21; Houston Thompson, 1; James W. Gerard, 42; George K. Shuler, 4; Mrs. Belle Miller, 3; Mrs. Maidee B. Renshaw, 3; Frederick D. Gardner, 1; William D. Upshaw, 1; Key H. Pittman, 6; Edwin T. Meredith, 2; Morton Clark, 1; Newton D. Baker, 7; Albert C. Ritchie, 1; Thomas J. Walsh, 16.
First ballot (after shift), pp. 1035-7.
e/ Other candidates: Alvin Owsley, 16; Silzer, 10; Mrs. Springs, 18; Greenway, 2; Gerard, 10; Flynn, 15; Clark, 41; Davis, 4; John F. Hylan, 6; Enright, 5; Baker, 7; Ritchie, 1; Upshaw, 1; Farrell, 1; Pittman, 6; Whitlock, 1; Mrs. Miller, 3; Mrs. Renshaw, 3.

Source: *Official Proceedings, 1928.*
Presidential. First ballot (before shift), pp. 212-4.
a/ Add two-thirds.
b/ Add one-third.
f/ Add two-thirds.
g/ Other candidates: Cordell Hull, 71 and five-sixths; Walter F. George, 52½; James A. Reed, 48; Atlee Pomerene, 47; Jesse H. Jones, 43; Evans Woollen, 32; Patrick Harrison, 20; William A. Ayres, 20; Richard C. Watts, 18; Gilbert M. Hitchcock, 16; Vic Donahey, 5; Houston Thompson, 2.
First ballot (after shift), pp. 215-7.
h/ Add one-sixth.
i/ Other candidates: George, 52½; Reed, 52; Hull, 50 and five-sixths; Jones, 43; Watts, 18; Harrison, 8½; Woollen, 7; Donahey, 5; Ayres, 3; Pomerene, 3; Hitchcock, 2; Thompson, 2; Theodore G. Bilbo, 1; not voting, 2½.

	1928 DEMOCRATIC Vice-Presidential					1932 DEMOCRATIC											
		First Ballot (before shift)		First (after shift)			Minority Report, Louisiana Credentials			Minority Report, Minnesota Credentials			Minority Report, Permanent Organization		Minority Plank on Prohibition		
Delegation	Votes	Robinson	Other	Robinson	Other	Votes	Yea	Nay	Not Voting	Yea	Nay	Not Voting	Yea	Nay	Yea	Nay	Not Voting
Alabama	24	2	22	2	22	24	...	24	...	...	24	...	4½	19½	21	3	...
Arizona	6	6	...	6	...	6	...	6	...	...	6	...	...	6	...	6	...
Arkansas	18	18	...	18	...	18	...	18	...	...	18	...	...	18	13	5	...
California	26	23	3	26	...	44	44	...	...	44	...	...	44	...	11	33	...
Colorado	12	12	...	12	...	12	...	12	...	...	12	...	...	12	1	11	...
Connecticut	14	14	...	14	...	16	9½	6½	...	9a	6b	...	9½	6½	c	15d	...
Delaware	6	6	...	6	...	6	1	5	...	...	6	...	1	5	4	2	...
Florida	12	3	9	3	9	14	3	11	...	...	14	...	...	14	1	13	...
Georgia	28	28	...	28	...	28	...	28	...	...	28	...	...	28	28	...	...
Idaho	8	...	8	8	...	8	...	8	...	...	8	...	...	8	...	8	...
Illinois	58	56	2	56	2	58	50e	7f	...	48	10	...	42	16	...	58	...
Indiana	30	19	11	19	11	30	30	...	...	30	...	...	30	...	...	30	...
Iowa	26	26	...	26	...	26	13	13	...	...	26	...	10	16	...	26	...
Kansas	20	10	10	10	10	20	...	20	...	...	20	...	6½	13½	12	8	...
Kentucky	26	...	26	26	...	26	...	26	...	...	26	...	...	26	...	26	...
Louisiana	20	20	...	20	...	20	...	20	...	...	20	...	...	20	3	17	...
Maine	12	12	...	12	...	12	6	6	...	6	6	...	7	5	2	10	...
Maryland	16	16	...	16	...	16	16	...	...	16	...	...	16	...	...	16	...
Massachusetts	36	34	2	36	...	36	36	...	...	36	...	...	36	...	...	36	...
Michigan	30	30	...	30	...	38	...	38	...	...	38	...	...	38	...	38	...
Minnesota	24	24	...	24	...	24	1	23	...	1	23	...	3	21	4	18	2
Mississippi	20	20	...	20	...	20	...	20	...	...	20	...	...	20	20	...	...
Missouri	36	15	21	36	...	36	16½	19½	...	16½	19½	...	16½	10½	7½	28½	...
Montana	8	8	...	8	...	8	...	8	...	...	8	...	...	8	...	8	...
Nebraska	16	16	...	16	...	16	...	16	...	...	16	...	1	15	5	9	2
Nevada	6	...	6	6	...	6	...	6	...	...	6	...	...	6	...	6	...
New Hampshire	8	7	1	8	...	8	...	8	...	...	8	...	...	8	...	8	...
New Jersey	28	28	...	28	...	32	32	...	...	32	...	...	32	...	...	32	...
New Mexico	6	6	...	6	...	6	...	6	...	...	6	...	3	3	1	5	...
New York	90	90	...	90	...	94	65	29	...	65	29	...	67	27	...	94	...
North Carolina	24	14g	9h	14g	9h	26	20½	5½	...	...	26	...	4	22	18	8	...
North Dakota	10	10	...	10	...	10	...	10	...	2½	7½	...	1	9	...	10	...
Ohio	48	34	14	48	...	52	40	11	1	48½	2½	1	49½	2½	2	49	1
Oklahoma	20	20	...	20	...	22	22	...	...	22	...	...	22	...	22	...	...
Oregon	10	9	1	10	...	10	...	10	...	...	10	...	1	9	3	7	...
Pennsylvania	76	75	1	76	...	76	20½	55½	...	25	49	2	27½	48½	...	76	...
Rhode Island	10	10	...	10	...	10	10	...	...	10	...	...	10	...	...	10	...
South Carolina	18	18	...	18	...	18	...	18	...	...	18	...	...	18	...	18	...
South Dakota	10	4	6	10	...	10	...	10	...	...	10	...	...	10	6	4	...
Tennessee	24	6½	17½	22½	1½	24	...	24	...	...	24	...	...	24	6	18	...
Texas	40	40	...	40	...	46	46	...	...	46	...	...	46	...	...	46	...
Utah	8	6	2	8	...	8	...	8	...	...	8	...	...	8	...	8	...
Vermont	8	8	...	8	...	8	...	8	...	...	8	...	...	8	...	8	...
Virginia	24	22	2	24	...	24	24	...	...	24	...	...	24	...	13	11	...
Washington	14	14	...	14	...	16	...	16	...	...	16	...	...	16	1½	14½	...
West Virginia	16	16	...	16	...	16	...	16	...	3	13	...	...	16	8½	7	½
Wisconsin	26	26	...	26	...	26	2	24	...	2	24	...	2	24	...	26	...
Wyoming	6	...	6	6	...	6	...	6	...	...	6	...	...	6	...	6	...
Alaska	6	6	...	6	...	6	...	6	...	...	6	...	6	...	...	6	...
Canal Zone	6	6	...	6	...	6	...	6	...	...	6	...	...	6	...	6	...
District of Columbia	6	6	...	6	...	6	...	6	...	...	6	...	...	6	...	6	...
Hawaii	6	6	...	6	...	6	...	6	...	...	6	...	...	6	...	6	...
Philippine Islands	6	...	6	6	...	6	6	...	...	6	...	...	6	...	...	6	...
Puerto Rico	6	6	...	6	...	6	...	6	...	...	6	...	...	6	...	6	...
Virgin Islands	2	2	...	2	...	2	...	2	...	...	2	...	...	2	...	2	...
Total	1100	914i	185j	1035k	64l	1154	514m	638n	1	492o	658p	3	528	626	213q	934r	5½

Source: *Official Proceedings, 1928.*
Vice-Presidential. First ballot (before shift), pp. 249-50.
g/ Add two-thirds.
h/ Add one-third.
i/ Add one-sixth.
j/ Other candidates: Alben W. Barkley, 77; Mrs. Nellie T. Ross, 31; Henry T. Allen, 28; George L. Berry, 17½; Dan Moody, 9 and one-third; Duncan U. Fletcher, 7; John H. Taylor, 6; Lewis G. Stevenson, 4; Evans Woollen, 2; Joseph P. Tumulty, 1; not voting, 1.
First ballot (after shift), pp. 251-2.
k/ Add one-sixth.
l/ Other candidates: Allen, 21; Berry, 11½; Moody, 9 and one-third; Barkley, 9; Fletcher, 7; Mrs. Ross, 2; Woollen, 2; Stevenson, 2; not voting, 1.

Source: *Official Proceedings, 1932.*
Minority report, Louisiana credentials, pp. 67-8.
e/ Add one-fourth.
f/ Add three-fourths.
m/ Add one-fourth.
n/ Add three-fourths.
Minority report, Minnesota credentials, pp. 78-9.
a/ Add one-fourth.
b/ Add three-fourths.
o/ Add three-fourths.
p/ Add three-fourths.
Minority report, permanent organization, pp. 133-4.
Minority plank on prohibition, pp. 188-9.
c/ Add one-fourth.
d/ Add three-fourths.
q/ Add three-fourths.
r/ Add three-fourths.

	1932 DEMOCRATIC																1936 DEM.
		Motion to Adjourn			Presidential												
					First Ballot			Second Ballot			Third Ballot			Fourth Ballot			
Delegation	Votes	Yea	Nay	Not Voting	Roosevelt	Smith	Other	Roosevelt	Smith	Other	Roosevelt	Smith	Other	Roosevelt	Smith	Other	Votes
Alabama	24	...	24	...	24	...	...	24	...	...	24	...	...	24	...	...	22
Arizona	6	...	6	...	6	...	...	6	...	...	6	...	...	6	...	...	6
Arkansas	18	...	18	...	18	...	...	18	...	...	18	...	...	18	...	...	18
California	44	44	...	...	...	...	44	...	...	44	...	...	44	44	...	...	44
Colorado	12	...	12	...	12	...	...	12	...	...	12	...	...	12	...	...	12
Connecticut	16	9½	6½	...	...	16	...	...	16	...	...	16	...	...	16	...	16
Delaware	6	...	5	1	6	...	...	6	...	...	6	...	...	6	...	...	6
Florida	14	...	14	...	14	...	...	14	...	...	14	...	...	14	...	...	14
Georgia	28	...	28	...	28	...	...	28	...	...	28	...	...	28	...	...	24
Idaho	8	...	8	...	8	...	...	8	...	...	8	...	...	8	...	...	8
Illinois	58	...	58	...	15[a]	2[b]	40½	15[a]	2[b]	40½	15[a]	2[b]	40½	58	...	...	58
Indiana	30	...	30	...	14	2	14	16	2	12	16	2	12	30	...	...	28
Iowa	26	...	26	...	26	...	...	26	...	...	26	...	...	26	...	...	22
Kansas	20	...	20	...	20	...	...	20	...	...	20	...	...	20	...	...	18
Kentucky	26	...	26	...	26	...	...	26	...	...	26	...	...	26	...	...	22
Louisiana	20	...	20	...	20	...	...	20	...	...	20	...	...	20	...	...	20
Maine	12	...	12	...	12	...	...	12	...	...	12	...	...	12	...	...	10
Maryland	16	16	...	...	...	...	16	...	...	16	...	...	16	16	...	...	16
Massachusetts	36	...	36	...	...	36	...	...	36	...	...	36	...	...	36	...	34
Michigan	38	...	38	...	38	...	...	38	...	...	38	...	...	38	...	...	38
Minnesota	24	5	19	...	24	...	...	24	...	...	24	...	...	24	...	...	22
Mississippi	20	...	20	...	20	...	...	20	...	...	20	...	...	20	...	...	18
Missouri	36	...	36	...	12	...	24	18	...	18	20½	...	15½	36	...	...	30
Montana	8	...	8	...	8	...	...	8	...	...	8	...	...	8	...	...	8
Nebraska	16	...	16	...	16	...	...	16	...	...	16	...	...	16	...	...	14
Nevada	6	...	6	...	6	...	...	6	...	...	6	...	...	6	...	...	6
New Hampshire	8	...	8	...	8	...	...	8	...	...	8	...	...	8	...	...	8
New Jersey	32	...	32	...	...	32	...	...	32	...	...	32	...	...	32	...	32
New Mexico	6	...	6	...	6	...	...	6	...	...	6	...	...	6	...	...	6
New York	94	67	27	...	28½	65½	...	29½	64½	...	31	63	...	31	63	...	94
North Carolina	26	...	26	...	26	...	...	26	...	...	25[c]	...	d	26	...	...	26
North Dakota	10	...	10	...	9	...	1	10	...	...	9	...	1	10	...	...	8
Ohio	52	44	8	...	...	...	52	½	...	51½	2½	...	49½	29	17	6	52
Oklahoma	22	22	...	...	...	...	22	...	...	22	...	...	22	22	...	...	22
Oregon	10	...	10	...	10	...	...	10	...	...	10	...	...	10	...	...	10
Pennsylvania	76	22	46	8	44½	30	1½	44½	23½	8	45½	21	9½	49	14½	12½	72
Rhode Island	10	...	10	...	...	10	...	...	10	...	...	10	...	...	10	...	8
South Carolina	18	...	18	...	18	...	...	18	...	...	18	...	...	18	...	...	16
South Dakota	10	...	10	...	10	...	...	10	...	...	10	...	...	10	...	...	8
Tennessee	24	...	24	...	24	...	...	24	...	...	24	...	...	24	...	...	22
Texas	46	46	...	...	...	...	46	...	...	46	...	...	46	46	...	...	46
Utah	8	...	8	...	8	...	...	8	...	...	8	...	...	8	...	...	8
Vermont	8	...	8	...	8	...	...	8	...	...	8	...	...	8	...	...	6
Virginia	24	...	24	...	...	...	24	...	...	24	...	...	24	24	...	...	22
Washington	16	...	16	...	16	...	...	16	...	...	16	...	...	16	...	...	16
West Virginia	16	...	16	...	16	...	...	16	...	...	16	...	...	16	...	...	16
Wisconsin	26	...	26	...	24	2	...	24	2	...	24	2	...	24	2	...	24
Wyoming	6	...	6	...	6	...	...	6	...	...	6	...	...	6	...	...	6
Alaska	6	...	6	...	5	...	1	6	...	...	6	...	...	6	...	...	6
Canal Zone	6	...	6	...	6	...	...	6	...	...	6	...	...	6	...	...	6
District of Columbia	6	...	6	...	6	...	...	6	...	...	6	...	...	6	...	...	6
Hawaii	6	...	6	...	6	...	...	6	...	...	6	...	...	6	...	...	6
Philippine Islands	6	6	...	...	...	6	...	...	6	...	...	6	...	6	...	...	6
Puerto Rico	6	...	6	...	6	...	...	6	...	...	6	...	...	6	...	...	6
Virgin Islands	2	...	2	...	2	...	...	2	...	...	2	...		2	...	...	2
Total	1154	281½	863½	9	666[e]	201[f]	286[g]	677[h]	194[i]	282[j]	682[k]	190[l]	280[m]	945	190½	18½[n]	1100

Source: *Official Proceedings, 1932.*
Motion to adjourn, pp. 270-1.
Presidential. First ballot, pp. 288-9.
a/ Add one-fourth.
b/ Add one-fourth.
e/ Add one-fourth.
f/ Add three-fourths.
g/ Other candidates: John N. Garner, 90 and one-fourth; Harry F. Byrd, 25; Melvin A. Traylor, 42 and one-fourth; Albert C. Ritchie, 21; James A. Reed, 24; George White, 52; William H. Murray, 23; Newton D. Baker, 8½.
Second ballot, pp. 301-2.
h/ Add three-fourths.
i/ Add one-fourth.
j/ Other candidates: Garner, 90 and one-fourth: Byrd, 24; Traylor, 40 and one-fourth; Ritchie, 23½; Reed, 18; White, 50½; Baker, 8; Will Rogers, 22; not voting, 5½.
Third ballot, pp. 315-6.
c/ Add four-hundredths.
d/ Add ninety-six-hundredths.
k/ Add seventy-nine-hundredths.
l/ Add one-fourth.
m/ Other candidates: Garner, 101 and one-fourth; Byrd, 24 and ninety-six-hundredths; Traylor, 40 and one-fourth; Ritchie, 23½; Reed, 27½; White, 52½; Baker, 8½; not voting, 2½.
Fourth ballot, pp. 324-5.
n/ Other candidates: Ritchie, 3½; White, 3; Baker, 5½; James M. Cox, 1; not voting, 5½.

Source: *Official Proceedings, 1936.*

Delegation	1940 DEMOCRATIC						1944 DEMOCRATIC											
		Presidential		Vice-Pres.				Presidential		Vice-Presidential								
		First Ballot		First Ballot				First Ballot		First Ballot			Second Ballot (before shift)			Second Ballot (after shift)		
	Votes	Roosevelt	Other	Bankhead	Wallace	Other	Votes	Roosevelt	Other	Wallace	Truman	Other	Wallace	Truman	Other	Wallace	Truman	Other
Alabama	22	20	2	22	...	...	24	22	2	...	...	24	2	...	22	...	24	...
Arizona	6	6	...	6	...	...	10	10	...	1	9	...	1	9	...	...	10	...
Arkansas	18	18	...	...	18	...	20	20	...	...	20	...	...	20	...	...	20	...
California	44	43	1	6½	35	2½	52	52	...	30	22	...	30	22	...	10	42	...
Colorado	12	12	...	...	½	11½	12	12	...	1	...	11	9½	2½	...	...	12	...
Connecticut	16	16	...	...	16	...	18	18	...	18	...	...	18	...	...	...	18	...
Delaware	6	6	...	...	4	2	8	8	...	8	...	...	...	8	...	...	8	...
Florida	14	12½	1½	2½	8½	3	18	14	4	9	2	7	9	6	3	...	18	...
Georgia	24	24	...	24	...	...	26	26	...	26	...	...	26	...	...	...	26	...
Idaho	8	8	...	...	...	8	10	10	...	5	5	...	5	5	...	...	10	...
Illinois	58	58	...	3	55	...	58	58	...	...	...	58	...	...	58	3	55	...
Indiana	28	28	...	8	20	...	26	26	...	5	...	21	6	1	19	2	24	...
Iowa	22	22	...	...	22	...	20	20	...	20	...	...	20	...	...	20	...	...
Kansas	18	18	...	...	18	...	16	16	...	16	...	...	16	...	...	...	16	...
Kentucky	22	22	...	11	11	...	24	24	...	...	...	24	...	...	24	...	24	...
Louisiana	20	20	...	20	...	...	22	...	22	...	22	...	...	22	...	...	22	...
Maine	10	10	...	3	3	4	10	10	...	1	5	4	4	6	...	...	10	...
Maryland	16	7½	8½	13	3	...	18	18	...	...	...	18	...	18	...	...	18	...
Massachusetts	34	21½	12½	5	22[a]	6[b]	34	34	...	12½	12	9½	11½	14½	8	...	34	...
Michigan	38	38	...	...	38	...	38	38	...	34	1	3	35	2	1	8	30	...
Minnesota	22	22	...	...	22	...	24	24	...	24	...	...	24	...	...	24	...	...
Mississippi	18	18	...	13½	4	½	20	...	20	...	...	20	...	20	...	...	20	...
Missouri	30	26½	3½	28½	1½	...	32	32	...	...	32	...	...	32	...	...	32	...
Montana	8	8	...	3½	3	1½	10	10	...	4	5	1	4	6	...	4	6	...
Nebraska	14	13	1	9	3	2	12	12	...	4	1	7	4	1	7	4	1	7
Nevada	6	2	4	4	½	1½	8	8	...	...	1	7	4	4	...	...	8	...
New Hampshire	8	8	...	...	4	4	10	10	...	2½	7	½	2½	7	½	...	10	...
New Jersey	32	32	...	...	32	...	34	34	...	10	24	...	10	24	...	...	34	...
New Mexico	6	6	...	...	6	...	10	10	...	...	10	...	...	10	...	...	10	...
New York	94	64½	29½	4½	47	42½	96	94½	1½	23	69½	3½	18	74½	3½	...	93	3
North Carolina	26	26	...	17[c]	4[d]	4[e]	30	30	...	...	...	30	...	...	30	...	30	...
North Dakota	8	8	...	...	8	...	8	8	...	8	...	...	8	...	...	8	...	...
Ohio	52	52	...	...	52	...	52	52	...	24½	19½	8	26½	21½	4	...	52	...
Oklahoma	22	22	...	...	...	22	22	22	...	...	...	22	...	22	...	...	22	...
Oregon	10	10	...	...	10	...	14	14	...	14	...	...	12	1	1	6	4	4
Pennsylvania	72	72	...	3	68	1	72	72	...	46½	23½	2	46	24	2	...	72	...
Rhode Island	8	8	...	...	5½	2½	10	10	...	...	10	...	...	10	...	...	10	...
South Carolina	16	16	...	4	9½	2½	18	14½	3½	...	...	18	...	16½	1½	...	18	...
South Dakota	8	3	5	...	8	...	8	8	...	7	1	...	7	1	...	...	8	...
Tennessee	22	22	...	22	...	...	26	26	...	...	...	26	...	...	26	...	...	26
Texas	46	...	46	46	...	...	48	36	12	...	1	47	27	21	...	...	48	...
Utah	8	8	...	2	6	...	10	10	...	...	...	10	10	...	...	...	10	...
Vermont	6	6	...	1	5	...	6	6	...	1½	4	½	2	4	...	...	6	...
Virginia	22	5[f]	16[g]	22	...	...	24	...	24	...	...	24	...	24	...	...	24	...
Washington	16	15	1	7½	1½	7	18	18	...	18	...	...	18	...	...	...	18	...
West Virginia	16	12	4	2	11	3	18	17	1	12	...	6	12	4	2	1	17	...
Wisconsin	24	21	3	5	15	4	26	26	...	25	1	...	25	1	...	13	13	...
Wyoming	6	6	...	3	3	...	8	8	...	...	...	8	...	...	8	...	8	...
Alaska	6	...	6	3	3	...	6	6	...	6	...	...	6	...	...	...	6	...
Canal Zone	6	...	6	1	5	...	6	6	...	3	2	1	3	3	...	...	6	...
District of Columbia	6	6	...	...	6	...	6	6	...	2	4	...	2	4	...	1	5	...
Hawaii	6	6	...	2	2	2	6	6	...	6	...	...	6	...	...	...	6	...
Philippine Islands	6	6	...	...	...	6	6	6	...	...	...	6	1	...	5	...	6	...
Puerto Rico	6	3	3	...	6	...	6	6	...	...	6	...	...	6	...	...	6	...
Virgin Islands	2	2	...	2	...	...	2	2	...	2	...	...	2	...	...	1	1	...
Total	1100	946[h]	153[i]	329[j]	626[k]	144[l]	1176	1086	90[m]	429½	319½	427[n]	473	477½	225½[o]	105	1031	40[p]

Source: *Official Proceedings, 1940.*

Presidential. First ballot, pp. 189-90.

f/ Add fourteen-fifteenths.

g/ Add one-fifteenth.

h/ Add thirteen-thirtieths.

i/ Other candidates: James A. Farley, 72 and nine-tenths; John N. Garner, 61; Millard E. Tydings, 9½; Cordell Hull, 5 and two-thirds; not voting, 4½.

Vice-Presidential. First ballot, pp. 240-1.

a/ Add two-thirds.

b/ Add one-third.

c/ Add one-tenth.

d/ Add one-fifth.

e/ Add seven-tenths.

j/ Add three-fifths.

k/ Add eleven-thirtieths.

l/ Other candidates: Jesse H. Jones, 5 and nine-tenths; Alva B. Adams, 11½; Paul V. McNutt, 68 and four-fifths; Prentiss M. Brown, 1; Bascom Timmons, 1; Scott W. Lucas, 1; James A. Farley, 7 and five-sixths; Joseph C. O'Mahoney, 3; Alben W. Barkley, 2; Louis A. Johnson, 1; David I. Walsh, ½; not voting, 40½.

Source: *Official Proceedings, 1944.*

Presidential. First ballot, p. 110.

m/ Other candidates: Harry F. Byrd, 89; James A. Farley, 1.

Vice-Presidential. First ballot, p. 256.

n/ Other candidates: J. Melville Broughton, 43; Scott W. Lucas, 61; Prentice Cooper, 26; Alben W. Barkley, 49½; John H. Bankhead, 98; Herbert S. O'Conor, 18; Elbert D. Thomas, 10; Joseph C. O'Mahoney, 27; Claude Pepper, 3; Frank Murphy, 2; Paul V. McNutt, 31; Robert S. Kerr, 23; Bascom Timmons, 1; Sam Rayburn, 2; not voting, 32½.

Second ballot (before shift), pp. 257-62.

o/ Other candidates: Bankhead, 23½; Pepper, 3; Lucas, 58; Barkley, 40; Kerr, 1; McNutt, 28; Broughton, 30; William O. Douglas, 1; Cooper, 26; O'Mahoney, 8; not voting, 7.

Second ballot (after shift), p. 270.

p/ Other candidates: McNutt, 1; Barkley, 6; Cooper, 26; Douglas, 4; not voting, 3.

	1948 DEMOCRATIC											1952 DEMOCRATIC						
		Moody Resolution on Civil Rights		Biemiller Resolution on Civil Rights		Presidential							Seating of Virginia Delegation			Table Motion to Adjourn		
						First Ballot (before shift)			First Ballot (after shift)									
Delegation	Votes	Yea	Nay	Yea	Nay	Truman	Russell	Other	Truman	Russell	Other	Votes	Yea	Nay	Not Voting	Yea	Nay	Not Voting
Alabama	26	26	...	...	26	...	26	...	...	26	...	22	22	...	...	13½	8½	...
Arizona	12	...	12	...	12	12	...	...	12	...	...	12	12	...	...	12	...	...
Arkansas	22	22	...	...	22	...	22	...	...	22	...	22	22	...	...	19	3	...
California	54	1½	52½	53	1	53½	...	½	54	...	...	68	4	61	3	...	68	...
Colorado	12	3	9	10	2	12	...	...	12	...	...	16	4½	11½	...	4	12	...
Connecticut	20	...	20	20	...	20	...	...	20	...	...	16	...	16	...	16	...	...
Delaware	10	...	10	...	10	10	...	...	10	...	...	6	6	...	...	6	...	...
Florida	20	20	...	...	20	...	19	1	...	20	...	24	24	...	...	19	5	...
Georgia	28	28	...	...	28	...	28	...	...	28	...	28	28	...	...	28	...	...
Idaho	12	...	12	...	12	12	...	...	12	...	...	12	12	...	...	...	12	...
Illinois	60	...	60	60	...	60	...	...	60	...	...	60	52	8	...	53	7	...
Indiana	26	...	26	17	9	25	...	1	26	...	...	26	14½	6½	5	25	1	...
Iowa	20	...	20	18	2	20	...	...	20	...	...	24	17	7	...	8	15	1
Kansas	16	...	16	16	...	16	...	...	16	...	...	16	...	16	...	16	...	...
Kentucky	26	...	26	...	26	26	...	...	26	...	...	26	26	...	...	26	...	...
Louisiana	24	24	...	...	24	...	24	...	...	24	...	20	20	...	...	20	...	...
Maine	10	...	10	3	7	10	...	...	10	...	...	10	2½	7½	...	4½	5½	...
Maryland	20	...	20	...	20	20	...	...	20	...	...	18	18	...	...	18	...	...
Massachusetts	36	...	36	36	...	36	...	...	36	...	...	36	16	19	1	30	4½	1½
Michigan	42	...	42	42	...	42	...	...	42	...	...	40	...	40	...	...	40	...
Minnesota	26	...	26	26	...	26	...	...	26	...	...	26	...	26	...	...	26	...
Mississippi	22	22	...	...	22	...	...	22	...	...	22	18	18	...	...	18	...	...
Missouri	34	...	34	...	34	34	...	...	34	...	...	34	34	...	...	29	5	...
Montana	12	...	12	1½	10½	12	...	...	12	...	...	12	...	12	...	12	...	...
Nebraska	12	...	12	3	9	12	...	...	12	...	...	12	8	3	1	...	12	...
Nevada	10	...	10	...	10	10	...	...	10	...	...	10	10	...	...	9½	½	...
New Hampshire	12	...	12	1	11	11	...	1	11	...	1	8	1	7	...	...	8	...
New Jersey	36	...	36	36	...	36	...	...	36	...	...	32	...	32	...	24	8	...
New Mexico	12	...	12	...	12	12	...	...	12	...	...	12	12	...	...	12	...	...
New York	98	...	98	98	...	83	...	15	98	...	...	94	7	87	...	5	89	...
North Carolina	32	32	...	...	32	13	19	...	13	19	...	32	32	...	...	32	...	...
North Dakota	8	...	8	...	8	8	...	...	8	...	...	8	8	...	...	8	...	...
Ohio	50	...	50	39	11	50	...	...	50	...	...	54	33½	14½	6	26	28	...
Oklahoma	24	...	24	...	24	24	...	...	24	...	...	24	24	...	...	24	...	...
Oregon	16	3	13	7	9	16	...	...	16	...	...	12	4	8	...	...	12	...
Pennsylvania	74	...	74	74	...	74	...	...	74	...	...	70	57	13	...	35	35	...
Rhode Island	12	...	12	...	12	12	...	...	12	...	...	12	10	2	...	10	2	...
South Carolina	20	20	...	...	20	...	20	...	...	20	...	16	...	...	16	...	...	16
South Dakota	8	...	8	8	...	8	...	...	8	...	...	8	...	8	...	...	8	...
Tennessee	28	28	...	...	28	...	28	...	...	28	...	28	...	28	...	...	28	...
Texas	50	50	...	...	50	...	50	...	...	50	...	52	52	...	...	52	...	...
Utah	12	...	12	...	12	12	...	...	12	...	...	12	3	9	...	...	12	...
Vermont	6	...	6	6	...	5½	...	½	5½	...	½	6	...	6	...	6	...	...
Virginia	26	26	...	...	26	...	26	...	...	26	...	28	...	...	28	28	...	...
Washington	20	...	20	20	...	20	...	...	20	...	...	22	12½	9½	...	3	10	...
West Virginia	20	...	20	7	13	15	4	1	20	...	...	20	13½	5	1½	10	9	1
Wisconsin	24	...	24	24	...	24	...	...	24	...	...	28	1	27	...	...	28	...
Wyoming	6	1½	4½	4	2	6	...	...	6	...	...	10	5½	4½	...	2½	7½	...
Alaska	6	3	3	2	4	6	...	...	6	...	...	6	...	6	...	...	6	...
Canal Zone	2	...	2	...	2	2	...	...	2	...	...	2	2	...	...	2	...	...
District of Columbia	6	...	6	6	...	6	...	...	6	...	...	6	...	6	...	...	6	...
Hawaii	6	...	6	6	...	6	...	...	6	...	...	6	...	6	...	4	2	...
Philippine Islands	...	...	...	...	...	...	...	...	...	...	...	...	...	...	...	...	...	...
Puerto Rico	6	...	6	6	...	6	...	...	6	...	...	6	2	4	...	1	5	...
Virgin Islands	2	...	2	2	...	2	...	...	2	...	...	2	...	2	...	...	2	...
Total	1234	310[a]	924[b]	651½	582½	926	266	42[c]	947½	263	23½[d]	1230	650½	518	61½	671	539½[e]	19½

Source: *Official Proceedings, 1948.*
Moody resolution on civil rights, pp. 196-201.
a/ Sum of column; proceedings record 309.
b/ Sum of column; proceedings record 925.
Biemiller resolution on civil rights, pp. 202-210.
Presidential. First ballot (before shift), pp. 270-280.
c/ Other candidates: Paul V. McNutt, 2½; James A. Roe, 15; Alben W. Barkley, 1; not voting, 23½.
First ballot (after shift), p. 280.
d/ Other candidates: McNutt, ½; not voting, 23.

Source: *Official Proceedings, 1952.*
Seating of Virginia delegation, p. 363.
Table motion to adjourn, p. 393.
e/ Sum of column; proceedings record 534.

		1952 DEMOCRATIC													
		Presidential													
		First Ballot					Second Ballot					Third Ballot			
Delegation	Votes	Harriman	Kefauver	Russell	Stevenson	Other	Harriman	Kefauver	Russell	Stevenson	Other	Kefauver	Russell	Stevenson	Other
Alabama	22	...	8	13	½	½	...	7½	14	½	...	7½	14	½	...
Arizona	12	...	...	...	...	12	...	...	12	...	...	...	12	...	...
Arkansas	22	...	...	...	...	22	1	1½	18	1½	...	1½	...	20½	...
California	68	...	68	...	...	...	...	68	...	...	...	68	...	...	...
Colorado	16	5	2	8½	½	...	5	5	2½	3½	...	4	3½	8½	...
Connecticut	16	...	...	...	16	...	...	...	...	16	...	...	...	16	...
Delaware	6	...	...	...	6	...	...	...	...	6	...	...	...	6	...
Florida	24	...	5	19	...	...	...	5	19	...	...	5	19	...	...
Georgia	28	...	...	28	...	...	...	...	28	...	...	...	28	...	...
Idaho	12	3½	3	1	1½	3	...	...	...	12	...	...	...	12	...
Illinois	60	1	3	...	53	3	...	3	...	54	3	3	...	54	3
Indiana	26	...	1	...	25	...	...	1	...	25	...	1	...	25	...
Iowa	24	½	8	2	8	5½	½	8½	3	9½	2½	8	3	10	3
Kansas	16	...	...	...	16	...	...	...	...	16	...	...	...	16	...
Kentucky	26	...	...	...	...	26	...	...	...	...	26	...	...	...	26
Louisiana	20	...	...	20	...	...	...	...	20	...	...	...	20	...	...
Maine	10	1½	1½	2½	3½	1	1	1	2½	4½	1	½	2½	7	...
Maryland	18	...	18	...	...	...	...	15½	2	...	½	8½	2½	6	1
Massachusetts	36	...	...	...	...	36	...	2½	...	...	33½	5	1	25	5
Michigan	40	...	40	...	...	...	...	40	...	...	...	...	...	40	...
Minnesota	26	...	...	...	...	26	1½	17	...	7½	...	13	...	13	...
Mississippi	18	...	...	18	...	...	...	...	18	...	...	...	18	...	...
Missouri	34	1½	2	...	18	12½	1½	2	...	19½	11	2	...	22	10
Montana	12	...	...	...	...	12	3	3	3	...	3	...	...	12	...
Nebraska	12	...	5	1	2	4	...	5	1	2	4	3	1	8	...
Nevada	10	...	½	8	1	½	...	½	7½	2	...	½	7½	2	...
New Hampshire	8	...	8	...	...	...	...	8	...	...	...	8	...	...	...
New Jersey	32	1	3	...	28	...	...	4	...	28	...	4	...	28	...
New Mexico	12	1	1½	4	1	4½	...	1½	6	4½	...	1½	3½	7	...
New York	94	83½	1	...	6½	3	84½	1	...	6½	2	4	...	86½	3½
North Carolina	32	...	...	26	5½	½	...	...	24	7	1	...	24	7½	½
North Dakota	8	...	2	2	2	2	...	...	...	...	8	...	...	8	...
Ohio	54	1	29½	7	13	3½	1	27½	8	17½	...	27	1	26	...
Oklahoma	24	...	...	...	...	24	...	...	...	...	24	...	...	...	24
Oregon	12	...	12	...	...	...	...	12	...	...	...	11	...	1	...
Pennsylvania	70	4½	22½	...	36	7	2½	21½	...	40	6	...	...	70	...
Rhode Island	12	1½	3½	...	5½	1½	...	4	...	8	...	...	...	12	...
South Carolina	16	...	...	16	...	...	...	...	16	...	...	...	16	...	...
South Dakota	8	...	8	...	...	...	...	8	...	...	...	8	...	...	...
Tennessee	28	...	28	...	...	...	...	28	...	...	...	28	...	...	...
Texas	52	...	...	52	...	...	...	...	52	...	...	...	52	...	...
Utah	12	6½	½	2	½	2½	9	1½	...	½	1	...	...	12	...
Vermont	6	...	½	...	5	½	...	½	½	5	...	...	½	5½	...
Virginia	28	...	...	28	...	...	...	...	28	...	...	...	28	...	...
Washington	22	1	12	½	6	2½	2	12½	½	6	1	11	½	10½	...
West Virginia	20	...	5½	7	1	6½	...	7½	6½	5½	½	7½	3½	9	...
Wisconsin	28	...	28	...	...	...	...	28	...	...	...	28	...	...	...
Wyoming	10	3½	1½	½	3	1½	2½	3	...	4½	...	...	...	10	...
Alaska	6	...	6	...	...	...	...	6	...	...	...	6	...	...	...
Canal Zone	2	...	...	2	...	...	...	...	2	...	...	...	...	2	...
District of Columbia	6	6	...	...	...	...	6	...	...	...	...	...	...	6	...
Hawaii	6	1	1	...	2	2	...	1	...	5	...	1	...	5	...
Philippine Islands	...	...	...	...	...	...	...	...	...	...	...	...	...	...	...
Puerto Rico	6	...	...	...	6	...	...	...	...	6	...	...	...	6	...
Virgin Islands	2	...	1	...	1	...	...	1	...	1	...	...	...	2	...
Total	1230	123½	340	268	273	225½[a]	121	362½	294	324½	128[b]	275½	261	617½	76[c]

Source: *Official Proceedings, 1952.*

Presidential. First ballot, p. 456.

a/ Other candidates: Alben W. Barkley, 48½; Robert S. Kerr, 65; J. William Fulbright, 22; Paul H. Douglas, 3; Oscar R. Ewing, 4; Paul A. Dever, 37½; Hubert H. Humphrey, 26; James E. Murray, 12; Harry S. Truman, 6; William O. Douglas, ½; not voting, 1.

Second ballot, p. 484.

b/ Other candidates: Barkley, 78½; Paul H. Douglas, 3; Kerr, 5½; Ewing, 3; Dever, 30½; Truman, 6; not voting, 1½.

Third ballot, p. 538.

c/ Other candidates: Barkley, 67½; Paul H. Douglas, 3: Dever, ½; Ewing, 3; not voting, 2.

Delegation	Votes	1956 DEMOCRATIC: Presidential, First Ballot: Stevenson	Harriman	Other	Vice-Presidential, First Ballot: Kefauver	Kennedy	Humphrey	Gore	Wagner	Other	Second Ballot (before shift): Kefauver	Kennedy	Other	Second Ballot (after shift): Kefauver	Kennedy	Other
Alabama	26	15½	...	10½	3½	1½	...	12½	...	8½	6	12½	7½	6	16½	3½
Arizona	16	16	...	...	16	...	...	...	...	...	16	...	...	16	...	...
Arkansas	26	26	...	...	...	...	...	26	...	...	...	26	...	...	26	...
California	68	68	...	...	33	10½	23½	...	...	1	37½	25	5½	50	18	...
Colorado	20	13½	6	½	15	2	3	...	...	...	15½	2	2½	20	...	...
Connecticut	20	20	...	...	...	20	...	...	...	...	...	20	...	...	20	...
Delaware	10	10	...	...	...	...	...	...	10	...	...	10	...	10	...	...
Florida	28	25	...	3	...	...	...	...	...	28	17	10½	½	23½	3½	1
Georgia	32	...	...	32	...	32	...	...	...	...	...	32	...	...	32	...
Idaho	12	12	...	...	12	...	...	...	...	...	12	...	...	12	...	...
Illinois	64	53½	8½	2	12½	46	...	...	3½	2	10½	49½	4	9½	54½	...
Indiana	26	21½	3	1½	22	2½	1½	...	...	...	20	3½	2½	20	3½	2½
Iowa	24	16½	7	½	15½	2	6	...	½	...	18½	4	1½	24	...	...
Kansas	16	16	...	...	16	...	...	...	...	...	16	...	...	16	...	...
Kentucky	30	...	...	30	...	...	...	...	...	30	...	...	30	...	30	...
Louisiana	24	24	...	...	...	24	...	...	...	...	...	24	...	...	24	...
Maine	14	10½	3½	...	6	7½	½	...	...	...	5	9	...	14	...	...
Maryland	18	18	...	...	18	...	...	...	...	...	18	...	...	18	...	...
Massachusetts	40	32	7½	½	...	40	...	...	...	...	...	40	...	...	40	...
Michigan	44	39	5	...	40	...	4	...	...	...	40	...	4	44	...	...
Minnesota	30	19	11	...	...	...	30	...	...	...	13½	...	16½	30	...	...
Mississippi	22	...	...	22	...	...	...	22	...	...	...	22	...	...	22	...
Missouri	38	...	...	38	1	2½	34½	...	...	...	3	2½	32½	36	1½	½
Montana	16	10	6	...	8	2½	4½	...	1	...	13½	1½	1	15	1	...
Nebraska	12	12	...	...	12	...	...	...	...	...	12	...	...	12	...	...
Nevada	14	5½	7	1½	2	11	...	...	1	...	½	13½	...	½	13½	...
New Hampshire	8	5½	1½	1	7½	½	...	...	...	...	8	...	...	8	...	...
New Jersey	36	36	...	...	4	½	...	...	31½	...	6	30	...	6	30	...
New Mexico	16	12	3½	½	...	...	...	...	...	16	9½	4½	2	9½	4½	2
New York	98	5½	92½	...	...	...	...	...	98	...	1½	96½	...	1½	96½	...
North Carolina	36	34½	1	½	...	...	...	...	...	36	9½	17½	9	9½	17½	9
North Dakota	8	8	...	...	8	...	...	...	...	...	8	...	...	8	...	...
Ohio	58	52	½	5½	50½	5½	...	...	...	2	51½	5½	1	57	...	1
Oklahoma	28	...	28	...	...	...	...	28	...	...	...	...	28	28	...	...
Oregon	16	16	...	...	16	...	...	...	...	...	16	...	...	16	...	...
Pennsylvania	74	67	7	...	54	9½	2	...	8½	...	64	8½	1½	74	...	...
Rhode Island	16	16	...	...	½	15½	...	...	...	...	½	15½	...	½	15½	...
South Carolina	20	2	...	18	...	6½	...	½	...	13	...	17	3	...	20	...
South Dakota	8	8	...	...	7	...	1	...	...	...	8	...	...	8	...	...
Tennessee	32	32	...	...	...	...	...	32	...	...	...	...	32	32	...	...
Texas	56	...	...	56	...	...	...	56	...	...	...	56	...	...	56	...
Utah	12	12	...	...	9	...	2½	...	½	...	11	...	1	12	...	...
Vermont	6	5½	½	...	...	6	...	...	...	...	...	6	...	...	6	...
Virginia	32	...	...	32	...	32	...	...	...	...	...	32	...	...	32	...
Washington	26	19½	6	½	24	½	1½	...	...	...	25	1	...	26	...	...
West Virginia	24	24	...	...	7	5	12	...	...	...	9	9	6	24	...	...
Wisconsin	28	22½	5	½	28	...	...	...	...	...	28	...	...	28	...	...
Wyoming	14	14	...	...	7	5	2	...	...	...	9½	4½	...	14	...	...
Alaska	6	6	...	...	6	...	...	...	...	...	6	...	...	6	...	...
Canal Zone	3	3	...	...	...	3	...	...	...	...	...	3	...	...	3	...
District of Columbia	6	6	...	...	3	...	3	...	...	...	3	...	3	6	...	...
Hawaii	6	6	...	...	1½	1	1½	1	1	...	2	2	2	2	2	2
Philippine Islands	...	...	...	...	...	...	...	...	...	...	...	...	...	...	...	...
Puerto Rico	6	6	...	...	...	...	...	...	6	...	...	...	6	...	...	6
Virgin Islands	3	3	...	...	1	...	1	...	1	...	1	2	...	3	...	...
Total	1372	905½	210	256½ [a]	466½	294½	134	178	162½	136½ [b]	551½	618	202½ [c]	755½	589	27½ [d]

Source: *Official Proceedings, 1956*

a/ Other Candidates: Lyndon B. Johnson, 80; James C. Davis, 33; Albert B. Chandler, 36½; John S. Battle, 32½; George B. Timmerman, 23½; W. Stuart Symington, 45½; Frank Lausche, 5½.

b/ Other Candidates: Luther B. Hodges, 40; P. T. Maner, 33; LeRoy P. Collins, 28½; Clinton P. Anderson, 16; Edmund G. Brown, 1; W. Stuart Symington, 1; Frank Clement, 13½; Lyndon B. Johnson, ½.

At the end of the roll call, Florida changed its vote. The totals for all candidates after this change were as follows: Kefauver, 483½, Kennedy, 304; Gore, 178; Wagner, 162½; Humphrey, 134½; Hodges, 40; Maner, 33; Anderson, 16; Clement, 13½; Collins, 1½; Brown, 1; Symington, 1; Johnson, ½; not cast, 3.

c/ Other Candidates: Hubert Humphrey, 74½; Albert Gore, 110½; Robert Wagner, 9½; Luther Hodges, ½; Frank Clement, ½; Edmund G. Brown, ½.

d/ Other Candidates: Gore, 13½; Wagner, 6; Humphrey, 2; Clement, ½; not cast, 5½.

| | 1960 DEMOCRATIC | | | | | | 1968 DEMOCRATIC | | | | | | | | | |
| | Presidential First ballot | | | | | | | Motion to delay credentials debate | | | Majority report Texas credentials | | | Minority report Georgia credentials | | |
Delegation	Votes	Kennedy	Johnson	Stevenson	Symington	Others	Votes	Yea	Nay	Not voting	Yea	Nay	Not voting	Yea	Nay	Not voting
Alabama	29	3½	20	½	3½	1½	32	½	31½	...	32	...	...	10	22	...
Alaska	9	9	...	...	...	...	22	...	22	...	17	5	...	5	17	...
Arizona	17	17	...	...	...	...	19	4½	14	½	1½	17	½	17	2	...
Arkansas	27	...	27	...	...	...	33	...	33	...	33	...	...	3	29	1
California	81	33½	7½	31½	8	½	174	173	1	...	1	173	...	173	1	...
Colorado	21	13½	...	5½	2	...	35	31	4	...	...	35	...	30	5	...
Connecticut	21	21	...	...	...	...	44	...	44	...	30	12	2	13	27	4
Delaware	11	...	11	...	...	...	22	...	21	1	21	...	1	3	18	1
Florida	29	...	...	...	...	29	63	5	58	...	58	4	1	9	54	...
Georgia	33	...	33	...	...	...	43	...	43a	....	...	...	43	...	...	43
Hawaii	9	1½	3	3½	1	...	26	...	26	...	26	...	...	4	22	...
Idaho	13	6	4½	½	2	...	25	2	23	...	22½	2½	...	4½	20½	...
Illinois	69	61½	...	2	5½	...	118	...	118	...	114	4	...	12	83	23
Indiana	34	34	...	...	...	...	63	13	48	2	34	10	19	25	38	...
Iowa	26	21½	½	2	½	1½	46	33½	12½	...	37½	8½	...	32	12	2
Kansas	21	21	...	...	...	...	38	...	38	...	38	...	...	3½	34½	...
Kentucky	31	3½	25½	1½	½	...	46	3	43	...	40½	5½	...	6	40	...
Louisiana	26	...	26	...	...	...	36	...	36	...	32	4	...	7	29	...
Maine	15	15	...	...	...	...	27	2	24	1	25	1	1	5	22	...
Maryland	24	24	...	...	...	...	49	5	44	...	46	3	...	3	46	...
Massachusetts	41	41	...	...	...	...	72	19	53	...	16	47	9	39	24	9
Michigan	51	42½	...	2½	6	...	96	20	69	7	70	23	3	35	58	3
Minnesota	31	...	...	...	...	31	52	16	32	4	34½	14½	3	16	33	3
Mississippi	23	...	...	...	...	23	24	24	...	...	2	18½	3½	18	2	4
Missouri	39	...	...	...	39	...	60	3	57	...	48	12	...	12	48	...
Montana	17	10	2	2½	2½	...	26	3	23	...	20	4	2	2½	21½	2
Nebraska	16	11	½	...	4	½	30	16	14	...	12	16	2	11	18	1
Nevada	15	5½	6½	2½	½	...	22	1	21	...	13	7	2	14	8	...
New Hampshire	11	11	...	...	...	...	26	21	4	1	6	20	...	23	2	1
New Jersey	41	...	...	...	...	41	82	20	62	...	43	25	14	22	51	9
New Mexico	17	4	13	...	...	...	26	11	15	...	13	13	...	11	15	...
New York	114	104½	3½	3½	2½	...	190	190	...	...	...	190	...	190	...	...
North Carolina	37	6	27½	3	...	½	59	3½	55½	...	54½	4½	...	3½	55½	...
North Dakota	11	11	...	...	...	...	25	6	17	2	17	5	3	5	17	3
Ohio	64	64	...	...	...	...	115	30	85	...	37½	27	50½	21	80	14
Oklahoma	29	...	29	...	...	...	41	5	36	...	40	1	...	1	40	...
Oregon	17	16½	...	½	...	...	35	21	13	1	10	23	2	32	...	3
Pennsylvania	81	68	4	7½	...	1½	130	24	102	4	80¾	42¼	7	31½	90½	8
Rhode Island	17	17	...	...	...	...	27	1½	25½	...	24½	2½	...	12	11	4
South Carolina	21	...	21	...	...	...	28	...	28	...	28	...	...	4	22	2
South Dakota	11	4	2	1	2½	1½	26	26	...	...	1	25	...	26	...	...
Tennessee	33	...	33	...	...	...	51	½	50½	...	48½	1	1½	...	51	...
Texas	61	...	61	...	...	...	104	...	104	...	...	...	104	2.55	101.45	...
Utah	13	8	3	...	1½	½	26	10	16	...	18	8	...	7	19	...
Vermont	9	9	...	...	...	...	22	14	7	1	5	13	4	17	4	1
Virginia	33	...	33	...	...	...	54	9	36	9	21½	22½	10	8½	35½	10
Washington	27	14½	2½	6½	3	½	47	13½	29½	4	31½	15½	...	18	29	...
West Virginia	25	15	5½	3	1½	...	38	15	17	6	19	12	7	8	22	8
Wisconsin	31	23	...	...	...	8	59	54	5	...	5	54	...	52	7	...
Wyoming	15	15	...	...	...	...	22	3½	18½	...	18½	3½	...	2	20	...
Canal Zone	4	...	4	...	...	...	5	1	3	1	4	...	1	2	3	...
Dist. of Columbia	9	9	...	...	...	...	23	21	1	1	...	22	1	22	...	1
Guam	...	...	...	...	...	...	5	...	5	...	4½	½	...	...	5	...
Puerto Rico	7	7	...	...	...	...	8	...	8	...	8	...	...	7½	...	½
Virgin Islands	4	4	...	...	...	...	5	...	5	...	5	...	...	2½	...	2½
Total	1521	806	409	79½	86	140½b	2622	875c	1701½d	45½	1368¼e	956¾f	297	1043.55g	1415.45h	163

Sources: *Official Proceedings, 1960*, p. 168. *Official Proceedings, 1968*, pp. 78-91, 136; pp. 119-36; and pp. 158-73.

a. Georgia vote later disallowed because cast before that state's own credentials dispute was settled.

b. Barnett, 23 (Mississippi); Smathers, 30 (29 in Florida, ½ in Alabama, ½ in North Carolina); Humphrey, 41½ (31 in Minnesota, 8 in Wisconsin, 1½ in South Dakota, ½ in Nebraska, ½ in Utah); Meyner, 43 (41 in New Jersey, 1½ in Pennsylvania, ½ in Alabama); Loveless, 1½ (Iowa); Faubus, ½ (Alabama); Brown, ½ (California); Rosellini, ½ (Washington).

c. Sum of column; proceedings record, 1691½ (sic).

d. Sum of column; proceedings record, 832 (sic).

e. Sum of column; proceedings record, 1368.

f. Sum of column; proceedings record, 955.

g. Sum of column; proceedings record, 1041½.

h. Sum of column; proceedings record, 1413.

		1968 DEMOCRATIC											
		Minority report Alabama credentials			Motion to end unit rule			Motion to enlarge National Committee			Platform minority report on Vietnam		
Delegation	Votes	Yea	Nay	Not voting	Yea	Nay	Not voting	Yea	Nay	Not voting	Yea	Nay	Not voting
Alabama	32	...	...	32	5½	24½	2	20½	9	2½	1½	30½	...
Alaska	22	14	8	...	22	...	...	22	...	...	10	12	...
Arizona	19	7½	11½	...	...	19	...	16½	2½	...	6½	12½	...
Arkansas	33	8	23	2	...	32	1	18	14	1	7	25	1
California	174	173	1	...	173	1	...	15	122	37	166	6	2
Colorado	35	34	1	...	35	...	...	19	16	...	21	14	...
Connecticut	44	21	21	2	9	30	5	...	44	...	13	30	1
Delaware	22	2	19	1	...	21	1	20	1	1	...	21	1
Florida	63	6	57	...	11	52	...	23	20	20	7	56	...
Georgia	43	25	17½	½	39	4	...	8½	34½	...	19½	23½	...
Hawaii	26	...	2	26	...	3	23	...	...	26	...	...	26	...
Idaho	25	2	23	...	1	24	...	11	11	3	10	15	...
Illinois	118	18	100	...	3	115	...	1	117	...	13	105	...
Indiana	63	13	41½	8½	63	...	...	61	2	...	15	47½	½
Iowa	46	24½	21½	...	46	...	...	43	3	...	36	10	...
Kansas	38	5½	31½	1	6	20	12	16	19	3	4½	33½	...
Kentucky	46	6½	39½	...	6½	39½	...	43½	2½	...	7	39	...
Louisiana	36	...	36	...	...	36	...	4	32	...	2½	33½	...
Maine	27	...	26	1	27	...	...	19	8	...	4½	22½	...
Maryland	49	2	47	...	49	...	...	48	1	...	12	37	...
Massachusetts	72	29	29	14	37	31	4	24	47	1	56	16	...
Michigan	96	26	67	3	43½	44½	8	19	61	16	52	44	...
Minnesota	52	23½	28½	...	16	33½	2½	11½	38	2½	16½	34½	1
Mississippi	24	12½	8½	3	21½	½	2	22	...	2	19½	2½	2
Missouri	60	8	52	...	60	...	...	4½	53½	2	10	50	...
Montana	26	3½	22½	...	12½	12	1½	17½	8	½	6	20	...
Nebraska	30	13	15	2	26	2	2	30	...	...	19	11	...
Nevada	22	12½	9½	...	22	...	...	19	3	...	3½	18½	...
New Hampshire	26	25	...	1	23	3	...	16	10	...	23	3	...
New Jersey	82	21	61	...	21	61	...	4	78	...	24	57	1
New Mexico	26	11	15	...	11	15	...	5½	20½	...	11½	14½	...
New York	190	80[a]	82[a]	28[a]	190	...	...	17	173	...	148	42	...
North Carolina	59	1	58	...	2	57	...	59	...	...	7	51	1
North Dakota	25	7	18	...	17	5	3	3	19	3	6	19	...
Ohio	115	30½	65	19½	23	92	...	113	2	...	48	67	...
Oklahoma	41	6½	34	½	6	35	...	...	41	...	4	37	...
Oregon	35	31	3	1	31	...	4	14	20	1	29	6	...
Pennsylvania	130	22¼	100½	7¼	39¾	79½	10¾	89¾	9¾	30½	35¼	92¼	2½
Rhode Island	27	2½	24½	...	3½	23½	...	...	27	...	5	22	...
South Carolina	28	...	28	...	4½	23½	...	18	10	...	1	27	...
South Dakota	26	24	2	...	26	...	...	2	23	1	26	...	...
Tennessee	51	½	49½	1	2½	46½	2	47	...	4	2	49	...
Texas	104	...	104	...	5	99	...	7½	84½	12	...	104	...
Utah	26	5	21	...	26	...	...	21	3	2	6	20	...
Vermont	22	14	7	1	22	...	...	10	12	...	17	5	...
Virginia	54	1	53	...	9½	43½	1	15	38	1	8	46	...
Washington	47	16	28	3	21½	25½	...	5	42	...	15½	31½	...
West Virginia	38	9	29	...	38	...	...	38	...	...	8	30	...
Wisconsin	59	54	4	1	58	1	...	40½	17½	1	52	7	...
Wyoming	22	6½	15½	...	3	19	...	2½	19½	...	3½	18½	...
Canal Zone	5	...	4	1	1	4	...	5	...	...	1½	3½	...
Dist. of Columbia	23	23	...	...	23	...	...	23	...	...	21	2	...
Guam	5	...	5	...	½	4½	...	½	4½	...	½	4½	...
Puerto Rico	8	...	8	...	1	7	...	8	...	...	...	8	...
Virgin Islands	5	...	5	...	5	...	...	5	...	...	...	5	...
Total	2622	880¾[b]	1607[c]	134¼	1351¼[d]	1209[e]	61¾	1125¾	1349¼	147	1041¼	1567¾	13

Source: *Official Proceedings, 1968*, pp. 225-42, 251; pp. 277-92, 303-09; pp. 310-22; and pp. 431-42.

a. New York vote announced after outcome of roll call.
b. Sum of column; proceedings record (without New York vote), 801½.
c. Sum of column; proceedings record (without New York), 1525.
d. Sum of column; proceedings record, 1350.
e. Sum of column; proceedings record, 1206.

Delegation	Votes	Presidential					Vice-presidential			
		Humphrey	McCarthy	McGovern	Phillips	Other	Muskie	Bond	Others	Not voting
Alabama	32	23	...	...	...	9	...	...	1½	30½
Alaska	22	17	2	3	...	...	...	...	...	22
Arizona	19	14½	2½	2	...	...	17½	1	...	½
Arkansas	33	30	2	...	...	1	32	...	...	1
California	174	14	91	51	17	1	...	...	...	174
Colorado	35	16½	10	5½	3	...	...	...	...	35
Connecticut	44	35	8	...	1	...	...	...	...	44
Delaware	22	21	...	...	...	1	21	...	...	1
Florida	63	58	5	...	...	...	56	5	...	2
Georgia	43	19½	13½	1	3	6	22	½	...	20½
Hawaii	26	26	...	...	...	...	25	...	1	...
Idaho	25	21	3½	½	...	...	25	...	...	...
Illinois	118	112	3	3	...	...	116	...	...	2
Indiana	63	49	11	2	1	...	63	...	...	...
Iowa	46	18½	19½	5	...	3	46	...	...	...
Kansas	38	34	1	3	...	...	38	...	...	...
Kentucky	46	41	5	...	...	...	46	...	...	...
Louisiana	36	35	...	...	...	1	36	...	...	...
Maine	27	23	4	...	...	...	27	...	...	...
Maryland	49	45	2	2	...	...	49	...	...	...
Massachusetts	72	2	70	...	...	...	72	...	...	...
Michigan	96	72½	9½	7½	6½	...	96	...	...	...
Minnesota	52	38	11½	...	2½	...	39½	12½	...	...
Mississippi	24	9½	6½	4	2	2	...	...	...	24
Missouri	60	56	3½	...	½	...	60	...	...	...
Montana	26	23½	2½	...	...	...	26	...	...	...
Nebraska	30	15	6	9	...	...	24	...	4	2
Nevada	22	18½	2½	1	...	...	19½	...	2½	...
New Hampshire	26	6	20	...	...	...	...	...	...	26
New Jersey	82	62	19	...	1	...	65	1	...	16
New Mexico	26	15	11	...	...	...	23½	...	...	2½
New York	190	96½	87	1½	2	3	100	...	...	90
North Carolina	59	44½	2	½	...	12	58	...	1	...
North Dakota	25	18	7	...	...	...	21	3	1	...
Ohio	115	94	18	2	...	1	115	...	...	...
Oklahoma	41	37½	2½	½	½	...	41	...	...	...
Oregon	35	...	35	...	...	...	...	...	...	35
Pennsylvania	130	103¾	21½	2½	1½	¾	118	...	2¼	9¾
Rhode Island	27	23½	2½	...	...	1	27	...	...	...
South Carolina	28	28	...	...	...	...	26½	...	1½	...
South Dakota	26	2	...	24	...	...	26	...	...	...
Tennessee	51	49½	½	1	...	...	51	...	...	...
Texas	104	100½	2½	...	1	...	104	...	...	...
Utah	26	23	2	...	1	...	25	1	...	...
Vermont	22	8	6	7	...	1	...	...	...	22
Virginia	54	42½	5½	...	2	4	50	3½	...	½
Washington	47	32½	8½	6	...	...	42	...	3	2
West Virginia	38	34	3	...	...	1	38	...	...	...
Wisconsin	59	8	49	1	1	...	8	...	9	42
Wyoming	22	18½	3½	...	...	...	22	...	...	...
Canal Zone	5	4	...	1	...	...	5	...	...	...
Dist. of Columbia	23	2	...	...	21	...	2	21	...	...
Guam	5	5	...	...	...	...	5	...	...	...
Puerto Rico	8	8	...	...	...	...	8	...	...	...
Virgin Islands	5	5	...	...	...	...	5	...	...	...
Total	2622	1759¼[a]	601	146½	67½	47¾[b]	1942½[c]	48½	26¾[d]	604¼

Source: *Official Proceedings, 1968,* pp. 536-56; and pp. 593-609.

a. Sum of column; proceedings record, 1761¾.

b. Moore, 17½ (12 in North Carolina, 3 in Virginia, 2 in Georgia, ½ in Alabama); Kennedy, 12¾ (proceedings record, 12½) (3½ in Alabama, 3 in Iowa, 3 in New York, 1 in Ohio, 1 in West Virginia, ¾ in Pennsylvania, ½ in Georgia); Bryant, 1½ (Alabama); Wallace, ½ (Alabama); Gray, ½ (Georgia). Not voting, 15 (3 in Alabama, 3 in Georgia, 2 in Mississippi, 1 in Arkansas, 1 in California, 1 in Delaware, 1 in Louisiana, 1 in Rhode Island, 1 in Vermont, 1 in Virginia).

c. Though all states were called, the roll call was never completed. Under suspension of the rules, Muskie was nominated by acclamation.

d. Hoeh, 4 (3 in Washington, 1 in Wisconsin); Kennedy, 3½ (2 in Wisconsin, 1½ in Nevada); McCarthy, 3 (2 in Nebraska, 1 in Hawaii); Ribicoff, 2 (Wisconsin); McGovern, 2 (1 in North Dakota, 1 in Wisconsin); Edwards, 2 (Nebraska); Daley, 1½ (Alabama); McNair, 1½ (South Carolina); Tate, 1½ (Pennsylvania); Sanford, 1 (North Carolina); Shriver, 1 (Nevada); Lowenstein, 1 (Wisconsin); Reuss, 1 (Wisconsin); O'Dwyer, 1 (Wisconsin); Ryan, ¾ (Pennsylvania).

Delegation	Votes	Minority report South Carolina credentials			Minority report California credentials			Sustain chair's ruling on California			Suspend rules for Illinois credentials compromise		
		Yea	Nay	Not voting	Yea	Nay	Not voting	Yea	Nay	Not voting	Yea	Nay	Not voting
California	271	120	151	...	120	...	151	120	...	151	123	106	42
South Carolina	32	...	9	23	3	29	...	3	29	...	1	31	...
Ohio	153	63	87	3	75	78	...	78	75	...	69	84	...
Canal Zone	3	1.50	1.50	...	3	...	...	3	...	...	3	...	...
Utah	19	10	8	1	13	6	...	14	5	...	15	4	...
Delaware	13	5.85	7.15	...	6.50	6.50	...	6.50	6.50	...	6.50	6.50	...
Rhode Island	22	20	2	...	22	...	...	22	...	...	17.27	3.36	1.36[b]
Texas	130	34	96	...	34	96	...	40	90	...	42	88	...
West Virginia	35	13	22	...	15	20	...	16	19	...	13	22	...
South Dakota	17	17	...	...	17	...	...	17	...	...	17	...	...
Kansas	35	17	18	...	18	17	...	18	17	...	13	22	...
New York	278	269	9	...	267	11	...	268	10	...	251	27	...
Virginia	53	34.50	18.50	...	38.50	14.50	...	38.50	13	1.50	36.50	16.50	...
Wyoming	11	2.20	8.80	...	4.40	6.60	...	6.05	4.95	...	3.30	7.70	...
Arkansas	27	13	14	...	8	19	...	10	17	...	16	11	...
Indiana	76	18	58	...	33	43	...	35	41	...	25	51	...
Puerto Rico	7	6.50	0.50	...	6.50	0.50	...	6.50	0.50	...	...	7	...
Tennessee	49	22	27	...	23	26	...	24	23	2	26	22	1
Pennsylvania	182	55.50	126	0.50	72	105	5	72	106	4	58	111.50	12.50
Mississippi	25	20	5	...	19	6	...	24	1	...	21	3	1
Wisconsin	67	39	28	...	55	12	...	56	11	...	44	23	...
Illinois	170	79	90	1	114.50	55.50	...	111.50	58.50	...	37.50	73	59.50
Maine	20	1	19	...	...	20	...	...	20	...	8	12	...
Florida	81	1	80	...	3	78	...	3	78	...	2	79	...
New Hampshire	18	13.50	4.50	...	9.90	8.10	...	12.60	5.40	...	9	9	...
Arizona	25	15	10	...	12	13	...	22	3	...	13	12	...
North Carolina	64	6	58	...	21	43	...	16	48	...	15	46	3
Massachusetts	102	97	5	...	97	5	...	98	4	...	48	54	...
Nebraska	24	14	9	1	20	4	...	20	4	...	22	2	...
Georgia	53	5.50	47.50	...	21.75	31.25	...	19.50	31.25	2.25	18.75	32.75	1.50
North Dakota	14	7	6.30	0.70	8.40	5.60	...	7.70	6.30	...	4.90	9.10	...
Maryland	53	24	29	...	27.83	25.17	...	34.17	18.83	...	33.83	19.17	...
New Jersey	109	79	29	1	85.50	22.50	1	83.50	23.50	2	78.50	28	2.50
Vermont	12	7	5	...	11	1	...	11	1	...	7.50	4	0.50
Nevada	11	5.75	5.25	...	5.75	5.25	...	5.75	5.25	...	6.25	4.75	...
Michigan	132	51	81	...	55	76	1	56.50	75.50	...	47	85	...
Iowa	46	23	23	...	27	19	...	32	13	1	28	18	...
Colorado	36	23	13	...	27	9	...	32	4	...	25	11	...
Alabama	37	1	36	...	1	36	...	2	35	...	1	36	...
Alaska	10	6.75	3.25	...	7.25	2.75	...	7.25	2.75	...	5.75	4.25	...
Hawaii	17	2	15	...	7	10	...	11	6	...	...	17	...
Washington	52	...	52	...	...	52	...	...	52	...	...	52	...
Minnesota	64	56	8	...	29	35	...	31	33	...	22	42	...
Louisiana	44	25	19	...	22.50	21.50	...	26.50	17.50	...	35.50	8.50	...
Idaho	17	12.50	4.50	...	11.50	5.50	...	12.50	4.50	...	9.50	7.50	...
Montana	17	10	7	...	14.50	1	1.50	15.50	1	0.50	15.50	1.50	...
Connecticut	51	8	43	...	21	30	...	31	20	...	20	30	1
Dist. of Columbia	15	12	3	...	13.50	1.50	...	13.50	1.50	...	15	...	...
Virgin Islands	3	1	2	...	2.50	0.50	...	2.50	0.50	...	3	...	...
Kentucky	47	10	37	...	11	36	...	14	33	...	8	33	6
Missouri	73	13.50	59.50	...	22.50	50.50	...	22.50	50.50	...	15.50	57.50	...
New Mexico	18	10	8	...	10	8	...	10	8	...	10	8	...
Guam	3	1.50	1.50	...	1.50	1.50	...	1.50	1.50	...	2.50	0.50	...
Oregon	34	16	18	...	33	1	...	34	...	...	33	1	...
Oklahoma	39	11	28	...	11	28	...	12	27	...	10	29	...
Total	3016	1429.05	1555.75	31.20	1618.28	1238.22	159.50	1689.52	1162.23	164.25	1411.05	1473.08[c]	131.86

Source: "Official Proceedings, 1972" (daily transcript of proceedings, July 1972; processed).

a. Delegations at this convention are listed in the order in which they voted. All fractional votes are expressed in decimals for consistency. For explanation of the new voting rules, see the text.

b. Figures do not add to total because of rounding.

c. Sum of column; proceedings record, 1483.08.

		1972 DEMOCRATIC								
		Minority report Illinois credentials			Minority report guaranteed income			Minority report women's rights		
Delegation	Votes	Yea	Nay	Not voting	Yea	Nay	Not voting	Yea	Nay	Not voting
California	271	84	136	51	131	114	26	167	96	8
South Carolina	32	31	1	...	4	21	7	2	30	...
Ohio	153	69	70	14	39	86	28	30	87	36
Canal Zone	3	1	2	...	2.50	0.50	...	2.50	...	0.50
Utah	19	5	14	...	8	11	...	6	12	1
Delaware	13	6.50	6.50	...	4.55	8.45	...	5.85	6.50	0.65
Rhode Island	22	7.09	14.91	...	10.86	11.14	...	9.50	12.50	...
Texas	130	96	34	...	15	115	...	7	114	9
West Virginia	35	24	11	...	3	32	...	2	25	8
South Dakota	17	...	17	...	1	16	...	1	16	...
Kansas	35	18	17	...	5	30	...	6	28	1
New York	278	20	256	2	152	118	8	186	75	17
Virginia	53	16.50	35.50	1	30	21	2	30.50	20.50	2
Wyoming	11	7.70	3.30	...	0.55	10.45	...	2.75	7.70	0.55
Arkansas	27	13	14	...	10	16	1	7	17	3
Indiana	76	53	23	...	17	56	3	8	64	4
Puerto Rico	7	0.50	6.50	...	4	3	...	1	6	...
Tennessee	49	20	29	...	21	27	1	27	21	1
Pennsylvania	182	106.50	62	13.50	49.50	117.50	15	46	92.50	43.50
Mississippi	25	...	25	...	22	...	3	16	7	2
Wisconsin	67	12	55	...	29	38	...	30	29	8
Illinois	170	76	30	64	59	95	16	66.50	62.50	41
Maine	20	13	7	...	1	19	...	8	12	...
Florida	81	80	1	...	4	77	...	16	54	11
New Hampshire	18	9	8.10	0.90	0.90	14.40	2.70	5.40	9	3.60
Arizona	25	4	21	...	6	19	...	7	17	1
North Carolina	64	39	23	2	17	47	...	46	11	7
Massachusetts	102	11	91	...	60	40	2	50	36	16
Nebraska	24	13	11	...	2	22	...	3	20	1
Georgia	53	24	27.50	1.50	10.50	34	8.50	14	21	18
North Dakota	14	2.10	11.90	...	1.40	10.50	2.10	4.20	9.10	0.70
Maryland	53	28.67	24.33	...	14.33	38.67	...	16.67	30.50	5.83
New Jersey	109	30	75.50	3.50	61.50	35.50	12	55.50	43	10.50
Vermont	12	2	10	...	4	8	...	3.50	8	0.50
Nevada	11	6.75	4.25	...	2.75	8.25	...	2.75	6.75	1.50
Michigan	132	85	47	...	30.50	96.50	5	35	86	11
Iowa	46	20	26	...	6	39	1	8	37	1
Colorado	36	5	31	...	15	21	...	13	18	5
Alabama	37	32	5	...	10	27	...	13	24	...
Alaska	10	4.75	5.25	...	3	5.50	1.50	3.75	4.75	1.50
Hawaii	17	17	...	...	1.50	15.50	...	3	11.50	2.50
Washington	52	52	...	...	1	51	...	12	34	6
Minnesota	64	32	32	...	28	33	3	33	30	1
Louisiana	44	9.50	32.50	2	22	20	2	20	19.75	4.25
Idaho	17	4	13	...	5	12	...	6.50	8.50	2
Montana	17	2.50	14.50	...	2	14	1	3	8.50	5.50
Connecticut	51	40	11	...	22	29	...	11	30	10
Dist. of Columbia	15	1.50	13.50	...	15	...	...	4.50	9.75	0.75
Virgin Islands	3	3	...	...	2.50	0.50	...	1	2	...
Kentucky	47	36	10	1	1	41	5	7	36	4
Missouri	73	59	13	1	12	55	6	3	53.50	16.50
New Mexico	18	8	10	...	3	15	...	3	11	4
Guam	3	...	3	...	...	3	...	1	1.50	0.50
Oregon	34	2	32	...	11	23	...	15	18	1
Oklahoma	39	29	9	1	5.50	31.50	2	14	22.50	2.50
Total	3016	1371.56[a]	1486.04[b]	158.40	999.34	1852.86	163.80	1101.37	1572.80	341.83

Source: "Official Proceedings, 1972."
a. Sum of column; proceedings record, 1371.55.
b. Sum of column; proceedings record, 1486.05.

		1972 DEMOCRATIC											
		Presidential (before shifts)						Presidential (after shifts)					
Delegation	Votes	McGovern	Jackson	Wallace	Chisholm	Sanford	Other	McGovern	Jackson	Wallace	Chisholm	Sanford	Others
California	271	271	...	...	...	...	...	271	...	...	...	...	...
South Carolina	32	6	10	6	4	6	...	10	9	6	...	6	1
Ohio	153	77	39	...	23	3	11	77	39	...	23	3	11
Canal Zone	3	3	...	...	...	...	...	3	...	...	...	...	...
Utah	19	14	1	...	...	3	1	14	1	...	...	3	1
Delaware	13	5.85	6.50	...	0.65	...	...	5.85	5.85	...	0.65	...	0.65
Rhode Island	22	22	...	...	...	...	...	22	...	...	...	...	...
Texas	130	54	23	48	4	...	1	54	23	48	4	...	1
West Virginia	35	16	14	1	...	4	...	16	14	1	...	4	...
South Dakota	17	17	...	...	...	...	...	17	...	...	...	...	...
Kansas	35	20	10	...	2	1	2	20	10	...	2	1	2
New York	278	263	9	...	6	...	...	278	...	...	...	...	...
Virginia	53	33.50	4	1	5.50	9	...	37	5	...	2.50	8.50	...
Wyoming	11	3.30	6.05	...	1.10	...	0.55	3.30	6.05	...	1.10	...	0.55
Arkansas	27	1	1	...	...	...	25	1	1	...	...	...	25
Indiana	76	26	20	26	1	...	3	28	19	25	...	...	4
Puerto Rico	7	7	...	...	...	...	...	7	...	...	...	...	...
Tennessee	49	...	...	33	10	...	6	5	...	32	7	...	5
Pennsylvania	182	81	86.50	2	9.50	1	2	81	86.50	2	9.50	1	2
Mississippi	25	10	...	...	12	3	...	23	...	...	2	...	...
Wisconsin	67	55	3	...	5	...	4	55	3	...	5	...	4
Illinois	170	119	30.50	0.50	4.50	2	13.50	155	6	...	1	...	8
Maine	20	5	...	...	...	...	15	5	...	...	...	...	15
Florida	81	2	...	75	2	...	2	4	...	75	1	...	1
New Hampshire	18	10.80	5.40	...	...	...	1.80	10.80	5.40	...	...	...	1.80
Arizona	25	21	3	...	...	1	...	22	3	...	...	...	...
North Carolina	64	...	...	37	...	27	...	...	...	37	...	27	...
Massachusetts	102	102	...	...	...	...	...	102	...	...	...	...	...
Nebraska	24	21	3	...	...	...	...	21	3	...	...	...	...
Georgia	53	14.50	14.50	11	12	1	...	14.50	14.50	11	12	1	...
North Dakota	14	8.40	2.80	0.70	0.70	...	1.40	10.50	2.10	...	0.70	...	0.70
Maryland	53	13	...	38	2	...	...	13	...	38	2	...	...
New Jersey	109	89	11.50	...	4	1.50	3	92.50	11	...	3.50	...	2
Vermont	12	12	...	...	...	...	...	12	...	...	...	...	...
Nevada	11	5.75	5.25	...	...	...	...	5.75	5.25	...	...	...	...
Michigan	132	50.50	7	67.50	3	1	3	51.50	7	67.50	2	1	3
Iowa	46	35	...	...	3	4	4	35	...	...	3	4	4
Colorado	36	27	...	...	7	...	2	29	2	...	5	...	...
Alabama	37	9	1	24	...	1	2	9	1	24	...	1	2
Alaska	10	6.50	3.25	...	...	...	0.25	6.50	3.25	...	...	...	0.25
Hawaii	17	6.50	8.50	...	1	...	1	6.50	8.50	...	1	...	1
Washington	52	...	52	...	...	...	...	...	52	...	...	...	...
Minnesota	64	11	...	...	6	...	47	43	...	...	4	1	16
Louisiana	44	10.25	10.25	3	18.50	2	...	25.75	5.25	3	4	1	5
Idaho.	17	12.50	2.50	...	2	...	...	12.50	2.50	...	2	...	...
Montana	17	16	...	...	1	...	...	16	...	...	1	...	...
Connecticut	51	30	20	...	...	1	...	30	20	...	...	1	...
Dist. of Columbia	15	13.50	1.50	...	...	...	...	13.50	1.50	...	...	...	...
Virgin Islands	3	1	1.50	...	0.50	...	...	1	1.50	...	0.50	...	...
Kentucky	47	10	35	...	...	2	...	10	35	...	...	2	...
Missouri	73	24.50	48.50	...	...	...	...	24.50	48.50	...	...	...	...
New Mexico	18	10	...	8	...	...	...	10	...	8	...	...	...
Guam	3	1.50	1.50	...	...	...	...	1.50	1.50	...	...	...	...
Oregon	34	34	...	...	...	...	...	34	...	...	...	...	...
Oklahoma	39	10.50	23.50	...	1	4	...	9.50	23.50	...	2	4	...
Total[a]	3016	1728.35	525.00	381.70	151.95	77.50	151.50[b]	1864.95	485.65	377.50	101.45	69.50	116.95[c]

Source: "Official Proceedings, 1972."

a. Total before shifts never announced in convention proceedings.

b. Humphrey, 66.70 (46 in Minnesota, 4 in Ohio, 4 in Wisconsin, 3 in Michigan, 2 in Indiana, 2 in Pennsylvania, 2 in Florida, 1 in Utah, 1 in Colorado, 1 in Hawaii, 0.70 in North Dakota); Mills, 33.80 (25 in Arkansas, 3 in Illinois, 3 in New Jersey, 2 in Alabama, 0.55 in Wyoming, 0.25 in Alaska); Muskie, 24.30 (15 in Maine, 5.50 in Illinois, 1.80 in New Hampshire, 1 in Texas, 1 in Colorado); Kennedy, 12.70 (4 in Iowa, 3 in Illinois, 2 in Ohio, 1 in Kansas, 1 in Indiana, 1 in Tennessee, 0.70 in North Dakota); Hays, 5 (Ohio); McCarthy, 2 (Illinois); Mondale, 1 (Kansas); Clark, 1 (Minnesota); not voting, 5 (Tennessee).

c. Humphrey, 35 (16 in Minnesota, 4 in Ohio, 4 in Wisconsin, 3 in Indiana, 3 in Michigan, 2 in Pennsylvania, 1 in Utah, 1 in Florida, 1 in Hawaii); Mills, 32.80 (25 in Arkansas, 2 in Illinois, 2 in New Jersey, 2 in Alabama, 1 in South Carolina, 0.55 in Wyoming, 0.25 in Alaska); Muskie, 20.80 (15 in Maine, 3 in Illinois, 1.80 in New Hampshire, 1 in Texas); Kennedy, 10.65 (4 in Iowa, 2 in Ohio, 1 in Kansas, 1 in Indiana, 1 in Tennessee, 1 in Illinois, 0.65 in Delaware); Hays, 5 (Ohio); McCarthy, 2 (Illinois); Mondale, 1 (Kansas).

		1972 DEMOCRATIC								
		Party charter resolution[a]			Vice-presidential[b]					
Delegation	Votes	Yea	Nay	Not voting	Eagleton	Farenthold	Gravel	Peabody	Smothers	Other
California	271	259	10	2	198	37	22	...	...	14
South Carolina	32	29	3	...	9	...	1	20	...	2
Ohio	153	137	16	...	104	4	35	3	...	7
Canal Zone	3	2	...	1	2.50	0.50	...	...	...	...
Utah	19	16	...	3	15	2	1	1	...	...
Delaware	13	13	...	...	6.50	...	0.65	5.20	...	0.65
Rhode Island	22	15.23	5.77	1	18.59	1.36	...	0.68	...	1.36
Texas	130	130	...	...	50	22	2	5	45	6
West Virginia	35	19	16	...	28	...	1	4	...	2
South Dakota	17	17	...	...	17	...	...	...	...	...
Kansas	35	35	...	...	35	...	...	...	...	...
New York	278	...	...	...	163	79	21	...	...	15
Virginia	53	44	8	1	25.50	14	4.50	1	...	8
Wyoming	11	11	...	...	8.25	1.10	...	...	...	1.65
Arkansas	27	26	1	...	7	19	...	...	...	1
Indiana	76	76	...	...	7	...	1	...	...	68
Puerto Rico	7	7	...	...	4	...	3	...	...	...
Tennessee	49	47	2	...	25	21	1	1	...	1
Pennsylvania	182	182	...	...	94.50	6	31	21.50	1	28
Mississippi	25	24	1	...	17	5	1	...	...	2
Wisconsin	67	52	5	10	38	17	2	2	...	8
Illinois	170	130	13.50	26.50	96	27	10.50	4	1	31.50
Maine	20	20	...	...	7	1	3	8	...	1
Florida	81	79	...	2	16	8	...	...	9	48
New Hampshire	18	18	...	...	1.80	6.30	2.70	6.30	...	0.90
Arizona	25	24	1	...	9	6	1	1	...	8
North Carolina	64	64	...	...	42	12	...	2	...	8
Massachusetts	102	56	2	44	52	27	7	5	...	11
Nebraska	24	24	...	...	19	4	...	...	...	1
Georgia	53	49.50	2	1.50	19	1	1	...	1	31
North Dakota	14	6.30	7	0.70	3.50	0.70	4.20	...	...	5.60
Maryland	53	50.17	2.83	...	43.67	2.83	1.83	3.83	...	0.83
New Jersey	109	77.50	24.50	7	22	10	12	...	...	65
Vermont	12	10	...	2	10	0.50	1	...	...	0.50
Nevada	11	11	...	...	4	1.75	0.50	4.75	...	...
Michigan	132	105.50	12	14.50	84.50	3	21.50	1.50	9	12.50
Iowa	46	46	...	...	34	...	...	...	...	12
Colorado	36	13	21	2	20	12	4	...	...	...
Alabama	37	37	...	...	37	...	...	...	...	...
Alaska	10	7.25	1.50	1.25	2.50	1.50	5.50	...	...	0.50
Hawaii	17	17	...	...	10	3	3	...	...	1
Washington	52	52	...	...	52	...	...	...	...	...
Minnesota	64	57	4	3	23	20	2	...	...	19
Louisiana	44	43	1	...	10.50	...	7	...	1	25.50
Idaho	17	16.50	0.50	...	13	3	...	...	...	1
Montana	17	16	1	...	13	1.50	1	...	...	1.50
Connecticut	51	33	18	...	45	4	1	...	...	1
Dist. of Columbia	15	15	...	...	15	...	...	...	...	...
Virgin Islands	3	3	...	...	1.50	...	...	...	...	1.50
Kentucky	47	37	...	10	34	3	3	6	...	1
Missouri	73	69.50	3.50	...	73	...	...	...	...	...
New Mexico	18	8	8	2	6	1	1	...	7	3
Guam	3	3	...	...	1	1	0.50	0.50	...	...
Oregon	34	33	1	...	15	14	2	...	...	3
Oklahoma	39	36	3	...	34	...	2	...	...	3
Total	3016	2408.45[c]	195.10	134.45	1741.81	404.04	225.38	107.26	74	463.49[d]

Source: "Official Proceedings, 1972."

a. By unanimous consent, the tally without New York was announced when that state remained in extended caucus and it was clear that the disposition of its votes would not affect the overall outcome.

b. Figures may not add to totals because of rounding. Total never announced; roll call suspended and in a voice vote Eagleton was nominated unanimously.

c. Sum of column; proceedings record, 2418.45.

d. Bayh, 62 (58 in Indiana, 1 in California, 1 in New York, 1 in New Jersey, 1 in Arizona); Rodino, 56.50 (51.50 in New Jersey, 2 in Ohio, 2 in Illinois, 1 in Hawaii); Jimmy Carter, 30 (27 in Georgia, 1 in California, 1 in Illinois, 1 in Wisconsin); Chisholm, 20 (6 in Massachusetts, 4 in Iowa, 3 in Minnesota, 2½ in Illinois, 2 in Louisiana, 1 in New York, 1 in Oregon, ½ in Vermont); Landrieu, 18½ (Louisiana); Breathitt, 18 (Pennsylvania); Kennedy, 15 (3 in Pennsylvania, 2 in California, 2 in Ohio, 2 in Wisconsin, 1 in New York, 1 in Illinois, 1 in Massachusetts, 1 in Georgia, 1 in Minnesota, 1 in Oregon); Harris, 14½ (3 in California, 3 in Oklahoma, 2 in Wisconsin, 1 in West Virginia, 1 in New York, 1 in Pennsylvania, 1 in Mississippi, 1 in Illinois, 1 in Maine, ½ in Virgin Islands); Hatcher, 11 (10 in Indiana, 1 in New Jersey); Hughes, 10 (8 in Iowa, 1 in South Carolina, 1 in Massachusetts); Montoya, 9 (6 in Arizona, 2 in Texas, 1 in Illinois); Stevenson, 8 (6 in Illinois, 1 in Maryland, 1 in Massachusetts); Guy, 7.10 (5.60 in North Dakota, 1.50 in Montana); Bergland, 5 (Minnesota); Hodding Carter, 5 (4 in Virginia, 1 in Mississippi); Chavez, 5 (3 in New Mexico, 2 in New York); Mills, 5 (3 in New Jersey, 1 in Tennessee, 1 in North Carolina); Anderson, 4 (Minnesota); Arnold, 4 (2 in Ohio, 1 in New York, 1 in Massachu- setts); Dellums, 4 (California); Houlihan, 4 (Illinois); Mondragon, 4 (3 in California, 1 in Idaho); Askew, 3 (2 in Florida, 1 in Illinois); McCarthy, 3 (1 in New York, 1 in Illinois, 1 in Massachusetts); Sanford, 3 (1 in Virginia, 1 in Pennsylvania, 1 in North Carolina); Pell, 2-15/22 (2 in Illinois, 15/22 in Rhode Island); Badillo, 2½ (New Jersey); Clark, 2 (New Jersey); Daley, 2 (1 in Florida, 1 in Michigan); DeCarlo, 2 (1 in Texas, 1 in Florida); Mudd, 2 (Wisconsin); Muskie, 2 (1 in New York, 1 in Minnesota); Pepper, 2 (Florida); Ribicoff, 2 (New York); Taylor, 2 (North Carolina); Woodcock, 2 (Virginia); Gruening, 1-4/22 (15/22 in Rhode Island, ½ in Alaska); Agnoli, 1 (New Jersey); Albright, 1 (Florida); Barrett, 1 (Illinois); Daniel Berrigan, 1 (New York); Philip Berrigan, 1 (Georgia); Bond, 1 (Georgia); Bonnetti, 1 (New Jersey); Bowles, 1 (North Carolina); Bunker, 1 (South Carolina); Burton, 1 (Virgin Islands); Chappell, 1 (Florida); Chiles, 1 (Florida); Church, 1 (Minnesota); Cook, 1 (Minnesota); Dowdy, 1 (Kentucky); Drinan, 1 (New York); Galifianakis, 1 (North Carolina); Goodrich, 1 (Ohio); Griffin, 1 (Florida); Griffiths, 1 (New York); Hamilton, 1 (West Virginia); Hunt, 1 (North Carolina); Inouye, 1 (Connecticut); Jackson, 1 (Texas); Kariss, 1 (Florida); Lowenstein, 1 (Minnesota); Eleanor McGovern, 1 (Oregon); Nader, 1 (Minnesota); Norcross, 1 (New Jersey); Rubin, 1 (New York); Seaman, 1 (Texas); Smith, 1 (Nebraska); Spock, 1 (New Jersey); Tavolacci, 1 (Michigan); Wallace, 1 (North Carolina); Mitchell, 5/6 (Maryland). Not voting, 74.70 (37 in Florida, 10.50 in Michigan, 8 in Illinois, 5 in Pennsylvania, 5 in Louisiana, 1.65 in Wyoming, 1 in Texas, 1 in Arkansas, 1 in Wisconsin, 1 in Arizona, 1 in Georgia, 1 in Minnesota, 0.90 in New Hampshire, 0.65 in Delaware).

Delegation	Votes	Clay	Davis	Fillmore	Freling-huysen	Sergeant	Davis	Fillmore	Freling-huysen	Sergeant	Davis	Fillmore	Freling-huysen	Other	Votes	Yea	Nay	Not Voting
		Pres. First Ballot	**Vice-Presidential**												**1848 WHIG Proxy Voting for Absent Delegates**			
			First Ballot				**Second Ballot**				**Third Ballot**							
Alabama	9	9	1	...	8	...	2	...	7	...	...	...	8	1	7	8	1	...
Arizona	...	...	...	...	...	...	...	...	...	...	...	...	...	...	...	...	...	...
Arkansas	3	3	...	...	3	...	...	...	3	...	...	...	3	...	3	3	...	...
California	...	...	...	...	...	...	...	...	...	...	...	...	...	...	...	...	...	...
Colorado	...	...	...	...	...	...	...	...	...	...	...	...	...	...	...	...	...	...
Connecticut	6	6	6	...	...	...	6	...	...	...	6	...	...	...	6	3	2	1
Delaware	3	3	...	...	...	3	...	...	3	...	...	...	3	...	3	1	2	...
Florida	...	...	...	...	...	...	...	...	...	...	...	...	...	...	3	3	...	...
Georgia	10	10	...	...	10	...	...	...	10	...	...	...	10	...	10	10	...	...
Idaho	...	...	...	...	...	...	...	...	...	...	...	...	...	...	...	...	...	...
Illinois	9	9	2	4	2	1	2	2	4	1	2	...	7	...	8	2	7	...
Indiana	12	12	7	4	...	1	6	2	4	...	5	...	7	...	12	6	6	...
Iowa	...	...	...	...	...	...	...	...	...	...	...	...	...	...	4	2	2	...
Kansas	...	...	...	...	...	...	...	...	...	...	...	...	...	...	...	...	...	...
Kentucky	12	12	5	3	2	2	5	3	3	1	6	3	3	...	12	11	1	...
Louisiana	6	6	...	...	6	...	...	...	6	...	...	...	6	...	6	6	...	...
Maine	9	9	9	...	...	...	9	...	...	...	9	...	...	...	9	5	4	...
Maryland	8	8	1	...	7	...	...	...	8	...	...	...	8	...	8	5	3	...
Massachusetts	12	12	12	...	...	...	12	...	...	...	12	...	...	...	12	...	12	...
Michigan	5	5	1	4	...	...	1	4	...	...	5	...	...	...	5	...	5	...
Minnesota	...	...	...	...	...	...	...	...	...	...	...	...	...	...	...	...	...	...
Mississippi	6	6	...	...	6	...	...	...	6	...	1	...	5	...	6	6	...	...
Missouri	7	7	4	1	2	...	2	...	6	1	...	...	7	...	7	7	...	...
Montana	...	...	...	...	...	...	...	...	...	...	...	...	...	...	...	...	...	...
Nebraska	...	...	...	...	...	...	...	...	...	...	...	...	...	...	...	...	...	...
Nevada	...	...	...	...	...	...	...	...	...	...	...	...	...	...	...	...	...	...
New Hampshire	6	6	6	...	...	...	6	...	...	...	3	...	3	...	6	3	3	...
New Jersey	7	7	...	...	7	...	...	...	7	...	...	...	7	...	7	3	4	...
New Mexico	...	...	...	...	...	...	...	...	...	...	...	...	...	...	...	...	...	...
New York	36	36	...	35	1	...	...	35	1	...	4	29	3	...	36	2	34	...
North Carolina	11	11	...	...	11	...	...	...	11	...	...	...	11	...	11	2	9	...
North Dakota	...	...	...	...	...	...	...	...	...	...	...	...	...	...	...	...	...	...
Ohio	23	23	20	2	...	1	19	4	...	...	19	3	1	...	23	...	23	...
Oklahoma	...	...	...	...	...	...	...	...	...	...	...	...	...	...	...	...	...	...
Oregon	...	...	...	...	...	...	...	...	...	...	...	...	...	...	...	...	...	...
Pennsylvania	26	26	...	...	...	26	...	...	...	26	3	4	18	1	26	8	17	1
Rhode Island	4	4	...	...	...	4	...	...	...	4	...	...	4	...	4	...	4	...
South Carolina	9	9	3	...	6	...	...	...	9	...	...	...	9	...	2	...	2	...
South Dakota	...	...	...	...	...	...	...	...	...	...	...	...	...	...	...	...	...	...
Tennessee	13	13	...	...	13	...	...	...	13	...	...	...	13	...	13	13	...	...
Texas	...	...	...	...	...	...	...	...	...	...	...	...	...	...	4	4	...	...
Utah	...	...	...	...	...	...	...	...	...	...	...	...	...	...	...	...	...	...
Vermont	6	6	6	...	...	...	5	1	...	...	4	1	1	...	6	...	6	...
Virginia	17	17	...	...	17	...	...	...	17	...	...	...	17	...	17	11	6	...
Washington	...	...	...	...	...	...	...	...	...	...	...	...	...	...	...	...	...	...
West Virginia	...	...	...	...	...	...	...	...	...	...	...	...	...	...	...	...	...	...
Wisconsin	...	...	...	...	...	...	...	...	...	...	...	...	...	...	4	2	2	...
Wyoming	...	...	...	...	...	...	...	...	...	...	...	...	...	...	...	...	...	...
Alaska	...	...	...	...	...	...	...	...	...	...	...	...	...	...	...	...	...	...
Canal Zone	...	...	...	...	...	...	...	...	...	...	...	...	...	...	...	...	...	...
District of Columbia	...	...	...	...	...	...	...	...	...	...	...	...	...	...	...	...	...	...
Hawaii	...	...	...	...	...	...	...	...	...	...	...	...	...	...	...	...	...	...
Philippine Islands	...	...	...	...	...	...	...	...	...	...	...	...	...	...	...	...	...	...
Puerto Rico	...	...	...	...	...	...	...	...	...	...	...	...	...	...	...	...	...	...
Virgin Islands	...	...	...	...	...	...	...	...	...	...	...	...	...	...	...	...	...	...
Total	275	275	83	53	101	38	75[a]	51	118	33	79	40	154[b]	2[c]	280[d]	126[e]	155[f]	2

Source: *Niles' Register, 1844.*
Presidential. First ballot, p. 147.
Vice-Presidential. First ballot, p. 236.
Second ballot, p. 236.
a/ Sum of column; proceedings record 74.
Third ballot, p. 236.
b/ Sum of column; proceedings record 155.
c/ Not voting, 2.

Source: *Niles' Register, 1848.*
Proxy voting for absent delegates, p. 356.
e/ Sum of column; proceedings record 120.
f/ Sum of column; proceedings record 156.

1848 WHIG

Delegation	Votes	First Ballot				Third Ballot				Fourth Ballot			
		Taylor	Clay	Scott	Other	Taylor	Clay	Scott	Other	Taylor	Clay	Scott	Other
Alabama	7	6	1	...	...	6	1	...	...	6	1	...	...
Arizona	...	...	...	...	...	...	...	...	...	...	...	...	...
Arkansas	3	3	...	...	...	3	...	...	...	3	...	...	...
California	...	...	...	...	...	...	...	...	...	...	...	...	...
Colorado	...	...	...	...	...	...	...	...	...	...	...	...	...
Connecticut	6	...	6	...	...	3	3	...	...	3	3	...	1
Delaware	3	...	...	...	3	1	...	1	1	2	...	1	...
Florida	3	3	...	...	...	3	...	...	...	3	...	...	...
Georgia	10	10	...	...	...	10	...	...	...	10	...	...	...
Idaho	...	...	...	...	...	...	...	...	...	...	...	...	...
Illinois	8	4	3	1	...	4	3	1	...	8	...	...	...
Indiana	12	1	2	9	...	5	1	6	...	7	1	4	...
Iowa	4	2	1	...	1	3	1	...	...	4	...	...	...
Kansas	...	...	...	...	...	...	...	...	...	...	...	...	...
Kentucky	12	7	5	...	...	7	5	...	...	11	1	...	...
Louisiana	6	5	1	...	...	6	...	...	...	6	...	...	...
Maine	9	5	1	...	3	5	...	2	2	5	...	3	1
Maryland	8	...	8	...	...	3	5	...	...	8	...	...	...
Massachusetts	12	...	...	...	12	1	...	2	9	1	...	2	9
Michigan	5	...	3	2	...	...	1	4	...	2	...	3	...
Minnesota	...	...	...	...	...	...	...	...	...	...	...	...	...
Mississippi	6	6	...	...	...	6	...	...	...	6	...	...	...
Missouri	7	6	...	...	1	6	...	...	1	7	...	...	...
Montana	...	...	...	...	...	...	...	...	...	...	...	...	...
Nebraska	...	...	...	...	...	...	...	...	...	...	...	...	...
Nevada	...	...	...	...	...	...	...	...	...	...	...	...	...
New Hampshire	6	...	...	...	6	...	...	...	6	2	...	...	4
New Jersey	7	3	4	...	...	4	3	...	...	4	3	...	...
New Mexico	...	...	...	...	...	...	...	...	...	...	...	...	...
New York	36	...	29	5	2	2	28	6	...	6	13	17	...
North Carolina	11	6	5	...	...	7	3	1	...	10	1	...	...
North Dakota	...	...	...	...	...	...	...	...	...	...	...	...	...
Ohio	23	1	1	20	1	1	1	21	...	1	1	21	...
Oklahoma	...	...	...	...	...	...	...	...	...	...	...	...	...
Oregon	...	...	...	...	...	...	...	...	...	...	...	...	...
Pennsylvania	26	8	12	6	...	12	4	10	...	12	4	10	...
Rhode Island	4	...	4	...	...	1	3	...	...	4	...	...	...
South Carolina	2	1	1	...	...	1	1	...	...	1	1	...	...
South Dakota	...	...	...	...	...	...	...	...	...	...	...	...	...
Tennessee	13	13	...	...	...	13	...	...	...	13	...	...	...
Texas	4	4	...	...	...	4	...	...	...	4	...	...	...
Utah	...	...	...	...	...	...	...	...	...	...	...	...	...
Vermont	6	1	5	...	...	1	5	...	...	2	2	2	...
Virginia	17	15	2	...	...	15	2	...	...	16	1	...	...
Washington	...	...	...	...	...	...	...	...	...	...	...	...	...
West Virginia	...	...	...	...	...	...	...	...	...	...	...	...	...
Wisconsin	4	1	3	...	...	...	4	...	...	4	...	...	...
Wyoming	...	...	...	...	...	...	...	...	...	...	...	...	...
Alaska	...	...	...	...	...	...	...	...	...	...	...	...	...
Canal Zone	...	...	...	...	...	...	...	...	...	...	...	...	...
District of Columbia	...	...	...	...	...	...	...	...	...	...	...	...	...
Hawaii	...	...	...	...	...	...	...	...	...	...	...	...	...
Philippine Islands	...	...	...	...	...	...	...	...	...	...	...	...	...
Puerto Rico	...	...	...	...	...	...	...	...	...	...	...	...	...
Virgin Islands	...	...	...	...	...	...	...	...	...	...	...	...	...
Total	280	111	97	43	29[a]	133	74	54	19[b]	171	32	63	14[c]

Source: *Niles' Register, 1848.*

No breakdown of the state by state vote is given for the Vice-Presidential nominations. The totals are as follows:

First Ballot: Millard Fillmore, 115; Abbot Lawrence, 109; Andrew Stewart, 14; T. M. T. McKennan, 13; George Evans, 6; John Sergeant, 6; John M. Clayton, 3; Hamilton Fish, 2; scattering, 6.

Second Ballot: Fillmore, 173; Lawrence, 87; Evans, 2; Sergeant, 1; Clayton, 3.

a/ Other Candidates: Daniel Webster, 22; John McLean, 2; John M. Clayton, 4.
b/ Other Candidates: Webster, 17; Clayton, 1.
c/ Other Candidate: Webster, 14.

1852 WHIG CONVENTION

Delegation	Votes	Formation of Resolutions Committee Aye	No	Amend. for Elect. Col. Voting in Resol. Ctte. Aye	No	Prov. Ques. Report of Cred. Ctte. Aye	Nay	Adoption of Platform Yea	Nay	1st Ballot Scott	Fillmore	Webster	7th Ballot Scott	Fillmore	Webster	46th Ballot Scott	Fillmore	Webster
Alabama	9	9	...	...	9	9	...	9	...	...	9	...	...	9	...	...	9	...
Arizona	...	...	...	...	...	...	...	...	...	...	...	...	...	...	...	...	...	...
Arkansas	4	4	...	...	4	4	...	4	...	...	4	...	...	4	...	...	4	...
California	4	4	...	2	2	1	2	4	...	2	1	1	3	...	1	3	...	1
Colorado	...	...	...	...	...	...	...	...	...	...	...	...	...	...	...	...	...	...
Connecticut	6	6	...	2	4	4	2	4	1	2	1	3	2	1	3	2	...	4
Delaware	3	3	...	3	...	...	3	3	...	3	...	...	3	...	...	3	...	...
Florida	3	3	...	...	3	3	...	3	...	...	3	...	...	3	...	...	3	...
Georgia	10	10	...	...	10	10	...	10	...	...	10	...	...	10	...	...	10	...
Idaho	...	...	...	...	...	...	...	...	...	...	...	...	...	...	...	...	...	...
Illinois	11	11	...	11	...	2	8	7	5	11	...	...	9	2	...	9	2	...
Indiana	13	...	13	13	...	7	6	7	6	13	...	...	13	...	...	13	...	...
Iowa	4	4	...	4	...	4	...	4	...	...	4	...	...	4	...	1	3	...
Kansas	...	...	...	...	...	...	...	...	...	...	...	...	...	...	...	...	...	...
Kentucky	12	12	...	...	12	12	...	12	...	...	12	...	...	12	...	...	12	...
Louisiana	6	6	...	...	6	6	...	6	...	...	6	...	...	6	...	...	6	...
Maine	8	...	8	8	...	...	8	4	4	8	...	...	8	...	...	8	...	...
Maryland	8	8	...	...	8	8	...	8	...	...	8	...	...	8	...	...	8	...
Massachusetts	13	13	...	3	10	12	1	13	...	2	...	11	2	...	11	2	...	11
Michigan	6	...	6	6	...	1	5	...	6	6	...	...	6	...	...	6	...	...
Minnesota	...	...	...	...	...	...	...	...	...	...	...	...	...	...	...	...	...	...
Mississippi	7	7	...	...	7	7	...	7	...	...	7	...	...	7	...	...	7	...
Missouri	9	9	...	6	2	5	...	9	...	...	9	...	...	9	...	1	8	...
Montana	...	...	...	...	...	...	...	...	...	...	...	...	...	...	...	...	...	...
Nebraska	...	...	...	...	...	...	...	...	...	...	...	...	...	...	...	...	...	...
Nevada	...	...	...	...	...	...	...	...	...	...	...	...	...	...	...	...	...	...
New Hampshire	5	5	...	1	4	5	...	5	...	1	...	4	1	...	4	1	...	4
New Jersey	7	...	7	7	...	1	6	7	...	7	...	...	7	...	...	7	...	...
New Mexico	...	...	...	...	...	...	...	...	...	...	...	...	...	...	...	...	...	...
New York	35	...	35	31	4	4	24	12	22	24	7	2	24	7	1[a]	24	7	2
North Carolina	10	10	...	...	10	10	...	10	...	...	10	...	...	10	...	...	10	...
North Dakota	...	...	...	...	...	...	...	...	...	...	...	...	...	...	...	...	...	...
Ohio	23	1	22	23	...	...	23	8	15	22	1	...	22	1	...	22	1	...
Oklahoma	...	...	...	...	...	...	...	...	...	...	...	...	...	...	...	...	...	...
Oregon	...	...	...	...	...	...	...	...	...	...	...	...	...	...	...	...	...	...
Pennsylvania	27	27	...	27	...	2	25	21	6	26	1	...	26	1	...	26	1	...
Rhode Island	4	4	...	...	4	4	...	4	...	1	1	2	1	1	2	1	1	2
South Carolina	8	8	...	...	8	8	...	8	...	...	8	...	...	8	...	...	8	...
South Dakota	...	...	...	...	...	...	...	...	...	...	...	...	...	...	...	...	...	...
Tennessee	12	12	...	...	12	12	...	12	...	...	12	...	...	12	...	...	12	...
Texas	4	4	...	...	4	4	...	4	...	...	4	...	...	4	...	...	4	...
Utah	...	...	...	...	...	...	...	...	...	...	...	...	...	...	...	...	...	...
Vermont	5	5	...	1	4	4	1	...	...	1	1	3	1	1	3	1	...	4
Virginia	15	15	...	...	14	12	1	15	...	1	13	...	9	12	b	3	10	...
Washington	...	...	...	...	...	...	...	...	...	...	...	...	...	...	...	...	...	...
West Virginia	...	...	...	...	...	...	...	...	...	...	...	...	...	...	...	...	...	...
Wisconsin	5	...	5	1	3	3	2	4	1	1	1	3	1	1	3	1	1	3
Wyoming	...	...	...	...	...	...	...	...	...	...	...	...	...	...	...	...	...	...
Alaska	...	...	...	...	...	...	...	...	...	...	...	...	...	...	...	...	...	...
Canal Zone	...	...	...	...	...	...	...	...	...	...	...	...	...	...	...	...	...	...
District of Columbia	...	...	...	...	...	...	...	...	...	...	...	...	...	...	...	...	...	...
Hawaii	...	...	...	...	...	...	...	...	...	...	...	...	...	...	...	...	...	...
Philippine Islands	...	...	...	...	...	...	...	...	...	...	...	...	...	...	...	...	...	...
Puerto Rico	...	...	...	...	...	...	...	...	...	...	...	...	...	...	...	...	...	...
Virgin Islands	...	...	...	...	...	...	...	...	...	...	...	...	...	...	...	...	...	...
Total	296	200	96	149	144	164	117	227	66	132	133	29	131	133		134	127	31

Source: *The Baltimore Sun*, Vol. **XXXI**, No. 28, June 17, 1852, No. 29, June 18, No. 30, June 19 and No. 31, June 21.

a/ Bates 1.
b/ One blank.

	1852 WHIG CONVENTION									
	Presidential Nomination									
		50th Ballot			52nd Ballot			53rd Ballot		
Delegation	Votes	Scott	Fillmore	Webster	Scott	Fillmore	Webster	Scott	Fillmore	Webster
Alabama	9	...	9	...	...	9	...	...	9	...
Arizona	...	...	...	...	...	...	...	...	...	...
Arkansas	4	...	4	...	...	4	...	...	4	...
California	4	3	1	...	3	...	1	3	...	...
Colorado	...	...	...	...	...	...	...	...	...	...
Connecticut	6	2	1	3	2	1	3	2	1	3
Delaware	3	3	...	...	3	...	...	3	...	...
Florida	3	...	3	...	...	3	...	...	3	...
Georgia	10	...	10	...	...	10	...	...	10	...
Idaho	...	...	...	...	...	...	...	...	...	...
Illinois	11	11	...	...	11	...	...	11	...	...
Indiana	13	13	...	...	13	...	...	13	...	...
Iowa	4	1	3	...	1	3	...	1	3	...
Kansas	...	...	...	...	...	...	...	...	...	...
Kentucky	12	...	12	...	...	12	...	...	11	...
Louisiana	6	...	6	...	...	6	...	...	6	...
Maine	8	8	...	...	8	...	...	8	...	...
Maryland	8	...	8	...	...	8	...	...	8	...
Massachusetts	13	2	...	11	2	...	11	2	...	11
Michigan	6	6	...	...	6	...	...	6	...	...
Minnesota	...	...	...	...	...	...	...	...	...	...
Mississippi	7	...	7	...	...	7	...	...	7	...
Missouri	9	3	6	...	1	6	...	3	6	...
Montana	...	...	...	...	...	...	...	...	...	...
Nebraska	...	...	...	...	...	...	...	...	...	...
Nevada	...	...	...	...	...	...	...	...	...	...
New Hampshire	5	...	...	4	1	...	4	5	...	...
New Jersey	7	7	...	...	7	...	...	7	...	...
New Mexico	...	...	...	...	...	...	...	...	...	...
New York	35	25	7	1	25	7	1	25	7	1
North Carolina	10	...	10	...	...	10	...	...	10	...
North Dakota	...	...	...	...	...	...	...	...	...	...
Ohio	23	23	...	...	23	...	...	23	...	...
Oklahoma	...	...	...	...	...	...	...	...	...	...
Oregon	...	...	...	...	...	...	...	...	...	...
Pennsylvania	27	26	1	...	27	...	...	27	...	...
Rhode Island	4	2	...	2	2	...	2	3	...	1
South Carolina	8	...	8	...	...	8	...	...	8	...
South Dakota	...	...	...	...	...	...	...	...	...	...
Tennessee	12.	...	12	...	4	8	...	3	9	...
Texas	4	...	4	...	...	4	...	...	4	...
Utah	...	...	...	...	...	...	...	...	...	...
Vermont	5	2	...	3	2	2	1	5	...	...
Virginia	15	3	10	...	3	10	...	8	6	...
Washington	...	...	...	...	...	...	...	...	...	...
West Virginia	...	...	...	...	...	...	...	...	...	...
Wisconsin	5	1	1	3	2	...	2	1	...	4
Wyoming	...	...	...	...	...	...	...	...	...	...
Alaska	...	...	...	...	...	...	...	...	...	...
Canal Zone	...	...	...	...	...	...	...	...	...	...
District of Columbia	...	...	...	...	...	...	...	...	...	...
Hawaii	...	...	...	...	...	...	...	...	...	...
Philippine Islands	...	...	...	...	...	...	...	...	...	...
Puerto Rico	...	...	...	...	...	...	...	...	...	...
Virgin Islands	...	...	...	...	...	...	...	...	...	...
Total	296	142	122	27	148	118	25	159	112	21

Source: *The Baltimore Sun*, Vol. XXXI, No. 28, June 17, 1852,
No. 29, June 18, No. 30, June 19 and No. 31, June 21.

Delegation	Votes	1856 REPUBLICAN										1860 REPUBLICAN						
		Presidential					Vice-Presidential					Votes	Recommit Report to Credentials Committee			Minority Report of Credentials Committee		
		Informal Ballot			Formal		Informal Ballot			Formal								
		Fremont	McLean	Other	Fremont	Other	Dayton	Lincoln	Other	Dayton	Other		Yea	Nay	Not Voting	Yea	Nay	Not Voting
Alabama	...	...	...	...	...	...	...	...	...	...	...	...	...	...	...	...	...	...
Arizona	...	...	...	...	...	...	...	...	...	...	...	...	...	...	...	...	...	...
Arkansas	...	...	...	...	...	...	...	...	...	...	...	...	...	...	...	...	...	...
California	12	12	...	...	12	...	...	12	...	12	...	8	4	2	2	8	...	...
Colorado	...	...	...	...	...	...	...	...	...	...	...	...	...	...	...	...	...	...
Connecticut	18	18	...	...	18	...	1	...	17	10	8	12	10	2	...	8	4	...
Delaware	9	...	9	...	9	...	9	...	...	9	...	6	1	5	...	6	...	...
Florida	...	...	...	...	...	...	...	...	...	...	...	...	...	...	...	...	...	...
Georgia	...	...	...	...	...	...	...	...	...	...	...	...	...	...	...	...	...	...
Idaho	...	...	...	...	...	...	...	...	...	...	...	...	...	...	...	...	...	...
Illinois	34	14	19	1	33	1	...	33	1	33	1	22	22	...	...	7	...	15
Indiana	39	18	21	...	39	...	13	26	...	39	...	26	26	...	...	25	1	...
Iowa	12	12	...	...	12	...	7	...	5	12	...	8	8	...	...	5	3	...
Kansas	10	9	...	1	9	1	...	...	10	9	1	6	...	...	6	6	...	...
Kentucky	5	5	...	...	5	...	...	...	5	5	...	23	24	...	...	10	9	4
Louisiana	...	...	...	...	...	...	...	...	...	...	...	...	...	...	...	...	...	...
Maine	24	13	11	...	24	...	20	1	3	24	...	16	3	13	...	16	...	...
Maryland	9	4	3	2	7	2	6	...	3	6	3	11	4	6	1	5	6	...
Massachusetts	39	39	...	...	39	...	25	7	7	39	...	26	13	9	4	22	3	1
Michigan	18	18	...	...	18	...	13	5	...	18	...	12	...	12	...	12	...	...
Minnesota	2	...	...	2	...	2	...	...	2	...	2	8	...	8	...	8	...	...
Mississippi	...	...	...	...	...	...	...	...	...	...	...	...	...	...	...	...	...	...
Missouri	...	...	...	...	...	...	...	...	...	...	...	18	4	14	...	...	18	...
Montana	...	...	...	...	...	...	...	...	...	...	...	...	...	...	...	...	...	...
Nebraska	...	...	...	...	...	...	...	...	...	...	...	6	...	...	6	6	...	...
Nevada	...	...	...	...	...	...	...	...	...	...	...	...	...	...	...	...	...	...
New Hampshire	15	15	...	...	15	...	7	8	...	15	...	10	9	1	...	10	...	...
New Jersey	21	7	14	...	21	...	21	...	...	21	...	14	...	14	...	12	1	1
New Mexico	...	...	...	...	...	...	...	...	...	...	...	...	...	...	...	...	...	...
New York	105	93	3	9	105	...	15	3	87	81	24	70	1	69	...	70	...	...
North Carolina	...	...	...	...	...	...	...	...	...	...	...	...	...	...	...	...	...	...
North Dakota	...	...	...	...	...	...	...	...	...	...	...	...	...	...	...	...	...	...
Ohio	69	30	39	...	55	14	65	2	2	68	1	46	46	...	...	32	9	5
Oklahoma	...	...	...	...	...	...	...	...	...	...	...	...	...	...	...	...	...	...
Oregon	...	...	...	...	...	...	...	...	...	...	...	5	...	5	...	3	2	...
Pennsylvania	81	10	71	...	57	24	28	11	42	77	4	54	53½	½	...	33½	20½	...
Rhode Island	12	12	...	...	12	...	8	2	2	12	...	8	8	...	...	4	4	...
South Carolina	...	...	...	...	...	...	...	...	...	...	...	...	...	...	...	...	...	...
South Dakota	...	...	...	...	...	...	...	...	...	...	...	...	...	...	...	...	...	...
Tennessee	...	...	...	...	...	...	...	...	...	...	...	...	...	...	...	...	...	...
Texas	...	...	...	...	...	...	...	...	...	...	...	6	...	...	6	6	...	...
Utah	...	...	...	...	...	...	...	...	...	...	...	...	...	...	...	...	...	...
Vermont	15	15	...	...	15	...	...	...	15	15	...	10	9	1	...	10	...	...
Virginia	...	...	...	...	...	...	...	...	3	3	...	23	30	...	...	13	8	2
Washington	...	...	...	...	...	...	...	...	...	...	...	...	...	...	...	...	...	...
West Virginia	...	...	...	...	...	...	...	...	...	...	...	...	...	...	...	...	...	...
Wisconsin	15	15	...	...	15	...	15	...	...	15	...	10	...	10	...	10	...	...
Wyoming	...	...	...	...	...	...	...	...	...	...	...	...	...	...	...	...	...	...
Alaska	...	...	...	...	...	...	...	...	...	...	...	...	...	...	...	...	...	...
Canal Zone	...	...	...	...	...	...	...	...	...	...	...	...	...	...	...	...	...	...
District of Columbia	3	...	...	3	...	3	...	...	3	...	3	2	...	...	2	2	...	...
Hawaii	...	...	...	...	...	...	...	...	...	...	...	...	...	...	...	...	...	...
Philippine Islands	...	...	...	...	...	...	...	...	...	...	...	...	...	...	...	...	...	...
Puerto Rico	...	...	...	...	...	...	...	...	...	...	...	...	...	...	...	...	...	...
Virgin Islands	...	...	...	...	...	...	...	...	...	...	...	...	...	...	...	...	...	...
Total	567	359	190	18[a]	520	47[b]	253	110	204[c]	523	44[d]	466	275½[e]	171½[f]	27	349½[g]	88½[h]	28

Source: *Official Proceedings, 1856.*

Presidential Ballots: Informal, p. 64; formal, p. 65.
Vice Presidential Ballots: Informal, p. 64; formal, p. 65.

a/ Other candidates: Nathaniel Banks, 1; Charles Sumner, 2; William Seward, 1; absent or not voting, 14.

b/ Other candidates: John McLean, 37; William Seward, 1; absent or not voting, 9.

c/ Other candidates: Nathaniel Banks, 46; David Wilmot, 43; John King, 9; Charles Sumner, 35; Thomas Ford, 7; Cassius Clay, 3; Jacob Collamer, 15; Joshua Giddings , 2; Whitfield Johnson, 2; H. C. Carey, 3; Aaron Pennington, 1; Henry Wilson, 1; Samuel Pomeroy, 8; absent or not voting, 29. Three votes are recorded for Virginia in the column, although Virginia was not included in the list of delegates submitted by the Committee on Credentials. These votes may have been cast by the District of Columbia delegation.

d/ Other candidates: Abraham Lincoln, 20; Nathaniel Banks, 6; John King, 1; Thomas Ford, 1; Charles Sumner, 3; absent or not voting, 13. Comment on Virginia in previous footnote applies here also.

Source: *Official Proceedings, 1860.*

Ballot to recommit report of Committee on Credentials, p. 123. Ballot on substitution of minority report of Committee on Credentials, p. 129.

e/ Total vote on this ballot exceeds authorized total convention strength by 8. Kentucky, 23 authorized votes, recorded as casting 24 votes Yea. Virginia, 23 authorized votes, recorded as casting 30 votes Yea.

f/ Sum of column; proceedings record 172½.
g/ Sum of column; proceedings record 358½.
h/ Sum of column; proceedings record 94½.

1860 REPUBLICAN — Presidential

Delegation	Votes	Previous Question on Report of Platform Committee			First Ballot						Second Ballot			Third Ballot (before shift)		
		Yea	Nay	Not Voting	Seward	Lincoln	Cameron	Bates	Chase	Other	Seward	Lincoln	Other	Seward	Lincoln	Other
Alabama	...	...	...	...	...	...	...	...	...	...	...	...	...	...	...	...
Arizona	...	...	...	...	...	...	...	...	...	...	...	...	...	...	...	...
Arkansas	...	...	...	...	...	...	...	...	...	...	...	...	...	...	...	...
California	8	...	8	...	8	...	...	...	...	...	8	...	...	8	...	...
Colorado	...	...	...	...	...	...	...	...	...	...	...	...	...	...	...	...
Connecticut	12	1	11	...	...	2	...	7	2	1	...	4	10	1	4	7
Delaware	6	4	2	...	...	...	...	6	...	...	...	6	...	...	6	...
Florida	...	...	...	...	...	...	...	...	...	...	...	...	...	...	...	...
Georgia	...	...	...	...	...	...	...	...	...	...	...	...	...	...	...	...
Idaho	...	...	...	...	...	...	...	...	...	...	...	...	...	...	...	...
Illinois	22	14	8	...	...	22	...	...	...	...	...	22	...	...	22	...
Indiana	26	20	6	...	...	26	...	...	...	...	...	26	...	...	26	...
Iowa	8	2	6	...	2	2	1	1	1	1	2	5	1	2	5½	½
Kansas	6	...	6	...	6	...	...	...	...	...	6	...	...	6	...	...
Kentucky	23	10	10	3	5	6	...	...	8	4	7	9	7	6	13	4
Louisiana	...	...	...	...	...	...	...	...	...	...	...	...	...	...	...	...
Maine	16	1	14	1	10	6	...	...	...	...	10	6	...	10	6	...
Maryland	11	...	11	...	3	...	...	8	...	...	3	...	8	2	9	...
Massachusetts	26	4	21	1	21	4	...	...	...	1	22	4	...	18	8	...
Michigan	12	8	4	...	12	...	...	...	...	...	12	...	...	12	...	...
Minnesota	8	...	8	...	8	...	...	...	...	...	8	...	...	8	...	...
Mississippi	...	...	...	...	...	...	...	...	...	...	...	...	...	...	...	...
Missouri	18	...	18	...	...	...	...	18	...	...	...	...	18	...	...	18
Montana	...	...	...	...	...	...	...	...	...	...	...	...	...	...	...	...
Nebraska	6	2	4	...	2	1	1	...	2	...	3	1	2	3	1	2
Nevada	...	...	...	...	...	...	...	...	...	...	...	...	...	...	...	...
New Hampshire	10	...	10	...	...	...	...	1	1	...	1	9	...	1	9	...
New Jersey	14	12½	1½	...	1	7	...	...	...	14	4	...	10	5	8	1
New Mexico	...	...	...	...	...	...	...	...	...	...	...	...	...	...	...	...
New York	70	25	45	...	70	...	...	...	...	...	70	...	...	70	...	...
North Carolina	...	...	...	...	...	...	...	...	...	...	...	...	...	...	...	...
North Dakota	...	...	...	...	...	...	...	...	...	...	...	...	...	...	...	...
Ohio	46	28	18	...	...	8	...	...	34	4	...	14	32	...	29	17
Oklahoma	...	...	...	...	...	...	...	...	...	...	...	...	...	...	...	...
Oregon	5	2	2	1	...	...	...	5	...	...	...	...	5	1	4	...
Pennsylvania	54	½	53½	...	1½	4	47½	...	...	1	2½	48	3½	...	52	2
Rhode Island	8	...	8	...	...	...	...	1	1	6	...	3	3	1	5	2
South Carolina	...	...	...	...	...	...	...	...	...	...	...	...	...	...	...	...
South Dakota	...	...	...	...	...	...	...	...	...	...	...	...	...	...	...	...
Tennessee	...	...	...	...	...	...	...	...	...	...	...	...	...	...	...	...
Texas	6	...	6	...	4	...	...	2	...	...	6	...	...	6	...	...
Utah	...	...	...	...	...	...	...	...	...	...	...	...	...	...	...	...
Vermont	10	...	10	...	...	...	...	...	...	10	...	10	...	...	10	...
Virginia	23	17	6	...	8	14	1	...	...	...	8	14	1	8	14	1
Washington	...	...	...	...	...	...	...	...	...	...	...	...	...	...	...	...
West Virginia	...	...	...	...	...	...	...	...	...	...	...	...	...	...	...	...
Wisconsin	10	8	2	...	10	...	...	...	...	...	10	...	...	10	...	...
Wyoming	...	...	...	...	...	...	...	...	...	...	...	...	...	...	...	...
Alaska	...	...	...	...	...	...	...	...	...	...	...	...	...	...	...	...
Canal Zone	...	...	...	...	...	...	...	...	...	...	...	...	...	...	...	...
District of Columbia	2	...	2	...	2	...	...	...	...	...	2	...	...	2	...	...
Hawaii	...	...	...	...	...	...	...	...	...	...	...	...	...	...	...	...
Philippine Islands	...	...	...	...	...	...	...	...	...	...	...	...	...	...	...	...
Puerto Rico	...	...	...	...	...	...	...	...	...	...	...	...	...	...	...	...
Virgin Islands	...	...	...	...	...	...	...	...	...	...	...	...	...	...	...	...
Total	466	159	301	6	173½	102	50½	48	49	43[a]	184½	181	100½[b]	180	231½	54½[c]

Source: *Official Proceedings, 1860.*

Ballot on Previous Question on Report of Platform Committee, p. 135. Presidential Ballots: First, p. 149; Second, p. 152; Third, p. 153.

a/ Other candidates: Benjamin F. Wade, 3; John McLean, 12; John M. Reed, 1; William L. Dayton, 14; Charles Sumner, 1; John C. Fremont, 1; Jacob Collamer, 10; absent and not voting, 1.

b/ Other candidates: Edward Bates, 35; Simon Cameron, 2; John McLean, 8; Salmon P. Chase, 42½; William L. Dayton, 10; Cassius M. Clay, 2; absent and not voting, 1.

c/ Other candidates: Edward Bates, 22; Salmon P. Chase, 24½; John McLean, 5; William L. Dayton, 1; Cassius M. Clay, 1; absent and not voting, 1.

	1860 REPUBLICAN												1864 REPUBLICAN			
	Presidential			Vice-Presidential									Admission of Missouri Delegation			
	Third Ballot (after shift)			First Ballot					Second Ballot							
Delegation	Votes	Seward	Lincoln	Other	Clay	Reeder	Hickman	Hamlin	Other	Clay	Hamlin	Other	Votes	Yea	Nay	Not Voting
Alabama	...	...	...	...	...	...	...	...	...	...	...	...	...	...	...	...
Arizona	...	...	...	...	...	...	...	...	...	...	...	...	...	...	...	...
Arkansas	...	...	...	...	...	...	...	...	...	...	...	...	10	...	...	10
California	8	3	5	...	...	...	8	...	...	1	7	...	10	10	...	...
Colorado	...	...	...	...	...	...	...	...	...	...	...	...	6	...	...	6
Connecticut	12	1	8	3	2	...	2	5	3	...	10	2	12	12	...	...
Delaware	6	...	6	...	3	...	1	2	...	...	6	...	6	6	...	...
Florida	...	...	...	...	...	...	...	...	...	...	...	...	...	...	...	...
Georgia	...	...	...	...	...	...	...	...	...	...	...	...	...	...	...	...
Idaho	...	...	...	...	...	...	...	...	...	...	...	...	...	...	...	...
Illinois	22	...	22	...	2	16	2	2	...	2	20	...	32	32	...	...
Indiana	26	...	26	...	18	...	...	8	...	14	12	...	26	26	...	...
Iowa	8	...	8	...	...	1	...	6	1	...	8	...	16	16	...	...
Kansas	6	...	6	...	...	...	6	...	...	1	2	3	6	6	...	...
Kentucky	23	...	23	...	23	...	...	...	...	23	...	...	22	21	1	...
Louisiana	...	...	...	...	...	...	...	...	...	...	...	...	14	...	...	14
Maine	16	...	16	...	...	...	...	16	...	...	16	...	14	14	...	...
Maryland	11	2	9	...	2	...	1	8	...	1	10	...	14	14	...	...
Massachusetts	26	18	8	...	...	1	1	1	23	...	26	...	24	24	...	...
Michigan	12	12	...	...	4	...	...	8	...	4	8	...	16	16	...	...
Minnesota	8	...	8	...	1	...	1	6	...	1	7	...	8	8	...	...
Mississippi	...	...	...	...	...	...	...	...	...	...	...	...	...	...	...	...
Missouri	18	...	18	...	...	...	9	...	9	5	13	...	22	...	...	22
Montana	...	...	...	...	...	...	...	...	...	...	...	...	...	...	...	...
Nebraska	6	...	6	...	1	...	5	...	...	...	...	6	6	...	...	6
Nevada	...	...	...	...	...	...	...	...	...	...	...	...	6	...	...	6
New Hampshire	10	...	10	...	...	...	...	10	...	...	10	...	10	10	...	...
New Jersey	14	5	8	1	1	7	...	6	...	...	14	...	14	14	...	...
New Mexico	...	...	...	...	...	...	...	...	...	...	...	...	...	...	...	...
New York	70	70	...	...	9	2	11	35	13	...	70	...	66	66	...	...
North Carolina	...	...	...	...	...	...	...	...	...	...	...	...	...	...	...	...
North Dakota	...	...	...	...	...	...	...	...	...	...	...	...	...	...	...	...
Ohio	46	...	46	...	...	...	...	46	...	...	46	...	42	42	...	...
Oklahoma	...	...	...	...	...	...	...	...	...	...	...	...	...	...	...	...
Oregon	5	...	5	...	...	...	3	1	1	...	3	2	6	6	...	...
Pennsylvania	54	½	53	½	4½	24	7	11	7½	...	54	...	52	49	3	...
Rhode Island	8	...	8	...	...	...	...	8	...	...	8	...	8	8	...	...
South Carolina	...	...	...	...	...	...	...	...	...	...	...	...	...	...	...	...
South Dakota	...	...	...	...	...	...	...	...	...	...	...	...	...	...	...	...
Tennessee	...	...	...	...	...	...	...	...	...	...	...	...	15	...	...	15
Texas	6	...	6	...	...	...	...	6	6	...	...	...	...	...	...	...
Utah	...	...	...	...	...	...	...	...	...	...	...	...	...	...	...	...
Vermont	10	...	10	...	...	...	...	10	...	...	10	...	10	10	...	...
Virginia	23	...	23	...	23	...	...	...	...	23	...	...	...	...	...	...
Washington	...	...	...	...	...	...	...	...	...	...	...	...	...	...	...	...
West Virginia	...	...	...	...	...	...	...	...	...	...	...	...	10	10	...	...
Wisconsin	10	10	...	...	5	...	...	5	...	5	5	...	16	16	...	...
Wyoming	...	...	...	...	...	...	...	...	...	...	...	...	...	...	...	...
Alaska	...	...	...	...	...	...	...	...	...	...	...	...	...	...	...	...
Canal Zone	...	...	...	...	...	...	...	...	...	...	...	...	...	...	...	...
District of Columbia	2	...	2	...	2	...	...	...	...	...	2	...	...	...	...	...
Hawaii	...	...	...	...	...	...	...	...	...	...	...	...	...	...	...	...
Philippine Islands	...	...	...	...	...	...	...	...	...	...	...	...	...	...	...	...
Puerto Rico	...	...	...	...	...	...	...	...	...	...	...	...	...	...	...	...
Virgin Islands	...	...	...	...	...	...	...	...	...	...	...	...	...	...	...	...
Total	466	121½	340[a]	4½[b]	100½[c]	51	57[d]	194	63½[e]	86	367[f]	13[g]	519	436[h]	4	79

Source: *Official Proceedings 1860.*
a/ Sum of column; proceedings record 364.
b/ Other candidates: Salmon P. Chase, 2; William L. Dayton, 1; Cassius M. Clay, 1; John McLean, ½.
c/ Sum of column; proceedings record 101½.
d/ Sum of column; proceedings record 58.
e/ Other candidates: Nathaniel P. Banks, 38½; H. Winter Davis, 8; Samuel Houston, 6; William L. Dayton, 3; John M Reed, 1; absent and not voting, 7.
f/ Sum of column; proceedings record 357.
g/ Other candidates; John Hickman, 13.

Source: *Official Proceedings 1864.*
h/ Sum of column; proceedings record 440.

		1864 REPUBLICAN														
		Division on King Amendment			Admission of Arkansas and Louisiana Delegations			Presidential			Vice-Presidential					
								First Ballot			First Ballot				Second Ballot	
Delegation	Votes	Yea	Nay	Not Voting	Yea	Nay	Not Voting	Lincoln	Grant	Not Voting	Johnson	Hamlin	Dickinson	Other	Johnson	Other
Alabama	...	...	...	...	...	...	...	...	...	...	...	...	...	...	...	...
Arizona	...	...	...	...	...	...	...	...	...	...	...	...	...	...	...	...
Arkansas	10	...	...	10	...	...	10	10	...	...	10	...	...	...	10	...
California	10	10	...	...	6	4	...	7	...	3	5	5	...	...	10	...
Colorado	6	...	...	6	...	...	6	6	...	...	...	...	6	...	6	...
Connecticut	12	10	2	...	10	2	...	12	...	...	12	...	...	...	12	...
Delaware	6	1	4	1	...	5	1	6	...	...	...	...	6	...	6	...
Florida	...	...	...	...	...	...	...	...	...	...	...	...	...	...	...	...
Georgia	...	...	...	...	...	...	...	...	...	...	...	...	...	...	...	...
Idaho	...	...	...	...	...	...	...	...	...	...	...	...	...	...	...	...
Illinois	32	32	...	...	32	...	...	32	...	...	...	32	...	...	32	...
Indiana	26	24	2	...	22	4	...	26	...	...	26	...	...	...	26	...
Iowa	16	9	7	...	14	2	...	16	...	...	16	...	...	...	16	...
Kansas	6	6	...	...	6	...	...	6	...	...	2	2	2	...	6	...
Kentucky	22	4	18	...	12	10	...	22	...	...	...	...	...	22	21	1
Louisiana	14	...	...	14	...	...	14	14	...	...	7	...	7	...	14	...
Maine	14	3	11	...	3	11	...	14	...	...	...	14	...	...	14	...
Maryland	14	1	13	...	1	13	...	14	...	...	2	1	11	...	14	...
Massachusetts	24	...	24	...	...	24	...	24	...	...	...	3	17	4	21	3
Michigan	16	2	14	...	10	6	...	16	...	...	...	16	...	...	16	...
Minnesota	8	1	7	...	...	8	...	8	...	...	...	5	3	...	...	8
Mississippi	...	...	...	...	...	...	...	...	...	...	...	...	...	...	...	...
Missouri	22	19	3	...	17	5	...	...	22	...	2	...	...	20	22	...
Montana	...	...	...	...	...	...	...	...	...	...	...	...	...	...	...	...
Nebraska	6	...	...	6	...	...	6	6	...	...	3	1	1	1	6	...
Nevada	6	...	...	6	...	...	6	6	...	...	6	...	...	...	6	...
New Hampshire	10	...	10	...	...	10	...	10	...	...	1	4	3	2	10	...
New Jersey	14	14	...	...	14	...	...	14	...	...	2	...	12	...	14	...
New Mexico	...	...	...	...	...	...	...	...	...	...	...	...	...	...	...	...
New York	66	66	...	...	61	3	2	66	...	...	32	6	28	...	66	...
North Carolina	...	...	...	...	...	...	...	...	...	...	...	...	...	...	...	...
North Dakota	...	...	...	...	...	...	...	...	...	...	...	...	...	...	...	...
Ohio	42	42	...	...	42	...	...	42	...	...	42	...	...	...	42	...
Oklahoma	...	...	...	...	...	...	...	...	...	...	...	...	...	...	...	...
Oregon	6	6	...	...	6	...	...	6	...	...	...	...	...	6	6	...
Pennsylvania	52	31	21	...	5	47	...	52	...	...	...	52	...	...	52	...
Rhode Island	8	2	6	...	1	7	...	8	...	...	...	3	1	4	7	1
South Carolina	...	...	...	...	...	...	...	...	...	...	...	...	...	...	...	...
South Dakota	...	...	...	...	...	...	...	...	...	...	...	...	...	...	...	...
Tennessee	15	...	...	15	15	...	...	15	...	...	15	...	...	...	15	...
Texas	...	...	...	...	...	...	...	...	...	...	...	...	...	...	...	...
Utah	...	...	...	...	...	...	...	...	...	...	...	...	...	...	...	...
Vermont	10	2	8	...	5	5	...	10	...	...	5	2	1	2	10	...
Virginia	...	...	...	...	...	...	...	...	...	...	...	...	...	...	...	...
Washington	...	...	...	...	...	...	...	...	...	...	...	...	...	...	...	...
West Virginia	10	10	...	...	10	...	...	10	...	...	10	...	...	...	10	...
Wisconsin	16	15	1	...	15	1	...	16	...	...	2	4	10	...	2	14
Wyoming	...	...	...	...	...	...	...	...	...	...	...	...	...	...	...	...
Alaska	...	...	...	...	...	...	...	...	...	...	...	...	...	...	...	...
Canal Zone	...	...	...	...	...	...	...	...	...	...	...	...	...	...	...	...
District of Columbia	...	...	...	...	...	...	...	...	...	...	...	...	...	...	...	...
Hawaii	...	...	...	...	...	...	...	...	...	...	...	...	...	...	...	...
Philippine Islands	...	...	...	...	...	...	...	...	...	...	...	...	...	...	...	...
Puerto Rico	...	...	...	...	...	...	...	...	...	...	...	...	...	...	...	...
Virgin Islands	...	...	...	...	...	...	...	...	...	...	...	...	...	...	...	...
Total	519	310	151	58	307	167	45	494[a]	22	3[b]	200	150	108	61[c]	492[d]	27[e]

Source: *Official Proceedings, 1864.*

a/ Sum of column; proceedings record 484.
b/ Absent and not voting, 3.
c/ Other candidates: Benjamin F. Butler, 28; Lovell H. Rousseau, 21; Schuyler P. Colfax, 6; Ambrose E. Burnside, 2; Joseph Holt, 2; David Tod, 1; John M. King, 1.
d/ Sum of column; proceedings record 494.
e/ Other candidates: Daniel S. Dickinson, 17; Hannibal Hamlin, 9; David Tod, 1.

1868 REPUBLICAN

Delegation	Votes	Pres. First Ballot — Grant	First Ballot					Second Ballot					Third Ballot				
			Wilson	Colfax	Wade	Fenton	Other	Wilson	Colfax	Wade	Fenton	Other	Wilson	Colfax	Wade	Fenton	Other
Alabama	18	18	4	4	2	2	4	11	1	1	2	...	11	1	2	2	...
Arizona	...	...	...	...	...	...	...	...	...	...	...	...	...	...	...	.1.	...
Arkansas	10	10	9	...	1	...	...	10	...	...	...	...	10	...	...	...	...
California	10	10	1	2	5	2	...	1	2	5	2	...	...	1	8	1	...
Colorado	6	6	...	6	...	...	...	...	6	...	...	...	...	6	...	...	...
Connecticut	12	12	4	2	2	4	...	4	1	3	4	...	...	3	2	7	...
Delaware	6	6	6	...	...	...	...	5	...	...	...	1	...	5	...	...	...
Florida	6	6	2	2	...	2	...	2	2	...	2	...	2	2	...	2	...
Georgia	18	18	6	2	3	6	1	2	2	7	7	...	...	4	6	8	...
Idaho	2	2	...	...	...	2	...	...	...	...	2	...	...	...	...	2	...
Illinois	32	32	...	3	15	3	11	...	3	15	3	11	...	4	17	3	8
Indiana	26	26	...	26	...	...	...	...	26	...	...	...	...	26	...	...	...
Iowa	16	16	...	...	...	...	16	...	4	...	10	2	...	8	...	8	...
Kansas	6	6	...	...	...	...	6	...	2	2	2	...	...	2	2	2	...
Kentucky	22	22	...	...	...	...	22	...	9	13	...	...	...	10	12	...	...
Louisiana	14	14	...	...	...	14	...	...	...	...	14	...	...	...	5	9	...
Maine	14	14	...	...	...	...	14	...	...	...	...	14	...	...	...	...	14
Maryland	14	14	...	...	1	...	13	1	2	10	...	1	1	2	10	...	1
Massachusetts	24	24	24	...	...	...	...	24	...	...	...	...	24	...	...	...	...
Michigan	16	16	...	16	...	...	...	...	16	...	...	...	...	16	...	...	...
Minnesota	8	8	...	...	8	...	...	...	...	8	...	...	1	...	7	...	...
Mississippi	14	14	5	...	5	4	...	5	...	5	4	...	4	1	4	5	...
Missouri	22	22	...	2	20	...	...	...	2	20	...	...	...	2	20	...	...
Montana	2	2	...	...	2	...	...	...	...	2	...	...	...	...	2	...	...
Nebraska	6	6	...	...	6	...	...	...	...	6	...	...	...	...	6	...	...
Nevada	6	6	...	...	2	4	...	...	...	2	4	...	...	...	2	4	...
New Hampshire	10	10	10	...	...	...	...	10	...	...	...	...	10	...	...	...	...
New Jersey	14	14	...	14	...	...	...	...	14	...	...	...	...	14	...	...	...
New Mexico	...	...	...	...	...	...	...	...	...	...	...	...	...	...	...	...	...
New York	66	66	...	...	...	66	...	...	...	...	66	...	...	...	...	66	...
North Carolina	18	18	...	...	18	...	...	9	...	9	...	...	9	...	9	...	...
North Dakota	2*	2	...	2	...	...	...	...	2	...	...	...	...	2	...	...	...
Ohio	42	42	...	...	42	...	...	...	4	38	...	...	...	5	37	...	...
Oklahoma	...	...	...	...	...	...	...	...	...	...	...	...	...	...	...	...	...
Oregon	6	6	...	6	...	...	...	...	6	...	...	...	...	6	...	...	...
Pennsylvania	52	52	...	1	3	...	48	...	3	5	...	44	...	5	7	...	40
Rhode Island	8	8	2	3	2	...	1	5	3	...	...	...	...	8	...	...	...
South Carolina	12	12	12	...	...	...	...	12	...	...	...	...	12	...	...	...	...
South Dakota	*	...	...	...	...	...	...	...	...	...	...	...	...	...	...	...	...
Tennessee	20	20	...	6	3	11	...	...	6	3	11	...	...	6	3	11	...
Texas	12	12	11	...	1	...	...	...	...	9	3	...	...	...	11	1	...
Utah	...	...	...	...	...	...	...	...	...	...	...	...	...	...	...	...	...
Vermont	10	10	...	10	...	...	...	...	10	...	...	...	...	10	...	...	...
Virginia	20	20	18	...	2	...	...	12	4	2	2	...	10	6	2	2	...
Washington	...	...	...	...	...	...	...	...	...	...	...	...	...	...	...	...	...
West Virginia	10	10	5	1	2	...	1	6	3	1	...	...	7	2	1	...	...
Wisconsin	16	16	7	...	6	...	4	...	7	1	6	2	...	8	1	5	2
Wyoming	...	...	...	...	...	...	...	...	...	...	...	...	...	...	...	...	...
Alaska	...	...	...	...	...	...	...	...	...	...	...	...	...	...	...	...	...
Canal Zone	...	...	...	...	...	...	...	...	...	...	...	...	...	...	...	...	...
District of Columbia	2	2	...	...	2	...	...	...	...	2	...	...	...	...	2	...	...
Hawaii	...	...	...	...	...	...	...	...	...	...	...	...	...	...	...	...	...
Philippine Islands	...	...	...	...	...	...	...	...	...	...	...	...	...	...	...	...	...
Puerto Rico	...	...	...	...	...	...	...	...	...	...	...	...	...	...	...	...	...
Virgin Islands	...	...	...	...	...	...	...	...	...	...	...	...	...	...	...	...	...
Total	650	650	119	115	147	126	141a	114	145	170	144	75b	101	165	178	139	65c

Source: *Official Proceedings, 1868.*
Presidential. First ballot, p. 96.
Vice-Presidential. First ballot, p. 118.
a/ Other candidates: Andrew G. Curtin, 51; Hannibal Hamlin, 28; James Speed, 22; James Harlan, 16; John A. J. Creswell, 14; Samuel C. Pomeroy, 6; William D. Kelley, 4.
Second ballot, p. 120.
b/ Other candidates: Curtin, 45; Hamlin, 30.
Third ballot, p. 122.
c/ Other candidates: Curtin, 40; Hamlin, 25.

* Dakota Territory, 2 votes.

	1868 REPUBLICAN														1872 REP.	
	Vice-Presidential														Pres.	
	Fourth Ballot					Fifth Ballot (before shift)					Fifth Ballot (after shift)				First Ballot	
Delegation	Votes	Wilson	Colfax	Wade	Fenton	Other	Wade	Colfax	Fenton	Wilson	Other	Fenton	Wade	Colfax	Other	Votes	Grant
Alabama	18	11	1	2	2	2	2	1	2	11	2	1	...	15	2	20	20
Arizona	...	...	...	...	...	...	...	...	...	...	...	...	...	...	...	2	2
Arkansas	10	8	...	2	...	...	2	...	...	8	...	...	...	10	...	12	12
California	10	...	1	7	2	...	8	1	1	...	...	...	...	10	...	12	12
Colorado	6	...	6	...	...	...	...	6	...	...	...	...	...	6	...	2	2
Connecticut	12	...	2	2	8	...	2	4	6	...	...	...	...	12	...	12	12
Delaware	6	...	5	...	1	...	2	4	...	...	...	...	...	6	...	6	6
Florida	6	2	2	...	2	...	...	1	5	...	...	...	...	6	...	8	8
Georgia	18	...	5	5	8	...	5	3	10	...	...	...	...	18	...	22	22
Idaho	2	...	...	...	2	...	...	...	2	...	...	2	...	...	...	2	2
Illinois	32	...	6	17	3	6	19	8	3	...	2	...	...	32	...	42	42
Indiana	26	...	26	...	...	...	...	26	...	...	...	...	...	26	...	30	30
Iowa	16	...	8	...	8	...	...	8	8	...	...	...	...	16	...	22	22
Kansas	6	...	2	2	2	...	2	2	2	...	...	...	...	6	...	10	10
Kentucky	22	...	10	12	...	...	12	10	...	...	...	...	...	22	...	24	24
Louisiana	14	...	...	5	9	...	5	...	9	...	...	...	...	14	...	16	16
Maine	14	...	...	...	...	14	...	...	...	...	14	...	...	14	...	14	14
Maryland	14	1	3	10	...	...	10	3	...	1	...	...	...	14	...	16	16
Massachusetts	24	24	...	...	...	...	...	...	...	24	...	...	...	24	...	26	26
Michigan	16	...	16	...	...	...	...	16	...	...	...	...	...	16	...	22	22
Minnesota	8	1	...	7	...	...	7	...	...	1	...	...	...	8	...	10	10
Mississippi	14	4	1	5	4	...	6	1	4	3	...	...	...	14	...	16	16
Missouri	22	...	2	20	...	...	20	2	...	...	...	...	...	22	...	30	30
Montana	2	...	...	2	...	...	2	...	...	...	...	...	2	...	...	2	2
Nebraska	6	...	...	6	...	...	6	...	...	...	...	...	...	6	...	6	6
Nevada	6	...	...	2	4	...	1	...	5	...	...	...	...	6	...	6	6
New Hampshire	10	10	...	...	...	...	9	...	1	...	...	...	...	10	...	10	10
New Jersey	14	...	14	...	...	...	...	14	...	...	...	...	...	14	...	18	18
New Mexico	...	...	...	...	...	...	...	...	...	...	...	...	...	...	...	2	2
New York	66	...	...	...	66	...	...	...	66	...	...	66	...	...	...	70	70
North Carolina	18	7	...	10	1	...	9	7	...	2	...	...	...	18	...	20	20
North Dakota	2	...	2	...	...	...	...	2	...	...	...	...	...	2	...	2*	2
Ohio	42	...	6	36	...	...	36	6	...	...	...	...	36	6	...	44	44
Oklahoma	...	...	...	...	...	...	...	...	...	...	...	...	...	...	...	...	...
Oregon	6	...	6	...	...	...	...	6	...	...	...	...	...	6	...	6	6
Pennsylvania	52	2	14	33	...	3	20	30	1	...	1	...	...	52	...	58	58
Rhode Island	8	...	6	2	...	...	...	8	...	...	...	...	...	8	...	8	8
South Carolina	12	7	...	...	5	...	2	...	7	3	...	...	...	12	...	14	14
South Dakota	...	...	...	...	...	...	...	...	...	...	...	...	...	...	...	*	
Tennessee	20	...	6	3	11	...	3	17	...	...	...	...	...	20	...	24	24
Texas	12	...	1	11	...	...	12	...	...	...	...	...	...	12	...	16	16
Utah	...	...	...	...	...	...	...	...	...	...	...	...	...	...	...	2	2
Vermont	10	...	10	...	...	...	...	10	...	...	...	...	...	10	...	10	10
Virginia	20	5	10	2	3	...	2	10	5	3	...	...	...	20	...	22	22
Washington	...	...	...	...	...	...	...	...	...	...	...	...	...	...	...	2	2
West Virginia	10	5	4	1	...	...	1	9	...	...	...	...	...	10	...	10	10
Wisconsin	16	...	11	...	3	2	...	11	2	...	3	...	...	16	...	20	20
Wyoming	...	...	...	...	...	...	...	...	...	...	...	...	...	...	...	2	2
Alaska	...	...	...	...	...	...	...	...	...	...	...	...	...	...	...	...	...
Canal Zone	...	...	...	...	...	...	...	...	...	...	...	...	2	...	...	...	...
District of Columbia	2	...	...	2	...	...	2	...	...	...	...	...	...	2	...	2	2
Hawaii	...	...	...	...	...	...	...	...	...	...	...	...	...	...	...	...	...
Philippine Islands	...	...	...	...	...	...	...	...	...	...	...	...	...	...	...	...	...
Puerto Rico	...	...	...	...	...	...	...	...	...	...	...	...	...	...	...	...	...
Virgin Islands	...	...	...	...	...	...	...	...	...	...	...	...	...	...	...	...	...
Total	650	87	186	206	144	27a	207	226	139	56	22b	69	38	541	2c	752	752

Source: *Official Proceedings, 1868.*
Fourth ballot, p. 124.
a/ Other candidates: Hamlin, 25; not voting, 2.
Fifth ballot (before shift), p. 126.
b/ Other candidates: Hamlin, 20; not voting, 2.
Fifth ballot (after shift), p. 131.
c/ Not voting, 2.

Source: *Official Proceedings 1872.*
Presidential. First ballot, p. 42.

* Dakota Territory, 2 votes.

| Delegation | 1872 REPUBLICAN Vice-Presidential | | | | | | | 1876 REPUBLICAN | | | | | | |
| | First Ballot (before shift) | | | First Ballot (after shift) | | | | Minority Report on Credentials | | | Mongolian Immigration Plank | | |
	Votes	Wilson	Colfax	Other	Wilson	Colfax	Other	Votes	Yea	Nay	Not Voting	Yea	Nay	Not Voting
Alabama	20	12	7	1	12	7	1	20	...	...	20	10	10	...
Arizona	2	...	2	...	...	2	...	2	2	...	...	...	2	...
Arkansas	12	12	...	...	12	...	...	12	11	1	...	8	4	...
California	12	12	...	...	12	...	...	12	5	7	...	...	12	...
Colorado	2	1	1	...	1	1	...	6	...	6	...	...	6	...
Connecticut	12	6	6	...	6	6	...	12	8	4	...	5	7	...
Delaware	6	...	6	...	...	6	...	6	...	6	...	2	4	...
Florida	8	5	3	...	5	3	...	8	7	1	...	...	8	...
Georgia	22	16	6	...	22	...	...	22	11	11	...	7	15	...
Idaho	2	...	2	...	...	2	...	2	...	2	...	...	2	...
Illinois	42	25	17	...	25	17	...	42	10	32	...	2	40	...
Indiana	30	...	30	...	...	30	...	30	30	...	...	10	20	...
Iowa	22	19	3	...	19	3	...	22	7	15	...	12	10	...
Kansas	10	10	...	...	10	...	...	10	...	10	...	...	10	...
Kentucky	24	4	20	...	4	20	...	24	...	24	...	14	10	...
Louisiana	16	5	11	...	5	11	...	16	9	7	...	5	8	3
Maine	14	4	10	...	4	10	...	14	...	14	...	6	8	...
Maryland	16	...	16	...	...	16	...	16	3	13	...	15	1	...
Massachusetts	26	26	...	...	26	...	...	26	...	26	...	20	6	...
Michigan	22	...	22	...	...	22	...	22	...	22	...	6	16	...
Minnesota	10	...	10	...	...	10	...	10	...	10	...	...	10	...
Mississippi	16	11	4	1	11	4	1	16	11	5	...	11	5	...
Missouri	30	27	2	1	27	2	1	30	21	9	...	12	17	1
Montana	2	...	2	...	...	2	...	2	...	2	...	2	...	...
Nebraska	6	2	4	...	2	4	...	6	...	6	...	...	6	...
Nevada	6	6	...	...	6	...	...	6	6	...	...	...	6	...
New Hampshire	10	10	...	...	10	...	...	10	4	6	...	2	8	...
New Jersey	18	...	18	...	...	18	...	18	3	15	...	...	18	...
New Mexico	2	2	...	...	2	...	...	2	...	2	...	...	2	...
New York	70	16	53	1	16	53	1	70	59	9	2	30	35	5
North Carolina	20	20	...	...	20	...	...	20	18	2	...	3	17	...
North Dakota	*2	½	1½	...	½	1½	...	*2	...	2	...	...	2	...
Ohio	44	30	14	...	30	14	...	44	15	25	4	19	25	...
Oklahoma	...	...	...	...	...	...	...	...	...	...	...	...	...	...
Oregon	6	...	6	...	...	6	...	6	6	...	...	...	6	...
Pennsylvania	58	58	...	...	58	...	...	58	58	...	...	...	58	...
Rhode Island	8	...	8	...	...	8	...	8	8	...	...	5	3	...
South Carolina	14	9	5	...	9	5	...	14	11	3	...	14	...	...
South Dakota	*	...	...	...	...	...	...	*	...	...	...	...	...	...
Tennessee	24	...	...	24	...	...	24	24	13	11	...	2	22	...
Texas	16	...	...	16	...	...	16	16	11	4	1	...	16	...
Utah	2	...	2	...	...	2	...	2	...	2	...	...	2	...
Vermont	10	...	10	...	...	10	...	10	...	10	...	4	6	...
Virginia	22	...	...	22	20	2	...	22	9	13	...	...	22	...
Washington	2	...	2	...	...	2	...	2	...	2	...	...	2	...
West Virginia	10	...	10	...	9	1	...	10	2	8	...	3	7	...
Wisconsin	20	15	5	...	15	5	...	20	2	18	...	...	20	...
Wyoming	2	1	1	...	1	1	...	2	...	2	...	...	2	...
Alaska	...	...	...	...	...	...	...	...	...	...	...	...	...	...
Canal Zone	...	...	...	...	...	...	...	...	...	...	...	...	...	...
District of Columbia	2	...	2	...	...	2	...	2	...	2	...	...	2	...
Hawaii	...	...	...	...	...	...	...	...	...	...	...	...	...	...
Philippine Islands	...	...	...	...	...	...	...	...	...	...	...	...	...	...
Puerto Rico	...	...	...	...	...	...	...	...	...	...	...	...	...	...
Virgin Islands	...	...	...	...	...	...	...	...	...	...	...	...	...	...
Total	752	364½	321½	66a	399½	308½	44b	756	360c	369d	27	229e	518f	9

Source: *Official Proceedings, 1872.*
Vice-Presidential. First ballot (before shift), p. 54-5.
a/ Other candidates: Horace Maynard, 26; John F. Lewis, 22; Edmund J. Davis, 16; Joseph R. Hawley, 1; Edward F. Noyes, 1.
First ballot (after shift), p. 55.
b/ Other candidates: Maynard, 26; Davis, 16; Hawley, 1; Noyes, 1.

Source: *Official Proceedings, 1876.*
Minority report on credentials, p. 55.
c/ Sum of column; proceedings record 354.
d/ Sum of column; proceedings record 375.
Mongolian Immigration plank, p. 68.
e/ Sum of column; proceedings record 215.
f/ Sum of column; proceedings record 532.

* Dakota Territory, 2 votes.

		1876 REPUBLICAN										Reconsider Vote Sustaining Chair, Penna. Vote			Question on Sustaining Chair, Penna. Vote		
		Presidential															
		First Ballot					Second Ballot										
Delegation	Votes	Blaine	Morton	Conkling	Bristow	Other	Blaine	Morton	Conkling	Bristow	Other	Yea	Nay	Not Voting	Yea	Nay	Not Voting
Alabama	20	10	...	...	7	3	16	...	...	4	...	...	20	...	20	...	...
Arizona	2	2	...	...	...	...	2	...	...	...	...	...	2	...	2	...	...
Arkansas	12	...	12	...	...	...	1	11	...	...	...	10	2	...	4	8	...
California	12	9	...	1	2	...	6	...	3	...	3	5	7	...	11	1	...
Colorado	6	6	...	...	...	...	6	...	...	...	...	...	6	...	6	...	...
Connecticut	12	...	...	...	2	10	2	...	...	9	1	10	2	...	3	9	...
Delaware	6	6	...	...	...	...	6	...	...	...	...	...	6	...	5	1	...
Florida	8	1	4	3	...	...	4	4	...	...	...	1	7	...	4	4	...
Georgia	22	5	6	8	3	...	9	4	6	3	...	17	5	...	9	13	...
Idaho	2	2	...	...	...	...	2	...	...	...	...	...	2	...	2	...	...
Illinois	42	38	...	...	3	1	35	...	...	6	1	10	32	...	38	4	...
Indiana	30	...	30	...	...	...	...	30	...	...	...	30	...	...	1	29	...
Iowa	22	22	...	...	...	...	22	...	...	...	...	...	22	...	22	...	...
Kansas	10	10	...	...	...	...	10	...	...	...	...	...	10	...	10	...	...
Kentucky	24	...	...	...	24	...	...	...	...	24	...	23	1	...	1	23	...
Louisiana	16	2	14	...	...	...	3	12	...	...	1	10	6	...	6	10	...
Maine	14	14	...	...	...	...	14	...	...	...	...	...	14	...	14	...	...
Maryland	16	16	...	...	...	...	16	...	...	...	...	...	16	...	16	...	...
Massachusetts	26	6	...	...	17	3	5	...	...	18	3	5	11	10	15	7	4
Michigan	22	8	...	1	9	4	8	...	1	9	4	21	1	...	3	19	...
Minnesota	10	10	...	...	...	...	9	...	...	...	1	2	8	...	7	3	...
Mississippi	16	...	11	1	3	1	1	6	3	6	...	8	8	...	9	6	1
Missouri	30	14	12	1	2	1	15	11	1	2	1	11	19	...	25	5	...
Montana	2	2	...	...	...	...	1	...	...	...	1	...	2	...	2	...	...
Nebraska	6	6	...	...	...	...	6	...	...	...	...	...	6	...	6	...	...
Nevada	6	...	...	2	3	1	...	...	2	...	4	6	...	...	...	6	...
New Hampshire	10	7	...	...	3	...	7	...	...	3	...	...	9	1	10	...	...
New Jersey	18	13	...	...	...	5	12	...	...	...	6	5	13	...	15	3	...
New Mexico	2	2	...	...	...	...	2	...	...	...	...	...	2	...	2	...	...
New York	70	...	...	69	1	...	...	...	69	1	...	56	12	2	15	54	1
North Carolina	20	9	2	7	1	1	8	2	3	1	6	12	7	1	6	13	1
North Dakota	*2	2	...	...	...	...	2	...	...	...	...	...	2	...	2	...	...
Ohio	44	...	...	...	...	44	...	...	...	...	44	24	20	...	14	30	...
Oklahoma	...	...	...	...	...	...	...	...	...	...	...	...	...	...	...	...	...
Oregon	6	6	...	...	...	...	6	...	...	...	...	...	6	...	6	...	...
Pennsylvania	58	...	...	...	...	58	4	...	...	...	54	58	...	...	1	57	...
Rhode Island	8	2	...	...	6	...	2	...	...	6	...	8	...	...	1	7	...
South Carolina	14	...	13	...	1	...	...	13	...	1	...	12	2	...	2	12	...
South Dakota	*																
Tennessee	24	4	10	...	10	...	8	8	...	8	...	8	16	...	19	5	...
Texas	16	2	5	3	6	...	2	12	1	1	...	11	5	...	4	12	...
Utah	2	2	...	...	...	...	2	...	...	...	...	...	2	...	2	...	...
Vermont	10	1	...	...	8	1	1	...	...	8	1	4	6	...	5	5	...
Virginia	22	16	3	3	...	...	14	4	4	...	...	6	15	1	19	2	1
Washington	2	2	...	...	...	...	2	...	...	...	...	...	2	...	2	...	...
West Virginia	10	8	...	...	...	2	8	...	...	...	2	2	8	...	10	...	...
Wisconsin	20	20	...	...	...	...	17	1	...	2	...	4	15	1	17	3	...
Wyoming	2	...	...	...	2	...	...	...	...	2	...	2	...	...	...	2	...
Alaska	...	...	...	...	...	...	...	...	...	...	...	...	...	...	...	...	...
Canal Zone	...	...	...	...	...	...	...	...	...	...	...	...	...	...	...	...	...
District of Columbia	2	...	2	...	...	...	...	2	...	...	...	...	2	...	2	...	...
Hawaii	...	...	...	...	...	...	...	...	...	...	...	...	...	...	...	...	...
Philippine Islands	...	...	...	...	...	...	...	...	...	...	...	...	...	...	...	...	...
Puerto Rico	...	...	...	...	...	...	...	...	...	...	...	...	...	...	...	...	...
Virgin Islands	...	...	...	...	...	...	...	...	...	...	...	...	...	...	...	...	...
Total	756	285	124	99	113	135a	296	120	93	114	133b	381	359	16	395	353	8

Source: *Official Proceedings, 1876.*

Presidential. First ballot, pp. 83-4.

a/ Other candidates: Rutherford B. Hayes, 61; John F. Hartranft, 58; Marshall Jewell, 11; William A. Wheeler, 3; not voting, 2.

Second ballot, pp. 86-7.

b/ Other candidates: Hayes, 64; Hartranft, 63; Wheeler, 3; Elihu B. Washburne, 1; not voting, 2.

Reconsider vote sustaining chair, Pennsylvania vote, p. 95.

Question on sustaining chair, Pennsylvania vote, p. 99.

* Dakota Territory, 2 votes.

1876 REPUBLICAN
Presidential

Delegation	Votes	Third Ballot Blaine	Bristow	Conkling	Morton	Other	Fourth Ballot Blaine	Bristow	Conkling	Morton	Other	Fifth Ballot Blaine	Bristow	Conkling	Hayes	Morton	Other
Alabama	20	15	4	1	...	...	16	4	...	...	...	16	4	...	...	...	...
Arizona	2	2	...	...	...	...	2	...	...	...	...	2	...	...	...	...	...
Arkansas	12	1	...	..	11	...	1	...	..	11	...	1	...	...	...	11	...
California	12	6	...	3	...	3	6	...	3	...	3	6	...	3	3	...	...
Colorado	6	6	...	...	...	...	6	...	...	...	...	6	...	...	...	...	...
Connecticut	12	2	8	...	...	2	2	9	...	...	1	2	8	...	2	...	...
Delaware	6	6	...	...	...	...	6	...	...	...	...	6	...	...	...	...	...
Florida	8	2	...	3	...	3	2	...	2	...	4	2	...	...	...	3	3
Georgia	22	9	3	6	4	...	9	2	6	4	1	8	2	6	...	5	1
Idaho	2	2	...	...	...	...	2	...	...	...	...	2	...	...	...	...	...
Illinois	42	35	6	...	...	1	35	5	...	...	2	33	5	...	3	...	1
Indiana	30	...	...	...	30	...	...	...	...	30	...	...	...	...	...	30	...
Iowa	22	22	...	...	...	...	21	...	1	...	...	21	...	1	...	...	...
Kansas	10	10	...	...	...	...	10	...	...	...	...	10	...	...	...	...	...
Kentucky	24	...	24	...	...	...	...	24	...	...	...	...	24	...	...	...	...
Louisiana	16	5	...	...	11	...	5	...	...	11	...	5	...	...	...	11	...
Maine	14	14	...	...	...	...	14	...	...	...	...	14	...	...	...	...	...
Maryland	16	16	...	...	...	...	16	...	...	...	...	16	...	...	...	...	...
Massachusetts	26	5	19	...	...	2	5	19	...	...	2	5	19	...	...	...	2
Michigan	22	8	10	...	...	4	6	11	...	...	5	...	...	...	22	...	...
Minnesota	10	8	1	...	...	1	8	1	...	...	1	9	...	...	...	...	1
Mississippi	16	...	7	2	5	2	...	7	2	4	3	...	8	2	2	4	...
Missouri	30	15	3	...	11	1	18	3	...	8	1	20	3	...	2	5	...
Montana	2	1	...	...	...	1	1	...	...	...	1	1	...	...	1	...	...
Nebraska	6	6	...	...	...	...	6	...	...	...	...	6	...	...	...	...	...
Nevada	6	...	2	2	...	2	...	1	2	...	3	...	1	2	1	...	2
New Hampshire	10	7	3	...	...	...	7	3	...	...	...	7	3	...	...	...	...
New Jersey	18	12	...	...	...	6	12	...	...	...	6	12	...	...	6	...	...
New Mexico	2	2	...	...	...	...	2	...	...	...	...	2	...	...	...	...	...
New York	70	...	1	69	...	...	...	2	68	...	...	...	2	68	...	...	...
North Carolina	20	9	1	1	...	9	9	...	...	1	10	...	...	...	12	1	7
North Dakota	*2	2	...	...	...	...	2	...	...	...	...	2	...	...	...	...	...
Ohio	44	...	...	...	...	44	...	...	...	...	44	...	...	...	44	...	...
Oklahoma	...	...	...	...	...	...	...	...	...	...	...	...	...	...	...	...	...
Oregon	6	6	...	...	...	...	6	...	...	...	...	6	...	...	...	...	...
Pennsylvania	58	3	...	...	...	55	3	...	...	...	55	5	...	...	...	...	53
Rhode Island	8	2	6	...	...	...	2	6	...	...	...	2	6	...	...	...	...
South Carolina	14	...	1	...	13	...	...	1	...	13	...	5	3	...	1	5	...
South Dakota	*	...	...	...	...	...	...	...	...	...	...	...	...	...	...	...	...
Tennessee	24	7	8	...	9	...	7	10	...	7	...	7	10	...	...	7	...
Texas	16	2	1	...	13	...	1	5	...	10	...	3	3	...	1	8	1
Utah	2	2	...	...	...	...	2	...	...	...	...	2	...	...	...	...	...
Vermont	10	1	8	...	...	1	...	8	...	...	2	...	8	...	2	...	...
Virginia	22	15	...	3	4	...	15	...	...	7	...	16	...	...	...	3	3
Washington	2	2	...	...	...	...	2	...	...	...	...	2	...	...	...	...	...
West Virginia	10	8	...	...	...	2	8	...	...	...	2	7	...	...	2	...	1
Wisconsin	20	16	3	...	1	...	16	3	...	1	...	16	3	...	...	1	...
Wyoming	2	...	2	...	...	...	...	2	...	...	...	...	2	...	...	...	...
Alaska	...	...	...	...	...	...	...	...	...	...	...	...	...	...	...	...	...
Canal Zone	...	...	...	...	...	...	...	...	...	...	...	...	...	...	...	...	...
District of Columbia	2	1	...	...	1	...	1	...	...	1	...	1	...	...	...	1	...
Hawaii	...	...	...	...	...	...	...	...	...	...	...	...	...	...	...	...	...
Philippine Islands	...	...	...	...	...	...	...	...	...	...	...	...	...	...	...	...	...
Puerto Rico	...	...	...	...	...	...	...	...	...	...	...	...	...	...	...	...	...
Virgin Islands	...	...	...	...	...	...	...	...	...	...	...	...	...	...	...	...	...
Total	756	293	121	90	113	139a	292	126	84	108	146b	286	114	82	104	95	75c

Source: *Official Proceedings, 1876.*
Third ballot, pp. 100-1.
a/ Other candidates: Hartranft, 68; Hayes, 67; Wheeler, 2; Washburne, 1; not voting, 1.
Fourth ballot, pp. 101-2.
b/ Other candidates: Hartranft, 71; Hayes, 68; Washburne, 3; Wheeler, 2; not voting, 2.
Fifth ballot, pp. 103-4.
c/ Other candidates: Hartranft, 69; Washburne, 3; Wheeler, 2; not voting, 1.

* Dakota Territory, 2 votes.

Delegation	Votes	Presidential Sixth Ballot						Presidential Seventh Ballot			Vice-Presidential First Ballot				
		Blaine	Morton	Conkling	Bristow	Hayes	Other	Blaine	Hayes	Other	Wheeler	Woodford	Jewell	Hawley	Freling-huysen
Alabama	20	15	...	...	4	1	...	17	...	3	17	...	3	...	...
Arizona	2	2	...	...	...	...	...	2	...	...	...	...	...	...	...
Arkansas	12	1	11	...	...	...	...	11	1	...	5	5	...	...	2
California	12	6	...	2	...	4	...	6	6	...	...	12	...	...	...
Colorado	6	6	...	...	...	...	...	6	...	...	6	...	...	...	...
Connecticut	12	2	...	...	7	3	...	2	3	7	1	...	11	...	...
Delaware	6	6	...	...	...	...	...	6	...	...	6	...	...	...	...
Florida	8	4	4	...	...	...	...	8	...	...	...	8	...	...	...
Georgia	22	9	4	6	2	...	1	14	7	1	...	...	22	...	...
Idaho	2	2	...	...	...	...	...	2	...	...	...	...	...	...	...
Illinois	42	32	...	...	5	3	2	35	2	5	42	...	...	...	...
Indiana	30	...	30	...	...	...	...	...	25	5	2	20	7	1	...
Iowa	22	21	...	...	...	1	...	22	...	...	22	...	...	...	...
Kansas	10	10	...	...	...	...	...	10	...	...	5	2	...	...	3
Kentucky	24	...	...	...	24	...	...	...	24	...	...	...	...	24	...
Louisiana	16	6	10	...	...	...	...	14	2	...	8	2	...	...	6
Maine	14	14	...	...	...	...	...	14	...	...	14	...	...	...	...
Maryland	16	16	...	...	...	...	...	16	...	...	...	...	16	...	...
Massachusetts	26	5	...	...	19	...	2	5	21	...	25	...	1	...	...
Michigan	22	...	...	...	...	22	...	...	22	...	22	...	...	...	...
Minnesota	10	9	...	...	...	...	1	9	1	...	10	...	...	...	...
Mississippi	16	1	5	2	4	4	...	...	16	...	1	15	...	...	...
Missouri	30	18	7	...	3	2	...	20	10	...	4	...	26	...	...
Montana	2	1	...	...	...	1	...	...	2	...	...	...	...	...	...
Nebraska	6	6	...	...	...	...	...	6	...	...	6	...	...	...	...
Nevada	6	...	...	2	2	1	1	...	6	...	...	6	...	...	...
New Hampshire	10	7	...	...	3	...	...	7	3	...	10	...	...	...	...
New Jersey	18	12	...	...	...	6	...	12	6	...	...	...	...	...	18
New Mexico	2	2	...	...	...	1	...	2	...	...	...	...	...	...	...
New York	70	...	...	68	2	...	...	9	61	...	70	...	...	...	...
North Carolina	20	12	1	...	...	1	6	...	20	...	20	...	...	...	...
North Dakota	*2	2	...	...	...	...	...	2	...	...	...	...	...	...	...
Ohio	44	...	...	...	...	44	...	...	44	...	44	...	...	...	...
Oklahoma	...	...	...	...	...	...	...	...	...	...	...	...	...	...	...
Oregon	6	6	...	...	...	...	...	6	...	...	6	...	...	...	...
Pennsylvania	58	14	...	...	...	...	44	30	28	...	...	...	...	...	58
Rhode Island	8	2	...	...	6	...	...	2	6	...	8	...	...	...	...
South Carolina	14	10	2	...	1	1	...	7	7	...	12	...	...	...	2
South Dakota	*	...	...	...	...	...	...	...	...	...	...	...	...	...	...
Tennessee	24	7	1	...	12	4	...	6	18	...	...	...	...	...	...
Texas	16	2	4	1	1	7	1	1	15	...	...	...	...	...	...
Utah	2	2	...	...	...	...	...	2	...	...	...	...	...	...	...
Vermont	10	...	...	...	8	2	...	...	10	...	...	...	...	...	...
Virginia	22	13	4	...	3	2	...	14	8	...	...	...	...	...	...
Washington	2	2	...	...	...	...	...	2	...	...	...	...	...	...	...
West Virginia	10	6	...	...	...	4	...	6	4	...	...	...	...	...	...
Wisconsin	20	16	1	...	3	...	...	16	4	...	...	...	...	...	...
Wyoming	2	...	...	...	2	...	...	...	2	...	...	...	...	...	...
Alaska	...	...	...	...	...	...	...	...	...	...	...	...	...	...	...
Canal Zone	...	...	...	...	...	...	...	...	...	...	...	...	...	...	...
District of Columbia	2	1	1	...	...	...	...	2	...	...	...	...	...	...	...
Hawaii	...	...	...	...	...	...	...	...	...	...	...	...	...	...	...
Philippine Islands	...	...	...	...	...	...	...	...	...	...	...	...	...	...	...
Puerto Rico	...	...	...	...	...	...	...	...	...	...	...	...	...	...	...
Virgin Islands	...	...	...	...	...	...	...	...	...	...	...	...	...	...	...
Total	756	308	85	81	111	113	58a	351	384	21b	366	70	86	25	89

Source: *Official Proceedings, 1876.*
Sixth ballot, pp. 105-6.
a/ Other candidates: Hartranft, 50; Washburne, 4; Wheeler, 2; not voting, 2.
Seventh ballot, pp. 108-9.
b/ Other candidates: Bristow, 21.
Vice-Presidential. First ballot, pp. 110-2.

* Dakota Territory, 2 votes.

Delegation	Votes	Substitute Credentials for Rules Report			Support Nominee			Minority Report, Alabama Credentials			Motion to Adjourn		Minority Report, Illinois 1st Dist.			Majority Report, Illinois 1st Dist.		
		Yea	Nay	Not Voting	Yea	Nay	Not Voting	Yea	Nay	Not Voting	Yea	Nay	Yea	Nay	Not Voting	Yea	Nay	Not Voting
Alabama	20	19	1	...	20	...	...	17	3	...	7	13	16	4	...	4	16	...
Arizona	2	...	2	...	2	...	...	...	2	...	...	2	...	2	...	2	...	...
Arkansas	12	12	...	...	12	...	...	12	...	...	...	12	12	...	...	...	12	...
California	12	...	12	...	12	...	...	...	12	...	...	12	...	12	...	12	...	...
Colorado	6	6	...	...	6	...	...	6	...	...	...	6	6	...	...	...	6	...
Connecticut	12	...	12	...	12	...	...	...	12	...	4	8	...	10	2	10	...	2
Delaware	6	...	6	...	6	...	...	...	6	...	...	6	...	6	...	6	...	...
Florida	8	8	...	...	8	...	...	8	...	...	8	...	8	...	...	...	8	...
Georgia	22	6	16	...	22	...	...	6	16	...	1	21	6	16	...	16	6	...
Idaho	2	...	2	...	...	...	2	...	2	...	...	2	...	2	...	2	...	...
Illinois	42	42	...	...	42	...	...	42	...	...	...	42	40	...	2	...	40	2
Indiana	30	6	23	1	30	...	...	4	26	...	...	30	5	25	...	25	5	...
Iowa	22	...	22	...	22	...	...	...	22	...	...	22	...	22	...	22	...	...
Kansas	10	...	10	...	10	...	...	...	10	...	...	10	...	...	10	...	...	10
Kentucky	24	20	4	...	24	...	...	20	4	...	...	24	21	3	...	3	21	...
Louisiana	16	...	...	16	14	...	16	8	8	...	...	16	8	8	...	8	8	...
Maine	14	...	14	...	14	...	...	...	14	...	...	14	...	14	...	14	...	...
Maryland	16	7	8	1	16	...	...	7	9	...	2	14	8	8	...	8	8	...
Massachusetts	26	7	17	2	26	...	...	2	23	1	26	...	4	22	...	22	4	...
Michigan	22	1	21	...	22	...	...	1	21	...	...	22	1	21	...	21	1	...
Minnesota	10	3	6	1	10	...	...	2	8	...	...	10	4	6	...	4	6	...
Mississippi	16	8	7	1	16	...	...	7	9	...	5	11	11	5	...	4	12	...
Missouri	30	29	1	...	30	...	...	29	1	...	...	30	29	1	...	1	29	...
Montana	2	...	2	...	...	...	2	...	2	...	...	2	...	2	...	2	...	...
Nebraska	6	...	6	...	6	...	...	...	6	...	...	6	...	6	...	6	...	...
Nevada	6	...	6	...	6	...	...	...	6	...	...	6	...	6	...	6	...	...
New Hampshire	10	...	10	...	10	...	...	...	10	...	...	10	...	10	...	10	...	...
New Jersey	18	...	18	...	18	...	...	...	18	...	...	18	...	18	...	18	...	...
New Mexico	2	...	2	...	2	...	...	...	2	...	...	2	...	2	...	2	...	...
New York	70	47	23	...	70	...	...	47	23	...	1	69	47	22	1	22	47	1
North Carolina	20	5	15	...	20	...	...	...	20	...	5	15	19	1	...	1	19	...
North Dakota	*2	1	1	...	2	...	...	1	1	...	1	1	.1	1	...	1	1	...
Ohio	44	3	41	...	44	...	...	...	44	...	22	22	16	28	...	28	16	...
Oklahoma	...	...	...	...	...	...	...	...	...	...	...	...	...	...	...	...	...	...
Oregon	6	...	6	...	6	...	...	...	6	...	...	6	...	6	...	6	...	...
Pennsylvania	58	31	23	4	58	...	...	35	23	...	...	58	34	24	...	24	34	...
Rhode Island	8	...	8	...	8	...	...	...	8	...	...	8	...	8	...	8	...	...
South Carolina	14	7	5	2	1	...	13	9	5	...	...	14	10	4	...	4	10	...
South Dakota	*	...	...	...	...	...	...	...	...	...	...	...	...	...	...	...	...	...
Tennessee	24	16	7	1	24	...	...	16	8	...	1	23	16	8	...	8	16	...
Texas	16	9	7	...	16	...	...	9	7	...	11	5	11	4	1	4	11	1
Utah	2	...	2	...	2	...	...	...	2	...	...	2	...	2	...	2	...	...
Vermont	10	10	...	...	10	...	...	4	6	...	...	10	4	6	...	6	4	...
Virginia	22	11	8	3	22	...	...	12	10	...	...	22	13	9	...	9	13	...
Washington	2	...	2	...	...	...	2	...	2	...	...	2	...	2	...	2	...	...
West Virginia	10	...	10	...	5	3	2	...	10	...	...	10	...	10	...	10	...	...
Wisconsin	20	2	18	...	20	...	...	1	19	...	1	19	1	19	...	19	1	...
Wyoming	2	...	2	...	2	...	...	1	1	...	...	2	1	1	...	1	1	...
Alaska	...	...	...	...	...	...	...	...	...	...	...	...	...	...	...	...	...	...
Canal Zone	...	...	...	...	...	...	...	...	...	...	...	...	...	...	...	...	...	...
District of Columbia	2	2	...	...	...	...	2	...	2	...	...	2	1	1	...	1	1	...
Hawaii	...	...	...	...	...	...	...	...	...	...	...	...	...	...	...	...	...	...
Philippine Islands	...	...	...	...	...	...	...	...	...	...	...	...	...	...	...	...	...	...
Puerto Rico	...	...	...	...	...	...	...	...	...	...	...	...	...	...	...	...	...	...
Virgin Islands	...	...	...	...	...	...	...	...	...	...	...	...	...	...	...	...	...	...
Total	756	318	406	32	714a	3	39	306	449	1	95b	661c	353	387	16	384	356	16

Source: *Official Proceedings, 1880.*
Substitute credentials for rules report, p. 31.
Support nominee, p. 35.
a/ Sum of column; proceedings record 716.
Minority report, Alabama credentials, p. 91.
Motion to adjourn, p. 119.
b/ Sum of column; proceedings record 103.
c/ Sum of column; proceedings record 653.
Minority report, Illinois 1st District, p. 120.
Majority report, Illinois 1st District, p. 121.

* Dakota Territory, 2 votes.

1880 REPUBLICAN

Delegation	Votes	Majority Report, Illinois 3rd Dist.			Majority Report, Illinois 4th Dist.			Majority Report, Kansas Credentials			Minority Report, West Virginia Credentials			Minority Report, Utah Credentials		
		Yea	Nay	Not Voting	Yea	Nay	Not Voting	Yea	Nay	Not Voting	Yea	Nay	Not Voting	Yea	Nay	Not Voting
Alabama	20	4	16	...	4	16	...	5	15	...	14	4	2	16	4	...
Arizona	2	2	...	...	2	...	...	2	...	...	...	2	...	...	2	...
Arkansas	12	...	12	...	...	12	...	...	12	...	12	...	...	12	...	...
California	12	12	...	...	12	...	...	12	...	...	...	12	...	...	12	...
Colorado	6	6	...	...	...	6	...	...	6	...	6	...	...	...	6	...
Connecticut	12	10	...	2	11	...	1	12	...	...	3	8	1	9	2	1
Delaware	6	6	...	...	6	...	...	6	...	...	...	6	...	6	...	...
Florida	8	...	8	...	...	8	...	...	8	...	8	...	...	8	...	...
Georgia	22	16	6	...	16	6	...	22	...	...	19	2	1	6	7	9
Idaho	2	2	...	...	2	...	...	2	...	...	...	2	...	...	2	...
Illinois	42	2	38	2	4	36	2	18	24	...	25	17	...	24	18	...
Indiana	30	25	5	...	25	5	...	27	3	...	8	22	...	4	26	...
Iowa	22	22	...	...	22	...	...	22	...	...	...	22	...	...	22	...
Kansas	10	...	...	10	...	...	10	5	5	...	4	6	...	4	6	...
Kentucky	24	3	21	...	3	21	...	4	20	...	20	4	...	22	2	...
Louisiana	16	8	8	...	8	8	...	16	...	...	4	12	...	6	10	...
Maine	14	14	...	...	14	...	...	14	...	...	...	14	...	...	14	...
Maryland	16	8	8	...	8	8	...	11	5	...	16	...	...	11	5	...
Massachusetts	26	22	4	...	22	4	...	24	1	1	26	...	...	26	...	...
Michigan	22	20	...	2	20	...	2	21	1	...	1	21	...	11	10	1
Minnesota	10	4	6	...	4	6	...	5	4	1	4	6	...	6	4	...
Mississippi	16	4	12	...	4	12	...	7	2	7	11	5	...	13	3	3
Missouri	30	1	29	...	1	29	...	1	...	29	30	...	...	29	...	1
Montana	2	2	...	...	2	...	...	2	...	...	...	2	...	...	2	...
Nebraska	6	6	...	...	6	...	...	6	...	...	...	6	...	...	6	...
Nevada	6	6	...	...	6	...	...	6	...	...	...	6	...	...	6	...
New Hampshire	10	10	...	...	10	...	...	10	...	...	...	10	...	...	10	...
New Jersey	18	18	...	...	18	...	...	18	...	...	...	18	...	...	18	...
New Mexico	2	2	...	...	2	...	...	2	...	...	...	2	...	...	2	...
New York	70	22	47	1	22	47	1	22	...	48	49	20	1	50	19	1
North Carolina	20	1	19	...	1	19	...	20	...	...	20	...	...	20	...	...
North Dakota	*2	1	1	...	1	1	...	1	1	...	...	2	...	1	1	...
Ohio	44	28	16	...	28	16	...	44	...	...	28	16	...	33	10	1
Oklahoma	...	...	...	...	...	...	...	...	...	...	...	...	...	...	...	...
Oregon	6	6	...	...	6	...	...	6	...	...	...	6	...	...	6	...
Pennsylvania	58	24	34	...	24	34	...	25	33	...	33	25	...	28	30	...
Rhode Island	8	8	...	...	8	...	...	8	...	...	...	8	...	...	8	...
South Carolina	14	4	10	...	4	10	...	3	11	...	11	3	...	11	3	...
South Dakota	*	...	...	...	...	...	...	...	...	...	...	...	...	...	...	...
Tennessee	24	8	16	...	8	16	...	8	16	...	16	8	...	19	5	...
Texas	16	4	11	1	4	11	1	4	11	1	11	3	2	11	4	1
Utah	2	2	...	...	2	...	...	2	...	...	...	2	...	...	...	2
Vermont	10	6	4	...	6	4	...	9	1	...	10	...	...	10	...	...
Virginia	22	9	13	...	9	13	...	11	2	9	16	6	...	10	12	...
Washington	2	2	...	...	2	...	...	2	...	...	...	2	...	1	1	...
West Virginia	10	10	...	...	10	...	...	10	...	...	...	8	2	1	8	1
Wisconsin	20	19	1	...	19	1	...	19	1	...	10	10	...	17	3	...
Wyoming	2	1	1	...	1	1	...	1	1	...	1	1	...	...	2	...
Alaska	...	...	...	...	...	...	...	...	...	...	...	...	...	...	...	...
Canal Zone	...	...	...	...	...	...	...	...	...	...	...	...	...	...	...	...
District of Columbia	2	1	1	...	1	1	...	1	1	...	1	1	...	1	1	...
Hawaii	...	...	...	...	...	...	...	...	...	...	...	...	...	...	...	...
Philippine Islands	...	...	...	...	...	...	...	...	...	...	...	...	...	...	...	...
Puerto Rico	...	...	...	...	...	...	...	...	...	...	...	...	...	...	...	...
Virgin Islands	...	...	...	...	...	...	...	...	...	...	...	...	...	...	...	...
Total	756	391a	347b	18	388	351	17	476	184	96	417	330	9	426	312	18

Source: *Official Proceedings, 1880.*
Majority report, Illinois 3rd District, p. 123.
a/ Sum of column; proceedings record 385.
b/ Sum of column; proceedings record 353.
Majority report, Illinois 4th District, p. 124.
Majority report, Kansas credentials, p. 135.
Minority report, West Virginia credentials, p. 143.
Minority report, Utah credentials, p. 150.

* Dakota Territory, 2 votes.

1880 REPUBLICAN

Delegation	Votes	Time Limit on Speeches			First Ballot				Eleventh Ballot				Twenty-first Ballot			
		Yea	Nay	Not Voting	Grant	Blaine	Sherman	Other	Grant	Blaine	Sherman	Other	Grant	Blaine	Sherman	Other
Alabama	20	15	5	...	16	1	3	...	17	...	3	...	16	1	3	...
Arizona	2	...	2	...	...	2	...	...	...	2	...	...	...	2	...	...
Arkansas	12	12	...	...	12	...	...	...	12	...	...	...	12	...	...	...
California	12	...	12	...	...	12	...	...	...	12	...	...	...	12	...	...
Colorado	6	6	...	...	6	...	...	...	6	...	...	...	6	...	...	...
Connecticut	12	...	12	...	...	3	...	9	...	3	...	9	...	3	...	9
Delaware	6	...	6	...	...	6	...	...	...	6	...	...	...	6	...	...
Florida	8	8	...	...	8	...	...	...	7	1	...	...	8	...	...	...
Georgia	22	6	16	...	6	8	8	...	6	8	8	...	7	7	8	...
Idaho	2	...	2	...	...	2	...	...	...	2	...	...	...	2	...	...
Illinois	42	24	18	...	24	10	...	8	24	10	...	8	24	10	...	8
Indiana	30	...	30	...	1	26	2	1	2	27	...	1	2	21	3	4
Iowa	22	...	22	...	...	22	...	...	...	22	...	...	...	22	...	...
Kansas	10	4	6	...	4	6	...	...	4	6	...	...	4	6	...	...
Kentucky	24	20	4	...	20	1	3	...	20	1	3	...	20	2	2	...
Louisiana	16	2	14	...	8	2	6	...	8	2	6	...	8	2	6	...
Maine	14	...	14	...	...	14	...	...	...	14	...	...	...	14	...	...
Maryland	16	7	9	...	7	7	2	...	8	5	2	1	7	5	4	...
Massachusetts	26	4	22	...	3	...	2	21	4	...	2	20	4	...	2	20
Michigan	22	1	21	...	1	21	...	...	1	21	...	...	1	21	...	...
Minnesota	10	...	10	...	...	...	...	10	...	...	...	10	...	...	...	10
Mississippi	16	5	11	...	6	4	6	...	6	4	6	...	6	4	6	...
Missouri	30	29	1	...	29	...	...	1	29	...	...	1	29	...	...	1
Montana	2	...	2	...	...	2	...	...	...	2	...	...	...	2	...	...
Nebraska	6	...	6	...	...	6	...	...	...	6	...	...	...	6	...	...
Nevada	6	...	6	...	...	6	...	...	...	6	...	...	...	6	...	...
New Hampshire	10	...	10	...	...	10	...	...	...	10	...	...	...	10	...	...
New Jersey	18	...	18	...	...	16	...	2	...	16	...	2	...	16	...	2
New Mexico	2	...	2	...	...	2	...	...	...	2	...	...	...	2	...	...
New York	70	48	22	...	51	17	2	...	51	17	2	...	50	18	2	...
North Carolina	20	4	16	...	6	...	14	...	5	...	15	...	5	...	15	...
North Dakota	*2	...	2	...	1	1	...	...	1	1	...	...	1	1	...	...
Ohio	44	...	44	...	...	9	34	1	...	9	34	1	...	9	34	1
Oklahoma	...	...	...	...	...	...	...	...	...	...	...	...	...	...	...	...
Oregon	6	...	6	...	...	6	...	...	...	6	...	...	...	6	...	...
Pennsylvania	58	31	27	...	32	23	3	...	34	22	1	1	34	21	1	2
Rhode Island	8	...	8	...	...	8	...	...	...	8	...	...	...	8	...	...
South Carolina	14	9	5	...	13	...	1	...	12	1	1	...	12	1	1	...
South Dakota	*	...	...	...	...	...	...	...	...	...	...	...	...	...	...	...
Tennessee	24	16	8	...	16	6	1	1	16	6	1	1	17	5	1	1
Texas	16	11	5	...	11	2	2	1	12	1	2	1	12	2	1	1
Utah	2	...	2	...	1	1	...	...	1	1	...	...	1	1	...	...
Vermont	10	...	10	...	...	...	...	10	...	...	...	10	...	...	...	10
Virginia	22	12	10	...	18	3	1	...	15	2	4	1	16	3	3	...
Washington	2	...	2	...	...	2	...	...	...	2	...	...	...	2	...	...
West Virginia	10	1	8	1	1	8	...	1	1	8	...	1	1	8	...	1
Wisconsin	20	1	19	...	1	7	3	9	1	7	3	9	1	7	3	9
Wyoming	2	...	2	...	1	1	...	...	1	1	...	...	1	1	...	...
Alaska	...	...	...	...	...	...	...	...	...	...	...	...	...	...	...	...
Canal Zone	...	...	...	...	...	...	...	...	...	...	...	...	...	...	...	...
District of Columbia	2	...	2	...	1	1	...	...	1	1	...	...	...	1	1	...
Hawaii	...	...	...	...	...	...	...	...	...	...	...	...	...	...	...	...
Philippine Islands	...	...	...	...	...	...	...	...	...	...	...	...	...	...	...	...
Puerto Rico	...	...	...	...	...	...	...	...	...	...	...	...	...	...	...	...
Virgin Islands	...	...	...	...	...	...	...	...	...	...	...	...	...	...	...	...
Total	756	276	479	1	304	284	93	75a	305	281	93	77b	305	276	96	79c

Source: *Official Proceedings, 1880.*

Time limit on speeches, p. 158.
Presidential. First ballot, p. 198.
a/ Other candidates: George F. Edmunds, 34; Elihu B. Washburne, 30; William Windom, 10; not voting, 1.
Eleventh ballot, pp. 218-9.
b/ Other candidates: Washburne, 32; Edmunds, 31; Windom, 10; James A. Garfield, 2; Rutherford B. Hayes, 1; not voting, 1.
Twenty-first ballot, pp. 237-8.
c/ Other candidates: Washburne, 35; Edmunds, 31; Windom, 10; Garfield, 1; John F. Hartranft, 1; not voting, 1.

* Dakota Territory, 2 votes.

Delegation	Votes	Motion to Adjourn			Twenty-ninth Ballot				Thirty-fourth Ballot				Thirty-fifth Ballot				
		Yea	Nay	Not Voting	Grant	Blaine	Sherman	Other	Grant	Blaine	Sherman	Other	Grant	Blaine	Sherman	Garfield	Other
Alabama	20	4	15	1	15	1	3	1	16	4	...	...	16	4	...	...	...
Arizona	2	2	...	...	...	2	...	...	...	2	...	...	...	2	...	...	...
Arkansas	12	...	12	...	12	...	...	...	12	...	...	...	12	...	...	...	...
California	12	12	...	...	...	12	...	...	...	12	...	...	6	...	...	...	...
Colorado	6	...	6	...	6	...	...	...	6	...	...	...	6	...	...	...	...
Connecticut	12	...	12	...	...	3	...	9	...	3	...	9	...	3	...	...	9
Delaware	6	6	...	...	...	6	...	...	...	6	...	...	...	6	...	...	...
Florida	8	...	8	...	7	...	1	...	8	...	...	...	8	...	...	...	...
Georgia	22	20	2	...	7	7	8	...	8	9	5	...	8	9	5	...	...
Idaho	2	2	...	...	...	2	...	...	...	2	...	...	...	2	...	...	...
Illinois	42	2	40	...	24	10	...	8	24	10	...	8	24	10	...	...	8
Indiana	30	24	4	2	2	21	3	4	2	20	2	6	1	2	...	27	...
Iowa	22	22	...	...	...	22	...	...	...	22	...	...	...	22	...	...	...
Kansas	10	6	4	...	4	6	...	...	4	6	...	...	4	6	...	...	...
Kentucky	24	2	22	...	20	1	3	...	20	1	3	...	20	1	3	...	...
Louisiana	16	14	2	...	8	4	4	...	8	4	4	...	8	4	4	...	...
Maine	14	14	...	...	...	14	...	...	...	14	...	...	...	14	...	...	...
Maryland	16	9	7	...	7	3	6	...	7	2	7	...	7	3	2	4	...
Massachusetts	26	21	5	...	4	...	21	1	4	...	21	1	4	...	21	...	1
Michigan	22	21	1	...	1	21	...	...	1	21	...	...	1	21	...	...	...
Minnesota	10	10	...	...	...	3	...	7	...	6	...	4	1	6	...	...	3
Mississippi	16	12	4	...	9	4	3	...	8	4	3	1	8	4	3	1	...
Missouri	30	...	30	...	29	...	...	1	29	...	...	1	29	...	...	...	1
Montana	2	2	...	...	...	2	...	...	...	2	...	...	...	2	...	...	...
Nebraska	6	6	...	...	...	6	...	...	...	6	...	...	...	6	...	...	...
Nevada	6	6	...	...	...	6	...	...	...	6	...	...	...	6	...	...	...
New Hampshire	10	10	...	...	...	10	...	...	...	10	...	...	...	10	...	...	...
New Jersey	18	18	...	...	...	16	...	2	...	14	2	2	...	14	2	...	2
New Mexico	2	2	...	...	...	2	...	...	...	2	...	...	...	2	...	...	...
New York	70	20	50	...	50	18	2	...	50	18	2	...	50	18	2	...	...
North Carolina	20	20	...	...	5	...	15	...	6	...	14	...	6	...	13	1	...
North Dakota	*2	2	...	...	1	1	...	...	1	1	...	...	1	1	...	...	...
Ohio	44	44	...	...	...	9	34	1	...	9	34	1	...	9	34	...	1
Oklahoma	...	...	...	...	...	...	...	...	...	...	...	...	...	...	...	...	...
Oregon	6	6	...	...	...	6	...	...	...	6	...	...	...	6	...	...	...
Pennsylvania	58	20	38	...	34	22	...	2	35	22	...	1	36	20	...	1	1
Rhode Island	8	8	...	...	...	8	...	...	...	8	...	...	...	8	...	...	...
South Carolina	14	10	3	1	12	1	1	...	11	1	2	...	11	1	2	...	...
South Dakota	*	...	...	...	...	...	...	...	...	...	...	...	...	...	...	...	...
Tennessee	24	8	16	...	16	5	2	1	17	4	3	...	17	4	3	...	...
Texas	16	8	7	1	12	1	2	1	13	1	1	1	13	1	1	...	1
Utah	2	2	...	...	1	1	...	...	1	1	...	...	1	1	...	...	...
Vermont	10	10	...	...	...	...	...	10	...	...	...	10	...	...	...	...	10
Virginia	22	10	11	1	16	3	3	...	16	3	3	...	16	3	3	...	...
Washington	2	2	...	...	...	2	...	...	...	2	...	...	...	2	...	...	...
West Virginia	10	6	3	1	1	8	1	...	1	8	1	...	1	8	1	...	...
Wisconsin	20	19	1	...	1	7	3	9	2	1	...	17	2	2	...	16	...
Wyoming	2	2	...	...	1	1	...	...	1	1	...	...	1	1	...	...	...
Alaska	...	...	...	...	...	...	...	...	...	...	...	...	...	...	...	...	...
Canal Zone	...	...	...	...	...	...	...	...	...	...	...	...	...	...	...	...	...
District of Columbia	2	2	...	...	...	1	1	...	1	1	...	...	1	1	...	...	...
Hawaii	...	...	...	...	...	...	...	...	...	...	...	...	...	...	...	...	...
Philippine Islands	...	...	...	...	...	...	...	...	...	...	...	...	...	...	...	...	...
Puerto Rico	...	...	...	...	...	...	...	...	...	...	...	...	...	...	...	...	...
Virgin Islands	...	...	...	...	...	...	...	...	...	...	...	...	...	...	...	...	...
Total	756	446	303	7	305	278	116	57[a]	312	275	107	62[b]	313	257	99	50	37[c]

Source: *Official Proceedings, 1880.*

Motion to adjourn, pp. 250-1.
Twenty-ninth ballot, pp. 252-3.
a/ Other candidates: Washburne, 35; Edmunds, 12;
Windom, 7; Garfield, 2; not voting, 1.
Thirty-fourth ballot, pp. 267-8.
b/ Other candidates: Washburne, 30; Garfield, 17;
Edmunds, 11; Windom, 4.
Thirty-fifth ballot, pp. 269-70.
c/ Other candidates: Washburne, 23; Edmunds, 11;
Windom, 3.

* Dakota Territory, 2 votes.

Delegation	1880 REPUBLICAN								1884 REPUBLICAN						
	Presidential Thirty-sixth Ballot				Vice-Presidential First Ballot					Temporary Chairman			Motion to Adjourn		
	Votes	Grant	Blaine	Garfield	Other	Arthur	Washburne	Other	Votes	Lynch	Clayton	Not Voting	Yea	Nay	Not Voting
Alabama	20	16	4	...	...	18	...	2	20	19	1	...	20	...	...
Arizona	2	...	...	2	...	...	...	2	2	...	2	...	2	...	...
Arkansas	12	12	...	...	...	12	...	...	14	1	13	...	14	...	...
California	12	...	12	...	...	...	12	...	16	...	16	...	16	...	...
Colorado	6	6	...	...	...	6	...	...	6	...	6	...	6	...	...
Connecticut	12	...	1	11	...	...	...	12	12	6	6	...	...	12	...
Delaware	6	...	6	...	...	6	...	...	6	1	5	...	3	1	2
Florida	8	8	...	...	...	8	...	...	8	7	1	...	...	8	...
Georgia	22	8	10	1	3	22	...	...	24	24	...	...	...	24	...
Idaho	2	...	...	2	...	...	2	...	2	2	...	...	1	1	...
Illinois	42	24	6	7	5	24	18	...	44	16	28	...	3	41	...
Indiana	30	1	...	29	...	5	11	14	30	10	20	...	23	7	...
Iowa	22	...	...	22	...	...	22	...	26	3	23	...	26	...	...
Kansas	10	4	...	6	...	10	...	...	18	4	14	...	14	4	...
Kentucky	24	20	1	3	...	24	...	...	26	20	6	...	8	18	...
Louisiana	16	8	...	8	...	10	...	6	16	11	4	1	7	8	1
Maine	14	...	...	14	...	...	...	14	12	...	12	...	12	...	...
Maryland	16	6	...	10	...	16	...	...	16	6	10	...	12	4	...
Massachusetts	26	4	...	22	...	2	22	2	28	24	4	...	...	28	...
Michigan	22	1	...	21	...	6	14	2	26	12	14	...	19	7	...
Minnesota	10	2	...	8	...	8	2	...	14	6	8	...	5	9	...
Mississippi	16	7	...	9	...	11	...	5	18	16	2	...	1	17	...
Missouri	30	29	...	1	...	30	...	...	32	14	16	2	9	20	3
Montana	2	...	...	2	...	1	1	...	2	1	1	...	...	2	...
Nebraska	6	...	...	6	...	...	6	...	10	2	8	...	8	2	...
Nevada	6	2	1	3	...	...	6	...	6	...	6	...	6	...	...
New Hampshire	10	...	...	10	...	3	3	4	8	8	...	...	1	7	...
New Jersey	18	...	...	18	...	3	14	1	18	9	9	...	18	...	...
New Mexico	2	...	...	2	...	2	...	...	2	2	...	...	...	2	...
New York	70	50	...	20	...	69	1	...	72	46	26	...	27	41	4
North Carolina	20	5	...	15	...	20	...	...	22	17	3	2	3	19	...
North Dakota	*2	...	...	2	...	2	...	...	*2	...	2	...	2	...	...
Ohio	44	...	...	43	1	42	2	...	46	22	23	1	23	23	...
Oklahoma	...	...	...	...	...	...	...	...	...	...	...	...	...	...	...
Oregon	6	...	...	6	...	6	...	...	6	...	6	...	6	...	...
Pennsylvania	58	37	...	21	...	47	11	...	60	13	45	2	42	17	1
Rhode Island	8	...	...	8	...	...	8	...	8	8	...	...	...	8	...
South Carolina	14	8	...	6	...	14	...	...	18	18	...	...	...	18	...
South Dakota	*	...	...	...	...	...	...	...	*	...	...	...	...	...	...
Tennessee	24	15	1	8	...	...	...	24	24	21	2	1	7	16	1
Texas	16	13	...	3	...	9	5	2	26	12	12	2	12	10	4
Utah	2	...	...	2	...	2	...	...	2	...	2	...	...	2	...
Vermont	10	...	...	10	...	4	5	1	8	8	...	...	...	8	...
Virginia	22	19	...	3	...	19	2	1	24	20	4	...	3	21	...
Washington	2	...	...	2	...	1	...	1	2	1	1	...	2	...	...
West Virginia	10	1	...	9	...	1	9	...	12	...	12	...	12	...	...
Wisconsin	20	...	...	20	...	2	16	2	22	11	10	1	18	4	...
Wyoming	2	...	...	2	...	2	...	...	2	2	...	...	...	1	1
Alaska	...	...	...	...	...	...	...	...	...	...	...	...	...	...	...
Canal Zone	...	...	...	...	...	...	...	...	...	...	...	...	...	...	...
District of Columbia	2	...	...	2	...	1	1	...	2	1	1	...	...	2	...
Hawaii	...	...	...	...	...	...	...	...	...	...	...	...	...	...	...
Philippine Islands	...	...	...	...	...	...	...	...	...	...	...	...	...	...	...
Puerto Rico	...	...	...	...	...	...	...	...	...	...	...	...	...	...	...
Virgin Islands	...	...	...	...	...	...	...	...	...	...	...	...	...	...	...
Total	756	306	42	399	9a	468	193	95b	820	424	384	12	391	412c	17

Source: *Official Proceedings, 1880.*
Thirty-sixth ballot, pp. 270-1.
a/ Other candidates: Washburne, 5; Sherman, 3; not voting, 1.
Vice-Presidential. First ballot, pp. 293-4.
b/ Other candidates: Marshall Jewell, 44; Horace Maynard, 30; Blanche K. Bruce, 8; James L. Alcorn, 4; Edmund J. Davis, 2; Stewart L. Woodford, 1; Thomas Settle, 1; not voting, 5.

Source: *Official Proceedings, 1884.*
Temporary Chairman, p. 17.
Motion to adjourn, p. 133.
c/ Sum of column; proceedings record 410.

* Dakota Territory, 2 votes.

* Dakota Territory, 2 votes.

Source: *Official Proceedings, 1884.*

		1884 REPUBLICAN																	
		Presidential											Motion to Adjourn			Presidential		
		First Ballot				Second Ballot				Third Ballot						Fourth Ballot		
Delegation	Votes	Arthur	Blaine	Edmunds	Other	Arthur	Blaine	Edmunds	Other	Arthur	Blaine	Other	Yea	Nay	Not Voting	Arthur	Blaine	Other
Alabama	20	17	1	...	2	17	2	...	1	17	2	1	17	3	...	12	8	...
Arizona	2	...	2	...	...	...	2	...	...	...	2	...	...	2	...	...	2	...
Arkansas	14	4	8	2	...	3	11	...	...	3	11	...	3	11	...	3	11	...
California	16	...	16	...	...	...	16	...	...	...	16	...	...	16	...	...	16	...
Colorado	6	...	6	...	...	...	6	...	...	...	6	...	...	6	...	...	6	...
Connecticut	12	...	...	...	12	...	...	...	12	...	...	12	...	12	...	...	...	12
Delaware	6	1	5	...	...	1	5	...	...	1	5	...	1	5	...	1	5	...
Florida	8	7	1	...	...	7	1	...	...	7	1	...	5	3	...	5	3	...
Georgia	24	24	...	...	...	24	...	...	...	24	...	...	24	...	...	24	...	...
Idaho	2	2	...	...	...	2	...	...	...	1	1	...	...	2	...	...	2	...
Illinois	44	1	3	...	40	1	3	...	40	1	3	40	31	13	...	3	34	7
Indiana	30	9	18	1	2	9	18	1	2	10	18	2	8	22	...	...	30	...
Iowa	26	...	26	...	...	...	26	...	...	...	26	...	2	24	...	2	24	...
Kansas	18	4	12	...	2	2	13	...	3	...	15	3	...	18	...	...	18	...
Kentucky	26	16	5½	...	4½	17	5	...	4	16	6	4	18	8	...	15	9	2
Louisiana	16	10	2	...	4	9	4	...	3	9	4	3	7	8	1	7	9	...
Maine	12	...	12	...	...	...	12	...	...	...	12	...	...	12	...	...	12	...
Maryland	16	6	10	...	...	4	12	...	...	4	12	...	4	12	...	1	15	...
Massachusetts	28	2	1	25	...	3	1	24	...	3	1	24	23	5	...	7	3	18
Michigan	26	2	15	7	2	4	15	5	2	4	18	4	8	18	...	...	26	...
Minnesota	14	1	7	6	...	1	7	6	...	2	7	5	...	14	...	...	14	...
Mississippi	18	17	1	...	...	17	1	...	...	16	1	1	17	1	...	16	2	...
Missouri	32	10	5	6	11	10	7	5	10	11	12	9	10	22	...	...	32	...
Montana	2	...	1	1	...	...	1	1	...	...	1	1	1	1	...	...	2	...
Nebraska	10	2	8	...	...	2	8	...	...	...	10	...	...	10	...	...	10	...
Nevada	6	...	6	...	...	...	6	...	...	...	6	...	...	6	...	...	6	...
New Hampshire	8	4	...	4	...	5	...	3	...	5	...	3	8	...	...	2	3	3
New Jersey	18	...	9	6	3	...	9	6	3	1	11	6	5	13	...	...	17	1
New Mexico	2	2	...	...	...	2	...	...	...	2	...	...	2	...	...	2	...	...
New York	72	31	28	12	1	31	28	12	1	32	28	12	42	29	1	30	29	13
North Carolina	22	19	2	...	1	18	3	...	1	18	4	...	14	6	2	12	8	2
North Dakota	*2	...	2	...	...	...	2	...	...	...	2	...	...	2	...	...	2	...
Ohio	46	...	21	...	25	...	23	...	23	...	25	21	17	28	1	...	46	...
Oklahoma	...	...	...	...	...	...	...	...	...	...	...	...	...	...	...	...	...	...
Oregon	6	...	6	...	...	...	6	...	...	...	6	...	...	6	...	...	6	...
Pennsylvania	60	11	47	1	1	11	47	1	1	8	50	2	11	48	1	8	51	1
Rhode Island	8	...	...	8	...	...	...	8	...	...	...	8	7	1	...	1	7	...
South Carolina	18	17	1	...	...	17	1	...	...	16	2	...	16	2	...	15	2	1
South Dakota	*	...	...	...	...	...	...	...	...	...	...	...	...	...	...	...	...	...
Tennessee	24	16	7	...	1	16	7	...	1	17	7	...	12	12	...	12	11	1
Texas	26	11	13	...	2	11	13	...	2	11	14	1	10	16	...	8	15	3
Utah	2	2	...	...	...	2	...	...	...	2	...	...	2	...	...	...	2	...
Vermont	8	...	...	8	...	...	...	8	...	...	...	8	...	8	...	...	...	8
Virginia	24	21	2	...	1	21	2	...	1	20	4	...	20	4	...	20	4	...
Washington	2	...	2	...	...	...	2	...	...	...	2	...	...	2	...	...	2	...
West Virginia	12	...	12	...	...	...	12	...	...	...	12	...	...	12	...	...	12	...
Wisconsin	22	6	10	6	...	6	11	5	...	10	11	1	10	12	...	...	22	...
Wyoming	2	2	...	...	...	2	...	...	...	2	...	...	...	2	...	...	2	...
Alaska	...	...	...	...	...	...	...	...	...	...	...	...	...	...	...	...	...	...
Canal Zone	...	...	...	...	...	...	...	...	...	...	...	...	...	...	...	...	...	...
District of Columbia	2	1	1	...	...	1	1	...	...	1	1	...	1	1	...	1	1	...
Hawaii	...	...	...	...	...	...	...	...	...	...	...	...	...	...	...	...	...	...
Philippine Islands	...	...	...	...	...	...	...	...	...	...	...	...	...	...	...	...	...	...
Puerto Rico	...	...	...	...	...	...	...	...	...	...	...	...	...	...	...	...	...	...
Virgin Islands	...	...	...	...	...	...	...	...	...	...	...	...	...	...	...	...	...	...
Total	820	278	334½	93	114½a	276	349	85	110b	274	375	171c	356d	458e	6	207	541	72f

Presidential. First ballot, pp. 138-42.

a/ Other candidates: John A. Logan, 63½; John Sherman, 30; Joseph R. Hawley, 13; Robert T. Lincoln, 4; William T. Sherman, 2; not voting, 2.

Second ballot, pp. 142-7.

b/ Other candidates: Logan, 61; John Sherman, 28; Hawley, 13; Lincoln, 4; William T. Sherman, 3; not voting, 1.

Third ballot, pp. 148-50.

c/ Other candidates: Edmunds, 69; Logan, 53; John Sherman, 25; Hawley, 13; Lincoln, 8; William T. Sherman, 2; not voting, 1.

Motion to adjourn, pp. 151-5.

d/ Sum of column; proceedings record 364.

e/ Sum of column; proceedings record 450.

Fourth ballot, pp. 156-63.

f/ Other candidates: Edmunds, 41; Hawley, 15; Logan, 7; Lincoln, 2; not voting, 7.

* Dakota Territory, 2 votes.

Delegation	1884 REPUBLICAN Vice-Pres. First Ballot			1888 REPUBLICAN Minority Report, Virginia Credentials				Presidential First Ballot						
	Votes	Logan	Other	Votes	Yea	Nay	Not Voting	Alger	Allison	Depew	Gresham	Harrison	Sherman	Other
Alabama	20	20	...	20	10	8	2	6	...	1	...	1	12	...
Arizona	2	2	...	2	...	2	...	2	...	...	...	...	...	...
Arkansas	14	14	...	14	...	14	...	...	...	...	1	1	2	10
California	16	16	...	16	...	16	...	...	1	...	...	...	...	16
Colorado	6	6	...	6	...	6	...	...	1	...	3	2	...	...
Connecticut	12	5	7	12	...	12	...	...	...	...	...	...	...	12
Delaware	6	6	...	6	...	6	...	...	...	...	...	6	...	...
Florida	8	8	...	8	4	4	...	...	...	...	...	1	4	3
Georgia	24	24	...	24	12½	4	7½	...	...	...	1	2	19	2
Idaho	2	2	...	2	...	2	...	...	1	...	1	...	...	...
Illinois	44	44	...	44	2	42	...	...	...	...	44	...	...	...
Indiana	30	30	...	30	...	30	...	...	...	...	1	29	...	...
Iowa	26	26	...	26	...	26	...	...	26	...	...	...	...	...
Kansas	18	18	...	18	...	18	...	...	...	...	...	...	...	18
Kentucky	26	26	...	26	1	25	...	4	...	1	5	4	12	...
Louisiana	16	16	...	16	9	7	...	2	3	1	1	...	9	...
Maine	12	12	...	12	...	12	...	3	2	3	1	2	1	...
Maryland	16	16	...	16	1	11	4	...	2	1	1	5	5	2
Massachusetts	28	12	16	28	6	19	3	6	2	1	2	4	9	4
Michigan	26	26	...	26	...	26	...	26	...	...	...	...	...	...
Minnesota	14	14	...	14	...	14	...	1	...	2	11	...	...	...
Mississippi	18	18	...	18	15	1	2	...	...	1	3	...	14	...
Missouri	32	30	2	32	4	23	5	6	3	2	11	3	6	1
Montana	2	2	...	2	...	2	...	...	1	...	1	...	...	...
Nebraska	10	10	...	10	6	4	...	2	3	...	1	...	3	1
Nevada	6	6	...	6	6	...	...	3	3	...	...	...	...	...
New Hampshire	8	8	...	8	...	3	5	...	4	...	4	...	...	...
New Jersey	18	18	...	18	4	12	2	...	...	...	...	...	...	18
New Mexico	2	2	...	2	...	2	...	1	...	...	...	...	...	1
New York	72	60	12	72	22	50	...	...	...	71	...	...	1	...
North Carolina	22	22	...	22	18	4	...	2	...	1	2	1	15	1
North Dakota	*2	2	...	*10	10	...	...	1	1	2	1	1	1	3
Ohio	46	46	...	46	19	19	8	...	...	...	...	...	46	...
Oklahoma	...	...	...	...	...	...	...	...	...	...	...	...	...	...
Oregon	6	6	...	6	...	6	...	...	...	...	4	1	...	1
Pennsylvania	60	59	1	60	56	4	...	1	...	5	...	...	29	25
Rhode Island	8	8	...	8	...	8	...	...	8	...	...	...	...	...
South Carolina	18	18	...	18	18	...	...	3	...	1	...	...	11	3
South Dakota	*	...	...	*	...	...	...	...	...	...	...	...	...	...
Tennessee	24	24	...	24	6	7	11	9	1	2	1	1	7	3
Texas	26	26	...	26	2	19	5	2	7	...	5	1	7	4
Utah	2	2	...	2	...	2	...	...	2	...	...	...	...	...
Vermont	8	8	...	8	...	8	...	...	...	...	...	8	...	...
Virginia	24	24	...	24	10	...	14	3	3	...	1	5	11	1
Washington	2	2	...	6	...	6	...	...	1	...	3	1	...	1
West Virginia	12	12	...	12	4	8	...	1	...	...	2	2	5	2
Wisconsin	22	19	3	22	3	19	...	...	...	...	...	...	...	22
Wyoming	2	2	...	2	1	1	...	...	2	...	...	...	...	...
Alaska	...	...	...	...	...	...	...	...	...	...	...	...	...	...
Canal Zone	...	...	...	...	...	...	...	...	...	...	...	...	...	...
District of Columbia	2	2	...	2	...	2	...	...	...	...	...	...	...	2
Hawaii	...	...	...	...	...	...	...	...	...	...	...	...	...	...
Philippine Islands	...	...	...	...	...	...	...	...	...	...	...	...	...	...
Puerto Rico	...	...	...	...	...	...	...	...	...	...	...	...	...	...
Virgin Islands	...	...	...	...	...	...	...	...	...	...	...	...	...	...
Total	820	779a	41b	832	249½	514	68½	84	72	99	107	85	229	156c

Source: *Official Proceedings, 1884.*
Vice-Presidential. First ballot, pp. 176-8.
a/ Sum of column; proceedings record 773.
b/ Other candidates: Walter Q. Gresham, 6; Joseph B. Foraker, 1; not voting, 34.

Source: *Official Proceedings, 1888.*
Minority report, Virginia credentials, p. 88.
Presidential. First ballot, pp. 152-60.
c/ Other candidates: James G. Blaine, 35; John J. Ingalls, 28; William W. Phelps, 25; Jeremiah M. Rusk, 25; Edwin H. Fitler, 24; Joseph R. Hawley, 13; Robert T. Lincoln, 3; William McKinley, 2; not voting, 1.

* Dakota Territory, 2 votes.

* Dakota Territory, 10 votes.

		1888 REPUBLICAN																
		Presidential													Motion to Adjourn		
		Second Ballot							Third Ballot								
Delegation	Votes	Alger	Allison	Depew	Gresham	Harrison	Sherman	Other	Alger	Allison	Depew	Gresham	Harrison	Sherman	Other	Yea	Nay	Not Voting
Alabama	20	7	...	1	...	1	11	...	7	...	1	...	2	10	...	19	1	...
Arizona	2	2	...	...	...	...	...	...	2	...	...	...	...	...	...	2	...	...
Arkansas	14	14	...	...	...	...	...	...	14	...	...	...	...	...	...	14	...	...
California	16	...	...	...	...	...	...	16	...	...	...	...	...	...	16	16	...	...
Colorado	6	...	1	...	3	2	...	...	...	1	...	5	...	...	...	6	...	...
Connecticut	12	1	4	6	1	...	...	...	1	5	...	6	...	...	...	4	8	...
Delaware	6	...	...	...	...	6	...	...	...	...	...	1	5	...	...	...	6	...
Florida	8	3	...	...	...	1	4	...	3	...	...	...	1	4	...	3	4	1
Georgia	24	...	...	...	1	2	19	2	...	...	...	2	2	18	2	21	1	2
Idaho	2	...	1	...	1	...	...	...	...	1	...	1	...	...	...	2	...	...
Illinois	44	...	...	...	44	...	...	...	...	...	...	44	...	...	...	30	12	2
Indiana	30	...	...	...	2	28	...	...	...	...	...	2	28	...	...	...	30	...
Iowa	26	...	26	...	...	...	...	...	...	26	...	...	...	...	...	26	...	...
Kansas	18	...	...	...	...	...	...	18	...	4	...	5	2	2	5	18	...	...
Kentucky	26	3	...	1	6	2	11	3	4	2	1	4	4	9	2	14	10	2
Louisiana	16	3	2	1	1	...	9	...	3	2	1	1	...	9	...	16	...	...
Maine	12	3	2	3	1	2	1	...	3	2	3	1	2	1	...	12	...	...
Maryland	16	...	3	...	1	6	6	...	...	4	...	1	6	5	...	8	8	...
Massachusetts	28	7	1	1	2	5	9	3	6	3	1	1	4	9	4	21	7	...
Michigan	26	26	...	...	...	...	...	...	26	...	...	...	...	...	...	25	1	...
Minnesota	14	1	...	2	11	...	...	...	1	...	2	11	...	...	...	10	4	...
Mississippi	18	...	...	1	3	...	14	...	...	...	1	3	...	14	...	18	...	...
Missouri	32	10	1	2	9	3	6	1	11	2	2	9	2	4	2	21	11	...
Montana	2	...	1	...	1	...	...	...	...	1	...	1	...	...	...	2	...	...
Nebraska	10	2	4	...	...	...	3	1	2	5	...	...	...	3	...	10	...	...
Nevada	6	3	3	...	...	...	...	...	4	2	...	...	...	...	...	6	...	...
New Hampshire	8	...	...	4	...	4	...	...	...	...	4	...	4	...	...	...	8	...
New Jersey	18	...	...	...	...	...	...	18	...	4	1	...	4	2	7	7	11	...
New Mexico	2	1	...	...	...	...	1	...	1	...	...	...	...	1	...	...	2	...
New York	72	...	...	71	...	...	...	1	...	...	71	...	...	...	1	10	61	1
North Carolina	22	4	...	...	...	2	15	1	5	...	...	1	15	1	...	19	3	...
North Dakota	*10	...	1	2	2	3	1	1	...	1	1	3	3	2	...	...	10	...
Ohio	46	...	...	...	...	...	46	...	...	...	...	...	...	46	...	46	...	...
Oklahoma	...	...	...	...	...	...	...	...	...	...	...	...	...	...	...	...	...	...
Oregon	6	...	...	...	4	1	...	1	...	...	...	4	1	...	1	3	3	...
Pennsylvania	60	2	...	1	...	4	53	...	1	...	1	...	5	53	...	50	10	...
Rhode Island	8	...	8	...	...	...	...	...	...	8	...	...	...	...	...	8	...	...
South Carolina	18	7	...	2	...	...	9	...	11	...	...	...	1	6	...	12	6	...
South Dakota	*	...	...	...	...	...	...	...	...	...	...	...	...	...	...	...	...	...
Tennessee	24	8	3	1	1	2	7	2	9	3	1	1	...	7	3	15	7	2
Texas	26	3	8	...	5	1	6	3	2	7	...	5	1	6	5	11	12	3
Utah	2	...	2	...	...	...	...	...	...	2	...	...	...	...	...	2	...	...
Vermont	8	...	...	...	...	8	...	...	...	...	...	...	8	...	...	...	8	...
Virginia	24	4	3	...	1	5	11	...	4	3	...	2	5	10	...	10	13	1
Washington	6	1	1	...	3	1	...	...	1	...	...	4	1	...	...	3	3	...
West Virginia	12	1	...	...	2	2	5	2	1	...	...	2	1	5	3	7	5	...
Wisconsin	22	...	...	...	3	...	...	19	...	...	...	4	1	1	16	...	22	...
Wyoming	2	...	...	...	...	...	2	...	...	...	...	...	...	2	...	2	...	...
Alaska	...	...	...	...	...	...	...	...	...	...	...	...	...	...	...	...	...	...
Canal Zone	...	...	...	...	...	...	...	...	...	...	...	...	...	...	...	...	...	...
District of Columbia	2	...	...	...	...	...	...	2	...	...	...	...	...	...	2	2	...	...
Hawaii	...	...	...	...	...	...	...	...	...	...	...	...	...	...	...	...	...	...
Philippine Islands	...	...	...	...	...	...	...	...	...	...	...	...	...	...	...	...	...	...
Puerto Rico	...	...	...	...	...	...	...	...	...	...	...	...	...	...	...	...	...	...
Virgin Islands	...	...	...	...	...	...	...	...	...	...	...	...	...	...	...	...	...	...
Total	832	116	75	99	108	91	249	94a	122	88	91	123	94	244	70b	531	287	14

Source: *Official Proceedings, 1888.*

Second ballot, pp. 160-3.
a/ Other candidates: Blaine, 33; Rusk, 20; Phelps, 18; Ingalls, 16; McKinley, 3; Lincoln, 2; not voting, 2.
Third ballot, pp. 163-7.
b/ Other candidates: Blaine, 35; Rusk, 16; McKinley, 8; Phelps, 5; Lincoln, 2; Samuel F. Miller, 2; not voting, 2.
Motion to adjourn, pp. 168-71.

* Dakota Territory, 10 votes.

		1888 REPUBLICAN														
		Presidential												Motion to Adjourn		
		Fourth Ballot						Fifth Ballot								
Delegation	Votes	Alger	Allison	Gresham	Harrison	Sherman	Other	Alger	Allison	Gresham	Harrison	Sherman	Other	Yea	Nay	Not Voting
Alabama	20	10	...	...	1	8	1	8	...	...	2	9	1	16	4	...
Arizona	2	2	...	...	...	...	...	2	...	...	...	...	...	2	...	...
Arkansas	14	14	...	...	...	...	...	14	...	...	...	...	...	14	...	...
California	16	...	...	...	...	...	16	...	...	...	...	...	16	16	...	...
Colorado	6	...	2	3	1	...	...	...	6	...	...	...	...	6	...	...
Connecticut	12	1	6	4	...	...	1	2	6	3	...	...	1	6	5	1
Delaware	6	...	...	1	5	...	...	...	1	1	3	...	1	2	4	...
Florida	8	4	...	...	2	2	...	5	...	...	1	2	...	8	...	...
Georgia	24	...	...	1	2	19	2	...	...	1	2	20	1	22	1	1
Idaho	2	1	...	...	1	...	...	...	1	1	...	...	...	...	2	...
Illinois	44	...	...	41	3	...	...	...	...	41	3	...	...	37	7	...
Indiana	30	...	...	...	30	...	...	...	...	1	29	...	...	...	30	...
Iowa	26	...	26	...	...	...	...	...	26	...	...	...	...	26	...	...
Kansas	18	...	2	3	8	...	5	...	2	3	8	...	5	18	...	...
Kentucky	26	3	2	2	6	10	3	8	...	2	8	7	1	4	16	6
Louisiana	16	3	2	2	...	9	...	3	2	2	...	9	...	16	...	...
Maine	12	3	4	1	2	2	...	3	5	1	2	1	...	12	...	...
Maryland	16	...	2	...	8	6	...	...	4	...	6	6	...	14	2	...
Massachusetts	28	8	2	1	8	7	2	4	3	1	10	5	5	14	12	2
Michigan	26	26	...	...	...	...	...	26	...	...	...	...	...	...	26	...
Minnesota	14	2	...	5	7	...	...	3	...	3	7	...	1	...	14	...
Mississippi	18	...	...	3	...	14	1	...	...	2	...	15	1	14	3	1
Missouri	32	13	1	11	3	2	2	14	1	10	2	1	4	15	13	4
Montana	2	...	1	1	...	...	...	...	1	1	...	...	...	2	...	...
Nebraska	10	2	5	...	...	3	...	2	5	...	...	3	...	10	...	...
Nevada	6	4	2	...	...	...	...	4	2	...	...	...	...	6	...	...
New Hampshire	8	1	1	1	1	5	...	1	...	...	...	8	...	1	7	...
New Jersey	18	...	3	2	7	2	4	...	5	2	4	1	6	18	...	...
New Mexico	2	1	...	...	...	1	...	1	...	...	...	1	...	...	2	...
New York	72	3	1	...	58	1	9	5	1	...	58	1	7	...	72	...
North Carolina	22	6	...	1	2	13	...	9	...	...	2	11	...	12	10	...
North Dakota	*10	...	3	1	4	2	...	...	3	1	5	1	...	...	10	...
Ohio	46	...	...	...	...	46	...	...	...	...	...	46	...	38	8	...
Oklahoma	...															
Oregon	6	...	...	4	1	...	1	...	...	4	1	...	1	...	6	...
Pennsylvania	60	...	...	...	7	53	...	...	...	...	7	53	...	55	5	...
Rhode Island	8	...	8	...	...	...	...	...	8	...	...	...	...	6	2	...
South Carolina	18	10	...	...	2	6	...	10	...	...	2	6	...	18	...	...
South Dakota	*															
Tennessee	24	9	1	...	2	8	4	10	1	...	2	5	6	17	4	3
Texas	26	3	9	3	1	7	3	2	11	3	2	7	1	26	...	...
Utah	2	...	2	...	...	...	...	...	2	...	...	...	...	2	...	...
Vermont	8	...	...	...	8	...	...	...	...	...	8	...	...	...	8	...
Virginia	24	3	3	...	8	10	...	3	3	...	6	10	2	10	14	...
Washington	6	2	...	3	1	...	...	3	...	2	1	...	...	2	4	...
West Virginia	12	1	...	2	3	2	4	2	...	...	3	2	5	1	9	2
Wisconsin	22	...	...	2	20	...	...	...	...	2	20	...	...	4	18	...
Wyoming	2	...	...	...	...	2	...	...	...	...	...	2	...	...	2	...
Alaska	...															
Canal Zone	...															
District of Columbia	2	...	...	...	...	...	2	...	...	...	...	...	2	2	...	...
Hawaii	...															
Philippine Islands	...															
Puerto Rico	...															
Virgin Islands	...															
Total	832	135	88	98	216	235	60a	143	99	87	212	224	67b	492	320	20

Source: *Official Proceedings, 1888.*

Fourth ballot, pp. 174-8.
a/ Other candidates: Blaine, 42; McKinley, 11; Lincoln, 1; Joseph B. Foraker, 1; Frederick Douglass, 1; not voting, 4.
Fifth ballot, pp. 179-80.
b/ Other candidates: Blaine, 48; McKinley, 14; not voting, 5.
Motion to adjourn, p. 184.

* Dakota Territory, 10 votes.

Delegation	Votes	Sixth Ballot Alger	Allison	Gresham	Harrison	Sherman	Other	Seventh Ballot Alger	Allison	Gresham	Harrison	Sherman	Other	Eighth Ballot Alger	Gresham	Harrison	Sherman	Other
Alabama	20	6	...	...	1	12	1	6	...	...	1	12	1	10	...	3	5	2
Arizona	2	2	...	...	...	...	...	2	...	...	...	...	...	...	...	2	...	...
Arkansas	14	14	...	...	...	...	...	14	...	...	...	...	...	14	...	...	...	...
California	16	...	...	...	...	...	16	1	...	...	15	...	...	...	...	15	...	1
Colorado	6	...	...	...	5	...	1	...	6	...	...	...	...	...	...	6	...	...
Connecticut	12	2	4	...	...	6	...	2	...	...	4	5	1	...	...	12	...	...
Delaware	6	...	...	1	5	...	...	...	...	1	5	...	...	...	...	6	...	...
Florida	8	5	...	...	1	1	1	3	...	...	4	1	...	4	...	2	2	...
Georgia	24	...	...	1	2	19	2	1	...	1	3	17	2	3	1	10	9	1
Idaho	2	...	...	2	...	...	...	...	...	2	...	...	...	...	...	2	...	...
Illinois	44	...	...	41	3	...	...	1	...	40	3	...	...	...	40	4	...	...
Indiana	30	...	...	1	29	...	...	...	...	1	29	...	...	...	1	29	...	...
Iowa	26	...	26	...	...	...	...	...	26	...	...	...	...	1	3	22	...	...
Kansas	18	2	3	3	6	1	3	1	3	...	12	1	1	1	...	16	...	1
Kentucky	26	6	...	2	7	9	2	3	...	2	10	9	2	1	2	15	7	1
Louisiana	16	3	2	2	...	9	...	3	2	2	...	9	...	4	...	9	3	...
Maine	12	2	1	2	1	3	3	1	2	2	2	1	4	...	1	5	3	3
Maryland	16	...	1	...	6	6	3	...	...	9	6	1	...	...	...	11	4	1
Massachusetts	28	8	2	1	5	11	1	2	3	1	9	11	2	1	...	25	2	...
Michigan	26	26	...	...	...	...	...	26	...	...	...	...	...	26	...	...	...	...
Minnesota	14	3	...	5	6	...	...	2	...	4	8	...	...	1	...	13	...	...
Mississippi	18	...	...	3	...	14	1	...	...	3	...	14	1	...	3	4	11	..
Missouri	32	15	1	11	2	2	1	14	...	12	3	2	1	15	8	7	2	..
Montana	2	...	1	1	...	...	...	...	1	1	...	...	...	...	...	2	...	...
Nebraska	10	2	5	...	...	3	...	2	5	...	2	1	...	1	...	9	...	...
Nevada	6	5	...	...	...	...	1	...	6	...	...	...	...	2	...	4	...	...
New Hampshire	8	...	1	...	6	1	...	...	...	...	8	...	...	...	...	8	...	...
New Jersey	18	...	...	1	14	...	3	1	...	1	10	1	5	...	...	18	...	...
New Mexico	2	1	...	...	...	1	...	1	...	...	...	1	...	...	...	2	...	...
New York	72	...	...	...	72	...	...	...	...	...	72	...	...	...	...	72	...	...
North Carolina	22	9	...	...	2	11	...	7	...	...	3	12	...	3	...	8	11	...
North Dakota	*10	...	...	...	10	...	...	...	...	...	10	...	...	...	...	10	...	...
Ohio	46	...	...	...	1	45	...	...	...	...	1	45	...	...	...	1	45	...
Oklahoma	...	...	...	...	...	...	...	...	...	...	...	...	...	...	...	...	...	...
Oregon	6	...	...	5	...	...	1	...	...	6	...	...	...	...	...	6	...	...
Pennsylvania	60	...	...	...	6	54	...	...	...	...	9	51	...	...	...	59	1	...
Rhode Island	8	...	8	...	...	...	...	...	6	...	2	...	...	...	...	8	...	...
South Carolina	18	11	...	...	1	6	...	11	...	...	1	6	...	10	...	4	4	...
South Dakota	*	...	...	...	...	...	...	...	...	...	...	...	...	...	...	...	...	...
Tennessee	24	6	1	...	1	8	8	9	1	...	3	5	6	3	...	20	...	1
Texas	26	3	8	3	1	7	4	2	8	1	3	7	5	...	...	26	...	...
Utah	2	...	2	...	...	...	...	...	2	...	...	...	...	...	...	2	...	...
Vermont	8	...	...	...	8	...	...	...	...	...	8	...	...	...	...	8	...	...
Virginia	24	3	5	...	6	10	...	3	5	...	6	10	...	...	...	15	9	...
Washington	6	1	...	4	1	...	...	1	...	4	1	...	...	...	...	6	...	...
West Virginia	12	1	...	1	2	5	3	...	...	5	3	1	3	...	...	12	...	...
Wisconsin	22	...	...	1	21	...	...	...	...	2	20	...	...	...	...	22	...	...
Wyoming	2	...	2	...	...	...	...	...	...	...	...	2	...	...	...	2	...	...
Alaska	...	...	...	...	...	...	...	...	...	...	...	...	...	...	...	...	...	...
Canal Zone	...	...	...	...	...	...	...	...	...	...	...	...	...	...	...	...	...	...
District of Columbia	2	1	...	...	...	...	1	1	...	...	...	...	1	...	...	2	...	...
Hawaii	...	...	...	...	...	...	...	...	...	...	...	...	...	...	...	...	...	...
Philippine Islands	...	...	...	...	...	...	...	...	...	...	...	...	...	...	...	...	...	...
Puerto Rico	...	...	...	...	...	...	...	...	...	...	...	...	...	...	...	...	...	...
Virgin Islands	...	...	...	...	...	...	...	...	...	...	...	...	...	...	...	...	...	...
Total	832	137	73	91	231	244	56a	120	76	91	279	230	36b	100	59	544	118	11c

Source: *Official Proceedings, 1888.*
Sixth ballot, pp. 187-90.
a/ Other candidates: Blaine, 40; McKinley, 12; Foraker, 1; Frederick D. Grant, 1; not voting, 2.
Seventh ballot, pp. 191-3.
b/ Other candidates: McKinley, 16; Blaine, 15; Lincoln, 2; Foraker, 1; Creed Haymond, 1; not voting, 1.
Eighth ballot, pp. 198-9.
c/ Other candidates: Blaine, 5; McKinley, 4; not voting, 2.

* Dakota Territory, 10 votes.

Delegation	1888 REPUBLICAN Vice-Presidential First Ballot				1892 REPUBLICAN	Minority Report, Alabama Credentials			Majority Report, Alabama Credentials			Presidential First Ballot			
	Votes	Bradley	Morton	Phelps	Other / Votes	Yea	Nay	Not Voting	Yea	Nay	Not Voting	Harrison	Blaine	McKinley	Other
Alabama	20	5	15	...	... / 22	13	5	4	5	13	4	15	...	7	...
Arizona	2	...	2	...	... / 2	1	1	...	1	1	...	1	1	...	...
Arkansas	14	...	14	...	... / 16	1	15	...	15	1	...	15	...	1	...
California	16	...	13	3	... / 18	10	8	...	8	10	...	8	9	1	...
Colorado	6	...	6	...	... / 8	8	...	...	...	8	...	...	8	...	...
Connecticut	12	...	12	...	... / 12	9	3	...	4	6	2	4	...	8	...
Delaware	6	...	6	...	... / 6	2	4	...	4	2	...	4	1	1	...
Florida	8	4	4	...	... / 8	...	8	...	8	...	...	8	...	...	...
Georgia	24	18	1	...	5 / 26	1	25	...	26	...	...	26	...	...	...
Idaho	2	...	2	...	... / 6	6	...	...	...	6	...	...	6	...	...
Illinois	44	2	27	15	... / 48	20	28	...	26	18	4	34	14	...	...
Indiana	30	...	30	...	... / 30	...	30	...	30	...	...	30	...	...	...
Iowa	26	2	10	14	... / 26	6	20	...	20	6	...	20	5	1	...
Kansas	18	1	17	...	... / 20	10	10	...	10	8	2	11	...	9	...
Kentucky	26	25	...	...	1 / 26	6	20	...	22	4	...	22	2	1	1
Louisiana	16	3	11	2	... / 16	11	2	3	3	11	2	8	8	...	...
Maine	12	...	7	5	... / 12	12	...	...	...	11	1	...	12	...	...
Maryland	16	1	12	3	... / 16	...	16	...	16	...	...	14	...	2	...
Massachusetts	28	...	28	...	... / 30	14	16	...	13	13	4	18	1	11	...
Michigan	26	9	15	2	... / 28	20	8	...	11	11	6	7	2	19	...
Minnesota	14	...	14	...	... / 18	11	7	...	6	8	4	8	9	1	...
Mississippi	18	3	5	3	7 / 18	6	10½	1½	11	5½	1½	13½	4½	...	...
Missouri	32	5	25	2	... / 34	14	19	1	24	8	2	28	4	2	...
Montana	2	...	2	...	... / 6	5	1	...	1	4	1	...	5	1	...
Nebraska	10	...	5	5	... / 16	6	10	...	10	6	...	15	...	1	...
Nevada	6	...	6	...	... / 6	6	...	...	...	6	...	...	6	...	...
New Hampshire	8	...	7	1	... / 8	2	6	...	5	1	2	4	2	...	2
New Jersey	18	...	...	18	... / 20	2	18	...	18	2	...	18	2	...	...
New Mexico	2	...	2	...	... / 6	...	6	...	6	...	...	6	...	...	...
New York	72	...	72	...	... / 72	45	27	...	28	44	...	27	35	10	...
North Carolina	22	3	14	5	... / 22	6½	13½	2	15	6	1	17e	2e	1	e
North Dakota	*10	...	10	...	... / 6	4	2	...	2	4	...	2	4	...	...
Ohio	46	8	30	8	... / 46	29	19	...	26	15	5	1	...	45	...
Oklahoma	...	...	...	...	... / 4	...	2	.2	2	...	2	3	1	...	...
Oregon	6	...	6	...	... / 8	6	2	...	2	6	...	1	...	7	...
Pennsylvania	60	...	52	8	... / 64	54	9	1	9	54	1	19	3	42	...
Rhode Island	8	...	8	...	... / 8	3	5	...	3	5	...	5	1	1	1
South Carolina	18	...	17	1	... / 18	6	12	...	15	3	...	13	3	2	...
South Dakota	*	...	...	...	... / 8	5	3	...	3	5	...	8	...	...	...
Tennessee	24	11	9	...	4 / 24	12	10	2	10	6	8	17	4	3	...
Texas	26	...	10	15	1 / 30	9	20	1	19	9	2	22	6	...	2
Utah	2	...	2	...	... / 2	1	1	...	1	1	...	2	...	...	...
Vermont	8	...	8	...	... / 8	5	3	...	2	...	6	8	...	...	...
Virginia	24	2	17	5	... / 24	15	9	...	8	15	1	9	13	2	...
Washington	6	...	5	1	... / 8	8	...	...	...	8	...	1	6	1	...
West Virginia	12	...	12	...	... / 12	2	10	...	10	2	...	12	...	...	...
Wisconsin	22	1	18	3	... / 24	9	15	...	14	9	1	19	2	3	...
Wyoming	2	...	2	...	... / 6	2	4	...	4	2	...	4	2	...	...
Alaska	...	...	...	...	... / 2	...	...	2	...	...	2	2	...	...	...
Canal Zone	...	...	...	...	...	...	...	...	...	...	...	...	...	...	...
District of Columbia	2	...	2	...	... / 2	2	...	...	...	2	...	...	2	...	...
Hawaii	...	...	...	...	...	...	...	...	...	...	...	...	...	...	...
Philippine Islands	...	...	...	...	...	...	...	...	...	...	...	...	...	...	...
Puerto Rico	...	...	...	...	...	...	...	...	...	...	...	...	...	...	...
Virgin Islands	...	...	...	...	...	...	...	...	...	...	...	...	...	...	...
Total	832	103	592	119	18a / 906	423½	463	19½	476	365½	64½	535b	182c	182	6d

Source: *Official Proceedings, 1888.*

Vice-Presidential. First ballot, pp. 232-3.
a/ Other candidates: Blanche K. Bruce, 11; Walter S. Thomas, 1; not voting, 6.

Source: *Official Proceedings, 1892.*

Minority report, Alabama credentials, p. 81.
Majority report, Alabama credentials, p. 84.
Presidential. First ballot, pp. 113-4.
b/ Add one-sixth.
c/ Add one-sixth.
d/ Other candidates: Thomas B. Reed, 4; Robert T. Lincoln, 1; not voting, 1 and two-thirds.
e/ Add two-thirds.

* Dakota Territory, 10 votes.

1876 REPUBLICAN

Delegation	Votes	Presidential									Vice-Presidential				
		Sixth Ballot						Seventh Ballot			First Ballot				
		Blaine	Morton	Conkling	Bristow	Hayes	Other	Blaine	Hayes	Other	Wheeler	Woodford	Jewell	Hawley	Freling-huysen
Alabama	20	15	...	...	4	1	...	17	...	3	17	...	3	...	...
Arizona	2	2	...	...	...	...	...	2	...	...	...	...	...	...	...
Arkansas	12	1	11	...	2	...	...	11	1	...	5	5	...	...	2
California	12	6	...	2	...	4	...	6	6	...	...	12	...	...	...
Colorado	6	6	...	...	...	...	...	6	...	...	6	...	...	...	...
Connecticut	12	2	...	...	7	3	...	2	3	7	1	...	11	...	...
Delaware	6	6	...	...	...	...	...	6	...	...	6	...	...	...	...
Florida	8	4	4	...	...	...	...	8	...	...	...	...	8	...	...
Georgia	22	9	4	6	2	...	1	14	7	1	...	...	22	...	...
Idaho	2	2	...	...	...	...	...	2	...	...	...	...	...	...	...
Illinois	42	32	...	...	5	3	2	35	2	5	42	...	...	...	...
Indiana	30	...	30	...	...	...	...	...	25	5	2	20	7	1	...
Iowa	22	21	...	...	...	1	...	22	...	...	22	...	...	...	...
Kansas	10	10	...	...	...	...	...	10	...	...	5	2	...	...	3
Kentucky	24	...	...	...	24	...	...	...	24	...	...	...	...	24	...
Louisiana	16	6	10	...	...	...	...	14	2	...	8	2	...	...	6
Maine	14	14	...	...	...	...	...	14	...	...	14	...	...	...	...
Maryland	16	16	...	...	...	...	...	16	...	...	...	...	16	...	...
Massachusetts	26	5	...	...	19	...	2	5	21	...	25	...	1	...	...
Michigan	22	...	...	...	...	22	...	...	22	...	22	...	...	...	...
Minnesota	10	9	...	...	...	...	1	9	1	...	10	...	...	...	...
Mississippi	16	1	5	2	4	4	...	...	16	...	1	15	...	...	...
Missouri	30	18	7	...	3	2	...	20	10	...	4	...	26	...	...
Montana	2	1	...	...	...	1	...	...	2	...	...	...	...	...	...
Nebraska	6	6	...	...	...	...	...	6	...	...	6	...	...	...	...
Nevada	6	...	...	2	2	1	1	...	6	...	...	6	...	...	...
New Hampshire	10	7	...	...	3	...	...	7	3	...	10	...	...	...	...
New Jersey	18	12	...	...	...	6	...	12	6	...	...	...	...	...	18
New Mexico	2	2	...	...	...	1	...	2	...	...	...	...	...	...	...
New York	70	...	...	68	2	...	...	9	61	...	70	...	...	...	...
North Carolina	20	12	1	...	...	1	6	...	20	...	20	...	...	...	...
North Dakota	*2	2	...	...	...	...	...	2	...	...	...	...	...	...	...
Ohio	44	...	...	...	...	44	...	...	44	...	44	...	...	...	...
Oklahoma	...	...	...	...	...	...	...	...	...	...	...	...	...	...	...
Oregon	6	6	...	...	...	...	...	6	...	...	6	...	...	...	...
Pennsylvania	58	14	...	...	...	...	44	30	28	...	...	...	...	...	58
Rhode Island	8	2	...	...	6	...	...	2	6	...	8	...	...	...	...
South Carolina	14	10	2	...	1	1	...	7	7	...	12	...	...	...	2
South Dakota	*	...	...	...	...	...	...	...	...	...	...	...	...	...	...
Tennessee	24	7	1	...	12	4	...	6	18	...	...	...	...	...	...
Texas	16	2	4	1	1	7	1	1	15	...	...	...	...	...	...
Utah	2	2	...	...	...	...	...	2	...	...	...	...	...	...	...
Vermont	10	...	...	...	8	2	...	...	10	...	...	...	...	...	...
Virginia	22	13	4	...	3	2	...	14	8	...	...	...	...	...	...
Washington	2	2	...	...	...	...	...	2	...	...	...	...	...	...	...
West Virginia	10	6	...	...	...	4	...	6	4	...	...	...	...	...	...
Wisconsin	20	16	1	...	3	...	...	16	4	...	...	...	...	...	...
Wyoming	2	...	...	...	2	...	...	...	2	...	...	...	...	...	...
Alaska	...	...	...	...	...	...	...	...	...	...	...	...	...	...	...
Canal Zone	...	...	...	...	...	...	...	...	...	...	...	...	...	...	...
District of Columbia	2	1	1	...	...	...	...	2	...	...	...	...	...	...	...
Hawaii	...	...	...	...	...	...	...	...	...	...	...	...	...	...	...
Philippine Islands	...	...	...	...	...	...	...	...	...	...	...	...	...	...	...
Puerto Rico	...	...	...	...	...	...	...	...	...	...	...	...	...	...	...
Virgin Islands	...	...	...	...	...	...	...	...	...	...	...	...	...	...	...
Total	756	308	85	81	111	113	58a	351	384	21b	366	70	86	25	89

Source: *Official Proceedings, 1876.*
Sixth ballot, pp. 105-6.
a/ Other candidates: Hartranft, 50; Washburne, 4;
Wheeler, 2; not voting, 2.
Seventh ballot, pp. 108-9.
b/ Other candidates: Bristow, 21.
Vice-Presidential. First ballot, pp. 110-2.

* Dakota Territory, 2 votes.

1880 REPUBLICAN

Delegation	Votes	Substitute Credentials for Rules Report			Support Nominee			Minority Report, Alabama Credentials			Motion to Adjourn		Minority Report, Illinois 1st Dist.			Majority Report, Illinois 1st Dist.		
		Yea	Nay	Not Voting	Yea	Nay	Not Voting	Yea	Nay	Not Voting	Yea	Nay	Yea	Nay	Not Voting	Yea	Nay	Not Voting
Alabama	20	19	1	...	20	...	...	17	3	...	7	13	16	4	...	4	16	...
Arizona	2	...	2	...	2	...	...	...	2	...	...	2	...	2	...	2	...	...
Arkansas	12	12	...	...	12	...	...	12	...	...	...	12	12	...	...	...	12	...
California	12	...	12	...	12	...	...	...	12	...	...	12	...	12	...	12	...	...
Colorado	6	6	...	...	6	...	...	6	...	...	...	6	6	...	...	...	6	...
Connecticut	12	...	12	...	12	...	...	...	12	...	4	8	...	10	2	10	...	2
Delaware	6	...	6	...	6	...	...	...	6	...	...	6	...	6	...	6	...	...
Florida	8	8	...	...	8	...	...	8	...	...	8	...	8	...	...	...	8	...
Georgia	22	6	16	...	22	...	...	6	16	...	1	21	6	16	...	16	6	...
Idaho	2	...	2	...	...	...	2	...	2	...	...	2	...	2	...	2	...	...
Illinois	42	42	...	...	42	...	...	42	...	...	...	42	40	...	2	...	40	2
Indiana	30	6	23	1	30	...	...	4	26	...	...	30	5	25	...	25	5	...
Iowa	22	...	22	...	22	...	...	...	22	...	...	22	...	22	...	22	...	...
Kansas	10	...	10	...	10	...	...	...	10	...	...	10	...	...	10	...	...	10
Kentucky	24	20	4	...	24	...	...	20	4	...	...	24	21	3	...	3	21	...
Louisiana	16	...	...	16	...	...	16	8	8	...	...	16	8	8	...	8	8	...
Maine	14	...	14	...	14	...	...	...	14	...	...	14	...	14	...	14	...	...
Maryland	16	7	8	1	16	...	...	7	9	...	2	14	8	8	...	8	8	...
Massachusetts	26	7	17	2	26	...	...	2	23	1	26	...	4	22	...	22	4	...
Michigan	22	1	21	...	22	...	...	1	21	...	...	22	1	21	...	21	1	...
Minnesota	10	3	6	1	10	...	...	2	8	...	...	10	4	6	...	4	6	...
Mississippi	16	8	7	1	16	...	...	7	9	...	5	11	11	5	...	4	12	...
Missouri	30	29	1	...	30	...	...	29	1	...	...	30	29	1	...	1	29	...
Montana	2	...	2	...	...	...	2	...	2	...	...	2	...	2	...	2	...	...
Nebraska	6	...	6	...	6	...	...	...	6	...	...	6	...	6	...	6	...	...
Nevada	6	...	6	...	6	...	...	...	6	...	...	6	...	6	...	6	...	...
New Hampshire	10	...	10	...	10	...	...	...	10	...	...	10	...	10	...	10	...	...
New Jersey	18	...	18	...	18	...	...	...	18	...	...	18	...	18	...	18	...	...
New Mexico	2	...	2	...	2	...	...	...	2	...	...	2	...	2	...	2	...	...
New York	70	47	23	...	70	...	...	47	23	...	1	69	47	22	1	22	47	1
North Carolina	20	5	15	...	20	...	...	...	20	...	5	15	19	1	...	1	19	...
North Dakota	*2	1	1	...	2	...	...	1	1	...	1	1	.1	1	...	1	1	...
Ohio	44	3	41	...	44	...	...	...	44	...	22	22	16	28	...	28	16	...
Oklahoma	...	...	...	...	...	...	...	...	...	...	...	...	...	...	...	...	...	...
Oregon	6	...	6	...	...	6	...	...	6	...	...	6	...	6	...	6	...	...
Pennsylvania	58	31	23	4	58	...	...	35	23	...	...	58	34	24	...	24	34	...
Rhode Island	8	...	8	...	8	...	...	...	8	...	...	8	...	8	...	8	...	...
South Carolina	14	7	5	2	1	...	13	9	5	...	...	14	10	4	...	4	10	...
South Dakota	*																	
Tennessee	24	16	7	1	24	...	...	16	8	...	1	23	16	8	...	8	16	...
Texas	16	9	7	...	16	...	...	9	7	...	11	5	11	4	1	4	11	1
Utah	2	...	2	...	2	...	...	...	2	...	...	2	...	2	...	2	...	...
Vermont	10	10	...	...	10	...	...	4	6	...	...	10	4	6	...	6	4	...
Virginia	22	11	8	3	22	...	...	12	10	...	...	22	13	9	...	9	13	...
Washington	2	...	2	...	...	...	2	...	2	...	...	2	...	2	...	2	...	...
West Virginia	10	...	10	...	5	3	2	...	10	...	...	10	...	10	...	10	...	...
Wisconsin	20	2	18	...	20	...	...	1	19	...	1	19	1	19	...	19	1	...
Wyoming	2	...	2	...	2	...	...	1	1	...	...	2	1	1	...	1	1	...
Alaska	...	...	...	...	...	...	...	...	...	...	...	...	...	...	...	...	...	...
Canal Zone	...	...	...	...	...	...	...	...	...	...	...	...	...	...	...	...	...	...
District of Columbia	2	2	...	...	...	...	2	...	2	...	...	2	1	1	...	1	1	...
Hawaii	...	...	...	...	...	...	...	...	...	...	...	...	...	...	...	...	...	...
Philippine Islands	...	...	...	...	...	...	...	...	...	...	...	...	...	...	...	...	...	...
Puerto Rico	...	...	...	...	...	...	...	...	...	...	...	...	...	...	...	...	...	...
Virgin Islands	...	...	...	...	...	...	...	...	...	...	...	...	...	...	...	...	...	...
Total	756	318	406	32	714a	3	39	306	449	1	95b	661c	353	387	16	384	356	16

Source: *Official Proceedings, 1880.*
Substitute credentials for rules report, p. 31.
Support nominee, p. 35.
a/ Sum of column; proceedings record 716.
Minority report, Alabama credentials, p. 91.
Motion to adjourn, p. 119.
b/ Sum of column; proceedings record 103.
c/ Sum of column; proceedings record 653.
Minority report, Illinois 1st District, p. 120.
Majority report, Illinois 1st District, p. 121.

* Dakota Territory, 2 votes.

Delegation	Votes	Majority Report, Illinois 3rd Dist.			Majority Report, Illinois 4th Dist.			Majority Report, Kansas Credentials			Minority Report, West Virginia Credentials			Minority Report, Utah Credentials		
		Yea	Nay	Not Voting	Yea	Nay	Not Voting	Yea	Nay	Not Voting	Yea	Nay	Not Voting	Yea	Nay	Not Voting
Alabama	20	4	16	...	4	16	...	5	15	...	14	4	2	16	4	...
Arizona	2	2	...	...	2	...	...	2	...	...	...	2	...	...	2	...
Arkansas	12	...	12	...	...	12	...	...	12	...	12	...	...	12	...	...
California	12	12	...	...	12	...	...	12	...	...	...	12	...	...	12	...
Colorado	6	6	...	...	...	6	...	...	6	...	6	...	...	...	6	...
Connecticut	12	10	...	2	11	...	1	12	...	...	3	8	1	9	2	1
Delaware	6	6	...	...	6	...	...	6	...	...	...	6	...	6	...	...
Florida	8	...	8	...	...	8	...	...	8	...	8	...	...	8	...	...
Georgia	22	16	6	...	16	6	...	22	...	...	19	2	1	6	7	9
Idaho	2	2	...	...	2	...	...	2	...	...	...	2	...	...	2	...
Illinois	42	2	38	2	4	36	2	18	24	...	25	17	...	24	18	...
Indiana	30	25	5	...	25	5	...	27	3	...	8	22	...	4	26	...
Iowa	22	22	...	...	22	...	...	22	...	...	...	22	...	...	22	...
Kansas	10	...	...	10	...	...	10	5	5	...	4	6	...	4	6	...
Kentucky	24	3	21	...	3	21	...	4	20	...	20	4	...	22	2	...
Louisiana	16	8	8	...	8	8	...	16	...	...	4	12	...	6	10	...
Maine	14	14	...	...	14	...	...	14	...	...	...	14	...	...	14	...
Maryland	16	8	8	...	8	8	...	11	5	...	16	...	...	11	5	...
Massachusetts	26	22	4	...	22	4	...	24	1	1	26	...	...	26	...	...
Michigan	22	20	...	2	20	...	2	21	1	...	1	21	...	11	10	1
Minnesota	10	4	6	...	4	6	...	5	4	1	4	6	...	6	4	...
Mississippi	16	4	12	...	4	12	...	7	2	7	11	5	...	13	3	3
Missouri	30	1	29	...	1	29	...	1	...	29	30	...	...	29	...	1
Montana	2	2	...	...	2	...	...	2	...	...	...	2	...	...	2	...
Nebraska	6	6	...	...	6	...	...	6	...	...	...	6	...	...	6	...
Nevada	6	6	...	...	6	...	...	6	...	...	...	6	...	...	6	...
New Hampshire	10	10	...	...	10	...	...	10	...	...	...	10	...	...	10	...
New Jersey	18	18	...	...	18	...	...	18	...	...	...	18	...	...	18	...
New Mexico	2	2	...	...	2	...	...	2	...	...	...	2	...	...	2	...
New York	70	22	47	1	22	47	1	22	...	48	49	20	1	50	19	1
North Carolina	20	1	19	...	1	19	...	20	...	...	20	...	...	20	...	...
North Dakota	*2	1	1	...	1	1	...	1	1	...	...	2	...	1	1	...
Ohio	44	28	16	...	28	16	...	44	...	...	28	16	...	33	10	1
Oklahoma	...	...	...	...	...	...	...	...	...	...	...	...	...	...	...	...
Oregon	6	6	...	...	6	...	...	6	...	...	...	6	...	...	6	...
Pennsylvania	58	24	34	...	24	34	...	25	33	...	33	25	...	28	30	...
Rhode Island	8	8	...	...	8	...	...	8	...	...	...	8	...	...	8	...
South Carolina	14	4	10	...	4	10	...	3	11	...	11	3	...	11	3	...
South Dakota	*	...	...	...	...	...	...	...	...	...	...	...	...	...	...	...
Tennessee	24	8	16	...	8	16	...	8	16	...	16	8	...	19	5	...
Texas	16	4	11	1	4	11	1	4	11	1	11	3	2	11	4	1
Utah	2	2	...	...	2	...	...	2	...	...	10	2	...	10	...	2
Vermont	10	6	4	...	6	4	...	9	1	...	10	...	...	10	...	...
Virginia	22	9	13	...	9	13	...	11	2	9	16	6	...	10	12	...
Washington	2	2	...	...	2	...	...	2	...	...	...	2	...	1	1	...
West Virginia	10	10	...	...	10	...	...	10	...	...	...	8	2	1	8	1
Wisconsin	20	19	1	...	19	1	...	19	1	...	10	10	...	17	3	...
Wyoming	2	1	1	...	1	1	...	1	1	...	1	1	...	...	2	...
Alaska	...	...	...	...	...	...	...	...	...	...	...	...	...	...	...	...
Canal Zone	...	...	...	...	...	...	...	...	...	...	...	...	...	...	...	...
District of Columbia	2	1	1	...	1	1	...	1	1	...	1	1	...	1	1	...
Hawaii	...	...	...	...	...	...	...	...	...	...	...	...	...	...	...	...
Philippine Islands	...	...	...	...	...	...	...	...	...	...	...	...	...	...	...	...
Puerto Rico	...	...	...	...	...	...	...	...	...	...	...	...	...	...	...	...
Virgin Islands	...	...	...	...	...	...	...	...	...	...	...	...	...	...	...	...
Total	756	391[a]	347[b]	18	388	351	17	476	184	96	417	330	9	426	312	18

Source: *Official Proceedings, 1880.*
Majority report, Illinois 3rd District, p. 123.
a/ Sum of column; proceedings record 385.
b/ Sum of column; proceedings record 353.
Majority report, Illinois 4th District, p. 124.
Majority report, Kansas credentials, p. 135.
Minority report, West Virginia credentials, p. 143.
Minority report, Utah credentials, p. 150.

* Dakota Territory, 2 votes.

1880 REPUBLICAN

Delegation	Votes	Time Limit on Speeches Yea	Nay	Not Voting	First Ballot Grant	Blaine	Sherman	Other	Eleventh Ballot Grant	Blaine	Sherman	Other	Twenty-first Ballot Grant	Blaine	Sherman	Other
Alabama	20	15	5	...	16	1	3	...	17	...	3	...	16	1	3	...
Arizona	2	...	2	...	...	2	...	...	...	2	...	...	...	2	...	...
Arkansas	12	12	...	...	12	...	...	...	12	...	...	...	12	...	...	...
California	12	...	12	...	...	12	...	...	...	12	...	...	...	12	...	...
Colorado	6	6	...	...	6	...	...	...	6	...	...	...	6	...	...	...
Connecticut	12	...	12	...	...	3	...	9	...	3	...	9	...	3	...	9
Delaware	6	...	6	...	...	6	...	...	...	6	...	...	...	6	...	...
Florida	8	8	...	...	8	...	...	...	7	1	...	...	8	...	...	...
Georgia	22	6	16	...	6	8	8	...	6	8	8	...	7	7	8	...
Idaho	2	...	2	...	...	2	...	...	...	2	...	...	...	2	...	...
Illinois	42	24	18	...	24	10	...	8	24	10	...	8	24	10	...	8
Indiana	30	...	30	...	1	26	2	1	2	27	...	1	2	21	3	4
Iowa	22	...	22	...	...	22	...	...	...	22	...	...	...	22	...	...
Kansas	10	4	6	...	4	6	...	...	4	6	...	...	4	6	...	...
Kentucky	24	20	4	...	20	1	3	...	20	1	3	...	20	2	2	...
Louisiana	16	2	14	...	8	2	6	...	8	2	6	...	8	2	6	...
Maine	14	...	14	...	...	14	...	...	...	14	...	...	...	14	...	...
Maryland	16	7	9	...	7	7	2	...	8	5	2	1	7	5	4	...
Massachusetts	26	4	22	...	3	...	2	21	4	...	2	20	4	...	2	20
Michigan	22	1	21	...	1	21	...	...	1	21	...	...	1	21	...	...
Minnesota	10	...	10	...	...	...	...	10	...	...	...	10	...	...	...	10
Mississippi	16	5	11	...	6	4	6	...	6	4	6	...	6	4	6	...
Missouri	30	29	1	...	29	...	...	1	29	...	...	1	29	...	...	1
Montana	2	...	2	...	...	2	...	...	...	2	...	...	...	2	...	...
Nebraska	6	...	6	...	...	6	...	...	...	6	...	...	...	6	...	...
Nevada	6	...	6	...	...	6	...	...	...	6	...	...	...	6	...	...
New Hampshire	10	...	10	...	...	10	...	...	...	10	...	...	...	10	...	...
New Jersey	18	...	18	...	...	16	...	2	...	16	...	2	...	16	...	2
New Mexico	2	...	2	...	...	2	...	...	...	2	...	...	...	2	...	...
New York	70	48	22	...	51	17	2	...	51	17	2	...	50	18	2	...
North Carolina	20	4	16	...	6	...	14	...	5	...	15	...	5	...	15	...
North Dakota	*2	...	2	...	1	1	...	...	1	1	...	...	1	1	...	...
Ohio	44	...	44	...	...	9	34	1	...	9	34	1	...	9	34	1
Oklahoma	...	...	...	...	...	...	...	...	...	...	...	...	...	...	...	...
Oregon	6	...	6	...	...	6	...	...	...	6	...	...	...	6	...	...
Pennsylvania	58	31	27	...	32	23	3	...	34	22	1	1	34	21	1	2
Rhode Island	8	...	8	...	...	8	...	...	...	8	...	...	...	8	...	...
South Carolina	14	9	5	...	13	...	1	...	12	1	1	...	12	1	1	...
South Dakota	*	...	...	...	...	...	...	...	...	...	...	...	...	...	...	...
Tennessee	24	16	8	...	16	6	1	1	16	6	1	1	17	5	1	1
Texas	16	11	5	...	11	2	2	1	12	1	2	1	12	2	1	1
Utah	2	...	2	...	1	1	...	...	1	1	...	...	1	1	...	...
Vermont	10	...	10	...	...	...	...	10	...	...	...	10	...	...	...	10
Virginia	22	12	10	...	18	3	1	...	15	2	4	1	16	3	3	...
Washington	2	...	2	...	...	2	...	...	...	2	...	...	...	2	...	...
West Virginia	10	1	8	1	1	8	...	1	1	8	...	1	1	8	...	1
Wisconsin	20	1	19	...	1	7	3	9	1	7	3	9	1	7	3	9
Wyoming	2	...	2	...	1	1	...	...	1	1	...	...	1	1	...	...
Alaska	...	...	...	...	...	...	...	...	...	...	...	...	...	...	...	...
Canal Zone	...	...	...	...	...	...	...	...	...	...	...	...	...	...	...	...
District of Columbia	2	...	2	...	1	1	...	...	1	1	...	...	...	1	1	...
Hawaii	...	...	...	...	...	...	...	...	...	...	...	...	...	...	...	...
Philippine Islands	...	...	...	...	...	...	...	...	...	...	...	...	...	...	...	...
Puerto Rico	...	...	...	...	...	...	...	...	...	...	...	...	...	...	...	...
Virgin Islands	...	...	...	...	...	...	...	...	...	...	...	...	...	...	...	...
Total	756	276	479	1	304	284	93	75a	305	281	93	77b	305	276	96	79c

Source: *Official Proceedings, 1880.*

Time limit on speeches, p. 158.

Presidential. First ballot, p. 198.

a/ Other candidates: George F. Edmunds, 34; Elihu B. Washburne, 30; William Windom, 10; not voting, 1.

Eleventh ballot, pp. 218-9.

b/ Other candidates: Washburne, 32; Edmunds, 31; Windom, 10; James A. Garfield, 2; Rutherford B. Hayes, 1; not voting, 1.

Twenty-first ballot, pp. 237-8.

c/ Other candidates: Washburne, 35; Edmunds, 31; Windom, 10; Garfield, 1; John F. Hartranft, 1; not voting, 1.

* Dakota Territory, 2 votes.

| Delegation | Votes | 1888 REPUBLICAN Presidential Fourth Ballot | | | | | | Fifth Ballot | | | | | | Motion to Adjourn | | |
		Alger	Allison	Gresham	Harrison	Sherman	Other	Alger	Allison	Gresham	Harrison	Sherman	Other	Yea	Nay	Not Voting
Alabama	20	10	...	...	1	8	1	8	...	...	2	9	1	16	4	...
Arizona	2	2	...	...	...	...	...	2	...	...	...	...	...	2	...	...
Arkansas	14	14	...	...	...	...	...	14	...	...	...	...	...	14	...	...
California	16	...	...	...	...	...	16	...	...	...	...	...	16	16	...	...
Colorado	6	...	2	3	1	...	...	...	6	...	...	...	...	6	...	...
Connecticut	12	1	6	4	...	...	1	2	6	3	...	...	1	6	5	1
Delaware	6	...	...	1	5	...	...	...	1	1	3	...	1	2	4	...
Florida	8	4	...	...	2	2	...	5	...	...	1	2	...	8	...	...
Georgia	24	...	...	1	2	19	2	...	...	1	2	20	1	22	1	1
Idaho	2	1	...	...	1	...	...	...	1	1	...	...	...	...	2	...
Illinois	44	...	...	41	3	...	...	...	...	41	3	...	...	37	7	...
Indiana	30	...	...	...	30	...	...	...	...	1	29	...	...	...	30	...
Iowa	26	...	26	...	...	...	...	...	26	...	...	...	...	26	...	...
Kansas	18	...	2	3	8	...	5	...	2	3	8	...	5	18	...	...
Kentucky	26	3	2	2	6	10	3	8	...	2	8	7	1	4	16	6
Louisiana	16	3	2	2	...	9	...	3	2	2	...	9	...	16	...	...
Maine	12	3	4	1	2	2	...	3	5	1	2	1	...	12	...	...
Maryland	16	...	2	...	8	6	...	...	4	...	6	6	...	14	2	...
Massachusetts	28	8	2	1	8	7	2	4	3	1	10	5	5	14	12	2
Michigan	26	26	...	...	...	...	...	26	...	...	...	...	...	26	...	...
Minnesota	14	2	...	5	7	...	...	3	...	3	7	...	1	...	14	...
Mississippi	18	...	...	3	...	14	1	...	...	2	...	15	1	14	3	1
Missouri	32	13	1	11	3	2	2	14	1	10	2	1	4	15	13	4
Montana	2	...	1	1	...	...	...	...	1	1	...	...	...	2	...	...
Nebraska	10	2	5	...	...	3	...	2	5	...	...	3	...	10	...	...
Nevada	6	4	2	...	...	...	...	4	2	...	...	...	...	6	...	...
New Hampshire	8	1	1	1	5	...	...	...	...	...	8	...	...	1	7	...
New Jersey	18	...	3	2	7	2	4	...	5	2	4	1	6	18	...	...
New Mexico	2	1	...	...	...	1	...	1	...	...	...	1	...	...	2	...
New York	72	3	1	...	58	1	9	5	1	...	58	1	7	...	72	...
North Carolina	22	6	...	1	2	13	...	9	...	...	2	11	...	12	10	...
North Dakota	*10	...	3	1	4	2	...	...	3	1	5	1	...	...	10	...
Ohio	46	...	...	...	...	46	...	...	...	...	...	46	...	38	8	...
Oklahoma	...															
Oregon	6	...	...	4	1	...	1	...	...	4	1	...	1	...	6	...
Pennsylvania	60	...	...	...	7	53	...	...	...	...	7	53	...	55	5	...
Rhode Island	8	...	8	...	...	...	...	...	8	...	...	...	...	6	2	...
South Carolina	18	10	...	...	2	6	...	10	...	...	2	6	...	18	...	...
South Dakota	*															
Tennessee	24	9	1	...	2	8	4	10	1	...	2	5	6	17	4	3
Texas	26	3	9	3	1	7	3	2	11	3	2	7	1	26	...	...
Utah	2	...	2	...	...	...	...	...	2	...	...	...	...	2	...	...
Vermont	8	...	...	...	8	...	...	...	...	...	8	...	...	...	8	...
Virginia	24	3	3	...	8	10	...	3	3	...	6	10	2	10	14	...
Washington	6	2	...	3	1	...	...	3	...	2	1	...	...	2	4	...
West Virginia	12	1	...	2	3	2	4	2	...	...	3	2	5	1	9	2
Wisconsin	22	...	...	2	20	...	...	...	...	2	20	...	...	4	18	...
Wyoming	2	...	...	...	...	2	...	...	...	...	...	2	...	...	2	...
Alaska	...															
Canal Zone	...															
District of Columbia	2	...	...	...	...	...	2	...	...	...	...	...	2	2	...	...
Hawaii	...															
Philippine Islands	...															
Puerto Rico	...															
Virgin Islands	...															
Total	832	135	88	98	216	235	60a	143	99	87	212	224	67b	492	320	20

Source: *Official Proceedings, 1888.*

Fourth ballot, pp. 174-8.
a/ Other candidates: Blaine, 42; McKinley, 11; Lincoln, 1; Joseph B. Foraker, 1; Frederick Douglass, 1; not voting, 4.
Fifth ballot, pp. 179-80.
b/ Other candidates: Blaine, 48; McKinley, 14; not voting, 5.
Motion to adjourn, p. 184.

* Dakota Territory, 10 votes.

Delegation	Votes	Second Ballot							Third Ballot							Motion to Adjourn		
		Alger	Allison	Depew	Gresham	Harrison	Sherman	Other	Alger	Allison	Depew	Gresham	Harrison	Sherman	Other	Yea	Nay	Not Voting
Alabama	20	7	...	1	...	1	11	...	7	...	1	...	2	10	...	19	1	...
Arizona	2	2	...	...	...	...	...	...	2	...	...	...	...	...	...	2	...	...
Arkansas	14	14	...	...	...	...	...	...	14	...	...	...	...	...	...	14	...	...
California	16	...	...	...	...	...	...	16	...	...	...	...	...	...	16	16	...	...
Colorado	6	...	1	...	3	2	...	...	...	1	...	5	...	...	...	6	...	...
Connecticut	12	1	4	6	1	...	...	...	1	5	...	6	...	...	...	4	8	...
Delaware	6	...	...	...	...	6	...	...	...	...	1	...	5	...	...	...	6	...
Florida	8	3	...	...	...	1	4	...	3	...	...	...	1	4	...	3	4	1
Georgia	24	...	...	...	1	2	19	2	...	...	...	2	2	18	2	21	1	2
Idaho	2	...	1	...	1	...	...	...	...	1	...	1	...	...	...	2	...	...
Illinois	44	...	...	...	44	...	...	...	...	...	...	44	...	...	...	30	12	2
Indiana	30	...	...	...	2	28	...	...	...	...	...	2	28	...	...	...	30	...
Iowa	26	...	26	...	...	...	...	...	...	26	...	...	...	...	...	26	...	...
Kansas	18	...	...	...	...	...	...	18	...	4	...	5	2	2	5	18	...	...
Kentucky	26	3	...	1	6	2	11	3	4	2	1	4	4	9	2	14	10	2
Louisiana	16	3	2	1	1	...	9	...	3	2	1	1	...	9	...	16	...	...
Maine	12	3	2	3	1	2	1	...	3	2	3	1	2	1	...	12	...	...
Maryland	16	...	3	...	1	6	6	...	...	4	...	1	6	5	...	8	8	...
Massachusetts	28	7	1	1	2	5	9	3	6	3	1	1	4	9	4	21	7	...
Michigan	26	26	...	...	...	...	...	...	26	...	...	...	...	...	...	25	1	...
Minnesota	14	1	...	2	11	...	...	...	1	...	2	11	...	...	...	10	4	...
Mississippi	18	...	...	1	3	...	14	...	...	...	1	3	...	14	...	18	...	...
Missouri	32	10	1	2	9	3	6	1	11	2	2	9	2	4	2	21	11	...
Montana	2	...	1	...	1	...	...	...	...	1	...	1	...	...	...	2	...	...
Nebraska	10	2	4	...	...	...	3	1	2	5	...	...	...	3	...	10	...	...
Nevada	6	3	3	...	...	...	...	...	4	2	...	...	...	...	...	6	...	...
New Hampshire	8	...	...	4	...	4	...	...	...	...	4	4	...	...	...	...	8	...
New Jersey	18	...	...	...	...	...	...	18	...	4	1	...	4	2	7	7	11	...
New Mexico	2	1	...	...	...	...	1	...	1	...	...	...	1	...	...	...	2	...
New York	72	...	...	71	...	...	...	1	...	...	71	...	...	...	1	10	61	1
North Carolina	22	4	...	...	...	2	15	1	5	...	...	1	15	...	1	19	3	...
North Dakota	*10	...	1	2	2	3	1	1	...	1	1	3	3	2	...	...	10	...
Ohio	46	...	...	...	...	...	46	...	...	...	...	...	...	46	...	46	...	...
Oklahoma	...	...	...	...	...	...	...	...	...	...	...	...	...	...	...	...	...	...
Oregon	6	...	...	...	4	1	...	1	...	...	...	4	1	...	1	3	3	...
Pennsylvania	60	2	...	1	...	4	53	...	1	...	1	5	...	53	...	50	10	...
Rhode Island	8	...	8	...	...	...	...	...	...	8	...	...	...	...	...	8	...	...
South Carolina	18	7	...	2	...	...	9	...	11	...	...	...	1	6	...	12	6	...
South Dakota	*	...	...	...	...	...	...	...	...	...	...	...	...	...	...	...	...	...
Tennessee	24	8	3	1	1	2	7	2	9	3	1	1	...	7	3	15	7	2
Texas	26	3	8	...	5	1	6	3	2	7	...	5	1	6	5	11	12	3
Utah	2	...	2	...	...	...	...	...	...	2	...	...	...	...	...	2	...	...
Vermont	8	...	...	...	...	8	...	...	...	...	...	8	...	...	...	...	8	...
Virginia	24	4	3	...	1	5	11	...	4	3	...	2	5	10	...	10	13	1
Washington	6	1	1	...	3	1	...	...	1	...	...	4	1	...	...	3	3	...
West Virginia	12	1	...	...	2	2	5	2	1	...	...	2	1	5	3	7	5	...
Wisconsin	22	...	...	...	3	...	...	19	...	...	...	4	1	1	16	...	22	...
Wyoming	2	...	...	...	...	...	2	...	...	...	...	...	2	...	...	2	...	...
Alaska	...	...	...	...	...	...	...	...	...	...	...	...	...	...	...	...	...	...
Canal Zone	...	...	...	...	...	...	...	...	...	...	...	...	...	...	...	...	...	...
District of Columbia	2	...	...	...	...	...	...	2	...	...	...	...	...	...	2	2	...	...
Hawaii	...	...	...	...	...	...	...	...	...	...	...	...	...	...	...	...	...	...
Philippine Islands	...	...	...	...	...	...	...	...	...	...	...	...	...	...	...	...	...	...
Puerto Rico	...	...	...	...	...	...	...	...	...	...	...	...	...	...	...	...	...	...
Virgin Islands	...	...	...	...	...	...	...	...	...	...	...	...	...	...	...	...	...	...
Total	832	116	75	99	108	91	249	94a	122	88	91	123	94	244	70b	531	287	14

Source: *Official Proceedings, 1888.*

Second ballot, pp. 160-3.

a/ Other candidates: Blaine, 33; Rusk, 20; Phelps, 18; Ingalls, 16; McKinley, 3; Lincoln, 2; not voting, 2.

Third ballot, pp. 163-7.

b/ Other candidates: Blaine, 35; Rusk, 16; McKinley, 8; Phelps, 5; Lincoln, 2; Samuel F. Miller, 2; not voting, 2.

Motion to adjourn, pp. 168-71.

* Dakota Territory, 10 votes.

1884 REPUBLICAN

Delegation	Votes	First Ballot				Second Ballot				Third Ballot			Motion to Adjourn			Presidential Fourth Ballot		
		Arthur	Blaine	Edmunds	Other	Arthur	Blaine	Edmunds	Other	Arthur	Blaine	Other	Yea	Nay	Not Voting	Arthur	Blaine	Other
Alabama	20	17	1	...	2	17	2	...	1	17	2	1	17	3	...	12	8	...
Arizona	2	...	2	...	...	...	2	...	...	...	2	...	...	2	...	...	2	...
Arkansas	14	4	8	2	...	3	11	...	...	3	11	...	3	11	...	3	11	...
California	16	...	16	...	...	...	16	...	...	...	16	...	...	16	...	...	16	...
Colorado	6	...	6	...	...	...	6	...	...	...	6	...	...	6	...	...	6	...
Connecticut	12	...	...	...	12	...	...	...	12	...	...	12	12	...	...	...	...	12
Delaware	6	1	5	...	...	1	5	...	...	1	5	...	1	5	...	1	5	...
Florida	8	7	1	...	...	7	1	...	...	7	1	...	5	3	...	5	3	...
Georgia	24	24	...	...	...	24	...	...	...	24	...	...	24	...	...	24	...	...
Idaho	2	2	...	...	...	2	...	...	...	1	1	...	...	2	...	...	2	...
Illinois	44	1	3	...	40	1	3	...	40	1	3	40	31	13	...	3	34	7
Indiana	30	9	18	1	2	9	18	1	2	10	18	2	8	22	...	...	30	...
Iowa	26	...	26	...	...	...	26	...	...	...	26	...	2	24	...	2	24	...
Kansas	18	4	12	...	2	2	13	...	3	...	15	3	...	18	...	...	18	...
Kentucky	26	16	5½	...	4½	17	5	...	4	16	6	4	18	8	...	15	9	2
Louisiana	16	10	2	...	4	9	4	...	3	9	4	3	7	8	1	7	9	...
Maine	12	...	12	...	...	...	12	...	...	...	12	...	...	12	...	...	12	...
Maryland	16	6	10	...	...	4	12	...	...	4	12	...	4	12	...	1	15	...
Massachusetts	28	2	1	25	...	3	1	24	...	3	1	24	23	5	...	7	3	18
Michigan	26	2	15	7	2	4	15	5	2	4	18	4	8	18	...	...	26	...
Minnesota	14	1	7	6	...	1	7	6	...	2	7	5	...	14	...	...	14	...
Mississippi	18	17	1	...	...	17	1	...	...	16	1	1	17	1	...	16	2	...
Missouri	32	10	5	6	11	10	7	5	10	11	12	9	10	22	...	...	32	...
Montana	2	...	1	1	...	...	1	1	...	...	1	1	1	1	...	...	2	...
Nebraska	10	2	8	...	...	2	8	...	...	...	10	...	...	10	...	...	10	...
Nevada	6	...	6	...	...	...	6	...	...	...	6	...	...	6	...	...	6	...
New Hampshire	8	4	...	4	...	...	5	...	3	...	5	3	8	...	...	2	3	3
New Jersey	18	...	9	6	3	...	9	6	3	1	11	6	5	13	...	...	17	1
New Mexico	2	2	...	...	...	2	...	...	...	2	...	...	2	...	...	2	...	...
New York	72	31	28	12	1	31	28	12	1	32	28	12	42	29	1	30	29	13
North Carolina	22	19	2	...	1	18	3	...	1	18	4	...	14	6	2	12	8	2
North Dakota	*2	...	2	...	...	...	2	...	...	...	2	...	...	2	...	...	2	...
Ohio	46	...	21	...	25	...	23	...	23	...	25	21	17	28	1	...	46	...
Oklahoma	...																	
Oregon	6	...	6	...	...	...	6	...	...	...	6	...	...	6	...	...	6	...
Pennsylvania	60	11	47	1	1	11	47	1	1	8	50	2	11	48	1	8	51	1
Rhode Island	8	...	...	8	...	...	...	8	...	...	...	8	7	1	...	1	7	...
South Carolina	18	17	1	...	...	17	1	...	...	16	2	...	16	2	...	15	2	1
South Dakota	*																	
Tennessee	24	16	7	...	1	16	7	...	1	17	7	...	12	12	...	12	11	1
Texas	26	11	13	...	2	11	13	...	2	11	14	1	10	16	...	8	15	3
Utah	2	2	...	...	...	2	...	...	...	2	...	...	2	...	...	...	2	...
Vermont	8	...	...	8	...	...	...	8	...	...	...	8	...	8	...	...	...	8
Virginia	24	21	2	...	1	21	2	...	1	20	4	...	20	4	...	20	4	...
Washington	2	...	2	...	...	...	2	...	...	...	2	...	...	2	...	...	2	...
West Virginia	12	...	12	...	...	...	12	...	...	...	12	...	...	12	...	...	12	...
Wisconsin	22	6	10	6	...	6	11	5	...	10	11	1	10	12	...	...	22	...
Wyoming	2	2	...	...	...	2	...	...	...	2	...	...	...	2	...	...	2	...
Alaska	...																	
Canal Zone	...																	
District of Columbia	2	1	1	...	...	1	1	...	...	1	1	...	1	1	...	1	1	...
Hawaii	...																	
Philippine Islands	...																	
Puerto Rico	...																	
Virgin Islands	...																	
Total	820	278	334½	93	114½a	276	349	85	110b	274	375	171c	356d	458e	6	207	541	72f

Source: *Official Proceedings, 1884.*

Presidential. First ballot, pp. 138-42.

a/ Other candidates: John A. Logan, 63½; John Sherman, 30; Joseph R. Hawley, 13; Robert T. Lincoln, 4; William T. Sherman, 2; not voting, 2.

Second ballot, pp. 142-7.

b/ Other candidates: Logan, 61; John Sherman, 28; Hawley, 13; Lincoln, 4; William T. Sherman, 3; not voting, 1.

Third ballot, pp. 148-50.

c/ Other candidates: Edmunds, 69; Logan, 53; John Sherman, 25; Hawley, 13; Lincoln, 8; William T. Sherman, 2; not voting, 1.

Motion to adjourn, pp. 151-5.

d/ Sum of column; proceedings record 364.

e/ Sum of column; proceedings record 450.

Fourth ballot, pp. 156-63.

f/ Other candidates: Edmunds, 41; Hawley, 15; Logan, 7; Lincoln, 2; not voting, 7.

* Dakota Territory, 2 votes.

	1884 REPUBLICAN Vice-Pres. First Ballot			1888 REPUBLICAN										
				Minority Report, Virginia Credentials				Presidential First Ballot						
Delegation	Votes	Logan	Other	Votes	Yea	Nay	Not Voting	Alger	Allison	Depew	Gresham	Harrison	Sherman	Other
Alabama	20	20	...	20	10	8	2	6	...	1	...	1	12	...
Arizona	2	2	...	2	...	2	...	2	...	...	...	...	...	...
Arkansas	14	14	...	14	...	14	...	...	...	...	1	1	2	10
California	16	16	...	16	...	16	...	...	...	...	...	...	...	16
Colorado	6	6	...	6	...	6	...	...	1	...	3	2	...	...
Connecticut	12	5	7	12	...	12	...	...	...	...	...	...	...	12
Delaware	6	6	...	6	...	6	...	...	...	...	...	6	...	...
Florida	8	8	...	8	4	4	...	...	...	...	...	1	4	3
Georgia	24	24	...	24	12½	4	7½	...	...	...	1	2	19	2
Idaho	2	2	...	2	...	2	...	...	1	...	1	...	...	...
Illinois	44	44	...	44	2	42	...	...	...	...	44	...	...	...
Indiana	30	30	...	30	...	30	...	...	...	...	1	29	...	...
Iowa	26	26	...	26	...	26	...	...	26	...	...	...	...	...
Kansas	18	18	...	18	...	18	...	...	...	...	...	...	...	18
Kentucky	26	26	...	26	1	25	...	4	...	1	5	4	12	...
Louisiana	16	16	...	16	9	7	...	2	3	1	1	...	9	...
Maine	12	12	...	12	...	12	...	3	2	3	1	2	1	...
Maryland	16	16	...	16	1	11	4	...	2	1	1	5	5	2
Massachusetts	28	12	16	28	6	19	3	6	2	1	2	4	9	4
Michigan	26	26	...	26	...	26	...	26	...	...	...	...	...	...
Minnesota	14	14	...	14	...	14	...	1	...	2	11	...	...	...
Mississippi	18	18	...	18	15	1	2	...	...	1	3	...	14	...
Missouri	32	30	2	32	4	23	5	6	3	2	11	3	6	1
Montana	2	2	...	2	...	2	...	...	1	...	1	...	...	...
Nebraska	10	10	...	10	6	4	...	2	3	...	1	...	3	1
Nevada	6	6	...	6	6	...	...	3	3	...	...	...	...	...
New Hampshire	8	8	...	8	...	3	5	...	...	4	...	4	...	...
New Jersey	18	18	...	18	4	12	2	...	...	...	...	...	...	18
New Mexico	2	2	...	2	...	2	...	1	...	...	...	...	...	1
New York	72	60	12	72	22	50	...	...	...	71	...	...	1	...
North Carolina	22	22	...	22	18	4	...	2	...	1	2	1	15	1
North Dakota	*2	2	...	*10	10	...	...	1	1	2	1	1	1	3
Ohio	46	46	...	46	19	19	8	...	...	...	...	...	46	...
Oklahoma	...	...	...	...	...	...	...	...	...	...	...	...	...	...
Oregon	6	6	...	6	...	6	...	...	...	...	4	1	...	1
Pennsylvania	60	59	1	60	56	4	...	1	...	5	...	...	29	25
Rhode Island	8	8	...	8	...	8	...	...	8	...	...	...	...	...
South Carolina	18	18	...	18	18	...	...	3	...	1	...	...	11	3
South Dakota	*	...	...	*	...	...	...	...	...	...	...	...	...	...
Tennessee	24	24	...	24	6	7	11	9	1	2	1	1	7	3
Texas	26	26	...	26	2	19	5	2	7	...	5	1	7	4
Utah	2	2	...	2	...	2	...	...	2	...	...	...	...	...
Vermont	8	8	...	8	...	8	...	...	...	...	...	8	...	...
Virginia	24	24	...	24	10	...	14	3	3	...	1	5	11	1
Washington	2	2	...	6	...	6	...	...	1	...	3	1	...	1
West Virginia	12	12	...	12	4	8	...	1	...	...	2	2	5	2
Wisconsin	22	19	3	22	3	19	...	...	...	...	...	...	...	22
Wyoming	2	2	...	2	1	1	...	...	2	...	...	...	...	...
Alaska	...	...	...	...	...	...	...	...	...	...	...	...	...	...
Canal Zone	...	...	...	...	...	...	...	...	...	...	...	...	...	...
District of Columbia	2	2	...	2	...	2	...	...	...	...	...	...	...	2
Hawaii	...	...	...	...	...	...	...	...	...	...	...	...	...	...
Philippine Islands	...	...	...	...	...	...	...	...	...	...	...	...	...	...
Puerto Rico	...	...	...	...	...	...	...	...	...	...	...	...	...	...
Virgin Islands	...	...	...	...	...	...	...	...	...	...	...	...	...	...
Total	820	779a	41b	832	249½	514	68½	84	72	99	107	85	229	156c

Source: *Official Proceedings, 1884.*
Vice-Presidential. First ballot, pp. 176-8.
a/ Sum of column; proceedings record 773.
b/ Other candidates: Walter Q. Gresham, 6; Joseph B. Foraker, 1; not voting, 34.

Source: *Official Proceedings, 1888.*
Minority report, Virginia credentials, p. 88.
Presidential. First ballot, pp. 152-60.
c/ Other candidates: James G. Blaine, 35; John J. Ingalls, 28; William W. Phelps, 25; Jeremiah M. Rusk, 25; Edwin H. Fitler, 24; Joseph R. Hawley, 13; Robert T. Lincoln, 3; William McKinley, 2; not voting, 1.

* Dakota Territory, 2 votes.

* Dakota Territory, 10 votes.

1896 REPUBLICAN

Delegation	Votes	Previous Question on Credentials			Table Minority Financial Plank		Majority Financial Plank			Presidential First Ballot						Vice-Presidential First Ballot		
		Yea	Nay	Not Voting	Yea	Nay	Yea	Nay	Not Voting	McKinley	Reed	Morton	Allison	Quay	Other	Hobart	Evans	Other
Alabama	22	19	3	...	15	7	19	3	...	19	2	1	...	...	...	10	11	1
Arizona	6	4	2	...	...	6	...	6	...	6	...	...	...	...	...	4	1	1
Arkansas	16	16	...	...	15	1	15	1	...	16	...	...	...	...	...	10	5	1
California	18	7	10	1	3	15	4	14	...	18	...	...	...	...	...	14	3	1
Colorado	8	...	8	...	...	8	...	8	...	...	...	...	...	...	8	...	...	8
Connecticut	12	...	12	...	12	...	12	...	...	7	5	...	...	...	...	...	...	12
Delaware	6	...	...	6	6	...	6	...	...	6	...	...	...	...	...	6	...	...
Florida	8	7	1	...	6	2	7	1	...	6	...	2	...	...	...	5	3	...
Georgia	26	20	6	...	23	3	25	1	...	22	2	...	...	2	...	5	21	...
Idaho	6	...	6	...	...	6	...	6	...	...	...	...	...	...	6	...	...	6
Illinois	48	30	18	...	47	1	46	2	...	46	2	...	...	...	...	44	4	...
Indiana	30	27	3	...	30	...	30	...	...	30	...	...	...	...	...	2	26	2
Iowa	26	...	26	...	26	...	26	...	...	...	...	...	26	...	...	8	5	13
Kansas	20	20	...	...	16	4	15	5	...	20	...	...	...	...	...	20	...	...
Kentucky	26	26	3	...	26	...	26	...	...	26	...	...	...	...	...	8	17	1
Louisiana	16	11	5	...	16	...	16	...	...	11	4	...	½	½	...	8	8	...
Maine	12	...	12	...	12	...	12	...	...	...	12	...	...	...	...	...	5	7
Maryland	16	...	16	...	16	...	16	...	...	15	1	...	...	...	...	14	1	1
Massachusetts	30	2	28	...	30	...	30	...	...	1	29	...	...	...	...	14	12	4
Michigan	28	28	...	...	27	1	25	3	...	28	...	...	...	...	...	21	7	...
Minnesota	18	18	...	...	18	...	18	...	...	18	...	...	...	...	...	6	12	...
Mississippi	18	12	6	...	18	...	18	...	...	17	...	...	1	...	...	13	5	...
Missouri	34	20	14	...	33	1	33	...	1	34	...	...	...	...	...	10	23	1
Montana	6	1	5	...	...	6	...	6	...	1	...	...	...	...	5	1	...	5
Nebraska	16	16	...	...	16	...	13	3	...	16	...	...	...	...	...	16	...	...
Nevada	6	1	5	...	...	6	...	6	...	3	...	...	...	...	3	3	...	3
New Hampshire	8	...	8	...	8	...	8	...	...	...	8	...	...	...	...	8	...	...
New Jersey	20	20	...	...	20	...	20	...	...	19	1	...	...	...	...	20	...	...
New Mexico	6	1	5	...	3	3	2	4	...	5	...	...	1	...	...	...	6	...
New York	72	19	52	1	72	...	72	...	...	17	...	55	...	...	...	72	...	...
North Carolina	22	16½	5½	...	7½	14½	7½	14½	...	19½	2½	...	...	...	...	1½	20½	...
North Dakota	6	6	...	...	6	...	6	...	...	6	...	...	...	...	...	3	3	...
Ohio	46	46	...	...	46	...	46	...	...	46	...	...	...	...	...	25	15	6
Oklahoma	*12	12	2	...	11	1	6	6	...	10	1	...	1	...	...	10	2	...
Oregon	8	...	8	...	8	...	8	...	...	8	...	...	...	...	...	8	...	...
Pennsylvania	64	5	59	...	64	...	64	...	...	6	...	...	...	58	...	64	...	...
Rhode Island	8	...	8	...	8	...	8	...	...	...	8	...	...	...	...	...	...	8
South Carolina	18	18	...	...	18	...	18	...	...	18	...	...	...	...	...	3	15	...
South Dakota	8	8	...	...	6	2	7	1	...	8	...	...	...	...	...	8	...	...
Tennessee	24	23	1	...	23	1	23	1	...	24	...	...	...	...	...	...	24	...
Texas	30	16	8	6	30	...	30	...	...	21	5	...	3	...	1	11	12	7
Utah	6	...	6	...	...	6	...	6	...	3	...	...	3	...	...	5	1	...
Vermont	8	4	3	1	8	...	8	...	...	8	...	...	...	...	...	8	...	...
Virginia	24	22	1	1	19	5	17	7	...	23	1	...	...	...	...	...	...	24
Washington	8	8	...	...	8	...	8	...	...	8	...	...	...	...	...	8	...	...
West Virginia	12	12	...	...	12	...	12	...	...	12	...	...	...	...	...	12	...	...
Wisconsin	24	24	...	...	24	...	24	...	...	24	...	...	...	...	...	3	20	...
Wyoming	6	6	...	...	...	6	...	6	...	6	...	...	...	...	...	6	...	...
Alaska	4	...	2	2	4	...	4	...	...	4	...	...	...	...	...	4	...	...
Canal Zone	...	...	...	...	...	...	...	...	...	...	...	...	...	...	...	...	...	...
District of Columbia	2	...	2	...	2	...	2	...	...	...	...	1	...	1	...	2	...	...
Hawaii	...	...	...	...	...	...	...	...	...	...	...	...	...	...	...	...	...	...
Philippine Islands	...	...	...	...	...	...	...	...	...	...	...	...	...	...	...	...	...	...
Puerto Rico	...	...	...	...	...	...	...	...	...	...	...	...	...	...	...	...	...	...
Virgin Islands	...	...	...	...	...	...	...	...	...	...	...	...	...	...	...	...	...	...
Total	924	551½	359½	18	818½	105½	812½	110½	1	661½	84½	58	35½	61½	23[a]	523½[b]	287½[c]	113[d]

Source: *Official Proceedings, 1896.*

Previous question on credentials, p. 51.
Table minority financial plank, p. 91.
Majority financial plank, p. 96.
Presidential. First ballot, p. 123.
a/ Other candidates: J. Donald Cameron, 1; not voting, 22.
Vice-Presidential. First ballot, p. 141.
b/ Sum of column; proceedings record 533½.
c/ Sum of column; proceedings record 280½.
d/ Other candidates: Morgan G. Bulkeley, 39; James A. Walker, 24; Charles W. Lippitt, 8; Thomas B. Reed, 3; Chauncey M. Depew, 3; John M. Thurston, 2; Frederick D. Grant, 2; Levi P. Morton, 1; not voting, 31.

* Including Indian Territory, 6 votes.

Delegation	1900 REPUBLICAN Pres. First Ballot Votes	McKinley	Vice-Pres First Ballot Roosevelt	Other	1904 REPUBLICAN Amendment to Rules, Hawaiian Delegation Votes	Yea	Nay	Not Voting	Pres. First Ballot Roosevelt	1908 REPUBLICAN Votes	Minority Report on Rules Yea	Nay	Not Voting	Minority Platform Yea	Nay	Minority Plank, Campaign Funds Yea	Nay	Not Voting
Alabama	22	22	22	...	22	4	18	...	22	22	...	22	...	...	22	...	22	...
Arizona	6	6	6	...	6	...	6	...	6	2	...	2	...	...	2	...	2	...
Arkansas	16	16	16	...	18	1	17	...	18	18	...	18	...	...	18	...	18	...
California	18	18	18	...	20	...	20	...	20	20	...	20	...	...	20	...	20	...
Colorado	8	8	8	...	10	...	10	...	10	10	10	...	...	...	10	...	10	...
Connecticut	12	12	12	...	14	...	14	...	14	14	14	...	...	...	14	...	14	...
Delaware	6	6	6	...	6	1	5	...	6	6	...	6	...	...	6	...	6	...
Florida	8	8	8	...	10	...	8	2	10	10	...	10	...	...	10	...	10	...
Georgia	26	26	26	...	26	...	26	...	26	26	...	26	...	...	26	...	26	...
Idaho	6	6	6	...	6	...	6	...	6	6	...	6	...	...	6	6	...	...
Illinois	48	48	48	...	54	34	20	...	54	54	54	...	...	...	54	...	54	...
Indiana	30	30	30	...	30	28	2	...	30	30	30	...	...	...	30	17	13	...
Iowa	26	26	26	...	26	...	26	...	26	26	6	20	...	...	26	...	26	...
Kansas	20	20	20	...	20	20	...	...	20	20	...	20	...	...	20	...	20	...
Kentucky	26	26	26	...	26	18	8	...	26	26	1	25	...	...	26	3	23	...
Louisiana	16	16	16	...	18	9	9	...	18	18	...	18	...	...	18	...	18	...
Maine	12	12	12	...	12	4	8	...	12	12	12	...	...	...	12	...	12	...
Maryland	16	16	16	...	16	16	...	...	16	16	...	16	...	...	16	1	15	...
Massachusetts	30	30	30	...	32	32	...	...	32	32	32	...	...	...	32	...	32	...
Michigan	28	28	28	...	28	14	14	...	28	28	18	10	...	...	28	...	28	...
Minnesota	18	18	18	...	22	...	22	...	22	22	10	11	1	...	22	...	22	...
Mississippi	18	18	18	...	20	...	20	...	20	20	...	20	...	...	20	...	20	...
Missouri	34	34	34	...	36	14	22	...	36	36	12	24	...	...	36	3	33	...
Montana	6	6	6	...	6	4	2	...	6	6	...	6	...	...	6	...	6	...
Nebraska	16	16	16	...	16	14	2	...	16	16	7	9	...	...	16	16	...	...
Nevada	6	6	6	...	6	6	...	...	6	6	...	6	...	...	6	...	6	...
New Hampshire	8	8	8	...	8	2	5	1	8	8	8	...	...	...	8	...	8	...
New Jersey	20	20	20	...	24	10	14	...	24	24	23	1	...	1	23	1	23	...
New Mexico	6	6	6	...	6	...	6	...	6	2	...	...	2	...	2	...	2	...
New York	72	72	71	1	78	71	7	...	78	78	78	...	...	...	78	6	66	6
North Carolina	22	22	22	...	24	12	12	...	24	24	...	24	...	...	24	...	24	...
North Dakota	6	6	6	...	8	...	8	...	8	8	...	8	...	...	8	...	8	...
Ohio	46	46	46	...	46	2	44	...	46	46	8	38	...	...	46	...	46	...
Oklahoma	*12	12	12	...	*12	2	10	...	12	14	...	14	...	...	14	...	14	...
Oregon	8	8	8	...	8	...	8	...	8	8	3	5	...	...	8	...	8	...
Pennsylvania	64	64	64	...	68	68	...	...	68	68	68	...	...	...	68	8	60	...
Rhode Island	8	8	8	...	8	8	...	...	8	8	8	...	...	...	8	...	8	...
South Carolina	18	18	18	...	18	9	9	...	18	18	...	18	...	...	18	...	18	...
South Dakota	8	8	8	...	8	...	8	...	8	8	8	...	...	2	6	6	2	...
Tennessee	24	24	24	...	24	17	7	...	24	24	...	24	...	...	24	...	24	...
Texas	30	30	30	...	36	1	35	...	36	36	...	36	...	...	36	...	36	...
Utah	6	6	6	...	6	1	5	...	6	6	6	...	...	...	6	...	6	...
Vermont	8	8	8	...	8	8	...	...	8	8	8	...	...	...	8	...	8	...
Virginia	24	24	24	...	24	24	...	...	24	24	...	24	...	...	24	...	24	...
Washington	8	8	8	...	10	...	10	...	10	10	4	6	...	...	10	...	10	...
West Virginia	12	12	12	...	14	14	...	...	14	14	14	...	...	...	14	2	12	...
Wisconsin	24	24	24	...	26	26	...	...	26	26	26	...	...	25	1	25	1	...
Wyoming	6	6	6	...	6	1	5	...	6	6	...	6	...	...	6	...	6	...
Alaska	4	4	4	...	6	...	6	...	6	2	2	...	...	...	2	...	2	...
Canal Zone	...	...	...	...	...	...	...	...	...	...	...	...	...	...	...	...	...	...
District of Columbia	2	2	2	...	2	...	2	...	2	2	1	1	...	...	2	...	2	...
Hawaii	2	2	2	...	6	...	...	6	6	2	...	2	...	...	2	...	2	...
Philippine Islands	...	...	...	...	2	...	2	...	2	2	...	2	...	...	2	...	2	...
Puerto Rico	...	...	...	...	2	...	2	...	2	2	...	2	...	...	2	...	2	...
Virgin Islands	...	...	...	...	...	...	...	...	...	...	...	...	...	...	...	...	...	...
Total	926	926	925	1a	994	495	490	9	994	980	471	506	3	28	952	94	880	6

Source: *Official Proceedings, 1900.*
Presidential. First ballot, p. 130.
Vice-Presidential. First ballot, p. 138.
a/ Not voting, 1.

Source: *Official Proceedings, 1904.*
Amendment to rules, Hawaiian delegation, p. 131.
Presidential. First ballot, p. 165.

Source: *Official Proceedings, 1908.*
Minority report on rules, pp. 109-10.
Minority platform, pp. 136-7.
Minority plank, campaign funds, pp. 138-9.

* Including Indian Territory, 6 votes.

Delegation	1908 REPUBLICAN									1912 REPUBLICAN						
	Votes	Minority Plank, Railroad Valuation		Minority Plank, Election of Senators		Pres. First Ballot		Vice-Pres. First Ballot		Votes	Temporary Chairman			Table Voting Rules, Credentials Committee		
		Yea	Nay	Yea	Nay	Taft	Other	Sherman	Other		Root	McGovern	Other	Yea	Nay	Not Voting
Alabama	22	...	22	...	22	22	...	19	3	24	22	2	...	22	2	...
Arizona	2	...	2	...	2	2	...	2	...	6	6	...	...	6	...	...
Arkansas	18	...	18	...	18	18	...	18	...	18	17	1	...	17	1	...
California	20	...	20	...	20	20	...	20	...	26	2	24	...	2	24	...
Colorado	10	...	10	...	10	10	...	9	1	12	12	...	...	12	...	...
Connecticut	14	...	14	...	14	14	...	...	14	14	14	...	...	14	...	...
Delaware	6	...	6	...	6	6	...	6	...	6	6	...	...	6	...	...
Florida	10	...	10	...	10	10	...	10	...	12	12	...	...	12	...	...
Georgia	26	...	26	...	26	17	9	26	...	28	22	6	...	24	4	...
Idaho	6	...	6	3	3	6	...	6	...	8	...	8	...	...	8	...
Illinois	54	...	54	1	53	3	51	51	3	58	9	49	...	7	51	...
Indiana	30	8	22	11	19	...	30	26	4	30	20	10	...	20	9	1
Iowa	26	...	26	1	25	26	...	15	11	26	16	10	...	16	10	...
Kansas	20	...	20	...	20	20	...	19	1	20	2	18	...	2	18	...
Kentucky	26	...	26	2	24	24	2	26	...	26	23	3	...	24	2	...
Louisiana	18	...	18	...	18	18	...	15	3	20	20	...	...	20	...	...
Maine	12	...	12	...	12	12	...	9	3	12	...	12	...	...	12	...
Maryland	16	...	16	1	15	16	...	16	...	16	8	8	...	9	7	...
Massachusetts	32	...	32	...	32	32	...	...	32	36	18	18	...	18	18	...
Michigan	28	...	28	5	23	27	1	20	8	30	19	10	1	20	10	...
Minnesota	22	...	22	...	22	22	...	22	...	24	...	24	...	...	24	...
Mississippi	20	...	20	...	20	20	...	19	1	20	16	4	...	16	4	...
Missouri	36	3	33	4	32	36	...	36	...	36	16	20	...	16	20	...
Montana	6	...	6	...	6	6	...	6	...	8	8	...	...	8	...	...
Nebraska	16	12	4	16	...	16	...	12	4	16	...	16	...	...	16	...
Nevada	6	...	6	...	6	6	...	6	...	6	6	...	...	6	...	...
New Hampshire	8	...	8	...	8	5	3	8	...	8	8	...	...	8	...	...
New Jersey	24	...	24	...	24	15	9	...	24	28	...	28	...	...	28	...
New Mexico	2	...	2	...	2	2	...	...	2	8	6	2	...	7	1	...
New York	78	3	75	...	78	10	68	78	...	90	76	13	1	75	15	...
North Carolina	24	...	24	...	24	24	...	24	...	24	3	21	...	2	22	...
North Dakota	8	...	8	...	8	8	...	8	...	10	...	9	1	2	8	...
Ohio	46	...	46	2	44	42	4	26	20	48	14	34	...	14	34	...
Oklahoma	14	...	14	14	...	14	...	14	...	20	4	16	...	4	16	...
Oregon	8	...	8	...	8	8	...	8	...	10	3	6	1	5	5	...
Pennsylvania	68	4	64	13	55	1	67	60	8	76	12	64	...	12	64	...
Rhode Island	8	...	8	...	8	8	...	8	...	10	10	...	...	10	...	...
South Carolina	18	...	18	...	18	13	5	17	1	18	11	7	...	11	6	1
South Dakota	8	8	...	8	...	8	...	8	...	10	...	10	...	...	10	...
Tennessee	24	...	24	...	24	24	...	24	...	24	23	1	...	23	1	...
Texas	36	...	36	...	36	36	...	36	...	40	31	8	1	29	9	2
Utah	6	...	6	2	4	6	...	6	...	8	7	1	...	7	1	...
Vermont	8	...	8	...	8	8	...	8	...	8	6	2	...	6	2	...
Virginia	24	...	24	...	24	21	3	24	...	24	22	2	...	21	3	...
Washington	10	...	10	...	10	10	...	10	...	14	14	...	...	14	...	...
West Virginia	14	...	14	5	9	14	...	13	1	16	...	16	...	...	16	...
Wisconsin	26	25	1	25	1	1	25	4	22	26	...	12	14	...	26	...
Wyoming	6	...	6	...	6	6	...	6	...	6	6	...	...	6	...	...
Alaska	2	...	2	...	2	2	...	2	...	2	2	...	...	2	...	...
Canal Zone	...	...	...	...	...	...	...	...	...	...	...	...	...	...	...	...
District of Columbia	2	...	2	...	2	1	1	2	...	2	2	...	...	2	...	...
Hawaii	2	...	2	1	1	2	...	2	...	6	...	6	...	6	...	...
Philippine Islands	2	...	2	...	2	2	...	2	...	2	2	...	...	2	...	...
Puerto Rico	2	...	2	...	2	2	...	2	...	2	2	...	...	2	...	...
Virgin Islands	...	...	...	...	...	...	...	...	...	...	...	...	...	...	...	...
Total	980	63	917	114	866	702	278[a]	816	164[b]	1078	558	501	19[c]	567	507	4

Source: *Official Proceedings, 1908.*

Minority plank, railroad valuation, p. 139.
Minority plank, election of Senators, p. 140.
Presidential. First ballot, p. 182.
a/ Other candidates: Philander C. Knox, 68; Charles E. Hughes, 67; Joseph G. Cannon, 58; Charles W. Fairbanks, 40; Robert M. LaFollette, 25; Joseph B. Foraker, 16; Theodore Roosevelt, 3; not voting, 1.
Vice-Presidential. First ballot, p. 196.
b/ Other candidates: Edward F. Murphy, 77; Curtis Guild, 75; George L. Sheldon, 10; Charles W. Fairbanks, 1; not voting, 1.

Source: *Official Proceedings, 1912.*

Temporary Chairman, pp. 61-88.
c/ Other candidates: W. S. Lauder, 12; Asle J. Gronna, 1; not voting, 6.
Table voting rules, credentials committee, p. 161.

Delegation	Votes	Table Voting Rules, Credentials Minority Report			Table Minority Report, Alabama Credentials			Table Minority Report, Arizona Credentials			Table Minority Report, California Credentials			Adoption of Platform			
		Yea	Nay	Not Voting	Yea	Nay	Not Voting	Yea	Nay	Not Voting	Yea	Nay	Not Voting	Yea	Nay	Present, Not Voting	Absent
Alabama	24	20	2	2	20	2	2	22	2	...	22	2	...	22	...	2	...
Arizona	6	6	...	...	6	...	...	...	...	6	6	...	...	6	...	...	...
Arkansas	18	17	1	...	17	1	...	17	1	...	17	1	...	17	1	...	...
California	26	2	24	...	2	24	...	2	24	...	...	24	2	2	...	24	...
Colorado	12	12	...	...	12	...	...	12	...	...	12	...	...	12	...	...	...
Connecticut	14	14	...	...	14	...	...	14	...	...	14	...	...	14	...	...	...
Delaware	6	6	...	...	6	...	...	6	...	...	6	...	...	6	...	...	...
Florida	12	12	...	...	12	...	...	12	...	...	12	...	...	12	...	...	...
Georgia	28	28	...	...	28	...	...	28	...	...	28	...	...	28	...	...	...
Idaho	8	...	8	...	...	8	...	...	8	...	...	8		8	...	...	...
Illinois	58	7	51	...	7	51	...	7	51	...	8	50	...	46	...	9	3
Indiana	30	20	9	1	20	10	...	20	10	...	20	10	...	21	2	7	...
Iowa	26	16	10	...	16	10	...	16	10	...	15	11	...	16	10	...	...
Kansas	20	2	18	...	2	18	...	2	18	...	2	18	...	2	...	18	...
Kentucky	26	24	2	...	24	2	...	24	2	...	23	3	...	26	...	...	...
Louisiana	20	20	...	...	20	...	...	20	...	...	20	...	...	20	...	...	...
Maine	12	...	12	...	...	12	...	...	12	...	...	12	...	...	...	12	...
Maryland	16	8	8	...	8	8	...	9	7	...	1	14	1	10	...	6	...
Massachusetts	36	18	18	...	18	18	...	18	18	...	18	18	...	20	...	14	2
Michigan	30	20	10	...	20	10	...	20	10	...	20	10	...	22	...	8	...
Minnesota	24	...	24	...	...	23	1	...	22	2	...	24	...	...	...	24	...
Mississippi	20	16	4	...	16	4	...	16	4	...	16	4	...	17	...	3	...
Missouri	36	16	20	...	16	20	...	16	20	...	16	20	...	36	...	...	...
Montana	8	8	...	...	8	...	...	8	...	...	8	...	...	8	...	...	...
Nebraska	16	...	16	...	...	16	...	...	16	...	...	16	...	...	...	16	...
Nevada	6	6	...	...	6	...	...	6	...	...	6	...	...	6	...	...	...
New Hampshire	8	8	...	...	8	...	...	8	...	...	8	...	...	8	...	...	...
New Jersey	28	...	28	...	...	28	...	...	28	...	...	28	...	...	...	28	...
New Mexico	8	7	1	...	7	1	...	8	...	...	6	2	...	8	...	...	...
New York	90	76	13	1	77	12	1	76	14	...	75	15	...	85	...	5	...
North Carolina	24	3	20	1	3	20	1	3	20	1	3	21	...	6	...	12	6
North Dakota	10	...	10	...	...	10	...	...	10	...	...	10	...	...	10	...	...
Ohio	48	14	34	...	14	34	...	14	34	...	14	34	...	14	...	34	...
Oklahoma	20	4	16	...	4	16	...	4	16	...	4	16	...	4	1	15	...
Oregon	10	5	5	...	6	4	...	5	1	4	...	10	...	4	2	2	2
Pennsylvania	76	12	64	...	12	64	...	12	64	...	12	64	...	12	...	63	1
Rhode Island	10	10	...	...	10	...	...	10	...	...	10	...	...	10	...	...	...
South Carolina	18	12	5	1	12	5	1	12	5	1	11	6	1	15	...	3	...
South Dakota	10	...	10	...	...	10	...	...	10	...	...	10	...	...	...	10	...
Tennessee	24	23	1	...	23	1	...	23	1	...	22	2	...	23	...	1	...
Texas	40	29	9	2	29	10	1	29	10	1	29	10	1	30	1	8	1
Utah	8	7	1	...	7	1	...	7	1	...	7	1	...	8	...	...	...
Vermont	8	6	2	...	6	2	...	6	2	...	5	3	...	6	...	2	...
Virginia	24	21	2	1	22	1	1	19	4	1	18	4	2	22	...	1	1
Washington	14	14	...	...	14	...	...	14	...	...	14	...	...	14	...	...	...
West Virginia	16	...	16	...	...	16	...	...	16	...	...	16	...	...	...	16	...
Wisconsin	26	...	25	1	25	...	1	...	26	...	...	26	...	...	26	...	...
Wyoming	6	6	...	...	6	...	...	6	...	...	6	...	...	6	...	...	...
Alaska	2	2	...	...	2	...	...	2	...	...	2	...	...	2	...	...	...
Canal Zone	...	...	...	...	...	...	...	...	...	...	...	...	...	...	...	...	...
District of Columbia	2	2	...	...	2	...	...	2	...	...	2	...	...	2	...	...	...
Hawaii	6	6	...	...	6	...	...	5	...	1	...	6		6	...	...	...
Philippine Islands	2	2	...	...	2	...	...	2	...	...	2	...	...	2	...	...	...
Puerto Rico	2	2	...	...	2	...	...	2	...	...	2	...	...	2	...	...	...
Virgin Islands	...	...	...	...	...	...	...	...	...	...	...	...	...	...	...	...	...
Total	1078	569	499	10	597[a]	472[b]	9	564	497	17	542	529	7	666	53	343	16

Source: *Official Proceedings, 1912.*

Table voting rules, credentials minority report, pp. 185-6.

Table minority report, Alabama credentials, pp. 189-90.

a/ Sum of column; proceedings record 605.

b/ Sum of column; proceedings record 464.

Table minority report, Arizona credentials, pp. 195-6.

Table minority report, California credentials, pp. 218-9.

Adoption of platform, pp. 373-4.

Delegation	Votes	1912 REPUBLICAN							Votes	1916 REPUBLICAN						
		Presidential First Ballot				Vice-Presidential First Ballot				Presidential						
										First Ballot				Second Ballot		
		Taft	Roosevelt	Present, Not Voting	Other	Sherman	Present, Not Voting	Other		Hughes	Root	Weeks	Other	Hughes	Root	Other
Alabama	24	22	...	2	...	22	2	...	16	8	...	3	5	9	...	7
Arizona	6	6	...	...	...	6	...	...	6	4	...	...	2	4	...	2
Arkansas	18	17	...	1	...	18	...	...	15	1	3	3	8	...	2	13
California	26	2	...	24	...	2	24	...	26	9	8	3	6	11	12	3
Colorado	12	12	...	...	...	12	...	...	12	...	5	...	7	...	5	7
Connecticut	14	14	...	...	...	14	...	...	14	5	5	1	3	5	7	2
Delaware	6	6	...	...	...	6	...	...	6	...	...	...	6	...	...	6
Florida	12	12	...	...	...	12	...	...	8	8	...	...	...	8	...	...
Georgia	28	28	...	...	...	28	...	...	17	5	...	6	6	6	...	11
Idaho	8	1	...	...	7	...	...	8	8	4	...	...	4	4	1	3
Illinois	58	2	53	1	2	9	17	32	58	...	...	...	58	...	...	58
Indiana	30	20	3	7	...	21	7	2	30	...	...	...	30	...	...	30
Iowa	26	16	...	...	10	16	...	10	26	...	...	...	26	...	...	26
Kansas	20	2	...	18	...	2	18	...	20	10	2	3	5	10	2	8
Kentucky	26	24	2	...	...	26	...	...	26	10	...	...	16	11	...	15
Louisiana	20	20	...	...	...	20	...	...	12	4	1	3	4	6	1	5
Maine	12	...	...	12	...	...	12	...	12	6	1	3	2	8	1	3
Maryland	16	1	9	5	1	8	3	5	16	7	1	5	3	7	1	8
Massachusetts	36	15	...	21	...	15	4	17	36	4	...	28	4	12	...	24
Michigan	30	20	9	1	...	20	6	4	30	...	...	...	30	28	...	2
Minnesota	24	...	...	24	...	...	24	...	24	...	...	...	24	...	...	24
Mississippi	20	17	...	3	...	17	3	...	12	4	...	1½	6½	4	...	8
Missouri	36	16	...	20	...	20	16	...	36	18	...	8	10	22	...	14
Montana	8	8	...	...	...	8	...	...	8	...	...	...	8	...	...	8
Nebraska	16	...	2	14	...	...	14	2	16	...	...	...	16	2	...	14
Nevada	6	6	...	...	...	6	...	...	6	4	2	...	...	4	2	...
New Hampshire	8	8	...	...	...	8	...	...	8	...	...	8	...	3	3	2
New Jersey	28	...	2	26	...	...	28	...	28	12	12	1	3	16	3	9
New Mexico	8	7	1	...	...	8	...	...	6	2	...	2	2	2	...	4
New York	90	76	8	6	...	87	3	...	87	42	43	...	2	43	42	2
North Carolina	24	1	1	22	...	6	1	17	21	6	2	3	10	6	2	13
North Dakota	10	...	...	...	10	...	10	...	10	...	...	...	10	...	...	10
Ohio	48	14	...	34	...	14	34	...	48	...	...	...	48	...	...	48
Oklahoma	20	4	1	15	...	4	16	...	20	5	1	6	8	5	1	14
Oregon	10	...	8	2	...	...	2	8	10	10	...	...	...	10	...	...
Pennsylvania	76	9	2	62	3	12	63	1	76	2	...	...	74	8	1	67
Rhode Island	10	10	...	...	...	10	...	...	10	10	...	...	...	10	...	...
South Carolina	18	16	...	1	1	15	3	...	11	2	1	3	5	4	...	7
South Dakota	10	...	5	...	5	...	10	...	10	...	...	...	10	...	...	10
Tennessee	24	23	1	...	...	23	1	...	21	9	...	3½	8½	8	½	12½
Texas	40	31	...	8	1	31	8	1	26	1	1	1	23	3	3	20
Utah	8	8	...	...	...	8	...	...	8	4	3	...	1	5	2	1
Vermont	8	6	...	2	...	6	2	...	8	8	...	...	...	8	...	...
Virginia	24	22	...	1	1	22	1	1	15	5½	3	3	3½	8½	5	1½
Washington	14	14	...	...	...	14	...	...	14	5	8	...	1	5	...	9
West Virginia	16	...	...	16	...	...	16	...	16	1	...	5	10	4	1	11
Wisconsin	26	...	...	...	26	...	4	22	26	11	...	...	15	11	...	15
Wyoming	6	6	...	...	...	6	...	...	6	6	...	...	...	6	...	...
Alaska	2	2	...	...	...	2	...	...	2	1	...	1	...	1	...	1
Canal Zone	...	...	...	...	...	...	...	...	...	...	...	...	...	...	...	...
District of Columbia	2	2	...	...	...	2	...	...	...	...	...	...	...	...	...	...
Hawaii	6	6	...	...	...	6	...	...	2	...	...	1	1	1	...	1
Philippine Islands	2	2	...	...	...	2	...	...	2	...	1	...	1	...	1	1
Puerto Rico	2	2	...	...	...	2	...	...	...	...	...	...	...	...	...	...
Virgin Islands	...	...	...	...	...	...	...	...	...	...	...	...	...	...	...	...
Total	1078	556a	107	348b	67c	596d	352	130e	987	253½	103	105	525½f	328½	98½	560g

Source: *Official Proceedings, 1912.*

Presidential. First ballot, pp. 402-3.
a/ Sum of column; proceedings record 561.
b/ Sum of column; proceedings record 349.
c/ Other candidates: Robert M. LaFollette, 41; Albert B. Cummins, 17; Charles E. Hughes, 2; absent and not voting, 7.
Vice-Presidential. First ballot, pp. 406-7.
d/ Sum of column; proceedings record 595.
e/ Other candidates: William E. Borah, 21; Charles H. Merriam, 20; Herbert S. Hadley, 14; Albert J. Beveridge, 2; Howard F. Gillette, 1; absent and not voting, 72.

Source: *Official Proceedings, 1916.*

Presidential. First ballot, pp. 181-2.
f / Other candidates: Albert B. Cummins, 85; Theodore E. Burton, 77½; Charles W. Fairbanks, 74½; Lawrence Y. Sherman, 66; Theodore Roosevelt, 65; Philander C. Knox, 36; Henry Ford, 32; Martin G. Brumbaugh, 29; Robert M. LaFollette, 25; William H. Taft, 14; Coleman du Pont, 12; Frank B. Willis, 4; William F. Borah, 2; Samuel W. McCall, 1; not voting, 2½.
Second ballot, pp. 184-5.
g/ Other candidates: Fairbanks, 88½; Cummins, 85; Roosevelt, 81; Weeks, 79; Burton, 76½; Sherman, 65; Knox, 36; LaFollette, 25; du Pont, 13; John Wanamaker, 5; Willis, 1; Leonard Wood, 1; Warren G. Harding, 1; McCall, 1; not voting, 2.

Delegation	Votes	Motion to Adjourn			Pres. Third Ballot		Vice-Presidential First Ballot			Votes	First Ballot				Second Ballot			
		Yea	Nay	Not Voting	Hughes	Other	Fairbanks	Burkett	Other		Wood	Lowden	Johnson	Other	Wood	Lowden	Johnson	Other
		1916 REPUBLICAN								**1920 REPUBLICAN Presidential**								
Alabama	16	5	11	...	16	...	15	1	...	14	4	6	3	1	4	6	3	1
Arizona	6	3	3	...	6	...	6	...	...	6	6	...	...	...	6	...	...	...
Arkansas	15	15	...	...	15	...	14	1	...	13	6	6	...	1	2½	10½	...	...
California	26	11	14	1	26	...	26	...	...	26	...	...	26	...	...	...	26	...
Colorado	12	12	...	...	12	...	12	...	...	12	9	2	...	1	9	2	...	1
Connecticut	14	9	5	...	14	...	14	...	...	14	...	14	...	...	...	13	1	...
Delaware	6	4	2	...	6	...	6	...	...	6	...	...	...	6	...	...	...	6
Florida	8	...	8	...	8	...	8	...	...	8	4½	2½	...	1	5½	2½	...	...
Georgia	17	12	5	...	17	...	17	...	...	17	8	9	...	...	8	9	...	...
Idaho	8	4	4	...	8	...	7	1	...	8	5	...	1	2	5	1	1	1
Illinois	58	58	...	...	58	...	56	1	1	58	14	41	3	...	...	41	17	...
Indiana	30	30	...	...	30	...	30	...	...	30	22	...	8	...	22	...	8	...
Iowa	26	26	...	...	26	...	...	26	...	26	...	26	...	...	...	26	...	...
Kansas	20	10	10	...	20	...	20	...	...	20	14	6	...	...	14	6	...	...
Kentucky	26	13½	11½	1	26	...	26	...	...	26	...	20	1	5	...	26	...	...
Louisiana	12	6	6	...	12	...	12	...	...	12	3	3	1	5	3	6	...	3
Maine	12	10	2	...	12	...	12	...	...	12	11	...	...	1	11	...	...	1
Maryland	16	10	6	...	15	1	16	...	...	16	16	...	...	...	16	...	...	...
Massachusetts	36	30	5	1	32	4	34	1	1	35	7	...	...	28	7	...	...	28
Michigan	30	...	30	...	30	...	30	...	...	30	...	...	30	...	...	...	30	...
Minnesota	24	22	2	...	24	...	12	5	7	24	19	3	2	...	19	3	2	...
Mississippi	12	6	6	...	8½	3½	12	...	...	12	4½	2	2	3½	5½	3½	1	2
Missouri	36	36	...	...	34	2	36	...	...	36	4½	18	3	10½	5	19	3	9
Montana	8	8	...	...	7	1	1	...	7	8	...	...	8	...	...	...	8	...
Nebraska	16	8	8	...	16	...	...	16	...	16	3	...	13	...	5	...	11	...
Nevada	6	5	...	1	6	...	6	...	...	6	2	1½	2	½	2	1½	2	½
New Hampshire	8	8	...	...	8	...	8	...	...	8	8	...	...	...	8	...	...	...
New Jersey	28	15	13	...	27	1	28	...	...	28	17	...	11	...	17	...	11	...
New Mexico	6	6	...	...	5	1	6	...	...	6	6	...	...	...	6	...	...	...
New York	87	45	42	...	87	...	76	11	...	88	10	2	...	76	19	16	4	49
North Carolina	21	17	3	1	14	7	19	2	...	22	...	...	1	21	2	10	...	10
North Dakota	10	10	...	...	10	...	...	10	...	10	2	...	8	...	3	1	6	...
Ohio	48	48	...	...	48	...	48	...	...	48	9	...	...	39	9	...	...	39
Oklahoma	20	16	4	...	19	1	19	1	...	20	1½	18½	...	...	2	18	...	...
Oregon	10	...	10	...	10	...	7	...	3	10	1	...	9	...	1	...	9	...
Pennsylvania	76	65	10	1	72	4	74	1	1	76	...	...	...	76	...	...	...	76
Rhode Island	10	...	10	...	10	...	10	...	...	10	10	...	...	...	...	...	...	76
South Carolina	11	8	3	...	6	5	9	2	...	11	...	8	...	3	...	10	...	1
South Dakota	10	10	...	...	10	...	...	10	...	10	10	...	...	...	10	...	...	...
Tennessee	21	12	9	...	18	3	21	...	...	20	20	...	...	...	17	2	1	...
Texas	26	21	5	...	26	...	26	...	...	23	8½	5	1½	8	9	7½	1	5½
Utah	8	6	2	...	7	1	8	...	...	8	5	2	...	1	5	2	...	1
Vermont	8	...	8	...	8	...	8	...	...	8	...	...	...	8	...	...	...	8
Virginia	15	14	1	...	15	...	15	...	...	15	3	12	...	...	3	12	...	...
Washington	14	10	4	...	14	...	14	...	...	14	...	...	...	14	...	...	...	14
West Virginia	16	9	7	...	16	...	16	...	...	16	...	...	...	16	1	...	...	15
Wisconsin	26	10	16	...	23	3	11	12	3	26	1	...	...	25	1	...	...	25
Wyoming	6	6	...	...	6	...	6	...	...	6	...	3	...	3	3	3	...	...
Alaska	2	1	1	...	2	...	2	...	...	2	...	...	...	2	1	1	...	...
Canal Zone	...	...	...	...	...	...	...	...	...	...	...	...	...	...	...	...	...	...
District of Columbia	...	...	...	...	...	...	...	...	...	2	2	...	...	...	2	...	...	...
Hawaii	2	2	...	...	2	...	2	...	...	2	...	...	...	2	...	...	1	1
Philippine Islands	2	2	...	...	2	...	2	...	...	2	2	...	...	...	2	...	...	...
Puerto Rico	...	...	...	...	...	...	...	...	...	2	1	1	...	...	1	1	...	...
Virgin Islands	...	...	...	...	...	...	...	...	...	2	...	...	...	...	...	...	...	...
Total	987	694½	286½	6	949½	37½[a]	863	108	16[b]	984	287½	211½	133½	351½[c]	289½	259½	146	289[d]

Source: *Official Proceedings, 1916.*
Motion to adjourn, p. 188.
Third ballot, p. 197.
a/ Other candidates: Roosevelt, 18½; LaFollette, 3; du Pont, 5; Henry Cabot Lodge, 7; Weeks, 3; not voting, 1.
Vice-Presidential. First ballot, pp. 211-2.
b/ Other candidates: Theodore E. Burton, 1; William E. Borah, 8; Hiram W. Johnson, 1; William G. Webster, 2; not voting, 4.

Source: *Official Proceedings, 1920.*
Presidential Ballots. First, pp. 184-5.
c/ Other candidates: Warren G. Harding, 65½; William C. Sproul, 84; Calvin Coolidge, 34; Herbert Hoover, 5½; Coleman du Pont, 7; Jeter C. Pritchard, 21; Robert M. LaFollette, 24; Howard Sutherland, 17; William E. Borah, 2; Charles B. Warren, 1; Miles Poindexter, 20; Nicholas M. Butler, 69½; not voting, 1.
Second ballot, pp. 187-8.
d/ Other candidates: Harding, 59; Sproul, 78½; Coolidge, 32; Hoover, 5½; du Pont, 7; Pritchard, 10; LaFollette, 24; Sutherland, 15; Borah, 1; Poindexter, 15; Butler, 41; Philander C. Knox, 1.

		1920 REPUBLICAN														
		Presidential Third Ballot				Motion to Adjourn			Presidential Fourth Ballot				Fifth Ballot			
Delegation	Votes	Wood	Lowden	Johnson	Other	Yea	Nay	Not Voting	Wood	Lowden	Johnson	Other	Wood	Lowden	Johnson	Other
Alabama	14	4	6	4	...	...	14	...	4	6	4	...	4	6	4	...
Arizona	6	6	...	...	...	...	6	...	6	...	...	...	6	...	...	...
Arkansas	13	2½	10½	...	...	...	13	...	2½	10½	...	...	1½	11½	...	...
California	26	...	...	26	...	26	...	...	...	...	26	...	...	...	26	...
Colorado	12	9	2	...	1	...	12	...	9	2	...	1	7	2	...	3
Connecticut	14	...	13	1	...	...	14	...	...	13	1	...	...	13	1	...
Delaware	6	...	1	...	5	6	...	...	...	2	...	4	...	...	...	6
Florida	8	5½	2½	...	...	...	8	...	6½	1½	...	...	6½	1½	...	...
Georgia	17	8	9	...	...	...	17	...	8	9	...	...	8	9	...	...
Idaho	8	5	1	1	1	...	8	...	5	1	1	1	5	1	1	1
Illinois	58	...	41	17	...	17	41	...	...	41	17	...	...	41	17	...
Indiana	30	18	2	8	2	10	20	...	18	3	6	3	18	3	5	4
Iowa	26	...	26	...	...	...	26	...	...	26	...	...	...	26	...	...
Kansas	20	14	6	...	...	...	20	...	14	6	...	...	10	6	...	4
Kentucky	26	...	26	...	...	...	26	...	...	26	...	...	...	26	...	...
Louisiana	12	3	6	...	3	...	12	...	3	6	...	3	3	7	...	2
Maine	12	11	...	...	1	...	12	...	11	...	...	1	11	...	...	1
Maryland	16	16	...	...	...	...	16	...	16	...	...	...	16	...	...	...
Massachusetts	35	13	...	...	22	2	33	...	16	...	...	19	13	...	...	22
Michigan	30	...	...	30	...	...	30	...	...	...	30	...	...	...	30	...
Minnesota	24	17	6	1	...	7	17	...	17	5	2	...	16	5	2	1
Mississippi	12	6½	3½	...	2	12	...	...	7½	2½	...	2	9	1½	...	1½
Missouri	36	4½	20	4	7½	14	17	5	8½	19	1	7½	3½	18½	1	13
Montana	8	...	...	8	...	8	...	...	...	...	8	...	...	...	8	...
Nebraska	16	6	...	10	...	...	16	...	6	...	10	...	6	...	10	...
Nevada	6	2	1½	2	½	4	2	...	2½	2	1½	...	1½	2	2½	...
New Hampshire	8	8	...	...	...	...	8	...	8	...	...	...	8	...	...	...
New Jersey	28	17	...	11	...	5	23	...	17	...	11	...	17	...	10	1
New Mexico	6	6	...	...	...	...	6	...	6	...	...	...	6	...	...	...
New York	88	23	26	5	34	36	50	2	20	32	5	31	24	42	3	19
North Carolina	22	2	15	4	1	1	21	...	3	15	2	2	3	17	1	1
North Dakota	10	3	1	6	...	4	6	...	3	1	6	...	3	2	5	...
Ohio	48	9	...	...	39	...	48	...	9	...	...	39	9	...	...	39
Oklahoma	20	2	18	...	...	...	20	...	2	18	...	...	2	18	...	...
Oregon	10	2	...	8	...	...	10	...	5	...	5	...	4	1	5	...
Pennsylvania	76	...	...	...	76	50	26	...	...	...	...	76	...	...	...	76
Rhode Island	10	10	...	...	...	...	10	...	10	...	...	...	10	...	...	...
South Carolina	11	...	10	...	1	...	11	...	...	11	...	...	...	11	...	...
South Dakota	10	10	...	...	...	...	10	...	10	...	...	...	10	...	...	...
Tennessee	20	19	1	...	...	...	20	...	19	1	...	...	18	2	...	...
Texas	23	9	8½	1	4½	12½	10½	...	8	9½	1	4½	6	10	1	6
Utah	8	5	2	...	1	...	8	...	5	2	...	1	5	2	...	1
Vermont	8	8	...	...	...	...	8	...	8	...	...	...	8	...	...	...
Virginia	15	3	12	...	...	...	15	...	3	12	...	...	3	12	...	...
Washington	14	...	...	...	14	14	...	...	...	...	...	14	...	...	...	14
West Virginia	16	6	...	1	9	15	1	...	8	...	1	7	9	...	1	6
Wisconsin	26	1	...	...	25	24	2	...	1	...	2	23	1	...	...	25
Wyoming	6	3	3	...	...	6	...	...	3	3	...	...	2	3	...	1
Alaska	2	1	...	...	1	2	...	...	1	...	...	1	1	...	...	1
Canal Zone	...	...	...	...	...	...	...	...	...	...	...	...	...	...	...	...
District of Columbia	2	2	...	...	...	...	2	...	2	...	...	...	2	...	...	...
Hawaii	2	...	2	...	...	...	2	...	...	2	...	...	...	2	...	...
Philippine Islands	2	2	...	...	...	...	2	...	2	...	...	...	2	...	...	...
Puerto Rico	2	1	1	...	...	...	2	...	1	1	...	...	1	1	...	...
Virgin Islands	...	...	...	...	...	...	...	...	...	...	...	...	...	...	...	...
Total	984	303	282½	148	250½[a]	275½	701½	7	314½	289	140½	240[b]	299	303	133½	248½[c]

Source: *Official Proceedings, 1920.*
Third Ballot, pp. 190-1.
a/ Other candidates: Harding, 58½; Sproul, 79½; Coolidge, 27; Hoover, 5½; du Pont, 2; LaFollette, 24; Sutherland, 9; Borah, 1; Poindexter, 15; Butler, 25; James E. Watson, 2; Knox, 2.
Motion to adjourn, p. 192.
Fourth ballot, pp. 193-4.
b/ Other candidates: Harding, 61½; Sproul, 79½; Coolidge, 25; Hoover, 5; du Pont, 2; LaFollette, 22; Sutherland, 3; Borah, 1; Poindexter, 15; Butler, 20; Watson, 4; Knox, 2.
Fifth ballot, pp. 200-1.
c/ Other candidates: Harding, 78; Sproul, 82½; Coolidge, 29; Poindexter, 15; LaFollette, 24; Sutherland, 1; du Pont, 6; Hoover, 6; Frank B. Kellogg, 1; Butler, 4; Knox, 1; William L. Ward, 1.

Delegation	Votes	1920 REPUBLICAN — Presidential — Sixth Ballot: Wood	Lowden	Johnson	Other	Seventh Ballot: Wood	Lowden	Harding	Johnson	Other	Eighth Ballot: Wood	Lowden	Harding	Other	Ninth Ballot: Wood	Lowden	Harding	Other
Alabama	14	4	6	4	...	4	6	2	2	...	4	6	4	...	4	6	4	...
Arizona	6	6	...	...	...	6	...	...	...	...	6	...	...	...	6	...	...	...
Arkansas	13	1½	11½	...	...	1½	11½	...	...	...	1½	11½	...	...	1½	10½	1	...
California	26	...	...	26	...	...	...	...	26	...	...	...	...	26	...	...	...	26
Colorado	12	6	3	...	3	6	3	3	...	...	6	3	3	...	6	1	5	...
Connecticut	14	...	13	1	...	1	12	...	1	...	1	11	...	2	...	...	13	1
Delaware	6	1	...	...	5	...	1	2	...	3	...	...	3	3	...	...	3	3
Florida	8	6½	1½	...	...	7	1	...	...	...	7	1	...	...	1	...	7	...
Georgia	17	8	9	...	...	8	9	...	...	...	8	9	...	...	8	8	1	...
Idaho	8	4	2	1	1	4	2	1	1	...	4	2	1	1	5	1	1	1
Illinois	58	...	41	17	...	...	41	...	17	...	...	41	...	17	...	41	...	17
Indiana	30	16	7	2	5	17	5	8	...	...	15	4	11	...	15	4	11	...
Iowa	26	...	26	...	...	...	26	...	...	...	...	26	...	...	...	26	...	...
Kansas	20	10	6	...	4	10	6	4	...	...	10	6	4	...	...	...	20	...
Kentucky	26	...	26	...	...	...	26	...	...	...	...	26	...	...	...	...	26	...
Louisiana	12	3	7	...	2	3	7	2	...	...	3	7	2	...	...	...	12	...
Maine	12	12	...	...	...	12	...	...	...	...	12	...	...	...	12	...	...	...
Maryland	16	16	...	...	...	16	...	...	...	...	16	...	...	...	16	...	...	...
Massachusetts	35	12	...	...	23	12	...	...	...	23	11	...	...	24	11	1	1	22
Michigan	30	11	1	18	...	13	1	...	16	...	13	7	...	10	15	6	1	8
Minnesota	24	16	5	2	1	16	5	...	2	1	16	5	...	3	17	5	...	2
Mississippi	12	9½	1½	...	1	9½	1½	1	...	...	8½	1½	2	...	7½	...	4½	...
Missouri	36	2½	18½	...	15	2½	16½	16	...	1	2½	15½	17	1	...	...	36	...
Montana	8	...	...	8	...	...	...	...	8	...	...	...	...	8	...	...	...	8
Nebraska	16	12	...	4	...	13	...	...	3	...	14	...	...	2	16	...	...	...
Nevada	6	2	2	2	...	2	2	...	2	...	1½	...	3½	1	1½	...	3½	1
New Hampshire	8	8	...	...	...	8	...	...	...	...	8	...	...	...	8	...	...	...
New Jersey	28	17	...	10	1	17	...	1	10	...	16	...	2	10	15	...	4	9
New Mexico	6	6	...	...	...	6	...	...	...	...	6	...	...	...	6	...	...	...
New York	88	23	44	3	18	24	45	8	...	11	23	45	8	12	5	4	66	13
North Carolina	22	2	16	1	3	3	15	3	1	...	2	16	4	...	3	...	18	1
North Dakota	10	3	3	3	1	3	4	...	3	...	3	4	...	3	3	4	...	3
Ohio	48	13	...	...	35	13	...	35	...	...	9	...	39	...	9	...	39	...
Oklahoma	20	2	18	...	...	2	18	...	...	...	2	18	...	...	½	...	18	1½
Oregon	10	4	...	5	1	4	...	1	5	...	4	...	1	5	4	...	1	5
Pennsylvania	76	...	...	...	76	...	...	...	...	76	...	...	...	76	...	...	...	76
Rhode Island	10	10	...	...	...	10	...	...	...	...	10	...	...	...	10	...	...	...
South Carolina	11	...	11	...	...	...	11	...	...	...	...	11	...	...	...	...	11	...
South Dakota	10	10	...	...	...	10	...	...	...	...	10	...	...	...	10	...	...	...
Tennessee	20	17	3	...	...	9½	7	2	1½	...	10	7	3	...	6	1	13	...
Texas	23	5½	8½	1	8	6	9	7	1	...	5	8½	8½	1	1	1	19½	1½
Utah	8	4	2	...	2	4	2	2	...	...	4	2	2	...	2	2	4	...
Vermont	8	8	...	...	...	8	...	...	...	...	8	...	...	...	8	...	...	...
Virginia	15	3	12	...	...	3	12	...	...	...	3	10	2	...	4	...	11	...
Washington	14	...	...	...	14	...	...	...	...	14	...	...	...	14	...	...	...	14
West Virginia	16	8	1	2	5	9	...	6	...	1	9	...	7	...	8	...	7	1
Wisconsin	26	1	...	...	25	1	...	...	...	25	1	...	...	25	1	...	...	25
Wyoming	6	2	3	...	1	2	3	1	...	...	...	...	6	...	...	...	6	...
Alaska	2	1	...	...	1	1	...	...	...	1	1	...	...	1	1	...	1	...
Canal Zone	...	...	...	...	...	...	...	...	...	...	...	...	...	...	...	...	...	...
District of Columbia	2	2	...	...	...	2	...	...	...	...	2	...	...	...	...	...	2	...
Hawaii	2	...	2	...	...	...	2	...	...	...	...	2	...	...	...	...	2	...
Philippine Islands	2	2	...	...	...	2	...	...	...	...	2	...	...	...	2	...	...	...
Puerto Rico	2	1	1	...	...	1	1	...	...	...	1	1	...	...	...	...	2	...
Virgin Islands	...	...	...	...	...	...	...	...	...	...	...	...	...	...	...	...	...	...
Total	984	311½	311½	110	251a	312	311½	105	99½	156b	299	307	133c	245d	249	121½	374½	239e

Source: *Official Proceedings, 1920.*
Sixth ballot, pp. 201-2.
a/ Other candidates: Harding, 89; Sproul, 77; Coolidge, 28; Poindexter, 15; LaFollette, 24; du Pont, 4; Hoover, 5; Kellogg, 1; Butler, 4; Knox, 1; Ward, 2; Watson, 1.
Seventh ballot, pp. 205-6.
b/ Other candidates: Coolidge, 28; du Pont, 3; Sproul, 76; Butler, 2; Poindexter, 15; Hoover, 4; Irvine L. Lenroot, 1; Kellogg, 1; LaFollette, 24; Ward, 1.
Eighth ballot, pp. 210-11.
c/ Sum of column; proceedings record 133½.
d/ Other candidates: Johnson, 87; Coolidge, 30; du Pont, 3; Kellogg, 1; LaFollette, 24; Poindexter, 15; Lenroot, 1; Hoover, 5; Butler, 2; Knox, 1; Sproul, 76.
Ninth ballot, pp. 213-4.
e/ Other candidates: Johnson, 82; Sproul, 78; Coolidge, 28; Hoover, 6; Lenroot, 1; Butler, 2; Knox, 1; LaFollette, 24; Poindexter, 14; Will H. Hays, 1; H. F. MacGregor, 1; not voting, 1.

Delegation	1920 REPUBLICAN										1924 REPUBLICAN							
		Presidential						Vice-Presidential				Presidential		Vice-Presidential				
		Tenth Ballot (before shift)			Tenth Ballot (after shift)			First Ballot				First Ballot		First Ballot				
	Votes	Wood	Harding	Other	Wood	Harding	Other	Coolidge	Lenroot	Other	Votes	Coolidge	Other	Lowden	Kenyon	Dawes	Burton	Other
Alabama	14	3	8	3	3	8	3	2	12	...	16	16	...	3	7	2	...	4
Arizona	6	6	...	...	...	6	...	6	...	...	9	9	...	9	...	...	...	...
Arkansas	13	...	13	...	...	13	...	13	...	...	14	14	...	...	...	...	...	14
California	26	...	...	26	...	...	26	19	...	7	29	29	...	10	2	1	10	6
Colorado	12	6	5	1	...	12	...	...	...	12	15	15	...	1	2	11	...	1
Connecticut	14	...	13	1	...	13	1	13	...	1	17	17	...	17	...	...	...	...
Delaware	6	...	6	...	...	6	...	1	5	...	9	9	...	9	...	...	...	...
Florida	8	½	7½	...	½	7½	...	8	...	...	10	10	...	9	...	...	...	1
Georgia	17	7	10	...	7	10	...	9	8	...	18	18	...	...	3	5	...	10
Idaho	8	3	2	3	3	2	3	8	...	...	11	11	...	...	...	...	...	11
Illinois	58	...	22[a]	35[b]	...	38[c]	19[d]	36	4	18	61	61	...	30	...	29	...	2
Indiana	30	8	20	2	9	21	...	16	11	3	33	33	...	...	...	...	...	33
Iowa	26	...	26	...	...	26	...	17½	3	5½	29	29	...	...	29	...	...	...
Kansas	20	1	18	1	1	18	1	...	...	20	23	23	...	...	...	...	...	23
Kentucky	26	...	26	...	...	26	...	1	24	1	26	26	...	26	...	...	...	...
Louisiana	12	...	12	...	...	12	...	12	...	...	13	13	...	5	...	1	...	7
Maine	12	12	...	...	12	...	...	12	...	...	15	15	...	2	5	5	3	...
Maryland	16	10	5	1	10	5	1	16	...	...	19	19	...	...	...	...	...	19
Massachusetts	35	17	17	1	17	17	1	35	...	...	39	39	...	3	11	3	4	18
Michigan	30	1	25	4	1	25	4	30	...	...	33	33	...	...	33	...	...	...
Minnesota	24	21	2	1	21	2	1	24	...	...	27	27	...	...	...	...	...	27
Mississippi	12	2½	9½	...	...	12	...	12	...	...	12	12	...	2	1	2	...	7
Missouri	36	...	36	...	...	36	...	8	21½	6½	39	39	...	...	...	1	...	38
Montana	8	...	...	8	...	...	8	1	7	...	11	11	...	...	...	...	...	11
Nebraska	16	5	4	7	5	4	7	16	...	...	19	19	...	...	...	19	...	...
Nevada	6	...	3½	2½	...	3½	2½	6	...	...	9	9	...	4	5	...	...	...
New Hampshire	8	8	...	...	8	...	...	8	...	...	11	11	...	...	2	4	5	...
New Jersey	28	15	5	8	15	5	8	25	2	1	31	31	...	...	...	31	...	...
New Mexico	6	6	...	...	...	6	...	1	5	...	9	9	...	9	...	...	...	...
New York	88	6	68	14	6	68	14	59	21	8	91	91	...	2	23	...	63	3
North Carolina	22	2	20	...	2	20	...	9	4	9	22	22	...	5	6	1	2	8
North Dakota	10	1	9	...	...	10	...	10	...	...	13	7	6	3	1	3	...	6
Ohio	48	...	48	...	...	48	...	10	9	29	51	51	...	...	...	...	50	1
Oklahoma	20	½	18	1½	½	18	1½	20	...	...	23	23	...	5	4	1	...	13
Oregon	10	3	2	5	3	2	5	10	...	...	13	13	...	13	...	...	...	...
Pennsylvania	76	14	60	2	14	60	2	76	...	...	79	79	...	...	...	...	...	79
Rhode Island	10	...	10	...	...	10	...	10	...	...	13	13	...	13	...	...	...	...
South Carolina	11	...	11	...	...	11	...	11	...	...	11	11	...	11	...	...	...	...
South Dakota	10	6	4	...	6	4	...	10	...	...	13	3	10	...	7	...	...	6
Tennessee	20	...	20	...	...	20	...	20	...	...	27	27	...	...	...	...	...	27
Texas	23	...	23	...	...	23	...	22	...	1	23	23	...	9	4	9	...	1
Utah	8	1	5	2	1	5	2	7	1	...	11	11	...	...	...	...	...	11
Vermont	8	8	...	...	8	...	...	8	...	...	11	11	...	11	...	...	...	...
Virginia	15	1	14	...	1	14	...	...	...	15	17	17	...	2	7	2	...	6
Washington	14	5	6	3	...	14	...	7	7	...	17	17	...	2	...	15	...	...
West Virginia	16	...	16	...	...	16	...	16	...	...	19	19	...	5	8	3	...	3
Wisconsin	26	...	1	25	...	1	25	...	2	24	29	1	28	...	...	1	...	28
Wyoming	6	...	6	...	...	6	...	6	...	...	9	9	...	...	9	...	...	...
Alaska	2	...	2	...	...	2	...	2	...	...	2	2	...	...	1	...	...	1
Canal Zone	...	...	...	...	...	...	...	...	...	...	...	...	...	...	...	...	...	...
District of Columbia	2	...	2	...	...	2	...	2	...	...	2	2	...	...	...	...	1	1
Hawaii	2	...	2	...	...	2	...	...	...	2	2	2	...	2	...	...	...	...
Philippine Islands	2	2	...	...	2	...	...	2	...	...	2	2	...	...	2	...	...	...
Puerto Rico	2	...	2	...	...	2	...	2	...	...	2	2	...	...	...	...	1	1
Virgin Islands	...	...	...	...	...	...	...	...	...	...	...	...	...	...	...	...	...	...
Total	984	181½	644[e]	157[f]	156	692[g]	135[h]	674½	146½	163[i]	1109	1065	44[j]	222	172	149	139	427[k]

Source: *Official Proceedings, 1920.*
Tenth ballot (before shift), pp. 220-1.
a/ Add one-fifth.
b/ Add four-fifths.
e/ Add seven-tenths.
f/ Other candidates: Lowden, 28; Johnson 80 and four-fifths; Hoover 10½; Coolidge, 5; Butler, 2; Lenroot, 1; Hays, 1; Knox, 1; LaFollette, 24; Poindexter, 2; not voting, 2½.
Tenth ballot (after shift), pp. 222-3.
c/ Add one-fifth.
d/ Add four-fifths.
g/ Add one-fifth.
h/ Other candidates: Lowden, 11; Johnson, 80 and four-fifths; Hoover, 9½; Coolidge, 5; Butler, 2; Lenroot, 1; Hays, 1; Knox, 1; LaFollette, 24; not voting, ½.
Vice-Presidential. First ballot, pp. 231-2.
i/ Other candidates: Jeter C. Pritchard, 11; Hiram W. Johnson, 22½; Asle J. Gronna, 24; Henry W. Anderson, 28; Henry J. Allen, 68½; not voting, 9.

Source: *Official Proceedings, 1924.*
Presidential. First ballot, p. 163.
j/ Other candidates: Robert M. LaFollette, 34; Hiram W. Johnson, 10.
Vice-Presidential ballots. First, p. 180.
k/ Other candidates: James E. Watson, 79; Charles Curtis, 56; Arthur M. Hyde, 55; Frank T. Hines, 29; Charles A. March, 28; George N. Norris, 35; James G. Harbord, 3; George S. Graham, 81; J. Will Taylor, 27; Albert J. Beveridge, 2; William Wrigley, Jr., 1; William P. Jackson, 23; not voting, 8.

Delegation	Votes	1924 REPUBLICAN Vice-Presidential Second Ballot (before shift)				Second Ballot (after shift)				Third Ballot			Votes	1928 REPUBLICAN Minority Report, Texas Credentials		
		Lowden	Dawes	Burton	Other	Lowden	Dawes	Burton	Other	Dawes	Hoover	Other		Yea	Nay	Not Voting
Alabama	16	11	1	2	2	11	1	2	2	2	14	...	15	1	14	...
Arizona	9	9	...	...	...	9	...	...	...	9	...	...	9	...	9	...
Arkansas	14	...	...	...	14	14	...	...	...	...	14	...	11	1	10	...
California	29	23	1	...	5	23	1	...	5	...	29	...	29	...	29	...
Colorado	15	1	10	3	1	15	...	...	...	15	...	...	15	1	14	...
Connecticut	17	17	...	...	...	17	...	...	...	1	16	...	17	17	...	...
Delaware	9	9	...	...	...	9	...	...	...	...	...	9	9	9	...	...
Florida	10	10	...	...	...	10	...	...	...	...	10	...	10	...	9	1
Georgia	18	...	...	17	1	...	...	17	1	2	15	1	16	2	14	...
Idaho	11	...	...	...	11	...	...	...	11	10	...	1	11	...	11	...
Illinois	61	60	...	...	1	60	...	...	1	53	2	6	61	61	...	...
Indiana	33	...	...	...	33	33	...	...	...	...	...	33	33	32	1	...
Iowa	29	...	...	...	29	...	...	...	29	...	...	29	29	21	8	...
Kansas	23	...	...	...	23	...	...	...	23	23	...	...	23	23	...	...
Kentucky	26	26	...	...	...	26	...	...	...	7	...	19	29	...	29	...
Louisiana	13	...	...	13	...	13	...	...	...	6	7	...	12	2	10	...
Maine	15	8	...	6	1	8	...	6	1	15	...	...	15	...	15	...
Maryland	19	17	2	...	...	19	...	...	...	17	2	...	19	...	19	...
Massachusetts	39	...	...	33	6	...	...	33	6	...	39	...	39	...	39	...
Michigan	33	33	...	...	...	33	...	...	...	32	1	...	33	...	33	...
Minnesota	27	24	...	...	3	27	...	...	...	25	...	2	27	16	11	...
Mississippi	12	...	...	12	...	...	...	12	...	...	12	...	12	...	12	...
Missouri	39	...	2	...	37	...	2	...	37	22½	15½	...	39	18	16	5
Montana	11	11	...	...	...	11	...	...	...	5	...	6	11	5½	5½	...
Nebraska	19	...	19	...	...	...	19	...	...	19	...	...	19	...	18	1
Nevada	9	9	...	...	...	9	...	...	...	9	...	...	9	...	9	...
New Hampshire	11	...	7	2	2	...	7	2	2	7	1	3	11	...	11	...
New Jersey	31	...	31	...	...	31	...	...	...	31	...	...	31	...	31	...
New Mexico	9	9	...	...	...	9	...	...	...	9	...	...	9	2	7	...
New York	91	16	4	49	22	86	...	1	4	60	4	27	90	59	31	...
North Carolina	22	3	...	17	2	3	...	17	2	18	...	4	20	13	7	...
North Dakota	13	7	...	...	6	7	...	...	6	6	...	7	13	11	2	...
Ohio	51	...	...	49	2	51	...	...	...	25	25	1	51	20	31	...
Oklahoma	23	13	...	...	10	22	...	...	1	22	1	...	20	20	...	...
Oregon	13	13	...	...	...	13	...	...	...	...	13	...	13	...	13	...
Pennsylvania	79	...	...	78	1	78	...	...	1	78	...	1	79	...	79	...
Rhode Island	13	...	13	...	...	13	...	...	...	13	...	...	13	...	13	...
South Carolina	11	11	...	...	...	11	...	...	...	11	...	...	11	11	...	...
South Dakota	13	...	...	...	13	...	...	...	13	...	...	13	13	13	...	...
Tennessee	27	24	...	3	...	24	...	3	...	13	14	...	19	5	14	...
Texas	23	...	...	...	23	...	...	...	23	23	...	...	26	...	4	22
Utah	11	...	...	...	11	11	...	...	...	11	...	...	11	...	11	...
Vermont	11	11	...	...	...	11	...	...	...	11	...	...	11	...	11	...
Virginia	17	7	2	1	7	16	...	...	1	16	...	1	15	...	15	...
Washington	17	17	...	...	...	17	...	...	...	17	...	...	17	...	17	...
West Virginia	19	...	19	...	...	...	19	...	...	19	...	...	19	16	3	...
Wisconsin	29	1	...	...	28	1	...	...	28	1	...	28	26	18	7	1
Wyoming	9	9	...	...	...	9	...	...	...	9	...	...	9	...	9	...
Alaska	2	...	...	...	2	...	...	...	2	2	...	...	2	2	...	...
Canal Zone	..	...	...	...	...	...	...	...	...	...	...	...	..	...	...	...
District of Columbia	2	...	...	1	1	...	...	1	1	2	...	...	2	...	2	...
Hawaii	2	2	...	...	...	2	...	...	...	2	...	...	2	...	2	...
Philippine Islands	2	2	...	...	...	2	...	...	...	2	...	...	2	...	2	...
Puerto Rico	2	...	...	2	...	2	...	...	...	2	...	...	2	...	2	...
Virgin Islands	...	...	...	...	...	...	...	...	...	...	...	...	...	...	...	...
Total	1109	413	111	288	297a	766	49	94	200b	682½	234½	192c	1089	399½	659½	30

Source: *Official Proceedings, 1924*.
Second ballot (before shift), p. 182.
a/ Other candidates: William S. Kenyon, 95; Watson, 55; Curtis, 31; Hines, 15; Hyde, 36; Joseph M. Dixon, 1; Smith W. Brookhart, 31; Charles B. Warren, 23; Norris, 2; Lee Coulter, 1; Wrigley, 1; not voting, 6.
Second ballot (after shift), p. 185.
b/ Other candidates: Kenyon, 68; Watson, 7; Curtis, 24; Hyde, 36; Dixon, 1; Brookhart, 31; Warren, 23; Norris, 2; Coulter, 1; Wrigley, 1; not voting, 6.
Third ballot, p. 191.
c/ Other candidates: Kenyon, 75; Watson, 45; Dixon, 6; Coleman du Pont, 11; Everett Saunders, 4; Wrigley, 1; Norris, 29; not voting, 21.

Source: *Official Proceedings, 1928*.
Minority report, Texas credentials, p. 68.

Delegation	Votes	Minority Farm Plank Yea	Nay	Not Voting	Presidential First Ballot Hoover	Other	Table Georgia Request Yea	Nay	Not Voting	Vice-Pres. First Ballot Curtis	Other	Votes	Minority Prohibition Plank Yea	Nay	Not Voting	Presidential First Ballot Hoover	Other
Alabama	15	1	14	...	15	...	...	15	...	15	...	19	...	19	...	19	...
Arizona	9	4	5	...	9	...	9	...	...	9	...	9	9	...	...	9	...
Arkansas	11	4	7	...	11	...	10	1	...	11	...	15	...	15	...	15	...
California	29	...	29	...	29	...	29	...	...	29	...	47	6	41	...	47	...
Colorado	15	...	15	...	15	...	15	...	...	15	...	15	1	14	...	15	...
Connecticut	17	...	17	...	17	...	17	...	...	17	...	19	19	...	...	19	...
Delaware	9	...	9	...	9	...	9	...	...	9	...	9	...	9	...	9	...
Florida	10	3	7	...	9	1	...	10	...	10	...	16	...	16	...	16	...
Georgia	16	...	16	...	15	1	...	...	16	16	...	16	2	14	...	16	...
Idaho	11	1	10	...	11	...	...	11	...	11	...	11	...	11	...	11	...
Illinois	61	61	...	...	24	37	60	1	...	61	...	61	45	15½	½	54½	6½
Indiana	33	30	3	...	...	33	33	...	...	33	...	31	28	3	...	31	...
Iowa	29	27	2	...	7	22	15	14	...	29	...	25	3	22	...	25	...
Kansas	23	6	17	...	...	23	23	...	...	23	...	21	4	17	...	21	...
Kentucky	29	...	29	...	29	...	...	29	...	29	...	25	15	10	...	25	...
Louisiana	12	...	12	...	11	1	12	...	...	12	...	12	...	12	...	12	...
Maine	15	...	15	...	15	...	15	...	...	15	...	13	5	8	...	13	...
Maryland	19	...	19	...	19	...	9	10	...	19	...	19	...	19	...	19	...
Massachusetts	39	...	39	...	39	...	39	...	...	39	...	34	16	17	1	34	...
Michigan	33	19	14	...	33	...	2	31	...	33	...	41	25½	15½	...	41	...
Minnesota	27	18	9	...	11	16	7	20	...	24	3	25	...	25	...	25	...
Mississippi	12	...	12	...	12	...	11	1	...	12	...	11	11	...	...	11	...
Missouri	39	2	33	4	28	11	35	4	...	39	...	33	8½	23c	d	33	...
Montana	11	5	6	...	10	1	11	...	...	11	...	11	...	11	...	11	...
Nebraska	19	9	10	...	11	8	10	7	2	19	...	17	1	16	...	17	...
Nevada	9	...	9	...	9	...	9	...	...	9	...	9	8	1	...	9	...
New Hampshire	11	...	11	...	11	...	11	...	...	11	...	11	...	11	...	11	...
New Jersey	31	...	31	...	31	...	31	...	...	31	...	35	35	...	...	35	...
New Mexico	9	1	8	...	7	2	4	5	...	9	...	9	2	7	...	8	1
New York	90	...	90	...	90	...	78	12	...	90	...	97	76	21	...	97	...
North Carolina	20	...	20	...	17	3	7	13	...	20	...	28	3	25	...	28	...
North Dakota	13	13	...	...	4	9	6	7	...	7	6	11	...	11	...	9	2
Ohio	51	12	39	...	36	15	32	19	...	51	...	55	12e	42f	...	55	...
Oklahoma	20	...	20	...	...	20	7	13	...	20	...	25	...	25	...	25	...
Oregon	13	...	13	...	13	...	13	...	...	13	...	13	3	10	...	9	4
Pennsylvania	79	2	77	...	79	...	79	...	...	79	...	75	51	23	1	73	2
Rhode Island	13	...	13	...	12	1	13	...	...	13	...	8	8	...	...	8	...
South Carolina	11	10	1	...	11	...	...	11	...	11	...	10	...	10	...	10	...
South Dakota	13	13	...	...	2	11	...	13	...	3	10	11	3	8	...	11	...
Tennessee	19	...	19	...	19	...	...	19	...	19	...	24	1	23	...	24	...
Texas	26	...	26	...	26	...	26	...	...	26	...	49	...	49	...	49	...
Utah	11	3	8	...	9	2	11	...	...	11	...	11	1	10	...	11	...
Vermont	11	...	11	...	11	...	11	...	...	11	...	9	9	...	...	9	...
Virginia	15	...	15	...	15	...	9	6	...	15	...	25	...	25	...	25	...
Washington	17	1	16	...	17	...	17	...	...	17	...	19	11	8	...	19	...
West Virginia	19	12	7	...	1	18	1	18	...	19	...	19	4	15	...	19	...
Wisconsin	26	18	7	1	9	17	9	15	2	8	18	27	22	5	...	15	12
Wyoming	9	...	9	...	9	...	9	...	...	9	...	9	9	...	...	9	...
Alaska	2	2	...	...	2	...	2	...	...	2	...	2	...	2	...	2	...
Canal Zone	...	...	...	...	...	...	...	...	...	...	...	...	...	...	...	...	...
District of Columbia	2	...	2	...	2	...	2	...	...	2	...	2	...	2	...	...	...
Hawaii	2	...	2	...	2	...	2	...	...	2	...	2	2	...	...	2	...
Philippine Islands	2	...	2	...	2	...	...	2	...	2	...	2	1	1	...	2	...
Puerto Rico	2	...	2	...	2	...	1	1	...	2	...	2	...	2	...	2	...
Virgin Islands	...	...	...	...	...	...	...	...	...	...	...	...	...	...	...	...	...
Total	1089	277	807	5	837	252a	761	308	20	1052	37b	1154	460g	690h	2i	1126½	27½j

Source: *Official Proceedings, 1928.*

Minority farm plank, p. 175.
Presidential. First ballot, p. 220
a/ Other candidates: Frank O. Lowden, 74; Charles Curtis, 64; James E. Watson, 45; George W. Norris, 24; Guy D. Goff, 18; Calvin Coolidge, 17; Charles G. Dawes, 4; Charles E. Hughes, 1; not voting, 5.
Table Georgia request, p. 233.
Vice-Presidential. First ballot, pp. 250-1.
b/ Other candidates: H. L. Ekern, 19; Charles G. Dawes, 13; Hanford MacNider, 2; not voting, 3.

Source: *Official Proceedings, 1932.*

Minority prohibition plank, pp. 160-1.
c/ Add three-fourths.
d/ Add one-fourth.
e/ Add two-ninths.
f/ Add two-ninths.
g/ Add two-ninths.
h/ Add nineteen-thirty-sixths.
i/ Add three-fourths.
Presidential. First ballot, pp. 198-9.
j/ Other candidates: John J. Blaine, 13; Calvin Coolidge, 4½; Joseph I. France, 4; Charles G. Dawes, 1; James W. Wadsworth, 1; not voting, 4.

	1932 REPUBLICAN Vice-Presidential First Ballot					1936 REPUBLICAN Presidential First Ballot			V.-P. First Ballot	1940 REPUBLICAN Presidential								
											First Ballot				Second Ballot			
Delegation	Votes	Curtis	MacNider	Harbord	Other	Votes	Landon	Other	Knox	Votes	Dewey	Taft	Willkie	Other	Dewey	Taft	Willkie	Other
Alabama	19	15	...	3	1	13	13	...	13	13	7	6	...	...	7	6	...	...
Arizona	9	9	...	...	...	6	6	...	6	6	...	...	...	6	...	...	...	6
Arkansas	15	12	...	1	2	11	11	...	11	12	2	7	2	1	3	6	2	1
California	47	47	...	...	...	44	44	...	44	44	7	7	7	23	8	9	9	18
Colorado	15	11	4	...	...	12	12	...	12	12	1	4	3	4	1	5	4	2
Connecticut	19	2	...	17	...	19	19	...	19	16	...	...	16	...	...	...	16	...
Delaware	9	9	...	...	...	9	9	...	9	6	...	1	3	2	...	2	4	...
Florida	16	...	...	...	16	12	12	...	12	12	6	1	...	5	9	1	...	2
Georgia	16	11	2	...	3	14	14	...	14	14	7	3	...	4	7	2	...	5
Idaho	11	4	1	3	3	8	8	...	8	8	8	...	...	...	8	...	...	...
Illinois	61	13½	33½	6	8	57	57	...	57	58	52	2	4	...	45	7	5	1
Indiana	31	31	...	...	...	28	28	...	28	28	7	7	9	5	7	6	12	3
Iowa	25	...	23	...	2	22	22	...	22	22	...	...	...	22	...	...	...	22
Kansas	21	21	...	...	...	18	18	...	18	18	...	...	...	18	...	...	...	18
Kentucky	25	25	...	...	...	22	22	...	22	22	12	8	...	2	11	10	...	1
Louisiana	12	12	...	...	...	12	12	...	12	12	5	5	...	2	6	6	...	...
Maine	13	6	7	...	...	13	13	...	13	13	...	...	...	13	3	1	9	...
Maryland	19	19	...	...	...	16	16	...	16	16	16	...	...	...	12	...	4	...
Massachusetts	34	...	...	...	34	33	33	...	33	34	...	...	1	33	...	1	8	25
Michigan	41	32	9	...	...	38	38	...	38	38	...	...	...	38	...	...	...	38
Minnesota	25	10	15	...	...	22	22	...	22	22	3	4	6	9	2	5	6	9
Mississippi	11	11	...	...	...	11	11	...	11	11	3	8	...	...	3	8	...	...
Missouri	33	21a	2b	3c	5d	30	30	...	30	30	10	3	6	11	8	4	13	5
Montana	11	2	9	...	...	8	8	...	8	8	8	...	...	...	8	...	...	...
Nebraska	17	14	3	...	...	14	14	...	14	14	14	...	...	...	5	2	2	5
Nevada	9	7	2	...	...	6	6	...	6	6	...	2	3	2	...	2	3	1
New Hampshire	11	...	...	...	11	11	11	...	11	8	...	...	...	8	...	...	...	8
New Jersey	35	8	3	21	3	32	32	...	32	32	20	...	12	...	14	1	17	...
New Mexico	9	3	...	...	6	6	6	...	6	6	3	1	2	...	2	1	3	...
New York	97	2	...	95	...	90	90	...	90	92	61	...	8	23	58	...	13	21
North Carolina	28	28	...	...	...	23	23	...	23	23	9	7	2	5	8	7	6	2
North Dakota	11	5	6	...	...	8	8	...	8	8	2	1	1	4	2	1	3	2
Ohio	55	27	15	5	8	52	52	...	52	52	...	52	...	...	...	52	...	...
Oklahoma	25	24	1	...	...	21	21	...	21	22	22	...	...	...	22	...	...	...
Oregon	13	12	...	...	1	10	10	...	10	10	...	...	...	10	...	...	...	10
Pennsylvania	75	75	...	...	...	75	75	...	75	72	1	...	1	70	2	...	5	65
Rhode Island	8	7	...	1	...	8	8	...	8	8	1	3	3	1	1	3	4	...
South Carolina	10	5	1	1	3	10	10	...	10	10	10	...	...	...	10	...	...	...
South Dakota	11	5	6	...	...	8	8	...	8	8	...	...	...	8	2	...	...	6
Tennessee	24	22	2	...	...	17	17	...	17	18	8	3	2	5	7	4	5	2
Texas	49	...	...	...	49	25	25	...	25	26	...	26	...	...	...	26	...	...
Utah	11	2	5	4	...	8	8	...	8	8	2	2	1	3	2	2	...	4
Vermont	9	1	1	...	7	9	9	...	9	9	1	3	3	2	2	3	4	...
Virginia	25	22	2	1	...	17	17	...	17	18	2	9	5	2	5	7	5	1
Washington	19	5	13	...	1	16	16	...	16	16	13	3	...	...	12	3	...	1
West Virginia	19	16	2	...	1	16	15	1	16	16	8	5	3	...	6	4	6	...
Wisconsin	27	2	14	...	11	24	6	18	24	24	24	...	...	...	24	...	...	...
Wyoming	9	8	1	...	...	6	6	...	6	6	1	1	2	2	2	1	2	1
Alaska	2	2	...	...	...	3	3	...	3	3	1	2	...	...	1	2	...	...
Canal Zone	...	...	...	...	...	...	...	...	...	...	...	...	...	...	...	...	...	...
District of Columbia	2	2	...	...	...	3	3	...	3	3	2	1	...	...	2	1	...	...
Hawaii	2	2	...	...	...	3	3	...	3	3	...	...	...	3	...	...	...	3
Philippine Islands	2	2	...	...	...	2	2	...	2	2	...	1	1	...	...	1	1	...
Puerto Rico	2	2	...	...	...	2	2	...	2	2	1	1	...	...	1	1	...	...
Virgin Islands	...	...	...	...	...	...	...	...	...	...	...	...	...	...	...	...	...	...
Total	1154	634e	182f	161g	175h	1003	984	19i	1003	1000	360	189	105	346j	338	203	171	288k

Source: *Official Proceedings, 1932.*

Vice-Presidential. First ballot, pp. 215-6.
a/ Add three-fourths.
b/ Add one-fourth.
c/ Add three-fourths.
d/ Add one-fourth.
e/ Add three-fourths.
f/ Add three-fourths.
g/ Add three-fourths.
h/ Other candidates: Alvan T. Fuller, 57; Bertrand H. Snell, 56; J. Leonard Replogle, 23 and three-fourths; James G. Couzens, 11; Charles G. Dawes, 9 and three-fourths; David S. Ingalls, 5; Patrick J. Hurley, 2; William S. Kenyon, 2; Hiram Bingham, 1; Edward Martin, 1; not voting, 6 and three-fourths.

Source: *Official Proceedings, 1936.*

Presidential. First ballot, pp. 177-8.
i/ Other candidates: William E. Borah, 19.
Vice-Presidential. First ballot, pp. 207-8.

Source: *Official Proceedings, 1940.*

Presidential. First ballot, pp. 279-80.
j/ Other candidates: Arthur H. Vandenberg, 76; Arthur H. James, 74; Joseph W. Martin, 44; Hanford MacNider, 34; Frank E. Gannett, 33; Styles Bridges, 28; Arthur Capper, 18; Herbert Hoover, 17; Charles L. McNary, 13; Harlan F. Bushfield, 9.
Second ballot, p. 285.
k/ Other candidates: Vandenberg, 73; James, 66; MacNider, 34; Gannett, 30; Martin, 26; Hoover, 21; Capper, 18; McNary, 10; Bridges, 9; Fiorello H. LaGuardia, 1.

1940 REPUBLICAN
Presidential

Delegation	Votes	Third Ballot Dewey	Taft	Willkie	Other	Fourth Ballot Dewey	Taft	Willkie	Other	Fifth Ballot Taft	Willkie	Other	Sixth Ballot (before shift) Taft	Willkie	Other	Sixth Ballot (after shift) Willkie	Other
Alabama	13	7	5	1	...	7	5	1	...	7	5	1	7	6	...	13	...
Arizona	6	...	...	6	...	...	...	6	...	...	6	...	...	6	...	6	...
Arkansas	12	3	7	2	...	3	7	2	...	10	2	...	10	2	...	12	...
California	44	10	11	8	15	9	11	10	14	12	9	23	22	17	5	44	...
Colorado	12	1	6	2	3	1	4	3	4	4	4	4	6	5	1	12	...
Connecticut	16	...	...	16	...	...	...	16	...	...	16	...	...	16	...	16	...
Delaware	6	...	...	6	...	...	...	6	...	...	6	...	...	6	...	6	...
Florida	12	9	1	...	2	9	2	...	1	3	7	2	2	10	...	12	...
Georgia	14	7	3	1	3	6	3	2	3	7	6	1	7	6	1	14	...
Idaho	8	8	...	...	...	8	...	...	...	7	...	1	6	2	...	8	...
Illinois	58	47	4	7	...	17	27	10	4	30	17	11	33	24	1	58	...
Indiana	28	6	5	14	3	5	6	15	2	7	20	1	5	23	...	28	...
Iowa	22	...	...	...	22	2	...	...	20	13	7	2	15	7	...	22	...
Kansas	18	11	2	4	1	11	2	5	...	...	18	...	...	18	...	18	...
Kentucky	22	9	11	...	2	9	13	...	...	22	...	...	22	...	...	22	...
Louisiana	12	6	6	...	...	6	6	...	...	12	...	...	12	...	...	12	...
Maine	13	3	1	9	...	2	2	9	...	...	13	...	...	13	...	13	...
Maryland	16	2	2	10	2	...	...	14	2	1	14	1	1	15	...	16	...
Massachusetts	34	...	2	28	4	...	2	28	4	2	28	4	2	30	2	34	...
Michigan	38	2	...	...	36	2	...	...	36	...	...	38	2	35	1	38	...
Minnesota	22	2	5	8	7	2	9	9	2	12	9	1	11	10	1	22	...
Mississippi	11	2	9	...	...	2	9	...	...	11	...	...	9	2	...	11	...
Missouri	30	6	3	16	5	4	3	18	5	7	21	2	4	26	...	30	...
Montana	8	4	2	2	...	3	3	2	...	4	4	...	4	4	...	8	...
Nebraska	14	3	4	3	4	2	5	5	2	9	5	...	6	8	...	14	...
Nevada	6	...	1	4	1	...	1	4	1	2	4	...	2	4	...	6	...
New Hampshire	8	...	...	4	4	...	...	4	4	2	6	...	2	6	...	8	...
New Jersey	32	7	1	19	5	6	1	23	2	1	26	5	...	32	...	32	...
New Mexico	6	1	1	4	...	1	1	4	...	2	4	...	1	5	...	6	...
New York	92	54	...	27	11	48	5	35	4	10	75	7	7	78	7	92	...
North Carolina	23	6	8	7	2	6	6	9	2	11	12	...	8	15	...	23	...
North Dakota	8	2	1	3	2	2	1	3	2	4	4	...	4	4	...	8	...
Ohio	52	...	52	...	...	...	52	...	...	52	...	...	52	...	...	52	...
Oklahoma	22	22	...	...	...	10	6	3	3	18	4	...	5	17	...	22	...
Oregon	10	...	...	...	10	1	...	1	8	...	1	9	3	7	...	10	...
Pennsylvania	72	...	...	15	57	...	...	19	53	...	21	51	...	72	...	72	...
Rhode Island	8	...	4	4	...	...	4	4	...	4	4	...	3	5	...	8	...
South Carolina	10	10	...	...	...	8	...	2	...	...	9	1	...	10	...	10	...
South Dakota	8	5	...	...	3	4	1	...	3	7	1	...	2	6	...	8	...
Tennessee	18	7	4	5	2	5	6	5	2	9	6	3	5	10	3	17	1
Texas	26	...	26	...	...	...	26	...	...	26	...	...	26	...	...	26	...
Utah	8	2	1	1	4	2	2	1	3	3	5	...	1	7	...	8	...
Vermont	9	1	3	5	...	1	3	5	...	3	6	...	2	7	...	9	...
Virginia	18	3	7	8	...	...	7	11	...	7	11	...	2	16	...	18	...
Washington	16	12	3	...	1	12	3	...	1	16	...	...	4	10	2	16	...
West Virginia	16	6	3	7	...	6	3	7	...	9	6	1	...	15	1	15	1
Wisconsin	24	24	...	...	...	24	...	...	...	...	...	24	2	20	2	24	...
Wyoming	6	3	2	1	...	3	2	1	...	3	3	...	...	6	...	6	...
Alaska	3	...	3	...	...	...	2	1	...	3	...	...	1	2	...	3	...
Canal Zone	...																
District of Columbia	3	1	1	1	...	...	1	2	...	1	2	...	...	3	...	3	...
Hawaii	3	...	...	...	3	...	...	...	3	1	1	1	...	3	...	3	...
Philippine Islands	2	...	1	1	...	...	1	1	...	1	1	...	...	2	...	2	...
Puerto Rico	2	1	1	...	...	1	1	...	...	2	...	...	...	2	...	2	...
Virgin Islands	...																
Total	1000	315	212	259	214a	250	254	306	190b	377	429	194c	318	655	27d	998	2e

Source: *Official Proceedings, 1940.*

Third ballot, pp. 289-90.
a/ Other candidates: Vandenberg, 72; James, 59; Hoover, 32; MacNider, 28; Gannett, 11; McNary, 10; Bridges, 1; not voting, 1.
Fourth ballot, p. 296.
b/ Other candidates: Vandenberg, 61; James, 56; Hoover, 31; MacNider, 26; McNary, 8; Gannett, 4; Bridges, 1; not voting, 3.
Fifth ballot, p. 302.
c/ Other candidates: James, 59; Dewey, 57; Vandenberg, 42; Hoover, 20; McNary, 9; MacNider, 4; Gannett, 1; not voting, 2.
Sixth ballot (before shift), pp. 307-18.
d/ Other candidates: Dewey, 11; Hoover, 10; Gannett, 1; McNary, 1; not voting, 4.
Sixth ballot (after shift), p. 320.
e/ Not voting, 2.

Delegation	1940 REPUBLICAN Vice-Presidential First Ballot				1944 REPUBLICAN Pres. First Ballot			1944 Vice-Pres. First Ballot		1948 REPUBLICAN Presidential	First Ballot				Second Ballot			
	Votes	McNary	Short	Other	Votes	Dewey	Other	Bricker	Other	Votes	Dewey	Stassen	Taft	Other	Dewey	Stassen	Taft	Other
Alabama	13	13	...	...	14	14	...	14	...	14	9	...	5	...	9	...	5	...
Arizona	6	6	...	...	8	8	...	8	...	8	3	2	3	...	4	2	2	...
Arkansas	12	7	5	...	12	12	...	12	...	14	3	4	7	...	3	4	7	...
California	44	44	...	...	50	50	...	50	...	53	...	...	...	53	...	...	...	53
Colorado	12	12	...	...	15	15	...	15	...	15	3	5	7	...	3	8	4	...
Connecticut	16	16	...	...	16	16	...	16	...	19	...	...	...	19	...	...	...	19
Delaware	6	4	2	...	9	9	...	9	...	9	5	1	2	1	6	1	2	...
Florida	12	12	...	...	15	15	...	15	...	16	6	4	6	...	6	4	6	...
Georgia	14	14	...	...	14	14	...	14	...	16	12	1	...	3	13	1	...	2
Idaho	8	8	...	...	11	11	...	11	...	11	11	...	...	...	11	...	...	...
Illinois	58	52	6	...	59	59	...	59	...	56	...	...	...	56	5	...	50	1
Indiana	28	28	...	...	29	29	...	29	...	29	29	...	...	...	29	...	...	...
Iowa	22	22	...	...	23	23	...	23	...	23	3	13	5	2	13	7	2	1
Kansas	18	18	...	...	19	19	...	19	...	19	12	1	2	4	14	1	2	2
Kentucky	22	21	1	...	22	22	...	22	...	25	10	1	11	3	11	1	11	2
Louisiana	12	10	2	...	13	13	...	13	...	13	6	...	7	...	6	...	7	...
Maine	13	13	...	...	13	13	...	13	...	13	5	4	1	3	5	7	...	1
Maryland	16	16	...	...	16	16	...	16	...	16	8	3	5	...	13	...	3	...
Massachusetts	34	29	5	...	35	35	...	35	...	35	17	1	2	15	18	1	3	13
Michigan	38	33	5	...	41	41	...	41	...	41	...	...	...	41	...	...	...	41
Minnesota	22	20	2	...	25	25	...	25	...	25	...	25	...	...	...	25	...	...
Mississippi	11	11	...	...	6	6	...	6	...	8	...	...	8	...	...	...	8	...
Missouri	30	...	30	...	30	30	...	30	...	33	17	6	8	2	18	6	7	2
Montana	8	8	...	...	8	8	...	8	...	11	5	3	3	...	6	2	3	...
Nebraska	14	10	4	...	15	15	...	15	...	15	2	13	...	...	6	9	...	...
Nevada	6	6	...	...	6	6	...	6	...	9	6	1	2	...	6	1	2	...
New Hampshire	8	8	...	...	11	11	...	11	...	8	6	2	...	...	6	2	...	...
New Jersey	32	32	...	...	35	35	...	35	...	35	...	...	...	35	24	6	2	3
New Mexico	6	6	...	...	8	8	...	8	...	8	3	2	3	...	3	2	3	...
New York	92	82	10	...	93	93	...	93	...	97	96	...	1	...	96	...	1	...
North Carolina	23	15	8	...	25	25	...	25	...	26	16	2	5	3	17	2	4	3
North Dakota	8	8	...	...	11	11	...	11	...	11	...	11	...	...	...	11	...	...
Ohio	52	36	16	...	50	50	...	50	...	53	...	9	44	...	1	8	44	...
Oklahoma	22	22	...	...	23	23	...	23	...	20	18	...	1	1	19	...	1	...
Oregon	10	10	...	...	15	15	...	15	...	12	12	...	...	...	12	...	...	...
Pennsylvania	72	72	...	...	70	70	...	70	...	73	41	1	28	3	40	1	29	3
Rhode Island	8	8	...	...	8	8	...	8	...	8	1	...	1	6	4	...	2	2
South Carolina	10	8	2	...	4	4	...	4	...	6	...	...	6	...	...	...	6	...
South Dakota	8	8	...	...	11	11	...	11	...	11	3	8	...	...	7	4	...	...
Tennessee	18	18	...	...	19	19	...	19	...	22	6	...	...	16	8	...	13	1
Texas	26	22	2	2	33	33	...	33	...	33	2	1	30	...	2	2	29	...
Utah	8	8	...	...	8	8	...	8	...	11	5	2	4	...	6	2	3	...
Vermont	9	9	...	...	9	9	...	9	...	9	7	2	...	...	7	2	...	...
Virginia	18	12	6	...	19	19	...	19	...	21	10	...	10	1	13	...	7	1
Washington	16	16	...	...	16	16	...	16	...	19	14	2	1	2	14	2	3	...
West Virginia	16	16	...	...	19	19	...	19	...	16	11	5	...	...	13	3	...	...
Wisconsin	24	24	...	...	24	23	1	24	...	27	...	19	...	8	2	19	...	6
Wyoming	6	4	2	...	9	9	...	9	...	9	4	3	2	...	6	3	...	...
Alaska	3	3	...	...	3	3	...	3	...	3	2	...	1	...	3	...	...	...
Canal Zone	...	...	...	...	...	...	...	...	...	...	...	...	...	...	...	...	...	...
District of Columbia	3	3	...	...	3	3	...	3	...	3	2	...	...	1	3	...	...	...
Hawaii	3	3	...	...	5	5	...	5	...	5	3	...	1	1	3	...	2	...
Philippine Islands	2	2	...	...	2	...	2	...	2	...	...	...	...	...	...	...	...	...
Puerto Rico	2	2	...	...	2	2	...	2	...	2	...	...	2	...	1	...	1	...
Virgin Islands	...	...	...	...	...	...	...	...	...	...	...	...	...	...	...	...	...	...
Total	1000	890	108	2a	1059	1056	3b	1057	2c	1094	434	157	224	279d	515	149	274	156e

Source: *Official Proceedings, 1940.*
Vice-Presidential. First ballot, pp. 336-7.
a/ Other candidates: Styles Bridges, 2.

Source: *Official Proceedings, 1944.*
Presidential. First ballot, pp. 204-5.
b/ Other candidates: Douglas MacArthur, 1; absent, 2.
Vice-Presidential. First ballot, pp. 216-7.
c/ Absent, 2.

Source: *Official Proceedings, 1948.*
Presidential. First ballot, pp. 257-8.
d/ Other candidates: Arthur H. Vandenberg, 62; Earl Warren, 59; Dwight H. Green, 56; Alfred E. Driscoll, 35; Raymond E. Baldwin, 19; Joseph W. Martin, 18; B. Carroll Reece, 15; Douglas MacArthur, 11; Everett M. Dirksen, 1; not voting, 3.
Second ballot, pp. 261-2.
e/ Other candidates: Vandenberg, 62; Warren, 57; Baldwin, 19; Martin, 10; MacArthur, 7; Reece, 1.

Delegation	1948 Third Ballot: Votes	1948: Dewey	1952: Votes	Brown Amendment, Contested Delegates: Yea	Brown: Nay	Minority Report, Georgia Contest: Yea	Minority: Nay	Minority: Not Voting	Adoption of Rules Committee Report: Yea	Adoption: Nay	Adoption: Not Voting	Presidential First Ballot (before shift): Eisenhower	Before: Taft	Before: Other	First Ballot (after shift): Eisenhower	After: Taft	After: Other
Alabama	14	14	14	9	5	5	9	...	...	14	...	5	9	...	14	...	...
Arizona	8	8	14	12	2	3	11	...	...	14	...	4	10	...	4	10	...
Arkansas	14	14	11	11	...	3	8	...	11	...	...	4	6	1	11	...	...
California	53	53	70	...	70	62	8	...	70	...	...	...	...	70	...	...	70
Colorado	15	15	18	1	17	17	1	...	18	...	...	15	2	1	17	1	...
Connecticut	19	19	22	2	20	21	1	...	22	...	...	21	1	...	22	...	...
Delaware	9	9	12	5	7	8	4	...	...	12	...	7	5	...	12	...	...
Florida	16	16	18	15	3	5	13	...	...	18	...	6	12	...	18	...	...
Georgia	16	16	17	17	...	...	...	17	16	1	...	14	2	1	16	1	...
Idaho	11	11	14	14	...	...	14	...	14	...	...	...	14	...	14	...	...
Illinois	56	56	60	58	2	1	59	...	...	60	...	1	59	...	1	59	...
Indiana	29	29	32	31	1	3	29	...	32	...	...	2	30	...	2	30	...
Iowa	23	23	26	11	15	16	10	...	24	1	1	16	10	...	20	6	...
Kansas	19	19	22	2	20	20	2	...	22	...	...	20	2	...	22	...	...
Kentucky	25	25	20	18	2	2	18	...	1	19	...	1	19	...	13	7	...
Louisiana	13	13	15	13	2	...	2	13	...	13	2	13	2	...	15	...	...
Maine	13	13	16	5	11	11	5	...	16	...	...	11	5	...	15	1	...
Maryland	16	16	24	5	19	15	9	...	24	...	...	16	8	...	24	...	...
Massachusetts	35	35	38	5	33	33	5	...	23	15	...	34	4	...	38	...	...
Michigan	41	41	46	1	45	32	14	...	44	2	...	35	11	...	35	11	...
Minnesota	25	25	28	...	28	28	...	...	28	...	...	9	...	19	28	...	...
Mississippi	8	8	5	5	...	...	5	...	...	5	...	...	5	...	5	...	...
Missouri	33	33	26	4	22	21	5	...	18	8	...	21	5	...	26	...	...
Montana	11	11	8	7	1	1	7	...	...	8	...	1	7	...	1	7	...
Nebraska	15	15	18	13	5	7	11	...	15	3	...	4	13	1	7	11	...
Nevada	9	9	12	7	5	2	10	...	2	10	...	5	7	...	10	2	...
New Hampshire	8	8	14	...	14	14	...	...	8	6	...	14	...	...	14	...	...
New Jersey	35	35	38	5	33	32	6	...	38	...	...	33	5	...	38	...	...
New Mexico	8	8	14	8	6	5	9	...	14	...	...	6	8	...	6	8	...
New York	97	97	96	1	95	92	4	...	96	...	...	92	4	...	95	1	...
North Carolina	26	26	26	14	12	10	16	...	...	26	...	12	14	...	26	...	...
North Dakota	11	11	14	11	3	3	11	...	14	...	...	4	8	2	5	8	1
Ohio	53	53	56	56	...	...	56	...	28	28	...	...	56	...	...	56	...
Oklahoma	20	20	16	10	6	4	12	...	...	16	...	4	7	5	8	4	4
Oregon	12	12	18	...	18	18	...	...	9	9	...	18	...	...	18	...	...
Pennsylvania	73	73	70	13	57	52	18	...	...	70	...	53	15	2	70	...	...
Rhode Island	8	8	8	2	6	6	2	...	1	1	6	6	1	1	8	...	...
South Carolina	6	6	6	5	1	1	5	...	...	6	...	2	4	...	6	...	...
South Dakota	11	11	14	14	...	...	14	...	...	14	...	...	14	...	7	7	...
Tennessee	22	22	20	20	...	...	20	...	...	20	...	...	20	...	20	...	...
Texas	33	33	38	22	16	...	...	38	14	...	...	33	5	...	38	...	...
Utah	11	11	14	14	...	...	14	...	14	...	...	...	14	...	...	14	...
Vermont	9	9	12	...	12	12	...	...	12	...	...	12	...	...	12	...	...
Virginia	21	21	23	13	10	7	16	...	...	23	...	9	14	...	19	4	...
Washington	19	19	24	4	20	19	5	...	24	...	...	20	4	...	21	3	...
West Virginia	16	16	16	15	1	1	15	...	1	15	...	1	14	1	3	13	...
Wisconsin	27	27	30	24	6	6	24	...	30	...	...	...	24	6	...	24	6
Wyoming	9	9	12	8	4	4	8	...	12	...	...	6	6	...	12	...	...
Alaska	3	3	3	3	...	...	3	...	...	3	...	1	2	...	3	...	...
Canal Zone	...	...	...	...	...	...	...	...	...	...	...	...	...	...	...	...	...
District of Columbia	3	3	6	6	...	...	6	...	...	6	...	...	6	...	6	...	...
Hawaii	5	5	8	7	1	3	5	...	8	...	...	3	4	1	4	4	...
Philippine Islands	...	...	...	...	...	...	...	...	...	...	...	...	...	...	...	...	...
Puerto Rico	2	2	3	2	1	1	2	...	...	3	...	...	3	...	1	2	...
Virgin Islands	...	...	1	...	1	1	...	...	1	...	...	1	...	...	1	...	...
Total	1094	1094	1206	548	658	607	531	68	683	513	10	595	500	111[a]	845	280	81[b]

Source: *Official Proceedings, 1948.*
Third ballot, pp. 275-6.

Source: *Official Proceedings, 1952.*
Brown amendment, contested delegates, pp. 48-9.
Minority report, Georgia contest, pp. 184-5.
Adoption of rules committee report, pp. 288-9.
Presidential. First ballot (before shift), pp. 388-99.
a/ Other candidates: Earl Warren, 81; Harold E. Stassen, 20; Douglas MacArthur, 10.
First ballot (after shift), pp. 405-6.
b/ Other candidates: Warren, 77; MacArthur, 4.

Delegation	1956 REPUBLICAN		
		Pres.	V.-P.
	Votes	Eisenhower	Nixon
Alabama	21	21	21
Arizona	14	14	14
Arkansas	16	16	16
California	70	70	70
Colorado.	18	18	18
Connecticut	22	22	22
Delaware	12	12	12
Florida.	26	26	26
Georgia	23	23	23
Idaho	14	14	14
Illinois	60	60	60
Indiana	32	32	32
Iowa.	26	26	26
Kansas	22	22	22
Kentucky.	26	26	26
Louisiana	20	20	20
Maine.	16	16	16
Maryland	24	24	24
Massachusetts	38	38	38
Michigan.	46	46	46
Minnesota	28	28	28
Mississippi.	15	15	15
Missouri.	32	32	32
Montana	14	14	14
Nebraska	18	18	18
Nevada	12	12	12
New Hampshire	14	14	14
New Jersey	38	38	38
New Mexico.	14	14	14
New York	96	96	96
North Carolina.	28	28	28
North Dakota	14	14	14
Ohio.	56	56	56
Oklahoma	22	22	22
Oregon	18	18	18
Pennsylvania	70	70	70
Rhode Island	14	14	14
South Carolina	16	16	16
South Dakota	14	14	14
Tennessee.	28	28	28
Texas.	54	54	54
Utah.	14	14	14
Vermont	12	12	12
Virginia	30	30	30
Washington	24	24	24
West Virginia	16	16	16
Wisconsin.	30	30	30
Wyoming.	12	12	12
Alaska	4	4	4
Canal Zone	...	...	...
District of Columbia .	6	6	6
Hawaii	10	10	10
Philippine Islands. . .	...	...	...
Puerto Rico.	3	3	3
Virgin Islands	1	1	1
Total	1323	1323	1323

Source: *Official Proceedings, 1956.*

Presidential. First ballot, pp. 288-9.
Vice-Presidential. First ballot, pp. 320-1.

Delegation	1960 REPUBLICAN				1964 REPUBLICAN											
	Presidential First ballot			Vice-pres. First ballot	Minority report civil rights			Presidential First ballot (before shifts)				Presidential First ballot (after shifts)				Vice-pres. First ballot
	Votes	Nixon	Goldwater	Lodge	Votes	Yea	Nay	Goldwater	Rockefeller	Scranton	Others	Goldwater	Rockefeller	Scranton	Other	Miller
Alabama	22	22	...	22	20	...	20	20	...	...	...	20	...	...	...	20
Alaska	6	6	...	6	12	12	...	...	...	8	4	...	...	8	4	12
Arizona	14	14	...	14	16	...	16	16	...	...	...	16	...	...	...	16
Arkansas	16	16	...	16	12	...	12	9	1	2	...	12	...	...	...	12
California	70	70	...	70	86	...	86	86	...	...	...	86	...	...	...	86
Colorado	18	18	...	18	18	...	18	15	...	3	...	18	...	...	...	18
Connecticut	22	22	...	22	16	11	5	4	...	12	...	16	...	...	...	16
Delaware	12	12	...	12	12	11	1	7	...	5	...	10	...	2	...	12
Florida	26	26	...	26	34	...	34	32	...	2	...	34	...	...	...	34
Georgia	24	24	...	24	24	...	24	22	...	2	...	24	...	...	...	24
Hawaii	12	12	...	12	8	4	4	4	...	...	4	8	...	...	...	8
Idaho	14	14	...	14	14	...	14	14	...	...	...	14	...	...	...	14
Illinois	60	60	...	60	58	4	54	56	2	...	...	56	2	...	...	58
Indiana	32	32	...	32	32	...	32	32	...	...	...	32	...	...	...	32
Iowa	26	26	...	26	24	2	22	14	...	10	...	24	...	...	...	24
Kansas	22	22	...	22	20	2	18	18	...	1	1	18	...	1	1	20
Kentucky	26	26	...	26	24	1	23	21	...	3	...	22	...	2	...	24
Louisiana	26	16	10	26	20	...	20	20	...	...	...	20	...	...	...	20
Maine	16	16	...	16	14	11	3	...	...	...	14	...	...	...	14	14
Maryland	24	24	...	24	20	17	3	6	1	13	...	7	1	12	...	20
Massachusetts	38	38	...	38	34	27	7	5	...	26	3	34	...	...	...	34
Michigan	46	46	...	46	48	37a	9	8	...	...	40	48	...	...	...	48
Minnesota	28	28	...	28	26	17	9	8	...	...	18	26	...	...	...	26
Mississippi	12	12	...	12	13	...	13	13	...	...	...	13	...	...	...	13
Missouri	26	26	...	26	24	1	23	23	...	1	...	24	...	...	...	24
Montana	14	14	...	14	14	...	14	14	...	...	...	14	...	...	...	14
Nebraska	18	18	...	18	16	...	16	16	...	...	...	16	...	...	...	16
Nevada	12	12	...	12	6	...	6	6	...	...	...	6	...	...	...	6
New Hampshire	14	14	...	14	14	14	...	...	...	14	...	...	...	14	...	14
New Jersey	38	38	...	38	40	40	...	20	...	20	...	38	...	2	...	40
New Mexico	14	14	...	14	14	...	14	14	...	...	...	14	...	...	...	14
New York	96	96	...	96	92	86	6	5	87	...	...	87	...	...	5	92
North Carolina	28	28	...	28	26	...	26	26	...	...	...	26	...	...	...	26
North Dakota	14	14	...	14	14	1	13	7	1	...	6	14	...	...	...	14
Ohio	56	56	...	56	58	...	58	57	...	...	1	58	...	...	...	58
Oklahoma	22	22	...	22	22	...	22	22	...	...	...	22	...	...	...	22
Oregon	18	18	...	18	18	10	8	...	18	...	...	16	...	...	2	18
Pennsylvania	70	70	...	70	64	62	2	4	...	60	...	64	...	...	...	64
Rhode Island	14	14	...	14	14	11	3	3	...	11	...	14	...	...	...	14
South Carolina	13	13	...	13	16	...	16	16	...	...	...	16	...	...	...	16
South Dakota	14	14	...	14	14	...	14	12	...	2	...	14	...	...	...	14
Tennessee	28	28	...	28	28	...	28	28	...	...	...	28	...	...	...	25b
Texas	54	54	...	54	56	...	56	56	...	...	...	56	...	...	...	56
Utah	14	14	...	14	14	...	14	14	...	...	...	14	...	...	...	14
Vermont	12	12	...	12	12	8	4	3	2	2	5	3	2	2	5	12
Virginia	30	30	...	30	30	...	30	29	...	1	...	30	...	...	...	30
Washington	24	24	...	24	24	1	23	22	...	1	1	22	...	1	1	24
West Virginia	22	22	...	22	14	4	10	10	2	2	...	12	1	1	...	14
Wisconsin	30	30	...	30	30	...	30	30	...	...	...	30	...	...	...	30
Wyoming	12	12	...	12	12	...	12	12	...	...	...	12	...	...	...	12
Dist. of Columbia	8	8	...	8	9	7	2	4	...	5	...	4	...	5	...	9
Puerto Rico	3	3	...	3	5	5	...	...	...	5	...	5	...	...	...	5
Virgin Islands	1	1	...	1	3	3	...	...	...	3	...	3	...	...	...	3
Total	1331	1321	10	1331	1308	409	897	883	114	214	97c	1220	6	50	32d	1305

Sources: *Official Proceedings, 1960*, pp. 301-02, 332-33. *Official Proceedings, 1964*, pp. 244-45, 366-67, 373-74, 397-98.

a. Two Michigan delegates not voting.

b. Three Tennessee delegates not voting.

c. Romney, 41 (40 in Michigan, 1 in Kansas); Smith, 27 (14 in Maine, 5 in Vermont, 3 in North Dakota, 2 in Alaska, 1 in Massachusetts, 1 in Ohio, 1 in Washington); Judd, 22 (18 in Minnesota, 3 in North Dakota, 1 in Alaska); Fong, 5 (4 in Hawaii, 1 in Alaska); Lodge, 2 (Massachusetts).

d. Smith, 22 (14 in Maine, 5 in Vermont, 2 in Alaska, 1 in Washington); Fong, 1 (Alaska); Judd, 1 (Alaska); Romney, 1 (Kansas); not voting, 7 (5 in New York, 2 in Oregon).

| | 1968 REPUBLICAN | | | | | | | | | | | 1972 REPUBLICAN | | | | | | | |
| | | Presidential (before shifts) | | | | Presidential (after shifts) | | | Vice-presidential | | | | Minority report rules | | | Presidential | | Vice-pres. | |
Delegation	Votes	Nixon	Nelson Rockefeller	Reagan	Others	Nixon	Nelson Rockefeller	Reagan	Agnew	Romney	Other	Votes	Yea	Nay	Not voting	Nixon	McCloskey	Agnew	Other
Alabama	26	14	...	12	...	26	...	...	25	...	1	18	...	18	...	18	...	18	...
Alaska	12	11	1	...	...	12	...	...	11	1	...	12	...	12	...	12	...	12	...
Arizona	16	16	...	...	...	16	...	...	16	...	...	18	...	18	...	18	...	18	...
Arkansas	18	...	...	...	18	18	...	...	9	9	...	18	...	18	...	18	...	17	1a
California	86	...	...	86	...	86	...	...	86	...	...	96	...	96	...	96	...	96	...
Colorado	18	14	3	1	...	18	...	...	14	4	...	20	...	20	...	20	...	20	...
Connecticut	16	4	12	...	...	16	...	...	16	...	...	22	21	1	...	22	...	22	...
Delaware	12	9	3	...	...	12	...	...	3	9	...	12	...	12	...	12	...	12	...
Florida	34	32	1	1	...	34	...	...	34	...	...	40	...	40	...	40	...	40	...
Georgia	30	21	2	7	...	30	...	...	29	1	...	24	...	24	...	24	...	24	...
Hawaii	14	...	...	...	14	14	...	...	14	...	...	14	...	14	...	14	...	14	...
Idaho	14	9	...	5	...	14	...	...	14	...	...	14	...	14	...	14	...	14	...
Illinois	58	50	5	3	...	58	...	...	56	...	2	58	8	50	...	58	...	58	...
Indiana	26	26	...	...	...	26	...	...	26	...	...	32	...	32	...	32	...	32	...
Iowa	24	13	8	3	...	24	...	...	18	6	...	22	12	10	...	22	...	22	...
Kansas	20	...	...	...	20	19	1	...	19	...	1	20	...	20	...	20	...	20	...
Kentucky	24	22	2	...	...	24	...	...	24	...	...	24	1	22	1	24	...	24	...
Louisiana	26	19	...	7	...	26	...	...	26	...	...	20	...	20	...	20	...	20	...
Maine	14	7	7	...	...	14	...	...	13	1	...	8	6	2	...	8	...	8	...
Maryland	26	18	8	...	...	26	...	...	26	...	...	26	7	19	...	26	...	26	...
Massachusetts	34	...	34	...	...	34	...	...	26	8	...	34	31	3	...	34	...	34	...
Michigan	48	4	...	...	44	48	...	...	5	43	...	48	47	1	...	48	...	48	...
Minnesota	26	9	15	...	2	26	...	...	4	22	...	26	22	4	...	26	...	26	...
Mississippi	20	20	...	...	...	20	...	...	20	...	...	14	...	14	...	14	...	14	...
Missouri	24	16	5	3	...	24	...	...	24	...	...	30	6	24	...	30	...	30	...
Montana	14	11	...	3	...	14	...	...	14	...	...	14	...	14	...	14	...	14	...
Nebraska	16	16	...	...	...	16	...	...	16	...	...	16	...	16	...	16	...	16	...
Nevada	12	9	3	...	...	12	...	...	11	1	...	12	...	12	...	12	...	12	...
New Hampshire	8	8	...	...	...	8	...	...	8	...	...	14	...	14	...	14	...	14	...
New Jersey	40	18	...	...	22	40	...	...	36	4	...	40	36	3	1	40	...	40	...
New Mexico	14	8	1	5	...	14	...	...	14	...	...	14	1	13	...	13	1	14	...
New York	92	4	88	...	...	4	88	...	84	8	...	88	88	...	...	88	...	88	...
North Carolina	26	9	1	16	...	26	...	...	22	...	4	32	...	32	...	32	...	32	...
North Dakota	8	5	2	1	...	8	...	...	8	...	...	12	...	12	...	12	...	12	...
Ohio	58	2	...	...	56	58	...	...	56	...	2	56	52	4	...	56	...	56	...
Oklahoma	22	14	1	7	...	22	...	...	22	...	...	22	...	22	...	22	...	22	...
Oregon	18	18	...	...	...	18	...	...	3	15	...	18	7	11	...	18	...	16	2b
Pennsylvania	64	22	41	1	...	64	...	...	30	24	10	60	58	2	...	60	...	60	...
Rhode Island	14	...	14	...	...	14	...	...	1	13	...	8	8	...	...	8	...	8	...
South Carolina	22	22	...	...	...	22	...	...	22	...	...	22	...	22	...	22	...	22	...
South Dakota	14	14	...	...	...	14	...	...	14	...	...	14	...	14	...	14	...	14	...
Tennessee	28	28	...	...	...	28	...	...	27	1	...	26	...	26	...	26	...	26	...
Texas	56	41	...	15	...	54	...	2	48	...	8	52	...	52	...	52	...	52	...
Utah	8	2	...	...	6	8	...	...	6	2	...	14	...	14	...	14	...	14	...
Vermont	12	9	3	...	...	12	...	...	12	...	...	12	3	9	...	12	...	12	...
Virginia	24	22	2	...	...	24	...	...	24	...	...	30	...	30	...	30	...	30	...
Washington	24	15	3	6	...	24	...	...	19	5	...	24	6	18	...	24	...	24	...
West Virginia	14	11	3	...	...	13	1	...	14	...	...	18	...	17	1	18	...	18	...
Wisconsin	30	30	...	...	...	30	...	...	25	5	...	28	10	17	1	28	...	28	...
Wyoming	12	12	...	...	...	12	...	...	12	...	...	12	...	12	...	12	...	12	...
Dist. of Columbia	9	6	3	...	...	6	3	...	5	4	...	9	...	9	...	9	...	9	...
Guam	...	...	...	...	...	...	...	...	...	...	...	3	1	2	...	3	...	3	...
Puerto Rico	5	...	5	...	...	5	...	...	5	...	...	5	...	5	...	5	...	5	...
Virgin Islands	3	2	1	...	...	3	...	...	3	...	...	3	3	...	...	3	...	3	...
Total	1333	692	277	182	182c	1238	93	2	1119	186	28d	1348	434	910	4	1347	1	1345	3

Sources: *Official Proceedings, 1968*, pp. 378-79, 388-89, 430-31. "Official Proceedings, 1972" (daily transcript of proceedings, August 1972; processed).

a. Abstention.

b. One abstention, one vote for David Brinkley.

c. Rhodes, 55 (Ohio); Romney, 50 (44 in Michigan, 6 in Utah); Case, 22 (New Jersey); Carlson, 20 (Kansas); Winthrop Rockefeller, 18 (Arkansas); Fong, 14 (Hawaii); Stassen, 2 (1 in Minnesota, 1 in Ohio); Lindsay, 1 (Minnesota).

d. Lindsay, 10 (Pennsylvania); Brooke, 1 (Ohio); Rhodes, 1 (Ohio); not voting, 16 (8 in Texas, 4 in North Carolina, 2 in Illinois, 1 in Alabama, 1 in Kansas).